W9-BUR-924

THE McGRAW-HILL
BOOK OF POETRY

THE McGRAW-HILL BOOK OF POETRY

Robert DiYanni

Pace University, Pleasantville

Kraft Rompf

Essex Community College

McGraw-Hill, Inc.

New York St. Louis San Francisco Auckland Bogotá
Caracas Lisbon London Madrid Mexico City Milan
Montreal New Delhi San Juan Singapore
Sydney Tokyo Toronto

This book was developed by STEVEN PENSINGER, Inc.

THE McGRAW-HILL BOOK OF POETRY

Copyright © 1993 by McGraw-Hill, Inc. All rights reserved.
Printed in the United States of America. Except as permitted under the
United States Copyright Act of 1976, no part of this publication may be
reproduced or distributed in any form or by any means, or stored in a data
base or retrieval system, without the prior written permission of the
publisher.

Acknowledgments appear on pages 1181–1203, and on this page by reference.

90 DOC DOC 0198

ISBN: 978-0-07-016944-9
MHID: 0-07-016944-6

This book was set in Galliard by ComCom, Inc.
The editors were Steve Pensinger and Scott Amerman;
the designer was Carol Couch;
the production supervisor was Richard A. Ausburn.
The photo researcher was Siva Bonatti.
R. R. Donnelley & Sons Company was printer and binder.

Cover: *Young Woman with a Water Jug,* Jan Vermeer, c. 1662
Oil on canvas, 18 × 16 inches
The Metropolitan Museum of Art, New York
Gift of Henry G. Marquand, 1889
Marquand Collection

Library of Congress Cataloging-in-Publication Data

DiYanni, Robert.
   The McGraw-Hill book of poetry / Robert DiYanni, Kraft Rompf.
      p.   cm.
   Includes bibliographical references and index.
   ISBN 0-07-016944-6
    1. Poetry—Collections.   2. College readers.   I. Rompf, Kraft.
II. McGraw-Hill, Inc.   III. Title.
PN6101.D59   1993
808.81—dc20   92-37243

Robert DiYanni is Professor of English and Director of Interdisciplinary Studies at Pace University, Pleasantville, New York, where he teaches courses in literature, writing, and humanities. He has also taught at Queens College of the City University of New York, at New York University in the Graduate Rhetoric Program, and most recently in the Expository Writing Program at Harvard University. He received his B.A. from Rutgers University (1968) and his Ph.D. from the City University of New York (1976).

Professor DiYanni has written articles and reviews on various aspects of literature, composition, and pedagogy. His books include *Literature; The Art of Reading; Women's Voices; Reading Poetry; Like Season'd Timber: New Essays on George Herbert;* and *Modern American Poets: Their Voices and Visions* (a text to accompany the Public Broadcasting Television series that aired in 1988). Current projects include a college handbook, an introduction to the humanities and with Kraft Rompf, *The McGraw-Hill Book of Fiction,* scheduled for publication in 1994.

Kraft Rompf is an Associate Professor of English at Essex Community College, a large suburban community college near Baltimore. He has had over twenty years' experience there helping students of all ages and backgrounds address the problems and pleasures of reading and writing poetry. A graduate of the Johns Hopkins University Writing Seminars, he was recently awarded a fellowship by the National Endowment for the Humanities.

Professor Rompf is the author of numerous publications, including two volumes of poetry, *Skunk Missal* and *Five Fingers*. He has read and discussed his poetry on National Public Radio, and he has given readings throughout the east, including visits to the Folger Shakespeare Library, Columbia University, and the Poetry Center at SUNY, Stony Brook.

FOR MARY AND SHIRLEY

CONTENTS

PART TWO: POEMS IN ENGLISH 111

PART THREE: POEMS FROM OTHER LANGUAGES 893

Hebrew Poetry 895

The McGraw-Hill Book of Poetry provides a rich selection of poems for students in college poetry courses and for general readers alike. The book is divided into three parts: (1) an introduction to reading poetry; (2) a collection of poems in English, largely by British and American poets, organized chronologically; (3) an anthology of poems from eighteen other languages, a number in both the original language and in facing English translations. Following these three major divisions is an appendix that presents comments on poetry from thirty-five poets and thinkers from ancient times to the present. A brief glossary of poetic terms concludes the book.

Each of the book's major sections offers one or more special features. The introduction, for example, while including a discussion of the elements of poetry, also approaches poems with a view to readers' experiences, values, and pleasures. Complementing the critical vocabulary of the elements' sections is an attention to readers' subjective responses to poems, their personal engagement with them, their acts of interpretation, and their cultural and aesthetic evaluation. In addition, the Introduction includes three special features: (1) a selection of visual poems, including concrete poetry along with emblem and pattern poems; (2) poems with color reproductions of the paintings that inspired them; (3) poems associated with music and song, a number of which include the music itself.

Part Two, the longest section of the book, collects a substantial number of poems by British and American poets from Caedmon to modern times. Practical limitations made it impossible to include critical introductions to every British and American poet included in this section of the book. Rather than provide brief headnotes for all the poets, we have written more extensive critical headnotes for twenty-five poets, selected for their cultural and literary importance. These introductory headnotes provide literary and historical contexts and identify central features of each poet's work. In addition to these basic features of Part Two, we have included some unusual features for a book of this kind. With our Chaucer selections, for example, we have included substantial excerpts from the General Prologue to *The Canterbury Tales* and the complete Pardoner's Tale, with its framing material. Both of these selections appear in Chaucer's Middle English coupled with a modern facing translation. This double presentation of Chaucer provides more experienced readers with access to Chaucer's language while permitting those encountering Middle English for the first time with a chance to experience his genius in translation.

And, of course, readers can alternate readily between the medieval text and its modern counterpart.

We have also selected our Shakespeare poems somewhat differently than editors of other poetry anthologies. In addition to a representative selection of sonnets followed by songs from five comedies, we have also included soliloquies from nine plays, representing comedy, tragedy, history, and romance. Readers will thus have readily available Shakespeare's poetic achievement across a wide range of genres.

Throughout Part Two, moreover, we have varied the poems selected. Thus John Donne is represented by song and sonnet, elegy and religious hymn; John Milton by elegy, sonnet, and paired poems, along with substantial excerpts from his epic, *Paradise Lost;* Alexander Pope by ode, epistle, philosophic satire, and mock epic. In these and other instances we have included as many long poems as we could accomodate. Some, like *The Rape of the Lock, The Wreck of the Deutschland,* and *The Waste Land,* appear complete. Others, such as *Paradise Lost, Song of Myself, Paterson,* and *The Cantos,* have been excerpted.

Readers can find in Part Two a broad selection of poems from the Middle Ages to the present. They will experience by turns the pleasure of renewed acquaintance with familiar works and the delight of encountering new poems in fresh voices. This is especially the case with the modern poems in this section of the book, though we have scattered some surprises earlier as well.

The most unusual and innovative section of the book, however, is Part Three, "Poems from Other Languages." In this section we have collected poems from nearly twenty languages (counting our African and Native American selections as one "language" each). The other languages range from ancient to modern. Poems from the Bible in Hebrew are followed by Hebrew poems from the Middle Ages and the twentieth century. Chinese and Japanese poets, like their Western counterparts in Greece and Rome, are represented by ancient and modern voices. Throughout these and the other foreign language sections in French, Italian, Spanish, German, and Russian, we have included long poems and short, coupling narrative excerpts with lyric poems in their entirety. Our selections from the Celtic and Scandinavian poetic traditions, moreover, include poems from various dialects, languages, and historical periods.

In addition, a number of foreign language poets receive multiple representation. Homer and Callimachus, Virgil and Catullus, Dante and Petrarch, Lorca and Paz, Baudelaire and Apollinaire, Goethe and Rilke, Senghor and Awoonor, along with many others contribute more than one poem. Nor have we neglected poems by women, whose work appears throughout our selection of foreign language poetry. Among the Greek poets included are the ancient Greek lyricist Sappho, along with the twentieth-century Myrtiotissa, represented by her stunning "Women of Suli"; the modern Hebrew poets Leah Goldberg, Yocheved Bat-Miriam, Rahel Bluwstein, and Dalia Ravikovich; the Chinese poets Li Ching-chao, Cheng Min, and Shen Yee-ping; the Japanese poets the Lady Ōtomo no Sakanoe, the Lady Kasa, Ono no Komachi, the Lady Izumi, and Tomioka Taeko; Italy's

Amelia Rosselli; Mexico's Sor Juana Inés de la Cruz and Chile's Gabriela Mistral; France's Marie de France; the German language poets Nelly Sachs and Annette von Droste-Hülshoff; the modern Russian poets Anna Akhmatova, Marina Tsvetayeva, and Bella Akhmadulina; the Welsh Emily Jane Pfeiffer and the Irish Eavan Boland; the Swedish Elsa Grave; from the Faeroe Islands, Gudrid Helmsdal-Nielsen; and, finally, the Native American poets Leslie Marmon Silko and Louise Erdrich.

Besides its historical range and cultural diversity "Poems from Other Languages" includes poems in a variety of different languages in their original form. Although we could not include all the poems in this section both in their original languages and in facing English translations, we have presented nearly forty poems that way. In some instances, as with certain poems of Petrarch, Rilke, Sappho, and Catullus, we have included more than one translation. Our selection from the Hebrew Bible's Book of Job, for example, appears in both the Revised Standard Version and in a recent translation by Stephen Mitchell.

Our goal in Part Three is to suggest the range and diversity of these other language traditions rather than to represent every aspect of their various historical and literary perspectives. A number of our choices of foreign language poems, moreover, connect with the English poetic tradition. Readers, consequently, have convenient opportunities to compare various schools of influence. Readers interested, for example, in particular strands of the Western European tradition could consider Milton's debt to Homer and Virgil in the epic vein while also seeing how Milton adapts the Petrarchan sonnet to English. English sonnets, in fact, appear abundantly in Parts Two and Three, and students interested in the sonnet tradition can thus consider both the Petrarchan and Shakespearean versions and their respective influences. Similarly, readers can trace back not only the metaphysical echoes of John Donne in the poetry of T. S. Eliot, but also Eliot's use of such French Symbolist masters as Charles Baudelaire and Stéphane Mallarmé. The influence of the image as worked by Chinese and Japanese can also be considered in the works of modernist poets such as William Carlos Williams and Ezra Pound, who also appears as a translator of Old English and Chinese poems. Numerous additional kinds of crosscutting within, between, and among traditions can be made, many of which are highlighted in the headnotes provided for each of the foreign language sections.

A word on dates: Dates have been supplied for English language poems in Part Two, where we have grouped them by author and arranged them chronogically. These dates represent the first publication in book form. Occasionally, however, for poets such as Emily Dickinson and Gerard Manley Hopkins, whose poetry was largely unpublished in their lifetimes, a date of composition is supplied. When two dates appear, the first is for composition and the second is for publication. Dates have not been included for the illustrative poems in the Introduction. Nor have they been provided for foreign language poems and translations; instead, foreign language poets and poems have been situated historically in their respective headnotes.

Instructor's Manual

Kraft Rompf has prepared a lively and informative *Instructor's Manual*. This useful teaching aid includes many practical suggestions for using *The McGraw-Hill Book of Poetry* in the classroom—in both literature and creative writing courses. The *Instructor's Manual* also contains observations, questions, interpretive leads, definitions of additional terms, and other kinds of background information helpful for teaching.

Acknowledgments

We would like to express our gratitude to those who encouraged us on this project. We could never have completed this book without the assistance of many people. First, thanks to Steve Pensinger, editor, publisher, and friend, who supported our work generously and graciously. Thanks also to the McGraw-Hill team, who converted our manuscript into a finished book, and a quite beautiful one, we might add; Scott Amerman, the editing supervisor; Carol Couch, the designer; and Rich Ausburn, the production supervisor.

We would also like to thank five reviewers, who offered sound criticism and valuable suggestions. Stephen C. Behrendt, University of Nebraska, Lincoln; Ralph Berets, University of Missouri, Kansas City; David Cowles, Brigham Young University, Utah; Mark Johnston, Quinnipiac College, Connecticut; and Ilene Rubenstein, California State University–Northridge.

We also wish to express our gratitude to our colleagues and friends, who advised us on various matters, especially on the foreign language poetry. Thanks to David and Hilda Rowe for their comments on our German poetry selections; to Susan and Joseph Gannon for their assistance with the Greek and Latin poems; to Michelle Newman and Adelia Williams for their response to our French selections, and again to Adelia Williams for her translations of Apollinaire's calligrammatic poems; to Noel Ortega and Boria Sax for their suggestions about Spanish and German poetry, respectively, and again to Boria Sax for his translation of Lutz Rathenow's "For Uwe Gressmann"; to Frank Greene and Michael Fallon for their suggestions about Celtic poetry; and to Peter Glassgold for his advice about both foreign poetry and modern American poetry, as well as for his Catullus translation.

We would like to acknowledge with appreciation the contribution of Suzanne Gilliard, whose still-life painting appears in Part One, coupled with the poem by Vinnie-Marie D'Ambrosio. Thanks to others who have contributed poems, especially Cathy Appel, Ruth F. Eisenberg, Roger Kamenetz, and Askold Melnyczuk. And a general word of thanks to all who have alerted us to poems we would otherwise have overlooked, poems such as May Swenson's "The Centaur," put forth by Jamieson Spencer; Abraham Cowley's "My Picture," suggested by Allan Casson; Kathleen Fraser's "Poem in Which My Legs Are Accepted," suggested by Judith Stanford; Sandra Schor's "At Point Hope on the Chukchi Sea" along with her translation of the modern Chinese poet Shen Yee-Ping, both provided by Esther

Schor; and Alice Fulton's "Dance Script with Electric Ballerina," called to our attention by Bill Hollinger.

Finally, we would like to thank our wives, Mary Hammond DiYanni and Shirley Johnsen Rompf, for their patience, encouragement, and love.

Robert DiYanni
Kraft Rompf

THE McGRAW-HILL
BOOK OF POETRY

INTRODUCTION

The Pleasures of Poetry

We read poetry for the many pleasures it offers—pleasures of sound and meaning, pleasures of image and symbol, pleasures of speech and feeling and thought. Some of these pleasures are intellectual, as when we enjoy a poet's witty wordplay or understand a poem's central idea. Other pleasures of poetry are emotional, as when a poem evokes sorrow or pity, fear or joy. Still others are physical, as when our skin tingles or we feel an impulse to tap our feet or nod in time to a poem's rhythmic beat. Emily Dickinson once suggested that she could tell she was reading poetry when she felt as if the top of her head was coming off. Although our own ways of acknowledging the power of poetry may not be as extravagant as Dickinson's, each of us experiences the pleasures of poetry in a meaningful way.

Poems may, at times, seem puzzling or mysterious. Yet mystery and confusion are not essential attributes of poetry. Nor is poetry simply dressed-up prose, statements that have been made to look good by being organized in stanzas and sound good by being arranged in patterns of rhythm and rhyme. And even though we can discuss poems' ideas, they can never be reduced to their intellectual content. Poems present experiences in language, experiences the poet creates for the reader to re-create. In reading poetry our experience involves more than considering the meanings of words. It includes our apprehension of a poem's form, its patterns of sound and sense, its controlled structure of thought. The meaning of any poem involves our total experience of reading it, an experience that includes intellectual understanding but that is not restricted to it.

Poetry sharpens our perception of the world around us since it draws its energy from the fresh observation of life. Poetry can reveal to us things we didn't know or knew only vaguely. It can excite our capacity for wonder, and it can enlarge our appreciation of beauty. It can make us feel more acutely and deeply, and it can make us more receptive to imaginative experience. Consider the following short poem.

ROBERT FROST

[1874–1963]

Dust of Snow

The way a crow
Shook down on me
The dust of snow
From a hemlock tree

Has given my heart   5
A change of mood
And saved some part
Of a day I had rued.

Part of our enjoyment of this poem comes from its brevity. It captures an experience and re-creates it in just a few words. The poem's quick stab of reality engages us, very likely sending us back for a second look almost immediately. We may be struck by the nature of the poem's action—a crow jounces a tree limb, which unloads its snow on a man beneath it. We may smile, considering that the crow's action may have been intentional. And we may reflect on the man's response—not anger or frustration, but a shift in his feelings, "a change of mood" (presumably from sorrow to something more joyous, elation perhaps).

The pleasure we take in "Dust of Snow" may include a consideration of our own experience—whether or not that experience duplicates either the poem's external action or the speaker's internal change. We may find ourselves thinking about how our moods change and about what prompts those changes. We may enjoy the surprising reversal of our expectations in reading how Frost's speaker responds to the situation, perhaps comparing what our own imagined response might be.

These experiential or imaginative pleasures, moreover, might very well be supplemented by the pleasure we take in the poem's sounds—especially its rhythm and rhyme. And they may extend to other details we observe about its structure and language. We may notice, for example, that though "Dust of Snow" is a single sentence, it is cast as two separate, nearly symmetrical stanzas. And we might ask ourselves how it would differ if arranged as one stanza or constructed of two sentences. Furthermore, we might enjoy Frost's use of "rued," which stands out in a context of more common and familiar language.

"Dust of Snow" may lead us to speculate not only about the narrative incident it recounts but about the event's larger significance. We might think about the relationship between human beings and the natural world that "Dust of Snow" implies. (That is, that nature can affect people in beneficial ways; that it can make us feel better. We may derive additional pleasure from considering other poems we have read by Frost or by others that seem to confirm or contradict the experience this poem displays.

THE ACT OF READING

We divide our preliminary discussion of understanding poetry into three parts: reading, interpretation, and evaluation. By **reading** we mean primarily our subjective experience of the poem; by **interpretation** we mean the process of analysis we engage in to understand the poem; and by **evaluation** we mean our estimation of the attitudes it conveys and the values it endorses. All three aspects of reading poetry can be used in measuring the extent to which any poem moves or touches us, stimulating us to see and think and wonder.

READING

We experience poems both intellectually and emotionally. This experience involves our feelings about a poem's speaker and situation, and it includes our desire to see how its poetic action is resolved. In *reading* we are thus concerned with our personal, subjective involvement in the poem. Instead of asking ourselves immediately what the poem means, we consider what it does to us and how it affects us—and why. To examine this dimension of our experience of poetry, read the following poem.

RAYMOND CARVER

[1939–1988]

Photograph of My Father in His Twenty-Second Year

October. Here in this dank, unfamiliar kitchen
I study my father's embarrassed young man's face.
Sheepish grin, he holds in one hand a string
of spiny yellow perch, in the other
a bottle of Carlsbad beer.   5

In jeans and denim shirt, he leans
against the front fender of a 1934 Ford.
He would like to pose bluff and hearty for his posterity,

wear his old hat cocked over his ear.
All his life my father wanted to be bold.   *10*

But the eyes give him away, and the hands
that limply offer the string of dead perch
and the bottle of beer. Father, I love you,
yet how can I say thank you, I who can't hold my liquor either,
and don't even know the places to fish?   *15*

We may never have seen a picture of our father holding a bottle of beer or a string of fish, but Carver's poem may trigger our memories nonetheless. In listening to the speaker describe the photograph of his father, we may think less about the picture and more about the man. Perhaps feelings about our own fathers will emerge as we listen to the speaker describing his.

We might be struck by particular details such as the father's lack of boldness or the way he seems to pose for posterity. Such observations may stimulate us to make connections with our own experience. Very likely, by the time we read the last stanza, we will respond to the speaker's direct expression of love for his father and perhaps also to his confession of inadequacy. That is, Carver's poem may raise questions about how we see our own fathers, and it may stimulate additional reflection about how we measure ourselves in relation to them. It might, moreover, tap a well of emotion, dredging up memories, and with them thoughts and feelings we didn't know we had.

Suppose, however, that we cannot relate the poem to a relationship between a father and son. Does the poem's focus on males, for example, deny female readers access to its pleasures? Not really, since in reading literature we typically make adjustments to accommodate such differences. Women experience strong feelings about their fathers, and they also judge them. Moreover, a female reader who couldn't relate the poem to her father might easily transpose it to reflect her way of seeing her mother, whether or not her mother fishes or drinks beer. Such adaptations form a normal part of our reading experience.

INTERPRETATION

When we interpret a poem, we explain it to ourselves. We make sense of it. If "reading" is viewed as primarily a subjective experience in which we satisfy our personal needs as readers, then "interpreting" directs us to more objective considerations. When we interpret a poem, we concern ourselves less with how it affects us and how it makes us feel than with what it means or suggests. Interpretation, in short, aims at understanding; it relies on intellectual comprehension and rational understanding rather than on emotional response.

The act of interpreting involves four essential acts of mind: observing, connecting, inferring, and concluding. To understand a poem, we first need to observe its details. We hear its rhythm and rhyme; we notice its pattern of organization; we envision the objects or experiences it describes. As we do these things, we begin to formulate a sense of the poem's focus, emphasis, and point. We arrive at this formulation, however tentative it may be, largely by making connections among its details. On the basis of these connections we make inferences, or interpretive hypotheses, about their significance. Finally, we come to some kind of provisional conclusion about the poem's meaning based on our observations, connections, and inferences.

About Raymond Carver's poem, for example, we might make the following observations:

The poem is constructed of three stanzas, each of five lines.

The first stanza is descriptive; the second adds an explanatory comment (about the father's desire to be bold), and the third asks a question and expresses the speaker's feelings.

The speaker talks to his father (or to his father's image in the photograph).

In the picture the father is younger than the speaker.

We might then begin to put our observations together and to notice how they are related, and thus begin to make inferences about the speaker and his relationship with his father. We might say, for example, that the speaker understands both his father's limitations and his father's abilities. He can "read" the photograph, interpreting his father's image because he remembers what his father was like, especially how he wanted to be perceived. From those things we might then conclude that in studying the photograph and thinking about his father, the speaker is expressing a sense of his own inadequacy about things his father did well, such as holding his liquor and fishing for perch. Beyond this, however, we might generalize about the speaker's desire to come to terms with his father's memory, seeing his father partly as a model and partly as a stimulus for evaluating his own manhood.

Our act of interpretation, moreover, continues while we read. We don't delay making inferences, for example, until after we have made and connected all our observations. Instead, we develop a tentative conclusion *as* we read and observe, *while* we make observations and develop inferences. We may change and adjust our inferences and provisional conclusion both *during* our reading of a poem and *afterward,* as we think back over its details. We do not, however, separate this intellectual process from our subjective reactions and emotional responses. Although here they are separated for convenience, the way we actually read combines emotional response and intellectual analysis. In the same way, the four interpretive actions of observing, connecting, inferring, and concluding occur together, sometimes simultaneously, and not in a series of neatly segregated, sequential stages.

Consider the following poem from the standpoint of interpretation.

EMILY DICKINSON

[1830–1886]

Much Madness is divinest Sense

Much Madness is divinest Sense—
To a discerning eye—
Much Sense—the starkest Madness—
'Tis the Majority
In this, as All, prevail—   5
Assent—and you are sane—
Demur—you're straightway dangerous—
And handled with a Chain—

What sense do you make of such a poem? How can you begin to interpret it? First, notice the way "sense" and "madness" are the dominant issues. Although opposites, Dickinson asserts their apparent equality, perhaps even their identity, in lines one and three. To be more precise, she ascribes the condition of one state to the other. Madness, the lines suggest, may not be what it appears to be. Although madness might look insane, it might really be quite sensible. Conversely, something may appear sane and sensible, but upon closer inspection turn out, instead, to be madness.

So far we have been simply unpacking Dickinson's tightly compressed lines, clarifying our sense of what her words mean, of what the lines suggest. We have not yet asked why or how madness can be sense and sense can be madness. Nor have we considered whether we agree with such an assertion. Our purpose in interpretation is to understand patiently and deliberately the meaning of the words.

You may have noticed, however, that in interpreting lines 1–3, we omitted important details. First, the lines assert that "much" madness (not all) is or may be sensible, and that "much" sense may also be madness. That is, Dickinson's lines do not insist that what appears to be madness never is, or that what appears sensible is never so. The word "much" qualifies her assertion to suggest that sometimes madness and sense masquerade as each other. Second, her lines also indicate that when "madness" is really "sense" it is "divinest" sense; and when "sense" is really madness, it is "starkest" madness. The superlative form of both words suggests that when madness and sense are interchanged, the reversal is complete, thorough, and absolute.

Dickinson bases her poem on *paradox,* a poetic device that describes an apparent contradiction: in this case, that madness can be sense and that sense can be madness. In a paradox, the apparent contradiction disappears with a shift in perspective. Thus, for example, from the standpoint of worldly wisdom, sacrificing everything else in life for money or power or prestige may be sensible. But from a religious standpoint, such as that of Buddhism or Christianity, such behavior is madness. To take another example, from the standpoint of finding employment upon graduating from college, majoring in business, perhaps in accounting or management, may seem eminently sensible. However, from an alternative standpoint that an undergraduate major should promote broad learning and assure an ability to learn how to learn, a major in a liberal arts subject such as history, English, or philosophy may be the better choice.

The second part of the poem (lines 4–8) moves on to something else—how sense and madness are defined by a social majority. Lines 4–8 suggest that if you go along with the majority opinion, you will be considered sane; if not, you may be considered a threat to the majority and branded odd, different, perhaps even crazy. As in the first part of the poem, Dickinson employs a pair of contrasting words to accentuate these contradictory responses: "Assent" (or agree) and "Demur" (or disagree). The poem suggests that it is dangerous to disagree, to diverge from the conventional ways of seeing and doing things. While recognizing this as a fact of life, the poem nevertheless questions the validity of such a view, and in fact undermines it by suggesting that it is often the majority in its seeming sensibleness that is mad and the individual in his seemingly eccentric madness who is really right and sane. By means of paradox Dickinson invites us to think about this prospect. And even though the poem ends with a touch of dark humor, it is a serious poem about a serious matter.

In reaching an interpretation of this or of any poem, we should be concerned less with finding the "right" answer than with arriving at a satisfying explanation. Nonetheless, some interpretations will be more satisfying than others. They will be more convincing, largely because they take into account more of the poem's details. Other interpretations, while perhaps not as convincing, may be valuable for the intellectual stimulation they provide. Still others may strain credibility. Because invariably we bring different experiences, different lives, and different selves to our reading of poems, we often see different things in them. The different things we see and the varying interpretations we make depend largely on our values, on our attitude toward what matters most to us. Through conversation and discussion we can debate the merits of those viewpoints and values while enriching our understanding of poems, and deepening our pleasure in reading them.

EVALUATION

We are not always aware—except perhaps in a vague, general way—why we respond to something as we do. We may know that we like or dislike it without bothering to think about why. We accept particular ideas, events, experiences, and works of art while rejecting others, sometimes almost instinctively. We may agree or disagree with the attitude toward madness and sanity expressed in Dickinson's poem. We may accept or reject the behavior displayed in Frost's "Dust of Snow." And we may approve or disapprove of the comments made by Carver's speaker in "Photograph of My Father in His Twenty-second Year." Yet however we assess these poems, we invariably measure their values and attitudes against our own. But even though part of our evaluation of a work is unconscious, we can make it more deliberate and more fully conscious.

When we evaluate a poem, we appraise it according to our own unique combination of cultural, moral, and aesthetic values. Our cultural values derive from our lives as members of families and societies. Our moral values reflect our ethical norms—what we consider to be good or evil, right or wrong. Our aesthetic values concern what we see as beautiful or ugly, well or ill made. Over time, through education and experience, our values may change. A poem we once valued for what it reveals about human experience or for its moral perspective may mean little to us later. Conversely, a work we once found uninteresting or disappointing may later engage us powerfully.

Our personal response to any poem's values is closely tied to our interpretation of it. Evaluation depends on interpretation; our judgment of a poem's values (and perhaps its value as a literary work as well) depends on how we understand it. Our evaluation, moreover, may be linked to our initial experience of the poem, with our first impressions and precritical reactions. If our reaction is unsympathetic to the poem as a whole or to the values it seems to endorse, we may be reluctant to change either our interpretation or our evaluation, even when we discover evidence convincing enough to warrant a reconsideration of both.

Consider "Dust of Snow" from this perspective. What values seem to animate the poem's speaker? What, for example, is his attitude toward nature? What does his very act of reflecting on the experience suggest about him? What does it suggest more generally about reflective habits of mind? And what does the poem (and perhaps the poet) suggest about the emotional experience of human beings? Is it good, for example, to experience such rapid changes of mood over such apparently trivial occurrences?

Consider also the implicit values of Carver's poem. Is Carver's speaker overly concerned with his image as a "man" who can "hold his liquor"? Does he somehow blame his father for passing on to him an inability to drink liquor without showing its effects? Is he too hard on himself for not measuring up to his father's ability to catch fish? In short, how should we evaluate the image of manhood the poem displays?

And of Dickinson's paradoxes you might ask whether she is right. Is apparent madness sometimes sensible, and apparent sense sometimes madness? Is Dickinson's speaker correct about majority opinion? Does it usually prevail, and if so, what do you think about that prevalence? What do you think about those who demur, who don't assent to the majority view, and who thereby may be labeled as mad? What are the dangers and virtues of going against the grain of conventional wisdom, of majority opinion? How important is it for you to be one of the majority? How important are other perspectives, alternate ways of seeing, thinking, and valuing—perspectives that run counter to the views of the majority?

Such are the kinds of questions we bring to bear on poems under the rubric of evaluation. Although we have isolated the processes of reading, interpretation, and evaluation, the three acts occur simultaneously in an intricate web of thinking and feeling. To derive the fullest pleasure from the poems we read, we should be alert for all three aspects of our experience in reading them. In doing so we will develop our skill as thoughtful, sensitive readers who know what we think, how we feel, and why. As you read Adrienne Rich's poem "Aunt Jennifer's Tigers," consider each of these three aspects of literary response.

ADRIENNE RICH

[b. 1929]

Aunt Jennifer's Tigers

Aunt Jennifer's tigers prance across a screen,
Bright topaz denizens of a world of green.
They do not fear the men beneath the tree;
They pace in sleek chivalric certainty.

Aunt Jennifer's fingers fluttering through her wool   5
Find even the ivory needle hard to pull.
The massive weight of Uncle's wedding band
Sits heavily upon Aunt Jennifer's hand.

When Aunt is dead, her terrified hands will lie
Still ringed with ordeals she was mastered by.   10
The tigers in the panel that she made
Will go on prancing, proud and unafraid.

QUESTIONS

Reading

What associations about your own aunts and uncles do you bring to the poem? Could the situation described in this poem apply to your parents rather than to your aunts and uncles? What words in the poem triggered your responses most strongly? Why?

Interpretation

What words and phrases recur, and what details do you see as significant? Why? What connections can you make and what inferences can you draw after reading the poem a few times? How do you interpret "Aunt Jennifer's Tigers"?

Evaluation

What values are associated with Aunt Jennifer? With the uncle? With the tigers? What is the relationship among the values associated with these three figures? How do your own values, beliefs, and convictions contradict or support those displayed in the poem?

Whatever our initial impressions of the poem's language and situation, we soon ascertain that the speaker is a woman (possibly the poet herself) who values her aunt's crocheted or embroidered tigers very much. We may or may not feel pity or sympathy for Aunt Jennifer; we may or may not think much about the nameless "Uncle" whose wedding ring is a symbolic burden for his wife. But we must certainly respond to the speaker's celebration of the tigers.

The poem begins and ends with the tigers, and they appear with Aunt Jennifer in the title. The tigers are thus associated with her; they somehow belong to her. The tigers "prance"; they also "pace," and they are unafraid of "the men" (hunters perhaps) depicted beneath the tree on Aunt Jennifer's wool picture. The tigers, moreover, are portrayed in bright colors. They appear as majestic creatures—vibrant, strong, certain, and very much alive. And they seem more interesting and more powerful than the men in the poem. This much we can glean from the opening stanza.

The second stanza shows Aunt Jennifer having difficulty making her stitches. Her heavy wedding band impedes her, inhibiting and slowing her progress. The wedding band is clearly symbolic, representing the oppressiveness of marriage to "Uncle," which weighs Aunt Jennifer down, keeping her in her place. How far we pursue such an interpretive lead will depend on our personal experience, our observation of the poem's details, our knowledge of Adrienne Rich's poetry in general, and our own values.

The third stanza leaps forward to a time after Aunt Jennifer's death. In death she lies "ringed with ordeals" that oppressed her in life. There seems to be no escape from the stultifying effects of traditional sociosexual relationships, her death notwithstanding. Even the rituals established for death have been sex stereotyped, and the perceptions of Aunt Jennifer by those who live on will be made in the context of her place as a woman and the wife of "Uncle." This is not to suggest that Uncle is necessarily the villain of the poem. He may, in fact, be a decent fellow. But he is clearly meant to represent an attitude that Rich's speaker considers destructive. And it is this larger, socially tolerated way of seeing women that Uncle typifies and the poem's speaker condemns.

Even though Aunt Jennifer maintains her place, and even though she remains "Aunt Jennifer" in death, her tigers continue to prance. They go on living, a product of her handiwork, representing an aspect of Aunt Jennifer that she could not display in life—freedom from male domination, freedom from fear. Through her art Aunt Jennifer creates an image of a power and vitality she herself could possess only in imagination. Thus, in a way, even though Aunt Jennifer is mastered by her fate, she nonetheless ultimately prevails through the imaginative vision displayed in her art.

In considering this poem's values, we need, then, to address questions about the power of men to control the lives of women. And we need to consider the presumed submission of women along with the reasons for their submission. On the other hand, we may want to shift perspective and not see submission here at all, but rather an acceptance of a natural and socially viable order. That is, although we need to consider the values attached to Uncle and to Aunt Jennifer as described by the speaker, we might consider whether Aunt Jennifer and Uncle would ever see themselves the way the speaker does. In addition, we certainly need to consider the role and value of art for the speaker, for the poet, and for the lives of people more generally. Such considerations lead us to examine the cultural assumptions, sexual stereotypes, and social dispositions suggested by the poem. They may lead to a consideration of whether Aunt Jennifer's woolwork is truly a form of "art" (and an implicit rebellion) or simply another example of how she (and women in general) have been limited to performing socially sanctioned acts in socially acceptable ways.

Elements of Poetry

The elements of a poem include its speaker and situation; its *diction* or selection of words; its *imagery* or details of sight, sound, taste, smell, and touch; its *figurative language,* especially *simile* and *metaphor;* its inclusion of *symbolism* and *allusion;* its *tone,* or the implied attitude of its speaker; its *syntax,* or order of words in phrase and sentence; its sound effects, especially *rhyme, assonance,* and *alliteration;* its rhythm and *meter,* or the pattern of accent and emphasis we hear in it; and its *structure,* or formal patterns of organization. All the elements of a poem together convey feeling and embody meaning.

SPEAKER AND SITUATION

In reading any poem, the first thing we hear is the voice of its speaker. In listening to the speaker we gain a sense of his or her circumstances and situation. We learn, that is, what the speaker is talking about, how he or she feels about it, and why. Our first concern, therefore, is to determine who we are listening to, what is happening, and how the speaker is affected by it.

In Frost's "Dust of Snow," for example, a speaker reflects on a recent experience. The speaker seems to take pleasure both in the experience and in his memory of it. In Carver's "Photograph of My Father in His Twenty-Second Year" the speaker is a man looking at a snapshot of his father holding a string of fish and a bottle of beer. The son remembers his father and measures himself against him. Expressing both his affection and appreciation, he also reveals differences between them that hint at the speaker's sense of his own inadequacy. Dickinson's "Much Madness is divinest Sense" gives us a confident speaker, one who neither reflects on experience like Frost's speaker nor questions it as Carver's does. Dickinson's speaker comments, instead, on what she has observed; from her observed experience she

14

generalizes an axiom or truth. And finally, the speaker in Rich's "Aunt Jennifer's Tigers" thinks about the relationship and values of her aunt and uncle, as she contemplates an embroidered pattern of tigers made by her aunt. We see the speaker celebrating the memory of her aunt through her aunt's handiwork; we note how the speaker's memory of her aunt and uncle suggest a set of cultural values the speaker herself identifies and evaluates.

Consider the speaker and situation in the following poem.

LANGSTON HUGHES

[1902–1967]

Mother to Son

Well, son, I'll tell you:
Life for me ain't been no crystal stair.
It's had tacks in it,
And splinters,
And boards torn up, 5
And places with no carpet on the floor—
Bare.
But all the time
I'se been a-climbin' on,
And reachin' landin's, 10
And turnin' corners,
And sometimes goin' in the dark
Where there ain't been no light.
So boy, don't you turn back.
Don't you set down on the steps 15
'Cause you finds it's kinder hard.
Don't you fall now—
For I'se still goin', honey,
I'se still climbin',
And life for me ain't been no crystal stair. 20

Even without the title ("Mother to Son") we can clearly see that the speaker is a parent giving advice to a child. We are not told the specific occasion. Nor are we provided with the particularities of their circumstances. Those things are left to our imagination. What we are given, however, is a general sense of their situation. The mother is encouraging her son to persist in his efforts, not to give up, not even to slow down, regardless of the difficulties she knows he will encounter. She presents herself, moreover, as a model for him to imitate. Although she is tired of her struggles in life, she is still "climbin'," still doing what she believes is necessary.

We hear a different speaker and voice in the next poem.

WALT WHITMAN

[1819–1892]

When I Heard the Learn'd Astronomer

When I heard the learn'd astronomer,
When the proofs, the figures, were ranged in columns before me,
When I was shown the charts and diagrams, to add, divide, and measure them,
When I sitting heard the astronomer where he lectured with much applause in the
   lecture-room,
How soon unaccountable I became tired and sick,   5
Till rising and gliding out I wander'd off by myself,
In the mystical moist night-air, and from time to time,
Look'd up in perfect silence at the stars.

Here the speaker is a student sitting in a lecture hall listening to a lecture. As the astronomer lectures, the speaker becomes increasingly discontented. Finally, when he can no longer stand it, he leaves the lecture hall and walks out into the starry night. Although the speaker does not give reasons for becoming tired and sick, we suspect it has something to do with a discrepancy between what he needs at the time and what he is experiencing. The lecture presumably bores him. Interestingly enough, others in the audience seem to enjoy it and applaud the lecturer approvingly. The speaker's experience, however, is different, and he goes off into the night, where he can commune silently, privately, mystically with nature. In this instance, the speaker's actions prove to be louder and more dramatic than the lecturer's words.

DICTION

Diction refers to the words of a poem, specifically to the selection of words the poet employs. We can speak of a poem's diction as being primarily abstract or concrete, formal or informal, general or specific. A word like "shovel," a general word, is less specific than "garden shovel" or "snow shovel," yet more specific than "garden tool" or "snow implement." Insofar as "shovel" is a concrete word, it refers to a concrete object rather than to an abstract idea. Words like "fear," "love," and "beauty," on the other hand, are abstract. They refer to concepts rather than things. To convey fear, a poet might describe "a tighter breathing" (Emily Dickinson's "A narrow Fellow in the Grass," p. 473); to portray love "two hearts beating as one" (Robert Browning's "Meeting at Night," p. 23); to illustrate beauty, "a red, red rose" (Robert Burns's "A Red, Red Rose," p. 327).

Formality and informality refer to the "social standing" of a word. Some words are more commonly used, more familiar, and hence more informal than others. "Talk," for example, is more common than its more formal counterpart "discourse." "Talk" is more likely to be used in everyday conversation, less likely to be reserved for formal situations.

The diction of the following poem, Robert Francis's "Pitcher," is more abstract than concrete, more general than specific, more formal than informal.

ROBERT FRANCIS

[1901–1987]

Pitcher

His art is eccentricity, his aim
How not to hit the mark he seems to aim at,

His passion how to avoid the obvious,
His technique how to vary the avoidance.

The others throw to be comprehended. He   5
Throws to be a moment misunderstood.

> Yet not too much. Not errant, arrant, wild,
> But every seeming aberration willed.
>
> Not to, yet still, still to communicate
> Making the batter understand too late.   *10*

Notice how Francis mixes polysyllabic words of Latin derivation with the monosyllabic, or one-syllable, words more typical of ordinary speech. Notice too how the relative formality, generality, and abstract vocabulary of "Pitcher" contrasts with the more informal, concrete, and specific language of the following excerpt from another baseball poem, "Cobb Would Have Caught It," by Robert Fitzgerald.

> In sunburnt parks where Sunday lies,
> Or the wide wastes beyond the cities,
> Teams in grey deploy through sunlight.
>
> Talk it up, boys, a little practice.
>
> Coming in stubby and fast, the baseman   *5*
> Gathers a grounder in fat green grass,
> Picks it stinging and clipped as wit
> Into the leather: a swinging step
> Wings it deadeye down to first.
> Smack. Oh, attaboy, attaoldboy. . . .   *10*

A striking aspect of Francis's poem is the abstract language he uses to describe a physical activity—a pitcher throwing a baseball to a catcher while a batter tries to hit it. Francis's choice of abstract words is a poetic strategy as eccentric as the pitcher's art. Both the pitcher's and the poet's "eccentricity" involve throwing "strikes"—hitting the mark each aims at—without doing it in an obvious or predictable way. The pitcher wants the batter to miss the ball. The poet tries to surprise the reader. He does so by reminding us that "eccentric" means off the center, where both pitcher and poet aim.

Fitzgerald's words are more specific and his images more concrete. He selects words that detail the action described, occasionally introducing the kind of talk one hears on a ballfield ("Talk it up, boys . . . Oh, attaboy, attaoldboy"). His selection of words is appropriate for his aims in the poem, as Francis's diction deftly defines his different poetic purpose.

In the following brief poem, Gwendolyn Brooks limits her speakers to monosyllables. The limitation, however, does not impoverish the poem's language. Instead it highlights the poet's ingenuity in recreating the rhythm and flavor of urban black speech, as she increases the stab of reality that language describes.

GWENDOLYN BROOKS

[b. 1917]

We Real Cool
The Pool Players. Seven at the Golden Shovel.

We real cool. We
Left school. We

Lurk late. We
Strike straight. We

Sing sin. We   5
Thin gin. We

Jazz June. We
Die soon.

CONNOTATION

In reading any poem it is necessary to know what the words mean, but it is equally important to understand what those words imply or suggest. The *denotation,* or dictionary meaning, of "dictator," for example, is "a person exercising absolute power, especially one who assumes absolute control without the free consent of the people." But "dictator" also carries additional *connotations,* or associations both personal and public. Beyond its dictionary meaning, "dictator" may suggest repressive force and tyrannical oppression; it may call up images of bloodbaths, purges, executions; it may trigger associations that prompt us to think of Hitler or Mussolini or "Papa Doc" Duvalier. The same kind of associative resonance occurs with a word like "vacation," the connotations of which far outstrip its dictionary definition: "A period of suspension of work, study, or other activity."

If words like "mother" or "vacation" are strongly connotative, words like "hypoteneuse" or "sodium bicarbonate" typically are not. Why? Because such mathematical and scientific terms are meant to express one and only one thing. They are deliberately devoid of feeling (as much as this is possible in language) in order to avoid the personal associations and emotional reverberations that other more connotatively charged words bear. As a rule, technical terms are often relatively barren of connotation. Their denotative meanings are far more important. The term "myocardial infarction," for example, refers to a particular kind of heart ailment in which the muscle tissue of the heart dies. "Coronary thrombosis" refers to a different kind of heart ailment in which a blood clot forms in the heart. Neither term, however, possesses for the nontechnical expert the imaginative power and emotional impact of "heart attack." "Heart attack" conjures up various images, feelings, and fears, perhaps even memories and other personal associations. It embodies a vivid image, especially in the word "attack." "Heart attack," moreover, is part of our linguistic and life experience in ways the more technical terms are not.

It isn't necessary to be a language expert to appreciate these distinctions between denotative and connotative meaning. Nor is it necessary to know everything about words before beginning to read poetry seriously. One pleasurable benefit of studying poetry, in fact, is an enrichment of our word hoard (an Anglo-Saxon term for vocabulary). One of the pleasures of reading poetry is seeing how poets play with the various meanings and resonances of words.

Consider, for example, the following excerpt from Emily Dickinson's "A narrow Fellow in the Grass." In these lines, in which a speaker describes a fear of snakes, the poet has selected her words for both their connotative impact and their etymological significance.

> Several of Nature's People
> I know, and they know me—
> I feel for them a transport
> Of cordiality—
>
> But never met this Fellow   5
> Attended, or alone
> Without a tighter breathing
> And Zero at the Bone—

Look first at Dickinson's description of the animals as "Nature's People," a term suggesting intimacy and friendly feeling. The word "feel" conveys the emotional character of the speaker's experience. But this feeling is intensified by the words "transport" and "cordiality." "Transport" suggests a state of being carried across or over something, usually a boundary (from the Latin *trans*, or "across," and *portare*, "to carry"). Crossing the boundary separating the human and animal worlds, the speaker experiences a feeling of "cordiality" (friendliness, or sincere fellow feeling). "Cordiality," moreover, derives from the Latin *corda*, meaning "heart." Cognates, or related derivations, occur in Italian (*cuore*), Spanish (*corazón*), and French (*cœur*)—all words for "heart." Furthermore, the connotations of "cordiality" include genuine warmth, a much closer and intimate form of feeling than would be indicated by, say, "approval" or "respect." Cordiality, then, connotes a sincere warmth of friendly feeling that is especially appropriate before the contrasting language describing the speaker's fear of snakes ("Zero at the Bone").

For poets, the "best words" are often those that do the most work: they convey feelings and imply ideas. Poets choose particular words because of their richness of implication and their range of suggestion. Consider the following poem as an example of such verbal resonance.

WILLIAM WORDSWORTH

[1770–1850]

I wandered lonely as a cloud

I wandered lonely as a cloud
That floats on high o'er vales and hills,
When all at once I saw a crowd,
A host, of golden daffodils;
Beside the lake, beneath the trees,   5
Fluttering and dancing in the breeze.

Continuous as the stars that shine
And twinkle on the milky way,
They stretched in never-ending line
Along the margin of a bay: 10
Ten thousand saw I at a glance,
Tossing their heads in sprightly dance.

The waves beside them danced; but they
Outdid the sparkling waves in glee:
A poet could not but be gay,   15
In such a jocund company:
I gazed—and gazed—but little thought
What wealth the show to me had brought:

For oft, when on my couch I lie
In vacant or in pensive mood,   20
They flash upon that inward eye
Which is the bliss of solitude;
And then my heart with pleasure fills,
And dances with the daffodils.

We can assure ourselves of the rightness or appropriateness of the poem's diction by considering the connotations of a few words. We can take lines 3 and 4 as examples.

When all at once I saw a crowd,
A host, of golden daffodils;

Suppose they had been written this way:

When all at once I spied a bunch,
A group of yellow daffodils;

Consider the connotations of each version. "Spied" may indicate something secretive or even prying about the speaker's looking. It may also suggest that he was looking for the flowers. In contrast, "saw" carries less intense and fewer connotations; it merely indicates that the speaker noticed the daffodils, and its tone is more matter-of-fact. The alternate version's "bunch" and "group" suggest, on the one hand, a smaller number than Wordsworth's corresponding "crowd" and, on the other, a less communal sense. "Crowd" and "host," moreover, carry connotations of a social gathering, of people congregated to share an experience or simply to enjoy one another's company. This implicit humanizing or personifying of the daffodils (identifying them with human actions and feelings) brings the daffodils to life: they are described as dancing and as "tossing their heads" (line 12), and they are called a "jocund company" (line 16). "Company" underscores the sociality of the daffodils and "jocund" indicates the human quality of being joyful.

This emphasis on the happiness of the daffodils and their large number serves to point up sharply the isolation and dispiritedness of the speaker. Their vast number is emphasized in the second stanza, where they are described as "continuous" and as stretching in a "never-ending line." (And, of course, in the count: "ten thousand.") But this important contrast between the isolation of the speaker and the solidarity of the daffodils, though continued into the second stanza, gives way in stanzas 3 and 4 as the speaker imagines himself among the daffodils rather than simply looking at them from a distance. More important, when he thinks about them later, he thinks about being "with" them, not literally but imaginatively.

But before we look at words in later stanzas that describe the speaker, we should return to the first adjective that describes the flowers: "golden" (line 4). Wordsworth uses "golden," not "yellow" or "amber" or "tawny," because "golden" suggests more than a color; it connotes light (it shines and glitters) and wealth (money and fortune). In fact, the speaker uses the word "wealth" in line 18 to indicate how important the experience of seeing the daffodils has been. And in the last two stanzas, we notice that the speaker uses in succession five words denoting "joy" ("glee," "gay," "jocund," "bliss," and "pleasure") in a crescendo that suggests the intensity of the speaker's happiness.

Although Wordsworth uses various words to indicate joy, he occasionally repeats rather than varies his diction. The repetitions of the words for seeing ("saw," "gazed") inaugurate and sustain the imagery of vision that is central to the poem's meaning; the forms of the verb "to dance" ("dancing," "danced," "dance," and "dances") suggest both that the various elements of nature are in harmony with one another and that nature is in harmony with man. The poet conveys this by bringing the elements of nature together in pairs: daffodils and wind (stanza 1); daffodils and water, daffodils and stars (stanza 2); water and wind (stanza 3). Nature and man come together explicitly in stanza 4, when the speaker says that his heart dances with the daffodils.

A different kind of repetition appears in the movement from the loneliness of line 1 to the solitude of line 22. Both words denote an aloneness, but they suggest a radical difference in the solitary person's attitude to his state of being alone. The poem moves from the sadly alienated separation felt by the speaker in the beginning to his joy in reimagining the natural scene, a movement framed by the words "loneliness" and "solitude." An analogous movement is suggested within the final stanza by the words "vacant" and "fills." The emptiness of the speaker's spirit is transformed into a fullness of feeling as he remembers the daffodils.

IMAGERY

We perceive the world through our senses. We see, hear, touch, taste, and smell. When poets use language in ways that stimulate our senses or our imaginative recall of sense experience, they do so by means of images. An image in poetry is thus a word or phrase that refers to a sensory experience—seeing a leaf fall, for example, or touching a marble surface. Images appeal to one or more of our senses and may be visual, auditory, olfactory, tactile, or gustatory; they refer, that is, to things seen, heard, smelled, touched, or tasted. In addition, images may be kinetic, suggesting movement, or synaesthetic, in which a single image appeals to two or more senses simultaneously.

Consider, for example, the following poem by Robert Browning, in which the poet describes a lover traveling to meet his beloved.

ROBERT BROWNING

[1812–1889]

Meeting at Night

The gray sea and the long black land;
And the yellow half-moon large and low;
And the startled little waves that leap
In fiery ringlets from their sleep,
As I gain the cove with pushing prow, *5*
And quench its speed i' the slushy sand.

Then a mile of warm sea-scented beach;
Three fields to cross till a farm appears;
A tap at the pane, the quick sharp scratch
And blue spurt of a lighted match, *10*
And a voice less loud, through its joys and fears,
Than the two hearts beating each to each!

Each line includes a specific image. In stanza 1, the imagery is largely visual (lines 1–4) and tactile (lines 5–6). We envision the sea, land, moon, and waves; we imagine the boat drag slowly across the sand. In stanza 2, images of sound (the tap at the pane, the sharp scratch of the match, the sound of speaking voice and beating hearts) accumulate to support and enrich a tactile image (the warm beach), an olfactory image (the scent of the beach), and visual images of field, farm, and blue-lit match flame. Taken together, the images allow us to imagine the experience the poet describes. In addition, they suggest the speaker's heightened awareness as he approaches his beloved. Ultimately, they convey how strongly the two lovers feel about one another, particularly in the familiar but fine image of their two hearts beating as one.

Images are not merely decorative. Poets employ them not only to stimulate our imagination, but also to convey feeling. Sometimes a poet will use a physical image to suggest an emotional experience. For example, the speaker of the following lines from William Butler Yeats's "The Lake Isle of Innisfree" describes an emotional experience in physical terms: he remembers a sound and associates it with his strong feelings for a place.

> I will arise and go now, for always night and day
> I hear lake water lapping with low sounds by the shore;
> While I stand on the roadway, or on the pavement gray,
> I hear it in the deep heart's core.

The speaker in Ezra Pound's "The River-Merchant's Wife: A Letter" describes things she sees and hears. As she awaits her husband's return from a journey, she makes us aware of her loneliness. The poet casts her thoughts in the form of a letter written to her husband.

> You went into far Ku-to-yen by the river of swirling eddies,
> And you have been gone five months.
> The monkeys make sorrowful noise overhead.
>
> You dragged your feet when you went out.
> By the gate now, the moss is grown, the different mosses   5
> Too deep to clear them away!
>
> The leaves fall early this autumn, in wind.
> The paired butterflies are already yellow with August,
> Over the grass in the West garden;
> They hurt me. I grow older.   10

The poet's images reveal the speaker's state of mind. In describing the monkeys' noise as "sorrowful," for example, the speaker provides an index of her own sorrow. This sorrow is further exemplified by her inability to clear away the deeply overgrown mosses, and even more poignantly by her description of the yellow butterflies, whose brief lives are nearly over. By noticing that the butterflies are "paired," the speaker reveals her own fear of growing old alone. The poet enriches our sense of the speaker's sadness with the image of leaves falling in autumn, which represents the twilight of life. Rather than making the speaker's feelings explicit, the poet allows his carefully chosen images to reveal her state of mind.

In our next example, the contemporary German poet Lutz Rathenow describes a heart in three different ways: as a leaf nearly destroyed by winter, as a bit of frozen snow, and as a foreign object in the body.

LUTZ RATHENOW

[b. 1952]

For Uwe Gressmann

TRANSLATED BY BORIA SAX

The heart a leaf—
It survives the Winter
crippled

Or remains ice cold—
a foreign object in the body   5
surrounded by blood

This bit of snow
that doesn't melt
that doesn't fall

Rathenow's images of the heart echo and reinforce one another. In the last stanza, in fact, the image of the heart as a bit of snow combines the images of the previous stanzas. And while it may not be strictly logical to say that the heart (or a bit of snow) "doesn't fall," Luthenow reveals the intensity of the speaker's lack of feeling and increases the intensity and power of the poem by bringing back the image of the withered leaf and linking it directly with that of the frozen heart.

In considering a poem's imagery, then, it is important to consider what the images imply—what ideas they suggest and what feelings they convey. Moreover, it is useful to look not only for relationships between images but also for patterns among them. For poets often present a unified expression of experience by means of a pattern of closely related images. Consider, for example, the relationship among the images in Wordsworth's "I wandered lonely as a cloud" (p. 21).

Although the poem's images are exclusively visual, Wordsworth is not interested in simply presenting a pretty picture of a natural scene. His images, that is, serve more than a pictorial purpose. Instead, they present an attitude toward nature that includes a belief in nature's power to restore the human spirit. And they also imply an intimacy that exists both within the natural world and between nature and man.

Wordsworth suggests the unity of nature by describing daffodils, yellow flowers that grow in clusters, fluttering in the breeze coming in off a lake. Nature here appears as wind or air, as water, and as flower (earth is implied since flowers grow in soil). Another natural element, fire, is also implied—though much more tenuously—in the daffodils' golden color, which can be related to the shining of the stars described in stanza 2. Other connections among the natural elements include that between the waves and the flowers (both dance in the wind); between the flowers and the stars (both are numerous); and between the stars and the waves (both sparkle and twinkle).

The primary concern of the poem, however, is not the unity of nature, but rather the power of nature to move the human spirit to joy. This movement occurs in three stages. First is the direct experience of nature, which the poet/speaker undergoes. Second is the poet/speaker's remembrance of that experience in all its imagistic particularity. And third is the realization of the importance of the experience, its wealth of meaning, its power to fill the heart with happiness. Wordsworth underscores the unity of the human and natural worlds in the last line, in which the speaker indicates that his heart "dances with the daffodils."

Unlike Wordsworth's poem, which, though alluding to other senses, heavily emphasizes sight and visual images, the following poem by Elizabeth Bishop includes a more extensive range of images and a more intricate set of relationships among them. Like Wordsworth's poem, however, Bishop's communicates meaning and conveys feeling by means of closely related images.

ELIZABETH BISHOP

[1911–1979]

First Death in Nova Scotia

In the cold, cold parlor
my mother laid out Arthur
beneath the chromographs:
Edward, Prince of Wales,
with Princess Alexandra,   5
and King George with Queen Mary.
Below them on the table

stood a stuffed loon
shot and stuffed by Uncle
Arthur, Arthur's father.   *10*

Since Uncle Arthur fired
a bullet into him,
he hadn't said a word.
He kept his own counsel
on his white, frozen lake,   *15*
the marble-topped table.
His breast was deep and white,
cold and caressable;
his eyes were red glass,
much to be desired.   *20*

"Come," said my mother,
"Come and say good-bye
to your little cousin Arthur."
I was lifted up and given
one lily of the valley   *25*
to put in Arthur's hand.
Arthur's coffin was
a little frosted cake,
and the red-eyed loon eyed it
from his white, frozen lake.   *30*

Arthur was very small.
He was all white, like a doll
that hadn't been painted yet.
Jack Frost had started to paint him
the way he always painted   *35*
the Maple Leaf (Forever).
He had just begun on his hair,
a few red strokes, and then
Jack Frost had dropped the brush
and left him white, forever.   *40*

The gracious royal couples
were warm in red and ermine;
their feet were well wrapped up
in the ladies' ermine trains.
They invited Arthur to be   *45*
the smallest page at court.
But how could Arthur go,
clutching his tiny lily,

> with his eyes shut up so tight
> and the roads deep in snow?   *50*

By means of images, specifically through what the young speaker sees and hears, Bishop describes a child's view of death. The poet renders the child speaker's incomprehension and confused feelings about the death of her cousin Arthur, filtering the child's perceptions through an adult sensibility. In a similar way, the poet combines a child's syntax with an adult's vocabulary, thus creating a complex double perspective through which we gain an understanding of the speaker's experience, vividly rendered in the poem's imagery.

Our first sense impression is tactile: we imagine "the cold, cold parlor." Immediately after, we see two things: a picture of the British royal family and a stuffed loon, which had been shot by the dead boy's father, also named Arthur. The second stanza describes the loon in more detail. It sits on a marble-topped table, a detail that conveys two tactile impressions, hardness and coldness. This imagery is emphasized in the description of the marble table top as the loon's "white, frozen lake."

These visual images are continued in the third stanza, in which the speaker sees her dead cousin in his coffin. She holds a long-stemmed white flower, which she puts into the dead boy's hand. The images of whiteness and cold (the frozen lake, the marble table top, and the dead, stuffed white loon of the previous stanzas) are continued: the speaker describes Arthur's coffin as a "frosted cake." The birthday cake image also indicates the limited extent of the speaker's comprehension of the reality and finality of death.

With the repeated details about the loon's red eyes and its frozen posture and base, the child unconsciously (and the poet consciously) associates the dead boy and the dead loon. This connection is further established, moreover, by the imagery of the fourth stanza, in which Arthur is described as "all white," with "a few red strokes" for his hair. Unlike the maple leaf with its complete and thorough redness, little Arthur is left "unpainted" by Jack Frost (another image of the cold) and is thus left white "forever." On the one hand, such a description clearly indicates the child's fantastic incomprehension of Arthur's death; on the other, it suggests that she intuitively senses that Arthur has been drained of color and of life. A similar combination of intuitive understanding and conscious ignorance is echoed in the speaker's comparison of Arthur with the doll. She sees how similar they look on the surface, but she does not consciously register their similar lifelessness.

The images of the final stanzas recall those of stanza 1. The royal couples of the chromographs are described as dressed in red clothes with white fur trim, details that connect directly with the dead loon. Moreover, the lily of the third stanza (white and short-lived like the boy) reappears clutched in Arthur's hand. The final image is one of whiteness and coldness: deep snow covers the cold ground where Arthur soon will lie.

The poem's concrete details, mostly visual and tactile images, strongly evoke the coldness and lifelessness of the dead child. But they suggest other things as well. The portrait of the royal family and the stuffed loon suggest something of the family's social identity—its conservatism and propriety in particular. More important, however, these details, along with the others noted above, reveal the limitation of the speaker's understanding. She sees the loon, for example, as quiet: "he hadn't said a word," and "He kept his own counsel." In addition, she fantasizes that the royal family (which she sees as very much alive in their warm furs) has invited little Arthur to serve as "the smallest page at court." Even though this may be the speaker's way of coping with death, the final two images of white lily and cold snow, and the tone in which she asks her final question, all point toward her near acknowledgment of the truth.

FIGURATIVE LANGUAGE

METAPHOR AND SIMILE

Language can conveniently be classified as either literal or figurative. When we speak literally, we mean exactly what each word conveys; when we use figurative language, we mean something other than the actual meaning of the words. "Go jump in the lake," for example, if meant literally, would be a command to leave (go) and jump (not dive or wade) into a lake (not a pond or a stream). Usually, however, such an expression is not meant literally. In telling someone to go jump in the lake we are telling them something, to be sure, but what we mean differs from the literal meaning of the words.

Of the more than two hundred fifty figures of speech, perhaps the most important for poetry are metaphor and simile. The heart of both these figures of speech is comparison, or making connections between normally unrelated things, seeing one thing in terms of another. More than 2,300 years ago Aristotle defined metaphor as "an intuitive perception of the similarity in dissimilars." And he suggested further that to be a "master of metaphor" is the greatest achievement of a writer. In our century, Robert Frost has echoed Aristotle by suggesting that metaphor is central to poetry and that poetry is essentially a way of "saying one thing and meaning another, saying one thing in terms of another."

Although both simile and metaphor involve comparisons between unlike things, simile establishes the comparison explicitly with the word *like* or *as.* Metaphor, on the other hand, employs no such explicit verbal clue. The comparison is implied in such a way that a figurative term is substituted for or identified with a literal one. "My son talks like an encyclopedia" is a simile; "my son devours ideas" is a metaphor. The difference involves more than the word *like;* the simile is more restricted in its comparative suggestion than is the metaphor. That is, the son's comparison with the encyclopedia is limited to the way he sounds when he talks. But in the more extensive metaphor of eating ideas, there is a suggestion that his appetite for ideas matches his appetite for food. It is a natural appetite, one necessary for survival.

Consider the opening line of Wordsworth's poem about the daffodils: "I wandered lonely as a cloud." The simile suggests the speaker's isolation, without indicating other ways cloud and speaker are related. The speaker later compares the daffodils with stars by means of a simile that accentuates the large number of both. In an additional comparison from the same poem, this time a metaphor, Wordsworth writes that the daffodils "flash" upon the "inward eye" of the speaker. "Flash" implies that the speaker envisions the flowers in his mind's eye, the "inward eye" of memory and imagination. Moreover, when he "sees" the daffodils in this "inward eye," the speaker realizes the "wealth" they have brought him. Here, "wealth" is also a figure of speech; Wordsworth uses it as a metaphor for joy.

Metaphor pervades language. It is so common that we can speak of "dead" metaphors—comparisons that have become so familiar we hardly notice them as metaphors at all. We speak, for example, of the legs of a table, the eye of a needle, the arms of a chair, the head of an organization. For us, roads "branch," checks "bounce," love "grows," musical instruments "sing." These metaphorical expressions are based on comparison, or analogy—the heart of metaphor.

Good poets employ metaphor and simile with skill and originality. The best of them use these figures of speech to help us see things in previously unrecognized ways. Gertrude Stein's one-line poem "A Petticoat" invites us to consider this undergarment in four different ways:

GERTRUDE STEIN

[1874–1946]

A Petticoat

A light white, a disgrace, an ink spot, a rosy charm.

And N. Scott Momaday, in a slightly longer, one-sentence poem calls our attention to the elaborate simile that governs it:

N. SCOTT MOMADAY

[b. 1934]

A Simile

What did we say to each other
that now we are as the deer
who walk in single file

with heads high
with ears forward 5
with eyes watchful
with hooves always placed on firm ground
in whose limbs there is latent flight

In addition to these examples, numerous others could be cited since simile and metaphor infuse so many poems. John Donne, in "A Valediction: Forbidding Mourning" (pp. 194–195), for example, compares the relationship between two lovers to planetary motion, to a geometrical compass, and to various properties of gold. Robert Wallace (p. 840) describes a baseball double play in terms of a dance, and in the process compares both dance and double play to a poem. Robert Frost (p. 553) compares a woman to a silken tent, describing both in language perfectly suitable for each. Robert Burns, in a famous example from "A Red, Red Rose," conveys through similes an impression of a woman and a speaker's feeling for her.

O my luve's like a red, red rose
  That's newly sprung in June;
O my luve's like the melodie
  That's sweetly played in tune.

And Sylvia Plath, in her riddling poem "Metaphors," invites us to guess the connections among her various metaphors so we can identify her poem's subject.

SYLVIA PLATH

[1932–1963]

Metaphors

I'm a riddle in nine syllables,
An elephant, a ponderous house,
A melon strolling on two tendrils.
O red fruit, ivory, fine timbers!
This loaf's big with its yeasty rising. 5
Money's new-minted in this fat purse.
I'm a means, a stage, a cow in calf.
I've a bag of green apples,
Boarded the train there's no getting off.

But these examples of simile and metaphor are fairly uncomplicated. For a more complex approach to metaphor, we can think about metaphor as *an image with implications*—imagery that conveys implied thought and feeling. Imagery shades into metaphor, as the following sonnet demonstrates.

WILLIAM SHAKESPEARE

[1564–1616]

That time of year thou may'st in me behold

That time of year thou may'st in me behold
When yellow leaves, or none, or few, do hang
Upon those boughs which shake against the cold,
Bare ruined choirs where late the sweet birds sang.
In me thou see'st the twilight of such day   5
As after sunset fadeth in the west,
Which by-and-by black night doth take away,
Death's second self that seals up all in rest.
In me thou see'st the glowing of such fire
That on the ashes of his youth doth lie,   10
As the deathbed whereon it must expire,
Consumed with that which it was nourished by.
　　This thou perceiv'st, which makes thy love more strong,
　　To love that well which thou must leave ere long.

Perhaps the first thing to mention about the poem's metaphorical language is that its images appeal to three senses: sight, hearing, and touch. Moreover, the images of the first four lines include appeals to each of these senses: we *see* the yellow leaves and bare branches; we *feel* the cold that shakes the boughs; we *hear* (in memory) the singing birds of summer.

But these concrete representations of sensory experience become more than images with emotional reverberations. They become metaphors, ways of talking about one thing in terms of something else. The first image extended into a metaphor is that of autumn, "that time of year" when leaves turn yellow and branches become bare. The fourth line extends the image by describing tree branches as a choir loft that birds have recently vacated. Because Shakespeare's speaker says that "you" (we) can behold autumn *in him* ("In me thou see'st the twilight of such day," line 5), we know that he is speaking of more than autumn. We realize that he is talking about one thing in terms of another—about ageing in terms of the seasons.

In the next four lines the metaphor of autumn gives way to another: that of twilight ending the day. The sun has set; night is coming on. The "black" night is described as taking away the sun's light (line 7); the sun's setting is seen as a dying of its light. The implied comparison of night with death is directly stated in line 8, where night is called "death's second self"; like death, night "seals up all in rest." Night's rest is, of course, temporary; death's, however, is final. The image or metaphor is both consoling (death is a kind of restful sleep) and frightening (death "seals up" life in a way that suggests there will be no unsealing).

So far we have noted two extended metaphors of autumn and of evening. Each comparison highlights the way death begins with a prelude: twilight precedes night; autumn precedes winter; illness precedes death. The speaker knows that he is in the autumn of his life, the twilight of his time. This metaphor is continued in a third image: the dying of the fire, which represents the dying out of the speaker's life. This third image emphasizes the dying out of light and the dying out of heat. Moreover, the speaker's youth is "ashes," which serve as the "deathbed" on which he will "expire" (line 11). Literally, the lines say that the fire will expire as it burns up the fuel that feeds it. As it does so, it glows with light and heat. The glowing fire is a metaphor for the speaker's life, which is presently still "glowing" but which is beginning to die out as it consumes itself. The speaker's youth, like the dying fire, has turned to ashes. We might notice that the fire will "expire," a word which means literally to "breathe out . . . to emit the last breath," an image that suggests the termination of breathing in the dying.

The final element of this image of the dying fire is given in line 12: "Consumed with that which it was nourished by." Literally, the fire consumes itself by using up its fuel, burning up logs. In its very glowing it burns toward its own extinction. Analogously, the speaker's youthful vitality consumes itself in living. His very living continues to be a dying.

OTHER FIGURES OF SPEECH

Some additional types of figurative language commonly used in poetry include *paradox,* or apparent contradiction; *hyperbole,* or overstatement; *litotes,* or understatement; *personification; synecdoche;* and *metonymy.* Paradox we have seen in Emily Dickinson's "Much Madness is divinest Sense" (p. 8), a line that seems contradictory but whose apparent contradiction can be explained. Hyperbole is found in many of John Donne's poems, including "The Sun Rising" (p. 192), in which the speaker directly addresses the sun (a figure of speech identified as *apostrophe*). The speaker tells the sun that by shining on him and his lover, the sun is shining everywhere, and in warming them, the sun is warming the entire world. The opposite of such hyperbolic overstatement is litotes, or understatement, a characteristic of some of Robert Frost's poems, including "Birches" (pp. 539–540), "Fire and Ice" (p. 543), and "Acquainted with the Night" (p. 548), among others. In litotes, poets seem to say less than they mean, leaving their readers to infer the larger implications of their deliberately played-down language. In the opening and closing lines of "Acquainted with the night," Frost's speaker says simply, "I have been one acquainted with the night." It sounds simple, as if he doesn't mean much by it. But the details of the poem suggest otherwise. By using such an understatement to counterpoint the poem's symbolic details, the poet achieves striking and memorable effects.

PERSONIFICATION

Personification is a type of comparison in which abstract concepts or inanimate objects are invested with human properties or characteristics. Examples include Wordsworth's daffodils "dancing in the breeze" and Rich's tigers "prancing un-afraid." The following brief poem illustrates personification.

WILLIAM CARLOS WILLIAMS

[1883–1963]

Winter Trees

All the complicated details
of the attiring and
the disattiring are completed!
A liquid moon
moves gently among   5
the long branches.
Thus having prepared their buds
against a sure winter
the wise trees
stand sleeping in the cold.   10

More elaborate examples of personification can be found in the odes of John Keats (pp. 370–374). This excerpt from his "Ode on Melancholy" can serve as illustration. In it, Keats personifies not an aspect of nature, like Williams, but a series of abstractions.

She [Melancholy] dwells with Beauty—Beauty that must die;
    And Joy, whose hand is ever at his lips
Bidding adieu; and aching Pleasure nigh,
    Turning to Poison while the bee-mouth sips . . .

Keats uses personification to make concrete abstract concepts such as "Beauty" and "Joy." Williams employs personification to suggest a way of thinking about the inevitability of natural processes.

SYNECDOCHE AND METONYMY

In synecdoche a part of something is substituted for the whole, as when we refer to workers as "hands," or to cars as "wheels." In metonymy one thing stands for something associated with it, as when we speak of "the oval office" to mean the president or use "the grave" to signify death.

Like other forms of comparison, synecdoche and metonymy shade into symbol. It isn't far from associating one thing with another to letting one thing stand for or represent another, which is the essence of symbolism. In fact, although we speak of image, metaphor, and symbol as discrete aspects of poetry, there is really a continuity among them. In discussing Shakespeare's sonnet "That time of year thou may'st in me behold," for example, we commented on how its images become metaphors for human experience. We can move one step further and see the poem as a symbol of human feeling. Its patterns of imagery and metaphor combine to produce a symbol of fading life. This symbolism is perhaps most powerfully evident in the image of the dying fire, which represents the speaker's life. The fire, burning toward its own extinction, symbolizes the speaker's glowing life, which is being consumed in his very living.

SYMBOL

Like metaphor, symbolism is a way of describing one thing in terms of another. A symbol is an object that stands for something beyond itself, a feeling perhaps, or an abstract idea, or an experience. A rose can represent beauty or love or mortality; a lily can stand for purity or innocence. Ashes can represent death; birds can symbolize freedom. Light and darkness can stand for life and death, knowledge and ignorance, joy and sorrow. The possibilities are nearly endless.

The meaning of a symbol is controlled by its context. Whether fire symbolizes lust, rage, destruction, or purification (or nothing beyond itself) is determinable only within the context of a particular poem. Nor is there any limit to how many symbolic meanings an object, character, or gesture may possess—even within the context of a single poem. In long poems especially, poets may shift the meanings of their symbols.

Deciding on the symbolic significance of a poetic detail is not always an easy matter. Even when we are confident that something is symbolic, it is not often easy to determine just what the symbol represents. Like all inferences we make in interpreting poetry, the decision to view something as symbolic depends partly on our skill in reading and partly on whether the poetic context invites and rewards a symbolic interpretation.

Consider, for example, the following poem from this standpoint.

ROBERT FROST

[1874–1963]

Nothing Gold Can Stay

Nature's first green is gold,
Her hardest hue to hold.
Her early leaf's a flower;
But only so an hour.
Then leaf subsides to leaf.   5
So Eden sank to grief,
So dawn goes down to day.
Nothing gold can stay.

Frost's examples seem to suggest that whatever gold symbolizes (the good, the true, the beautiful), it does not remain; it does not last. Traditionally, however, gold has represented wealth and value; it has stood for those things we hold dear. Since poets do not explain their symbols, Frost does not specify precisely what "gold" symbolizes in the poem. The poem's overall concern, however, is with transience, with the ephemerality of things precious and valuable. Yet we might consider the poem's symbolism and meaning another way: that the most transient things are most valuable *because* they don't last. We value them because we can't retain them forever.

Frost's examples are drawn mostly from nature: "dawn," which begins the day in golden splendor, diminishes to the mere ordinariness of "day." The initial golden green of a tree's first blossom is quickly followed by a greener leaf, with the golden flower lasting only a brief time. And as in nature, so in the story of Eden—one of the myths of the "golden age," a time of perfection, innocence, and harmony. These few, carefully selected examples imply that the "golden" aspects of human experience are equally ephemeral. Specifically what these may be, however, Frost leaves for us to decide. It seems reasonable, however, to assume that "life" itself is one of them, one we treasure all the more for our short hold on it.

ALLUSION

"Nothing Gold Can Stay" contains an allusion, or reference, to the biblical story of the Garden of Eden. This story of humankind's fall from grace and banishment from

Paradise is found in the second chapter of Genesis. For most readers of Frost's poem this allusion poses no problem; they know the story and can recognize the allusion. But consider the allusions in the following poem.

W I L L I A M   B L A K E

[1757–1827]

Mock on, Mock on, Voltaire, Rousseau

Mock on, Mock on, Voltaire, Rousseau;
Mock on, Mock on, 'tis all in vain.
You throw the sand against the wind,
And the wind blows it back again.

And every sand becomes a Gem   5
Reflected in the beams divine;
Blown back, they blind the mocking Eye,
But still in Israel's paths they shine.

The atoms of Democritus
And Newton's Particles of light   10
Are sands upon the Red Sea shore,
Where Israel's tents do shine so bright.

Blake mingles biblical references to the Israelites with allusions to four historical figures: the French writer Voltaire (1694–1778); the French philosopher Rousseau (1712–1778); the English physicist and mathematician Newton (1642–1727); and the Greek philosopher Democritus (c. 460–c. 370 B.C.). Without some knowledge of both the biblical allusions and the philosophical and scientific ideas associated with these historical figures, interpreting Blake's poem is difficult. At the very least, readers need to know that Democritus's philosophy centers on the theory that the world and everything in it is composed of atoms, the smallest constituent particles of matter. Democritus was a materialist, for whom spiritual properties simply did not exist. Newton described nature in terms of inanimate particles of light. Like Democritus, his science attempted to explain the mystery of the universe in scientific terms. Voltaire and Rousseau, though not scientist–philosophers like Democritus and Newton, were thinkers who had little if any use for religious belief and spiritual vision. Both diminished faith and exalted reason.

Blake thus alludes to those who mock religious faith and spiritual vision. He also alludes to God's chosen people, the Israelites, who crossed the Red Sea (line 11) when God miraculously parted its waters, a story recounted in the book of

Exodus. Knowing what these allusions refer to enables readers to make the connections necessary to understand the poem. In simple terms, Blake celebrates the power of God and things spiritual while indicting the inadequacy of human reason to arrive at truth.

TONE

When we read a poem or listen to it read aloud, we hear a particular tone, or implied attitude that the poet and/or speaker takes toward its subject. Tone is an abstraction we make from the details of a poem's language. We derive our sense of the poem's tone, or its implied attitude toward its subject, from the poet's inclusion of certain kinds of details and the exclusion of other kinds; from the use of meter and rhyme; from choices of words and sentence patterns; from particular uses of imagery and figures of speech. In listening to a poem's language, in hearing its voice tones, we catch its feeling and, ultimately, its meaning.

The range of tones we find in poems is as diverse and complex as the range of voices and attitudes we discern in everyday experience. Moreover, some poems maintain a consistent tone throughout, as does this brief poem by the modern Greek poet C. P. Cavafy.

C. P. CAVAFY

[1863–1933]

As Much As You Can

TRANSLATED BY RAE DALVEN

And if you cannot make your life as you want it,
at least try this
as much as you can: do not disgrace it
in the crowding contact with the world
in the many movements and all the talk.   5

Do not disgrace it by taking it,
dragging it around often and exposing it
to the daily folly
of relationships and associations,
till it becomes like an alien burdensome life.   10

The speaker's tone remains resigned yet admonitory. He accepts a diminution of his life's prospects while encouraging the person addressed to retain his or her dignity.

In contrast to the consistent tone of "As Much As You Can," some poems include changes in tone, as does this brief lyric by the Russian poet Alexander Pushkin.

ALEXANDER PUSHKIN

[1799–1837]

Old Man

TRANSLATED BY BABETTE DEUTSCH

I am no more the ardent lover
Who caused the world such vast amaze:
My spring is past, my summer over,
And dead the fires of other days.
Oh, Eros, god of youth! your servant   5
Was loyal—that you will avow.
Could I be born again this moment,
Ah, with what zest I'd serve you now!

The first four lines sound matter-of-fact, even resigned. But in line five, the speaker's "Oh" indicates a dramatic shift of feeling. This exclamation introduces a new and more complex tone that combines regret for lost opportunities with something approximating hope—or at least an imaginative pleasure in thinking about how the speaker's life might have been different.

Whether a poem's tone changes or remains constant, tone is an important dimension of its meaning. Sometimes, however, it is not so easy to determine just what that tone is. Consider the tone of the following poem.

THEODORE ROETHKE

[1908–1963]

My Papa's Waltz

The whiskey on your breath
Could make a small boy dizzy;
But I hung on like death:
Such waltzing was not easy.

We romped until the pans   *5*
Slid from the kitchen shelf;
My mother's countenance
Could not unfrown itself.

The hand that held my wrist
Was battered on one knuckle;   *10*
At every step you missed
My right ear scraped a buckle.

You beat time on my head
With a palm caked hard by dirt,
Then waltzed me off to bed   *15*
Still clinging to your shirt.

The speaker, now a man, remembers when as a boy, his father would "waltz" him around the house rather roughly en route to putting him to bed. The dance is described as a romp through the house by father and son, while the mother watches, her frown indicating disapproval. The dance is rough because the boy's father presumably has been drinking. The boy is described as "clinging" to his father's shirt, but the language doesn't clarify whether that clinging is characterized by fear or joy—or both. It's not entirely clear, that is, whether the rough dance exemplifies an intimate and characteristic expression of male affection. The speaker's memory of his father as "papa" coupled with the poem's energetic and high-spirited rhythm seem to counter any indication that the father's drinking or the son's fear are its central concerns. The speaker's response seems more complex than either of those explanations suggests.

IRONY

One of the more important tones found in poems is that of irony. Irony is not so much an element of poetry as a tone of voice and an attitude found in it. Irony may appear in poetry in three ways: in a poem's language, in its description of incident, and in its point of view. But in whatever form it appears, irony always involves a contrast or discrepancy between one thing and another. The contrast may be between what is said and what is meant, a form of verbal irony; between what happens and what is expected to happen, a form of situational irony; between what a character sees and what readers see, a form of dramatic irony.

Verbal irony appears in Stephen Crane's "War Is Kind," in which the speaker's words seem to say one thing (that war is kind) but actually mean the opposite (that war is actually brutal). Crane accentuates the opposition between what the words say literally and what they mean figuratively (ironically) by including numerous details that depict the horrors of war.

STEPHEN CRANE

[1871–1900]

War Is Kind

Do not weep, maiden, for war is kind.
Because your lover threw wild hands toward the sky
And the affrighted steed ran on alone,
Do not weep.
War is kind.   5

       Hoarse, booming drums of the regiment,
       Little souls who thirst for fight,
       These men were born to drill and die.
       The unexplained glory flies above them,
       Great is the battle god, great, and his kingdom   10
       A field where a thousand corpses lie.

Do not weep, babe, for war is kind.
Because your father tumbled in the yellow trenches,
Raged at his breast, gulped and died,
Do not weep.   15
War is kind.

       Swift blazing flag of the regiment,
       Eagle with crest of red and gold,
       These men were born to drill and die.
       Point for them the virtue of slaughter,   20
       Make plain to them the excellence of killing
       And a field where a thousand corpses lie.

Mother whose heart hung humble as a button
On the bright splendid shroud of your son,
Do not weep.   25
War is kind.

How do we know that the speaker's attitude towards war is not what his words indicate, that his words are ironic? We know because the details of death in battle are antithetical to the consoling refrain of stanzas 1, 3, and 5: "Do not weep. / War is kind." Moreover, the details of stanzas 2 and 4 also work toward the same ironic end, but in a different way. Instead of the ironic consoling voice of stanzas 1, 3, and 5 (which of course offers no real consolation given the brutality described), stanzas 2 and 4 sound more supportive of military glory: Crane uses a marchlike rhythm along with words connoting military glory in a context that makes them sound hollow and false.

Situational irony, also known as irony of circumstance, can be illustrated with A. E. Housman's "Is my team plowing." Housman's speaker has died and speaks from beyond death to ask about events occurring in the world of the living. He wonders, for example, about his fiancée's happiness, imagining her still to be mourning his death. This dead speaker is answered by another, living one, his friend, who answers each of the first speaker's questions. His answer to the dead speaker's final question contains a surprising revelation. For there we discover something that the dead speaker neither desired nor suspected. Moreover, it is not clear whether he fully understands the implications of what the living speaker is telling him. For the reader, however, the implications are unmistakably ironic.

A. E. HOUSMAN

[1859–1936]

Is my team plowing

"Is my team plowing,
    That I was used to drive
And hear the harness jingle
    When I was man alive?"

Ay, the horses trample,   5
    The harness jingles now;
No change though you lie under
    The land you used to plow.

"Is football playing
    Along the river shore,   10
With lads to chase the leather,
    Now I stand up no more?"

Ay, the ball is flying,
    The lads play heart and soul;
The goal stands, up, the keeper   15
    Stands up to keep the goal.

"Is my girl happy,
    That I thought hard to leave,
And has she tired of weeping
    As she lies down at eve?"   20

Ay, she lies down lightly,
    She lies not down to weep:
Your girl is well contented.
    Be still, my lad, and sleep.

"Is my friend hearty,   25
    Now I am thin and pine,
And has he found to sleep in
    A better bed than mine?"

Yes, lad, I lie easy,
    I lie as lads would choose;   30
I cheer a dead man's sweetheart,
    Never ask me whose.

Dramatic irony occurs when the perceptions of characters differ from those of readers. In dramatic irony characters see and understand things one way while readers see and understand them in a different, often opposite way. Dramatic irony can be illustrated by Thomas Hardy's "The Ruined Maid," in which two friends meet and discuss their different lives. Hardy lets the reader see 'Melia's situation differently than either she sees herself or her companion sees her.

THOMAS HARDY

[1840–1928]

The Ruined Maid

"O 'Melia, my dear, this does everything crown!
Who could have supposed I should meet you in Town?
And whence such fair garments, such prosperi-ty?"
"O didn't you know I'd been ruined?" said she.

"You left us in tatters, without shoes or socks,   5
Tired of digging potatoes, and spudding up docks;
And now you've gay bracelets and bright feathers three!"
"Yes: that's how we dress when we're ruined," said she.

"At home in the barton you said 'thee' and 'thou,'
And 'thik oon,' and 'theäs oon,' and 't'other'; but now   10
Your talking quite fits 'ee for high compa-ny!"
"Some polish is gained with one's ruin," said she.

"Your hands were like paws then, your face blue and bleak
But now I'm bewitched by your delicate cheek,
And your little gloves fit as on any la-dy!"   15
"We never do work when we're ruined," said she.

"You used to call home-life a hag-ridden dream,
And you'd sigh, and you'd sock; but at present you seem
To know not of megrims° or melancho-ly!"   *low spirits*
"True. One's pretty lively when ruined," said she.   20

"I wish I had feathers, a fine sweeping gown,
And a delicate face, and could strut about Town!"
"My dear—a raw country girl, such as you be,
Cannot quite expect that. You ain't ruined," said she.

As in Housman's "Is my team plowing," Hardy's "The Ruined Maid" in-
cludes two speakers. The first speaker is a poor unnamed country girl; the second
is Amelia, or, as the speaker calls her, 'Melia. 'Melia has left her little country village
for the splendors of the larger life of the town. There, according to the perspective
of the first speaker, 'Melia has achieved "prosperi-ty." 'Melia's prosperity, however,
has been achieved by becoming "ruined," by selling her body in prostitution,
perhaps by being kept as a rich man's mistress. Part of the poem's irony resides in
the first speaker's lack of understanding of just what 'Melia has given up to achieve
her new position. The poor country girl wants nothing more than to wear fine
clothes and strut about town like her former country friend. Her last comment in
the final stanza suggests as much. But following this last remark of the country girl,
Hardy turns the irony against the town girl, whose ungrammatical country speech
reveals her as one who is still very much the raw, rustic girl she sees her old friend
as being. Hardy, in short, sees 'Melia differently than she sees herself. And so,
ultimately, do we.

SYNTAX

Syntax is the order or sequence of words in a sentence. Poets occasionally alter the
normal syntactic order for such purposes as creating a powerful emotional stimulus,
effecting a sense of movement, or imitating the action the words of the poem
describe. Poets may invert normal word order, as Robert Frost does in the opening
line of "Stopping by Woods on a Snowy Evening": "Whose woods these are I think
I know." By reversing the two units of four words (I think I know; whose woods
these are) Frost avoids the conventional word order of everyday speech. At the same
time, however, he keeps close to the sounds of colloquial speech. The effect is thus
to lift the line a bit above everyday speech without making it sound unduly "poetic."
And perhaps most important, Frost's inverted syntax creates an emphasis the normal
word order lacks.

Emily Dickinson's inversions of normal word order create a different effect: usually one of compression, as in these lines:

> Tell all the Truth but tell it slant—
> Success in Circuit lies
> Too bright for our infirm Delight
> The Truth's superb surprise

Dickinson inverts normal syntax in the second line after establishing it in line 1. She then alters word order more dramatically by reversing the order of lines 3 and 4. The difference is apparent upon comparing a reconstruction of Dickinson's lines in a more conventional syntactic arrangement:

> Tell all the Truth but tell it slant
> [For] Success lies in Circuit.
> The superb surprise [of] Truth's
> Too bright for our infirm delight.

With the more conventional syntax we lose the steady rhythm that beats in Dickinson's original lines. We also lose her rhyme and emphasis. The alternative rendering of her lines also requires the inclusion of additional words to make sense. And finally, Dickinson's original inverted syntax illustrate what the lines say. Her word order makes a significant difference.

Other forms of syntactic structuring poets use include balance and symmetry, as illustrated by Alexander Pope's "An Essay on Man." In balanced syntax, words are arranged so that phrases, lines, or parts of lines are set off against one another. Such pairings of phrases and lines may parallel one another so that one line or phrase echoes or repeats the idea of another. Or the pairings may be contrastive so that one line or phrase stands in opposition to another. Lines exhibit symmetry when the syntactic balance is exact, as in lines 5–6 of the following example. Pope employs both parallel and contrastive balances.

ALEXANDER POPE

[1688–1744]

from *An Essay on Man*

> Know then thyself, presume not God to scan;
> The proper study of mankind is Man.
> Placed on this isthmus of a middle state,
> A being darkly wise, and rudely great:
> With too much knowledge for the skeptic side,   5
> With too much weakness for the Stoic's pride,

He hangs between; in doubt to act, or rest,
In doubt to deem himself a god, or beast;
In doubt his mind or body to prefer,
Born but to die, and reasoning but to err. . . .   *10*
Created half to rise, and half to fall;
Great lord of all things, yet a prey to all;
Sole judge of truth, in endless error hurled:
The glory, jest, and riddle of the world!

Pope's balanced syntax neatly captures man's dual nature. On the one hand, man is a great lord of creation, the glory of the world, a rational, wise, godlike creature. On the other, he is not great but rude, not possessed of certain knowledge but adrift in uncertainty and ignorance. He is less a master than a victim of creation, less the glory of the world than something to be puzzled over and laughed at. In employing a syntactic structure so well suited to his subject, Pope employs what we can call mimetic syntax—a word order that imitates what it describes.

A variant of mimetic syntax is fractured or broken syntax, in which the poet reorders the conventional arrangement of subject, verb, and object not so much to imitate the idea expressed but to alter our experience in reading the rearranged words. Consider the use of fractured syntax in the following poem:

E. E. CUMMINGS

[1894–1962]

Me up at does

Me up at does

out of the floor
quietly Stare

a poisoned mouse
still who alive   *5*

is asking What
have i done that

You wouldn't have

In order to make sense of this poem, we must first rearrange it in conventional syntax. We can begin with the subject of the sentence in something like the following manner: "A poisoned mouse, who, still alive, is asking what have i done that you wouldn't have, does quietly stare out of the floor up at me." By inverting and fracturing syntax the way he does, Cummings surprises us into looking more closely not only at his language, but at the experience it conveys. The emotional and intellectual experiences of reading Cummings's original poem and our revision differ significantly. Cummings's redistribution of words on the page and his unusual syntactic arrangement compel us to look more deliberately at his subject. We are made to see much more clearly the mouse's point of view. Instead of a speaker looking down at a dying mouse, Cummings creates a perspective in which the mouse is looking up at his executioner. Cummings emphasizes this perspective by reversing the order of subject and predicate and by dispersing phrases in short poetic lines that focus on one aspect of the experience at a time. The poet further emphasizes the unusual relationship between mouse and speaker by using conventional word order in the last three lines.

Poets use other syntactic patterns, including ordering words to reflect the mental associations of a poem's speaker—as in T. S. Eliot's "The Love Song of J. Alfred Prufrock" (pp. 642–646). In such poems, sentences may be interrupted by words that refer to something in the past while the speaker is speaking of something else in the present. Syntax may also follow patterns of rhetorical persuasiveness, as in Alfred, Lord Tennyson's "Ulysses" (pp. 395–397). In such poems, lines, phrases, and sentences suggest a carefully worded argument, a speech given to persuade an audience to take a particular course of action. Syntax may also be arranged to create continuity, as in Robert Frost's "The Silken Tent" (p. 553), or to imitate the ruptured halting quality of broken speech, as in Thomas Hardy's "The Man He Killed" (pp. 478–479). In the first case, Frost spins out one single, smoothly flowing sentence over fourteen lines of a sonnet. In the second instance, Hardy uses interrupted words—included between dashes—to suggest the speaker's confusion. These and other deviations from normal sentence patterns are expressive. They intensify our experience of reading poetry; they sharpen our appreciation of the power of language and the beauty of form.

SOUNDS

The most familiar element of poetry is *rhyme*, which can be defined as the matching of final vowel and consonant sounds in two or more words. When the corresponding sounds occur at the ends of lines, we have *end rhyme*; when they occur within lines, we have *internal rhyme*. The opening stanza of Edgar Allan Poe's "The Raven" illustrates both:

> Once upon a midnight dreary, while I pondered weak and weary,
> Over many a quaint and curious volume of forgotten lore—
> While I nodded nearly napping, suddenly there came a tapping,
> As of some one gently rapping, rapping at my chamber door.
> " 'Tis some visiter," I muttered, "tapping at my chamber door—   5
> Only this and nothing more."

For the reader rhyme is a pleasure, for the poet a challenge. Part of its pleasure for the reader is in anticipating and hearing a poem's echoing song. Part of its challenge for the poet is in rhyming naturally, without forcing the rhythm, the syntax, or the sense. When the challenge is met successfully, the poem is a pleasure to listen to; it sounds natural to the ear. An added bonus is that rhyme makes it easier to remember.

Robert Frost's "Stopping by Woods on a Snowy Evening" is one such rhyming success. Reread it a few times, preferably aloud, and listen to its music.

ROBERT FROST

[1874–1963]

Stopping by Woods on a Snowy Evening

Whose woods these are I think I know.
His house is in the village, though;
He will not see me stopping here
To watch his woods fill up with snow.

My little horse must think it queer   5
To stop without a farmhouse near
Between the woods and frozen lake
The darkest evening of the year.

He gives his harness bells a shake
To ask if there is some mistake.   10
The only other sound's the sweep
Of easy wind and downy flake.

The woods are lovely, dark, and deep,
But I have promises to keep,
And miles to go before I sleep,   15
And miles to go before I sleep.

Notice how in each of the first three stanzas, three of the four lines rhyme (lines 1, 2, and 4). Frost picks up the nonrhymed sound of the third line of each stanza and links it with the rhyming sound of the stanza that follows it, until the fourth stanza, when he closes with four matching rhymes. Part of our pleasure in Frost's rhyming may derive from the pattern of departure and return it voices. Part may stem also from the way the rhyme pattern supports the poem's meaning. The speaker is caught between his desire to remain still, peacefully held by the serene beauty of the woods, and his contrasting need to leave, to return to his responsibilities. In a similar way, the poem's rhyme is caught between a surge forward toward a new sound and a return to a sound repeated earlier. The pull and counterpull of the rhyme reflect the speaker's ambivalence.

The rhymes in Frost's poem are *exact* or *perfect rhymes:* that is, the rhyming words share corresponding sounds and stresses and a similar number of syllables. While Frost's poem contains perfect rhymes ("know," "though," and "snow," for example), we sometimes hear in poems a less exact, *imperfect, approximate,* or *slant rhyme.* Emily Dickinson's "Crumbling is not an instant's Act" (p. 61) includes both exact rhyme ("dust"–"rust") and slant rhyme ("slow"–"law"). Theodore Roethke's "My Papa's Waltz" (pp. 39–40) contains a slant rhyme on ("*dizzy*"–"*easy*"), which also exemplifies *feminine rhyme.* In feminine rhyme the final syllable of a rhymed word is unstressed; in *masculine rhyme* the final syllable is stressed—or the words rhymed are each of only one syllable.

Besides rhyme, two other forms of sound play prevail in poetry: *alliteration,* or the repetition of consonant sounds, especially at the beginning of words, and *assonance,* or the repetition of vowel sounds. In his witty guide to poetic technique, *Rhyme's Reason,* John Hollander describes alliteration and assonance like this:

> Assonance is the spirit of a rhyme,
> A common vowel, hovering like a sigh
> After its consonantal body dies. . . .
>
> . . . .
>
> Alliteration lightly links
> Stressed syllables with common consonants.

Walt Whitman's "When I Heard the Learn'd Astronomer," (p. 16) though it does not include end rhyme, possesses a high degree of assonance. The long *i*'s in lines 1, 3, and 4 accumulate and gather force as the poem glides into its last four lines: "*I*," "*tired*," "*rising*," "*gliding*," "*I*," "*myself*," "*night*," "*time to time*," and "*silence*." This assonance sweetens the sound of the poem, highlighting its shift of action and feeling.

Both alliteration and assonance are clearly audible in "Stopping by Woods," particularly in the third stanza:

> He gives his harness bells a shake
> To ask if there is some mistake.
> The only other sound's the sweep
> Of easy wind and downy flake.

Notice that the long *e* of "sweep" is echoed in "*easy*" and "*downy*," and that the *ow* of "*downy*" echoes the same sound in "*sound's*." These repetitions of sound accentuate the images the words embody, aural images (wind-blow and snowfall), tactile images (the soft fluff of down and the feel of the gently blowing wind), and visual images (the white flakes of snow).

The alliterative *s*'s in "*some*," "*sound*," and "*sweep*" are supported by the internal and terminal *s*'s: "Gives," "his," "harness bells," and "is," and also by midword *s*'s: "a*s*k," "mi*s*take," and "ea*s*y." There is a difference in the weight of these sounds; some are heavier than others—the two similar heavy *s*'s of "ea*s*y" and "hi*s*" contrast with the lighter, softer "*s*" in "harne*ss*" and "mi*s*take."

In the following playful poem Helen Chasin gets her mouth around the sound of the word "plum." Notice how Chasin sounds the letters of the word as she captures the experience of eating a plum along with the experience of pronouncing the word. To do this she relies heavily on assonance and alliteration.

HELEN CHASIN

[b. 1938]

The Word Plum

The word *plum* is delicious

pout and push, luxury of
self-love, and savoring murmur

full in the mouth and falling
like fruit   5

taut skin
pierced, bitten, provoked into
juice, and tart flesh

question
and reply, lip and tongue   10
of pleasure.

For a more elaborate and intricate display of sound effects, listen to the music of the following poem.

GERARD MANLEY HOPKINS

[1844–1889]

In the Valley of the Elwy

I remember a house where all were good
To me, God knows, deserving no such thing:
Comforting smell breathed at very entering,

Fetched fresh, as I suppose, off some sweet wood.
That cordial air made those kind people a hood   5
   All over, as a bevy of eggs the mothering wing
   Will, or mild nights the new morsels of Spring:
Why, it seemed of course; seemed of right it should.

Lovely the woods, waters, meadows, combes, vales,
All the air things wear that build this world of Wales;   10
   Only the inmate does not correspond:

God, lover of souls, swaying considerate scales,
Complete thy creature dear O where it fails,
   Being mighty a master, being a father and fond.

We note first that the rhyme scheme reveals a Petrarchan sonnet: *abba, abba, ccd, ccd* (see p. 1055). We might note, too, that its rhyme pattern corresponds to its sentence structure: the octave splits into two sentences, lines 1–4 and 5–8; the sestet, though only one sentence, splits into two equal parts, lines 9–11 and 12–14. Hopkins's use of the Italian rhyme scheme keeps similar sounds repeating throughout: *good, wood, hood, should; thing, entering, wing, Spring; vales, Wales, scales, fails; correspond, fond.* (The rhyme pattern of the Shakespearean or English sonnet, by contrast, as heard in "That time of year"—page 32—contains fewer rhyming repetitions, as it uses a greater number of different sounds.)

Besides extensive rhyme, Hopkins uses alliteration and assonance—lightly in the octave and more heavily in the sestet. Lines 3–6, for example, collect short *e*'s in "sm*e*ll," "v*e*ry," "*e*ntering," "f*e*tched" and "fr*e*sh," "b*e*vy" and "*e*ggs." Lines 4–8 begin an alliterative use of *w*, which is more elaborately sounded in lines 9–10 of the sestet; in lines 4–8 we hear: "*sw*eet *w*ood," "*w*ing *W*ill," and "*w*hy." In addition, in line 7 "m*i*ld n*i*ghts" picks up the long *i* of "Why," which finds an echo in the rhyme on "r*i*ght." This seventh line also contains what we might call a reversed or crisscrossed alliteration in "*m*ild *n*ights" and "*n*ew *m*orsels."

But these sound effects are only a pale indication of what we hear in the sestet. Perhaps the most musical lines of the entire poem are the opening lines of the sestet (lines 9–10). *L*'s frame both of these lines: "*L*ovely . . . va*l*es" and "A*ll* . . . Wa*l*es." *L*'s are further sounded in "bui*l*d this wor*l*d." The *w*, which as we noted ended the octave, is carried into the sestet in "*w*oods," "*w*aters," "meado*w*s," "*w*ear," "*w*orld," and "*W*ales." The sestet also includes a variety of vowels: l*o*vely, w*oo*ds, w*a*ter, m*ea*d*o*ws, c*o*mbes, v*a*les, *a*ll, *ai*r, w*ea*r, th*a*t, b*ui*ld, th*i*s, w*o*rld, W*a*les.

Hopkins sounds a similarly varied vowel music in the last line, where he also uses alliteration and repetition to call attention to important attributes of God:

    Being mighty a master, being a father and fond.

One line, however, in particular lacks music: line 11. Coming amid such splendid sounds, it stands out even more sharply:

Only the inmate does not correspond.

This expressive use of sound variation supports the idea that the line conveys: that in this beautiful natural world, the "inmate," the speaker in the guise of prisoner, does not fit. He feels out of place, out of harmony with his environment. In the lines that follow (12–14), he asks God to "complete" him, to make him whole, to integrate him into the world. And he prays in language that immediately picks up the sound play of assonance and alliteration that had been momentarily suspended in line 11. The speaker's harmony and wholeness are thus restored in the poem's beauty of sound.

RHYTHM AND METER

Rhythm is the pulse, or beat, we feel in a line of prose, poetry, or music. Rhythm is a pattern of regularly recurring accents, or stresses, on the syllables of words in poem or song. We are familiar with such rhythmic patterning from patriotic songs such as "America the Beautiful," whose accented, or stressed, syllables we have capitalized.

> oh BEAUtiFUL for SPAcious SKIES
> for AMber WAVES of GRAIN
> for PURple MOUNtains' MAJesTY
> aBOVE the FRUIted PLAIN
>
> aMERiCA aMERiCA   5
> God SHED his GRACE on THEE
> and CROWN thy GOOD with BROtherHOOD
> from SEA to SHIning SEA.

An alternative and more conventional way to represent accented or stressed syllables is with a diagonal slash over the syllable: ′. Unaccented syllables are marked with a short line curving upward: ◡. We can mark the syllables of words to indicate stress in any text, whether poetry or prose. Here, for example, is the opening sentence of Charles Dickens's novel *A Tale of Two Cities* with stress markings:

It was the best of times; it was the worst of times

And here are portions of two familiar nursery rhymes, also with their accented syllables identified.

Baa, baa black sheep! Have you any wool?
London Bridge is falling down
Falling down, falling down,
London Bridge is falling down
My fair lady.

Poets rely on rhythm to express meaning and convey feeling. The following couplet by Robert Frost uses rhythm expressively.

ROBERT FROST

[1874–1963]

The Span of Life

The old dog barks backward without getting up.
I can remember when he was a pup.

The first line is slower than the second. It is harder to pronounce and takes longer to say because Frost clusters the hard consonant sounds—*d, k,* and *g*—in the first line, and because the first line contains seven stresses to the four of line 2. Three of the seven stresses in the first line fall at the beginning, which gets it off to a halting start, whereas the accents of the second line are more evenly spaced. The contrasting rhythms of the lines reinforce their contrasting images and sound effects. More important, however, the differences in sound and rhythm echo the lines' contrast of youth and age, which is the poem's theme, as suggested by its title, "The Span of Life."

The following poem, Louis Simpson's "The Heroes," marches to a different beat, grouping syllables in threes rather than twos. Its rhythm conveys both meaning and tone.

LOUIS SIMPSON

[b. 1923]

The Heroes

I dreamed of war-heroes, of wounded war-heroes
With just enough of their charms shot away
To make them more handsome. The women moved nearer
To touch their brave wounds and their hair streaked with grey.

I saw them in long ranks ascending the gang-planks;   5

The girls with the doughnuts were cheerful and gay.

They minded their manners and muttered their thanks;

The chaplain advised them to watch and to pray.

They shipped these rapscallions, these sea-sick battalions

To a patriotic and picturesque spot;   10

They gave them new bibles and marksmen's medallions,

compasses, maps, and committed the lot.

A fine dust has settled on all that scrap metal.

The heroes were packaged and sent home in parts

To pluck at a poppy and sew on a petal   15

And count the long night by the stroke of their hearts.

But we cannot proceed any further in this discussion without introducing more precise terms to refer to the patterns of accent we hear in poems. If rhythm is the pulse or beat we hear in the poetic line, then we can define *meter* as the measure or patterned count of accent or syllable group in the line. Just as music is divided into measures with accented and unaccented beats, so too language is divided into patterns of stressed and unstressed syllables. The basic unit of meter in poetry is called the foot. Depending upon where the stresses fall, a poetic foot may be iambic, trochaic, anapestic, or dactylic. An iambic foot, or iamb ($\smile\prime$), is a two-syllable foot consisting of an unaccented syllable followed by an accented one, as in the words helLO and goodBYE. If we reverse the order of accented and unaccented syllables, placing the stress on the first syllable, we have a trochaic foot, or trochee ($\prime\smile$), as in the words STOry and MUsic. Because both iambic and trochaic feet contain two syllables per foot, they are called duple (or double) meters. These duple meters are distinguished from the triple meters (three-syllable feet) of anapestic and dactylic meters. An anapestic foot, or anapest ($\smile\smile\prime$), consists of two unaccented syllables followed by an accented one, as in obsoLETE and interJECT. A dactylic foot, or dactyl ($\prime\smile\smile$), reverses the anapest's order of accents and consists of an accented syllable followed by two unaccented ones. DANgerous and CHEERfully are examples. So is the word ANapest.

Three additional points must be noted about poetic meter. First, anapestic ($\smile\smile\prime$) and iambic ($\smile\prime$) meters move from an unstressed syllable to a stressed one. For this reason they are called *rising* meters (they "rise" to the stressed syllable). Lines in anapestic or iambic meter almost always end with a stressed syllable. Trochaic ($\prime\smile$) and dactylic ($\prime\smile\smile$) meters, on the other hand, are said to be *falling* meters because they begin with a stressed syllable (they "fall" in pitch and emphasis). Thus, syllables at the ends of trochaic and dactylic lines are generally unstressed.

Second, we give names to lines of poetry based on the number of feet they contain. An eight-syllable, or octosyllabic, line composed of four iambic feet is called iambic tetrameter. "Iambic" describes the metrical pattern; "tetrameter" indicates the number of feet in each line (from the Greek word *tetra,* meaning "four"). Robert Frost's "Stopping by Woods on a Snowy Evening" (p. 48) is one poem written in iambic tetrameter. His sonnet "The Silken Tent" (p. 553), which contains ten-syllable lines in an iambic meter, is described as being in iambic pentameter (from the Greek *penta,* meaning "five"). Sonnets, in fact, are written in iambic pentameter.

Third, the regularity of a poem's meter is usually flexible. In a predominantly iambic or trochaic poem, not every line will conform exactly to the metrical pattern. Metrical variation is evident in Simpson's "The Heroes" (lines 5 and 12), in Shakespeare's "That time of year thou may'st in me behold" (lines 4, 8, 11, and 13), in Roethke's "My Papa's Waltz" (lines 6 and 14), and in Whitman's "When I Heard the Learn'd Astronomer," in which the iambic pentameter of the final line contrasts with its absence in all previous lines.

The following chart summarizes the various meters and poetic feet.

	Foot	Meter	Example
Rising or ascending feet	iamb	iambic	hello
	anapest	anapestic	obsolete
Falling or descending feet	trochee	trochaic	story
	dactyl	dactylic	anxiously
Substitute feet	spondee	spondaic	knick-knack
	pyrrhic	pyrrhic	pick of the day
Duple meters:	two syllables per foot: iambic and trochaic		
Triple meters:	three syllables per foot: anapestic and dactylic		

Number of Feet Per Line	
one foot	monometer
two feet	dimeter
three feet	trimeter
four feet	tetrameter
five feet	pentameter
six feet	hexameter
seven feet	heptameter
eight feet	octameter

In determining a poem's prevailing meter, it is important to retain a sense of the logic of its sentences. That is, it is necessary to hear the metrical beat while simultaneously accenting words of a line because of their position and importance in a sentence rather than merely as part of a metrical pattern of stressed and unstressed syllables. In reading a sonnet, for example, we need to feel its iambic pulse. But we should also hear the sense made by its sentences. Sometimes metrical accent and sentence emphasis will coincide. At other times there will be tension between them. In such cases readers may feel pulled in two directions at once.

We confront a similar problem of emphasis in reading poems with *enjambed,* or run-on, lines. *End-stopped* lines contain a pause or stop at the end of the line, indicated by a punctuation mark. When there is no mark of punctuation, and where the sense of the sentence remains incomplete until the next line, we experience a double commitment. On the one hand, we are inclined to stop at the end of the line (after all, it is a poem with lines and perhaps rhymes clearly indicated). On the other hand, we are also propelled past the end of the line, rhyme or not, since the sense of the sentence demands completion in the line or lines that follow it. Preserving a balance between such competing impulses is one of the challenges of writing poetry and one of the pleasures of reading it.

STRUCTURE: CLOSED FORM AND OPEN FORM

Basically, poetic structures can be either open or closed. Poems written in open forms do not follow a prescribed pattern of rhyme or stanzaic structure. They are freer, looser, less constrained than poems written in closed or fixed forms, which adhere more closely to prescribed requirements concerning line length, rhyme, and stanzaic structure.

The difference is readily apparent when you look at the following poems, one in closed form, the other in open.

LANGSTON HUGHES

[1902–1967]

My People

The night is beautiful,
So the faces of my people.

The stars are beautiful,
So the eyes of my people.

Beautiful, also, is the sun.   5
Beautiful, also, are the souls of my people.

I, too, sing America

I, too, sing America.

I am the darker brother.
They send me to eat in the kitchen
When company comes,
But I laugh,   5
And eat well,
And grow strong.

Tomorrow,
I'll be at the table
When company comes.   10
Nobody'll dare
Say to me,
"Eat in the kitchen,"
Then.

Besides,   15
They'll see how beautiful I am
And be ashamed—

I, too, am America.

The first poem is written according to a tighter formal structure than the second. Its three stanzas are couplets or two-line units, with the second line of each couplet ending with the words "of my people." This parallel language is supported by many other doublings of language: "The night . . . The stars" . . . "So the faces . . . So the eyes" . . . "Beautiful, also . . . Beautiful, also." There is, moreover, a gradual intensification of light as the poem moves from night through stars to sun, and a corresponding crescendo of interiority as it goes from faces through eyes to souls. Hughes's other poem, however, is not formless. Yet even though it is framed by a near-exact repetition in its opening and closing lines, its remaining sixteen lines are spun out over three stanzas of differing numbers of lines of varying lengths, some with only one word. The effect is much freer in form.

In comparison with the strictness of traditional fixed poetic forms, however, both of Hughes's poems exhibit a comparatively free structure. Neither follows the strict formal constraints of a form such as the sonnet, for example, with its fourteen lines arranged according to a carefully prescribed sequence of rhymes and an additional pattern of accented and unaccented syllables. The *Shakespearean*, or *English*, sonnet consists of three quatrains, or four-line sections, with the rhyme pattern *abab cdcd efef* followed by a rhymed couplet *gg*. The following poem exemplifies the English, or Shakespearean, sonnet form:

EDNA ST. VINCENT MILLAY

[1892–1950]

Love is not all: it is not meat nor drink

Love is not all: it is not meat nor drink	a
Nor slumber nor a roof against the rain;	b
Nor yet a floating spar to men that sink	a
And rise and sink and rise and sink again;	b
Love can not fill the thickened lung with breath,	c 5
Nor clean the blood, nor set the fractured bone;	d
Yet many a man is making friends with death	c
Even as I speak, for lack of love alone.	d
It well may be that in a difficult hour,	e
Pinned down by pain and moaning for release,	f 10
Or nagged by want past resolution's power,	e
I might be driven to sell your love for peace,	f
Or trade the memory of this night for food.	g
It well may be. I do not think I would.	g

The rhymes of Millay's sonnet clearly follow the Shakespearean pattern. We have represented the sounds of the rhyming words by letters, with repeated sounds designated by the same letters. The rhymes, moreover, approximate the poem's logical structure. Lines 1–4 form a clear unit of thought about the limitations of love. Lines 5–8 define love's limits by referring to physical needs that love cannot satisfy and to adverse circumstances it cannot alter. Midway through this second set of lines, however, the speaker suggests that even though the power of love is restricted, its presence is necessary. This counterimpulse suggests the power and prominence of love. Instead of repeating the idea of the first quatrain in the second, Millay introduces a complication that qualifies the initial statement. The result is a tension between the poem's structure of rhyme and its organization of thought.

In the third quatrain the poem turns from generalized statements about love to the speaker's personal situation. Here, too, the poem's rhyme pattern is slightly at odds with its structure of thought. Why? Because the idea of the third quatrain (that the speaker might trade love for peace or abandon love for food) continues into the concluding couplet. The second half of the couplet, however, swerves to counter this notion. The change in tone and rhythm of the poem's final line signals a shift in the speaker's thought and feeling. This shift undermines the idea that some things are more important than love.

An alternative to the Shakespearean sonnet is the *Petrarchan*, or *Italian*, sonnet, which typically falls into two parts: an *octave* of eight lines and a *sestet* of six. The octave rhyme pattern is *abba abba*, with the rhymes of the sestet more variable. The sestet may rhyme according to one of the following patterns: *cde cde; cde ced; cd cd cd* (or some other minor variation). The following sonnet, again by Edna St. Vincent Millay, exemplifies this form.

EDNA ST. VINCENT MILLAY

[1892–1950]

What lips my lips have kissed, and where, and why

What lips my lips have kissed, and where, and why,	a	
I have forgotten, and what arms have lain	b	
Under my head till morning; but the rain	b	
Is full of ghosts tonight, that tap and sigh	a	
Upon the glass and listen for reply,	a	5
And in my heart there stirs a quiet pain	b	
For unremembered lads that not again	b	
Will turn to me at midnight with a cry.	a	
Thus in the winter stands the lonely tree,	c	
Nor knows what birds have vanished one by one,	d	10
Yet knows its boughs more silent than before:	e	
I cannot say what loves have come and gone,	d	
I only know that summer sang in me	c	
A little while, that in me sings no more.	e	

Composed as two sentences of eight and six lines respectively, this sonnet breaks neatly into syntactic units that parallel the two-part structure of the Italian sonnet. It also adheres to the form's rhyme scheme: *abba abba; cde dce* (with a slight variation in the rhymes of the sestet).

The octave describes the speaker's feelings as she remembers her former lovers. And although she doesn't recall specific details, she feels their loss, as she is presumably now alone. In line 9 the poem turns to an image of a tree in which birds once sang but which is now abandoned. The shift to this image after the personal exposition in lines 1–8 is characteristic of the Petrarchan sonnet, which frequently changes direction in the first line of the sestet. In the second half of the sestet (lines

12–14) the poet explicitly compares the speaker's lonely predicament with that of the birdless tree.

These two sonnet forms offer different possibilities for poets. The Shakespearean sonnet is particularly well suited to theme and variations, in which an idea expressed in the first quatrain is followed by variations in the second and third quatrains. The sonnet then concludes with a summarizing couplet that may be ironic. The Petrarchan form, on the other hand, is especially well suited to a problem-resolution structure, in which the octet states a problem, which the sestet resolves. The Petrarchan form also functions well to capture radical shifts of direction, especially contrasts in tone, idea, and feeling. Millay's sonnets exploit the possibilities inherent in both forms.

We discern form in poetry largely by noticing recurring patterns, recognizing shifts of emphasis, observing changes of tone and mood, and considering the relationship of one part of a poem to another. If a poem is arranged in two stanzas, for instance, it is important to consider how the two sections are related. Look, for example, at Ben Jonson's "Still to be neat, still to be dressed" (p. 205), Robert Herrick's "Upon Julia's Clothes" (p. 210), and Walt Whitman's "A noiseless patient spider" (p. 451). If a poem is arranged in three stanzas, it is necessary to notice what happens in each, to see how the parts are related, and to consider the changes that occur from one stanza to another. Multiple stanzas may suggest a shifting perspective on experience (John Donne's "Song," p. 191), a changing set of attitudes (Philip Larkin's "A Study of Reading Habits," p. 763), a movement from description to reflection to feeling (William Wordsworth's "The Solitary Reaper," pp. 336–337)—or something else.

Conversely, if a poem displays no discernible large-scale structural units like stanzas or verse paragraphs, it may be useful to create them yourself. Walt Whitman's "When I Heard the Learn'd Astronomer" (p. 16), Gwendolyn Brooks's "The Mother" (pp. 750–751), and Robert Frost's "Birches" (pp. 539–540), for example, are all written without stanza breaks. Yet each contains plausible natural divisions. In reading any or all of these poems readers must decide for themselves where the poem shifts direction and what that shift signifies.

Form is thus necessary for poetic art. It makes poetry expressive. It makes it memorable and meaningful. Ultimately, moreover, it is form that makes it poetry.

THEME

Theme is an abstraction or generalization drawn from the details of a literary work. It refers to an idea or meaning inherent and implicit in the work. Arriving at a poem's theme can be more difficult than simply stating a general idea about the poem's significance—for any idea that "explains" the poem necessarily substitutes a generalization for our experience of reading the poem itself. To some extent, of course, such substitution is unavoidable when describing a poem's theme. So too is the prospect of oversimplifying or even distorting the poem. We can minimize these potential dangers, however, by taking into account as much of the poem's language and structure as we can when describing its theme.

Consider the following poems and the accompanying discussion of their themes.

EMILY DICKINSON

[1830–1886]

Crumbling is not an instant's Act

Crumbling is not an instant's Act,
A fundamental pause
Dilapidation's processes
Are organized Decays.

'Tis first a Cobweb on the Soul,   5
A Cuticle of Dust,
A Borer in the Axis,
An Elemental Rust—

Ruin is formal—Devil's work,
Consecutive and slow—   10
Fail in an instant, no man did
Slipping—is Crash's law.

The central idea of the poem is expressed in its opening line. We might paraphrase it this way: crumbling does not happen instantaneously; it is a gradual process, occurring slowly, cumulatively over time. The remainder of the first stanza further establishes this idea by accenting how "crumbling" is a consequence of dilapidation, which is a result of "decay." The deterioration that results is progressive; it is an organized, systematic process: one stage of decay leads to the next until destruction inevitably follows.

The gradual nature of decay is further emphasized by the statement that no one ever failed in an "instant," that the catastrophe occurs after, and as a consequence of, a series of failures. We can thus read the poem as a statement about the process of ruin (personal, emotional, financial) as well as a description of the process of decay. And we can summarize its theme thus: failure and destruction can be traced to small-scale elements that precede and cause them.

This theme is further extended in the second stanza, which contains four images of decay: cobweb, rust, dust, and the borer in the axis. These images are all accompanied by bits of specifying detail. The dust is a "cuticle," an image with suggestions of something at the "edges," of something on the outside and also of something human; the "cobweb on the soul" suggests spiritual deterioration ("cobwebs" suggest neglect); the "elemental" rust puts decay at the heart of things, at the center and vital core where the "borer" is operating. The poet applies each of these images of decay to a person, particularly to his or her soul: the dust encircling it, the cobweb netting it, the borer eating into it, and the rust corrupting it. Such an emphasis on spiritual decay seems further warranted by the first line of the third stanza: "Ruin is formal—Devil's work." "Ruin" is perhaps the word most strongly suggestive of human and spiritual collapse; "Devil's work" speaks for itself. Thus, a statement of the poem's theme must accommodate the idea of spiritual decay.

ELIZABETH BISHOP

[1911–1979]

One Art

The art of losing isn't hard to master;
so many things seem filled with the intent
to be lost that their loss is no disaster.

Lose something every day. Accept the fluster
of lost door keys, the hour badly spent.   5
The art of losing isn't hard to master.

Then practice losing farther, losing faster:
places, and names, and where it was you meant
to travel. None of these will bring disaster.

I lost my mother's watch. And look! my last, or   10
next-to-last, of three loved houses went.
The art of losing isn't hard to master.

I lost two cities, lovely ones. And, vaster,
some realms I owned, two rivers, a continent.
I miss them, but it wasn't a disaster.   15

—Even losing you (the joking voice, a gesture
I love) I shan't have lied. It's evident
the art of losing's not too hard to master
though it may look like *(Write it!)* like disaster.

The central idea of "One Art" is expressed in its opening line: that "the art of losing isn't hard to master." In other words, losing isn't merely something that happens, but is instead an "art" that one can learn. The line is repeated three times, once with a slight variation. An additional line, line 3, also repeated with slightly greater variations, strengthens the point of the first, that loss is no disaster. Taken together, these two lines and ideas sum up the poem's theme, which we can paraphrase as follows: human loss is inescapable; we all experience it frequently. Because of our repeated practice at losing, we can learn to accept our losses, however great; no loss is too overwhelming for us.

Although this is what the poem says, it's not what it means, or at least it's not the poem's only meaning. We can offer a fuller explanation of its meaning based on a closer look at its details and a consideration of its *tone* (the writer's implied attitude toward the subject).

Besides making the central points outlined in our initial interpretation, the opening stanza implies that things get lost of their own inclination. The implication of this hyperbolic suggestion is that we can't do much, if anything, to prevent their loss. From this we move to the advice of stanzas 2 and 3: practice losing things; learn to accept the inconvenience and frustration of doing without them.

In stanza 4 we are given a glimpse of lost things that seems to undercut the flat statement that loss is easy to take. The loss of one's mother's watch, while not necessarily a disaster, could be gravely disappointing if one attached sentimental value to it. The lost houses, too, could represent not merely the loss of a residence, easily enough replaced, but possibly of a spouse or of a segment of one's life. The same can be said for the losses described in stanza 5: cities, a river, a continent. Though the speaker claims that these losses weren't significant, she does miss them, rather more, we expect, than she misses a lost hour or set of keys. Finally, in the last stanza, we are shown a much greater loss—the loss of someone the speaker loves. Here, too, we read that the loss can be accommodated, that the speaker can come to terms with it, presumably without too much trouble.

As we make our way through the poem, perhaps near the end, perhaps upon a second reading, we may begin to wonder whether the speaker's repeated claims that losing is neither difficult nor consequential are not a bit too heavily pressed. That is, the speaker's insistently repeated claim may suggest the opposite of what she explicitly says. We wonder whether she may be trying to talk herself into accepting what her words literally say. We may suspect that the opposite case more nearly approximates reality: that losing is indeed difficult to master—if it can ever be mastered—and that it may cause, at times, very real disasters.

The poem can thus be read two ways: literally or ironically. In a literal reading, we accept the speaker's words for what they state. In an ironic reading, we reverse the literal meaning of her claim and realize that the speaker has not mastered the art of losing.

Centering on a poem's theme then, we work toward understanding a poem's significance—what it says, what it implies, what it means. As we have suggested previously, our sense of a poem's significance may change as we reread it. Moreover, our understanding of any poem's theme depends on our experience—both our literary experience and our experience in living—and as these develop so will our understanding and appreciation of poetry.

VISUAL POETRY

As early as the sixteenth century, poets were writing poems in forms that combined visual emblems with words. One type of such visual poetry, in fact, was called "emblem poetry," and it was practiced by the seventeenth-century Briton Francis Quarles. The emblem poem consisted of a print that represented a religious belief accompanied by a scriptural quotation and a poem that elaborated on the the print and the biblical quote. Additional quotations from various religious authorities might also be included. The whole package concluded with an epigram.

This is a typical example.

My Beloued is mine and I am his, He feedeth among the Lillies. Cant: 2.16.

Will: ſimpſon. ſculp:

FRANCIS QUARLES

[1592–1644]

Emblem III

Canticles 2:16

My beloved is mine, and I am his; he feedeth among the lilies.

Ev'n like two little bank-dividing brooks
   That wash the pebbles with their wanton streams,
And having ranged and searched a thousand nooks,
   Meet both at length in silver-breasted Thames,
      Where in a greater current they conjoin,   5
So I my best beloved's am; so He is mine.

Ev'n so we met, and after long pursuit,
   Ev'n so we joined; we both became entire.
No need for either to renew a suit,
   For I was flax, and He was flames of fire.   10
      Our firm-united souls did more than twine;
So I my best beloved's am; so He is mine.

If all those glitt'ring monarchs that command
   The servile quarters of this earthly ball
Should tender, in exchange, their shares of land,   15
   I would not change my fortunes for them all;
      Their wealth is but a counter to my coin;
The world's but theirs; but my beloved's mine.

Nay more, if the fair Thespian ladies all
   Should heap together their diviner treasure,   20
That treasure should be deemed a price too small
   To buy a minute's lease of half my pleasure.
      'Tis not the sacred wealth of all the Nine
Can buy my heart from Him, or His from being mine.

Nor time, nor place,, nor chance, nor death, can bow   25
   My least desires unto the least remove;
He's firmly mine by oath, I His by vow;
   He's mine by faith, and I am His by love;
    He's mine by water, I am His by wine;
Thus I my best beloved's am; thus He is mine.   30

He is my altar; I His holy place;
   I am His guest, and He my living food;
I'm His by penitence, He mine by grace;
   I'm His by purchase, He is mine by blood.
    He's my supporting elm, and I His vine;   35
Thus I my best beloved's am; thus He is mine.

He gives me wealth, I give him all my vows;
   I give Him songs, He gives me length of days;
With wreaths of grace He crowns my conq'ring brows,
   And I His temples with a crown of praise;   40
    Which He accepts as an everlasting sign
That I my best beloved's am, that He is mine.

Epigram 3

Sing, Hymen, to my soul: what, lost and found?
Welcomed, espoused, enjoyed so soon and crowned!
He did but climb the cross, and then came down   45
To th' gates of hell; triumphed, and fetched a crown.

During this time a number of poets wrote another kind of visual poetry as well—poems in the shape of an object. One of the more accomplished of these poets was George Herbert, an Angelican priest whose book, *The Temple,* includes a variety of visually arresting poems. Two of his best known are "Easter Wings," which is shaped like a pair of angels wings tilted sideways, and "The Altar," which takes the shape of the object described. What is interesting about "The Altar," however, is the way Herbert uses the altar's shape as a visual metaphor for his real subject—the human heart.

GEORGE HERBERT

[1593–1633]

The Altar

A broken ALTAR, Lord, thy servant rears,
Made of a heart, and cemented with tears:
  Whose parts are as thy hand did frame:
  No workman's tool hath touched the same.
        A HEART alone
        Is such a stone,
        As nothing but
        Thy pow'r doth cut.
        Wherefore each part
        Of my hard heart
        Meets in this frame,
        To praise thy name.
  That, if I chance to hold my peace,
  These stones to praise thee may not cease.
O let thy blessed SACRIFICE be mine,
And sanctify this ALTAR to be thine.

It is clear that both George Herbert and Francis Quarles have more in mind than simply portraying an object in words or using the visual image to illustrate a text. Both poets use visual images to reveal thought and express feeling. Both poets dramatize particular religious attitudes and beliefs with their visual wordplay. And both make repeated use of Christian religious ideals in emphatically meditative poems.

There, however, the similarities end, for Herbert's poem is less a commentary on a verbal text visually illustrated than a shaping of language into a visual emblem of a state of spiritual feeling. Herbert's poem is less a depiction of an altar (or a commentary on the Biblical text that inspired it) than a prayer for communion of the speaker with God. Herbert's poem, moreover, is much less predictable than Quarles's is and far more intricate imagistically. Herbert's altar, for example, is both the table at which the priest performs religious rituals and the speaker's hardened and broken heart. In addition, the altar is an image on the page, constructed with words, the speaker-poet's metaphorical stones. Herbert's poem is thus a visual embodiment of the prayerful sentiment expressed in it.

For a decidedly different and much more modern example of a visual hieroglyph, or image that visually enacts what it describes verbally, look at the following unusual poem:

E. E. CUMMINGS

[1894–1962]

l(a

```
            l(a

            le
            af
            fa

            ll

            s)
            one
            l

            iness
```

Perhaps the first things to notice are the lack of capital letters and the absence of punctuation (except for the parentheses). What we don't see is as important as what we do. We don't see any recognizable words or sentences, to say nothing of traditional stanzas or lines of poetry. The poem strikes the eye as a series of letters that stream down the page, for the most part two to a line. Rearranging the letters horizontally, we find these words: *(a leaf falls) loneliness.* [The first *l* of *loneliness* appears before the parenthesis, like this: *l(a leaf falls)oneliness;* to get *loneliness* you have to move the *l* in front of *oneliness.*]

A single falling leaf is a traditional symbol of loneliness; this image is not new. What is new, however, is the way Cummings has coupled the concept with the image, the way he has formed and shaped them into a nontraditional poem. But what has the poet gained by arranging his poem this way? By breaking the horizontal line of verse into a series of fragments (from the horizontal viewpoint), Cummings illustrates visually the separation that is the primary cause of loneliness. Both the word "loneliness" and the image described in "a leaf falls" are broken apart, separated in this way. In addition, by splitting the initial letter from "loneliness," the poet has revealed the hidden "one" in the word. It's as if he is saying: loneliness is *one*-liness. This idea is further enforced by the visual ambiguity of "l." Initially we are not sure whether this symbol "l" is a number—"*one*"—or the letter *l.* By shaping and arranging his poem this way, Cummings unites form and content, structure and idea. In addition, he invites us to play the poetry game with him by remaking the poem as we put its pieces together. In doing so we step back and see in the design of the poem a leaf falling down the page.

By positioning the letters as he does, Cummings pictures a leaf falling:

le
af
fa
ll
s.

Visual poems come in other forms and are put to other purposes as well. Consider the two poems below, each in a familiar shape, though in a foreign language. We have provided a translation of the Eiffel Tower poem. The apple and worm poem needs less a translation than a patient scrutiny to find the apple's intruder. We have added an additional concrete poem and given it in both the original French and an English translation.

REINHOLD DÖHL

(*b.* 1934)

Pattern Poem with an Elusive Intruder

Apple/Worm

GUILLAUME APOLLINAIRE

[1880–1918]

La Tour Eiffel

The Eiffel Tower

TRANSLATED BY ADELIA WILLIAMS

```
        S                              H
        A                              E
       LUT                            LLO
        M                              W
        O N                           OR
        D E                           LD
       DONT                         WHERE
      JE SUIS                      I     AM
      LA LAN                      THE  ELO
      GUE É                      QUENT  T
     LOQUEN                      O N G U E
    TE QUESA                     WH   OSE
    B O U C H E                  MOUT   H
     O PARIS                      OH PARIS
  TIRE ET TIRERA                WILL STICKOUT
  TOU        JOURS              FOR        EVER
  AUX      A  L                 AT         THE
  LEM        ANDS               GER        MANS
```

Miroir

Mirror

TRANSLATED BY ADELIA WILLIAMS

```
        DANS                           IN
    FLETS    CE                   CTIONS    THIS
   RE         MI                   LE         MIR
  LES         ROIR                REF          ROR
  SONT         JE                 THE           I
 MB            SUIS               ARE           AM
 COM    Guillaume    EN           AS    Guillaume   EN
NON                  CLOS         NOT                CLOS
 ET                  VI           AND                ED
  GES  Apollinaire   VANT          GELS  Apollinaire  ALI
   AN               ET             AN                 VE
   LES            VRAI            THE               AND
    NE            COM             NES               TRUE
    GI            ME              GI                AS
    MA     ON                     MA     ONE
         I                               I
```

Consider also the next visual poem, depicting an animal.

JOHN HOLLANDER

[b. 1929]

Swan and Shadow

```
                    Dusk
                  Above the
               water hang the
                   loud
                   flies                              5
                   Here
                   O so
                   gray
                   then
                 What              A pale signal will appear    10
                 When          Soon before its shadow fades
                 Where         Here in this pool of opened eye
                 In us       No Upon us As at the very edges
                of where we take shape in the dark air
                   this object bares its image awakening     15
                  ripples of recognition that will
                     brush darkness up into light
even after this bird this hour both drift by atop the perfect sad instant now
                       already passing out of sight
                   toward yet-untroubled reflection          20
                  this image bears its object darkening
               into memorial shades Scattered bits of
                 light      No of water Or something across
                 water        Breaking up No Being regathered
                 soon           Yet by then a swan will have   25
                  gone            Yes out of mind into what
                   vast
                    pale
                    hush
                    of a                                       30
                    place
                    past
               sudden dark as
                if a swan
                    sang                                       35
```

We conclude this section with an invitation to consider the symbolic implications of a wave.

MAY SWENSON

[b. 1919]

How Everything Happens

(BASED ON A STUDY OF THE WAVE)

```
                                                happen.
                                              to
                                            up
                                        stacking
                                    is
                              something
      When nothing is happening
      When it happens
                        something
                              pulls
                                  back
                                    not
                                      to
                                        happen.
      When                     has happened.
            pulling back         stacking up
                  happens
            has happened          stacks up.
      When it        something          nothing
                              pulls back while
      Then nothing is happening.
                              happens.
                            and
                          forward
                        pushes
                      up
                  stacks
            something
      Then
```

POETRY AND ART

In Roman times and again during the Renaissance, poems were characterized as speaking pictures and painting as silent poetry. A poem, that is, was seen as a visual image given speech, a painting as a silent visual poem. Earlier, in our discussion of structure, we noted that the shape of a poem, its arrangement on the page, is an important dimension of its meaning and effect. In this connection, you might look at May Swenson's "Women" and John Hollander's "Swan and Shadow" (in addition to the other poems displayed in our section on visual poetry).

Here, however, we will consider another dimension of the relationship between words and visual images. On the pages that follow you will find poems paired with the paintings that inspired them. As you consider each pairing, spend some time looking carefully at the painting. Take an inventory of its details; observe its use of color and line, organization and perspective. Think about the implications of its title and examine the action or scene it depicts. Then read the accompanying poem as an interpretation of the painting. Notice what the poets include, what they omit, what they alter. Consider whether the poems can stand alone without their corresponding paintings. And finally, consider how each poet has transformed the painting to create a new and distinctive work.

Part of our pleasure in viewing paintings and their corresponding poems resides in watching what poets do with language and form in describing, translating, or interpreting the paintings. Consider, for example, how Stephen Mitchell's rendering of Vermeer's *Woman* and William Carlos Williams's depiction of Breughel's *Icarus* help us better see those paintings. Mitchell and Williams point to details we might have overlooked or perhaps considered insignificant. In rendering the paintings in words, Mitchell and Williams do more than merely describe or transcribe visual images verbally. They also capture the paintings' temper and spirit—Mitchell by capturing Vermeer's serenity, Williams by highlighting Breughel's concealment of Icarus.

Another dimension of our pleasure in considering poem-painting relationships emerges when we compare poems inspired by the same painting. Consider, for example, how differently Robert Fagles and Anne Sexton treat van Gogh's *Starry Night*. Sexton and Fagles make very different looking and sounding poems while focusing on a similar dimension of van Gogh's art—the energy and passion revealed in the thick brush strokes and swirling images. Unlike Mitchell and Williams, whose poetic rendering of painting is primarily descriptive, Sexton and Fagles have responses to van Gogh that are strongly interpretive.

In fact, however, every translation of painting into poems involves interpretation to some degree. W. H. Auden's and Anne Sexton's poems on Breughel's *Icarus* illustrate this strong interpretive emphasis. Both Auden and Sexton use Breughel's painting to exemplify an idea, though their ideas differ. We might remark additionally, here, that Brueghel's painting is itself an interpretation—of the myth of Daedalus and Icarus, as described in Ovid's *Metamorphoses*.

FROM "SONGS OF EXPERIENCE," 1794, THE HUNTINGTON LIBRARY, SAN MARINO, CALIFORNIA.

William Blake, *The Sick Rose.*

WILLIAM BLAKE
[1757–1827]
The Sick Rose

O Rose, thou art sick.
The invisible worm,
That flies in the night
In the howling storm:

Has found out thy bed
Of crimson joy:
And his dark secret love
Does thy life destroy.

74

X. J. KENNEDY

[b. 1929]

Nude Descending a Staircase

Toe upon toe, a snowing flesh,
A gold of lemon, root and rind,
She sifts in sunlight down the stairs
With nothing on. Nor on her mind.

We spy beneath the banister
A constant thresh of thigh on thigh—
Her lips imprint the swinging air
That parts to let her parts go by.

One-woman waterfall, she wears
Her slow descent like a long cape
And pausing, on the final stair
Collects her motions into shape.

PHILADELPHIA MUSEUM OF ART, LOUISE AND WALTER ARENSBERG COLLECTION.

Marcel Duchamp, *Nude Descending a Staircase,* No. 2, 1912.
Oil on canvas, 58 × 35 inches.

I am that I am it cries   *10*
it lifts me up the nightfall   up
the cloudrack coiling like a dragon's flanks
a third of the stars of heaven wheeling in its wake
wheels in wheels around the moon that cradles round the sun

and if I can only trail these whirling eternal stars   *15*
with one sweep of the brush like Michael's sword if I can
cut the life out of the beast—safeguard the mother and the son
all heaven will hymn in conflagration blazing down
          the night the mountain ranges down
the claustrophobic valleys of the mad   *20*

                          Madness
          is what I have instead of heaven
          God deliver me—help me now deliver
          all this frenzy back into your hands
          our brushstrokes burning clearer into dawn   *25*

Vincent van Gogh, *The Starry Night*, 1889. Oil on canvas, 29 × 36¼ inches.

COLLECTION, THE MUSEUM OF MODERN ART, NEW YORK. ACQUIRED THROUGH THE LILLIE P. BLISS BEQUEST.

ANNE SEXTON

[1928–1975]

The Starry Night

That does not keep me from having a terrible need of—shall I say the word—religion. Then I go out at night to paint the stars.

VINCENT VAN GOGH *in a letter to his brother*

The town does not exist
except where one black-haired tree slips
up like a drowned woman into the hot sky.
The town is silent. The night boils with eleven stars
Oh starry starry night! This is how   5
I want to die.

It moves. They are all alive.
Even the moon bulges in its orange irons
to push children, like a god, from its eye.
The old unseen serpent swallows up the stars.   10
Oh starry starry night! This is how
I want to die:

into that rushing beast of the night,
sucked up by that great dragon, to split
from my life with no flag,   15
no belly,
no cry.

ROBERT FAGLES

[b. 1933]

The Starry Night

Long as I paint
I feel myself
less mad
the brush in my hand
a lightning rod to madness   5

But never ground that madness
execute it   ride the lightning up
from these benighted streets and steeple   up
with the cypress   look its black is burning green

NATALIE SAFIR
[b. 1935]

Matisse's Dance

A break in the circle dance of naked women,
dropped stitch between the hands
of the slender figure stretching too hard
to reach her joyful sisters.

Spirals of glee sail from the arms   5
of the tallest woman. She pulls
the circle around with her fire.
What has she found that she doesn't
keep losing, her torso
a green-burning torch?   10

Grass mounds curve ripely beneath
two others who dance beyond the blue.
Breasts swell and multiply and
rhythms rise to a gallop.

Hurry, frightened one and grab on—before   15
the stitch is forever lost, before the dance
unravels and a black sun swirls from that space.

COLLECTION, THE MUSEUM OF MODERN ART, NEW YORK. GIFT OF NELSON A. ROCKEFELLER IN HONOR OF ALFRED H. BARR, JR.

Henri Matisse, *The Dance*. (first version), Paris, March 1909. Oil on canvas, 8 feet, 6½ inches × 12 feet, 9½ inches.

THE METROPOLITAN MUSEUM OF ART, GIFT OF HENRY G. MARQUAND, 1889, MARQUAND COLLECTION.

Jan Vermeer, *Young Woman with a Water Jug,* c. 1662.
Oil on canvas, 18 × 16 inches.

STEPHEN MITCHELL

[b. 1943]

Vermeer

Quia respexit humilitatem ancillae suae.
Luke I:48

She stands by the table, poised
at the center of your vision,
with her left hand
just barely on
the pitcher's handle, and her right   5
lightly touching the windowframe.
Serene as a clear sky, luminous
in her blue dress and many-toned
white cotton wimple, she is looking
nowhere. Upon her lips   10
is the subtlest and most lovely
of smiles, caught
for an instant
like a snowflake in a warm hand.

How weightless her body feels
as she stands, absorbed, within this
fulfillment that has brought more
than any harbinger could.
She looks down with an infinite
tenderness in her eyes,
as though the light at the window
were a newborn child
and her arms open enough
to hold it on her breast, forever.

15

20

WILLIAM CARLOS WILLIAMS

[1883–1963]

Landscape with the Fall of Icarus

According to Breughel
when Icarus fell
it was spring

a farmer was ploughing
his field
the whole pageantry

5

of the year was
awake tingling
near

the edge of the sea
concerned
with itself

10

sweating in the sun
that melted
the wings' wax

15

unsignificantly
off the coast
there was

a splash quite unnoticed
this was
Icarus drowning

20

Pieter Breughel the Elder, *Landscape with the Fall of Icarus*, c. 1558.

W. H. AUDEN

[1907–1973]

Musée des Beaux Arts

About suffering they were never wrong,
The Old Masters: how well they understood
Its human position; how it takes place
While someone else is eating or opening a window or just walking dully along;
How, when the aged are reverently, passionately waiting   5
For the miraculous birth, there always must be
Children who did not specially want it to happen, skating
On a pond at the edge of the wood:
They never forgot
That even the dreadful martyrdom must run its course   10
Anyhow in a corner, some untidy spot
Where the dogs go on with their doggy life and the torturer's horse
Scratches its innocent behind on a tree.

In Breughel's *Icarus,* for instance: how everything turns away
Quite leisurely from the disaster; the ploughman may   15
Have heard the splash, the forsaken cry,
But for him it was not an important failure; the sun shone
As it had to on the white legs disappearing into the green
Water; and the expensive delicate ship that must have seen
Something amazing, a boy falling out of the sky,   20
Had somewhere to get to and sailed calmly on.

81

ANNE SEXTON
[1928–1974]

To a Friend Whose Work Has Come to Triumph

Consider Icarus, pasting those sticky wings on,
testing that strange little tug at his shoulder blade,
and think of that first flawless moment over the lawn
of the labyrinth. Think of the difference it made!
There below are the trees, as awkward as camels;   5
and here are the shocked starlings pumping past
and think of innocent Icarus who is doing quite well:
larger than a sail, over the fog and the blast
of the plushy ocean, he goes. Admire his wings!
Feel the fire at his neck and see how casually   10
he glances up and is caught, wondrously tunneling
into that hot eye. Who cares that he fell back to the sea?
See him acclaiming the sun and come plunging down
while his sensible daddy goes straight into town.

OVID
[43 B.C.–17 A.D.]

The Story of Daedalus and Icarus

TRANSLATED BY ROLFE HUMPHRIES

Homesick for homeland, Daedalus hated Crete
And his long exile there, but the sea held him.
"Though Minos blocks escape by land or water,"
Daedalus said, "surely the sky is open,
And that's the way we'll go. Minos' dominion   5
Does not include the air." He turned his thinking
Toward unknown arts, changing the laws of nature.
He laid out feathers in order, first the smallest,
A little larger next it, and so continued,
The way that pan-pipes rise in gradual sequence.   10
He fastened them with twine and wax, at middle,
At bottom, so, and bent them, gently curving,
So that they looked like wings of birds, most surely.
And Icarus, his son, stood by and watched him,
Not knowing he was dealing with his downfall,   15
Stood by and watched, and raised his shiny face
To let a feather, light as down, fall on it,
Or stuck his thumb into the yellow wax,
Fooling around, the way a boy will, always,
Whenever a father tries to get some work done.   20
Still, it was done at last, and the father hovered,
Poised, in the moving air, and taught his son:

"I warn you, Icarus, fly a middle course:
Don't go too low, or water will weigh the wings down;
Don't go too high, or the sun's fire will burn them.   *25*
Keep to the middle way. And one more thing,
No fancy steering by star or constellation,
Follow my lead!" That was the flying lesson,
And now to fit the wings to the boy's shoulders.
Between the work and warning the father found   *30*
His cheeks were wet with tears, and his hands trembled.
He kissed his son (*Good-bye*, if he had known it),
Rose on his wings, flew on ahead, as fearful
As any bird launching the little nestlings
Out of high nest into thin air. *Keep on,*   *35*
Keep on, he signals, *follow me!* He guides him
In flight—O fatal art!—and the wings move
And the father looks back to see the son's wings moving.
Far off, far down, some fisherman is watching
As the rod dips and trembles over the water,   *40*
Some shepherd rests his weight upon his crook,
Some ploughman on the handles of the ploughshare,
And all look up, in absolute amazement,
At those air-borne above. They must be gods!
They were over Samos, Juno's sacred island,   *45*
Delos and Paros toward the left, Lebinthus
Visible to the right, and another island,
Calymne, rich in honey. And the boy
Thought *This is wonderful!* and left his father,
Soared higher, higher, drawn to the vast heaven,   *50*
Nearer the sun, and the wax that held the wings
Melted in that fierce heat, and the bare arms
Beat up and down in air, and lacking oarage
Took hold of nothing. *Father!* he cried, and *Father!*   *55*
Until the blue sea hushed him, the dark water
Men call the Icarian now. And Daedalus,
Father no more, called "Icarus, where are you!
Where are you, Icarus? Tell me where to find you!"   *60*
And saw the wings on the waves, and cursed his talents,
Buried the body in a tomb, and the land
Was named for Icarus.
                          During the burial
A noisy partridge, from a muddy ditch,   *65*
Looked out, drummed with her wings in loud approval.
No other bird, those days, was like the partridge,
Newcomer to the ranks of birds; the story
Reflects no credit on Daedalus. His sister,
Ignorant of the fates, had sent her son   *70*
To Daedalus as apprentice, only a youngster,
Hardly much more than twelve years old, but clever,
With an inventive turn of mind. For instance,
Studying a fish's backbone for a model,

He had notched a row of teeth in a strip of iron,   *75*
Thus making the first saw, and he had bound
Two arms of iron together with a joint
To keep them both together and apart,
One standing still, the other traversing
In a circle, so men came to have the compass.   *80*
And Daedalus, in envy, hurled the boy
Headlong from the high temple of Minerva,
And lied about it, saying he had fallen
Through accident, but Minerva, kind protectress
Of all inventive wits, stayed him in air,   *85*
Clothed him with plumage; he still retained his aptness
In feet and wings, and kept his old name, Perdix,
But in the new bird-form, Perdix, the partridge,
Never flies high, nor nests in trees, but flutters
Close to the ground, and the eggs are laid in hedgerows.   *90*
The bird, it seems, remembers, and is fearful
Of all high places.

VINNIE-MARIE D'AMBROSIO

[b. 1928]

The Painter Yearning for Her Lake

(TO SUZANNE GILLIARD)

Daffodils
grow from her fingernails.
A handshake—and they languish.

This is no slight
slough she's in,   *5*
because she's generous,
and phlox and orchids shoot
from her eyes,
and the city's sights
don't suit them.   *10*

If we could just halt the truckers
and pedestrians, just
pluck some salesmen
out from the shadows—she'd
haunt them, in a sylvan way.   *15*

Yet here she serves all elixir-makings,
like a yeoman,
busy, and stretching her green scenes
breathes flux
into our office.   *20*

Poets, when next we
open shop blinds
and catch dawn flashing
on the concrete walks,

I'll bet you a sestina that   *25*
our susurrous work-pot
will be swirling with her
dampening orchids' and
daffodils' petals, her

wild gardens staining   *30*
the vortex of our spreading poems.

PRIVATE COLLECTION.

Suzanne Gilliard, *Still Life with Tiger Lillies.*

[1875–1926]

Archaic Torso of Apollo

TRANSLATED BY STEPHEN MITCHELL

We cannot know his legendary head
with eyes like ripening fruit. And yet his torso
is still suffused with brilliance from inside,
like a lamp, in which his gaze, now turned to low,

gleams in all its power. Otherwise   5
the curved breast could not dazzle you so, nor could
a smile run through the placid hips and thighs
to that dark center where procreation flared.

Otherwise this stone would seem defaced
beneath the translucent cascade of the shoulders   10
and would not glisten like a wild beast's fur:

would not, from all the borders of itself,
burst like a star: for here there is not place
that does not see you. You must change your life.

JORIE GRAHAM
[b. 1951]

San Sepolcro

In this blue light
        I can take you there,
snow having made me
        a world of bone
seen through to. This   5
        is my house,

my section of Etruscan
        wall, my neighbor's
lemontrees, and, just below
        the lower church,   10
the airplane factory.
        A rooster

crows all day from mist
        outside the walls.
There's milk on the air,   15
        ice on the oily
lemonskins. How clean
        the mind is,

Piero della Francesca, *Madonna del Parto.*

CEMETERY CHAPEL, MONTERCHI, SANSEPOLCRO. SCALA/ART RESOURCE.

holy grave. It is this girl
    by Piero   *20*
della Francesca, unbuttoning
    her blue dress,
her mantle of weather,
    to go into

labor. Come, we can go in.   *25*
    It is before
the birth of god. No-one
    has risen yet
to the museums, to the assembly
    line—bodies   *30*

and wings—to the open air
    market. This is
what the living do: go in.
    It's a long way.
And the dress keeps opening   *35*
    from eternity

to privacy, quickening.
    Inside, at the heart,
is tragedy, the resent moment

forever stillborn,
but going in, each breath
    is a button

coming undone, something terribly
    nimble-fingered
finding all of the stops.

Coventry Cathedral

Nothing prepared us for it
Not the lookalike streets
traffic snorting and stopping
punks hanging outside the pubs
pints in hand celebrating Sunday

Some people hate the structure
Even the guide books hedge

We climb a rise
note smooth red walls, tall slit windows
Saint Michael slaying the devil
A lady of good works selling raffles
Children in mummer's costumes
Nothing prepares you

For the lurch of heart,
the spurting tear
as we swallow whole
the skeletal shell
empty apse and altar
a charred wood cross
crudely tied

Two words on the wall:
Father forgive

Nothing prepares us
The wall of light
clear etched glass
antic angels dancing and trumpeting
the glory of faith and the faithful

The effulgent flood
of stained glass, of gold light

40

45

5

10

15

20

25

Windows from Coventry Cathedral.

At Chartres the eye is drawn up   *30*
through a far distant window
toward heaven

At Coventry heaven swathes earth
and we share the radiance
in this tabernacle   *35*
whose cement is love
whose foundation is forgiveness

CATHY SONG
[b. 1955]

Girl Powdering Her Neck

From a ukiyo-e print by Utamaro

The light is the inside
sheen of an oyster shell,
sponged with talc and vapor,
moisture from a bath.

89

A pair of slippers
are placed outside
the rice-paper doors.
She kneels at a low table
in the room,
her legs folded beneath her
as she sits on a buckwheat pillow.

Her hair is black
with hints of red,
the color of seaweed
spread over rocks.

Morning begins the ritual
wheel of the body,
the application of translucent skins.
She practices pleasure:
the pressure of three fingertips
applying powder.
Fingerprints of pollen
some other hand will trace.

The peach-dyed kimono
patterned with maple leaves
drifting across the silk,
falls from right to left
in a diagonal, revealing
the nape of her neck

MUSÉE GUIMET, PARIS. © R.M.N.

Kitagawa Utamaro, *Girl Powdering Her Neck.*

and the curve of a shoulder   *30*
like the slope of a hill
set deep in snow in a country
of huge white solemn birds.
Her face appears in the mirror,
a reflection in a winter pond,   *35*
rising to meet itself.

She dips a corner of her sleeve
like a brush into water
to wipe the mirror;
she is about to paint herself.   *40*
The eyes narrow
in a moment of self-scrutiny.
The mouth parts
as if desiring to disturb
the placid plum face;   *45*
break the symmetry of silence.
But the berry-stained lips,
stenciled into the mask of beauty,
do not speak.

Two chrysanthemums   *50*
touch in the middle of the lake
and drift apart.

POETRY AND MUSIC

Poetry and music have long been associated. In ancient Greece, poems were chanted and sung to the accompaniment of the lyre, an ancient stringed instrument. Throughout the centuries, but especially during the Middle Ages, liturgical poetry based on biblical texts has been chanted and sung in synagogues and churches in many languages, but especially in Hebrew, Latin, Greek, and Russian (according to the liturgical rites followed). In Renaissance England and Italy poems were set to music and sung, often as madrigals for multiple voices and frequently accompanied by the lute. Up to our own time, song and poetry have continued to be associated as writers of popular song lyrics have sometimes aspired to poetry and conversely as numerous modern and contemporary poems have been set to music.

We provide here a few examples of poetry and music to suggest something of this scope and variety. Our selections range from the Middle English lyric "Sumer is icumen in" to the contemporary song "Vincent." We have included Renaissance lyric poems about love that were set to music as songs in their own time (Campion's "There Is a Garden in Her Face" and Jonson's "To Celia") as well as more modern poems that have not actually been set to music but which reflect particular musical styles (Langston Hughes's "Same in Blues").

Two of our modern selections, Paul Simon's "Richard Cory" and Pete Seeger's "Turn! Turn! Turn!" are based on earlier texts. Simon's derives from E. A. Robinson's poem of the same title while Seeger's song reworks a passage from the Bible. Perhaps the most familiar example, however, is the classic song setting of Robert Burns' famous poem "Auld Lang Syne."

"Sumer is icumen in," the most famous of Middle English lyrics, is one of several songs at the beginning of a monks' commonplace book compiled at Reading Abbey and now in the British Museum (MS. Harley 978, f. 11^b). This poem has usually been dated about 1240, but some musicologists believe that a date seventy years later is more likely. Reproduced by permission of the Trustees of the British Museum.

ANONYMOUS

Sumer is icumen in

Sumer is icumen in,
Lhude° sing, cuccu!°   loudly / cuckoo
Groweth sed° and bloweth° med°   seed / blooms / meadow
And springth the wude° nu.°   forest / now
Sing, cuccu!

Awe° bleteth after lomb,   *ewe*
Lhouth° after calve° cu,°   *lows / calf / cow*
Bulluc sterteth,° bucke ferteth.°   *leaps / breaks wind*
Murie° sing, cuccu!   *merrily*
Cuccu, cuccu,

Wel singes thu, cuccu.
Ne swik° thu naver° nu!   *cease/never*

Sing cuccu nu, sing cuccu!
Sing cuccu, sing cuccu nu!

ANONYMOUS
Barbara Allan

1

It was in and about the Martinmas time,
  When the green leaves were a-falling,
That Sir John Græme, in the West Country,
  Fell in love with Barbara Allan.

2

He sent his man down through the town,   5
  To the place where she was dwelling:
"O haste and come to my master dear,
  Gin° ye be Barbara Allan."   *If*

3

O hooly°, hooly rose she up,   *softly*
  To the place where he was lying,   10
And when she drew the curtain by:
  "Young man, I think you're dying."

4

"O it's I'm sick, and very, very sick,
  And 'tis a' for Barbara Allan."
"O the better for me ye s' never be,   15
  Though your heart's blood were a-spilling.

5

"O dinna ye mind, young man," said she,
  "When ye was in the tavern a-drinking,
That ye made the healths gae° round and round,   *go*
  And slighted Barbara Allan?"   20

BARBARA ALLAN   ¹**Martinmas time**   feast of St. Martin, November 11th.   ¹⁷**dinna ye mind** don't
you remember?

He turned his face unto the wall,
   And death was with him dealing:
"Adieu, adieu, my dear friends all,
   And be kind to Barbara Allan."

And slowly, slowly raise she up,   *25*
   And slowly, slowly left him,
And sighing said, she could not stay,
   Since death of life had reft him.

She had not gane a mile but twa°,   *gone / two*
   When she heard the dead-bell ringing,   *30*
And every jow° that the dead-bell geid°,   *beat / gave*
   It cried, "Woe to Barbara Allan!"

"O mother, mother, make my bed!
   O make it saft and narrow!
Since my love died for me to-day,   *35*
   I'll die for him to-morrow."

THOMAS CAMPION
[1567–1601]

There Is a Garden in Her Face

There is a garden in her face
   Where roses and white lilies grow;
A heavenly paradise is that place,
   Wherein these pleasant fruits do flow.
There cherries grow which none may buy,   *5*
Till "Cherry-ripe" themselves do cry.

These cherries fairly do enclose
   Of orient pearl a double row,
Which when her lovely laughter shows,
   They look like rose-buds filled with snow;   *10*
Yet them no peer nor prince can buy,
Till "Cherry-ripe" themselves do cry.

Her eyes like angels watch them still;
   Her brows like bended bows do stand,
Threatening with piercing shafts to kill   *15*
   All that presume with eye or hand
Those sacred cherries to come nigh,
Till "Cherry-ripe" themselves do cry.

*This is Campion's own setting, for lute and voice, of the preceding poem. The little melodic fragment to
"cherry ripe ripe ripe" was the street-cry actually sung to these words by London cherry vendors, and
Campion works it into the vocal part just as he works the words into the conceit of his text.*

BEN JONSON

[1572–1637]

To Celia

Drink to me only with thine eyes,
 And I will pledge with mine;
Or leave a kiss but in the cup,
 And I'll not ask for wine.
The thirst that from the soul doth rise   5
 Doth ask a drink divine;
But might I of Jove's nectar sup,
 I would not change for thine.

I sent thee late a rosy wreath,
 Not so much honoring thee   10
As giving it a hope that there
 It could not withered be.
But thou thereon didst only breathe,
 And sent'st it back to me;
Since when it grows, and smells, I swear,   15
 Not of itself but thee.

ISAAC WATTS

[1674–1748]

Our God, our help

Our God, our help in ages past,
    Our hope for years to come,
Our shelter from the stormy blast,
    And our eternal home:

Under the shadow of thy throne   5
    Thy saints have dwelt secure;
Sufficient is thine arm alone,
    And our defense is sure.

Before the hills in order stood
    Or earth received her frame,   10
From everlasting thou art God,
    To endless years the same.

Thy word commands our flesh to dust,
    "Return, ye sons of men";
All nations rose from earth at first,   15
    And turn to earth again.

A thousand ages in thy sight
    Are like an evening gone;
Short as the watch that ends the night
    Before the rising sun.   20

The busy tribes of flesh and blood,
    With all their lives and cares,
Are carried downwards by thy flood,
    And lost in following years.

Time, like an ever-rolling stream,   25
    Bears all its sons away;
They fly forgotten, as a dream
    Dies at the opening day.

Like flowery fields the nations stand,
    Pleased with the morning light;   30
The flowers beneath the mower's hand
    Lie withering e'er 'tis night.

Our God, our help in ages past,
    Our hope for years to come,
Be thou our guard while troubles last,   35
    And our eternal home.

ROBERT BURNS

[1759–1796]

Auld Lang Syne

Should auld acquaintance be forgot,
  And never brought to min'?
Should auld acquaintance be forgot,
  And days o' lang syne?

Chorus

For auld lang syne, my dear,   5
  For auld lang syne,
We'll tak a cup o' kindness yet,
  For auld lang syne.

We twa hae run about the braes°.   *slopes*
  And pu'd the gowans° fine,   *daisies* 10
But we've wandered mony a weary foot,
  Sin' auld lang syne.

(Chorus)

We twa hae paidled i' the burn,°   *stream*
  From morning sun till dine°,   *dinner, noon*
But seas between us braid° hae roared, *broad* 15
  Sin' auld lang syne.

(Chorus)

And there's a hand, my trusty fiere°,   *friend*
  And gie's a hand o' thine;
And we'll tak a right gude-willie waught,
  For auld lang syne.   20

(Chorus)

And surely ye'll be° your pint-stowp°, *pay for / pint cup*
  And surely I'll be mine;
And we'll tak a cup o' kindness yet,
  For auld lang syne.

(Chorus)

AULD LANG SYNE   long ago.   [19]**waught** a very hearty swig.

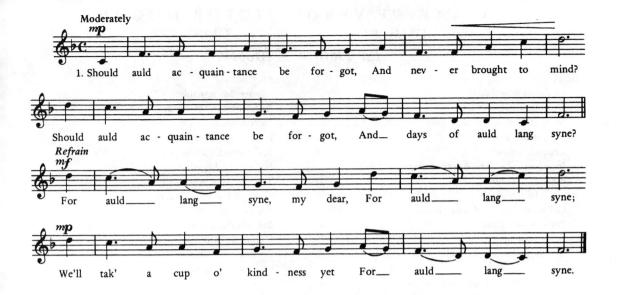

Moderately *mp*

1. Should auld ac-quain-tance be for-got, And nev-er brought to mind?

Should auld ac-quain-tance be for-got, And days of auld lang syne?

Refrain *mf*

For auld lang syne, my dear, For auld lang syne;

mp

We'll tak' a cup o' kind-ness yet For auld lang syne.

JOHN NEWTON
[1725–1807]

Amazing Grace

Amazing grace (how sweet the sound)
That saved a wretch like me!
I once was lost, but now am found,
Was blind, but now I see.

'Twas grace that taught my heart to fear,   5
And grace my fears relieved;
How precious did that grace appear
The hour I first believed!

Through many dangers, toils, and snares
I have already come;   *10*
'Tis grace has brought me safe thus far,
And grace will lead me home.

The Lord has promised good to me,
His word my hope secures;
He will my shield and portion be   *15*
As long as life endures.

The earth shall soon dissolve like snow,
The sun forbear to shine;
But God, who call'd me here below,
Will be forever mine.   *20*

GIUSEPPE VERDI/VICTOR HUGO
[1813–1901]   [1802–1885]
La Donna È Mobile

DUCA

La donna è mobile
Qual piuma al vento,
Muto d'accento—e di pensier.
Sempre un' amabile
Leggiadro viso,   5
In pianto o in riso—è menzogner.
È sempre misero,
Chi a lei s'affida,
Chi le confida—mal caute il cor!
Pur mai non sentesi   10
Felice appieno
Chi su quel seno—non liba amor.

DUKE

Women are unstable
As feathers in the wind,
Each moment change their mind.
In tears, or even smiles,
Yes, woman's lovely face,
For ever us beguiles!
The man that is so mad
To trust a woman's heart
For ever must be sad,
But still there is no bliss,
Upon this earth compared
To that of a sweet kiss!

EDWIN ARLINGTON ROBINSON

[1869–1935]

Richard Cory

Whenever Richard Cory went down town,
We people on the pavement looked at him:
He was a gentleman from sole to crown,
Clean favored and imperially slim.

And he was always quietly arrayed,   5
And he was always human when he talked,
But still he fluttered pulses when he said,
"Good-morning," and he glittered when he walked.

And he was rich—yes, richer than a king—
And admirably schooled in every grace: 10
In fine, we thought that he was everything
To make us wish that we were in his place.

So on we worked, and waited for the light,
And went without the meat and cursed the bread;
And Richard Cory, one calm summer night,   15
Went home and put a bullet through his head.

PAUL SIMON

[b. 1942]

Richard Cory

They say that Richard Cory owns one-half of this whole town,
With political connections to spread his wealth around.
Born into society, a banker's only child,
He had everything a man could want: power, grace and style.

But I work in his factory,   5
And I curse the life I'm living,
And I curse my poverty
And I wish that I could be
Richard Cory.

The papers print his picture almost everywhere he goes,   10
Richard Cory at the opera, Richard Cory at the show,
And the rumor of his parties, and the orgies on his yacht;
Oh, he surely must be happy with everything he's got.

But I work in his factory,
And I curse the life I'm living,
And I curse my poverty
And I wish that I could be
Richard Cory.

     15

He freely gave to charity, he had the common touch,
And they were grateful for his patronage, and they thanked him very much.   20
So my mind was filled with wonder, when the evening headlines read:
"Richard Cory went home last night and put a bullet through his head."

But I work in his factory,
And I curse the life I'm living,
And I curse my poverty
And I wish that I could be
Richard Cory.

     25

LANGSTON HUGHES
[1902–1967]
Same in Blues

I said to my baby,
Baby, take it slow.
I can't, she said, I can't!
I got to go!

    There's a certain   5
    amount of traveling
    in a dream deferred.

Lulu said to Leonard,
I want a diamond ring.
Leonard said to Lulu,   10
You won't get a goddamn thing!

    A certain
    amount of nothing
    in a dream deferred.

Daddy, daddy, daddy,   15
All I want is you.
You can have me, baby—
but my lovin' days is through.

    A certain
    amount of impotence   20
    in a dream deferred.

Three parties
On my party line—
But that third party,
Lord, ain't mine!   25

  There's liable
  to be confusion
  in a dream deferred.

From river to river
Uptown and down,   30
There's liable to be confusion
when a dream gets kicked around.

  You talk like
  they don't kick
  dreams around   35
  Downtown.

I expect they do—
But I'm talking about
Harlem to you!
Harlem to you!   40
Harlem to you!
Harlem to you!

ARTHUR HERZOG JR. AND BILLIE HOLIDAY

[1915–1959]

God Bless the Child

Them that's got shall get,
Them that's not shall lose,
So the Bible said,
And it still is news;

Refrain

  Mama may have,   5
  Papa may have,
  But God bless' the child
  That's got his own!
  That's got his own.

Yes, the strong gets more,   10
While the weak ones fade,
Empty pockets don't ever make the grade;

Money, you got lots o' friends,
Crowdin' 'round the door,
When you're gone and spendin' ends—   15
They don't come no more.

Rich relations give,
Crust of bread, and such
You can help yourself,
But don't take too much!   20

(Refrain)

Them that's got shall get, Them that's not shall lose, So the Bi-ble said, And it still is news;

Ma-ma may have, Pa-pa may have, But God bless' the child That's got his own! That's got his own.

Yes, the strong gets more, While the weak ones fade, Emp-ty pock-ets don't ev-er make the grade;

Ma-ma may have, Pa-pa may have, But God bless' the child That's got his own! That's got his own.

Mon-ey, you got lots o' friends, Crow-din' 'round the door, When you're gone and

spend-in' ends,— They don't come no more. Rich re-la-tions give, Crust of

bread, and such, You can help your-self, But don't take too much! Ma-ma may have,

Pa-pa may have, But God bless' the child That's got his own! That's got his own.___

BESSIE SMITH

[1894–1937]

Lost Your Head Blues

I was with you baby when you did not have a dime.
I was with you baby when you did not have a dime.
Now since you got plenty money you have throw'd your good gal down.

Once ain't for always, two ain't for twice.
Once ain't for always, two ain't for twice.   5
When you get a good gal you better treat her nice.

When you were lonesome I tried to treat you kind.
When you were lonesome I tried to treat you kind.
But since you've got money, it's done changed your mind.

I'm going to leave baby, ain't going to say goodbye.   10
I'm going to leave baby, ain't going to say goodbye.
But I'll write you and tell you the reason why.

Days are lonesome, nights are long.
Days are lonesome, nights are so long.
I'm a good old gal, but I've just been treated wrong.   15

WOODY GUTHRIE

[1912–1967]

This Land Is Your Land

This land is your land, this land is my land
From California to the New York Island,
From the Redwood forest, to the Gulf stream waters,
   This land was made for you and me.*

As I went walking that ribbon of highway   5
And saw above me the endless skyway
And saw below me that golden valley, I said
   This land was made for you and me.

I roamed and rambled and followed my footsteps
To the sparkling sands of her diamond deserts   10
And all around me, a voice was sounding:
   This land was made for you and me.

*In the original version of the song the last line of each stanza read. God blessed this land for you and me.

106

Was a big high wall there that tried to stop me
A sign was painted said: Private Property.
But on the back side, it didn't say nothing—   15
    This land was made for you and me.

When the sun come shining, then I was strolling
In the wheat fields waving, and dust clouds rolling
The voice was chanting as the fog was lifting:
    This land was made for you and me.   20

One bright sunny morning in the shadow of the steeple
By the relief office I saw my people—
As they stood there hungry, I stood there wondering if
    This land was made for you and me.

Ecclesiastes 3:1–8.

To every thing there is a season

To every *thing there is* a season,
and a time to every purpose under the heaven:
A time to be born, and a time to die;
a time to plant, and a time to pluck up *that which is* planted;
A time to kill, and a time to heal;
a time to break down, and a time to build up;
A time to weep, and a time to laugh;
a time to mourn, and a time to dance;
A time to cast away stones, and a time to gather stones together;
a time to embrace, and a time to refrain from embracing;
A time to get, and a time to lose;
a time to keep, and a time to cast away;
A time to rend, and a time to sew;
a time to keep silence, and a time to speak;
A time to love, and a time to hate;
a time of war, and a time of peace.

PETE SEEGER

[b. 1919]

Turn! Turn! Turn!

To everything,
Turn, turn, turn,
There is a season,
Turn, turn, turn,
And a time to every purpose under heaven.   5

A time to be born, a time to die,
A time to plant, a time to reap,
A time to kill, a time to heal,
A time to laugh, a time to weep.

To everything,   10
Turn, turn, turn,
There is a season,
Turn, turn, turn,
And a time to every purpose under heaven.

A time to build up, a time to break down,   15
A time to get, a time to want,
A time to cast away stones, a time to gather stones together.

To everything,
Turn, turn, turn,
There is a season,   20
Turn, turn, turn,
And a time to every purpose under heaven.

A time of love, a time of hate,
A time of war, a time of peace,
A time you may embrace, a time to refrain from embracing.   25

To everything,
Turn, turn, turn,
There is a season,
Turn, turn, turn,
And a time to every purpose under heaven.   30

A time to gain, a time to lose,
A time to rend, a time to sew,
A time for love, a time for hate,
A time for peace, I swear it's not too late.

DON MacLEAN

[b. 1945]

Vincent

Starry, starry night,
Paint your palette blue and gray.
Look out on a summer's day,
With eyes that know the darkness in my soul.

Shadows on the hills,   5
Sketch the trees and the daffodils,
Catch the breeze and the winter chills,
In colors on the snowy linen land.

Now I understand
What you tried to say to me,   10
How you suffered for your sanity,
How you tried to set them free.

They would not listen.
They did not know how.
Perhaps they'll listen now.   15

Starry, starry night,
Flaming flow'rs that brightly blaze,
Swirling clouds in violet haze
Reflect in Vincent's eyes of China blue.

Colors changing hue,   20
Morning fields of amber grain,
Weathered faces lined in pain
Are soothed beneath the artist's loving hand.

Now I understand
What you tried to say to me,   25
How you suffered for your sanity
How you tried to set them free.

They would not listen.
They did not know how.
Perhaps they'll listen now.   30

For they could not love you,
But still your love was true.
And when no hope was left in sight
On that starry, starry night,
You took your life, as lovers often do.   35

But I could have told you, Vincent,
This world was never meant
For one as beautiful as you.

Starry, starry night
Portraits hung in empty halls,   40
Frameless heads on nameless walls,
With eyes that watch the world and can't forget.

Like the strangers that you've met,
The ragged men in ragged clothes,

The silver thorn of bloody rose,   45
Lie crushed and broken on the virgin snow.

Now I think I know
What you tried to say to me,
How you suffered for your sanity
How you tried to set them free.   50

They would not listen.
They're not list'ning still.
Perhaps they never will.

POEMS IN ENGLISH

CAEDMON

[7th century]

*Caedmon's Hymn**

TRANSLATED BY E. TALBOT DONALDSON

Nu sculon herigean	heofonrices Weard
Now we must praise	heaven-kingdom's Guardian,
Meotodes meahte	and his modgeþane
the Measurer's might	and his mind-plans,
weorc Wuldor-Fæder	swa he wundra gehwæs
the work of the Glory-Father,	when he of wonders of every one,
ece Drihten	or onstealde
eternal Lord,	the beginning established.
He ærest sceop	ielda bearnum
He first created	for men's sons
hèofon to hrofe	halig Scyppend
heaven as a roof,	holy Creator;
ða middangeard	moncynnes Weard
then middle-earth	mankind's Guardian,
ece Drihten	æfter teode
eternal Lord,	afterwards made—
firum foldan	Frea ælmihtig
for men earth,	Master almighty.

*This Old English poem has been printed to emphasize the caesura or break in the middle of each line. The translation is printed directly beneath the original.

113

ANONYMOUS

The Seafarer

FROM THE ANGLO-SAXON

TRANSLATED BY EZRA POUND

May I for my own self song's truth reckon,
Journey's jargon, how I in harsh days
Hardship endured oft.
Bitter breast-cares have I abided,
Known on my keel many a care's hold,   5
And dire sea-surge, and there I oft spent
Narrow nightwatch nigh the ship's head
While she tossed close to cliffs. Coldly afflicted,
My feet were by frost benumbed.
Chill its chains are; chafing sighs   10
Hew my heart round and hunger begot
Mere-weary° mood. Lest man know not   *sea-weary*
That he on dry land loveliest liveth,
List how I, care-wretched, on ice-cold sea,
Weathered the winter, wretched outcast   15
Deprived of my kinsmen;
Hung with hard ice-flakes, where hail-scur° flew,   *hailstones*
There I heard naught save the harsh sea
And ice-cold wave, at whiles the swan cries,
Did for my games the gannet's clamor,   20
Sea-fowls' loudness was for me laughter,
The mews' singing all my mead-drink.
Storms, on the stone-cliffs beaten, fell on the stern
In icy feathers; full oft the eagle screamed
With spray on his pinion.
                              Not any protector   25
May make merry man faring needy.
This he little believes, who aye in winsome life
Abides 'mid burghers some heavy business,
Wealthy and wine-flushed, how I weary oft
Must bide above brine.   30
Neareth nightshade, snoweth from north,
Frost froze the land, hail fell on earth then,
Corn of the coldest. Nathless° there knocketh now   *notwithstanding*
The heart's thought that I on high streams

The salt-wavy tumult traverse alone.   35
Moaneth alway my mind's lust
That I fare forth, that I afar hence
Seek out a foreign fastness.
For this there's no mood-lofty man over earth's midst,
Not though he be given his good, but will have in his youth greed;   40
Nor his deed to the daring, nor his king to the faithful
But shall have his sorrow for sea-fare
Whatever his lord will.
He hath not heart for harping, nor in ring-having
Nor winsomeness to wife, nor world's delight   45
Nor any whit else save the wave's slash,
Yet longing comes upon him to fare forth on the water.
Bosque° taketh blossom, cometh beauty of berries,   *grove*
Fields to fairness, land fares brisker,
All this admonisheth man eager of mood,   50
The heart turns to travel so that he then thinks
On flood-ways to be far departing.
Cuckoo calleth with gloomy crying,
He singeth summerward, bodeth sorrow,
The bitter heart's blood. Burgher knows not—   55
He the prosperous man—what some perform
Where wandering them widest draweth.
So that but now my heart burst from my breastlock,
My mood 'mid the mere-flood,°   *sea flood*
Over the whale's acre, would wander wide.   60
On earth's shelter cometh oft to me,
Eager and ready, the crying lone-flyer,
Whets for the whale-path the heart irresistibly,
O'er tracks of ocean; seeing that anyhow
My lord deems to me this dead life   65
On loan and on land, I believe not
That any earth-weal eternal standeth
Save there be somewhat calamitous
That, ere a man's tide go, turn it to twain.
Disease or oldness or sword-hate   70
Beats out the breath from doom-gripped body.
And for this, every earl whatever, for those speaking after—
Laud of the living, boasteth some last word,
That he will work ere he pass onward,
Frame on the fair earth 'gainst foes his malice,   75
Daring ado°, . . .   *brave deeds*
So that all men shall honor him after
And his laud beyond them remain 'mid the English,

Aye, for ever, a lasting life's-blast,
Delight 'mid the doughty.
                              Days little durable,   *80*
And all arrogance of earthen riches,
There come now no kings nor Cæsars
Nor gold-giving lords like those gone.
Howe'er in mirth most magnified,
Whoe'er lived in life most lordliest,   *85*
Drear all this excellence, delights undurable!
Waneth the watch, but the world holdeth.
Tomb hideth trouble. The blade is layed low.
Earthly glory ageth and seareth.
No man at all going the earth's gait,   *90*
But age fares against him, his face paleth,
Gray-haired he groaneth, knows gone companions,
Lordly men, are to earth o'ergiven,
Nor may he then the flesh-cover, whose life ceaseth,
Nor eat the sweet nor feel the sorry,   *95*
Nor stir hand nor think in mid heart,
And though he strew the grave with gold,
His born brothers, their buried bodies
Be an unlikely treasure hoard.

[c. 9th century]

GEOFFREY CHAUCER

[c. 1343–1400]

Geoffrey Chaucer had the unusual experience, for a man of the Middle Ages, of living among different social classes. Born into a middle-class family as the son of a wine merchant, Chaucer spent his early years among commoners in the merchandising quarter of London. In his teens, however, he was sent to Antwerp, where he served as a page in the aristocratic household of a son of the English king, Edward III. There Chaucer became associated with the relatives of courtly families, including the future English kings Richard II and Henry IV. The young Chaucer's experience of living in both worlds became an element he drew upon in developing into a gifted and versatile poet.

Chaucer's duties in service of the aristocracy included travel to Italy and France as a trade ambassador. He was also responsible for collecting taxes on wool, England's largest trade commodity. Throughout his adult life, Chaucer held a number of posts and appointments, including deputy forester of one of the King's game preserves and Clerk of the King's Works. During these years, Chaucer became familiar with issues important to intellectuals of his time. He was well versed in French language and literature, and in fact is believed to have translated an important medieval French poem, the *Romance of the Rose*. Sometime in the 1360s, Chaucer was at work on what was to become his first major poetic achievement, the *Book of the Duchess*.

As a well-educated medieval intellectual, Chaucer was familiar with Latin literature, history, and philosophy. He read both Ovid and Virgil in their original language. Other Latin writers he probably read in French translations. Like Shakespeare, Chaucer did not know much if any Greek, though he became familiar with Greek myth, literature, and history through his knowledge of the Latin writers.

The most important influence on Chaucer's work, however, was not Latin but Italian. Chaucer's trip to Italy in 1372 is thought to have been a springboard to his immersion in Italian literature, especially the works of Dante and Boccaccio. Chaucer is known to have admired Dante's *Commedia* and to have appreciated if not deeply loved the poems of Petrarch. More important than either of these writers to Chaucer, however, was Giovanni Boccaccio, whose satiric temper was more attuned to Chaucer's. In fact, a number of Chaucer's *Canterbury Tales* derive from the tales of Boccaccio's *Decameron*. Even more important was the influence of Boccaccio's *Il Filostrato* (The Love Stricken) on Chaucer's longest completed poem, *Troilus and Criseide*, from about 1385. But it is neither *Troilus and Criseide*, as highly regarded as it is, nor Chaucer's other poetry that has made him such an admired and much-enjoyed poet. That honor belongs to his most famous work, *The Canterbury Tales*.

Although the *Tales* were unfinished at the time of his death in 1400, Chaucer had been working on them for nearly fifteen years, since about 1386. By this time Chaucer's many years of experience working with a wide range of people from different social classes had partially prepared him to write *The Canterbury Tales*. The *Tales*, in fact, are sometimes described as a medieval portrait gallery, since they include depictions of medieval figures from the highest and lowest social classes as well as from the three estates—the secular, the military, and the religious. But this descriptive range is only part of what Chaucer includes in the *Tales*. For although readers can learn a good deal about medieval social life from this work, *The Canterbury Tales* is primarily a work of literary art rather than one of social history. Its distinctiveness resides in Chaucer's ability to select the right details to portray his characters sharply and the appropriate combination of description, dialogue, and action to enable them to reveal themselves memorably.

Chaucer had originally planned to write 120 tales (or so at least the Host tells us in the General Prologue), two for each of his thirty pilgrims to tell on the pilgrimage to Canterbury and two for the return trip. (The pilgrims were making the journey to pay homage at the shrine of St. Thomas à Becket, who was martyred in Canterbury Cathedral in 1170.) Chaucer completed twenty-two tales and composed fragments of two others. He also prefaced the tales with a General Prologue that has been described as a "frame" for the tales, providing them with a realistic basis in fact. Beyond this important function, the General Prologue introduces the characters, who will later tell their own tales. Chaucer continues his characterization of these figures by ascribing to each a convincingly appropriate tale. That is, the character of the teller is further revealed by the nature and the manner of the tale he or she tells. In addition, Chaucer composed a series of "links," or brief interludes between tales, to join one to another and to further reveal the characters of the tellers.

It is clear from his selection of detail that Chaucer's attitude toward the various characters depicted in the General Prologue differs widely. Some he depicts as models, or ideals, to emulate; others he portrays as negative models, with their warts (both literal and figurative) showing. Chaucer uses the narrator as a conduit through which to channel his ironic and satiric portraits of the other pilgrims. Some critics have chosen to call the narrator "Chaucer the pilgrim" to distinguish him from "Chaucer the poet," the mastermind behind the literary performance of the whole work. However we choose to describe this dual Chaucer, the distinction is important, for as is clear at a number of points in the General Prologue, the narrator admires characters like the Pardoner and the Summoner in ways that differ from his admiration for the Clerk, the Parson, and the Knight. The "naive" narrator fails to discriminate between good and evil manifestations of human behavior; he also fails to distinguish between the ideals certain of the characters are supposed to strive for and the less admirable realities they substitute—as in the cases of the Monk and the Prioress.

In such instances of characterization, Chaucer employs acute irony as an instrument of equally trenchant satire. Chaucer's wit and observation are evident throughout the entire work, though we can see them perhaps most clearly and readily in the General Prologue. Evident in both the General Prologue and the *Tales* overall, moreover, is a vitality and gusto that reveal a remarkable appreciation of life, from its lowest and bawdiest examples to its most elegant and spiritual manifestations.

Although all this and more is evident in the General Prologue, one dimension of Chaucer's genius is not available in that introductory section of the work: his dramatic genius. For although *The Canterbury Tales* is essentially a collection of narratives in rhymed couplets, Chaucer has not overlooked the relationships among the pilgrims he portrays. These relationships are subtle and complex, but they can be suggested by the sections that precede and conclude Chaucer's description of the Pardoner—the words between the host and the Pardoner that precede and follow the Pardoner's Prologue and Tale. The way in which the Host, Harry Bailey, comments on the tale that precedes the Pardoner's, and the way Chaucer describes the Host as inviting the next pilgrim to begin his tale, reveal the writer's concern for the thematic and dramatic unity of his work. This is further illustrated in the Host's words to the Pardoner and in the Pardoner's own comments to his fellow pilgrims once his tale has been concluded. In fact, the entire description of the Pardoner's relationship to the pilgrims reveals Chaucer's understanding of the Pardoner's skill in manipulating the fears of his audience and an equally astute understanding of precisely how the Pardoner operates.

Two additional things must be noted. First, although generally cast in the form of iambic pentameter couplets, *The Canterbury Tales* are just that—a series of narratives, of stories well told. Our interest in them as literature thus is dual, for we need to consider both their narrative technique and their language. Second, Chaucer's medieval English differs in significant ways from Modern English, even from the Modern English that began to exist a generation before Shakespeare. Although we do not want to exaggerate the extent of this difference (since Chaucer's English is clearly recognizable as English and not a foreign language) we believe that some readers with little or no experience in reading Middle English will appreciate some help. We have therefore provided a facing translation into Modern English. Reading either Chaucer's language or the translator's modern version will unequivocally demonstrate why Chaucer is one of the greatest of English poets and also one of the best loved.

The Canterbury Tales

The General Prologue

Whan that Aprill with his shoures soote		When in April the sweet showers fall
The droghte of March hath perced to the roote,		And pierce the drought of March to the root, and all
And bathed every veyne in swich licour		The veins are bathed in liquor of such power
Of which vertu engendred is the flour;		As brings about the engendering of the flower,
Whan Zephirus eek with his sweete breeth	5	When also Zephyrus with his sweet breath
Inspired hath in every holt and heeth		Exhales an air in every grove and heath
The tendre croppes, and the yonge sonne		Upon the tender shoots, and the young sun
Hath in the Ram his half cours yronne,		His half course in the sign of the *Ram* has run,
And smale foweles maken melodye,		And the small fowl are making melody
That slepen al the nyght with open ye	10	That sleep away the night with open eye
(So priketh hem nature in hir corages),		(So nature pricks them and their heart engages)
Thanne longen folk to goon on pilgrimages,		Then people long to go on pilgrimages
And palmeres for to seken straunge strondes,		And palmers long to seek the stranger strands
To ferne halwes, kowthe in sondry londes;		Of far-off saints, hallowed in sundry lands,
And specially from every shires ende	15	And specially, from every shire's end
Of Engelond to Caunterbury they wende,		Of England, down to Canterbury they wend
The hooly blisful martir for to seke,		To seek the holy blissful martyr, quick
That hem hath holpen whan that they were seeke.		To give his help to them when they were sick.
Bifil that in that seson on a day,		It happened in that season that one day
In Southwerk at the Tabard as I lay	20	In Southwark, at *The Tabard*, as I lay
Redy to wenden on my pilgrymage		Ready to go on pilgrimage and start
To Caunterbury with ful devout corage,		For Canterbury, most devout at heart,
At nyght was come into that hostelrye		At night there came into that hostelry
Wel nyne and twenty in a compaignye		Some nine and twenty in a company
Of sondry folk, by aventure yfalle	25	Of sundry folk happening then to fall
In felaweshipe, and pilgrimes were they alle,		In fellowship, and they were pilgrims all
That toward Caunterbury wolden ryde.		That toward Canterbury meant to ride.
The chambres and the stables weren wyde,		The rooms and stables of the inn were wide;
And wel we weren esed atte beste.		They made us easy, all was of the best.
And shortly, whan the sonne was to reste,	30	And, briefly, when the sun had gone to rest,

So hadde I spoken with hem everichon
That I was of hir felaweshipe anon,
And made forward erly for to ryse,
To take oure wey ther as I yow devyse.

But nathelees, whil I have tyme and space,
Er that I ferther in this tale pace,
Me thynketh it acordaunt to resoun
To telle yow al the condicioun
Of ech of hem, so as it semed me,
And whiche they weren, and of what degree   40
And eek in what array that they were inne;
And at a knyght than wol I first bigynne.

A KNYGHT ther was, and that a worthy man,
That fro the tyme that he first bigan
To riden out, he loved chivalrie,   45
Trouthe and honour, fredom and curteisie.
Ful worthy was he in his lordes werre,
And therto hadde he riden, no man ferre,
As wel in cristendom as in hethenesse,
And evere honoured for his worthynesse;   50
At Alisaundre he was whan it was wonne.
Ful ofte tyme he hadde the bord bigonne
Aboven alle nacions in Pruce;
In Lettow hadde he reysed and in Ruce,
No Cristen man so ofte of his degree.   55
In Gernade at the seege eek hadde he be
Of Algezir, and riden in Belmarye.
At Lyeys was he and at Satalye,
Whan they were wonne, and in the Grete See
At many a noble armee hadde he be.   60
At mortal batailles hadde he been fiftene,
And foughten for oure feith at Tramyssene
In lystes thries, and ay slayn his foo.

This ilke worthy knyght hadde been also
Somtyme with the lord of Palatye   65
Agayn another hethen in Turkye;
And everemoore he hadde a sovereyn prys.
And though that he were worthy, he was wys,
And of his port as meeke as is a mayde.
He nevere yet no vileynye ne sayde   70
In al his lyf unto no maner wight.
He was a verray, parfit gentil knyght.
But for to tellen yow of his array,
His hors were goode, but he was nat gay.
Of fustian he wered a gypon   75
Al bismotered with his habergeon,

I'd spoken to them all upon the trip
And was soon one with them in fellowship,
Pledged to rise early and to take the way
To Canterbury, as you heard me say.

But nonetheless, while I have time and space,
Before my story takes a further pace,
It seems a reasonable thing to say
What their condition was, the full array
Of each of them, as it appeared to me,
According to profession and degree,
And what apparel they were riding in;
And at a Knight I therefore will begin.

There was a *Knight,* a most distinguished man,
Who from the day on which he first began
To ride abroad had followed chivalry,
Truth, honor, generousness and courtesy.
He had done nobly in his sovereign's war
And ridden into battle, no man more,
As well in Christian as in heathen places,
And ever honored for his noble graces;
     When we took Alexandria, he was there.
He often sat at table in the chair
Of honor, above all nations, when in Prussia.
In Lithuania he had ridden, and Russia,
No Christian man so often, of his rank.
When, in Granada, Algeciras sank
Under assault, he had been there, and in
North Africa, raiding Benamarin;
In Anatolia he had been as well
And fought when Ayas and Attalia fell,
For all along the Mediterranean coast
He had embarked with many a noble host.
In fifteen mortal battles he had been
And jousted for our faith at Tramissene
Thrice in the lists, and always killed his man.
This same distinguished knight had led the van
Once with the Bey of Balat, doing work
For him against another heathen Turk;
He was of sovereign value in all eyes.
And though so much distinguished, he was wise
And in his bearing modest as a maid.
He never yet a boorish thing had said
In all his life to any, come what might;
He was a true, a perfect gentle-knight.
     Speaking of his equipment, he possessed
Fine horses, but he was not gaily dressed.
He wore a fustian tunic stained and dark
With smudges where his armor had left mark;

For he was late ycome from his viage,
And wente for to doon his pilgrymage.

    With hym ther was his sone, a yong SQUIER,
A lovyere and a lusty bacheler,   80
With lokkes crulle as they were leyd in presse.
Of twenty yeer of age he was, I gesse.
Of his stature he was of evene lengthe,
And wonderly delyvere, and of greet strengthe.
And he hadde been somtyme in chyvachie   85
In Flaundres, in Artoys, and Pycardie,
And born hym weel, as of so litel space,
In hope to stonden in his lady grace.
Embrouded was he, as it were a meede
Al ful of fresshe floures, whyte and reede.   90
Syngynge he was, or floytynge, al the day;
He was as fressh as is the month of May.
Short was his gowne, with sleves longe and wyde.
Wel koude he sitte on hors and faire ryde.
He koude songes make and wel endite,   95
Juste and eek daunce, and weel purtreye and write.
So hoote he lovede that by nyghtertale
He sleep namoore than dooth a nyghtyngale.
Curteis he was, lowely, and servysable,
And carf biforn his fader at the table.   100

    A YEMAN hadde he and servantz namo
At that tyme, for hym liste ride so,
And he was clad in cote and hood of grene.
A sheef of pecok arwes, bright and kene,
Under his belt he bar ful thriftily   105
(Wel koude he dresse his takel yemanly;
His arwes drouped noght with fetheres lowe),
And in his hand he baar a myghty bowe.
A not heed hadde he, with a broun visage.
Of wodecraft wel koude he al the usage.   110
Upon his arm he baar a gay bracer,
And by his syde a swerd and a bokeler,
And on that oother syde a gay daggere
Harneised wel and sharp as point of spere;
A Cristopher on his brest of silver sheene.   115
An horn he bar, the bawdryk was of grene;
A forster was he, soothly, as I gesse.

    Ther was also a Nonne, a PRIORESSE,
That of hir smylyng was ful symple and coy;
Hire gretteste ooth was but by Seinte Loy;   120
And she was cleped madame Eglentyne.
Ful weel she soong the service dyvyne,

Just home from service, he had joined our ranks
To do his pilgrimage and render thanks.

    He had his son with him, a fine young *Squire,*
A lover and cadet, a lad of fire
With locks as curly as if they had been pressed.
He was some twenty years of age, I guessed.
In stature he was of a moderate length,
With wonderful agility and strength.
He'd seen some service with the cavalry
In Flanders and Artois and Picardy
And had done valiantly in little space
Of time, in hope to win his lady's grace.
He was embroidered like a meadow bright
And full of freshest flowers, red and white.
Singing he was, or fluting all the day;
He was as fresh as is the month of May.
Short was his gown, the sleeves were long and wide;
He knew the way to sit a horse and ride.
He could make songs and poems and recite,
Knew how to joust and dance, to draw and write.
He loved so hotly that till dawn grew pale
He slept as little as a nightingale.
Courteous he was, lowly and serviceable,
And carved to serve his father at the table.

    There was a *Yeoman* with him at his side,
No other servant; so he chose to ride.
This Yeoman wore a coat and hood of green,
And peacock-feathered arrows, bright and keen
And neatly sheathed, hung at his belt the while
—For he could dress his gear in yeoman style,
His arrows never drooped their feathers low—
And in his hand he bore a mighty bow.
His head was like a nut, his face was brown.
He knew the whole of woodcraft up and down.
A saucy brace was on his arm to ward
It from the bowstring, and a shield and sword
Hung at one side, and at the other slipped
A jaunty dirk, spear-sharp and well equipped.
A medal of St. Christopher he wore
Of shining silver on his breast, and bore
A hunting-horn, well slung and burnished clean,
That dangled from a baldrick of bright green.
He was a proper forester, I guess.

    There also was a *Nun,* a Prioress,
Her way of smiling very simple and coy.
Her greatest oath was only "By St. Loy!"
And she was known as Madam Eglantyne.
And well she sang a service, with a fine

Entuned in hir nose ful semely;
And Frenssh she spak ful faire and fetisly,
After the scole of Stratford atte Bowe,   125
For Frenssh of Parys was to hire unknowe.
At mete wel ytaught was she with alle;
She leet no morsel from hir lippes falle,
Ne wette hir fyngres in hir sauce depe;
Wel koude she carie a morsel and wel kepe   130
That no drope ne fille upon hire brest.
In curteisie was set ful muchel hir lest.
Hir over-lippe wyped she so clene
That in hir coppe ther was no ferthyng sene
Of grece, whan she dronken hadde hir draughte.   135
Ful semely after hir mete she raughte.
And sikerly she was of greet desport,
And ful plesaunt, and amyable of port,
And peyned hire to countrefete cheere
Of court, and to been estatlich of manere,   140
And to ben holden digne of reverence.
But for to speken of hire conscience,
She was so charitable and so pitous
She wolde wepe, if that she saugh a mous
Kaught in a trappe, if it were deed or bledde.   145
Of smale houndes hadde she that she fedde
With rosted flessh, or milk and wastel-breed.
But soore wepte she if oon of hem were deed,
Or if men smoot it with a yerde smerte;
And al was conscience and tendre herte.   150
Ful semyly hir wympul pynched was,
Hir nose tretys, hir eyen greye as glas,
Hir mouth ful smal, and therto softe and reed.
But sikerly she hadde a fair forheed;
It was almoost a spanne brood, I trowe;   155
For, hardily, she was nat undergrowe.
Ful fetys was hir cloke, as I was war.
Of smal coral aboute hire arm she bar
A peire of bedes, gauded al with grene,
And theron heng a brooch of gold ful sheene,   160
On which ther was first write a crowned A,
And after *Amor vincit omnia.*
    Another NONNE with hire hadde she,
That was hir chapeleyne, and preestes thre.
    A MONK ther was, a fair for the maistrie,   165
An outridere, that lovede venerie,
A manly man, to been an abbot able.
Ful many a deyntee hors hadde he in stable,
And whan he rood, men myghte his brydel heere
Gynglen in a whistlynge wynd als cleere   170
And eek as loude as dooth the chapel belle

Intoning through her nose, as was most seemly,
And she spoke daintily in French, extremely,
After the school of Stratford-at-Bowe;
French in the Paris style she did not know.
At meat her manners were well taught withal;
No morsel from her lips did she let fall,
Nor dipped her fingers in the sauce too deep;
But she could carry a morsel up and keep
The smallest drop from falling on her breast.
For courtliness she had a special zest,
And she would wipe her upper lip so clean
That not a trace of grease was to be seen
Upon the cup when she had drunk; to eat,
She reached a hand sedately for the meat.
She certainly was very entertaining,
Pleasant and friendly in her ways, and straining
To counterfeit a courtly kind of grace,
A stately bearing fitting to her place,
And to seem dignified in all her dealings.
As for her sympathies and tender feelings,
She was so charitably solicitous
She used to weep if she but saw a mouse
Caught in a trap, if it were dead or bleeding.
And she had little dogs she would be feeding
With roasted flesh, or milk, or fine white bread.
And bitterly she wept if one were dead
Or someone took a stick and made it smart;
She was all sentiment and tender heart.
Her veil was gathered in a seemly way,
Her nose was elegant, her eyes glass-grey;
Her mouth was very small, but soft and red,
Her forehead, certainly, was fair of spread,
Almost a span across the brows, I own;
She was indeed by no means undergrown.
Her cloak, I noticed, had a graceful charm.
She wore a coral trinket on her arm,
A set of beads, the gaudies tricked in green,
Whence hung a golden brooch of brightest sheen
On which there first was graven a crowned A,
And lower, *Amor vincit omnia.*
    Another *Nun,* the secretary at her cell,
Was riding with her, and *three Priests* as well.
    A *Monk* there was, one of the finest sort
Who rode the country; hunting was his sport.
A manly man, to be an Abbot able;
Many a dainty horse he had in stable.
His bridle, when he rode, a man might hear
Jingling in a whistling wind as clear,
Aye, and as loud as does the chapel bell

Ther as this lord was kepere of the celle.
The reule of Seint Maure or of Seint Beneit—
By cause that it was old and somdel streit
This ilke Monk leet olde thynges pace,   175
And heeld after the newe world the space.
He yaf nat of that text a pulled hen,
That seith that hunters ben nat hooly men,
Ne that a monk, whan he is recchelees,
Is likned til a fissh that is waterlees—   180
This is to seyn, a monk out of his cloystre.
But thilke text heeld he nat worth an oystre;
And I seyde his opinion was good.
What sholde he studie and make hymselven wood,
Upon a book in cloystre alwey to poure,   185
Or swynken with his handes, and laboure,
As Austyn bit? How shal the world be served?
Lat Austyn have his swynk to hym reserved!
Therfore he was a prikasour aright:
Grehoundes he hadde as swift as fowel in flight;   190
Of prikyng and of huntyng for the hare
Was al his lust, for no cost wolde he spare.
I seigh his sleves purfiled at the hond
With grys, and that the fyneste of a lond;
And for to festne his hood under his chyn,   195
He hadde of gold ywroght a ful curious pyn;
A love-knotte in the gretter ende ther was.
His heed was balled, that shoon as any glas,
And eek his face, as he hadde been enoynt.
He was a lord ful fat and in good poynt;   200
His eyen stepe, and rollynge in his heed,
That stemed as a forneys of a leed;
His bootes souple, his hors in greet estaat.
Now certeinly he was a fair prelaat;
He was nat pale as a forpyned goost.   205
A fat swan loved he best of any roost.
His palfrey was as broun as is a berye.
    A FRERE ther was, a wantowne and a merye,
A lymytour, a ful solempne man.
In alle the ordres foure is noon that kan   210
So muchel of daliaunce and fair langage.
He hadde maad ful many a mariage
Of yonge wommen at his owene cost.
Unto his ordre he was a noble post.
Ful wel biloved and famulier was he   215
With frankeleyns over al in his contree,
And eek with worthy wommen of the toun;
For he hadde power of confessioun,
As seyde hymself, moore than a curat,
For of his ordre he was licenciat.   220

Where my lord Monk was Prior of the cell.
The Rule of good St. Benet or St. Maur
As old and strict he tended to ignore;
He let go by the things of yesterday
And took the modern world's more spacious way.
He did not rate that text at a plucked hen
Which says that hunters are not holy men
And that a monk uncloistered is a mere
Fish out of water, flapping on the pier,
That is to say a monk out of his cloister.
That was a text he held not worth an oyster;
And I agreed and said his views were sound;
Was he to study till his head went round
Poring over books in cloisters? Must he toil
As Austin bade and till the very soil?
Was he to leave the world upon the shelf?
Let Austin have his labor to himself.
    This Monk was therefore a good man to horse;
Greyhounds he had, as swift as birds, to course.
Hunting a hare or riding at a fence
Was all his fun, he spared for no expense.
I saw his sleeves were garnished at the hand
With fine grey fur, the finest in the land,
And on his hood, to fasten it at his chin
He had a wrought-gold cunningly fashioned pin;
Into a lover's knot it seemed to pass.
His head was bald and shone like looking glass;
So did his face, as if it had been greased.
He was a fat and personable priest;
His prominent eyeballs never seemed to settle.
They glittered like the flames beneath a kettle;
Supple his boots, his horse in fine condition.
He was a prelate fit for exhibition,
He was not pale like a tormented soul.
He liked a fat swan best, and roasted whole.
His palfrey was as brown as is a berry.
    There was a *Friar,* a wanton one and merry,
A Limiter, a very festive fellow.
In all Four Orders there was none so mellow,
So glib with gallant phrase and well-turned speech.
He'd fixed up many a marriage, giving each
Of his young women what he could afford her.
He was a noble pillar to his Order.
Highly beloved and intimate was he
With County folk within his boundary,
And city dames of honor and possessions;
For he was qualified to hear confessions,
Or so he said, with more than priestly scope;
He had a special license from the Pope.

Ful swetely herde he confessioun,
And plesaunt was his absolucioun:
He was an esy man to yeve penaunce,
Ther as he wiste to have a good pitaunce.
For unto a povre ordre for to yive   225
Is signe that a man is wel yshryve;
For if he yaf, he dorste make avaunt,
He wiste that a man was repentaunt;
For many a man so hard is of his herte,
He may nat wepe, althogh hym soore smerte.   230
Therfore in stede of wepynge and preyeres
Men moote yeve silver to the povre freres.
His typet was ay farsed ful of knyves
And pynnes, for to yeven faire wyves.
And certeinly he hadde a murye note: 235
Wel koude he synge and pleyen on a rote;
Of yeddynges he baar outrely the pris.
His nekke whit was as the flour-de-lys;
Therto he strong was as a champioun.
He knew the tavernes wel in every toun   240
And everich hostiler and tappestere
Bet than a lazar or a beggestere,
For unto swich a worthy man as he
Acorded nat, as by his facultee,
To have with sike lazars aqueyntaunce.   245
It is nat honest; it may nat avaunce,
For to deelen with no swich poraille,
But al with riche and selleres of vitaille.
And over al, ther as profit sholde arise,
Curteis he was and lowely of servyse;   250
Ther nas no man nowher so vertuous.
He was the beste beggere in his hous;
[And yaf a certeyn ferme for the graunt;   252ᵃ
Noon of his bretheren cam ther in his haunt;]   252ᵇ
For thogh a wydwe hadde noght a sho,
So plesaunt was his *"In principio,"*
Yet wolde he have a ferthyng, er he wente.   255
His purchas was wel bettre than his rente.
And rage he koude, as it were right a whelp.
In love-dayes ther koude he muchel help,
For ther he was nat lyk a cloysterer
With a thredbare cope, as is a povre scoler,   260
But he was lyk a maister or a pope.
Of double worstede was his semycope,
That rounded as a belle out of the presse.
Somwhat he lipsed, for his wantownesse,
To make his Englissh sweete upon his tonge;   265
And in his harpyng, whan that he hadde songe,
His eyen twynkled in his heed aryght
As doon the sterres in the frosty nyght.

Sweetly he heard his penitents at shrift
With pleasant absolution, for a gift.
He was an easy man in penance giving
Where he could hope to make a decent living;
It's a sure sign whenever gifts are given
To a poor Order that a man's well shriven,
And should he give enough he knew in verity
The penitent repented in sincerity.
For many a fellow is so hard of heart
He cannot weep, for all his inward smart.
Therefore instead of weeping and of prayer
One should give silver for a poor Friar's care.
He kept his tippet stuffed with pins for curls,
And pocket knives, to give to pretty girls.
And certainly his voice was gay and sturdy,
For he sang well and played the hurdy-gurdy.
At singsongs he was champion of the hour.
His neck was whiter than a lily flower
But strong enough to butt a bruiser down.
He knew the taverns well in every town
And every innkeeper and barmaid too
Better than lepers, beggars and that crew,
For in so eminent a man as he
It was not fitting with the dignity
Of his position, dealing with a scum
Of wretched lepers; nothing good can come
Of commerce with such slum-and-gutter dwellers,
But only with the rich and victual sellers.
But anywhere a profit might accrue
Courteous he was and lowly of service too.
Natural gifts like his were hard to match.
He was the finest beggar of his batch,
And, for his begging district, paid a rent;
His brethren did no poaching where he went.
For though a widow mightn't have a shoe,
So pleasant was his holy how-d'ye-do
He got his farthing from her just the same
Before he left, and so his income came
To more than he laid out. And how he romped,
Just like a puppy! He was ever prompt
To arbitrate disputes on settling days
(For a small fee) in many helpful ways,
Not then appearing as your cloistered scholar
With threadbare habit hardly worth a dollar,
But much more like a Doctor or a Pope.
Of double worsted was the semicope
Upon his shoulders, and the swelling fold
About him, like a bell about its mold
When it is casting, rounded out his dress.
He lisped a little out of wantonness

This worthy lymytour was cleped Huberd.

A MARCHANT was ther with a forked berd,   *270*
In mottelee, and hye on horse he sat;
Upon his heed a Flaundryssh bever hat,
His bootes clasped faire and fetisly.
His resons he spak ful solempnely,
Sownynge alwey th'encrees of his wynnyng   *275*
He wolde the see were kept for any thyng
Bitwixe Middelburgh and Orewelle.
Wel koude he in eschaunge sheeldes selle.
This worthy man ful wel his wit bisette:
Ther wiste no wight that he was in dette,   *280*
So estatly was he of his governaunce
With his bargaynes and with his chevyssaunce.
For sothe he was a worthy man with alle,
But, sooth to seyn, I noot how men hym calle.

A CLERK ther was of Oxenford also,   *285*
That unto logyk hadde longe ygo.
As leene was his hors as is a rake,
And he nas nat right fat, I undertake,
But looked holwe, and therto sobrely.
Ful thredbare was his overeste courtepy,   *290*
For he hadde geten hym yet no benefice,
Ne was so worldly for to have office.
For hym was levere have at his beddes heed
Twenty bookes, clad in blak or reed,
Of Aristotle and his philosophie   *295*
Than robes riche, or fithele, or gay sautrie.
But al be that he was a philosophre,
Yet hadde he but litel gold in cofre;
But al that he myghte of his freendes hente,
On bookes and on lernynge he it spente,   *300*
And bisily gan for the soules preye
Of hem that yaf hym wherwith to scoleye.
Of studie took he moost cure and moost heede.
Noght o word spak he moore than was neede,
And that was seyd in forme and reverence,   *305*
And short and quyk and ful of hy sentence;
Sownynge in moral vertu was his speche,
And gladly wolde he lerne and gladly teche.

. . . .

A good WIF was ther OF biside BATHE,
But she was somdel deef, and that was scathe.   *310*
Of clooth-makyng she hadde swich an haunt
She passed hem of Ypres and of Gaunt.
In al the parisshe wif ne was ther noon

To make his English sweet upon his tongue,
When he had played his harp, or having sung,
His eyes would twinkle in his head as bright
As any star upon a frosty night.
This worthy's name was Hubert, it appeared.

There was a *Merchant* with a forking beard
And motley dress; high on his horse he sat,
Upon his head a Flemish beaver hat
And on his feet daintily buckled boots.
He told of his opinions and pursuits
In solemn tones, he harped on his increase
Of capital; there should be sea-police
(He thought) upon the Harwich–Holland ranges;
He was expert at dabbling in exchanges.
This estimable Merchant so had set
His wits to work, none knew he was in debt,
He was so stately in administration,
In loans and bargains and negotiation.
He was an excellent fellow all the same;
To tell the truth I do not know his name.

An *Oxford Cleric,* still a student though,
One who had taken logic long ago,
Was there; his horse was thinner than a rake,
And he was not too fat, I undertake,
But had a hollow look, a sober stare;
The thread upon his overcoat was bare.
He had found no preferment in the church
And he was too unworldly to make search
For secular employment. By his bed
He preferred having twenty books in red
And black, of Aristotle's philosophy,
Than costly clothes, fiddle or psaltery.
Though a philosopher, as I have told,
He had not found the stone for making gold.
Whatever money from his friends he took
He spent on learning or another book
And prayed for them most earnestly, returning
Thanks to them thus for paying for his learning.
His only care was study, and indeed
He never spoke a word more than was need,
Formal at that, respectful in the extreme,
Short, to the point, and lofty in his theme.
A tone of moral virtue filled his speech
And gladly would he learn, and gladly teach.

. . . .

A worthy *woman* from beside *Bath* city
Was with us, somewhat deaf, which was a pity.
In making cloth she showed so great a bent
She bettered those of Ypres and of Ghent.
In all the parish not a dame dared stir

That to the offrynge bifore hire sholde goon;
And if ther dide, certeyn so wrooth was she   315
That she was out of alle charitee.
Hir coverchiefs ful fyne weren of ground;
I dorste swere they weyeden ten pound
That on a Sonday weren upon hir heed.
Hir hosen weren of fyn scarlet reed,   320
Ful streite yteyd, and shoes ful moyste and newe.
Boold was hir face, and fair, and reed of hewe.
She was a worthy womman al hir lyve:
Housbondes at chirche dore she hadde fyve,
Withouten oother compaignye in youthe—   325
But thereof nedeth nat to speke as nowthe.
And thries hadde she been at Jerusalem;
She hadde passed many a straunge strem;
At Rome she hadde been, and at Boloigne,
In Galice at Seint-Jame, and at Coloigne.   330
She koude muchel of wandrynge by the weye.
Gat-tothed was she, soothly for to seye.
Upon an amblere esily she sat,
Ywympled wel, and on hir heed an hat
As brood as is a bokeler or a targe;   335
A foot-mantel aboute hir hipes large,
And on hir feet a paire of spores sharpe.
In felaweshipe wel koude she laughe and carpe.
Of remedies of love she knew per chaunce,
For she koude of that art the olde daunce.   340
   A good man was ther of religioun,
And was a povre PERSOUN OF A TOUN,
But riche he was of hooly thoght and werk.
He was also a lerned man, a clerk,
That Cristes gospel trewely wolde preche;   345
His parisshens devoutly wolde he teche.
Benygne he was, and wonder diligent,
And in adversitee ful pacient,
And swich he was ypreved ofte sithes.
Ful looth were hym to cursen for his tithes,   350
But rather wolde he yeven, out of doute,
Unto his povre parisshens aboute
Of his offryng and eek of his substaunce.
He koude in litel thyng have suffisaunce.
Wyd was his parisshe, and houses fer asonder,   355
But he ne lefte nat, for reyn ne thonder,
In siknesse nor in meschief to visite
The ferreste in his parisshe, muche and lite,
Upon his feet, and in his hand a staf.
This noble ensample to his sheep he yaf,   360
That first he wroghte, and afterward he taughte.
Out of the gospel he tho wordes caughte,
And this figure he added eek therto,

Towards the altar steps in front of her,
And if indeed they did, so wrath was she
As to be quite put out of charity.
Her kerchiefs were of finely woven ground;
I dared have sworn they weighed a good ten pound,
The ones she wore on Sunday, on her head.
Her hose were of the finest scarlet red
And gartered tight; her shoes were soft and new.
Bold was her face, handsome, and red in hue.
A worthy woman all her life, what's more
She'd had five husbands, all at the church door,
Apart from other company in youth;
No need just now to speak of that, forsooth.
And she had thrice been to Jerusalem,
Seen many strange rivers and passed over them;
She'd been to Rome and also to Boulogne,
St. James of Compostella and Cologne,
And she was skilled in wandering by the way.
She had gap teeth, set widely, truth to say.
Easily on an ambling horse she sat
Well wimpled up, and on her head a hat
As broad as is a buckler or a shield;
She had a flowing mantle that concealed
Large hips, her heels spurred sharply under that.
In company she liked to laugh and chat
And knew the remedies for love's mischances,
An art in which she knew the oldest dances.
   A holy-minded man of good renown
There was, and poor, the *Parson* to a town,
Yet he was rich in holy thought and work.
He also was a learned man, a clerk,
Who truly knew Christ's gospel and would preach it
Devoutly to parishioners, and teach it.
Benign and wonderfully diligent,
And patient when adversity was sent
(For so he proved in much adversity)
He hated cursing to extort a fee,
Nay, rather he preferred beyond a doubt
Giving to poor parishioners round about
Both from church offerings and his property;
He could in little find sufficiency.
Wide was his parish, with houses far asunder,
Yet he neglected not in rain or thunder,
In sickness or in grief, to pay a call
On the remotest, whether great or small,
Upon his feet, and in his hand a stave.
This noble example to his sheep he gave
That first he wrought, and afterwards he taught;
And it was from the Gospel he had caught
Those words, and he would add this figure too,

That if gold ruste, what shal iren do?
For if a preest be foul, on whom we truste,   *365*
No wonder is a lewed man to ruste;
And shame it is, if a prest take keep,
A shiten shepherde and a clene sheep.
Wel oghte a preest ensample for to yive,
By his clennesse, how that his sheep sholde lyve.   *370*
He sette nat his benefice to hyre
And leet his sheep encombred in the myre
And ran to Londoun unto Seinte Poules
To seken hym a chaunterie for soules,
Or with a bretherhed to been withholde;   *375*
But dwelte at hoom, and kepte wel his folde,
So that the wolf ne made it nat myscarie;
He was a shepherde and noght a mercenarie.
And though he hooly were and vertuous,
He was to synful men nat despitous,   *380*
Ne of his speche daungerous ne digne,
But in his techyng discreet and benygne.
To drawen folk to hevene by fairnesse,
By good ensample, this was his bisynesse.
But it were any persone obstinat,   *385*
What so he were, of heigh or lough estat,
Hym wolde he snybben sharply for the nonys.
A bettre preest I trowe that nowher noon ys.
He waited after no pompe and reverence,
Ne maked him a spiced conscience,   *390*
But Cristes loore and his apostles twelve
He taughte; but first he folwed it hymselve.
    With hym ther was a PLOWMAN, was his brother,
That hadde ylad of dong ful many a fother;
A trewe swynkere and a good was he,   *395*
Lyvynge in pees and parfit charitee.
God loved he best with al his hoole herte
At alle tymes, thogh him gamed or smerte,
And thanne his neighebor right as hymselve.
He wolde thresshe, and therto dyke and delve,   *400*
For Cristes sake, for every povre wight,
Withouten hire, if it lay in his myght.
His tithes payde he ful faire and wel,
Bothe of his propre swynk and his catel.
In a tabard he rood upon a mere.   *405*

Ther was also a REVE, and a MILLERE,
A SOMNOUR, and a PARDONER also,

A MAUNCIPLE, and myself—ther were namo.

That if gold rust, what then will iron do?
For if a priest be foul in whom we trust
No wonder that a common man should rust;
And shame it is to see—let priests take stock—
A shitten shepherd and a snowy flock.
The true example that a priest should give
Is one of cleanness, how the sheep should live.
He did not set his benefice to hire
And leave his sheep encumbered in the mire
Or run to London to earn easy bread
By singing masses for the wealthy dead,
Or find some Brotherhood and get enrolled.
He stayed at home and watched over his fold
So that no wolf should make the sheep miscarry.
He was a shepherd and no mercenary.
Holy and virtuous he was, but then
Never contemptuous of sinful men,
Never disdainful, never too proud or fine,
But was discreet in teaching and benign.
His business was to show a fair behavior
And draw men thus to Heaven and their Savior,
Unless indeed a man were obstinate;
And such, whether of high or low estate,
He put to sharp rebuke, to say the least.
I think there never was a better priest.
He sought no pomp or glory in his dealings,
No scrupulosity had spiced his feelings.
Christ and His Twelve Apostles and their lore
He taught, but followed it himself before.
    There was a *Plowman* with him there, his brother;
Many a load of dung one time or other
He must have carted through the morning dew.
He was an honest worker, good and true,
Living in peace and perfect charity,
And, as the gospel bade him, so did he,
Loving God best with all his heart and mind
And then his neighbor as himself, repined
At no misfortune, slacked for no content,
For steadily about his work he went
To thrash his corn, to dig or to manure
Or make a ditch; and he would help the poor
For love of Christ and never take a penny
If he could help it, and, as prompt as any,
He paid his tithes in full when they were due
On what he owned, and on his earnings too.
He wore a tabard smock and rode a mare.
    There was a *Reeve*, also a *Miller,* there,
A College *Manciple* from the Inns of Court,
A papal *Pardoner* and, in close consort,
A Church Court *Summoner,* riding at a trot,

The MILLERE was a stout carl for the nones;
Ful byg he was of brawn, and eek of bones.   410
That proved wel, for over al there he cam,
At wrastlynge he wolde have alwey the ram.
He was short-sholdred, brood, a thikke knarre;
Ther was no dore that he nolde heve of harre,
Or breke it at a rennyng with his heed.   415
His berd as any sowe or fox was reed,
And therto brood, as though it were a spade.
Upon the cop right of his nose he hade
A werte, and theron stood a toft of herys,
Reed as the brustles of a sowes erys;   420
His nosethirles blake were and wyde.
A swerd and a bokeler bar he by his syde.
His mouth as greet was as a greet forneys.
He was a janglere and a goliardeys,
And that was moost of synne and harlotries.   425
Wel koude he stelen corn and tollen thries;
And yet he hadde a thombe of gold, pardee.
A whit cote and a blew hood wered he.
A baggepipe wel koude he blowe and sowne
And therwithal he broghte us out of towne.   430

A gentil MAUNCIPLE was ther of a temple
Of which achatours myghte take exemple
For to be wise in byynge of vitaille;
For wheither that he payde or took by taille,
Algate he wayted so in his achaat   435
That he was ay biforn and in good staat.
Now is nat that of God a ful fair grace
That swich a lewed mannes wit shal pace
The wisdom of an heep of lerned men?
Of maistres hadde he mo than thries ten,   440
That weren of lawe expert and curious,
Of which ther were a duszeyne in that hous
Worthy to been stywardes of rente and lond
Of any lord that is in Engelond,
To make hym lyve by his propre good   445
In honour dettelees (but if he were wood),
Or lyve as scarsly as hym list desire;
And able for to helpen al a shire
In any caas that myghte falle or happe.
And yet this Manciple sette hir aller cappe.   450

. . . .

A SOMONOUR was ther with us in that place,
That hadde a fyr-reed cherubynnes face,
For saucefleem he was, with eyen narwe.

And finally myself—that was the lot.
    The *Miller* was a chap of sixteen stone,
A great stout fellow big in brawn and bone.
He did well out of them, for he could go
And win the ram at any wrestling show.
Broad, knotty and short-shouldered, he would boast
He could heave any door off hinge and post,
Or take a run and break it with his head.
His beard, like any sow or fox, was red
And broad as well, as though it were a spade;
And, at its very tip, his nose displayed
A wart on which there stood a tuft of hair
Red as the bristles in an old sow's ear.
His nostrils were as black as they were wide.
He had a sword and buckler at his side,
His mighty mouth was like a furnace door.
A wrangler and buffoon, he had a store
Of tavern stories, filthy in the main.
His was a master hand at stealing grain.
He felt it with his thumb and thus he knew
Its quality and took three times his due—
A thumb of gold, by God, to gauge an oat!
He wore a hood of blue and a white coat.
He liked to play his bagpipes up and down
And that was how he brought us out of town.
    The *Manciple* came from the Inner Temple;
All caterers might follow his example
In buying victuals; he was never rash
Whether he bought on credit or paid cash.
He used to watch the market most precisely
And got in first, and so he did quite nicely.
Now isn't it a marvel of God's grace
That an illiterate fellow can outpace
The wisdom of a heap of learned men?
His masters—he had more than thirty then—
All versed in the abstrusest legal knowledge,
Could have produced a dozen from their College
Fit to be stewards in land and rents and game
To any Peer in England you could name,
And show him how to live on what he had
Debt-free (unless of course the Peer were mad)
Or be as frugal as he might desire,
And make them fit to help about the Shire
In any legal case there was to try;
And yet this Manciple could wipe their eye.

. . . .

    There was a *Summoner* with us at that Inn,
His face on fire, like a cherubim,
For he had carbuncles. His eyes were narrow,

As hoot he was and lecherous as a sparwe,
With scalled browes blake and piled berd.   455
Of his visage children were aferd.
Ther nas quyk-silver, lytarge, ne brymstoon,
Boras, ceruce, ne oille of tartre noon,
Ne oynement that wolde clense and byte,
That hym myghte helpen of his whelkes white,   460
Nor of the knobbes sittynge on his chekes.
Wel loved he garleek, oynons, and eek lekes,
And for to drynken strong wyn, reed as blood;
Thanne wolde he speke and crie as he were wood.
And whan that he wel dronken hadde the wyn,   465
Thanne wolde he speke no word but Latyn.
A fewe termes hadde he, two or thre,
That he had lerned out of som decree—
No wonder is, he herde it al the day;
And eek ye knowen wel how that a jay   470
Kan clepen "Watte" as wel as kan the pope.
But whoso koude in oother thyng hym grope,
Thanne hadde he spent al his philosophie;
Ay *"Questio quid iuris"* wolde he crie.
He was a gentil harlot and a kynde;   475
A bettre felawe sholde men noght fynde.
He wolde suffre for a quart of wyn
A good felawe to have his concubyn
A twelf month, and excuse hym atte fulle;
Ful prively a fynch eek koude he pulle.   480
And if he foond owher a good felawe,
He wolde techen him to have noon awe
In swich caas of the ercedekenes curs,
But if a mannes soule were in his purs;
For in his purs he sholde ypunysshed be.   485
"Purs is the ercedekenes helle," seyde he.
But wel I woot he lyed right in dede;
Of cursyng oghte ech gilty man him drede,
For curs wol slee right as assoillyng savith,
And also war hym of a *Significavit*.   490
In daunger hadde he at his owene gise
The yonge girles of the diocise,
And knew hir conseil, and was al hir reed.
A gerland hadde he set upon his heed,
As greet as it were for an ale-stake.   495
A bokeleer hadde he maad hym of a cake.

   With hym ther rood a gentil PARDONER
Of Rouncivale, his freend and his compeer,
That streight was comen fro the court of Rome.
Ful loude he soong "Com hider, love, to me!"   500

He was as hot and lecherous as a sparrow.
Black scabby brows he had, and a thin beard.
Children were afraid when he appeared.
No quicksilver, lead ointment, tartar creams,
No brimstone, no boracic, so it seems,
Could make a salve that had the power to bite,
Clean up or cure his whelks of knobby white,
Or purge the pimples sitting on his cheeks.
Garlic he loved, and onions too, and leeks,
And drinking strong red wine till all was hazy.
Then he would shout and jabber as if crazy,
And wouldn't speak a word except in Latin
When he was drunk, such tags as he was pat in;
He only had a few, say two or three,
That he had mugged up out of some decree;
No wonder, for he heard them every day.
And, as you know, a man can teach a jay
To call out "Walter" better than the Pope.
But had you tried to test his wits and grope
For more, you'd have found nothing in the bag.
Then *"Questio quid juris"* was his tag.
He was a noble varlet and a kind one,
You'd meet none better if you went to find one.
Why, he'd allow—just for a quart of wine—
Any good lad to keep a concubine
A twelvemonth and dispense him altogether!
And he had finches of his own to feather:
And if he found some rascal with a maid
He would instruct him not to be afraid
In such a case of the Archdeacon's curse
(Unless the rascal's soul were in his purse)
For in his purse the punishment should be.
"Purse is the good Archdeacon's Hell," said he.
But well I know he lied in what he said;
A curse should put a guilty man in dread,
For curses kill, as shriving brings, salvation.
We should beware of excommunication.
Thus, as he pleased, the man could bring duress
On any young fellow in the diocese.
He knew their secrets, they did what he said.
He wore a garland set upon his head
Large as the holly bush upon a stake
Outside an alehouse, and he had a cake,
A round one, which it was his joke to wield
As if it were intended for a shield.

   He and a gentle *Pardoner* rode together,
A bird from Charing Cross of the same feather,
Just back from visiting the Court of Rome.
He loudly sang "Come hither, love, come home!"

This Somonour bar to hym a stif burdoun;
Was nevere trompe of half so greet a soun.
This Pardoner hadde heer as yelow as wex,
But smothe it heeng as dooth a strike of flex;
By ounces henge his lokkes that he hadde,   505
And therwith he his shuldres overspradde;
But thynne it lay, by colpons oon and oon.
But hood, for jolitee, wered he noon,
For it was trussed up in his walet.
Hym thoughte he rood al of the newe jet;   510
Dischevelee, save his cappe, he rood al bare.
Swiche glarynge eyen hadde he as an hare.
A vernycle hadde he sowed upon his cappe.
His walet, biforn hym in his lappe,
Bretful of pardoun comen from Rome al hoot.   515
A voys he hadde as smal as hath a goot.
No berd hadde he, ne nevere sholde have;
As smothe it was as it were late shave.
I trowe he were a geldyng or a mare.
But of his craft, fro Berwyk into Ware   520
Ne was ther swich another pardoner.
For in his male he hadde a pilwe-beer,
Which that he seyde was Oure Lady veyl;
He seyde he hadde a gobet of the seyl
That Seint Peter hadde, whan that he wente   525
Upon the see, til Jhesu Crist hym hente.
He hadde a croys of latoun ful of stones,
And in a glas he hadde pigges bones.
But with thise relikes, whan that he fond
A povre person dwellynge upon lond,   530
Upon a day he gat hym moore moneye
Than that the person gat in monthes tweye;
And thus, with feyned flaterye and japes,
He made the person and the peple his apes.
But trewely to tellen atte laste,   535
He was in chirche a noble ecclesiaste.
Wel koude he rede a lessoun or a storie,
But alderbest he song an offertorie;
For wel he wiste, whan that song was songe,
He moste preche and wel affile his tonge   540
To wynne silver, as he ful wel koude;
Therefore he song the murierly and loude.
    Now have I toold you soothly, in a clause,
Th'estaat, th'array, the nombre, and eek the cause
Why that assembled was this compaignye   545
In Southwerk at this gentil hostelrye
That highte the Tabard, faste by the Belle.
But now is tyme to yow for to telle
How that we baren us that ilke nyght,
Whan we were in that hostelrie alyght;   550

The Summoner sang deep seconds to this song,
No trumpet ever sounded half so strong.
This Pardoner had hair as yellow as wax,
Hanging down smoothly like a hank of flax.
In driblets fell his locks behind his head
Down to his shoulders which they overspread;
Thinly they fell, like rattails, one by one.
He wore no hood upon his head, for fun;
The hood inside his wallet had been stowed,
He aimed at riding in the latest mode;
But for a little cap his head was bare
And he had bulging eyeballs, like a hare.
He'd sewed a holy relic on his cap;
His wallet lay before him on his lap,
Brimful of pardons come from Rome, all hot.
He had the same small voice a goat has got.
His chin no beard had harbored, nor would harbor,
Smoother than ever chin was left by barber.
I judge he was a gelding, or a mare.
As to his trade, from Berwick down to Ware
There was no pardoner of equal grace,
For in his trunk he had a pillowcase
Which he asserted was Our Lady's veil.
He said he had a gobbet of the sail
St. Peter had the time when he made bold
To walk the waves, till Jesus Christ took hold.
He had a cross of metal set with stones
And, in a glass, a rubble of pigs' bones.
And with these relics, any time he found
Some poor upcountry parson to astound,
In one short day, in money down, he drew
More than the parson in a month or two,
And by his flatteries and prevarication
Made monkeys of the priest and congregation.
But still to do him justice first and last
In church he was a noble ecclesiast.
How well he read a lesson or told a story!
But best of all he sang an Offertory,
For well he knew that when that song was sung
He'd have to preach and tune his honey tongue
And (well he could) win silver from the crowd.
That's why he sang so merrily and loud.
    Now I have told you shortly, in a clause,
The rank, the array, the number and the cause
Of our assembly in this company
In Southwark, at that high-class hostelry
Known as *The Tabard*, close beside *The Bell*.
And now the time has come for me to tell
How we behaved that evening; I'll begin
After we had alighted at the Inn,

And after wol I telle of our viage
And al the remenaunt of oure pilgrimage.
But first I pray yow, of youre curteisye,
That ye n'arette it nat my vileynye,
Thogh that I pleynly speke in this mateere,   555
To telle yow hir wordes and hir cheere,
Ne thogh I speke hir wordes proprely.
For this ye knowen al so wel as I:
Whoso shal telle a tale after a man,
He moot reherce as ny as evere he kan   560
Everich a word, if it be in his charge,
Al speke he never so rudeliche and large,
Or ellis he moot telle his tale untrewe,
Or feyne thyng, or fynde wordes newe.
He may nat spare, althogh he were his brother;   565
He moot as wel seye o word as another.
Crist spak hymself ful brode in hooly writ,
And wel ye woot no vileynye is it.
Eek Plato seith, whoso kan hym rede,
The wordes moote be cosyn to the dede.   570
Also I prey yow to foryeve it me,
Al have I nat set folk in hir degree
Heere in this tale, as that they sholde stonde.
My wit is short, ye may wel understonde.

   Greet chiere made oure Hoost us everichon,   575
And to the soper sette he us anon.
He served us with vitaille at the beste;
Strong was the wyn, and wel to drynke us leste.
A semely man OURE HOOSTE was withalle
For to been a marchal in an halle.   580
A large man he was with eyen stepe—
A fairer burgeys was ther noon in Chepe—
Boold of his speche, and wys, and wel ytaught,
And of manhod hym lakkede right naught.
Eek therto he was right a myrie man;   585
And after soper pleyen he bigan,
And spak of myrthe amonges othere thynges,
Whan that we hadde maad oure rekenynges,
And seyde thus: "Now, lordynges, trewely,
Ye been to me right welcome, hertely;   590
For by my trouthe, if that I shal nat lye,
I saugh nat this yeer so myrie a compaignye
Atones in this herberwe as is now.
Fayn wolde I doon yow myrthe, wiste I how.
And of a myrthe I am right now bythoght,   595
To doon yow ese, and it shal coste noght.

   "Ye goon to Caunterbury—God yow speede,
The blisful martir quite yow youre meede!
And wel I woot, as ye goon by the weye,
Ye shapen yow to talen and to pleye;   600

Then I'll report our journey, stage by stage,
All the remainder of our pilgrimage.
But first I beg of you, in courtesy,
Not to condemn me as unmannerly
If I speak plainly and with no concealings
And give account of all their words and dealings,
Using their very phrases as they fell.
For certainly, as you all know so well,
He who repeats a tale after a man
Is bound to say, as nearly as he can,
Each single word, if he remembers it,
However rudely spoken or unfit,
Or else the tale he tells will be untrue,
The things pretended and the phrases new.
He may not flinch although it were his brother,
He may as well say one word as another.
And Christ Himself spoke broad in Holy Writ,
Yet there is no scurrility in it,
And Plato says, for those with power to read,
"The word should be as cousin to the deed."
Further I beg you to forgive it me
If I neglect the order and the degree
And what is due to rank in what I've planned.
I'm short of wit as you will understand.

   Our *Host* gave us great welcome; everyone
Was given a place and supper was begun.
He served the finest victuals you could think,
The wine was strong and we were glad to drink.
A very striking man our Host withal,
And fit to be a marshal in a hall.
His eyes were bright, his girth a little wide;
There is no finer burgess in Cheapside.
Bold in his speech, yet wise and full of tact,
There was no manly attribute he lacked,
What's more he was a merry-hearted man.
After our meal he jokingly began
To talk of sport, and, among other things
After we'd settled up our reckonings,
He said as follows: "Truly, gentlemen,
You're very welcome and I can't think when
—Upon my word I'm telling you no lie—
I've seen a gathering here that looked so spry,
No, not this year, as in this tavern now.
I'd think you up some fun if I knew how.
And, as it happens, a thought has just occurred
To please you, costing nothing, on my word.
You're off to Canterbury—well, Godspeed!
Blessed St. Thomas answer to your need!
And I don't doubt, before the journey's done
You mean to while the time in tales and fun.

For trewely, confort ne myrthe is noon
To ride by the weye doumb as a stoon;
And therfore wol I maken yow disport,
As I seyde erst, and doon yow som confort.
And if yow liketh alle by oon assent   605
For to stonden at my juggement,
And for to werken as I shal yow seye,
Tomorwe, whan ye riden by the weye,
Now, by my fader soule that is deed,
But ye be myrie, I wol yeve yow myn heed!   610
Hoold up youre hondes, withouten moore
    speche."
   Oure conseil was nat longe for to seche.
Us thoughte it was noght worth to make it wys,
And graunted hym withouten moore avys,
And bad him seye his voirdit as hym leste.   615
"Lordynges," quod he, "now herkneth for the
    beste;
But taak it nought, I prey yow, in desdeyn.
This is the poynt, to speken short and pleyn,
That ech of yow, to shorte with oure weye,
In this viage shal telle tales tweye   620
To Caunterbury-ward, I mene it so,
And homward he shal tellen othere two,
Of aventures that whilom han bifalle.
And which of yow that bereth hym best of alle—
That is to seyn, that telleth in this caas   625
Tales of best sentence and moost solaas—
Shal have a soper at oure aller cost
Heere in this place, sittynge by this post,
Whan that we come agayn fro Caunterbury.
And for to make yow the moore mury,   630
I wol myselven goodly with yow ryde,
Right at myn owene cost, and be youre gyde;
And whoso wole my juggement withseye
Shal paye al that we spenden by the weye.
And if ye vouche sauf that it be so,   635
Tel me anon, withouten wordes mo,
And I wol erly shape me therfore."
   This thyng was graunted, and oure othes
    swore
With ful glad herte, and preyden hym also
That he wolde vouche sauf for to do so,   640
And that he wolde been oure governour,
And of oure tales juge and reportour,
And sette a soper at a certeyn pris,
And we wol reuled been at his devys
In heigh and lough; and thus by oon assent   645
We been acorded to his juggement.
And therupon the wyn was fet anon;

Indeed, there's little pleasure for your bones
Riding along and all as dumb as stones.
So let me then propose for your enjoyment,
Just as I said, a suitable employment.
And if my notion suits and you agree
And promise to submit yourselves to me
Playing your parts exactly as I say
Tomorrow as you ride along the way,
Then by my father's soul (and he is dead)
If you don't like it you can have my head!
Hold up your hands, and not another word."

   Well, our opinion was not long deferred,
It seemed not worth a serious debate;
We all agreed to it at any rate
And bade him issue what commands he would.
"My lords," he said, "now listen for
    your good,
And please don't treat my notion with disdain.
This is the point, I'll make it short and plain.
Each one of you shall help to make things slip
By telling two stories on the outward trip
To Canterbury, that's what I intend,
And, on the homeward way to journey's end
Another two, tales from the days of old;
And then the man whose story is best told,
That is to say who gives the fullest measure
Of good morality and general pleasure,
He shall be given a supper, paid by all,
Here in this tavern, in this very hall,
When we come back again from Canterbury.
And in the hope to keep you bright and merry
I'll go along with you myself and ride
All at my own expense and serve as guide.
I'll be the judge, and those who won't obey
Shall pay for what we spend upon the way.
Now if you all agree to what you've heard
Tell me at once without another word,
And I will make arrangements early for it."
   Of course we all agreed, in fact we
    swore it
Delightedly, and made entreaty too
That he should act as he proposed to do,
Become our Governor, in short, and be
Judge of our tales and general referee,
And set the supper at a certain price.
We promised to be ruled by his advice
Come high, come low; unanimously thus
We set him up in judgment over us.
More wine was fetched, the business being done;

We dronken, and to reste wente echon,
Withouten any lenger taryynge.

    Amorwe, whan that day bigan to sprynge, *650*
Up roos oure Hoost, and was oure aller cok,
And gadrede us togidre alle in a flok,
And forth we riden a litel moore than paas
Unto the Wateryng of Seint Thomas;
And there oure Hoost bigan his hors areste *655*
And seyde, "Lordynges, herkneth, if yow leste.
Ye woot youre foreward, and I it yow recorde.
If even-song and morwe-song accorde,
Lat se now who shal telle the firste tale.
As evere mote I drynke wyn or ale, *660*
Whoso be rebel to my juggement
Shal paye for al that by the wey is spent.
Now draweth cut, er that we ferrer twynne;
He which that hath the shorteste shal bigynne.
Sire Knyght," quod he, "my mayster and my lord, *665*
Now draweth cut, for that is myn accord.
Cometh neer," quod he, "my lady Prioresse.
And ye, sire Clerk, lat be youre shamefastnesse,
Ne studieth noght; ley hond to, every man!"
Anon to drawen every wight bigan, *675*
And shortly for to tellen as it was,
Were it by aventure, or sort, or cas,
The sothe is this: the cut fil to the Knyght,
Of which ful blithe and glad was every wyght,
And telle he moste his tale, as was resoun, *680*
By foreward and by composicioun,
As ye han herd; what nedeth wordes mo?
And whan this goode man saugh that it was so,
As he that wys was and obedient
To kepe his foreward by his free assent, *685*
He seyde, "Syn I shal bigynne the game,
What, welcome be the cut, a Goddes name!
Now lat us ryde, and herkneth what I seye."
And with that word we ryden forth oure weye,
And he bigan with right a myrie cheere *690*
His tale anon, and seyde as ye may heere.

We drank it off and up went everyone
To bed without a moment of delay.

    Early next morning at the spring of day
Up rose our Host and roused us like a cock,
Gathering us together in a flock,
And off we rode at slightly faster pace
Than walking to St. Thomas' watering place;
And there our Host drew up, began to ease
His horse, and said, "Now, listen if you please,
My lords! Remember what you promised me.
If evensong and matins will agree
Let's see who shall be first to tell a tale.
And as I hope to drink good wine and ale
I'll be your judge. The rebel who disobeys,
However much the journey costs, he pays.
Now draw for cut and then we can depart;
The man who draws the shortest cut shall start.
My Lord the Knight," he said, "step up to me
And draw your cut, for that is my decree.
And come you near, my Lady Prioress,
And you, Sir Cleric, drop your shamefastness,
No studying now! A hand from every man!"
Immediately the draw for lots began
And to tell shortly how the matter went,
Whether by chance or fate or accident,
The truth is this, the cut fell to the Knight,
Which everybody greeted with delight.
And tell his tale he must, as reason was
Because of our agreement and because
He too had sworn. What more is there to say?
For when this good man saw how matters lay,
Being by wisdom and obedience driven
To keep a promise he had freely given,
He said, "Since it's for me to start the game,
Why, welcome be the cut in God's good name!
Now let us ride, and listen to what I say."
And at the word we started on our way
And in a cheerful style he then began
At once to tell his tale, and thus it ran.

The Pardoner

Words of the Host to the Physician and to the Pardoner

    Oure Hooste gan to swere as he were wood;
"Harrow!" quod he, "by nayles and by blood!
This was a fals cherl and a fals justise.
As shameful deeth as herte may devyse

    Our Host began a violent tirade.
"God's nails and blood," he said, "alas, poor maid!
What a low blackguard! What a treacherous judge!
Death to all lawyers that will bribe and fudge

Come to thise juges and hire advocatz!   5
Algate this sely mayde is slayn, allas!
Allas, to deere boughte she beautee!
Wherfore I seye al day that men may see
That yiftes of Fortune and of Nature
Been cause of deeth to many a creature.   10
Hire beautee was hire deth, I dar wel sayn.
Allas, so pitously as she was slayn!
Of bothe yiftes that I speke of now
Men han ful ofte moore for harm than prow.
But trewely, myn owene maister deere,   15
This is a pitous tale for to heere.
But nathelees, passe over; is no fors.
I pray to God so save thy gentil cors,
And eek thyne urynals and thy jurdones,
Thyn ypocras, and eek thy galiones,   20
And every boyste ful of thy letuarie;
God blesse hem, and oure lady Seinte Marie!
So moot I theen, thou art a propre man,
And lyk a prelat, by Seint Ronyan!
Seyde I nat wel? I kan nat speke in terme;   25
But wel I woot thou doost myn herte to erme,
That I almoost have caught a cardynacle.
By corpus bones! but I have triacle,
Or elles a draughte of moyste and corny ale,
Or but I heere anon a myrie tale,   30
Myn herte is lost for pitee of this mayde.
Thou beel amy, thou Pardoner," he sayde,
"Telle us som myrthe or japes right anon."

   "It shal be doon," quod he, "by Seint Ronyon!
But first," quod he, "heere at this alestake   35
I wol bothe drynke and eten of a cake."

   But right anon thise gentils gonne to crye,
"Nay, lat hym telle us of no ribaudye!
Telle us som moral thyng, that we may leere
Som wit, and thanne wol we gladly heere."   40

   "I graunte, ywis," quod he, "but I moot thynke
Upon som honest thyng while that I drynke."

To trap you, be they judge or advocate!
Well, the poor girl was killed at any rate.
Alas, her beauty cost her all too dear!
Just as I always say, it's pretty clear
The handsome gifts that fate and nature lend us
Are very often those that least befriend us.
Her beauty was her death as one might say;
How pitifully she was made away!
Those gifts that I was mentioning just now
Do us more harm than good, one must allow.
Well, my dear sir, if I may speak sincere,
Your tale was truly pitiful to hear.
Nevertheless, pass on. No sense in fretting.
God's blessing on you, Doctor, not forgetting
Your various urinals and chamberpots,
Bottles, medicaments and cordial tots
And boxes brimming all with panaceas,
God's blessing on them all and St. Maria's!
You look a proper fellow! Pills and pellets!
St. Ronyan, you've a figure like a prelate's!
Don't I say well?—although I lack the art
To talk like you; your story touched my heart,
It gave me heart disease, or very near.
By corpus bones! I'll need a dose, I fear,
Or else a good wet draught of malted ale
If someone doesn't tell a cheerful tale;
I'm lost in pity for that poor girl dead.
Come on, old chum and Pardoner," he said,
"Tell us a funny story, break a joke!"

   "Right, by St. Ronyan! but I'll have a soak
First at this pub. I've got a thirst to slake,"
Said he, "I'll drink and eat a bit of cake."

   Outcry arose among the gentlefolk.
"No, no, don't let him tell a dirty joke!
Tell something with a moral, something clear
And profitable, and we'll gladly hear."

   "Granted," he said, "but first I'll have to think;
I'll ponder something decent while I drink."

The Pardoner's Prologue

"Lordynges," quod he, "in chirches whan I
      preche
I peyne me to han an hauteyn speche,
And rynge it out as round as gooth a belle,   45
For I kan al by rote that I telle.
My theme is alwey oon, and evere was—
Radix malorum est Cupiditas.

"My lords," he said, "in churches where
      I preach
I cultivate a haughty kind of speech
And ring it out as roundly as a bell;
I've got it all by heart, the tale I tell.
I have a text, it always is the same
And always has been, since I learnt the game,
Old as the hills and fresher than the grass,
Radix malorum est cupiditas.

"First I pronounce whennes that I come,
And thanne my bulles shewe I, alle and some.   50
Oure lige lordes seel on my patente,
That shewe I first, my body to warente,
That no man be so boold, ne preest ne clerk,
Me to destourbe of Cristes hooly werk.
And after that thanne telle I forth my tales;   55
Bulles of popes and of cardynales,
Of patriarkes and bishopes I shewe,
And in Latyn I speke a wordes fewe,
To saffron with my predicacioun,
And for to stire hem to devocioun.   60
Thanne shewe I forth my longe cristal stones,
Ycrammed ful of cloutes and of bones—
Relikes been they, as wenen they echoon.
Thanne have I in latoun a sholder-boon
Which that was of an hooly Jewes sheep.   65
'Goode men,' I seye, 'taak of my wordes keep
If that this boon be wasshe in any welle,
If cow, or calf, or sheep, or oxe swelle
That any worm hath ete, or worm ystonge,
Taak water of that welle and wassh his tonge,   70
And it is hool anon; and forthermoore,
Of pokkes and of scabbe, and every soore
Shal every sheep be hool that of this welle
Drynketh a draughte. Taak kep eek what I telle:
If that the good-man that the beestes oweth   75
Wol every wyke, er that the cok hym croweth,
Fastynge, drynken of this welle a draughte,
As thilke hooly Jew oure eldres taughte,
His beestes and his stoor shal multiplie.
'And, sires, also it heeleth jalousie;   80
For though a man be falle in jalous rage,
Lat maken with this water his potage,
And nevere shal he moore his wyf mystriste,
Though he the soothe of hir defaute wiste,
Al had she taken prestes two or thre.   85
'Heere is a miteyn eek, that ye may se.
He that his hand wol putte in this mitayn,
He shal have multipliyng of his grayn,
Whan he hath sowen, be it whete or otes,
So that he offre pens, or elles grotes.   90
'Goode men and wommen, o thyng warne I
  yow:
If any wight be in this chirche now
That hath doon synne horrible, that he
Dar nat, for shame, of it yshryven be,
Or any womman, be she yong or old,   95
That hath ymaked hir housbonde cokewold,
Swich folk shal have no power ne no grace

"But first I make pronouncement whence I come,
Show them my bulls in detail and in sum.
And flaunt the papal seal for their inspection
As warrant for my bodily protection,
That none may have the impudence to irk
Or hinder me in Christ's most holy work.
Then I tell stories, as occasion calls,
Showing forth bulls from popes and cardinals,
From patriarchs and bishops; as I do,
I speak some words in Latin—just a few—
To put a saffron tinge upon my preaching
And stir devotion with a spice of teaching.
Then I bring all my long glass bottles out
Cram-full of bones and ragged bits of clout,
Relics they are, at least for such are known.
Then, cased in metal, I've a shoulder bone,
Belonging to a sheep, a holy Jew's.
"Good men," I say, 'take heed, for here is news.
Take but this bone and dip it in a well;
If cow or calf, if sheep or ox should swell
From eating snakes or that a snake has stung,
Take water from that well and wash its tongue,
And it will then recover. Furthermore,
Where there is pox or scab or other sore,
All animals that water at that well
Are cured at once. Take note of what I tell.
If the good man—the owner of the stock—
Goes once a week, before the crow of cock,
Fasting, and takes a draught of water too,
Why then, according to that holy Jew,
He'll find his cattle multiply and sell.
" 'And it's a cure for jealousy as well;
For though a man be given to jealous wrath,
Use but this water when you make his broth,
And never again will he mistrust his wife,
Though he knew all about her sinful life,
Though two or three clergy had enjoyed her love.
"Now look; I have a mitten here, a glove.
Whoever wears this mitten on his hand
Will multiply his grain. He sows his land
And up will come abundant wheat or oats,
Providing that he offers pence or groats.
" 'Good men and women, here's a word of
  warning;
If there is anyone in church this morning
Guilty of sin, so far beyond expression
Horrible, that he dare not make confession,
Or any woman, whether young or old,
That's cuckolded her husband, be she told
That such as she shall have no power or grace

To offren to my relikes in this place.
And whoso fyndeth hym out of swich blame,
He wol come up and offre a Goddes name,   100
And I assoille him by the auctoritee
Which that by bulle ygraunted was to me.'
    "By this gaude have I wonne, yeer by yeer,
An hundred mark sith I was pardoner.
I stonde lyk a clerk in my pulpet,   105
And whan the lewed peple is doun yset,
I preche so as ye han herd bifoore
And telle an hundred false japes moore.
Thanne peyne I me to strecche forth the nekke,
And est and west upon the peple I bekke,   110
As dooth a dowve sittynge on a berne.
Myne handes and my tonge goon so yerne
That it is joye to se my bisynesse.
Of avarice and of swich cursednesse
Is al my prechyng, for to make hem free   115
To yeven hir pens, and namely unto me.
For myn entente is nat but for to wynne,
And nothyng for correccioun of synne.
I rekke nevere, whan that they been beryed,
Though that hir soules goon a-blakeberyed!   120
For certes, many a predicacioun
Comth ofte tyme of yvel entencioun;
Som for plesance of folk and flaterye,
To been avaunced by ypocrisye,
And som for veyne glorie, and som for hate.   125
For whan I dar noon oother weyes debate,
Thanne wol I stynge hym with my tonge smerte
In prechyng, so that he shal nat asterte
To been defamed falsly, if that he
Hath trespased to my bretheren or to me.   130
For though I telle noght his propre name,
Men shal wel knowe that it is the same,
By signes, and by othere circumstances.
Thus quyte I folk that doon us displesances;
Thus spitte I out my venym under hewe   135
Of hoolynesse, to semen hooly and trewe.
    "But shortly myn entente I wol devyse:
I preche of no thyng but for coveityse.
Therfore my theme is yet, and evere was,
Radix malorum est Cupiditas.   140
Thus kan I preche agayn that same vice
Which that I use, and that is avarice.
But though myself be gilty in that synne,
Yet kan I maken oother folk to twynne
From avarice and soore to repente.   145
But that is nat my principal entente;

To offer to my relics in this place.
But those who can acquit themselves of blame
Can all come up and offer in God's name,
And I will shrive them by the authority
Committed in this papal bull to me.'
    "That trick's been worth a hundred marks a year
Since I became a Pardoner, never fear.
Then, priestlike in my pulpit, with a frown,
I stand, and when the yokels have sat down,
I preach, as you have heard me say before,
And tell a hundred lying mockeries more.
I take great pains, and stretching out my neck
To east and west I crane about and peck
Just like a pigeon sitting on a barn.
My hands and tongue together spin the yarn
And all my antics are a joy to see.
The curse of avarice and cupidity
Is all my sermon, for it frees the pelf.
Out come the pence, and specially for myself,
For my exclusive purpose is to win
And not at all to castigate their sin.
Once dead what matter how their souls may fare?
They can go blackberrying, for all I care!
"Believe me, many a sermon or devotive
Exordium issues from an evil motive.
Some to give pleasure by their flattery
And gain promotion through hypocrisy,
Some out of vanity, some out of hate;
Or when I dare not otherwise debate
I'll put my discourse into such a shape,
My tongue will be a dagger; no escape
For him from slandering falsehood shall there be.
If he has hurt my brethren or me.
For though I never mention him by name
The congregation guesses all the same
From certain hints that everybody knows,
And so I take revenge upon our foes
And spit my venom forth, while I profess
Holy and true—or seeming holiness.
    "But let me briefly make my purpose plain;
I preach for nothing but for greed of gain
And use the same old text, as bold as brass,
Radix malorum est cupiditas.
And thus I preach against the very vice
I make my living out of—avarice.
And yet however guilty of that sin
Myself, with others I have power to win
Them from it, I can bring them to repent;
But that is not my principal intent.

I preche nothyng but for coveitise.
Of this mateere it oghte ynogh suffise.

    "Thanne telle I hem ensamples many oon
Of olde stories longe tyme agoon.   *150*
For lewed peple loven tales olde;
Swiche thynges kan they wel reporte and holde.
What, trowe ye, that whiles I may preche,
And wynne gold and silver for I teche,
That I wol lyve in poverte wilfully?   *155*
Nay, nay, I thoghte it nevere, trewely!
For I wol preche and begge in sondry landes;
I wol nat do no labour with myne handes,
Ne make baskettes and lyve therby,
By cause I wol nat beggen ydelly.   *160*
I wol noon of the apostles countrefete;
I wol have moneie, wolle, chese, and whete,
Al were it yeven of the povereste page,
Or of the povereste wydwe in a village,
Al sholde hir children sterve for famyne.   *165*
Nay, I wol drynke licour of the vyne
And have a joly wenche in every toun.
But herkneth, lordynges, in conclusioun:
Youre likyng is that I shal telle a tale.
Now have I dronke a draughte of corny ale,   *170*
By God, I hope I shal yow telle a thyng
That shal by reson been at youre likyng.
For though myself be a ful vicious man,
A moral tale yet I yow telle kan,
Which I am wont to preche for to wynne.   *175*
Now hoold youre pees! My tale I wol bigynne."

Covetousness is both the root and stuff
Of all I preach. That ought to be enough.

    "Well, then I give examples thick and fast
From bygone times, old stories from the past.
A yokel mind loves stories from of old,
Being the kind it can repeat and hold.
What! Do you think, as long as I can preach
And get their silver for the things I teach,
That I will live in poverty, from choice?
That's not the counsel of my inner voice!
No! Let me preach and beg from kirk to kirk
And never do an honest job of work,
No, nor make baskets, like St. Paul, to gain
A livelihood. I do not preach in vain.
There's no apostle I would counterfeit;
I mean to have money, wool and cheese and wheat
Though it were given me by the poorest lad
Or poorest village widow, though she had
A string of starving children, all agape.
No, let me drink the liquor of the grape
And keep a jolly wench in every town!

    "But listen, gentlemen; to bring things down
To a conclusion, would you like a tale?
Now as I've drunk a draft of corn-ripe ale,
By God, it stands to reason I can strike
On some good story that you all will like.
For though I am a wholly vicious man
Don't think I can't tell moral tales. I can!
Here's one I often preach when out for winning;
Now please be quiet. Here is the beginning."

The Pardoner's Tale

    In Flaundres whilom was a compaignye
Of yonge folk that haunteden folye,
As riot, hasard, stywes, and tavernes,
Where as with harpes, lutes, and gyternes,   *180*
They daunce and pleyen at dees bothe day and
    nyght,
And eten also and drynken over hir myght,
Thurgh which they doon the devel sacrifise
Withinne that develes temple in cursed wise
By superfluytee abhomynable.   *185*
Hir othes been so grete and so dampnable
That it is grisly for to heere hem swere.
Oure blissed Lordes body they totere—
Hem thoughte that Jewes rente hym noght
    ynough—
And ech of hem at otheres synne lough.   *190*

    In Flanders once there was a company
Of youngsters haunting vice and ribaldry,
Riot and gambling, stews and public houses
Where each with harp, guitar or lute carouses,
Dancing and dicing day and night,
    and bold
To eat and drink far more than they can hold,
Doing thereby the devil sacrifice
Within that devil's temple of cursed vice,
Abominable in superfluity,
With oaths so damnable in blasphemy
That it's a grisly thing to hear them swear.
Our dear Lord's body they will rend and tear
As if the Jews had rent Him not enough;

And at the sin of others every tough

And right anon thanne comen tombesteres
Fetys and smale, and yonge frutesteres,
Syngeres with harpes, baudes, wafereres,
Whiche been the verray develes officeres
To kyndle and blowe the fyr of lecherye,   *195*
That is annexed unto glotonye.
The hooly writ take I to my witnesse
That luxurie is in wyn and dronkenesse.
    Lo, how that dronken Looth, unkyndely,
Lay by his doghtres two, unwityngly;   *200*
So dronke he was, he nyste what he wroghte.
    Herodes, whoso wel the stories soghte,
Whan he of wyn was repleet at his feeste,
Right at his owene table he yaf his heeste
To sleen the Baptist John, ful giltelees.   *205*
    Senec seith a good word doutelees;
He seith he kan no difference fynde
Bitwix a man that is out of his mynde
And a man which that is dronkelewe,
But that woodnesse, yfallen in a shrewe,   *210*
Persevereth lenger than doth dronkenesse.
O glotonye, ful of cursednesse!
O cause first of oure confusioun!
O original of oure dampnacioun,
Til Crist hadde boght us with his blood agayn!   *215*
Lo, how deere, shortly for to sayn,
Aboght was thilke cursed vileynye!
Corrupt was al this world for glotonye.
    Adam oure fader, and his wyf also,
Fro Paradys to labour and to wo   *220*
Were dryven for that vice, it is no drede.
For whil that Adam fasted, as I rede,
He was in Paradys; and whan that he
Eet of the fruyt deffended on the tree,
Anon he was out cast to wo and peyne.   *225*
O glotonye, on thee wel oghte us pleyne!
O, wiste a man how manye maladyes
Folwen of excesse and of glotonyes,
He wolde been the moore mesurable
Of his diete, sittynge at his table.   *230*
Allas, the shorte throte, the tendre mouth,
Maketh that est and west and north and south,
In erthe, in eir, in water, men to swynke
To gete a glotoun deyntee mete and drynke!
Of this matiere, O Paul, wel kanstow trete: *235*
"Mete unto wombe, and wombe eek unto mete,
Shal God destroyen bothe," as Paulus seith.
Allas, a foul thyng is it, by my feith,

Will laugh, and presently the dancing girls,
Small pretty ones, come in and shake their curls,
With youngsters selling fruit, and ancient bawds,
And girls with cakes and music, devil's gauds
To kindle and blow the fires of lechery
That are so close annexed to gluttony.
Witness the Bible, which is most express
That lust is bred of wine and drunkenness.
    Look how the drunken and unnatural Lot
Lay with his daughters, though he knew it not;
He was too drunk to know what he was doing.
    Take Herod, too, his tale is worth pursuing.
Replete with wine and feasting, he was able
To give the order at his very table
To kill the innocent Baptist, good St. John.
    Seneca has a thought worth pondering on;
No difference, he says, that he can find
Between a madman who has lost his mind
And one who is habitually mellow
Except that madness when it takes a fellow
Lasts longer, on the whole, than drunkenness.
O cursed gluttony, our first distress!
Cause of our first confusion, first temptation,
The very origin of our damnation,
Till Christ redeemed us with his blood again!
O infamous indulgence! Cursed stain
So dearly bought! And what has it been worth?
Gluttony has corrupted all the earth.
    Adam, our father, and his wife as well,
From Paradise to labor and to Hell
Were driven for that vice, they were indeed.
While she and Adam fasted, so I read,
They were in Paradise; when he and she
Ate of the fruit of that forbidden tree
They were at once cast forth in pain and woe.
O gluttony, it is to thee we owe
Our griefs! O if we knew the maladies
That follow on excess and gluttonies,
Sure we would diet, we would temper pleasure
In sitting down at table, show some measure!
Alas, the narrow throat, the tender mouth!
Men labor east and west and north and south
In earth, in air, in water—Why, d'you think?
To get a glutton dainty meat and drink!
How well of this St. Paul's Epistle treats!
"Meats for the belly, belly for the meats,
But God shall yet destroy both it and them."
Alas, the filth of it! If we condemn

To seye this word, and fouler is the dede,
Whan man so drynketh of the white and rede   240
That of his throte he maketh his pryvee
Thurgh thilke cursed superfluitee.
  The apostel wepyng seith ful pitously,
"Ther walken manye of whiche yow toold have I—
I seye it now wepyng, with pitous voys—   245
They been enemys of Cristes croys,
Of whiche the ende is deeth; wombe is hir god!"
O wombe! O bely! O stynkyng cod,
Fulfilled of dong and of corrupcioun!
At either ende of thee foul is the soun.   250
How greet labour and cost is thee to fynde!
Thise cookes, how they stampe, and streyne, and
     grynde,
And turnen substaunce into accident
To fulfille al thy likerous talent!
Out of the harde bones knokke they   255
The mary, for they caste noght awey
That may go thurgh the golet softe and swoote.
Of spicerie of leef, and bark, and roote
Shal been his sauce ymaked by delit,
To make hym yet a newer appetit.   260
But, certes, he that haunteth swiche delices
Is deed, whil that he lyveth in tho vices.
  A lecherous thyng is wyn, and dronkenesse
Is ful of stryvyng and of wrecchednesse.
O dronke man, disfigured is thy face,   265
Sour is thy breeth, foul artow to embrace,
And thurgh thy dronke nose semeth the soun
As though thou seydest ay "Sampsoun, Samp-
     soun!"
And yet, God woot, Sampsoun drank nevere no
     wyn.
Thou fallest as it were a styked swyn;   270
Thy tonge is lost, and al thyn honeste cure,
For dronkenesse is verray sepulture
Of mannes wit and his discrecioun.
In whom that drynke hath dominacioun
He kan no conseil kepe; it is no drede.   275
Now kepe yow fro the white and fro the rede,
And namely fro the white wyn of Lepe
That is to selle in Fysshstrete or in Chepe.
This wyn of Spaigne crepeth subtilly
In othere wynes, growynge faste by,   280
Of which ther ryseth swich fumositee
That whan a man hath dronken draughtes thre,
And weneth that he be at hoom in Chepe,

The name, how far more filthy is the act!
A man who swills down vintages in fact
Makes a mere privy of his throat, a sink
For cursed superfluities of drink!
  So the Apostle said, whom tears could soften:
"Many there are, as I have told you often,
And weep to tell, whose gluttony sufficed
To make them enemies of the cross of Christ,
Whose ending is destruction and whose God
Their belly!" O thou belly! stinking pod
Of dung and foul corruption, that canst send
Thy filthy music forth at either end,
What labor and expense it is to find
Thy sustenance! These cooks that strain
     and grind
And bray in mortars, transubstantiate
God's gifts into a flavor on a plate,
To please a lecherous palate. How they batter
Hard bones to put some marrow on your platter,
Spicery, root, bark, leaf—they search and cull it
In the sweet hope of flattering a gullet!
Nothing is thrown away that could delight
Or whet anew lascivious appetite.
Be sure a man whom such a fare entices
Is dead indeed, though living in his vices.
  Wine is a lecherous thing and drunkenness
A squalor of contention and distress.
O drunkard, how disfigured is thy face,
How foul thy breath, how filthy thy embrace!
And through thy drunken nose a stertorous snort
Like *"samson-samson"*—something of the sort.

Yet Samson never was a man to swig.

You totter, lurch and fall like a stuck pig,
Your manhood's lost, your tongue is in a burr.
Drunkenness is the very sepulcher
Of human judgment and articulation.
He that is subject to the domination
Of drink can keep no secrets, be it said.
Keep clear of wine, I tell you, white or red,
Especially Spanish wines which they provide
And have on sale in Fish Street and Cheapside.
That wine mysteriously finds its way
To mix itself with others—shall we say
Spontaneously!—that grow in neighboring regions.
Out of the mixture fumes arise in legions,
So when a man has had a drink or two

He is in Spaigne, right at the toune of Lepe—
Nat at the Rochele, ne at Burdeux toun—   285
And thanne wol he seye "Sampsoun, Sampsoun!"

But herkneth, lordynges, or word, I yow preye,
That alle the sovereyn actes, dar I seye,
Of victories in the Olde Testament,
Thurgh verray God, that is omnipotent,   290
Were doon in abstinence and in preyere.
Looketh the Bible, and ther ye may it leere.
    Looke, Attilla, the grete conquerour,
Deyde in his sleep, with shame and dishonour,
Bledynge ay at his nose in dronkenesse.   295
A capitayn sholde lyve in sobrenesse.
And over al this, avyseth yow right wel
What was comaunded unto Lamuel—
Nat Samuel, but Lemuel, seye I;
Redeth the Bible, and fynde it expresly   300
Of wyn-yevyng to hem that han justise.
Namoore of this, for it may wel suffise.
    And now that I have spoken of glotonye,
Now wol I yow deffenden hasardrye.
Hasard is verray mooder of lesynges,   305
And of deceite, and cursed forswerynges,
Blaspheme of Crist, manslaughtre, and wast also
Of catel and of tyme; and forthermo,
It is repreeve and contrarie of honour
For to ben holde a commune hasardour.   310
And ever the hyer he is of estaat,
The moore is he yholden desolaat.
If that a prynce useth hasardrye,
In alle governaunce and policye
He is, as by commune opinioun,   315
Yholde the lasse in reputacioun.
    Stilboun, that was a wys embassadour,
Was sent to Corynthe in ful greet honour
Fro Lacidomye to make hire alliaunce.
And whan he cam, hym happede, par chaunce,   320
That alle the gretteste that were of that lond,
Pleyynge atte hasard he hem fond.
For which, as soone as it myghte be,
He stal hym hoom agayn to his contree,
And seyde, "Ther wol I nat lese my name,   325
Ne I wol nat take on me so greet defame,
Yow for to allie unto none hasardours.
Sendeth othere wise embassadours;
For, by my trouthe, me were levere dye
Than I yow sholde to hasardours allye.   330

Though he may think he is at home with you
In Cheapside, I assure you he's in Spain
Where it was made, at Lepe I maintain,
Not at Bordeaux. He's soon elate
And very near the *"samson-samson"* state.
    But seriously, my lords, attention, pray!
All the most notable acts, I dare to say,
And victories in the Old Testament,
Won under God who is omnipotent,
Were won in abstinence, were won in prayer.
Look in the Bible, you will find it there.
    Or else take Attila the Conqueror;
Died in his sleep, a manner to abhor,
In drunken shame and bleeding at the nose.
A general should live sober, I suppose.
Moreover call to mind and ponder well
What was commanded unto Lemuel
—Not Samuel, but Lemuel, I said—
Read in the Bible, that's the fountainhead,
And see what comes of giving judges drink.
No more of that. I've said enough, I think.
    Having put gluttony in its proper setting
I wish to warn you against dice and betting.
Gambling's the very mother of robbed purses,
Lies, double dealing, perjury, and curses,
Manslaughter, blasphemy of Christ, and waste
Of time and money. Worse, you are debased
In public reputation, put to shame.
"A common gambler" is a nasty name.
    The more exalted such a man may be
So much the more contemptible is he.
A gambling prince would be incompetent
To frame a policy of government,
And he will sink in general opinion
As one unfit to exercise dominion.
    Stilbon, that wise ambassador whose mission
Took him to Corinth, was of high position;
Sparta had sent him with intent to frame
A treaty of alliance. When he came,
Hoping for reinforcement and advice,
It happened that he found them all at dice,
Their very nobles; so he quickly planned
To steal away, home to his native land.
He said, "I will not lose my reputation,
Or compromise the honor of my nation,
By asking dicers to negotiate,
Send other wise ambassadors of state,
For on my honor I would rather die
Than be a means for Sparta to ally

For ye, that been so glorious in honours,
Shul nat allyen yow with hasardours
As by my wyl, ne as by my tretee."
This wise philosophre, thus seyde hee.

Looke eek that to the kyng Demetrius   *335*
The kyng of Parthes, as the book seith us,
Sente him a paire of dees of gold in scorn,
For he hadde used hasard ther-biforn;
For which he heeld his glorie or his renoun
At no value or reputation.   *340*
Lordes may fynden oother maner pley
Honest ynough to dryve the day awey.

Now wol I speke of othes false and grete
A word or two, as olde bookes trete.
Gret sweryng is a thyng abhominable,   *345*
And fals sweryng is yet moore reprevable.
The heighe God forbad sweryng at al,
Witnesse on Mathew; but in special
Of sweryng seith the hooly Jeremye,
"Thou shalt swere sooth thyne othes, and
        nat lye,   *350*
And swere in doom and eek in rightwisnesse";
But ydel sweryng is a cursednesse.
Bihoold and se that in the firste table
Of heighe Goddes heestes honurable,
Hou that the seconde heeste of hym is this: *355*
"Take nat my name in ydel or amys."
Lo, rather he forbedeth swich sweryng
Than homycide or many a cursed thyng;
I seye that, as by ordre, thus it stondeth;
This knoweth, that his heestes understondeth,   *360*
How that the seconde heeste of God is that.
And forther over, I wol thee telle al plat
That vengeance shal nat parten from his house
That of his othes is to outrageous.
"By Goddes precious herte," and "By
        his nayles,"   *365*
And "By the blood of Crist that is in Hayles,
Sevene is my chaunce, and thyn is cynk and treye!"
"By Goddes armes, if thou falsly pleye,
This daggere shal thurghout thyn herte go!"—
This fruyt cometh of the bicched bones two,   *370*
Forsweryng, ire, falsnesse, homycide.
Now, for the love of Crist, that for us dyde,
Lete youre othes, bothe grete and smale.
But, sires, now wol I telle forth my tale.

Thise riotoures thre of whiche I telle,   *375*
Longe erst er prime rong of any belle,
Were set hem in a taverne to drynke,

With gamblers; Sparta, glorious in honour,
Shall take no such alliances upon her
As dicers make, by any act of mine!"
He showed his sense in taking such a line.

Again, consider King Demetrius;
The King of Parthia—history has it thus—
Sent him a pair of golden dice in scorn,
To show he reckoned him a gambler born
Whose honor, if unable to surmount
The vice of gambling, was of no account.
Lords can amuse themselves in other ways
Honest enough, to occupy their days.

Now let me speak a word or two of swearing
And perjury; the Bible is unsparing.
It's an abominable thing to curse
And swear, it says; but perjury is worse.
Almighty God has said, "Swear not at all,"
Witness St. Matthew, and you may recall
The words of Jeremiah, having care
To what he says of lying: "Thou shalt swear

In truth, in judgement and in righteousness."
But idle swearing is a sin, no less.
Behold and see the tables of the Law
Of God's Commandments, to be held in awe;
Look at the third where it is written plain,
"Thou shalt not take the name of God in vain."
You see He has forbidden swearing first;
Not murder, no, nor other thing accurst
Comes before that, I say, in God's commands.
That is the order; he who understands
Knows that the third commandment is just that.
And in addition, let me tell you flat,
Vengeance on him and all his house shall fall
That swears outrageously, or swears at all.
"God's precious heart and passion, by
        God's nails
And by the blood of Christ that is at Hailes,
Seven's my luck, and yours is five and three;
God's blessed arms! If you play false with me
I'll stab you with my dagger!" Overthrown
By two small dice, two bitching bits of bone,
Their fruit is perjury, rage and homicide.
O for the love of Jesus Christ who died
For us, abandon curses, small or great!
But, sirs, I have a story to relate.

It's of three rioters I have to tell
Who, long before the morning service bell,
Were sitting in a tavern for a drink.

And as they sat, they herde a belle clynke
Biforn a cors, was caried to his grave.
That oon of hem gan callen to his knave: 380
"Go bet," quod he, "and axe redily
What cors is this that passeth heer forby;
And looke that thou reporte his name weel."
    "Sire," quod this boy, "it nedeth never-a-deel;
It was me toold er ye cam heer two houres.   385
He was, pardee, an old felawe of youres,
And sodeynly he was yslayn to-nyght,
Fordronke, as he sat on his bench upright.
Ther cam a privee theef men clepeth Deeth,
That in this contree al the peple sleeth,   390
And with his spere he smoot his herte atwo,
And wente his wey withouten wordes mo.
He hath a thousand slayn this pestilence.
And, maister, er ye come in his presence,
Me thynketh that it were necessarie   395
For to be war of swich an adversarie.
Beth redy for to meete hym everemoore;
Thus taughte me my dame; I sey namoore."
    "By Seinte Marie!" seyde this taverner,
"The child seith sooth, for he hath slayn
            this yeer,   400
Henne over a mile, withinne a greet village,
Bothe man and womman, child, and hyne, and
            page;
I trowe his habitacioun be there.
To been avysed greet wysdom it were,
Er that he dide a man a dishonour."   405
    "Ye, Goddes armes!" quod this riotour,
"Is it swich peril with hym for to meete?
I shal hym seke by wey and eek by strete,
I make avow to Goddes digne bones!
Herkneth, felawes, we thre been al ones;   410
Lat ech of us holde up his hand til oother,
And ech of us bicomen otheres brother,
And we wol sleen this false traytour Deeth.
He shal be slayn, he that so manye sleeth,
By Goddes dignitee, er it be nyght!"   415
    Togidres han thise thre hir trouthes plight
To lyve and dyen ech of hem for oother,
As though he were his owene ybore brother.
And up they stirte, al dronken in this rage,
And forth they goon towardes that village   420
Of which the taverner hadde spoke biforn.
And many a grisly ooth thanne han they sworn,
And Cristes blessed body they torente—
Deeth shal be deed, if that they may hym hente!

And as they sat, they heard the hand bell clink
Before a coffin going to the grave;
One of them called the little tavern knave
And said "Go and find out at once—look spry!—
Whose corpse is in that coffin passing by;
And see you get the name correctly too."
    "Sir," said the boy, "no need, I promise you;
Two hours before you came here I was told.
He was a friend of yours in days of old,
And suddenly, last night, the man was slain,
Upon his bench, face up, dead drunk again.
There came a privy thief, they call him Death,
Who kills us all round here, and in a breath
He speared him through the heart, he never stirred.
And then Death went his way without a word.
He's killed a thousand in the present plague,
And, sir, it doesn't do to be too vague
If you should meet him; you had best be wary.
Be on your guard with such an adversary,
Be primed to meet him everywhere you go,
That's what my mother said. It's all I know."
    The publican joined in with, "By St. Mary,
What the child says is right; you'd best be wary,

This very year he killed, in a large village
A mile away, man, woman, serf at tillage,

Page in the household, children—all there were.
Yes, I imagine that he lives round there.
It's well to be prepared in these alarms,
He might do you dishonor. "Huh, God's arms!"
The rioter said, "Is he so fierce to meet?
I'll search for him, by Jesus, street by street.
God's blessed bones! I'll register a vow!
Here, chaps! The three of us together now,
Hold up your hands, like me, and we'll be brothers
In this affair, and each defend the others,
And we will kill this traitor Death, I say!
Away with him as he has made away
With all our friends. God's dignity! Tonight!"
    They made their bargain, swore with appetite,
These three, to live and die for one another
As brother-born might swear to his born brother.
And up they started in their drunken rage
And made toward this village which the page
And publican had spoken of before.
Many and grisly were the oaths they swore,
Tearing Christ's blessed body to a shred;
"If we can only catch him, Death is dead!"

Whan they han goon nat fully half a mile,   425
Right as they wolde han troden over a stile,
An oold man and a povre with hem mette.
This olde man ful mekely hem grette,
And seyde thus, "Now, lordes, God yow see!"
    The proudeste of thise riotoures three   430
Answerde agayn, "What, carl, with sory grace!
Why artow al forwrapped save thy face?
Why lyvestow so longe in so greet age?"
    This olde man gan looke in his visage,
And seyde thus: "For I ne kan nat fynde   435
A man, though that I walked into Ynde,
Neither in citee ne in no village,
That wolde chaunge his youthe for myn age;
And therfore moot I han myn age stille,
As longe tyme as it is Goddes wille.   440
Ne Deeth, allas, ne wol nat han my lyf.
Thus walke I, lyk a restelees kaityf,
And on the ground, which is my moodres gate,
I knokke with my staf, bothe erly and late,
And seye 'Leeve mooder, leet me in!   445
Lo how I vanysshe, flessh, and blood, and skyn!
Allas, whan shul my bones been at reste?
Mooder, with yow wolde I chaunge my cheste
That in my chambre longe tyme hath be,
Ye, for an heyre clowt to wrappe me!'   450
But yet to me she wol nat do that grace,
For which ful pale and welked is my face.

    "But, sires, to yow it is no curteisye
To speken to an old man vileynye,
But he trespasse in word or elles in dede.   455
In Hooly Writ ye may yourself wel rede:
'Agayns an oold man, hoor upon his heed,
Ye sholde arise; wherfore I yeve yow reed,
Ne dooth unto an oold man noon harm now,
Namoore than that ye wolde men did to yow   460
In age, if that ye so longe abyde.
And God be with yow, where ye go or ryde!
I moot go thider as I have to go."
    "Nay, olde cherl, by God, thou shalt nat so,"
Seyde this oother hasardour anon;   465
"Thou partest nat so lightly, by Seint John!
Thou spak right now of thilke traytour Deeth.
That in this contree alle oure freendes sleeth.
Have heer my trouthe, as thou art his espye,
Telle where he is or thou shalt it abye,   470
By God and by the hooly sacrement!

When they had gone not fully half a mile,
Just as they were about to cross a stile,
They came upon a very poor old man
Who humbly greeted them and thus began,
"God look to you, my lords, and give you quiet!"
To which the proudest of these men of riot
Gave back the answer, "What, old fool? Give place!
Why are you all wrapped up except your face?
Why live so long? Isn't it time to die?"
    The old, old fellow looked him in the eye
And said, "Because I never yet have found,
Though I have walked to India, searching round
Village and city on my pilgrimage,
One who would change his youth to have my age.
And so my age is mine and must be still
Upon me, for such time as God may will.
    "Not even Death, alas, will take my life;
So, like a wretched prisoner at strife
Within himself, I walk alone and wait
About the earth, which is my mother's gate,
Knock-knocking with my staff from night to noon
And crying, 'Mother, open to me soon!
Look at me, Mother, won't you let me in?
See how I wither, flesh and blood and skin!
Alas! When will these bones be laid to rest?
Mother, I would exchange—for that were best—
The wardrobe in my chamber, standing there
So long, for yours! Aye, for a shirt of hair
To wrap me in!' She has refused her grace,
Whence comes the pallor of my withered face.
    "But it dishonored you when you began
To speak so roughly, sir, to an old man,
Unless he had injured you in word or deed.
It says in holy writ, as you may read,
'Thou shalt rise up before the hoary head
And honor it.' And therefore be it said
'Do no more harm to an old man than you,
Being now young, would have another do
When you are old'—if you should live till then.
And so may God be with you, gentlemen,
For I must go whither I have to go."
    "By God," the gambler said, "you shan't do so,
You don't get off so easy, by St. John!
I heard you mention, just a moment gone,
A certain traitor Death who singles out
And kills the fine young fellows hereabout.
And you're his spy, by God! You wait a bit.
Say where he is or you shall pay for it,
By God and by the Holy Sacrament!

For soothly thou art oon of his assent
To sleen us younge folk, thou false theef!"
  "Now, sires," quod he, "if that yow be so leef
To fynde Deeth, turne up this croked wey,   475
For in that grove I lafte hym, by my fey,
Under a tree, and there he wole abyde;
Noght for youre boost he wole him no thyng hyde.
Se ye that ook? Right there ye shal hym fynde.
God save yow, that boghte agayn mankynde,   480
And yow amende!" Thus seyde this olde man;
And everich of thise riotoures ran
Til he cam to that tree, and ther they founde
Of floryns fyne of gold ycoyned rounde
Wel ny an eighte busshels, as hem thoughte.   485
No lenger thanne after Deeth they soughte,
But ech of hem so glad was of that sighte,
For that the floryns been so faire and brighte,
That doun they sette hem by this precious hoord.
The worste of hem, he spak the firste word.   490
  "Bretheren," quod he, "taak kep what that I
       seye;
My wit is greet, though that I bourde and pleye.
This tresor hath Fortune unto us yiven
In myrthe and jolitee oure lyf to lyven,
And lightly as it comth, so wol we spende.   495
Ey, Goddes precious dignitee! Who wende
To-day that we sholde han so fair a grace?
But myghte this gold be caried fro this place
Hoom to myn hous, or elles unto youres—
For wel ye woot that al this gold is oures—   500
Thanne were we in heigh felicitee.
But trewely, by daye it may nat bee.
Men wolde seyn that we were theves stronge,
And for oure owene tresor doon us honge.
This tresor moste ycaried be by nyghte   505
As wisely and as slyly as it myghte.
Wherfore I rede that cut among us alle
Be drawe, and lat se wher the cut wol falle;
And he that hath the cut with herte blithe
Shal renne to the town, and that ful swithe,   510
And brynge us breed and wyn ful prively.
And two of us shul kepen subtilly
This tresor wel; and if he wol nat tarie,
Whan it is nyght, we wol this tresor carie,
By oon assent, where as us thynketh best."   515
That oon of hem the cut broghte in his fest,
And bad hem drawe and looke where it wol falle;
And it fil on the yongeste of hem alle,

I say you've joined together by consent
To kill us younger folk, you thieving swine!"
  "Well, sirs," he said, "if it be your design
To find out Death, turn up this crooked way
Toward that grove, I left him there today
Under a tree, and there you'll find him waiting.
He isn't one to hide for all your prating.
You see that oak? He won't be far to find.
And God protect you that redeemed mankind,
Aye, and amend you!" Thus that ancient man.
  At once the three young rioters began
To run, and reached the tree, and there they found
A pile of golden florins on the ground,
New-coined, eight bushels of them as they thought.
No longer was it Death those fellows sought,
For they were all so thrilled to see the sight,
The florins were so beautiful and bright,
That down they sat beside the precious pile.
The wickedest spoke first after a while.
"Brothers," he said, "you listen to what I say.

I'm pretty sharp although I joke away.
It's clear that Fortune has bestowed this treasure
To let us live in jollity and pleasure.
Light come, light go! We'll spend it as we ought.
God's precious dignity! Who would have thought
This morning was to be our lucky day?
  "If one could only get the gold away,
Back to my house, or else to yours, perhaps—
For as you know, the gold is ours, chaps—
We'd all be at the top of fortune, hey?
But certainly it can't be done by day.
People would call us robbers—a strong gang,
So our own property would make us hang.
No, we must bring this treasure back by night
Some prudent way, and keep it out of sight.
And so as a solution I propose
We draw for lots and see the way it goes;
The one who draws the longest, lucky man,
Shall run to town as quickly as he can
To fetch us bread and wine—but keep things dark—
While two remain in hiding here to mark
Our heap of treasure. If there's no delay,
When night comes down we'll carry it away,
All three of us, wherever we have planned."
  He gathered lots and hid them in his hand
Bidding them draw for where the luck should fall.
It fell upon the youngest of them all,

And forth toward the toun he wente anon.
And also soone as that he was gon,   520
That oon of hem spak thus unto that oother:
"Thow knowest wel thou art my sworen, brother;
Thy profit wol I telle thee anon.
Thou woost wel that oure felawe is agon.
And heere is gold, and that ful greet plentee,   525
That shal departed been among us thre.
But nathelees, if I kan shape it so
That it departed were among us two,
Hadde I nat doon a freendes torn to thee?"
      That oother answerde, "I noot hou that
            may be.   530
He woot that the gold is with us tweye;
What shal we doon? What shal we to hym seye?"
      "Shal it be conseil?" seyde the firste shrewe
"And I shal tellen in a wordes fewe
What we shal doon, and brynge it wel aboute."   535
      "I graunte," quod that oother, "out of doute,
That, by my trouthe, I wol thee nat biwreye."
      "Now," quod the firste, "thou woost wel we be
            tweye,
And two of us shul strenger be than oon.
Looke whan that he is set, that right anoon   540
Arys as though thou woldest with hym pleye,
And I shal ryve hym thurgh the sydes tweye
Whil that thou strogelest with hym as in game,
And with thy daggere looke thou do the same;
And thanne shal al this gold departed be,   545
My deere freend, bitwixen me and thee.
Thanne may we bothe oure lustes all fulfille,
And pleye at dees right at oure owene wille."
And thus acorded been thise shrewes tweye
To sleen the thridde, as ye han herd me seye.   550
      This yongeste, which that wente to the toun,
Ful ofte in herte he rolleth up and doun
The beautee of thise floryns newe and brighte.
"O Lord!" quod he, "if so were that I myghte
Have all this tresor to myself allone,   555
Ther is no man that lyveth under the trone
Of God that sholde lyve so murye as I!"
And atte laste the feend, oure enemy,
Putte in his thought that he sholde poyson beye,
With which he myghte sleen his felawes tweye;   560
For-why the feend foond hym in swich lyvynge
That he hadde leve him to sorwe brynge.
For this was outrely his fulle entente,
To sleen hem bothe and nevere to repente.

And off he ran at once toward the town.
      As soon as he had gone the first sat down
And thus began a parley with the other:
"You know that you can trust me as a brother;
Now let me tell you where your profit lies;
You know our friend has gone to get supplies
And here's a lot of gold that is to be
Divided equally amongst us three.
Nevertheless, if I could shape things thus
So that we shared it out—the two of us—
Wouldn't you take it as a friendly act?"
      "But how?" the other said. "He knows the fact

That all the gold was left with me and you;
What can we tell him? What are we to do?"
      "Is it a bargain," said the first, "or no?
For I can tell you in a word or so
What's to be done to bring the thing about."
      "Trust me," the other said, "you needn't doubt
My word. I won't betray you, I'll be true."
      "Well," said his friend, "you see that we
            are two,
And two are twice as powerful as one.
Now look; when he comes back, get up in fun
To have a wrestle; then, as you attack,
I'll up and put my dagger through his back
While you and he are struggling, as in game;
Then draw your dagger too and do the same.
Then all this money will be ours to spend,
Divided equally, of course, dear friend.
Then we can gratify our lusts and fill
The day with dicing at our own sweet will."
Thus these two miscreants agreed to slay
The third and youngest, as you heard me say.
      The youngest, as he ran towards the town,
Kept turning over, rolling up and down
Within his heart the beauty of those bright
New florins, saying, "Lord, to think I might
Have all that treasure to myself alone!
Could there be anyone beneath the throne
Of God so happy as I then should be?"
      And so the Fiend, our common enemy,
Was given power to put it in his thought
That there was always poison to be bought,
And that with poison he could kill his friends.
To men in such a state the Devil sends
Thoughts of this kind, and has a full permission
To lure them on to sorrow and perdition;

And forth he gooth, no lenger wolde he tarie,   565
Into the toun, unto a pothecarie,
And preyde hym that he hym wolde selle
Som poyson, that he myghte his rattes quelle;
And eek ther was a polcat in his hawe,
That, as he seyde, his capouns hadde yslawe,   570
And fayn he wolde wreke hym, if he myghte,
On vermyn that destroyed hym by nyghte.

The pothecarie answerde, "And thou shalt have
A thyng that, also God my soule save,
In al this world ther is no creature   575
That eten or dronken hath of this confiture
Noght but the montance of a corn of whete,
That he ne shal his lif anon forlete;
Ye, sterve he shal, and that in lasse while
Than thou wolt goon a paas nat but a mile,   580
This poysoun is so strong and violent."
This cursed man hath in his hond yhent
This poysoun in a box, and sith he ran
Into the nexte strete unto a man,
And borwed [of] hym large botelles thre,   585
And in the two his poyson poured he;
The thridde he kepte clene for his drynke.
For al the nyght he shoop hym for to swynke
In cariynge of the gold out of that place.
And whan this riotour, with sory grace,   590
Hadde filled with wyn his grete botels thre,
To his felawes agayn repaireth he.
What nedeth it to sermone of it moore?
For right as they hadde cast his deeth bifoore,
Right so they han hym slayn, and that anon.   595
And whan that this was doon, thus spak that oon:
"Now lat us sitte and drynke, and make us merie,
And afterward we wol his body berie."
And with that word it happed hym, par cas,
To take the botel ther the poyson was,   600
And drank, and yaf his felawe drynke also,
For which anon they storven bothe two.
But certes, I suppose that Avycen
Wroot nevere in no canon, ne in no fen,
Mo wonder signes of empoisonyng   605
Than hadde thise wrecches two, er hir endyng.
Thus ended been thise homycides two,
And eek the false empoysonere also.
O cursed synne of alle cursednesse!
O traytours homycide, O wikkednesse!   610

For this young man was utterly content
To kill them both and never to repent.
    And on he ran, he had no thought to tarry,
Came to the town, found an apothecary
And said, "Sell me some poison if you will,
I have a lot of rats I want to kill
And there's a polecat too about my yard
That takes my chickens and it hits me hard;
But I'll get even, as is only right,
With vermin that destroy a man by night."
    The chemist answered, "I've a preparation
Which you shall have, and by my soul's salvation
If any living creature eat or drink
A mouthful, ere he has the time to think,
Though he took less than makes a grain of wheat,
You'll see him fall down dying at your feet;
Yes, die he must, and in so short a while
You'd hardly have the time to walk a mile,
The poison is so strong, you understand."
    This cursed fellow grabbed into his hand
The box of poison and away he ran
Into a neighboring street, and found a man
Who lent him three large bottles. He withdrew
And deftly poured the poison into two.
He kept the third one clean, as well he might,
For his own drink, meaning to work all night
Stacking the gold and carrying it away.
And when this rioter, this devil's clay,
Had filled his bottles up with wine, all three,
Back to rejoin his comrades sauntered he.
    Why make a sermon of it? Why waste breath?
Exactly in the way they'd planned his death
They fell on him and slew him, two to one.
Then said the first of them when this was done,
"Now for a drink. Sit down and let's be merry,
For later on there'll be the corpse to bury."
And, as it happened, reaching for a sup,
He took a bottle full of poison up
And drank; and his companion, nothing loth,
Drank from it also, and they perished both.
    There is, in Avicenna's long relation
Concerning poison and its operation,
Trust me, no ghastlier section to transcend
What these two wretches suffered at their end.
Thus these two murderers received their due,
So did the treacherous young poisoner too.
    O cursed sin! O blackguardly excess!
O treacherous homicide! O wickedness!

O glotonye, luxurie, and hasardrye!
Thou blasphemour of Crist with vileynye
And others grete, of usage and of pride!
Allas, mankynde, how may it bitide
That to thy creatour, which that the wroghte   615
And with his precious herte-blood thee boghte,
Thou art so fals and so unkynde, allas?
   Now, goode men, God foryeve yow youre
      trespas,
And ware yow fro the synne of avarice!
Myn hooly pardoun may yow alle warice,   620
So that ye offre nobles or sterlynges,
Or elles silver broches, spoones, rynges.
Boweth youre heed under this hooly bulle!
Cometh up, ye wyves, offreth of youre wolle!
Youre names I entre heer in my rolle anon;   625
Into the blisse of hevene shul ye gon.
I yow assoille, by myn heigh power,
Yow that wol offre, as clene and eek as cleer
As ye were born.—And lo, sires, thus I preche.
And Jhesu Crist, that is oure soules leche,   630
So graunte yow his pardoun to receyve,
For that is best; I wol yow nat deceyve.
   But, sires, o word forgat I in my tale:
I have relikes and pardoun in my male,
As faire as any man in Engelond,   635
Whiche were me yeven by the popes hond.
If any of yow wole, of devocion,
Offren and han myn absolucion,
Com forth anon, and kneleth heere adoun,   640
And mekely receyveth my pardoun;
Or elles taketh pardoun as ye wende,
Al newe and fressh at every miles ende,
So that ye offren, alwey newe and newe,
Nobles or pens, whiche that be goode and trewe.
It is an honour to everich that is heer   645
That ye mowe have a suffisant pardoneer
T'assoille yow in contree as ye ryde,
For aventures whiche that may bityde.
Paraventure ther may fallen oon or two
Doun of his hors and breke his nekke atwo.   650
Looke which a seuretee is it to yow alle
That I am in youre felaweshipe yfalle,
That may assoille yow, bothe moore and lasse,
Whan that the soule shal fro the body passe.
I rede that oure Hoost heere shal bigynne,   655
For he is moost envoluped in synne.
Com forth, sire Hoost, and offre first anon,

O gluttony that lusted on and diced!
O blasphemy that took the name of Christ
With habit-hardened oaths that pride began!
Alas, how comes it that a mortal man,
That thou, to thy Creator, Him that wrought thee,
That paid His precious blood for thee and bought thee,
Art so unnatural and false within?
   Dearly beloved, God forgive your sin

And keep you from the vice of avarice!
My holy pardon frees you all of this,
Provided that you make the right approaches,
That is with sterling, rings, or silver brooches.
Bow down your heads under this holy bull!
Come on, you women, offer up your wool!
I'll write your name into my ledger; so!
Into the bliss of Heaven you shall go.
For I'll absolve you by my holy power,
You that make offering, clean as at the hour
When you were born. . . . That, sirs, is how I preach.
And Jesu Christ, soul's healer, aye, the leech
Of every soul, grant pardon and relieve you
Of sin, for that is best, I won't deceive you.
   One thing I should have mentioned in my tale,
Dear people. I've some relics in my bale
And pardons too, as full and fine, I hope,
As any in England, given me by the Pope.
If there be one among you that is willing
To have my absolution for a shilling
Devoutly given, come! and do not harden
Your hearts but kneel in humbleness for pardon;
Or else, receive my pardon as we go.
You can renew it every town or so
Always provided that you still renew
Each time, and in good money, what is due.
It is an honor to you to have found
A pardoner with his credentials sound
Who can absolve you as you ply the spur
In any accident that may occur.
For instance—we are all at Fortune's beck—
Your horse may throw you down and break your neck.
What a security it is to all
To have me here among you and at call
With pardon for the lowly and the great
When soul leaves body for the future state!
And I advise our Host here to begin,
The most enveloped of you all in sin.
Come forward, Host, you shall be the first to pay,

And thou shalt kisse the relikes everychon,
Ye, for a grote! Unbokele anon thy purs."
  "Nay, nay!" quod he, "thanne have I Cristes
          curs!   660
Lat be," quod he, "it shal nat be, so theech!
Thou woldest make me kisse thyn olde breech,
And swere it were a relyk of a seint,
Though it were with thy fundement depeint!
But, by the croys which that Seint Eleyne fond,   665
I wolde I hadde thy coillons in myn hond
In stide of relikes or of seintuarie.
Lat kutte hem of, I wol thee helpe hem carie;
They shul be shryned in an hogges toord!"
  This Pardoner answerde nat a word;   670
So wrooth he was, no word ne wolde he seye.
  "Now," quod oure Hoost, "I wol no lenger
          pleye
With thee, ne with noon oother angry man."
But right anon the worthy Knyght bigan,
Whan that he saugh that al the people lough,   675
"Namoore of this, for it is right ynough!
Sire Pardoner, be glad and myrie of cheere;
And ye, sire Hoost, that been to me so deere,
I prey yow that ye kisse the Pardoner.
And Pardoner, I prey thee, drawe thee neer   680
And, as we diden, lat us laughe and pleye."
Anon they kiste, and ryden forth hir weye.

And kiss my holy relics right away.
Only a groat. Come on, unbuckle your purse!"
  "No, no," said he, "not I, and may the curse
Of Christ descend upon me if I do!
You'll have me kissing your old breeches too
And swear they were the relic of a saint
Although your fundament supplied the paint!
Now by St. Helen and the Holy Land
I wish I had your ballocks in my hand
Instead of relics in a reliquarium;
Have them cut off and I will help to carry 'em.
We'll have them shrined for you in a hog's turd."
  The Pardoner said nothing, not a word;
He was so angry that he couldn't speak.
  "Well," said our Host, "if you're for
          showing pique,
I'll joke no more, not with an angry man."
  The worthy Knight immediately began,
Seeing the fun was getting rather rough,
And said, "No more, we've all had quite enough.
Now, Master Pardoner, perk up, look cheerly!
And you, Sir Host, whom I esteem so dearly,
I beg of you to kiss the Pardoner.
  "Come, Pardoner, draw nearer, my dear sir.
Let's laugh again and keep the ball in play."
They kissed, and we continued on our way.

[1386–1399]

ANONYMOUS

Adam lay ibounden

Adam lay ibounden,°   bound
    Bounden in a bond,
Foure thousand winter
    Thoght he not too long;
And al was for an appil,   5
    An appil that he tok,
As clerkes finden
    Wreten in here° bok.   their

Ne hadde the appil take ben,   *10*
    The appil taken ben,
Ne hadde never our lady
    A ben° hevene quene;   *have been*
Blessed be the time
    That appil take was!   *15*
Therfore we moun° singen   *may*
    "Deo gracias."

ANONYMOUS

I sing of a mayden

I sing of a mayden
    That is makeles;°   *matchless*
King of alle kinges
    To° her son she ches.°   *for/chose*

He cam also stille   *5*
    Ther his moder was,
As dew in Aprille
    That falleth on the gras.

He cam also stille
    To his moderes bowr,   *10*
As dew in Aprille
    That falleth on the flowr.

He cam also stille
    Ther his moder lay,
As dew in Aprille   *15*
    That falleth on the spray.

Moder and maiden
    Was never none but she;
Wel may swich a lady
    Godes moder be.   *20*

ADAM LAY IBOUNDEN   ***Deo gracias.***   Latin for "Thanks be to God."

ANONYMOUS

Westron wynde/Western wind

Westron wynde when wyll thow blow
the smalle rayne downe can rayne
Chryst yf my love were in my armys
and I yn my bed agayne

Western wind, when will thou blow,
　The small rain down can rain?
Christ, if my love were in my arms
　And I in my bed again!

ANONYMOUS

Edward

1

"Why does your brand° sae° drap wi' bluid,   *sword/so*
　Edward, Edward,
Why does your brand sae drap wi' bluid,
　And why sae sad gang° ye, O?"   *go*
"O I ha'e killed my hawk sae guid,   5
　Mither, mither,
O I ha'e killed my hawk sae guid,
　And I had nae mair but he, O."

2

"Your hawke's bluid was never sae reid,°   *red*
　Edward, Edward,   10
Your hawke's bluid was never sae reid,
　My dear son I tell thee, O."
"O I ha'e killed my reid-roan steed,
　Mither, mither,
O I ha'e killed my reid-roan steed,   15
　That erst was sae fair and free, O."

3

"Your steed was auld, and ye ha'e gat mair,
　Edward, Edward,
Your steed was auld, and ye ha'e gat mair,
　Some other dule° ye drie,° O."   *grief/suffer* 20

"O I ha'e killed my fader dear,
    Mither, mither,
O I ha'e killed my fader dear,
  Alas, and wae° is me, O!"   *woe*

4

"And whatten° penance wul ye drie for that,   *what sort of* 25
    Edward, Edward?
And whatten penance wul ye drie for that,
  My dear son, now tell me O?"
"I'll set my feet in yonder boat,
    Mither, mither,   30
I'll set my feet in yonder boat,
  And I'll fare over the sea, O."

5

"And what wul ye do wi' your towers and your ha',
    Edward, Edward?
And what wul ye do wi' your towers and your ha',   35
  That were sae fair to see, O?"
"I'll let them stand tul they down fa',
    Mither, mither,
I'll let them stand tul they down fa',
  For here never mair maun° I be, O."   *must* 40

6

"And what wul ye leave to your bairns° and your wife,   *children*
    Edward, Edward?
And what wul ye leave to your bairns and your wife,
  Whan ye gang over the sea, O?"
"The warlde's room, let them beg thrae° life,   *through* 45
    Mither, mither,
The warlde's room, let them beg thrae life,
  For them never mair wul I see, O."

7

"And what wul ye leave to your ain mither dear,
    Edward, Edward?   50
And what wul ye leave to your ain mither dear,
  My dear son, now tell me, O?"
"The curse of hell frae° me sall° ye bear,   *from/shall*
    Mither, mither,
The curse of hell frae me sall ye bear,   55
  Sic° counsels ye gave to me, O."   *such*

ANONYMOUS

The Three Ravens

There were three ravens sat on a tree,
Down a downe, hay down, hay downe,
There were three ravens sat on a tree,
With a downe;

There were three ravens sat on a tree,   5
They were as blacke as they might be,
With a downe derrie, derrie, derrie, downe, downe.

The one of them said to his make,°   *mate*
Where shall we our breakfast take?

Downe in yonder greene field   *10*
There lies a knight slain under his shield.

His hounds they lie downe at his feete,
So well they can their master keepe.

His hawkes they flie so eagerly°   *fiercely*
There's no fowle dare him come nie.   *15*

Downe there comes a fallow doe
As great with yong as she might goe.

She lift up his bloody hed
And kist his wounds that were so red.

She got him up upon her back   *20*
And carried him to earthen lake.°   *pit*

She buried him before the prime,°   *sunrise*
She was dead her selfe ere even-song time.

God send every gentleman
Such hawkes, such hounds, and such a leman.°   *lover/sweetheart 25*

JOHN SKELTON

[1460–1529]

To Mistress Margaret Hussey

Merry Margaret,
  As midsummer flower,
  Gentle as falcon
  Or hawk of the tower:
With solace and gladness,   5
Much mirth and no madness,
All good and no badness;
    So joyously,
    So maidenly,
    So womanly   10
    Her demeaning
    In every thing,
    Far, far passing
    That I can indite,°   *say*
    Or suffice to write   15
Of Merry Margaret
  As midsummer flower,
  Gentle as falcon
  Or hawk of the tower.
  As patient and still   20
And as full of good will
As fair Isaphill,
Coriander,
Sweet pomander,
Good Cassander,   25
Steadfast of thought,
Well made, well wrought,
Far may be sought
Ere that ye can find
So courteous, so kind   30
As Merry Margaret,
  This midsummer flower,
  Gentle as falcon
  Or hawk of the tower.

[1495, 1523]

TO MISTRESS MARGARET HUSSEY   ²²**Isaphill**   Hypsipyle, queen of an island in the Aegean Sea (Lemnos). Famed for her devotion to her father and children.   ²³**coriander**   an aromatic medicinal herb. ²⁴**pomander**   a perfumed ball.   ²⁵**Cassander**   Cassandra, a steadfast prophet.

THOMAS WYATT

[1503–1542]

They flee from me

They flee from me, that sometime did me seek,
With naked foot stalking in my chamber.
I have seen them, gentle, tame, and meek,
That now are wild, and do not remember
That sometime they put themselves in danger   5
To take bread at my hand; and now they range,
Busily seeking with a continual change.

Thanked be Fortune it hath been otherwise,
Twenty times better; but once in special,
In thin array, after a pleasant guise,   10
When her loose gown from her shoulders did fall,
And she me caught in her arms long and small,
And therewith all sweetly did me kiss
And softly said, "Dear heart, how like you this?"

It was no dream, I lay broad waking.   15
But all is turned, thorough my gentleness,
Into a strange fashion of forsaking;
And I have leave to go, of her goodness,
And she also to use newfangleness.
But since that I so kindely am served,   20
I fain would know what she hath deserved.

[1557]

Whoso list to hunt

Whoso list to hunt, I know where is an hind,
   But as for me, alas, I may no more;
   The vain travail hath wearied me so sore,
   I am of them that furthest come behind.
Yet may I by no means my wearied mind   5
   Draw from the deer, but as she fleeth afore
   Fainting I follow; I leave off therefore,
   Since in a net I seek to hold the wind.

Who list her hunt, I put him out of doubt,
   As well as I, may spend his time in vain.   *10*
   And graven with diamonds in letters plain,
There is written her fair neck round about,
   "Noli me tangere, for Caesar's I am,
   And wild for to hold, though I seem tame."

                                             [1557]

HENRY HOWARD, EARL OF SURREY

[1517–1547]

The soote season

The soote° season, that bud and bloom forth brings,	*sweet*
With green hath clad the hill and eke° the vale;	*also*
The nightingale with feathers new she sings;	
The turtle° to her make° hath told her tale.	*turtledove/mate*
Summer is come, for every spray now springs;	*5*
The hart hath hung his old head on the pale;	
The buck in brake his winter coat he flings,	
The fishes float with new repairéd scale;	
The adder all her slough away she slings,	
The swift swallow pursueth the flies small;	*10*
The busy bee her honey now she mings.°	*remembers*
Winter is worn, that was the flowers' bale.°	*harm*
And thus I see among these pleasant things,	
Each care decays, and yet my sorrow springs.	

                                             [1557]

QUEEN ELIZABETH I

[1533–1603]

When I was fair and young

When I was fair and young, and favor gracéd me,
Of many was I sought, their mistress for to be;
But I did scorn them all, and answered them therefore,

"Go, go, go seek some otherwhere!
    Importune me no more!"   *5*

How many weeping eyes I made to pine with woe,
How many sighing hearts, I have no skill to show;
Yet I the prouder grew, and answered them therefore,
    "Go, go, go seek some otherwhere!
    Importune me no more!"   *10*

Then spake fair Venus' son, that proud victorious boy,
And said, "Fine dame, since that you be so coy,
I will so pluck your plumes that you shall say no more,
    'Go, go, go seek some otherwhere!
    Importune me no more!"   *15*

When he had spake these words, such change grew in my breast
That neither night nor day since that, I could take any rest.
Then lo! I did repent that I had said before,
    "Go, go, go seek some otherwhere!
    Importune me no more!"   *20*

                                            [c. 1575]

EDMUND SPENSER

[1552–1599]

One day I wrote her name upon the strand

One day I wrote her name upon the strand,°   *beach*
But came the waves and washéd it away;
Agayne I wrote it with a second hand,
But came the tyde, and made my paynes his pray.
"Vayne man," sayd she, "that doest in vaine assay,   *5*
A mortall thing so to immortalize,
For I my selve shall lyke to this decay,
And eek° my name bee wypéd out lykewize."   *also*
"Not so," quod° I, "let baser things devize°   *said / devise*
To dy in dust, but you shall live by fame: *10*
My verse your vertues rare shall eternize,
And in the hevens wryte your glorious name.

Where whenas death shall all the world subdew,
Our love shall live, and later life renew."

[1595]

SIR WALTER RALEGH

[c. 1552–1618]

The Nymph's Reply to the Shepherd

If all the world and love were young,
And truth in every shepherd's tongue,
These pretty pleasures might me move
To live with thee and be thy love.

Time drives the flocks from field to fold   5
When rivers rage and rocks grow cold,
And Philomel becometh dumb;
The rest complains of cares to come.

The flowers do fade, and wanton fields
To wayward winter reckoning yields;   10
A honey tongue, a heart of gall,
Is fancy's spring, but sorrow's fall.

Thy gowns, thy shoes, thy beds of roses,
Thy cap, thy kirtle,° and thy posies   *long dress*
Soon break, soon wither, soon forgotten—   15
In folly ripe, in reason rotten.

Thy belt of straw and ivy buds,
Thy coral clasps and amber studs,
All these in me no means can move
To come to thee and be thy love.   20

But could youth last and love still breed,
Had joys no date° nor age no need,   *end*

THE NYMPH'S REPLY TO THE SHEPHERD   7**Philomel**   the nightingale. According to Ovid's *Metamor-phoses*, Philomel's brother-in-law Tereus had her tongue cut out to prevent her from revealing that he had raped her. Ralegh's poem is a reply to Christopher Marlowe's "The Passionate Shepherd to His Love" (p. 161).

Then these delights my mind might move
To live with thee and be thy love.

[1600]

SIR PHILIP SIDNEY

[1554–1586]

Loving in truth

from Astrophel and Stella

1

Loving in truth, and fain° in verse my love to show,	*eager*
That she dear she might take some pleasure of my pain,	
Pleasure might cause her read, reading might make her know,	
Knowledge might pity win, and pity grace obtain,	
I sought fit words to paint the blackest face of woe:	*5*
Studying inventions fine, her wits to entertain,	
Oft turning others' leaves, to see if thence would flow	
Some fresh and fruitful showers upon my sunburned brain.	
But words came halting forth, wanting Invention's stay;	
Invention, Nature's child, fled stepdame Study's blows;	*10*
And others' feet still seemed but strangers in my way.	
Thus, great with child to speak, and helpless in my throes,	
Biting my truant pen, beating myself for spite:	
"Fool," said my Muse to me, "look in thy heart, and write."	

[1591]

Thou blind man's mark

Thou blind man's mark,° thou fool's self-chosen snare,	*target*
Fond° fancy's scum, and dregs of scattered thought,	*foolish*
Bands of all evils, cradle of causeless care,	
Thou web of will whose end is never wrought;	
Desire, Desire, I have too dearly bought	*5*
With prize of mangled mind thy worthless ware!	
Too long, too long asleep thou hast me brought	
Who should my mind to higher things prepare.	

But yet in vain thou hast my ruin sought;
In vain thou madest me to vain things aspire;   *10*
In vain thou kindlest all thy smoky fire.

For Virtue hath this better lesson taught:
Within myself to seek my only hire,°   *payment*
Desiring nought but how to kill desire.

[1591]

CHIDIOCK TICHBORNE

[c. 1558–1586]

Tichborne's Elegy

WRITTEN WITH HIS OWN HAND IN THE TOWER BEFORE HIS EXECUTION

My prime of youth is but a frost of cares,
My feast of joy is but a dish of pain,
My crop of corn° is but a field of tares,°   *wheat/weeds*
And all my good is but vain hope of gain;   *5*
The day is past, and yet I saw no sun,
And now I live, and now my life is done.

My tale was heard and yet it was not told,
My fruit is fallen and yet my leaves are green,
My youth is spent and yet I am not old,
I saw the world and yet I was not seen;   *10*
My thread is cut and yet it is not spun,
And now I live, and now my life is done.

I sought my death and found it in my womb,
I looked for life and saw it was a shade,
I trod the earth and knew it was my tomb,   *15*
And now I die, and now I was but made;
My glass is full, and now my glass is run,
And now I live, and now my life is done.

[1586]

TICHBORNE'S ELEGY   Tichborne was hanged for plotting to murder Queen Elizabeth I.   [11]**My thread
is cut** . . .   the three Fates spun, measured, and cut the thread of men's lives.

ROBERT SOUTHWELL

[c. 1561–1595]

The Burning Babe

As I in hoary winter's night stood shivering in the snow,
Surprised I was with sudden heat which made my heart to glow;
And lifting up a fearful eye to view what fire was near,
A pretty babe all burning bright did in the air appear;
Who, scorchéd with excessive heat, such floods of tears did shed   5
As though his floods should quench his flames which with his tears were fed.
"Alas," quoth he, "but newly born in fiery heats I fry,
Yet none approach to warm their hearts or feel my fire but I!
My faultless breast the furnace is, the fuel wounding thorns,
Love is the fire, and sighs the smoke, the ashes shame and scorns;   10
The fuel justice layeth on, and mercy blows the coals,
The metal in this furnace wrought are men's defiléd souls,
For which, as now on fire I am to work them to their good,
So will I melt into a bath to wash them in my blood."
With this he vanished out of sight and swiftly shrunk away,   15
And straight I calléd unto mind that it was Christmas day.

[1602]

MICHAEL DRAYTON

[1563–1631]

Since there's no help, come let us kiss and part

Since there's no help, come let us kiss and part;
Nay, I have done, you get no more of me,
And I am glad, yea glad with all my heart
That thus so cleanly I myself can free;
Shake hands forever, cancel all our vows,   5
And when we meet at any time again,
Be it not seen in either of our brows
That we one jot of former love retain.
Now at the last gasp of love's latest breath,
When, his pulse failing, passion speechless lies,   10
When faith is kneeling by his bed of death,

And innocence is closing up his eyes,
Now if thou wouldst, when all have given him over,
From death to life thou mightst him yet recover.

[1619]

CHRISTOPHER MARLOWE

[1564–1593]

The Passionate Shepherd to His Love

Come live with me and be my love,
And we will all the pleasures prove°   *try*
That valleys, groves, hills, and fields,
Woods, or steepy mountain yields.

And we will sit upon the rocks,   5
Seeing the shepherds feed their flocks,
By shallow rivers to whose falls
Melodious birds sing madrigals.

And I will make thee beds of roses
And a thousand fragrant posies,   10
A cap of flowers, and a kirtle°   *gown*
Embroidered all with leaves of myrtle;

A gown made of the finest wool
Which from our pretty lambs we pull;
Fair lined slippers for the cold,   15
With buckles of the purest gold;

A belt of straw and ivy buds,
With coral clasps and amber studs:
And if these pleasures may thee move,
Come live with me, and be my love.   20

The shepherds' swains shall dance and sing
For thy delight each May morning:
If these delights thy mind may move,
Then live with me and be my love.

[1600]

THE PASSIONATE SHEPHERD TO HIS LOVE   See Sir Walter Ralegh's reply on p. 157.

WILLIAM SHAKESPEARE

[1564–1616]

William Shakespeare, without doubt the most famous English writer, also remains one of the most popular. His fame and popularity, however, rest on his plays more than on his nondramatic poetry—though his sonnets remain perennially in fashion. Entire libraries have been devoted to exploring Shakespeare's literary genius. Moreover, one does not have to go to a specialized library to find either his works or interpretations of them. Many public libraries, however modest their holdings, include both.

What makes Shakespeare such a literary phenomenon? Why are readers so drawn to his work? We offer two simple explanations: (1) his revelation of human character, especially his exploration of complex states of mind and feeling; (2) his explosive and exuberant language, particularly the richness and variety of his metaphors. Both of these literary virtues abound in the sequence of 154 sonnets Shakespeare wrote in the 1590s. Both also consistently appear in his thirty-seven plays, particularly in the soliloquies, those inward meditative speeches of the major characters. The richness of Shakespeare's language is also apparent in the songs from the plays, largely from the comedies. In fact, throughout his poetic and dramatic writing, Shakespeare added nearly two thousand words to the English language, many of which are still in use today. Some examples include *assassination, barefaced, courtship, dwindle, dislocate, eventful, lackluster,* and *premeditated.*

Another source of Shakespeare's popularity is his immense quotability. Shakespeare's plays and poems provide a repository of familiar sayings and recognizable quotations. From *Hamlet* alone we glean the following:

In my mind's eye

To the manner born

There are more things in heaven and earth

Hold the mirror up to nature

I must be cruel only to be kind.

Brevity is the soul of wit.

To be, or not to be: that is the question.

Frailty, thy name is woman.

Neither a borrower nor a lender be.

Get thee to a nunnery.

Something's rotten in the state of Denmark.

What a piece of work is man.

There is special providence in the fall of a sparrow.

Good night, sweet prince. And flights of angels sing thee to thy rest.

To reduce Shakespeare's appeal to his most famous quotes, however, is to ignore other important dimensions of his popularity. It is, moreover, to get things backward—to put the cart before the horse. Shakespeare is not a great writer because he is quotable; he is quotable because he is a great writer. And it is his manipulation of language and his revelation of character that have made him both widely read and deeply revered.

Very little about Shakespeare's life is known with certainty. Scholars, however, have determined the following basic outline of fact. He was born in Stratford-on-Avon in April 1564. He attended the local grammar school, where he would have studied Latin and perhaps a little Greek. His formal education did not include attendance at a university—in his day either Oxford or Cambridge. Instead, at eighteen, he married Anne Hathaway, who bore three children in as many years, a daughter in 1583 and twins, a boy and a girl, in 1585. We also know that Shakespeare wrote and acted in plays, for by 1592 he was known in London as both actor and playwright.

Shakespeare was initially known as a poet, first of a pair of narrative poems on mythological subjects ("Venus and Adonis" and "The Rape of Lucrece") and later and more importantly of an original and brilliant sonnet sequence. Shakespeare's fame as a poet, in fact, rests mostly on his sonnets, which represent his commitment to what was then a popular poetic fashion. The sonnets display dramatic power and narrative drive as well as melodic lyricism. Their range of emotional experience is wide, including melancholy, despair, hope, shame, guilt, fear, jealousy, and exhilaration. Written during the 1590s, they were not published until 1609—though Nos. 138 and 144 were printed in a 1599 collection, *The Passionate Pilgrim,* apparently without Shakespeare's authorization. Like John Donne's poems, Shakespeare's sonnets circulated in manuscript before publication. And also like Donne's poems, according to contemporary testimony, they were much admired.

There has been considerable conjecture as to whether the sonnets are autobiographical, and much speculation about the identity of those described in them. Without pursuing this biographical line of inquiry to any significant extent, we can at least acknowledge that in addition to the poet-speaker, three other characters appear in the sonnets: a friend, a mistress, and a rival poet. One of Shakespeare's boldest and most original strokes was to address many of his sonnets to a friend rather than to a mistress (as did many of his contemporaries in their sonnets). Of those sonnets Shakespeare did address to a mistress—his "dark lady" of sonnets nos. 127 to 152—there has been even more interest in identifying her than the friend of the earlier sonnets.

What matters ultimately, however, is the power and beauty of the sonnets' language, not the identity of those described in them. Consider sonnet no. 116:

Let me not to the marriage of true minds
Admit impediments; love is not love
Which alters when it alteration finds,
Or bends with the remover to remove.
Oh no, it is an ever-fixed mark
That looks on tempests and is never shaken;
It is the star to every wandering bark
Whose worth's unknown, though his height be taken.
Love's not time's fool, though rosy lips and cheeks
Within his bending sickle's compass come;
Love alters not with his brief hours and weeks,
But bears it out even to the edge of doom.
    If this be error and upon me proved,
    I never writ, nor no man ever loved.

Shakespeare's eloquence appears in the opening lines' echo of the Anglican marriage ceremony from the Book of Common Prayer; in the repetitions of "love," "alters," "alteration," "remove," and "remover"; in the imagery of fixedness and eternity; in its blend of crisp Saxon monosyllabic diction with polysyllabic Latinate words like "impediment"; in the sound play at the turn in lines 9–10; in the rhythmic shifts in the sestet, particularly in the slowing down of the verse in line 12; and finally in the elegance and witty argument of the concluding couplet.

But Shakespeare's eloquence manifests itself with even greater variety in the soliloquies from the plays. Written predominantly in blank verse, each of the plays, but especially the tragedies, contains poetry of grandeur. We will illustrate with one example—a soliloquy from *Macbeth*. Macbeth, the usurping king of Scotland, his hands reddened with the blood of many—including the rightful king, Duncan, whose kingship Macbeth has stolen—speaks the following soliloquy upon discovering that his wife, Lady Macbeth, has killed herself.

Tomorrow, and tomorrow, and tomorrow
Creeps in this petty pace from day to day,
To the last syllable of recorded time;
And all our yesterdays have lighted fools
The way to dusty death. Out, out, brief candle!
Life's but a walking shadow, a poor player
That struts and frets his hour upon the stage
And then is heard no more. It is a tale
Told by an idiot, full of sound and fury
Signifying nothing.

In this soliloquy Shakespeare reveals Macbeth's state of mind. The opening words suggest Macbeth's boredom and frustration at his perceived slowness of time's passing. Even more important, however, is the series of metaphors that reveal Macbeth's attitude toward life. First, the brevity of life is emphasized in the implied comparison with a candle, which doesn't last very long and which is subject to being snuffed out. Second, life is compared with a shadow, an insubstantial, dark reflection of the real thing. Third comes the more elaborate comparison of life with the situation of an actor, whose theatrical existence is confined to the duration of the play. Shakespeare's metaphor resonates to suggest that in a way "all the world's a stage," that we are all actors who one moment are proudly and confidently strutting through life only to fret anxiously the next over lost opportunities and brute realities we may be powerless to change. And then, quite simply, we die. All this Macbeth now understands. All this Shakespeare has him express through his densely metaphorical blank verse.

Although the soliloquies contain Shakespeare's most intensely dramatic poetry, his lyrical gift is displayed in the many fine songs that appear in the plays, predominantly in the comedies and romances. Even though we can fully appreciate the songs and soliloquies only in their dramatic contexts, we can nonetheless admire their poetic achievement outside those contexts. The songs and soliloquies, moreover, are also important because later poets such as T. S. Eliot alluded to them. But most important, they are beautiful in their own right, and they remind us of the origin of poetry as a musical art, not merely a verbal one.

Many tributes have been paid to Shakespeare. One, however, stands above the rest: his contemporary Ben Jonson's judgment: "He is not for an age, but for all time."

THE SONNETS

Shall I compare thee to a summer's day?

Shall I compare thee to a summer's day?
Thou art more lovely and more temperate.
Rough winds do shake the darling buds of May,
And summer's lease hath all too short a date.
Sometime too hot the eye of heaven shines,   5
And often is his gold complexion dimmed;
And every fair from fair sometime declines,
By chance, or nature's changing course, untrimmed;
But thy eternal summer shall not fade,
Nor lose possession of that fair thou ow'st,°   *ownest* 10
Nor shall Death brag thou wand'rest in his shade,
When in eternal lines to time thou grow'st.
  So long as men can breathe or eyes can see,
  So long lives this, and this gives life to thee.

[#18, 1609]

SHALL I COMPARE THEE   ⁸**untrimmed**   stripped or divested of beauty.

When, in disgrace with Fortune and men's eyes

When, in disgrace with Fortune and men's eyes,
I all alone beweep my outcast state,
And trouble deaf heaven with my bootless° cries,   *fruitless*
And look upon myself and curse my fate,
Wishing me like to one more rich in hope,   5
Featured like him, like him with friends possessed,
Desiring this man's art, and that man's scope,
With what I most enjoy contented least;
Yet in these thoughts myself almost despising,
Haply I think on thee, and then my state,   10
Like to the lark at break of day arising
From sullen earth, sings hymns at heaven's gate;
    For thy sweet love rememb'red such wealth brings,
    That then I scorn to change my state with kings.

[#29, 1609]

Not marble, nor the gilded monuments

Not marble, nor the gilded monuments
Of princes, shall outlive this pow'rful rhyme,
But you shall shine more bright in these contents
Than unswept stone, besmeared with sluttish° time.   *dirty*
When wasteful war shall statues overturn,   5
And broils root out the work of masonry,
Nor Mars his sword nor war's quick fire shall burn
The living record of your memory.
'Gainst death and all oblivious enmity
Shall you pace forth; your praise shall still find room   10
Even in the eyes of all posterity
That wear this world out to the ending doom.°   *judgment day*
    So, till the judgment that yourself arise,
    You live in this, and dwell in lovers' eyes.

[#15, 1609]

Since brass, nor stone, nor earth, nor boundless sea

Since brass, nor stone, nor earth, nor boundless sea,
But sad mortality o'ersways their power,
How with this rage shall beauty hold a plea,

Whose action is no stronger than a flower?
O, how shall summer's honey breath hold out   5
Against the wrackful siege of batt'ring days,
When rocks impregnable are not so stout,
Nor gates of steel so strong but Time decays?
O, fearful meditation, where, alack,
Shall Time's best jewel from Time's chest lie hid?   10
Or what strong hand can hold his swift foot back,
Or who his spoil of beauty can forbid?
    O, none, unless this miracle have might,
    That in black ink my love may still shine bright.

                                       [#65, 1609]

No longer mourn for me when I am dead

No longer mourn for me when I am dead
Than you shall hear the surly sullen bell
Give warning to the world that I am fled
From this vile world with vilest worms to dwell.
Nay, if you read this line, remember not   5
The hand that writ it, for I love you so
That I in your sweet thoughts would be forgot,
If thinking on me then should make you woe.
O, if, I say, you look upon this verse,
When I, perhaps, compounded am with clay,   10
Do not so much as my poor name rehearse,
But let your love even with my life decay,
    Lest the wise world should look into your moan,
    And mock you with me after I am gone.

                                       [#71, 1609]

They that have pow'r to hurt and will do none

They that have pow'r to hurt and will do none,
That do not do the thing they most do show,
Who, moving others, are themselves as stone,
Unmovèd, cold, and to temptation slow;
They rightly do inherit heaven's graces   5
And husband nature's riches from expense;°   *expenditure*
They are the lords and owners of their faces,
Others but stewards of their excellence.

The summer's flow'r is to the summer sweet,
Though to itself it only live and die;   *10*
But if that flow'r with base infection meet,
The basest weed outbraves° his dignity: *exceeds*
   For sweetest things turn sourest by their deeds;
   Lilies that fester smell far worse than weeds.

                                                        [#94, 1609]

Th' expense of spirit in a waste of shame

Th' expense of spirit in a waste of shame
Is lust in action; and, till action, lust
Is perjured, murd'rous, bloody, full of blame,
Savage, extreme, rude, cruel, not to trust;
Enjoyed no sooner but despisèd straight;   *5*
Past reason hunted, and no sooner had,
Past reason hated as a swallowed bait
On purpose laid to make the taker mad;
Mad in pursuit, and in possession so;
Had, having, and in quest to have, extreme;   *10*
A bliss in proof, and proved, a very woe,
Before, a joy proposed; behind, a dream.
   All this the world well knows, yet none knows well
   To shun the heaven that leads men to this hell.

                                                       [#129, 1609]

My mistress' eyes are nothing like the sun

My mistress' eyes are nothing like the sun;
Coral is far more red than her lips' red;
If snow be white, why then her breasts are dun;°   *grayish brown*
If hairs be wires, black wires grow on her head.
I have seen roses damasked, red and white,   *5*
But no such roses see I in her cheeks,
And in some perfumes is there more delight
Than in the breath that from my mistress reeks.
I love to hear her speak, yet well I know
That music hath a far more pleasing sound.   *10*

TH' EXPENSE OF SPIRIT   **in proof** during the experience.
MY MISTRESS' EYES   **damasked** mixed red and white; pink.

I grant I never saw a goddess go;
My mistress when she walks treads on the ground.
　　And yet, by heaven, I think my love as rare
　　As any she belied with false compare.

[#130, 1609]

Poor soul, the center of my sinful earth

Poor soul, the center of my sinful earth,
My sinful earth these rebel pow'rs that thee array,°   *dress*
Why dost thou pine within and suffer dearth,
Painting thy outward walls so costly gay?
Why so large cost, having so short a lease,   5
Dost thou upon thy fading mansion spend?
Shall worms, inheritors of this excess,
Eat up thy charge°? Is this thy body's end?   *expense*
Then, soul, live thou upon thy servant's loss,
And let that pine to aggravate° thy store;   *increase* 10
Buy terms divine in selling hours of dross;
Within be fed, without be rich no more:
　　So shalt thou feed on Death, that feeds on men,
　　And Death once dead, there's no more dying then.

[#146, 1609]

SONGS

When daisies pied

Spring

When daisies pied and violets blue
　　And ladysmocks all silver-white
And cuckoobuds of yellow hue
　　Do paint the meadows with delight,
The cuckoo then, on every tree,   5
Mocks married men for thus sings he,
　　　　Cuckoo;

POOR SOUL, THE CENTER　　¹**my sinful earth** the body.　　⁴**outword walls** the body.
WHEN DAISIES PIED　　from *Love's Labors Lost*, conclusion.　　¹**pied** multicolored.　　²**ladysmocks**
spring flowers.　　⁶**Mocks married men** "cuckoo" was similar in sound to "cuckold," a derisive term for a man
whose wife is unfaithful to him.

Cuckoo, cuckoo: Oh word of fear,
Unpleasing to a married ear!

When shepherds pipe on oaten straws,   10
  And merry larks are plowmen's clocks,
When turtles tread,° and rooks, and daws,   *mate*
  And maidens bleach their summer smocks,
The cuckoo then, on every tree,
Mocks married men; for thus sings he,   15
       Cuckoo;
Cuckoo, cuckoo: Oh word of fear,
Unpleasing to a married ear!

      Winter

When icicles hang by the wall
And Dick the shepherd blows his nail   20
And Tom bears logs into the hall,
  And milk comes frozen home in pail.
When blood is nipped and ways be foul,
Then nightly sings the staring owl,
       Tu-who;   25
Tu-whit, tu-who: a merry note,
While greasy Joan doth keel° the pot.   *stir*

When all aloud the wind doth blow,
  And coughing drowns the parson's saw,°   *wise saying*
And birds sit brooding in the snow,   30
  And Marian's nose looks red and raw,
When roasted crabs° hiss in the bowl,   *crab apples*
Then nightly sings the staring owl,
       Tu-who;
Tu-whit, tu-who: a merry note   35
While greasy Joan doth keel the pot.

                  [1595?, 1598]

Under the greenwood tree

    Under the greenwood tree
    Who loves to lie with me,
    And turn his merry note
    Unto the sweet bird's throat,

UNDER THE GREENWOOD TREE   from *As You Like It*, II, v.

Come hither, come hither, come hither: 5
    Here shall he see
    No enemy
But winter and rough weather.

    Who doth ambition shun
    And loves to live i' the sun, 10
    Seeking the food he eats,
    And pleased with what he gets,
Come hither, come hither, come hither:
    Here shall he see
    No enemy 15
But winter and rough weather.

[1599?, 1623]

Blow, blow, thou winter wind

Blow, blow, thou winter wind,
Thou art not so unkind
    As man's ingratitude;
Thy tooth is not so keen,
Because thou art not seen, 5
    Although thy breath be rude.
Heigh-ho! sing, heigh-ho! unto the green holly:
Most friendship is feigning, most loving mere folly:
    Then, heigh-ho, the holly!
    This life is most jolly. 10

Freeze, freeze, thou bitter sky,
That dost not bite so nigh
    As benefits forgot:
Though thou the waters warp,
Thy sting is not so sharp 15
    As friend remembered not.
Heigh-ho! sing, . . .

[1599?, 1623]

It was a lover and his lass

It was a lover and his lass,
    With a hey, and a ho, and a hey nonino,
That o'er the green corn field did pass
    In springtime, the only pretty ring time,

BLOW, BLOW, THOU WINTER WIND   from *As You Like It,* II, vii.
IT WAS A LOVER AND HIS LASS   from *As You Like It,* V, iii.

When birds do sing, hey ding a ding, ding: *5*
Sweet lovers love the spring.

Between the acres of the rye,
    With a hey, and a ho, and a hey nonino,
These pretty country folks would lie,
    In springtime, . . .   *10*

This carol they began that hour,
    With a hey, and a ho, and a hey nonino,
How that a life was but a flower
    In springtime, . . .

And therefore take the present time,   *15*
    With a hey, and a ho, and a hey nonino;
For love is crownéd with the prime
    In springtime, . . .

[1599?, 1623]

Oh mistress mine!

Oh mistress mine! where are you roaming?
Oh! stay and hear; your true love's coming,
    That can sing both high and low.
Trip no further, pretty sweeting;
Journeys end in lovers meeting,   *5*
    Every wise man's son doth know.

What is love? 'tis not hereafter;
Present mirth hath present laughter;
    What's to come is still unsure:
In delay there lies no plenty;   *10*
Then come kiss me, sweet and twenty,
    Youth's a stuff will not endure.

[1602, 1623]

When that I was and a little tiny boy

When that I was and a little tiny boy,
    With hey, ho, the wind and the rain,
A foolish thing was but a toy,
    For the rain it raineth every day.

OH MISTRESS MINE!   from *Twelfth Night*, II, iii.
WHEN THAT I WAS   from *Twelfth Night*, conclusion.

But when I came to man's estate,   5
    With hey, ho, . . .
'Gainst knaves and thieves men shut their gate,
    For the rain, . . .

But when I came, alas! to wive,
    With hey, ho, . . .   10
By swaggering could I never thrive,
    For the rain, . . .

But when I came unto my beds,
    With hey, ho, . . .
With toss-pots still had drunken heads,   15
    For the rain, . . .

A great while ago the world begun,
    With hey, ho, . . .
But that's all one, our play is done,
    And we'll strive to please you every day.   20

                                                            [1602, 1623]

Fear no more the heat o' the sun

Fear no more the heat o' the sun,
    Nor the furious winter's rages;
Thou thy worldly task hast done,
    Home art gone, and ta'en thy wages:
Golden lads and girls all must,   5
As chimney-sweepers, come to dust.

Fear no more the frown o' the great;
    Thou art past the tyrant's stroke;
Care no more to clothe and eat;
    To thee the reed is as the oak: 10
The scepter, learning, physic, must
All follow this, and come to dust.

Fear no more the lightning flash,
    Nor the all-dreaded thunder stone,°   *thunderbolt*
Fear not slander, censure rash;   15
    Thou hast finished joy and moan:

FEAR NO MORE   from *Cymbeline,* IV, ii.

All lovers young, all lovers must
Consign to thee, and come to dust.

No exorciser harm thee!
Nor no witchcraft charm thee!   20
Ghost unlaid forbear thee!
Nothing ill come near thee!
Quiet consummation have;
And renownéd be thy grave!

[1609, 1623]

Full fathom five

Full fathom five thy father lies;
    Of his bones are coral made;
Those are pearls that were his eyes:
    Nothing of him that doth fade,
But doth suffer a sea change   5
Into something rich and strange.
Sea nymphs hourly ring his knell:
    Ding-dong.
Hark! now I hear them—Ding-dong, bell.

[1611, 1623]

SOLILOQUIES

All the world's a stage

Jaques.   All the world's a stage,
And all the men and women merely players;
They have their exits and their entrances,
And one man in his time plays many parts,
His acts being seven ages. At first, the infant,   5
Mewling° and puking° in the nurse's arms.   *crying/vomiting*
Then the whining schoolboy, with his satchel
And shining morning face, creeping like snail
Unwillingly to school. And then the lover,
Sighing like furnace, with a woeful ballad   10

FULL FATHOM FIVE   from *The Tempest*, I, ii.
ALL THE WORLD'S A STAGE   from *As You Like It*, II, vii, 139–166.

Made to his mistress' eyebrow. Then a soldier,
Full of strange oaths and bearded like the pard,°   *leopard*
Jealous° in honor, sudden° and quick in quarrel,   *zealous/rash*
Seeking the bubble reputation
Even in the cannon's mouth. And then the justice,   *15*
In fair round belly with good capon lined,
With eyes severe and beard of formal cut,
Full of wise saws° and modern instances;°   *maxims/examples*
And so he plays his part. The sixth age shifts
Into the lean and slippered pantaloon,   *20*
With spectacles on nose and pouch on side;
His youthful hose, well saved, a world too wide
For his shrunk shank, and his big manly voice,
Turning again toward childish treble, pipes
And whistles in his° sound. Last scene of all,   *its   25*
That ends this strange eventful history,
Is second childishness and mere oblivion,
Sans teeth, sans eyes, sans taste, sans everything.

                                        [1599, 1623]

Now is the winter of our discontent

Richard. Now is the winter of our discontent
   Made glorious summer by this sun of York;
   And all the clouds that loured upon our house
   In the deep bosom of the ocean buried.
   Now are our brows bound with victorious wreaths,   *5*
   Our bruisèd arms hung up for monuments,°   *memorials*
   Our stern alarums° changed to merry meetings,   *alarms*
   Our dreadful marches to delightful measures.°   *dances*
   Grim-visaged War hath smoothed his wrinkled front,°   *forehead*
   And now, instead of mounting barbèd steeds   *10*
   To fright the souls of fearful adversaries,
   He capers nimbly in a lady's chamber
   To the lascivious pleasing of a lute.
   But I, that am not shaped for sportive tricks
   Nor made to court an amorous looking glass;   *15*
   I, that am rudely stamped, and want° love's majesty   *lack*
   To strut before a wanton ambling nymph;

ALL THE WORLD'S A STAGE   ¹⁶**capon lined**   a capon is a bribe offered to a judge.   ²⁰**pantaloon**   a
figure in the Italian *commedia dell'arte;* a ridiculous old man.   ²⁸**Sans**   French for "without."
NOW IS THE WINTER OF OUR DISCONTENT   from *Richard III,* I, i, 1–41.

I, that am curtailed of this fair proportion,
Cheated of feature° by dissembling Nature,   *bodily form*
Deformed, unfinished, sent before my time   20
Into this breathing world scarce half made up,
And that so lamely and unfashionable
That dogs bark at me as I halt by them;
Why, I, in this weak piping time of peace,
Have no delight to pass away the time,   25
Unless to spy my shadow in the sun
And descant on mine own deformity.
And therefore, since I cannot prove a lover
To entertain these fair well-spoken days,
I am determinèd to prove a villain   30
And hate the idle pleasures of these days.
Plots have I laid, inductions° dangerous,   *plans*
By drunken prophecies, libels, and dreams,
To set my brother Clarence and the King
In deadly hate the one against the other;   35
And if King Edward be as true and just
As I am subtle, false, and treacherous,
This day should Clarence closely be mewed up°   *imprisoned*
About a prophecy which says that *G*
Of Edward's heirs the murderer shall be.   40
Dive, thoughts, down to my soul.

[1592, 1623]

O mighty Caesar!

Antony. O mighty Caesar! Dost thou lie so low?
Are all thy conquests, glories, triumphs, spoils,
Shrunk to this little measure? Fare thee well.
I know not, gentlemen, what you intend,
Who else must be let blood,° who else is rank.°   *killed/diseased* 5
If I myself, there is no hour so fit
As Caesar's death's hour, nor no instrument
Of half that worth as those your swords, made rich
With the most noble blood of all this world.
I do beseech ye, if you bear me hard,°   *a grudge* 10
Now, whilst your purpled° hands do reek and smoke,   *bloodied*

NOW IS THE WINTER OF OUR DISCONTENT   ²⁴**piping . . . peace** The pipe, or wooden flute, was associated with peacetime.   ²⁷**descant** a musical term meaning "to compose variations on a theme."
O MIGHTY CAESAR!   from *Julius Caesar*, III, i, 148–163.   ¹¹**reek and smoke** steam with warm blood.

Fulfill your pleasure. Live a thousand years,
I shall not find myself so apt° to die;   *ready*
No place will please me so, no mean° of death,   *manner*
As here by Caesar, and by you cut off,   15
The choice and master spirits of this age.

[1599, 1623]

Friends, Romans, countrymen

Antony. Friends, Romans, countrymen, lend me your ears;
I come to bury Caesar, not to praise him.
The evil that men do lives after them,
The good is oft interrèd with their bones;
So let it be with Caesar. The noble Brutus   5
Hath told you Caesar was ambitious.
If it were so, it was a grievous fault,
And grievously hath Caesar answered it.
Here, under leave of Brutus and the rest
(For Brutus is an honorable man,   10
So are they all, all honorable men),
Come I to speak in Caesar's funeral.
He was my friend, faithful and just to me;
But Brutus says he was ambitious,
And Brutus is an honorable man.   15
He hath brought many captives home to Rome,
Whose ransoms did the general coffers° fill;   *treasury*
Did this in Caesar seem ambitious?
When that the poor have cried, Caesar hath wept;
Ambition should be made of sterner stuff.   20
Yet Brutus says he was ambitious;
And Brutus is an honorable man.
You all did see that on the Lupercal
I thrice presented him a kingly crown,
Which he did thrice refuse. Was this ambition?   25
Yet Brutus says he was ambitious;
And sure he is an honorable man.
I speak not to disprove what Brutus spoke,
But here I am to speak what I do know.
You all did love him once, not without cause;   30

O MIGHTY CAESAR!   ¹²**Live**   If I should live.
FRIENDS, ROMANS, COUNTRYMEN   from *Julius Caesar*, III, ii, 75–109.   ⁸**answered**   paid the penalty.

What cause withholds you then to mourn for him?
O judgment, thou art fled to brutish beasts,
And men have lost their reason! Bear with me;
My heart is in the coffin there with Caesar,
And I must pause till it come back to me.   35

[1599, 1623]

Once more unto the breach

King. Once more unto the breach, dear friends, once more;
   Or close the wall up with our English dead!
   In peace there's nothing so becomes a man
   As modest stillness and humility;
   But when the blast of war blows in our ears,   5
   Then imitate the action of the tiger:
   Stiffen the sinews, conjure up the blood,
   Disguise fair nature with hard-favored rage;
   Then lend the eye a terrible aspect:
   Let it pry through the portage° of the head   *portholes* 10
   Like the brass cannon; let the brow o'erwhelm it
   As fearfully as doth a gallèd° rock   *eroded*
   O'erhang and jutty his confounded base,
   Swilled° with the wild and wasteful ocean.   *consumed*
   Now set the teeth, and stretch the nostril wide,   15
   Hold hard the breath, and bend up every spirit
   To his full height! On, on, you noble English,
   Whose blood is fet° from fathers of war-proof;°   *derived/war-tested*
   Fathers that like so many Alexanders
   Have in these parts from morn till even fought   20
   And sheathed their swords for lack of argument.°   *opposition*
   Dishonor not your mothers; now attest
   That those whom you called fathers did beget you!
   Be copy now to men of grosser blood
   And teach them how to war! And you, good yeomen,   25
   Whose limbs were made in England, show us here
   The mettle of your pasture. Let us swear
   That you are worth your breeding; which I doubt not,
   For there is none of you so mean and base
   That hath not noble luster in your eyes.   30
   I see you stand like greyhounds in the slips,°   *leashes*

ONCE MORE UNTO THE BREACH   from *Henry V*, III, i, 1–34.   ¹³**jutty his confounded base**   jut
over its ruined base.   ²⁷**mettle of your pasture**   quality of your rearing.

Straining upon the start. The game's afoot!
Follow your spirit; and upon this charge,
Cry, "God for Harry, England and Saint George!"

[1599, 1623]

If we are marked to die

King Henry. If we are marked to die, we are enow
    To do our country loss; and if to live,
    The fewer men, the greater share of honor.
    God's will! I pray thee wish not one man more.
    By Jove, I am not covetous for gold,   5
    Nor care I who doth feed upon my cost;
    It earns° me not if men my garments wear;   *moves, grieves*
    Such outward things dwell not in my desires:
    But if it be a sin to covet honor,
    I am the most offending soul alive.   10
    No, faith, my coz, wish not a man from England.
    God's peace! I would not lose so great an honor
    As one man more methinks would share from me
    For the best hope I have. O, do not wish one more!
    Rather proclaim it, Westmoreland, through my host,   15
    That he which hath no stomach to this fight,
    Let him depart; his passport shall be made,
    And crowns for convoy put into his purse;
    We would not die in that man's company
    That fears his fellowship to die with us.   20
    This day is called the Feast of Crispian
    He that outlives this day, and comes safe home,
    Will stand a-tiptoe when this day is named,
    And rouse him at the name of Crispian.
    He that shall see this day, and live old age,   25
    Will yearly on the vigil feast his neighbors
    And say, "Tomorrow is Saint Crispian."
    Then will he strip his sleeve and show his scars,
    And say, "These wounds I had on Crispin's day."
    Old men forget; yet all shall be forgot,   30
    But he'll remember, with advantages,°   *embellishments*
    What feats he did that day. Then shall our names,

ONCE MORE UNTO THE BREACH   [34]**Saint George** patron saint of England, famed for his proverbial dragon slaying.
IF WE ARE MARKED TO DIE   from *Henry V,* IV, iii, 20–67.   [1–2]**enow to do** Enough to cause.
[21]**Feast of Crispian** October 25. The brothers Crispinus and Crispianus were martyred in 487.

Familiar in his mouth as household words—
Harry the King, Bedford and Exeter,
Warwick and Talbot, Salisbury and Gloucester—   *35*
Be in their flowing cups freshly rememb'red.
This story shall the good man teach his son;
And Crispin Crispian shall ne'er go by,
From this day to the ending of the world,
But we in it shall be rememberèd—   *40*
We few, we happy few, we band of brothers;
For he today that sheds his blood with me
Shall be my brother; be he ne'er so vile,°   *lowborn*
This day shall gentle his condition
And gentlemen in England, now abed,   *45*
Shall think themselves accursed they were not here;
And hold their manhoods cheap whiles any speaks
That fought with us upon Saint Crispin's day.

                                                       [1599, 1623]

Is this a dagger which I see before me

Macbeth. Is this a dagger which I see before me,
    The handle toward my hand? Come, let me clutch thee.
    I have thee not, and yet I see thee still.
    Art thou not, fatal vision, sensible°   *perceptible*
    To feeling as to sight, or art thou but   *5*
    A dagger of the mind, a false creation,
    Proceeding from the heat-oppressèd brain?
    I see thee yet, in form as palpable
    As this which now I draw.
    Thou marshal'st me the way that I was going;   *10*
    And such an instrument I was to use.
    Mine eyes are made the fools o'th' other senses,
    Or else worth all the rest. I see thee still;
    And on thy blade and dudgeon° gouts° of blood,   *hilt/blobs*
    Which was not so before. There's no such thing.   *15*
    It is the bloody business which informs°   *creates impressions*
    Thus to mine eyes. Now o'er the one half-world
    Nature seems dead, and wicked dreams abuse°   *deceive, trick*
    The curtained sleep; witchcraft celebrates
    Pale Hecate's offerings; and withered murder,   *20*

IF WE ARE MARKED TO DIE   **⁴⁴gentle his condition**   achieve the status of gentility.
IS THIS A DAGGER WHICH I SEE   from *Macbeth*, II, i, 33–64.   **²⁰Hecate's offerings**   given in worship
of Hecate, goddess of sorcery.

Alarumed° by his sentinel, the wolf,   *signaled*
Whose howl's his watch, thus with his stealthy pace,
With Tarquin's ravishing strides, towards his design
Moves like a ghost. Thou sure and firm-set earth,
Hear not my steps, which way they walk, for fear   25
Thy very stones prate of my whereabout,
And take the present horror from the time,
Which now suits with it. Whiles I threat, he lives:
Words to the heat of deeds too cold breath gives.

A bell rings.

I go, and it is done: the bell invites me.   30
Hear it not, Duncan, for it is a knell
That summons thee to heaven, or to hell.

                                                    [1606, 1623]

It is the cause, it is the cause

Othello. It is the cause, it is the cause, my soul.
  Let me not name it to you, you chaste stars.
  It is the cause. Yet I'll not shed her blood,
  Nor scar that whiter skin of hers than snow,
  And smooth as monumental alabaster.   5
  Yet she must die, else she'll betray more men.
  Put out the light, and then put out the light.
  If I quench thee, thou flaming minister,°   *servant*
  I can again thy former light restore,
  Should I repent me; but once put out thy light,   10
  Thou cunning'st pattern of excelling nature,
  I know not where is that Promethean heat°   *divine fire*
  That can thy light relume.° When I have plucked the rose,   *relight*
  I cannot give it vital° growth again;   *living*
  It needs must wither. I'll smell thee on the tree.   15

He kisses her.

O balmy breath, that dost almost persuade
Justice to break her sword. One more, one more!
Be thus when thou art dead, and I will kill thee,
And love thee after. One more, and that's the last!

IS THIS A DAGGER WHICH I SEE   ²³**Tarquin** a Roman tyrant.
IT IS THE CAUSE   from *Othello*, V, ii, 1–22.

So sweet was ne'er so fatal. I must weep,   *20*
But they are cruel tears. This sorrow's heavenly;
It strikes where it doth love. She wakes.

[1604, 1623]

O that this too too sullied flesh would melt

Hamlet. O that this too too sullied flesh would melt,
  Thaw, and resolve itself into a dew,
  Or that the Everlasting had not fixed
  His canon° 'gainst self-slaughter. O God, God,   *law*
  How weary, stale, flat, and unprofitable   *5*
  Seem to me all the uses of this world!
  Fie on't, ah, fie, 'tis an unweeded garden
  That grows to seed. Things rank and gross in nature
  Possess it merely.° That it should come to this: *completely*
  But two months dead, nay, not so much, not two,   *10*
  So excellent a king, that was to this
  Hyperion to a satyr, so loving to my mother
  That he might not beteem° the winds of heaven   *allow*
  Visit her face too roughly. Heaven and earth,
  Must I remember? Why, she would hang on him   *15*
  As if increase of appetite had grown
  By what it fed on; and yet within a month—
  Let me not think on't; frailty, thy name is woman—
  A little month, or ere those shoes were old
  With which she followed my poor father's body   *20*
  Like Niobe, all tears, why she, even she—
  O God, a beast that wants discourse of reason
  Would have mourned longer—married with my uncle,
  My father's brother, but no more like my father
  Than I to Hercules. Within a month,   *25*
  Ere yet the salt of most unrighteous tears
  Had left the flushing in her gallèd eyes,
  She married. O, most wicked speed, to post
  With such dexterity to incestuous sheets!
  It is not, nor it cannot come to good.   *30*
  But break my heart, for I must hold my tongue.

[1601, 1623]

O THAT THIS TOO TOO SULLIED FLESH WOULD MELT   from *Hamlet,* I, iii, 129–159.
[12]**Hyperion** the sun god.   [21]**Niobe** proud mother whose children were slain by Apollo and Artemis. Niobe was transformed into a stone that continually wept tears.   [29]**incestuous sheets** Hamlet thinks of his mother sleeping with his father's brother.

To be, or not to be

Hamlet. To be, or not to be: that is the question:
Whether 'tis nobler in the mind to suffer
The slings and arrows of outrageous fortune,
Or to take arms against a sea of troubles,
And by opposing end them. To die, to sleep— 5
No more—and by a sleep to say we end
The heartache, and the thousand natural shocks
That flesh is heir to! 'Tis a consummation
Devoutly to be wished. To die, to sleep—
To sleep—perchance to dream: ay, there's the rub,°   *obstacle* 10
For in that sleep of death what dreams may come
When we have shuffled off this mortal coil,
Must give us pause. There's the respect°   *consideration*
That makes calamity of so long life:
For who would bear the whips and scorns of time, 15
Th' oppressor's wrong, the proud man's contumely,
The pangs of despised love, the law's delay,
The insolence of office, and the spurns
That patient merit of th' unworthy takes,
When he himself might his quietus° make   *settlement* 20
With a bare bodkin°? Who would fardels° bear,   *dagger/burdens*
To grunt and sweat under a weary life,
But that the dread of something after death,
The undiscovered country, from whose bourn°   *region*
No traveler returns, puzzles the will, 25
And makes us rather bear those ills we have,
Than fly to others that we know not of?
Thus conscience does make cowards of us all,
And thus the native hue of resolution
Is sicklied o'er with the pale cast of thought, 30
And enterprises of great pitch and moment,
With this regard° their currents turn awry,   *consideration*
And lose the name of action.—Soft you now,
The fair Ophelia!—Nymph, in thy orisons°   *prayers*
Be all my sins remembered. 35

[1601–1623]

TO BE, OR NOT TO BE   from *Hamlet,* III, i, 56–90.

O reason not the need!

Lear. O reason not the need! Our basest beggars
    Are in the poorest thing superfluous.
    Allow not nature more than nature needs,
    Man's life is cheap as beast's. Thou art a lady:
    If only to go warm were gorgeous,   5
    Why, nature needs not what thou gorgeous wear'st,
    Which scarcely keeps thee warm. But, for true need—
    You heavens, give me that patience, patience I need.
    You see me here, you gods, a poor old man,
    As full of grief as age, wretched in both.   10
    If it be you that stirs these daughters' hearts
    Against their father, fool° me not so much   *humiliate*
    To bear it tamely; touch me with noble anger,
    And let not women's weapons, water drops,
    Stain my man's cheeks. No, you unnatural hags!   15
    I will have such revenges on you both
    That all the world shall—I will do such things—
    What they are, yet I know not; but they shall be
    The terrors of the earth. You think I'll weep.
    No, I'll not weep.   20

                Storm and tempest.

    I have full cause of weeping, but this heart
    Shall break into a hundred thousand flaws°   *fragments*
    Or ere° I'll weep. O Fool, I shall go mad!   *before*

                             [1605, 1623]

Our revels now are ended

Ariel. Our revels now are ended. These our actors,
    As I foretold you, were all spirits and
    Are melted into air, into thin air;
    And, like the baseless fabric of this vision,
    The cloud-capped towers, the gorgeous palaces,   5

O REASON NOT THE NEED!   from *King Lear,* II, iv, 263–285.
OUR REVELS NOW ARE ENDED   from *The Tempest,* IV, i, 148–163.

The solemn temples, the great globe itself,
Yea, all which it inherit,° shall dissolve.   *occupy it*
And, like this insubstantial pageant faded,
Leave not a rack° behind. We are such stuff   *wisp of cloud*
As dreams are made on, and our little life   10
Is rounded with a sleep. Sir, I am vexed.
Bear with my weakness; my old brain is troubled.
Be not disturbed with my infirmity.
If you be pleased, retire into my cell
And there repose. A turn or two I'll walk   15
To still my beating mind.

[1611–1623]

THOMAS CAMPION

[1567–1620]

I care not for these ladies

I care not for these ladies,
That must be wooed and prayed:
Give me kind Amaryllis,
The wanton country maid.
Nature art disdaineth,   5
Her beauty is her own.
   Who when we court and kiss,
   She cries, "Forsooth, let go!"
   But when we come where comfort is,
   She never will say no.   10

If I love Amaryllis,
She gives me fruit and flowers:
But if we love these ladies,
We must give golden showers.
Give them gold, that sell love,   15
Give me the nut-brown lass,
   Who, when we court and kiss,
   She cries, "Forsooth, let go!"
   But when we come where comfort is,
   She never will say no.   20

These ladies must have pillows,
And beds by strangers wrought;
Give me a bower of willows,
Of moss and leaves unbought,
And fresh Amaryllis,   25
With milk and honey fed;
    Who, when we court and kiss,
    She cries, "Forsooth, let go!"
    But when we come where comfort is,
    She never will say no.   30

[1601]

My Sweetest Lesbia, let us live and love

My sweetest Lesbia, let us live and love,
And though the sager sort our deeds reprove,
Let us not weigh them. Heaven's great lamps do dive
Into their west, and straight again revive;
But, soon as once set is our little light,   5
Then must we sleep one ever-during night.

If all would lead their lives in love like me,
Then bloody swords and armour should not be;
No drum nor trumpet peaceful sleeps should move,
Unless alarm came from the camp of love.   10
But fools do live and waste their little light,
And seek with pain their ever-during night.

When timely death my life and fortune ends,
Let not my hearse be vexed with mourning friends;
But let all lovers, rich in triumph, come   15
And with sweet pastimes grace my happy tomb:
And, Lesbia, close up thou my little light,
And crown with love my ever-during night.

[1601]

I CARE NOT FOR THESE LADIES   ²⁵**Amaryllis** Following the classical tradition popularized by Virgil, the
name Amaryllis was typically used for an attractive shepherd girl.
MY SWEETEST LESBIA   The opening stanza translates the first six lines of Catullus's *Vivamus Lesbia et
amemus*. Thereafter, in stanzas 2 & 3 of Catullus's poem, Campion departs from his Latin model.

THOMAS NASHE

[1567–1601]

A Litany in Time of Plague

Adieu, farewell, earth's bliss;
This world uncertain is;
Fond° are life's lustful joys;   *foolish*
Death proves them all but toys;°   *trifles*
None from his darts can fly;   5
I am sick, I must die.
    Lord, have mercy on us!

Rich men, trust not in wealth,
Gold cannot buy you health;
Physic himself must fade.   10
All things to end are made,
The plague full swift goes by;
I am sick, I must die.
    Lord, have mercy on us!

Beauty is but a flower   15
Which wrinkles will devour;
Brightness falls from the air;
Queens have died young and fair;
Dust hath closed Helen's eye.
I am sick, I must die.   20
    Lord, have mercy on us!

Strength stoops unto the grave,
Worms feed on Hector brave;
Swords may not fight with fate,
Earth still holds ope her gate.   25
"Come, come!" the bells do cry.
I am sick, I must die.
    Lord, have mercy on us.

Wit with his wantonness
Tasteth death's bitterness;   30
Hell's executioner
Hath no ears for to hear
What vain art can reply.

I am sick, I must die.
   Lord, have mercy on us.   *35*

Haste, therefore, each degree,
To welcome destiny;
Heaven is our heritage,
Earth but a player's stage;
Mount we unto the sky.   *40*
I am sick, I must die.
   Lord, have mercy on us.

[1600]

JOHN DONNE

[1572–1631]

John Donne's poetry speaks to twentieth-century readers in ways unusual for poetry of his era. Without minimizing the extent to which Donne was a Renaissance poet, we can read him as a poet who shares the interests of many modern readers, particularly in his love poems. Among modern readers, T. S. Eliot had much to do with enhancing Donne's reputation. Along with Sir Herbert Grierson, who edited a 1912 collection of metaphysical poems, Eliot was among the first to appreciate Donne's unique poetic gifts. In his "The Metaphysical Poets" Eliot suggested that Donne was the preeminent metaphysical poet because he was able to relate poetic thought and emotion in previously unimagined ways. Eliot was so impressed by Donne's fusion of thought and feeling that he proclaimed Donne the greatest poet of his age.

Donne's poetry departs in significant ways from the lyric poetry of his time. While employing many of the conventions of Elizabethan love poetry, Donne frequently exaggerates and occasionally parodies them. We can find in his poems, for example, the conventional sighing and weeping of Petrarchan lovers. But Donne's use of those conventions in poems such as "A Valediction: Of Weeping" and "A Valediction: Forbidding Mourning" is more to dismiss than to endorse what they traditionally represent. Taking for granted a familiarity with conventions such as sighing lovers and bleeding hearts and such familiar decorative images as pearllike teeth and roselike cheeks, Donne freshens them by treating them in unexpected ways—by parodying the convention, for example, or by developing an image in an extensive and intellectually concentrated manner (as he does with the compass image in "A Valediction: Forbidding Mourning").

But more than his deviation from certain Petrarchan poetic conventions, Donne introduced a bold, aggressive intellectuality into English verse. Many of his poems develop as arguments, displaying carefully reasoned positions. In poems such as "The Flea," for example, the developing argument is deliberately outrageous, whereas in others such as "A Valediction: Forbidding Mourning," intellectual positions are advanced with seeming conviction. The intellectual nature of Donne's poems, moreover, includes more than the use of syllogistic reasoning or dialectical structure. It includes his extensive range of allusion to a wide variety of subjects including astronomy, metallurgy, mathematics, philosophy, classics, divinity, and law. Notably absent from Donne's poems are all but occasional mythological references, the kind of allusions inordinately popular in Elizabethan verse of the late 1500s.

To suggest, however, that Donne is an intellectual poet with a wide-ranging and inquiring mind is not to indicate that he is either a forbidding poet or an abstract one. He uses his knowledge and his intelligence to explore the nature of love in all its complexity—of thought and feeling, of intellectual reasoning, of emotional disposition, and of psychological experience. Donne describes, moreover, two kinds of love. In his divine poems he explores the religious person's love of God; in the erotic poems he probes the love between men and women. Donne engages in both these explorations in serious but witty ways, often using the language of religion to describe erotic love and the language of sexual experience to describe the relationship between the human and the divine. As a result, Donne's poetry is neither coldly intellectual nor philosophically abstract. His ideas are meant to be felt, to be experienced. As T. S. Eliot has noted, "a thought to Donne was an experience; it modified his sensibility."

In reading Donne's poetry it is necessary to distinguish between the serious love poems and the playful ones, between jest and earnest. Jesting poems such as "Woman's Constancy" and "The Indifferent" represent a playful, witty side of Donne's imagination that finds more serious expression in poems such as "The Canonization" and "The Anniversary." "Lovers' Infiniteness" occupies a middle ground in its combination of playfulness and seriousness. Essentially an argument about the nature of love, "Lovers' Infiniteness" playfully delineates a series of paradoxes that provokes its readers to decide what it means to have "all" of someone's love, and in fact whether one can ever have it all. Like a number of Donne's poems, this one presents one point of view only to counter it with another, then to abandon that perspective in a search for an increasingly adequate and accurate way to characterize the experience and nature of love.

But love wasn't the only subject that interested Donne. Religion permeated Donne's life, affecting it in crucial ways at important junctures. He was born into a Roman Catholic family at a time when anti-Catholic sentiment in England was strong. Although Donne was well educated, having attended both Oxford and Cambridge universities in addition to Lincoln's Inn, where he received legal training, his Catholicism made it difficult for him to obtain a position at court. Moreover, his decision to marry the seventeen-year-old Anne More, niece of Lady Egerton, wife to Lord Keeper Sir Thomas Egerton, who had appointed Donne his private secretary, further diminished his opportunities. Donne's secret marriage effectively closed the doors of court preferment that had been only partway open to him before. It also resulted in Donne's dismissal from his post as Egerton's secretary and, additionally, in a brief imprisonment.

About the time of his marriage in 1601, however, Donne converted to Anglicanism. And though he had ruined his chances for court preferment, Donne did retain many friends among those who resided at court and among poets and clergy as well. Even with such friends, however, Donne struggled through a financially difficult and psychologically stressful middle period of his life. In fact, one of the works he wrote during this period, *Biathanatos,* was a treatise on suicide.

Up through these first two periods of Donne's life, the years of his education and the early years of his marriage, he continued to write poetry, which circulated in manuscript among his friends and acquaintances. In 1615 Donne consented to become ordained as an Anglican minister, thereby acceding to the wishes of King James I, who thought Donne would make a brilliant preacher. In 1621 Donne became Dean of St. Paul's Cathedral in London, where he preached numerous sermons, many of which survive. During this period—the last dozen years of his life—Donne wrote, in addition to more than 160 sermons, a series of religious poems and a set of meditations on mortality, *The Devotions upon Emergent Occasions.* Donne's prose is characterized by the same intellectual curiosity, restlessness of mind, and metaphorical richness as his poetry. In reading both Donne's early poetry and his later verse and prose, we often have the sense that we are observing a mind in the act of thinking, a heart in the midst of feeling.

Donne's influence extends to other religious poets and other writers of amorous verse, especially those later characterized as "metaphysical poets" partly because of their philosophical preoccupations and partly because of their extensive use of complex images or "conceits." Donne, in fact, was roundly criticized by John Dryden for a "tendency to perplex the minds of the fair sex with nice speculations of philosophy, when he should engage their hearts, and entertain them with the softnesses of love." But Donne was also soundly praised by poets such as Thomas Carew, whose "Elegy" celebrates Donne as a "king that ruled as he thought fit / The universal monarchy of wit."

Besides Carew, other poets of the "School of Donne" include George Herbert, whose poetic voice and vision are less dramatic and theatrical than Donne's; Richard Crashaw, whose images are more elaborate and excessive; and Andrew Marvell, whose poetry combines, as T. S. Eliot has remarked, "a tough reasonableness beneath a slight lyric grace." These and other metaphysical poets were later censured by the eighteenth-century man of letters Samuel Johnson for their "heterogeneous ideas . . . yoked by violence together." But even Johnson acknowledged that to read their poems well it was necessary to read carefully and to think.

The twentieth century has seen a consistent strengthening of Donne's poetic reputation. From Grierson to Eliot to Helen Gardner, who prepared careful editions of the poems in the 1950s, '60s, and '70s, Donne has maintained a secure position as one of the major poets of his time and one who continues to speak eloquently to our own.

Song (Go, and catch a falling star)

Go, and catch a falling star,
    Get with child a mandrake root,
Tell me, where all past years are,
    Or who cleft the devil's foot,
Teach me to hear mermaids singing   5
Or to keep off envy's stinging,
        And find
        What wind
Serves to advance an honest mind.

If thou beest born to strange sights,   10
    Things invisible to see,
Ride ten thousand days and nights,
    Till age snow white hairs on thee;
Thou, when thou return'st, wilt tell me
All strange wonders that befell thee,   15
        And swear,
        No where
Lives a woman true, and fair.

If thou find'st one, let me know:
    Such a pilgrimage were sweet.   20
Yet do not, I would not go,
    Though at next door we might meet:
Though she were true when you met her,
And last till you write your letter,
        Yet she   25
        Will be
False, ere I come, to two, or three.

                                             [1633]

The Indifferent

I can love both fair and brown;
Her whom abundance melts, and her whom want betrays;
Her who loves loneness best, and her who masks and plays;

SONG   ²**mandrake root** Resembling a human body, the forked root of the mandrake was used as a medicine to induce conception.

Her whom the country formed, and whom the town;
Her who believes, and her who tries;   5
Her who still weeps with spongy eyes,
And her who is dry cork and never cries.
I can love her, and her, and you, and you;
I can love any, so she be not true.

Will no other vice content you?   10
Will it not serve your turn to do as did your mothers?
Or have you all old vices spent, and now would find out others?
Or doth a fear that men are true torment you?
Oh, we are not; be not you so;
Let me, and do you, twenty know.   15
Rob me, but bind me not, and let me go.
Must I, who came to travail thorough you,
Grow your fixed subject because you are true?

Venus heard me sigh this song,
And by love's sweetest part, variety, she swore   20
She heard not this till now, and that is should be so no more.
She went, examined, and returned ere long,
And said, "Alas! some two or three
Poor heretics in love there be,
Which think to 'stablish dangerous constancy.
But I have told them 'Since you will be true,
You shall be true to them who are false to you.' "

The Sun Rising

Busy old fool, unruly sun,
Why dost thou thus,
Through windows, and through curtains call on us?
Must to thy motions lovers' seasons run?
Saucy pedantic wretch, go chide   5
Late schoolboys, and sour prentices,
Go tell court-huntsmen that the King will ride,
Call country ants to harvest offices;
Love, all alike, no season knows, nor clime,
Nor hours, days, months, which are the rags of time.   10

Thy beams, so reverend and strong
Why shouldst thou think?
I could eclipse and cloud them with a wink,

But that I would not lose her sight so long;
    If her eyes have not blinded thine,   *15*
     Look, and tomorrow late, tell me
   Whether both the Indias of spice and mine
   Be where thou left'st them, or lie here with me.
Ask for those kings whom thou saw'st yesterday,   *20*
And thou shalt hear, All here in one bed lay.

     She's all states, and all princes, I,
      Nothing else is.
Princes do but play us; compared to this,
All's honor's mimic, all wealth alchemy.
     Thou, sun, art half as happy as we,   *25*
      In that the world's contracted thus;
   Thine age asks ease, and since thy duties be
    To warm the world, that's done in warming us.
Shine here to us, and thou art everywhere;
This bed thy center is, these walls, thy sphere.   *30*
               [1633]

The Anniversary

  All kings, and all their favorites,
   All glory' of honors, beauties, wits,
The sun itself, which makes times, as they pass,
Is elder by a year, now, than it was
When thou and I first one another saw:
All other things to their destruction draw,
   Only our love hath no decay;
This, no tomorrow hath, nor yesterday;
Running it never runs from us away,
But truly keeps his first, last, everlasting day.

  Two graves must hide thine and my corse;°   *corpse*
If one might, death were no divorce:
Alas, as well as other princes, we
(Who prince enough in one another be)
Must leave at last in death, these eyes, and ears,
Oft fed with true oaths, and with sweet salt tears;
   But souls where nothing dwells but love
(All other thoughts being inmates) then shall prove
This, or a love increaséd there above,
When bodies to their graves, souls from their graves remove.

And then we shall be throughly° blest,   *thoroughly*
   But we no more than all the rest;
Here upon earth, we're kings, and none but we
Can be such kings, nor of such subjects be;
Who is so safe as we, where none can do
Treason to us, except one of us two?
   True and false fears let us refrain,
Let us love nobly, and live, and add again
Years and years unto years, till we attain
To write threescore, this is the second of our reign.

                                              [1633]

A Valediction: Forbidding Mourning

As virtuous men pass mildly away,
   And whisper to their souls to go,
Whilst some of their sad friends do say,
   "The breath goes now," and some say, "No,"

So let us melt, and make no noise,   5
   No tear-floods, nor sigh-tempests move;
'Twere profanation of our joys
   To tell the laity our love.

Moving of the earth° brings harms and fears,   *earthquakes*
   Men reckon what it did and meant;   10
But trepidation of the spheres,
   Though greater far, is innocent.

Dull sublunary° lovers' love   *earthly*
   (Whose soul is sense) cannot admit
Absence, because it doth remove   15
   Those things which elemented° it.   *composed*

But we, by a love so much refined
   That our selves know not what it is,
Inter-assured of the mind,
   Care less, eyes, lips, and hands to miss.   20

A VALEDICTION   ¹¹trepidation of the spheres   movement in the outermost of the heavenly spheres. In Ptolemy's astronomy these outer spheres caused others to vary from their orbits.

Our two souls therefore, which are one,
    Though I must go, endure not yet
A breach, but an expansion,
    Like gold to airy thinness beat.

If they be two, they are two so   25
    As stiff twin compasses are two:
Thy soul, the fixed foot, makes no show
    To move, but doth, if the other do;

And though it in the center sit,
    Yet when the other far doth roam,   30
It leans, and hearkens after it,
    And grows erect, as that comes home.

Such wilt thou be to me, who must,
    Like the other foot, obliquely run;
Thy firmness makes my circle just,   35
    And makes me end where I begun.

                                            [1633]

A Nocturnal upon St. Lucy's Day, Being the Shortest Day

'Tis the year's midnight, and it is the day's,
Lucy's, who scarce seven hours herself unmasks;
    The sun is spent, and now his flasks
    Send forth light squibs, no constant rays;
        The world's whole sap is sunk;   5
The general balm th' hydroptic° earth hath drunk,   *thirsty*
Whither, as to the bed's-feet, life is shrunk,
Dead and interred; yet all these seem to laugh,
Compared with me, who am their epitaph.

Study me then, you who shall lovers be   10
At the next world, that is, at the next spring:
    For I am every dead thing,
    In whom love wrought new alchemy.
        For his art did express
A quintessence even from nothingness,   15

A NOCTURNAL   In Donne's time St. Lucy's Day, December 13, fell close to the winter solstice, the shortest day of the year, with a late sunrise and early sunset.

From dull privations, and lean emptiness;
He ruined me, and I am re-begot
Of absence, darkness, death; things which are not.

All others, from all things, draw all that's good,
Life, soul, form, spirit, whence they being have;   *20*
   I, by love's limbeck, am the grave
    Of all that's nothing. Oft a flood
     Have we two wept, and so
Drowned the whole world, us two; oft did we grow
To be two chaoses, when we did show   *25*
Care to aught else; and often absences
Withdrew our souls, and made us carcasses.

But I am by her death (which word wrongs her)
Of the first nothing the elixir grown;
   Were I a man, that I were one   *30*
    I needs must know; I should prefer,
     If I were any beast,
Some ends, some means; yea plants, yea stones detest,
And love; all, all some properties invest;
If I an ordinary nothing were,   *35*
As shadow, 'a light and body must be here.

But I am none; nor will my Sun renew.
You lovers, for whose sake the lesser sun
   At this time to the Goat is run
    To fetch new lust, and give it you,   *40*
     Enjoy your summer all;
Since she enjoys her long night's festival,
Let me prepare towards her, and let me call
This hour her Vigil, and her Eve, since this
Both the year's, and the day's deep midnight is.   *45*

[1633]

The Canonization

For God's sake hold your tongue, and let me love,
   Or chide my palsy, or my gout,
My five gray hairs, or ruined fortune, flout,
   With wealth your state, your mind with arts improve,

A NOCTURNAL   [39]**Goat** proverbially lustful animal.

Take you a course,° get you a place,°   *direction/appointment* 5
    Observe His Honor, or His Grace,
Or the King's real, or his stampéd face°   *on a coin*
    Contémplate; what you will, approve,°   *try*
        So you will let me love.

Alas, alas, who's injured by my love?   10
    What merchant's ships have my sighs drowned?
Who says my tears have overflowed his ground?
    When did my colds a forward spring remove?
        When did the heats which my veins fill
        Add one more to the plaguy bill°?   *list of victims* 15
Soldiers find wars, and lawyers find out still
        Litigious men, which quarrels move,
        Though she and I do love.

Call us what you will, we're made such by love;
    Call her one, me another fly,   20
We're tapers too, and at our own cost die,
    And we in us find th' eagle and the dove
        The phoenix riddle hath more wit°   *sense*
        By us: we two being one, are it.
So, to one neutral thing both sexes fit.   25
We die and rise the same, and prove
Mysterious by this love.

We can die by it, if not live by love,
    And if unfit for tombs and hearse
Our legend be, it will be fit for verse;   30
    And if no piece of chronicle we prove,
        We'll build in sonnets pretty rooms;
        As well a well-wrought urn becomes
The greatest ashes, as half-acre tombs;
        And by these hymns, all shall approve   35
        Us canonized for love:

And thus invoke us: You whom reverend love
    Made one another's hermitage;
You, to whom love was peace, that now is rage;
    Who did the whole world's soul contract, and drove   40
        Into the glasses of your eyes
        (So made such mirrors, and such spies,

THE CANONIZATION   ²¹**at our own cost die**   Death was a metaphor for sexual intercourse; each act of
sexual congress supposedly shortened one's life by a day   ²³**the phoenix riddle**   the phoenix is a mythological
bird, the only one of its kind. It is consumed in fire and then resurrected from the ashes to begin life anew.

That they did all to you epitomize)
   Countries, towns, courts: Beg from above
   A pattern of your love!

[1633]

Lovers' Infiniteness

If yet I have not all thy love,
Dear, I shall never have it all;
I cannot breathe one other sigh to move,
Nor can entreat one other tear to fall;
All my treasure, which should purchase thee,   5
Sighs, tears, and oaths, and letters, I have spent.
Yet no more can be due to me
Than at the bargain made was meant;
If then thy gift of love were partial,
That some to me, some should to others fall,   10
   Dear, I shall never have thee all.

Or if then thou gavest me all,
All was but all which thou hadst then;
But if in thy heart since there be or shall
New love created be by other men,   15
Which have their stocks entire, and can in tears,
In sighs, in oaths, and letters outbid me,
This new love may beget new fears,
For this love was not vowed by thee.
And yet it was, thy gift being general;   20
The ground, thy heart, is mine; whatever shall
   Grow there, dear, I should have it all.

Yet I would not have all yet.
He that hath all can have no more;
And since my love doth every day admit   25
New growth, thou shouldst have new rewards in store.
Thou canst not every day give me thy heart;
If thou canst give it, then thou never gavest it.
Love's riddles are, that though thy heart depart,
It stays at home, and thou with losing savest it.   30
But we will have a way more liberal
Than changing hearts, to join them; so we shall
   Be one, and one another's all.

[1633]

The Flea

Mark but this flea, and mark in this
How little that which thou deny'st me is;
It sucked me first, and now sucks thee,
And in this flea our two bloods mingled be;
Thou know'st that this cannot be said   5
A sin, nor shame, nor loss of maidenhead;
    Yet this enjoys before it woo,
    And pampered swells with one blood made of two,
    And this, alas, is more than we would do.

Oh stay, three lives in one flea spare,   10
Where we almost, yea, more than married are.
This flea is you and I, and this
Our marriage bed and marriage temple is;
Though parents grudge, and you, we are met
And cloistered in these living walls of jet.   15
    Though use° make you apt to kill me,   *custom*
    Let not to that, self-murder added be,
    And sacrilege, three sins in killing three.

Cruel and sudden, hast thou since
Purpled thy nail in blood of innocence?   20
Wherein could this flea guilty be,
Except in that drop which it sucked from thee?
Yet thou triumph'st and say'st that thou
Find'st not thyself, nor me the weaker now.
    'Tis true. Then learn how false fears be: 25
    Just so much honor, when thou yield'st to me,
    Will waste, as this flea's death took life from thee.

        [1633]

The Ecstasy

    Where, like a pillow on a bed.
      A pregnant bank swelled up to rest
    The violet's reclining head,
      Sat we two, one another's best.

THE ECSTASY   For Donne's contemporaries the word implies not wild delight as it commonly does nowadays, but a standing apart, a movement of the soul outside of the body.

Our hands were firmly cemented   *5*
    With a fast balm, which thence did spring.
Our eye-beams twisted, and did thread
    Our eyes upon one double string,
So to intergraft our hands, as yet
    Was all our means to make us one;   *10*
And pictures in our eyes to get
    Was all our propagation.
As 'twixt two equal armies, Fate
    Suspends uncertain victory,
Our souls (which to advance their state,   *15*
    Were gone out) hung 'twixt her and me.
And whilst our souls negotiate there,
    We like sepulchral statues lay;
All day the same our postures were,
    And we said nothing all the day.   *20*
If any, so by love refined
    That he soul's language understood,
And by good love were grown all mind,
    Within convenient distance stood,
He (though he know not which soul spake,   *25*
    Because both meant, both spake the same)
Might thence a new concoction take,
    And part far purer than he came.
This ecstasy doth unperplex,
    We said, and tell us what we love;   *30*
We see by this it was not sex;
    We see we saw not what did move;
But as all several souls contain
    Mixture of things, they know not what,
Love these mixed souls doth mix again,   *35*
    And makes both one, each this and that.
A single violet transplant,
    The strength, the color, and the size
(All which before was poor, and scant)
    Redoubles still, and multiplies.   *40*
When love, with one another so
    Interinanimates two souls,
That abler soul, which thence doth flow,
    Defects of loneliness controls.
We then, who are this new soul, know,   *45*
    Of what we are composed, and made,
For, th' atomies° of which we grow,   *atoms*
    Are souls, whom no change can invade.

---

²⁷**concoction**   a mixture of elements that has been purified in fire.

But O alas, so long, so far
    Our bodies why do we forbear?   *50*
They are ours, though they are not we; we are
    The intelligences, they the sphere.
We owe them thanks because they thus,
    Did us to us at first convey,
Yielded their forces, sense, to us,   *55*
    Nor are dross to us, but allay.°   *alloy*
On man heaven's influence works not so
    But that it first imprints the air,
So soul into the soul may flow,
    Though it to body first repair.   *60*
As our blood labors to beget
    Spirits as like souls as it can,
Because such fingers need to knit
    That subtle knot which makes us man:
So must pure lovers' souls descend   *65*
    T' affections, and to faculties
Which sense may reach and apprehend;
    Else a great Prince in prison lies.
To our bodies turn we then, that so
    Weak men on love revealed may look;   *70*
Love's mysteries in souls do grow,
    But yet the body is his book.
And if some lover, such as we,
    Have heard this dialogue of one,
Let him still mark us; he shall see   *75*
    Small change when we are to bodies gone.

                                  [1633]

Elegy XIX: To His Mistress Going to Bed

Come, madam, come, all rest my powers defy,
Until I labor, I in labor lie.
The foe oft-times having the foe in sight,
Is tired with standing though he never fight.
Off with that girdle, like heaven's zone glistering,   *5*
But a far fairer world encompassing.
Unpin that spangled breastplate which you wear,

THE ECSTASY   ⁵²**intelligences . . . sphere** According to medieval theologians, the heavenly bodies were controlled and moved by angels ("intelligences").   ⁵⁸**the air** the medium through which influences of the heavenly bodies ("the spheres") were believed to be transmitted.   ⁶²**blood . . . can** It was once thought that blood gave rise to animal spirits, wich mediated between body and soul.

That th' eyes of busy fools may be stopped there.
Unlace yourself, for that harmonious chime
Tells me from you that now it is bed time.   10
Off with that happy busk,° which I envy,   *corset*
That still can be, and still can stand so nigh.
Your gown, going off, such beauteous state reveals,
As when from flowry meads th' hill's shadow steals.
Off with that wiry coronet and show   15
The hairy diadem which on you doth grow:
Now off with those shoes, and then safely tread
In this love's hallowed temple, this soft bed.
In such white robes, heaven's angels used to be
Received by men; thou, Angel, bring'st with thee   20
A heaven like Mahomet's Paradise; and though
Ill spirits walk in white, we easily know
By this these angels from an evil sprite:
Those set our hairs, but these our flesh upright.
    License my roving hands, and let them go   25
Before, behind, between, above, below.
O my America! my new-found-land,
My kingdom, safeliest when with one man manned,
My mine of precious stones, my empery,°   *empire*
How blest am I in this discovering thee!   30
To enter in these bonds is to be free;
Then where my hand is set, my seal shall be.
    Full nakedness! All joys are due to thee,
As souls unbodied, bodies unclothed must be
To taste whole joys. Gems which you women use   35
Are like Atlanta's balls, cast in men's views,
That when a fool's eye lighteth on a gem,
His earthly soul may covet theirs, not them.
Like pictures, or like books' gay coverings made
For lay-men, are all women thus arrayed;   40
Themselves are mystic books, which only we
(Whom their imputed grace will dignify)
Must see revealed. Then, since that I may know,
As liberally as to a midwife, show
Thyself: cast all, yea, this white linen hence,   45
There is no penance due to innocence.
    To teach thee, I am naked first; why than,°   *then*
What needst thou have more covering than a man?

                                                    [1633]

ELEGY XIX   [36]**Atlanta's balls**   While she was running a race, Atlanta stopped to pick up some beautiful
golden apples strewn in her path by Hippomenes, who would be allowed to marry her if he could beat her in a
foot race.

Batter my heart, three-personed God

Batter my heart, three-personed God; for You
As yet but knock, breathe, shine, and seek to mend;
That I may rise and stand, o'erthrow me, and bend
Your force to break, blow, burn, and make me new.
I, like an usurped town, to another due,   5
Labor to admit You, but O, to no end;
Reason, Your viceroy in me, me should defend,
But is captíved, and proves weak or untrue.
Yet dearly I love You, and would be lovéd fain,°   *gladly*
But am betrothed unto Your enemy.   10
Divorce me, untie or break that knot again;
Take me to You, imprison me, for I,
Except You enthrall me, never shall be free,
Nor ever chaste, except You ravish me.

[1633]

Death, be not proud

Death, be not proud, though some have called thee
Mighty and dreadful, for thou are not so;
For those whom thou think'st thou dost overthrow
Die not, poor Death, nor yet canst thou kill me.
From rest and sleep, which but thy pictures be,   5
Much pleasure; then from thee much more must flow,
And soonest our best men with thee do go,
Rest of their bones, and soul's delivery.
Thou art slave to fate, chance, kings, and desperate men,
And dost with poison, war, and sickness dwell,   10
And poppy or charms can make us sleep as well
And better than thy stroke; why swell'st thou then?
One short sleep past, we wake eternally
And death shall be no more; Death, thou shalt die.

[1633]

Hymn to God the Father

1

Wilt thou forgive that sin where I begun,
    Which was my sin though it were done before?

Wilt thou forgive that sin through which I run,
    And do run still, though still I do deplore?
        When thou hast done, thou hast not done,   *5*
        For I have more.

2

Wilt thou forgive that sin by which I've won
    Others to sin, and made my sin their door?
Wilt thou forgive that sin which I did shun
    A year or two, but wallowed in a score?   *10*
        When thou hast done, thou hast not done,
        For I have more.

3

I have a sin of fear, that when I've spun
    My last thread, I shall perish on the shore;
But swear by thyself that at my death thy son   *15*
    Shall shine as he shines now, and heretofore;
        And having done that, Thou hast done;
        I fear no more.

        [1633]

Hymn to God My God, in My Sickness

Since I am coming to that holy room
    Where, with Thy choir of saints for evermore,
I shall be made Thy music; as I come
    I tune the instrument here at the door,
    And what I must do then, think here before.   *5*

Whilst my physicians by their love are grown
    Cosmographers, and I their map, who lie
Flat on this bed, that by them may be shown
    That this is my southwest discovery
    Per fretum febris, by these straits to die.   *10*

I joy, that in these straits, I see my West
    For, though their currents yield return to none,
What shall my West hurt me? As West and East
    In all flat maps (and I am one) are one,
    So death doth touch the resurrection.   *15*

HYMN TO GOD MY GOD   *9***southwest discovery**   the Strait of Magellan, discovered in 1520.
*10***Per fretum febris**   through the strait of fever.

Is the Pacific Sea my home? Or are
   The Eastern riches? Is Jerusalem?
Anyan, and Magellan, and Gibraltar,
   All straits, and none but straits, are ways to them,
   Whether where Japhet dwelt, or Cham, or Shem.   *20*

We think that Paradise and Calvary,
   Christ's cross, and Adam's tree, stood in one place;
Look, Lord, and find both Adams met in me;
   As the first Adam's sweat surrounds my face,
   May the last Adam's blood my soul embrace.   *25*

So, in his purple wrapped, receive me, Lord;
   By these his thorns give me his other crown;
And, as to others' souls I preached Thy word,
   Be this my text, my sermon to mine own;
   Therefore that he may raise the Lord throws down.   *30*

           [1635]

BEN JONSON

[1573–1637]

Still to be neat, still to be dressed

Still to be neat, still to be dressed,
As you were going to a feast;
Still to be powdered, still perfumed:
Lady, it is to be presumed,
Though art's hid causes are not found,   *5*
All is not sweet, all is not sound.

Give me a look, give me a face,
That makes simplicity a grace;
Robes loosely flowing, hair as free:
Such sweet neglect more taketh me   *10*
Than all the adulteries of art;
They strike mine eyes, but not my heart.

           [1609]

HYMN TO GOD MY GOD   **18Anyan**   the Bering strait.   **20Japhet . . . Shem**   The three sons of Noah,
whose descendants repopulated the world after the great flood.

Come, my Celia

Come, my Celia, let us prove,°   *experience*
While we can, the sports of love;
Time will not be ours forever;
He at length our good will sever.
Spend not then his gifts in vain.   5
Suns that set may rise again;
But if once we lose this light,
'Tis with us perpetual night.
Why should we defer our joys?
Fame and rumor are but toys.   10
Cannot we delude the eyes
Of a few poor household spies,
Or his easier ears beguile,
So removéd by our wile?
'Tis no sin love's fruit to steal;   15
But the sweet thefts to reveal,
To be taken, to be seen,
These have crimes accounted been.

[1606]

On My First Daughter

Here lies, to each her parents' ruth,°   *sadness*
Mary, the daughter of their youth;
Yet all heaven's gifts being heaven's due,
It makes the father less to rue.
At six months' end she parted hence
With safety of her innocence;
Whose soul heaven's queen, whose name she bears,
In comfort of her mother's tears,
Hath placed amongst her virgin-train:
Where, while that severed doth remain,
This grave partakes the fleshly birth;
Which cover lightly, gentle earth!

[1616]

On My First Son

Farewell, thou child of my right hand, and joy;
My sin was too much hope of thee, loved boy:
Seven years thou wert lent to me, and I thee pay,
Exacted by thy fate, on the just day.
O could I lose all father now! for why   5
Will man lament the state he should envý,
To have so soon 'scaped world's and flesh's rage,
And, if no other misery, yet age?
Rest in soft peace, and asked, say, "Here doth lie
Ben Jonson his best piece of poetry."   10
For whose sake henceforth all his vows be such
As what he loves may never like too much.

                                                                    [1616]

To Penshurst

Thou art not, Penshurst, built to envious show,
Of touch° or marble; nor canst boast a row   *touchstone, basanite*
Of polished pillars, or a roof of gold;
Thou hast no lantern, whereof tales are told,
Or stair, or courts; but stand'st an ancient pile,   5
And, these grudged at, art reverenced the while.
Thou joy'st in better marks, of soil, of air,
Of wood, of water; therein thou art fair.
Thou hast thy walks for health, as well as sport;
Thy mount, to which the dryads° do resort,   *wood nymphs*   10
Where Pan and Bacchus their high feasts have made,
Beneath the broad beech and the chestnut shade;
That taller tree, which of a nut was set
At his great birth where all the Muses met.
There in the writhéd bark are cut the names   15
Of many a sylvan,° taken with his flames;   *forest dweller*
And thence the ruddy satyrs oft provoke

ON MY FIRST SON   ¹**child of my right hand**   the literal meaning, in Hebrew, of Benjamin, the boy's name.
Jonson's son died on his seventh birthday.
TO PENSHURST   Penshurst was the country estate of the Sidney family in Kent, England.   ¹⁴**At his great
birth**   the birth of Sir Philip Sidney on November 30, 1554.

The lighter fauns to reach thy Lady's Oak.
Thy copse too, named of Gamage, thou hast there,
That never fails to serve thee seasoned deer   *20*
When thou wouldst feast or exercise thy friends.
The lower land, that to the river bends,
Thy sheep, thy bullocks, kine, and calves do feed;
The middle grounds thy mares and horses breed.
Each bank doth yield thee conies;° and the tops,   *rabbits* 25
Fertile of wood, Ashore and Sidney's copse,
To crown thy open table, doth provide
The purpled pheasant with the speckled side;
The painted partridge lies in every field,
And for thy mess is willing to be killed.   *30*
And if the high-swollen Medway fail thy dish,
Thou hast thy ponds, that pay thee tribute fish,
Fat aged carps that run into thy net,
And pikes, now weary their own kind to eat,
As loath the second draught or cast to stay,°   *await* 35
Officiously° at first themselves betray;   *dutifully*
Bright eels that emulate them, and leap on land
Before the fisher, or into his hand.
Then hath thy orchard fruit, thy garden flowers,
Fresh as the air, and new as are the hours.   *40*
The early cherry, with the later plum,
Fig, grape, and quince, each in his time doth come;
The blushing apricot and woolly peach
Hang on thy walls, that every child may reach.
And though thy walls be of the country stone,   *45*
They're reared with no man's ruin, no man's groan;
There's none that dwell about them wish them down;
But all come in, the farmer and the clown,°   *countryman*
And no one empty-handed, to salute
Thy lord and lady, though they have no suit.   *50*
Some bring a capon, some a rural cake,
Some nuts, some apples; some that think they make
The better cheeses bring them, or else send
By their ripe daughters, whom they would commend
This way to husbands, and whose baskets bear   *55*
An emblem of themselves in plum or pear.
But what can this (more than express their love)
Add to thy free provisions, far above
The need of such? whose liberal board doth flow
With all that hospitality doth know;   *60*

---

[19]**named of Gamage**   reference to the wife of Sir Philip Sidney's younger brother.   [31]**Medway**   a river.

Where comes no guest but is allowed to eat,
Without his fear, and of thy lord's own meat;
Where the same beer and bread, and selfsame wine,
That is his lordship's shall be also mine,
And I not fain° to sit (as some this day   *obliged*   65
At great men's tables), and yet dine away.
Here no man tells° my cups; nor, standing by,   *counts*
A waiter doth my gluttony envý,
But gives me what I call, and lets me eat;
He knows below he shall find plenty of meat.   70
Thy tables hoard not up for the next day;
Nor, when I take my lodging, need I pray
For fire, or lights, or livery;° all is there,   *provisions*
As if thou then wert mine, or I reigned here:
There's nothing I can wish, for which I stay.   75
That found King James when, hunting late this way
With his brave son, the prince, they saw thy fires
Shine bright on every hearth, as the desires
Of thy Penates had been set on flame
To entertain them; or the country came   80
With all their zeal to warm their welcome here.
What (great I will not say, but) sudden cheer
Didst thou then make 'em! and what praise was heaped
On thy good lady then, who therein reaped
The just reward of her high housewifery;   85
To have her linen, plate, and all things nigh,
When she was far; and not a room but dressed
As if it had expected such a guest!
These, Penshurst, are thy praise, and yet not all.
Thy lady's noble, fruitful, chaste withal.   90
His children thy great lord may call his own,
A fortune in this age but rarely known.
They are, and have been, taught religion; thence
Their gentler spirits have sucked innocence.
Each morn and even they are taught to pray,   95
With the whole household, and may, every day,
Read in their virtuous parents' noble parts
The mysteries of manners, arms, and arts.
Now, Penshurst, they that will proportion° thee   *compare*
With other edifices, when they see   100
Those proud, ambitious heaps, and nothing else,
May say their lords have built, but thy lord dwells.

[1616]

⁷⁹**Penates**   household gods of the Romans.

ROBERT HERRICK

[1591–1674]

Delight in Disorder

A sweet disorder in the dress
Kindles in clothes a wantonness.
A lawn° about the shoulders thrown   *fine linen*
Into a fine distractiön;
An erring lace, which here and there   5
Enthralls the crimson stomacher;
A cuff neglectful, and thereby
Ribbons to flow confusedly;
A winning wave, deserving note,
In the tempestuous petticoat;   10
A careless shoestring, in whose tie
I see a wild civility;
Do more bewitch me than when art
Is too precise in every part.

[1648]

Upon Julia's Clothes

Whenas in silks my Julia goes,
Then, then, methinks, how sweetly flows
That liquefaction of her clothes.

Next, when I cast mine eyes, and see
That brave vibration, each way free,   5
O, how that glittering taketh me!

[1648]

To the Virgins, to Make Much of Time

Gather ye rosebuds while ye may,
    Old time is still a-flying;
And this same flower that smiles today
    Tomorrow will be dying.

The glorious lamp of heaven, the sun,   5
    The higher he's a-getting,
The sooner will his race be run,
    And nearer he's to setting.

That age is best which is the first,
    When youth and blood are warmer;   10
But being spent, the worse, and worst
    Times still succeed the former.

Then be not coy, but use your time,
    And, while ye may, go marry;
For, having lost but once your prime,   15
    You may forever tarry.

                                 [1648]

HENRY KING

[1592–1669]

The Exequy

Accept, thou shrine of my dead saint,
Instead of dirges, this complaint;
And for sweet flowers to crown thy hearse,
Receive a strew of weeping verse
From thy grieved friend, whom thou might'st see   5
Quite melted into tears for thee.

Dear loss! since thy untimely fate
My task hath been to meditate
On thee, on thee; thou art the book,
The library whereon I look,   10
Though almost blind. For thee, loved clay,
I languish out, not live, the day,
Using no other exercise
But what I practice with mine eyes;
By which wet glasses I find out   15
How lazily time creeps about
To one that mourns: this, only this,

THE EXEQUY   a funeral rite.

My exercise and business is.
So I compute the weary hours
With sighs dissolvéd into showers.   *20*

Nor wonder if my time go thus
Backward and most preposterous;
Thou hast benighted me, thy set
This eve of blackness did beget,
Who wast my day, though overcast   *25*
Before thou hadst thy noontide passed;
And I remember must in tears,
Thou scarce hadst seen so many years
As day tells hours. By thy clear sun
My love and fortune first did run;   *30*
But thou wilt never more appear
Folded within my hemisphere,
Since both thy light and motiön
Like a fled star is fallen and gone;
And 'twixt me and my soul's dear wish   *35*
An earth now interposéd is,
Which such a strange eclipse doth make
As ne'er was read in almanac.

I could allow thee for a time
To darken me and my sad clime;   *40*
Were it a month, a year, or ten,
I would thy exile live till then,
And all that space my mirth adjourn,
So thou wouldst promise to return;
And putting off thy ashy shroud,   *45*
At length disperse this sorrow's cloud.

But woe is me! the longest date
Too narrow is to calculate
These empty hopes; never shall I
Be so much blest as to descry   *50*
A glimpse of thee, till that day come
Which shall the earth to cinders doom,
And a fierce fever must calcine
The body of this world—like thine,
My little world! That fit of fire   *55*
Once off, our bodies shall aspire
To our souls' bliss; then we shall rise

[53]**calcine**   burn to dust.

And view ourselves with clearer eyes
In that calm region where no night
Can hide us from each other's sight. 60

Meantime, thou hast her, earth: much good
May my harm do thee. Since it stood
With heaven's will I might not call
Her longer mine, I give thee all
My short-lived right and interest 65
In her whom living I loved best;
With a most free and bounteous grief
I give thee what I could not keep.
Be kind to her, and prithee look
Thou write into thy doomsday book 70
Each parcel of this rarity
Which in thy casket shrined doth lie.
See that thou make thy reckoning straight,
And yield her back again by weight;
For thou must audit on thy trust 75
Each grain and atom of this dust,
As thou wilt answer Him that lent,
Not gave thee, my dear monument.

So close the ground, and 'bout her shade
Black curtains draw; my bride is laid. 80

Sleep on, my love, in thy cold bed,
Never to be disquieted!
My last good-night! Thou wilt not wake
Till I thy fate shall overtake;
Till age, or grief, or sickness must 85
Marry my body to that dust
It so much loves; and fill the room
My heart keeps empty in thy tomb.
Stay for me there; I will not fail
To meet thee in that hollow vale. 90
And think not much of my delay;
I am already on the way,
And follow thee with all the speed
Desire can make, or sorrows breed.
Each minute is a short degree, 95
And every hour a step towards thee.
At night when I betake to rest,
Next morn I rise nearer my west
Of life, almost by eight hours' sail,

Than when sleep breathed his drowsy gale.   *100*
Thus from the sun my bottom° steers,   *vessel*
And my day's compass downward bears;
Nor labor I to stem the tide
Through which to thee I swiftly glide.

'Tis true, with shame and grief I yield,   *105*
Thou like the van° first took'st the field,   *vanguard*
And gotten hast the victory
In thus adventuring to die
Before me, whose more years might crave
A just precédence in the grave.   *110*
But hark! my pulse like a soft drum
Beats my approach, tells thee I come;
And slow howe'er my marches be,
I shall at last sit down by thee.

The thought of this bids me go on,   *115*
And wait my dissolutïon
With hope and comfort. Dear (forgive
The crime), I am content to live
Divided, with but half a heart,
Till we shall meet and never part.   *120*

                                                                          [1657]

GEORGE HERBERT

[1593–1633]

The Pulley

When God at first made man,
Having a glass of blessings standing by,
    "Let us," said he, "pour on him all we can:
Let the world's riches, which dispersed lie,
    Contract into a span."   *5*

    So Strength first made a way;
Then Beauty flowed; then Wisdom, Honor, Pleasure.
    When almost all was out, God made a stay,
Perceiving that alone of all his treasure
    Rest in the bottom lay.   *10*

"For if I should," said he,
"Bestow this jewel also on my creature,
    He would adore my gifts instead of me,
And rest in Nature, not the God of Nature;
    So both should losers be. 15

    "Yet let him keep the rest,
But keep them with repining restlessness:
    Let him be rich and weary, that at least,
If goodness lead him not, yet weariness
    May toss him to my breast." 20

[1633]

The Collar

I struck the board° and cried, "No more;   *table*
    I will abroad!
What? shall I ever sigh and pine?
My lines and life are free, free as the road,
    Loose as the wind, as large as store.°   *abundance* 5
       Shall I be still in suit?
Have I no harvest but a thorn
To let me blood, and not restore
What I have lost with cordial° fruit?   *life-giving*
      Sure there was wine   10
Before my sighs did dry it; there was corn
    Before my tears did drown it.
Is the year only lost to me?
    Have I no bays to crown it,
No flowers, no garlands gay? All blasted?   15
      All wasted?
Not so, my heart; but there is fruit,
      And thou hast hands.
Recover all thy sigh-blown age
On double pleasures: leave thy cold dispute   20
Of what is fit and not. Forsake thy cage,
      Thy rope of sands,
Which petty thoughts have made, and made to thee
    Good cable, to enforce and draw,
      And be thy law,   25
While thou didst wink and wouldst not see.
      Away! take heed;
      I will abroad.

Call in thy death's-head there; tie up thy fears.
He that forbears   30
To suit and serve his need,
Deserves his load."
But as I raved and grew more fierce and wild
At every word,
Methought I heard one calling, *Child!*   35
And I replied, *My Lord.*

[1633]

Denial

When my devotions could not pierce
Thy silent ears,
Then was my heart broken, as was my verse;
My breast was full of fears
And disorder.   5

My bent thoughts, like a brittle bow,
Did fly asunder:
Each took his way; some would to pleasures go,
Some to the wars and thunder
Of alarms.   10

As good go anywhere, they say,
As to benumb
Both knees and heart, in crying night and day,
Come, come, my God, O come!
But no hearing.   15

O that thou shouldst give dust a tongue
To cry to thee,
And then not hear it crying! All day long
My heart was in my knee,
But no hearing.   20

Therefore my soul lay out of sight,
Untuned, unstrung:
My feeble spirit, unable to look right,
Like a nipped blossom, hung
Discontented.   25

O cheer and tune my heartless breast,
Defer no time;

That so thy favors granting my request,
    They and my mind may chime,
        And mend my rhyme.   30

                                      [1633]

Virtue

Sweet day, so cool, so calm, so bright,
    The bridal of the earth and sky:
The dew shall weep thy fall tonight;
        For thou must die.

Sweet rose, whose hue, angry and brave,   5
    Bids the rash gazer wipe his eye:
Thy root is ever in its grave,
        And thou must die.

Sweet spring, full of sweet days and roses,
    A box where sweets° compacted lie;   *perfumes* 10
My music shows ye have your closes,°   *musical cadences*
        And all must die.

Only a sweet and virtuous soul,
    Like seasoned timber, never gives;
But though the whole world turn to coal,   15
        Then chiefly lives.

                                        [1633]

JAMES SHIRLEY

[1596–1666]

The glories of our blood and state

The glories of our blood and state
Are shadows, not substantial things;
There is no armor against fate;
Death lays his icy hand on kings.
    Scepter and crown   5
    Must tumble down
And in the dust be equal made
With the poor crooked scythe and spade.

Some men with swords may reap the field
And plant fresh laurels where they kill,   *10*
But their strong nerves at last must yield;
They tame but one another still.
   Early or late
   They stoop to fate
And must give up their murmuring breath,   *15*
When they, pale captives, creep to death.

The garlands wither on your brow,
Then boast no more your mighty deeds;
Upon death's purple altar now
See where the victor-victim bleeds.   *20*
   Your heads must come
   To the cold tomb;
Only the actions of the just
Smell sweet and blossom in their dust.

                                       [1659]

THOMAS CAREW

[c. 1598 – c. 1640]

Song (Ask me no more where Jove bestows)

Ask me no more where Jove bestows,
When June is past, the fading rose;
For in your beauty's orient deep,
These flowers, as in their causes, sleep.

Ask me no more whither do stray   *5*
The golden atoms of the day;
For in pure love heaven did prepare
Those powders to enrich your hair.

Ask me no more whither doth haste
The nightingale when May is past;   *10*
For in your sweet dividing throat
She winters, and keeps warm her note.

Ask me no more where those stars light,
That downwards fall in dead of night;

For in your eyes they sit, and there   *15*
Fixéd become, as in their sphere.

Ask me no more if east or west
The phoenix builds her spicy nest;
For unto you at last she flies,
And in your fragrant bosom dies.   *20*

[1640]

EDMUND WALLER
[1606–1687]

Song (Go, lovely rose!)

Go, lovely rose!
Tell her that wastes her time and me
That now she knows,
When I resemble° her to thee,   *liken*
How sweet and fair she seems to be.   *5*

Tell her that's young,
And shuns to have her graces spied,
That hadst thou sprung
In deserts, where no men abide,
Thou must have uncommended died.   *10*

Small is the worth
Of beauty from the light retired;
Bid her come forth,
Suffer herself to be desired,
And not blush so to be admired.   *15*

Then die! that she
The common fate of all things rare
May read in thee;
How small a part of time they share
That are so wondrous sweet and fair!   *20*

[1645]

ASK ME NO MORE   ¹⁸**phoenix**   mythical bird that lived for five hundred years, was consumed in fire, then
rose from its own ashes.

JOHN MILTON

[1608–1674]

No poet more than John Milton exemplifies the ideal of a poetic vocation. Milton believed that one didn't become a poet simply by writing poems. Much more was necessary. A man had to prepare himself to become a poet intellectually and spiritually through disciplined study and prayer. For great art could be written only by a great man, one whose mind and soul were prepared for the enormous challenge the poetic vocation entailed.

What kind of poetry would be produced by a poet considered from such a standpoint? And what specific kinds of preparation were necessary for Milton? The poetry itself would be erudite, based on the writings of the great classical writers of ancient Greece and Rome. Homer and Virgil, Ovid and Theocritus would be its inspiration. It would also be serious in outlook and grand in manner, as befitting one who wanted to "leave something so written to aftertimes as they should not willingly let it die." In addition to the Greek and Latin writers just mentioned, Spenser in English and Ariosto in Italian would add their inspiring voices. Milton's view of the poetic vocation, of himself as poet, and of the preparation necessary to undertake such a vocation was both grand and noble, a nobility and grandeur that was to characterize both his life and his work. It would involve, moreover, nothing less than a careful reading of the entire literature of Greece and Rome in their original languages along with the complete Bible in its original languages as well.

From the early apprentice work to the later epics, *Paradise Lost* and *Paradise Regained*, Milton's poetry was grounded in the ideals of classical humanism and biblical morality. Combining these two influential Western traditions more thoroughly and more profoundly than any other writer in English, Milton presents a fuller and more decisive summation of Renaissance art and Christian humanism than that of any other poet. From the Greeks and Romans Milton derived a sense of civic responsibility. Like his forebears, Milton believed that a primary function of art was to teach, and one of its primary lessons was civic responsibility. Milton himself was steeped in the tradition that valued great statesmen, who by virtue of their own nobility, intellectuality, and vision could ensure the survival of civilized, humane, and spiritual values. And in fact, in later life Milton found his ideal statesman in the Puritan leader Oliver Cromwell, for whom Milton wrote a series of prose works.

Milton's life can be divided into three parts. First were the years of education during which Milton prepared himself for his poetic vocation, a period that culminated in the publication of "Lycidas" in 1637 and a two-year tour of the continent. Milton's second stage includes the years of his political involvement, a twenty-year span from about 1640 to 1660, during which he wrote prose rather than poetry. Placing himself in the service of the Puritan cause, Milton wrote pamphlets and tracts on various theological and ecclesiastical issues such as antiepiscopacy and divorce. The third and final stage includes the last decade and a half of his life, in which he wrote and published his greatest and most ambitious works, those for which he had been preparing all his life: *Paradise Lost* (1667), *Paradise Regained* (1671), and *Samson Agonistes* (1671).

At St. Paul's School Milton mastered Latin, Greek, and Hebrew in addition to several modern languages, the most important of which was Italian. Following his years of study at Cambridge University, where he took both a B.A. and an M.A., Milton retired to his father's private estate at Horton to read and study for six more years. He is said to have memorized nearly all of the Bible and to have read every important work in four languages: Latin, Greek, Italian, and English.

Milton was married three times—first to Mary Powell, from whom he was separated for three years. During this separation he wrote his tract *The Doctrine and Discipline of Divorce*. Reconciled, John and Mary Powell Milton had four children, one of whom became the poet's amanuensis, or scribe, in 1652, when his wife died and he became blind. Four years later Milton married Katherine Woodcock, who died in childbirth fifteen months later. Finally, in 1663 he married Katherine Minshull, who outlived him.

Milton spent the last two decades of his life in blindness brought on in part by his heroic and exhausting efforts during the 1640s in the service of the Puritan cause. With the restoration of the English monarchy to the Stuarts, Milton was imprisoned and his property confiscated. Set free a short time later, he lived out his remaining years in relative isolation working on his great epic poems. The image we have of him is that of an old blind prophet dictating his iambic pentameter lines to his daughter, who faithfully copied them down.

In these poems, especially in *Paradise Lost,* Milton attempted, in his words, "to justify the ways of God to man." This justification, of course, would reflect Milton's own blend of Puritan theology and classical humanism. It would reinterpret the crucial event of Genesis, humankind's fall into sin, its loss of primeval innocence, and its banishment from the Garden of Eden together with all the woe that resulted from Adam and Eve's disobedience of God's commandment. In his epic, Milton would emphasize the central theological belief of Christianity: the incarnation of God as man in Jesus Christ, who came to atone for the sin of our first parents and restore humankind to the place of favor it had lost through original sin. Christ's sacrifice thus balanced the scales of almighty justice, thereby gaining for human beings the chance to gain eternal life—providing, of course, that they lived their lives in accord with biblical teachings and values.

This brief sketch of the theological underpinnings of Milton's epic merely suggests that it is the poetry rather than the theology that matters most to us today. Regardless of our religious beliefs, *Paradise Lost* impresses us with its remarkable drama, especially its descriptions of the battle in heaven between the faithful and the rebellious angels; its presentation of the debate in hell among the various fallen angels about how best to proceed against their common enemy, God; and its temptation scene, in which Satan tempts Eve to eat the forbidden fruit. These and other aspects of the epic are stamped with Milton's peculiar grandeur of style and conception. They echo and interpret Genesis without simply repeating the story of the Fall of Man recounted there.

Like the poetry of John Donne, Milton's poetry is challenging to read and difficult to understand. Besides the challenge presented by Milton's enormous erudition, which is repeatedly manifested in frequent classical allusions, there is also the problem of his style. Milton's sentence structure is Latinate, with the usual delaying of predication that he had become accustomed to in his reading of Roman writers. Moreover, his sentences are often quite long. One, in fact—the first sentence of *Paradise Lost*—runs to twenty-six lines and nearly a hundred words. The style thus takes some getting used to. But the effort and time are well worthwhile since no other poem in English (and few in any language) matches *Paradise Lost* for grandeur of conception and magnificence of execution.

To emphasize Milton's epic is not to diminish his achievement in smaller forms. He is author of one of the most original elegies in the language, "Lycidas," written as a memorial to his college friend Edward King, who died at sea. And he has left some of the most memorable sonnets in English, including one on his deceased wife and one on his blindness. In these and other sonnets, Milton honored Petrarch rather than Shakespeare by employing the Italian pattern of octave and sestet rather than the English form of three quatrains and a couplet.

As powerful as Milton's sonnets are, however, it is *Paradise Lost* that contains his most majestic and glorious poetry. It is that greatest of English epics by which we measure Milton's poetic achievement and rank him among the supreme poets of our language.

Lycidas

IN THIS MONODY THE AUTHOR BEWAILS A LEARNED FRIEND, UNFORTUNATELY DROWNED IN HIS PASSAGE FROM CHESTER ON THE IRISH SEAS, 1637. AND BY OCCASION FORETELLS THE RUIN OF OUR CORRUPTED CLERGY, THEN IN THEIR HEIGHT.

> Yet once more, O ye laurels, and once more
> Ye myrtles brown, with ivy never sere
> I come to pluck your berries harsh and crude°   *unripe*
> And with forced fingers rude,
> Shatter your leaves before the mellowing year.   5
> Bitter constraint, and sad occasion dear,
> Compels me to disturb your season due;
> For Lycidas is dead, dead ere his prime,
> Young Lycidas, and hath not left his peer.
> Who would not sing for Lycidas? He knew   10
> Himself to sing, and build the lofty rhyme.
> He must not float upon his watery bier

LYCIDAS   a pastoral elegy in the tradition of Theocritus, Virgil, and Petrarch The poem was occasioned by the death of Edward King, a fellow student of Milton at Cambridge.   **monody** In Greek drama, a song sung by a single voice.   1-2**laurels . . . ivy** laurel, myrtle, and ivy are all evergreens associated with poetic inspiration.

Unwept, and welter to the parching wind,
Without the meed° of some melodious tear.   *reward*
   Begin then, sisters of the sacred well   15
That from beneath the seat of Jove doth spring,
Begin, and somewhat loudly sweep the string.
Hence with denial vain, and coy excuse;
So may some gentle Muse
With lucky words favor my destined urn,   20
And as he passes turn,
And bid fair peace be to my sable shroud.
For we were nursed upon the selfsame hill,
Fed the same flock, by fountain, shade, and rill.
   Together both, ere the high lawns° appeared   *pastures* 25
Under the opening eyelids of the morn,
We drove afield, and both together heard
What time the grayfly winds her sultry horn.
Battening° our flocks with the fresh dews of night,   *feeding*
Oft till the star that rose at evening bright   30
Toward Heaven's descent had sloped his westering wheel.
Meanwhile the rural ditties were not mute,
Tempered to th' oaten flute,
Rough satyrs danced, and fauns with cloven heel
From the glad sound would not be absent long,   35
And old Damoetas loved to hear our song.
   But O the heavy change, now thou art gone,
Now thou art gone, and never must return!
Thee, shepherd, thee the woods and desert caves,
With wild thyme and the gadding° vine o'ergrown,   *struggling* 40
And all their echoes mourn.
The willows and the hazel copses green
Shall now no more be seen,
Fanning their joyous leaves to thy soft lays.
As killing as the canker° to the rose,   *cankerworm* 45
Or taint-worm to the weanling herds that graze,
Or frost to flowers that their gay wardrobe wear,
When first the white thorn blows;°   *blossoms*
Such, Lycidas, thy loss to shepherd's ear.
   Where were ye, nymphs,° when the remorseless deep   *river deities* 50
Closed o'er the head of your loved Lycidas?
For neither were ye playing on the steep,
Where your old Bards, the famous Druids lie,
Nor on the shaggy top of Mona high,

---

¹⁵**sisters . . . well** The nine sacred muses reputedly dwelled near springs.   ³⁶**Damoetas** a characteristic name
of a generic pastoral shepherd.   ⁵³**Druids** priest-kings of Celtic Britain who worshiped the forces of nature.
⁵⁴⁻⁵⁵**Mona . . . Deva** Mona: Anglesey Island; Deva: the river Dee.

Nor yet where Deva spreads her wizard stream: 55
Ay me! I fondly dream—
Had ye been there—for what could that have done?
What could the Muse herself that Orpheus bore,
The Muse herself, for her inchanting son
Whom universal Nature did lament,   60
When by the rout that made the hideous roar,
His gory visage down the stream was sent,
Down the swift Hebrus to the Lesbian shore?

    Alas! What boots° it with incessant care   *profits*
To tend the homely slighted shepherd's trade,   65
And strictly meditate the thankless Muse?
Were it not better done as others use,
To sport with Amaryllis in the shade,
Or with the tangles of Neaera's hair?
Fame is the spur that the clear spirit doth raise   70
(That last infirmity of noble mind)
To scorn delights, and live laborious days;
But the fair guerdon° when we hope to find,   *reward*
And think to burst out into sudden blaze,
Comes the blind Fury with th' abhorréd shears,   75
And slits the thin spun life. "But not the praise,"
Phoebus replied, and touched my trembling ears;
"Fame is no plant that grows on mortal soil,
Not in the glistering foil
Set off to th' world, nor in broad rumor lies,   80
But lives and spreads aloft by those pure eyes,
And perfect witness of all-judging Jove;
As he pronounces lastly on each deed,
Of so much fame in Heaven expect thy meed."

    O fountain Arethuse, and thou honored flood,   85
Smooth-sliding Mincius, crowned with vocal reeds,
That strain I heard was of a higher mood.
But now my oat° proceeds,   *pipe, flute*
And listens to the herald of the sea°   *Triton*
That came in Neptune's plea.   90
He asked the waves, and asked the felon winds,
"What hard mishap hath doomed this gentle swain?"
And questioned every gust of rugged wings

---

⁵⁸**Muse**   the muse of epic poetry, Calliope.   ⁶¹⁻⁶³**rout . . . shore**   Orpheus was dismembered by a mob of
screaming, frenzied Thracian women.   ⁶⁶**meditate . . . Muse**   work at writing poetry.   ⁶⁸⁻⁶⁹**Amaryllis
. . . Neaera**   conventional names for pretty young women in pastoral poems.   ⁷⁵**Fury**   Atropos, one of the
three Fates. Atropos cuts the thread of life.   ⁷⁷**Phoebus**   Apollo, god of the sun and poetic inspiration.
⁸⁵**Arethuse**   Arethusa, a fountain in Sicily. In mythology, Arethusa was a nymph who, to escape the river god,
Alpheus, enamored of her, was changed into a fountain.   ⁸⁶**Mincius**   a river in Italy.

That blows from off each beakéd promontory;
They knew not of his story, 95
And sage Hippotades their answer brings,
That not a blast was from his dungeon strayed,
The air was calm, and on the level brine,
Sleek Panope with all her sisters played.
It was that fatal and perfidious bark 100
Built in th' eclipse, and rigged with curses dark,
That sunk so low that sacred head of thine.

    Next Camus, reverend sire, went footing slow,
His mantle hairy, and his bonnet sedge,
Inwrought with figures dim, and on the edge 105
Like to that sanguine flower inscribed with woe.
"Ah! who hath reft," quoth he, "my dearest pledge?"
Last came and last did go
The pilot of the Galilean lake,
Two massy keys he bore of metals twain 110
(The golden opes, the iron shuts amain).
He shook his mitered locks, and stern bespake:
"How well could I have spared for thee, young swain,
Enow° of such as for their bellies' sake, *Enough*
Creep and intrude, and climb into the fold! 115
Of other care they little reckoning make,
Than how to scramble at the shearers' feast,
And shove away the worthy bidden guest.
Blind mouths! That scarce themselves know how to hold
A sheep-hook,° or have learned aught else the least *crozier* 120
That to the faithful herdsman's art belongs!
What recks it them? What need they? They are sped;
And when they list,° their lean and flashy songs *choose*
Grate on their scrannel° pipes of wretched straw. *meager*
The hungry sheep look up, and are not fed, 125
But swoln with wind, and the rank mist they draw,
Rot inwardly, and foul contagion spread,
Besides what the grim wolf with privy paw
Daily devours apace, and nothing said.
But that two-handed engine at the door 130
Stands ready to smite once, and smite no more."

    Return, Alpheus, the dread voice is past,
That shrunk thy streams; return, Sicilian muse,

---

⁹⁶**Hippotades** Aeolus, god of winds, son of Hippotas.   ⁹⁹**Panope** a sea nymph or Nereid.   ¹⁰³**Camus** god of the river Cam(granta); represents Cambridge University.   ¹⁰⁴⁻¹⁰⁶**bonnet . . . flower** Camus's hat is associated with the hyacinth's woe. According to Ovid, Apollo accidentally killed the youth Hyacinth and from his blood created the flower, whose leaves he inscribed with *AI, AI* as words of woe.   ¹⁰⁹⁻¹¹⁰**pilot . . . keys** St. Peter, the fisherman apostle, who became the first Pope. His keys open and close the gates of heaven.

And call the vales, and bid them hither cast
Their bells and flowerets of a thousand hues.   135
Ye valleys low where the mild whispers use,°   *are heard*
Of shades and wanton winds, and gushing brooks,
On whose fresh lap the swart star sparely looks,
Throw hither all your quaint enameled eyes,
That on the green turf suck the honeyed showers,   140
And purple all the ground with vernal flowers.
Bring the rathe° primrose that forsaken dies.   *early*
The tufted crow-toe, and pale jessamine,
The white pink, and the pansy freaked° with jet,   *flecked*
The glowing violet,   145
The musk-rose, and the well attired woodbine.
With cowslips wan that hang the pensive head,
And every flower that sad embroidery wears:
Bid amaranthus all his beauty shed,
And daffadillies fill their cups with tears,   150
To strew the laureate hearse where Lycid lies.
For so to interpose a little ease,
Let our frail thoughts dally with false surmise.
Ay me! Whilst thee the shores and sounding seas
Wash far away, where'er thy bones are hurled,   155
Whether beyond the stormy Hebrides,
Where thou perhaps under the whelming tide
Visit'st the bottom of the monstrous world;
Or whether thou, to our moist vows denied,
Sleep'st by the fable of Bellerus old,   160
Where the great vision of the guarded mount
Looks toward Namancos and Bayona's hold;
Look homeward angel now, and melt with ruth:°   *grief, sorrow*
And, O ye dolphins, waft the hapless youth.
     Weep no more, woeful shepherds, weep no more,   165
For Lycidas your sorrow is not dead,
Sunk though he be beneath the watery floor,
So sinks the day-star° in the ocean bed,   *the sun*
And yet anon repairs his drooping head,
And tricks° his beams, and with new-spangled ore,   *dresses*   170
Flames in the forehead of the morning sky:
So Lycidas sunk low, but mounted high,
Through the dear might of him that walked the waves,

---

[138]**swart star**   Sirius, the dog star.   [151]**laureate hearse**   a bier decked with laurels.   [156]**Hebrides**   islands off the coast of Scotland.   [160]**Bellerus**   legendary giant.   [161-162]**mount . . . hold**   St. Michael the archangel is considered to be poised atop a mountain in Cornwall, England, looking out over the Atlantic Ocean to Bayona and Aamancos in Spain.   [164]**dolphins**   Legend has it that dolphins carried humans, poets especially, to safety when in peril of the sea.

Where other groves, and other streams along,
With nectar pure his oozy locks he laves,   *175*
And hears the unexpressive nuptial song,
In the blest kingdoms meek of joy and love.
There entertain him all the saints above,
In solemn troops and sweet societies
That sing, and singing in their glory move,   *180*
And wipe the tears forever from his eyes.
Now, Lycidas, the shepherds weep no more;
Henceforth thou art the genius° of the shore,   *guardian spirit*
In thy large recompense, and shalt be good
To all that wander in that perilous flood.   *185*
    Thus sang the uncouth swain° to th' oaks and rills,   *shepherd*
While the still morn went out with sandals gray;
He touched the tender stops of various quills,°   *pipes, flutes*
With eager thought warbling his Doric° lay: *rustic*
And now the sun had stretched out all the hills,   *190*
And now was dropped into the western bay;
At last he rose, and twitched his mantle blue:
Tomorrow to fresh woods, and pastures new.

                                               [1637]

L'Allegro

Hence loathéd Melancholy
   Of Cerberus and blackest midnight born,
In Stygian cave forlorn
   'Mongst horrid shapes, and shrieks, and sights unholy,
Find out some uncouth cell,   *5*
   Where brooding Darkness spreads his jealous wings,
And the night-raven sings;
   There under ebon shades, and low-browed rocks,
As ragged as thy locks,
   In dark Cimmerian desert ever dwell.   *10*
But come thou goddess fair and free,
In Heaven yclept° Euphrosyne,   *called*
And by men, heart-easing Mirth,

L'ALLEGRO   The title suggests a happy, contented, sociable man, who is contrasted with the character and spirit of the man portrayed in the companion poem, "Il Penseroso," which follows this one.   **²Cerberus** three-headed dog that guards the gate of the underworld.   **³Stygian cave** located near the river Styx in the underworld   **¹⁰Cimmerian** It was once believed that the Cimmerians, early Crimeans, lived in darkness at the edge of the world.   **¹²Euphrosyne** with Aglaia and Thalia, one of the three Graces, goddesses of great beauty.

Whom lovely Venus at a birth
With two sister Graces more   15
To ivy-crownéd Bacchus bore;
Or whether (as some sager sing)
The frolic wind that breathes the spring,
Zephyr with Aurora playing,
As he met her once a-Maying,   20
There on beds of violets blue,
And fresh-blown° roses washed in dew,   *blossomed*
Filled her with thee a daughter fair,
So buxom,° blithe, and debonair.   *lively*
Haste thee nymph, and bring with thee   25
Jest and youthful Jollity,
Quips and Cranks,° and wanton Wiles,   *jokes*
Nods, and Becks,° and wreathéd Smiles,   *curtseys*
Such as hang on Hebe's cheek,
And love to live in dimple sleek;   30
Sport that wrinkled Care derides,
And Laughter, holding both his sides.
Come, and trip it as ye go
On the light fantastic toe,
And in thy right hand lead with thee,   35
The mountain nymph, sweet Liberty;
And if I give thee honor due,
Mirth, admit me of thy crew
To live with her and live with thee,
In unreprovéd pleasures free;   40
To hear the lark begin his flight,
And, singing, startle the dull night,
From his watch-tower in the skies,
Till the dappled dawn doth rise;
Then to come in spite of sorrow,   45
And at my window bid good morrow,
Through the sweetbriar, or the vine,
Or the twisted eglantine.
While the cock with lively din,
Scatters the rear of darkness thin,   50
And to the stack, or the barn door,
Stoutly struts his dames before;
Oft listening how the hounds and horn
Cheerly rouse the slumbering morn,
From the side of some hoar hill,   55
Through the high wood echoing shrill.

---

[16]**Bacchus**   god of wine and revelry.   [29]**Hebe**   goddess of youth

Sometime walking not unseen
By hedgerow elms, on hillocks green,
Right against the eastern gate,
Where the great sun begins his state,°   *procession* 60
Robed in flames, and amber light,
The clouds in thousand liveries dight,°   *dressed*
While the plowman near at hand,
Whistles o'er the furrowed land,
And the milkmaid singeth blithe,   65
And the mower whets his scythe,
And every shepherd tells his tale,
Under the hawthorn in the dale.
Straight mine eye hath caught new pleasures
Whilst the landscape round it measures,   70
Russet lawns and fallows gray,
Where the nibbling flocks do stray,
Mountains on whose barren breast
The laboring clouds do often rest;
Meadows trim with daisies pied,°   *speckled* 75
Shallow brooks, and rivers wide.
Towers and battlements it sees
Bosomed high in tufted trees,
Where perhaps some beauty lies,
The cynosure of neighboring eyes.   80
Hard by, a cottage chimney smokes,
From betwixt two aged oaks,
Where Corydon and Thyrsis met,
Are at their savory dinner set
Of herbs, and other country messes,   85
Which the neat-handed Phyllis dresses;
And then in haste her bower she leaves,
With Thestylis to bind the sheaves;
Or if the earlier season lead
To the tanned haycock in the mead.   90
Sometimes with secure delight
The upland hamlets will invite,
When the merry bells ring round
And the jocund rebecks° sound   *fiddles*
To many a youth and many a maid,   95
Dancing in the checkered shade;
And young and old come forth to play
On a sunshine holiday,
Till the livelong daylight fail;

---

[83]**Corydon and Thyrsis**   traditional shepherd's names—as are Phyllis and Thestylis.

Then to the spicy nut-brown ale,   100
With stories told of many a feat,
How fairy Mab the junkets eat;
She was pinched and pulled, she said,
And he, by Friar's lantern led,
Tells how the drudging goblin sweat   105
To earn his cream-bowl, duly set,
When in one night, ere glimpse of morn,
His shadowy flail hath threshed the corn
That ten day-laborers could not end;
Then lies him down the lubber fiend,   110
And, stretched out all the chimney's length,
Basks at the fire his hairy strength;
And crop-full out of doors he flings
Ere the first cock his matin rings.
Thus done the tales, to bed they creep,   115
By whispering winds soon lulled asleep.
Towered cities please us then,
And the busy hum of men,
Where throngs of knights and barons bold,
In weeds° of peace high triumphs hold,   *garments*   120
With store of ladies, whose bright eyes
Rain influence, and judge the prize
Of wit, or arms, while both contend
To win her grace, whom all commend.
There let Hymen oft appear   125
In saffron robe, with taper clear,
And pomp, and feast, and revelry,
With masque, and antique pageantry;
Such sights as youthful poets dream
On summer eves by haunted stream.   130
Then to the well-trod stage anon,
If Jonson's learned sock be on,
Or sweetest Shakespeare, fancy's child,
Warble his native wood-notes wild.
And ever against eating cares   135
Lap me in soft Lydian airs,°   *sensual music*
Married to immortal verse
Such as the meeting soul may pierce
In notes, with many a winding bout

---

[102]**Mab**   wife of Oberon, king of the fairies.   [104]**Friar's lantern**   will-o'-the-wisp.   [105]**goblin**   Robin
Goodfellow, better known as Puck.   [125]**Hymen**   god of marriage.   [132]**Jonson's learned sock**   a slipper
worn by actors in classical comedy, in contrast to the buskin, or boot, appropriate for tragedy. Ben Jonson was a
learned poet.   [139]**winding bout**   a musical passage, a run.

Of linkéd sweetness long drawn out,   *140*
With wanton heed, and giddy cunning,
The melting voice through mazes running;
Untwisting all the chains that tie
The hidden soul of harmony;
That Orpheus' self may heave his head   *145*
From golden slumber on a bed
Of heaped Elysian flowers, and hear
Such strains as would have won the ear
Of Pluto, to have quite set free
His half-regained Eurydice.   *150*
These delights if thou canst give,
Mirth, with thee I mean to live.

[c. 1631, 1645]

Il Penseroso

Hence vain deluding Joys,
   The brood of Folly without father bred.
How little you bestead,°   *help*
   Or fill the fixéd mind with all your toys;°   *trifles*
Dwell in some idle brain,   *5*
   And fancies fond° with gaudy shapes possess,   *foolish*
As thick and numberless
   As the gay motes that people the sunbeams,
Or likest hovering dreams,
   The fickle pensioners° of Morpheus' train.   *followers* 10
But hail thou Goddess, sage and holy,
Hail, divinest Melancholy,
Whose saintly visage is too bright
To hit the sense of human sight;
And therefore to our weaker view,   *15*
O'erlaid with black, staid Wisdom's hue.
Black, but such as in esteem,
Prince Memnon's sister might beseem,
Or that starred Ethiope queen that strove

L'ALLEGRO ¹⁴⁵**Orpheus' self** Orpheus went down to the underworld to rescue his wife, Eurydice. As they were leaving, Orpheus violated a condition he had agreed to for her release. (He looked back at her as she followed him out of Hades.) He thus lost her once more.
IL PENSEROSO A sad, melancholy, pensive man; contrasts "L'Allegro." ¹⁰**Morpheus** the god of sleep.
¹⁸**Prince Memnon's sister** Henera, sister of an Ethiopian prince who fought for Troy in the Trojan War.
¹⁹**Ethiope queen** Cassiopeia, who was turned into a constellation when she boasted that her daughter Andromeda was more beautiful than the sea nymphs.

To set her beauty's praise above   *20*
The sea nymphs, and their powers offended.
Yet thou art higher far descended;
Thee bright-haired Vesta long of yore
To solitary Saturn bore;
His daughter she (in Saturn's reign   *25*
Such mixture was not held a stain).
Oft in glimmering bowers and glades
He met her, and in secret shades
Of woody Ida's inmost grove,
While yet there was no fear of Jove.   *30*
Come pensive nun, devout and pure,
Sober, steadfast, and demure,
All in a robe of darkest grain,°   *color*
Flowing with majestic train,
And sable stole of cypress lawn   *35*
Over thy decent shoulders drawn.
Come, but keep thy wonted state,
With even step and musing gait,
And looks commercing with the skies,
Thy rapt soul sitting in thine eyes: *40*
There held in holy passion still,
Forget thyself to marble, till
With a sad leaden downward cast,
Thou fix them on the earth as fast.
And join with thee calm Peace and Quiet,   *45*
Spare Fast, that oft with gods doth diet,
And hears the Muses in a ring
Aye round about Jove's altar sing.
And add to these retired Leisure,
That in trim gardens takes his pleasure;   *50*
But first, and chiefest, with thee bring,
Him that yon soars on golden wing,
Guiding the fiery-wheeléd throne,
The cherub Contemplation;
And the mute Silence hist° along   *summon 55*
'Less Philomel will deign a song,
In her sweetest, saddest plight,
Smoothing the rugged brow of night,
While Cynthia checks her dragon yoke
Gently o'er th' accustomed oak;   *60*
Sweet bird that shunn'st the noise of folly,

---

[23]**Vesta** goddess of purity.   [35]**cypress lawn** a dark, fragile, semitransparent, gauzelike cloth.   [56]**Philomel** the nightingale.   [59]**Cynthia** goddess of the moon.

Most musical, most melancholy!
Thee chantress oft the woods among,
I woo to hear thy evensong;
And missing thee, I walk unseen   65
On the dry smooth-shaven green,
To behold the wandering moon,
Riding near her highest noon,
Like one that had been led astray
Through the Heaven's wide pathless way;   70
And oft as if her head she bowed,
Stooping through a fleecy cloud.
Oft on a plat° of rising ground,   *plot*
I hear the far-off curfew sound,
Over some wide-watered shore,   75
Swinging slow with sullen roar;
Or if the air will not permit,
Some still removéd place will fit,
Where glowing embers through the room
Teach light to counterfeit a gloom   80
Far from all resort of mirth,
Save the cricket on the hearth,
Or the bellman's drowsy charm,
To bless the doors from nightly harm;
Or let my lamp at midnight hour   85
Be seen in some high lonely tower,
Where I may oft outwatch the Bear,
With thrice great Hermes, or unsphere
The spirit of Plato to unfold
What worlds, or what vast regions hold   90
The immortal mind that hath forsook
Her mansion in this fleshly nook;
And of those demons° that are found   *god–men*
In fire, air, flood, or underground,
Whose power hath a true consent   95
With planet, or with element.
Some time let gorgeous Tragedy
In sceptered pall° come sweeping by,   *royal robe*
Presenting Thebes', or Pelops' line,
Or the tale of Troy divine.   100
Or what (though rare) of later age
Ennobled hath the buskined stage.
But, O sad virgin, that thy power

---

⁸⁷**Bear**   Ursa Major, a constellation that never sets.   ⁸⁸**Hermes**   here the Egyptian god Thoth, who later, under the name of Hermes Trismegistus, was considered a patron of magic.

Might raise Musaeus from his bower,
Or bid the soul of Orpheus sing   *105*
Such notes as, warbled to the string,
Drew iron tears down Pluto's cheek,
And made Hell grant what Love did seek.
Or call up him that left half told
The story of Cambuscan bold,   *110*
Of Camball, and of Algarsife,
And who had Canacee to wife,
That owned the virtuous° ring and glass,   *magical*
And of the wondrous horse of brass,
On which the Tartar king did ride;   *115*
And if aught else great bards beside
In sage and solemn tunes have sung,
Of tourneys and of trophies hung,
Of forests and enchantments drear,
Where more is meant than meets the ear.   *120*
Thus, Night, oft see me in thy pale career,
Till civil-suited morn appear,
Not tricked° and frounced° as she was wont,   *adorned/ornamented*
With the Attic boy to hunt,
But kerchiefed in a comely cloud,   *125*
While rocking winds are piping loud,
Or ushered with a shower still,
When the gust hath blown his fill,
Ending on the rustling leaves,
With minute-drops from off the eaves.   *130*
And when the sun begins to fling
His flaring beams, me, Goddess, bring
To archéd walks of twilight groves,
And shadows brown that Sylvan loves
Of pine or monumental oak,   *135*
Where the rude ax with heavéd stroke,
Was never heard the nymphs to daunt,
Or fright them from their hallowed haunt.
There in close covert by some brook,
Where no profaner eye may look,   *140*
Hide me from day's garish eye,
While the bee with honeyed thigh,
That at her flowery work doth sing,
And the waters murmuring

---

[104]**Musaeus** legendary poet-priest, reputedly the son of Orpheus.   [109]**him** Geoffrey Chaucer in "The Squire's Tale" from the *Canterbury Tales*.   [123–124]**she . . . Attic boy** Aurora, goddess of the dawn, used to meet Cephalus and hunt with him.

With such consort° as they keep,   *company* 145
Entice the dewy-feathered sleep;
And let some strange mysterious dream,
Wave at his wings in airy stream,
Of lively portraiture displayed,
Softly on my eyelids laid.   *150*
And as I wake, sweet music breathe
Above, about, or underneath,
Sent by some spirit to mortals good,
Or th' unseen genius° of the wood.   *guardian spirit*
But let my due feet never fail   155
To walk the studious cloister's pale,°   *enclosure*
And love the high embowéd roof,
With antic pillars massy proof,
And storied windows richly dight,°   *dressed*
Casting a dim religious light.   *160*
There let the pealing organ blow,
To the full-voiced choir below,
In service high, and anthems clear,
As may with sweetness, through mine ear,
Dissolve me into ecstasies,   *165*
And bring all heaven before mine eyes.
And may at last my weary age
Find out the peaceful hermitage,
The hairy gown and mossy cell,
Where I may sit and rightly spell°   *study* 170
Of every star that Heaven doth show,
And every herb that sips the dew
Till old experience do attain
To something like prophetic strain.
These pleasures, Melancholy, give,   *175*
And I with thee will choose to live.

                        [1645]

When I consider how my light is spent

When I consider how my light is spent
    Ere half my days, in this dark world and wide,
    And that one talent which is death to hide,
    Lodged with me useless, though my soul more bent

IL PENSEROSO   [159]**storied windows**   stained-glass windows, which visually display biblical stories

To serve therewith my Maker, and present   5
    My true account, lest he returning chide;
    "Doth God exact day-labor, light denied?"
    I fondly° ask; but Patience to prevent°   *foolishly/forestall*
That murmur, soon replies, "God doth not need
    Either man's work or his own gifts; who best   10
    Bear his mild yoke, they serve him best. His state
Is kingly. Thousands at his bidding speed
    And post o'er land and ocean without rest:
    They also serve who only stand and wait."

                                                        [1673]

On the Late Massacre in Piedmont

Avenge, O Lord, thy slaughtered saints, whose bones
    Lie scattered on the Alpine mountains cold,
    Even them who kept thy truth so pure of old
    When all our fathers worshiped stocks° and stones   *idols*
Forget not: in thy book record their groans   5
    Who were thy sheep and in their ancient fold
    Slain by the bloody Piedmontese that rolled
    Mother with infant down the rocks. Their moans
The vales redoubled to the hills, and they
    To Heaven. Their martyred blood and ashes sow   10
    O'er all th' Italian fields where still doth sway
The triple tyrant: that from these may grow
    A hundredfold, who having learnt thy way
    Early may fly the Babylonian woe.

                                                        [1673]

Methought I saw my late espoused saint

Methought I saw my late espoused saint
    Brought to me like Alcestis from the grave,
    Whom Jove's great son to her glad husband gave,
    Rescued from death by force though pale and faint.

ON THE LATE MASSACRE   The Duke of Savoy in 1655 massacred 1,700 Waldensians, members of a
Protestant sect.   ¹²**The triple tyrant** the pope, whose tiara contains three crowns.
METHOUGHT I SAW   ²**Alcestis** Hercules rescued her from the underworld.

Mine, as whom washed from spot of childbed taint,   5
   Purification in the old law did save,
   And such, as yet once more I trust to have
   Full sight of her in Heaven without restraint,
Came vested all in white, pure as her mind.
   Her face was veiled, yet to my fancied sight,   10
   Love, sweetness, goodness, in her person shined
So clear, as in no face with more delight.
   But O, as to embrace me she inclined,
   I waked, she fled, and day brought back my night.

                                    [1673]

Paradise Lost
from Book I

Of man's first disobedience, and the fruit
Of that forbidden tree whose mortal taste
Brought death into the world, and all our woe,
With loss of Eden, till one greater Man
Restore us, and regain the blissful seat,   5
Sing, Heavenly Muse, that, on the secret top
Of Oreb, or of Sinai, didst inspire
That shepherd who first taught the chosen seed
In the beginning how the Heavens and Earth
Rose out of Chaos: or, if Sion hill   10
Delight thee more, and Siloa's brook that flowed
Fast° by the oracle of God, I thence   *close*
Invoke thy aid to my adventurous song,
That with no middle flight intends to soar
Above th' Aonian mount, while it pursues   15
Things unattempted yet in prose or rhyme.
And chiefly thou, O Spirit, that dost prefer
Before all temples th' upright heart and pure,
Instruct me, for thou know'st; thou from the first
Wast present, and, with mighty wings outspread,   20

METHOUGHT I SAW   ⁶**Purification . . . save** ancient biblical law prescribed ritual purification of a woman after she bore a child.

PARADISE LOST, BOOK I   Genesis 1–3 describes the creation of Eden and its inhabitants, Adam and Eve, who are expelled from paradise for disobeying God's commandment not to eat the fruit of a particular tree. ⁴**Man** Christ, the second Adam. ⁶**Muse** Urania, the Greek mythological Muse, or source of inspiration for epic poets, is here Judaeo-Christianized with references to Mount Sinai and the Holy Spirit, who provided inspiration for biblical authors. ¹⁵**Aonian mount** Helicon mountain, home of the Muses.

Dovelike sat'st brooding on the vast abyss,
And mad'st it pregnant: what in me is dark
Illumine; what is low, raise and support;
That, to the height of this great argument,°   *theme*
I may assert Eternal Providence,   25
And justify the ways of God to men.

    Say first (for Heaven hides nothing from thy view,
Nor the deep tract of Hell), say first what cause
Moved our grand parents, in that happy state,
Favored of Heaven so highly, to fall off   30
From their Creator, and transgress his will
For one restraint, lords of the world besides?
Who first seduced them to that foul revolt?

    Th' infernal serpent; he it was, whose guile,
Stirred up with envy and revenge, deceived   35
The mother of mankind, what time his pride
Had cast him out from Heaven, with all his host
Of rebel angels, by whose aid, aspiring
To set himself in glory above his peers,
He trusted to have equaled the Most High,   40
If he opposed; and with ambitious aim
Against the throne and monarchy of God,
Raised impious war in Heaven and battle proud,
With vain attempt. Him the Almighty Power
Hurled headlong flaming from th' ethereal sky,   45
With hideous ruin and combustion, down
To bottomless perdition, there to dwell
In adamantine chains and penal fire,
Who durst defy th' Omnipotent to arms.

    Nine times the space that measures day and night   50
To mortal men, he with his horrid crew,
Lay vanquished, rolling in the fiery gulf,
Confounded though immortal. But his doom
Reserved him to more wrath; for now the thought
Both of lost happiness and lasting pain   55
Torments him; round he throws his baleful eyes,
That witnessed huge affliction and dismay,
Mixed with obdúrate pride and steadfast hate.
At once, as far as angels ken,° he views   *sight*
The dismal situation waste and wild: 60
A dungeon horrible, on all sides round,
As one great furnace flamed; yet from those flames
No light, but rather darkness visible

---

²¹**Dovelike . . . brooding** Compare with Genesis 1·2 and Luke 3:22

Served only to discover sights of woe,
Regions of sorrow, doleful shades, where peace   *65*
And rest can never dwell, hope never comes
That comes to all, but torture without end
Still urges, and a fiery deluge, fed
With ever-burning sulphur unconsumed.
Such place Eternal Justice had prepared   *70*
For those rebellious; here their prison ordained
In utter darkness, and their portion set,
As far removed from God and light of Heaven
As from the center° thrice to th' utmost pole.   *the earth*
O how unlike the place from whence they fell!   *75*
There the companions of his fall, o'erwhelmed
With floods and whirlwinds of tempestuous fire,
He soon discerns; and, weltering by his side,
One next himself in power, and next in crime,
Long after known in Palestine, and named   *80*
Beëlzebub. To whom th' arch-enemy,
And thence in Heaven called Satan with bold words
Breaking the horrid silence, thus began:
    "If thou beëst he—but O how fallen! how changed
From him who, in the happy realms of light   *85*
Clothed with transcendent brightness, didst outshine
Myriads, though bright! if he whom mutual league,
United thoughts and counsels, equal hope
And hazard in the glorious enterprise,
Joined with me once, now misery hath joined   *90*
In equal ruin; into what pit thou seest
From what height fallen, so much the stronger proved
He with his thunder: and till then who knew
The force of those dire arms? Yet not for those,
Nor what the potent Victor in his rage   *95*
Can else inflict, do I repent, or change,
Though changed in outward luster, that fixed mind,
And high disdain from sense of injured merit,
That with the Mightiest raised me to contend,
And to the fierce contentions brought along   *100*
Innumerable force of spirits armed,
That durst dislike his reign, and, me preferring,
His utmost power with adverse power opposed
In dubious battle on the plains of Heaven,
And shook his throne. What though the field be lost?   *105*
All is not lost: the unconquerable will,

---

[81]**Beëlzebub**   lord of the flies, prince of devils.   [82]**Satan**   Hebrew for "adversary."

And study° of revenge, immortal hate,   *pursuit*
And courage never to submit or yield:
And what is else not to be overcome?
That glory never shall his wrath or might   *110*
Extort from me. To bow and sue for grace
With suppliant knee, and deify his power
Who, from the terror of this arm, so late
Doubted his empire—that were low indeed;
That were an ignominy and shame beneath   *115*
This downfall; since, by fate, the strength of gods,
And this empyreal° substance, cannot fail;   *heavenly*
Since, through experience of this great event,
In arms not worse, in foresight much advanced,
We may with more successful hope resolve   *120*
To wage by force or guile eternal war,
Irreconcilable to our grand Foe,
Who now triúmphs, and in th' excess of joy
Sole reigning holds the tyranny of Heaven."
    So spake th' apostate angel, though in pain,   *125*
Vaunting aloud, but racked with deep despair;
And him thus answered soon his bold compeer:°   *equal*
    "O prince, O chief of many thronéd powers,
That led th' embattled seraphim to war
Under thy conduct, and, in dreadful deeds   *130*
Fearless, endangered Heaven's perpetual King,
And put to proof his high supremacy,
Whether upheld by strength, or chance, or fate!
Too well I see and rue the dire event°   *outcome*
That with sad overthrow and foul defeat   *135*
Hath lost us Heaven, and all this mighty host
In horrible destruction laid thus low,
As far as gods and heavenly essences
Can perish: for the mind and spirit remains
Invincible, and vigor soon returns,   *140*
Though all our glory extinct, and happy state
Here swallowed up in endless misery.
But what if he our Conqueror (whom I now
Of force° believe almighty, since no less   *necessity*
Than such could have o'erpowered such force as ours)   *145*
Have left us this our spirit and strength entire,
Strongly to suffer and support our pains,
That we may so suffice° his vengeful ire,   *satisfy*
Or do him mightier service as his thralls

---

[129]**seraphim**   one of the nine orders of angels.

By right of war, whate'er his business be,   *150*
Here in the heart of Hell to work in fire,
Or do his errands in the gloomy deep?
What can it then avail though yet we feel
Strength undiminished, or eternal being
To undergo eternal punishment?"   *155*
    Whereto with speedy words th' arch-fiend replied:
"Fallen cherub, to be weak is miserable,
Doing or suffering; but of this be sure,
To do aught good never will be our task,
But ever to do ill our sole delight,   *160*
As being the contrary to his high will
Whom we resist. If then his providence
Out of our evil seek to bring forth good,
Our labor must be to pervert that end,
And out of good still to find means of evil;   *165*
Which oft times may succeed, so as perhaps
Shall grieve him, if I fail not, and disturb
His inmost counsels from their destined aim.
But see! the angry Victor hath recalled
His ministers of venegeance and pursuit   *170*
Back to the gates of Heaven; the sulphurous hail,
Shot after us in storm, o'erblown hath laid
The fiery surge that from the precipice
Of Heaven received us falling; and the thunder,
Winged with red lightning and impetuous rage,   *175*
Perhaps hath spent his shafts, and ceases now
To bellow through the vast and boundless deep.
Let us not slip th' occasion, whether scorn
Or satiate fury yield it from our Foe.
Seest thou yon dreary plain, forlorn and wild,   *180*
The seat of desolation, void of light,
Save what the glimmering of these livid flames
Casts pale and dreadful? Thither let us tend
From off the tossing of these fiery waves;
There rest, if any rest can harbor there;   *185*
And, reassembling our afflicted powers,°   *armies*
Consult how we may henceforth most offend
Our enemy, our own loss how repair,
How overcome this dire calamity,
What reinforcement we may gain from hope,   *190*
If not, what resolution from despair."
    Thus Satan, talking to his nearest mate,
With head uplift above the wave, and eyes
That sparkling blazed; his other parts besides,

Prone on the flood, extended long and large,   *195*
Lay floating many a rood, in bulk as huge
As whom the fables name of monstrous size,
Titanian or Earth-born, that warred on Jove,
Briareos or Typhon, whom the den
By ancient Tarsus held, or that sea beast   *200*
Leviathan, which God of all his works
Created hugest that swim th' ocean-stream.
Him, haply, slumbering on the Norway foam,
The pilot of some small night-foundered skiff,
Deeming some island, oft, as seamen tell,   *205*
With fixéd anchor in his scaly rind,
Moors by his side under the lee, while night
Invests° the sea, and wishéd morn delays.   *covers*
So stretched out huge in length the arch-fiend lay,
Chained on the burning lake; nor ever thence   *210*
Had risen or heaved his head, but that the will
And high permission of all-ruling Heaven
Left him at large to his own dark designs,
That with reiterated crimes he might
Heap on himself damnation, while he sought   *215*
Evil to others, and enraged might see
How all his malice served but to bring forth
Infinite goodness, grace, and mercy shown
On man by him seduced, but on himself
Treble confusion, wrath, and vengeance poured.   *220*
    Forthwith upright he rears from off the pool
His mighty stature; on each hand the flames
Driven backward slope their pointing spires, and, rolled
In billows, leave i' th' midst a horrid vale.
Then with expanded wings he steers his flight   *225*
Aloft, incumbent on the dusky air,
That felt unusual weight; till on dry land
He lights, if it were land that ever burned
With solid, as the lake with liquid fire,
And such appeared in hue; as when the force   *230*
Of subterranean wind transports a hill
Torn from Pelorus, or the shattered side
Of thundering Etna, whose combustible
And fueled entrails, thence conceiving fire,
Sublimed° with mineral fury, aid the winds,   *vaporized* 235

---

¹⁹⁶**rood**   a unit of measure equaling six to eight yards.   ¹⁹⁹**Briareos or Typhon**   leaders, respectively, of the Titans and the Giants who fought against Jove, the chief god.   ²⁰¹**Leviathan**   sea monster. Compare Job 41 ²³²⁻²³³**Pelorus . . . Etna**   volcanoes in Sicily.

And leave a singéd bottom all involved°   *wrapped*
With stench and smoke. Such resting found the sole
Of unblest feet. Him followed his next mate,
Both glorying to have 'scaped the Stygian flood
As gods, and by their own recovered strength,   240
Not by the sufferance° of supernal power.   *permission*
   "Is this the region, this the soil, the clime,"
Said then the lost archangel, "this the seat
That we must change for Heaven? this mournful gloom
For that celestial light? Be it so, since he   245
Who now is sovereign can dispose and bid
What shall be right: farthest from him is best,
Whom reason hath equaled, force hath made supreme
Above his equals. Farewell, happy fields,
Where joy forever dwells! Hail, horrors! hail,   250
Infernal world! and thou, profoundest Hell,
Receive thy new possessor, one who brings
A mind not to be changed by place or time.
The mind is its own place, and in itself
Can make a Heaven of Hell, a Hell of Heaven.   255
What matter where, if I be still the same,
And what I should be, all but less than he
Whom thunder hath made greater? Here at least
We shall be free; th' Almighty hath not built
Here for his envy, will not drive us hence: 260
Here we may reign secure; and, in my choice,
To reign is worth ambition, though in Hell:
Better to reign in Hell than serve in Heaven.

from Book III

   Hail, holy Light, offspring of Heaven first-born!
Or of th' Eternal coeternal beam,
May I express thee unblamed? since God is light,
And never but in unapproachéd light
Dwelt from eternity, dwelt then in thee,   5
Bright effluence of bright essence increate°!   *eternal*
Or hear'st thou rather pure ethereal stream,
Whose fountain who shall tell? Before the sun,
Before the heavens, thou wert, and at the voice
Of God, as with a mantle, didst invest°   *occupy* 10

PARADISE LOST, BOOK I   ²³⁹**Stygian**   associated with the river Styx in the Greek mythological underworld.

The rising world of waters dark and deep,
Won from the void and formless infinite!
Thee I revisit now with bolder wing,
Escaped the Stygian pool, though long detained
In that obscure sojourn, while in my flight,   *15*
Through utter and through middle darkness° borne,   *chaos, hell*
With other notes than to th' Orphean lyre
I sung of Chaos and eternal Night;
Taught by the Heavenly Muse° to venture down   *Urania*
The dark descent, and up to reascend,   *20*
Though hard and rare. Thee I revisit safe,
And feel thy sovereign vital lamp; but thou
Revisit'st not these eyes, that roll in vain
To find thy piercing ray, and find no dawn;
So thick a drop serene hath quenched their orbs,   *25*
Or dim suffusion veiled. Yet not the more
Cease I to wander where the Muses haunt
Clear spring, or shady grove, or sunny hill,
Smit with the love of sacred song; but chief
Thee, Sion, and the flowery brooks beneath,   *30*
That wash thy hallowed feet, and warbling flow,
Nightly I visit: nor sometimes forget
Those other two equaled with me in fate,
So were I equaled with them in renown,
Blind Thamyris and blind Maeonides,   *35*
And Tiresias and Phineus, prophets old:
Then feed on thoughts that voluntary move
Harmonious numbers: as the wakeful bird
Sings darkling,° and, in shadiest covert hid.   *at night*
Tunes her nocturnal note. Thus with the year   *40*
Seasons return; but not to me returns
Day, or the sweet approach of even or morn,
Or sight of vernal bloom, or summer's rose,
Or flocks, or herds, or human face divine;
But cloud instead and ever-during dark   *45*
Surrounds me, from the cheerful ways of men
Cut off, and, for the book of knowledge fair,
Presented with a universal blank
Of Nature's works, to me expunged and rased,°   *erased*
And wisdom at one entrance quite shut out.   *50*

PARADISE LOST, BOOK III   [30]**Sion**   mountain of Biblical inspiration.   [35]**Thamyris . . . Maeonides**
Thamyris was a pre-Homeric Thracian poet "Maeonides" refers to Homer. Both poets were reputedly blind.
[36]**Tiresias and Phineus**   Tiresias was a blind prophet, Phineus a blind soothsayer.   [38]**wakeful bird**   the
nightingale.

So much the rather thou, Celestial Light,
Shine inward, and the mind through all her powers
Irradiate; there plant eyes; all mist from thence
Purge and disperse, that I may see and tell
Of things invisible to mortal sight.   55

from Book IV

O for that warning voice, which he who saw
Th' Apocalypse heard cry in Heaven aloud,
Then when the dragon, put to second rout,
Came furious down to be revenged on men,
Woe to the inhabitants on Earth! that now,   5
While time was, our first parents had been warned
The coming of their secret foe, and scaped,
Haply so scaped, his mortal snare! For now
Satan, now first inflamed with rage, came down,
The tempter, ere th' accuser, of mankind,   10
To wreak on innocent frail man his loss
Of that first battle, and his flight to hell.
Yet not rejoicing in his speed, though bold
Far off and fearless, nor with cause to boast,
Begins his dire attempt; which, nigh the birth   15
Now rolling, boils in his tumultuous breast,
And like a devilish engine back recoils
Upon himself. Horror and doubt distract
His troubled thoughts, and from the bottom stir
The Hell within him; for within him Hell   20
He brings, and round about him, nor from Hell
One step, no more than from himself, can fly
By change of place. Now conscience wakes despair
That slumbered; wakes the bitter memory
Of what he was, what is, and what must be   25
Worse; of worse deeds worse sufferings must ensue
Sometimes towards Eden, which now in his view
Lay pleasant, his grieved look he fixes sad;
Sometimes towards heaven and the full-blazing sun,
Which now sat high in his meridian tower: 30
Then, much revolving, thus in sighs began:—
    "O thou that, with surpassing glory crowned,
Look'st from thy sole dominion like the god

PARADISE LOST, BOOK IV   [5]**woe . . . Earth**   Compare with Revelation 12.

Of this new world—at whose sight all the stars
Hide their diminished heads—to thee I call,   35
But with no friendly voice, and add thy name,
O sun, to tell thee how I hate thy beams,
That bring to my remembrance from what state
I fell, how glorious once above thy sphere,
Till pride and worse ambition threw me down,   40
Warring in Heaven against Heaven's matchless king!
Ah, wherefore? He deserved no such return
From me, whom he created what I was
In that bright eminence, and with his good
Upbraided none; nor was his service hard.   45
What could be less than to afford him praise,
The easiest recompense, and pay him thanks,
How due! Yet all his good proved ill in me,
And wrought but malice. Lifted up so high,
I 'sdained° subjection, and thought one step higher   disdained, scorned 50
Would set me highest, and in a moment quit°   acquit
The debt immense of endless gratitude,
So burdensome, still paying, still to owe;
Forgetful what from him I still received;
And understood not that a grateful mind   55
By owing owes not, but still pays, at once
Indebted and discharged—what burden then?
Oh, had his powerful destiny ordained
Me some inferior angel, I had stood
Then happy; no unbounded hope had raised   60
Ambition. Yet why not? Some other power
As great might have aspired, and me, though mean,
Drawn to his part. But other powers as great
Fell not, but stand unshaken, from within
Or from without to all temptations armed!   65
Hadst thou the same free will and power to stand?
Thou hadst. Whom hast thou then, or what, to accuse,
But Heaven's free love dealt equally to all?
Be then his love accursed, since, love or hate,
To me alike it deals eternal woe.   70
Nay, cursed be thou; since against his thy will
Chose freely what it now so justly rues.
Me miserable! which way shall I fly
Infinite wrath and infinite despair?
Which way I fly is Hell; myself am Hell;   75
And, in the lowest deep, a lower deep
Still threatening to devour me opens wide,
To which the Hell I suffer seems a Heaven.

O, then, at last relent! Is there no place
Left for repentance, none for pardon left?   *80*
None left but by submission; and that word
Disdain forbids me, and my dread of shame
Among the spirits beneath, whom I seduced
With other promises and other vaunts
Than to submit, boasting I could subdue   *85*
Th' omnipotent. Ay me! they little know
How dearly I abide that boast so vain,
Under what torments inwardly I groan.
While they adore me on the throne of Hell,
With diadem and scepter high advanced,   *90*
The lower still I fall, only supreme
In misery: such joy ambition finds!
But say I could repent, and could obtain,
By act of grace my former state, how soon
Would height recall high thoughts, how soon unsay   *95*
What feigned submission swore! Ease would recant
Vows made in pain, as violent and void
For never can true reconcilement grow
Where wounds of deadly hate have pierced so deep;
Which would but lead me to a worse relapse   *100*
And heavier fall: so should I purchase dear
Short intermission, bought with double smart.
This knows my punisher; therefore as far
From granting he, as I from begging, peace.
All hope excluded thus, behold, instead   *105*
Of us, outcast, exiled, his new delight,
Mankind, created, and for him this world!
So farewell hope, and, with hope, farewell fear,
Farewell remorse! All good to me is lost;
Evil, be thou my good: by thee at least   *110*
Divided empire with Heaven's king I hold,
By thee, and more than half perhaps will reign;
As man ere long, and this new world, shall know."
    Thus while he spake, each passion dimmed his face,
Thrice changed with pale—ire, envy, and despair;   *115*
Which marred his borrowed visage, and betrayed
Him counterfeit, if any eye beheld:
For heavenly minds from such distempers foul
Are ever clear. Whereof he soon aware
Each perturbation smoothed with outward calm,   *120*
Artificer of fraud; and was the first
That practiced falsehood under saintly show,
Deep malice to conceal, couched with revenge:

Yet not enough had practiced to deceive
Uriel, once warned; whose eye pursued him down   *125*
The way he went, and on th' Assyrian mount
Saw him disfigured, more than could befall
Spirit of happy sort: his gestures fierce
He marked and mad demeanor, then alone,
As he supposed, all unobserved, unseen.   *130*
    So on he fares, and to the border comes.
Of Eden, where delicious Paradise,
Now nearer, crowns with her enclosure green,
As with a rural mound, the champaign° head   *open countryside*
Of a steep wilderness, whose hairy sides   *135*
With thicket overgrown, grotesque° and wild,   *picturesque*
Access denied; and overhead up grew
Insuperable height of loftiest shade,
Cedar, and pine, and fir, and branching palm,
A sylvan scene, and, as the ranks ascend   *140*
Shade above shade, a woody theater
Of stateliest view. Yet higher than their tops
The verdurous wall of Paradise up sprung;
Which to our general sire° gave prospect large   *Adam*
Into his nether empire neighboring round.   *145*
And higher than that wall a circling row
Of goodliest trees, laden with fairest fruit,
Blossoms and fruits at once of golden hue,
Appeared, with gay enameled colors mixed;
On which the sun more glad impressed his beams   *150*
Than in fair evening cloud, or humid bow,°   *rainbow*
When God hath showered the earth: so lovely seemed
That landscape. And of pure now purer air
Meets his approach, and to the heart inspires
Vernal delight and joy, able to drive°   *scatter* *155*
All sadness but despair. Now gentle gales,
Fanning their odoriferous wings, dispense
Native perfumes, and whisper whence they stole
Those balmy spoils. As when to them who sail
Beyond the Cape of Hope, and now are past   *160*
Mozambic, off at sea northeast winds blow
Sabean odors from the spicy shore
Of Araby the Blest, with such delay
Well pleased they slack their course, and many a league
Cheered with the grateful smell old Ocean smiles;   *165*
So entertained those odorous sweets the fiend

---

[141]**Shade . . . theater**   the trees are arranged in rows.

Who came their bane, though with them better pleased
Than Asmodëus with the fishy fume
That drove him, though enamored, from the spouse
Of Tobit's son, and with a vengeance sent 170
From Media post to Egypt, there fast bound.
    Now to th' ascent of that steep savage° hill *wooded*
Satan had journeyed on, pensive and slow;
But further way found none; so thick entwined,
As one continued brake, the undergrowth 175
Of shrubs and tangling bushes had perplexed
All path of man or beast that passed that way.
One gate there only was, and that looked east
On th' other side. Which when th' arch-felon saw,
Due entrance he disdained, and, in contempt, 180
At one slight bound high overleaped all bound
Of hill or highest wall, and sheer within
Lights on his feet. As when a prowling wolf,
Whom hunger drives to seek new haunt for prey,
Watching where shepherds pen their flocks at eve, 185
In hurdled cotes amid the field secure,
Leaps o'er the fence with ease into the fold;
Or as a thief, bent to unhoard the cash
Of some rich burgher, whose substantial doors,
Cross-barred and bolted fast, fear no assault, 190
In at the window climbs, or o'er the tiles;
So clomb° this first grand thief into God's fold: *climbed*
So since into his church lewd hirelings climb.
Thence up he flew, and on the Tree of Life,
The middle tree and highest there that grew, 195
Sat like a cormorant; yet not true life
Thereby regained, but sat devising death
To them who lived; nor on the virtue thought
Of that life-giving plant, but only used
For prospect,° what, well used, had been the pledge *perspective, view* 200
Of immortality. So little knows
Any, but God alone, to value right
The good before him, but perverts best things
To worst abuse, or to their meanest use.
    Beneath him, with new wonder, now he views, 205
To all delight of human sense exposed,
In narrow room Nature's whole wealth; yea, more,
A Heaven on Earth; for blissful Paradise

---

[170]**Tobit's son**   married Sara and on the advice of Raphael was able to drive away a devil by creating a fishy smell.
[186]**cotes**   pens made of woven reeds.

Of God the garden was, by him in the east
Of Eden planted. Eden stretched her line   210
From Auran eastward to the royal towers
Of great Seleucia, built by Grecian kings,
Or where the sons of Eden long before
Dwelt in Telassar. In this pleasant soil
His far more pleasant garden God ordained.   215
Out of the fertile ground he caused to grow
All trees of noblest kind for sight, smell, taste;
And all amid them stood the Tree of Life,
High eminent, blooming ambrosial fruit
Of vegetable gold; and next to life,   220
Our death, the Tree of Knowledge, grew fast by—
Knowledge of good, bought dear by knowing ill.

SIR JOHN SUCKLING

[1609–1642]

Out upon it!

Out upon it! I have loved
   Three whole days together;
And am like to love three more,
   If it prove fair weather.

Time shall molt away his wings,   5
   Ere he shall discover
In the whole wide world again
   Such a constant lover.

But the spite on 't is, no praise
   Is due at all to me: 10
Love with me had made no stays
   Had it any been but she.

Had it any been but she,
   And that very face,
There had been at least ere this   15
   A dozen dozen in her place.

                                          [1659]

PARADISE LOST, BOOK IV   211–214**Auran . . . Telassar**   Auran is in Syria, Seleucia in Iraq, and Telassar on
the eastern bank of the Euphrates River.

ANNE BRADSTREET

[1612–1672]

Before the Birth of One of Her Children

All things within this fading world hath end,
Adversity doth still our joys attend;
No ties so strong, no friends so dear and sweet,
But with death's parting blow is sure to meet.
The sentence past is most irrevocable,   *5*
A common thing, yet oh, inevitable.
How soon, my Dear, death may my steps attend,
How soon't may be thy lot to lose thy friend,
We both are ignorant, yet love bids me
These farewell lines to recommend to thee,   *10*
That when that knot's untied that made us one,
I may seem thine, who in effect am none.
And if I see not half my days that's due,
What nature would, God grant to yours and you;
The many faults that well you know I have   *15*
Let be interred in my oblivious grave;
If any worth or virtue were in me,
Let that live freshly in thy memory
And when thou feel'st no grief, as I no harms,
Yet love thy dead, who long lay in thine arms.   *20*
And when thy loss shall be repaid with gains
Look to my little babes, my dear remains.
And if chance to thine eyes shall bring this verse,
With some sad sighs honor my absent hearse;
And kiss this paper for thy love's dear sake,   *25*
Who with salt tears this last farewell did take.

[1678]

ABRAHAM COWLEY

[1618–1667]

My Picture

Here, take my likeness with you, whilst 'tis so;
    For when from hence you go,
    The next sun's rising will behold

Me pale and lean and old.
The man who did this picture draw   5
Will swear next day my face he never saw.

I really believe, within a while,
If you upon this shadow smile,
Your presence will such vigor give
(Your presence which makes all things live)   10
And absence so much alter me,
This will the substance, I the shadow be.

When from your well-wrought cabinet you take it,
And your bright looks awake it,
Ah, be not frighted, if you see   15
The new-soul'd picture gaze on thee,
And hear it breath a sigh or two;
For those are the first things that it will do.

My rival-image will be then thought blest,
And laugh at me as dispossest;   20
But thou, who (if I know thee right)
I'th' substance does not much delight,
Wilt rather send again for me,
Who then shall but my picture's picture be.

[1668]

RICHARD LOVELACE

[1618–1657]

To Althea, from Prison

When Love with unconfinéd wings
Hovers within my gates,
And my divine Althea brings
To whisper at the grates;
When I lie tangled in her hair   5
And fettered to her eye,
The birds that wanton in the air
Know no such liberty.

When flowing cups run swiftly round,
With no allaying Thames,   *10*
Our careless heads with roses bound,
Our hearts with loyal flames;
When thirsty grief in wine we steep,
When healths and draughts go free,
Fishes, that tipple in the deep,   *15*
Know no such liberty.

When, like committed° linnets, I   *caged*
With shriller throat shall sing
The sweetness, mercy, majesty,
And glories of my King;   *20*
When I shall voice aloud how good
He is, how great should be,
Enlargéd winds, that curl the flood,
Know no such liberty.

Stone walls do not a prison make,   *25*
Nor iron bars a cage;
Minds innocent and quiet take
That for an hermitage.
If I have freedom in my love,
And in my soul am free,   *30*
Angels alone, that soar above,
Enjoy such liberty.

                                                     [1649]

ANDREW MARVELL

[1621–1678]

A Dialogue Between the Soul and Body

Soul

Oh, who shall from this dungeon raise
A soul enslaved so many ways?
With bolts of bones that fettered stands
In feet, and manacled in hands;
Here blinded with an eye, and there   *5*
Deaf with the drumming of an ear;
A soul hung up, as 'twere, in chains

Of nerves and arteries and veins;
Tortured, besides each other part,
In a vain head and double heart.   10

Body

Oh, who shall me deliver whole
From bonds of this tyrannic soul?
Which stretched upright, impales me so
That mine own precipice I go,
And warms and moves this needless frame—   15
A fever could but do the same—
And, wanting where its spite to try,
Has made me live to let me die:
A body that could never rest,
Since this ill spirit it possessed.   20

Soul

What magic could me thus confine
Within another's grief to pine?
Where whatsoever it complain,
I feel, that cannot feel, the pain,
And all my care itself employs,   25
That to preserve which me destroys,
Constrained not only to endure
Diseases, but, what's worse, the cure;
And ready oft the port° to gain,   *heaven*
And shipwrecked into health again.   30

Body

But physic° yet could never reach   *medicine*
The maladies thou me dost teach:
Whom first the cramp of hope does tear,
And then the palsy shakes of fear;
The pestilence of love does heat,   35
Or hatred's hidden ulcer eat;
Joy's cheerful madness does perplex,
Or sorrow's other madness vex;
Which knowledge forces me to know,
And memory will not forgo.   40
What but a soul could have the wit
To build me up for sin so fit?
So architects do square and hew
Green trees that in the forest grew.

[1681]

The Definition of Love

My Love is of a birth as rare
As 'tis, for object, strange and high;
It was begotten by Despair
Upon Impossibility.

Magnanimous Despair alone   5
Could show me so divine a thing,
Where feeble Hope could ne'er have flown
But vainly flapped its tinsel wing.

And yet I quickly might arrive
Where my extended soul is fixed;   10
But Fate does iron wedges drive,
And always crowds itself betwixt.

For Fate with jealous eye does see
Two perfect loves, nor lets them close;°   *unite*
Their union would her ruin be,   15
And her tyrannic power depose.

And therefore her decrees of steel
Us as the distant poles have placed
(Though Love's whole world on us doth wheel),
Not by themselves to be embraced,   20

Unless the giddy heaven fall,
And earth some new convulsion tear,
And, us to join, the world should all
Be cramped into a planisphere.

As lines, so loves oblique may well   25
Themselves in every angle greet;
But ours, so truly parallel,
Though infinite, can never meet.

Therefore the love which us doth bind,
But Fate so enviously debars,   30
Is the conjunction of the mind,
And opposition of the stars.

[1681]

THE DEFINITION OF LOVE   24**planisphere**   a sphere projected onto a flat surface.

To His Coy Mistress

Had we but world enough, and time,
This coyness, lady, were no crime.
We would sit down, and think which way
To walk, and pass our long love's day.
Thou by the Indian Ganges' side   5
Shoudst rubies find; I by the tide
Of Humber would complain. I would
Love you ten years before the flood,
And you should, if you please, refuse
Till the conversion of the Jews.   10
My vegetable love should grow
Vaster than empires and more slow;
An hundred years should go to praise
Thine eyes, and on thy forehead gaze;
Two hundred to adore each breast,   15
But thirty thousand to the rest;
An age at least to every part,
And the last age should show your heart.
For, lady, you deserve this state,
Nor would I love at lower rate.   20
    But at my back I always hear
Time's winged chariot hurrying near;
And yonder all before us lie
Deserts of vast eternity.
Thy beauty shall no more be found;   25
Nor, in thy marble vault, shall sound
My echoing song; then worms shall try
That long-preserved virginity,
And your quaint° honor turn to dust,   *overscrupulous*
And into ashes all my lust: 30
The grave's a fine and private place,
But none, I think, do there embrace.
    Now therefore, while the youthful hue
Sits on thy skin like morning dew
And while thy willing soul transpires°   *breathes forth* 35
At every pore with instant fires,
Now let us sport us while we may,
And now, like amorous birds of prey,
Rather at once our time devour

TO HIS COY MISTRESS   °rubies   associated with virginity.   ⁷Humber   the river that runs through
Marvell's native town, Hull.   ¹⁰the conversion of the Jews   supposedly to occur at the end of time.
¹¹vegetable love   a reference to the idea that vegetables have the power to grow but lack consciousness.

Than languish in his slow-chapped° power.   *slow-jawed*   40
Let us roll all our strength and all
Our sweetness up into one ball,
And tear our pleasures with rough strife
Thorough the iron gates of life:
Thus, though we cannot make our sun   45
Stand still, yet we will make him run.

                                                          [1681]

The Garden

How vainly men themselves amaze°   *perplex*
To win the palm, the oak, or bays,
And their incessant labors see
Crowned from some single herb, or tree,
Whose short and narrow-vergéd shade   5
Does prudently their toils upbraid;
While all flowers and all trees do close
To weave the garlands of repose!

Fair Quiet, have I found thee here,
And Innocence, thy sister dear?   10
Mistaken long, I sought you then
In busy companies of men.
Your sacred plants,° if here below,   *cuttings*
Only among the plants will grow;
Society is all but rude°   *savage, primitive* 15
To this delicious solitude.

No white nor red was ever seen
So amorous as this lovely green.
Fond lovers, cruel as their flame,
Cut in these trees their mistress' name;   20
Little, alas, they know or heed
How far these beauties hers exceed!
Fair trees, wheresoe'er your barks I wound,
No name shall but your own be found.

When we have run our passion's heat,°   *course*   25
Love hither makes his best retreat.

THE GARDEN   ²**palm . . . bays** wreaths made of these leaves were awarded for military or athletic feats, for civic or political accomplishment, or for poetic achievement.   ⁵**narrow-vergéd** confined in a small space.

The gods, that mortal beauty chase,
Still in a tree did end their race:
Apollo hunted Daphne so,
Only that she might laurel grow;   30
And Pan did after Syrinx speed,
Not as a nymph, but for a reed.

   What wondrous life is this I lead!
Ripe apples drop about my head;
The luscious clusters of the vine   35
Upon my mouth do crush their wine;
The nectarine and curious° peach   *exquisite*
Into by hands themselves do reach;
Stumbling on melons, as I pass,
Insnared with flowers, I fall on grass.   40

   Meanwhile the mind, from pleasure less,
Withdraws into its happiness;
The mind, that ocean where each kind
Does straight its own resemblance find;
Yet it creates, transcending these,   45
Far other worlds and other seas,
Annihilating all that's made
To a green thought in a green shade.

   Here at the fountain's sliding foot,
Or at some fruit tree's mossy root,   50
Casting the body's vest° aside,   *garment*
My soul into the boughs does glide:
There, like a bird, it sits and sings,
Then whets and combs its silver wings,
And, till prepared for longer flight,   55
Waves in its plumes the various light.

   Such was that happy garden-state,
While man there walked without a mate:
After a place so pure and sweet,
What other help could yet be meet!   60
But 'twas beyond a mortal's share
To wander solitary there:
Two paradises 'twere in one
To live in paradise alone.

[29-32]**Apollo . . . reed**   Ovid's *Metamorphoses* describes how Daphne, when pursued and about to be overtaken by Apollo, was changed into a laurel tree. Pursued by Pan, Syrinx escaped him by being transformed into a reed.
[43-44]**ocean . . . find**   referring to the notion that for every land creature there was thought to be a corresponding marine equivalent.

How well the skillful gardener drew 65
Of flowers and herbs this dial new,
Where, from above, the milder sun
Does through a fragrant zodiac run;
And as it works, th' industrious bee
Computes its time as well as we! 70
How could such sweet and wholesome hours
Be reckoned but with herbs and flowers?

[1681]

HENRY VAUGHAN

[1621–1695]

They are all gone into the world of light!

They are all gone into the world of light!
  And I alone sit lingering here;
Their very memory is fair and bright,
  And my sad thoughts doth clear.

It glows and glitters in my cloudy breast 5
  Like stars upon some gloomy grove,
Or those faint beams in which this hill is dressed
  After the sun's remove.

I see them walking in an air of glory,
  Whose light doth trample on my days; 10
My days, which are at best but dull and hoary,
  Mere glimmering and decays.

O holy hope, and high humility,
  High as the heavens above!
These are your walks, and you have showed them me 15
  To kindle my cold love.

Dear, beauteous death! the jewel of the just,
  Shining nowhere but in the dark;
What mysteries do lie beyond thy dust,
  Could man outlook that mark°! *boundary* 20

THE GARDEN   ⁶⁶**dial** flowers and plants arranged in the shape of a sundial.

He that hath found some fledged bird's nest may know
    At first sight if the bird be flown;
But what fair well or grove he sings in now,
    That is to him unknown.

And yet, as angels in some brighter dreams   *25*
    Call to the soul when man doth sleep,
So some strange thoughts transcend our wonted themes,
    And into glory peep.

If a star were confined into a tomb,
    Her captive flames must needs burn there;   *30*
But when the hand that locked her up gives room,
    She'll shine through all the sphere.

O Father of eternal life, and all
    Created glories under Thee!
Resume° Thy spirit from this world of thrall   *take back* *35*
    Into true liberty!

Either disperse these mists, which blot and fill
    My perspective° still as they pass;   *telescope*
Or else remove me hence unto that hill
    Where I shall need no glass.   *40*

                         [1655]

JOHN DRYDEN

[1631–1700]

A Song for St. Cecilia's Day

1

From harmony, from heavenly harmony
    This universal frame began:
    When Nature underneath a heap
        Of jarring atoms lay,
        And could not heave her head,   *5*
    The tuneful voice was heard from high:
        "Arise, ye more than dead."

A SONG FOR ST. CECILIA'S DAY   St. Cecilia was a Roman martyr and a patron saint of music.
³**Nature**   created nature.

Then cold, and hot, and moist, and dry,
In order to their stations leap,
        And Music's power obey.   *10*
From harmony, from heavenly harmony
     This universal frame began:
     From harmony to harmony
Through all the compass of the notes it ran,
The diapason closing full in man.   *15*

2

What passion cannot Music raise and quell!
     When Jubal struck the corded shell,°   *lyre*
    His listening brethren stood around,
    And, wondering, on their faces fell
    To worship that celestial sound.   *20*
Less than a god they thought there could not dwell
     Within the hollow of that shell
     That spoke so sweetly and so well.
What passion cannot Music raise and quell!

3

    The trumpet's loud clangor   *25*
      Excites us to arms,
   With shrill notes of anger,
      And mortal alarms.
    The double double double beat
      Of the thundering drum   *30*
Cries: "Hark! the foes come;
Charge, charge, 'tis too late to retreat."

4

    The soft complaining flute
    In dying notes discovers
    The woes of hopeless lovers,   *35*
Whose dirge is whispered by the warbling lute.

5

    Sharp violins proclaim
Their jealous pangs, and desperation,
Fury, frantic indignation,
Depth of pains, and height of passion,   *40*
     For the fair, disdainful dame.

---

[15]**diapason**   an octave consonance, harmony.   [17]**Jubal**   father of the harp and organ (Genesis 4:21).

6

But O! what art can teach,
What human voice can reach,
The sacred organ's praise?
　　Notes inspiring holy love,　　　　　　　　　45
Notes that wing their heavenly ways
　　To mend the choirs above.

7

Orpheus could lead the savage race;
And trees unrooted left their place,
　　Sequacious° of the lyre;　　　　　　　*following*　50
But bright Cecilia raised the wonder higher:
When to her organ vocal breath was given,
An angel heard, and straight appeared,
　　Mistaking earth for heaven.

Grand Chorus　　　　　　　　　　　55
As from the power of sacred lays
*　The spheres began to move,*
And sung the great Creator's praise
*　To all the blest above;*
So, when the last and dreadful hour　　　60
This crumbling pageant shall devour,
The trumpet shall be heard on high,
The dead shall live, the living die,
And Music shall untune the sky.

[1687]

ANNE FINCH,
COUNTESS OF WINCHILSEA

[1661–1720]

A Nocturnal Reverie

In such a night, when every louder wind
Is to its distant cavern safe confined;
And only gentle Zephyr fans his wings,
And lonely Philomel, still waking, sings;

A SONG FOR ST. CECILIA'S DAY　　　⁴⁸**Orpheus**　In classical mythology, Orpheus was famed for his power
to enchant with music.

Or from some tree, famed for the owl's delight,   *5*
She, hollowing clear, directs the wanderer right:
In such a night, when passing clouds give place,
Or thinly veil the heavens' mysterious face;
When in some river, overhung with green,
The waving moon and trembling leaves are seen;   *10*
When freshened grass now bears itself upright,
And makes cool banks to pleasing rest invite,
Whence springs the woodbind, and the bramble-rose,
And where the sleepy cowslip sheltered grows;
Whilst now a paler hue the foxglove takes,   *15*
Yet checkers still with red the dusky brakes.°   *thickets*
When scattered glow-worms, but in twilight fine,
Show trivial beauties watch their hour to shine;
Whilst Salisbury stands the test of every light,
In perfect charms, and perfect virtue bright: *20*
When odors, which declined repelling day,
Through temperate air uninterrupted stray;
When darkened groves their softest shadows wear,
And falling waters we distinctly hear;
When through the gloom more venerable shows   *25*
Some ancient fabric,° awful in repose,   *building*
While sunburnt hills their swarthy looks conceal,
And swelling haycocks thicken up the vale:
When the loosed horse now, as his pasture leads,
Comes slowly grazing through the adjoining meads,   *30*
Whose stealing pace, and lengthened shade we fear,
Till torn-up forage in his teeth we hear:
When nibbling sheep at large pursue their food,
And unmolested kine rechew the cud;
When curlews° cry beneath the village walls,   *shore birds* 35
And to her straggling brood the partridge calls;
Their shortlived jubilee the creatures keep,
Which but endures, whilst tyrant man does sleep;
When a sedate content the spirit feels,
And no fierce light disturbs, whilst it reveals;   *40*
But silent musings urge the mind to seek
Something, too high for syllables to speak;
Till the free soul to a composedness charmed,
Finding the elements of rage disarmed,
O'er all below a solemn quiet grown,   *45*
Joys in the inferior° world, and thinks it like her own: *lower*
In such a night let me abroad remain,

---

[19]**Salisbury** Lady Salisbury, renowned for her beauty.

Till morning breaks, and all's confused again;
Our cares, our toils, our clamors are renewed,
Or pleasures, seldom reached, again pursued.   50

[1713]

JONATHAN SWIFT

[1667–1745]

A Description of the Morning

Now hardly here and there a hackney-coach
Appearing, showed the ruddy morn's approach.
Now Betty from her master's bed had flown,
And softly stole to discompose her own;
The slip-shod 'prentice from his master's door   5
Had pared the dirt and sprinkled round the floor.
Now Moll had whirled her mop with dext'rous airs,
Prepared to scrub the entry and the stairs.
The youth with broomy stumps began to trace
The kennel-edge, where wheels had worn the place.   10
The small-coal man was heard with cadence deep,
Till drowned in shriller notes of chimney-sweep:
Duns° at his lordship's gate began to meet;   *bill collectors*
And brickdust Moll had screamed through half the street.
The turnkey° now his flock returning sees,   *jailer* 15
Duly let out a-nights to steal for fees:
The watchful bailiffs° take their silent stands,   *deputies*
And schoolboys lag with satchels in their hands.

[1709]

The Lady's Dressing Room

Five hours, (and who can do it less in?)
By haughty Celia spent in dressing;
The goddess from her chamber issues,
Arrayed in lace, brocades and tissues.
    Strephon, who found the room was void,   5

A DESCRIPTION OF THE MORNING   ¹⁴brickdust Moll   a woman who sold powdered brick, used to
sharpen knives.

And Betty otherwise employed,
Stole in, and took a strict survey,
Of all the litter as it lay;
Whereof, to make the matter clear,
An inventory follows here.   10
   And first a dirty smock appeared,
Beneath the armpits well besmeared.
Strephon, the rogue, displayed it wide,
And turned it round on every side.
On such a point few words are best,   15
And Strephon bids us guess the rest,
But swears how damnably the men lie,
In calling Celia sweet and cleanly.
Now listen while he next produces
The various combs for various uses,   20
Filled up with dirt so closely fixt,
No brush could force a way betwixt.
A paste of composition rare,
Sweat, dandruff, powder, lead and hair;
A forehead cloth with oil upon't   25
To smooth the wrinkles on her front;
Here alum flower to stop the steams,
Exhaled from sour unsavory streams,
There night-gloves made of Tripsy's hide,
Bequeathed by Tripsy when she died,   30
With puppy water, beauty's help
Distilled from Tripsy's darling whelp;
Here gallypots and vials placed,
Some filled with washes, some with paste,
Some with pomatum, paints and slops,   35
And ointments good for scabby chops.
Hard by a filthy basin stands,
Fouled with the scouring of her hands;
The basin takes whatever comes
The scrapings of her teeth and gums,   40
A nasty compound of all hues,
For here she spits, and here she spews.
But oh! it turned poor Strephon's bowels,
When he beheld and smelled the towels,
Begummed, bemattered, and beslimed   45
With dirt, and sweat, and earwax grimed.
No object Strephon's eye escapes,
Here petticoats in frowzy heaps;
Nor be the handkerchiefs forgot

---

[24]**lead** used to make hair shine. [33]**gallypots** jars for medicines or cosmetics.

All varnished o'er with snuff and snot.   50
The stockings why should I expose,
Stained with the marks of stinking toes;
Or greasy coifs and pinners° reeking,   *headwear*
Which Celia slept at least a week in?
A pair of tweezers next he found   55
To pluck her brows in arches round,
Or hairs that sink the forehead low,
Or on her chin like bristles grow.
    The virtues we must not let pass,
Of Celia's magnifying glass.   60
When frighted Strephon cast his eye on't
It showed visage of a giant.
A glass that can to sight disclose,
The smallest worm in Celia's nose,
And faithfully direct her nail   65
To squeeze it out from head to tail;
For catch it nicely by the head,
It must come out alive or dead.
    Why Strephon will you tell the rest?
And must you needs describe the chest?   70
That careless wench! no creature warn her
To move it out from yonder corner;
But leave it standing full in sight
For you to exercise your spite.
In vain the workman showed his wit   75
With rings and hinges counterfeit
To make it seem in this disguise
A cabinet to vulgar eyes;
For Strephon ventured to look in,
Resolved to go through thick and thin;   80
He lifts the lid, there needs no more,
He smelled it all the time before.
As from within Pandora's box,
When Epimetheus op'd the locks,
A sudden universal crew   85
Of human evils upwards flew;
He still was comforted to find
That Hope at last remained behind;
So Strephon lifting up the lid,
To view what in the chest was hid.   90

[83-84]**Pandora's box . . . Epimetheus**   Pandora, created by the Greek gods as the first human woman, brought with her to earth a box containing all human ills which, when it was opened, were released into the world, leaving only Hope behind. Epimetheus, brother of Prometheus, was her husband.

The vapors flew from out the vent,
But Strephon cautious never meant
The bottom of the pan to grope,
And foul his hands in search of Hope.
O never may such vile machine   95
Be once in Celia's chamber seen!
O may she better learn to keep
Those "secrets of the hoary deep!"
   As mutton cutlets, prime of meat,
Which though with art you salt and beat   100
As laws of cookery require,
And toast them at the clearest fire;
If from adown the hopeful chops
The fat upon a cinder drops,
To stinking smoke it turns the flame   105
Pois'ning the flesh from whence it came,
And up exhales a greasy stench,
For which you curse the careless wench;
So things, which must not be expressed,
When plumped into the reeking chest,   110
Send up an excremental smell
To taint the parts from whence they fell.
The petticoats and gown perfume,
Which waft a stink round every room.
Thus finishing his grand survey,   115
Disgusted Strephon stole away
Repeating in his amorous fits,
Oh! Celia, Celia, Celia shits!
   But Vengeance, goddess never sleeping
Soon punished Strephon for his peeping;   120
His foul imagination links
Each Dame he sees with all her stinks:
And, if unsavory odors fly,
Conceives a lady standing by:
All women his description fits,   125
And both ideas jump like wits:
By vicious fancy coupled fast,
And still appearing in contrast.
I pity wretched Strephon blind
To all the charms of female kind;   130
Should I the queen of love refuse,
Because she rose from stinking ooze?
To him that looks behind the scene,
Satira's but some pocky quean.°   *whore*
When Celia in her glory shows,   135

If Strephon would but stop his nose
(Who now so impiously blasphemes
Her ointments, daubs, and paints and creams,
Her washes, slops, and every clout,°   *rag*
With which he makes so foul a rout°)   *fuss*   140
He soon would learn to think like me,
And bless his ravished sight to see
Such order from confusion sprung,
Such gaudy tulips raised from dung.

[1730]

ALEXANDER POPE

[1688–1744]

Alexander Pope was so splendid a poet and so prominent a literary personage that the first half of the eighteenth century in England is referred to as the "Age of Pope." By the time he was twenty-eight Pope had published two works that earned him fortune and renown. His translation of Homer's *Iliad* provided Pope with financial security such that he became the first important English poet to live solely on his earnings from his work as a writer. Four years before the initial volumes of his *Iliad* (1715) began to appear, Pope published his first major poem, *An Essay on Criticism* (1711), which established his reputation as a skillful master of meter and rhyme. This was quickly followed by *The Rape of the Lock* (shorter version, 1712; longer version, 1714).

Composed in iambic pentameter couplets, *An Essay on Criticism* outlines Pope's poetic theory. The poem is notable for its memorable expression of commonly accepted poetic ideas of the time, thus serving as a source of eighteenth-century literary taste. Famous for some of its most successful couplets, the poem should be read, however, as more than a treasure trove of aphoristic wisdom and pleasing lines, though it is difficult not to appreciate the elegance and good sense of lines like the following.

A little learning is a dangerous thing.

To err is human; to forgive, divine.

True ease in writing comes from art, not chance.

The sound must seem an echo to the sense.

True wit is Nature to advantage dressed,
What oft was thought, but ne'er so well expressed.

One important animus of Pope's writing was to express consummately what was considered generally accepted truth—what many believed or had frequently thought, but which only the poet could express memorably. Pope's goal was thus not so much to create something new, to be original, as to perfect what already existed. Unlike the poets of the later part of the century, beginning with William Blake (1757–1827), Pope was not a revolutionary thinker or writer. Rather than introducing a new poetic style or altering prevailing poetic forms, he instead polished the elegant style of the rhymed couplet, using it in a variety of verse paragraphs in both satiric and elegiac modes, often in the form of the verse letter. Like Mozart, who perfected eighteenth-century musical style, Pope perfected the style of eighteenth-century English poetry, particularly in the form of the heroic couplet.

Like his predecessor, Ben Jonson (pp. 205–209), Pope was largely a moral and didactic poet, one who felt compelled to instruct his readers, to warn them of the dangers of vice while encouraging them to pursue truth and goodness. These virtues Pope located in the wisdom of the past, especially in Greek and Latin literature, in Christian teaching, and in nature. Pope's debt to ancient Greek and Latin writers is evident everywhere in his poetry—in the frequent allusions to episodes and lines, in his imitations and parodies, in his assumption of their moral principles, and in his translations, especially of Homer's *Iliad* and *Odyssey*. Pope's appreciation of nature is evident in the earliest of his poems, especially in "Windsor Forest," which celebrates the estate where Pope grew up, and the "Ode on Solitude," which he wrote while a teenager and which encapsulates the eighteenth-century pastoral ideal. It is this ideal of nature's purity, simplicity, and innocence that Pope counterpointed against the corruption of city and court life. Nature, for Pope, meant both the physical beauty of the external world and, even more important, its enduring, universal moral power. If Pope celebrated the ideal of nature less explicitly, less persistently, and less extravagantly than his Romantic poetic successors, he nonetheless valued nature as a stable and harmonious whole against which to measure the limitations and failures of human behavior. Pope, however, was primarily concerned with human attitudes and actions rather than nature in and of itself. His most consistent approach was didactic, moral, and satiric.

If *An Essay on Criticism* established Pope's reputation as a learned and elegant formulator of "what oft was thought, but ne'er so well expressed," *The Rape of the Lock* solidified his reputation by revealing a gift for wit and satire. Based on an actual incident in which a young man from a prominent family clipped a lock of hair from one Miss Arabella Fermor, an event that caused consternation among her family, Pope's poem was written at the request of a friend of both families who hoped that Pope's poetic effort might reconcile them through laughter. Pope's original, shorter two-canto version achieved this reconciliation, and with such success that he expanded the poem to five cantos two years later. In this extended version, *The Rape of the Lock* gains its effects largely through playful manipulation of epic conventions. The poem treats a trivial incident in a heroic manner and style suitable to the traditional epic subjects of war and nation building. The effect is comical. As readers, we marvel at Pope's ingenuity and inventiveness in adapting to his material epic gestures and conventions such as the extensive simile. In Pope's mock-epic poem, the heroes and heroines of Homer and Virgil's Trojan War become gentlemen and ladies of polite society. The "war" itself is one of physically harmless deeds and of words between the sexes. These and other epic details are described in a high style suitable for heroic action on a grand scale, and thus are comical when applied to a charming and frivolous world of snuffboxes, chinaware, and cosmetics.

Alexander Pope was born into a Roman Catholic family at a time when anti-Catholic sentiment was unusually high. In fact, during the year of Pope's birth William of Orange established free elections to Parliament and ensured a Protestant successor to the English throne vacated by the Catholic king, James III, who abandoned his throne and fled to France. William implemented measures that strictly controlled the lives of Catholics, who were not allowed to practice their religion openly or to live within a ten-mile radius of London. Nor could they purchase land, hold public office, or obtain a university degree. Young Alexander Pope, consequently, was educated at home by a series of private tutors, a number of them Catholic priests. At the age of twelve, Pope taught himself Greek and Latin; a few years later he learned French and Italian. In this he resembled John Milton, who also learned modern languages as a form of recreation from his more vigorous scholarly labors and who, like Pope, had the benefit of years of leisure to read and study in a secluded country residence.

Besides his education and learning, another important element of Pope's life was his physical debility. He was small and sickly and suffered from severe headaches. More important and more disabling, however, was the deformation he suffered from spinal tuberculosis, which crippled him for life. Although his Catholicism denied him access to formal education and his illness limited his opportunities for employment, Pope found solace in reading and writing. His literary precociousness was abundantly evident, and as a result he acquired the friendship of prominent men such as Sir William Trumbull, a retired foreign secretary, and Jacob Tonon, the most important publisher in London. Both men helped Pope bring his work before the public.

With the publication of his translation of Homer's *Iliad,* Pope entered into a literary warfare from which he never emerged. "The life of a wit is a warfare on earth," he once remarked. And for most of his life, Pope was either being attacked in the writings of others or lampooning them in his own. Although some of Pope's criticism of other poets appears in mild form in early poems, his most caustic satire of his enemies appears in *The Dunciad,* originally published in three books in 1728 but expanded to four in 1742. The first three books of *The Dunciad* satirize Pope's critics, especially Lewis Theobald, who had criticized Pope's edition of Shakespeare (1725). The fourth book contains a darker and more disturbing satiric vision—of political, social, educational, and religious disintegration.

Before composing *The Dunciad,* Pope had written "Eloisa to Abelard," an imaginative precursor of the later dramatic monologue. The poem reads, by turns, like a love letter and like a debate, and it shares features with the dramatic soliloquy. "Eloisa to Abelard" is Pope's most dramatic and passionate poem, though not as successful as his more satiric and philosophical poems. *An Essay on Man* is without doubt his most philosophical poem. Containing a highly optimistic view of man and his place in the world, *An Essay on Man* emphasizes the various kinds of harmony Pope believed to be necessary for happiness. Celebrating virtue and reason as twin sources of stability and harmony, this elaborate poem assured Pope's poetic reputation as the greatest poet of his age, though it too was followed by still other philosophical and satiric epistles that continued to express Pope's moral teachings with grace, elegance, and wit.

Pope's rage for order and his regard for reason, along with his insistence on the need for social and moral virtue, were matched only by his equally strong passion for gardening. Pope inherited his love of gardening from his father, who raised his son on a rural estate. After his father's death, Pope leased a villa at Twickenham, twelve miles outside London. There he lived and wrote until his death, persistently defending the moral, cosmic, and aesthetic order he so valued against the corrupting influences of his time.

Ode on Solitude

Happy the man whose wish and care
  A few paternal acres bound,
Content to breathe his native air,
        In his own ground.

Whose herds with milk, whose fields with bread,   5
  Whose flocks supply him with attire,
Whose trees in summer yield him shade,
        In winter fire.

Blest, who can unconcernedly find
  Hours, days, and years slide soft away,   10
In health of body, peace of mind,
        Quiet by day,

Sound sleep by night; study and ease,
  Together mixed; sweet recreation;
And innocence, which most does please   15
        With meditation.

Thus let me live, unseen, unknown;
  Thus unlamented let me die;
Steal from the world, and not a stone
        Tell where I lie.   20

[1717]

from *An Essay on Criticism*

Part 1

'Tis hard to say, if greater want of skill
Appear in writing or in judging ill;
But of the two less dangerous is the offense
To tire our patience than mislead our sense.
Some few in that, but numbers err in this,   5
Ten censure° wrong for one who writes amiss;   *judge*
A fool might once himself alone expose,
Now one in verse makes many more in prose.
    'Tis with our judgments as our watches, none
Go just alike, yet each believes his own.   10
In poets as true genius is but rare,
True taste as seldom is the critic's share;
Both must alike from Heaven derive their light,
These born to judge, as well as those to write.
Let such teach others who themselves excel,   15
And censure freely who have written well.
Authors are partial to their wit, 'tis true,
But are not critics to their judgment too?
    Yet if we look more closely, we shall find
Most have the seeds of judgment in their mind: 20
Nature affords at least a glimmering light;
The lines, though touched but faintly, are drawn right.
But as the slightest sketch, if justly traced, ⎫
Is by ill coloring but the more disgraced,   ⎬
So by false learning is good sense defaced: ⎭   25
Some are bewildered in the maze of schools,
And some made coxcombs Nature meant but fools.
In search of wit these lose their common sense,
And then turn critics in their own defense:
Each burns alike, who can, or cannot write,   30
Or with a rival's or an eunuch's spite.
All fools have still an itching to deride,
And fain would be upon the laughing side.
If Maevius scribble in Apollo's spite,
There are who judge still worse than he can write.   35
    Some have at first for wits, then poets passed,
Turned critics next, and proved plain fools at last.

AN ESSAY ON CRITICISM   [27]**coxcombs** pretenders to learning.   [34]**Maevius** a Latin poet ridiculed
by Virgil and Horace.

Some neither can for wits nor critics pass,
As heavy mules are neither horse nor ass.
Those half-learn'd witlings, numerous in our isle,   40
As half-formed insects on the banks of Nile;
Unfinished things, one knows not what to call,
Their generation's so equivocal:
To tell them would a hundred tongues require,
Or one vain wit's, that might a hundred tire.   45
    But you who seek to give and merit fame,
And justly bear a critic's noble name,
Be sure yourself and your own reach to know,
How far your genius, taste, and learning go;
Launch not beyond your depth, but be discreet,   50
And mark that point where sense and dullness meet.
    Nature to all things fixed the limits fit,
And wisely curbed proud man's pretending wit.
As on the land while here the ocean gains,
In other parts it leaves wide sandy plains;   55
Thus in the soul while memory prevails,
The solid power of understanding fails;
Where beams of warm imagination play,
The memory's soft figures melt away.
One science only will one genius fit,   60
So vast is art, so narrow human wit.
Not only bounded to peculiar arts,
But oft in those confined to single parts.
Like kings we lose the conquests gained before,
By vain ambition still to make them more;   65
Each might his several province well command,
Would all but stoop to what they understand.
    First follow Nature, and your judgment frame
By her just standard, which is still the same;
Unerring Nature, still divinely bright,   70
One clear, unchanged, and universal light,
Life, force, and beauty must to all impart,
At once the source, and end, and test of art.
Art from that fund each just supply provides,
Works without show, and without pomp presides.   75
In some fair body thus the informing soul
With spirits feeds, with vigor fills the whole,
Each motion guides, and every nerve sustains;
Itself unseen, but in the effects remains.
Some, to whom Heaven in wit has been profuse,   80

---

⁴¹**insects . . . Nile**   It was believed that some forms of life were spontaneously generated in the Nile River's mud.

Want as much more to turn it to its use;
For wit and judgment often are at strife,
Though meant each other's aid, like man and wife.
'Tis more to guide than spur the Muse's steed,
Restrain his fury than provoke his speed;   85
The winged courser, like a generous° horse,   *spirited*
Shows most true mettle when you check his course.
    Those rules of old discovered, not devised,
Are Nature still, but Nature methodized;
Nature, like liberty, is but restrained   90
By the same laws which first herself ordained. . . .

Part 2

    Of all the causes which conspire to blind
Man's erring judgment, and misguide the mind,
What the weak head with strongest bias rules,
Is pride, the never-failing vice of fools.   95
Whatever Nature has in worth denied,
She gives in large recruits° of needful pride;   *supplies*
For as in bodies, thus in souls, we find
What wants in blood and spirits swelled with wind:
Pride, where wit fails, steps in to our defense,   100
And fills up all the mighty void of sense.
If once right reason drives that cloud away,
Truth breaks upon us with resistless day.
Trust not yourself: but your defects to know,
Make use of every friend—and every foe.   105
    A little learning is a dangerous thing;
Drink deep, or taste not the Pierian spring.
There shallow draughts intoxicate the brain,
And drinking largely sobers us again.
Fired at first sight with what the Muse imparts,   110
In fearless youth we tempt the heights of arts,
While from the bounded level of our mind
Short views we take, nor see the lengths behind;
But more advanced, behold with strange surprise
New distant scenes of endless science rise!   115
So pleased at first the towering Alps we try,
Mount o'er the vales, and seem to tread the sky,
The eternal snows appear already past,
And the first clouds and mountains seem the last;
But, those attained, we tremble to survey   120

---

[86]**winged courser** Pegasus, winged horse associated with poetic inspiration   [107]**Pierian spring** on Mount Piera, sacred to the Muses.

The growing labors of the lengthened way,
The increasing prospect tires our wandering eyes,
Hills peep o'er hills, and Alps on Alps arise!
    A perfect judge will read each work of wit
With the same spirit that its author writ: *125*
Survey the whole, nor seek slight faults to find
Where Nature moves, and rapture warms the mind;
Nor lose, for that malignant dull delight,
The generous pleasure to be charmed with wit.
But in such lays as neither ebb nor flow,   *130*
Correctly cold, and regularly low,
That, shunning faults, one quite tenor keep,
We cannot blame indeed—but we may sleep.
In wit, as nature, what affects our hearts
Is not the exactness of peculiar parts;   *135*
'Tis not a lip, or eye, we beauty call,
But the joint force and full result of all.
Thus when we view some well-proportioned dome
(The world's just wonder, and even thine, O Rome!),
No single parts unequally surprise,   *140*
All comes united to the admiring eyes:
No monstrous height, or breadth, or length appear;
The whole at once is bold and regular.
    Whoever thinks a faultless piece to see,
Thinks what ne'er was, nor is, nor e'er shall be.   *145*
In every work regard the writer's end,
Since none can compass more than they intend;
And if the means be just, the conduct true,
Applause, in spite of trivial faults, is due.
As men of breeding, sometimes men of wit,   *150*
To avoid great errors must the less commit,
Neglect the rules each verbal critic lays,
For not to know some trifles is a praise.
Most critics, fond of some subservient art,
Still make the whole depend upon a part: *155*
They talk of principles, but notions prize,
And all to one loved folly sacrifice.
    Once on a time La Mancha's knight, they say,
A certain bard encountering on the way,
Discoursed in terms as just, with looks as sage,   *160*
As e'er could Dennis, of the Grecian stage;
Concluding all were desperate sots and fools

---

[139]**wonder . . . Rome** the dome of St. Peter's Cathedral in Rome, designed by Michelangelo.   [158]**La Mancha's Knight** Don Quixote.   [161]**Dennis** the poet John Dennis (1657–1734).

Who durst depart from Aristotle's rules.
Our author, happy in a judge so nice,
Produced his play, and begged the knight's advice;   *165*
Made him observe the subject and the plot,
The manners, passions, unities; what not?
All which exact to rule were brought about,
Were but a combat in the lists left out.
"What! leave the combat out?" exclaims the knight.   *170*
"Yes, or we must renounce the Stagirite."
"Not so, by Heaven!" he answers in a rage,
"Knights, squires, and steeds must enter on the stage."
"So vast a throng the stage can ne'er contain."
"Then build a new, or act it in a plain."   *175*

    Thus critics of less judgment than caprice,
Curious,° not knowing, not exact, but nice,°   *careful/precise*
Form short ideas, and offend in arts
(As most in manners), by a love to parts.
    Some to conceit° alone their taste confine,   *wit* *180*
And glittering thoughts struck out at every line;
Pleased with a work where nothing's just or fit,
One glaring chaos and wild heap of wit.
Poets, like painters, thus unskilled to trace
The naked nature and the living grace,   *185*
With gold and jewels cover every part,
And hide with ornaments their want of art.
    True wit is Nature to advantage dressed,
What oft was thought, but ne'er so well expressed;
Something whose truth convinced at sight we find,   *190*
That gives us back the image of our mind.
As shades more sweetly recommend the light,
So modest plainness sets off sprightly wit;
For works may have more wit than does them good,
As bodies perish through excess of blood.   *195*
    Others for language all their care express,
And value books, as women men, for dress.
Their praise is still—the style is excellent;
The sense they humbly take upon content.°   *acquiescence*
Words are like leaves; and where they most abound,   *200*
Much fruit of sense beneath is rarely found.
False eloquence, like the prismatic glass,
Its gaudy colors spreads on every place;
The face of Nature we no more survey,
All glares alike, without distinction gay.   *205*

²⁰²**prismatic glass**   A reference to Newton's *Optics,* published in 1704.

But true expression, like the unchanging sun, ⎫
Clears and improves whate'er it shines upon; ⎬
It gilds all objects, but it alters none. ⎭
Expression is the dress of thought, and still
Appears more decent as more suitable.   210
A vile conceit in pompous words expressed
Is like a clown° in regal purple dressed: *a rustic*
For different styles with different subjects sort,
As several garbs with country, town, and court.
Some by old words to fame have made pretense,   215
Ancients in phrase, mere moderns in their sense.
Such labored nothings, in so strange a style,
Amaze the unlearn'd, and make the learned smile;
Unlucky as Fungoso in the play, ⎫
These sparks with awkward vanity display ⎬   220
What the fine gentleman wore yesterday; ⎭
And but so mimic ancient wits at best,
As apes our grandsires in their doublets dressed.
In words as fashions the same rule will hold,
Alike fantastic if too new or old: 225
Be not the first by whom the new are tried,
Nor yet the last to lay the old aside.
    But most by numbers° judge a poet's song,   *poetic meter*
And smooth or rough with them is right or wrong.
In the bright Muse though thousand charms conspire,   230
Her voice is all these tuneful fools admire,
Who haunt Parnassus but to please their ear, ⎫
Not mend their minds; as some to church repair, ⎬
Not for the doctrine, but the music there. ⎭
These equal syllables alone require,   235
Though oft the ear the open vowels tire
While expletives their feeble aid do join,
And ten low words oft creep in one dull line:
While they ring round the same unvaried chimes,
With sure returns of still expected rhymes;   240
Where'er you find "the cooling western breeze,"
In the next line, it "whispers through the trees";
If crystal streams "with pleasing murmurs creep,"
The reader's threatened (not in vain) with "sleep";
Then, at the last and only couplet fraught   245
With some unmeaning thing they call a thought,
A needless Alexandrine ends the song

[219]**Fungoso**   character in a play by Ben Jonson, *Every Man Out of His Humor* (1599).   [247]**Alexandrine**   A line of verse containing six iambic feet. Line 248 is an Alexandrine.

That, like a wounded snake, drags its slow length along.
Leave such to tune their own dull rhymes, and know
What's roundly smooth or languishingly slow;   250
And praise the easy vigor of a line
Where Denham's strength and Waller's sweetness join.
True ease in writing comes from art, not chance,
As those move easiest who have learned to dance.
'Tis not enough no harshness gives offense,   255
The sound must seem an echo to the sense.
Soft is the strain when Zephyr gently blows,
And the smooth stream in smoother numbers flows;
But when loud surges lash the sounding shore,
The hoarse, rough verse should like the torrent roar.   260
When Ajax strives some rock's vast weight to throw,
The line too labors, and the words move slow;
Not so when swift Camilla scours the plain,
Flies o'er the unbending corn, and skims along the main.
Hear how Timotheus' varied lays surprise,   265
And bid alternate passions fall and rise!
While at each change the son of Libyan Jove
Now burns with glory, and then melts with love;
Now his fierce eyes with sparkling fury glow,
Now sighs steal out, and tears begin to flow: 270
Persians and Greeks like turns of nature found
And the world's victor stood subdued by sound!
The power of music all our hearts allow,
And what Timotheus was is Dryden now.
    Avoid extremes; and shun the fault of such   275
Who still are pleased too little or too much.
At every trifle scorn to take offense:
That always shows great pride, or little sense.
Those heads, as stomachs, are not sure the best,
Which nauseate all, and nothing can digest.   280
Yet let not each gay turn thy rapture move;
For fools admire,° but men of sense approve:°   *wonder/judge*
As things seem large which we through mists descry,
Dullness is ever apt to magnify.
    Some foreign writers, some our own despise;   285
The ancients only, or the moderns prize.
Thus wit, like faith, by each man is applied
To one small sect, and all are damned beside.
Meanly they seek the blessing to confine,

---

²⁵²**Denham . . . Waller** Sir John Denham (1615–1669) and Edmund Waller (1606–1687), poets admired by Pope and by John Dryden (1631–1700).   ²⁶⁵**Timotheus**   musician in John Dryden's "Alexander's Feast." ²⁶⁷**Libyan Jove** Alexander the Great

And force that sun but on a part to shine,   *290*
Which not alone the southern wit sublimes,
But ripens spirits in cold northern climes;
Which from the first has shone on ages past,
Enlights the present, and shall warm the last;
Though each may feel increases and decays,   *295*
And see now clearer and now darker days.
Regard not then if wit be old or new,
But blame the false and value still the true.
  Some ne'er advance a judgment of their own,
But catch the spreading notion of the town;   *300*
They reason and conclude by precedent,
And own stale nonsense which they ne'er invent.
Some judge of authors' names, not works, and then
Nor praise nor blame the writings, but the men.
Of all this servile herd the worst is he   *305*
That in proud dullness joins with quality,
A constant critic at the great man's board,
To fetch and carry nonsense for my lord.
What woeful stuff this madrigal would be
In some starved hackney sonneteer or me!   *310*
But let a lord once own the happy lines,
How the wit brightens! how the style refines!
Before his sacred name flies every fault,
And each exalted stanza teems with thought!
  The vulgar thus through imitation err;   *315*
As oft the learn'd by being singular;
So much they scorn the crowd, that if the throng
By chance go right, they purposely go wrong.
So schismatics the plain believers quit,
And are but damned for having too much wit.   *320*
Some praise at morning what they blame at night,
But always think the last opinion right.
A Muse by these is like a mistress used,
This hour she's idolized, the next abused;
While their weak heads like towns unfortified,   *325*
'Twixt sense and nonsense daily change their side.
Ask them the cause; they're wiser still, they say;
And still tomorrow's wiser than today.
We think our fathers fools, so wise we grow;
Our wiser sons, no doubt, will think us so.   *330*
Once school divines this zealous isle o'erspread;
Who knew most sentences was deepest read.

---

[319]**schismatics** those who cause schism, or division, usually within the Roman Catholic church. [331]**divines** Medieval scholastic Theologians.

Faith, Gospel, all seemed made to be disputed,
And none had sense enough to be confuted.
Scotists and Thomists now in peace remain   335
Amidst their kindred cobwebs in Duck Lane.
If faith itself has different dresses worn,
What wonder modes in wit should take their turn?
Oft, leaving what is natural and fit,
The current folly proves the ready wit;   340
And authors think their reputation safe,
Which lives as long as fools are pleased to laugh.

[1711]

The Rape of the Lock
An Heroi-Comical Poem

Nolueram, Belinda, tuos violare capillos;
sed juvat hoc precibus me tribuisse tuis.
—Martial

TO MRS. ARABELLA FERMOR

MADAM,
It will be in vain to deny that I have some regard for this piece, since I dedicate it
to you. Yet you may bear me witness, it was intended only to divert a few young
ladies, who have good sense and good humor enough to laugh not only at their sex's
little unguarded follies, but at their own. But as it was communicated with the air
of a secret, it soon found its way into the world. An imperfect copy having been
offered to a bookseller, you had the good nature for my sake to consent to the
publication of one more correct; this I was forced to, before I had executed half my
design, for the machinery was entirely wanting to complete it.

The machinery, Madam, is a term invented by the critics, to signify that part
which the deities, angels, or demons are made to act in a poem; for the ancient poets
are in one respect like many modern ladies: let an action be never so trivial in itself,
they always make it appear of the utmost importance. These machines I determined
to raise on a very new and odd foundation, the Rosicrucian doctrine of spirits.

I know how disagreeable it is to make use of hard words before a lady; but 'tis
so much the concern of a poet to have his works understood, and particularly by
your sex, that you must give me leave to explain two or three difficult terms.

The Rosicrucians are a people I must bring you acquainted with. The best

AN ESSAY ON CRITICISM   336Duck Lane Street where secondhand books were sold.
THE RAPE OF THE LOCK   Nolueram . . . tuis Latin for "I was unwilling, Belinda, to ravish your locks;
but I rejoice to have conceded this to your prayers."

account I know of them is in a French book called *Le Comte de Gabalis,* which both in its title and size is so like a novel, that many of the fair sex have read it for one by mistake. According to these gentlemen, the four elements are inhabited by spirits, which they call Sylphs, Gnomes, Nymphs, and Salamanders. The Gnomes or Demons of earth delight in mischief; but the Sylphs, whose habitation is in the air, are the best-conditioned creatures imaginable. For they say, any mortals may enjoy the most intimate familiarities with these gentle spirits, upon a condition very easy to all true adepts, an inviolate preservation of chastity.

As to the following cantos, all the passages of them are as fabulous as the vision at the beginning, or the transformation at the end; (except the loss of your hair, which I always mention with reverence). The human persons are as fictitious as the airy ones; and the character of Belinda, as it is now managed, resembles you in nothing but in beauty.

If this poem had as many graces as there are in your person, or in your mind, yet I could never hope it should pass through the world half so uncensured as you have done. But let its fortune be what it will, mine is happy enough, to have given me this occasion of assuring you that I am, with the truest esteem,

MADAM,

Your most obedient, humble servant,

A. POPE

Canto 1

What dire offense from amorous causes springs,
What mighty contests rise from trivial things,
I sing—This verse to Caryll, Muse! is due:
This, even Belinda may vouchsafe to view:
Slight is the subject, but not so the praise,   5
If she inspire, and he approve my lays.
   Say what strange motive, Goddess! could compel
A well-bred lord to assault a gentle belle?
Oh, say what stranger cause, yet unexplored,
Could make a gentle belle reject a lord?   10
In tasks so bold can little men engage,
And in soft bosoms dwells such mighty rage?
   Sol through white curtains shot a timorous ray,
And oped those eyes that must eclipse the day.
Now lapdogs give themselves the rousing shake,   15
And sleepless lovers just at twelve awake:
Thrice rung the bell, the slipper knocked the ground,
And the pressed watch returned a silver sound.
Belinda still her downy pillow pressed,
Her guardian Sylph prolonged the balmy rest: 20
'Twas he had summoned to her silent bed

The morning dream that hovered o'er her head.
A youth more glittering than a birthnight beau
(That even in slumber caused her cheek to glow)
Seemed to her ear his winning lips to lay,   25
And thus in whispers said, or seemed to say:
    "Fairest of mortals, thou distinguished care
Of thousand bright inhabitants of air!
If e'er one vision touched thy infant thought,
Of all the nurse and all the priest have taught,   30
Of airy elves by moonlight shadows seen,
The silver token, and the circled green,
Or virgins visited by angel powers,
With golden crowns and wreaths of heavenly flowers,
Hear and believe! thy own importance know,   35
Nor bound thy narrow views to things below.
Some secret truths, from learned pride concealed,
To maids alone and children are revealed:
What though no credit doubting wits may give?
The fair and innocent shall still believe.   40
Know, then, unnumbered spirits round thee fly,
The light militia of the lower sky:
These, though unseen, are ever on the wing,
Hang o'er the box, and hover round the Ring.
Think what an equipage thou hast in air,   45
And view with scorn two pages and a chair
As now your own, our beings were of old,
And once enclosed in woman's beauteous mold;
Thence, by a soft transition, we repair
From earthly vehicles to these of air.   50
Think not, when woman's transient breath is fled,
That all her vanities at once are dead:
Succeeding vanities she still regards,
And though she plays no more, o'erlooks the cards.
Her joy in gilded chariots, when alive,   55
And love of ombre, after death survive.
For when the Fair in all their pride expire,
To their first elements their souls retire:
The sprites of fiery termagants in flame
Mount up, and take a Salamander's name.   60
Soft yielding minds to water glide away,

---

³¹⁻³²**elves . . . silver token**   It was believed by some that elves skimmed off the cream from jugs of milk left standing overnight, leaving a silver coin as payment.   ⁴⁴**Ring**   fashionable circular drive in Hyde Park, London.   ⁵⁶**ombre**   popular card game.   ⁵⁸**elements**   The four elements—earth, air, fire, and water—which supposedly constituted all things.   ⁶⁰**Salamander's name**   The salamander, a lizardlike creature, is associated with the element of fire in the Rosicrucian mystical system.

And sip, with Nymphs, their elemental tea.
The graver prude sinks downward to a Gnome,
In search of mischief still on earth to roam.
The light coquettes in Sylphs aloft repair,   65
And sport and flutter in the fields of air.
   "Know further yet; whoever fair and chaste
Rejects mankind, is by some Sylph embraced:
For spirits, freed from mortal laws, with ease
Assume what sexes and what shapes they please.   70
What guards the purity of melting maids,
In courtly balls, and midnight masquerades,
Safe from the treacherous friend, the daring spark,
The glance by day, the whisper in the dark,
When kind occasion prompts their warm desires,   75
When music softens, and when dancing fires?
'Tis but their Sylph, the wise Celestials know,
Though Honor is the word with men below.
   "Some nymphs there are, too conscious of their face,
For life predestined to the Gnomes' embrace.   80
These swell their prospects and exalt their pride,
When offers are disdained, and love denied:
Then gay ideas crowd the vacant brain,
While peers, and dukes, and all their sweeping train,
And garters, stars, and coronets appear,   85
And in soft sounds, 'your Grace' salutes their ear.
'Tis these that early taint the female soul,
Instruct the eyes of young coquettes to roll,
Teach infant cheeks a bidden blush to know,
And little hearts to flutter at a beau.   90
   "Oft, when the world imagine women stray,
The Sylphs through mystic mazes guide their way,
Through all the giddy circle they pursue,
And old impertinence° expel by new.   *trifle*
What tender maid but must a victim fall   95
To one man's treat, but for another's ball?
When Florio speaks what virgin could withstand,
If gentle Damon did not squeeze her hand?
With varying vanities, from every part,
They shift the moving toyshop of their heart;   100
Where wigs with wigs, with sword-knots sword-knots strive,
Beaux banish beaux, and coaches coaches drive.
This erring mortals levity may call;
Oh, blind to truth! the Sylphs contrive it all.
   "Of these am I, who thy protection claim,   105
A watchful sprite, and Ariel is my name.

Late, as I ranged the crystal wilds of air,
In the clear mirror of thy ruling star
I saw, alas! some dread event impend,
Ere to the main this morning sun descend,   110
But Heaven reveals not what, or how, or where:
Warned by the Sylph, O pious maid, beware!
This to disclose is all thy guardian can:
Beware of all, but most beware of Man!"
    He said; when Shock, who thought she slept too long,   115
Leaped up, and waked his mistress with his tongue.
'Twas then, Belinda, if report say true,
Thy eyes first opened on a billet-doux;
Wounds, charms, and ardors were no sooner read,
But all the vision vanished from thy head.   120
    And now, unveiled, the toilet stands displayed,
Each silver vase in mystic order laid.
First, robed in white, the nymph intent adores,
With head uncovered, the cosmetic powers.
A heavenly image in the glass° appears;   mirror 125
To that she bends, to that her eyes she rears.
The inferior priestess, at her altar's side,
Trembling begins the sacred rites of Pride.
Unnumbered treasures ope at once, and here
The various offerings of the world appear;   130
From each she nicely culls with curious toil,
And decks the goddess with the glittering spoil.
This casket India's glowing gems unlocks,
And all Arabia breathes from yonder box.
The tortoise here and elephant unite,   135
Transformed to combs, the speckled and the white.
Here files of pins extend their shining rows,
Puffs, powders, patches, Bibles, billet-doux.
Now awful Beauty puts on all its arms;
The fair each moment rises in her charms,   140
Repairs her smiles, awakens every grace,
And calls forth all the wonders of her face;
Sees by degrees a purer blush arise,
And keener lightnings quicken in her eyes.
The busy Sylphs surround their darling care,   145
These set the head, and those divide the hair,
Some fold the sleeve, whilst others plait the gown;
And Betty's praised for labors not her own.

---

[115]**Shock** a longhaired poodle, Belinda's lapdog   [118]**billet-doux** love letter   [148]**Betty** Belinda's maid.

Canto 2

Not with more glories, in the ethereal plain,
The sun first rises o'er the purpled main,
Than, issuing forth, the rival of his beams
Launched on the bosom of the silver Thames.
Fair nymphs and well-dressed youths around her shone,   5
But every eye was fixed on her alone.
On her white breast a sparkling cross she wore,
Which Jews might kiss, and infidels adore.
Her lively looks a sprightly mind disclose,
Quick as her eyes, and as unfixed as those: 10
Favors to none, to all she smiles extends;
Oft she rejects, but never once offends.
Bright as the sun, her eyes the gazers strike,
And, like the sun, they shine on all alike.
Yet graceful ease, and sweetness void of pride,   15
Might hide her faults, if belles had faults to hide:
If to her share some female errors fall,
Look on her face, and you'll forget 'em all.
   This nymph, to the destruction of mankind,
Nourished two locks which graceful hung behind   20
In equal curls, and well conspired to deck
With shining ringlets the smooth ivory neck.
Love in these labyrinths his slaves detains,
And mighty hearts are held in slender chains.
With hairy springes we the birds betray,   25
Slight lines of hair surprise the finny prey,
Fair tresses man's imperial race ensnare,
And beauty draws us with a single hair.
   The adventurous Baron the bright locks admired,
He saw, he wished, and to the prize aspired.   30
Resolved to win, he meditates the way,
By force to ravish, or by fraud betray;
For when success a lover's toil attends,
Few ask if fraud or force attained his ends.
   For this, ere Phoebus° rose, he had implored   *the sun* 35
Propitious Heaven, and every power adored,
But chiefly Love—to Love an altar built,
Of twelve vast French romances, neatly gilt.
There lay three garters, half a pair of gloves,
And all the trophies of his former loves.   40
With tender billet-doux he lights the pyre,
And breathes three amorous sighs to raise the fire.

Then prostrate falls, and begs with ardent eyes
Soon to obtain, and long possess the prize:
The powers gave ear, and granted half his prayer,   45
The rest the winds dispersed in empty air.
    But now secure the painted vessel glides,
The sunbeams trembling on the floating tides,
While melting music steals upon the sky,
And softened sounds along the waters die.   50
Smooth flow the waves, the zephyrs gently play,
Belinda smiled, and all the world was gay.
All but the Sylph—with careful thoughts oppressed,
The impending woe sat heavy on his breast.
He summons straight his denizens of air;   55
The lucid squadrons round the sails repair:
Soft o'er the shrouds aërial whispers breathe
That seemed but zephyrs to the train beneath.
Some to the sun their insect-wings unfold,
Waft on the breeze, or sink in clouds of gold.   60
Transparent forms too fine for mortal sight,
Their fluid bodies half dissolved in light,
Loose to the wind their airy garments flew,
Thin glittering textures of the filmy dew,
Dipped in the richest tincture of the skies,   65
Where light disports in ever-mingling dyes,
While every beam new transient colors flings,
Colors that change whene'er they wave their wings.
Amid the circle, on the gilded mast,
Superior by the head was Ariel placed;   70
His purple pinions opening to the sun,
He raised his azure wand, and thus begun:
    "Ye Sylphs and Sylphids, to your chief give ear!
Fays, Fairies, Genii, Elves, and Daemons, hear!
Ye know the spheres and various tasks assigned   75
By laws eternal to the aërial kind.
Some in the fields of purest ether play,
And bask and whiten in the blaze of day.
Some guide the course of wandering orbs on high,
Or roll the planets through the boundless sky.   80
Some less refined, beneath the moon's pale light
Pursue the stars that shoot athwart the night,
Or suck the mists in grosser air below,
Or dip their pinions in the painted bow,
Or brew fierce tempests on the wintry main,   85
Or o'er the glebe° distill the kindly rain.   *cultivated field*
Others on earth o'er human race preside,

Watch all their ways, and all their actions guide:
Of these the chief the care of nations own,
And guard with arms divine the British Throne.   90
    "Our humbler province is to tend the Fair,
Not a less pleasing, though less glorious care:
To save the powder from too rude a gale,
Nor let the imprisoned essences exhale;
To draw fresh colors from the vernal flowers;   95
To steal from rainbows e'er they drop in showers
A brighter wash°; to curl their waving hairs,   *a cosmetic*
Assist their blushes, and inspire their airs,
Nay oft, in dreams invention we bestow,
To change a flounce, or add a furbelow.   100
    "This day black omens threat the brightest fair,
That e'er deserved a watchful spirit's care;
Some dire disaster, or by force or slight,
But what, or where, the Fates have wrapped in night:
Whether the nymph shall break Diana's law,   105
Or some frail china jar receive a flaw,
Or stain her honor or her new brocade,
Forget her prayers, or miss a masquerade,
Or lose her heart, or necklace, at a ball;
Or whether Heaven has doomed that Shock must fall.   110
Haste, then, ye spirits! to your charge repair:
The fluttering fan be Zephyretta's care;
The drops° to thee, Brillante, we consign;   *diamond earrings*
And, Momentilla, let the watch be thine;
Do thou, Crispissa, tend her favorite Lock;   115
Ariel himself shall be the guard of Shock.
    "To fifty chosen Sylphs, of special note,
We trust the important charge, the petticoat;
Oft have we known that sevenfold fence to fail,
Though stiff with hoops, and armed with ribs of whale.   120
Form a strong line about the silver bound,
And guard the wide circumference around.
    "Whatever spirit, careless of his charge,
His post neglects, or leaves the fair at large,
Shall feel sharp vengeance soon o'ertake his sins,   125
Be stopped in vials, or transfixed with pins,
Or plunged in lakes of bitter washes lie,
Or wedged whole ages in a bodkin's eye;
Gums and pomatums shall his flight restrain,
While clogged he beats his silken wings in vain,   130

---

[105]**Diana** goddess of chastity.   [128]**bodkin** a blunt needle.

Or alum styptics with contracting power
Shrink his thin essence like a riveled° flower: *wrinkled*
Or, as Ixion fixed, the wretch shall feel
The giddy motion of the whirling mill,
In fumes of burning chocolate shall glow,   *135*
And tremble at the sea that froths below!''
    He spoke; the spirits from the sails descend;
Some, orb in orb, around the nymph extend;
Some thread the mazy ringlets of her hair;
Some hang upon the pendants of her ear: *140*
With beating hearts the dire event they wait,
Anxious, and trembling for the birth of Fate.

Canto 3

    Close by those meads, forever crowned with flowers,
Where Thames with pride surveys his rising towers,
There stands a structure of majestic frame,
Which from the neighboring Hampton takes its name.
Here Britain's statesmen oft the fall foredoom   *5*
Of foreign tyrants and of nymphs at home;
Here thou, great Anna! whom three realms obey,
Dost sometimes counsel take—and sometimes tea.
    Hither the heroes and the nymphs resort,
To taste awhile the pleasures of a court;   *10*
In various talk the instructive hours they passed,
Who gave the ball, or paid the visit last;
One speaks the glory of the British Queen,
And one describes a charming Indian screen;
A third interprets motions, looks, and eyes;   *15*
At every word a reputation dies.
Snuff, or the fan, supply each pause of chat,
With singing, laughing, ogling, and all that.
    Meanwhile, declining from the noon of day,
The sun obliquely shoots his burning ray;   *20*
The hungry judges soon the sentence sign,
And wretches hang that jurymen may dine;
The merchant from the Exchange° returns in peace,   *stock market*
And the long labors of the toilet cease.
Belinda now, whom thirst of fame invites,   *25*
Burns to encounter two adventurous knights,
At ombre singly to decide their doom,
And swells her breast with conquests yet to come.

°**Hampton**   Hampton Court, the royal palace about fifteen miles from London.

Straight the three bands prepare in arms to join,
Each band the number of the sacred nine.   30
Soon as she spreads her hand, the aërial guard
Descend, and sit on each important card:
First Ariel perched upon a Matadore,
Then each according to the rank they bore;
For Sylphs, yet mindful of their ancient race,   35
Are, as when women, wondrous fond of place.
    Behold, four Kings in majesty revered,
With hoary whiskers and a forky beard;
And four fair Queens whose hands sustain a flower,
The expressive emblem of their softer power;   40
Four Knaves in garbs succinct, a trusty band,
Caps on their heads, and halberts in their hand;
And parti-colored troops, a shining train,
Draw forth to combat on the velvet plain.
    The skillful nymph reviews her force with care; 45
"Let Spades be trumps!" she said, and trumps they were.
    Now move to war her sable Matadores,
In show like leaders of the swarthy Moors.
Spadillio first, unconquerable lord!
Led off two captive trumps, and swept the board.   50
As many more Manillio forced to yield,
And marched a victor from the verdant field.
Him Basto followed, but his fate more hard
Gained but one trump and one plebeian card.
With his broad saber next, a chief in years,   55
The hoary Majesty of Spades appears,
Puts forth one manly leg, to sight revealed,
The rest his many-colored robe concealed.
The rebel Knave, who dares his prince engage,
Proves the just victim of his royal rage.   60
Even mighty Pam, that kings and queens o'erthrew
And mowed down armies in the fights of loo,
Sad chance of war! now destitute of aid,
Falls undistinguished by the victor Spade.
    Thus far both armies to Belinda yield;   65
Now to the Baron fate inclines the field.
His warlike amazon her host invades,
The imperial consort of the crown of Spades.
The Club's black tyrant first her victim died,
Spite of his haughty mien and barbarous pride.   70
What boots the regal circle on his head,
His giant limbs, in state unwieldy spread?
That long behind he trails his pompous robe,

And of all monarchs only grasps the globe?
    The Baron now his Diamonds pours apace;   *75*
The embroidered King who shows but half his face,
And his refulgent Queen, with powers combined
Of broken troops an easy conquest find.
Clubs, Diamonds, Hearts, in wild disorder seen,
With throngs promiscuous strew the level green.   *80*
Thus when dispersed a routed army runs,
Of Asia's troops, and Afric's sable sons,
With like confusion different nations fly,
Of various habit,° and of various dye,°   *dress/color*
The pierced battalions disunited fall   *85*
In heaps on heaps; one fate o'erwhelms them all.
    The Knave of Diamonds tries his wily arts,
And wins (oh, shameful chance!) the Queen of Hearts.
At this, the blood the virgin's cheek forsook,
A livid paleness spreads o'er all her look;   *90*
She sees, and trembles at the approaching ill,
Just in the jaws of ruin, and Codille,
And now (as oft in some distempered state)
On one nice trick depends the general fate.
An Ace of Hearts steps forth: the King unseen   *95*
Lurked in her hand, and mourned his captive Queen.
He springs to vengeance with an eager pace,
And falls like thunder on the prostrate Ace.
The nymph exulting fills with shouts the sky,
The walls, the woods, and long canals reply.   *100*
    O thoughtless mortals! ever blind to fate,
Too soon dejected, and too soon elate:
Sudden these honors shall be snatched away,
And cursed forever this victorious day.
    For lo! the board with cups and spoons is crowned,   *105*
The berries crackle, and the mill turns round;
On shining altars of Japan° they raise   *lacquer*
The silver lamp; the fiery spirits blaze:
From silver spouts the grateful liquors glide,
While China's earth receives the smoking tide.   *110*
At once they gratify their scent and taste,
And frequent cups prolong the rich repast.
Straight hover round the fair her airy band;
Some, as she sipped, the fuming liquor fanned,
Some o'er her lap their careful plumes displayed,   *115*
Trembling, and conscious of the rich brocade.

---

⁹²**Codille**   a losing hand in cards.

Coffee (which makes the politician wise,
And see through all things with his half-shut eyes)
Sent up in vapors to the Baron's brain
New stratagems, the radiant Lock to gain.   120
Ah, cease, rash youth! desist ere 'tis too late,
Fear the just Gods, and think of Scylla's fate!
Changed to a bird, and sent to flit in air,
She dearly pays for Nisus' injured hair!
    But when to mischief mortals bend their will,   125
How soon they find fit instruments of ill!
Just then, Clarissa drew with tempting grace
A two-edged weapon from her shining case:
So ladies in romance assist their knight,
Present the spear, and arm him for the fight.   130
He takes the gift with reverence, and extends
The little engine on his fingers' ends;
This just behind Belinda's neck he spread,
As o'er the fragrant steams she bends her head.
Swift to the Lock a thousand sprites repair,   135
A thousand wings, by turns, blow back the hair,
And thrice they twitched the diamond in her ear,
Thrice she looked back, and thrice the foe drew near.
Just in that instant, anxious Ariel sought
The close recesses of the virgin's thought;   140
As on the nosegay in her breast reclined,
He watched the ideas rising in her mind,
Sudden he viewed, in spite of all her art,
An earthly lover lurking at her heart.
Amazed, confused, he found his power expired,   145
Resigned to fate, and with a sigh retired.
    The Peer now spreads the glittering forfex° wide,   *scissors*
To enclose the Lock; now joins it, to divide.
Even then, before the fatal engine closed,
A wretched Sylph too fondly interposed;   150
Fate urged the shears, and cut the Sylph in twain
(But airy substance soon unites again):
The meeting points the sacred hair dissever
From the fair head, forever, and forever!
    Then flashed the living lightning from her eyes,   155
And screams of horror rend the affrighted skies.
Not louder shrieks to pitying heaven are cast,
When husbands, or when lapdogs breathe their last;
Or when rich china vessels fallen from high,

---

[122]**Scylla's fate**   Scylla was turned into a sea bird for cutting a lock of her father's hair on which his safety depended.

In glittering dust and painted fragments lie!   160
"Let wreaths of triumph now my temples twine,"
The victor cried, "the glorious prize is mine!
While fish in streams, or birds delight in air,
Or in a coach and six the British Fair,
As long as *Atalantis* shall be read,   165
Or the small pillow grace a lady's bed,
While visits shall be paid on solemn days,
When numerous wax-lights in bright order blaze,
While nymphs take treats, or assignations give,
So long my honor, name, and praise shall live!   170
What Time would spare, from Steel receives its date,°   *termination*
And monuments, like men, submit to fate!
Steel could the labor of the Gods destroy,
And strike to dust the imperial towers of Troy;
Steel could the works of mortal pride confound,   175
And hew triumphal arches to the ground.
What wonder then, fair nymph! thy hairs should feel,
The conquering force of unresisted Steel?"

Canto 4

But anxious cares the pensive nymph oppressed,
And secret passions labored in her breast.
Not youthful kings in battle seized alive,
Not scornful virgins who their charms survive,
Not ardent lovers robbed of all their bliss,   5
Not ancient ladies when refused a kiss,
Not tyrants fierce that unrepenting die,
Not Cynthia when her manteau's° pinned awry,   *negligée*
E'er felt such rage, resentment, and despair,
As thou, sad virgin! for thy ravished hair.   10
    For, that sad moment, when the Sylphs withdrew
And Ariel weeping from Belinda flew,
Umbriel, a dusky, melancholy sprite
As ever sullied the fair face of light,
Down to the central earth, his proper scene,   15
Repaired to search the gloomy Cave of Spleen.
    Swift on his sooty pinions flits the Gnome,
And in a vapor reached the dismal dome.
No cheerful breeze this sullen region knows,
The dreaded east is all the wind that blows.   20
Here in a grotto, sheltered close from air,
And screened in shades from day's detested glare,
She sighs forever on her pensive bed,

Pain at her side, and Megrim° at her head.   *headache*
    Two handmaids wait the throne: alike in place   25
But differing far in figure and in face.
Here stood Ill-Nature like an ancient maid,
Her wrinkled form in black and white arrayed;
With store of prayers for mornings, nights, and noons,
Her hand is filled; her bosom with lampoons.   30
    There Affectation, with a sickly mien,
Shows in her cheek the roses of eighteen,
Practiced to lisp, and hang the head aside,
Faints into airs, and languishes with pride,
On the rich quilt sinks with becoming woe,   35
Wrapped in a gown, for sickness and for show.
The fair ones feel such maladies as these,
When each new nightdress gives a new disease.
    A constant vapor o'er the palace flies,
Strange phantoms rising as the mists arise;   40
Dreadful as hermit's dreams in haunted shades,
Or bright as visions of expiring maids.
Now glaring fiends, and snakes on rolling spires,°   *coils*
Pale specters, gaping tombs, and purple fires;
Now lakes of liquid gold, Elysian scenes,   45
And crystal domes, and angels in machines.
    Unnumbered throngs on every side are seen
Of bodies changed to various forms by Spleen.
Here living teapots stand, one arm held out,
One bent; the handle this, and that the spout: 50
A pipkin° there, like Homer's tripod, walks;   *earthen pot*
Here sighs a jar, and there a goose pie talks;
Men prove with child, as powerful fancy works,
And maids, turned bottles, call aloud for corks.
    Safe passed the Gnome through this fantastic band,   55
A branch of healing spleenwort in his hand.
Then thus addressed the Power: "Hail, wayward Queen!
Who rule the sex to fifty from fifteen:
Parent of vapors and of female wit,
Who give the hysteric or poetic fit,   60
On various tempers act by various ways,
Make some take physic, others scribble plays;
Who cause the proud their visits to delay,
And send the godly in a pet to pray.
A nymph there is that all your power disdains,   65

---

⁴⁶**machines**   mechanical devices employed in theaters for purposes of spectacle.   ⁵⁶**spleenwort**   herb that was
supposed to counter the effects of spleen.

And thousands more in equal mirth maintains.
But oh! if e'er thy Gnome could spoil a grace,
Or raise a pimple on a beauteous face,
Like citron-waters matrons' cheeks inflame,
Or change complexions at a losing game;   *70*
If e'er with airy horns I planted heads,
Or rumpled petticoats, or tumbled beds,
Or caused suspicion when no soul was rude,
Or discomposed the headdress of a prude,
Or e'er to costive lapdog gave disease,   *75*
Which not the tears of brightest eyes could ease,
Hear me, and touch Belinda with chagrin:°   *annoyance*
That single act gives half the world the spleen."
    The Goddess with a discontented air
Seems to reject him though she grants his prayer.   *80*
A wondrous bag with both her hands she binds,
Like that where once Ulysses held the winds;
There she collects the force of female lungs,
Sighs, sobs, and passions, and the war of tongues.
A vial next she fills with fainting fears,   *85*
Soft sorrows, melting griefs, and flowing tears.
The Gnome rejoicing bears her gifts away,
Spreads his black wings, and slowly mounts to day.
    Sunk in Thalestris' arms the nymph he found,
Her eyes dejected and her hair unbound.   *90*
Full o'er their heads the swelling bag he rent,
And all the Furies issued at the vent.
Belinda burns with more than mortal ire,
And fierce Thalestris fans the rising fire.
"O wretched maid!" she spread her hands, and cried   *95*
(While Hampton's echoes, "Wretched maid!" replied),
"Was it for this you took such constant care
The bodkin, comb, and essence to prepare?
For this your locks in paper durance bound,
For this with torturing irons wreathed around?   *100*
For this with fillets strained your tender head,
And bravely bore the double loads of lead?
Gods! shall the ravisher display your hair,
While the fops envy, and the ladies stare!
Honor forbid! at whose unrivaled shrine   *105*

---

⁶⁹**citron-waters** orange brandy.   ⁷¹**horns** symbol of the cuckold, a man whose wife has been sexually unfaithful.   ⁸¹**wondrous bag** The wind god, Aeolus, enabled Odysseus to contain unfavorable winds in a bag. His companions, however, opened the bag, and storms broke loose   ⁸⁹**Thalestris** an Amazon said to have traveled thirty days to conceive a child by Alexander the Great.

Ease, pleasure, virtue, all, our sex resign.
Methinks already I your tears survey,
Already hear the horrid things they say,
Already see you a degraded toast,
And all your honor in a whisper lost!   110
How shall I, then, your helpless fame defend?
'Twill then be infamy to seem your friend!
And shall this prize, the inestimable prize,
Exposed through crystal to the gazing eyes,
And heightened by the diamond's circling rays,   115
On that rapacious hand forever blaze?
Sooner shall grass in Hyde Park Circus grow,
And wits take lodgings in the sound of Bow;
Sooner let earth, air, sea, to chaos fall,
Men, monkeys, lapdogs, parrots, perish all!"   120
   She said; then raging to Sir Plume repairs,
And bids her beau demand the precious hairs
(Sir Plume of amber snuffbox justly vain,
And the nice conduct of a clouded cane),
With earnest eyes, and round unthinking face,   125
He first the snuffbox opened, then the case,
And thus broke out—"My Lord, why, what the devil!
Z———ds! damn the lock! 'fore Gad, you must be civil!
Plague on 't! 'tis past a jest—nay prithee, pox!
Give her the hair"—he spoke, and rapped his box.   130
   "It grieves me much," replied the Peer again,
"Who speaks so well should ever speak in vain.
But by this Lock, this sacred Lock I swear
(Which never more shall join its parted hair;
Which never more its honors shall renew,   135
Clipped from the lovely head where late it grew),
That while my nostrils draw the vital air,
This hand, which won it, shall forever wear."
He spoke, and speaking, in proud triumph spread
The long-contended honors° of her head.   *ornaments*   140
   But Umbriel, hateful Gnome, forebears not so;
He breaks the vial whence the sorrows flow.
Then see! the nymph in beauteous grief appears,
Her eyes half languishing, half drowned in tears;
On her heaved bosom hung her drooping head,   145
Which with a sigh she raised, and thus she said:
   "Forever cursed be this detested day,

---

¹¹⁸**in the sound of Bow**   to live within the sound of the bells of Bowchurch was to live in an unfashionable London district.

Which snatched my best, my favorite curl away!
Happy! ah, ten times happy had I been,
If Hampton Court these eyes had never seen!   *150*
Yet am not I the first mistaken maid,
By love of courts to numerous ills betrayed.
Oh, had I rather unadmired remained
In some lone isle, or distant northern land;
Where the gilt chariot never marks the way,   *155*
Where none learn ombre, none e'er taste bohea°!   *costly tea*
There kept my charms concealed from mortal eye,
Like roses that in deserts bloom and die.
What moved my mind with youthful lords to roam?
Oh, had I stayed, and said my prayers at home!   *160*
'Twas this the morning omens seemed to tell,
Thrice from my trembling hand the patch box fell;
The tottering china shook without a wind,
Nay, Poll sat mute, and Shock was most unkind!
A Sylph too warned me of the threats of fate,   *165*
In mystic visions, now believed too late!
See the poor remnants of these slighted hairs!
My hands shall rend what e'en thy rapine spares.
These in two sable ringlets taught to break,
Once gave new beauties to the snowy neck;   *170*
The sister lock now sits uncouth, alone,
And in its fellow's fate foresees its own;
Uncurled it hangs, the fatal shears demands,
And tempts once more thy sacrilegious hands.
Oh, hadst thou, cruel! been content to seize   *175*
Hairs less in sight, or any hairs but these!''

Canto 5

She said: the pitying audience melt in tears.
But Fate and Jove had stopped the Baron's ears.
In vain Thalestris with reproach assails,
For who can move when fair Belinda fails?
Not half so fixed the Trojan could remain,   *5*
While Anna begged and Dido raged in vain.
Then grave Clarissa graceful waved her fan;
Silence ensued, and thus the nymph began:
   "Say why are beauties praised and honored most,
The wise man's passion, and the vain man's toast?   *10*
Why decked with all that land and sea afford,
Why angels called, and angel-like adored?

---

[162]**patch box**   for ornamental patches to accent the face   [5]**Trojan**   Aeneas, who forsook Queen Dido of
Carthage to fulfill his destiny of founding Rome.

Why round our coaches crowd the white-gloved beaux,
Why bows the side box from its inmost rows?
How vain are all these glories, all our pains,   *15*
Unless good sense preserve what beauty gains;
That men may say when we the front box grace,
'Behold the first in virtue as in face!'
Oh! if to dance all night, and dress all day,
Charmed the smallpox, or chased old age away,   *20*
Who would not scorn what housewife's cares produce,
Or who would learn one earthly thing of use?
To patch, nay ogle, might become a saint,
Nor could it sure be such a sin to paint.
But since, alas! frail beauty must decay,   *25*
Curled or uncurled, since locks will turn to gray;
Since painted, or not painted, all shall fade,
And she who scorns a man must die a maid;
What then remains but well our power to use,
And keep good humor still whate'er we lose?   *30*
And trust me, dear, good humor can prevail
When airs, and flights, and screams, and scolding fail.
Beauties in vain their pretty eyes may roll;
Charms strike the sight, but merit wins the soul."
    So spoke the dame, but no applause ensued;   *35*
Belinda frowned, Thalestris called her prude.
"To arms, to arms!" the fierce virago cries,
And swift as lightning to the combat flies.
All side in parties, and begin the attack;
Fans clap, silks rustle, and tough whalebones crack;   *40*
Heroes' and heroines' shouts confusedly rise,
And bass and treble voices strike the skies.
No common weapons in their hands are found,
Like Gods they fight, nor dread a mortal wound.
    So when bold Homer makes the Gods engage,   *45*
And heavenly breasts with human passions rage;
'Gainst Pallas, Mars; Latona, Hermes arms;
And all Olympus rings with loud alarms:
Jove's thunder roars, heaven trembles all around,
Blue Neptune storms, the bellowing deeps resound: *50*
Earth shakes her nodding towers, the ground gives way,
And the pale ghosts start at the flash of day!
    Triumphant Umbriel on a sconce's height
Clapped his glad wings, and sat to view the fight:
Propped on the bodkin spears, the sprites survey   *55*
The growing combat, or assist the fray.
    While through the press enraged Thalestris flies,
And scatters death around from both her eyes,

A beau and witling perished in the throng,
One died in metaphor, and one in song.   60
"O cruel nymph! a living death I bear,"
Cried Dapperwit, and sunk beside his chair.
A mournful glance Sir Fopling upwards cast,
"Those eyes are made so killing"—was his last.
Thus on Maeander's flowery margin lies   65
The expiring swan, and as he sings he dies.
    When bold Sir Plume had drawn Clarissa down,
Chloe stepped in, and killed him with a frown;
She smiled to see the doughty hero slain,
But, at her smile, the beau revived again.   70
    Now Jove suspends his golden scales in air,
Weighs the men's wits against the lady's hair;
The doubtful beam long nods from side to side;
At length the wits mount up, the hairs subside.
    See, fierce Belinda on the Baron flies,   75
With more than usual lightning in her eyes;
Nor feared the chief the unequal fight to try,
Who sought no more than on his foe to die.
    But this bold lord with manly strength endued,
She with one finger and a thumb subdued: 80
Just where the breath of life his nostrils drew,
A charge of snuff the wily virgin threw;
The Gnomes direct, to every atom just,
The pungent grains of titillating dust.
Sudden, with starting tears each eye o'erflows,   85
And the high dome re-echoes to his nose.
    "Now meet thy fate," incensed Belinda cried,
And drew a deadly bodkin° from her side.   *ornamental pin*
(The same, his ancient personage to deck,
Her great-great-grandsire wore about his neck,   90
In three seal rings; which after, melted down,
Formed a vast buckle for his widow's gown:
Her infant grandame's whistle next it grew,
The bells she jingled, and the whistle blew;
Then in a bodkin graced her mother' hairs,   95
Which long she wore, and now Belinda wears.)
    "Boast not my fall," he cried, "insulting foe!
Thou by some other shalt be laid as low.
Nor think to die dejects my lofty mind:
All that I dread is leaving you behind!   100
Rather than so, ah, let me still survive,
And burn in Cupid's flames—but burn alive."
    "Restore the Lock!" she cries; and all around

"Restore the Lock!" the vaulted roofs rebound.
Not fierce Othello in so loud a strain   105
Roared for the handkerchief that caused his pain.
But see how oft ambitious aims are crossed,
And chiefs contend till all the prize is lost!
The lock, obtained with guilt, and kept with pain,
In every place is sought, but sought in vain: 110
With such a prize no mortal must be blessed,
So Heaven decrees! with Heaven who can contest?
    Some thought it mounted to the lunar sphere,
Since all things lost on earth are treasured there.
There heroes' wits are kept in ponderous vases,   115
And beaux' in snuffboxes and tweezer cases.
There broken vows and deathbed alms are found,
And lovers' hearts with ends of riband bound,
The courtier's promises, and sick man's prayers,
The smiles of harlots, and the tears of heirs,   120
Cages for gnats, and chains to yoke a flea,
Dried butterflies, and tomes of casuistry.
    But trust the Muse—she saw it upward rise,
Though marked by none but quick, poetic eyes
(So Rome's great founder to the heavens withdrew,)   125
To Proculus alone confessed in view);
A sudden star, it shot through liquid air,
And drew behind a radiant trail of hair.
Not Berenice's locks first rose so bright,
The heavens bespangling with disheveled light.   130
The Sylphs behold it kindling as it flies,
And pleased pursue its progress through the skies.
    This the beau monde shall from the Mall survey,
And hail with music its propitious ray.
This the blest lover shall for Venus take,   135
And send up vows from Rosamonda's Lake.
This Partridge soon shall view in cloudless skies,
When next he looks through Galileo's eyes;°   *telescope*
And hence the egregious wizard shall foredoom
The fate of Louis, and the fall of Rome.   140
    Then cease, bright nymph! to mourn thy ravished hair,
Which adds new glory to the shining sphere!

[105-106]**Othello . . . handkerchief** see *Othello*, III, iv.   [125]**Rome's great founder** Romulus, who was borne heavenward in a storm cloud and later deified.   [129]**Berenice's locks** Berenice, wife of the Egyptian astronomer Ptolemy, dedicated locks of her hair to the gods for her husband's safety. The locks were said to have been transformed into a constellation.   [133]**the Mall** a walkway in St. James's Park, in London.   [136]**Rosamonda's Lake** in St. James's Park; associated with unhappy lovers.   [137]**Partridge** John Partridge, an eighteenth-century astrologer.

Not all the tresses that fair head can boast,
Shall draw such envy as the Lock you lost.
For, after all the murders of your eye,   *145*
When, after millions slain, yourself shall die:
When those fair suns shall set, as set they must,
And all those tresses shall be laid in dust,
This Lock the Muse shall consecrate to fame,
And 'midst the stars inscribe Belinda's name.   *150*

[1714]

Epistle to Miss Blount
On Her Leaving the Town, After the Coronation

As some fond virgin, whom her mother's care
Drags from the town to wholesome country air,
Just when she learns to roll a melting eye,
And hear a spark,° yet think no danger nigh;   *a bean*
From the dear man unwilling she must sever,   *5*
Yet takes one kiss before she parts forever:
Thus from the world fair Zephalinda flew,
Saw others happy, and with sighs withdrew;
Not that their pleasures caused her discontent;
She sighed not that they stayed, but that she went.   *10*
  She went to plain-work,° and to purling brooks,   *needlework*
Old-fashioned halls, dull aunts, and croaking rooks:
She went from opera, park, assembly, play,
To morning walks, and prayers three hours a day;
To part her time 'twixt reading and bohea,°   *a costly tea* *15*
To muse, and spill her solitary tea,
Or o'er cold coffee trifle with the spoon,
Count the slow clock, and dine exact at noon;
Divert her eyes with pictures in the fire,
Hum half a tune, tell stories to the squire;   *20*
Up to her godly garret after seven,
There starve and pray, for that's the way to heaven.
  Some squire, perhaps, you take delight to rack,
Whose game is whist, whose treat a toast in sack;
Who visits with a gun, presents you birds,   *25*

EPISTLE TO MISS BLOUNT   Teresa Blount, sister of Pope's friend Martha Blount.   [18]**dine exact at noon**   a sign of rusticity, as the fashionable London dining hour was four.

Then gives a smacking buss, and cries—"No words!"
Or with his hounds comes hollowing from the stable,
Makes love with nods and knees beneath a table;
Whose laughs are hearty, though his jests are coarse,
And loves you best of all things—but his horse.   30
    In some fair evening, on your elbow laid,
You dream of triumphs in the rural shade;
In pensive thought recall the fancied scene,
See coronations rise on every green:
Before you pass the imaginary sights   35
Of lords and earls and dukes and gartered knights,
While the spread fan o'ershades your closing eyes;
Then gives one flirt, and all the vision flies.
Thus vanish scepters, coronets, and balls,
And leave you in lone woods, or empty walls!   40
    So when your slave, at some dear idle time
(Not plagued with headaches or the want of rhyme)
Stands in the streets, abstracted from the crew,
And while he seems to study, thinks of you;
Just when his fancy points° your sprightly eyes,   *notices* 45
Or sees the blush of soft Parthenia rise,
Gay pats my shoulder, and you vanish quite;
Streets, chairs,° and coxcombs° rush upon my sight;   *sedan chairs/dandies*
Vexed to be still in town, I knit my brow,
Look sour, and hum a tune—as you may now.   50

[1717]

from *An Essay on Man*

TO HENRY ST. JOHN, LORD BOLINGBROKE

Epistle 1. Of the Nature and State of Man, With Respect to the Universe

Awake, my St. John! leave all meaner things
To low ambition, and the pride of kings.
Let us (since life can little more supply
Than just to look about us and to die)
Expatiate free o'er all this scene of man;   5
A mighty maze! but not without a plan;
A wild, where weeds and flowers promiscuous shoot,
Or garden, tempting with forbidden fruit.

EPISTLE TO MISS BLOUNT   ⁴⁶**Parthenia** Martha Blount.   ⁴⁷**Gay** Pope's friend John Gay.

Together let us beat this ample field,
Try what the open, what the covert yield;   *10*
The latent tracts, the giddy heights, explore
Of all who blindly creep, or sightless soar;
Eye Nature's walks, shoot folly as it flies,
And catch the manners living as they rise;
Laugh where we must, be candid° where we can;   *kindly* *15*
But vindicate the ways of God to man.

    1. Say first, of God above, or man below,
What can we reason, but from what we know?
Of man, what see we but his station here,
From which to reason, or to which refer?   *20*
Through worlds unnumbered though the God be known,
'Tis ours to trace him only in our own.
He, who through vast immensity can pierce,
See worlds on worlds compose one universe,
Observe how system into system runs,   *25*
What other planets circle other suns,
What varied being peoples every star,
May tell why Heaven has made us as we are.
But of this frame the bearings, and the ties,
The strong connections, nice dependencies,   *30*
Gradations just, has thy pervading soul
Looked through? or can a part contain the whole?
   Is the great chain, that draws all to agree,
And drawn supports, upheld by God, or thee?

    2. Presumptuous man! the reason wouldst thou find,   *35*
Why formed so weak, so little, and so blind?
First, if thou canst, the harder reason guess,
Why formed no weaker, blinder, and no less!
Ask of thy mother earth, why oaks are made
Taller or stronger than the weeds they shade?   *40*
Or ask of yonder argent fields above,
Why Jove's satellites are less than Jove?
   Of systems possible, if 'tis confessed
That Wisdom Infinite must form the best,
Where all must full or not coherent be,   *45*
And all that rises, rise in due degree;
Then, in the scale of reasoning life, 'tis plain,
There must be, somewhere, such a rank as man:
And all the question (wrangle e'er so long)
Is only this, if God has placed him wrong?   *50*
   Respecting man, whatever wrong we call,

May, must be right, as relative to all.
In human works, though labored on with pain,
A thousand movements scarce one purpose gain;
In God's, one single can its end produce; 55
Yet serves to second too some other use.
So man, who here seems principal alone,
Perhaps acts second to some sphere unknown,
Touches some wheel, or verges to some goal;
'Tis but a part we see, and not a whole. 60
    When the proud steed shall know why man restrains
His fiery course, or drives him o'er the plains;
When the dull ox, why now he breaks the clod,
Is now a victim, and now Egypt's god:
Then shall man's pride and dullness comprehend 65
His actions', passions', being's use and end;
Why doing, suffering, checked, impelled; and why
This hour a slave, the next a deity.
    Then say not man's imperfect, Heaven in fault;
Say rather, man's as perfect as he ought; 70
His knowledge measured to his state and place,
His time a moment, and a point his space.
If to be perfect in a certain sphere,
What matter, soon or late, or here or there?
The blest today is as completely so, 75
As who began a thousand years ago.

    3. Heaven from all creatures hides the book of Fate,
All but the page prescribed, their present state:
From brutes what men, from men what spirits know:
Or who could suffer being here below? 80
The lamb thy riot dooms to bleed today,
Had he thy reason, would he skip and play?
Pleased to the last, he crops the flowery food,
And licks the hand just raised to shed his blood.
O blindness to the future! kindly given, 85
That each may fill the circle marked by Heaven:
Who sees with equal eye, as God of all,
A hero perish, or a sparrow fall,
Atoms or systems into ruin hurled,
And now a bubble burst, and now a world. 90
    Hope humbly then; with trembling pinions soar;
Wait the great teacher Death, and God adore!
What future bliss, he gives not thee to know,
But gives that hope to be thy blessing now.
Hope springs eternal in the human breast: 95

Man never is, but always to be blest:
The soul, uneasy and confined from home,
Rests and expatiates in a life to come.
   Lo! the poor Indian, whose untutored mind
Sees God in clouds, or hears him in the wind;   *100*
His soul proud Science never taught to stray
Far as the solar walk, or milky way;
Yet simple Nature to his hope has given,
Behind the cloud-topped hill, an humbler heaven;
Some safer world in depth of woods embraced,   *105*
Some happier island in the watery waste,
Where slaves once more their native land behold,
No fiends torment, no Christians thirst for gold!
To be, contents his natural desire,
He asks no angel's wing, no seraph's fire;   *110*
But thinks, admitted to that equal sky,
His faithful dog shall bear him company.

   4. Go, wiser thou! and, in thy scale of sense,
Weigh thy opinion against Providence;
Call imperfection what thou fancy'st such,   *115*
Say, here he gives too little, there too much;
Destroy all creatures for thy sport or gust,
Yet cry, if man's unhappy, God's unjust;
If man alone engross not Heaven's high care,
Alone made perfect here, immortal there: *120*
Snatch from his hand the balance and the rod,
Rejudge his justice, be the God of God!
In pride, in reasoning pride, our error lies;
All quit their sphere, and rush into the skies.
Pride still is aiming at the blest abodes,   *125*
Men would be angels, angels would be gods.
Aspiring to be gods, if angels fell,
Aspiring to be angels, men rebel:
And who but wishes to invert the laws
Of order, sins against the Eternal Cause.   *130*

   5. Ask for what end the heavenly bodies shine,
Earth for whose use? Pride answers, " 'Tis for mine:
For me kind Nature wakes her genial power,
Suckles each herb, and spreads out every flower;
Annual for me, the grape, the rose renew   *135*
The juice nectareous, and the balmy dew;
For me, the mine a thousand treasures brings;
For me, health gushes from a thousand springs;

Seas roll to waft me, suns to light me rise;
My footstool earth, my canopy the skies." 140
　　But errs not Nature from this gracious end,
From burning suns when livid deaths descend,
When earthquakes swallow, or when tempests sweep
Towns to one grave, whole nations to the deep?
"No," 'tis replied, "the first Almighty Cause 145
Acts not by partial, but by general laws;
The exceptions few; some change since all began,
And what created perfect?"—Why then man?
If the great end be human happiness,
Then Nature deviates; and can man do less? 150
As much that end a constant course requires
Of showers and sunshine, as of man's desires;
As much eternal springs and cloudless skies,
As men forever temperate, calm, and wise.
If plagues or earthquakes break not Heaven's design, 155
Why then a Borgia, or a Catiline?
Who knows but he whose hand the lightning forms,
Who heaves old ocean, and who wings the storms,
Pours fierce ambition in a Caesar's mind,
Or turns young Ammon loose to scourge mankind? 160
From pride, from pride, our very reasoning springs;
Account for moral, as for natural things:
Why charge we Heaven in those, in these acquit?
In both, to reason right is to submit.
　　Better for us, perhaps, it might appear, 165
Were there all harmony, all virtue here;
That never air or ocean felt the wind;
That never passion discomposed the mind:
But ALL subsists by elemental strife;
And passions are the elements of life. 170
The general ORDER, since the whole began,
Is kept in Nature, and is kept in man.

　　6. What would this man? Now upward will he soar,
And little less than angel, would be more;
Now looking downwards, just as grieved appears 175
To want the strength of bulls, the fur of bears.
Made for his use all creatures if he call,
Say what their use, had he the powers of all?

---

[156]**Borgia . . . Catiline**　The Borgias were a notorious Renaissance Italian family both ruthless and powerful. The most famous is Cesare Borgia (c. 1476–1507), son of Pope Alexander VI. Lucius Sergius Catiline (c. 108–62 B.C.) conspired against Rome and was denounced in a famous oration by the Roman orator Cicero.　[160]**Ammon** Alexander the Great.

Nature to these, without profusion, kind,
The proper organs, proper powers assigned;   *180*
Each seeming want compènsated of course,
Here with degrees of swiftness, there of force;
All in exact proportion to the state;
Nothing to add, and nothing to abate.
Each beast, each insect, happy in its own;   *185*
Is Heaven unkind to man, and man alone?
Shall he alone, whom rational we call,
Be pleased with nothing, if not blessed with all?
    The bliss of man (could pride that blessing find)
Is not to act or think beyond mankind;   *190*
No powers of body or of soul to share,
But what his nature and his state can bear.
Why has not man a microscopic eye?
For this plain reason, man is not a fly.
Say what the use, were finer optics given,   *195*
To inspect a mite, not comprehend the heaven?
Or touch, if tremblingly alive all o'er,
To smart and agonize at every pore?
Or quick effluvia darting through the brain,
Die of a rose in aromatic pain?   *200*
If nature thundered in his opening ears,
And stunned him with the music of the spheres,
How would he wish that Heaven had left him still
The whispering zephyr, and the purling rill?
Who finds not Providence all good and wise,   *205*
Alike in what it gives, and what denies?

    7. Far as creation's ample range extends,
The scale of sensual,° mental powers ascends: *sensory*
Mark how it mounts, to man's imperial race,
From the green myriads in the peopled grass: *210*
What modes of sight betwixt each wide extreme,
The mole's dim curtain, and the lynx's beam:
Of smell, the headlong lioness between,
And hound sagacious on the tainted green:
Of hearing, from the life that fills the flood,   *215*
To that which warbles through the vernal wood:
The spider's touch, how exquisitely fine!
Feels at each thread, and lives along the line:
In the nice° bee, what sense so subtly true   *exact*

---

[199]**effluvia . . . brain** According to a seventeenth-century theory, the senses are bombarded by streams of effluvia, tiny images of objects.   [212]**beam** Some theories of vision held that the eye casts a beam of light that enables us to see objects

From poisonous herbs extracts the healing dew: 220
How instinct varies in the groveling swine,
Compared, half-reasoning elephant, with thine!
'Twixt that, and reason, what a nice barrier,
Forever separate, yet forever near!
Remembrance and reflection how allied; 225
What thin partitions sense from thought divide:
And middle natures, how they long to join,
Yet never pass the insuperable line!
Without this just gradation, could they be
Subjected, these to those, or all to thee? 230
The powers of all subdued by thee alone,
Is not thy reason all these powers in one?

    8. See, through this air, this ocean, and this earth,
All matter quick, and bursting into birth.
Above, how high progressive life may go! 235
Around, how wide! how deep extend below!
Vast Chain of Being! which from God began,
Natures ethereal, human, angel, man,
Beast, bird, fish, insect, what no eye can see,
No glass can reach! from Infinite to thee, 240
From thee to nothing.—On superior powers
Were we to press, inferior might on ours:
Or in the full creation leave a void,
Where, one step broken, the great scale's destroyed:
From Nature's chain whatever link you strike, 245
Tenth or ten thousandth, breaks the chain alike.
    And, if each system in gradation roll
Alike essential to the amazing Whole,
The least confusion but in one, not all
That system only, but the Whole must fall. 250
Let earth unbalanced from her orbit fly,
Planets and suns run lawless through the sky,
Let ruling angels from their spheres be hurled,
Being on being wrecked, and world on world,
Heaven's whole foundations to their center nod, 255
And Nature tremble to the throne of God:
All this dread ORDER break—for whom? for thee?
Vile worm!—oh, madness, pride, impiety!

    9. What if the foot, ordained the dust to tread,
Or hand, to toil, aspired to be the head? 260
What if the head, the eye, or ear repined
To serve mere engines to the ruling Mind?
Just as absurd, to mourn the tasks or pains,

The great directing MIND OF ALL ordains.
    All are but parts of one stupendous whole,   265
Whose body Nature is, and God the soul;
That, changed through all, and yet in all the same,
Great in the earth, as in the ethereal frame,
Warms in the sun, refreshes in the breeze,
Glows in the stars, and blossoms in the trees,   270
Lives through all life, extends through all extent,
Spreads undivided, operates unspent,
Breathes in our soul, informs our mortal part,
As full, as perfect, in a hair as heart;
As full, as perfect, in vile man that mourns,   275
As the rapt seraph that adores and burns;
To him no high, no low, no great, no small;
He fills, he bounds, connects, and equals all.

    10. Cease then, nor ORDER imperfection name:
Our proper bliss depends on what we blame.   280
Know thy own point: this kind, this due degree
Of blindness, weakness, Heaven bestows on thee.
Submit—In this, or any other sphere,
Secure to be as blest as thou canst bear:
Safe in the hand of one disposing Power,   285
Or in the natal, or the mortal hour.
All Nature is but art, unknown to thee;
All chance, direction, which thou canst not see;
All discord, harmony not understood;
All partial evil, universal good: 290
And, spite of pride, in erring reason's spite,
One truth is clear: Whatever IS, is RIGHT.

                                 [1733]

THOMAS GRAY

[1716–1771]

Elegy Written in a Country Churchyard

The curfew tolls the knell of parting day,
    The lowing herd wind slowly o'er the lea,
The plowman homeward plods his weary way,
    And leaves the world to darkness and to me.

Now fades the glimmering landscape on the sight,   *5*
    And all the air a solemn stillness holds,
Save where the beetle wheels his droning flight,
    And drowsy tinklings lull the distant folds;

Save that from yonder ivy-mantled tower
    The moping owl does to the moon complain   *10*
Of such, as wandering near her secret bower,
    Molest her ancient solitary reign.

Beneath those rugged elms, that yew tree's shade,
    Where heaves the turf in many a moldering heap,
Each in his narrow cell forever laid,   *15*
    The rude° forefathers of the hamlet sleep.   *rustic*

The breezy call of incense-breathing morn,
    The swallow twittering from the straw-built shed,
The cock's shrill clarion, or the echoing horn,°   *hunter's horn*
    No more shall rouse them from their lowly bed.   *20*

For them no more the blazing hearth shall burn,
    Or busy housewife ply her evening care;
No children run to lisp their sire's return,
    Or climb his knees the envied kiss to share.

Oft did the harvest to their sickle yield,   *25*
    Their furrow oft the stubborn glebe° has broke;   *soil*
How jocund did they drive their team afield!
    How bowed the woods beneath their sturdy stroke!

Let not Ambition mock their useful toil,
    Their homely joys, and destiny obscure;   *30*
Nor Grandeur hear with a disdainful smile
    The short and simple annals of the poor.

The boast of heraldry, the pomp of power,
    And all that beauty, all that wealth e'er gave,
Awaits alike the inevitable hour.   *35*
    The paths of glory lead but to the grave.

Nor you, ye proud, impute to these the fault,
    If Memory o'er their tomb no trophies raise,
Where through the long-drawn aisle and fretted° vault   *ornamented*
    The pealing anthem swells the note of praise.   *40*

Can storied urn or animated° bust   *lifelike*
    Back to its mansion call the fleeting breath?
Can Honor's voice provoke° the silent dust,   *call forth*
    Or Flattery soothe the dull cold ear of Death?

Perhaps in this neglected spot is laid   *45*
    Some heart once pregnant with celestial fire;
Hands that the rod of empire might have swayed,
    Or waked to ecstasy the living lyre.

But Knowledge to their eyes her ample page
    Rich with the spoils of time did ne'er unroll;   *50*
Chill Penury repressed their noble rage,°   *ardor*
    And froze the genial current of the soul.

Full many a gem of purest ray serene,
    The dark unfathomed caves of ocean bear:
Full many a flower is born to blush unseen,   *55*
    And waste its sweetness on the desert air.

Some village Hampden, that with dauntless breast
    The little tyrant of his fields withstood;
Some mute inglorious Milton here may rest,
    Some Cromwell guiltless of his country's blood.   *60*

The applause of listening senates to command,
    The threats of pain and ruin to despise,
To scatter plenty o'er a smiling land,
    And read their history in a nation's eyes,

Their lot forbade: nor circumscribed alone   *65*
    Their growing virtues, but their crimes confined;
Forbade to wade through slaughter to a throne,
    And shut the gates of mercy on mankind,

The struggling pangs of conscious truth to hide,
    To quench the blushes of ingenuous shame,   *70*
Or heap the shrine of Luxury and Pride
    With incense kindled at the Muse's flame.

Far from the madding° crowd's ignoble strife,   *milling*
    Their sober wishes never learned to stray;

---

[41]**storied urn**   an urn giving a person's history in a descriptive epitaph.   [57]**Hampden**   John Hampden expressed opposition to a tax levied by Charles I, one of the events leading to civil war.

Along the cool sequestered vale of life   75
    They kept the noiseless tenor of their way.

Yet even these bones from insult to protect
    Some frail memorial still erected nigh,
With uncouth rhymes and shapeless sculpture decked,
    Implores the passing tribute of a sigh.   80

Their name, their years, spelt by the unlettered Muse,
    The place of fame and elegy supply:
And many a holy text around she strews,
    That teach the rustic moralist to die.

For who to dumb Forgetfulness a prey,   85
    This pleasing anxious being e'er resigned,
Left the warm precincts of the cheerful day,
    Nor cast one longing lingering look behind?

On some fond breast the parting soul relies,
    Some pious drops the closing eye requires;   90
Even from the tomb the voice of Nature cries,
    Even in our ashes live their wonted fires.

For thee, who mindful of the unhonored dead
    Cost in these lines their artless tale relate;
If chance, by lonely contemplation led,   95
    Some kindred spirit shall inquire thy fate,

Haply some hoary-headed swain may say,
    "Oft have we seen him at the peep of dawn
Brushing with hasty steps the dews away
    To meet the sun upon the upland lawn.   100

"There at the foot of yonder nodding beech
    That wreathes its old fantastic roots so high,
His listless length at noontide would he stretch,
    And pore upon the brook that babbles by.

"Hard by yon wood, now smiling as in scorn,   105
    Muttering his wayward fancies he would rove,
Now drooping, woeful wan, like one forlorn,
    Or crazed with care, or crossed in hopeless love.

"One morn I missed him on the customed hill,
    Along the heath and near his favorite tree;   110

Another came; nor yet beside the rill,
    Nor up the lawn, nor at the wood was he;

"The next with dirges due in sad array
    Slow through the churchway path we saw him borne.
Approach and read (for thou canst read) the lay,   115
    Graved on the stone beneath yon aged thorn."

The Epitaph

Here rests his head upon the lap of Earth
    A youth to Fortune and to Fame unknown.
Fair Science° frowned not on his humble birth,   learning
    And Melancholy marked him for her own.   120

Large was his bounty, and his soul sincere,
    Heaven did a recompense as largely send:
He gave to Misery all he had, a tear,
    He gained from Heaven ('twas all he wished) a friend.

No farther seek his merits to disclose,   125
    Or draw his frailties from their dread abode
(There they alike in trembling hope repose),
    The bosom of his Father and his God.

[1751]

OLIVER GOLDSMITH

[1730–1774]

When lovely woman stoops to folly

When lovely woman stoops to folly,
    And finds too late that men betray,
What charm can soothe her melancholy,
    What art can wash her guilt away?

The only art her guilt to cover,   5
    To hide her shame from every eye,
To give repentance to her lover,
    And wring his bosom—is to die.

[1766]

WILLIAM BLAKE

[1757–1827]

Dismissed as mad by his contemporaries, William Blake has endured the partiality of an age, for he is now considered, as Coleridge once privately acknowledged, "a man of Genius." A major poet and one of England's finest visual artists, Blake saw himself as both a religious and a social prophet. He wrote, "One power alone makes a poet: Imagination, the Divine Vision." Questioning every accepted artistic value of the period, he prefaced the great rebellion against neoclassicism and against poets who "knew enough of artifice, but little of art."

Because Blake saw himself as a prophet, he drew heavily on both the Hebrew and the Christian Bible. Nevertheless, it would be misleading to call Blake a Christian in any orthodox sense of the word. For example, if we look at his "The Everlasting Gospel," he states:

> The Vision of Christ that thou dost see
> Is my Vision's Greatest Enemy: . . .

> Thine is the friend of all Mankind,
> Mine speaks in parables to the Blind:
> Thine loves the same world that mine hates,
> Thy Heaven doors are my Hell gates.

As a prophet, Blake was more interested in proving the ways of man to man than in demonstrating the ways of the Deity. To restate this without religious overtones, he was, as T. S. Eliot writes, "a man with a profound interest in human emotions, and a profound knowledge of them."

Without a sense of the underlying design of Blake's poetry, however, we might easily perceive him as the most simple of lyric poets or as an artist of hermetic impenetrability. At the core, Blake frames two contrary archetypal states of the human soul: innocence and experience. Humanity's vicissitudes between these states are the focus of nearly all his poetry.

The first tendency of human nature Blake projects might best be suggested by "The Lamb," taken from his *Songs of Innocence*. With its nursery-rhyme qualities and simple rhythms, the poem implies a child's perception of God and world and humanity as one harmonious configuration.

> For he calls himself a Lamb:
> He is meek & he is mild.
> He became a little child:
> I a child & thou a lamb,
> We are calléd by his name.
>   Little Lamb God bless thee.

This seems direct enough, but Blake uses irony to great effect: despite the poem's Edenic echoes, we should remember that the adult world would also perceive the lamb as commodities—mutton and wool. As is often the case with Blake, innocence implies its opposite, experience, as surely as the "Lamb" (or Christ) implies the crucifixion.

Conversely, the second state Blake points to, experience, as indicated by the "The Tyger" in *Songs of Experience,* appears to reflect only the terrifying cataclysms of Genesis unleashed as fire and flood.

> Tyger! Tyger! burning bright
> In the forests of the night,
> What immortal hand or eye
> Could frame thy fearful symmetry?

However, as innocence implies experience, so experience implies *its* polar opposite. True, the tiger terrifies, but as Blake comments, its "Passion & Expression is Beauty Itself." According to Blake, "Everything that lives is holy." Our failure to see either the lamb or the tiger clearly is a failure of imagination. Blake would have us fashion a creative whole out of the tiger and lamb both, for "All deities reside in the human breast."

Because Blake saw himself as prophet as well as poet, he stressed that innocence and experience are psychological states that also carry political implications. For example, in "The Chimney Sweeper" in *Songs of Innocence,* we encounter a young boy who rationalizes his misery and naively declares that "if all do their duty, they need not fear harm." Historically, nothing could have been further from the truth. Young "sweeps" who dutifully accepted forced labor rarely lived to reach adulthood. Master chimney sweepers found these children (some as young as four years old) perfectly suited to climb up chimneys and scour them. Reluctant sweeps were often prodded and poked with rods and pins as they climbed, naked, up chimneys below which fires were still burning. Young sweeps who did not die trapped in these "coffins of black" died of lung ailments and related diseases. Those who survived were social outcasts, forbidden even to attend church. Because the sweep is innocent, the irony of his final pronouncement escapes the young boy as he confronts the horrors of the Industrial Revolution.

In *Songs of Experience,* however, we face another chimney sweep who has also been taught "to sing the notes of woe," but who has something of the tiger about him. He knows who has "clothed" him in the "clothes of death"—his parents and ". . . God & his Priest & King, / Who make up a heaven of our misery." Here Blake, as prophet, directly attacks the "dark Satanic Mills" of industry. And yet even as the sweep stands in the harsh snow of experience, we can see the traces of innocence that allow him to preserve enough of himself to "dance & sing" despite neglect and cruelty.

Himself a product of the industrial slums, William Blake was born in poverty on November 28, 1757. Unable to attend school, he taught himself by reading widely and studying engravings from paintings by such Renaissance masters as

Raphael, Dürer, and Michelangelo. Samuel Palmer remembers how Blake "saw everything through art, finding sources of delight throughout the whole range of art." At age twenty-two Blake entered the Royal Academy as an engraving student, but unsettling clashes over artistic differences returned him to a life of nonconformist study. A ferocious supporter of the American and French revolutions, he moved in a circle of radical thinkers including William Godwin, Thomas Paine, Joseph Priestley, and Mary Wollstonecraft Shelley. In 1780 he joined in the Gordon Riots and the burning of Newgate Prison.

On August 18, 1782, Blake married Catherine Boucher, an illiterate daughter of a Battersea market gardener, and taught her to read and write. She in turn helped him with his engravings. He had begun integrating images expressly created for each poem with the text. In doing so he invented a special technique of relief etching he termed "illuminated painting." Each page was printed in monochrome from an engraved plate incorporating both text and illustration. In these books word and image combine in rhythmic contours to fashion a creative and harmonic whole. Blake or Catherine then colored the pages by hand and bound them in paper covers.

Because Blake insisted his "great task" as poet was to "open the Eternal Worlds, to open the immortal Eyes of Man inwards into the Worlds of Thought," he stressed a poetry of revelation, not technique. It is therefore easy to overlook Blake's skill as a poet. Discarding the heroic couplet, he reexamined and reintroduced Elizabethan biblical cadences. Also, in searching for new ways to use old forms, Blake experimented with free verse, the free septenary, and unrhymed trimeter. But it was his ability to see beyond the physical, what he called his "double vision," that fueled Blake's poetic imagination. As W. H. Auden wrote in "New Year Letter,"

Self-educated Blake . . .
Spoke to Isaiah in the Strand
And heard inside each mortal thing
Its holy emanation sing.

Throughout his life, Blake continued to make a meager living on commissions for designs and engravings, as a printer, or under the patronage of his few admirers. Ironically, he spent his last years engraving a series of illustrations for the Book of Job. Blake died at age sixty-nine literally singing heaven's praises and was buried in Bunhill Fields, the dissenters' cemetery.

The Ecchoing Green

The Sun does arise,
And make happy the skies.
The merry bells ring

To welcome the Spring.
The sky-lark and thrush,   5
The birds of the bush,
Sing louder around,
To the bells chearful sound.
While our sports shall be seen
On the Ecchoing Green.   10

Old John with white hair
Does laugh away care,
Sitting under the oak,
Among the old folk,
They laugh at our play,   15
And soon they all say.
Such such were the joys.
When we all girls & boys,
In our youth-time were seen,
On the Ecchoing Green.   20

Till the little ones weary
No more can be merry
The sun does descend,
And our sports have an end:
Round the laps of their mothers,   25
Many sisters and brothers,
Like birds in their nest,
Are ready for rest;
And sport no more seen,
On the darkening Green.   30

[1789]

The Lamb

Little Lamb, who made thee?
  Dost thou know who made thee?
Gave thee life & bid thee feed,
By the stream & o'er the mead;
Gave thee clothing of delight,   5
Softest clothing wooly bright;
Gave thee such a tender voice,
Making all the vales rejoice!

Little Lamb who made thee?
Dost thou know who made thee? 10

  Little Lamb I'll tell thee,
  Little Lamb I'll tell thee!
He is calléd by thy name,
For he calls himself a Lamb:
He is meek & he is mild, 15
He became a little child:
I a child & thou a lamb,
We are calléd by his name.
  Little Lamb God bless thee.
  Little Lamb God bless thee. 20

[1789]

The Chimney Sweeper (Innocence)

When my mother died I was very young,
And my father sold me while yet my tongue,
Could scarcely cry " 'weep! 'weep! 'weep! 'weep!"
So your chimneys I sweep & in soot I sleep.

There's little Tom Dacre, who cried when his head 5
That curl'd like a lamb's back, was shav'd, so I said.
"Hush Tom never mind it, for when your head's bare,
You know that the soot cannot spoil your white hair."

And so he was quiet, & that very night,
As Tom was a-sleeping he had such a sight, 10
That thousands of sweepers Dick, Joe, Ned & Jack,
Were all of them lock'd up in coffins of black;

And by came an Angel who had a bright key,
And he open'd the coffins & set them all free;
Then down a green plain leaping laughing they run, 15
And wash in a river and shine in the Sun.

Then naked & white, all their bags left behind,
They rise upon clouds, and sport in the wind.
And the Angel told Tom if he'd be a good boy,
He'd have God for his father & never want joy. 20

And so Tom awoke and we rose in the dark
And got with our bags & our brushes to work.
Tho' the morning was cold, Tom was happy & warm;
So if all do their duty, they need not fear harm.

[1789]

The Chimney Sweeper (Experience)

A little black thing among the snow:
Crying " 'weep, 'weep," in notes of woe!
"Where are thy father & mother? say?"
"They are both gone up to the church to pray.

"Because I was happy upon the heath,   5
And smil'd among the winter's snow:
They clothed me in the clothes of death,
And taught me to sing the notes of woe.

"And because I am happy, & dance & sing,
They think they have done me no injury: 10
And are gone to praise God & his Priest & King
Who make up a heaven of our misery."

[1794]

The Tyger

Tyger! Tyger! burning bright
In the forests of the night,
What immortal hand or eye
Could frame thy fearful symmetry?

In what distant deeps or skies   5
Burnt the fire of thine eyes?
On what wings dare he aspire?
What the hand, dare seize the fire?

And what shoulder, & what art,
Could twist the sinews of thy heart?   10
And when thy heart began to beat,
What dread hand? & what dread feet?

What the hammer? what the chain?
In what furnace was thy brain?
What the anvil? what dread grasp   *15*
Dare its deadly terrors clasp?

When the stars threw down their spears,
And water'd heaven with their tears,
Did he smile his work to see?
Did he who made the Lamb make thee?   *20*

Tyger! Tyger! burning bright
In the forests of the night,
What immortal hand or eye
Dare frame thy fearful symmetry?

                                                        [1794]

The Clod & the Pebble

"Love seeketh not Itself to please,
Nor for itself hath any care;
But for another gives its ease,
And builds a Heaven in Hell's despair."

    So sang a little Clod of Clay,   *5*
    Trodden with the cattle's feet;
    But a Pebble of the brook,
    Warbled out these metres meet:

"Love seeketh only Self to please,
To bind another to its delight,   *10*
Joys in another's loss of ease,
And builds a Hell in Heaven's despite."

                                                        [1794]

The Garden of Love

I went to the Garden of Love,
And saw what I never had seen:
A Chapel was built in the midst,
Where I used to play on the green.

And the gates of this Chapel were shut,   5
And "Thou shalt not" writ over the door;
So I turn'd to the Garden of Love,
That so many sweet flowers bore,

And I saw it was filled with graves,
And tomb-stones where flowers should be: 10
And Priests in black gowns were walking their rounds,
And binding with briars my joys & desires.

[1794]

A Poison Tree

I was angry with my friend:
I told my wrath, my wrath did end.
I was angry with my foe:
I told it not, my wrath did grow.

And I water'd it in fears,   5
Night & morning with my tears;
And I sunnéd it with smiles,
And with soft deceitful wiles.

And it grew both day and night,
Till it bore an apple bright.   10
And my foe beheld it shine,
And he knew that it was mine,

And into my garden stole,
When the night had veil'd the pole;
In the morning glad I see   15
My foe outstretch'd beneath the tree.

[1794]

London

I wander thro' each charter'd street,
Near where the charter'd Thames does flow,
And mark in every face I meet
Marks of weakness, marks of woe.

In every cry of every Man,   5
In every Infant's cry of fear,
In every voice, in every ban,
The mind-forg'd manacles I hear.

How the Chimney-sweeper's cry
Every black'ning Church appalls;   10
And the hapless Soldier's sigh
Runs in blood down Palace walls.

But most thro' midnight streets I hear
How the youthful Harlot's curse
Blasts the new born Infant's tear,   15
And blights with plagues the Marriage hearse.

[1794]

from *The Marriage of Heaven and Hell*
Proverbs of Hell

In seed time learn, in harvest teach, in winter enjoy.
Drive your cart and your plow over the bones of the dead.
The road of excess leads to the palace of wisdom.
Prudence is a rich ugly old maid courted by Incapacity.
He who desires but acts not, breeds pestilence.   5
The cut worm forgives the plow.
Dip him in the river who loves water.
A fool sees not the same tree that a wise man sees.
He whose face gives no light, shall never become a star.
Eternity is in love with the productions of time.   10
The busy bee has no time for sorrow.
The hours of folly are measur'd by the clock; but of wisdom,
    no clock can measure.
All wholsom food is caught without a net or a trap.
Bring out number, weight, & measure in a year of dearth.
No bird soars too high, if he soars with his own wings. 15
A dead body revenges not injuries.
The most sublime act is to set another before you.
If the fool would persist in his folly he would become wise.

Folly is the cloke of knavery.
Shame is Pride's cloke.   *20*

Prisons are built with stones of Law, Brothels with bricks of Religion.
The pride of the peacock is the glory of God.
The lust of the goat is the bounty of God.
The wrath of the lion is the wisdom of God.
The nakedness of woman is the work of God.   *25*
Excess of sorrow laughs. Excess of joy weeps.
The roaring of lions, the howling of wolves, the raging of the stormy sea, and the
    destructive sword, are portions of eternity too great for the eye of man.
The fox condemns the trap, not himself.
Joys impregnate. Sorrows bring forth.
Let man wear the fell of the lion, woman the fleece of the sheep.   *30*
The bird a nest, the spider a web, man friendship.
The selfish smiling fool & the sullen frowning fool shall be both thought wise,
    that they may be a rod.
What is now proved was once only imagin'd.
The rat, the mouse, the fox, the rabbit watch the roots; the lion, the tyger,
    the horse, the elephant, watch the fruits.
The cistern contains; the fountain overflows.   *35*
One thought fills immensity.
Always be ready to speak your mind, and a base man will avoid you.
Every thing possible to be believ'd is an image of truth.
The eagle never lost so much time as when he submitted to learn of the crow.

The fox provides for himself, but God provides for the lion.   *40*
Think in the morning, Act in the noon, Eat in the evening, Sleep in the night.
He who has sufferd you to impose on him knows you.
As the plow follows words, so God rewards prayers.
The tygers of wrath are wiser than the horses of instruction.
Expect poison from the standing water.   *45*
You never know what is enough unless you know what is more than enough.
Listen to the fool's reproach! it is a kingly title!
The eyes of fire, the nostrils of air, the mouth of water, the beard of earth.
The weak in courage is strong in cunning.
The apple tree never asks the beech how he shall grow, nor the lion the horse,
    how he shall take his prey.   *50*
The thankful reciever bears a plentiful harvest.
If others had not been foolish, we should be so.
The soul of sweet delight can never be defil'd.
When thou seest an Eagle, thou seest a portion of Genius; lift up thy head!
As the catterpiller chooses the fairest leaves to lay her eggs on, so the priest
    lays his curse on the fairest joys.   *55*

To create a little flower is the labour of ages.
Damn braces; Bless relaxes.
The best wine is the oldest, the best water the newest.
Prayers plow not! Praises reap not!
Joys laugh not! Sorrows weep not!   60

The head Sublime, the heart Pathos, the genitals Beauty,
   the hands & feet Proportion.
As the air to a bird or the sea to a fish, so is contempt to the contemptible.
The crow wish'd every thing was black, the owl that every thing was white.
Exuberance is Beauty.
If the lion was advised by the fox, he would be cunning.   65
Improvement makes strait roads, but the crooked roads without Improvement
   are roads of Genius.
Sooner murder an infant in its cradle than nurse unacted desires.
Where man is not, nature is barren.
Truth can never be told so as to be understood, and not be believ'd.
        Enough! or Too much.   70

                             [1790–1793]

from *Milton: And did those feet*

    And did those feet in ancient time
    Walk upon England's mountains green?
    And was the holy Lamb of God
    On England's pleasant pastures seen?

    And did the Countenance Divine   5
    Shine forth upon our clouded hills?
    And was Jerusalem builded here,
    Among these dark Satanic Mills?

    Bring me my Bow of burning gold:
    Bring me my Arrows of desire: 10
    Bring me my Spear: O clouds unfold!
    Bring me my Chariot of fire!

I will not cease from Mental Fight,
Nor shall my Sword sleep in my hand,
Till we have built Jerusalem   *15*
In England's green & pleasant Land.

[1804–1810]

Auguries of Innocence

To see a World in a Grain of Sand
And a Heaven in a Wild Flower
Hold Infinity in the palm of your hand
And Eternity in an hour
A Robin Red breast in a Cage   *5*
Puts all Heaven in a Rage
A dove house filld with doves & Pigeons
Shudders Hell thro all its regions
A dog starvd at his Masters Gate
Predicts the ruin of the State   *10*
A Horse misusd upon the Road
Calls to Heaven for Human blood
Each outcry of the hunted Hare
A fibre from the Brain does tear
A Skylark wounded in the wing   *15*
A Cherubim does cease to sing
The Game Cock clipd & armd for fight
Does the Rising Sun affright
Every Wolfs & Lions howl
Raises from Hell a Human Soul   *20*
The wild deer wandring here & there
Keeps the Human Soul from Care
The Lamb misusd breeds Public strife
And yet forgives the Butchers Knife
The Bat that flits at close of Eve   *25*
Has left the Brain that wont Believe
The Owl that calls upon the Night
Speaks the Unbelievers fright
He who shall hurt the little Wren
Shall never be belovd by Men   *30*
He who the Ox to wrath has movd
Shall never be by Woman lovd
The wanton Boy that kills the Fly

Shall feel the Spiders enmity
He who torments the Chafers sprite   35
Weaves a Bower in endless Night
The Catterpiller on the Leaf
Repeats to thee thy Mothers grief
Kill not the Moth nor Butterfly
For the Last Judgment draweth nigh   40
He who shall train the Horse to War
Shall never pass the Polar Bar
The Beggers Dog & Widows Cat
Feed them & thou wilt grow fat
The Gnat that sings his Summers song   45
Poison gets from Slanders tongue
The poison of the Snake & Newt
Is the sweat of Envys Foot
The Poison of the Honey Bee
Is the Artists Jealousy   50
The Princes Robes & Beggars Rags
Are Toadstools on the Misers Bags
A truth thats told with bad intent
Beats all the Lies you can invent
It is right it should be so   55
Man was made for Joy & Woe
And when this we rightly know
Thro the World we safely go
Joy & Woe are woven fine
A Clothing for the Soul divine   60
Under every grief & pine
Runs a joy with silken twine
The Babe is more than swadling Bands
Throughout all these Human Lands
Tools were made & Born were hands   65
Every Farmer Understands
Every Tear from Every Eye
Becomes a Babe in Eternity
This is caught by Females bright
And returnd to its own delight   70
The Bleat the Bark Bellow & Roar
Are Waves that Beat on Heavens Shore
The Babe that weeps the Rod beneath
Writes Revenge in realms of death
The Beggars Rags fluttering in Air   75
Does to Rags the Heavens tear
The Soldier armd with Sword & Gun

Palsied strikes the Summers Sun
The poor Mans Farthing is worth more
Than all the Gold on Africs Shore   *80*
One Mite wrung from the Labrers hands
Shall buy & sell the Misers Lands
Or if protected from on high
Does that whole Nation sell & buy
He who mocks the Infants Faith   *85*
Shall be mock'd in Age & Death
He who shall teach the Child to Doubt
The rotting Grave shall neer get out
He who respects the Infants faith
Triumphs over Hell & Death   *90*
The Childs Toys & the Old Mans Reasons
Are the Fruits of the Two seasons
The Questioner who sits so sly
Shall never know how to Reply
He who replies to words of Doubt   *95*
Doth put the Light of Knowledge out
The Strongest Poison ever known
Came from Caesars Laurel Crown
Nought can deform the Human Race
Like to the Armours iron brace   *100*
When Gold & Gems adorn the Plow
To peaceful Arts shall Envy Bow
A Riddle or the Crickets Cry
Is to Doubt a fit Reply
The Emmets Inch & Eagles Mile   *105*
Make Lame Philosophy to smile
He who Doubts from what he sees
Will neer Believe do what you Please
If the Sun & Moon should doubt
Theyd immediately Go out   *110*
To be in a Passion you Good may do
But no Good if a Passion is in you
The Whore & Gambler by the State
Licencd build that Nations Fate
The Harlots cry from Street to Street   *115*
Shall weave Old Englands winding Sheet
The Winners Shout the Losers Curse
Dance before dead Englands Hearse
Every Night & every Morn
Some to Misery are Born   *120*
Every Morn & every Night

Some are Born to sweet delight
Some are Born to sweet delight
Some are Born to Endless Night
We are led to Believe a Lie   *125*
When we see not Thro the Eye
Which was Born in a Night to perish in a Night
When the Soul Slept in Beams of Light
God Appears & God is Light
To those poor Souls who dwell in Night   *130*
But does a Human Form Display
To those who Dwell in Realms of day

[1803]

ROBERT BURNS

[1759–1796]

A Red, Red Rose

O my luve's like a red, red rose,
    That's newly sprung in June;
O my luve's like the melodie
    That's sweetly played in tune.

As fair art thou, my bonnie lass,   *5*
    So deep in luve am I;
And I will luve thee still, my dear,
    Till a' the seas gang° dry.   *go*

Till a' the seas gang dry, my dear,
    And the rocks melt wi' the sun: *10*
O I will love thee still, my dear,
    While the sands o' life shall run.

And fare thee weel, my only luve,
    And fare thee weel awhile!
And I will come again, my luve,   *15*
    Though it were ten thousand mile.

[1796]

WILLIAM WORDSWORTH

[1770–1850]

Perhaps more than any other poet of his time, William Wordsworth helped to foster a poetry of the individual, of the inner life and "the essential passions of the heart." Taking himself as subject, he delved deep within the self to discover a universal "we." In doing so, Wordsworth became one of the most representative of the English Romantics, because he embodied the "Spirit of the Age."

Tracing the autonomous imagination as it focuses on nature, on daily life, and finally on itself, Wordsworth wrote his poetry in what he termed a "language really used by men." As his Preface to *Lyrical Ballads* clarified, a poet is only "a man speaking to other men." Wordsworth rebelled against the current penchant for "canned" metaphors such as "denizens of the deep" or "finny tribe," preferring the direct and simple "fish." He also avoided stylized expression choosing to link his poetry directly to experience rather than connecting it with any literary tradition. Consequently, he also embraced everyday subjects for his poetry.

Wordsworth's "Lines Composed a Few Miles above Tintern Abbey" illustrates these points. The poem opens with the speaker and his sister walking by the River Wye near the ruined abbey. The speaker's voice is both austere and genuine as he views his surroundings after a five-year absence. Weaving autobiography and perception into a lyrical and meditative blank verse, the poet–speaker comes to realize that his youthful, unthinking harmony with nature has transformed itself into a more profound empathy with "the still, sad music of humanity." For Wordsworth, such poetry was not a function of wit. Poetry's "object is truth . . . carried alive into the heart by passion." Poetry is "the spontaneous overflow of powerful feelings originating in emotion recollected in tranquility."

Because of Wordsworth's inclination toward inwardly directed explorations, many modern critics have come to see him as one of the first great poets of the "inner life." His is often a poetry of psychological insight focusing on self-realization, and the birth and growth of the individual. His familiar "My Heart Leaps Up" makes his point of view clear:

> My heart leaps up when I behold
>   A rainbow in the sky:
> So was it when my life began;
> So is it now I am a man;
> So be it when I shall grow old,
>   Or let me die!

Central to Wordsworth's sense of humanity is not just an appreciation of natural beauty; Wordsworth is more than a poet of the "scenic view." The speaker's response to the rainbow—his leaping heart—is life itself. Implied within his "Or let me die!" is the underlying knowledge: or I shall die. For Wordsworth, we are most alive and most ourselves when we experience nature, and we experience nature most clearly through the imagination.

Exactly how the imagination delineates its strong sense of place in nature, and by extension in daily reality, also underlies Wordsworth's lyric, "I Wandered Lonely as a Cloud" (p. 21). According to his sister Dorothy's journal of April 15, 1802, he and Dorothy had gone for a walk "in the woods beyond Gowbarrow Park." Together they stumbled upon a stretch of daffodils that "grew among the mossy stones . . . some rested their heads upon these stones as on a pillow for weariness; and the rest tossed and reeled and danced, and seemed as if they verily laughed with the wind, that flew upon them over the Lake; they looked so gay, ever glancing, ever changing."

Personified, the daffodils of Wordsworth's poem are the same daffodils of Dorothy's journal entry, but in the end brother and sister witness different events. While Dorothy draws pleasure from her walk among the flowers, her brother's attention becomes fixed on how the imagination interacts with nature. True, Wordsworth takes pleasure in his walk, but the "wealth" that the poem refers to is only brought into focus through the "inward eye" of the imagination.

The poet who was to choose the personal life as the subject of his poetry was himself remarkably human. He was born on April 7, 1790, in the English Lake District. His mother died when he was eight, and his father five years later. The young Wordsworth was considered to be a self-absorbed and somewhat moody child who once slashed a family portrait in anger and at another time, having considered himself ill treated, locked himself in the attic, threatening suicide. Rather than socializing or studying, he spent considerable time outdoors, walking the mountains and meadows by himself. He explains in "The Tables Turned" that book learning was a poor substitute for nature's revelations:

One impulse from a vernal wood
May teach you more of man
Of moral evil and of good,
Than all the sages can.

At college Wordsworth proved himself an average student, though he disliked school and found few friends. As the years passed, he turned more and more to his younger sister, Dorothy, for support. Eventually he would marry her best friend, Mary Hutchinson, but it would be his sister who called him "beloved."

In 1791 he traveled to France and fell in love with Annette Vallon, with whom he had a child, Caroline. Later he would write of his early years as a political radical living in France on the eve of the revolution:

Bliss was it in that dawn to be alive,
But to be young was very heaven!

Wordsworth, however, soon became disillusioned with the revolution and its Reign of Terror. Political circumstances as well as personal and financial considerations brought him back to England.

In 1795 Wordsworth met Samuel Taylor Coleridge, with whom he would publish *Lyrical Ballads.* Coleridge tells us in the fourteenth chapter of *Biographia Literaria* that they had agreed that Wordsworth would contribute poems about ordinary people in natural situations while Coleridge would contribute poems that focused on the "supernatural, or at least romantic" characters and situations that nevertheless contained a "semblance of truth sufficient to procure for these shadows of imagination that willing suspension of disbelief for the moment, which constitutes poetic faith." The friendship and collaborative efforts of Coleridge and Dorothy Wordsworth (consult her *Alfoxden Journal* and *Grasmere Journal*), who met each other almost daily for years, proved invaluable to Wordsworth.

In 1843 Wordsworth was appointed Poet Laureate, the culmination of a fifty-year poetic career. He died in 1850, the year the final version of his long autobiographical work, *The Prelude,* was published. Because he helped redefine what poetry would be, Wordsworth is still considered a major poet. Fresh insights concerning diction, metaphor, tone, and subject, as well as his theories on nature and the imagination contribute to his achievement as one of England's finest poets.

Lines

COMPOSED A FEW MILES ABOVE TINTERN ABBEY ON REVISITING THE BANKS OF THE WYE DURING A TOUR. JULY 13, 1798

Five years have passed; five summers, with the length
Of five long winters! and again I hear
These waters, rolling from their mountain-springs
With a soft inland murmur. Once again
Do I behold these steep and lofty cliffs,   *5*
That on a wild secluded scene impress
Thoughts of more deep seclusion; and connect
The landscape with the quiet of the sky.
The day is come when I again repose
Here, under this dark sycamore, and view   *10*
These plots of cottage ground, these orchard tufts,
Which at this season, with their unripe fruits,
Are clad in one green hue, and lose themselves
'Mid groves and copses.° Once again I see   *thickets*
These hedgerows, hardly hedgerows, little lines   *15*
Of sportive wood run wild; these pastoral farms,
Green to the very door; and wreaths of smoke
Sent up, in silence, from among the trees!
With some uncertain notice, as might seem

Of vagrant dwellers in the houseless woods, 20
Or of some Hermit's cave, where by his fire
The Hermit sits alone.

                  These beauteous forms,
Through a long absence, have not been to me
As is a landscape to a blind man's eye;
But oft, in lonely rooms, and 'mid the din 25
Of towns and cities, I have owed to them,
In hours of weariness, sensations sweet,
Felt in the blood, and felt along the heart;
And passing even into my purer mind
With tranquil restoration—feelings too 30
Of unremembered pleasure; such, perhaps,
As have no slight or trivial influence
On that best portion of a good man's life,
His little, nameless, unremembered acts
Of kindness and of love. Nor less, I trust, 35
To them I may have owed another gift,
Of aspect more sublime; that blessed mood,
In which the burthen of the mystery,
In which the heavy and the weary weight
Of all this unintelligible world, 40
Is lightened—that serene and blessed mood,
In which the affections gently lead us on—
Until, the breath of this corporeal frame
And even the motion of our human blood
Almost suspended, we are laid asleep 45
In body, and become a living soul;
While with an eye made quiet by the power
Of harmony, and the deep power of joy,
We see into the life of things.

                       If this
Be but a vain belief, yet, oh! how oft— 50
In darkness and amid the many shapes
Of joyless daylight; when the fretful stir
Unprofitable, and the fever of the world,
Have hung upon the beatings of my heart—
How oft, in spirit, have I turned to thee, 55
O sylvan Wye! thou wanderer through the woods,
How often has my spirit turned to thee!

    And now, with gleams of half-extinguished thought,
With many recognitions dim and faint,

And somewhat of a sad perplexity,   60
The picture of the mind revives again;
While here I stand, not only with the sense
Of present pleasure, but with pleasing thoughts
That in this moment there is life and food
For future years. And so I dare to hope,   65
Though changed, no doubt, from what I was when first
I came among these hills; when like a roe
I bounded o'er the mountains, by the sides
Of the deep rivers, and the lonely streams,
Wherever nature led—more like a man   70
Flying from something that he dreads than one
Who sought the thing he loved. For nature then
(The coarser pleasures of my boyish days,
And their glad animal movements all gone by)
To me was all in all.—I cannot paint   75
What then I was. The sounding cataract
Haunted me like a passion; the tall rock,
The mountain, and the deep and gloomy wood,
Their colors and their forms, were then to me
An appetite; a feeling and a love,   80
That had no need of a remoter charm,
By thought supplied, nor any interest
Unborrowed from the eye.—That time is past,
And all its aching joys are now no more,
And all its dizzy raptures. Not for this   85
Faint I, nor mourn nor murmur; other gifts
Have followed; for such loss, I would believe,
Abundant recompense. For I have learned
To look on nature, not as in the hour
Of thoughtless youth, but hearing oftentimes   90
The still, sad music of humanity,
Nor harsh nor grating, though of ample power
To chasten and subdue. And I have felt
A presence that disturbs me with the joy
Of elevated thoughts; a sense sublime   95
Of something far more deeply interfused,
Whose dwelling is the light of setting suns,
And the round ocean and the living air,
And the blue sky, and in the mind of man:
A motion and a spirit, that impels   100
All thinking things, all objects of all thought,
And rolls through all things. Therefore am I still
A lover of the meadows and the woods,
And mountains; and of all that we behold

From this green earth; of all the mighty world   *105*
Of eye, and ear—both what they half create,
And what perceive; well pleased to recognize
In nature and the language of the sense
The anchor of my purest thoughts, the nurse,
The guide, the guardian of my heart, and soul   *110*
Of all my moral being.

              Nor perchance,
If I were not thus taught, should I the more
Suffer my genial spirits° to decay: *powers*
For thou art with me here upon the banks
Of this fair river; thou my dearest Friend,   *115*
My dear, dear Friend; and in thy voice I catch
The language of my former heart, and read
My former pleasures in the shooting lights
Of thy wild eyes. Oh! yet a little while
May I behold in thee what I was once,   *120*
My dear, dear Sister! and this prayer I make,
Knowing that Nature never did betray
The heart that loved her; 'tis her privilege,
Through all the years of this our life, to lead
From joy to joy: for she can so inform°   *give form to* *125*
The mind that is within us, so impress
With quietness and beauty, and so feed
With lofty thoughts, that neither evil tongues,
Rash judgments, nor the sneers of selfish men,
Nor greetings where no kindness is, nor all   *130*
The dreary intercourse of daily life,
Shall e'er prevail against us, or disturb
Our cheerful faith, that all which we behold
Is full of blessings. Therefore let the moon
Shine on thee in thy solitary walk;   *135*
And let the misty mountain winds be free
To blow against thee: and, in after years,
When these wild ecstasies shall be matured
Into a sober pleasure; when thy mind
Shall be a mansion for all lovely forms,   *140*
Thy memory be as a dwelling place
For all sweet sounds and harmonies; oh! then,
If solitude, or fear, or pain, or grief
Should be thy portion, with what healing thoughts
Of tender joy wilt thou remember me,   *145*

[115]**Friend**   Wordsworth's sister, Dorothy.

And these my exhortations! Nor, perchance—
If I should be where I no more can hear
Thy voice, nor catch from thy wild eyes these gleams
Of past existence—wilt thou then forget
That on the banks of this delightful stream   *150*
We stood together; and that I, so long
A worshiper of Nature, hither came
Unwearied in that service; rather say
With warmer love—oh! with far deeper zeal
Of holier love. Nor wilt thou then forget,   *155*
That after many wanderings, many years
Of absence, these steep woods and lofty cliffs,
And this green pastoral landscape, were to me
More dear, both for themselves and for thy sake!

                                                               [1798]

To My Sister

It is the first mild day of March;
Each minute sweeter than before,
The redbreast sings from the tall larch
That stands beside our door.

There is a blessing in the air,   *5*
Which seems a sense of joy to yield
To the bare trees, and mountains bare,
And grass in the green field.

My sister! ('tis a wish of mine)
Now that our morning meal is done,   *10*
Make haste, your morning task resign;
Come forth and feel the sun.

Edward will come with you; —and, pray,
Put on with speed your woodland dress;
And bring no book: for this one day   *15*
We'll give to idleness.

No joyless forms shall regulate
Our living calendar:
We from to-day, my Friend, will date
The opening of the year.   *20*

Love, now a universal birth,
From heart to heart is stealing.
From earth to man, from man to earth:
—It is the hour of feeling.

One moment now may give us more   25
Than years of toiling reason:
Our minds shall drink at every pore
The spirit of the season.

Some silent laws our hearts will make,
Which they shall long obey: 30
We for the year to come may take
Our temper from to-day.

And from the blessèd power that rolls
About, below, above,
We'll frame the measure of our souls: 35
They shall be tuned to love.

Then come, my Sister! come, I pray,
With speed put on your woodland dress;
And bring no book: for this one day
We'll give to idleness.   40

[1798]

She dwelt among the untrodden ways

She dwelt among the untrodden ways
    Beside the springs of Dove.
A Maid whom there were none to praise
    And very few to love;

A violet by a mossy stone   5
    Half hidden from the eye!
—Fair as a star, when only one
    Is shining in the sky.

She lived unknown, and few could know
    When Lucy ceased to be;   10
But she is in her grave, and, oh,
    The difference to me!

[1800]

A slumber did my spirit seal

A slumber did my spirit seal;
  I had no human fears:
She seemed a thing that could not feel
  The touch of earthly years.

No motion has she now, no force;   5
  She neither hears nor sees;
Rolled round in earth's diurnal course,
  With rocks, and stones, and trees.

[1800]

My heart leaps up

My heart leaps up when I behold
  A rainbow in the sky:
So was it when my life began;
So is it now I am a man;
So be it when I shall grow old,   5
  Or let me die!
The Child is father of the Man;
And I could wish my days to be
Bound each to each by natural piety.

[1807]

The Solitary Reaper

Behold her, single in the field,
Yon solitary Highland Lass!
Reaping and singing by herself;
Stop here, or gently pass!
Alone she cuts and binds the grain,   5
And sings a melancholy strain;
O listen! for the Vale profound
Is overflowing with the sound.

No Nightingale did ever chaunt
More welcome notes to weary bands   10
Of travelers in some shady haunt,
Among Arabian sands;
A voice so thrilling ne'er was heard
In springtime from the Cuckoo bird,
Breaking the silence of the seas   15
Among the farthest Hebrides.

Will no one tell me what she sings?—
Perhaps the plaintive numbers flow
For old, unhappy, far-off things,
And battles long ago;   20
Or is it some more humble lay,
Familiar matter of today?

Some natural sorrow, loss, or pain,
That has been, and may be again?
Whate'er the theme, the Maiden sang   25
As if her song could have no ending;
I saw her singing at her work,
And o'er the sickle bending—
I listened, motionless and still;
And, as I mounted up the hill,   30
The music in my heart I bore,
Long after it was heard no more.

                                                              [1807]

The world is too much with us

The world is too much with us; late and soon,
Getting and spending, we lay waste our powers;
Little we see in Nature that is ours;
We have given our hearts away, a sordid boon°!   *gift*
This Sea that bares her bosom to the moon,   5
The winds that will be howling at all hours,
And are up-gathered now like sleeping flowers,
For this, for everything, we are out of tune;
It moves us not.—Great God! I'd rather be
A Pagan suckled in a creed outworn;   10
So might I, standing on this pleasant lea,
Have glimpses that would make me less forlorn;

Have sight of Proteus rising from the sea;
Or hear old Triton blow his wreathéd horn.

[1807]

It is a beauteous evening

It is a beauteous evening, calm and free,
The holy time is quiet as a Nun
Breathless with adoration; the broad sun
Is sinking down in its tranquility;
The gentleness of heaven broods o'er the Sea: 5
Listen! the mighty Being is awake,
And doth with his eternal motion make
A sound like thunder—everlastingly.
Dear Child! dear Girl! that wakest with me here,
If thou appear untouched by solemn thought,   10
Thy nature is not therefore less divine:
Thou liest in Abraham's bosom all the year,
And worship'st at the Temple's inner shrine,
God being with thee when we know it not.

[1807]

She was a Phantom of delight

She was a Phantom of delight
When first she gleamed upon my sight;
A lovely Apparition, sent
To be a moment's ornament;
Her eyes as stars of Twilight fair;   5
Like Twilight's, too, her dusky hair;
But all things else about her drawn
From May-time and the cheerful Dawn;
A dancing Shape, an Image gay,
To haunt, to startle, and way-lay.   10

THE WORLD IS TOO MUCH WITH US   13-14**Proteus . . . Triton**   classical sea gods Triton's conch-shell
horn calmed the waves.

I saw her upon nearer view,
A Spirit, yet a Woman too!
Her household motions light and free,
And steps of virgin-liberty;
A countenance in which did meet   15
Sweet records, promises as sweet;
A Creature not too bright or good
For human nature's daily food;
For transient sorrows, simple wiles,
Praise, blame, love, kisses, tears, and smiles.   20

And now I see with eye serene
The very pulse of the machine;
A Being breathing thoughtful breath,
A Traveller between life and death;
The reason firm, the temperate will,   25
Endurance, foresight, strength, and skill;
A perfect Woman, nobly planned,
To warn, to comfort, and command;
And yet a Spirit still, and bright
With something of angelic light.   30

[1807]

Ode

Intimations of Immortality from Recollections of Early Childhood

The Child is father of the Man;
And I could wish my days to be
Bound each to each by natural piety.

1

There was a time when meadow, grove, and stream,
The earth, and every common sight,
To me did seem
Appareled in celestial light,
The glory and the freshness of a dream.   5
It is not now as it hath been of yore—
Turn whereso'er I may,
By night or day,
The things which I have seen I now can see no more.

2

The Rainbow comes and goes,   *10*
And lovely is the Rose,
The Moon doth with delight
Look round her when the heavens are bare,
Waters on a starry night
Are beautiful and fair;   *15*
The sunshine is a glorious birth;
But yet I know, where'er I go,
That there hath passed away a glory from the earth.

3

Now, while the birds thus sing a joyous song,
And while the young lambs bound   *20*
As to the tabor's sound,
To me alone there came a thought of grief:
A timely utterance gave that thought relief,
And I again am strong:
The cataracts blow their trumpets from the steep;   *25*
No more shall grief of mine the season wrong;
I hear the Echoes through the mountains throng,
The Winds come to me from the fields of sleep,
And all the earth is gay;
Land and sea   *30*
Give themselves up to jollity,
And with the heart of May
Doth every Beast keep holiday—
Thou Child of Joy,
Shout round me, let me hear thy shouts, thou happy Shepherd-boy!   *35*

4

Ye blessèd Creatures, I have heard the call
Ye to each other make; I see
The heavens laugh with you in your jubilee;
My heart is at your festival,
My head hath its coronal,   *40*
The fullness of your bliss, I feel—I feel it all.
Oh, evil day! if I were sullen
While Earth herself is adorning,
This sweet May morning,
And the Children are culling   *45*
On every side,

In a thousand valleys far and wide,
Fresh flowers; while the sun shines warm,
And the Babe leaps up on his Mother's arm—
I hear, I hear, with joy I hear! 50
—But there's a Tree, of many, one,
A single Field which I have looked upon,
Both of them speak of something that is gone:
The Pansy at my feet
Doth the same tale repeat: 55
Whither is fled the visionary gleam?
Where is it now, the glory and the dream?

5

Our birth is but a sleep and a forgetting:
The Soul that rises with us, our life's Star,
Hath had elsewhere its setting, 60
And cometh from afar:
Not in entire forgetfulness,
And not in utter nakedness,
But trailing clouds of glory do we come
From God, who is our home: 65
Heaven lies about us in our infancy!
Shades of the prison-house begin to close
Upon the growing Boy
But he
Beholds the light, and whence it flows, 70
He sees it in his joy;
The Youth, who daily farther from the east
Must travel, still is Nature's Priest,
And by the vision splendid
Is on his way attended; 75
At length the Man perceives it die away,
And fade into the light of common day.

6

Earth fills her lap with pleasures of her own;
Yearnings she hath in her own natural kind,
And, even with something of a Mother's mind, 80
And no unworthy aim,
The homely° Nurse doth all she can   *simple, kindly*
To make her foster child, her Inmate Man,
Forget the glories he hath known,
And that imperial palace whence he came. 85

7

Behold the Child among his newborn blisses,
A six-years' Darling of a pygmy size!
See, where 'mid work of his own hand he lies,
Fretted° by sallies of his mother's kisses,   *vexed*
With light upon him from his father's eyes!   90
See, at his feet, some little plan or chart,
Some fragment from his dream of human life,
Shaped by himself with newly-learnéd art;
    A wedding or a festival,
    A mourning or a funeral;   95
      And this hath now his heart,
    And unto this he frames his song;
      Then will he fit his tongue
To dialogues of business, love, or strife;
    But it will not be long   100
    Ere this be thrown aside,
    And with new joy and pride
The little Actor cons another part;
Filling from time to time his "humorous stage"
With all the Persons, down to palsied Age,   105
That Life brings with her in her equipage;
    As if his whole vocation
    Were endless imitation.

8

Thou, whose exterior semblance doth belie
    Thy Soul's immensity;   110
Thou best Philosopher, who yet dost keep
Thy heritage, thou Eye among the blind,
That, deaf and silent, read'st the eternal deep,
Haunted forever by the eternal mind—
    Mighty Prophet! Seer blest!   115
    On whom those truths do rest,
Which we are toiling all our lives to find,
In darkness lost, the darkness of the grave;
Thou, over whom thy Immortality
Broods like the Day, a Master o'er a Slave,   120
A Presence which is not to be put by;
Thou little Child, yet glorious in the might

---

¹⁰⁴**"humorous stage"**   refers to the various temperaments, called "humors" during the Renaissance.

Of heaven-born freedom on thy being's height,
Why with such earnest pains dost thou provoke
The years to bring the inevitable yoke, 125
Thus blindly with thy blessedness at strife?
Full soon thy Soul shall have her earthly freight,
And custom lie upon thee with a weight,
Heavy as frost, and deep almost as life!

9

O joy! that in our embers 130
Is something that doth live,
That nature yet remembers
What was so fugitive!
The thought of our past years in me doth breed
Perpetual benediction: not indeed 135
For that which is most worthy to be blest;
Delight and liberty, the simple creed
Of Childhood, whether busy or at rest,
With new-fledged hope still fluttering in his breast—
Not for these I raise 140
The song of thanks and praise;
But for those obstinate questionings
Of sense and outward things,
Fallings from us, vanishings;
Blank misgivings of a Creature 145
Moving about in worlds not realized,
High instincts before which our mortal Nature
Did tremble like a guilty Thing surprised;
But for those first affections,
Those shadowy recollections, 150
Which, be they what they may,
Are yet the fountain light of all our day,
Are yet a master light of all our seeing;
Uphold us, cherish, and have power to make
Our noisy years seem moments in the being 155
Of the eternal Silence: truths that wake,
To perish never;
Which neither listlessness, nor mad endeavor,
Nor Man nor Boy,
Nor all that is at enmity with joy, 160
Can utterly abolish or destroy!
Hence in a season of calm weather
Though inland far we be,

Our Souls have sight of that immortal sea
        Which brought us hither,   *165*
        Can in a moment travel thither,
And see the Children sport upon the shore,
And hear the mighty waters rolling evermore.

10

Then sing, ye Birds, sing, sing a joyous song!
        And let the young Lambs bound   *170*
        As to the tabor's sound!
We in thought will join your throng,
        Ye that pipe and ye that play,
        Ye that through your hearts today
        Feel the gladness of the May!   *175*
What though the radiance which was once so bright
Be now forever taken from my sight,
        Though nothing can bring back the hour
Of splendor in the grass, of glory in the flower;
        We will grieve not, rather find   *180*
        Strength in what remains behind;
        In the primal sympathy
        Which having been must ever be;
        In the soothing thoughts that spring
        Out of human suffering;   *185*
        In the faith that looks through death,
In years that bring the philosophic mind.

11

And O, ye Fountains, Meadows, Hills, and Groves,
Forebode not any severing of our loves!
Yet in my heart of hearts I feel your might;   *190*
I only have relinquished one delight
To live beneath your more habitual sway.
I love the Brooks which down their channels fret,
Even more than when I tripped lightly as they;
The innocent brightness of a newborn Day   *195*
        Is lovely yet;
The clouds that gather round the setting sun
Do take a sober coloring from an eye
That hath kept watch o'er man's mortality;
Another race hath been, and other palms°
    are won.   *symbols of victory* 200
Thanks to the human heart by which we live,
Thanks to its tenderness, its joys, and fears,

To me the meanest° flower that blows° can give   *most ordinary/blooms*
Thoughts that do often lie too deep for tears.

[1807]

from *The Prelude*

from Book I (Fair Seed-time)

Fair seed-time had my soul, and I grew up
Fostered alike by beauty and by fear:
Much favoured in my birth-place, and no less
In that beloved Vale to which erelong
We were transplanted—there were we let loose   5
For sports of wider range. Ere I had told
Ten birth-days, when among the mountain slopes
Frost, and the breath of frosty wind, had snapped
The last autumnal crocus, 'twas my joy
With store of springes o'er my shoulder hung   10
To range the open heights where woodcocks run
Along the smooth green turf. Through half the night,
Scudding away from snare to snare, I plied
That anxious visitation;—moon and stars
Were shining o'er my head. I was alone,   15
And seemed to be a trouble to the peace
That dwelt among them. Sometimes it befel
In these night wanderings, that a strong desire
O'erpowered my better reason, and the bird
Which was the captive of another's toil   20
Became my prey; and when the deed was done
I heard among the solitary hills
Low breathings coming after me, and sounds
Of undistinguishable motion, steps
Almost as silent as the turf they trod.   25

Nor less when spring had warmed the cultured Vale,
Moved we as plunderers where the mother-bird
Had in high places built her lodge; though mean
Our object and inglorious, yet the end
Was not ignoble. Oh! when I have hung   30
Above the raven's nest, by knots of grass

THE PRELUDE   ⁴**Vale** the valley of Esthwaite, a lake in the English Lake District. Wordsworth attended
school in the nearby village of Hawkshead.   ¹⁰**springes** bird traps.   ²⁶**cultured** cultivated.

And half-inch fissures in the slippery rock
But ill sustained, and almost (so it seemed)
Suspended by the blast that blew amain,
Shouldering the naked crag, oh, at that time   35
While on the perilous ridge I hung alone,
With what strange utterance did the loud dry wind
Blow through my ear! the sky seemed not a sky
Of earth—and with what motion moved the clouds!

    Dust as we are, the immortal spirit grows   40
Like harmony in music; there is a dark
Inscrutable workmanship that reconciles
Discordant elements, makes them cling together
In one society. How strange that all
The terrors, pains, and early miseries,   45
Regrets, vexations, lassitudes interfused
Within my mind, should e'er have borne a part,
And that a needful part, in making up
The calm existence that is mine when I
Am worthy of myself! Praise to the end!   50
Thanks to the means which Nature deigned to employ;
Whether her fearless visitings, or those
That came with soft alarm, like hurtless light
Opening the peaceful clouds; or she may use
Severer interventions, ministry   55
More palpable, as best might suit her aim.

    One summer evening (led by her) I found
A little boat tied to a willow tree
Within a rocky cave, its usual home.
Straight I unloosed her chain, and stepping in   60
Pushed from the shore. It was an act of stealth
And troubled pleasure, nor without the voice
Of mountain-echoes did my boat move on;
Leaving behind her still, on either side,
Small circles glittering idly in the moon,   65
Until they melted all into one track
Of sparkling light. But now, like one who rows,
Proud of his skill, to reach a chosen point
With an unswerving line, I fixed my view
Upon the summit of a craggy ridge,   70
The horizon's utmost boundary; far above
Was nothing but the stars and the grey sky.

---

[52]**fearless**   causing no fear.

She was an elfin pinnace; lustily
I dipped my oars into the silent lake,
And, as I rose upon the stroke, my boat   75
Went heaving through the water like a swan;
When, from behind that craggy steep till then
The horizon's bound, a huge peak, black and huge,
As if with voluntary power instinct
Upreared its head. I struck and struck again,   80
And growing still in stature the grim shape
Towered up between me and the stars, and still,
For so it seemed, with purpose of its own
And measured motion like a living thing,
Strode after me. With trembling oars I turned,   85
And through the silent water stole my way
Back to the covert of the willow tree;
There in her mooring-place I left my bark,—
And through the meadows homeward went, in grave
And serious mood; but after I had seen   90
That spectacle, for many days, my brain
Worked with a dim and undetermined sense
Of unknown modes of being; o'er my thoughts
There hung a darkness, call it solitude
Or blank desertion. No familiar shapes   95
Remained, no pleasant images of trees,
Of sea or sky, no colors of green fields;
But huge and mighty forms, that do not live
Like living men, moved slowly through the mind
By day and were a trouble to my dreams.   100

from Book V (The Boy of Winander)

There was a Boy: ye knew him well, ye cliffs
And islands of Winander!—many a time
At evening, when the earliest stars began
To move along the edges of the hills,
Rising or setting, would he stand alone   5
Beneath the trees or by the glimmering lake,
And there, with fingers interwoven, both hands
Pressed closely palm to palm, and to his mouth
Uplifted, he, as through an instrument,

THE PRELUDE   ⁷³**pinnace**   small boat.
BOOK V   ²**Winander**   another name for Windermere, the largest lake in the Lake District of northern England.

Blew mimic hootings to the silent owls,   *10*
That they might answer him; and they would shout
Across the watery vale, and shout again,
Responsive to his call, with quivering peals,
And long halloos and screams, and echoes loud,
Redoubled and redoubled, concourse wild   *15*
Of jocund din; and, when a lengthened pause
Of silence came and baffled his best skill,
Then sometimes, in that silence while he hung
Listening, a gentle shock of mild surprise
Has carried far into his heart the voice   *20*
Of mountain torrents; or the visible scene
Would enter unawares into his mind,
With all its solemn imagery, its rocks,
Its woods, and that uncertain heaven, received
Into the bosom of the steady lake.   *25*

from Book XII (Spots of Time)

There are in our existence spots of time,
That with distinct pre-eminence retain
A renovating virtue, whence, depressed
By false opinion and contentious thought,
Or aught of heavier or more deadly weight,   *5*
In trivial occupations, and the round
Of ordinary intercourse, our minds
Are nourished and invisibly repaired;
A virtue, by which pleasure is enhanced,
That penetrates, enables us to mount,   *10*
When high, more high, and lifts us up when fallen.
This efficacious spirit chiefly lurks
Among those passages of life that give
Profoundest knowledge to what point, and how,
The mind is lord and master—outward sense   *15*
The obedient servant of her will. Such moments
Are scattered everywhere, taking their date
From our first childhood. I remember well,
That once, while yet my inexperienced hand
Could scarcely hold a bridle, with proud hopes   *20*
I mounted, and we journeyed towards the hills:
An ancient servant of my father's house
Was with me, my encourager and guide:

We had not traveled long, ere some mischance
Disjoined me from my comrade; and, through fear   25
Dismounting, down the rough and stony moor
I led my horse, and, stumbling on, at length
Came to a bottom, where in former times
A murderer had been hung in iron chains.
The gibbet-mast had moldered down, the bones   30
And iron case were gone; but on the turf,
Hard by, soon after that fell deed was wrought,
Some unknown hand had carved the murderer's name.
The monumental letters were inscribed
In times long past; but still, from year to year,   35
By superstition of the neighborhood,
The grass is cleared away, and to this hour
The characters are fresh and visible:
A casual glance had shown them, and I fled,
Faltering and faint, and ignorant of the road: 40
Then, reascending the bare common, saw
A naked pool that lay beneath the hills,
The beacon on the summit, and, more near,
A girl, who bore a pitcher on her head,
And seemed with difficult steps to force her way   45
Against the blowing wind. It was, in truth,
An ordinary sight; but I should need
Colors and words that are unknown to man,
To paint the visionary dreariness
Which, while I looked all round for my lost guide,   50
Invested moorland waste, and naked pool,
The beacon crowning the lone eminence,
The female and her garments vexed and tossed
By the strong wind. When, in the blessed hours
Of early love, the loved one at my side,   55
I roamed, in daily presence of this scene,
Upon the naked pool and dreary crags,
And on the melancholy beacon fell
A spirit of pleasure and youth's golden gleam;
And think ye not with radiance more sublime   60
For these remembrances, and for the power
They had left behind? So feeling comes in aid
Of feeling, and diversity of strength
Attends us, if but once we have been strong.
Oh! mystery of man, from what a depth   65

<hr>

[55]**loved one**   Wordsworth's future wife, Mary Hutchinson

Proceed thy honors. I am lost, but see
In simple childhood something of the base
On which thy greatness stands; but this I feel,
That from thyself it comes, that thou must give,
Else never canst receive. The days gone by   *70*
Return upon me almost from the dawn
Of life; the hiding-places of man's power
Open; I would approach them, but they close.
I see by glimpses now; when age comes on,
May scarcely see at all; and I would give,   *75*
While yet we may, as far as words can give,
Substance and life to what I feel, enshrining,
Such is my hope, the spirit of the Past
For future restoration.

                                                    [1798–1805, 1850]

SAMUEL TAYLOR COLERIDGE

[1772–1834]

Kubla Khan

Or a Vision in a Dream. A Fragment

In Xanadu did Kubla Khan
A stately pleasure dome decree:
Where Alph, the sacred river, ran
Through caverns measureless to man
   Down to a sunless sea.   *5*
So twice five miles of fertile ground
With walls and towers were girdled round:
And there were gardens bright with sinuous rills,
Where blossomed many an incense-bearing tree;
And here were forests ancient as the hills,   *10*
Enfolding sunny spots of greenery.

But oh! that deep romantic chasm which slanted
Down the green hill athwart a cedarn cover!

KUBLA KHAN   the first ruler of the Mongol dynasty in thirteenth-century China. Coleridge's topography and
place names are imaginary.

A savage place! as holy and enchanted
As e'er beneath a waning moon was haunted   *15*
By woman wailing for her demon lover!
And from this chasm, with ceaseless turmoil seething,
As if this earth in fast thick pants were breathing,
A mighty fountain momently was forced:
Amid whose swift half-intermitted burst   *20*
Huge fragments vaulted like rebounding hail,
Or chaffy grain beneath the thresher's flail:
And 'mid these dancing rocks at once and ever
It flung up momently the sacred river.
Five miles meandering with a mazy motion   *25*
Through wood and dale the sacred river ran,
Then reached the caverns measureless to man,
And sank in tumult to a lifeless ocean:
And 'mid this tumult Kubla heard from far
Ancestral voices prophesying war!   *30*

    The shadow of the dome of pleasure
    Floated midway on the waves;
    Where was heard the mingled measure
    From the fountain and the caves.
It was a miracle of rare device,   *35*
A sunny pleasure dome with caves of ice!

    A damsel with a dulcimer
    In a vision once I saw:
    It was an Abyssinian maid,
    And on her dulcimer she played,   *40*
    Singing of Mount Abora.
Could I revive within me
Her symphony and song,
To such a deep delight 'twould win me,
That with music loud and long,   *45*
I would build that dome in air,
That sunny dome! those caves of ice!
And all who heard should see them there,
And all should cry, Beware! Beware!
His flashing eyes, his floating hair!   *50*
Weave a circle round him thrice,
And close your eyes with holy dread,
For he on honey-dew hath fed,
And drunk the milk of Paradise.

                                                                  [1798]

Dejection: An Ode

Late, late yestreen I saw the new Moon,
With the old Moon in her arms;
And I fear, I fear, my master dear!
We shall have a deadly storm.
—Ballad of Sir Patrick Spence

1

Well! If the bard was weather-wise, who made
  The grand old ballad of Sir Patrick Spence,
  This night, so tranquil now, will not go hence
Unroused by winds, that ply a busier trade
Than those which mold yon cloud in lazy flakes,   5
Or the dull sobbing draft, that moans and rakes
Upon the strings of this Aeolian lute,
    Which better far were mute.
    For lo! the New-moon winter-bright!
  And overspread with phantom light,   10
  (With swimming phantom light o'erspread
  But rimmed and circled by a silver thread)
I see the old Moon in her lap, foretelling
  The coming-on of rain and squally blast.
And oh! that even now the gust were swelling,   15
    And the slant night shower driving loud and fast!
Those sounds which oft have raised me, whilst they awed,
    And sent my soul abroad,
Might now perhaps their wonted° impulse give,   *usual*
Might startle this dull pain, and make it move and live!   20

2

A grief without a pang, void, dark, and drear,
  A stifled, drowsy, unimpassioned grief,
  Which finds no natural outlet, no relief,
    In word, or sigh, or tear—
O Lady! in this wan and heartless mood,   25
To other thoughts by yonder throstle wooed,
  All this long eve, so balmy and serene,

---

⁷**Aeolian lute**   The wind-harp (named after Aeolus, classical god of winds) has a sounding board equipped with a set of strings that vibrate in response to air currents.

Have I been gazing on the western sky,
  And its peculiar tint of yellow green:
And still I gaze—and with how blank an eye!   30
And those thin clouds above, in flakes and bars,
That give away their motion to the stars;
Those stars, that glide behind them or between,
Now sparkling, now bedimmed, but always seen:
Yon crescent Moon, as fixed as if it grew   35
In its own cloudless, starless lake of blue;
I see them all so excellently fair,
I see, not feel, how beautiful they are!

3

    My genial spirits° fail;   *vital energies*
      And what can these avail   40
To lift the smothering weight from off my breast?
      It were a vain endeavor,
        Though I should gaze forever
On that green light that lingers in the west:
I may not hope from outward forms to win   45
The passion and the life, whose fountains are within.

4

O Lady! we receive but what we give,
And in our life alone does Nature live:
Ours is her wedding garment, ours her shroud!
    And would we aught behold, of higher worth,   50
Than that inanimate cold world allowed
To the poor loveless ever-anxious crowd,
    Ah! from the soul itself must issue forth
A light, a glory, a fair luminous cloud
      Enveloping the Earth—   55
And from the soul itself must there be sent
    A sweet and potent voice, of its own birth,
Of all sweet sounds the life and element!

5

O pure of heart! thou need'st not ask of me
What this strong music in the soul may be!   60
What, and wherein it doth exist,
This light, this glory, this fair luminous mist,
This beautiful and beauty-making power.
    Joy, virtuous Lady! Joy that ne'er was given,

Save to the pure, and in their purest hour,   65
Life, and Life's effluence, cloud at once and shower,
Joy, Lady! is the spirit and the power,
Which wedding Nature to us gives in dower
    A new Earth and new Heaven,
Undreamnt of by the sensual and the proud—   70
Joy is the sweet voice, Joy the luminous cloud—
      We in ourselves rejoice!
And thence flows all that charms or ear or sight,
    All melodies the echoes of that voice,
All colors a suffusion from that light.   75

6

There was a time when, though my path was rough,
    This joy within me dallied with distress,
And all misfortunes were but as the stuff
    Whence Fancy made me dreams of happiness:
For hope grew round me, like the twining vine,   80
And fruits, and foliage, not my own, seemed mine.
But now afflictions bow me down to earth:
Nor care I that they rob me of my mirth;
      But oh! each visitation
Suspends what nature gave me at my birth,   85
    My shaping spirit of Imagination.

For not to think of what I needs must feel,
    But to be still and patient, all I can;
And happly by abstruse research to steal
    From my own nature all the natural man—   90
    This was my sole resource, my only plan:
Till that which suits a part infects the whole,
And now is almost grown the habit of my soul.

7

Hence, viper thoughts, that coil around my mind,
    Reality's dark dream!   95
I turn from you, and listen to the wind,
    Which long has raved unnoticed. What a scream
Of agony by torture lengthened out
That lute sent forth! Thou Wind, that rav'st without,
    Bare crag, or mountain tairn,° or blasted tree,   *pool*   100
Or pine grove whither woodman never clomb,

Or lonely house, long held—the witches' home,
   Methinks were fitter instruments for thee,
Mad lutanist! who in this month of showers,
Of dark-brown gardens, and of peeping flowers,   *105*
Mak'st devils' yule, with worse than wintry song,
The blossoms, buds, and timorous leaves among.
    Thou actor, perfect in all tragic sounds!
Thou mighty poet, e'en to frenzy bold!
      What tell'st thou now about?   *110*
       'Tis of the rushing of an host in rout,
   With groans, of trampled men, with smarting wounds—
At once they groan with pain, and shudder with the cold!
But hush! there is a pause of deepest silence!
    And all that noise, as of a rushing crowd,   *115*
With groans, and tremulous shudderings—all is over—
   It tells another tale, with sounds less deep and loud!
      A tale of less affright,
      And tempered with delight,
As Otway's self had framed the tender lay—   *120*
      'Tis of a little child
      Upon a lonesome wild,
Not far from home, but she hath lost her way:
And now moans low in bitter grief and fear,
And now screams loud, and hopes to make her mother hear.   *125*

8

'Tis midnight, but small thoughts have I of sleep:
Full seldom may my friend such vigils keep!
Visit her, gentle Sleep! with wings of healing,
   And may this storm be but a mountain birth,
May all the stars hang bright above her dwelling,   *130*
   Silent as though they watched the sleeping Earth!
      With light heart may she rise,
      Gay fancy, cheerful eyes,
   Joy lift her spirit, joy attune her voice;
To her may all things live, from pole to pole,   *135*
Their life the eddying of her living soul!
    O simple spirit, guided from above,
Dear Lady! friend devoutest of my choice,
Thus mayest thou ever, evermore rejoice.

[1802, 1817]

---

[106]**devils' yule** a winter storm in spring; hence, an unnatural or "devils'" Christmas   [120]**Otway (1652–1685)** dramatist known for creating scenes of pathos in his tradgedies.

GEORGE GORDON, LORD BYRON

[1788–1824]

She walks in beauty

1

She walks in beauty, like the night
  Of cloudless climes and starry skies;
And all that's best of dark and bright
  Meet in her aspect and her eyes:
Thus mellowed to that tender light   5
  Which heaven to gaudy day denies.

2

One shade the more, one ray the less,
  Had half impaired the nameless grace
Which waves in every raven tress;
  Or softly lightens o'er her face;   10
Where thoughts serenely sweet express
  How pure, how dear their dwelling place.

3

And on that cheek, and o'er that brow,
  So soft, so calm, yet eloquent,
The smiles that win, the tints that glow,   15
  But tell of days in goodness spent,
A mind at peace with all below,
  A heart whose love is innocent!

[1815]

The Destruction of Sennacherib

The Assyrian came down like the wolf on the fold,
And his cohorts were gleaming in purple and gold;
And the sheen of their spears was like stars on the sea,
When the blue wave rolls nightly on deep Galilee.

THE DESTRUCTION OF SENNACHERIB   Sennacherib was an eighth-century-B C. Assyrian king.

Like the leaves of the forest when summer is green, 5
That host with their banners at sunset were seen:
Like the leaves of the forest when autumn hath blown,
That host on the morrow lay withered and strown.

For the Angel of Death spread his wings on the blast,
And breathed in the face of the foe as he passed; 10
And the eyes of the sleepers waxed deadly and chill,
And their hearts but once heaved—and for ever grew still!

And there lay the steed with his nostril all wide,
But through it there rolled not the breath of his pride;
And the foam of his gasping lay white on the turf, 15
And cold as the spray of the rock-beating surf.

And there lay the rider distorted and pale,
With the dew on his brow, and the rust on his mail;
And the tents were all silent, the banners alone,
The lances unlifted, the trumpet unblown. 20

And the widows of Ashur are loud in their wail,
And the idols are broke in the temple of Baal;
And the might of the Gentile, unsmote by the sword,
Hath melted like snow in the glance of the Lord!

[1815]

PERCY BYSSHE SHELLEY

[1792–1822]

Ozymandias

I met a traveler from an antique land
Who said: Two vast and trunkless legs of stone
Stand in the desert . . . Near them, on the sand,
Half sunk, a shattered visage lies, whose frown,
And wrinkled lip, and sneer of cold command, 5
Tell that its sculptor well those passions read
Which yet survive, stamped on these lifeless things,
The hand that mocked them, and the heart that fed:

OZYMANDIAS   Greek name for the Egyptian ruler Rameses II, who erected a huge statue in his own likeness.

And on the pedestal these words appear:
"My name is Ozymandias, king of kings: 10
Look on my works, ye Mighty, and despair!"
Nothing beside remains. Round the decay
Of that colossal wreck, boundless and bare
The lone and level sands stretch far away.

[1818]

To a Skylark

Hail to thee, blithe Spirit!
  Bird thou never wert,
That from Heaven, or near it,
  Pourest thy full heart
In profuse strains of unpremeditated art.   5

Higher still and higher
  From the earth thou springest
Like a cloud of fire;
  The blue deep thou wingest,
And singing still dost soar, and soaring ever singest.   10

In the golden lightning
  Of the sunken sun,
O'er which clouds are bright'ning,
  Thou dost float and run;
Like an unbodied joy whose race is just begun.   15

The pale purple even
  Melts around thy flight;
Like a star of Heaven,
  In the broad daylight
Thou art unseen, but yet I hear thy shrill delight,   20

Keen as are the arrows
  Of that silver sphere,°   *star*
Whose intense lamp narrows
  In the white dawn clear
Until we hardly see—we feel that it is there.   25

All the earth and air
  With thy voice is loud,

As, when night is bare,
　　From one lonely cloud
The moon rains out her beams, and Heaven is overflowed.　　　　30

What thou art we know not;
　　What is most like thee?
From rainbow clouds there flow not
　　Drops so bright to see
As from thy presence showers a rain of melody.　　　　35

Like a Poet hidden
　　In the light of thought,
Singing hymns unbidden,
　　Till the world is wrought
To sympathy with hopes and fears it heeded not:　　　　40

Like a high-born maiden
　　In a palace tower,
Soothing her love-laden
　　Soul in secret hour
With music sweet as love, which overflows her bower:　　　　45

Like a glowworm golden
　　In a dell of dew,
Scattering unbeholden
　　Its aërial hue
Among the flowers and grass, which screen it from the view!　　　　50

Like a rose embowered
　　In its own green leaves,
By warm winds deflowered,
　　Till the scent it gives
Makes faint with too much sweet those heavy-wingéd thieves:　　　　55

Sound of vernal showers
　　On the twinkling grass,
Rain-awakened flowers,
　　All that ever was
Joyous, and clear, and fresh, thy music doth surpass:　　　　60

Teach us, Sprite° or Bird,　　　　　　　　　　*spirit*
　　What sweet thoughts are thine:
I have never heard
　　Praise of love or wine
That panted forth a flood of rapture so divine.　　　　65

Chorus Hymeneal,
    Or triumphal chant,
Matched with thine would be all
    But an empty vaunt,
A thing wherein we feel there is some hidden want.   70

What objects are the fountains
    Of thy happy strain?
What fields, or waves, or mountains?
    What shapes of sky or plain?
What love of thine own kind? what ignorance of pain?   75

With thy clear keen joyance
    Languor cannot be:
Shadow of annoyance
    Never came near thee:
Thou lovest—but ne'er knew love's sad satiety.   80

Waking or asleep,
    Thou of death must deem
Things more true and deep
    Than we mortals dream,
Or how could thy notes flow in such a crystal stream?   85

We look before and after,
    And pine for what is not:
Our sincerest laughter
    With some pain is fraught;
Our sweetest songs are those that tell of saddest thought.   90

Yet if we could scorn
    Hate, and pride, and fear;
If we were things born
    Not to shed a tear,
I know not how thy joy we ever should come near.   95

Better than all measures
    Of delightful sound,
Better than all treasures
    That in books are found,
Thy skill to poet were, thou scorner of the ground!   100

66Hymeneal   reference to Hymen, the Greek god of marriage. Hence, pertaining to a wedding.

Teach me half the gladness
  That thy brain must know,
Such harmonious madness
  From my lips would flow
The world should listen then—as I am listening now.   105

[1820]

Ode to the West Wind

1

O wild West Wind, thou breath of Autumn's being,
Thou, from whose unseen presence the leaves dead
Are driven, like ghosts from an enchanter fleeing,

Yellow, and black, and pale, and hectic red,
Pestilence-stricken multitudes: O thou,   5
Who chariotest to their dark wintry bed

The wingéd seeds, where they lie cold and low,
Each like a corpse within its grave, until
Thine azure sister of the Spring shall blow

Her clarion° o'er the dreaming earth, and fill   *trumpet call* 10
(Driving sweet buds like flocks to feed in air)
With living hues and odors plain and hill:

Wild Spirit, which art moving everywhere;
Destroyer and preserver; hear, oh, hear!

2

Thou on whose stream, mid the steep sky's commotion,   15
Loose clouds like earth's decaying leaves are shed,
Shook from the tangled boughs of Heaven and Ocean,

Angels° of rain and lightning: there are spread   *messengers*
On the blue surface of thine aëry surge,
Like the bright hair uplifted from the head   20

Of some fierce Maenad, even from the dim verge
Of the horizon to the zenith's height,
The locks of the approaching storm. Thou dirge

Of the dying year, to which this closing night
Will be the dome of a vast sepulcher,   25
Vaulted with all thy congregated might

Of vapors, from whose solid atmosphere
Black rain, and fire, and hail will burst: oh, hear!

3

Thou who didst waken from his summer dreams
The blue Mediterranean, where he lay,   30
Lulled by the coil of his crystálline streams,

Beside a pumice isle in Baiae's bay,
And saw in sleep old palaces and towers
Quivering within the wave's intenser day,

All overgrown with azure moss and flowers   35
So sweet, the sense faints picturing them! Thou
For whose path the Atlantic's level powers

Cleave themselves into chasms, while far below
The sea-blooms and the oozy woods which wear
The sapless foliage of the ocean, know   40

Thy voice, and suddenly grow gray with fear,
And tremble and despoil themselves: oh, hear!

4

If I were a dead leaf thou mightest bear;
If I were a swift cloud to fly with thee;
A wave to pant beneath thy power, and share   45

The impulse of thy strength, only less free
Than thou, O uncontrollable! If even
I were as in my boyhood, and could be

The comrade of thy wanderings over Heaven,
As then, when to outstrip thy skyey speed   50
Scarce seemed a vision; I would ne'er have striven

---

²¹**Maenad**   frenzied female worshipper of Dionysus, god of wine and revelry.

As thus with thee in prayer in my sore need.
Oh, lift me as a wave, a leaf, a cloud!
I fall upon the thorns of life! I bleed!

A heavy weight of hours has chained and bowed   55
One too like thee: tameless, and swift, and proud.

5

Make me thy lyre,° even as the forest is: *small harp*
What if my leaves are falling like its own!
The tumult of thy mighty harmonies

Will take from both a deep, autumnal tone,   60
Sweet though in sadness. Be thou, Spirit fierce,
My spirit! Be thou me, impetuous one!

Drive my dead thoughts over the universe
Like withered leaves to quicken a new birth!
And, by the incantation of this verse,   65

Scatter, as from an unextinguished hearth
Ashes and sparks, my words among mankind!
Be through my lips to unawakened earth

The trumpet of a prophecy! O Wind,
If Winter comes, can Spring be far behind?   70

[1820]

JOHN KEATS

[1795–1821]

As remarkable an achievement as Keats's poetry is, it is still less a wonder than his
life. As Douglas Bush once commented: "No other English poet of the century had
his poetic endowment, and no other strove so intensely." Keats's career as a poet
spanned four brief years: all his poetry is "early Keats." But his poems and letters
chronicle such a rapid growth of insight that when he died at twenty-six, he died a
fully mature poet.

Keats's first great sonnet, "On First Looking into Chapman's Homer," written when he was only twenty years old, indicates his aspirations as poet: to write a poetry of epic proportions in the manner of Homer, Virgil, Spenser, and Milton. *Endymion: A Poetic Romance,* his first truly ambitious undertaking, is a lengthy allegory that draws heavily on classical mythology. Moreover, Keats's final publication—*Lamia, Isabella, The Eve of St. Agnes, and Other Poems*—shows that he never abandoned these ambitions. "Hyperion" (later revised as "The Fall of Hyperion") reflects his continuing determination to "speak out loud and bold" in the grand manner. Similarly, the motif of classical allusion that animates so much of Keats's imagery springs from his study of the classics. Though early nineteenth-century and Victorian critics centered their study on Keats's longer works, we cannot overlook Keats's sonnets, nor the narratives, nor his incomparable ballad "La Belle Dame sans Merci." Most modern critics, however, focus on the great odes. While fully assuring Keats's artistic mastery, the odes also record his struggle with the essential questions of life and art, especially the relationship between beauty and truth. Keats himself describes their simple and yet stunning equation in an 1817 letter to his friend Benjamin Bailey: "I am certain of nothing but of the holiness of the Heart's affections and the truth of Imagination—What the Imagination seizes as Beauty must be truth."

Though little is known of Keats's earliest years, we do know that his father died after being thrown from a horse when the poet was eight. Shortly after the death of her husband, Keats's mother deserted the family, only to return six years later to die of tuberculosis. Despite a sizable inheritance, Keats led a life of relative poverty under the guardianship of the unimaginative and parsimonious Richard Abbey, who insisted that the adolescent Keats enter an apprenticeship with a surgeon, Thomas Hammond. By age twenty-one, however, over Abbey's objections, Keats abandoned medicine for poetry. At age twenty-three and already well trained for the task, Keats nursed his brother Tom, who soon died of tuberculosis. Although Keats found some pleasure in the company of his fiancée, the young Fanny Brawne, he could take little enjoyment in the reviews his poetry received. The leading journals dismissed the young poet as a "Cockney" upstart reaching beyond his station and cited his long poem *Endymion* as "drivelling idiocy." A year later Keats contracted the disease that had already claimed his mother and brother. Moving to Italy in hope of a cure, he died within a few months. At his request, no name marks the tombstone that reads "Here lies one whose name is writ in water."

The constant presence of death underscores Keats's poetry and keeps him alive to what is possible. Like Wordsworth, he presumes the vitality of sensation but does not limit himself to sight and sound. Keats's poetry also includes the senses of smell, taste, and touch. ("Touch," Keats wrote, "has a memory.") Often blurring sense imagery, Keats uses one sense in place of another, thus creating synesthesia. Keats writes of "fragrant and enwreathed light," "pale and silver silence," "scarlet pain," and "the touch of scent." In his "Ode to a Nightingale," the speaker complains:

> I cannot see what flowers are at my feet,
> Nor what soft incense hangs upon the boughs.

A dense flow of concrete particulars infuses Keats's poetry with cinematic close-ups, pans, distant shots, and fade-outs that vivify the narratives, sonnets, and odes. In "Ode to a Nightingale," the speaker mimics the bird's ecstatic cry: "Already with thee!" Here long and short vowels mirror the trill of the nightingale as the poem fades, cuts, and dissolves into an exquisite montage of the inner life that leaves the speaker dazed. In "Ode on Melancholy" we *see* the momentary "rainbow" but *taste* and *touch* the poised "salt sand-wave." The closing stanza continues to stress taste and touch with its

> *aching* Pleasure nigh,
> Turning to Poison while the *bee-mouth sips* . . .
> Though seen of none save him whose *strenuous tongue*
> Can *burst* Joy's *grape against his palate fine* . . .

Infusing a poetry of sensation, Keats's images register on palate and fingertip as well as on ear and eye. And so the world, the poet, and the poem become one through sensation. This blurring of borders reflects the empathic power Keats termed "negative capability." In essence, it was the poet's ability to remain "content with half-knowledge" while composing poetry, enabling the poet to assume other characters or entities, living or imagined, animate or inanimate. Free of his own life, "the chameleon poet" could then move among "uncertainties, mysteries, [and] doubts, without any irritable reaching after fact and reason." Negative capability was, for Keats, a way of emptying or "annulling" the self, and as such, a way of making room for his subject. As he wrote, "If a sparrow come before my window, I take part in its existence and pick about the gravel." According to his friend Richard Woodhouse, Keats even "affirmed that he can conceive of a billiard Ball that it may have a sense of delight from its own roundness, smoothness, volubility & the rapidity of its motion." Perhaps the most affecting of young Keats's efforts at negative capability is "This Living Hand," written shortly before he died:

> This living hand, now warm and capable
> Of earnest grasping, would, if it were cold
> And in the icy silence of the tomb,
> So haunt thy days and chill thy dreaming nights
> That thou wouldst wish thine own heart dry of blood
> So in my veins red life might stream again,
> And thou be conscience-calmed—see here it is—
> I hold it towards you.

Many of Keats's insights into the making of poetry are recorded in the poetry itself and in his letters, which T. S. Eliot called "the most important ever written by an English poet." His highly personal tone and strong sense of intimacy combine with the characteristic poetics of his best efforts—the dignity and sensitivity of his lines, the concreteness of description in which all the senses combine to re-create the encounter with experience—and place him among the very best of the English poets.

On First Looking into Chapman's Homer

Much have I traveled in the realms of gold
    And many goodly states and kingdoms seen;
    Round many western islands have I been
Which bards in fealty° to Apollo hold.   *allegiance*
Oft of one wide expanse had I been told   5
    That deep-browed Homer ruled as his demesne;°   *realm*
    Yet never did I breathe its pure serene
Till I heard Chapman speak out loud and bold:
Then felt I like some watcher of the skies
    When a new planet swims into his ken;   10
Or like stout Cortez when with eagle eyes
    He stared at the Pacific—and all his men
Looked at each other with a wild surmise—
    Silent, upon a peak in Darien.

                     [1816]

On Sitting Down to Read King Lear Once Again

O golden-tongued Romance with serene lute!
    Fair pluméd Siren°! Queen of far away!   *enchantress*
    Leave melodizing on this wintry day,
Shut up thine olden pages, and be mute:
Adieu! for once again the fierce dispute   5
    Betwixt damnation and impassioned clay
    Must I burn through; once more humbly assay
The bitter-sweet of this Shakespearean fruit.
Chief Poet! and ye clouds of Albion,
    Begetters of our deep eternal theme,   10
When through the old oak forest I am gone,
    Let me not wander in a barren dream,

ON FIRST LOOKING INTO CHAPMAN'S HOMER   Chapman's *Homer* was an Elizabethan translation of Homer.   **¹¹Cortez**   Keats mistakes Cortez for Balboa, who was the first Spanish *conquistador* to discover the Pacific, at Darien, Panama.
ON SITTING DOWN . . .   **⁹Albion**   ancient Britain.

But when I am consuméd in the fire,
Give me new Phoenix wings to fly at my desire.

[1818, 1838]

Why did I laugh tonight?

Why did I laugh tonight? No voice will tell:
    No God, no Demon of severe response,
Deigns to reply from Heaven or from Hell.
    Then to my human heart I turn at once.
Heart! Thou and I are here sad and alone;   5
    I say, why did I laugh? O mortal pain!
O Darkness! Darkness! ever must I moan,
    To question Heaven and Hell and Heart in vain.
Why did I laugh? I know this Being's lease,
    My fancy to its utmost blisses spreads;   10
Yet would I on this very midnight cease,
    And the world's gaudy ensigns see in shreds;
Verse, Fame, and Beauty are intense indeed,
But Death intenser—Death is Life's high meed.

[1819, 1848]

Bright Star

Bright star! would I were steadfast as thou art—
    Not in lone splendor hung aloft the night
And watching, with eternal lids apart
    Like Nature's patient sleepless Eremite,
The moving waters at their priestlike task   5
    Of pure ablution round earth's human shores,
Or gazing on the new soft fallen mask
    Of snow upon the mountains and the moors—
No—yet still steadfast, still unchangeable,
    Pillowed upon my fair love's ripening breast,   10
To feel forever its soft fall and swell,
    Awake forever in a sweet unrest,

¹⁴**Phoenix**   mythological bird that bursts into flame upon death and then rises from its ashes.

Still, still to hear her tender-taken breath,
And so live ever—or else swoon to death.

[1819, 1838]

When I have fears that I may cease to be

When I have fears that I may cease to be
   Before my pen has gleaned my teeming brain,
Before high-piléd books, in charact'ry,°   *written symbols*
   Hold like rich garners the full-ripened grain;
When I behold, upon the night's starred face,   *5*
   Huge cloudy symbols of a high romance,
And think that I may never live to trace
   Their shadows, with the magic hand of chance;
And when I feel, fair creature of an hour,
   That I shall never look upon thee more,   *10*
Never have relish in the faery° power   *magical*
   Of unreflecting love!—then on the shore
Of the wide world I stand alone, and think
Till Love and Fame to nothingness do sink.

[1818, 1848]

La Belle Dame sans Merci

O what can ail thee, Knight at arms,
   Alone and palely loitering?
The sedge has withered from the Lake
   And no birds sing!

O what can ail thee, Knight at arms,   *5*
   So haggard, and so woebegone?
The squirrel's granary is full
   And the harvest's done.

I see a lily on thy brow
   With anguish moist and fever dew,   *10*
And on thy cheeks a fading rose
   Fast withereth too.

LA BELLE DAME SANS MERCI   French for "the beautiful lady without mercy."

"I met a Lady in the Meads,°   *meadows*
    Full beautiful, a faery's child,
Her hair was long, her foot was light   15
    And her eyes were wild.

"I made a Garland for her head,
    And bracelets too, and fragrant Zone;°   *girdle, sash*
She looked at me as she did love
    And made sweet moan.   20

"I set her on my pacing steed
    And nothing else saw all day long,
For sidelong would she bend and sing
    A faery's song.

"She found me roots of relish sweet,   25
    And honey wild, and manna dew,
And sure in language strange she said
    'I love thee true.'

"She took me to her elfin grot
    And there she wept and sighed full sore,   30
And there I shut her wild wild eyes
    With kisses four.

"And there she lulléd me asleep,
    And there I dreamed, Ah Woe betide!
The latest dream I ever dreamt   35
    On the cold hill side.

"I saw pale Kings, and Princes too,
    Pale warriors, death-pale were they all;
They cried, 'La belle dame sans merci
    Hath thee in thrall!'   40

"I saw their starved lips in the gloam
    With horrid warning gapéd wide,
And I awoke, and found me here
    On the cold hill's side.

"And this is why I sojourn here,   45
    Alone and palely loitering;
Though the sedge is withered from the Lake
    And no birds sing."

                                                    [1819, 1888]

Ode to a Nightingale

1

My heart aches, and a drowsy numbness pains
  My sense, as though of hemlock I had drunk,
Or emptied some dull opiate to the drains°   *dregs*
  One minute past, and Lethe-wards had sunk:
'Tis not through envy of thy happy lot,   5
  But being too happy in thine happiness—
    That thou, light-wingéd Dryad° of the trees,   *tree nymph*
    In some melodious plot
  Of beechen green, and shadows numberless,
    Singest of summer in full-throated ease.   10

2

O, for a draught of vintage! that hath been
  Cooled a long age in the deep-delvéd earth,
Tasting of Flora and the country green,
  Dance, and Provençal song, and sunburnt mirth!
O for a beaker full of the warm South,   15
  Full of the true, the blushful Hippocrene,
    With beaded bubbles winking at the brim,
    And purple-stainéd mouth;
  That I might drink, and leave the world unseen,
    And with thee fade away into the forest dim: 20

3

Fade far away, dissolve, and quite forget
  What thou among the leaves hast never known,
The weariness, the fever, and the fret
  Here, where men sit and hear each other groan;
Where palsy shakes a few, sad, last gray hairs,   25
  Where youth grows pale, and specter-thin, and dies,
    Where but to think is to be full of sorrow
    And leaden-eyed despairs,
  Where Beauty cannot keep her lustrous eyes,
    Or new Love pine at them beyond tomorrow.   30

ODE TO A NIGHTINGALE   ²**hemlock** opiate; poisonous in large quantities.   ⁴**Lethe-wards** towards Lethe, the river of forgetfulness.   ¹³**Flora** goddess of the flowers.   ¹⁴**Provençal song** Provence, in southern France, home of the troubadours.   ¹⁶**true . . . Hippocrene** wine. A fountain on Mount Helicon in Greece, whose waters reputedly stimulated poetic imagination.

4

Away! away! for I will fly to thee,
  Not charioted by Bacchus and his pards,
But on the viewless° wings of Poesy,   *invisible*
  Though the dull brain perplexes and retards:
Already with thee! tender is the night,   *35*
  And haply° the Queen-Moon is on her throne,   *perhaps*
    Clustered around by all her starry Fays;°   *fairies*
      But here there is no light,
Save what from heaven is with the breezes blown
    Through verdurous glooms and winding mossy ways.   *40*

5

I cannot see what flowers are at my feet,
  Nor what soft incense hangs upon the boughs,
But, in embalméd° darkness, guess each sweet   *scented*
  Wherewith the seasonable month endows
The grass, the thicket, and the fruit tree wild;   *45*
  White hawthorn, and the pastoral eglantine°;   *sweetbriar*
    Fast fading violets covered up in leaves;
      And mid-May's eldest child,
The coming musk-rose, full of dewy wine,
    The murmurous haunt of flies on summer eves.   *50*

6

Darkling° I listen; and for many a time   *in darkness*
  I have been half in love with easeful Death,
Called him soft names in many a muséd rhyme,
  To take into the air my quiet breath;
Now more than ever seems it rich to die,   *55*
  To cease upon the midnight with no pain,
    While thou art pouring forth thy soul abroad
      In such an ecstasy!
Still wouldst thou sing, and I have ears in vain—
  To thy high requiem become a sod.   *60*

7

Thou wast not born for death, immortal Bird!
  No hungry generations tread thee down;
The voice I hear this passing night was heard
  In ancient days by emperor and clown:

---

³²**Bacchus . . . pards** the god of wine and revelry and the leopards who drew his chariot.

Perhaps the selfsame song that found a path   *65*
   Through the sad heart of Ruth, when, sick for home,
     She stood in tears amid the alien corn;
       The same that ofttimes hath
   Charmed magic casements, opening on the foam
     Of perilous seas, in faery lands forlorn.   *70*

8

Forlorn! the very word is like a bell
   To toll me back from thee to my sole self!
Adieu! the fancy cannot cheat so well
   As she is famed to do, deceiving elf.
Adieu! adieu! thy plaintive anthem fades   *75*
   Past the near meadows, over the still stream,
     Up the hill side; and now 'tis buried deep
       In the next valley-glades:
Was it a vision, or a waking dream?
     Fled is that music:—Do I wake or sleep?   *80*

Ode on a Grecian Urn

1

Thou still unravished bride of quietness,
   Thou foster child of silence and slow time,
Sylvan° historian, who canst thus express   *woodland*
   A flowery tale more sweetly than our rhyme:
What leaf-fringed legend haunts about thy shape   *5*
   Of deities or mortals, or of both,
     In Tempe or the dales of Arcady?
     What men or gods are these? What maidens loath?
What mad pursuit? What struggle to escape?
     What pipes and timbrels? What wild ecstasy?   *10*

2

Heard melodies are sweet, but those unheard
   Are sweeter; therefore, ye soft pipes, play on;
Not to the sensual ear, but, more endeared,
   Pipe to the spirit ditties of no tone:
Fair youth, beneath the trees, thou canst not leave   *15*
   Thy song, nor ever can those trees be bare;
     Bold Lover, never, never canst thou kiss,

ODE ON A GRECIAN URN   ⁷**Tempe . . . Arcady** beautiful rural regions of Greece.

Though winning near the goal—yet, do not grieve;
    She cannot fade, though thou hast not thy bliss,
    Forever wilt thou love, and she be fair!   *20*

3

Ah, happy, happy boughs! that cannot shed
    Your leaves, nor ever bid the Spring adieu;
And, happy melodist, unweariéd,
    Forever piping songs forever new;
More happy love! more happy, happy love!   *25*
    Forever warm and still to be enjoyed,
        Forever panting, and forever young;
All breathing human passion far above,
    That leaves a heart high-sorrowful and cloyed,
        A burning forehead, and a parching tongue.   *30*

4

Who are these coming to the sacrifice?
    To what green altar, O mysterious priest,
Lead'st thou that heifer lowing at the skies,
    And all her silken flanks with garlands dressed?
What little town by river or sea shore,   *35*
    Or mountain-built with peaceful citadel,
        Is emptied of this folk, this pious morn?
And, little town, thy streets forevermore
    Will silent be; and not a soul to tell
        Why thou art desolate, can e'er return.   *40*

5

O Attic shape! Fair attitude! with brede°   *woven pattern*
    Of marble men and maidens overwrought,°   *ornamented*
With forest branches and the trodden weed;
    Thou, silent form, dost tease us out of thought
As doth eternity: Cold Pastoral!   *45*
    When old age shall this generation waste,
        Thou shalt remain, in midst of other woe
Than ours, a friend to man, to whom thou say'st,
"Beauty is truth, truth beauty,"—that is all
    Ye know on earth, and all ye need to know.   *50*

[1819, 1820]

⁴¹**Attic**   Attica, the region of Greece in which Athens is located.

Ode on Melancholy

1

No, no, go not to Lethe, neither twist
    Wolfsbane, tight-rooted, for its poisonous wine;
Nor suffer thy pale forehead to be kissed
    By nightshade, ruby grape of Proserpine;
Make not your rosary of yew-berries,   5
    Nor let the beetle, nor the death-moth be
        Your mournful Psyche, nor the downy owl
    A partner in your sorrow's mysteries;
    For shade to shade will come too drowsily,
        And drown the wakeful anguish of the soul.   10

2

But when the melancholy fit shall fall
    Sudden from heaven like a weeping cloud,
That fosters the droop-headed flowers all,
    And hides the green hill in an April shroud;
Then glut thy sorrow on a morning rose,   15
    Or on the rainbow of the salt sand-wave,
        Or on the wealth of globéd peonies;
Or if thy mistress some rich anger shows,
    Imprison her soft hand, and let her rave,
        And feed deep, deep upon her peerless eyes.   20

3

She dwells with Beauty—Beauty that must die;
    And Joy, whose hand is ever at his lips
Bidding adieu; and aching Pleasure nigh,
    Turning to Poison while the bee-mouth sips:
Aye, in the very temple of Delight   25
    Veiled Melancholy has her sov'reign shrine,
        Though seen of none save him whose strenuous tongue
    Can burst Joy's grape against his palate fine;
His soul shall taste the sadness of her might,
        And be among her cloudy trophies hung.   30

[1819, 1820]

ODE ON MELANCHOLY   [1]**Lethe**   river of forgetfulness in the Greek mythological underworld.
[2]**Wolfsbane** a poisonous plant.   [4]**nightshade** a poisonous plant.   **Proserpine**   queen of the under-
world.   [7]**Psyche**   In ancient times, Psyche (the soul) was occasionally represented by a butterfly.

To Autumn

1

Season of mists and mellow fruitfulness,
   Close bosom-friend of the maturing sun;
Conspiring with him how to load and bless
   With fruit the vines that round the thatch-eaves run;
To bend with apples the mossed cottage-trees,   *5*
   And fill all fruit with ripeness to the core;
      To swell the gourd, and plump the hazel shells
   With a sweet kernel; to set budding more,
And still more, later flowers for the bees,
   Until they think warm days will never cease,   *10*
      For Summer has o'er-brimmed their clammy cells.

2

Who hath not seen thee oft amid thy store?
   Sometimes whoever seeks abroad may find
Thee sitting careless on a granary floor,
   Thy hair soft-lifted by the winnowing wind;   *15*
Or on a half-reaped furrow sound asleep,
   Drowsed with the fume of poppies, while thy hook°   *sickle*
      Spares the next swath and all its twinéd flowers:
And sometimes like a gleaner thou dost keep
   Steady thy laden head across a brook;   *20*
   Or by a cider-press, with patient look,
      Thou watchest the last oozings hours by hours.

3

Where are the songs of Spring? Aye, where are they?
   Think not of them, thou hast thy music too—
While barréd clouds bloom the soft-dying day,   *25*
   And touch the stubble-plains with rosy hue;
Then in a wailful choir the small gnats mourn
   Among the river sallows,° borne aloft   *low-growing willows*
   Or sinking as the light wind lives or dies;
And full-grown lambs loud bleat from hilly bourn;°   *field 30*
   Hedge crickets sing; and now with treble soft
   The redbreast whistles from a garden-croft;°   *small garden*
      And gathering swallows twitter in the skies.

[1819, 1820]

RALPH WALDO EMERSON

[1803–1882]

Brahma

If the red slayer think he slays,
  Or if the slain think he is slain,
They know not well the subtle ways
  I keep, and pass, and turn again.

Far or forgot to me is near;   5
  Shadow and sunlight are the same;
The vanished gods to me appear;
  And one to me are shame and fame.

They reckon ill who leave me out;
  When me they fly, I am the wings;   10
I am the doubter and the doubt,
  And I the hymn the Brahmin sings.

The strong gods pine for my abode,
  And pine in vain the sacred Seven,
But thou, meek lover of the good!   15
  Find me, and turn thy back on heaven.

                                                            [1857]

ELIZABETH BARRETT BROWNING

[1806–1861]

How do I love thee? Let me count the ways

How do I love thee? Let me count the ways.
I love thee to the depth and breadth and height
My soul can reach, when feeling out of sight
For the ends of Being and ideal Grace.
I love thee to the level of everyday's   5
Most quiet need, by sun and candle-light.
I love thee freely, as men strive for Right;
I love thee purely, as they turn from Praise.

I love thee with the passion put to use
In my old griefs, and with my childhood's faith.
I love thee with a love I seemed to lose
With my lost saints—I love thee with the breath,
Smiles, tears, of all my life!—and, if God choose,
I shall but love thee better after death.

10

[1850]

E D W A R D   F I T Z G E R A L D

[1809–1883]

from *The Rubáiyát of Omar Khayyám*

1

Wake! For the Sun, who scattered into flight
The Stars before him from the Field of Night,
    Drives Night along with them from Heav'n, and strikes
The Sultán's Turret with a Shaft of Light.

7

Come, fill the Cup, and in the fire of Spring
Your Winter-garment of Repentance fling:
    The Bird of Time has but a little way
To flutter—and the Bird is on the Wing.

5

12

A Book of Verses underneath the Bough,
A Jug of Wine, a Loaf of Bread—and Thou
    Beside me singing in the Wilderness—
Oh, Wilderness were Paradise enow!

10

16

The Worldly Hope men set their Hearts upon
Turns Ashes—or it prospers; and anon,
    Like Snow upon the Desert's dusty Face,
Lighting a little hour or two—is gone.

15

THE RUBÁIYÁT OF OMAR KHAYYÁM   Omar Khayyám (c. 1050–c. 1132) was a Persian poet whose quatrains Fitzgerald translated no less than five times. Our selection samples Fitzgerald's more famous verses from his fourth edition.

24

Ah, make the most of what we yet may spend,
Before we too into the Dust descend;
   Dust into Dust, and under Dust to lie,
Sans Wine, sans Song, sans Singer, and sans End!   20

42

And if the Wine you drink, the Lip you press,
End in what All begins and ends in—Yes;
   Think then you are TODAY what YESTERDAY
You were—TOMORROW you shall not be less.

54

Waste not your Hour, nor in the vain pursuit   25
Of This and That endeavor and dispute;
   Better be jocund with the fruitful Grape
Than sadden after none, or bitter, Fruit.

63

Oh threats of Hell and Hopes of Paradise!
One thing at least is certain—*This* Life flies;   30
   One thing is certain and the rest is Lies;
The Flower that once has blown for ever dies.

71

The Moving Finger writes; and, having writ,
Moves on: nor all your Piety nor Wit
   Shall lure it back to cancel half a Line,   35
Nor all your Tears wash out a Word of it.

74

YESTERDAY *This* Day's Madness did prepare;
TOMORROW's Silence, Triumph, or Despair:
   Drink! for you know not whence you came, nor why:
Drink! for you know not why you go, nor where.   40

100

Yon rising Moon that looks for us again—
How oft hereafter will she wax and wane;
   How oft hereafter rising look for us
Through this same Garden—and for *one* in vain!

101

And when like her, oh Sákí, you shall pass   45
Among the Guests Star-scattered on the Grass,
   And in your joyous errand reach the spot
Where I made One—turn down an empty Glass!

TAMÁM

[1859, 1879]

OLIVER WENDELL HOLMES

[1809–1894]

The Chambered Nautilus

This is the ship of pearl, which, poets feign,
   Sails the unshadowed main,
   The venturous bark that flings
On the sweet summer wind its purpled wings
In gulfs enchanted, where the Siren sings,   5
   And coral reefs lie bare,
Where the cold sea-maids rise to sun their streaming hair.

Its webs of living gauze no more unfurl;
   Wrecked is the ship of pearl!
   And every chambered cell,   10
Where its dim dreaming life was wont to dwell,
As the frail tenant shaped his growing shell,
   Before thee lies revealed,
Its irised ceiling rent, its sunless crypt unsealed!

Year after year beheld the silent toil   15
   That spread his lustrous coil;
   Still, as the spiral grew,
He left the past year's dwelling for the new,
Stole with soft step its shining archway through,
   Built up its idle door,   20
Stretched in his last-found home, and knew the old no more.

THE RUBÁIYÁT OF OMAR KHAYYÁM   ⁴⁹**Tamám** It is ended.
THE CHAMBERED NAUTILUS   a mollusk found in the South Pacific whose webbed appendages were
thought to function as a sail.

Thanks for the heavenly message brought by thee,
    Child of the wandering sea,
    Cast from her lap, forlorn!
From thy dead lips a clearer note is born   25
Than ever Triton blew from wreathéd horn!
    While on mine ear it rings,
Through the deep caves of thought I hear a voice that sings:

Build thee more stately mansions, O my soul,
    As the swift seasons roll!   30
    Leave thy low-vaulted past!
Let each new temple, nobler than the last,
Shut thee from heaven with a dome more vast,
    Till thou at length art free,
Leaving thine outgrown shell by life's unresting sea!   35

[1858]

EDGAR ALLAN POE

[1809–1849]

To Helen

Helen, thy beauty is to me
    Like those Nicean barks° of yore,   *ships*
That gently, o'er a perfumed sea,
    The weary, way-worn wanderer bore
    To his own native shore.   5

On desperate seas long wont to roam,
    Thy hyacinth hair, thy classic face,
Thy Naiad airs have brought me home
    To the glory that was Greece
And the grandeur that was Rome.   10

Lo! in yon brilliant window-niche
    How statue-like I see thee stand!
    The agate lamp within thy hand,
Ah! Psyche from the regions which
    Are Holy Land!   15

[1831, 1845]

THE CHAMBERED NAUTILUS   ²⁶**Triton** Greek sea god who blew on a trumpet made of a conch shell.
TO HELEN   ⁷**hyacinth hair** allusion to the curled hair of the slain youth Hyacinthus, beloved of Apollo.
⁸**Naiad** water nymph.

The Raven

Once upon a midnight dreary, while I pondered, weak and weary,
Over many a quaint and curious volume of forgotten lore—
While I nodded, nearly napping, suddenly there came a tapping,
As of some one gently rapping, rapping at my chamber door—
" 'Tis some visiter," I muttered, "tapping at my chamber door—   5
    Only this and nothing more."

Ah, distinctly I remember it was in the bleak December;
And each separate dying ember wrought its ghost upon the floor.
Eagerly I wished the morrow;—vainly I had sought to borrow
From my books surcease of sorrow—sorrow for the lost Lenore—   10
For the rare and radiant maiden whom the angels name Lenore—
    Nameless *here* for evermore.

And the silken, sad, uncertain rustling of each purple curtain
Thrilled me—filled me with fantastic terrors never felt before;
So that now, to still the beating of my heart, I stood repeating   15
" 'Tis some visiter entreating entrance at my chamber door—
Some late visiter entreating entrance at my chamber door;—
    This it is and nothing more."

Presently my soul grew stronger; hesitating then no longer,
"Sir," said I, "or Madam, truly your forgiveness I implore;   20
But the fact is I was napping, and so gently you came rapping,
And so faintly you came tapping, tapping at my chamber door,
  That I scarce was sure I heard you"—here I opened wide the door;—
    Darkness there and nothing more.

Deep into that darkness peering, long I stood there wondering, fearing,   25
Doubting, dreaming dreams no mortal ever dared to dream before;
But the silence was unbroken, and the stillness gave no token,
And the only word there spoken was the whispered word, "Lenore!"
This I whispered, and an echo murmured back the word, "Lenore!"
    Merely this and nothing more.   30

Back into the chamber turning, all my soul within me burning,
Soon again I heard a tapping somewhat louder than before.
"Surely," said I, "surely that is something at my window lattice;
Let me see, then, what thereat is, and this mystery explore—
Let my heart be still a moment and this mystery explore;—   35
    'Tis the wind and nothing more!"

Open here I flung the shutter, when, with many a flirt and flutter,
In there stepped a stately Raven of the saintly days of yore;

Not the least obeisance made he; not a minute stopped or stayed he;
But, with mien of lord or lady, perched above my chamber door—   40
Perched upon a bust of Pallas just above my chamber door—
    Perched, and sat, and nothing more.

Then this ebony bird beguiling my sad fancy into smiling,
By the grave and stern decorum of the countenance it wore,
"Though thy crest be shorn and shaven, thou," I said, "art sure no craven,   45
Ghastly grim and ancient Raven wandering from the Nightly shore—
Tell me what thy lordly name is on the Night's Plutonian shore!"
    Quoth the Raven "Nevermore."

Much I marvelled this ungainly fowl to hear discourse so plainly,
Though its answer little meaning—little relevancy bore;   50
For we cannot help agreeing that no living human being
Ever yet was blessed with seeing bird above his chamber door—
Bird or beast upon the sculptured bust above his chamber door,
    With such name as "Nevermore."

But the Raven, sitting lonely on the placid bust, spoke only   55
That one word, as if his soul in that one word he did outpour.
Nothing farther then he uttered—not a feather then he fluttered—
Till I scarcely more than muttered "Other friends have flown before—
On the morrow *he* will leave me, as my Hopes have flown before."
    Then the bird said "Nevermore."   60

Startled at the stillness broken by reply so aptly spoken,
"Doubtless," said I, "what it utters is its only stock and store
Caught from some unhappy master whom unmerciful Disaster
Followed fast and followed faster till his songs one burden bore—
Till the dirges of his Hope that melancholy burden bore   65
    Of 'Never—nevermore.' "

But the Raven still beguiling my sad fancy into smiling,
Straight I wheeled a cushioned seat in front of bird, and bust and door;
Then, upon the velvet sinking, I betook myself to linking
Fancy unto fancy, thinking what this ominous bird of yore—   70
What this grim, ungainly, ghastly, gaunt, and ominous bird of yore
    Meant in croaking "Nevermore."

Thus I sat engaged in guessing, but no syllable expressing
To the fowl whose fiery eyes now burned into my bosom's core;
This and more I sat divining, with my head at ease reclining   75

---

⁴¹Pallas   Pallas Athena, patron goddess of Athens   **⁴⁷Plutonian**   Pluto, god of the underworld.

On the cushion's velvet lining that the lamp-light gloated o'er,
But whose velvet-violet lining with the lamp-light gloating o'er,
    She shall press, ah, nevermore!

Then, methought, the air grew denser, perfumed from an unseen censer
Swung by seraphim whose foot-falls tinkled on the tufted floor.   *80*
"Wretch," I cried, "thy God hath lent thee—by these angels he hath sent thee
Respite—respite and nepenthe from thy memories of Lenore;
Quaff, oh quaff this kind nepenthe and forget this lost Lenore!"
    Quoth the Raven "Nevermore."

"Prophet!" said I, "thing of evil!—prophet still, if bird or devil!—   *85*
Whether Tempter sent, or whether tempest tossed thee here ashore,
Desolate yet all undaunted, on this desert land enchanted—
Oh this home by Horror haunted—tell me truly, I implore—
Is there—*is* there balm in Gilead?—tell me—tell me, I implore!"
    Quoth the Raven "Nevermore."   *90*

"Prophet!" said I, "thing of evil!—prophet still, if bird or devil!
By that Heaven that bends above us—by that God we both adore—
Tell this soul with sorrow laden if, within the distant Aidenn,
It shall clasp a sainted maiden whom the angels name Lenore—
Clasp a rare and radiant maiden whom the angels name Lenore."   *95*
    Quoth the Raven "Nevermore."

"Be that word our sign of parting, bird or fiend!" I shrieked, upstarting—
"Get thee back into the tempest and the Night's Plutonian shore!
Leave no black plume as a token of that lie thy soul hath spoken!
Leave my loneliness unbroken!—quit the bust above my door!   *100*
Take thy beak from out my heart, and take thy form from off my door!"
    Quoth the Raven "Nevermore."

And the Raven, never flitting, still is sitting, *still* is sitting
On the pallid bust of Pallas just above my chamber door;
And his eyes have all the seeming of a demon's that is dreaming,   *105*
And the lamp-light o'er him streaming throws his shadow on the floor;
And my soul from out that shadow that lies floating on the floor
    Shall be lifted—nevermore!

                                                          [1845]

Annabel Lee

    It was many and many a year ago,
        In a kingdom by the sea,
    That a maiden there lived whom you may know
        By the name of Annabel Lee;

And this maiden she lived with no other thought   5
    Than to love and be loved by me.

She was a child and *I* was a child,
    In this kingdom by the sea,
But we loved with a love that was more than love—
    I and my Annabel Lee—   10
With a love that the wingéd seraphs of Heaven
    Coveted her and me.

And this was the reason that, long ago,
    In this kingdom by the sea,
A wind blew out of a cloud by night   15
    Chilling my Annabel Lee;
So that her highborn kinsmen came
    And bore her away from me,
To shut her up in a sepulchre
    In this kingdom by the sea.   20

The angels, not half so happy in Heaven,
    Went envying her and me:
Yes! that was the reason (as all men know,
    In this kingdom by the sea)
That the wind came out of the cloud, chilling   25
    And killing my Annabel Lee.

But our love it was stronger by far than the love
    Of those who were older than we—
    Of many far wiser than we—
And neither the angels in Heaven above   30
    Nor the demons down under the sea,
Can ever dissever my soul from the soul
    Of the beautiful Annabel Lee:

For the moon never beams without bringing me dreams
    Of the beautiful Annabel Lee;   35
And the stars never rise but I see the bright eyes
    Of the beautiful Annabel Lee;
And so, all the night-tide, I lie down by the side
Of my darling, my darling, my life and my bride,
    In her sepulchre there by the sea—   40
    In her tomb by the side of the sea.

                                                          [1850]

ALFRED, LORD TENNYSON

[1809–1892]

Like Walt Whitman, his near contemporary, Alfred Tennyson has come to represent the consummate poet. Both Whitman and Tennyson became recognized as great poets as well as popular ones. Both were honored, especially in their later years, Whitman by contemporary writers, who paid tribute by visiting him at his Camden home; Tennyson by the establishment, who made him poet laureate in 1850 following the death of William Wordsworth, the previous recipient of that august honor.

Public images aside, however, Whitman and Tennyson were radically different poets. Whitman, a revolutionary poet, initiated a set of poetic experiments with form and line length, opening both to new possibilities and inaugurating a new age of poetic experimentation that continues today. Although he too experimented with different styles and forms throughout his long career, Tennyson is a more conservative poet best known and most highly regarded for his lyric achievement in forms that look back to classical models. He is especially revered for the music of his verse, for its rich melody and its intricate rhythmic patterns, which could not be more different from Whitman's "barbaric yawp."

Moreover, Tennyson's poetry, unlike Whitman's, reflects the taste and values of his time. A Victorian poet through and through, Tennyson explored issues that troubled many during the mid to late nineteenth century. Prominent among such concerns was the problem of religious faith. During a period when scientific discoveries were being made, especially in biology and geology, the faith of many people was being clouded by these issues and by social problems such as child labor, poverty, and industrialism. Susceptible to protracted periods of doubt and despair, the melancholic Tennyson wrestled personally with the problem of belief. His poems, though characterized by the Romanticist spirit of affirmation and hope, frequently include heavy doses of skepticism and doubt. Tennyson himself embodied in mind and poetic output the doubts that had been cast on traditional philosophical explanations, the skepticism that had undermined previous religious certainties, and developments such as Darwin's theory of natural selection that had altered scientific understanding. Hope and despair, faith and doubt coexist in many of Tennyson's poems. Moreover, as T. S. Eliot has suggested, Tennyson wrote at his best when depicting skepticism and doubt. Eliot remarked about *In Memoriam,* in fact, that it "is not religious because of the quality of its faith, but because of the quality of its doubt."

Alfred Tennyson was the fourth of twelve children. He was born into a complex family with its share of problems. His father was a clergyman by default, working at a career he disliked largely because he had been disinherited of a minor fortune by his own father. Alfred Tennyson's father expressed his resentment in melancholic brooding and in regular bouts of drunken rage. One of his children became an opium addict; another was confined to an asylum for life. Counterbalancing these desperate facts, however, was the senior Tennyson's learning. He was well educated, particularly in languages, and he taught his sons ancient and modern languages in preparation for attendance at Cambridge University.

During his years at Cambridge, Tennyson was recognized by a group known as the "Apostles," who encouraged him to write and who sought publication venues for his work. Among the group was Arthur Hallam, two years Tennyson's junior, who became his best friend and greatest advocate. Tennyson was deprived of Hallam's companionship when in 1831 Alfred had to leave Cambridge following his father's death. Two years later Arthur Hallam died, leaving Tennyson near despair. Bereft of his closest and only dear friend, lacking money, and suffering from both family tensions and the poor critical reception of his first book of poems, Tennyson nonetheless embarked upon a series of elegies in memory of Hallam. Begun in 1833, the year of Hallam's death, the collection of 131 elegiac poems was completed and published anonymously in 1850 as *In Memoriam A.H.H.* A set of reflections on man's relationship to God and the natural world, the poems range in length from a few brief stanzas to longer meditative lyrics extending to 144 lines. By turns affirmative and skeptical, hopeful and doubtful, the elegies express Tennyson's intense love for his friend and his deep suffering at his loss. To some extent the elegies of *In Memoriam,* for which Tennyson devised a special four-line stanza rhyming *abba,* were therapeutic. He came to accept not only the loss of his friend but also the place of suffering in human life. It was this quality of acceptance and faith that Queen Victoria recognized in the work and for which she selected Tennyson to be her poet laureate. Moreover, along with the marked rise in his critical reputation occasioned by publication of *In Memoriam* was the financial boost it gave Tennyson, providing him with a substantial income and the financial resources to marry.

Although he is perhaps best known for *In Memoriam,* Tennyson also composed many other important works, some of them very well known. Among his early poems is "Mariana," which describes the pain of loneliness as Mariana waits alone, near despair, for her lover to arrive. In "Mariana" we can discern the poetic qualities for which Tennyson is most admired: the use of symbolic landscape, which he uses more masterfully in the elegies of *In Memoriam;* the use of images to convey emotional states, perhaps the central achievement of another famous lyric, "Break, break, break"; and the poetic music, which appears at its most splendid in three songs from *The Princess:* "Tears, idle tears"; "Now sleeps the crimson petal"; and "Come down, O maid." These lyrics are justly considered among the most beautiful in English for their visual imagery as well as for their music. As in the best of Tennyson's poems, the descriptions of nature in these lyrics is more than scene-setting picturesqueness; it reflects, instead, the psychological state of the speaker while evoking an emotional response from the reader. Scenery is linked to states of mind; feelings are summoned up and symbolized at the same time. Tennyson accomplishes this rich fusion of sound and symbol both in brief lyrics and in longer choral odes like "The Lotos-Eaters."

Less musical than these poems are Tennyson's dramatic monologues, including "Ulysses," which, though not without its poetic beauties, is more a poetry of statement than a poetry of song. Like "Tithonus," with which it forms an interesting contrastive pair, "Ulysses" illustrates Tennyson's fondness for the classical past. (So steeped was Tennyson in Latin and Greek that his father would not let him leave for college until he could recite all the odes of Horace by heart.) What is interesting about these two dramatic monologues, however, is how Tennyson characterizes these classical figures, something his contemporary Robert Browning also excelled at.

Tennyson has been described as having the finest ear of any poet writing in English. He has also been described as among the stupidest of English poets. Both characterizations hold more than a grain of truth, though calling Tennyson stupid reflects as much a disagreement with his ideas as an opinion that he had none. Whatever evaluation we finally make of Tennyson's mind, it is clear that he is less a poet of reflection, like William Wordsworth, than a poet of sensation, such as John Keats, with whom Tennyson is sometimes compared. Tennyson, moreover, is more a poet of the past than of the present (although he did write some poems, such as "The Charge of the Light Brigade," that were occasioned by contemporary events).

Tennyson was honored in his own time by the great and loved by the common people for his poetry of hope, for the heroic ideals and traditional virtues his poems celebrate. As his friend Arthur Hallam wrote in an essay celebrating the 1830 volume, *Poems, Chiefly Lyrical,* Tennyson's poems "communicate the love of beauty to the heart." Today Tennyson is recognized as a great poet less for the values he endorses than for his sheer mastery of language. And though he was very much a poet for his age, one who reigned supreme for half a century, his music still sounds in his sensuous and elegant verse.

Mariana

> *Mariana in the moated grange.*
> *Measure for Measure*

> With blackest moss the flower-plots
>   Were thickly crusted, one and all;
> The rusted nails fell from the knots
>   That held the pear to the gable wall.
> The broken sheds looked sad and strange: 5
>   Unlifted was the clinking latch;
>   Weeded and worn the ancient thatch
> Upon the lonely moated grange.

MARIANA   In Shakespeare's *Measure for Measure* 3.1.277, Mariana waits in a grange (an outlying farmhouse) for her lover who has deserted her.

She only said, "My life is dreary,
   He cometh not," she said;   10
She said, "I am aweary, aweary,
   I would that I were dead!"

Her tears fell with the dews at even;
   Her tears fell ere the dews were dried;
She could not look on the sweet heaven,   15
   Either at morn or eventide.
After the flitting of the bats,
   When thickest dark did trance° the sky,   *cross*
   She drew her casement curtain by,
And glanced athwart the glooming flats.   20
   She only said, "The night is dreary,
      He cometh not," she said;
   She said, "I am aweary, aweary,
      I would that I were dead!"

Upon the middle of the night,   25
   Waking she heard the nightfowl crow;
The cock sung out an hour ere light;
   From the dark fen the oxen's low
Came to her; without hope of change,
   In sleep she seemed to walk forlorn,   30
   Till cold winds woke the gray-eyed morn
About the lonely moated grange.
   She only said, "The day is dreary,
      He cometh not," she said;
   She said, "I am aweary, aweary,   35
      I would that I were dead!"

About a stonecast from the wall
   A sluice with blackened waters slept,
And o'er it many, round and small,
   The clustered marish-mosses crept.   40
Hard by a poplar shook alway,
   All silver-green with gnarlèd bark:
   For leagues no other tree did mark
The level waste, the rounding gray.
   She only said, "My life is dreary,   45
      He cometh not," she said;

---

⁴⁰**marish-mosses**   "The little marsh-moss lumps that float on the surface of water" [Tennyson's comment].

She said, "I am aweary, aweary,
        I would that I were dead!"

And ever when the moon was low,
    And the shrill winds were up and away,   50
In the white curtain, to and fro,
    She saw the gusty shadow sway.
But when the moon was very low,
    And wild winds bound within their cell,
    The shadow of the poplar fell   55
Upon her bed, across her brow.
        She only said, "The night is dreary,
            He cometh not," she said;
        She said, "I am aweary, aweary,
            I would that I were dead!"   60

All day within the dreamy house,
    The doors upon their hinges creaked;
The blue fly sung in the pane; the mouse
    Behind the moldering wainscot shrieked,
Or from the crevice peered about.   65
    Old faces glimmered through the doors,
    Old footsteps trod the upper floors,
Old voices called her from without.
        She only said, "My life is dreary,
            He cometh not," she said;   70
        She said, "I am aweary, aweary,
            I would that I were dead!"

The sparrow's chirrup on the roof,
    The slow clock ticking, and the sound
Which to the wooing wind aloof   75
    The poplar made, did all confound
Her sense; but most she loathed the hour
    When the thick-moted sunbeam lay
    Athwart the chambers, and the day
Was sloping toward his western bower.   80
        Then, said she, "I am very dreary,
            He will not come," she said;
        She wept, "I am aweary, aweary,
            Oh God, that I were dead!"

                                                    [1830]

The Lotos-Eaters

"Courage!" he said, and pointed toward the land,
"This mounting wave will roll us shoreward soon."
In the afternoon they came unto a land
In which it seeméd always afternoon.
All round the coast the languid air did swoon,   5
Breathing like one that hath a weary dream.
Full-faced above the valley stood the moon;
And, like a downward smoke, the slender stream
Along the cliff to fall and pause and fall did seem.

A land of streams! some, like a downward smoke,   10
Slow-dropping veils of thinnest lawn, did go;
And some through wavering lights and shadows broke,
Rolling a slumbrous sheet of foam below.
They saw the gleaming river seaward flow
From the inner land; far off, three mountain-tops,   15
Three silent pinnacles of aged snow,
Stood sunset-flushed; and, dewed with showery drops,
Up-clomb the shadowy pine above the woven copse.

The charméd sunset lingered low adown
In the red West; through mountain clefts the dale   20
Was seen far inland, and the yellow down
Bordered with palm, and many a winding vale
And meadow, set with slender galingale;
A land where all things always seemed the same!
And round about the keel with faces pale,   25
Dark faces pale against that rosy flame,
The mild-eyed melancholy Lotos-eaters came.

Branches they bore of that enchanted stem,
Laden with flower and fruit, whereof they gave
To each, but whoso did receive of them   30
And taste, to him the gushing of the wave
Far far away did seem to mourn and rave
On alien shores; and if his fellow spake,
His voice was thin, as voices from the grave;

THE LOTOS-EATERS   Tennyson's poem expands an episode from Homer's *Odyssey* (Book nine). Homer
depicts a group of Greek warriors being tempted to abandon their homeward voyage following the Trojan War.
¹he said   Ulysses (Odysseus).

And deep-asleep he seemed, yet all awake,   35
And music in his ears his beating heart did make.

They sat them down upon the yellow sand,
Between the sun and moon upon the shore;
And sweet it was to dream of fatherland,
Of child, and wife, and slave; but evermore   40
Most weary seemed the sea, weary the oar,
Weary the wandering fields of barren foam.
Then someone said, "We will return no more;"
And all at once they sang, "Our island home
Is far beyond the wave; we will no longer roam."   45

Choric Song
1

There is sweet music here that softer falls
Than petals from blown roses on the grass,
Or night-dews on still waters between walls
Of shadowy granite, in a gleaming pass;
Music that gentlier on the spirit lies,   50
Than tired eyelids upon tired eyes;
Music that brings sweet sleep down from the blissful skies.
Here are cool mosses deep,
And through the moss the ivies creep,
And in the stream the long-leaved flowers weep,   55
And from the craggy ledge the poppy hangs in sleep.

2

Why are we weighed upon with heaviness,
And utterly consumed with sharp distress,
While all things else have rest from weariness?
All things have rest: why should we toil alone,   60
We only toil, who are the first of things,
And make perpetual moan,
Still from one sorrow to another thrown;
Nor ever fold our wings,
And cease from wanderings,   65
Nor steep our brows in slumber's holy balm;
Nor harken what the inner spirit sings,
"There is no joy but calm!"—
Why should we only toil, the roof and crown of things?

"Our island home Ithaca.

3

Lo! in the middle of the wood,   *70*
The folded leaf is wooed from out the bud
With winds upon the branch, and there
Grows green and broad, and takes no care,
Sun-steeped at noon, and in the moon
Nightly dew-fed; and turning yellow   *75*
Falls, and floats adown the air.
Lo! sweetened with the summer light,
The full-juiced apple, waxing over-mellow,
Drops in a silent autumn night.
All its allotted length of days   *80*
The flower ripens in its place,
Ripens and fades, and falls, and hath no toil,
Fast-rooted in the fruitful soil.

4

Hateful is the dark-blue sky,
Vaulted o'er the dark-blue sea.   *85*
Death is the end of life; ah, why
Should life all labor be?
Let us alone. Time driveth onward fast
And in a little while our lips are dumb.
Let us alone. What is it that will last?   *90*
All things are taken from us, and become
Portions and parcels of the dreadful past.
Let us alone. What pleasure can we have
To war with evil? Is there any peace
In ever climbing up the climbing wave?   *95*
All things have rest, and ripen toward the grave
In silence—ripen, fall, and cease:
Give us long rest or death, dark death, or dreamful ease.

5

How sweet it were, hearing the downward stream,
With half-shut eyes ever to seem   *100*
Falling asleep in a half-dream!
To dream and dream, like yonder amber light,
Which will not leave the myrrh-bush on the height;
To hear each other's whispered speech;
Eating the Lotos day by day,   *105*
To watch the crisping° ripples on the beach,   **curling**
And tender curving lines of creamy spray;

To lend our hearts and spirits wholly
To the influence of mild-minded melancholy;
To muse and brood and live again in memory,   110
With those old faces of our infancy
Heaped over with a mound of grass,
Two handfuls of white dust, shut in an urn of brass!

6

Dear is the memory of our wedded lives,
And dear the last embraces of our wives   115
And their warm tears; but all hath suffered change;
For surely now our household hearths are cold,
Our sons inherit us, our looks are strange,
And we should come like ghosts to trouble joy.
Or else the island princes over-bold   120
Have eat our substance, and the minstrel sings
Before them of the ten years' war in Troy,
And our great deeds, as half-forgotten things.
Is there confusion in the little isle?
Let what is broken so remain.   125
The Gods are hard to reconcile;
'Tis hard to settle order once again.
There *is* confusion worse than death,
Trouble on trouble, pain on pain,
Long labor unto aged breath,   130
Sore tasks to hearts worn out by many wars
And eyes grown dim with gazing on the pilot stars.

7

But, propt on beds of amaranth and moly,
How sweet—while warm airs lull us, blowing lowly—
With half-dropt eyelid still,   135
Beneath a heaven dark and holy,
To watch the long bright river drawing slowly
His waters from the purple hill—
To hear the dewy echoes calling
From cave to cave through the thick-twined vine—   140
To watch the emerald-colored water falling
Through many a woven acanthus-wreath divine!
Only to hear and see the far-off sparkling brine,
Only to hear were sweet, stretched out beneath the pine.

[120]**the island princes** suitors of Ulysses' wife, Penelope. [133]**amaranth and moly** flowers; amaranth was a legendary unfading flower, and moly a flower that Homer describes as possessing magical properties.

8

The Lotos blooms below the barren peak,   *145*
The Lotos blows by every winding creek;
All day the wind breathes low with mellower tone;
Through every hollow cave and alley lone
Round and round the spicy downs the yellow Lotos-dust is blown.
We have had enough of action, and of motion we,   *150*
Rolled to starboard, rolled to larboard, when the surge was seething free,
Where the wallowing monster spouted his foam-fountains in the sea.
Let us swear an oath, and keep it with an equal mind,
In the hollow Lotos-land to live and lie reclined
On the hills like Gods together, careless of mankind.   *155*
For they lie beside their nectar, and the bolts are hurled
Far below them in the valleys, and the clouds are lightly curled
Round their golden houses, girdled with the gleaming world;
Where they smile in secret, looking over wasted lands,
Blight and famine, plague and earthquake, roaring deeps and fiery sands, *160*
Clanging fights, and flaming towns, and sinking ships, and praying hands.
But they smile, they find a music centered in a doleful song
Steaming up, a lamentation and an ancient tale of wrong,
Like a tale of little meaning though the words are strong;
Chanted from an ill-used race of men that cleave the soil,   *165*
Sow the seed, and reap the harvest with enduring toil,
Storing yearly little dues of wheat, and wine and oil;
Till they perish and they suffer—some, 'tis whispered—down in hell
Suffer endless anguish, others in Elysian valleys dwell,
Resting weary limbs at last on beds of asphodel.   *170*
Surely, surely, slumber is more sweet than toil, the shore
Than labor in the deep mid-ocean, wind and wave and oar;
O, rest ye, brother mariners, we will not wander more.

[1832, 1842]

Break, break, break

Break, break, break,
  On thy cold gray stones, O Sea!
And I would that my tongue could utter
  The thoughts that arise in me.

O, well for the fisherman's boy,   5
  That he shouts with his sister at play!

O, well for the sailor lad,
   That he sings in his boat on the bay!

And the stately ships go on
   To their haven under the hill;   10
But O for the touch of a vanished hand,
   And the sound of a voice that is still!

Break, break, break,
   At the foot of thy crags, O Sea!
But the tender grace of a day that is dead   15
   Will never come back to me.

                            [1834, 1842]

Ulysses

It little profits that an idle king,
By this still hearth, among these barren crags,
Matched with an aged wife, I mete and dole
Unequal laws unto a savage race,
That hoard, and sleep, and feed, and know not me.   5
I cannot rest from travel; I will drink
Life to the lees. All times I have enjoyed
Greatly, have suffered greatly, both with those
That loved me, and alone; on shore, and when
Through scudding drifts the rainy Hyades   10
Vext the dim sea. I am become a name;
For always roaming with a hungry heart
Much have I seen and known—cities of men
And manners,° climates, councils, governments,   *customs*
Myself not least, but honored of them all,—   15
And drunk delight of battle with my peers,
Far on the ringing plains of windy Troy.
I am a part of all that I have met;
Yet all experience is an arch wherethrough
Gleams that untraveled world whose margin fades   20
For ever and for ever when I move.
How dull it is to pause, to make an end,

ULYSSES   According to Dante (in *The Inferno*, Canto 26) Ulysses, having been away for ten years during the Trojan War, is restless upon returning to his island kingdom of Ithaca, and he persuades a band of followers to accompany him on a journey.   [10]**Hyades** a constellation of stars whose rising with the sun forecasts rain.

To rust unburnished, not to shine in use!
As though to breathe were life! Life piled on life
Were all too little, and of one to me   25
Little remains; but every hour is saved
From that eternal silence, something more,
A bringer of new things; and vile it were
For some three suns to store and hoard myself,
And this gray spirit yearning in desire   30
To follow knowledge like a sinking star,
Beyond the utmost bound of human thought.
    This is my son, mine own Telemachus,
To whom I leave the scepter and the isle,
Well-loved of me, discerning to fulfill   35
This labor, by slow prudence to make mild
A rugged people, and through soft degrees
Subdue them to the useful and the good.
Most blameless is he, centered in the sphere
Of common duties, decent° not to fail   proper 40
In offices° of tenderness, and pay   duties
Meet° adoration to my household gods,   appropriate
When I am gone. He works his work, I mine.
    There lies the port; the vessel puffs her sail;
There gloom the dark, broad seas. My mariners,   45
Souls that have toiled, and wrought, and thought with me,
That ever with a frolic welcome took
The thunder and the sunshine, and opposed
Free hearts, free foreheads—you and I are old;
Old age hath yet his honor and his toil.   50
Death closes all; but something ere the end,
Some work of noble note, may yet be done,
Not unbecoming men that strove with gods.
The lights begin to twinkle from the rocks;
The long day wanes; the slow moon climbs; the deep   55
Moans round with many voices. Come, my friends,
'Tis not too late to seek a newer world.
Push off, and sitting well in order smite
The sounding furrows; for my purpose holds
To sail beyond the sunset, and the baths   60
Of all the western stars, until I die.
It may be that the gulfs will wash us down;
It may be we shall touch the Happy Isles,
And see the great Achilles, whom we knew.
Though much is taken, much abides; and though   65

°³**Happy Isles** the abode after death of those favored by the gods.

We are not now that strength which in old days
Moved earth and heaven, that which we are, we are,
One equal temper of heroic hearts,
Made weak by time and fate, but strong in will
To strive, to seek, to find, and not to yield.   *70*

[1842]

Tithonus

The woods decay, the woods decay and fall,
The vapors weep their burthen to the ground,
Man comes and tills the field and lies beneath,
And after many a summer dies the swan.
Me only cruel immortality   *5*
Consumes; I wither slowly in thine arms,
Here at the quiet limit of the world,
A white-haired shadow roaming like a dream
The ever-silent spaces of the East,
Far-folded mists, and gleaming halls of morn.   *10*
    Alas! for this gray shadow, once a man—
So glorious in his beauty and thy choice,
Who madest him thy chosen, that he seemed
To his great heart none other than a God!
I asked thee, "Give me immortality."   *15*
Then didst thou grant mine asking with a smile,
Like wealthy men who care not how they give.
But thy strong Hours indignant worked their wills,
And beat me down and marred and wasted me,
And though they could not end me, left me maimed   *20*
To dwell in presence of immortal youth.
Immortal age beside immortal youth,
And all I was in ashes. Can thy love,
Thy beauty, make amends, though even now,
Close over us, the silver star° thy guide,   *morning star* 25
Shines in those tremulous eyes that fill with tears
To hear me? Let me go; take back thy gift.
Why should a man desire in any way
To vary from the kindly° race of men,   *natural*
Or pass beyond the goal of ordinance   *30*

TITHONUS   a Trojan prince loved by the dawn goddess, Eos, who asked her for immortality but not for eternal youth.

Where all should pause, as is most meet° for all?   *fitting*
 A soft air fans the cloud apart; there comes
A glimpse of that dark world where I was born.
Once more the old mysterious glimmer steals
From thy pure brows, and from thy shoulders pure,   35
And bosom beating with a heart renewed.
Thy cheek begins to redden through the gloom,
Thy sweet eyes brighten slowly close to mine,
Ere yet they blind the stars, and the wild team
Which love thee, yearning for thy yoke, arise,   40
And shake the darkness from their loosened manes,
And beat the twilight into flakes of fire.
 Lo! ever thus thou growest beautiful
In silence, then before thine answer given
Departest, and thy tears are on my cheek.   45
 Why wilt thou ever scare me with thy tears,
And make me tremble lest a saying learnt,
In days far-off, on that dark earth, be true?
"The Gods themselves cannot recall their gifts."
 Ay me! ay me! with what another heart   50
In days far-off, and with what other eyes
I used to watch—if I be he that watched—
The lucid outline forming round thee; saw
The dim curls kindle into sunny rings;
Changed with thy mystic change, and felt my blood   55
Glow with the glow that slowly crimsoned all
Thy presence and thy portals, while I lay,
Mouth, forehead, eyelids, growing dewy-warm
With kisses balmier than half-opening buds
Of April, and could hear the lips that kissed   60
Whispering I knew not what of wild and sweet,
Like that strange song I heard Apollo sing,
While Ilion like a mist rose into towers.
 Yet hold me not for ever in thine East;
How can my nature longer mix with thine?   65
Coldly thy rosy shadows bathe me, cold
Are all thy lights, and cold my wrinkled feet
Upon thy glimmering thresholds, when the steam
Floats up from those dim fields about the homes
Of happy men that have the power to die,   70
And grassy barrows of the happier dead.
Release me, and restore me to the ground.
Thou seest all things, thou wilt see my grave;

---

⁶²**Like that . . . Apollo sing** The walls of Troy (Ilion) rose to the music of Apollo.

Thou wilt renew thy beauty morn by morn,
I earth in earth forget these empty courts,   75
And thee returning on thy silver wheels.

[1860]

Tears, idle tears

Tears, idle tears, I know not what they mean,
Tears from the depth of some divine despair
Rise in the heart, and gather to the eyes,
In looking on the happy autumn-fields,
And thinking of the days that are no more.   5

Fresh as the first beam glittering on a sail,
That brings our friends up from the underworld,
Sad as the last which reddens over one
That sinks with all we love below the verge;
So sad, so fresh, the days that are no more.   10

Ah, sad and strange as in dark summer dawns
The earliest pipe of half-awakened birds
To dying ears, when unto dying eyes
The casement slowly grows a glimmering square;
So sad, so strange, the days that are no more.   15

Dear as remembered kisses after death,
And sweet as those by hopeless fancy feigned
On lips that are for others; deep as love,
Deep as first love, and wild with all regret;
O Death in Life, the days that are no more!   20

[1847]

Now sleeps the crimson petal

Now sleeps the crimson petal, now the white;
Nor waves the cypress in the palace walk;
Nor winks the gold fin in the porphyry font.
The firefly wakens; waken thou with me.

Now droops the milk-white peacock like a ghost,   *5*
And like a ghost she glimmers on to me.

Now lies the Earth all Danaë to the stars,
And all thy heart lies open unto me.

Now slides the silent meteor on, and leaves
A shining furrow, as thy thoughts in me.   *10*

Now folds the lily all her sweetness up,
And slips into the bosom of the lake.
So fold thyself, my dearest, thou, and slip
Into my bosom and be lost in me.

[1847]

Come down, O maid

Come down, O maid, from yonder mountain height.
What pleasure lives in height (the shepherd sang),
In height and cold, the splendor of the hills?
But cease to move so near the heavens, and cease
To glide a sunbeam by the blasted pine,   *5*
To sit a star upon the sparkling spire;
And come, for Love is of the valley, come,
For Love is of the valley, come thou down
And find him; by the happy threshold, he,
Or hand in hand with Plenty in the maize,   *10*
Or red with spirted purple of the vats,
Or foxlike in the vine; nor cares to walk
With Death and Morning on the Silver Horns,°   *mountain peaks*
Nor wilt thou snare him in the white ravine,
Nor find him dropped upon the firths of ice,°   *glaciers* 15
That huddling slant in furrow-cloven falls
To roll the torrent out of dusky doors
But follow; let the torrent dance thee down
To find him in the valley; let the wild
Lean-headed eagles yelp alone, and leave   *20*
The monstrous ledges there to slope, and spill
Their thousand wreaths of dangling water-smoke,
That like a broken purpose waste in air.
So waste not thou, but come; for all the vales
Await thee; azure pillars of the hearth   *25*
Arise to thee; the children call, and I

Thy shepherd pipe, and sweet is every sound,
Sweeter thy voice, but every sound is sweet;
Myriads of rivulets hurrying through the lawn,
The moan of doves in immemorial elms,   30
And murmuring of innumerable bees.

[1847]

from *In Memoriam A.H.H.*

7

Dark house, by which once more I stand
  Here in the long unlovely street,
  Doors, where my heart was used to beat
So quickly, waiting for a hand,

A hand that can be clasped no more—   5
  Behold me, for I cannot sleep,
  And like a guilty thing I creep
At earliest morning to the door.

He is not here; but far away
  The noise of life begins again,   10
  And ghastly through the drizzling rain
On the bald street breaks the blank day.

11

Calm is the morn without a sound,
  Calm as to suit a calmer grief,
  And only through the faded leaf
The chestnut pattering to the ground;

Calm and deep peace on this high wold,°   *high open country* 5
  And on these dews that drench the furze,
  And all the silvery gossamers
That twinkle into green and gold;

Calm and still light on yon great plain
  That sweeps with all its autumn bowers,   10
  And crowded farms and lessening towers,
To mingle with the bounding main;

IN MEMORIAM A.H.H.   Arthur Henry Hallam (1811–1833), Tennyson's close friend.

Calm and deep peace in this wide air,
  These leaves that redden to the fall,
  And in my heart, if calm at all,   *15*
If any calm, a calm despair;

Calm on the seas, and silver sleep,
  And waves that sway themselves in rest,
  And dead calm in that noble breast
Which heaves but with the heaving deep.   *20*

34

My own dim life should teach me this,
  That life shall live forevermore,
  Else earth is darkness at the core,
And dust and ashes all that is;

This round of green, this orb of flame,   *5*
  Fantastic beauty; such as lurks
  In some wild poet, when he works
Without a conscience or an aim.

What then were God to such as I?
  'Twere hardly worth my while to choose   *10*
  Of things all mortal, or to use
A little patience ere I die;

'Twere best at once to sink to peace,
  Like birds the charming serpent draws,
  To drop head-foremost in the jaws   *15*
Of vacant darkness and to cease.

119

Doors, where my heart was used to beat
  So quickly, not as one that weeps
  I come once more; the city sleeps;
I smell the meadow in the street;

I hear a chirp of birds; I see   *5*
  Betwixt the black fronts long-withdrawn
  A light-blue lane of early dawn,
And think of early days and thee,

And bless thee, for thy lips are bland,
  And bright the friendship of thine eyes;   *10*
  And in my thoughts with scarce a sigh
I take the pressure of thine hand.

130

Thy voice is on the rolling air;
   I hear thee where the waters run;
   Thou standest in the rising sun,
And in the setting thou art fair.

What are thou then? I cannot guess;   5
   But though I seem in star and flower
   To feel thee some diffusive power,
I do not therefore love thee less.

My love involves the love before;
   My love is vaster passion now;   10
   Though mixed with God and Nature thou,
I seem to love thee more and more.

Far off thou art, but ever nigh;
   I have thee still, and I rejoice;
   I prosper, circled with thy voice;   15
I shall not lose thee though I die.

                                [1850]

The Eagle: A Fragment

He clasps the crag with crooked hands;
Close to the sun in lonely lands,
Ringed with the azure world, he stands.

The wrinkled sea beneath him crawls;
He watches from his mountain walls,   5
And like a thunderbolt he falls.

                                [1851]

Crossing the Bar

Sunset and evening star,
   And one clear call for me!
And may there be no moaning of the bar,
   When I put out to sea,

But such a tide as moving seems asleep,   5
   Too full for sound and foam,
When that which drew from out the boundless deep
   Turns again home.

Twilight and evening bell,
   And after that the dark!   10
And may there be no sadness of farewell,
   When I embark;

For though from out our bourne of Time and Place
   The flood may bear me far,
I hope to see my Pilot face to face   15
   When I have crossed the bar.

[1889]

ROBERT BROWNING

[1812–1889]

Though most critics agree that Robert Browning's mature writing moves from the subjective to a poetry that is dramatic in principle, some modern critics hold that Browning's monologues are equally lyrical and subjective. According to Harold Bloom, Browning's "company of ruined questers, imperfect poets, self-sabotaged artists, failed lovers, inspired fanatics, charlatans, monomaniacs, and self-deceiving confidence men all have a certain family resemblance." As such, it may be fair to conclude that Browning's monologues scan the future as well as the past, anticipating the monologues of Ezra Pound (pp. 604–625), T. S. Eliot (pp. 639–671), Robert Lowell (pp. 746–750), and Sylvia Plath (pp. 821–837).

Born into that complex era of British history that would be irrevocably shaken by the revolutionary theories of Sigmund Freud, Charles Darwin, and Karl Marx, Robert Browning was a product of the urban middle class when even the Queen of England and her husband were considered models of middle-class domesticity. Fully aware of the social impact of the industrial and intellectual revolutions of his day, Browning went on to express the energy, the delight in striving, and the acquisitive temperament of his age. The descendant of monied bureaucrats, Browning rejected a formal education, preferring to read at home as he saw fit in a library of over six thousand books. As a young man he took learnedness for granted, claiming to have become acquainted with "Paracelsus, Faustus, and even Talmudic personages, personally." Approaching middle age and traveling through Italy in 1844, Browning stumbled on a poem titled "Lady Geraldine's Courtship" that alluded to a poem of his own. Unused to such attention, Browning responded to the author in a letter:

"I love your verses with all my heart, dear Miss Barrett." Then he added, "and I love you, too." Less than a year later he called on Elizabeth Barrett, and on September 12, 1846, they eloped to Italy. Upon her marriage, Elizabeth gained vitality and began leading a fully active social life for the first time, and because Elizabeth was a widely accepted and admired poet at that time, Robert Browning gracefully bore the title of "Mrs. Browning's husband."

In 1867 Browning stated that his "poetry was always dramatic in principle," that it was "so many utterances of so many imaginary persons not mine." Often taking Shakespeare's soliloquies (pp. 174–185) as models, Browning perfected the short monologue in which a character, dramatically set in daily life, discloses an essential, psychologically complex aspect of his or her inner life through natural speech. Browning often chose his characters from history or placed fictional characters within an imagined historical moment. By distancing himself from the characters in this manner, Browning hoped to make the shift from subjective lyric to dramatic monologue complete.

"My Last Duchess," for example, Browning's best-known dramatic monologue, characterizes the Duke of Ferrara as a man who prefers inanimate objects that mirror his inflated sense of self to a living wife who finds grace and beauty almost everywhere, even in the company of servant painters and "officious" fools. Unable to tolerate the ubiquitous warmth and spontaneous affection of his last duchess, the duke "gave commands" and has, at least temporarily, found a solution that suits him: she is dead, and her portrait is safely tucked behind a curtain only he may open. But now he wishes to marry again. The poem begins as the duke discusses his previous duchess with a silent envoy from the count.

The historical figures often cited as the sources of this poem are Alfonso II of the House of Este, Duke of Ferrara, who was negotiating for the niece of the Count of Tyrol in 1564. His last duchess was believed to have been poisoned in 1561 when she was seventeen. Few would argue that the duke, like Shakespeare's Richard III (p. 175), is not a monster. But like Richard, the duke is an interesting monster. Browning uses the technique of concise character revelation and indirect ironic exposure to develop the character of the duke in subtle ways. For example, we note the duke's use of the personal pronoun and its important placement at the conclusion of the monologue. We also note the revealing subject of Claus of Innsbruck's sculpture (Neptune *taming* a sea-horse) and how it is significant in light of the duke's arrogant, vain, and icy nature. Adding to the character's complexity, however, is the duke's revelation of the murder to the envoy. Is it to warn the count on how to instruct his daughter? Or is it simply meant matter-of-factly, as if to suggest that any nobleman with a "nine-hundred-years-old name" would act in a similar manner? The duke claims he never stoops, and yet he addresses the envoy as if he were an equal, saying, "Nay, we'll go / Together down, sir." Is the duke flattering the envoy who would normally be expected to walk behind? Is the envoy about to warn the count? Is the duke calling him back? Browning is ambiguous, and the ambiguity enhances the poem.

We may also consider the character of Andrea del Sarto, the "tolerant, idealizing" artist whose only vice appears to be domestic fidelity. Still, the "perfect painter" now brings nothing to his art but an exquisite technique. We hear him blame himself and blame his wife who cuckolds him with a "cousin" and realize that he is prone to human fallibility as well as to nobility of spirit.

The historical Andrea d'Angelo di Francesca (1486–1531), known as Andrea del Sarto, was renowned for the perfection of his work. The model for Browning's character study was suggested by the painter's biography in Giorgio Vasari's *Lives of the Painters* and by Andrea d'Angelo di Francesca's own portrait of himself and his wife in the Pitti Palace, Florence. Once again we see how Browning's character grows in psychological complexity, typifying Browning's paradoxical view of "failure in success." The son of a Florentine tailor, del Sarto rose to become regarded as "the faultless painter." His student Vasari, however, notes how the master "in whom art and nature combined to show all that may be done in painting, when design, colouring and invention unite . . . [also showed] a certain timidity of mind, a sort of diffidence and want of force in his nature." Paralleling his model's character, Browning's del Sarto masochistically resigns himself to his own personality as fate. He accepts his wife's insistence on a life inimical to his talents as a painter as apprehensively as he accepts her betrayal, nevertheless accepting both. He blames her, and he blames himself but does nothing. Unable to realize his promise fully, del Sarto, nevertheless, still reaches for his ideal:

> Ah, but a man's reach should exceed his grasp,
> Or what's a heaven for?

Having won fame with the series of psychological portraits that became his monologues, Browning is now remembered as a bold, inventive technician, working for freedom of expression and vitality during the decorous Victorian era. As Rupert Brooke once suggested, no poet before Browning could have begun a poem with "G-r-r—there go, my heart's abhorrence!" Integrating humor with the sublime, discord with harmony, Browning influenced modern poetry more than any other Victorian poet except Gerard Manley Hopkins.

My Last Duchess

Ferrara

That's my last Duchess painted on the wall,
Looking as if she were alive. I call
That piece a wonder, now; Frà Pandolf's hands
Worked busily a day, and there she stands.
Will 't please you sit and look at her? I said   5
"Frà Pandolf" by design, for never read
Strangers like you that pictured countenance,
The depth and passion of its earnest glance,
But to myself they turned (since none puts by

The curtain I have drawn for you, but I)   10
And seemed as they would ask me, if they durst,
How such a glance came there; so, not the first
Are you to turn and ask thus. Sir, 'twas not
Her husband's presence only, called that spot
Of joy into the Duchess' cheek; perhaps   15
Frà Pandolf chanced to say, "Her mantle laps
Over my lady's wrist too much," or "Paint
Must never hope to reproduce the faint
Half-flush that dies along her throat." Such stuff
Was courtesy, she thought, and cause enough   20
For calling up that spot of joy. She had
A heart—how shall I say?—too soon made glad,
Too easily impressed; she liked whate'er
She looked on, and her looks went everywhere.
Sir, 'twas all one! My favor at her breast,   25
The dropping of the daylight in the West,
The bough of cherries some officious fool
Broke in the orchard for her, the white mule
She rode with round the terrace—all and each
Would draw from her alike the approving speech,   30
Or blush, at least. She thanked men,—good! but thanked
Somehow—I know not how—as if she ranked
My gift of a nine-hundred-years-old name
With anybody's gift. Who'd stoop to blame
This sort of trifling? Even had you skill   35
In speech—which I have not—to make your will
Quite clear to such an one, and say "Just this
Or that in you disgusts me; here you miss,
Or there exceed the mark"—and if she let
Herself be lessoned so, nor plainly set   40
Her wits to yours, forsooth, and made excuse—
E'en then would be some stooping; and I choose
Never to stoop. Oh sir, she smiled, no doubt,
Whene'er I passed her; but who passed without
Much the same smile? This grew; I gave commands;   45
Then all smiles-stopped together. There she stands
As if alive. Will 't please you rise? We'll meet
The company below, then. I repeat,
The Count your master's known munificence
Is ample warrant that no just pretense   50
Of mine for dowry will be disallowed;
Though his fair daughter's self, as I avowed
At starting, is my object. Nay, we'll go
Together down, sir. Notice Neptune, though,

Taming a sea-horse, thought a rarity,   55
Which Claus of Innsbruck cast in bronze for me!

[1842]

Porphyria's Lover

The rain set early in tonight,
    The sullen wind was soon awake,
It tore the elm-tops down for spite,
    And did its worst to vex the lake:
    I listened with heart fit to break.   5
When glided in Porphyria; straight
    She shut the cold out and the storm,
And kneeled and made the cheerless grate
    Blaze up, and all the cottage warm;
    Which done, she rose, and from her form   10
Withdrew the dripping cloak and shawl,
    And laid her soiled gloves by, untied
Her hat and let the damp hair fall,
    And, last, she sat down by my side
    And called me. When no voice replied,   15
She put my arm about her waist,
    And made her smooth white shoulder bare,
And all her yellow hair displaced,
    And, stooping, made my cheek lie there,
    And spread, o'er all, her yellow hair,   20
Murmuring how she loved me—she
    Too weak, for all her heart's endeavor,
To set its struggling passion free
    From pride, and vainer ties dissever,
    And give herself to me forever.   25
But passion sometimes would prevail,
    Nor could tonight's gay feast restrain
A sudden thought of one so pale
    For love of her, and all in vain:
    So, she was come through wind and rain.   30
Be sure I looked up at her eyes
    Happy and proud; at last I knew
Porphyria worshiped me: surprise
    Made my heart swell, and still it grew
    While I debated what to do.   35
That moment she was mine, mine, fair,
    Perfectly pure and good: I found

A thing to do, and all her hair
    In one long yellow string I wound
    Three times her little throat around,   *40*
And strangled her. No pain felt she;
    I am quite sure she felt no pain.
As a shut bud that holds a bee,
    I warily oped her lids: again
    Laughed the blue eyes without a stain.   *45*
And I untightened next the tress
    About her neck; her cheek once more
Blushed bright beneath my burning kiss:
    I propped her head up as before,
    Only, this time my shoulder bore   *50*
Her head, which droops upon it still:
    The smiling rosy little head,
So glad it has its utmost will,
    That all it scorned at once is fled,
    And I, its love, am gained instead!   *55*
Porphyria's love: she guessed not how
    Her darling one wish would be heard.
And thus we sit together now,
    And all night long we have not stirred,
    And yet God has not said a word!   *60*

[1842]

Soliloquy of the Spanish Cloister

1

Gr-r-r—there go, my heart's abhorrence!
    Water your damned flower-pots, do!
If hate killed men, Brother Lawrence,
    God's blood, would not mine kill you!
What? your myrtle-bush wants trimming?   *5*
    Oh, that rose has prior claims—
Needs its leaden vase filled brimming?
    Hell dry you up with its flames!

2

At the meal we sit together:
    Salve tibi! I must hear   *10*

SOLILOQUY OF THE SPANISH CLOISTER   ¹⁰**Salve tibi!** Hail to thee!

Wise talk of the kind of weather,
    Sort of season, time of year:
Not a plenteous cork-crop: scarcely
    Dare we hope oak-galls, I doubt:
What's the Latin name for "parsley"?   15
    What's the Greek name for Swine's Snout?

3

Whew! We'll have our platter burnished,
    Laid with care on our own shelf!
With a fire-new spoon we're furnished,
    And a goblet for ourself,   20
Rinsed like something sacrificial
    Ere 'tis fit to touch our chaps—
Marked with L for our initial!
    (He-he! There his lily snaps!)

4

Saint, forsooth! While brown Dolores   25
    Squats outside the Convent bank
With Sanchicha, telling stories,
    Steeping tresses in the tank,
Blue-black, lustrous, thick like horsehairs,
    —Can't I see his dead eye glow,   30
Bright as 'twere a Barbary corsair's?
    (That is, if he'd let it show!)

5

When he finishes refection,°   *dinner*
    Knife and fork he never lays
Cross-wise, to my recollection,   35
    As do I, in Jesu's praise.
I the Trinity illustrate,
    Drinking watered orange-pulp—
In three sips the Arian frustrate;
    While he drains his at one gulp.   40

---

[14]**oak-galls** growths produced on oak leaves by gallflies. [31]**Barbary corsair's** pirate's. [39]**Arian** Arius, a fourth-century heretic, denied the doctrine of the Trinity.

6

Oh, those melons? If he's able
    We're to have a feast! so nice!
One goes to the Abbot's table,
    All of us get each a slice.
How go on your flowers? None double?   45
    Not one fruit-sort can you spy?
Strange! And I, too, at such trouble,
    Keep them close-nipped on the sly!

7

There's a great text in Galatians,
    Once you trip on it, entails   50
Twenty-nine distinct damnations,
    One sure, if another fails:
If I trip him just a-dying,
    Sure of heaven as sure can be,
Spin him around and send him flying   55
    Off to hell, a Manichee?

8

Or, my scrofulous French novel
    On grey paper with blunt type!
Simply glance at it, you grovel
    Hand and foot in Belial's gripe: 60
If I double down its pages
    At the woeful sixteenth print,
When he gathers his greengages,
    Ope a sieve and slip it in't?

9

Or, there's Satan! one might venture   65
    Pledge one's soul to him, yet leave
Such a flaw in the indenture
    As he'd miss till, past retrieve,
Blasted lay that rose-acacia
    We're so proud of! *Hy, Zy, Hine* . . .   70
'St, there's vespers! *Plena gratiâ*
    Ave, Virgo! Gr-r-r—you swine!

                        [1842]

---

[49]**Galatians** a New Testament epistle of St. Paul; see Chapters 5:14–15, and 5:16–24. [56]**Manichee** The Manichean heresy divided the world into two equally powerful forces of darkness (evil) and light (good). [60]**in Belial's gripe** in the devil's grip [70]**Hy, Zy, Hine** an incantation. [71-72]**Plena gratiâ Ave, Virgo!** Full of grace Hail, Virgin! (reverses the opening words of the *Ave Maria*).

The Bishop Orders His Tomb at Saint Praxed's Church

ROME, 15—

Vanity, saith the preacher, vanity!
Draw round my bed: is Anselm keeping back?
Nephews—sons mine . . . ah God, I know not! Well—
She, men would have to be your mother once,
Old Gandolf envied me, so fair she was!   5
What's done is done, and she is dead beside,
Dead long ago, and I am Bishop since,
And as she died so must we die ourselves,
And thence ye may perceive the world's a dream.
Life, how and what is it? As here I lie   10
In this state chamber, dying by degrees,
Hours and long hours in the dead night, I ask
"Do I live, am I dead?" Peace, peace seems all.
Saint Praxed's ever was the church for peace;
And so, about this tomb of mine. I fought   15
With tooth and nail to save my niche, ye know:
—Old Gandolf cozened° me, despite my care;   *swindled*
Shrewd was that snatch from out the corner south
He graced his carrion with, God curse the same!
Yet still my niche is not so cramped but thence   20
One sees the pulpit o' the epistle side,
And somewhat of the choir, those silent seats,
And up into the aery dome where live
The angels, and a sunbeam's sure to lurk:
And I shall fill my slab of basalt there,   25
And 'neath my tabernacle° take my rest,   *canopy*
With those nine columns round me, two and two,
The odd one at my feet where Anselm stands:
Peach-blossom marble all, the rare, the ripe
As fresh-poured red wine of a mighty pulse.°   *strength* 30
—Old Gandolf with his paltry onion-stone,
Put me where I may look at him! True peach,
Rosy and flawless: how I earned the prize!
Draw close: that conflagration of my church
—What then? So much was saved if aught were missed!   35

THE BISHOP ORDERS HIS TOMB   **Saint Praxed's Church**   named after a second-century Roman virgin
who donated her wealth to destitute Christians.   [1]**vanity** Ecclesiastes 1:2.   [21]**epistle side** right side of the
altar.   [25]**basalt** a shadowy igneous rock.   [31]**onion-stone** a lesser marble that flakes.

My sons, ye would not be my death? Go dig
The white-grape vineyard where the oil-press stood,
Drop water gently till the surface sink,
And if ye find . . . Ah God, I know not, I! . . .
Bedded in store of rotten fig leaves soft,   40
And corded up in a tight olive-frail,
Some lump, ah God, of *lapis lazuli,*
Big as a Jew's head cut off at the nape,
Blue as a vein o'er the Madonna's breast . . .
Sons, all have I bequeathed you, villas, all,   45
That brave Frascati villa with its bath,
So, let the blue lump poise between my knees,
Like God the Father's globe on both his hands
Ye worship in the Jesu° Church so gay,   *Jesuit*
For Gandolf shall not choose but see and burst!   50
Swift as a weaver's shuttle fleet our years:
Man goeth to the grave, and where is he?
Did I say basalt for my slab, sons? Black—
'Twas ever antique-black I meant! How else
Shall ye contrast my frieze to come beneath?   55
The bas-relief in bronze ye promised me,
Those Pans and Nymphs ye wot of, and perchance
Some tripod, thyrsus, with a vase or so,
The Saviour at his sermon on the mount,
Saint Praxed in a glory, and one Pan   60
Ready to twitch the Nymph's last garment off,
And Moses with the tables . . . but I know
Ye mark me not! What do they whisper thee,
Child of my bowels, Anselm? Ah, ye hope
To revel down my villas while I gasp   65
Bricked o'er with beggar's moldy travertine
Which Gandolf from his tomb-top chuckles at!
Nay, boys, ye love me—all of jasper, then!
'Tis jasper ye stand pledged to, lest I grieve
My bath must needs be left behind, alas!   70
One block, pure green as a pistachio nut,
There's plenty jasper somewhere in the world—
And have I not Saint Praxed's ear to pray
Horses for ye, and brown Greek manuscripts,
And mistresses with great smooth marbly limbs?   75

---

⁴¹**olive-frail** basket for carrying olives.   ⁴²**lapis lazuli** expensive blue-tinged stone.   ⁴⁶**Frascati** Italian
suburban resort.   ⁵¹**Swift . . . years** allusion to Job.   ⁵³**Black** a kind of marble.   ⁵⁵**frieze** an
uninterrupted band of sculpture.   ⁵⁹⁻⁶²**The Saviour . . . tables** inappropriate mixture of Christian, Judaic, and
pagan imagery.   ⁶⁶**travertine** Italian limestone.

—That's if ye carve my epitaph aright
Choice Latin, picked phrase, Tully's every word,
No gaudy ware like Gandolf's second line—
Tully, my masters? Ulpian serves his need!
And then how I shall lie through centuries,   *80*
And hear the blessed mutter of the mass,
And see God made and eaten all day long,
And feel the steady candle flame, and taste
Good strong thick stupefying incense-smoke!
For as I lie here, hours of the dead night,   *85*
Dying in state and by such slow degrees,
I fold my arms as if they clasped a crook,
And stretch my feet forth straight as stone can point,
And let the bedclothes, for a mortcloth, drop
Into great laps and folds of sculptor's-work: *90*
And as yon tapers dwindle, and strange thoughts
Grow, with a certain humming in my ears,
About the life before I lived this life,
And this life too, popes, cardinals, and priests,
Saint Praxed at his sermon on the mount,   *95*
Your tall pale mother with her talking eyes,
And new-found agate urns as fresh as day,
And marble's language, Latin pure, discreet
—Aha, ELUCESCEBAT quoth our friend?
No Tully, said I, Ulpian at the best!   *100*
Evil and brief hath been my pilgrimage.
All *lapis*, all, sons! Else I give the Pope
My villas! Will ye ever eat my heart?
Ever your eyes were as a lizard's quick,
They glitter like your mother's for my soul,   *105*
Or ye would heighten my impoverished frieze,
Piece out its starved design, and fill my vase
With grapes, and add a vizor and a Term,
And to the tripod ye would tie a lynx
That in his struggle throws the thyrsus down,   *110*
To comfort me on my entablature°   *platform*
Whereon I am to lie till I must ask
"Do I live, am I dead?" There, leave me, there!
For ye have stabbed me with ingratitude
To death—ye wish it—God, ye wish it! Stone—   *115*

---

[77]**Tully's** Cicero's.   [79]**Ulpian** a second-rate Latin writer   [82]**And see . . . long** allusion to the Catholic
doctrine of transubstantiation   [87]**crook** the bishop's staff.   [89]**mortcloth** covering over a dead body.
[99]**ELUCESCEBAT** "He was illustrious" . . . the bishop considers the expression in bad taste.   [108]**Term** a
pedestal holding a bust.

Gritstone, a-crumble! Clammy squares which sweat
As if the corpse they keep were oozing through—
And no more *lapis* to delight the world!
Well go! I bless ye. Fewer tapers there,
But in a row: and, going, turn your backs 120
—Aye, like departing altar-ministrants,
And leave me in my church, the church for peace,
That I may watch at leisure if he leers—
Old Gandolf, at me, from his onion-stone,
As still he envied me, so fair she was! 125

[1845]

Andrea del Sarto
(Called "The Faultless Painter")

But do not let us quarrel any more,
No, my Lucrezia; bear with me for once:
Sit down and all shall happen as you wish.
You turn your face, but does it bring your heart?
I'll work then for your friend's friend, never fear, 5
Treat his own subject after his own way,
Fix his own time, accept too his own price,
And shut the money into this small hand
When next it takes mine. Will it? tenderly?
Oh, I'll content him—but tomorrow, Love! 10
I often am much wearier than you think,
This evening more than usual, and it seems
As if—forgive now—should you let me sit
Here by the window with your hand in mine
And look a half-hour forth on Fiesole, 15
Both of one mind, as married people use,
Quietly, quietly the evening through,
I might get up tomorrow to my work
Cheerful and fresh as ever. Let us try.
Tomorrow, how you shall be glad for this! 20
Your soft hand is a woman of itself,
And mine the man's bared breast she curls inside.
Don't count the time lost, neither; you must serve
For each of the five pictures we require:

ANDREA DEL SARTO   a gifted painter who never realized his promise; taken from Giorgio Vasari's *The Lives of the Painters*.   15**Fiesole** hill town near Florence.

It saves a model. So! keep looking so—   25
My serpentining beauty, rounds on rounds!
—How could you ever prick those perfect ears,
Even to put the pearl there! oh, so sweet—·
My face, my moon, my everybody's moon,
Which everybody looks on and calls his,   30
And, I suppose, is looked on by in turn,
While she looks—no one's: very dear, no less.
You smile? why, there's my picture ready made,
There's what we painters call our harmony!
A common grayness silvers everything—   35
All in a twilight, you and I alike
—You, at the point of your first pride in me
(That's gone you know)—but I, at every point;
My youth, my hope, my art, being all toned down
To yonder sober pleasant Fiesole.   40
There's the bell clinking from the chapel top;
That length of convent wall across the way
Holds the trees safer, huddled more inside;
The last monk leaves the garden; days decrease,
And autumn grows, autumn in everything.   45
Eh? the whole seems to fall into a shape
As if I saw alike my work and self
And all that I was born to be and do,
A twilight-piece. Love, we are in God's hand.
How strange now, looks the life he makes us lead;   50
So free we seem, so fettered fast we are!
I feel he laid the fetter: let it lie!
This chamber for example—turn your head—
All that's behind us! You don't understand
Nor care to understand about my art,   55
But you can hear at least when people speak:
And that cartoon, the second from the door
—It is the thing, Love! so such things should be—
Behold Madonna!—I am bold to say.
I can do with my pencil what I know,   60
What I see, what at bottom of my heart
I wish for, if I ever wish so deep—
Do easily, too—when I say, perfectly,
I do not boast, perhaps: yourself are judge,
Who listened to the Legate's talk last week,   65
And just as much they used to say in France.
At any rate 'tis easy, all of it!

---

⁵⁷**cartoon** outline, drawing.   ⁶⁵**Legate's** church official's.

No sketches first, no studies, that's long past:
I do what many dream of, all their lives,
—Dream? strive to do, and agonize to do,   *70*
And fail in doing. I could count twenty such
On twice your fingers, and not leave this town,
Who strive—you don't know how the others strive
To paint a little thing like that you smeared
Carelessly passing with your robes afloat—   *75*
Yet do much less, so much less, Someone says
(I know his name, no matter)—so much less!
Well, less is more, Lucrezia: I am judged.
There burns a truer light of God in them,
In their vexed beating stuffed and stopped-up brain,   *80*
Heart, or whate'er else, than goes on to prompt
This low-pulsed forthright craftsman's hand of mine.
Their works drop groundward, but themselves, I know,
Reach many a time a heaven that's shut to me,
Enter and take their place there sure enough,   *85*
Though they come back and cannot tell the world.
My works are nearer heaven, but I sit here.
The sudden blood of these men! at a word—
Praise them, it boils, or blame them, it boils too.
I, painting from myself and to myself,   *90*
Know what I do, am unmoved by men's blame
Or their praise either. Somebody remarks
Morello's outline there is wrongly traced,
His hue mistaken; what of that? or else,
Rightly traced and well ordered; what of that?   *95*
Speak as they please, what does the mountain care?
Ah, but a man's reach should exceed his grasp,
Or what's a heaven for? All is silver-gray
Placid and perfect with my art: the worse!
I know both what I want and what might gain,   *100*
And yet how profitless to know, to sigh
"Had I been two, another and myself,
Our head would have o'erlooked the world!" No doubt.
Yonder's a work now, of that famous youth
The Urbinate who died five years ago.   *105*
('Tis copied, George Vasari sent it me.)
Well, I can fancy how he did it all,
Pouring his soul, with kings and popes to see,
Reaching, that heaven might so replenish him,
Above and through his art—for it gives way;   *110*

---

[105]**The Urbinate**   the painter Raphael (1483–1520).

That arm is wrongly put—and there again—
A fault to pardon in the drawing's lines,
Its body, so to speak: its soul is right,
He means right—that, a child may understand.
Still, what an arm! and I could alter it: *115*
But all the play, the insight and the stretch—
Out of me, out of me! And wherefore out?
Had you enjoined them on me, given me soul,
We might have risen to Rafael, I and you!
Nay, Love, you did give all I asked, I think—   *120*
More than I merit, yes, by many times.
But had you—oh, with the same perfect brow,
And perfect eyes, and more than perfect mouth,
And the low voice my soul hears, as a bird
The fowler's pipe, and follows to the snare—   *125*
Had you, with these the same, but brought a mind!
Some women do so. Had the mouth there urged
"God and the glory! never care for gain.
The present by the future, what is that?
Live for fame, side by side with Agnolo!   *130*
Rafael is waiting: up to God, all three!"
I might have done it for you. So it seems:
Perhaps not. All is as God overrules.
Beside, incentives come from the soul's self;
The rest avail not. Why do I need you?   *135*
What wife had Rafael, or has Agnolo?
In this world, who can do a thing, will not;
And who would do it, cannot, I perceive:
Yet the will's somewhat—somewhat, too, the power—
And thus we half-men struggle. At the end,   *140*
God, I conclude, compensates, punishes.
'Tis safer for me, if the award be strict,
That I am something underrated here.
Poor this long while, despised, to speak the truth.
I dared not, do you know, leave home all day,   *145*
For fear of chancing on the Paris lords.
The best is when they pass and look aside;
But they speak sometimes; I must bear it all.
Well may they speak! That Francis, that first time,
And that long festal year at Fontainebleau!   *150*
I surely then could sometimes leave the ground,
Put on the glory, Rafael's daily wear,
In that humane great monarch's golden look—

[125]**fowler's pipe**   a hunter's lure.   [130]**Agnolo**   Michelangelo (1475–1564).   [149]**Francis**   a king of France.

One finger in his beard or twisted curl
Over his mouth's good mark that made the smile,   155
One arm about my shoulder, round my neck,
The jingle of his gold chain in my ear,
I painting proudly with his breath on me,
All his court round him, seeing with his eyes,
Such frank French eyes, and such a fire of souls   160
Profuse, my hand kept plying by those hearts—
And, best of all, this, this, this face beyond,
This in the background, waiting on my work,
To crown the issue with a last reward!
A good time, was it not, my kingly days?   165
And had you not grown restless . . . but I know—
'Tis done and past; 'twas right, my instinct said;
Too live the life grew, golden and not gray,
And I'm the weak-eyed bat no sun should tempt
Out of the grange whose four walls make his world.   170
How could it end in any other way?
You called me, and I came home to your heart.
The triumph was—to reach and stay there; since
I reached it ere the triumph, what is lost?
Let my hands frame your face in your hair's gold,   175
You beautiful Lucrezia that are mine!
"Rafael did this, Andrea painted that;
The Roman's is the better when you pray,
But still the other's Virgin was his wife—"
Men will excuse me. I am glad to judge   180
Both pictures in your presence; clearer grows
My better fortune, I resolve to think.
For, do you know, Lucrezia, as God lives,
Said one day Agnolo, his very self,
To Rafael . . . I have known it all these years . . .   185
(When the young man was flaming out his thoughts
Upon a palace wall for Rome to see,
Too lifted up in heart because of it)
"Friend, there's a certain sorry little scrub
Goes up and down our Florence, none cares how,   190
Who, were he set to plan and execute
As you are, pricked on by your popes and kings,
Would bring the sweat into that brow of yours!"
To Rafael's—And indeed the arm is wrong.
I hardly dare . . . yet, only you to see,   195
Give the chalk here—quick, thus the line should go!
Aye, but the soul! he's Rafael! rub it out!

---

[170]**grange**   farm outbuilding.

Still, all I care for, if he spoke the truth,
(What he? why, who but Michel Agnolo?
Do you forget already words like those?)   200
If really there was such a chance, so lost—
Is, whether you're—not grateful—but more pleased.
Well, let me think so. And you smile indeed!
This hour has been an hour! Another smile?
If you would sit thus by me every night   205
I should work better, do you comprehend?
I mean that I should earn more, give you more.
See, it is settled dusk now; there's a star;
Morello's gone, the watch-lights show the wall,
The cue-owls speak the name we call them by.   210
Come from the window, love—come in, at last,
Inside the melancholy little house
We built to be so gay with. God is just.
King Francis may forgive me: oft at nights
When I look up from painting, eyes tired out,   215
The walls become illumined, brick from brick
Distinct, instead of mortar, fierce bright gold,
That gold of his I did cement them with!
Let us but love each other. Must you go?
That Cousin here again? he waits outside?   220
Must see you—you, and not with me? Those loans?
More gaming debts to pay? you smiled for that?
Well, let smiles buy me! have you more to spend?
While hand and eye and something of a heart
Are left me, work's my ware, and what's it worth?   225
I'll pay my fancy. Only let me sit
The gray remainder of the evening out,
Idle, you call it, and muse perfectly
How I could paint, were I but back in France,
One picture, just one more—the Virgin's face,   230
Not yours this time! I want you at my side
To hear them—that is, Michel Agnolo—
Judge all I do and tell you of its worth.
Will you? Tomorrow, satisfy your friend.
I take the subjects for his corridor,   235
Finish the portrait out of hand—there, there,
And throw him in another thing or two
If he demurs; the whole should prove enough
To pay for this same Cousin's freak. Beside,
What's better and what's all I care about,   240
Get you the thirteen scudi for the ruff!

---

[220]**Cousin** euphemism for lover.   [241]**scudi** monetary unit.

Love, does that please you? Ah, but what does he,
The Cousin! What does he to please you more?

I am grown peaceful as old age tonight.
I regret little, I would change still less.　　　　　　245
Since there my past life lies, why alter it?
The very wrong to Francis!—it is true
I took his coin, was tempted and complied,
And built this house and sinned, and all is said.
My father and my mother died of want.　　　　　　250
Well, had I riches of my own? you see
How one gets rich! Let each one bear his lot.
They were born poor, lived poor, and poor they died:
And I have labored somewhat in my time
And not been paid profusely. Some good son　　　　255
Paint my two hundred pictures—let him try!
No doubt, there's something strikes a balance. Yes,
You loved me quite enough, it seems tonight.
This must suffice me here. What would one have?
In heaven, perhaps, new chances, one more chance—　260
Four great walls in the New Jerusalem,
Meted on each side by the angel's reed,
For Leonard, Rafael, Agnolo and me
To cover—the three first without a wife,
While I have mine! So—still they overcome　　　　265
Because there's still Lucrezia—as I choose.

Again the Cousin's whistle! Go, my Love.

　　　　　　　　　　　　　　　　　　　　　　[1855]

EDWARD LEAR

[1812–1888]

The Owl and the Pussy-cat

1

The Owl and the Pussy-cat went to sea
　　In a beautiful pea-green boat,
They took some honey, and plenty of money,
　　Wrapped up in a five-pound note.

ANDREA DEL SARTO　　²⁶¹**New Jerusalem**　from Revelation 21:10–21.　　²⁶³**Leonard**　Leonardo da
Vinci.

The Owl looked up to the stars above,   5
   And sang to a small guitar,
"O lovely Pussy! O Pussy, my love,
    What a beautiful Pussy you are,
       You are,
       You are!   10
   What a beautiful Pussy you are!"

2

Pussy said to the Owl, "You elegant fowl!
   How charmingly sweet you sing!
O let us be married! too long we have tarried:
   But what shall we do for a ring?"   15
They sailed away, for a year and a day,
   To the land where the Bong-tree grows
And there in a wood a Piggy-wig stood
   With a ring at the end of his nose,
       His nose,   20
       His nose,
   With a ring at the end of his nose.

3

"Dear Pig, are you willing to sell for one shilling
   Your ring?" Said the Piggy, "I will."
So they took it away, and were married next day   25
   By the Turkey who lives on the hill.
They dined on mince, and slices of quince,
   Which they ate with a runcible spoon
And hand in hand, on the edge of the sand,
   They danced by the light of the moon,   30
       The moon,
       The moon,
   They danced by the light of the moon.

[1871]

EMILY BRONTË

[1818–1848]

Remembrance

Cold in the earth—and the deep snow piled above thee,
Far, far removed, cold in the dreary grave!

Have I forgot, my only Love, to love thee,
Severed at last by Time's all-severing wave?

Now, when alone, do my thoughts no longer hover   5
Over the mountains, on that northern shore,
Resting their wings where heath and fern leaves cover
Thy noble heart forever, ever more?

Cold in the earth—and fifteen wild Decembers,
From those brown hills, have melted into spring;   10
Faithful, indeed, is the spirit that remembers
After such years of change and suffering!

Sweet Love of youth, forgive, if I forget thee,
While the world's tide is bearing me along;
Other desires and other hopes beset me,   15
Hopes which obscure, but cannot do thee wrong!

No later light has lightened up my heaven,
No second morn has ever shone for me;
All my life's bliss from thy dear life was given,
All my life's bliss is in the grave with thee.   20

But, when the days of golden dreams had perished,
And even Despair was powerless to destroy,
Then did I learn how existence could be cherished,
Strengthened, and fed without the aid of joy.

Then did I check the tears of useless passion—   25
Weaned my young soul from yearning after thine;
Sternly denied its burning wish to hasten
Down to that tomb already more than mine.

And, even yet, I dare not let it languish,
Dare not indulge in memory's rapturous pain;   30
Once drinking deep of that divinest anguish,
How could I seek the empty world again?

[1846]

WALT WHITMAN

[1819–1892]

Walt Whitman is important to American poetry for two reasons: he was a great poet, and he was a seminal influence. As a poet, Whitman revolutionized American verse, inaugurating a poetic tradition remarkable for its energy, diversity, and resilience. Whitman broke new ground in subject matter, form, and style. After Whitman, American poets could take as subjects of their poems any aspect of life. Whitman excluded nothing from his poems. One of his important achievements was to extend the range of poetic subjects to encompass the common, the ordinary, the seemingly unimportant and inconsequential. One result of this change was a renewed interest in the familiar, in things often overlooked or taken for granted such as insects, individual blades of grass, even our own hearing and breathing.

Whitman took as his self-appointed task "to write up America." He did this by making the American land and people his essential subject, celebrating both in a style and set of poetic forms notable for their departure from the prevailing tendencies in British and American poetry of the time. For example, instead of using iambic pentameter, the reigning poetic meter, Whitman wrote verse free of metrical regularity. Instead of closed couplets and tightly symmetrical stanzas, he developed more open, fluid forms. Rather than employing an archaic poetic diction, both formalized and conventional, he used a more familiar and informal language. He also experimented by mixing exalted language with common speech. The result was, as he remarked, a "new style . . . necessitated by new theories, new themes," theories and themes far removed from European models. Whitman's stylistic innovation in *Leaves of Grass,* which he once described as "a language experiment," formed part of his ambition "to give something to our literature which will be our own . . . strengthening and intensifying the national."

Social values and political ideals animate nearly all of Whitman's work. Whitman envisioned a democratic brotherhood of people that cuts across barriers of class, race, and creed. His poetry emphasizes the fundamental equality of human beings, an equality rooted in the intrinsic worth of all living things. Coupled with his concerns for social solidarity and the value of life is an emphasis on self-reliance and individualism, ideas heralded by Emerson, who made reliance on the self a philosophic ideal.

Whitman saw America itself as a great poem. He considered his poetry as analogous to that of the epic bard who mythologizes the distinctive social and cultural characteristics of a country and its people. Epic, too, are the grandeur and sweep of Whitman's subject and tone. Whitman chanted the praises of an expanding country, singing of progress, democracy, freedom, individualism, and brotherhood. His characteristic tone was one of celebration. His characteristic manner of celebration was to name. By naming things American, Whitman called them to the attention of his readers, acknowledging them as worthy of notice and appreciation.

Whitman was something of a prophet—a seer whose vision transcended that of ordinary people, but whose sympathy and imagination united him in spirit with everyone. Allied with Whitman's visionary capacity and his sympathetic imagination is his tendency to embrace and absorb all he comes in contact with. He is the most inclusive of poets, accepting into his embrace all aspects of experience, good and bad, common and unusual. His poetry, moreover, attempts to transcend time and place. It strives to break down boundaries, to abolish differences, eliminate separateness. In "Crossing Brooklyn Ferry," for example, Whitman speaks directly to us across the century that separates him from us. He collapses temporal distinctions and breaks down spatial barriers, making all places a central everywhere and all times a continuous eternal present. Furthermore, his poetry relates people to the natural world and connects them with one another. Its prevailing impulse is to unite, making Whitman one of the most receptive, affirmative, and democratic of poets.

We can illustrate some of these attitudes and values so fundamental to Whitman's poetic vision by quoting a short poem from the "Inscriptions" section of *Leaves of Grass.*

One's Self I Sing

One's Self I sing, a simple separate person,
Yet utter the word Democratic, the word En-Masse.

Of physiology from top to toe I sing,
Not physiognomy alone nor brain alone is worthy for the Muse,
  I say the form complete is worthier far,
The Female equally with the Male I sing.

Of Life immense in passion, pulse, and power,
Cheerful, for freest action form'd under the laws divine,
The Modern Man I sing.

These optimistic, affirmative lines celebrate life, especially its vitality, energy, and physicality. Whitman's lines embrace male and female, body and soul, separateness and togetherness. They announce the arrival of a new man, the nineteenth-century American whom Whitman celebrates throughout *Leaves of Grass,* which he saw through no less than nine editions beginning in 1855 and concluding in the famous deathbed edition of 1892. This book of poems was, as Whitman himself said, an attempt "to put a *Person,* a human being (myself in the latter half of the Nineteenth Century, in America) freely, fully, and truly on record."

Whitman has had both a wide influence and a strong impact. Many modern American poets have benefited from his revolutionary poetics. William Carlos Williams, for example, was influenced by Whitman's attention to the commonplace and by his experiments with the poetic line. Wallace Stevens displays the meditative and philosophical cast found in poems such as Whitman's "Crossing Brooklyn Ferry." E. E. Cummings echoes Whitman's affirmation and celebration of life as well as his frank avowal of the erotic. These and many other poets have made and continue to make Whitman's legacy a living poetic reality.

The facts of Whitman's life can only hint at the range of his experience and the impulses that animate his poetry. He was born in 1819 on Long Island—in Huntington, New York—and was educated in the Brooklyn public schools. In his youth he worked successively as an office boy and clerk for a doctor, lawyer, and printer. He taught school from 1836 to 1841. His journalistic career involved, at various stages, writing, typesetting, and editing, and included the editorship of the Brooklyn *Daily Eagle,* the New Orleans *Crescent,* the Brooklyn *Freeman,* and the Brooklyn *Daily Times.* Whitman also worked as a carpenter, building a house for himself and his family. During the Civil War he served as a nurse and worked briefly as a clerk in the Bureau of Indian Affairs. He also worked in the attorney general's office in Washington, until he suffered a paralytic stroke. He spent the last two decades of his life in Camden, New Jersey, where he died quietly in 1892, shortly after he prepared the deathbed edition of his life's work.

In reading Whitman's poems it helps to know not only the salient facts of his life but also something about both his reading and his poetic intentions. One of the chief stumbling blocks for readers unfamiliar with Whitman is the largeness of his claims. He seems to boast, to brag about his status, his vision, his amplitude. He seems to claim for himself exemption from the limitations of time and space. Once we realize, however, that the "I" of poems such as *Song of Myself* is not the autobiographical I, that it is not the historical Walt Whitman, we minimize this potential difficulty. The "I" we hear throughout *Leaves of Grass* is the American self—the larger-than-life embodiment of the American spirit that Whitman employs to establish and sustain his vision of America. The "I" who speaks in Whitman's poems is confident, assertive, and authoritative. It possesses knowledge acquired partly from living, partly through observing, but largely through intuition. Whitman's "I" sees and knows all—or nearly all. His "I" shares in the participatory divinity he believed was common to all people. Whitman sees human beings as immortal and eternal, with the potential of transcending the finite boundaries of their physical beings.

As an American poet living in an age of progress and expansionism, Whitman valued material reality as much as its spiritual counterpart. Whitman's spiritualizing of man and nature did not require a corresponding rejection of physical experience. His attitude toward sex, for example, runs counter to the celibate ascetic ideal of Oriental mysticism. But Whitman, like Emerson before him, sees the value of looking beyond appearances, beyond the physical and material differences that separate human beings from one another to the ties of spiritual essence that bind them. Whitman's unifying view extends to the natural world as well as the social one. Nature figures prominently in Whitman's poetry not only as inspiration and symbol but as an important dimension of the way spirit is manifested in the external world.

An additional aspect of Whitman's poetry is his tendency to contradict himself. On one hand, he celebrates the single and simple separate person, praising the virtues of originality and self-reliance. At the same time, however, he urges the claims of community, fraternity, and solidarity. These emphases for Whitman, however, are less contradictory than complementary. "Do I contradict myself?" he asks in *Song of Myself.* "Very well then," he answers, "I contradict myself, (I am large. I contain multitudes.)" Whitman's solution to contradiction was an all-encompassing embrace and a spiritual perspective on the unity of life. He accepted both his own diversity and that of the world.

One additional item of interest is the way Whitman's poetry mirrors the cultural situation of his time. In an important book on Whitman's life and art, *Walt Whitman: The Making of the Poet,* Paul Zweig describes the influence of Whitman's milieu on his work. Zweig recounts Whitman's transformation from an undistinguished journalist into a profoundly original poet, whose journalistic experience and ambitions became part of his poems. Zweig also describes Whitman's love for the theater, suggesting that the relationship between actor and audience provided a model for the relationship Whitman tried to establish with his readers. Whitman's insistent presence in his poems and his effort to assume many roles and speak in other voices, along with his repeated use of direct address, exemplify this attempt.

Besides theater, music also influenced Whitman's poetry. He passionately loved opera, which he describes as "a new world—a liquid world—[that] rushes like a torrent through you." He spoke of dating a new era in his development from his introduction to opera. One aspect of that development affected the structure of his poems. Longer poems like *Song of Myself,* and "When lilacs last in the dooryard bloom'd," exhibit a symphonic rather than a logical structure. They use repetition and refrain, and they blend speech and song in the manner of operatic aria and recitative.

One additional social reality had a decisive impact on Whitman's life and art: the Civil War. It was not as a soldier that Whitman served but as a nurse. On hearing that his brother George had been wounded in battle, Whitman hurried to the military hospital in Washington. Although his brother had not been seriously injured, Whitman, deeply moved by the suffering of the soldiers, remained for twelve years. He nursed the wounded and wrote letters and ran errands for them, giving of his immense reserves of sympathy and compassion. Out of his experience came the series of poems entitled *Drum-Taps,* which contains some of his most affecting poetry.

Finally, we should mention how the cultural conventions and moral attitudes of Whitman's time prevented his poetry from receiving the recognition it deserved. Many contemporary readers were shocked by the frankly erotic quality of some of his poems. Condemned as obscene, vulgar, and depraved, Whitman's poems were considered by many as violations of the morals of the day. Such readers were unprepared for his frank celebration of physical love. They were also unprepared for his inclusion of physical details such as sweating and belching. Not until the twentieth century did the cultural and moral climate change sufficiently for readers to see Whitman's celebration of the body as liberating.

Whitman was a poet who drew sustenance from his culture while rebelling against its stultifying conventions. His poems serve both as journalistic reports of his time and as an imaginative transformation of its raw data into art. His greatest poems transcend their time and place to become universal statements about intensely felt experiences. He remains the greatest and most representative of American poets.

There was a child went forth every day

There was a child went forth every day,
And the first object he looked upon and received with wonder or pity or love or dread,
    that object he became,
And that object became part of him for the day or a certain part of the day . . . .
    or for many years or stretching cycles of years.

The early lilacs became part of this child,
And grass, and white and red morningglories, and white and red clover, and the song
    of the phoebe-bird,   5
And the March-born lambs, and the sow's pink-faint litter, and the mare's foal, and
    the cow's calf, and the noisy brood of the barnyard or by the mire of the pondside . .
    and the fish suspending themselves so curiously below there . . and the beautiful
    curious liquid . . and the water-plants with their graceful flat heads . . all became
    part of him.

And the field-sprouts of April and May became part of him . . . . wintergrain sprouts,
    and those of the light-yellow corn, and of the esculent roots of the garden,
And the appletrees covered with blossoms, and the fruit afterward . . . . and
    woodberries . . and the commonest weeds by the road;
And the old drunkard staggering home from the outhouse of the tavern whence he
    had lately risen,
And the schoolmistress that passed on her way to the school . . and the friendly boys
    that passed . . and the quarrelsome boys . . and the tidy and freshcheeked girls . .
    and the barefoot negro boy and girl,   10
And all the changes of city and country wherever he went.

His own parents . . he that had propelled the fatherstuff at night, and fathered him . .
    and she that conceived him in her womb and birthed him . . . . they gave this
    child more of themselves than that,
They gave him afterward every day . . . . they and of them became part of him.

The mother at home quietly placing the dishes on the suppertable,
The mother with mild words . . . . clean her cap and gown . . . . a wholesome odor
    falling off her person and clothes as she walks by: 15
The father, strong, selfsufficient, manly, mean, angered, unjust,
The blow, the quick loud word, the tight bargain, the crafty lure,
The family usages, the language, the company, the furniture . . . . the yearning and
    swelling heart,

Affection that will not be gainsayed . . . . The sense of what is real . . . . the thought
    if after all it should prove unreal,
The doubts of daytime and the doubts of nighttime . . . the curious whether
    and how,   20
Whether that which appears so is so . . . . Or is it all flashes and specks?
Men and women crowding fast in the streets . . if they are not flashes and specks
    what are they?
The streets themselves, and the facades of houses . . . . the goods in the windows,
Vehicles . . teams . . the tiered wharves, and the huge crossing at the ferries;
The village on the highland seen from afar at sunset . . . . the river between,   25
Shadows . . aureola and mist . . light falling on roofs and gables of white or brown,
    three miles off,
The schooner near by sleepily dropping down the tide . . the little boat slacktowed
    astern,
The hurrying tumbling waves and quickbroken crests and slapping;
The strata of colored clouds . . . . the long bar of maroontint away solitary by itself
     . . . . the spread of purity it lies motionless in,
The horizon's edge, the flying seacrow, the fragrance of saltmarsh and shoremud;   30
These became part of that child who went forth every day, and who now goes and
    will always go forth every day,
And these become of him or her that peruses them now.

                                                  [1855]

from *Song of Myself*

1

I celebrate myself, and sing myself,
And what I assume you shall assume,
For every atom belonging to me as good belongs to you.

I loafe and invite my soul,
I lean and loafe at my ease observing a spear of summer grass.   5

My tongue, every atom of my blood, form'd from this soil, this air,
Born here of parents born here from parents the same, and their parents the same,
I, now thirty-seven years old in perfect health begin,
Hoping to cease not till death.

Creeds and schools in abeyance,   10
Retiring back a while sufficed at what they are, but never forgotten,

SONG OF MYSELF   This poem was untitled in the first edition of *Leaves of Grass;* in the second edition it was
called "Poem of Walt Whitman, an American", and finally, in 1881–1882, it became "Song of Myself."

I harbor for good or bad, I permit to speak at every hazard,
Nature without check with original energy.

2

Houses and rooms are full of perfumes, the shelves are crowded with perfumes,
I breathe the fragrance myself and know it and like it,   *15*
The distillation would intoxicate me also, but I shall not let it.

The atmosphere is not a perfume, it has no taste of the distillation, it is odorless,
It is for my mouth forever, I am in love with it,
I will go to the bank by the wood and become undisguised and naked,
I am mad for it to be in contact with me.   *20*

The smoke of my own breath,
Echoes, ripples, buzz'd whispers, love-root, silk-thread, crotch and vine,
My respiration and inspiration, the beating of my heart, the passing of blood and air
    through my lungs,
The sniff of green leaves and dry leaves, and of the shore and dark-color'd sea-rocks,
    and of hay in the barn,
The sound of the belch'd words of my voice loos'd to the eddies of the wind,   *25*
A few light kisses, a few embraces, a reaching around of arms,
The play of shine and shade on the trees as the supple boughs wag,
The delight alone or in the rush of the streets, or along the fields and hill-sides,
The feeling of health, the full-noon trill, the song of me rising from bed and meeting
    the sun.

Have you reckon'd a thousand acres much? have you reckon'd the earth much?   *30*
Have you practis'd so long to learn to read?
Have you felt so proud to get at the meaning of poems?

Stop this day and night with me and you shall possess the origin of all poems,
You shall possess the good of the earth and sun, (there are millions of suns left,)
You shall no longer take things at second or third hand, nor look through the eyes
    of the dead, nor feed on the spectres in books,   *35*
You shall not look through my eyes either, nor take things from me,
You shall listen to all sides and filter them from your self.

3

I have heard what the talkers were talking, the talk of the beginning and the end,
But I do not talk of the beginning or the end.

There was never any more inception than there is now,   *40*
Nor any more youth or age than there is now,

And will never be any more perfection than there is now,
Nor any more heaven or hell than there is now.

Urge and urge and urge,
Always the procreant urge of the world.   *45*

Out of the dimness opposite equals advance, always substance and increase, always sex,
Always a knit of identity, always distinction, always a breed of life.

To elaborate is no avail, learn'd and unlearn'd feel that it is so.

Sure as the most certain sure, plumb in the uprights, well entretied, braced in the
     beams,
Stout as a horse, affectionate, haughty, electrical,   *50*
I and this mystery here we stand.

Clear and sweet is my soul, and clear and sweet is all that is not my soul.

Lack one lacks both, and the unseen is proved by the seen,
Till that becomes unseen and receives proof in its turn.

Showing the best and dividing it from the worst age vexes age,   *55*
Knowing the perfect fitness and equanimity of things, while they discuss I am silent,
     and go bathe and admire myself.

Welcome is every organ and attribute of me, and of any man hearty and clean,
Not an inch nor a particle of an inch is vile, and none shall be less familiar than
     the rest.

I am satisfied—I see, dance, laugh, sing;
As the hugging and loving bed-fellow sleeps at my side through the night, and
     withdraws at the peep of the day with stealthy tread,   *60*
Leaving me baskets cover'd with white towels swelling the house with their plenty,
Shall I postpone my acceptation and realization and scream at my eyes,
That they turn from gazing after and down the road,
And forthwith cipher and show me to a cent,
Exactly the value of one and exactly the value of two, and which is ahead?   *65*

4

Trippers and askers surround me,
People I meet, the effect upon me of my early life or the ward and city I live in,
     or the nation,
The latest dates, discoveries, inventions, societies, authors old and new,
My dinner, dress, associates, looks, compliments, dues,

The real or fancied indifference of some man or woman I love,   70
The sickness of one of my folks or of myself, or ill-doing or loss or lack of money,
    or depressions or exaltations,
Battles, the horrors of fratricidal war, the fever of doubtful news, the fitful events;
These come to me days and nights and go from me again,
But they are not the Me myself.

Apart from the pulling and hauling stands what I am,   75
Stands amused, complacent, compassionating, idle, unitary,
Looks down, is erect, or bends an arm on an impalpable certain rest,
Looking with side-curved head curious what will come next,
Both in and out of the game and watching and wondering at it.

Backward I see in my own days where I sweated through fog with linguists and
    contenders,   80
I have no mockings or arguments, I witness and wait.

5

I believe in you my soul, the other I am must not abase itself to you,
And you must not be abased to the other.

Loaf with me on the grass, loose the stop from your throat,
Not words, not music or rhyme I want, not custom or lecture, not even the best,   85
Only the lull I like, the hum of your valvèd voice.

I mind how once we lay such a transparent summer morning,
How you settled your head athwart my hips and gently turn'd over upon me,
And parted the shirt from my bosom-bone, and plunged your tongue to my
    bare-stript heart,
And reach'd till you felt my beard, and reach'd till you held my feet.   90

Swiftly arose and spread around me the peace and knowledge that pass all the
    argument of the earth,
And I know that the hand of God is the promise of my own,
And I know that the spirit of God is the brother of my own,
And that all the men ever born are also my brothers, and the women my sisters and
    lovers,
And that a kelson of the creation is love,   95
And limitless are leaves stiff or drooping in the fields,
And brown ants in the little wells beneath them,
And mossy scabs of the worm fence, heap'd stones, elder, mullein and poke-weed.

6

A child said *What is the grass?* fetching it to me with full hands;
How could I answer the child? I do not know what it is any more than he.   100

I guess it must be the flag of my disposition, out of hopeful green stuff woven.

Or I guess it is the handkerchief of the Lord,
A scented gift and remembrancer designedly dropt,
Bearing the owner's name someway in the corners, that we may see and remark,
    and say *Whose?*

Or I guess the grass is itself a child, the produced babe of the vegetation.   *105*

Or I guess it is a uniform hieroglyphic,
And it means, Sprouting alike in broad zones and narrow zones,
Growing among black folks as among white,
Kanuck, Tuckahoe, Congressman, Cuff, I give them the same, I receive them
    the same.

And now it seems to me the beautiful uncut hair of graves.   *110*

Tenderly will I use you curling grass,
It may be you transpire from the breasts of young men,
It may be if I had known them I would have loved them,
It may be you are from old people, or from offspring taken soon out of their
    mothers' laps,
And here you are the mothers' laps.   *115*

This grass is very dark to be from the white heads of old mothers,
Darker than the colorless beards of old men,
Dark to come from under the faint red roofs of mouths.

O I perceive after all so many uttering tongues,
And I perceive they do not come from the roofs of mouths for nothing.   *120*

I wish I could translate the hints about the dead young men and women,
And the hints about old men and mothers, and the offspring taken soon out
    of their laps.
What do you think has become of the young and old men?
And what do you think has become of the women and children?

They are alive and well somewhere,   *125*
The smallest sprout shows there is really no death,
And if ever there was it led forward life, and does not wait at the end to arrest it,
And ceas'd the moment life appear'd.

---

[109]**Kanuck . . . Cuff** "Kanuck" denotes a French Canadian; "Tuckahoe," a Virginian who lived on poor lands in the tidewater region and ate tuckahoe, a fungus; and "Cuff," a black.

All goes onward and outward, nothing collapses,
And to die is different from what any one supposed, and luckier.   *130*

11

Twenty-eight young men bathe by the shore,
Twenty-eight young men and all so friendly;
Twenty-eight years of womanly life and all so lonesome.

She owns the fine house by the rise of the bank,
She hides handsome and richly drest aft the blinds of the window.   *135*

Which of the young men does she like the best?
Ah the homeliest of them is beautiful to her.

Where are you off to, lady? for I see you,
You splash in the water there, yet stay stock still in your room.

Dancing and laughing along the beach came the twenty-ninth bather,   *140*
The rest did not see her, but she saw them and loved them.

The beards of the young men glisten'd with wet, it ran from their long hair,
Little streams pass'd all over their bodies.

An unseen hand also pass'd over their bodies,
It descended trembling from their temples and ribs.   *145*

The young men float on their backs, their white bellies bulge to the sun, they
        do not ask who seizes fast to them,
They do not know who puffs and declines with pendant and bending arch,
They do not think whom they souse with spray.

24

Walt Whitman, a kosmos, of Manhattan the son,
Turbulent, fleshly, sensual, eating, drinking and breeding,   *150*
No sentimentalist, no stander above men and women or apart from them,
No more modest than immodest.

Unscrew the locks from the doors!
Unscrew the doors themselves from their jambs!

Whoever degrades another degrades me,   *155*
And whatever is done or said returns at last to me.

Through me the afflatus surging and surging, through me the current and index.

[157]**afflatus**   Latin for "a strong wind or blast," figuratively "inspiration."

I speak the pass-word primeval, I give the sign of democracy,
By God! I will accept nothing which all cannot have their counterpart of on the
    same terms.

Through me many long dumb voices, 160
Voices of the interminable generations of prisoners and slaves,
Voices of the diseas'd and despairing and of thieves and dwarfs,
Voices of cycles of preparation and accretion,
And of the threads that connect the stars, and of wombs and of the father-stuff,
And of the rights of them the others are down upon, 165
Of the deform'd, trivial, flat, foolish, despised,
Fog in the air, beetles rolling balls of dung.

Through me forbidden voices,
Voices of sexes and lusts, voices veil'd and I remove the veil,
Voices indecent by me clarified and transfigur'd. 170

I do not press my fingers across my mouth,
I keep as delicate around the bowels as around the head and heart,
Copulation is no more rank to me than death is.

I believe in the flesh and the appetites,
Seeing, hearing, feeling, are miracles, and each part and tag of me is a miracle. 175

Divine am I inside and out, and I make holy whatever I touch or am touch'd from,
The scent of these arm-pits aroma finer than prayer,
This head more than churches, bibles, and all the creeds.

If I worship one thing more than another it shall be the spread of my own body,
    or any part of it,
Translucent mould of me it shall be you! 180
Shaded ledges and rests it shall be you!
Firm masculine colter it shall be you!
Whatever goes to the tilth of me it shall be you!
You my rich blood! your milky stream pale strippings of my life!
Breast that presses against other breasts it shall be you! 185
My brain it shall be your occult convolutions!
Root of wash'd sweet-flag! timorous pond-snipe! nest of guarded duplicate eggs!
    it shall be you!
Mix'd tussled hay of head, beard, brawn, it shall be you!
Trickling sap of maple, fibre of manly wheat, it shall be you!
Suns so generous it shall be you! 190
Vapors lighting and shading my face it shall be you!
You sweaty brooks and dews it shall be you!
Winds whose soft-tickling genitals rub against me it shall be you!

Broad muscular fields, branches of live oak, loving lounger in my winding paths, it
    shall be you!
Hands I have taken, face I have kiss'd, mortal I have ever touch'd, it shall be you.   *195*

I dote on myself, there is that lot of me and all so luscious,
Each moment and whatever happens thrills me with joy,
I cannot tell how my ankles bend, nor whence the cause of my faintest wish,
Nor the cause of the friendship I emit, nor the cause of the friendship I take again.

That I walk up my stoop, I pause to consider if it really be,   *200*
A morning-glory at my window satisfies me more than the metaphysics of books.

To behold the day-break!
The little light fades the immense and diaphanous shadows,
The air tastes good to my palate.

Hefts of the moving world at innocent gambols silently rising, freshly exuding,   *205*
Scooting obliquely high and low.

Something I cannot see puts upward libidinous prongs,
Seas of bright juice suffuse heaven.

The earth by the sky staid with, the daily close of their junction,
The heav'd challenge from the east that moment over my head,   *210*
The mocking taunt. See then whether you shall be master!

32

I think I could turn and live with animals, they are so placid and self-contain'd,
I stand and look at them long and long.

They do not sweat and whine about their condition,
They do not lie awake in the dark and weep for their sins,   *215*
They do not make me sick discussing their duty to God,
Not one is dissatisfied, not one is demented with the mania of owning things,
Not one kneels to another, nor to his kind that lived thousands of years ago,
Not one is respectable or unhappy over the whole earth.

So they show their relations to me and I accept them,   *220*
They bring me tokens of myself, they evince them plainly in their possession.

I wonder where they get those tokens,
Did I pass that way huge times ago and negligently drop them?

Myself moving forward then and now and forever,
Gathering and showing more always and with velocity,   *225*
Infinite and omnigenous, and the like of these among them,

Not too exclusive toward the reachers of my remembrancers,
Picking out here one that I love, and now go with him on brotherly terms.

A gigantic beauty of a stallion, fresh and responsive to my caresses,
Head high in the forehead, wide between the ears,   230
Limbs glossy and supple, tail dusting the ground,
Eyes full of sparkling wickedness, ears finely cut, flexibly moving.

His nostrils dilate as my heels embrace him,
His well-built limbs tremble with pleasure as we race around and return.

I but use you a minute, then I resign you, stallion,   235
Why do I need your paces when I myself out-gallop them?
Even as I stand or sit passing faster than you.

46

I know I have the best of time and space, and was never measured and never will
    be measured.

I tramp a perpetual journey, (come listen all!)
My signs are a rain-proof coat, good shoes, and a staff cut from the woods,   240
No friend of mine takes his ease in my chair,
I have no chair, no church, no philosophy,
I lead no man to a dinner-table, library, exchange,
But each man and each woman of you I lead upon a knoll,
My left hand hooking you round the waist,   245
My right hand pointing to landscapes of continents and the public road.

Not I, not any one else can travel that road for you,
You must travel it for yourself.
It is not far, it is within reach,
Perhaps you have been on it since you were born and did not know,   250
Perhaps it is everywhere on water and on land.

Shoulder your duds dear son, and I will mine, and let us hasten forth,
Wonderful cities and free nations we shall fetch as we go.

If you tire, give me both burdens, and rest the chuff of your hand on my hip,
And in due time you shall repay the same service to me,   255
For after we start we never lie by again.

This day before dawn I ascended a hill and look'd at the crowded heaven,
And I said to my spirit *When we become the enfolders of those orbs, and the pleasure*
    and knowledge of every thing in them, shall we be fill'd and satisfied then?
And my spirit said *No, we but level that lift to pass and continue beyond.*

You are also asking me questions and I hear you,   260
I answer that I cannot answer, you must find out for yourself.

Sit a while dear son,
Here are biscuits to eat and here is milk to drink,
But as soon as you sleep and renew yourself in sweet clothes, I kiss you with a
    good-by kiss and open the gate for your egress hence.

Long enough have you dream'd contemptible dreams,   265
Now I wash the gum from your eyes,
You must habit yourself to the dazzle of the light and of every moment of your life.

Long have you timidly waded holding a plank by the shore,
Now I will you to be a bold swimmer,
To jump off in the midst of the sea, rise again, nod to me, shout, and laughingly
    dash with your hair.   270

47

I am the teacher of athletes,
He that by me spreads a wider breast than my own proves the width of my own,
He most honors my style who learns under it to destroy the teacher.

The boy I love, the same becomes a man not through derived power, but in his
    own right,
Wicked rather than virtuous out of conformity or fear,   275
Fond of his sweetheart, relishing well his steak,
Unrequited love or a slight cutting him worse than sharp steel cuts,
First-rate to ride, to fight, to hit the bull's eye, to sail a skiff, to sing a song or
    play on the banjo,
Preferring scars and the beard and faces pitted with small-pox over all latherers,
And those well-tann'd to those that keep out of the sun.   280

I teach straying from me, yet who can stray from me?
I follow you whoever you are from the present hour,
My words itch at your ears till you understand them.

I do not say these things for a dollar or to fill up the time while I wait for a boat,
(It is you talking just as much as myself, I act as the tongue of you,   285
Tied in your mouth, in mine it begins to be loosen'd.)

I swear I will never again mention love or death inside a house,
And I swear I will never translate myself at all, only to him or her who privately stays
    with me in the open air.

If you would understand me go to the heights or water-shore,
The nearest gnat is an explanation, and a drop or motion of waves a key,   290
The maul, the oar, the hand-saw, second my words.

No shutter'd room or school can commune with me,
But roughs and little children better than they.

The young mechanic is closest to me, he knows me well,
The woodman that takes his axe and jug with him shall take me with him all day,   295
The farm-boy ploughing in the field feels good at the sound of my voice,
In vessels that sail my words sail, I go with fishermen and seamen and love them.

The soldier camp'd or upon the march is mine,
On the night ere the pending battle many seek me, and I do not fail them,
On that solemn night (it may be their last) those that know me seek me.   300

My face rubs to the hunter's face when he lies down alone in his blanket,
The driver thinking of me does not mind the jolt of his wagon,
The young mother and old mother comprehend me,
The girl and the wife rest the needle a moment and forget where they are,
They and all would resume what I have told them.   305

48

I have said that the soul is not more than the body,
And I have said that the body is not more than the soul,
And nothing, not God, is greater to one than one's self is,
And whoever walks a furlong without sympathy walks to his own funeral drest in his
    shroud,
And I or you pocketless of a dime may purchase the pick of the earth,   310
And to glance with an eye or show a bean in its pod confounds the learning
    of all times
And there is no trade or employment but the young man following it may
    become hero,
And there is no object so soft but it makes a hub for the wheel'd universe,
And I say to any man or woman, Let your soul stand cool and composed before a
    million universes.

And I say to mankind, Be not curious about God,   315
For I who am curious about each am not curious about God,
(No array of terms can say how much I am at peace about God and about death.)

I hear and behold God in every object, yet understand God not in the least,
Nor do I understand who there can be more wonderful than myself.

Why should I wish to see God better than this day?   320
I see something of God each hour of the twenty-four, and each moment then,
In the faces of men and women I see God, and in my own face in the glass,
I find letters from God dropt in the street, and every one is sign'd by God's name,
And I leave them where they are, for I know that wheresoe'er I go
Others will punctually come for ever and ever.   325

49

And as to you Death, and you bitter hug of mortality, it is idle to try to alarm me.

To his work without flinching the accoucheur° comes,   *midwife*
I see the elder-hand pressing receiving supporting,
I recline by the sills of the exquisite flexible doors,
And mark the outlet, and mark the relief and escape.   330

And as to you Corpse I think you are good manure, but that does not offend me,
I smell the white roses sweet-scented and growing.
I reach to the leafy lips, I reach to the polish'd breasts of melons.

And as to you Life I reckon you are the leavings of many deaths,
(No doubt I have died myself ten thousand times before.)   335

I hear you whispering there O stars of heaven,
O suns—O grass of graves—O perpetual transfers and promotions,
If you do not say any thing how can I say any thing?

Of the turbid pool that lies in the autumn forest,
Of the moon that descends the steeps of the soughing twilight,   340
Toss, sparkles of day and dusk—toss on the black stems that decay in the muck,
Toss to the moaning gibberish of the dry limbs.

I ascend from the moon, I ascend from the night,
I perceive that the ghastly glimmer is noonday sunbeams reflected,
And debouch to the steady and central from the offspring great or small.   345

50

There is that in me—I do not know what it is—but I know it is in me.

Wrench'd and sweaty—calm and cool then my body becomes,
I sleep—I sleep long.

I do not know it—it is without name—it is a word unsaid,
It is not in any dictionary, utterance, symbol.   350

Something it swings on more than the earth I swing on,
To it the creation is the friend whose embracing awakes me.

Perhaps I might tell more. Outlines! I plead for my brothers and sisters.

Do you see O my brothers and sisters?
It is not chaos or death—it is form, union, plan—it is eternal life—it is
  Happiness.   355

51

The past and present wilt—I have fill'd them, emptied them,
And proceed to fill my next fold of the future.

Listener up there! what have you to confide to me?
Look in my face while I snuff the sidle of evening,
(Talk honestly, no one else hears you, and I stay only a minute longer.)   360

Do I contradict myself?
Very well then I contradict myself,
(I am large, I contain multitudes.)

I concentrate toward them that are nigh, I wait on the door-slab.

Who has done his day's work? who will soonest be through with his supper?   365
Who wishes to walk with me?

Will you speak before I am gone? will you prove already too late?

52

The spotted hawk swoops by and accuses me, he complains of my gab and
  my loitering.

I too am not a bit tamed, I too am untranslatable,
I sound my barbaric yawp over the roofs of the world.   370

The last scud of day holds back for me,
It flings my likeness after the rest and true as any on the shadow'd wilds,
It coaxes me to the vapor and the dusk.

I depart as air, I shake my white locks at the runaway sun,
I effuse my flesh in eddies, and drift it in lacy jags.   375

I bequeath myself to the dirt to grow from the grass I love,
If you want me again look for me under your boot-soles.

You will hardly know who I am or what I mean,
But I shall be good health to you nevertheless,
And filter and fibre your blood.   *380*

Failing to fetch me at first keep encouraged,
Missing me one place search another,
I stop somewhere waiting for you.

[1855, 1881–1882]

Crossing Brooklyn Ferry

1

Flood-tide below me! I see you face to face!
Clouds of the west—sun there half an hour high—I see you also face to face.

Crowds of men and women attired in the usual costumes, how curious you are to me!
On the ferry-boats the hundreds and hundreds that cross, returning home, are more
    curious to me than you suppose,
And you that shall cross from shore to shore years hence are more to me, and more
    in my meditations, than you might suppose.   *5*

2

The impalpable sustenance of me from all things at all hours of the day,
The simple, compact, well-join'd scheme, myself disintegrated, every one disintegrated
    yet part of the scheme,
The similitudes of the past and those of the future,
The glories strung like beads on my smallest sights and hearings, on the walk in the
    street and the passage over the river,
The current rushing so swiftly and swimming with me far away,   *10*
The others that are to follow me, the ties between me and them,
The certainty of others, the life, love, sight, hearing of others.

Others will enter the gates of the ferry and cross from shore to shore,
Others will watch the run of the flood-tide,
Others will see the shipping of Manhattan north and west, and the heights of
    Brooklyn to the south and east,   *15*
Others will see the islands large and small;
Fifty years hence, others will see them as they cross, the sun half an hour high,
A hundred years hence, or ever so many hundred years hence, others will see them,
Will enjoy the sunset, the pouring-in of the flood-tide, the falling-back to the sea
    of the ebb-tide.

3

It avails not, time nor place—distance avails not, 20
I am with you, you men and women of a generation, or ever so many generations
hence,
Just as you feel when you look on the river and sky, so I felt,
Just as any of you is one of a living crowd, I was one of a crowd,
Just as you are refresh'd by the gladness of the river and the bright flow, I was
refresh'd,
Just as you stand and lean on the rail, yet hurry with the swift current, I stood yet
was hurried, 25
Just as you look on the numberless masts of ships and the thick-stemm'd pipes of
steamboats, I look'd.

I too many and many a time cross'd the river of old,
Watched the Twelfth-month sea-gulls, saw them high in the air floating with
motionless wings, oscillating their bodies,
Saw how the glistening yellow lit up parts of their bodies and left the rest in strong
shadow,
Saw the slow-wheeling circles and the gradual edging toward the south, 30
Saw the reflection of the summer sky in the water,
Had my eyes dazzled by the shimmering track of beams,
Look'd at the fine centrifugal spokes of light round the shape of my head in the
sunlit water,
Look'd on the haze on the hills southward and south-westward,
Look'd on the vapor as it flew in fleeces tinged with violet, 35
Look'd toward the lower bay to notice the vessels arriving,
Saw their approach, saw aboard those that were near me,
Saw the white sails of schooners and sloops, saw the ships at anchor,
The sailors at work in the rigging or out astride the spars,
The round masts, the swinging motion of the hulls, the slender serpentine
pennants, 40
The large and small steamers in motion, the pilots in their pilot-houses,
The white wake left by the passage, the quick tremulous whirl of the wheels,
The flags of all nations, the falling of them at sunset,
The scallop-edged waves in the twilight, the ladled cups, the frolicsome crests and
glistening,
The stretch afar growing dimmer and dimmer, the gray walls of the granite
storehouses by the docks, 45
On the river the shadowy group, the big steam-tug closely flank'd on each side
by the barges, the hay-boat, the belated lighter,
On the neighboring shore the fires from the foundry chimneys burning high and
glaringly into the night,
Casting their flicker of black contrasted with wild red and yellow light over the tops
of houses, and down into the clefts of streets.

4

These and all else were to me the same as they are to you,
I loved well those cities, loved well the stately and rapid river,   *50*
The men and women I saw were all near to me,
Others the same—others who look back on me because I look'd forward to them,
(The time will come, though I stop here to-day and to-night.)

5

What is it then between us?
What is the count of the scores of hundreds of years between us?   *55*

Whatever it is, it avails not—distance avails not, and place avails not,
I too lived, Brooklyn of ample hills was mine,
I too walk'd the streets of Manhattan island, and bathed in the waters around it,
I too felt the curious abrupt questionings stir within me,
In the day among crowds of people sometimes they came upon me,   *60*
In my walks home late at night or as I lay in my bed they came upon me,
I too had been struck from the float forever held in solution,
I too had receiv'd identity by my body,
That I was I knew was of my body, and what I should be I knew I should be
    of my body.

6

It is not upon you alone the dark patches fall,   *65*
The dark threw its patches down upon me also,
The best I had done seem'd to me blank and suspicious,
My great thoughts as I supposed them, were they not in reality meagre?
Nor is it you alone who know what it is to be evil,
I am he who knew what it was to be evil,   *70*
I too knitted the old knot of contrariety,
Blabb'd, blush'd, resented, lied, stole, grudg'd,
Had guile, anger, lust, hot wishes I dared not speak,
Was wayward, vain, greedy, shallow, sly, cowardly, malignant,
The wolf, the snake, the hog, not wanting in me,   *75*
The cheating look, the frivolous word, the adulterous wish, not wanting,
Refusals, hates, postponements, meanness, laziness, none of these wanting,
Was one with the rest, the days and haps of the rest,
Was call'd by my nighest name by clear loud voices of young men as they saw me
    approaching or passing,
Felt their arms on my neck as I stood, or the negligent leaning of their flesh against
    me as I sat,   *80*
Saw many I loved in the street or ferry-boat or public assembly, yet never told them
    a word,

Lived the same life with the rest, the same old laughing, gnawing, sleeping,
Play'd the part that still looks back on the actor or actress,
The same old role, the role that is what we make it, as great as we like,
Or as small as we like, or both great and small.   85

7

Closer yet I approach you,
What thought you have of me now, I had as much of you—I laid in my stores in
    advance,
I consider'd long and seriously of you before you were born.

Who was to know what should come home to me?
Who knows but I am enjoying this?   90
Who knows, for all the distance, but I am as good as looking at you now, for all
    you cannot see me?

8

Ah, what can ever be more stately and admirable to me than mast-hemm'd Manhattan?
River and sunset and scallop-edg'd waves of flood-tide?
The sea-gulls oscillating their bodies, the hay-boat in the twilight, and the belated
    lighter?
What gods can exceed these that clasp me by the hand, and with voices I love call
    me promptly and loudly by my nighest name as I approach?   95
What is more subtle than this which ties me to the woman or man that looks in my
    face?
Which fuses me into you now, and pours my meaning into you?

We understand then do we not?
What I promis'd without mentioning it, have you not accepted?
What the study could not teach—what the preaching could not accomplish is
    accomplish'd, is it not?   100

9

Flow on, river! flow with the flood-tide, and ebb with the ebb-tide!
Frolic on, crested and scallop-edg'd waves!
Gorgeous clouds of the sunset! drench with your splendor me, or the men and
    women generations after me!
Cross from shore to shore, countless crowds of passengers!
Stand up, tall masts of Mannahatta! stand up, beautiful hills of Brooklyn!   105
Throb, baffled and curious brain! throw out questions and answers!
Suspend here and everywhere, eternal float of solution!
Gaze, loving and thirsting eyes, in the house or street or public assembly!
Sound out, voices of young men! loudly and musically call me by my nighest name!

Live, old life! play the part that looks back on the actor or actress!   *110*
Play the old role, the role that is great or small according as one makes it!
Consider, you who peruse me, whether I may not in unknown ways be looking
     upon you;
Be firm, rail over the river, to support those who lean idly, yet haste with the
     hasting current;
Fly on, sea-birds! fly sideways, or wheel in large circles high in the air;
Receive the summer sky, you water, and faithfully hold it till all downcast eyes have
     time to take it from you!   *115*
Diverge, fine spokes of light, from the shape of my head, or any one's head, in the
     sunlit water!
Come on, ships from the lower bay! pass up or down, white-sail'd schooners,
     sloops, lighters!
Flaunt away, flags of all nations! be duly lower'd at sunset!
Burn high your fires, foundry chimneys! cast black shadows at nightfall!
     cast red and yellow light over the tops of the houses!
Appearances, now or henceforth, indicate what you are,   *120*
You necessary film, continue to envelop the soul,
About my body for me, and your body for you, be hung our divinest aromas,
Thrive, cities—bring your freight, bring your shows, ample and sufficient rivers,
Expand, being than which none else is perhaps more spiritual,
Keep your places, objects than which none else is more lasting.   *125*

You have waited, you always wait, you dumb, beautiful ministers,
We receive you with free sense at last, and are insatiate henceforward,
Not you any more shall be able to foil us, or withhold yourselves from us,
We use you, and do not cast you aside—we plant you permanently within us,
We fathom you not—we love you—there is perfection in you also,   *130*
You furnish your parts toward eternity,
Great or small, you furnish your parts toward the soul.

                                                     [1856, 1892]

Cavalry Crossing a Ford

A line in long array where they wind betwixt green islands,
They take a serpentine course, their arms flash in the sun—hark to the musical clank,
Behold the silvery river, in it the splashing horses loitering stop to drink,
Behold the brown-faced men, each group, each person a picture, the negligent rest
     on the saddles,
Some emerge on the opposite bank, others are just entering the ford—while,   *5*
Scarlet and blue and snowy white,
The guidon flags flutter gayly in the wind.

                                                     [1865]

Bivouac on a Mountain Side

I see before me now a traveling army halting,
Below a fertile valley spread, with barns and the orchards of summer,
Behind, the terraced sides of a mountain, abrupt, in places rising high,
Broken, with rocks, with clinging cedars, with tall shapes dingily seen,
The numerous camp-fires scatter'd near and far, some away up on the mountain,   5
The shadowy forms of men and horses, looming, large-sized, flickering,
And over all the sky—the sky! far, far out of reach, studded, breaking out, the
    eternal stars.

            [1865]

Vigil strange I kept on the field one night

Vigil strange I kept on the field one night;
When you my son and my comrade dropt at my side that day,
One look I but gave which your dear eyes return'd with a look I shall never forget,
One touch of your hand to mine O boy, reach'd up as you lay on the ground,
Then onward I sped in the battle, the even-contested battle,   5
Till late in the night reliev'd to the place at last again I made my way,
Found you in death so cold dear comrade, found your body son of responding
    kisses, (never again on earth responding,)
Bared your face in the starlight, curious the scene, cool blew the moderate
    night-wind,
Long there and then in vigil I stood, dimly around me the battle-field spreading,
Vigil wondrous and vigil sweet there in the fragrant silent night,   10
But not a tear fell, not even a long-drawn sigh, long, long I gazed,
Then on the earth partially reclining sat by your side leaning my chin in my hands,
Passing sweet hours, immortal and mystic hours with you dearest comrade—not
    a tear, not a word,
Vigil of silence, love and death, vigil for you my son and my soldier,
As onward silently stars aloft, eastward new ones upward stole,   15
Vigil final for you brave boy, (I could not save you, swift was your death,
I faithfully loved you and cared for you living, I think we shall surely meet again,)
Till at latest lingering of the night, indeed just as the dawn appear'd,
My comrade I wrapt in his blanket, envelop'd well his form,
Folded the blanket well, tucking it carefully over head and carefully under feet,   20
And there and then and bathed by the rising sun, my son in his grave, in his
    rude-dug grave I deposited,
Ending my vigil strange with that, vigil of night and battle-field dim,

Vigil for boy of responding kisses, (never again on earth responding,)
Vigil for comrade swiftly slain, vigil I never forget, how as day brighten'd,
I rose from the chill ground and folded my soldier well in his blanket,   *25*
And buried him where he fell.

[1865]

A sight in camp in the daybreak gray and dim

A sight in camp in the daybreak gray and dim,
As from my tent I emerge so early sleepless,
As slow I walk in the cool fresh air the path near by the hospital tent,
Three forms I see on stretchers lying, brought out there untended lying,
Over each the blanket spread, ample brownish woolen blanket,   *5*
Gray and heavy blanket, folding, covering all.

Curious I halt and silent stand,
Then with light fingers I from the face of the nearest the first just lift the blanket;
Who are you elderly man so gaunt and grim, with well-gray'd hair, and flesh
    all sunken about the eyes?
Who are you my dear comrade?   *10*

Then to the second I step—and who are you my child and darling?
Who are you sweet boy with cheeks yet blooming?

Then to the third—a face nor child nor old, very calm, as of beautiful yellow-white
    ivory;
Young man I think I know you—I think this face is the face of the Christ himself,
Dead and divine and brother of all, and here again he lies.   *15*

[1865]

The Wound-Dresser

1

An old man bending I come among new faces,
Years looking backward resuming in answer to children,
Come tell us old man, as from young men and maidens that love me,
(Arous'd and angry, I'd thought to beat the alarum, and urge relentless war,
But soon my fingers fail'd me, my face droop'd and I resign'd myself,   *5*

To sit by the wounded and soothe them, or silently watch the dead;)
Years hence of these scenes, of these furious passions, these chances,
Of unsurpass'd heroes, (was one side so brave? the other was equally brave;)
Now be witness again, paint the mightiest armies of earth,
Of those armies so rapid so wondrous what saw you to tell us?   10
What stays with you latest and deepest? of curious panics
Of hard-fought engagements or sieges tremendous what deepest remains?

2

O maidens and young men I love and that love me,
What you ask of my days those the strangest and sudden your talking recalls,
Soldier alert I arrive after a long march cover'd with sweat and dust,   15
In the nick of time I come, plunge in the fight, loudly shout in the rush of
    successful charge,
Enter the captur'd works—yet lo, like a swift-running river they fade,
Pass and are gone they fade—I dwell not on soldiers' perils or soldiers' joys,
(Both I remember well—many the hardships, few the joys, yet I was content.)

But in silence, in dreams' projections,   20
While the world of gain and appearance and mirth goes on,
So soon what is over forgotten, and waves wash the imprints off the sand,
With hinged knees returning I enter the doors, (while for you up there,
Whoever you are, follow without noise and be of strong heart.)

Bearing the bandages, water and sponge,   25
Straight and swift to my wounded I go,
Where they lie on the ground after the battle brought in,
Where their priceless blood reddens the grass the ground,
Or to the rows of the hospital tent, or under the roof'd hospital,
To the long rows of cots up and down each side I return,   30
To each and all one after another I draw near, not one do I miss,

An attendant follows holding a tray, he carries a refuse pail,
Soon to be fill'd with clotted rags and blood, emptied, and fill'd again.

I onward go, I stop,
With hinged knees and steady hand to dress wounds,   35
I am firm with each, the pangs are sharp yet unavoidable,
One turns to me his appealing eyes—poor boy! I never knew you,
Yet I think I could not refuse this moment to die for you, if that would save you.

3

On, on I go, (open doors of time! open hospital doors!)
The crush'd head I dress, (poor crazed hand tear not the bandage away,)   40

The neck of the cavalry-man with the bullet through and through I examine,
Hard the breathing rattles, quite glazed already the eye, yet life struggles hard,
(Come sweet death! be persuaded O beautiful death!
In mercy come quickly.)

From the stump of the arm, the amputated hand,   *45*
I undo the clotted lint, remove the slough, wash off the matter and blood,
Back on his pillow the soldier bends with curv'd neck and side-falling head,
His eyes are closed, his face is pale, he dares not look on the bloody stump,
And has not yet look'd on it.

I dress a wound in the side, deep, deep,   *50*
But a day or two more, for see the frame all wasted and sinking,
And the yellow-blue countenance see.

I dress the perforated shoulder, the foot with the bullet-wound,
Cleanse the one with a gnawing and putrid gangrene, so sickening, so offensive,
While the attendant stands behind aside me holding the tray and pail.   *55*

I am faithful, I do not give out,
The fractur'd thigh, the knee, the wound in the abdomen,
These and more I dress with impassive hand, (yet deep in my breast a fire, a
    burning flame.)

4

Thus in silence in dreams' projections,
Returning, resuming, I thread my way through the hospitals,   *60*
The hurt and wounded I pacify with soothing hand,
I sit by the restless all the dark night, some are so young,
Some suffer so much, I recall the experience sweet and sad,
(Many a soldier's loving arms about this neck have cross'd and rested,
Many a soldier's kiss dwells on these bearded lips.)   *65*

[1865]

The Dalliance of the Eagles

Skirting the river road, (my forenoon walk, my rest,)
Skyward in air a sudden muffled sound, the dalliance of the eagles,
The rushing amorous contact high in space together,
The clinching interlocking claws, a living, fierce, gyrating wheel,
Four beating wings, two beaks, a swirling mass tight grappling,   *5*

In tumbling turning clustering loops, straight downward falling,
Till o'er the river pois'd, the twain yet one, a moment's lull,
A motionless still balance in the air, then parting, talons loosing,
Upward again on slow-firm pinions slanting, their separate diverse flight,
She hers, he his, pursuing.   *10*

[1881]

A noiseless patient spider

A noiseless patient spider,
I mark'd where on a little promontory it stood isolated,
Mark'd how to explore the vacant vast surrounding,
It launch'd forth filament, filament, filament, out of itself,
Ever unreeling them, ever tirelessly speeding them.   *5*

And you O my soul where you stand,
Surrounded, detached, in measureless oceans of space,
Ceaselessly musing, venturing, throwing, seeking the spheres to connect them,
Till the bridge you will need be form'd, till the ductile anchor hold,
Till the gossamer thread you fling catch somewhere, O my soul.   *10*

[1881]

When lilacs last in the dooryard bloom'd

1

When lilacs last in the dooryard bloom'd,
And the great star early droop'd in the western sky in the night,
I mourn'd, and yet shall mourn with ever-returning spring.

Ever-returning spring, trinity sure to me you bring,
Lilac blooming perennial and drooping star in the west,   *5*
And thought of him I love.

2

O powerful western fallen star!
O shades of night—O moody, tearful night!
O great star disappear'd—O the black murk that hides the star!

O cruel hands that hold me powerless—O helpless soul of me!   10
O harsh surrounding cloud that will not free my soul.

3

In the dooryard fronting an old farm-house near the white-wash'd palings,
Stands the lilac-bush tall-growing with heart-shaped leaves of rich green,
With many a pointed blossom rising delicate, with the perfume strong I love,
With every leaf a miracle—and from this bush in the dooryard,   15
With delicate-color'd blossoms and heart-shaped leaves of rich green,
A sprig with its flower I break.

4

In the swamp in secluded recesses,
A shy and hidden bird is warbling a song.

Solitary the thrush,   20
The hermit withdrawn to himself, avoiding the settlements,
Sings by himself a song.

Song of the bleeding throat,
Death's outlet song of life, (for well dear brother I know,
If thou wast not granted to sing thou would'st surely die.)   25

5

Over the breast of the spring, the land, amid cities,
Amid lanes and through old woods, where lately the violets peep'd from the ground,
     spotting the gray debris,
Amid the grass in the fields each side of the lanes, passing the endless grass,
Passing the yellow-spear'd wheat, every grain from its shroud in the
     dark-brown fields uprisen,
Passing the apple-tree blows of white and pink in the orchards,   30
Carrying a corpse to where it shall rest in the grave,
Night and day journeys a coffin.

6

Coffin that passes through lanes and streets,
Through day and night with the great cloud darkening the land,
With the pomp of the inloop'd flags with the cities draped in black,   35
With the show of the States themselves as of crape-veil'd women standing,
With processions long and winding and the flambeaus of the night,
With the countless torches lit, with the silent sea of faces and the unbared heads,
With the waiting depot, the arriving coffin, and the sombre faces,
With dirges through the night, with the thousand voices rising strong and solemn,   40

With all the mournful voices of the dirges pour'd around the coffin,
The dim-lit churches and the shuddering organs—where amid these you journey,
With the tolling tolling bells' perpetual clang,
Here, coffin that slowly passes,
I give you my sprig of lilac.   45

7

(Nor for you, for one alone,
Blossoms and branches green to coffins all I bring,
For fresh as the morning, thus would I chant a song for you O sane and sacred death.

All over bouquets of roses,
O death, I cover you over with roses and early lilies,   50
But mostly and now the lilac that blooms the first,
Copious I break, I break the sprigs from the bushes,
With loaded arms I come, pouring for you,
For you and the coffins all of you O death.)

8

O western orb sailing the heaven,   55
Now I know what you must have meant as a month since I walk'd,
As I walk'd in silence the transparent shadowy night,
As I saw you had something to tell as you bent to me night after night,
As you droop'd from the sky low down as if to my side, (while the other stars
    all look'd on,)
As we wander'd together the solemn night, (for something I know not what
    kept me from sleep,)   60
As the night advanced, and I saw on the rim of the west how full you were of woe,
As I stood on the rising ground in the breeze in the cool transparent night,
As I watch'd where you pass'd and was lost in the netherward black of the night,
As my soul in its trouble dissatisfied sank, as where you sad orb,
Concluded, dropt in the night; and was gone.   65

9

Sing on there in the swamp,
O singer bashful and tender, I hear your notes, I hear your call,
I hear, I come presently, I understand you,
But a moment I linger, for the lustrous star has detain'd me,
The star my departing comrade holds and detains me.   70

10

O how shall I warble myself for the dead one there I loved?
And how shall I deck my song for the large sweet soul that has gone?
And what shall my perfume be for the grave of him I love?

Sea-winds blown from east and west,
Blown from the Eastern sea and blown from the Western sea, till there on
   the prairies meeting, *75*
These and with these and the breath of my chant,
I'll perfume the grave of him I love.

11

O what shall I hang on the chamber walls?
And what shall the pictures be that I hang on the walls,
To adorn the burial-house of him I love? *80*

Pictures of growing spring and farms and homes,
With the Fourth-month eve at sundown, and the gray smoke lucid and bright,
With floods of the yellow gold of the gorgeous, indolent, sinking sun, burning,
   expanding the air,
With the fresh sweet herbage under foot, and the pale green leaves of the trees
   prolific,
In the distance the flowing glaze, the breast of the river, with a wind-dapple here
   and there, *85*
With ranging hills on the banks, with many a line against the sky, and shadows,
And the city at hand with dwellings so dense, and stacks of chimneys,
And all the scenes of life and the workshops, and the workmen homeward returning.

12

Lo, body and soul—this land,
My own Manhattan with spires, and the sparkling and hurrying tides, and the ships, *90*
The varied and ample land, the South and the North in the light, Ohio's shores and
   flashing Missouri,
And ever the far-spreading prairies cover'd with grass and corn.

Lo, the most excellent sun so calm and haughty,
The violet and purple morn with just-felt breezes,
The gentle soft-born measureless light, *95*
The miracle spreading bathing all, the fulfill'd noon,
The coming eve delicious, the welcome night and the stars,
Over my cities shining all, enveloping man and land.

13

Sing on, sing on you gray-brown bird,
Sing from the swamps, the recesses, pour your chant from the bushes, *100*
Limitless out of the dusk, out of the cedars and pines.

Sing on dearest brother, warble your reedy song,
Loud human song, with voice of uttermost woe.

O liquid and free and tender!
O wild and loose to my soul!—O wondrous singer!   105
You only I hear—yet the star holds me, (but will soon depart,)
Yet the lilac with mastering odor holds me.

14

Now while I sat in the day and look'd forth,
In the close of the day with its light and the fields of spring, and the farmers
    preparing their crops,
In the large unconscious scenery of my land with its lakes and forests,   110
In the heavenly aerial beauty, (after the perturb'd winds and the storms,)
Under the arching heavens of the afternoon swift passing, and the voices of
    children and women,
The many-moving sea-tides, and I saw the ships how they sail'd,
And the summer approaching with richness, and the fields all busy with labor,
And the infinite separate houses, how they all went on, each with its meals and
    minutia of daily usages,   115
And the streets how their throbbings throbb'd, and the cities pent—lo, then
    and there,
Falling upon them all and among them all, enveloping me with the rest,
Appear'd the cloud, appear'd the long black trail,
And I knew death, its thought, and the sacred knowledge of death.

Then with the knowledge of death as walking one side of me,   120
And the thought of death close-walking the other side of me,
And I in the middle as with companions, and as holding the hands of companions,
I fled forth to the hiding receiving night that talks not,
Down to the shores of the water, the path by the swamp in the dimness,
To the solemn shadowy cedars and ghostly pines so still.   125

And the singer so shy to the rest receiv'd me,
The gray-brown bird I know receiv'd us comrades three,
And he sang the carol of death, and a verse for him I love.

From deep secluded recesses,
From the fragrant cedars and the ghostly pines so still,   130
Came the carol of the bird.

And the charm of the carol rapt me,
As I held as if by their hands my comrades in the night,
And the voice of my spirit tallied the song of the bird.

Come lovely and soothing death,   135
Undulate round the world, serenely arriving, arriving,
In the day, in the night, to all, to each,
Sooner or later delicate death.

Prais'd be the fathomless universe,
For life and joy, and for objects and knowledge curious,   140
And for love, sweet love—but praise! praise! praise!
For the sure-enwinding arms of cool-enfolding death.

Dark mother always gliding near with soft feet,
Have none chanted for thee a chant of fullest welcome?
Then I chant it for thee, I glorify thee above all,   145
I bring thee a song that when thou must indeed come, come unfalteringly.

Approach strong deliveress,
When it is so, when thou hast taken them I joyously sing the dead,
Lost in the loving floating ocean of thee,
Laved in the flood of thy bliss O death.   150

From me to thee glad serenades,
Dances for thee I propose saluting thee, adornments and feastings for thee,
And the sights of the open landscape and the high-spread sky are fitting,
And life and the fields, and the huge and thoughtful night.

The night in silence under many a star,   155
The ocean shore and the husky whispering wave whose voice I know,
And the soul turning to thee O vast and well-veil'd death,
And the body gratefully nestling close to thee.

Over the tree-tops I float thee a song,
Over the rising and sinking waves, over the myriad fields and the prairies wide,   160
Over the dense-pack'd cities all and the teeming wharves and ways,
I float this carol with joy, with joy to thee O death.

15

To the tally of my soul,
Loud and strong kept up the gray-brown bird,
With pure deliberate notes spreading filling the night.   165

Loud in the pines and cedars dim,
Clear in the freshness moist and the swamp-perfume,
And I with my comrades there in the night.

While my sight that was bound in my eyes unclosed,
As to long panoramas of visions.   170

And I saw askant the armies,
I saw as in noiseless dreams hundreds of battle-flags,
Borne through the smoke of the battles and pierc'd with missiles I saw them,
And carried hither and yon through the smoke, and torn and bloody,
And at last but a few shreds left on the staffs, (and all in silence,)   175
And the staffs all splinter'd and broken.

I saw battle-corpses, myriads of them,
And the white skeletons of young men, I saw them,
I saw the debris and debris of all the slain soldiers of the war,
But I saw they were not as was thought,   180
They themselves were fully at rest, they suffer'd not,
The living remain'd and suffer'd, the mother suffer'd,
And the wife and the child and the musing comrade suffer'd,
And the armies that remain'd suffer'd.

16

Passing the visions, passing the night,   185
Passing, unloosing the hold of my comrades' hands,
Passing the song of the hermit bird and the tallying song of my soul,
Victorious song, death's outlet song, yet varying ever-altering song,
As low and wailing, yet clear the notes, rising and falling, flooding the night,
Sadly sinking and fainting, as warning and warning, and yet again bursting
    with joy,   190
Covering the earth and filling the spread of the heaven,
As that powerful psalm in the night I heard from recesses,
Passing, I leave thee lilac with heart-shaped leaves,
I leave thee there in the door-yard, blooming, returning with spring.

I cease from my song for thee,   195
From my gaze on thee in the west, fronting the west, communing with thee,
O comrade lustrous with silver face in the night.

Yet each to keep and all, retrievements out of the night,
The song, the wondrous chant of the gray-brown bird,
And the tallying chant, the echo arous'd in my soul,   200
With the lustrous and drooping star with the countenance full of woe,
With the holders holding my hand nearing the call of the bird,
Comrades mine and I in the midst, and their memory ever to keep, for the dead
    I loved so well,
For the sweetest, wisest soul of all my days and lands—and this for his dear sake,
Lilac and star and bird twined with the chant of my soul,   205
There in the fragrant pines and the cedars dusk and dim.

                                                                              [1881]

Good-bye my Fancy!

Good-bye my Fancy!
Farewell dear mate, dear love!
I'm going away, I know not where,
Or to what fortune, or whether I may ever see you again,
So Good-bye my Fancy.   5

Now for my last—let me look back a moment;
The slower fainter ticking of the clock is in me,
Exit, nightfall, and soon the heart-thud stopping.

Long have we lived, joy'd, caress'd together;
Delightful!—now separation—Good-bye my Fancy.   10

Yet let me not be too hasty,
Long indeed have we lived, slept, filter'd, become really
    blended into one;
Then if we die we die together, (yes, we'll remain one,)
If we go anywhere we'll go together to meet what happens,
May-be we'll be better off and blither, and learn something,   15
May-be it is yourself now really ushering me to the
    true songs, (who knows?)
May-be it is you the mortal knob really undoing, turning—
    so now finally,
Good-bye—and hail! my Fancy.

[1891]

MATTHEW ARNOLD

[1822–1888]

Dover Beach

The sea is calm tonight.
The tide is full, the moon lies fair
Upon the straits; on the French coast the light
Gleams and is gone; the cliffs of England stand,
Glimmering and vast, out in the tranquil bay.   5
Come to the window, sweet is the night-air!
Only, from the long line of spray
Where the sea meets the moon-blanched land,

Listen! you hear the grating roar
Of pebbles which the waves draw back, and fling, 10
At their return, up the high strand,
Begin, and cease, and then again begin,
With tremulous cadence slow, and bring
The eternal note of sadness in.

Sophocles long ago 15
Heard it on the Aegean, and it brought
Into his mind the turbid ebb and flow
Of human misery; we
Find also in the sound a thought,
Hearing it by this distant northern sea. 20

The Sea of Faith
Was once, too, at the full, and round earth's shore
Lay like the folds of a bright girdle furled.
But now I only hear
Its melancholy, long, withdrawing roar, 25
Retreating, to the breath
Of the night-wind, down the vast edges drear
And naked shingles of the world.

Ah, love, let us be true
To one another! for the world, which seems 30
To lie before us like a land of dreams,
So various, so beautiful, so new,
Hath really neither joy, nor love, nor light,
Nor certitude, nor peace, nor help for pain;
And we are here as on a darkling plain 35
Swept with confused alarms of struggle and flight,
Where ignorant armies clash by night.

[1867]

GEORGE MEREDITH

[1828–1909]

Lucifer in Starlight

On a starred night Prince Lucifer uprose.
Tired of his dark dominion swung the fiend
Above the rolling ball in cloud part screened,
Where sinners hugged their specter of repose.

Poor prey to his hot fit of pride were those.   5
And now upon his western wing he leaned,
Now his huge bulk o'er Afric's sands careened,
Now the black planet shadowed Arctic snows.
Soaring through wider zones that pricked his scars
With memory of the old revolt from Awe,   10
He reached a middle height, and at the stars,
Which are the brain of heaven, he looked, and sank.
Around the ancient track marched, rank on rank,
The army of unalterable law.

[1883]

DANTE GABRIEL ROSSETTI

[1828–1882]

Barren Spring

Once more the changed year's turning wheel returns:
    And as a girl sails balanced in the wind,
    And now before and now again behind
Stoops as it swoops, with cheek that laughs and burns—
So Spring comes merry towards me here, but earns   5
    No answering smile from me, whose life is twined
    With the dead boughs that winter still must bind,
And whom to-day the Spring no more concerns.

Behold, this crocus is a withering flame;
    This snowdrop, snow; this apple-blossom's part   10
    To breed the fruit that breeds the serpent's art.
Nay, for these Spring-flowers, turn thy face from them,
Nor gaze till on the year's last lily-stem
    The white cup shrivels round the golden heart.

[1870, 1881]

CHRISTINA GEORGINA ROSSETTI

[1830–1894]

Remember

Remember me when I am gone away,
    Gone far away into the silent land;
    When you can no more hold me by the hand,

Nor I half turn to go yet turning stay.
Remember me when no more day by day   5
    You tell me of our future that you planned:
    Only remember me; you understand
It will be late to counsel then or pray.
Yet if you should forget me for a while
    And afterwards remember, do not grieve: 10
    For if the darkness and corruption leave
A vestige of the thoughts that once I had,
Better by far you should forget and smile
    Than that you should remember and be sad.

[1862]

EMILY DICKINSON

[1830–1886]

Emily Dickinson's external life was remarkably circumscribed. Born in 1830 in Amherst, Massachusetts, and educated at Amherst Academy, she lived there her entire life, except for a brief stay at what was later to become Mount Holyoke College. She lived a life of seclusion, leaving Massachusetts only once and rarely leaving her father's house during the last fifteen years of her life. She died in the house where she was born.

If Dickinson's external life was unadventurous, her interior life was not. Her mind was anything but provincial. She read widely in English literature and thought deeply about what she read. She expressed a particular fondness for the poetry of John Keats and Robert Browning, the prose of John Ruskin and Sir Thomas Browne, and the novels of George Eliot and Charlotte and Emily Brontë. And although she disclaimed knowledge of Whitman's work, she treasured a book that significantly influenced both Whitman's poetry and her own: the King James translation of the Bible. She especially liked the Book of Revelation.

Dickinson is often bracketed with Whitman as a cofounder of modern American poetry. Each brought to poetry something new, fresh, and strikingly original. But their poems, however prototypically modern, could not be more different. A mere glance at the page reveals a significant visual difference. Whitman's poems are large and expansive. The lines are long and the poems are typically ample and open. Dickinson's poems, by contrast, are highly compressed. They squeeze moments of intensely felt life and thought into tight four-line stanzas that compress feeling and condense thought.

The openness of Whitman's form is paralleled by the openness of his stance, his public outgoing manner. Dickinson's poetry is much more private, tending toward inwardness. Hers is a more meditative poetry than Whitman's, a poetry rooted partly in the metaphysical poetry of such seventeenth-century writers as John

Donne and George Herbert. More directly influential on Dickinson's poetry than the metaphysical poets, however, was the tradition of Protestant hymnology. Her poems frequently employ the meter of hymns and follow their typical stanzaic pattern. Here, for example, is the opening verse of "Our God, Our Help in Ages Past," its accented syllables marked with '.

> Our God, our help in ages past,
> Our hope for years to come,
> Our shelter from the stormy blast,
> And our eternal home.

The hymn's meter and formal structure are highly regular. The first and third lines are in iambic tetrameter, the second and fourth in iambic trimeter. The lack of metrical variation results in a steady, predictable rhythm, essential for singing. Dickinson varies this standard pattern to suit her poetic purpose. Her numerous variations amply testify to the ingenious and stunning uses to which she put this familiar meter. Consider, for example, "I felt a Funeral, in my Brain," "I like a look of Agony," "I died for Beauty—but was scarce," and "I heard a Fly buzz—when I died."

Dickinson's adaptation of hymn meter accords with her adaptation of the traditional religious doctrines of orthodox Christianity. For although her poems reflect a Calvinist heritage—particularly in their probing self-analysis, in which an intensely religious disposition intersects with profound psychological experience— she was not an orthodox Christian. Her religious ideas, like her life and poetry, were distinctive and individual. And even when her views tend toward orthodox teaching, as in her attitude toward immortality, her literary expression of such a belief is strikingly original. In addition, Dickinson's mischievous wit contrasts sharply with the brooding solemnity characteristic of much Calvinist-inspired religious writing. Finally, her love for nature separates her from her Puritan precursors, allying her instead with such transcendentalist contemporaries as Emerson, Whitman, and Thoreau, though her vision of life is starker than theirs.

Dickinson's poetry requires repeated and careful readings. Her diction is frequently surprising. Her elliptical syntax occasionally departs from the normal pattern. Readers must consequently fill in the gaps her language creates. Her taut lines need to be loosened; her tight poems need to be opened up. Words, phrases, lines cry out for the expansion of interpretive paraphrase.

Though a dictionary is necessary to identify the meanings of many of the words in Dickinson's poems, we need to attend to their richness of connotation as well. In "A narrow Fellow in the Grass," for example, we can explore the connotations of "Fellow," "transport," "cordiality," and "Zero at the Bone," considering how they fuse thought and feeling. In "The Bustle in a House," we can be alert for the fresh treatment of metaphor in the second stanza and attentive to the connotations of "industries," "Morning," and "Enacted" from the opening lines. And in "Tell all the Truth but tell it slant," we can discover the general idea implied by the poem and then apply it to specific areas of our experience. In doing so we will discover how

Dickinson treats both nature and human experience obliquely and indirectly. To read her poems requires, in addition, a willingness to wait for the poem's possibilities of meaning to reveal themselves. Since many of her poems are cast as riddles, we must be willing to accept uncertainty, ambiguity, and partial understanding in interpreting them.

We also have to extend our notion of what constitutes acceptable poetic technique—something her contemporaries found nearly impossible. Dickinson was criticized for using inexact rhymes, rough rhythms, and colloquial diction, and for taking liberties with grammar. Her odd punctuation—heavy on dashes—and her peculiar use of capitalization were also unappreciated. But Dickinson exploited these and other poetic resources to convey complex states of mind and feeling. She employed these and other poetic idiosyncrasies not for their own sake, but for emotional and psychological impact.

In his extensive biography of Dickinson, Richard B. Sewall describes her resolve to portray the state of her mind and being in all their unorthodox complexity. He also describes Dickinson's early and futile hopes for publication and appreciation as well as her resignation to what she termed her "barefoot rank: of anonymity." Sewall also reveals her determination to pursue truth and to make poems her way. When Thomas Wentworth Higginson, an influential contemporary critic, advised her to write a more polite poetry, less indirect and metaphoric, smoother in rhythm and rhyme, simpler in thought, and less colloquial in idiom, she replied with a poem. Her answer is that although she could have written otherwise, she chose to write as she did.

I cannot dance upon my Toes

I cannot dance upon my Toes—
No Man instructed me—
But oftentimes, among my mind,
A Glee possesseth me,

That had I Ballet knowledge—
Would put itself abroad
In Pirouette to blanch a Troupe—
Or lay a Prima, mad,

And though I had no Gown of Gauze—
No ringlet, to my Hair,
Nor hopped to Audiences—like Birds,
One claw upon the Air,

Nor tossed my shape in Eider Balls,
Nor rolled on wheels of snow

Till I was out of sight, in sound,
The House encore me so—

Nor any know I know the Art
I mention—easy—Here—
Nor any Placard boast me—
It's full as Opera

[#326, c. 1862, 1929]

Sewall describes how Dickinson's poems reflect her poetic vocation. He demonstrates how basic religious texts such as the Bible and Thomas à Kempis's *The Imitation of Christ* sustained her both spiritually and poetically. Though allowing that Dickinson's decision to cloister herself in her chamber could have had its roots in neurosis, he argues that her firm resolve was motivated by a commitment to the art of poetry akin to the ascetic discipline of religious devotion. In fact, he cites one of her more famous poems—one usually interpreted as a love poem—to suggest that it be read as a dedication to the spiritual or poetic life. It can also be read as a celebration of individual choice.

The Soul selects her own Society

The Soul selects her own Society—
Then—shuts the Door—
To her divine Majority—
Present no more—

Unmoved—she notes the Chariots—pausing—
At her low Gate—
Unmoved—an Emperor be kneeling
Upon her Mat—

I've known her—from an ample nation—
Choose One—
Then—close the Valves of her attention—
Like Stone—

[#303, c. 1862, 1890]

Sewall's central point about the relationship between Dickinson's life and art is that although we may not be certain which interpretation to favor when considering this and many other poems, we can remain satisfied with our uncertainty because such ambiguity is central to her art. She writes metaphorically, concealing as much as she reveals. As readers we share in apprehending the nature of the experience she describes—in the poem above, the experience of making a decisive choice involving commitment and renunciation. In doing so, however, we also supply specific details from our own lives to render the decision specific and significant. Dickinson's poetry, in other words, conveys the essence of an experience, its heart and core. Her poems, as Sewall aptly notes, do not tell us so much how to live as what it feels like to be alive.

Emily Dickinson's poems do not encompass a wide range of experience; instead they probe deeply into a few of life's major experiences—love, death, doubt, and faith. In examining her experience, Dickinson makes a scrupulous effort to tell the truth, but she tells it "slant." Part of her originality and artistry includes the way she invites us to share in her search for truth. The qualified assertions we frequently find in her poems, their riddles and uncertainties, and their questioning stance demand our participation and response. In considering her representation of intensely felt moments of consciousness, we experience for ourselves her explosive power. And in learning to share Dickinson's acute perceptions and feelings, we also come to understand our own.

I'm "wife"—I've finished that

I'm "wife"—I've finished that—
That other state—
I'm Czar—I'm "Woman" now—
It's safer so—

How odd the Girl's life looks   5
Behind this soft Eclipse—
I think that Earth feels so
To folks in Heaven—now—

This being comfort—then
That other kind—was pain—   10
But why compare?
I'm "Wife"! Stop there!

[#199, 1860, 1890]

I like a look of Agony

I like a look of Agony,
Because I know it's true—
Men do not sham Convulsion,
Nor simulate, a Throe—

The Eyes glaze once—and that is Death—   *5*
Impossible to feign
The Beads upon the Forehead
By homely Anguish strung.

[#241, 1861, 1890]

Wild Nights—Wild Nights!

Wild Nights—Wild Nights!
Were I with thee
Wild Nights should be
Our luxury!

Futile—the Winds—   *5*
To a Heart in port—
Done with the Compass—
Done with the Chart!

Rowing in Eden—
Ah, the Sea!   *10*
Might I but moor—Tonight—
In Thee!

[#249, 1861, 1891]

There's a certain Slant of light

There's a certain Slant of light,
Winter Afternoons—
That oppresses, like the Heft
Of Cathedral Tunes—

Heavenly Hurt, it gives us—   *5*
We can find no scar,
But internal difference,
Where the Meanings, are—

None may teach it—Any—
'Tis the Sea Despair—   *10*
An imperial affliction
Sent us of the Air—

When it comes, the Landscape listens—
Shadows—hold their breath—
When it goes, 'tis like the Distance   *15*
On the look of Death—

[#258, 1861, 1890]

I felt a Funeral, in my Brain

I felt a Funeral, in my Brain,
And Mourners to and fro
Kept treading—treading—till it seemed
That Sense was breaking through—

And when they all were seated,   *5*
A Service, like a Drum—
Kept beating—beating—till I thought
My Mind was going numb—

And I heard them lift a Box
And creak across my Soul   *10*
With those same Boots of Lead, again,
Then Space—began to toll,

As all the Heavens were a Bell,
And Being, but an Ear,
And I, and Silence, some strange Race   *15*
Wrecked, solitary, here—

And then a Plank in Reason, broke,
And I dropped down, and down—
And hit a World, at every plunge,
And Finished knowing—then—   *20*

[#280, 1861, 1896]

After great pain, a formal feeling comes

After great pain, a formal feeling comes—
The Nerves sit ceremonious, like Tombs—

The stiff Heart questions was it He, that bore,
And Yesterday, or Centuries before?

The Feet, mechanical, go round—   5
Of Ground, or Air, or Ought—
A Wooden way
Regardless grown,
A Quartz contentment, like a stone—

This is the Hour of Lead—   10
Remembered, if outlived,
As Freezing persons, recollect the Snow—
First—Chill—then Stupor—then the letting go—

[#341, 1862, 1929]

We grow accustomed to the Dark

We grow accustomed to the Dark—
When Light is put away—
As when the Neighbor holds the Lamp
To witness her Goodbye—

A Moment—We uncertain step   5
For newness of the night—
Then—fit our Vision to the Dark—
And meet the Road—erect—

And so of larger—Darknesses—
Those Evenings of the Brain—   10
When not a Moon disclose a sign—
Or Star—come out—within—

The Bravest—grope a little—
And sometimes hit a Tree
Directly in the Forehead—   15
But as they learn to see—

Either the Darkness alters—
Or something in the sight
Adjusts itself to Midnight—
And Life steps almost straight.   20

[#419, 1862, 1935]

I died for Beauty—but was scarce

I died for Beauty—but was scarce
Adjusted in the Tomb
When One who died for Truth, was lain
In an adjoining Room—

He questioned softly "Why I failed"?   5
"For Beauty", I replied—
"And I—for Truth—Themself are One—
We Brethren, are", He said—

And so, as Kinsmen, met a Night—
We talked between the Rooms—   10
Until the Moss had reached our lips—
And covered up—our names—

[#449, 1862, 1890]

I heard a Fly buzz—when I died

I heard a Fly buzz—when I died—
The Stillness in the Room
Was like the Stillness in the Air—
Between the Heaves of Storm—

The Eyes around—had wrung them dry—   5
And Breaths were gathering firm
For the last Onset—when the King
Be witnessed—in the Room—

I willed my Keepsakes—Signed away
What portion of me be   10
Assignable—and then it was
There interposed a Fly—

With Blue—uncertain stumbling Buzz—
Between the light—and me—
And then the Windows failed—and then   15
I could not see to see—

[#465, 1862, 1896]

The Heart asks Pleasure—first

The Heart asks Pleasure—first—
And then—Excuse from Pain—
And then—those little Anodynes
That deaden suffering—

And then—to go to sleep—   5
And then—if it should be
The will of its Inquisition
The privilege to die—

[#536, 1862, 1890]

There is a pain—so utter

There is a pain—so utter—
It swallows substance up—
Then covers the Abyss with Trance—
So Memory can step
Around—across—upon it—   5
As one within a Swoon—
Goes safely—where an open eye—
Would drop Him—Bone by Bone.

[#599, 1862, 1929]

Pain—has an Element of Blank

Pain—has an Element of Blank—
It cannot recollect
When it begun—or if there were
A time when it was not—

It has no Future—but itself—   5
Its Infinite contain
Its Past—enlightened to perceive
New Periods—of Pain.

[#650, 1862, 1890]

Because I could not stop for Death

Because I could not stop for Death—
He kindly stopped for me—
The Carriage held but just Ourselves—
And Immortality.

We slowly drove—He knew no haste   5
And I had put away
My labor and my leisure too,
For His Civility—

We passed the School, where Children strove
At Recess—in the Ring—   10
We passed the Fields of Gazing Grain—
We passed the Setting Sun—

Or rather—He passed Us—
The Dews drew quivering and chill—
For only Gossamer, my Gown—   15
My Tippet°—only Tulle—   scarf, stole

We paused before a House that seemed
A Swelling of the Ground—
The Roof was scarcely visible—
The Cornice—in the Ground—   20

Since then—'tis Centuries—and yet
Feels shorter than the Day
I first surmised the Horses' Heads
Were toward Eternity—

[#712, 1863, 1890]

Remorse—is Memory—awake

Remorse—is Memory—awake—
Her Parties all astir—
A Presence of Departed Acts—
At window—and at Door—

Its Past—set down before the Soul   5
And lighted with a Match—
Perusal—to facilitate—
And help Belief to stretch—

Remorse is cureless—the Disease
Not even God—can heal—   10
For 'tis His institution—and
The Adequate of Hell—

[#744, 1863, 1891]

My Life had stood—a Loaded Gun

My Life had stood—a Loaded Gun—
In Corners—till a Day
The Owner passed—identified—
And carried Me away—

And now We roam in Sovereign Woods—   5
And now We hunt the Doe—
And every time I speak for Him—
The Mountains straight reply—

And do I smile, such cordial light
Upon the Valley glow—   10
It is as a Vesuvian face
Had let its pleasure through—

And when at Night—Our good Day done—
I guard My Master's Head—
'Tis better than the Eider-Duck's   15
Deep Pillow—to have shared—

To foe of His—I'm deadly foe—
None stir the second time—
On whom I lay a Yellow Eye—
Or an emphatic Thumb—   20

Though I than He—may longer live
He longer must—than I—
For I have but the power to kill,
Without—the power to die—

[#754, 1863, 1929]

A narrow Fellow in the Grass

A narrow Fellow in the Grass
Occasionally rides—
You may have met Him—did you not
His notice sudden is—

The Grass divides as with a Comb—   .   5
A spotted shaft is seen—
And then it closes at your feet
And opens further on—

He likes a Boggy Acre
A floor too cool for Corn—   10
Yet when a Boy, and Barefoot—
I more than once at Noon
Have passed, I thought, a Whip lash
Unbraiding in the Sun
When stooping to secure it   15
It wrinkled, and was gone—

Several of Nature's People
I know, and they know me—
I feel for them a transport
Of cordiality—   20

But never met this Fellow
Attended, or alone
Without a tighter breathing
And Zero at the Bone—

                              [#986, 1865, 1866]

The Bustle in a House

The Bustle in a House
The Morning after Death
Is solemnest of industries
Enacted upon Earth—

The Sweeping up the Heart   5
And putting Love away
We shall not want to use again
Until Eternity.

                                    [#1078, 1866, 1890]

The last Night that She lived

The last Night that She lived
It was a Common Night
Except the Dying—this to Us
Made Nature different

We noticed smallest things—   5
Things overlooked before
By this great light upon our Minds
Italicized—as 'twere.

As We went out and in
Between Her final Room   10
And Rooms where Those to be alive
Tomorrow were, a Blame

That Others could exist
While She must finish quite
A Jealousy for Her arose   15
So nearly infinite—

We waited while She passed—
It was a narrow time—
Too jostled were Our Souls to speak
At length the notice came.   20

She mentioned, and forgot—
Then lightly as a Reed
Bent to the Water, struggled scarce—
Consented, and was dead—

And We—We placed the Hair—   25
And drew the Head erect—
And then an awful leisure was
Belief to regulate—

                                    [#1100, 1866, 1890]

Tell all the Truth but tell it slant

Tell all the Truth but tell it slant—
Success in Circuit lies
Too bright for our infirm Delight
The Truth's superb surprise

As Lightning to the Children eased   5
With explanation kind
The Truth must dazzle gradually
Or every man be blind—

[#1129, 1868, 1945]

Apparently with no surprise

Apparently with no surprise
To any happy Flower
The Frost beheads it at its play—
In accidental power—
The blonde Assassin passes on—   5
The Sun proceeds unmoved
To measure off another Day
For an Approving God.

[#1624, 1884, 1890]

My life closed twice before its close

My life closed twice before its close—
It yet remains to see
If Immortality unveil
A third event to me

So huge, so hopeless to conceive   5
As these that twice befell.
Parting is all we know of heaven,
And all we need of hell.

[#1732, 1896]

LEWIS CARROLL
(CHARLES LUTWIDGE DODGSON)

[1832–1898]

Jabberwocky

'Twas brillig, and the slithy toves
   Did gyre and gimble in the wabe:
All mimsy were the borogoves,
   And the mome raths outgrabe.

"Beware the Jabberwock, my son!   5
   The jaws that bite, the claws that catch!
Beware the Jubjub bird, and shun
   The frumious Bandersnatch!"

He took his vorpal sword in hand:
   Long time the manxome foe he sought—   10
So rested he by the Tumtum tree,
   And stood awhile in thought.

And, as in uffish thought he stood,
   The Jabberwock, with eyes of flame,
Came whiffling through the tulgey wood,   15
   And burbled as it came!

One, two! One, two! And through and through
   The vorpal blade went snicker-snack!
He left it dead, and with its head
   He went galumphing back.   20

"And hast thou slain the Jabberwock?
   Come to my arms, my beamish boy!
O frabjous day! Callooh! Callay!"
   He chortled in his joy.

'Twas brillig, and the slithy toves   25
   Did gyre and gimble in the wabe:
All mimsy were the borogoves,
   And the mome raths outgrabe.

[1871]

THOMAS HARDY

[1840–1928]

Neutral Tones

We stood by a pond that winter day,
And the sun was white, as though chidden of God,
And a few leaves lay on the starving sod;
   —They had fallen from an ash, and were gray.

Your eyes on me were as eyes that rove   5
Over tedious riddles of years ago;
And some words played between us to and fro
   On which lost the more by our love.

The smile on your mouth was the deadest thing
Alive enough to have strength to die;   10
And a grin of bitterness swept thereby
   Like an ominous bird a-wing. . . .

Since then, keen lessons that love deceives,
And wrings with wrong, have shaped to me
Your face, and the God-curst sun, and a tree,   15
   And a pond edged with grayish leaves.

                                              [1898]

Channel Firing

That night your great guns, unawares,
Shook all our coffins as we lay,
And broke the chancel window-squares,
We thought it was the Judgment-day

And sat upright. While drearisome   5
Arose the howl of wakened hounds:
The mouse let fall the altar-crumb,
The worms drew back into the mounds,

The glebe° cow drooled. Till God called, "No;   *small field*
It's gunnery practice out at sea   10

Just as before you went below;
The world is as it used to be:

"All nations striving strong to make
Red war yet redder. Mad as hatters
They do no more for Christés sake   *15*
Than you who are helpless in such matters.

"That this is not the judgment-hour
For some of them's a blessed thing,
For if it were they'd have to scour
Hell's floor for so much threatening. . . .   *20*

"Ha, ha. It will be warmer when
I blow the trumpet (if indeed
I ever do; for you are men,
And rest eternal sorely need)."

So down we lay again. "I wonder,   *25*
Will the world ever saner be,"
Said one, "than when He sent us under
In our indifferent century!"

And many a skeleton shook his head.
"Instead of preaching forty year,"   *30*
My neighbor Parson Thirdly said,
"I wish I had stuck to pipes and beer."

Again the guns disturbed the hour,
Roaring their readiness to avenge,
As far inland as Stourton Tower,   *35*
And Camelot, and starlit Stonehenge.

[1914]

The Man He Killed

"Had he and I but met
By some old ancient inn,
We should have sat us down to wet
Right many a nipperkin!

CHANNEL FIRING   ³⁶**Stonehenge**   a circular grouping of stone monuments near Salisbury, England, dating back to the Bronze Age.

"But ranged as infantry, 5
   And staring face to face,
I shot at him as he at me,
   And killed him in his place.

"I shot him dead because—
   Because he was my foe, 10
Just so: my foe of course he was;
   That's clear enough; although

"He thought he'd 'list, perhaps,
   Off-hand-like—just as I—
Was out of work—had sold his traps— 15
   No other reason why.

"Yes; quaint and curious war is!
   You shoot a fellow down
You'd treat if met where any bar is,
   Or help to half-a-crown." 20

[1914]

The Oxen

Christmas Eve, and twelve of the clock.
   "Now they are all on their knees,"
An elder said as we sat in a flock
   By the embers in hearthside ease.

We pictured the meek mild creatures where 5
   They dwelt in their strawy pen,
Nor did it occur to one of us there
   To doubt they were kneeling then.

So fair a fancy few would weave
   In these years! Yet, I feel, 10
If someone said on Christmas Eve,
   "Come; see the oxen kneel,

"In the lonely barton° by yonder coomb°   *farm/valley*
   Our childhood used to know,"
I should go with him in the gloom,   *15*
   Hoping it might be so.

                                     [1917]

During Wind and Rain

They sing their dearest songs—
He, she, all of them—yea,
Treble and tenor and bass,
   And one to play;
With the candles mooning each face. . . .   *5*
   Ah, no; the years O!
How the sick leaves reel down in throngs!

They clear the creeping moss—
Elders and juniors—aye,
Making the pathway neat   *10*
   And the garden gay;
And they build a shady seat. . . .
   Ah, no; the years, the years;
See, the white stormbirds wing across!

They are blithely breakfasting all—   *15*
Men and maidens—yea,
Under the summer tree,
   With a glimpse of the bay,
While pet fowl come to the knee. . . .
   Ah, no; the years O!   *20*
And the rotten rose is ripped from the wall.

They change to a high new house,
He, she, all of them—aye,
Clocks and carpets, and chairs
   On the lawn all day,   *25*
And brightest things that are theirs. . . .
   Ah, no; the years, the years;
Down their carved names the rain drop ploughs.

                                     [1917]

GERARD MANLEY HOPKINS

[1844–1889]

Gerard Manley Hopkins was both a strikingly original English poet and a Jesuit priest. Unlike George Herbert (pp. 214–217), an Anglican priest, whose poetry was a comfortable accessory to his priesthood, Hopkins struggled to reconcile the conflicting directions of his poetic inclination with the demands of his priestly vocation. Hopkins was unable to create more than an uneasy alliance between writing poems and performing his priestly ministry. For the most part, Hopkins never really moved beyond the tension he expressed in a letter to his friend R. W. Dixon.

> My vocation puts before me a standard so high that a higher can be found nowhere else. The question then for me is not whether I am willing . . . to make a sacrifice of hopes of fame. . . . but whether I am not to undergo a severe judgment from God for the lothness I have shewn in making it, for the waste of time the very compositions you admire may have caused and their preoccupation of the mind which belonged to more sacred or more binding duties.

From the perspective of readers of his work, however, Hopkins's agonized struggle for reconciliation of his poetic desire with his priestly responsibilities provided a necessary condition for the writing of his most powerfully affecting poems.

But this is not the only conflict to appear in Hopkins's work. A second and very different kind of tension inheres in the kind of poet he was. On one hand, Hopkins was clearly a poet of his time—a Victorian poet with strong Romanticist inclinations. On the other hand, Hopkins is a modern poet, his poems differing radically in diction and syntax from the other poetry of his time. His ideas, subjects, and ideals, infused with the beliefs of his Jesuit Catholic priestly life, are typical of the nineteenth century. His poetic style, however, represents a radical departure from the language of nineteenth-century verse. It is more inventive and experimental than the poetic language of most of his contemporaries. Hopkins's poetry revels in the play of sound, especially tightly packed alliteration and the resonant echoing of assonance.

It might be argued, however, that other nineteenth-century poets made extensive use of these poetic devices—John Keats, Alfred, Lord Tennyson, Christina Rossetti, and Robert Browning, among many others. What makes Hopkins's use of language and sound different? Three things at least: his diction, his syntax, and his poetic rhythms. Hopkins's diction inclines toward original word coinages such as "twindles" in "Inversnaid," a word that apparently means twists and dwindles. Or from "As kingfishers catch fire, dragonflies draw flame," "selves" used as a verb rather than a noun. Or from "Spring and Fall: To a Young Child," "Goldengrove" used to describe a grove of trees in autumn that are "unleaving" or dropping their leaves. In the same poem we find "wanwood," meaning pale or bloodless, and "leafmeal," created on the order of piecemeal. In addition, Hopkins's syntax or word order can be unconventional and sometimes requires disentangling. "Spring and Fall," for example, includes this syntactic inversion: "Leaves, like the things of man, you / With your fresh thoughts care for, can you?" And Hopkins's sonnet on despair, "Carrion Comfort," begins with still another unconventional syntactic arrangement: "Not, I'll not, carrion comfort, Despair, not feast on thee; / Not untwist—slack they may be—these last strands of man / In me or, most weary, cry *I can no more*. I can." In this instance the repeated words along with the interruption create a halting rhythm that combines with the unusual syntax to slow the line and dramatize the agonized feeling it expresses.

It is Hopkins's use of what he called "sprung rhythm," however, that was perhaps his most distinctive technical achievement. Sprung rhythm relies for its effects on the number of stressed sounds in a line rather than on the number of syllables. A typical sonnet by Shakespeare, for example, will contain a pentameter, or ten-syllable, line with five stresses. In his own sonnets Hopkins retained the five stresses, but sometimes added additional syllables since his concern was with the music and rhythm of the line and not with preserving an iambic metrical pattern. In emphasizing the number of stresses in the line and ignoring the number of syllables, Hopkins was returning to the roots of English poetry in Anglo-Saxon alliterative verse. (See *Caedmon's Hymn*, p. 113.)

One example of Hopkins's use of sprung rhythm occurs in "Pied Beauty," which begins this way:

> Glory be to God for dappled things—
>   For skies of couple-colour as a brinded cow;
>   For rose-moles all in stipple upon trout that swim;
> Fresh-firecoal chestnut-falls; finches' wings;
>   Landscape plotted and pieced—fold, fallow, and plough;
>   And all trades, their gear and tackle and trim.

We have marked the stressed syllables as we hear them. Also notable, however, are Hopkins's heavy use of alliteration (an Anglo-Saxon poetic device); his use of caesuras, or pauses, in the midst of lines 4, 5, and 6; and his combining of words, which in his original handwritten manuscript lacked the hyphens put in by his editor when the poems were first published thirty years after Hopkins's death.

To these technical matters we must add an additional consideration: Hopkins's ideas about individuation, expressed in his notions of *instress* and *inscape*. Instress and inscape together describe the distinctive and individual beauty of a thing, usually the particular and special quality of natural phenomena that Hopkins cherished— trees, clouds, waves, flowers, birds. But inscape is more than merely the flower or cloud or bird in and of itself; it is, rather, the living essence and action of things— clouds forming, flowers blooming or withering, a falcon flying. The special "this- ness" of the flying falcon, for example, is its "inscape"—its unified pattern of attributes that make it what it is. The "instress" of the falcon is the force or stress of energy that holds its inscape together. Hopkins's poetry attempts to capture the special beauty of the natural phenomena he describes and to communicate its distinctiveness in such a way that it suddenly explodes in the reader's consciousness. We see with Hopkins the beauty and magnificence of the falcon, and we share his joy in imagining its flight. And further, as with many of Hopkins's poems, in our amazement at the sheer beauty of the bird, we are brought to an appreciation of its creator. In fact, since God is centrally important as inspiration and focus of most of Hopkins's poetry, it is important to recognize that the distinctiveness shown forth in every aspect of nature has been created by Him. For Hopkins, thus, inscape also involves God as maker of each thing's "thisness," whose distinctive stamp shows in each "selving." As the first line of "God's Grandeur" has it: "The world is charged with the grandeur of God." And as the curtal or truncated sonnet "Pied Beauty" puts it:

> All things counter, original, spare, strange; . . .
> He fathers-forth whose beauty is past change: . . .

Hopkins's life can be outlined simply. Born in London in 1844, Hopkins was educated there at Highgate school. After converting to Catholicism in 1866 while studying at Oxford and graduating with a rare "double first" in Classics in 1867, he entered the Jesuit novitiate to prepare for his ordination to the Roman Catholic priesthood in 1877. For five years (1877–1882) Hopkins worked among the poor as a parish priest, mostly in Liverpool and Glasgow, work he was unsuited for physically, intellectually, and temperamentally. He spent the last five years of his life at University College, Dublin, where he was professor of Greek. During these years he suffered greatly both because, being deeply patriotic, he missed Britain, and because he was far from the natural inscapes he loved, especially those of Wales as described in "Inversnaid" and "In the Valley of the Elwy."

What this outline omits is the sense of strain under which Hopkins conducted his life. The tension began before he became a priest and began agonizing over his poetry. It began when he struggled with his decision to convert to Catholicism against the wishes of his family and against the advice of his friends. It continued through the early years of his priesthood, when he abandoned the writing of poetry until, encouraged by his Jesuit superiors, he wrote "The Wreck of the Deutschland," his first significant poetic effort following a seven-year self-imposed silence. To Hopkins's dismay, the poem was rejected by the Jesuit magazine *The Month,* due in part to its metrical eccentricities. But it opened the door for Hopkins to continue writing poems. It is in the poems that followed "Deutschland" that we learn of the spiritual crises Hopkins endured. These crises are most powerfully dramatized in his late, dark sonnets with their imagery of sterility and their sense of urgency, intensity, and anguish. These "terrible" sonnets, as Hopkins described them, recount his deep depression, his sense of failure in what for him was indeed a "dark night of the soul." However, it is important to note two things about Hopkins's experience of spiritual desolation: (1) he did partially regain his sense of spiritual equilibrium; and (2) he never seemed to question his belief in God.

Hopkins's distinctive poetic voice and vision have been only mildly influential. Of twentieth-century poets, the one who resembles Hopkins most and perhaps loved him best is Dylan Thomas, the Welsh poet who enthusiastically celebrated Hopkins's poetic innovations, especially his experiments with sound and rhythm. We should mention, moreover, that Hopkins was heavily influenced in his language experiments by both Anglo-Saxon and Welsh poetry. Hopkins's penchant for compounding words is one thing he derives from Anglo-Saxon poetry. Another is his reliance on alliteration. From Welsh, which Hopkins initially learned in order to be able to perform his priestly duties among the Welsh people, Hopkins learned the beauties of *cynghanedd,* or internal rhyme. Hopkins's innovations, however, and his double image as both a late Romantic and early modern poet, are not his only sources of appeal. Paul Mariani perhaps best describes what draws readers to him: "a poetic voice at once distinctive and filled with a broad, deep caritas [charity]. It is perhaps this fine humanity of spirit which endears him, finally, to so many."

God's Grandeur

The world is charged with the grandeur of God.
  It will flame out, like shining from shook foil;
  It gathers to a greatness, like the ooze of oil
Crushed. Why do men then now not reck his rod?
Generations have trod, have trod, have trod;   *5*
  And all is seared with trade; bleared, smeared with toil;
  And wears man's smudge and shares man's smell: the soil
Is bare now, nor can foot feel, being shod.

And for all this, nature is never spent;
  There lives the dearest freshness deep down things;   *10*
And though the last lights off the black West went
  Oh, morning, at the brown brink eastward, springs—
Because the Holy Ghost over the bent
  World broods with warm breast and with ah! bright wings.

                                     [1877, 1895]

The Windhover

TO CHRIST OUR LORD

I caught this morning morning's minion,° kingdom of   *darling*
    daylight's dauphin,° dapple-dawn-drawn Falcon, in his riding   *prince*
Of the rolling level underneath him steady air, and striding

GOD'S GRANDEUR   ²**foil** In a letter to Robert Bridges (January 4, 1883), Hopkins wrote, "I mean foil in its sense of leaf or tinsel. . . . Shaken goldfoil gives off broad glares like sheet lightning and also . owing to its zigzag dints and crossings and network of many small cornered facets, a sort of fork lightning too."
⁴**reck his rod** heed his rule.
THE WINDHOVER   the kestrel, a small falcon or hawk that hovers in the air with its head into the wind.

High there, how he rung upon the rein of a wimpling° wing   *rippling*
In his ecstasy! then off, off forth on swing,
   As a skate's heel sweeps smooth on a bow-bend: the hurl and gliding   5
   Rebuffed the big wind. My heart in hiding
Stirred for a bird,—the achieve of, the mastery of the thing!

Brute beauty and valour and act, oh, air, pride, plume, here
   Buckle! AND the fire that breaks from thee then, a billion
Times told lovelier, more dangerous, O my chevalier°!   *knight, champion* 10

   No wonder of it: shéer plód makes plough down sillion°   *furrow*
Shine, and blue-bleak embers, ah my dear,
   Fall, gall themselves, and gash gold-vermilion.

                                       [1877, 1918]

Pied Beauty

Glory be to God for dappled things—
   For skies of couple-colour as a brinded° cow;   *streaked, spotted*
      For rose-moles all in stipple upon trout that swim;
Fresh-firecoal chestnut-falls; finches' wings;
   Landscape plotted and pieced—fold, fallow, and plough;   5
      And áll trádes, their gear and tackle and trim.
All things counter, original, spare,° strange;   *rare*
   Whatever is fickle, freckled (who knows how?)
      With swift, slow; sweet, sour; adazzle, dim;
He fathers-forth whose beauty is past change: 10
            Praise him.

                                       [1877, 1918]

Spring

Nothing is so beautiful as spring—
   When weeds, in wheels, shoot long and lovely and lush;
   Thrush's eggs look little low heavens, and thrush
Through the echoing timber does so rinse and wring
The ear, it strikes like lightnings to hear him sing;   5

PIED BEAUTY   "Pied" means spotted, variegated patches of color.

The glassy peartree leaves and blooms, they brush
    The descending blue; that blue is all in a rush
With richness; the racing lambs too have fair their fling.

What is all this juice and all this joy?
    A strain of the earth's sweet being in the beginning   10
In Eden garden.—Have, get, before it cloy,
    Before it cloud, Christ, lord, and sour with sinning,
Innocent mind and Mayday in girl and boy,
    Most, O maid's child, thy choice and worthy the winning.

                                                    [1877, 1918]

The Wreck of the Deutschland

To the
happy memory of five Franciscan Nuns
exiled by the Falk Laws
drowned between midnight and morning of
Dec. 7th, 1876

Part the First
1

        Thou mastering me
    God! giver of breath and bread;
    World's strand, sway of the sea;
        Lord of living and dead;
Thou hast bound bones and veins in me, fastened me flesh,   5
And after it almost unmade, what with dread,
        Thy doing: and dost thou touch me afresh?
Over again I feel thy finger and find thee.

2.

        I did say yes
    O at lightning and lashed rod;   10
    Thou heardst me truer than tongue confess
        Thy terror, O Christ, O God;
    Thou knowest the walls, altar and hour and night:

THE WRECK OF THE DEUTSCHLAND   Deutschland, or "Germany," was the name of a ship.
Falk Laws   laws designed to diminish the power of the Roman Catholic Church, including the dissolution of
religious orders of nuns and priests, named after their sponsor, Adalbert Falk, the Prussian minister of culture

The swoon of a heart that the sweep and the hurl of thee trod
   Hard down with a horror of height: 15
And the midriff astrain with leaning of, laced with fire of stress.

3

    The frown of his face
     Before me, the hurtle of hell
    Behind, where, where was a, where was a place?
     I whirled out wings that spell   20
And fled with a fling of the heart to the heart of the Host.
My heart, but you were dovewinged, I can tell,
    Carrier-witted, I am bold to boast,
To flash from the flame to the flame then, tower from the grace to the grace.

4

    I am soft sift   25
     In an hourglass—at the wall
Fast, but mined with a motion, a drift,
     And it crowds and it combs to the fall;
I steady as a water in a well, to a poise, to a pane,
But roped with, always, all the way down from the tall   30
    Fells or flanks of the voel,° a vein   *bare hill*
Of the gospel proffer, a pressure, a principle, Christ's gift.

5

    I kiss my hand
     To the stars, lovely-asunder
    Starlight, wafting him out of it; and   35
     Glow, glory in thunder;
Kiss my hand to the dappled-with-damson° west: *purple plum*
Since, tho' he is under the world's splendour and wonder
    His mystery must be instressed,° stressed;   *realized*
For I greet him the days I meet him, and bless when I understand.   40

6

    Not out of his bliss
     Springs the stress felt
    Nor first from heaven (and few know this)
     Swings the stroke dealt—
Stroke and a stress that stars and storms deliver,   45
That guilt is hushed by, hearts are flushed by and melt—
    But it rides time like riding a river
(And here the faithful waver, the faithless fable and miss).

7

It dates from day
    Of his going in Galilee;
   Warm-laid grave of a womb-life grey;   *50*
     Manger, maiden's knee;
The dense and the driven Passion, and frightful sweat;
Thence the discharge of it, there its swelling to be,
     Though felt before, though in high flood yet—   *55*
What none would have known of it, only the heart, being hard at bay.

8

Is out with it! Oh,
    We lash with the best or worst
   Word last! How a lush-kept plush-capped sloe°   *plum*
    Will, mouthed to flesh-burst,   *60*
Gush!—flush the man, the being with it, sour or sweet,
Brim, in a flash, full!—Hither then, last or first,
    To hero of Calvary, Christ's feet—
Never ask if meaning it, wanting it, warned of it—men go.

9

Be adored among men,
    God, three-numberèd form;   *65*
   Wring thy rebel, dogged in den,
     Man's malice, with wrecking and storm.
Beyond saying sweet, past telling of tongue,
Thou art lightning and love, I found it, a winter and warm;   *70*
    Father and fondler of heart thou hast wrung:
Hast thy dark descending and most art merciful then.

10

With an anvil-ding
    And with fire in him forge thy will
   Or rather, rather then, stealing as Spring   *75*
    Through him, melt him but master him still:
Whether at once, as once at a crash Paul,
Or as Austin, a lingering-out swéet skill,
    Make mercy in all of us, out of us all
Mastery, but be adored, but be adored King.   *80*

[77-78]**Paul . . . Austin**   refers to St. Paul's sudden conversion on the road to Damascus and the more leisurely conversion of St. Augustine.

Part the Second

11

'Some find me a sword; some
      The flange and the rail; flame,
Fang, or flood' goes Death on drum,
      And storms bugle his fame.
But wé dream we are rooted in earth—Dust!   85
Flash falls within sight of us, we, though our flower the same,
      Wave with the meadow, forget that there must
The sour scythe cringe, and the blear share come.

12

On Saturday sailed from Bremen,
      American-outward-bound,   90
Take settler and seamen, tell men with women,
      Two hundred souls in the round—
O Father, not under thy feathers nor ever as guessing
The goal was a shoal, of a fourth the doom to be drowned;
      Yet did the dark side of the bay of thy blessing   95
Not vault them, the millions of rounds of thy mercy not reeve° even   *rope together*
      them in?

13

Into the snows she sweeps,
      Hurling the haven behind,
The Deutschland, on Sunday; and so the sky keeps,
      For the infinite air is unkind,   100
And the sea flint-flake, black-backed in the regular blow,
Sitting Eastnortheast, in cursed quarter, the wind;
      Wiry and white-fiery and whirlwind-swivellèd snow
Spins to the window-making unchilding unfathering deeps.

14

She drove in the dark to leeward,   105
      She struck—not a reef or a rock
But the combs of a smother of sand: night drew her
      Dead to the Kentish Knock;
And she beat the bank down with her bows and the ride of her keel:
The breakers rolled on her beam with ruinous shock;   110
      And canvas and compass, the whorl° and the wheel   *propeller*
Idle for ever to waft her or wind her with, these she endured.

---

[108]**Kentish Knock**   a sandbank near the mouth of the Thames.

15

Hope had grown grey hairs,
Hope had mourning on,
Trenched with tears, carved with cares,   *115*
Hope was twelve hours gone;
And frightful a nightfall folded rueful a day
Nor rescue, only rocket and lightship, shone,
And lives at last were washing away:
To the shrouds they took,—they shook in the hurling and horrible airs.   *120*

16

One stirred from the rigging to save
The wild woman-kind below,
With a rope's end round the man, handy and brave—
He was pitched to his death at a blow,
For all his dreadnought breast and braids of thew: *125*
They could tell him for hours, dandled the to and fro
Through the cobbled foam-fleece. What could he do
With the burl° of the fountains of air, buck and the flood of the wave?   *vortex*

17

They fought with God's cold—
And they could not and fell to the deck   *130*
(Crushed them) or water (and drowned them) or rolled
With the sea-romp over the wreck.
Night roared, with the heart-break hearing a heart-broke rabble,
The woman's wailing, the crying of child without check—
Till a lioness arose breasting the babble,   *135*
A prophetess towered in the tumult, a virginal tongue told.

18

Ah, touched in your bower of bone.
Are you! turned for an exquisite smart,
Have you! make words break from me here all alone,
Do you!—mother of being in me, heart.   *140*
O unteachably after evil, but uttering truth,
Why, tears! is it? tears; such a melting, a madrigal start!
Never-eldering revel and river of youth,
What can it be, this glee? the good you have there of your own?

19

Sister, a sister calling   *145*
A master, her master and mine!—

And the inboard seas run swirling and hawling;
The rash smart sloggering brine
Blinds her; but she that weather sees one thing, one;
Has one fetch in her: she rears herself to divine   150
Ears, and the call of the tall nun
To the men in the tops and the tackle rode over the storm's brawling.

20

She was first of a five and came
Of a coifèd sisterhood.
(O Deutschland, double a desperate name!   155
O world wide of its good!
But Gertrude, lily, and Luther, are two of a town
Christ's lily and beast of the waste wood:
From life's dawn it is drawn down,
Abel is Cain's brother and breasts they have sucked the same.)   160

21

Loathed for a love men knew in them,
Banned by the land of their birth,
Rhine refused them, Thames would ruin them;
Surf, snow, river and earth
Gnashed: but thou art above, thou Orion of light;   165
Thy unchancelling° poising palms were weighing the worth,   *exiling*
Thou martyr-master: in thy sight
Storm flakes were scroll-leaved flowers, lily showers—sweet heaven was astrew in them.

22

Five! The finding and sake
And cipher of suffering Christ.   170
Mark, the mark is of man's make
And the word of it Sacrificed.
But he scores it in scarlet himself on his own bespoken,
Before-time-taken, dearest prizèd and priced—
Stigma, signal, cinquefoil token   175
For lettering of the lamb's fleece, ruddying of the rose-flake.

23

Joy fall to thee, father Francis,
Drawn to the Life that died,

---

¹⁵⁷**Gertrude . . . Luther**   St. Gertrude lived in Eisleben, near the birthplace of Martin Luther.

With the gnarls of the nails in thee, niche of the lance, his
          Lovescape crucified   *180*
And seal of his seraph-arrival! and these thy daughters
And five-livèd and leavèd favour and pride,
          Are sisterly sealed in wild waters,
To bathe in his fall-gold mercies, to breathe in his all-fire glances.

24

          Away in the loveable west,   *185*
          On a pastoral forehead of Wales,
     I was under a roof here, I was at rest,
          And they the prey of the gales;
She to the black-about air, to the breaker, the thickly
Falling flakes, to the throng that catches and quails   *190*
     Was calling 'O Christ, Christ, come quickly':
The cross to her she calls Christ to her, christens her wild-worst Best.

25

          The majesty! what did she mean?
          Breathe, arch and original Breath.°   *Holy Spirit*
     Is it love in her of the being as her lover had been?   *195*
          Breathe, body of lovely Death.
They were else-minded then, altogether, the men
Woke thee with a *we are perishing* in the weather of Gennesareth.
          Or is it that she cried for the crown then,
The keener to come at the comfort for feeling the combating keen?   *200*

26

          For how to the heart's cheering
          The down-dugged ground-hugged grey
     Hovers off, the jay-blue heavens appearing
          Of pied and peeled May!
Blue-beating and hoary-glow height; or night, still higher,   *205*
With belled fire and the moth-soft Milky Way.
     What by your measure is the heaven of desire,
The treasure never eyesight got, nor was ever guessed what for the hearing?

27

          No, but it was not these.
          The jading and jar of the cart,   *210*

---

[198]**Gennesareth**   the Sea of Galilee. See Matthew 8:23–27, which describes Christ's calming of a stormy sea.
[204]**peeled May**   when flowers lose their petals.

Time's tasking, it is fathers that asking for ease
    Of the sodden-with-its-sorrowing heart,
  Not danger, electrical horror; then further it finds
  The appealing of the Passion is tenderer in prayer apart:
    Other, I gather, in measure her mind's   215
Burden, in wind's burly and beat of endragonèd seas.

28

    But how shall I . . . make me room there:
    Reach me a . . . Fancy, come faster—
  Strike you the sight of it? look at it loom there,
    Thing that she . . . there then! the Master,   220
Ipse, the only one, Christ, King, Head:
  He was to cure the extremity where he had cast her;
    Do, deal, lord it with living and dead;
Let him ride, her pride, in his triumph, despatch and have done with his doom there.

29

    Ah! there was a heart right   225
    There was single eye!
  Read the unshapeable shock night
    And knew the who and the why;
  Wording it how but by him that present and past,
  Heaven and earth are word of, worded by?—   230
    The Simon Peter of a soul! to the blast
Tarpeian-fast, but a blown beacon of light.

30

    Jesu, heart's light,
    Jesu, maid's son,   235
  What was the feast followed the night
    Thou hadst glory of this nun?—
  Feast of the one woman without stain.
  For so conceivèd, so to conceive thee is done;
    But here was heart-throe, birth of a brain,
Word, that heard and kept thee and uttered thee outright.   240

31

    Well, she has thee for the pain, for the
    Patience; but pity of the rest of them!

---

[221]**Ipse** Latin for "Himself."   [231]**Simon Peter** The lead, or principal, apostle.   [232]**Tarpeian** Roman hills from which condemned criminals were thrown to their deaths.

Heart, go and bleed at a bitterer vein for the
    Comfortless unconfessed of them—
No not uncomforted: lovely-felicitous Providence   245
Finger of a tender of, O of a feathery delicacy, the breast of the
    Maiden could obey so, be a bell to, ring of it, and
Startle the poor sheep back! is the shipwrack then a harvest, does tempest
    carry the grain for thee?

32

I admire thee, master of the tides,
    Of the Yore-flood, of the year's fall;   250
The recurb and the recovery of the gulf's sides,
    The girth of it and the wharf of it and the wall;
Stanching, quenching ocean of a motionable mind;
Ground of being, and granite of it: past all
    Grasp God, throned behind   255
Death with a sovereignty that heeds but hides, bodes but abides;

33

With a mercy that outrides
    The all of water, an ark
For the listener; for the lingerer with a love glides
    Lower than death and the dark;   260
A vein for the visiting of the past-prayer, pent in prison,
The-last-breath penitent spirits—the uttermost mark
    Our passion-plungèd giant risen,
The Christ of the Father compassionate, fetched in the storm of his strides.

34

Now burn, new born to the world,   265
    Doubled-naturèd name,
The heaven-flung, heart-fleshed, maiden-furled
    Miracle-in-Mary-of-flame,
Mid-numberèd He in three of the thunder-throne!
Not a dooms-day dazzle in his coming nor dark as he came;   270
    Kind, but royally reclaiming his own;
A released shower, let flash to the shire, not a lightning of fire hard-hurled.

35

Dame, at our door
    Drowned, and among our shoals,

---

[269]**Mid-numberèd He in three**   Christ, who comes after the Father and before the Holy Ghost in the Christian
Holy Trinity.

Remember us in the roads, the heaven-haven of the reward: *275*
    Our King back, oh, upon English souls!
Let him easter in us, be a dayspring to the dimness of us, be a crimson-cresseted
    east,
More brightening her, rare-dear Britain, as his reign rolls,
    Pride, rose, prince, hero of us, high-priest,
Our hearts' charity's hearth's fire, our thoughts' chivalry's throng's Lord.   *280*

                                      [1876, 1918]

Spring and Fall
To a Young Child

Márgarét, áre you gríeving
Over Goldengrove unleaving?
Leáves, líke the things of man, you
With your fresh thoughts care for, can you?
Áh! ás the heart grows older   *5*
It will come to such sights colder
By and by, nor spare a sigh
Though worlds of wanwood leafmeal lie;
And yet you *will* weep and know why.
Now no matter, child, the name: *10*
Sórrow's spríngs áre the same.
Nor mouth had, no nor mind, expressed
What heart heard of, ghost° guessed: *spirit, soul*
It ís the blight man was born for,
It is Margaret you mourn for.   *15*

                                      [1880, 1918]

Binsey Poplars

Felled 1879

My aspens dear, whose airy cages quelled,°   *subdued*
Quelled or quenched in leaves the leaping sun,
All felled, felled, are all felled;

THE WRECK OF THE DEUTSCHLAND   [275] **roads** sheltered waters.
SPRING AND FALL   [8] **wanwood** pale or dim woods.   [8] **leafmeal** on the order of "piecemeal."

Of a fresh and following folded rank
       Not spared, not one   5
        That dandled a sandalled
    Shadow that swam or sank
On meadow and river and wind-wandering weed-winding bank.

  O if we but knew what we do
      When we delve or hew—   10
    Hack and rack the growing green!
       Since country is so tender
    To touch, her being só slender,
    That, like this sleek and seeing ball
    But a prick will make no eye at all,   15
    Where we, even where we mean
       To mend her we end her,
    When we hew or delve:
After-comers cannot guess the beauty been.
Ten or twelve, only ten or twelve   20
  Strokes of havoc únselve
      The sweet especial scene,
  Rural scene, a rural scene,
  Sweet especial rural scene.

                                      [1879, 1918]

Inversnaid

This darksome burn,° horseback brown,   *stream*
His rollrock highroad roaring down,
In coop° and in comb° the fleece of his foam   *hollow/crest*
Flutes and low to the lake falls home.

A windpuff-bonnet of fáwn-fróth   5
Turns and twindles over the broth
Of a pool so pitchblack, féll-frówning,
It rounds and rounds Despair to drowning.

Degged° with dew, dappled with dew   *sprinkled*
Are the groins of the braes° that the brook treads through,   *hills* 10
Wiry heathpacks, flitches° of fern,   *clumps*
And the beadbonny ash that sits over the burn.

INVERSNAID   A Scottish town near a stream and a waterfall.

What would the world be, once bereft
Of wet and of wildness? Let them be left,
O let them be left, wildness and wet;   15
Long live the weeds and the wilderness yet.

[1881, 1918]

As kingfishers catch fire, dragonflies draw flame

As kingfishers catch fire, dragonflies draw flame;
   As tumbled over rim in roundy wells
   Stones ring; like each tucked° string tells, each hung bell's *touched, plucked*
Bow swung finds tongue to fling out broad its name;
Each mortal thing does one thing and the same: 5
   Deals out that being indoors each one dwells;
   Selves—goes itself; *myself* it speaks and spells,
Crying *What I do is me: for that I came.*

Í say more: the just man justices;
   Keeps gráce: thát keeps all his goings graces;   10
Acts in God's eye what in God's eye he is—
   Chríst. For Christ plays in ten thousand places,
Lovely in limbs, and lovely in eyes not his
   To the Father through the features of men's faces.

[1882, 1918]

I wake and feel the fell of dark, not day

I wake and feel the fell of dark, not day.
What hours, O what black hoürs we have spent
This night! what sights you, heart, saw; ways you went!
And more must, in yet longer light's delay.

With witness I speak this. But where I say   5
Hours I mean years, mean life. And my lament
Is cries countless, cries like dead letters sent
To dearest him that lives alas! away.

AS KINGFISHERS CATCH FIRE   ⁷**Selves** (verb) expresses individuality and distinctiveness.

I am gall, I am heartburn. God's most deep decree
Bitter would have me taste: my taste was me;   *10*
Bones built in me, flesh filled, blood brimmed the curse.

Selfyeast of spirit a dull dough sours. I see
The lost are like this, and their scourge to be
As I am mine, their sweating selves, but worse.

[1885, 1918]

Carrion Comfort

Not, I'll not, carrion comfort, Despair, not feast on thee;
Not untwist—slack they may be—these last strands of man
In me ór, most weary, cry *I can no more*. I can;
Can something, hope, wish day come, not choose not to be.

But ah, but O thou terrible, why wouldst thou rude on me   *5*
Thy wring-world right foot rock? lay a lionlimb against me? scan
With darksome devouring eyes my bruisèd bones? and fan,
O in turns of tempest, me heaped there; me frantic to avoid thee and flee?

Why? That my chaff might fly; my grain lie, sheer and clear.
Nay in all that toil, that coil, since (seems) I kissed the rod,   *10*
Hand rather, my heart lo! lapped strength, stole joy, would laugh, chéer.
Cheer whom though? The hero whose heaven-handling flung me, fóot tród
Me? or me that fought him? O which one? is it each one? That night, that year
Of now done darkness I wretch lay wrestling with (my God!) my God.

[1885, 1918]

No worst, there is none

No worst, there is none. Pitched past pitch of grief,
More pangs will, schooled at forepangs, wilder wring.
Comforter, where, where is your comforting?
Mary, mother of us, where is your relief?
My cries heave, herds-long; huddle in a main, a chief-   *5*
woe, world-sorrow; on an age-old anvil wince and sing—
Then lull, then leave off. Fury had shrieked 'No ling-
ering! Let me be fell:° force° I must be brief.'   *fierce/perforce*
    O the mind, mind has mountains; cliffs of fall

Frightful, sheer, no-man-fathomed. Hold them cheap   *10*
May who ne'er hung there. Nor does long our small
Durance° deal with that steep or deep. Here! creep,   *endurance*
Wretch, under a comfort serves in a whirlwind: all
Life death does end and each day dies with sleep.

[1885, 1918]

Thou art indeed just, Lord

Justus quidem tu es, Domine, si disputem tecum: verumtamen
justa loquar ad te: Quare via impiorum prosperatur?

Thou art indeed just, Lord, if I contend
With thee; but, sir, so what I plead is just.
Why do sinners' ways prosper? and why must
Disappointment all I endeavour end?
Wert thou my enemy, O thou my friend,   *5*
How wouldst thou worse, I wonder, than thou dost
Defeat, thwart me? Oh, the sots and thralls of lust
Do in spare hours more thrive than I that spend,

Sir, life upon thy cause. See, banks and brakes
Now, leavèd how thick! lacèd they are again   *10*
With fretty chervil, look, and fresh wind shakes
Them; birds build—but not I build; no, but strain,
Time's eunuch, and not breed one work that wakes.
Mine, O thou lord of life, send my roots rain.

[1889, 1918]

A. E. HOUSMAN

[1859–1936]

To an Athlete Dying Young

The time you won your town the race
We chaired you through the market-place;
Man and boy stood cheering by,
And home we brought you shoulder-high.

THOU ART INDEED JUST, LORD   Epigraph. The first three lines (up to *"prosper"*) translate the Latin.
¹¹**chervil** an herb with curled leaves.

To-day, the road all runners come,   *5*
Shoulder-high we bring you home,
And set you at your threshold down,
Townsman of a stiller town.

Smart lad, to slip betimes away
From fields where glory does not stay   *10*
And early though the laurel grows
It withers quicker than the rose.

Eyes the shady night has shut
Cannot see the record cut,
And silence sounds no worse than cheers   *15*
After earth has stopped the ears:

Now you will not swell the rout
Of lads that wore their honours out,
Runners whom renown outran
And the name died before the man.   *20*

So set, before its echoes fade,
The fleet foot on the sill of shade,
And hold to the low lintel up
The still-defended challenge-cup.

And round that early-laurelled head   *25*
Will flock to gaze the strengthless dead
And find unwithered on its curls
The garland briefer than a girl's.

                                    [1896]

With rue my heart is laden

With rue my heart is laden
    For golden friends I had,
For many a rose-lipt maiden
    And many a lightfoot lad.

By brooks too broad for leaping   *5*
    The lightfoot boys are laid;
The rose-lipt girls are sleeping
    In fields where roses fade.

                                    [1896]

WILLIAM BUTLER YEATS

[1865–1939]

Poet, dramatist, Irish nationalist, and winner of the Nobel Prize for Literature in 1923, William Butler Yeats is often considered not only Ireland's greatest poet, but the greatest poet of the modern age. As an artist, Yeats wished to revive the culture of a lost Ireland, more pagan than Christian, that fixed the poet at the center of the universe, for Yeats believed that "whatever the great poets had affirmed in their finest moments was the nearest we could come to an authoritative religion, and that their mythology, their spirits of water and wind, were but literal truth."

For Yeats, such truth was always associated with what he called "personal utterance," as the writings of great poets frequently drew heavily on their own lives. As a young poet, Yeats once commented, "If I can be sincere and make my language natural . . . I shall, if good luck or bad luck make my life interesting, be a great poet." In Yeats's poetry we encounter the likenesses of the people he knew. Maude Gonne, the passionate love of his life, appears in many of his poems, as does her husband in the poem "Easter 1916." Lady Gregory's son, Robert Gregory, appears in "An Irish Airman Foresees His Death." But these poems are not purely biographical. It is important to stress that Yeats's universality as a poet is mediated through personal history, because counterbalancing Yeats's insights into "personal utterance" was his suspicion that "all that is personal soon rots; it must be packed in ice or salt."

Yeats's technique for moving beyond the self, moving beyond biography and personal utterance, was his theory of the mask, which enabled him to objectify experience. The mask, or *persona* (Greek for "mask"), allowed Yeats to voice an alter ego, thereby engendering a tension between the poet's true self and the role played while wearing the mask. For Yeats, pure experience was as misleading as an empty mask. Reality, or universal truth, as Yeats saw it, could exist only in the tension between the poet's true self and the mask he or she wore. In "Crazy Jane Talks with the Bishop," for example, we must be aware of the clash between Jane and the Bishop—their obvious disagreement. But we must also be aware of the tension that drew the poet to each of these two masks to begin with. Yeats would want us to remember that it is the *poet* who explores the conflicts between vision and corporeal realities, between the "artifice of eternity" and the world of "mire and blood," and that it is also the poet who plays these opposites against each other to form a creative whole—the poems themselves.

Heir to the eighteenth-century Protestant Anglo-Irish tradition of such writers as Jonathan Swift and Oliver Goldsmith, Yeats nevertheless chose to explore the Irish Celtic tradition (pp. 950–958). Moreover, his choice of a visionary art further allies him with poets like Dante (pp. 1051–1054), Milton (pp. 220–250), and Blake (pp. 313–327). Drawing on translations of Celtic mythology, Yeats's earliest poems often focus on Irish folklore and legend, as in his "The Song of Wandering Aengus." In time, however, Yeats's poetry expanded to include meditations on the relationships between imagination and history. What many of his readers have found remarkable is that Yeats was able to present even the political struggle for Irish independence as if it were taking place within a distant mythological setting. Rather than present political struggle directly, Yeats drew his own life and the lives of those around him into a poetry that echoes what he termed the "wonder and terror of history."

One of Yeats's best-known lyrics, "Easter 1916," illustrates this point. Though it is a poem about political struggle, it is not really a political poem. As Yeats himself suggested:

> Players and painted stage took
> all my love,
> And not those things that they
> were emblems of.

For Yeats, it was the tension between mask and poet that revealed truth, not the political events themselves. From his perspective, even political reality was visible only on the "painted stage," in art. The moment as experienced in history could only disclose itself. Art fixed the moment within the cycle of eternity.

For Yeats, as for the ancient Celts, the artist stood at the center of the universe, and his quest for poetic truth was the most important enterprise imaginable and the fundamental subject matter of any great art. In short, Yeats literally saw the poet as magician and the poem as a kind of magic spell. There was, however, little magic in Yeats's writing habits. For Yeats, the actual process of putting words to paper was stunningly slow. Even at the height of his poetic powers, he struggled to produce six lines a week. All his poetry was taken through an exhaustive drafting process, and many times the later versions do not bear the slightest resemblance to the poem's first draft. Often charged with overwriting, Yeats responded:

> The friends that have it I do wrong
> When ever I remake a song,
> Should know what issue is at stake:
> It is myself that I remake.

In his maturity, Yeats adopted the dramatic lyric as his most characteristic form of expression. Under the influence of Ezra Pound (who worked as Yeats's secretary for two years) Yeats simplified his diction and modified his syntax to more closely resemble modern speech. He wrote, "I cast off traditional metaphors and loosened my rhythm, and recognizing that all criticism of life known to me was alien and English, became as emotional as possible but with an emotion I described to myself as cold." In addition to poetry, Yeats also wrote plays, fiction, criticism, philosophy, essays, and an autobiography. As a dramatist, he wanted to create plays that were symbolic and stark. Drawing on Japanese Nō plays, Yeats experimented with stylized ritual, symbolic action, and the use of masks, and as such anticipated modern abstract theater.

Despite such experimentation, Yeats's structures are more traditional than modern. Like Frost, he used conventional formal qualities to allow the reader to work through the expected patterns of a sustained composition. And though his insights are often paradoxical and his allusions esoteric, Yeats is not the poet of mystics and scholars. Most of his images are accessible to the average reader, who generally appreciates the music and polish of Yeats's language as that of a virtuoso.

Born in Dublin on June 13, 1865, to Susan Pollexfen, the daughter of a prosperous Sligo merchant, and John Butler Yeats, a painter, William Butler Yeats spent a lonely, unhappy childhood. Yeats's father was the dominant intellectual influence on the young poet's life. Upon his father's death in 1922, Yeats wrote to Olivia Shakespeare: "I find it hard to realize my father's death, he has so long been a mind to me, that mind seems to me still thinking and writing." Yeats received no formal education until he was eleven years old. He was a disappointing student: impulsive in his studies, given to fantasy, and poor at sports. He tells us that it was out of love of Sligo and its people in the west of Ireland as well as out of love for the ancient Irish legends that he began writing lyrics as a young man.

On January 30, 1889, Yeats met and fell passionately and obsessively in love with Maude Gonne, a political activist in the cause of Irish nationalism and a woman to whom Yeats proposed marriage at various times. He wrote, "I had never thought to see in a living woman so great beauty. It belonged to famous pictures, to poetry, to some legendary past." In 1896 Lady Augusta Gregory, a patron of the arts as well as a poet and playwright, invited Yeats to dine at her estate, Coole Park. She became intrigued by the poet and decided to help his work by bringing order and harmony into his life. She became a central figure in his life, and their relationship lasted until her death.

Having yet another proposal of marriage rejected by Maude Gonne, Yeats proposed marriage to her daughter, Iseult. She also rejected him, and a few weeks later, on October 20, 1917, Yeats married Georgie Hyde-Lees, who took a keen interest in her husband's work. Later, Yeats revealed that his wife's automatic spirit writing was the chief source for his study on the cyclical relationship among the imagination, magic, and history presented in his philosophical work *A Vision*.

In 1922, as Ireland headed into civil war, Yeats was appointed a member of the first Irish Senate. In 1923 he began his active role in establishing an Irish Academy of Letters and to have the Abbey Theatre officially adopted as the Irish State Theatre. In 1922 he was awarded an honorary degree from Trinity College, and in 1923 he was named a Nobel Prize laureate. He died on January 28, 1939, and is buried under Ben Bulben in his ancestral churchyard at Drumcliff. His epitaph, taken from "Under Ben Bulben," reads:

Cast a cold eye
On life, on death.
Horseman, pass by!

The Lake Isle of Innisfree

I will arise and go now, and go to Innisfree,
And a small cabin build there, of clay and wattles° made: *interwoven twigs*

THE LAKE ISLE OF INNISFREE   **Innisfree**   a small island in the west of Ireland. "Innisfree," in Irish, means "Heather Island."

Nine bean-rows will I have there, a hive for the honey-bee,
And live alone in the bee-loud glade.

And I shall have some peace there, for peace comes dropping slow,   *5*
Dropping from the veils of the morning to where the cricket sings;
There midnight's all a glimmer, and noon a purple glow,
And evening full of the linnet's wings.

I will arise and go now, for always night and day
I hear lake water lapping with low sounds by the shore;   *10*
While I stand on the roadway, or on the pavements gray,
I hear it in the deep heart's core.

[1892]

When you are old

When you are old and grey and full of sleep,
And nodding by the fire, take down this book,
And slowly read, and dream of the soft look
Your eyes had once, and of their shadows deep;

How many loved your moments of glad grace,   *5*
And loved your beauty with love false or true,
But one man loved the pilgrim soul in you,
And loved the sorrows of your changing face;

And bending down beside the glowing bars,
Murmur, a little sadly, how Love fled   *10*
And paced upon the mountains overhead
And hid his face amid a crowd of stars.

[1892]

The Song of Wandering Aengus

I went out to the hazel wood,
Because a fire was in my head,
And cut and peeled a hazel wand,
And hooked a berry to a thread;
And when white moths were on the wing,   *5*

And moth-like stars were flickering out,
I dropped the berry in a stream
And caught a little silver trout.

When I had laid it on the floor
I went to blow the fire aflame,   *10*
But something rustled on the floor,
And some one called me by my name:
It had become a glimmering girl
With apple blossom in her hair
Who called me by my name and ran   *15*
And faded through the brightening air.

Though I am old with wandering
Through hollow lands and hilly lands,
I will find out where she has gone,
And kiss her lips and take her hands;   *20*
And walk among long dappled grass,
And pluck till time and times are done
The silver apples of the moon
The golden apples of the sun.

                                           [1897]

Adam's Curse

We sat together at one summer's end
That beautiful mild woman your close friend
And you and I, and talked of poetry.
I said, "A line will take us hours maybe,
Yet if it does not seem a moment's thought   *5*
Our stitching and unstitching has been naught.
Better go down upon your marrow bones
And scrub a kitchen pavement, or break stones
Like an old pauper in all kinds of weather;
For to articulate sweet sounds together   *10*
Is to work harder than all these and yet
Be thought an idler by the noisy set
Of bankers, schoolmasters, and clergymen
The martyrs call the world."

                      That woman then   *15*
Murmured with her young voice, for whose mild sake

There's many a one shall find out all heartache
In finding that it's young and mild and low.
"There is one thing that all we women know
Although we never heard of it at school,   *20*
That we must labour to be beautiful."

I said, "It's certain there is no fine thing
Since Adam's fall but needs much labouring.
There have been lovers who thought love should be
So much compounded of high courtesy   *25*
That they would sigh and quote with learned looks
Precedents out of beautiful old books;
Yet now it seems an idle trade enough."

We sat grown quiet at the name of love.
We saw the last embers of daylight die   *30*
And in the trembling blue-green of the sky
A moon, worn as if it had been a shell
Washed by time's waters as they rose and fell
About the stars and broke in days and years.

I had a thought for no one's but your ears;   *35*
That you were beautiful and that I strove
To love you in the old high way of love;
That it had all seemed happy, and yet we'd grown
As weary hearted as that hollow moon.

[1903]

No Second Troy

Why should I blame her that she filled my days
With misery, or that she would of late
Have taught to ignorant men most violent ways,
Or hurled the little streets upon the great,
Had they but courage equal to desire?   *5*
What could have made her peaceful with a mind
That nobleness made simple as a fire,
With beauty like a tightened bow, a kind
That is not natural in an age like this,
Being high and solitary and most stern?   *10*
Why, what could she have done, being what she is?
Was there another Troy for her to burn?

[1910]

A Coat

I made my song a coat
Covered with embroideries
Out of old mythologies
From heel to throat;
But the fools caught it,   *5*
Wore it in the world's eyes
As though they'd wrought it.
Song, let them take it,
For there's more enterprise
In walking naked.   *10*

[1914]

The Scholars

Bald heads forgetful of their sins,
Old, learned, respectable bald heads
Edit and annotate the lines
That young men, tossing on their beds,
Rhymed out in love's despair   *5*
To flatter beauty's ignorant ear.

All shuffle there; all cough in ink;
All wear the carpet with their shoes;
All think what other people think;
All know the man their neighbour knows.   *10*
Lord, what would they say
Did their Catullus walk that way?

[1915]

The Wild Swans at Coole

The trees are in their autumn beauty,
The woodland paths are dry,
Under the October twilight the water
Mirrors a still sky;

Upon the brimming water among the stones   5
Are nine-and-fifty swans.

The nineteenth autumn has come upon me
Since I first made my count;
I saw before I had well finished,
All suddenly mount   10
And scatter wheeling in great broken rings
Upon their clamorous wings.

I have looked upon those brilliant creatures,
And now my heart is sore.
All's changed since I, hearing at twilight,   15
The first time on this shore,
The bell-beat of their wings above my head,
Trod with a lighter tread.

Unwearied still, lover by lover,
They paddle in the cold   20
Companionable streams or climb the air;
Their hearts have not grown old;
Passion or conquest, wander where they will,
Attend upon them still.

But now they drift on the still water,   25
Mysterious, beautiful;
Among what rushes will they build,
By what lake's edge or pool
Delight men's eyes when I awake some day
To find they have flown away?   30

[1917]

An Irish Airman Foresees His Death

I know that I shall meet my fate
Somewhere among the clouds above;
Those that I fight I do not hate,
Those that I guard I do not love;
My country is Kiltartan Cross,   5

AN IRISH AIRMAN FORESEES HIS DEATH   ³⁻⁴**Those that I fight . . . I do not love.**   Yeats is referring
to the Germans and the English, respectively; the war is World War I.

My countrymen Kiltartan's poor,
No likely end could bring them loss
Or leave them happier than before.
Nor law, nor duty bade me fight,
Nor public men, nor cheering crowds,   *10*
A lonely impulse of delight
Drove to this tumult in the clouds;
I balanced all, brought all to mind,
The years to come seemed waste of breath,
A waste of breath the years behind   *15*
In balance with this life, this death.

[1919]

Easter 1916

I have met them at close of day
Coming with vivid faces
From counter or desk among gray
Eighteenth-century houses.
I have passed with a nod of the head   *5*
Or polite meaningless words,
Or have lingered awhile and said
Polite meaningless words,
And thought before I had done
Of a mocking tale or a gibe   *10*
To please a companion
Around the fire at the club,
Being certain that they and I
But lived where motley is worn:
All changed, changed utterly: *15*
A terrible beauty is born.

That woman's days were spent
In ignorant good will,
Her nights in argument
Until her voice grew shrill.   *20*
What voice more sweet than hers
When, young and beautiful,

EASTER 1916   The title refers to an insurrection of Irish nationalists on Easter Monday, 1916; the four leaders
mentioned were executed by the English. The first two lines echo lines from Thomas Wyatt's "They flee from me,"
p. 154.   ¹⁴**motley** fool's costume.

She rode to harriers°?   *hounds*
This man had kept a school
And rode our wingéd horse;   25
This other his helper and friend
Was coming into his force;
He might have won fame in the end,
So sensitive his nature seemed,
So daring and sweet his thought.   30
This other man I had dreamed
A drunken, vainglorious lout.
He had done most bitter wrong
To some who are near my heart,
Yet I number him in the song;   35
He, too, has resigned his part
In the casual comedy;
He, too, has been changed in his turn,
Transformed utterly:
A terrible beauty is born.   40

Hearts with one purpose alone
Through summer and winter seem
Enchanted to a stone
To trouble the living stream.
The horse that comes from the road,   45
The rider, the birds that range
From cloud to tumbling cloud,
Minute by minute they change;
A shadow of cloud on the stream
Changes minute by minute;   50
A horse-hoof slides on the brim,
And a horse plashes within it;
The long-legged moor-hens dive,
And hens to moor-cocks call;
Minute by minute they live: 55
The stone's in the midst of all.

Too long a sacrifice
Can make a stone of the heart.
O when may it suffice?
That is Heaven's part, our part   60
To murmur name upon name,
As a mother names her child
When sleep at last has come
On limbs that had run wild.
What is it but nightfall?   65

No, no, not night but death;
Was it needless death after all?
For England may keep faith
For all that is done and said.
We know their dream; enough   *70*
To know they dreamed and are dead;
And what if excess of love
Bewildered them till they died?
I write it out in a verse—
MacDonagh and MacBride   *75*
And Connolly and Pearse
Now and in time to be,
Wherever green is worn,
Are changed, changed utterly:
A terrible beauty is born.   *80*

[1920]

The Second Coming

Turning and turning in the widening gyre°   *spiral*
The falcon cannot hear the falconer;
Things fall apart; the center cannot hold;
Mere anarchy is loosed upon the world,
The blood-dimmed tide is loosed, and everywhere   *5*
The ceremony of innocence is drowned;
The best lack all conviction, while the worst
Are full of passionate intensity.

Surely some revelation is at hand;
Surely the Second Coming is at hand;   *10*
The Second Coming! Hardly are those words out
When a vast image out of *Spiritus Mundi*
Troubles my sight: somewhere in sands of the desert
A shape with lion body and the head of a man,
A gaze blank and pitiless as the sun,   *15*
Is moving its slow thighs, while all about it
Reel shadows of the indignant desert birds.
The darkness drops again; but now I know

THE SECOND COMING   The title alludes to the prophesied return of Jesus Christ and also to the beast of the Apocalypse. See Matthew 24 and Revelation.   ¹²**Spiritus Mundi**   for Yeats, a common storehouse of images, a communal human memory.

That twenty centuries of stony sleep
Were vexed to nightmare by a rocking cradle,   *20*
And what rough beast, its hour come round at last,
Slouches towards Bethlehem to be born?

                                                                     [1921]

A Prayer for My Daughter

Once more the storm is howling, and half hid
Under this cradle-hood and coverlid
My child sleeps on. There is no obstacle
But Gregory's wood and one bare hill
Whereby the haystack- and roof-leveling wind,   *5*
Bred on the Atlantic, can be stayed;
And for an hour I have walked and prayed
Because of the great gloom that is in my mind.

I have walked and prayed for this young child an hour
And heard the sea-wind scream upon the tower,   *10*
And under the arches of the bridge, and scream
In the elms above the flooded stream;
Imagining in excited reverie
That the future years had come,
Dancing to a frenzied drum,   *15*
Out of the murderous innocence of the sea.

May she be granted beauty and yet not
Beauty to make a stranger's eye distraught,
Or hers before a looking glass, for such,
Being made beautiful overmuch,   *20*
Consider beauty a sufficient end,
Lose natural kindness and maybe
The heart-revealing intimacy
That chooses right, and never find a friend.

Helen being chosen found life flat and dull   *25*
And later had much trouble from a fool,
While that great Queen, that rose out of the spray,

A PRAYER FOR MY DAUGHTER   ²⁵**Helen**   Helen of Troy, whose beauty was legendary.   ²⁷**Queen**
Aphrodite, Greek goddess of love.

Being fatherless could have her way
Yet chose a bandy-leggèd smith for man.
It's certain that fine women eat 30
A crazy salad with their meat,
Whereby the Horn of Plenty is undone.

In courtesy I'd have her chiefly learned;
Hearts are not had as a gift but hearts are earned
By those that are not entirely beautiful; 35
Yet many, that have played the fool
For beauty's very self, has charm made wise,
And many a poor man that has roved,
Loved and thought himself beloved,
From a glad kindness cannot take his eyes. 40

May she become a flourishing hidden tree
That all her thoughts may like the linnet° be,   *small bird*
And have no business but dispensing round
Their magnanimities of sound,
Nor but in merriment begin a chase, 45
Nor but in merriment a quarrel.
Oh, may she live like some green laurel
Rooted in one dear perpetual place.

My mind, because the minds that I have loved,
The sort of beauty that I have approved, 50
Prosper but little, has dried up of late,
Yet knows that to be choked with hate
May well be of all evil chances chief.
If there's no hatred in a mind
Assault and battery of the wind 55
Can never tear the linnet from the leaf.

An intellectual hatred is the worst,
So let her think opinions are accursed.
Have I not seen the loveliest woman born
Out of the mouth of Plenty's horn, 60
Because of her opinionated mind
Barter that horn and every good
By quiet natures understood
For an old bellows full of angry wind?

Considering that, all hatred driven hence, 65
The soul recovers radical innocence

And learns at last that it is self-delighting,
Self-appeasing, self-affrighting,
And that its own sweet will is Heaven's will;
She can, though every face should scowl   70
And every windy quarter howl
Or every bellows burst, be happy still.

And may her bridegroom bring her to a house
Where all's accustomed, ceremonious;
For arrogance and hatred are the wares   75
Peddled in the thoroughfares.
How but in custom and in ceremony
Are innocence and beauty born?
Ceremony's a name for the rich horn,
And custom for the spreading laurel tree.

[1921]

Sailing to Byzantium

1

That is no country for old men. The young
In one another's arms, birds in the trees
—Those dying generations—at their song,
The salmon-falls, the mackerel-crowded seas,
Fish, flesh, or fowl, commend all summer long   5
Whatever is begotten, born, and dies.
Caught in that sensual music all neglect
Monuments of unaging intellect.

2

An aged man is but a paltry thing,
A tattered coat upon a stick, unless   10
Soul clap its hands and sing, and louder sing
For every tatter in its mortal dress,
Nor is there singing school but studying
Monuments of its own magnificence;
And therefore I have sailed the seas and come   15
To the holy city of Byzantium.

SAILING TO BYZANTIUM   Byzantium was the capital of the eastern Roman Empire and an important center
of art and architecture.

3

O sages standing in God's holy fire
As in the gold mosaic of a wall,
Come from the holy fire, perne° in a gyre,°   *descend/spiral*
And be the singing-masters of my soul.   20
Consume my heart away; sick with desire
And fastened to a dying animal
It knows not what it is; and gather me
Into the artifice of eternity.

4

Once out of nature I shall never take   25
My bodily form from any natural thing,
But such a form as Grecian goldsmiths make
Of hammered gold and gold enameling
To keep a drowsy Emperor awake;
Or set upon a golden bough to sing
To lords and ladies of Byzantium
Of what is past, or passing, or to come.

      [1927]

Leda and the Swan

A sudden blow: the great wings beating still
Above the staggering girl, her thighs caressed
By the dark webs, her nape caught in his bill,
He holds her helpless breast upon his breast.

How can those terrified vague fingers push   5
The feathered glory from her loosening thighs?
And how can body, laid in that white rush,
But feel the strange heart beating where it lies?

A shudder in the loins engenders there
The broken wall, the burning roof and tower   10
And Agamemnon dead.

LEDA AND THE SWAN   Zeus, in the guise of a swan, raped Leda, Queen of Sparta. Helen, their daughter, married Menelaus, King of Sparta, but ran off with Paris, son of Priam, King of Troy. A ten-year siege of Troy by the Greeks ensued to bring Helen back.

>   Being so caught up,
> So mastered by the brute blood of the air,
> Did she put on his knowledge with his power
> Before the indifferent beak could let her drop?   15

[1928]

Among School Children

I

I walk through the long schoolroom questioning;
A kind old nun in a white hood replies;
The children learn to cipher and to sing,
To study reading-books and history,
To cut and sew, be neat in everything   5
In the best modern way—the children's eyes
In momentary wonder stare upon
A sixty-year-old smiling public man.

II

I dream of a Ledaean body, bent
Above a sinking fire, a tale that she   10
Told of a harsh reproof, or trivial event
That changed some childish day to tragedy—
Told, and it seemed that our two natures blent
Into a sphere from youthful sympathy,
Or else, to alter Plato's parable,   15
Into the yolk and white of the one shell.

III

And thinking of that fit of grief or rage
I look upon one child or t'other there
And wonder if she stood so at that age—
For even daughters of the swan can share   20
Something of every paddler's heritage—
And had that colour upon cheek or hair,
And thereupon my heart is driven wild:
She stands before me as a living child.

AMONG SCHOOL CHILDREN   ¹**I walk . . . questioning** As an Irish Senator Yeats visited various schools
⁹**Ledaean body**   a reference to Leda, mother of Helen of Troy.   ¹⁵**Plato's parable**   allusion to Plato's
Symposium on the androgenous origins of man

IV

Her present image floats into the mind—   25
Did Quattrocento finger fashion it
Hollow of cheek as though it drank the wind
And took a mess of shadows for its meat?
And I though never of Ledaean kind
Had pretty plumage once—enough of that,   30
Better to smile on all that smile, and show
There is a comfortable kind of old scarecrow.

V

What youthful mother, a shape upon her lap
Honey of generation had betrayed,
And that must sleep, shriek, struggle to escape   35
As recollection or the drug decide,
Would think her son, did she but see that shape
With sixty or more winters on its head,
A compensation for the pang of his birth,
Or the uncertainty of his setting forth?   40

VI

Plato thought nature but a spume° that plays   *froth*
Upon a ghostly paradigm° of things;   *pattern*
Solider Aristotle played the taws
Upon the bottom of a king of kings;
World-famous golden-thighed Pythagoras   45
Fingered upon a fiddle-stick or strings
What a star sang and careless muses heard:
Old clothes upon old sticks to scare a bird.

VII

Both nuns and mothers worship images,
But those the candles light are not as those   50
That animate a mother's reveries,
But keep a marble or a bronze repose.
And yet they too break hearts—O Presences
That passion, piety or affection knows,
And that all heavenly glory symbolise—   55
O self-born mockers of man's enterprise;

[26]**Quattrocento finger** with great painterly skill, an allusion to fifteenth-century Italian art.   [43]**played the
taws** spanked   [45]**Pythagoras** Greek philosopher once described as having a golden thigh

VIII

Labour is blossoming or dancing where
The body is not bruised to pleasure soul,
Nor beauty born out of its own despair,
Nor blear-eyed wisdom out of midnight oil.   60
O chestnut-tree, great-rooted blossomer,
Are you the leaf, the blossom or the bole?
O body swayed to music, O brightening glance,
How can we know the dancer from the dance?

[1928]

Byzantium

The unpurged images of day recede;
The Emperor's drunken soldiery are abed;
Night resonance recedes, night-walkers' song
After great cathedral gong;
A starlit or a moonlit dome disdains   5
All that man is,
All mere complexities,
The fury and the mire of human veins.

Before me floats an image, man or shade,
Shade more than man, more image than a shade;   10
For Hades' bobbin bound in mummy-cloth
May unwind the winding path;
A mouth that has no moisture and no breath
Breathless mouths may summon;
I hail the superhuman;   15
I call it death-in-life and life-in-death.

Miracle, bird or golden handiwork,
More miracle than bird or handiwork,
Planted on the star-lit golden bough,
Can like the cocks of Hades crow,   20
Or, by the moon embittered, scorn aloud
In glory of changeless metal
Common bird or petal
And all complexities of mire or blood.

BYZANTIUM   See "Sailing to Byzantium" (p 514).   11Hades   the underworld in Greek mythology.

At midnight on the Emperor's pavement flit   *25*
Flames that no faggot feeds, nor steel has lit,
Nor storm disturbs, flames begotten of flame,
Where blood-begotten spirits come
And all complexities of fury leave,
Dying into a dance,   *30*
An agony of trance,
An agony of flame that cannot singe a sleeve.

Astraddle on the dolphin's mire and blood,
Spirit after spirit. The smithies break the flood,
The golden smithies of the Emperor!   *35*
Marbles of the dancing floor
Break bitter furies of complexity,
Those images that yet
Fresh images beget,
That dolphin-torn, that gong-tormented sea.

[1932]

Crazy Jane Talks with the Bishop

I met the Bishop on the road
And much said he and I.
"Those breasts are flat and fallen now,
Those veins must soon be dry;
Live in a heavenly mansion,   *5*
Not in some foul sty."

"Fair and foul are near of kin,
And fair needs foul," I cried.
"My friends are gone, but that's a truth
Nor grave nor bed denied,   *10*
Learned in bodily lowliness
And in the heart's pride.

"A woman can be proud and stiff
When on love intent;
But Love has pitched his mansion in   *15*
The place of excrement;
For nothing can be sole or whole
That has not been rent."

[1932]

Lapis Lazuli

(FOR HARRY CLIFTON)

I have heard that hysterical women say
They are sick of the palette and fiddle-bow,
Of poets that are always gay,
For everybody knows or else should know
That if nothing drastic is done   5
Aeroplane and Zeppelin will come out,
Pitch like King Billy bomb-balls in
Until the town lie beaten flat.

All perform their tragic play,
There struts Hamlet, there is Lear,   10
That's Ophelia, that Cordelia;
Yet they, should the last scene be there,
The great stage curtain about to drop,
If worthy their prominent part in the play,
Do not break up their lines to weep.   15
They know that Hamlet and Lear are gay;
Gaiety transfiguring all that dread.
All men have aimed at, found and lost;
Black out; Heaven blazing into the head:
Tragedy wrought to its uttermost.   20
Though Hamlet rambles and Lear rages,
And all the drop-scenes drop at once
Upon a hundred thousand stages,
It cannot grow by an inch or an ounce.

On their own feet they came, or on shipboard,   25
Camel-back, horse-back, ass-back, mule-back,
Old civilisations put to the sword.
Then they and their wisdom went to rack:
No handiwork of Callimachus,
Who handled marble as if it were bronze,   30
Made draperies that seemed to rise
When sea-wind swept the corner, stands;

LAPIS LAZULI   a precious blue-colored stone.   ¹I have . . . say   a foreshadowing of World War II.
⁶Zeppelin   a German dirigible that could carry bombs.   ⁷King Billy   William III, who overwhelmed James
II in 1690 at the Battle of Boyne in Ireland.   ²⁹Callimachus   Greek sculptor, fifth century B.C.

His long lamp-chimney shaped like the stem
Of a slender palm, stood but a day;
All things fall and are built again, 35
And those that build them again are gay.

Two Chinamen, behind them a third,
Are carved in lapis lazuli,
Over them flies a long-legged bird,
A symbol of longevity; 40
The third, doubtless a serving-man,
Carries a musical instrument.

Every discoloration of the stone,
Every accidental crack or dent,
Seems a water-course or an avalanche. 45
Or lofty slope where it still snows
Though doubtless plum or cherry-branch
Sweetens the little half-way house
Those Chinamen climb towards, and I
Delight to imagine them seated there; 50
There, on the mountain and the sky,
On all the tragic scene they stare.
One asks for mournful melodies;
Accomplished fingers begin to play.
Their eyes mid many wrinkles, their eyes, 55
Their ancient, glittering eyes, are gay.

[1938]

The Circus Animals' Desertion

I

I sought a theme and sought for it in vain,
I sought it daily for six weeks or so.
Maybe at last, being but a broken man,
I must be satisfied with my heart, although
Winter and summer till old age began 5
My circus animals were all on show,
Those stilted boys, that burnished chariot,
Lion and woman and the Lord knows what.

II

What can I but enumerate old themes?
First that sea-rider Oisin led by the nose   *10*
Through three enchanted islands, allegorical dreams,
Vain gaiety, vain battle, vain repose,
Themes of the embittered heart, or so it seems,
That might adorn old songs or courtly shows;
But what cared I that set him on to ride,   *15*
I, starved for the bosom of his faery bride?

And then a counter-truth filled out its play,
The Countess Cathleen was the name I gave it;
She, pity-crazed, had given her soul away,
But masterful Heaven had intervened to save it.   *20*
I thought my dear must her own soul destroy,
So did fanaticism and hate enslave it,
And this brought forth a dream and soon enough
This dream itself had all my thought and love.

And when the Fool and Blind Man stole the bread   *25*
Cuchulain fought the ungovernable sea;
Heart-mysteries there, and yet when all is said
It was the dream itself enchanted me:
Character isolated by a deed
To engross the present and dominate memory.   *30*
Players and painted stage took all my love,
And not those things that they were emblems of.

III

Those masterful images because complete
Grew in pure mind, but out of what began?
A mound of refuse or the sweepings of a street,   *35*
Old kettles, old bottles, and a broken can,
Old iron, old bones, old rags, that raving slut
Who keeps the till. Now that my ladder's gone,
I must lie down where all the ladders start,
In the foul rag-and-bone shop of the heart.   *40*

[1939]

THE CIRCUS ANIMALS' DESERTION   ¹¹**three enchanted islands**   allusion to Irish mythology: the Islands of Delight, of Many Fears, and of Forgetfulness.   ²⁶**Cuchulain . . . sea**   An allusion to events that occur in Yeat's play, *On Baile's Strand*.

Long-Legged Fly

That civilisation may not sink,
Its great battle lost,
Quiet the dog, tether the pony
To a distant post;
Our master Caesar is in the tent   5
Where the maps are spread,
His eyes fixed upon nothing;
A hand under his head.
Like a long-legged fly upon the stream
His mind moves upon silence.   10

That the topless towers be burnt
And men recall that face,
Move most gently if move you must
In this lonely place.
She thinks, part woman, three parts a child,   15
That nobody looks; her feet
Practise a tinker shuffle
Picked up on a street.
Like a long-legged fly upon the stream
Her mind moves upon silence.   20

That girls at puberty may find
The first Adam in their thought,
Shut the door of the Pope's chapel,
Keep those children out.
There on that scaffolding reclines   25
Michael Angelo.
With no more sound than the mice make
His hand moves to and fro.
Like a long-legged fly upon the stream
His mind moves upon silence.   30

[1939]

Politics

In our time the destiny of man presents its meaning in political terms.
                                                    —*Thomas Mann*

How can I, that girl standing there,
My attention fix
On Roman or on Russian
Or on Spanish politics?

Yet here's a travelled man that knows   *5*
What he talks about,
And there's a politician
That has read and thought,
And maybe what they say is true
Of war and war's alarms,   *10*
But O that I were young again
And held her in my arms!

[1939]

ERNEST DOWSON

[1867–1900]

Non sum qualis eram bonae sub regno Cynarae

Last night, ah, yesternight, betwixt her lips and mine
There fell thy shadow, Cynara! thy breath was shed
Upon my soul between the kisses and the wine;
And I was desolate and sick of an old passion,
   Yea, I was desolate and bowed my head: *5*
I have been faithful to thee, Cynara! in my fashion.

All night upon mine heart I felt her warm heart beat,
Night-long within mine arms in love and sleep she lay;
Surely the kisses of her bought red mouth were sweet;
But I was desolate and sick of an old passion,   *10*
   When I awoke and found the dawn was gray:
I have been faithful to thee, Cynara! in my fashion.

I have forgot much, Cynara! gone with the wind,
Flung roses, roses riotously with the throng,
Dancing, to put thy pale, lost lilies out of mind;   *15*
But I was desolate and sick of an old passion,
   Yea, all the time, because the dance was long:
I have been faithful to thee, Cynara! in my fashion.

NON SUM QUALIS ERAM BONAE SUB REGNO CYNARAE   a quote from Horace, *Odes,* IV, 1 Horace's
Latin can be translated as "I am not what I was under the reign of the good Cynara."

I cried for madder music and for stronger wine,
But when the feast is finished and the lamps expire,   *20*
Then falls thy shadow, Cynara! the night is thine;
And I am desolate and sick of an old passion,
   Yea hungry for the lips of my desire:
I have been faithful to thee, Cynara! in my fashion.

                                   [1896]

EDWIN ARLINGTON ROBINSON

[1869–1935]

Miniver Cheevy

Miniver Cheevy, child of scorn,
   Grew lean while he assailed the seasons;
He wept that he was ever born,
   And he had reasons.

Miniver loved the days of old   *5*
   When swords were bright and steeds were prancing;
The vision of a warrior bold
   Would set him dancing.

Miniver sighed for what was not,
   And dreamed, and rested from his labors;   *10*
He dreamed of Thebes and Camelot,
   And Priam's neighbors.

Miniver mourned the ripe renown
   That made so many a name so fragrant;
He mourned Romance, now on the town,   *15*
   And Art, a vagrant.

Miniver loved the Medici,
   Albeit he had never seen one;

MINIVER CHEEVY   [11]**Thebes** Greek city famous in history and legend.   [11]**Camelot** the seat of King Arthur's court.   [12]**Priam** King of Troy during the Trojan war.   [17]**The Medici** family of powerful merchants and bankers, rulers of Florence in the fourteenth, fifteenth, and sixteenth centuries who were known for their patronage of the arts.

He would have sinned incessantly
   Could he have been one.   *20*

Miniver cursed the commonplace
   And eyed a khaki suit with loathing;
He missed the mediæval grace
   Of iron clothing.

Miniver scorned the gold he sought,   *25*
   But sore annoyed was he without it;
Miniver thought, and thought, and thought,
   And thought about it.

Miniver Cheevy, born too late,
   Scratched his head and kept on thinking;   *30*
Miniver coughed, and called it fate,
   And kept on drinking.

                                                  [1906]

PAUL LAURENCE DUNBAR

[1872–1906]

We wear the mask

We wear the mask that grins and lies,
It hides our cheeks and shades our eyes—
This debt we pay to human guile;
With torn and bleeding hearts we smile,
And mouth with myriad subtleties.   *5*

Why should the world be over-wise,
In counting all our tears and sighs?
Nay, let them only see us, while
      We wear the mask.

We smile, but, O great Christ, our cries   *10*
To thee from tortured souls arise.
We sing, but oh the clay is vile

Beneath our feet, and long the mile;
But let the world dream otherwise,
We wear the mask! 15

[1896]

WALTER DE LA MARE

[1873–1956]

The Listeners

"Is there anybody there?" said the Traveler,
   Knocking on the moonlit door;
And his horse in the silence champed the grasses
   Of the forest's ferny floor:
And a bird flew up out of the turret, 5
   Above the Traveler's head:
And he smote upon the door again a second time;
   "Is there anybody there?" he said.
But no one descended to the Traveler;
   No head from the leaf-fringed sill 10
Leaned over and looked into his gray eyes,
   Where he stood perplexed and still.
But only a host of phantom listeners
   That dwelt in the lone house then
Stood listening in the quiet of the moonlight 15
   To that voice from the world of men:
Stood thronging the faint moonbeams on the dark stair,
   That goes down to the empty hall,
Hearkening in an air stirred and shaken
   By the lonely Traveler's call. 20
And he felt in his heart their strangeness,
   Their stillness answering his cry,
While his horse moved, cropping the dark turf,
   'Neath the starred and leafy sky;
For he suddenly smote on the door, even 25
   Louder, and lifted his head:—
"Tell them I came, and no one answered,
   That I kept my word," he said.

Never the least stir made the listeners,
    Though every word he spake   *30*
Fell echoing through the shadowiness of the still house
    From the one man left awake:
Ay, they heard his foot upon the stirrup,
    And the sound of iron on stone,
And how the silence surged softly backward,   *35*
    When the plunging hoofs were gone.

                                    [1912]

AMY LOWELL

[1874–1925]

Patterns

I walk down the garden-paths,
And all the daffodils
Are blowing, and the bright blue squills.
I walk down the patterned garden-paths
In my stiff, brocaded gown.   *5*
With my powdered hair and jeweled fan,
I too am a rare
Pattern. As I wander down
The garden-paths.

My dress is richly figured,   *10*
And the train
Makes a pink and silver stain
On the gravel, and the thrift
Of the borders.
Just a plate of current fashion,   *15*
Tripping by in high-heeled, ribboned shoes.
Not a softness anywhere about me,
Only whalebone and brocade.
And I sink on a seat in the shade
Of a lime tree. For my passion   *20*
Wars against the stiff brocade.
The daffodils and squills
Flutter in the breeze

As they please.
And I weep;   25
For the lime-tree is in blossom
And one small flower has dropped upon my bosom.

And the plashing of waterdrops
In the marble fountain
Comes down the garden-paths.   30
The dripping never stops.
Underneath my stiffened gown
Is the softness of a woman bathing in a marble basin,
A basin in the midst of hedges grown
So thick, she cannot see her lover hiding,   35
But she guesses he is near,
And the sliding of the water
Seems the stroking of a dear
Hand upon her.
What is Summer in a fine brocaded gown!   40
I should like to see it lying in a heap upon the ground.
All the pink and silver crumpled up on the ground.
I would be the pink and silver as I ran along the paths,
And he would stumble after,
Bewildered by my laughter.   45
I should see the sun flashing from his sword-hilt and the buckles on his shoes.
I would choose
To lead him in a maze along the patterned paths,
A bright and laughing maze for my heavy-booted lover.
Till he caught me in the shade,   50
And the buttons of his waistcoat bruised my body as he clasped me,
Aching, melting, unafraid.
With the shadows of the leaves and the sundrops,
And the plopping of the waterdrops,
All about us in the open afternoon—   55
I am very like to swoon
With the weight of this brocade,
For the sun sifts through the shade.

Underneath the fallen blossom
In my bosom   60
Is a letter I have hid.
It was brought to me this morning by a rider from the Duke.
"Madam, we regret to inform you that Lord Hartwell
Died in action Thursday se'ennight."
As I read it in the white, morning sunlight,   65

The letters squirmed like snakes.
"Any answer, Madam," said my footman.
"No," I told him.
"See that the messenger takes some refreshment.
No, no answer."   70
And I walked into the garden,
Up and down the patterned paths,
In my stiff, correct brocade.
The blue and yellow flowers stood up proudly in the sun,
Each one.   75
I stood upright too,
Held rigid to the pattern
By the stiffness of my gown;
Up and down I walked,
Up and down: 80

In a month he would have been my husband.
In a month, here, underneath this lime,
We would have broke the pattern;
He for me, and I for him,
He as Colonel, I as Lady,   85
On this shady seat.
He had a whim
That sunlight carried blessing.
And I answered, "It shall be as you have said."
Now he is dead.   90

In Summer and in Winter I shall walk
Up and down
The patterned garden-paths.
The squills and daffodils
Will give place to pillared roses, and to asters, and to snow. 95
I shall go
Up and down
In my gown.
Gorgeously arrayed,
Boned and stayed.   100
And the softness of my body will be guarded from embrace
By each button, hook, and lace.
For the man who should loose me is dead,
Fighting with the Duke in Flanders,
In a pattern called a war.   105
Christ! What are patterns for?

                                                        [1916]

ROBERT FROST
[1874–1963]

Like Walt Whitman before him, Robert Frost yearned to become America's foremost poet. Aiming for both critical and popular acclaim, Frost hoped to achieve recognition as a major poet and to reach the widest possible audience. And although he did succeed in becoming a popular poet (perhaps the most popular in America's history), in the minds of some readers his very popularity diminished his critical stature. Frost himself, however, was partly responsible for this. The image he projected—folksy, lovable, homespun—undercut his reputation as a major poet. Even today, with Frost's poetic stature amply acknowledged, he is occasionally seen as a less serious, less impressive, less demanding, and hence less important poet than his contemporaries Ezra Pound, T. S. Eliot, and Wallace Stevens.

There is a measure of truth in this assessment, perhaps, but only a small measure. Frost's poems are easier to read than those of Pound, Eliot, or Stevens: his familiar vocabulary and traditional forms enhance their accessibility. But his poems are neither simple nor easy to understand. Their diction is more richly allusive and connotative than at first may appear. Their paraphrasable thought is subtler and more profound than an initial reading might suggest. Moreover, their form, though traditional, is more intricately wrought and more decisively experimental than is generally recognized. Before turning to consider these claims, we should be aware of the course of Frost's poetic career, particularly of his popularity as an honored national poet, who, ironically, was first recognized abroad rather than at home.

Although Robert Frost is considered a New England farmer–poet who captures in his verse the tang of Yankee speech, he was born in San Francisco and lived there until the age of eleven, when his family moved to Lawrence, Massachusetts. He attended high school in Lawrence and was covaledictorian of his graduating class with Elinor White, whom he later married. Frost continued his education at Dartmouth College, where he remained for only one term, and later at Harvard University, where he studied for two years without taking a degree. After working at a succession of odd jobs including farming and factory work, Frost taught at Pinkerton Academy, where from 1906 to 1910 he reformed the English syllabus, directed theatrical productions, and wrote many of the poems later included in his first book, *A Boy's Will.*

In 1911, in an attempt to attract the attention of prominent and influential members in the literary world, he sold his farm in Derry, New Hampshire, and moved with his family to England. There he met and received the support of Ezra Pound, who helped secure publication of his first two volumes of poems, and of Edward Thomas, who reviewed them perceptively. Having launched his career, Frost returned to America in 1915 and quickly secured an American publisher— Henry Holt and Co.—for the two books published in England, *A Boy's Will* (1913) and *North of Boston* (1914), and for subsequent volumes as well. With the publication in 1916 of *Mountain Interval,* Frost's fame grew. In 1917, and periodically thereafter, he was poet in residence at Amherst College and served in a similar capacity at various other colleges and universities including Dartmouth, Wesleyan, Michigan, Harvard, and Yale. Frost received awards and prizes, among them the Bollingen Poetry Prize (1963) and four Pulitzer Prizes (1924, 1931, 1937, and 1943). In addition many honorary degrees, including ones from Oxford and Cambridge universities, were conferred on him. Although Frost was fond of joking that he could make a blanket of the many academic hoods he had acquired, he valued them, particularly those from the British institutions. Later in his life Frost was appointed goodwill emissary to South America and the Soviet Union. He was also the only American poet honored with an invitation to read his work at a presidential inauguration. In January 1961, at the inauguration of John F. Kennedy, Frost read "The Gift Outright," and another poem he had composed for the occasion.

This brief summary of Frost's career, however, oversimplifies what was in reality a more complex and arduous process. Initially an obscure writer, Frost experienced difficulty in breaking into print in a significant way. He later struggled with the decline of his poetic powers, most of his best work being produced when he was younger. And more tragically, he suffered the deaths of his wife and three of his children, one of whom committed suicide. He also saw his sister and one of his daughters succumb to mental illness. And finally, despite his many prizes and awards, Frost was bitter that he never won a Nobel Prize. He died in 1963, two weeks short of his eighty-ninth birthday.

What accounts for Frost's fame and popularity? Three things, at least: his shrewd management of his career, including the cultivation of his poetic image; his use of familiar subjects, especially the natural world and people engaged in recognizable activities; his accessible language and apparent simplicity of thought. From the beginning, Frost skillfully managed his poetic career, going abroad to England to win the approval of the prominent poets and critics of his day. Frost, of course, did not plan every step of his rise to fame; rather he trusted to his highly developed instinct for sizing up opportunities and capitalizing on them. As William Pritchard explains in *Robert Frost: A Literary Life Reconsidered,* Frost retrospectively structured his literary life as one of adversity overcome. The most important aspect of this biographical semifictionalizing was Frost's portrayal of himself as a literary exile unappreciated in his home country. Allied with this biographical myth-making was Frost's control over his public image. He refused, for example, to read his darker, more skeptical poems in public, preferring instead to reveal his more congenial, folksy side. And he carefully masked from public exposure his hunger for fame and an occasional nasty denigration of those poets he considered his strongest rivals.

More important to his popularity than his masterly manipulation of his public persona, however, is the readability of his poetry. Frost avoids obscure language, preferring the familiar word and the idiomatic phrase. He also shuns foreign words and shies away from all but the scantiest of references to economic, literary, and political history. And instead of the structural openness, fragmentation, and discontinuity favored by some of his contemporaries, Frost used traditional poetic forms characterized by coherence and continuity.

That Frost's poems are relatively easy to read does not mean that they are necessarily easy to understand. Frost is a master of concealment, of saying one thing in terms of another, especially of saying two or more things simultaneously. Even his most accessible poems such as "Birches," "Mending Wall," and "The Road Not Taken" contain clear invitations to consider their symbolic ramifications. The symbolic nature of these poems doesn't manifest itself immediately. To appreciate the fullness of Frost's achievement, we need to read with attention to their symbolic detail, whether we are reading the meditative blank verse of "Birches" or "Mending Wall" or the lyrical descriptions of "Desert Places" or "Stopping by Woods on a Snowy Evening" (p. 48).

It is also a mistake to assume, on the basis of a familiarity with a few of Frost's more famous lyrics, that his poetry lacks either drama or humor. "Departmental" reveals Frost's humorous side, while "Home Burial" shows him at work in a longer, more dramatic form. Though his poems are certainly serious, they are not solemn. This is as true of "Stopping by Woods" and "The Road Not Taken" as it is for "The Silken Tent," a witty extended comparison between a woman and a pitched tent; "Provide, Provide," a pragmatic set of admonitions about how to get on in the world; and "A Considerable Speck," a satirical jab at human limitations, particularly the performances of writers. Moreover, Frost himself warned us against taking him too seriously. Although we cannot completely trust him in such matters since he enjoyed teasing his audiences, we can at least regard his work as a mixture of playfulness and seriousness. "If it is with outer seriousness," he once remarked, "it must with inner humor; if with inner seriousness, then with outer humor."

Complicating matters further is Frost's view of nature. More often than not, nature appears as a powerful, dangerous, and cruel force, its purpose and design not immediately apparent. Frost avoids a simple representation of the relationship between the natural and human worlds. He does not share Emerson's belief in nature as a moral teacher. He does not believe, for example, that in reading nature we discover moral and spiritual truths. That romantic view is questioned in poems like "Desert Places" and "The Most of It," where nature seems to express "nothing" to the human observer. Frost's response to nature, essentially, is to question its meaning for human beings, to wonder skeptically just how much it does express. A poem like "Tree at my window" explores this issue in a way that may at first appear familiar but that changes as the poem progresses. This poem seems to suggest that there are definite connections between trees and people—that the human and the natural worlds intersect. But it also points to radical differences between the two worlds, differences that separate them more than their similarities bind them. At stake in this and many of Frost's other nature poems are the Emersonian and Whitmanesque transcendentalist ideas, in which nature and man form part of a harmonious whole, a unity exemplified by poems such as "The Tuft of Flowers" and "Two Look at Two."

The complexity and richness of Frost's vision of nature are paralleled by the subtlety of his technical achievement. Though he worked in traditional forms—sonnet, heroic couplet, blank verse, four-line stanza—the effects he wrought in them are remarkable for their range and versatility. To take just one example, consider his sonnets, which include poems in both of the traditional forms, Shakespearean and Petrarchan. "Putting in the Seed" is constructed according to the Shakespearean, or English, pattern with three quatrains and a concluding couplet (though Frost alters the rhyme pattern slightly). "Design" follows the Petrarchan model: an octave of eight lines followed by a sestet of six. The octave of "Design" describes a natural scene (a white spider finding on a white flower a white moth that it kills and devours). The sestet explores the significance of the event. Though conventional in logical organization, "Design" exhibits a variation from the Petrarchan rhyme scheme: *abba abba cde cde* (or *cd cd cd*). Frost's poem uses only three rhymes throughout both octave and sestet: *abba abba acc caa*.

Frost's sonnets often diverge in some way from the traditional sonnet and thus make something new and fresh of the form. "Mowing," for example, while composed according to the Petrarchan structure, contains a strong concluding couplet more characteristic of the Shakespearean sonnet. It also varies from the rhyme scheme of both traditional patterns, though using the same number of different sounds as the Shakespearean form: *abca bdec dfeg fg*. The poem displays a curious use of overlapping sound effects that Frost worked out more elaborately and systematically in other lyrics. Other sonnet variations appear in "The Silken Tent," which is constructed as a single sentence spun out over the fourteen lines in a Shakespearean pattern. Working against that rhyme scheme, however, is a logical structure more characteristic of the Petrarchan division into two major sections, with a turn at the ninth line. Such hybrid sonnets are accompanied by other sonnet experiments such as "Once by the Pacific," in seven couplets rhyming *aa bb cc dd ee ff gg*, and "Acquainted with the Night," composed in the interlocking rhymes of *terza rima: aba bcb cdc ded ee*.

Frost was a skilled wordsmith who cared about the sounds of his sentences. He noted more than once how "the sentence sound says more than the words"; how "tones of voice" can "mean more than words." In such voice tones Frost heard the sounds of sense and captured them in his verse, heightening their expressiveness by combining the inflections of ordinary speech with the measured regularity of meter. Because Frost's achievement in this regard surpasses that of most other modern American poets, we should be particularly attentive to the way he makes poetry out of the spoken word. His poems often mask the most elegant and subtle of his technical accomplishments. Perhaps the best way to read Frost's poems is to approach them as performances, as poetic acts of skillful daring, of risks taken, of technical dangers overcome. In doing so we may share the pleasure Frost took in poetic performance. In addition, we can see how Frost's poetry often "begins in delight and ends in wisdom," offering along the way what he called "a momentary stay against confusion."

Mowing

There was never a sound beside the wood but one,
And that was my long scythe whispering to the ground.
What was it it whispered? I knew not well myself;
Perhaps it was something about the heat of the sun,

Something, perhaps, about the lack of sound— 5
And that was why it whispered and did not speak.
It was no dream of the gift of idle hours,
Or easy gold at the hand of fay or elf:
Anything more than the truth would have seemed too weak
To the earnest love that laid the swale in rows, 10
Not without feeble-pointed spikes of flowers
(Pale orchises), and scared a bright green snake.
The fact is the sweetest dream that labor knows.
My long scythe whispered and left the hay to make.

[1913]

The Tuft of Flowers

I went to turn the grass once after one
Who mowed it in the dew before the sun.

The dew was gone that made his blade so keen
Before I came to view the leveled scene.

I looked for him behind an isle of trees; 5
I listened for his whetstone in the breeze.

But he had gone his way, the grass all mown,
And I must be, as he had been,—alone,

"As all must be," I said within my heart,
"Whether they work together or apart." 10

But as I said it, swift there passed me by
On noiseless wing a bewildered butterfly,

Seeking with memories grown dim o'er night
Some resting flower of yesterday's delight.

And once I marked his flight go round and round, 15
As where some flower lay withering on the ground.

And then he flew as far as eye could see,
And then on tremulous wing came back to me.

I thought of questions that have no reply,
And would have turned to toss the grass to dry; 20

But he turned first, and led my eye to look
At a tall tuft of flowers beside a brook,

A leaping tongue of bloom the scythe had spared
Beside a reedy brook the scythe had bared.

The mower in the dew had loved them thus,   25
By leaving them to flourish, not for us,

Nor yet to draw one thought of ours to him,
But from sheer morning gladness at the brim.

The butterfly and I had lit upon,
Nevertheless, a message from the dawn,   30

That made me hear the wakening birds around,
And hear his long scythe whispering to the ground,

And feel a spirit kindred to my own;
So that henceforth I worked no more alone;

But glad with him, I worked as with his aid,   35
And weary, sought at noon with him the shade;

And dreaming, as it were, held brotherly speech
With one whose thought I had not hoped to reach.

"Men work together," I told him from the heart,
"Whether they work together or apart."   40

                                                        [1913]

Mending Wall

Something there is that doesn't love a wall,
That sends the frozen-ground-swell under it,
And spills the upper boulders in the sun;
And makes gaps even two can pass abreast.
The work of hunters is another thing: 5
I have come after them and made repair
Where they have left not one stone on a stone,
But they would have the rabbit out of hiding,
To please the yelping dogs. The gaps I mean,
No one has seen them made or heard them made,   10
But at spring mending-time we find them there.
I let my neighbor know beyond the hill;
And on a day we meet to walk the line

And set the wall between us once again.
We keep the wall between us as we go.   15
To each the boulders that have fallen to each.
And some are loaves and some so nearly balls
We have to use a spell to make them balance:
"Stay where you are until our backs are turned!"
We wear our fingers rough with handling them.   20
Oh, just another kind of outdoor game,
One on a side. It comes to little more:
There where it is we do not need the wall:
He is all pine and I am apple orchard.
My apple trees will never get across   25
And eat the cones under his pines, I tell him.
He only says, "Good fences make good neighbors."
Spring is the mischief in me, and I wonder
If I could put a notion in his head:
"*Why* do they make good neighbors? Isn't it   30
Where there are cows? But here there are no cows.
Before I built a wall I'd ask to know
What I was walling in or walling out,
And to whom I was like to give offense.
Something there is that doesn't love a wall,   35
That wants it down." I could say "Elves" to him,
But it's not elves exactly, and I'd rather
He said it for himself. I see him there
Bringing a stone grasped firmly by the top
In each hand, like an old-stone savage armed.   40
He moves in darkness as it seems to me,
Not of woods only and the shade of trees.
He will not go behind his father's saying,
And he likes having thought of it so well
He says again, "Good fences make good neighbors."   45

[1914]

After Apple-Picking

My long two-pointed ladder's sticking through a tree
Toward heaven still,
And there's a barrel that I didn't fill
Beside it, and there may be two or three
Apples I didn't pick upon some bough.   5
But I am done with apple-picking now.
Essence of winter sleep is on the night,

The scent of apples: I am drowsing off.
I cannot rub the strangeness from my sight
I got from looking through a pane of glass   *10*
I skimmed this morning from the drinking trough
And held against the world of hoary grass.
It melted, and I let it fall and break.
But I was well
Upon my way to sleep before it fell,   *15*
And I could tell
What form my dreaming was about to take.
Magnified apples appear and disappear,
Stem end and blossom end,
And every fleck of russet showing clear.   *20*
My instep arch not only keeps the ache,
It keeps the pressure of a ladder-round.
I feel the ladder sway as the boughs bend.
And I keep hearing from the cellar bin
The rumbling sound   *25*
Of load on load of apples coming in.
For I have had too much
Of apple-picking: I am overtired
Of the great harvest I myself desired.
There were ten thousand thousand fruit to touch,   *30*
Cherish in hand, lift down, and not let fall.
For all
That struck the earth,
No matter if not bruised or spiked with stubble,
Went surely to the cider-apple heap   *35*
As of no worth.
One can see what will trouble
This sleep of mine, whatever sleep it is.
Were he not gone,
The woodchuck could say whether it's like his   *40*
Long sleep, as I describe its coming on,
Or just some human sleep.

                                                   [1914]

The Road Not Taken

Two roads diverged in a yellow wood,
And sorry I could not travel both
And be one traveler, long I stood

And looked down one as far as I could
To where it bent in the undergrowth;   5

Then took the other, as just as fair,
And having perhaps the better claim,
Because it was grassy and wanted wear;
Though as for that, the passing there
Had worn them really about the same,   10

And both that morning equally lay
In leaves no step had trodden black.
Oh, I kept the first for another day!
Yet knowing how way leads on to way,
I doubted if I should ever come back.   15

I shall be telling this with a sigh
Somewhere ages and ages hence:
Two roads diverged in a wood, and I—
I took the one less traveled by,
And that has made all the difference.   20

[1916]

Birches

When I see birches bend to left and right
Across the lines of straighter darker trees,
I like to think some boy's been swinging them.
But swinging doesn't bend them down to stay
As ice-storms do. Often you must have seen them   5
Loaded with ice a sunny winter morning
After a rain. They click upon themselves
As the breeze rises, and turn many-colored
As the stir cracks and crazes their enamel.
Soon the sun's warmth makes them shed crystal shells   10
Shattering and avalanching on the snow-crust—
Such heaps of broken glass to sweep away
You'd think the inner dome of heaven had fallen.
They are dragged to the withered bracken by the load,
And they seem not to break; though once they are bowed   15
So low for long, they never right themselves:

You may see their trunks arching in the woods
Years afterwards, trailing their leaves on the ground
Like girls on hands and knees that throw their hair
Before them over their heads to dry in the sun.   20
But I was going to say when Truth broke in
With all her matter-of-fact about the ice-storm,
I should prefer to have some boy bend them
As he went out and in to fetch the cows—
Some boy too far from town to learn baseball,   25
Whose only play was what he found himself,
Summer or winter, and could play alone.
One by one he subdued his father's trees
By riding them down over and over again
Until he took the stiffness out of them,   30
And not one but hung limp, not one was left
For him to conquer. He learned all there was
To learn about not launching out too soon
And so not carrying the tree away
Clear to the ground. He always kept his poise   35
To the top branches, climbing carefully
With the same pains you use to fill a cup
Up to the brim, and even above the brim.
Then he flung outward, feet first, with a swish,
Kicking his way down through the air to the ground.   40
So was I once myself a swinger of birches.
And so I dream of going back to be.
It's when I'm weary of considerations,
And life is too much like a pathless wood
Where your face burns and tickles with the cobwebs   45
Broken across it, and one eye is weeping
From a twig's having lashed across it open.
I'd like to get away from earth awhile
And then come back to it and begin over.
May no fate willfully misunderstand me   50
And half grant what I wish and snatch me away
Not to return. Earth's the right place for love:
I don't know where it's likely to go better.
I'd like to go by climbing a birch tree,
And climb black branches up a snow-white trunk   55
Toward heaven, till the tree could bear no more,
But dipped its top and set me down again.
That would be good both going and coming back.
One could do worse than be a swinger of birches.

[1916]

Hyla Brook

By June our brook's run out of song and speed.
Sought for much after that, it will be found
Either to have gone groping underground
(And taken with it all the Hyla breed
That shouted in the mist a month ago,   *5*
Like ghost of sleigh bells in a ghost of snow)—
Or flourished and come up in jewelweed,
Weak foliage that is blown upon and bent
Even against the way its waters went.
Its bed is left a faded paper sheet   *10*
Of dead leaves stuck together by the heat—
A brook to none but who remember long.
This as it will be seen is other far
Than with brooks taken otherwhere in song.
We love the things we love for what they are.   *15*

[1916]

The Oven Bird

There is a singer everyone has heard,
Loud, a mid-summer and a mid-wood bird,
Who makes the solid tree trunks sound again.
He says that leaves are old and that for flowers
Mid-summer is to spring as one to ten.   *5*
He says the early petal-fall is past,
When pear and cherry bloom went down in showers
On sunny days a moment overcast;
And comes that other fall we name the fall.
He says the highway dust is over all.   *10*
The bird would cease and be as other birds
But that he knows in singing not to sing.
The question that he frames in all but words
Is what to make of a diminished thing.

[1916]

"Out, Out—"

The buzz saw snarled and rattled in the yard
And made dust and dropped stove-length sticks of wood,
Sweet-scented stuff when the breeze drew across it.
And from there those that lifted eyes could count
Five mountain ranges one behind the other   5
Under the sunset far into Vermont.
And the saw snarled and rattled, snarled and rattled,
As it ran light, or had to bear a load.
And nothing happened: day was all but done.
Call it a day, I wish they might have said   10
To please the boy by giving him the half hour
That a boy counts so much when saved from work.
His sister stood beside them in her apron
To tell them "Supper." At the word, the saw,
As if to prove saws knew what supper meant,   15
Leaped out at the boy's hand, or seemed to leap—
He must have given the hand. However it was,
Neither refused the meeting. But the hand!
The boy's first outcry was a rueful laugh,
As he swung toward them holding up the hand,   20
Half in appeal, but half as if to keep
The life from spilling. Then the boy saw all—
Since he was old enough to know, big boy
Doing a man's work, though a child at heart—
He saw all spoiled. "Don't let him cut my hand off—   25
The doctor, when he comes. Don't let him, sister!"
So. But the hand was gone already.
The doctor put him in the dark of ether.
He lay and puffed his lips out with his breath.
And then—the watcher at his pulse took fright.   30
No one believed. They listened at his heart.
Little—less—nothing!—and that ended it.
No more to build on there. And they, since they
Were not the one dead, turned to their affairs.

[1916]

Putting in the Seed

You come to fetch me from my work tonight
When supper's on the table, and we'll see

If I can leave off burying the white
Soft petals fallen from the apple tree
(Soft petals, yes, but not so barren quite,   5
Mingled with these, smooth bean and wrinkled pea),
And go along with you ere you lose sight
Of what you came for and become like me,
Slave to a springtime passion for the earth.
How Love burns through the Putting in the Seed   10
On through the watching for that early birth
When, just as the soil tarnishes with weed,
The sturdy seedling with arched body comes
Shouldering its way and shedding the earth crumbs.

[1916]

Fire and Ice

Some say the world will end in fire,
Some say in ice.
From what I've tasted of desire
I hold with those who favor fire.
But if it had to perish twice,   5
I think I know enough of hate
To say that for destruction ice
Is also great
And would suffice.

[1923]

For Once, Then, Something

Others taunt me with having knelt at well-curbs
Always wrong to the light, so never seeing
Deeper down in the well than where the water
Gives me back in a shining surface picture
Me myself in the summer heaven godlike   5
Looking out of a wreath of fern and cloud puffs.
Once, when trying with chin against a well-curb,
I discerned, as I thought, beyond the picture,
Through the picture, a something white, uncertain,
Something more of the depths—and then I lost it.   10

Water came to rebuke the too clear water.
One drop fell from a fern, and lo, a ripple
Shook whatever it was lay there at bottom,
Blurred it, blotted it out. What was that whiteness?
Truth? A pebble of quartz? For once, then, something.   15

[1923]

To Earthward

Love at the lips was touch
As sweet as I could bear;
And once that seemed too much;
I lived on air

That crossed me from sweet things,   5
The flow of—was it musk
From hidden grapevine springs
Downhill at dusk?

I had the swirl and ache
From sprays of honeysuckle   10
That when they're gathered shake
Dew on the knuckle.

I craved strong sweets, but those
Seemed strong when I was young;
The petal of the rose   15
It was that stung.

Now no joy but lacks salt,
That is not dashed with pain
And weariness and fault;
I crave the stain   20

Of tears, the aftermark
Of almost too much love,
The sweet of bitter bark
And burning clove.

When stiff and sore and scarred   25
I take away my hand
From leaning on it hard
In grass and sand,

The hurt is not enough:
I long for weight and strength   30
To feel the earth as rough
To all my length.

[1923]

The Need of Being Versed in Country Things

The house had gone to bring again
To the midnight sky a sunset glow.
Now the chimney was all of the house that stood,
Like a pistil after the petals go.

The barn opposed across the way,   5
That would have joined the house in flame
Had it been the will of the wind, was left
To bear forsaken the place's name.

No more it opened with all one end
For teams that came by the stony road   10
To drum on the floor with scurrying hoofs
And brush the mow with the summer load.

The birds that came to it through the air
At broken windows flew out and in,
Their murmur more like the sigh we sigh   15
From too much dwelling on what has been.

Yet for them the lilac renewed its leaf,
And the aged elm, though touched with fire;
And the dry pump flung up an awkward arm;
And the fence post carried a strand of wire.   20

For them there was really nothing sad.
But though they rejoiced in the nest they kept,

One had to be versed in country things
Not to believe the phoebes wept.

[1923]

Two Look at Two

Love and forgetting might have carried them
A little further up the mountainside
With night so near, but not much further up.
They must have halted soon in any case
With thoughts of the path back, how rough it was   5
With rock and washout, and unsafe in darkness;
When they were halted by a tumbled wall
With barbed-wire binding. They stood facing this,
Spending what onward impulse they still had
In one last look the way they must not go,   10
On up the failing path, where, if a stone
On earthside moved at night, it moved itself;
No footstep moved it. "This is all," they sighed,
"Good-night to woods." But not so; there was more.
A doe from round a spruce stood looking at them   15
Across the wall, as near the wall as they.
She saw them in their field, they her in hers.
The difficulty of seeing what stood still,
Like some up-ended boulder split in two,
Was in her clouded eyes: they saw no fear there.   20
She seemed to think that two thus they were safe.
Then, as if they were something that, though strange,
She could not trouble her mind with too long,
She sighed and passed unscared along the wall.
"This, then, is all. What more is there to ask?"   25
But no, not yet. A snort to bid them wait.
A buck from round the spruce stood looking at them
Across the wall, as near the wall as they.
This was an antlered buck of lusty nostril,
Not the same doe come back into her place.   30
He viewed them quizzically with jerks of head,
As if to ask, "Why don't you make some motion?
Or give some sign of life? Because you can't.
I doubt if you're as living as you look."
Thus till he had them almost feeling dared   35

To stretch a proffering hand—and a spell-breaking.
Then he too passed unscared along the wall.
Two had seen two, whichever side you spoke from.
"This *must* be all." It was all. Still they stood,
A great wave from it going over them,   *40*
As if the earth in one unlooked-for favor
Had made them certain earth returned their love.

[1923]

Once by the Pacific

The shattered water made a misty din.
Great waves looked over others coming in,
And thought of doing something to the shore
That water never did to land before.
The clouds were low and hairy in the skies,   *5*
Like locks blown forward in the gleam of eyes.
You could not tell, and yet it looked as if
The shore was lucky in being backed by cliff,
The cliff in being backed by continent;
It looked as if a night of dark intent   *10*
Was coming, and not only a night, an age.
Someone had better be prepared for rage.
There would be more than ocean-water broken
Before God's last *Put out the Light* was spoken.

[1928]

On Looking Up by Chance at the Constellations

You'll wait a long, long time for anything much
To happen in heaven beyond the floats of cloud
And the Northern Lights that run like tingling nerves.
The sun and moon get crossed, but they never touch,
Nor strike out fire from each other, nor crash out loud.   *5*
The planets seem to interfere in their curves,
But nothing ever happens, no harm is done.
We may as well go patiently on with our life,
And look elsewhere than to stars and moon and sun

For the shocks and changes we need to keep us sane.   10
It is true the longest drouth will end in rain,
The longest peace in China will end in strife.
Still it wouldn't reward the watcher to stay awake
In hopes of seeing the calm of heaven break
On his particular time and personal sight.   15
That calm seems certainly safe to last tonight.

[1928]

Acquainted with the Night

I have been one acquainted with the night.
I have walked out in rain—and back in rain.
I have outwalked the furthest city light.

I have looked down the saddest city lane.
I have passed by the watchman on his beat   5
And dropped my eyes, unwilling to explain.

I have stood still and stopped the sound of feet
When far away an interrupted cry
Came over houses from another street,

But not to call me back or say good-by;   10
And further still at an unearthly height
One luminary clock against the sky

Proclaimed the time was neither wrong nor right.
I have been one acquainted with the night.

[1928]

Tree at my window

Tree at my window, window tree,
My sash is lowered when night comes on;

But let there never be curtain drawn
Between you and me.

Vague dream-head lifted out of the ground,   *5*
And thing next most diffuse to cloud,
Not all your light tongues talking aloud
Could be profound.

But, tree, I have seen you taken and tossed,
And if you have seen me when I slept,   *10*
You have seen me when I was taken and swept
And all but lost.

That day she put our heads together,
Fate had her imagination about her,
Your head so much concerned with outer,   *15*
Mine with inner, weather.

                                                        [1928]

Departmental

An ant on the tablecloth
Ran into a dormant moth
Of many times his size.
He showed not the least surprise.
His business wasn't with such.   *5*
He gave it scarcely a touch,
And was off on his duty run.
Yet if he encountered one
Of the hive's enquiry squad
Whose work is to find out God   *10*
And the nature of time and space,
He would put him onto the case.
Ants are a curious race;
One crossing with hurried tread
The body of one of their dead   *15*
Isn't given a moment's arrest—
Seems not even impressed.
But he no doubt reports to any
With whom he crosses antennae,
And they no doubt report   *20*

To the higher up at court.
Then word goes forth in Formic:
"Death's come to Jerry McCormic,
Our selfless forager Jerry.
Will the special Janizary   25
Whose office it is to bury
The dead of the commissary
Go bring him home to his people.
Lay him in state on a sepal.
Wrap him for shroud in a petal.   30
Embalm him with ichor of nettle.
This is the word of your Queen."
And presently on the scene
Appears a solemn mortician:
And taking formal position   35
With feelers calmly atwiddle,
Seizes the dead by the middle,
And heaving him high in the air,
Carries him out of there.
No one stands round to stare.   40
It is nobody else's affair.

It couldn't be called ungentle.
But how thoroughly departmental.

[1936]

Desert Places

Snow falling and night falling fast, oh, fast
In a field I looked into going past,
And the ground almost covered smooth in snow,
But a few weeds and stubble showing last.

The woods around it have it—it is theirs.   5
All animals are smothered in their lairs.
I am too absent-spirited to count;
The loneliness includes me unawares.

And lonely as it is, that loneliness
Will be more lonely ere it will be less—   10

A blanker whiteness of benighted snow
With no expression, nothing to express.

They cannot scare me with their empty spaces
Between stars—on stars where no human race is.
I have it in me so much nearer home   15
To scare myself with my own desert places.

[1936]

Design

I found a dimpled spider, fat and white,
On a white heal-all, holding up a moth
Like a white piece of rigid satin cloth—
Assorted characters of death and blight
Mixed ready to begin the morning right,   5
Like the ingredients of a witches' broth—
A snow-drop spider, a flower like froth,
And dead wings carried like a paper kite.

What had that flower to do with being white,
The wayside blue and innocent heal-all?   10
What brought the kindred spider to that height,
Then steered the white moth thither in the night?
What but design of darkness to appall?—
If design govern in a thing so small.

[1936]

Neither Out Far Nor in Deep

The people along the sand
All turn and look one way.
They turn their back on the land.
They look at the sea all day.

As long as it takes to pass   5
A ship keeps raising its hull;
The wetter ground like glass
Reflects a standing gull.

The land may vary more;
But wherever the truth may be—   *10*
The water comes ashore,
And the people look at the sea.

They cannot look out far.
They cannot look in deep.
But when was that ever a bar   *15*
To any watch they keep?

[1936]

Provide, Provide

The witch that came (the withered hag)
To wash the steps with pail and rag,
Was once the beauty Abishag,

The picture pride of Hollywood.
Too many fall from great and good   *5*
For you to doubt the likelihood.

Die early and avoid the fate.
Or if predestined to die late,
Make up your mind to die in state.

Make the whole stock exchange your own!   *10*
If need be occupy a throne,
Where nobody can call *you* crone.

Some have relied on what they knew;
Others on being simply true.
What worked for them might work for you.   *15*

No memory of having starred
Atones for later disregard
Or keeps the end from being hard.

Better to go down dignified
With boughten friendship at your side   *20*
Than none at all. Provide, provide!

[1936]

The Silken Tent

She is as in a field a silken tent
At midday when a sunny summer breeze
Has dried the dew and all its ropes relent,
So that in guys it gently sways at ease,
And its supporting central cedar pole,   5
That is its pinnacle to heavenward
And signifies the sureness of the soul,
Seems to owe naught to any single cord,
But strictly held by none, is loosely bound
By countless silken ties of love and thought   10
To everything on earth the compass round,
And only by one's going slightly taut
In the capriciousness of summer air
Is of the slightest bondage made aware.

[1942]

The Most of It

He thought he kept the universe alone;
For all the voice in answer he could wake
Was but the mocking echo of his own
From some tree-hidden cliff across the lake.
Some morning from the boulder-broken beach   5
He would cry out on life, that what it wants
Is not its own love back in copy speech,
But counter-love, original response.
And nothing ever came of what he cried
Unless it was the embodiment that crashed   10
In the cliff's talus on the other side,
And then in the far-distant water splashed,
But after a time allowed for it to swim,
Instead of proving human when it neared
And someone else additional to him,   15
As a great buck it powerfully appeared,
Pushing the crumpled water up ahead,
And landed pouring like a waterfall,

And stumbled through the rocks with horny tread,
And forced the underbrush—and that was all.   *20*

[1942]

JOHN MASEFIELD

[1878–1967]

Cargoes

Quinquireme of Nineveh from distant Ophir,
Rowing home to haven in sunny Palestine,
With a cargo of ivory,
And apes and peacocks,
Sandalwood, cedarwood, and sweet white wine.   *5*

Stately Spanish galleon coming from the Isthmus,
Dipping through the Tropics by the palm-green shores,
With a cargo of diamonds,
Emeralds, amethysts,
Topazes, and cinnamon, and gold moidores.   *10*

Dirty British coaster with a salt-caked smoke-stack,
Butting through the Channel in the mad March days,
With a cargo of Tyne coal,
Road-rails, pig-lead,
Firewood, iron-ware, and cheap tin trays.   *15*

[1910]

CARL SANDBURG

[1878–1967]

Chicago

Hog Butcher for the World,
Tool Maker, Stacker of Wheat,
Player with Railroads and the Nation's Freight Handler;

Stormy, husky, brawling,
City of the Big Shoulders: 5

They tell me you are wicked and I believe them, for I have seen your painted women
    under the gas lamps luring the farm boys.
And they tell me you are crooked and I answer: Yes, it is true I have seen the gunman
    kill and go free to kill again.
And they tell me you are brutal and my reply is: On the faces of women and children
    I have seen the marks of wanton hunger.
And having answered so I turn once more to those who sneer at this my city, and
    I give them back the sneer and say to them:
Come and show me another city with lifted head singing so proud to be alive and
    coarse and strong and cunning.   10
Flinging magnetic curses amid the toil of piling job on job, here is a tall bold slugger
    set vivid against the little soft cities;
Fierce as a dog with tongue lapping for action, cunning as a savage pitted against the
    wilderness,
      Bareheaded,
      Shoveling,
      Wrecking,
      Planning,   15
      Building, breaking, rebuilding,
Under the smoke, dust all over his mouth, laughing with white teeth,
Under the terrible burden of destiny laughing as a young man laughs,
Laughing even as an ignorant fighter laughs who has never lost a battle,
Bragging and laughing that under his wrist is the pulse, and under his ribs
    the heart of the people,   20
          Laughing!
Laughing the stormy, husky, brawling laughter of Youth, half-naked, sweating, proud
    to be Hog Butcher, Tool Maker, Stacker of Wheat, Player with Railroads and
    Freight Handler to the Nation.

                                          [1916]

WALLACE STEVENS

[1879–1955]

The poetry of Wallace Stevens is animated by the mind's quest for meaning. As his poem "Of Modern Poetry" suggests, Stevens's work reveals the mind "in the act of finding / What will suffice." Primarily reflective, his poems voice two fundamental questions: (1) What is the relationship between the external world and the human mind, between reality and the imagination? (2) What can human beings substitute for the consolations of traditional religion as a way of giving meaning to their experience? The answer to the first question, briefly put, is that imagination transforms reality; human beings perceive and create the reality they contemplate. Perception, for Stevens, is an imaginative act, not a mere registering or transcribing of what's "out there." The answer to the second question is related to that of the first. For Stevens, the creation of art and the perception of beauty in the natural world order experience and endow it with meaning and value. For Stevens, art in general and poetry in particular thus become necessary fictions. Poetry is a "fiction" because it is an imaginative construct; it is a "necessary" fiction because human beings need order, value, and meaning in their lives, and art provides them best.

These ideas appear in many of Stevens's poems, including "The Idea of Order at Key West" and his deservedly famous "Sunday Morning." In both poems the speaker discovers and creates meaning through the agency of the imagination. Stevens's speakers note the beauty of the natural world, especially its nuances of shape, sound, and color. This is not surprising for a poet who once noted that "the greatest poverty is not to live in a physical world." We can see this tendency in the final stanza of "Sunday Morning," in which we also notice the symbolic reverberations of its closing details:

> Deer walk upon our mountains, and the quail
> Whistle about us their spontaneous cries;
> Sweet berries ripen in the wilderness;
> And, in the isolation of the sky,
> At evening, casual flocks of pigeons make
> Ambiguous undulations as they sink,
> Downward to darkness, on extended wings.

In "The Idea of Order at Key West," Stevens's speaker serves as the model of the artist–poet, the maker who endows the natural world with form and hence with significance. The speaker's singing gives order and meaning to "the dark voice of the sea," to "the outer voice of sky/And cloud," and especially to "The meaningless plungings of water and the wind." For as Stevens notes, the speaker's song is an image of the artist's "Blessed rage for order . . . The maker's rage to order words." As the poem indicates, the artist is

> . . . the single artificer of the world
> In which she sang. And when she sang, the sea,
> Whatever self it had, became the self
> That was her song, for she was the maker
> . . . there never was a world for her
> Except the one she sang and, singing, made.

Stevens's poetry can be compared with that of William Carlos Williams in its attention to pictorial detail. The opening of Stevens's "The Poems of Our Climate" sounds something like Williams, though with more repetition than Williams customarily employed.

The Poems of Our Climate

I

Clear water in a brilliant bowl,
Pink and white carnations. the light
In the room more like a snowy air,
Reflecting snow. A newly-fallen snow
At the end of winter when afternoons return.
Pink and white carnations.

From this descriptive scene painting, however, the rest of Stevens's first stanza moves into his more characteristic meditative mode:

. . . One desires
So much more than that. The day itself
Is simplified: a bowl of white,
Cold, a cold porcelain, low and round,
With nothing more than the carnations there.

Such lines indicate the characteristic restlessness of mind common in Stevens's work, their explanatory touch being alien to Williams. So, too, is the invitation to speculate on the significance of flowers, bowl, and water. In the poem's two remaining stanzas we see Stevens's tendency to accept an imperfect world while reshaping it in the language of art:

II

Say even that this complete simplicity
Stripped one of all one's torments, concealed
The evilly compounded, vital I
And made it fresh in a world of white,
A world of clear water, brilliant edged,
Still one would want more, one would need more,
More than a world of white and snowy scents.

III

There would still remain the never-resting mind,
So that one would want to escape, come back
To what had been so long composed.
The imperfect is our paradise.
Note that, in this bitterness, delight,
Since the imperfect is so hot in us,
Lies in flawed words and stubborn sounds.

[1942]

Throughout "The Poems of Our Climate," Stevens explores the relationship between the external world and the human mind, especially as the poet's artistic intelligence finds meaning and solace in the eternity of art.

Like Stevens's poems, his life was contemplative, meditative, quiet. Relatively uneventful, both his life and his poems lack the external drama and emotional intensity of the lives and work of Frost, Whitman, or Pound. Born in Reading, Pennsylvania, in 1879, Stevens studied at Harvard (without obtaining a degree), graduated from the New York University School of Law, and practiced law privately before joining the Hartford Accident and Indemnity Company, where he later became a vice president. In college Stevens wrote poetry and served as president of the literary magazine and the literary society. During his years of practicing law and working as an insurance company executive, Stevens wrote many poems. Although his first volume, *Harmonium,* was not published until 1923, he had been publishing poems in literary magazines for ten years. His *Collected Poems,* published in 1955, the year of his death, won both the Pulitzer Prize and the National Book Award.

Perhaps the most difficult thing about Stevens's poetry is its privacy. In reading Stevens we are invited to share the perceptions and reflections of a finely nuanced imagination. We are shown the poet's imaginative life, and we observe him creating meanings out of the recalcitrant details of external reality. We are, however, only witnesses to Stevens's meaning making, not participants in it. His finely modulated discriminations of thought and feeling may prevent us from sharing broadly in his experience. But if we familiarize ourselves with Stevens's characteristic manner and central concerns, we can share his delicate perceptions.

Another aspect of Stevens's poetry that requires some attention is his wide-ranging vocabulary. By turns familiar and exotic, Stevens's diction is continuously surprising, whether in the nonsense words that appear in much of his early works or the eloquent sound play he often indulges in. For an initial sampling of Stevens's diction, look at "Bantams in Pine-Woods" and "Peter Quince at the Clavier." In these poems, as in some others, Stevens is something of a showman; he seems to enjoy displaying his linguistic virtuosity. And he revels in the sounds of his poems.

A final consideration in reading Stevens is to be aware that his poems center around a single idea or feeling that is frequently illustrated in multiple ways. Stevens's characteristic form is a theme and variations or a theme and accompanying set of meditative qualifications. A delightful example is "Thirteen Ways of Looking at a Blackbird," in which we are presented with multiple images of a single subject. More important than the blackbird in and of itself is what the poet makes of it. Stevens's imaginative transformations of the blackbird and the ways we perceive it are central to the poem's action and meaning. "Blackbird" also illustrates Stevens's penchant for innuendo, suggestion, and implication; the various images of the blackbird occasionally hint at their varied implications, but the thirteen images remain unexplained. The poem illustrates Stevens's belief in the power of the imagination to create meaning and to delight in that creation.

Although Stevens's poems lack the more democratic virtues of such other modern American poets as Whitman, Williams, and Frost, his poetry emerges just as powerfully from the same Emersonian tradition. Like his Romantic forebears

Wordsworth and Keats in England and Whitman and Emerson in America, Stevens wrestles with questions about the individual's relationship to external reality. And like the responses of his modern poetic counterparts, especially Robert Frost, Stevens's answers diverge from those of his Romanticist predecessors. Among modern American poets, his imaginative force and sheer rhetorical brilliance are unequaled. Perhaps more than any other American poet, he reveals and explores how poetry can be a speculative instrument that transforms reality, orders the world, and composes the self.

Peter Quince at the Clavier

I

Just as my fingers on these keys
Make music, so the self same sounds
On my spirit make a music, too.

Music is feeling, then, not sound;
And thus it is that what I feel,   5
Here in this room, desiring you,

Thinking of your blue-shadowed silk,
Is music. It is like the strain
Waked in the elders by Susanna.

Of a green evening, clear and warm,   10
She bathed in her still garden, while
The red-eyed elders watching, felt

The basses of their beings throb
In witching chords, and their thin blood
Pulse pizzicati of Hosanna.   15

II

In the green water, clear and warm,
Susanna lay.
She searched
The touch of springs,
And found   20
Concealed imaginings.
She sighed,
For so much melody.

Upon the bank, she stood
In the cool   25
Of spent emotions.
She felt, among the leaves,
The dew
Of old devotions.

She walked upon the grass,   30
Still quavering.
The winds were like her maids,
On timid feet,
Fetching her woven scarves,
Yet wavering.   35

A breath upon her hand
Muted the night.
She turned—
A cymbal crashed,
And roaring horns.   40

III

Soon, with a noise like tambourines
Came her attendant Byzantines

They wondered why Susanna cried
Against the elders by her side;

And as they whispered, the refrain   45
Was like a willow swept by rain.

Anon, their lamps' uplifted flame
Revealed Susanna and her shame.

And then, the simpering Byzantines
Fled, with a noise like tambourines,   50

IV

Beauty is momentary in the mind—
The fitful tracing of a portal;
But in the flesh it is immortal.

The body dies; the body's beauty lives.
So evenings die, in their green going,   55
A wave, interminably flowing.

So gardens die, their meek breath scenting
The cowl of winter, done repenting.
So maidens die, to the auroral
Celebration of a maiden's choral.   *60*

Susanna's music touched the bawdy strings
Of those white elders; but, escaping,
Left only Death's ironic scraping.
Now, in its immortality, it plays
On the clear viol of her memory,   *65*
And makes a constant sacrament of praise.

     [1923]

Sunday Morning

I

Complacencies of the peignoir and late
Coffee and oranges in a sunny chair,
And the green freedom of a cockatoo
Upon a rug mingle to dissipate
The holy hush of ancient sacrifice.   *5*
She dreams a little, and she feels the dark
Encroachment of that old catastrophe,
As a calm darkens among water-lights.
The pungent oranges and bright, green wings
Seem things in some procession of the dead,   *10*
Winding across wide water, without sound.
The day is like wide water, without sound,
Stilled for the passing of her dreaming feet
Over the seas, to silent Palestine,
Dominion of the blood and sepulchre.   *15*

II

Why should she give her bounty to the dead?
What is divinity if it can come
Only in silent shadows and in dreams?
Shall she not find in comforts of the sun,
In pungent fruit and bright, green wings, or else   *20*
In any balm or beauty of the earth,
Things to be cherished like the thought of heaven?
Divinity must live within herself:

Passions of rain, or moods in falling snow;
Grievings in loneliness, or unsubdued   25
Elations when the forest blooms; gusty
Emotions on wet roads on autumn nights;
All pleasures and all pains, remembering
The bough of summer and the winter branch.
These are the measures destined for her soul.   30

III

Jove in the clouds had his inhuman birth.
No mother suckled him, no sweet land gave
Large-mannered motions to his mythy mind
He moved among us, as a muttering king,
Magnificent, would move among his hinds,   35
Until our blood, commingling, virginal,
With heaven, brought such requital to desire
The very hind discerned it, in a star.
Shall our blood fail? Or shall it come to be
The blood of paradise? And shall the earth   40
Seem all of paradise that we shall know?
The sky will be much friendlier then than now,
A part of labor and a part of pain,
And next in glory to enduring love,
Not this dividing and indifferent blue.   45

IV

She says, "I am content when wakened birds,
Before they fly, test the reality
Of misty fields, by their sweet questionings;
But when the birds are gone, and their warm fields
Return no more, where, then, is paradise?"   50
There is not any haunt of prophecy,
Nor any old chimera of the grave,
Neither the golden underground, nor isle
Melodious, where spirits gat them home,
Nor visionary south, nor cloudy palm   55
Remote on heaven's hill, that has endured
As April's green endures; or will endure
Like her remembrance of awakened birds,
Or her desire for June and evening, tipped
By the consummation of the swallow's wings.   60

---

[31]**Jove** Roman name of Zeus, chief god of the pantheon.   [52]**chimera** in Greek mythology, a monster with a lion's head; more generally a fanciful image.

V

She says, "But in contentment I still feel
The need of some imperishable bliss."
Death is the mother of beauty; hence from her,
Alone, shall come fulfilment to our dreams
And our desires. Although she strews the leaves   65
Of sure obliteration on our paths,
The path sick sorrow took, the many paths
Where triumph rang its brassy phrase, or love
Whispered a little out of tenderness,
She makes the willow shiver in the sun   70
For maidens who were wont to sit and gaze
Upon the grass, relinquished to their feet.
She causes boys to pile new plums and pears
On disregarded plate. The maidens taste
And stray impassioned in the littering leaves.   75

VI

Is there no change of death in paradise?
Does ripe fruit never fall? Or do the boughs
Hang always heavy in that perfect sky,
Unchanging, yet so like our perishing earth,
With rivers like our own that seek for seas   80
They never find, the same receding shores
That never touch with inarticulate pang?
Why set the pear upon those river-banks
Or spice the shores with odors of the plum?
Alas, that they should wear our colors there,   85
The silken weavings of our afternoons,
And pick the strings of our insipid lutes!
Death is the mother of beauty, mystical,
Within whose burning bosom we devise
Our earthly mothers waiting, sleeplessly.   90

VII

Supple and turbulent, a ring of men
Shall chant in orgy on a summer morn
Their boisterous devotion to the sun,
Not as a god, but as a god might be,
Naked among them, like a savage source.   95
Their chant shall be a chant of paradise,
Out of their blood, returning to the sky;
And in their chant shall enter, voice by voice,

The windy lake wherein their lord delights,
The trees, like serafin, and echoing hills,   *100*
That choir among themselves long afterward.
They shall know well the heavenly fellowship
Of men that perish and of summer morn.
And whence they came and whither they shall go
The dew upon their feet shall manifest.   *105*

VIII

She hears, upon that water without sound,
A voice that cries, "The tomb in Palestine
Is not the porch of spirits lingering.
It is the grave of Jesus, where he lay."
We live in an old chaos of the sun,   *110*
Or old dependency of day and night,
Or island solitude, unsponsored, free,
Of that wide water, inescapable.
Deer walk upon our mountains, and the quail
Whistle about us their spontaneous cries;   *115*
Sweet berries ripen in the wilderness;
And, in the isolation of the sky,
At evening, casual flocks of pigeons make
Ambiguous undulations as they sink,
Downward to darkness, on extended wings.   *120*

[1923]

The Snow Man

One must have a mind of winter
To regard the frost and the boughs
Of the pine-trees crusted with snow;

And have been cold a long time
To behold the junipers shagged with ice,   *5*
The spruces rough in the distant glitter

Of the January sun; and not to think
Of any misery in the sound of the wind,
In the sound of a few leaves,

SUNDAY MORNING   ¹⁰⁰**serafin**   seraphim, an order of high-ranking angels close to God.

Which is the sound of the land   *10*
Full of the same wind
That is blowing in the same bare place

For the listener, who listens in the snow,
And, nothing himself, beholds
Nothing that is not there and the nothing that is.   *15*

[1923]

Anecdote of the Jar

I placed a jar in Tennessee,
And round it was, upon a hill.
It made the slovenly wilderness
Surround that hill.

The wilderness rose up to it,   *5*
And sprawled around, no longer wild.
The jar was round upon the ground
And tall and of a port in air.

It took dominion everywhere.
The jar was gray and bare.   *10*
It did not give of bird or bush,
Like nothing else in Tennessee.

[1923]

Thirteen Ways of Looking at a Blackbird

1

Among twenty snowy mountains,
The only moving thing
Was the eye of the blackbird.

2

I was of three minds,
Like a tree   *5*
In which there are three blackbirds.

3

The blackbird whirled in the autumn winds.
It was a small part of the pantomime.

4

A man and a woman
Are one.   10
A man and a woman and a blackbird
Are one.

5

I do not know which to prefer,
The beauty of inflections
Or the beauty of innuendoes,   15
The blackbird whistling
Or just after.

6

Icicles filled the long window
With barbaric glass.
The shadow of the blackbird   20
Crossed it to and fro.
The mood
Traced in the shadow
An indecipherable cause.

7

O thin men of Haddam,   25
Why do you imagine golden birds?
Do you not see how the blackbird
Walks around the feet
Of the women about you?

8

I know noble accents   30
And lucid, inescapable rhythms;
But I know, too,
That the blackbird is involved
In what I know.

9

When the blackbird flew out of sight,   35
It marked the edge
Of one of many circles.

10

At the sight of blackbirds
Flying in a green light,
Even the bawds of euphony   40
Would cry out sharply.

11

He rode over Connecticut
In a glass coach.
Once, a fear pierced him,
In that he mistook   45
The shadow of his equipage
For blackbirds.

12

The river is moving.
The blackbird must be flying.

13

It was evening all afternoon.   50
It was snowing
And it was going to snow.
The blackbird sat
In the cedar-limbs.

[1923]

Bantams in Pine-Woods

Chieftain Iffucan of Azcan in caftan
Of tan with henna hackles, halt!

Damned universal cock, as if the sun
Was blackamoor to bear your blazing tail.

Fat! Fat! Fat! Fat! I am the personal.   5
Your world is you. I am my world.

You ten-foot poet among inchlings. Fat!
Begone! An inchling bristles in these pines,

Bristles, and points their Appalachian tangs,
And fears not portly Azcan nor his hoos.   *10*

[1923]

The Idea of Order at Key West

She sang beyond the genius of the sea.
The water never formed to mind or voice,
Like a body wholly body, fluttering
Its empty sleeves; and yet its mimic motion
Made constant cry, caused constantly a cry,   *5*
That was not ours although we understood,
Inhuman, of the veritable ocean.

The sea was not a mask. No more was she.
The song and water were not medleyed sound
Even if what she sang was what she heard,   *10*
Since what she sang was uttered word by word.
It may be that in all her phrases stirred
The grinding water and the gasping wind;
But it was she and not the sea we heard.

For she was the maker of the song she sang.   *15*
The ever-hooded, tragic-gestured sea
Was merely a place by which she walked to sing.
Whose spirit is this? we said, because we knew
It was the spirit that we sought and knew
That we should ask this often as she sang.   *20*

If it was only the dark voice of the sea
That rose, or even colored by many waves;
If it was only the outer voice of sky
And cloud, of the sunken coral water-walled,
However clear, it would have been deep air,   *25*
The heaving speech of air, a summer sound
Repeated in a summer without end
And sound alone. But it was more than that,
More even than her voice, and ours, among

The meaningless plungings of water and the wind,   *30*
Theatrical distances, bronze shadows heaped
On high horizons, mountainous atmospheres
Of sky and sea.
              It was her voice that made
The sky acutest at its vanishing.   *35*
She measured to the hour its solitude.
She was the single artificer of the world
In which she sang. And when she sang, the sea,
Whatever self it had, became the self
That was her song, for she was the maker. Then we,   *40*
As we beheld her striding there alone,
Knew that there never was a world for her
Except the one she sang and, singing, made.

Ramon Fernandez tell me, if you know,
Why, when the singing ended and we turned   *45*
Toward the town, tell why the glassy lights,
The lights in the fishing boats at anchor there,
As the night descended, tilting in the air,
Mastered the night and portioned out the sea,
Fixing emblazoned zones and fiery poles,   *50*
Arranging, deepening, enchanting night.

Oh! Blessed rage for order, pale Ramon,
The maker's rage to order words of the sea,
Words of the fragrant portals, dimly-starred,
And of ourselves and of our origins,   *55*
In ghostlier demarcations, keener sounds.

                           [1936]

from *The Man with the Blue Guitar*

I

The man bent over his guitar,
A shearsman of sorts. The day was green.

They said, "You have a blue guitar,
You do not play things as they are."

The man replied, "Things as they are   *5*
Are changed upon the blue guitar."

And they said then, "But play, you must,
A tune beyond us, yet ourselves,

A tune upon the blue guitar
Of things exactly as they are."   *10*

II

I cannot bring a world quite round,
Although I patch it as I can.

I sing a hero's head, large eye
And bearded bronze, but not a man,

Although I patch him as I can   *15*
And reach through him almost to man.

If to serenade almost to man
Is to miss, by that, things as they are,

Say that it is the serenade
Of a man that plays a blue guitar.   *20*

III

Ah, but to play man number one,
To drive the dagger in his heart,

To lay his brain upon the board
And pick the acrid colors out,

To nail his thought across the door,   *25*
Its wings spread wide to rain and snow,

To strike his living hi and ho,
To tick it, tock it, turn it true,

To bang it from a savage blue,
Jangling the metal of the strings . . .   *30*

IV

So that's life, then: things as they are?
It picks its way on the blue guitar.

A million people on one string?
And all their manner in the thing,

And all their manner, right and wrong,   35
And all their manner, weak and strong?

The feelings crazily, craftily call,
Like a buzzing of flies in autumn air,

And that's life, then: things as they are,
This buzzing of the blue guitar.   40

V

Do not speak to us of the greatness of poetry,
Of the torches wisping in the underground,

Of the structure of vaults upon a point of light.
There are no shadows in our sun,

Day is desire and night is sleep.   45
There are no shadows anywhere.

The earth, for us, is flat and bare.
There are no shadows. Poetry

Exceeding music must take the place
Of empty heaven and its hymns,   50

Ourselves in poetry must take their place,
Even in the chattering of your guitar.

VI

A tune beyond us as we are,
Yet nothing changed by the blue guitar;

Ourselves in the tune as if in space,   55
Yet nothing changed, except the place

Of things as they are and only the place
As you play them, on the blue guitar,

Placed, so, beyond the compass of change,
Perceived in a final atmosphere;   60

For a moment final, in the way
The thinking of art seems final when

The thinking of god is smoky dew.
The tune is space. The blue guitar

Becomes the place of things as they are,   65
A composing of senses of the guitar.

[1937]

Of Modern Poetry

The poem of the mind in the act of finding
What will suffice. It has not always had
To find: the scene was set; it repeated what
Was in the script.
               Then the theatre was changed   5
To something else. Its past was a souvenir.
It has to be living, to learn the speech of the place.
It has to face the men of the time and to meet
The women of the time. It has to think about war
And it has to find what will suffice. It has   10
To construct a new stage. It has to be on that stage
And, like an insatiable actor, slowly and
With meditation, speak words that in the ear,
In the delicatest ear of the mind, repeat,
Exactly, that which it wants to hear, at the sound   15
Of which, an invisible audience listens,
Not to the play, but to itself, expressed
In an emotion as of two people, as of two
Emotions becoming one. The actor is
A metaphysician in the dark, twanging   20
An instrument, twanging a wiry string that gives
Sounds passing through sudden rightnesses, wholly
Containing the mind, below which it cannot descend,
Beyond which it has no will to rise.
                   It must   25
Be the finding of a satisfaction, and may
Be of a man skating, a woman dancing, a woman
Combing. The poem of the act of the mind.

[1942]

The house was quiet and the world was calm

The house was quiet and the world was calm.
The reader became the book; and summer night

Was like the conscious being of the book.
The house was quiet and the world was calm.

The words were spoken as if there was no book,   *5*
Except that the reader leaned above the page,

Wanted to lean, wanted much most to be
The scholar to whom his book is true, to whom

The summer night is like a perfection of thought.
The house was quiet because it had to be.   *10*

The quiet was part of the meaning, part of the mind:
The access of perfection to the page.

And the world was calm. The truth in a calm world,
In which there is no other meaning, itself

Is calm, itself is summer and night, itself   *15*
Is the reader leaning late and reading there.

[1947]

WILLIAM CARLOS WILLIAMS

[1883–1963]

Although William Carlos Williams pursued a full-time career as a physician (he was a general practitioner with a specialty in pediatrics), he was equally devoted to literature. Born in Rutherford, New Jersey, in 1883, Williams attended preparatory schools in New York and Switzerland before studying medicine at the University of Pennsylvania, where he met Ezra Pound, who encouraged him to continue writing. Although Williams took Pound's advice and began publishing his poetry, he did not abandon his medical education. He interned in a New York City hospital, did his pediatric training in Leipzig, Germany, then returned to New Jersey to start his own medical practice. He worked there as both a poet and a doctor until his death in 1963.

Like his major contemporaries, Williams received a number of awards for his work, including a National Book Award (1950), a Bollingen Prize (1953), and a Pulitzer Prize (1962). His poetry is infused with the qualities that characterized him as a man: warmth, kindness, gaiety, candor, and a healthy affirmation of life. His poems are noteworthy for their openness of form, imagistic concreteness, and a lack of discursive explanation. They exhibit qualities, moreover, that put them at odds with the poems of his most famous contemporary, T. S. Eliot. Although Williams sought to write innovative poems to make American poetry new, Williams's way was not Eliot's way. Where Eliot had raided history for allusion and illustration, and where he had used a variety of foreign languages in his poems, Williams avoided allusion and eschewed foreign linguistic borrowings. In fact, in his *Autobiography* Williams wrote that Eliot's highly allusive and erudite poems "returned us to the classroom at a time when American poetry was developing a different aesthetic rooted in the local, the present, and the familiar."

Like the poetry of his most illustrious American poetic forebear, Walt Whitman, Williams's poetry celebrates the common and the ordinary. According to Williams, any object or subject can be regarded poetically. Nothing is too odd or trivial not to be granted the appreciative and illuminating gaze of the poet. A woman standing on a street corner munching plums, a cat tipping over a flowerpot, a red wheelbarrow besides some white chickens—Williams made these and other seemingly inconsequential actions and objects fitting subjects for poems.

More important than the ordinariness of his subjects, however, is the way Williams defamiliarizes and reenvisions them. His poems invite observation, not abstract thinking. Williams is remembered for a credo that came to be associated with the poetic movement of Imagism, which favored concrete detail over discursive explanation. "No ideas but in things," he once wrote. Williams valued an idea as much as Eliot, Frost, or Stevens did. His motto, however, summarizes an aesthetic that does not so much rule out thought as insist that it be embodied in images. By omitting discursive explanation, Williams wrote poems that do not insist on a "meaning." Instead, his poems shape and organize language aesthetically. Such poems present imagistic pictures; more important, they also become objects made of words, aesthetic forms to be contemplated. One example is the following brief poem:

The Red Wheelbarrow

so much depends
upon

a red wheel
barrow

glazed with rain   5
water

beside the white
chickens.

To focus on the poem's paraphrasable meaning is to severely limit our enjoyment of it. We could ask, of course, just what does depend upon the red wheelbarrow. Although our answers will assuredly vary, to stop with that question is to avoid looking *at* the poem in an attempt to look *through* it.

Looking at Williams's "The Red Wheelbarrow" we see a miniature painting in the primary colors of red and white. Like its colors, its objects are basic, common, familiar. In inspecting the poem this way, we view it as a representation of something. But even this painterly way of seeing the work ignores the fact that it is "a machine made out of words," which is one way Williams once defined a poem. Perhaps we can see just what kind of machine Williams has made by altering it as follows: "So much depends upon a red wheelbarrow glazed with rainwater beside the white chickens."

Without considering the meaning of the statement, we can clearly see that this altered version lacks the formal qualities of Williams's poem. This alternative version does not invite consideration as a poem because its words are not arranged to form a poetic image. By arranging the words as he does, however, Williams challenges us to treat this text *as* a poem, to read it the way we read other, more traditional poems. In doing so, we notice a series of patterns: four two-line stanzas; a single two-syllable word as the second line of each stanza; a highly regularized syllable count in the lines of the poem—4/2, 3/2, 3/2, 4/2. We also see that each of the short lines contains one accented syllable and each of the long ones, two. In addition to this metrical regularity, we hear the poem's sound play in line 5—"gl*a*zed with r*ai*n"—and in line 7: "bes*i*de the wh*i*te."

Williams calls our attention to a familiar subject by organizing language and shaping it aesthetically. As a result, we look more closely at the objects depicted in the poem and at the poem itself as an aesthetic object. Beyond this, Williams invites us to listen to his language as well. Perhaps the most remarkable thing about this work is the way Williams splits the two compound words: wheel/barrow and rain/water; he not only splits them into their constituent parts, he does so by breaking them across the poetic line. In doing this, he makes the words new and thereby makes a poem that sees commonplace words in a fresh way.

The simplicity of Williams's verse forms, the matter-of-factness of his subjects, and the ordinariness of much of his language should not blind us to his poetic resourcefulness. His most successful poems, whether "seeing" poems like "Queen Anne's Lace" or "talking" poems like "Danse Russe," possess the power to surprise, to reveal things we hadn't seen quite that way before. Like Wallace Stevens, Williams had great respect for the power of the imagination. And like English Romantic writers such as William Wordsworth and Samuel Taylor Coleridge, for whom the imagination was a primary epistemological instrument, Williams never tired of celebrating its importance.

Williams reveals an intensely imaginative vision in his most memorable poems: the poetic suite *Pictures from Breughel,* inspired by Pieter Breughel the Elder, his complex epic poem *Paterson,* and his shorter lyrics. This vision also appears in prose works such as *In the Money* and *In the American Grain,* in which Williams scathingly criticizes habitual failures of the American imagination, especially its brutishness, violence, and Puritanical suspicion of pleasure.

Like Whitman before him, Williams performs, through his poetry, acts of reconciliation. He wanted, as he put it in "A Sort of a Song,"

—through metaphor to reconcile
the people and the stones.

Danse Russe

If when my wife is sleeping
and the baby and Kathleen
are sleeping
and the sun is a flame-white disc
in silken mists   5
above shining trees,—
if I in my north room
dance naked, grotesquely
before my mirror
waving my shirt round my head   10
and singing softly to myself:
"I am lonely, lonely.
I was born to be lonely,
I am best so!"
If I admire my arms, my face,   15
my shoulders, flanks, buttocks
against the yellow drawn shades,—

Who shall say I am not
the happy genius of my household?

                                                          [1917]

January Morning

SUITE:

I

I have discovered that most of
the beauties of travel are due to
the strange hours we keep to see them:

the domes of the Church of
the Paulist Fathers in Weehawken   5
against a smoky dawn—the heart stirred—
are beautiful as Saint Peters
approached after years of anticipation.

II

Though the operation was postponed
I saw the tall probationers   10
in their tan uniforms
                     hurrying to breakfast!

III

—and from basement entries
neatly coiffed, middle aged gentlemen
with orderly moustaches and   15
well-brushed coats

IV

—and the sun, dipping into the avenues
streaking the tops of
the irregular red houselets,
                   and   20
the gay shadows dropping and dropping.

V

—and a young horse with a green bed-quilt
on his withers shaking his head:
bared teeth and nozzle high in the air!

VI

—and a semicircle of dirt-colored men   25
about a fire bursting from an old
ash can,

VII

        —and the worn,
blue car rails (like the sky!)
gleaming among the cobbles!   30

VIII

—and the rickety ferry-boat "Arden"!
What an object to be called "Arden"

among the great piers,—on the
ever new river!
                    "Put me a Touchstone   35
at the wheel, white gulls, and we'll
follow the ghost of the *Half Moon*
to the North West Passage—and through!
(at Albany!) for all that!"

IX

Exquisite brown waves—long   40
circlets of silver moving over you!
enough with crumbling ice crusts among you!
The sky has come down to you,
lighter than tiny bubbles, face to
face with you!   45
                    His spirit is
a white gull with delicate pink feet
and a snowy breast for you to
hold to your lips delicately!

X

The young doctor is dancing with happiness   50
in the sparkling wind, alone
at the prow of the ferry! He notices
the curdy barnacles and broken ice crusts
left at the slip's base by the low tide
and thinks of summer and green   55
shell-crusted ledges among
                    the emerald eel-grass!

XI

Who knows the Palisades as I do
knows the river breaks east from them
above the city—but they continue south   60
—under the sky—to bear a crest of
little peering houses that brighten
with dawn behind the moody
water-loving giants of Manhattan.

XII

Long yellow rushes bending   65
above the white snow patches;
purple and gold ribbon

of the distant wood:
             what an angle
you make with each other as   *70*
you lie there in contemplation.

XIII

Work hard all your young days
and they'll find you too, some morning
staring up under
your chiffonier at its warped   *75*
bass-wood bottom and your soul—
out!
—among the little sparrows
behind the shutter.

XIV

—and the flapping flags are at   *80*
half mast for the dead admiral.

XV

All this—
             was for you, old woman.
I wanted to write a poem
that you would understand.   *85*
For what good is it to me
if you can't understand it?
             But you got to try hard—
But—
    Well, you know how   *90*
the young girls run giggling
on Park Avenue after dark
when they ought to be home in bed?
Well,
that's the way it is with me somehow.   *95*

                                               [1917]

The Last Words of My English Grandmother

There were some dirty plates
and a glass of milk
beside her on a small table
near the rank, disheveled bed—

Wrinkled and nearly blind   5
she lay and snored
rousing with anger in her tones
to cry for food,

Gimme something to eat—
They're starving me—   10
I'm all right I won't go
to the hospital. No, no, no

Give me something to eat
Let me take you
to the hospital, I said   15
and after you are well

you can do as you please.
She smiled, Yes
you do what you please first
then I can do what I please—   20

Oh, oh, oh! she cried
as the ambulance men lifted
her to the stretcher—
Is this what you call

making me comfortable?   25
By now her mind was clear—
Oh you think you're smart
you young people,

she said, but I'll tell you
you don't know anything.   30
Then we started.
On the way

we passed a long row
of elms. She looked at them
awhile out of   35
the ambulance window and said,

What are all those
fuzzy-looking things out there?
Trees? Well, I'm tired
of them and rolled her head away.   40

[1920]

Queen Anne's Lace

Her body is not so white as
anemone petals nor so smooth—nor
so remote a thing. It is a field
of the wild carrot taking
the field by force; the grass   5
does not raise above it.
Here is no question of whiteness,
white as can be, with a purple mole
at the center of each flower.
Each flower is a hand's span   10
of her whiteness. Wherever
his hand has lain there is
a tiny purple blemish. Each part
is a blossom under his touch
to which the fibres of her being   15
stem one by one, each to its end,
until the whole field is a
white desire, empty, a single stem,
a cluster, flower by flower,
a pious wish to whiteness gone over—   20
or nothing.

[1921]

To Elsie

The pure products of America
go crazy—
mountain folk from Kentucky

or the ribbed north end of
Jersey   5
with its isolate lakes and

valleys, its deaf-mutes, thieves
old names
and promiscuity between

devil-may-care men who have taken   10
to railroading
out of sheer lust of adventure—

and young slatterns, bathed
in filth
from Monday to Saturday   15

to be tricked out that night
with gauds
from imaginations which have no

peasant traditions to give them
character   20
but flutter and flaunt

sheer rags—succumbing without
emotion
save numbed terror

under some hedge of choke-cherry   25
or viburnum—
which they cannot express—

Unless it be that marriage
perhaps
with a dash of Indian blood   30

will throw up a girl so desolate
so hemmed round
with disease or murder

that she'll be rescued by an
agent—   35
reared by the state and

sent out at fifteen to work in
some hard-pressed
house in the suburbs—

some doctor's family, some Elsie—   40
voluptuous water
expressing with broken

brain the truth about us—
her great
ungainly hips and flopping breasts   45

addressed to cheap
jewelry
and rich young men with fine eyes

as if the earth under our feet
were   50
an excrement of some sky

and we degraded prisoners
destined
to hunger until we eat filth

while the imagination strains   55
after deer
going by fields of goldenrod in

the stifling heat of September
Somehow
it seems to destroy us   60

It is only in isolate flecks that
something
is given off

No one
to witness   65
and adjust, no one to drive the car

[1923]

Spring and All

By the road to the contagious hospital
under the surge of the blue
mottled clouds driven from the
northeast—a cold wind. Beyond, the
waste of broad, muddy fields   5
brown with dried weeds, standing and fallen

patches of standing water
the scattering of tall trees

All along the road the reddish
purplish, forked, upstanding, twiggy   10
stuff of bushes and small trees
with dead, brown leaves under them
leafless vines—

Lifeless in appearance, sluggish
dazed spring approaches—   15

They enter the new world naked,
cold, uncertain of all
save that they enter. All about them
the cold, familiar wind—

Now the grass, tomorrow   20
the stiff curl of wildcarrot leaf
One by one objects are defined—
It quickens: clarity, outline of leaf

But now the stark dignity of
entrance—Still, the profound change   25
has come upon them: rooted, they
grip down and begin to awaken

                                                        [1923]

At the Ball Game

The crowd at the ball game
is moved uniformly

by a spirit of uselessness
which delights them—

all the exciting detail   5
of the chase

and the escape, the error
the flash of genius—

all to no end save beauty
the eternal—   10

So in detail they, the crowd,
are beautiful
for this
to be warned against

saluted and defied—   15
It is alive, venomous

it smiles grimly
its words cut—

The flashy female with her
mother, gets it—   20

The Jew gets it straight—it
is deadly, terrifying—

It is the Inquisition, the
Revolution

It is beauty itself   25
that lives

day by day in them
idly—

This is
the power of their faces   30

It is summer, it is the solstice
the crowd is

cheering, the crowd is laughing
in detail

permanently, seriously   35
without thought

[1923]

This Is Just to Say

I have eaten
the plums
that were in
the icebox

and which
you were probably   5
saving
for breakfast

Forgive me
they were delicious
so sweet
and so cold   10

[1934]

To a Poor Old Woman

munching a plum on
the street a paper bag
of them in her hand

They taste good to her
They taste good   5
to her. They taste
good to her

You can see it by
the way she gives herself
to the one half   10
sucked out in her hand

Comforted
a solace of ripe plums
seeming to fill the air
They taste good to her   15

[1934]

Nantucket

Flowers through the window
lavender and yellow

changed by white curtains—
Smell of cleanliness—

Sunshine of late afternoon—   5
On the glass tray

a glass pitcher, the tumbler
turned down, by which

a key is lying—And the
immaculate white bed   10

[1934]

The Young Housewife

At ten A.M. the young housewife
moves about in negligee behind
the wooden walls of her husband's house.
I pass solitary in my car.

Then again she comes to the curb   5
to call the ice-man, fish-man, and stands
shy, uncorseted, tucking in
stray ends of hair, and I compare her
to a fallen leaf.

The noiseless wheels of my car   10
rush with a crackling sound over
dried leaves as I bow and pass smiling.

[1938]

The Dance

In Breughel's great picture, The Kermess,
the dancers go round, they go round and

around, the squeal and the blare and the
tweedle of bagpipes, a bugle and fiddles
tipping their bellies (round as the thick-   5
sided glasses whose wash they impound)
their hips and their bellies off balance
to turn them. Kicking and rolling about
the Fair Grounds, swinging their butts, those
shanks must be sound to bear up under such   10
rollicking measures, prance as they dance
in Breughel's great picture, The Kermess.

[1944]

A Sort of a Song

Let the snake wait under
his weed
and the writing
be of words, slow and quick, sharp
to strike, quiet to wait,   5
sleepless.
—through metaphor to reconcile
the people and the stones.
Compose. (No ideas
but in things) Invent!   10
Saxifrage is my flower that splits
the rocks.

[1944]

The Sparrow

(TO MY FATHER)

This sparrow
            who comes to sit at my window
                    is a poetic truth
more than a natural one.
            His voice,   5
                    his movements.

his habits—
      how he loves to
            flutter his wings
in the dust—   *10*
      all attest it;
            granted, he does it
to rid himself of lice
      but the relief he feels
            makes him   *15*
cry out lustily—
      which is a trait
            more related to music
than otherwise.
      Wherever he finds himself   *20*
            in early spring,
on back streets
      or beside palaces,
            he carries on
unaffectedly   *25*
      his amours.
            It begins in the egg,
his sex genders it:
      What is more pretentiously
            useless   *30*
or about which   ·
      we more pride ourselves?
            It leads as often as not
to our undoing.
      The cockerel, the crow   *35*
            with their challenging voices
cannot surpass
      the insistence
            of his cheep!
Once   *40*
      at El Paso
            toward evening,
I saw—and heard!—
      ten thousand sparrows
            who had come in from   *45*
the desert
      to roost. They filled the trees
            of a small park. Men fled
(with ears ringing!)
      from their droppings,   *50*
            leaving the premises

to the alligators
     who inhabit
          the fountain. His image
is familiar   55
     as that of the aristocratic
          unicorn, a pity
there are not more oats eaten
     nowadays
          to make living easier   60
for him.
     At that,
          his small size,
keen eyes,
     serviceable beak   65
          and general truculence
assure his survival—
     to say nothing
          of his innumerable
brood.   70
     Even the Japanese
          know him
and have painted him
     sympathetically,
          with profound insight   75
into his minor
     characteristics.
          Nothing even remotely
subtle
     about his lovemaking.   80
          He crouches
before the female,
     drags his wings,
          waltzing,
throws back his head   85
     and simply—
          yells! The din
is terrific.
     The way he swipes his bill
          across a plank   90
to clean it,
     is decisive.
          So with everything
he does. His coppery
     eyebrows   95
          give him the air

of being always
      a winner—and yet
            I saw once,
the female of his species   100
      clinging determinedly
            to the edge of
a water pipe,
      catch him
            by his crown-feathers   105
to hold him
      silent,
            subdued,
hanging above the city streets
      until   110
            she was through with him.
What was the use
      of that?
            She hung there
herself,   115
      puzzled at her success.
            I laughed heartily.
Practical to the end,
      it is the poem
            of his existence   120
that triumphed
      finally;
            a wisp of feathers
flattened to the pavement,
      wings spread symmetrically   125
            as if in flight,
the head gone,
      the black escutcheon of the breast
            undecipherable,
an effigy of a sparrow,   130
      a dried wafer only,
            left to say
and it says it
      without offense,
            beautifully;   135
This was I,
      a sparrow.
            I did my best;
farewell.

                            [1954]

from *Paterson, Book II:*
Sunday in the Park

I

Outside

    outside myself

                  there is a world,
he rumbled, subject to my incursions
—a world   .   5

    (to me) at rest,
      which I approach

concretely—

    The scene's the Park
    upon the rock,   10
    female to the city

—upon whose body Paterson instructs his thoughts
(concretely)

      —late spring,
    a Sunday afternoon!   15

—and goes by the footpath to the cliff (counting:
the proof)

    himself among the others,
—treads there the same stones
on which their feet slip as they climb,   20
paced by their dogs!

laughing, calling to each other—

      Wait for me!

. . the ugly legs of the young girls,
pistons too powerful for delicacy! .   25

the men's arms, red, used to heat and cold,
to toss quartered beeves and   .

                    Yah! Yah! Yah! Yah!

—over-riding
                    the risks: *30*
                              pouring down!
For the flower of a day!

Arrived breathless, after a hard climb he,
looks back (beautiful but expensive!) to
the pearl-grey towers! Re-turns   *35*
and starts, possessive, through the trees,

                    —that love,
that is not, is not in those terms
to which I'm still the positive
in spite of all;   *40*
the ground dry,—passive-possessive

Walking —

        Thickets gather about groups of squat sand-pine,
        all but from bare rock   .

        —a scattering of man-high cedars (sharp cones),   *45*
        antlered sumac   .

        —roots, for the most part, writhing
        upon the surface

                    (so close are we to ruin every

        day!)   *50*
        searching the punk-dry rot

Walking—

The body is tilted slightly forward from the basic standing
position and the weight thrown on the ball of the foot,
while the other thigh is lifted and the leg and opposite   *55*
arm are swung forward (fig. 6b). Various muscles, aided   .

Despite my having said that I'd never write to you again, I do so now because I find, with the passing of time, that the outcome of my failure with you has been the complete damming up of all my creative capacities in a particularly disastrous manner such as I have never before experienced.

For a great many weeks now (whenever I've tried to write poetry) every thought I've had, even every feeling, has been struck off some surface crust of myself which began gathering when I first sensed that you were ignoring the real contents of my last letters to you, and which finally congealed into some impenetrable substance when you asked me to quit corresponding with you altogether without even an explanation.

That kind of blockage, exiling one's self from one's self—have you ever experienced it? I dare say you have, at moments; and if so, you can well understand what a serious psychological injury it amounts to when turned into a permanent day-to-day condition.

How do I love you? These!

(He hears! Voices . indeterminate! Sees them
moving, in groups, by twos and fours—filtering
off by way of the many bypaths.)   60

I asked him, What do you do?

*He smiled patiently, The typical American question.
In Europe they would ask, What are you doing? Or,
What are you doing now?*

*What do I do? listen, to the water falling. (No   65
sound of it here but with the wind!) This is my entire
occupation.*

No fairer day ever dawned anywhere than May 2, 1880, when the German Singing Societies of Paterson met on Garret Mountain, as they did many years before on the first Sunday in May.

However the meeting of 1880 proved a fatal day, when William Dalzell, who owned a piece of property near the scene of the festivities, shot John Joseph Van Houten. Dalzell claimed that the visitors had in previous years walked over his garden and was determined that this year he would stop them from crossing any part of his grounds.

Immediately after the shot the quiet group of singers was turned into an infuriated mob who would take Dalzell into their own hands. The mob then proceeded to burn the barn into which Dalzell had retreated from the angry group.

Dalzell fired at the approaching mob from a window in the barn and one of the bullets struck a little girl in the cheek. . . . Some of the Paterson Police rushed Dalzell out of the barn [to] the house of John Ferguson some half furlong away.

The crowd now numbered some ten thousand,

"a great beast!"

*for many had come from the city to join the conflict. The case
looked serious, for the Police were greatly outnumbered. The crowd then tried to
burn the Ferguson house and Dalzell went to the house of John McGuckin. While
in this house it was that Sergeant John McBride suggested that it might be well
to send for William McNulty, Dean of Saint Joseph's Catholic Church.*

*In a moment the Dean set on a plan. He proceeded to the scene in a hack.
Taking Dalzell by the arm, in full view of the infuriated mob, he led the man to
the hack and seating himself by his side, ordered the driver to proceed. The crowd
hesitated, bewildered between the bravery of the Dean and   .*

Signs everywhere of birds nesting, while
in the air, slow, a crow zigzags
with heavy wings before the wasp-thrusts   *70*
of smaller birds circling about him
that dive from above stabbing for his eyes

Walking—

he leaves the path, finds hard going
across-field, stubble and matted brambles   *75*
seeming a pasture—but no pasture
—old furrows, to say labor sweated or
had sweated here   .

                         a flame,

spent.   *80*

       The file-sharp grass   .

When! from before his feet, half tripping,
picking a way, there starts
       a flight of empurpled wings!
—invisibly created (their   *85*
jackets dust-grey) from the dust kindled
to sudden ardor!

       They fly away, churring! until
their strength spent they plunge
to the coarse cover again and disappear   *90*
—but leave, livening the mind, a flashing
of wings and a churring song   .
AND a grasshopper of red basalt, boot-long,
tumbles from the core of his mind,
a rubble-bank disintegrating beneath a   *95*
tropic downpour

Chapultepec! grasshopper hill!

—a matt stone solicitously instructed
to bear away some rumor
of the living presence that has preceded   *100*
it, out-precedented its breath   .

These wings do not unfold for flight—
no need!
the weight (to the hand) finding
a counter-weight or counter buoyancy   *105*
by the mind's wings   .

He is afraid! What then?

Before his feet, at each step, the flight
is renewed. A burst of wings, a quick
churring sound   :   *110*

     couriers to the ceremonial of love!

—aflame in flight!
     —aflame only in flight!

     No flesh but the caress!

He is led forward by their announcing wings.   *115*

*If that situation with you (your ignoring those particular letters and then your
final note) had belonged to the inevitable lacrimae rerum (as did, for instance,
my experience with Z.) its result could not have been (as it has been) to destroy
the validity for me myself of myself, because in that case nothing to do with my
sense of personal identity would have been maimed—the cause of one's frustrations
in such instances being not in one's self nor in the other person but merely in the
sorry scheme of things. But since your ignoring those letters was not "natural" in
that sense (or rather since to regard it as unnatural I am forced, psychologically,
to feel that what I wrote you about, was sufficiently trivial and unimportant and
absurd to merit your evasion) it could not but follow that that whole side of life
connected with those letters should in consequence take on for my own self that same
kind of unreality and inaccessibility which the inner lives of other people often have
for us.*

          —his mind a red stone carved to be
          endless flight   .
          Love that is a stone endlessly in flight,
          so long as stone shall last bearing
          the chisel's stroke   .   *120*
          . . and is lost and covered

with ash, falls from an undermined bank
and—begins churring!
AND DOES, the stone after the life!

The stone lives, the flesh dies   *125*
—we know nothing of death.

—boot long
window-eyes that front the whole head,
        Red stone! as if
a light still clung in them .   *130*

Love

        combating sleep
        ———————
        the sleep

piecemeal

                                    [1958]

D. H. LAWRENCE

[1885–1930]

Love on the Farm

What large, dark hands are those at the window
Grasping in the golden light
Which weaves its way through the evening wind
   At my heart's delight?
Ah, only the leaves! But in the west   *5*
I see a redness suddenly come
Into the evening's anxious breast—
    'Tis the wound of love goes home!

The woodbine° creeps abroad   *honeysuckle*
Calling low to her lover: *10*
   The sun-lit flirt who all the day
   Has poised above her lips in play

LOVE ON THE FARM   This poem was originally titled "Cruelty and Love."

And stolen kisses, shallow and gay
Of pollen, now has gone away—
    She woos the moth with her sweet, low word: *15*
And when above her his moth-wings hover
Then her bright breast she will uncover
And yield her honey-drop to her lover.

Into the yellow, evening glow
Saunters a man from the farm below;   *20*
Leans, and looks in at the low-built shed
Where the swallow has hung her marriage bed.
    The bird lies warm against the wall.
    She glances quick her startled eyes
    Towards him, then she turns away   *25*
    Her small head, making warm display
    Of red upon the throat. Her terrors sway
    Her out of the nest's warm, busy ball,
    Whose plaintive cry is heard as she flies
    In one blue stoop from out the sties°   *animal pens* *30*
    Into the twilight's empty hall.
Oh, water-hen, beside the rushes
Hide your quaintly scarlet blushes,
Still your quick tail, lie still as dead,
Till the distance folds over his ominous tread!   *35*

The rabbit presses back her ears,
Turns back her liquid, anguished eyes
And crouches low; then with wild spring
Spurts from the terror of *his* oncoming;
To be choked back, the wire ring   *40*
Her frantic effort throttling:
    Piteous brown ball of quivering fears!
Ah, soon in his large, hard hands she dies,
And swings all loose from the swing of his walk!
Yet calm and kindly are his eyes   *45*
And ready to open in brown surprise
Should I not answer to his talk
Or should he my tears surmise.

I hear his hand on the latch, and rise from my chair
Watching the door open; he flashes bare   *50*
His strong teeth in a smile, and flashes his eyes
In a smile like triumph upon me; then careless-wise
He flings the rabbit soft on the table board
And comes towards me: ah! the uplifted sword

Of his hand against my bosom! and oh, the broad   *55*
Blade of his glance that asks me to applaud
His coming! With his hand he turns my face to him
And caresses me with his fingers that still smell grim
Of the rabbit's fur! God, I am caught in a snare!
I know not what fine wire is round my throat;   *60*
I only know I let him finger there
My pulse of life, and let him nose like a stoat°   *weasel*
Who sniffs with joy before he drinks the blood.

And down his mouth comes to my mouth! and down
His bright dark eyes come over me, like a hood   *65*
Upon my mind! his lips meet mine, and a flood
Of sweet fire sweeps across me, so I drown
Against him, die, and find death good.

                                                                    [1913]

Piano

Softly, in the dusk, a woman is singing to me;
Taking me back down the vista of years, till I see
A child sitting under the piano, in the boom of the tingling strings
And pressing the small, poised feet of a mother who smiles as she sings.

In spite of myself, the insidious mastery of song   *5*
Betrays me back, till the heart of me weeps to belong
To the old Sunday evenings at home, with winter outside
And hymns in the cosy parlour, the tinkling piano our guide.

So now it is vain for the singer to burst into clamour
With the great black piano appassionato. The glamour   *10*
Of childish days is upon me, my manhood is cast
Down in the flood of remembrance, I weep like a child for the past.

                                                                    [1918]

Snake

A snake came to my water-trough
On a hot, hot day, and I in pajamas for the heat,
To drink there.

In the deep, strange-scented shade of the great dark carob-tree
I came down the steps with my pitcher   5
And must wait, must stand and wait, for there he was at the trough before me.

He reached down from a fissure in the earth-wall in the gloom
And trailed his yellow-brown slackness soft-bellied down, over the edge of the stone
    trough
And rested his throat upon the stone bottom,
And where the water had dripped from the tap, in a small clearness,   10
He sipped with his straight mouth,
Softly drank through his straight gums, into his slack long body,
Silently.
Someone was before me at my water-trough,
And I, like a second comer, waiting.   15
He lifted his head from his drinking, as cattle do,
And looked at me vaguely, as drinking cattle do,
And flickered his two-forked tongue from his lips, and mused a moment,
And stooped and drank a little more,
Being earth-brown, earth-golden from the burning bowels of the earth   20
On the day of Sicilian July, with Etna smoking.

The voice of my education said to me
He must be killed,
For in Sicily the black, black snakes are innocent, the gold are venomous.

And voices in me said, If you were a man   25
You would take a stick and break him now, and finish him off.

But must I confess how I liked him,
How glad I was he had come like a guest in quiet, to drink at my water-trough

And depart peaceful, pacified, and thankless,
Into the burning bowels of this earth?   30

Was it cowardice, that I dared not kill him?
Was it perversity, that I longed to talk to him?
Was it humility, to feel so honored?
I felt so honored.

And yet those voices:
If you were not afraid, you would kill him!   35

And truly I was afraid, I was most afraid,
But even so, honored still more

That he should seek my hospitality
From out the dark door of the secret earth.

He drank enough   *40*
And lifted his head, dreamily, as one who has drunken,
And flickered his tongue like a forked night on the air, so black,
Seeming to lick his lips,
And looked around like a god, unseeing, into the air,
And slowly turned his head,   *45*
And slowly, very slowly, as if thrice adream,
Proceeded to draw his slow length curving round
And climb again the broken bank of my wall-face.

And as he put his head into that dreadful hole,
And as he slowly drew up, snake-easing his shoulders, and entered farther,   *50*
A sort of horror, a sort of protest against his withdrawing into that horrid black hole,
Deliberately going into the blackness, and slowly drawing himself after,
Overcame me now his back was turned.

I looked round, I put down my pitcher,
I picked up a clumsy log   *55*
And threw it at the water-trough with a clatter.

I think it did not hit him,
But suddenly that part of him that was left behind convulsed in undignified haste.
Writhed like lightning, and was gone
Into the black hole, the earth-lipped fissure in the wall-front,   *60*
At which, in the intense still noon, I stared with fascination.

And immediately I regretted it.
I thought how paltry, how vulgar, what a mean act!
I despised myself and the voices of my accursed human education.

And I thought of the albatross   *65*
And I wished he would come back, my snake.

For he seemed to me again like a king,
Like a king in exile, uncrowned in the underworld,
Now due to be crowned again.

And so, I missed my chance with one of the lords   *70*
Of life.
And I have something to expiate;
A pettiness.

                                                                    [1923]

The Elephant Is Slow to Mate—

The elephant, the huge old beast,
        is slow to mate;
he finds a female, they show no haste,
        they wait

for the sympathy in their vast shy hearts   5
        slowly, slowly to rouse
as they loiter along the river-beds
        and drink and browse

and dash in panic through the brake
        of forest with the herd,   10
and sleep in massive silence, and wake
        together, without a word.

So slowly the great hot elephant hearts
        grow full of desire,
and the great beasts mate in secret at last,   15
        hiding their fire.

Oldest they are and the wisest of beasts
        so they know at last
how to wait for the loneliest of feasts
        for the full repast.   20

They do not snatch, they do not tear;
        their massive blood
moves as the moon-tides, near, more near,
        till they touch in flood.

                                          [1923]

Humming-bird

I can imagine, in some other world
Primeval-dumb, far back
In that most awful stillness, that only gasped and hummed,
Humming-birds raced down the avenues.

Before anything had a soul,   5
While life was a heave of Matter, half inanimate,
This little bit chipped off in brilliance
And went whizzing through the slow, vast, succulent stems.

I believe there were no flowers then,
In the world where the humming-bird flashed ahead of creation.   10
I believe he pierced the slow vegetable veins with his long beak.

Probably he was big
As mosses, and little lizards, they say, were once big.
Probably he was a jabbing, terrifying monster.

We look at him through the wrong end of the long telescope of Time,   15
Luckily for us.

[1923]

When I read Shakespeare

When I read Shakespeare I am struck with wonder
that such trivial people should muse and thunder
in such lovely language.

Lear, the old buffer, you wonder his daughters
didn't treat him rougher,   5
the old chough, the old chuffer°!   *imposter*

And Hamlet, how boring, how boring to live with,
so mean and self-conscious, blowing and snoring
his wonderful speeches, full of other folks' whoring!

And Macbeth and his Lady, who should have been choring,   10
such suburban ambition, so messily goring
old Duncan with daggers!

How boring, how small Shakespeare's people are!
Yet the language so lovely! like the dyes from gas-tar.

[1929]

WHEN I READ SHAKESPEARE   °**chough**   a chattering jackdaw or crow.

EZRA POUND

[1885–1972]

It has been said of Ezra Pound that modern poetry would be substantially poorer without him, that he is the single most important influence on the history of poetry in our century. And although some might disagree with the largeness of this claim, few would deny Pound an important place in modern literary history. Why? Partly because of his own poetry, which consistently sought to find ways to revitalize the past, to make it relevant to the modern world. Partly also because of his prolific output of nearly one hundred volumes, including critical manifestos, anthologies of poems, translations, and literary criticism. In part, finally, because of his generous intervention on behalf of young writers whose works he championed (and sometimes influenced) in an effort to secure their initial publication; among the more famous writers he assisted were T. S. Eliot, Robert Frost, Marianne Moore, William Carlos Williams, Ernest Hemingway, and James Joyce.

Pound's poetry is animated by a desire to retain and renew the great literature of the past. As an editor, critic, and translator, he restored an appreciation of the achievements not only of individual poets such as Homer and Propertius, but also of specific literary genres such as the troubadour poetry of twelfth-century Provence. Pound's cultural impetus was evident in his support of and friendship with artists such as the French sculptor Henri Gaudier-Brzeska and the violinist Olga Rudge, with whom he later lived.

For Pound, art was a way of both preserving history and making it. He considered works of art to be embodiments of their historical moment, bearing signs of their cultural identity and their creator's individuality. Pound also believed that true artists passionately devote themselves to their own specific craft but also exhibit a love of other arts as well. Pound himself exemplified this ideal. Besides his friendship with artists, he contributed art and music reviews to *The New Age*, wrote a book on the American composer George Antheil, and composed an opera, *Villon*. At one point he defined poetry as a composition of words set to music; at another he condemned poets uninterested in art and music as bad poets.

The literary movements with which Pound has most often been associated are Imagism and Vorticism. Imagism, the more important, was less a revolutionary than a purificatory movement in poetry. Reacting against tendencies in late nineteenth-century and early twentieth-century Victorian and Edwardian verse—such as verbosity, didacticism, excessive ornamentation, and metrical regularity—the Imagists advocated precision and concreteness of detail, concentration of language, and a freshness of rhythmic cadence. Pound saw the image as the poet's pigment, the artist's way of making an impression visually, intellectually, and emotionally.

Pound's imagistic tendencies were strongly manifested in his works. Counseling poets to fear abstraction, Pound summed up his principles of Imagism as a set of guidelines in "A Few Dont's for an Imagist":

1. To present a direct treatment of the thing described.
2. To use absolutely no word that does not contribute to the presentation of the image.
3. To compose on the order of musical cadence and phrasing, not according to strict, unvarying rhythms.

But even though the Imagism of early Pound and H.D., Amy Lowell, William Carlos Williams, and others contributed to a revitalized American poetry, the movement had its limits. Its central limitation was one of its outstanding strengths—its pictorial precision. Imagistic poems tend to be static; they lack movement and tension. Pound's images, however, generally avoid this static pictorialism. Consider, for example, his most famous Imagist poem:

In a Station of the Metro

The apparition of these faces in the crowd;
Petals on a wet, black bough.

In *The Pound Era,* Hugh Kenner has described in illuminating detail the genesis of this poem. He argues that Pound's poem is not merely a static image or pictorial representation, however sharp, of something seen, preserved through memory, and later recorded in verse. Kenner quotes Pound's description of the stimulus for the poem: on a visit to Paris, he emerged from the Metro (Parisian subway) and "saw suddenly a beautiful face, and then another and another, and then a beautiful child's face, and then another beautiful woman, and I tried all that day to find words for what they had meant to me, and I could not find any words that seemed to me worthy, or as lovely as that sudden emotion."

Pound's final words ("that sudden emotion") provide the key to his initial experience and to his poetic intention and achievement. For Pound desired to translate his experience into an imagistic poem that would be the equivalent of an abstract painting—not a verbal portrait of what he had seen, but rather, as Kenner notes, "an abstract equivalent for it, reduced, intensified." Pound wrote a thirty-line poem, which he destroyed; six months later he produced another, shorter poem, which he also destroyed. Then, a year later, he completed the twenty words (title included) of "In a Station of the Metro."

The poem nicely illustrates Pound's definition of an image as "that which presents an intellectual and emotional complex in an instant of time." In calling it a "cluster" and a "VORTEX, from which and through which, and into which, ideas are constantly rushing," Pound went beyond the static Imagism of his contemporaries, moving toward a dynamic Imagism, which he soon termed Vorticism, a short-lived movement he inaugurated with the painter and writer Wyndham Lewis. Its central feature was the vortex or whirlpool of energy that the artist drew on to invent new forms and measures, rather than imitate old ones. But as we have seen, Pound's Imagism also actively sets things into relation with and against one another. "In a Station of the Metro," as Kenner has suggested, exhibits an act of mind by discovering a connection and devising a form of compressed metaphor to express this resemblance and its emotional significance.

There are additional problems, however, with the work of some Imagist poems: a lack of discursiveness, an avoidance of transitions, and an emphasis on particular poetic moments, all of which made it difficult for Imagist poets to sustain a long poem. T. S. Eliot partly solved this problem in *The Waste Land* (pp. 650–664) by using a musical structure that includes repetition, thematic variation, and ironic juxtaposition of images. Pound employed similar techniques in "Hugh Selwyn Mauberley." "Mauberley" has been seen as a collection of fragments comparable to those in Eliot's *The Waste Land*. But whereas the images in Eliot's poem seem to offer a hopeful restoration of meaning to life, Pound's images hold out no such possibility. Instead, the speaker of "Mauberley" ironically depicts the loss of coherence in society, the futility of poetic ambition, the destructive consequences of materialism, and the general cultural decay of modern civilization, especially the British empire. (Some have seen these, however, as basic themes in *The Waste Land*, as well.) Like Eliot's "Gerontion," "Mauberley" anticipates some of the technical devices of *The Waste Land*, especially its shifts of perspective, its amalgam of unidentified quotations in different languages, and its discontinuous structure. It differs from *The Waste Land*, however, and more closely approximates "Gerontion" and "The Love Song of J. Alfred Prufrock" in its focus on a single consciousness, though its scope and ambition have more in common with Eliot's longer poem.

Before "Mauberley," Pound was occupied with translations of poems from Chinese and Provençal, especially the troubadour poetry of Bertrans de Born. In both *Cathay* and *Personae* Pound employed the technique of speaking from behind a mask, speaking in the voice of another. From Provençal, Pound adapted de Born's "Sestina: Altaforte," capturing its vigorous energy and feverish lust for battle. The poem's repetitive structure creates a crescendo of emotional power, well suited to the intensity of the speaker's martial obsession. From the Chinese of Li Po, Pound created versions of poems that were less strictly translations than adaptations. Pound based his versions on the notes of the American Sinologist Ernest Fenollosa, who, like Pound, could not read Chinese, but who had had the poems translated by Japanese scholars. This fact accounts in large measure for Pound's use of Japanese spellings of place names in poems like "The River-Merchant's Wife: A Letter" and for its attribution to Rihaku, the Japanese name of Li Po. What perhaps fascinated Pound most about Chinese was the imagistic quality not only of the poems he adapted, but of the Chinese characters, which embody words and images simultaneously. Later, Pound explored the problems of life and love in the modern world by adapting the persona of the classical Roman poet Sextus Propertius.

Though Pound's poetic activity took him well beyond the land and culture of his birth, his background was distinctively American. He was born in Idaho in 1885 and was educated at Hamilton College and the University of Pennsylvania, from which he earned a B.A. and an M.A., respectively. He taught briefly at Wabash

College in Indiana but soon left to travel and live abroad, settling in London (1908–1920), Paris (1920–1924), and Rapallo, Italy (1924–1945). Pound was exceptionally active in literary pursuits of all sorts, particularly in founding and editing literary journals. He was the London editor of *Poetry* (1912–1919) and of *The Little Review* (1917–1919), the cofounder and editor of *The Exile* (1927–1928), and the Paris correspondent for *The Dial.* In 1914, he married Dorothy Shakespear, with whom he lived at Rapallo in alternation with Olga Rudge, by whom he had a child and with whom he lived in Venice.

Pound was more conservative in politics than in literature. For him the measure of a society's political integrity was the degree to which it allowed art to flourish. Pound saw capitalism as evil, and he viewed banking as a curse, associating it with usury, which he believed was contrary to nature. Ideas like these led Pound toward anti-Semitism, which was apparent in a series of broadcasts he made over Italian radio during the Second World War. The broadcasts were savagely critical of American policy and of Jews and were later deemed traitorous by a postwar tribunal. Arrested and imprisoned near Pisa in 1945, Pound was found unfit for trial by reason of insanity and was committed to St. Elizabeth's Hospital in Washington, D.C. He was released in 1958, due largely to the persistent efforts of other American poets, including Robert Frost and Archibald MacLeish. Pound returned to Italy, where he lived until his death in 1972.

When Pound was awarded the prestigious Bollingen Poetry Prize in 1948, a heated debate arose about his worthiness to receive it. Those who considered a poet's life and work as inextricably united were angered by the award. Others, separating the writer's politics from his poetry, felt that Pound's poetic achievement had been justly acknowledged. Still others were understandably ambivalent about the tribute. Disputes about this issue are still aired occasionally, though Pound's reputation as a preeminent Modernist poet–critic has been secured.

Pound's most ambitious and complex work of poetry is *The Cantos,* his attempt to write a modern epic. *The Cantos* make sustained and complex use of literary allusion to call up the context of literary works and historical events. Like Eliot, with whom he shared a propensity for learned reference, Pound expected his readers to be conversant with a broad range of humanistic knowledge, including a variety of languages and literatures both classical and modern, along with Italian art, Chinese philosophy, and modern American economic theory. These are among the subjects that appear in *The Cantos,* which together form a body of 117 separate poems and several fragments that combine description, reminiscence, meditation, quotation, and speculation in a complex amalgamation of forms, meters, and voices.

The Cantos occupied Pound for more than fifty years, from 1917 to 1968. Animating the poems is a set of beliefs about the importance and dignity of honest labor, whether that labor is channeled into making poems or furniture, and a corollary notion that what destroys societies is greed. These impulses are most clearly discernible in two of the more accessible *Cantos,* XLV and LXXXI (pp. 622–626). Although there is widespread disagreement about how effectively Pound has achieved his aims in *The Cantos,* and although his repugnant acts during World War II stained his reputation, there is no doubt that he has been a considerable force in modern poetry. In giving us the fragments of his poems, he assembled, as Donald Hall has suggested, "the best of himself and of the cultures he loved."

The White Stag

I ha' seen them 'mid the clouds on the heather.
Lo! they pause not for love nor for sorrow,
Yet their eyes are as the eyes of a maid to her lover,
When the white hart breaks his cover
And the white wind breaks the morn.   5
     " 'Tis the white stag, Fame, we're a-hunting,
     Bid the world's hounds come to horn!"

                                                       [1908]

Sestina: Altaforte

LOQUITUR: En Bertrans de Born. Dante Alighieri put this man in hell for that he was a stirrer up of strife. Eccovi! Judge ye! Have I dug him up again? The scene is at his castle, Altaforte. "Papiols" is his jongleur. "The Leopard," the device of Richard Cœur de Lion.

I

Damn it all! all this our South stinks peace.
You whoreson dog, Papiols, come! Let's to music!
I have no life save when the swords clash.
But ah! when I see the standards gold, vair, purple, opposing
And the broad fields beneath them turn crimson,   5
Then howl I my heart nigh mad with rejoicing.

II

In hot summer have I great rejoicing
When the tempests kill the earth's foul peace,
And the lightnings from black heav'n flash crimson,
And the fierce thunders roar me their music   10
And the winds shriek through the clouds mad, opposing,
And through all the riven skies God's swords clash.

III

Hell grant soon we hear again the swords clash!
And the shrill neighs of destriers in battle rejoicing,

Spiked breast to spiked breast opposing!   15
Better one hour's stour than a year's peace
With fat boards, bawds, wine and frail music!
Bah! there's no wine like the blood's crimson!

IV

And I love to see the sun rise blood-crimson.
And I watch his spears through the dark clash   20
And it fills all my heart with rejoicing
And pries wide my mouth with fast music
When I see him so scorn and defy peace,
His lone might 'gainst all darkness opposing.

V

The man who fears war and squats opposing   25
My words for stour, hath no blood of crimson
But is fit only to rot in womanish peace
Far from where worth's won and the swords clash
For the death of such sluts I go rejoicing;
Yea, I fill all the air with my music.   30

VI

Papiols, Papiols, to the music!
There's no sound like to swords swords opposing,
No cry like the battle's rejoicing
When our elbows and swords drip the crimson
And our charges 'gainst "The Leopard's" rush clash.   35
May God damn for ever all who cry "Peace!"

VII

And let the music of the swords make them crimson!
Hell grant soon we hear again the swords clash!
Hell blot black for alway the thought "Peace!"

[1908]

Portrait d'une Femme

Your mind and you are our Sargasso Sea,
London has swept about you this score years
And bright ships left you this or that in fee:

Ideas, old gossip, oddments of all things,
Strange spars of knowledge and dimmed wares of price.   *5*
Great minds have sought you—lacking someone else.
You have been second always. Tragical?
No. You preferred it to the usual thing:
One dull man, dulling and uxorious,
One average mind—with one thought less, each year.   *10*
Oh, you are patient, I have seen you sit
Hours, where something might have floated up.
And now you pay one. Yes, you richly pay.
You are a person of some interest, one comes to you
And takes strange gain away: *15*
Trophies fished up; some curious suggestion;
Fact that leads nowhere; and a tale or two,
Pregnant with mandrakes, or with something else
That might prove useful and yet never proves,
That never fits a corner or shows use,   *20*
Or finds its hour upon the loom of days:
The tarnished, gaudy, wonderful old work;
Idols and ambergris and rare inlays,
These are your riches, your great store; and yet
For all this sea-hoard of deciduous things,   *25*
Strange woods half sodden, and new brighter stuff:
In the slow float of different light and deep,
No! there is nothing! In the whole and all,
Nothing that's quite your own.
                    Yet this is you.

                                        [1912]

The Return

See, they return; ah, see the tentative
Movements, and the slow feet,
The trouble in the pace and the uncertain
Wavering!

See, they return, one, and by one,   *5*
With fear, as half-awakened;
As if the snow should hesitate
And murmur in the wind,
                    and half turn back;

These were the "Wing'd-with-Awe,"   *10*
          Inviolable,

Gods of the wingèd shoe!
With them the silver hounds,
          sniffing the trace of air!

Haie! Haie!   *15*
          These were the swift to harry;
These the keen-scented;
These were the souls of blood.

Slow on the leash,
          pallid the leash-men!   *20*

                                        [1912]

Epitaphs

Fu I
Fu I loved the high cloud and the hill,
Alas, he died of alcohol.

Li Po
And Li Po also died drunk.
He tried to embrace a moon
In the Yellow River.   *5*

                                        [1916]

The River-Merchant's Wife: A Letter

While my hair was still cut straight across my forehead
I played about the front gate, pulling flowers.
You came by on bamboo stilts, playing horse,
You walked about my seat, playing with blue plums.
And we went on living in the village of Chokan: *5*
Two small people, without dislike or suspicion.

At fourteen I married My Lord you.
I never laughed, being bashful.
Lowering my head, I looked at the wall.
Called to, a thousand times, I never looked back.   *10*

At fifteen I stopped scowling,
I desired my dust to be mingled with yours
Forever and forever and forever.
Why should I climb the look out?
At sixteen you departed,   *15*
You went into far Ku-to-yen by the river of swirling eddies,
And you have been gone five months.
The monkeys make sorrowful noise overhead.

You dragged your feet when you went out.
By the gate now, the moss is grown, the different mosses   *20*
Too deep to clear them away!

The leaves fall early this autumn, in wind.
The paired butterflies are already yellow with August,
Over the grass in the West garden;
They hurt me. I grow older.   *25*
If you are coming down through the narrows of the river Kiang,
Please let me know beforehand,
And I will come out to meet you
        As far as Cho-fu-Sa.

                                        By Rihaku
                                        [1916]

The Garden

En robe de parade.
        —Samain

Like a skein of loose silk blown against a wall
She walks by the railing of a path in Kensington Gardens,
And she is dying piece-meal
        of a sort of emotional anæmia.

THE GARDEN   **En robe de parade**   French for "dressed as for a state occasion." From "The Infanta" by
Albert Samain (1858–1900).

And round about there is a rabble 5
Of the filthy, sturdy, unkillable infants of the very poor.
They shall inherit the earth.

In her is the end of breeding.
Her boredom is exquisite and excessive.
She would like some one to speak to her, 10
And is almost afraid that I
        will commit that indiscretion.

[1916]

A Pact

I make a pact with you, Walt Whitman—
I have detested you long enough.
I come to you as a grown child
Who has had a pig-headed father;
I am old enough now to make friends. 5
It was you that broke the new wood,
Now is a time for carving.
We have one sap and one root—
Let there be commerce between us.

[1916]

from *Hugh Selwyn Mauberley*
(Life and Contacts)

E. P. Ode pour l'election de Son Sepulchre

"Vocat Aestus in Umbram"
        —*Nemesianus, Ec. IV*

For three years, out of key with his time,
He strove to resuscitate the dead art

HUGH SELWYN MAUBERLEY   Pound described this poem as "a farewell to London . . . a study in form, an attempt to condense the James novel." He also remarked about the poem's speaker: "I'm no more Mauberley than Eliot is Prufrock."   **Ode pour . . . Son Sepulchre** French for "Ode on the choice of his tomb." An adaptation of the title of a poem by Pierre de Ronsard (1524–1585).   **Vocat aestus in umbram** Latin for "Heat summons us into the shade." Nemesianus was a third-century Roman poet.

Of poetry; to maintain "the sublime"
In the old sense. Wrong from the start—

No, hardly, but seeing he had been born   5
In a half savage country, out of date;
Bent resolutely on wringing lilies from the acorn;
Capaneus, trout for factitious bait;

"Ἴδμεν γάρ τοι πάνθ᾽, ὅσ᾽ ἐνὶ Τροίη"
Caught in the unstopped ear;   10
Giving the rocks small lee-way
The chopped seas held him, therefore, that year.

His true Penelope was Flaubert,
He fished by obstinate isles;
Observed the elegance of Circe's hair   15
Rather than the mottoes on sun-dials.

Unaffected by "the march of events,"
He passed from men's memory in *l'an trentiesme*
De son eage, the case presents
No adjunct to the Muses' diadem.   20

II

The age demanded an image
Of its accelerated grimace,
Something for the modern stage,
Not, at any rate, an Attic grace;

Not, not certainly, the obscure reveries   25
Of the inward gaze;
Better mendacities
Than the classics in paraphrase!

---

⁸Capaneus   one of the seven warriors who attacked Thebes, who after swearing an oath against Zeus, was struck dead with a thunderbolt   **⁹**This Greek is from Homer's *Odyssey.* It means "For we know all the things that are in Troy." Part of the song of the Sirens, which was so powerfully seductive that Odysseus plugged the ears of his sailors with wax and lashed himself to the mast of his ship to prevent them all from jumping into the sea. **¹³Penelope**   wife of Odysseus, who faithfully awaited his return for twenty years.   **Flaubert**   French novelist (1821–1880).   **¹⁵Circe**   sorceress from Homer's *Odyssey* with whom Odysseus spent a year.   **¹⁸⁻¹⁹l'an trentiesme de son eage**   medieval French for "the thirtieth year of his age," an adaptation of the opening line of the *Grand Testament* of François Villon (1431–?): "In the thirtieth year of my life."

The "age demanded" chiefly a mold in plaster,
Made with no loss of time,   *30*
A prose kinema, not, not assuredly, alabaster
Or the "sculpture" of rhyme.

III

The tea-rose tea-grown, etc.
Supplants the mousseline of Cos,
The pianola "replaces"   *35*
Sappho's barbitos.

Christ follows Dionysus,
Phallic and ambrosial
Made way for macerations:
Caliban casts out Ariel.   *40*

All things are a flowing,
Sage Heracleitus says;
But a tawdry cheapness
Shall outlast our days.

Even the Christian beauty   *45*
Defects—after Samothrace;
We see τὸ καλόυ
Decreed in the market place.

Faun's flesh is not to us,
Nor the saint's vision.   *50*
We have the press for wafer;
Franchise for circumcision.

All men, in law, are equals.
Free of Pisistratus,
We choose a knave or an eunuch   *55*
To rule over us.

---

[32]**kinema** Greek for "movement" or "motion." [34]**Cos** a Greek island famous for its fabric, especially muslin. [36]**barbitos** a lyrelike instrument played by the Greek poet Sappho (c. 600 B.C.–?). [37]**Dionysus** Greek god of fertility and revelry. [39]**macerations** fasting. [40]**Caliban, Ariel** contrasting characters from Shakespeare's *The Tempest*. Caliban is associated with the earthly and the ugly; Ariel, with the ethereal and the beautiful. [42]**Heracleitus** Greek philosopher (c. 550 B.C.—?) who taught that life is in a constant state of flux or change. [46]**Samothrace** a Greek island. [47]The Greek characters mean "the beautiful." [54]**Pisistratus** Athenian tyrant (d. 527 B.C.).

O bright Apollo,
τίν' ἄυδρα, τίυ' ἥρωα, τίυα θεόυ
What god, man, or hero
Shall I place a tin wreath upon!   60

IV

These fought in any case,
and some believing,

            pro domo, in any case . . .

Some quick to arm,
some for adventure,   65
some from fear of weakness,
some from fear of censure,
some for love of slaughter, in imagination,
learning later . . .
some in fear, learning love of slaughter;   70

Died some, pro patria,
            non "dulce" non "et decor" . . .
walked eye-deep in hell
believing in old men's lies, then unbelieving
came home, home to a lie,   75
home to many deceits,
home to old lies and new infamy;
usury age-old and age-thick
and liars in public places.

Daring as never before, wastage as never before.   80
Young blood and high blood,
fair cheeks, and fine bodies;

fortitude as never before

frankness as never before,
disillusions as never told in the old days,   85
hysterias, trench confessions,
laughter out of dead bellies.

---

[58]The Greek is from Pindar (c. 518–c. 438 B.C.) and means: "What man, what hero, what god." [63]**pro domo** Latin for "for the home." [71-72]**pro patria . . . non "et decor"** Latin, adapted from Horace, *Odes,* III, ii, 138. Horace's line translates "it is sweet and glorious to die for one's country"; Pound's, "for one's native land, not sweetly, not gloriously."

Envoi (1919)

Go, *dumb-born book,*
Tell her that sang me once that song of Lawes:
Hadst thou but song
As thou has subjects known,
Then were there cause in thee that should condone
Even my faults that heavy upon me lie,
And build her glories their longevity.

Tell her that sheds
Such treasure in the air,
Recking naught else but that her graces give
Life to the moment,
I would bid them live
As roses might, in magic amber laid,
Red overwrought with orange and all made
One substance and one color
Braving time.

Tell her that goes
With song upon her lips
But sings not out the song, nor knows
The maker of it, some other mouth,
May be as fair as hers,
Might, in new ages, gain her worshippers,
When our two dusts with Waller's shall be laid,
Siftings on siftings in oblivion,
Till change hath broken down
All things save Beauty alone.

[1920]

Canto I: And then went down to the ship

And then went down to the ship,
Set keel to breakers, forth on the godly sea, and
We set up mast and sail on that swart ship,

HUGH SELWYN MAUBERLEY   [89]**Lawes** Henry Lawes (1596–1662) Composer who set to music the poems of Edmund Waller (1606–1687). This poem is influenced by Waller's "Song: Go Lovely Rose" (p. 219).
CANTO I   Lines 1–68 adapt Book XI of the *Odyssey,* in which Homer describes Odysseus's voyage to the Underworld.

Bore sheep aboard her, and our bodies also
Heavy with weeping, and winds from sternward   5
Bore us out onward with bellying canvas,
Circe's this craft, the trim-coifed goddess.
Then sat we amidships, wind jamming the tiller,
Thus with stretched sail, we went over sea till day's end.
Sun to his slumber, shadows o'er all the ocean,   10
Came we then to the bounds of deepest water,
To the Kimmerian lands, and peopled cities
Covered with close-webbed mist, unpierced ever
With glitter of sun-rays
Nor with stars stretched, nor looking back from heaven   15
Swartest night stretched over wretched men there.
The ocean flowing backward, came we then to the place
Aforesaid by Circe.
Here did they rites, Perimedes and Eurylochus,
And drawing sword from my hip   20
I dug the ell-square pitkin;°   *a small pit*
Poured we libations unto each the dead,
First mead and then sweet wine, water mixed with white flour.
Then prayed I many a prayer to the sickly death's-heads;
As set in Ithaca, sterile bulls of the best   25
For sacrifice, heaping the pyre with goods,
A sheep to Tiresias only, black and a bell-sheep.
Dark blood flowed in the fosse,
Souls out of Erebus, cadaverous dead, of brides
Of youths and of the old who had borne much;   30
Souls stained with recent tears, girls tender,
Men many, mauled with bronze lance heads,
Battle spoil, bearing yet dreory° arms,   *bloody*
These many crowded about me; with shouting,
Pallor upon me, cried to my men for more beasts;   35
Slaughtered the herds, sheep slain of bronze;
Poured ointment, cried to the gods,
To Pluto the strong, and praised Proserpine;
Unsheathed the narrow sword,
I sat to keep off the impetuous impotent dead,   40
Till I should hear Tiresias.
But first Elpenor came, our friend Elpenor,

---

¹²**Kimmerian** for a mythical people who lived at the edge of the world. ¹⁹**Perimedes and Eurylochus**
companions of Odysseus. ²⁹**Erebus** the land of the dead. ³⁸**Proserpine** wife of Pluto, the god of the
Underworld. ⁴²**Elpenor** Odysseus's companion who was left unburied after dying in a fall from the roof of
Circe's house.

Unburied, cast on the wide earth,
Limbs that we left in the house of Circe,
Unwept, unwrapped in sepulchre, since toils urged other.   45
Pitiful spirit. And I cried in hurried speech:
"Elpenor, how art thou come to this dark coast?
Cam'st thou afoot, outstripping seamen?"

            And he in heavy speech:
"Ill fate and abundant wine. I slept in Circe's ingle.°   *corner* 50
Going down the long ladder unguarded,
I fell against the buttress,
Shattered the nape-nerve, the soul sought Avernus.
But thou, O King, I bid remember me, unwept, unburied,
Heap up mine arms, be tomb by sea-bord, and inscribed: 55
A man of no fortune, and with a name to come.
And set my oar up, that I swung mid fellows."

And Anticlea came, whom I beat off, and then Tiresias Theban,
Holding his golden wand, knew me, and spoke first:
"A second time? why? man of ill star,   60
Facing the sunless dead and this joyless region?
Stand from the fosse, leave me my bloody bever
For soothsay."
            And I stepped back.
And he strong with the blood, said then: "Odysseus   65
Shalt return through spiteful Neptune, over dark seas,
Lose all companions." And then Anticlea came.
Lie quiet Divus. I mean, that is Andreas Divus,
In officina Wecheli, 1538, out of Homer.
And he sailed, by Sirens and thence outward and away   70
And unto Circe.
            Venerandam,
In the Cretan's phrase, with the golden crown, Aphrodite,
Cypri munimenta sortita est, mirthful, orichalchi, with golden
Girdles and breast bands, thou with dark eyelids   75
Bearing the golden bough of Argicida. So that:

                                                            [1917]

---

[53]**Avernus** entrance to the Underworld.   [58]**Anticlea** mother of Odysseus.   [62]**bever** a libation or offering to the gods.   [66]**Neptune** god of the sea.   [68]**Andreas Divus** Pound used a Latin translation of Homer by Andrus Divus made in 1538.   [72]**Venerandam** Latin for "commanding reverence," a phrase describing Aphrodite, the Greek goddess of love.   [74]**Cypri munimenta sortita est** Latin for "The fortresses of Cyprus were her appointed realm."   **orichalchi** Latin for "of copper."   [76]**Argicida** the Greek god Hermes, who slew the many-eyed Argus.

Canto XIII: Kung walked

Kung walked
        by the dynastic temple
And into the cedar grove,
        and then out by the lower river,
And with him Khieu, Tchi   5
        and Tian the low speaking
And "we are unknown," said Kung,
"You will take up charioteering?
        Then you will become known,
Or perhaps I should take up charioteering, or archery?   10
Or the practice of public speaking?"
And Tseu-lou said, "I would put the defences in order,"
And Khieu said, "If I were lord of a province
I would put it in better order than this is."
And Tchi said, "I would prefer a small mountain temple,   15
With order in the observances,
        with a suitable performance of the ritual,"
And Tian said, with his hand on the strings of his lute
The low sounds continuing
        after his hand left the strings,   20
And the sound went up like smoke, under the leaves,
And he looked after the sound:
        "The old swimming hole,
And the boys flopping off the planks,
Or sitting in the underbrush playing mandolins."   25
        And Kung smiled upon all of them equally.
And Thseng-sie desired to know:
        "Which had answered correctly?"
And Kung said, "They have all answered correctly,
That is to say, each in his nature."   30
And Kung raised his cane against Yuan Jang,
        Yuan Jang being his elder,
For Yuan Jang sat by the roadside pretending
        to be receiving wisdom.
And Kung said   35
        "You old fool, come out of it,

CANTO XIII   [1]**Kung** Confucius, Kung Fu-tze (551–479 B C.), the great Chinese wise man who founded
Confucianism.   [5-6]**Khieu, Tchi and Tian** three disciples of Confucius.

Get up and do something useful."
        And Kung said
"Respect a child's faculties
From the moment it inhales the clear air,   *40*
But a man of fifty who knows nothing
        Is worthy of no respect."
And "When the prince has gathered about him
All the savants and artists, his riches will be fully employed."
And Kung said, and wrote on the bo leaves: *45*
        If a man have not order within him
He can not spread order about him;
And if a man have not order within him
His family will not act with due order;
        And if the prince have not order within him   *50*
He can not put order in his dominions.
And Kung gave the words "order"
And "brotherly deference"
And said nothing of the "life after death."
And he said   *55*
        "Anyone can run to excesses,
It is easy to shoot past the mark,
It is hard to stand firm in the middle."
And they said: If a man commit murder
        Should his father protect him, and hide him?   *60*
And Kung said:
        He should hide him.

And Kung gave his daughter to Kong-Tch'ang
        although Kong-Tch'ang was in prison.
And he gave his niece to Nan-Young   *65*
        although Nan-Young was out of office.
And Kung said "Wan ruled with moderation,
        In his day the State was well kept,
And even I can remember
A day when the historians left blanks in their writings,   *70*
I mean for things they didn't know,
But that time seems to be passing."
And Kung said, "Without character you will
        be unable to play on that instrument
Or to execute the music fit for the Odes.   *75*
The blossoms of the apricot
        blow from the east to the west,
And I have tried to keep them from falling."

        [1925]

from *Canto XLV: With usura*

With usura hath no man a house of good stone
each block cut smooth and well fitting
that design might cover their face,
with usura
hath no man a painted paradise on his church wall   5
harpes et luz°   *harps and lutes*
or where virgin receiveth message
and halo projects from incision,
with usura
seeth no man Gonzaga his heirs and his concubines   10
no picture is made to endure nor to live with
but it is made to sell and sell quickly
with usura, sin against nature,
is thy bread ever more of stale rags
is thy bread dry as paper,   15
with no mountain wheat, no strong flour
with usura the line grows thick
with usura is no clear demarcation
and no man can find site for his dwelling.
Stone-cutter is kept from his stone   20
weaver is kept from his loom
WITH USURA
wool comes not to market
sheep bringeth no gain with usura
Usura is a murrain,° usura   *a plague*   25
blunteth the needle in the maid's hand
and stoppeth the spinner's cunning. Pietro Lombardo
came not by usura
Duccio came not by usura
nor Pier della Francesca; Zuan Bellin' not by usura   30
nor was "La Calunnia" painted.
Came not by usura Angelico; came not Ambrogio Praedis,
Came no church of cut stone signed: *Adamo me fecit.*

CANTO XLV   ¹⁰**Gonzaga** Luigi Gonzaga (1267–1360), a ruler of Mantua.
USURY: A charge for the use of purchasing power, levied without regard to production; often without regard to the possibilities of production. (Hence the failure of the Medici bank.) [Pound's note]
²⁷⁻³¹**Pietro Lombardo . . . "La Calunnia" painted** Pietro Lombardo, Italian sculptor (1435–1515); Duccio de Buoninsegna (c. 1260–c. 1318); Piero della Francesca (c 1420–c 1492), Giovanni Bellini (c 1445–1516)—all Italian painters; *La Calunnia (Rumor),* a painting by Sandro Botticelli (1445–1510).   ³²**Angelico . . . Ambrogio Praedis** Fra Angelico (1387–1445), Ambrogio Praedis (1445–1506), Italian painters.   ³³**Adamo me fecit** Latin for "Adam made me." These words were carved into the façade of the church of San Zeno Maggiore in Verona.

Not by usura St. Trophime
Not by usura Saint Hilaire,   *35*
Usura rusteth the chisel
It rusteth the craft and the craftsman
It gnaweth the thread in the loom
None learneth to weave gold in her pattern;
Azure hath a canker by usura; cramoisi is unbroidered   *40*
Emerald findeth no Memling
Usura slayeth the child in the womb
It stayeth the young man's courting
It hath brought palsey to bed, lyeth
between the young bride and her bridegroom   *45*
            CONTRA NATURAM
They have brought whores for Eleusis
Corpses are set to banquet
at behest of usura.

                                   [1937]

from *Canto LXXXI: Yet/Ere the season died a-cold*

Yet
Ere the season died a-cold
Borne upon a zephyr's° shoulder   *west wind's*
I rose through the aureate sky
   Lawes and Jenkins guard thy rest   *5*
   Dolmetsch ever be thy guest,
Has he tempered the viol's wood
To enforce both the grave and the acute?
Has he curved us the bowl of the lute?
   Lawes and Jenkins guard thy rest   *10*
   Dolmetsch ever be thy guest
Hast 'ou fashioned so airy a mood
   To draw up leaf from the root?
Hast 'ou found a cloud so light
   As seemed neither mist nor shade?   *15*

CANTO XLV   **34–35St. Trophime . . . Saint Hilaire** medieval French churches.   **40cramoisi** in French, a heavy crimson cloth.   **46CONTRA NATURAM** Latin for "against nature."   **47Eleusis** ancient Greek city, the home of secret fertility rites honoring Demeter and Persephone.
CANTO LXXXI   This poem is one of the *Pisan Cantos,* written during Pound's imprisonment as he awaited trial for allegedly treasonous wartime broadcasts.   **5Lawes and Jenkins . . . be thy guest** Henry Lawes (1596–1662) and John Jenkins (1592–1678), English composers; Arnold Dolmetsch (1858–1940), musicologist with a special interest in rebuilding old instruments.

Then resolve me, tell me aright
If Waller sang or Dowland played.

Your eyen two wol sleye me sodenly
I may the beauté of hem nat susteyne

And for 180 years almost nothing.   20

Ed ascoltando al leggier mormorio
        there came new subtlety of eyes into my tent,
whether of spirit or hypostasis,
        but what the blindfold hides
or at carneval   25
                nor any pair showed anger
        Saw but the eyes and stance between the eyes,
colour, diastasis,
        careless or unaware it had not the
        whole tent's room   30
nor was place for the full Ειδως
interpass, penetrate
        casting but shade beyond the other lights
            sky's clear
            night's sea   35
            green of the mountain pool
            shone from the unmasked eyes in half-mask's space.
What thou lovest well remains,
                the rest is dross
What thou lov'st well shall not be reft from thee   40
What thou lov'st well is thy true heritage
Whose world, or mine or theirs
                or is it of none?
First came the seen, then thus the palpable
        Elysium, though it were in the halls of hell,   45
What thou lovest well is thy true heritage

The ant's a centaur in his dragon world.
Pull down thy vanity, it is not man
Made courage, or made order, or made grace,
        Pull down thy vanity, I say pull down.   50

---

[17]**Waller**   Edmund Waller (1601–1687), English poet, whose "Go Lovely Rose" Lawes set to music and Pound adapted poetically in the *Envoi* to "Mauberley."   **Dowland**   John Dowland (1563–1626), composer and lutenist.   [18-19]**Your eyen . . . nat susteyne**   the lines come from the poem "Merciles Beaute" by Geoffrey Chaucer (c. 1343–1400): "Your two eyes will slay me quickly; I may not withstand their beauty."   [21]**Ed ascoltando al leggier mormorio**   Italian for "and listening to the light murmur."   [23]**hypostasis**   Greek for "the essential part of something."   [28]**diastasis**   Greek for "separation."   Ειδως   Greek for "image."   [45]**Elysium**   Greek mythological heaven for the good.

Learn of the green world what can be thy place
In scaled invention or true artistry,
Pull down thy vanity,
                Paquin pull down!
The green casque has outdone your elegance.   *55*

"Master thyself, then others shall thee beare"
      Pull down thy vanity
Thou art a beaten dog beneath the hail,
A swollen magpie in a fitful sun,
Half black half white   *60*
Nor knowst'ou wing from tail
Pull down thy vanity
         How mean thy hates
Fostered in falsity,
         Pull down thy vanity,   *65*
Rathe to destroy, niggard in charity,
Pull down thy vanity,
         I say pull down.

But to have done instead of not doing
         this is not vanity   *70*
To have, with decency, knocked
That a Blunt should open
         To have gathered from the air a live tradition
or from a fine old eye the unconquered flame
This is not vanity.   *75*
      Here error is all in the not done,
all in the diffidence that faltered . . .

                           [1948]

H.D. (HILDA DOOLITTLE)

[1886–1961]

Heat

O wind, rend open the heat,
   cut apart the heat,
   rend it to tatters.

CANTO LXXXI   **54Paquin** Parisian dress designer.   **56"Master thyself . . . thee beare"** adapted from Geoffrey Chaucer's poem "Truth." Chaucer's line reads "Control thyself, who controls the deeds of others."   **66Rathe** Middle English for "quick."   **72Blunt** Wilfred Blunt (1840–1922), poet and political writer.

Fruit cannot drop
through this thick air—   5
fruit cannot fall into heat
that presses up and blunts
the points of pears
and rounds the grapes.

Cut the heat—   10
plow through it,
turning it on either side
of your path.

[1916]

Helen

All Greece hates
the still eyes in the white face,
the lustre as of olives
where she stands,
and the white hands.   5

All Greece reviles
the wan face when she smiles,
hating it deeper still
when it grows wan and white,
remembering past enchantments   10
and past ills.

Greece sees unmoved,
God's daughter, born of love,
the beauty of cool feet
and slenderest knees,   15
could love indeed the maid,
only if she were laid,
white ash amid funereal cypresses.

[1924]

HELEN   Helen of Troy, abducted by Paris for her beauty.   ²**God's . . . love** Helen was the daughter of
Leda, a mortal, and Zeus, the Greek head god.

MARIANNE MOORE

[1887–1972]

With one of the freshest voices in twentieth-century American poetry, Marianne Moore brought an intellectual sense of play and an emotional sincerity to a poetry that thrives on hope, accuracy, and delight. Avoiding conventional poetic subjects, Moore wrote about animals and works of art, people and places, sports and society in eclectic and unpredictable ways. She valued in her animals and athletes their unconsciousness, their quirkiness, their elegant simplicity of action, and their surprising, sometimes astonishing behavior.

In addition to their singular subjects, Moore's poems are characterized by a wide-ranging diction and imagistic concreteness, unusual rhythms, unexpected rhymes, and stanzaic intricacy. Commenting on the diction in her familiar poem "Poetry," she states that a poet should not "discriminate against 'business documents and / school-books.' " T. S. Eliot suggests that her word choice is brilliant, precise, and at times a refinement of the speech that characterizes the American language and inspires "both the jargon of the laboratory and the slang of the comic strip." As such, Moore was as capable of describing a mussel shell

> opening and shutting itself like
> an
> injured fan

as she was capable of writing jargon such as "a liability rather than an asset," or "diminished vitality." This sense of diction, combined with her sense of a poem's possible rhythms, catches some readers off guard. Somehow it doesn't seem "poetic." We find no driving meter, no poetic rhetoric, only the cool, controlled illusion of everyday American speech. Moore's rhythms are spoken rhythms, but not the rhythms of the oral tradition. We find none of Whitman's biblical lists, no long chant-like invocations, no theatrical gestures. Her lines sound cleanly spoken, almost written, in a voice free of connectives. As Hugh Kenner remarks, her diction is "urbane without slickness and brisk without imprecision."

"I have a passion for rhythm and accent," Marianne Moore once told an interviewer, "and so I blundered into versifying." She enjoyed what she termed "inconspicuous rhymes and unpompous conspicuous rhymes" and considered the stanza, not the line, as the unit of poetry and "thus came to hazard hyphens at the end of the line." This stylistic feature is evident in one of her best poems, "The Fish," whose title is made up of its opening words. Notice the uneven line lengths within each stanza and the symmetry between stanzas. Notice, too, how the rhymes are sometimes hidden, displaced from accented syllables to less obtrusive words.

The Fish

wade
through black jade.
   Of the crow-blue mussel-shells, one keeps
   adjusting the ash-heaps;
      opening and shutting itself like   5

an
injured fan.
   The barnacles which encrust the side
   of the wave, cannot hide
      there for the submerged shafts of the   10

sun,
split like spun
   glass, move themselves with spotlight swiftness
   into the crevices—
      in and out, illuminating   15

the
turquoise sea
   of bodies. The water drives a wedge
   of iron through the iron edge
      of the cliff; whereupon the stars,   20

pink
rice-grains, ink-
   bespattered jelly-fish, crabs like green
   lilies, and submarine
      toadstools, slide each on the other.   25

All
external
   marks of abuse are present on this
   defiant edifice—
      all the physical features of   30

ac-
cident—lack
   of cornice, dynamic grooves, burns, and

hatchet strokes, these things stand
    out on it; the chasm-side is   35

dead.
Repeated
    evidence has proved that it can live
    on what can not revive
        its youth. The sea grows old in it.   40

                            [1921]

"The Fish" highlights more than Moore's stylistic virtuosity, poetic ingenuity, and linguistic extravagance. Beyond these admirable qualities, "The Fish" demonstrates an aptness of phrase and form suited to the scope of the subject, which one critic has identified as the "scars of experience."

Moore returns, as Bonnie Costello has noted, to premodernist assumptions about the moral value of poetry, particularly its capacity for teaching human values. And while her poems are not laced with didacticism, many do offer advice in the form of witty parables and of examples drawn from natural history. Unlike Robert Frost and Thomas Hardy, whose poetry is modernist in its philosophical premises while being cast in traditional poetic forms, Moore is modern in technique but traditional, even classical, in disposition and values. Her poetry is an original blend of classical reserve and modern candor. Her poems are "imaginary gardens with real toads in them."

Born in Missouri in 1887, Marianne Moore was educated at Bryn Mawr College in Pennsylvania, receiving her B.A. in 1909. She then taught commercial subjects at Carlisle Commercial College (1911–1915), where her pupils included the famous Native American athlete, Jim Thorpe. She began editing *The Dial*, an influential literary journal, from 1925 until it ceased publication in 1929. Her early poems appeared in the literary magazines *The Egoist*, *Poetry*, and *Others*, all of which published experimental modernist work. Her published writings also include a play, translations from the French and German, and the collections of critical essays *Predilections* (1955) and *Poetry and Criticism* (1965). She has received several prestigious honors, including the National Book Award (1952), the Bollinger Poetry Prize (1953), and the National Medal for Literature (1968) as well as honorary doctorates from eight universities.

In her later years she became a celebrity. In 1955 the Ford Motor Company engaged her help in the naming of Ford's then-new car, the Edsel. In 1968 at the invitation of the team's owners she opened the baseball season at Yankee Stadium. She appeared on television. Even people who had never read a poem could identify her by her flowing black cape and tricorn hat.

Moore's poetry testifies to the joy she took in life. She loved animals, slang, jargon—she loved to tango. Focusing her attention on the less exalted aspects of ordinary life, she wrote a poetry as Byzantine and explosive as the game of baseball she so admired. Gracefully muscling each line to the page, she created from these subjects, as T. S. Eliot has suggested, "part of the durable poetry written in our time."

Poetry

I, too, dislike it: there are things that are important beyond all this fiddle.
   Reading it, however, with a perfect contempt for it, one discovers in
   it after all, a place for the genuine.
      Hands that can grasp, eyes
        that can dilate, hair that can rise   5
          if it must, these things are important not because a

high-sounding interpretation can be put upon them but because they are
   useful. When they become so derivative as to become unintelligible,
   the same thing may be said for all of us, that we
      do not admire what   10
        we cannot understand: the bat
          holding on upside down or in quest of something to

eat, elephants pushing, a wild horse taking a roll, a tireless wolf under
   a tree, the immovable critic twitching his skin like a horse that feels a flea, the base-
   ball fan, the statistician—   15
      nor is it valid
        to discriminate against "business documents and

school-books"; all these phenomena are important. One must make a distinction
   however: when dragged into prominence by half poets, the result is not poetry,
   nor till the poets among us can be   20
      "literalists of
      the imagination"—above
        insolence and triviality and can present

for inspection, "imaginary gardens with real toads in them," shall we have
   it. In the meantime, if you demand on the one hand,   25
   the raw material of poetry in
      all its rawness and
      that which is on the other hand
        genuine, you are interested in poetry.

[1921]

Critics and Connoisseurs

There is a great amount of poetry in unconscious
  fastidiousness. Certain Ming
    products, imperial floor-coverings of coach-
wheel yellow, are well enough in their way but I have seen something
      that I like better—a   5
        mere childish attempt to make an imperfectly bal-
          lasted animal stand up,
        similar determination to make a pup
          eat his meat from the plate.

I remember a swan under the willows in Oxford,   10
  with flamingo-colored, maple-
    leaflike feet. It reconnoitered like a battle-
ship. Disbelief and conscious fastidiousness were
      ingredients in its
        disinclination to move. Finally its hardihood was   15
          not proof against its
        proclivity to more fully appraise such bits
          of food as the stream

bore counter to it; it made away with what I gave it
  to eat. I have seen this swan and   20
    I have seen you; I have seen ambition without
understanding in a variety of forms. Happening to stand
    by an ant-hill, I have
        seen a fastidious ant carrying a stick north, south,
          east, west, till it turned on   25
        itself, struck out from the flower-bed into the lawn,
          and returned to the point

from which it had started. Then abandoning the stick as
  useless and overtaxing its
    jaws with a particle of whitewash—pill-like but   30
heavy, it again went through the same course of procedure.
        What is
    there in being able
        to say that one has dominated the stream in an attitude of self-defense;
        in proving that one has had the experience   35
          of carrying a stick?

                          [1924]

The Steeple-Jack

Dürer would have seen a reason for living
    in a town like this, with eight stranded whales
to look at; with the sweet sea air coming into your house
on a fine day, from water etched
    with waves as formal as the scales   5
on a fish.

One by one in two's and three's, the seagulls keep
    flying back and forth over the town clock,
or sailing around the lighthouse without moving their wings—
rising steadily with a slight   10
    quiver of the body—or flock
mewing where

a sea the purple of the peacock's neck is
    paled to greenish azure as Dürer changed
the pine green of the Tyrol to peacock blue and guinea   15
gray. You can see a twenty-five-
    pound lobster; and fish nets arranged
to dry. The

whirlwind fife-and-drum of the storm bends the salt
    marsh grass, disturbs stars in the sky and the   20
star on the steeple; it is a privilege to see so
much confusion. Disguised by what
    might seem the opposite, the sea-
side flowers and

trees are favored by the fog so that you have   25
    the tropics at first hand: the trumpet vine,
fox-glove, giant snap-dragon, a salpiglossis that has
spots and stripes; morning-glories, gourds,
    or moon-vines trained on fishing-twine
at the back door;   30

cat-tails, flags, blueberries and spiderwort,
    striped grass, lichens, sunflowers, asters, daisies—
yellow and crab-claw ragged sailors with green bracts—toad-plant,

---

THE STEEPLE-JACK   [1]**Dürer**   Albrecht Dürer (1471–1528), German painter and engraver known for his meticulously detailed renderings of animals.

petunias, ferns; pink lilies, blue
      ones, tigers; poppies; black sweet-peas.   *35*
The climate

is not right for the banyan, frangipani, or
      jack-fruit trees; or for exotic serpent
life. Ring lizard and snake-skin for the foot, if you see fit;
but here they've cats, not cobras, to   *40*
      keep down the rats. The diffident
little newt

with white pin-dots on black horizontal spaced-
      out bands lives here; yet there is nothing that
ambition can buy or take away. The college student   *45*
named Ambrose sits on the hillside
      with his not-native books and hat
and sees boats

at sea progress white and rigid as if in
      a groove. Liking an elegance of which   *50*
the source is not bravado, he knows by heart the antique
sugar-bowl shaped summer-house of
      interlacing slats, and the pitch
of the church

spire, not true, from which a man in scarlet lets   *55*
      down a rope as a spider spins a thread;
he might be part of a novel, but on the sidewalk a
sign says C. J. Poole, Steeple-Jack,
      in black and white; and one in red
and white says   *60*

Danger. The church portico has four fluted
      columns, each a single piece of stone, made
modester by white-wash. This would be a fit haven for
waifs, children, animals, prisoners,
      and presidents who have repaid   *65*
sin-driven

senators by not thinking about them. The
      place has a school-house, a post-office in a
store, fish-houses, hen-houses, a three-masted schooner on   *70*
the stocks. The hero, the student,
      the steeple-jack, each in his way,
is at home.

It could not be dangerous to be living
    in a town like this, of simple people,
who have a steeple-jack placing danger-signs by the church   *75*
while he is gilding the solid-
    pointed star, which on a steeple
stands for hope.

        [1935]

To a Snail

If "compression is the first grace of style,"
you have it. Contractility is a virtue
as modesty is a virtue.
It is not the acquisition of any one thing
that is able to adorn,   *5*
or the incidental quality that occurs
as a concomitant of something well said,
that we value in style,
but the principle that is hid:
in the absence of feet, "a method of conclusions";   *10*
"a knowledge of principles,"
in the curious phenomenon of your occipital horn.

        [1935]

The Past Is the Present

If external action is effete
    and rhyme is outmoded,
      I shall revert to you,
    Habakkak, as when in a Bible class
      the teacher was speaking of unrhymed verse.   *5*
He said—and I think I repeat his exact words,
    "Hebrew poetry is prose
with a sort of heightened consciousness." Ecstasy affords
    the occasion and expediency determines the form.

        [1935]

The Monkeys

winked too much and were afraid of snakes. The zebras, supreme in
their abnormality; the elephants with their fog-colored skin
  and strictly practical appendages
    were there, the small cats; and the parakeet—
      trivial and humdrum on examination, destroying   *5*
    bark and portions of the food it could not eat.

I recall their magnificence, now not more magnificent
than it is dim. It is difficult to recall the ornament,
  speech, and precise manner of what one might
    call the minor acquaintances twenty   *10*
      years back; but I shall not forget him—that Gilgamesh among
    the hairy carnivora—that cat with the

wedge-shaped, slate-gray marks on its forelegs and the resolute tail,
astringently remarking, "They have imposed on us with their pale
  half-fledged protestations, trembling about   *15*
    in inarticulate frenzy, saying
      it is not for us to understand art; finding it
    all so difficult, examining the thing

as if it were inconceivably arcanic, as symmet-
rically frigid as if it had been carved out of chrysoprase   *20*
  or marble—strict with tension, malignant
    in its power over us and deeper
      than the sea when it proffers flattery in exchange for hemp,
    rye, flax, horses, platinum, timber, and fur."

                                                      [1935]

The Mind Is an Enchanting Thing

        is an enchanted thing
           like the glaze on a
      katydid-wing
           subdivided by sun
             till the nettings are legion.   *5*
      Like Gieseking playing Scarlatti;

THE MONKEYS   [11]**Gilgamesh**   legendary Sumerian king and hero of ancient epics.

like the apteryx-awl
        as a beak, or the
kiwi's rain-shawl
            of haired feathers, the mind   10
                feeling its way as though blind,
walks along with its eyes on the ground.

It has memory's ear
        that can hear without
having to hear.   15
            Like the gyroscope's fall,
                truly unequivocal
because trued by regnant certainty,

it is a power of
        strong enchantment. It   20
is like the dove-
            neck animated by
                sun; it is memory's eye;
it's conscientious inconsistency.

It tears off the veil; tears   25
        the temptation, the
mist the heart wears,
            from its eyes—if the heart
                has a face; it takes apart
dejection. It's fire in the dove-neck's   30

iridescence; in the
        inconsistencies
of Scarlatti.
            Unconfusion submits
                its confusion to proof; it's   35
not a Herod's oath that cannot change.

                                              [1941]

Nevertheless

you've seen a strawberry
        that's had a struggle; yet
        was, where the fragments met,

a hedgehog or a star-
    fish for the multitude 5
    of seeds. What better food

than apple-seeds—the fruit
    within the fruit—locked in
    like counter-curved twin

hazel-nuts? Frost that kills 10
    the little rubber-plant-
    leaves of *kok-saghyz*-stalks, can't

harm the roots; they still grow
    in frozen ground. Once where
    there was a prickly-pear- 15

leaf clinging to barbed wire,
    a root shot down to grow
    in earth two feet below;

as carrots form mandrakes
    or a ram's-horn root some- 20
    times. Victory won't come

to me unless I go
    to it; a grape-tendril
    ties a knot in knots till

knotted thirty times,—so 25
    the bound twig that's under-
    gone and over-gone, can't stir.

The weak overcomes its
    menace, the strong over-
    comes itself. What is there 30

like fortitude! What sap
    went through that little thread
    to make the cherry red!

[1944]

Propriety

is some such word
    as the chord
        Brahms had heard
        from a bird,

sung down near the root of the throat;   5
it's the little downy woodpecker
    spiraling a tree—
    up up up like mercury;

  a not long
  sparrow-song   10
    of hayseed
    magnitude—
a tuned reticence with rigor
from strength at the source. Propriety is
    Bach's Solfegietto—   15
    harmonica and basso.

  The fish-spine
  on firs, on
    somber trees
    by the sea's   20
walls of wave-worn rock—have it; and
a moonbow and Bach's cheerful firmness
    in a minor key.
    It's an owl-and-a-pussy-

  both-content   25
  agreement.
    Come, come. It's
    mixed with wits;
it's not a graceful sadness. It's
resistance with bent head, like foxtail   30
    millet's. Brahms and Bach,
    no; Bach and Brahms. To thank Bach

  for his song
  first, is wrong.
    Pardon me;   35
    both are the
unintentional pansy-face
uncursed by self-inspection; blackened
    because born that way.

        [1951]

T. S. ELIOT

[1888–1965]

Some readers believe that T. S. Eliot was more English than American, not only since he lived in England for much of his life and converted to its state religion, Anglicanism, but also because he subscribed to its cultural values. His description of himself as a "royalist in politics, classicist in literature, and Anglo-Catholic in religion" seems to support this view. So too does Eliot's assumption of British citizenship in 1927. Yet rather than losing his American cultural identity, Eliot seems to have grafted a British one onto it. Eliot thus became a poet of two worlds rather than one.

Ezra Pound and Thomas Stearns Eliot are generally recognized as the founders of modernist poetry in English (with Walt Whitman and Emily Dickinson serving as their American precursors). Their influence has been far greater than that of any other modern American poet. What made their poetry so important for modernism? Why did it become so prominent? And what distinguished it from the work of other modern poets writing in English? Three things at least: its difficulty; its technical innovation; its thematic preoccupations.

Both Eliot and Pound are considered "difficult" poets whose major works present formidable obstacles for all but the most experienced readers. The difficulty in reading Eliot's poems is attributable primarily to three factors: its heavy use of allusion, its borrowings from foreign languages, and its use of juxtaposed images. When considering Eliot's late religious poems, especially *Four Quartets,* one must also reckon with mystical and paradoxical ideas about time, death, and spirituality. Like Pound's work, much of Eliot's poetry includes numerous references to history, philosophy, and literature—especially medieval and Renaissance drama and the classical literature of Greece and Rome. Eliot expected his readers to be familiar with Greek mythology, to recognize references to Dante, Shakespeare, and Wagner (among others), and to make sense of the allusions by considering them in the context of the poem. Even if we cannot recognize all of Eliot's literary allusions or historical references, we can, nevertheless, gain a sense of the poem's meaning, intention, and power by attending to its images, especially by establishing connections among them.

Another dragon guarding the gate of Eliot's poetry is the apparent lack of connection among sections, stanzas, lines, and sentences. Eliot's poems are often highly imagistic. In *The Waste Land,* for example, he makes the image an instrument of ironic commentary by juxtaposing details of the present with more idealized images of the past. The images may be included as part of brief dramatic scenes, as in the typist's encounter with the "young man carbuncular." They may be presented as static pictorial details, as in the many examples of dryness and sterility. Or they may be primarily allusive, as in the references to the mythological rape of Philomel.

Eliot's poems employ fragmentation as a deliberate structural principle, one consequence of which is that their coherence must be inferred by the reader. One advantage, in fact, of poems that eschew discursive explanation is increased intensity and compression. Another is that they demand readers' active participation in making sense of a fragmented structure. Still another benefit is an opportunity for the poet to create new structural patterns, new ways to organize forms. Many of Eliot's poems, for example, employ musical structures. *The Waste Land,* to cite one example, is arranged in movements much like a symphony.

An additional reason that Eliot's poems are seen as difficult derives from his belief that poetry, especially modern poetry, *should be* difficult. In *The Use of Poetry and the Use of Criticism* he discusses his reason: "The difficulty in reading some poems is caused by the author's having left something out that the reader is used to finding; so that the reader, bewildered, gropes about for what is absent." Alongside this remark we should place Eliot's notion that great poetry need not be understood in every line and detail. Eliot believed that readers could apprehend poems in languages they could neither read nor translate. Eliot also believed that poetry should reflect the complexities and ambiguities of experience. His poetic forms typify the fragmentation, disconnection, and confusion at the heart of modern history, which he once described as an "immense panorama of futility and anarchy."

Thomas Stearns Eliot's life reflects some of the tensions and divisions of his poetry. He was born in St. Louis, Missouri, in 1888. Though raised in the South-west, his family had its roots in New England, and they vacationed at a summer home in Gloucester, Massachusetts. Solidifying this aspect of Eliot's life was his education at Harvard University (1906–1910), where he edited *The Harvard Advocate* and earned both bachelor's and master's degrees. Eliot then went abroad to attend the Sorbonne and to Merton College, Oxford, where he studied philosophy. He wrote his master's thesis there on the British philosopher F. H. Bradley and was working toward a doctorate in philosophy and an academic career when the outbreak of World War I prevented his return from England to complete his degree at Harvard.

Instead of pursuing an academic life, Eliot turned to business and to poetry. Eliot's employment ranged from teaching at the High Wycombe and Highgate schools (1915–1917) through working as a clerk for Lloyd's Bank of London (1917–1925) to serving as editor and later as director of Faber and Faber, a London publishing house (1926–1965). In addition, Eliot founded *The Criterion,* an important literary quarterly that flourished from 1922 to 1939. He received many distinctions and awards, including the Nobel Prize for Literature (1948), the New York Drama Critics Circle Award (1950), the Dante Gold Medal, Florence (1959), and the Order of Merit, Bonn (1959). He also received seventeen honorary doctorates from the most prestigious universities in six countries, including Harvard, Yale, Oxford, and Cambridge.

Eliot's most influential poem, *The Waste Land,* burst upon the literary scene in 1922. Nearly fifty years later, in 1971, a facsimile edition of this important document of literary modernism was published with transcripts of Eliot's original drafts, including extensive annotations made by Ezra Pound. Edited by Eliot's widow, this edition revealed the extent of Eliot's debt to Pound and the degree of Pound's editorial skill and judgment. Pound advised Eliot to revise the poem by excising discursive explanation and cutting seventy-two lines of rhymed couplets at the beginning of "The Fire Sermon." Pound also dissuaded Eliot from using "Gerontion" as a preface to the poem and suggested numerous small-scale alterations that resulted in a more unified poem. In gratitude Eliot dedicated *The Waste Land* to Pound, designating him *il miglior fabbro* ("the better craftsman"). *The Waste Land* is important not only as a poetic achievement but also as a remarkable influence exerted on an entire generation of poets, both those who were converted to Eliot's techniques and those who, like William Carlos Williams, resisted them.

Eliot's poetic output included a 1936 volume that collected his verse of 1906–1935 and a larger collection, *The Collected Poems 1909–1962*. This final book featured Eliot's last major poetic enterprise, *Four Quartets*, originally published in 1943. In addition to this modest poetic production, Eliot also wrote five plays and a collection of humorous verse, *Old Possum's Book of Practical Cats*, which inspired the musical *Cats*.

His literary criticism includes brief books on Dante, George Herbert, Elizabethan drama, and seventeenth-century poetry, among many essays. Eliot's criticism reflects an effort to find solutions to his own poetic problems. Like his plays, his criticism is interesting for the light it sheds on his own poetry, especially his emphasis on the poem itself rather than on the personality of the poet. His criticism is perhaps even more important for its influential revaluation of seventeenth-century literature, especially the poetry of John Donne and Andrew Marvell, and the plays of a number of Elizabethan and Jacobean dramatists.

Eliot's most popular and best-known poem after *The Waste Land* is "The Love Song of J. Alfred Prufrock." It portrays an inhibited, timid man who is unable to declare his feelings for a woman. In a series of self-deprecating excuses, he reveals his fear of human connection, identifying himself as a diminished, ineffectual person. Considered by some readers to be a dramatic monologue, "Prufrock" lacks the steady narrative drive and consistent voice characteristic of the form as practiced by Robert Browning and Alfred, Lord Tennyson. With its ironies, its fragmentation, and its elaborate conceits, "Prufrock" displays the influence of both the seventeenth-century metaphysical poets and the French Symbolists. The poem also exhibits Eliot's lifelong concern with human relationships.

The Waste Land, however, is Eliot's modernist masterpiece. It is the single most widely read and most frequently analyzed American poem of the twentieth century. Much celebrated as a modernist document, it offers an account of the dismal state of the world following World War I. The world of *The Waste Land* lacks value and meaning. Human relationships are based on misuse and self-gratification. The poem's various voices depict a place devoid of faith, hope, and love. Read with a biographical emphasis, *The Waste Land* reflects aspects of Eliot's personal problems, particularly his unhappy first marriage. From a historical perspective, the poem offers a critique of a world without an ultimate purpose. From a mythic standpoint, it suggests how heroic virtues and traditional cultural and religious values are necessary to restore a more vital, hopeful world. To see the poem as "only the relief of a personal and insignificant grouse against life" (as Eliot once described it) or to emphasize too heavily its connections with the Grail legend and fertility rituals (directions Eliot also suggested) is to restrict our understanding and impoverish our experience of it. *The Waste Land* shares with other ambitious American poems a multiplicity of facets. It is partly a language experiment, partly an ambiguous allegory, partly a puzzle, partly a game of wit. It is, for many, the most challenging poem of the century, and certainly the most famous.

Eliot was only thirty-four when *The Waste Land* was published. It would be more than twenty years before he would publish his next major poetic work, *Four Quartets,* a series of expansive meditations on time, change, age, suffering, love, spirituality, and history. Even more explicitly than *The Waste Land,* each of the quartets assumes a musical structure. Each contains five movements varied in rhythm; each contains themes or statements followed by counterthemes, repetitions, and variations of the original statements.

The last of the quartets, "Little Gidding," presents an opportunity to see Eliot in a more hopeful, less critical mode than is characteristic of his earlier work. In "Little Gidding," as in the other quartets, Eliot offers a positive image of community and an encouraging vision of life. Although generally recognized as a major achievement, the *Quartets* have never captured the imagination of readers the way *The Waste Land* has. It was *The Waste Land* that spread Eliot's fame and influence. And it was *The Waste Land,* along with the critical theory Eliot developed to support it, that largely created the taste of the age, a taste that would ultimately judge Eliot the supreme poet of his time.

The Love Song of J. Alfred Prufrock

S'io credesse che mia risposta fosse
A persona che mai tornasse al mondo,
Questa fiamma staria senza più scosse.
Ma perciocche giammai di questo fondo
Non tornò vivo alcun, s'i'odo il vero,
Senza tema d'infamia ti rispondo.

Let us go then, you and I,
When the evening is spread out against the sky
Like a patient etherized upon a table;
Let us go, through certain half-deserted streets,
The muttering retreats   5
Of restless nights in one-night cheap hotels
And sawdust restaurants with oyster-shells:

THE LOVE SONG OF J. ALFRED PRUFROCK   Epigraph from Dante's Inferno, canto XXVII, 61–66. The words are spoken by Guido da Montefeltro when asked to identify himself: "If I thought my answer were given to anyone who could ever return to the world, this flame would shake no more; but since none ever did return above from this depth, if what I hear is true, without fear of infamy I answer thee."

Streets that follow like a tedious argument
Of insidious intent
To lead you to an overwhelming question . . .   10
Oh, do not ask, "What is it?"
Let us go and make our visit.

In the room the women come and go
Talking of Michelangelo.

The yellow fog that rubs its back upon the window-panes,   15
The yellow smoke that rubs its muzzle on the window-panes,
Licked its tongue into the corners of the evening,
Lingered upon the pools that stand in drains,
Let fall upon its back the soot that falls from chimneys,
Slipped by the terrace, made a sudden leap,   20
And seeing that it was a soft October night,
Curled once about the house, and fell asleep.

And indeed there will be time
For the yellow smoke that slides along the street
Rubbing its back upon the window-panes;   25
There will be time, there will be time
To prepare a face to meet the faces that you meet;
There will be time to murder and create,
And time for all the works and days of hands
That lift and drop a question on your plate;   30
Time for you and time for me,
And time yet for a hundred indecisions,
And for a hundred visions and revisions,
Before the taking of a toast and tea.

In the room the women come and go   35
Talking of Michelangelo.

And indeed there will be time
To wonder, "Do I dare?" and, "Do I dare?"
Time to turn back and descend the stair,
With a bald spot in the middle of my hair—   40
(They will say: "How his hair is growing thin!")
My morning coat, my collar mounting firmly to the chin,
My necktie rich and modest, but asserted by a simple pin—
(They will say: "But how his arms and legs are thin!")

[29]**works and days**   *Works and Days* is the title of a poem by the Greek poet Hesiod (eighth century B.C.) that combines moral teaching with an account of an agrarian life.

Do I dare   *45*
Disturb the universe?
In a minute there is time
For decisions and revisions which a minute will reverse.

For I have known them all already, known them all—
Have known the evenings, mornings, afternoons,   *50*
I have measured out my life with coffee spoons;
I know the voices dying with a dying fall
Beneath the music from a farther room.
    So how should I presume?

And I have known the eyes already, known them all—   *55*
The eyes that fix you in a formulated phrase,
And when I am formulated, sprawling on a pin,
When I am pinned and wriggling on the wall,
Then how should I begin
To spit out all the butt-ends of my days and ways?   *60*
    And how should I presume?

And I have known the arms already, known them all—
Arms that are braceleted and white and bare
(But in the lamplight, downed with light brown hair!)
Is it perfume from a dress   *65*
That makes me so digress?
Arms that lie along a table, or wrap about a shawl.
    And should I then presume?
    And how should I begin?

    .   .   .   .   .

Shall I say, I have gone at dusk through narrow streets   *70*
And watched the smoke that rises from the pipes
Of lonely men in shirt-sleeves, leaning out of windows? . . .

I should have been a pair of ragged claws
Scuttling across the floors of silent seas.

    .   .   .   .

And the afternoon, the evening, sleeps so peacefully!   *75*
Smoothed by long fingers,
Asleep . . . tired . . . or it malingers,
Stretched on the floor, here beside you and me.
Should I, after tea and cakes and ices,
Have the strength to force the moment to its crisis?   *80*

---

[52]**I know . . . dying fall**   echoes Shakespeare's *Twelfth Night,* I, i, 1–4 "If music be the food of love, play on; / Give me excess of it, that, surfeiting / The appetite may sicken, and so die. / That strain again! it had a dying fall."

But though I have wept and fasted, wept and prayed,
Though I have seen my head (grown slightly bald) brought in upon a platter,
I am no prophet—and here's no greater matter;
I have seen the moment of my greatness flicker,
And I have seen the eternal Footman hold my coat, and snicker,   85
And in short, I was afraid.

And would it have been worth it, after all,
After the cups, the marmalade, the tea,
Among the porcelain, among some talk of you and me,
Would it have been worth while,   90
To have bitten off the matter with a smile,
To have squeezed the universe into a ball
To roll it towards some overwhelming question,
To say: "I am Lazarus, come from the dead,
Come back to tell you all, I shall tell you all"—   95
If one, settling a pillow by her head,
     Should say: "That is not what I meant at all.
     That is not it, at all."

And would it have been worth it, after all,
Would it have been worth while,   100
After the sunsets and the dooryards and the sprinkled streets,
After the novels, after the teacups, after the skirts that trail along the floor—
And this, and so much more?—
It is impossible to say just what I mean!
But as if a magic lantern threw the nerves in patterns on a screen: 105
Would it have been worth while
If one, settling a pillow or throwing off a shawl,
And turning toward the window, should say:
    "That is not it at all,
    That is not what I meant, at all."   110

    . . . . . .

No! I am not Prince Hamlet, nor was meant to be;
Am an attendant lord, one that will do
To swell a progress, start a scene or two,
Advise the prince; no doubt, an easy tool,
Deferential, glad to be of use,   115

[82]**my head . . . upon a platter**   John the Baptist was beheaded at the order of King Herod to please his wife, Herodias, and daughter, Salome. See Matthew 14:1–11.   [91–92]**To have bitten . . . into a ball**   An allusion to Andrew Marvell's poem "To His Coy Mistress": Let us roll all our strength and all / Our sweetness up into one ball / And tear our pleasures with rough strife / Thorough the iron gates of life." Eliot also alludes to the first line of Marvell's poem, "Had we world enough and time," in line 23. "And indeed there will be time."   [94]**Lazarus**   a man whom Jesus raised from the dead   See John 11:1–44   [113]**progress**   a procession or royal journey made by members of the court.

Politic, cautious, and meticulous;
Full of high sentence, but a bit obtuse;
At times, indeed, almost ridiculous—
Almost, at times, the Fool.

I grow old . . . I grow old . . .   *120*
I shall wear the bottoms of my trousers rolled.

Shall I part my hair behind? Do I dare to eat a peach?
I shall wear white flannel trousers, and walk upon the beach.
I have heard the mermaids singing, each to each.

I do not think that they will sing to me.   *125*

I have seen them riding seaward on the waves
Combing the white hair of the waves blown back
When the wind blows the water white and black.

We have lingered in the chambers of the sea
By sea-girls wreathed with seaweed red and brown   *130*
Till human voices wake us, and we drown.

    [1917]

Preludes

I

The winter evening settles down
With smell of steaks in passageways.
Six o'clock.
The burnt-out ends of smoky days.
And now a gusty shower wraps   *5*
The grimy scraps
Of withered leaves about your feet
And newspapers from vacant lots;
The showers beat
On broken blinds and chimney-pots,   *10*
And at the corner of the street
A lonely cab-horse steams and stamps.
And then the lighting of the lamps.

II

The morning comes to consciousness
Of faint stale smells of beer   *15*

From the sawdust-trampled street
With all its muddy feet that press
To early coffee-stands.
With the other masquerades
That time resumes,   *20*
One thinks of all the hands
That are raising dingy shades
In a thousand furnished rooms.

III

You tossed a blanket from the bed,
You lay upon your back, and waited;   *25*
You dozed, and watched the night revealing
The thousand sordid images
Of which your soul was constituted;
They flickered against the ceiling.
And when all the world came back   *30*
And the light crept up between the shutters
And you heard the sparrows in the gutters,
You had such a vision of the street
As the street hardly understands;
Sitting along the bed's edge, where   *35*
You curled the papers from your hair,
Or clasped the yellow soles of feet
In the palms of both soiled hands.

IV

His soul stretched tight across the skies
That fade behind a city block,   *40*
Or trampled by insistent feet
At four and five and six o'clock;
And short square fingers stuffing pipes,
And evening newspapers, and eyes
Assured of certain certainties,   *45*
The conscience of a blackened street
Impatient to assume the world.

I am moved by fancies that are curled
Around these images, and cling:
The notion of some infinitely gentle   *50*
Infinitely suffering thing.

Wipe your hand across your mouth, and laugh;
The worlds revolve like ancient women
Gathering fuel in vacant lots.

[1917]

Gerontion

Thou hast nor youth nor age
But as it were an after dinner sleep
Dreaming of both.

Here I am, an old man in a dry month,
Being read to by a boy, waiting for rain.
I was neither at the hot gates
Nor fought in the warm rain
Nor knee deep in the salt-marsh, heaving a cutlass,   5
Bitten by flies, fought.
My house is a decayed house,
And the Jew squats on the window sill, the owner,
Spawned in some estaminet of Antwerp,
Blistered in Brussels, patched and peeled in London.   10
The goat coughs at night in the field overhead;
Rocks, moss, stonecrop, iron, merds.
The woman keeps the kitchen, makes tea,
Sneezes at evening, poking the peevish gutter.
                    I an old man,   15
A dull head among windy spaces.

Signs are taken for wonders. "We would see a sign!"
The word within a word, unable to speak a word,
Swaddled with darkness. In the juvescence of the year
Came Christ the tiger   20

In depraved May, dogwood and chestnut, flowering judas,
To be eaten, to be divided, to be drunk
Among whispers; by Mr. Silvero

GERONTION   The title is coined from the Greek geron, or "old man" The epigraph is from Shakespeare's *Measure for Measure*, III, i, 32–34.   [3]hot gates   an allusion to Thermopylae (Greek for "hot gates"), the mountain pass where the Spartans defeated the Persians in 480 B.C   [12]merds   French for "dung." [17]"We would see a sign!"   See Matthew 12:38: "Master, we would see a sign from you," in which the disciples asked Jesus for an indication of his divinity. And also Luke 2:12: "And this will be a sign for you; you will find a babe wrapped in swaddling cloths and lying in a manger "   [18]The word . . . a word   see John 1:1, 14: "In the beginning was the Word, and the Word was with God, and the Word was God . . . And the Word became flesh and dwelt among us." Lines 17–18 also allude to a sermon by Lancelot Andrewes (1555–1626) in which Andrewes discusses the gospel and the life of Jesus as signs and wonders and refers to the infant Jesus as "*verbum infans,* the Word without a word; the eternal Word not able to speak a word."   [19]juvescence   juvenescence, or youth.   [21]depraved May   a reference to Henry Adams's autobiography, *The Education of Henry Adams,* Chapter 18, in which he describes the "passionate depravity that marked the Maryland May."

With caressing hands, at Limoges
Who walked all night in the next room;   25

By Hakagawa, bowing among the Titians;
By Madame de Tornquist, in the dark room
Shifting the candles; Fräulein von Kulp
Who turned in the hall, one hand on the door. Vacant shuttles
Weave the wind. I have no ghosts,   30
An old man in a draughty house
Under a windy knob.

After such knowledge, what forgiveness? Think now
History has many cunning passages, contrived corridors
And issues, deceives with whispering ambitions,   35
Guides us by vanities. Think now
She gives when our attention is distracted
And what she gives, gives with such supple confusions
That the giving famishes the craving. Gives too late
What's not believed in, or is still believed,   40
In memory only, reconsidered passion. Gives too soon
Into weak hands, what's thought can be dispensed with
Till the refusal propagates a fear. Think
Neither fear nor courage saves us. Unnatural vices
Are fathered by our heroism. Virtues   45
Are forced upon us by our impudent crimes.

These tears are shaken from the wrath-bearing tree.

The tiger springs in the new year. Us he devours. Think at last
We have not reached conclusion, when I
Stiffen in a rented house. Think at last   50
I have not made this show purposelessly
And it is not by any concitation
Of the backward devils.

I would meet you upon this honestly.
I that was near your heart was removed therefrom   55
To lose beauty in terror, terror in inquisition.
I have lost my passion: why should I need to keep it
Since what is kept must be adulterated?
I have lost my sight, smell, hearing, taste and touch:
How should I use them for your closer contact?   60

[23-28]**Mr. Silvero . . . Fräulein von Kulp** Eliot invented these names.   [52]**concitation** stirring up.

These with a thousand small deliberations
Protract the profit of their chilled delirium,
Excite the membrane, when the sense has cooled,
With pungent sauces, multiply variety
In a wilderness of mirrors. What will the spider do,   65
Suspend its operations, will the weevil
Delay? De Bailhache, Fresca, Mrs. Cammel, whirled
Beyond the circuit of the shuddering Bear
In fractured atoms. Gull against the wind, in the windy straits
. Of Belle Isle, or running on the Horn.   70
White feathers in the snow, the Gulf claims,
And an old man driven by the Trades
To a sleepy corner.

Tenants of the house,
Thoughts of a dry brain in a dry season.   75

[1920]

The Waste Land

"Nam Sibyllam quidem Cumis ego ipse oculis meis vidi in ampulla pendere, et cum illi pueri dicerent:
Σιβνλλα τί θελεις; *respondebat illa:* αποθανειν θελω.*"*

FOR EZRA POUND
IL MIGLIOR FABBRO.

I. The Burial of the Dead

April is the cruellest month, breeding
Lilacs out of the dead land, mixing
Memory and desire, stirring

GERONTION   67-68**De Bailhache . . . shuddering Bear**   unidentified, perhaps invented, persons who will be hurled around Polaris, the pole star, the outermost star in the handle of the Little Dipper.
THE WASTE LAND   Eliot acknowledged that the poem's title, plan, and symbolism were influenced by Jesse L. Weston's book on the Grail legend, *From Ritual to Romance* (1920). He also recognized the importance for the poem of *The Golden Bough* (1890–1915), especially the portions that concern vegetation myths and fertility rituals. Eliot's fifty-two footnotes are incorporated among those of the editors and identified as his. The epigraph quotes Petronius's *Satyricon* (first century A.D.: "For with my own eyes I saw the Sibyl hanging in a jar at Cumae, and when the boys said to her, 'Sibyl, what do you want'? she replied, 'I want to die.' " The Sibyl, a prophetess, had been granted immortal life but not immortal youth by Apollo. Her shriveled form was kept in a jar in the temple of Hercules at Cumae. Eliot's dedication acknowledges the editorial assistance of Ezra Pound, whom he designates "the better craftsman." The Italian quotation is taken from Dante's *Purgatorio*, XXVI, 17, in which Guido Guinizelli pays tribute to the Provençal poet Arnaut Daniel as a better maker of poems.   **The Burial of the Dead**   a phrase from the Anglican burial service.

Dull roots with spring rain.
Winter kept us warm, covering   5
Earth in forgetful snow, feeding
A little life with dried tubers.
Summer surprised us, coming over the Starnbergersee
With a shower of rain; we stopped in the colonnade,
And went on in sunlight, into the Hofgarten,   10
And drank coffee, and talked for a hour.
Bin gar keine Russin, stamm' aus Litauen, echt deutsch.
And when we were children, staying at the arch-duke's,
My cousin's, he took me out on a sled,
And I was frightened. He said, Marie,   15
Marie, hold on tight. And down we went.
In the mountains, there you feel free.
I read, much of the night, and go south in the winter.

What are the roots that clutch, what branches grow
Out of this stony rubbish? Son of man,   20
You cannot say, or guess, for you know only
A heap of broken images, where the sun beats,
And the dead tree gives no shelter, the cricket no relief,
And the dry stone no sound of water. Only
There is shadow under this red rock,   25
(Come in under the shadow of this red rock),
And I will show you something different from either
Your shadow at morning striding behind you
Or your shadow at evening rising to meet you;
I will show you fear in a handful of dust.   30
> *Frisch weht der Wind*
> *Der Heimat zu*
> *Mein Irisch Kind,*
> *Wo weilest du?*
"You gave me hyacinths first a year ago;   35
They called me the hyacinth girl."
—Yet when we came back, late, from the hyacinth garden,
Your arms full, and your hair wet, I could not
Speak, and my eyes failed, I was neither

8Starnbergersee a resort lake near Munich.   **10Hofgarten** a public park that had once been a royal palace garden.   **12Bin gar keine . . . echt deutsch** German for "I'm not Russian; I come from Lithuania, a true German."   **20Son of man** Eliot's note: "Cf. Ezekiel II, i: 'Son of man, stand upon thy feet, and I will speak to thee.'"   **23the cricket no relief** Eliot's note: "Cf. Ecclesiastes XII, v: 'the grasshopper shall be a burden, and desire shall fail.'"   **24-25And the dry stone . . . under this red rock** The prophet Isaiah had foretold the coming of a Messiah who would be "a river of water in a dry place, as the shadow of a great rock in a weary land." **31-34Frisch weht der Wind . . . Wo weilest du?** Eliot's note: *"V[ide]* [see] *Tristan und Isolde,* I, verses 5–8." The lines mean "Fresh blows the wind, to the homeland, my Irish child, where do you tarry?" It is sung in Wagner's opera by a sailor who thinks about his beloved.

Living nor dead, and I knew nothing,   *40*
Looking into the heart of light, the silence.
Oed' und leer das Meer.

Madame Sosostris, famous clairvoyante,
Had a bad cold, nevertheless
Is known to be the wisest woman in Europe,   *45*
With a wicked pack of cards. Here, said she,
Is your card, the drowned Phoenician Sailor,
(Those are pearls that were his eyes. Look!)
Here is Belladonna, the Lady of the Rocks,
The lady of situations.   *50*
Here is the man with three staves, and here the Wheel,
And here is the one-eyed merchant, and this card,
Which is blank, is something he carries on his back,
Which I am forbidden to see. I do not find
The Hanged Man. Fear death by water.   *55*
I see crowds of people, walking round in a ring.
Thank you. If you see dear Mrs. Equitone,
Tell her I bring the horoscope myself:
One must be so careful these days.

Unreal City,   *60*
Under the brown fog of a winter dawn,
A crowd flowed over London Bridge, so many
I had not thought death had undone so many.
Sighs, short and infrequent, were exhaled,
And each man fixed his eyes before his feet.   *65*

---

⁴²Oed' und leer das Meer   Eliot's note: "Id.[em] [the same] III, verse 24." In Wagner's *Tristan und Isolde,* this line is sung by a shepherd looking out to sea for a sign of Isolde's ship, which Tristan eagerly awaits. Tristan lies wounded at his castle. The line translates "Empty and waste is the sea."   **⁴⁶wicked pack of cards**   Tarot cards have been used for fortunetelling. Eliot's note on the passage reads: "I am not familiar with the exact constitution of the Tarot pack of cards, from which I have obviously departed to suit my own convenience. The Hanged Man, a member of the traditional pack, fits my purpose in two ways: because he is associated in my mind with the Hanged God of Frazer, and because I associate him with the hooded figure in the passage of the disciples to Emmaus in Part V. The Phoenician Sailor and the Merchant appear later; also the 'crowds of people,' and Death by Water is executed in Part IV. The Man with Three Staves (an authentic member of the Tarot pack) I associate, quite arbitrarily, with the Fisher King himself."   **⁴⁸Those are pearls that were his eyes**   a quotation from Shakespeare's *The Tempest,* I, ii, 398. Prince Ferdinand, who has been shipwrecked with his father on an island, is told falsely that his father has died. The line suggests that the supposed death involved a miraculous change into something rich and beautiful.   **⁴⁹Belladonna**   Literally "beautiful lady," belladonna also refers to nightshade, a poisonous plant.   **⁶⁰Unreal City**   Eliot's note: "Cf Baudelaire: *'Fourmillante cité, cité pleine de rêves / Où le spectre en plein jour raccroche le passant.'* "   The lines can be translated "Swarming city, city full of dreams, / Where the specter in broad daylight accosts the passersby."   **⁶³I had not thought . . . so many**   Eliot's note: "Cf. *Inferno,* III, 55–57." Eliot quotes the Italian, which can be translated "so long a train of people that I would never have believed death had undone so many."   **⁶⁴Sighs . . . were exhaled**   Eliot's note: "Cf. *Inferno,* IV, 25–27." Eliot again refers to the Italian, which translates "Here, to my hearing, there was no weeping, but sighs which caused the eternal air to tremble."

Flowed up the hill and down King William Street,
To where Saint Mary Woolnoth kept the hours
With a dead sound on the final stroke of nine.
There I saw one I knew, and stopped him, crying: "Stetson!
"You who were with me in the ships at Mylae!   *70*
"That corpse you planted last year in your garden,
"Has it begun to sprout? Will it bloom this year?
"Or has the sudden frost disturbed its bed?
"O keep the Dog far hence, that's friend to men,
"Or with his nails he'll dig it up again!   *75*
"You! hypocrite lecteur!—mon semblable,—mon frère!"

II. A Game of Chess

The Chair she sat in, like a burnished throne,
Glowed on the marble, where the glass
Held up by standards wrought with fruited vines
From which a golden Cupidon peeped out   *80*
(Another hid his eyes behind his wing)
Doubled the flames of sevenbranched candelabra
Reflecting light upon the table as
The glitter of her jewels rose to meet it,
From satin cases poured in rich profusion.   *85*
In vials of ivory and coloured glass
Unstoppered, lurked her strange synthetic perfumes,
Unguent, powdered, or liquid—troubled, confused
And drowned the sense in odours; stirred by the air
That freshened from the window, these ascended   *90*
In fattening the prolonged candle-flames,
Flung their smoke into the laquearia,
Stirring the pattern on the coffered ceiling.
Huge sea-wood fed with copper
Burned green and orange, framed by the coloured stone,   *95*
In which sad light a carvèd dolphin swam.

66-68King William Street . . . stroke of nine: Eliot's note: "A phenomenon which I have often noticed " The church of St. Mary Woolnoth is in London's financial district.   **70Mylae** site of a naval battle in the Punic War (260 B.C.).   **74-75"O keep the Dog . . . dig it up again!"** Eliot's note: "Cf. the dirge in Webster's *White Devil,* V, iv, 97–98 which reads 'But keep the wolf far thence, that's foe to man, / For with his nails he'll dig them up again.' "   **76"You! . . . mon frère!"** Eliot's note· "V. Baudelaire, Preface to *Fleurs du Mal.*" The last line of Baudelaire's introductory poem "To the Reader" can be translated "Hypocrite reader!—my likeness—my brother!"   **A Game of Chess** Thomas Middleton's play (1627) The title alludes to another play in which a seduction occurring on one part of the stage parallels a game of chess on another.   **77-78The Chair she sat in . . . Glowed on the marble:** Eliot's note: "Cf. *Antony and Cleopatra,* II, ii, 190 " The allusion is to Cleopatra's barge, which is described by the Roman soldier Enobarbus. "The barge she sat in, like a burnish'd throne, / Burn'd on the water."   **91-93In fattening . . . the coffered ceiling:** Eliot's note: "V. *Aeneid,* I, 726 " The reference is to Virgil's description of the banquet given by Dido, Queen of Carthage, for her Trojan lover, Aeneas. Eliot quotes two lines, which may be translated "Blazing torches hang from the golden paneled ceiling, and the torches conquer the night with flames."

Above the antique mantel was displayed
As though a window gave upon the sylvan scene
The change of Philomel, by the barbarous king
So rudely forced; yet there the nightingale   100
Filled all the desert with inviolable voice
And still she cried, and still the world pursues,
"Jug Jug" to dirty ears.
And other withered stumps of time
Were told upon the walls; staring forms   105
Leaned out, leaning, hushing the room enclosed.
Footsteps shuffled on the stair.
Under the firelight, under the brush, her hair
Spread out in fiery points
Glowed into words, then would be savagely still.   110

"My nerves are bad to-night. Yes, bad. Stay with me.
"Speak to me. Why do you never speak. Speak.
　　"What are you thinking of? What thinking? What?
"I never know what you are thinking. Think."

I think we are in rats' alley   115
Where the dead men lost their bones.

"What is that noise?"
　　　　　　　The wind under the door.
"What is that noise now? What is the wind doing?"
　　　　　Nothing again nothing.   120
　　　　　　　　　　"Do
"You know nothing? Do you see nothing? Do you remember
"Nothing?"

　　　I remember
Those are pearls that were his eyes.   125
"Are you alive, or not? Is there nothing in your head?"
　　　　　　　　But
O O O O that Shakespeherian Rag—
It's so elegant

---

⁹⁸**As though . . . the sylvan scene** Eliot's note: "V. Milton, *Paradise Lost,* IV, 140." Milton's description is of Satan looking at Eden.　⁹⁹⁻¹⁰⁰**The change of Philomel . . . there the nightingale** Eliot's note: "V. Ovid, *Metamorphoses,* VI, Philomela. "King Tereus raped Philomela, his wife's sister, and cut out her tongue. Procne, his wife, found out and revenged herself on Tereus by killing his son Itys and serving him to the king as food. Philomela was transformed into a nightingale by the gods.　¹¹⁵**rats' alley** Eliot's note: "Cf. Part III, line 195."　¹¹⁸**The wind under the door** Eliot's note: "Cf Webster: 'Is the wind in that door still?' "

So intelligent   130
"What shall I do now? What shall I do?"
"I shall rush out as I am, and walk the street
"With my hair down, so. What shall we do tomorrow?
"What shall we ever do?"
                              The hot water at ten.   135
And if it rains, a closed car at four.
And we shall play a game of chess,
Pressing lidless eyes and waiting for a knock upon the door.

When Lil's husband got demobbed, I said—
I didn't mince my words, I said to her myself,   140
HURRY UP PLEASE ITS TIME
Now Albert's coming back, make yourself a bit smart.
He'll want to know what you done with that money he gave you
To get yourself some teeth. He did, I was there.
You have them all out, Lil, and get a nice set,   145
He said, I swear, I can't bear to look at you.
And no more can't I, I said, and think of poor Albert,
He's been in the army four years, he wants a good time,
And if you don't give it him, there's others will, I said.
Oh is there, she said. Something o' that, I said.   150
Then I'll know who to thank, she said, and give me a straight look.
HURRY UP PLEASE ITS TIME
If you don't like it you can get on with it, I said.
Others can pick and choose if you can't.
But if Albert makes off, it won't be for lack of telling.   155
You ought to be ashamed, I said, to look so antique.
(And her only thirty-one.)
I can't help it, she said, pulling a long face,
It's them pills I took, to bring it off, she said.
(She's had five already, and nearly died of young George.)   160
The chemist said it would be all right, but I've never been the same.
You *are* a proper fool, I said.
Well, if Albert won't leave you alone, there it is, I said,
What you get married for if you don't want children?
HURRY UP PLEASE ITS TIME   165
Well, that Sunday Albert was home, they had a hot gammon,
And they asked me in to dinner, to get the beauty of it hot—
HURRY UP PLEASE ITS TIME
HURRY UP PLEASE ITS TIME
Goonight Bill. Goonight Lou. Goonight May. Goonight.   170

---

[139]**demobbed**   demobilized from the army after World War I.   [141]Hurry up please its time   barkeeper's call
at closing time in a British pub.   [161]**chemist**   pharmacist.   [166]**gammon**   ham.

Ta ta. Goonight. Goonight.
Good night, ladies, good night, sweet ladies, good night, good night.

III. The Fire Sermon

The river's tent is broken; the last fingers of leaf
Clutch and sink into the wet bank. The wind
Crosses the brown land, unheard. The nymphs are departed.   *175*
Sweet Thames, run softly, till I end my song.
The river bears no empty bottles, sandwich papers,
Silk handkerchiefs, cardboard boxes, cigarette ends
Or other testimony of summer nights. The nymphs are departed.
And their friends, the loitering heirs of City directors;   *180*
Departed, have left no addresses.
By the waters of Leman I sat down and wept . . .
Sweet Thames, run softly till I end my song,
Sweet Thames, run softly, for I speak not loud or long.
But at my back in a cold blast I hear   *185*
The rattle of the bones, and chuckle spread from ear to ear.

A rat crept softly through the vegetation
Dragging its slimy belly on the bank
While I was fishing in the dull canal
On a winter evening round behind the gashouse   *190*
Musing upon the king my brother's wreck
And on the king my father's death before him.
White bodies naked on the low damp ground
And bones cast in a little low dry garret,
Rattled by the rat's foot only, year to year.   *195*
But at my back from time to time I hear
The sound of horns and motors, which shall bring
Sweeney to Mrs. Porter in the spring.
O the moon shone bright on Mrs. Porter
And on her daughter   *200*

---

[172]**Good night, ladies . . . good night**   allusions to the popular song "Good Night, Ladies" and to Shakespeare's *Hamlet*, IV, v, 72, in which Ophelia sings her mad song before drowning herself.   **The Fire Sermon**   an allusion to Buddha's Fire Sermon, which urges the elimination of desire, the fire of passion.   [176]**Sweet Thames . . . end my song**   Eliot's note: "V. Spenser, *Prothalamion.*" The line is the refrain of Spenser's poem celebrating marriage.   [182]**By the waters . . . wept**   In Psalm 137, the exiled Jews lament the loss of their homeland: "By the waters of Babylon, there we sat down, yea, we wept, when we remembered Zion."   [185]**But at my back . . . I hear**   an echo of Andrew Marvell (1621–1678) in "To His Coy Mistress": "But at my back I always hear / Time's winged chariot hurrying near, / And yonder all before us lie / Deserts of vast eternity." Also echoed in line 196.   [192]**And on the king . . . before him**   Eliot's note: "Cf. *The Tempest*, I, ii "   [197-198]**The sound of horns . . . Mrs. Porter in the spring**   Eliot's note "Cf. Day, *Parliament of Bees:* 'When of the sudden, listening, you shall hear, / A noise of horns and hunting, which shall bring Actaeon to Diana in the spring, / Where all shall see her naked skin.' "   [200-201]**And on her daughter . . . soda water**   Eliot's note: "I do not know the origin of the ballad from which these lines are taken. it was reported to me from Sydney, Australia."

They wash their feet in soda water
Et O ces voix d'enfants, chantant dans la coupole!

Twit twit twit
Jug jug jug jug jug
So rudely forc'd.   205
Tereu

Unreal City
Under the brown fog of a winter noon
Mr. Eugenides, the Smyrna merchant
Unshaven, with a pocket full of currants   210
C.i.f. London: documents at sight,
Asked me in demotic French
To luncheon at the Cannon Street Hotel
Followed by a weekend at the Metropole.

At the violet hour, when the eyes and back   215
Turn upward from the desk, when the human engine waits
Like a taxi throbbing waiting,
I Tiresias, though blind, throbbing between two lives,
Old man with wrinkled female breasts, can see
At the violet hour, the evening hour that strives   220
Homeward, and brings the sailor home from sea,
The typist home at teatime, clears her breakfast, lights
Her stove, and lays out food in tins.
Out of the window perilously spread
Her drying combinations touched by the sun's last rays,   225
On the divan are piled (at night her bed)
Stockings, slippers, camisoles, and stays.
I Tiresias, old man with wrinkled dugs
Perceived the scene, and foretold the rest—

[202]**Et O ces voix . . . dans la coupole!** Eliot's note: "V. Verlaine, *Parsifal.*" The last line of the poem by Paul Verlaine (1844–1896) can be translated "And O those children's voices singing in the dome." [206]**Tereu** Tereus; along with "jug," it is a way of alluding to the nightingale's song. See note on lines 99–100. [211]**C.i.f. London: documents at sight** Eliot's note: "The currants were quoted at a price 'cost insurance and freight to London'; and the Bill of Lading, etc., were to be handed to the buyer upon payment of the sight draft " [218]**Tiresias** Eliot's note: "Tiresias, although a mere spectator and not indeed a 'character,' is yet the most important personage in the poem, uniting all the rest. Just as the one-eyed merchant, seller of currants, melts into the Phoenician Sailor, and the latter is not wholly distinct from Ferdinand, Prince of Naples, so all the women are one woman, and the two sexes meet in Tiresias. What Tiresias *sees*, in fact, is the substance of the poem. The whole passage from Ovid is of great anthropological interest. . . ." [221]**and brings the sailor home from sea** Eliot's note: "This may not appear as exact as Sappho's lines, but I had in mind the 'longshore' or 'dory' fisherman, who returns at nightfall." Eliot echoes both the Greek poet Sappho (c. 610–580 B.C.) and the Scottish writer Robert Louis Stevenson (1850–1894), who wrote in "Requiem," "Home is the sailor, home from the sea "

I too awaited the expected guest.   *230*
He, the young man carbuncular, arrives,
A small house agent's clerk, with one bold stare,
One of the low on whom assurance sits
As a silk hat on a Bradford millionaire.
The time is now propitious, as he guesses,   *235*
The meal is ended, she is bored and tired,
Endeavours to engage her in caresses
Which still are unreproved, if undesired.
Flushed and decided, he assaults at once;
Exploring hands encounter no defence;   *240*
His vanity requires no response,
And makes a welcome of indifference.
(And I Tiresias have foresuffered all
Enacted on this same divan or bed;
I who have sat by Thebes below the wall   *245*
And walked among the lowest of the dead.)
Bestows one final patronising kiss,
And gropes his way, finding the stairs unlit.

She turns and looks a moment in the glass,
Hardly aware of her departed lover;   *250*
Her brain allows one half-formed thought to pass:
"Well now that's done: and I'm glad it's over."
When lovely woman stoops to folly and
Paces about her room again, alone,
She smoothese her hair with automatic hand,   *255*
And puts a record on the gramophone.

"This music crept by me upon the waters"
And along the Strand, up Queen Victoria Street.
O City city, I can sometimes hear
Beside a public bar in Lower Thames Street,   *260*
The pleasant whining of a mandoline
And a clatter and a chatter from within
Where fishmen lounge at noon: where the walls
Of Magnus Martyr hold
Inexplicable splendour of Ionian white and gold.   *265*

---

[234]**Bradford millionaire**   The manufacturers of Bradford, an English industrial city, were reputed to have profited handsomely from the war industry in World War I   [253–256]**When lovely woman stoops . . . on the gramophone**   Eliot's note: "V. Goldsmith, the song in *The Vicar of Wakefield*." The seduced woman's song reads "When lovely woman stoops to folly / And finds too late that men betray / What charm can soothe her melancholy, / What art can wash her guilt away?"   [257]**'This music . . . upon the waters'**   Eliot's note: "V *The Tempest,* as above."   [263–265]**where the walls / Of Magnus Martyr . . . Ionian white and gold**   Eliot's note "The interior of St. Magnus Martyr is to my mind one of the finest among Wren's interiors"

The river sweats
Oil and tar
The barges drift
With the turning tide
Red sails   270
Wide
To leeward, swing on the heavy spar.
The barges wash
Drifting logs
Down Greenwich reach   275
Past the Isle of Dogs.
      Weialala leia
      Wallala leialala

Elizabeth and Leicester
Beating oars   280
The stern was formed
A gilded shell
Red and gold
The brisk swell
Rippled both shores   285
Southwest wind
Carried down stream
The peal of bells
White towers
      Weialala leia   290
      Wallala leialala

"Trams and dusty trees.
Highbury bore me. Richmond and Kew
Undid me. By Richmond I raised my knees
Supine on the floor of a narrow canoe."   295

"My feet are at Moorgate, and my heart
Under my feet. After the event

[275-276]**Greenwich reach . . . Dogs** a bend in the River Thames that forms a peninsula called the Isle of Dogs
[279]**Elizabeth and Leicester** refers to the love affair of Queen Elizabeth and the Earl of Leicester. Eliot's note quotes the historian J. A. Froude's *Elizabeth*, Vol. I, chapter 4, letter of De Quadra to Philip of Spain: "In the afternoon we were in a barge, watching the games on the river. [The queen] was alone with Lord Robert and myself on the poop, when they began to talk nonsense, and went so far that Lord Robert at last said, as I was on the spot there was no reason why they should not be married if the queen pleased." [292-305]**"Trams and dusty trees . . . people who expect / Nothing."** Eliot's note: "The Song of the (three) Thames daughters begins here. From lines 292 to 305 inclusive they speak in turn. V. *Gotterdammerung*, III, i: the Rhinedaughters." In Wagner's opera, the Rhine maidens attempt to seduce the hero, Siegfried, and threaten and implore him to retrieve their stolen gold. Eliot quotes their refrain. [293-294]**Highbury . . . Undid me.** Eliot's note: "Cf. *Purgatorio*, V, 133." Eliot quotes the Italian, which translates as "Remember me, who am La Pia. / Siena made me, Maremma undid me." Highbury is a London neighborhood; Richmond and Kew, boating places on the Thames. [296]**Moorgate** a London slum.

He wept. He promised 'a new start.'
I made no comment. What should I resent?"

"On Margate Sands.   *300*
I can connect
Nothing with nothing.
The broken fingernails of dirty hands.
My people humble people who expect
Nothing."   *305*
      la la

To Carthage then I came

Burning burning burning burning
O Lord Thou pluckest me out
O Lord Thou pluckest   *310*

burning

IV. Death by Water

Phlebas the Phoenician, a fortnight dead,
Forgot the cry of gulls, and the deep sea swell
And the profit and loss.
            A current under sea   *315*
Picked his bones in whispers. As he rose and fell
He passed the stages of his age and youth
Entering the whirlpool.
            Gentile or Jew
O you who turn the wheel and look to windward,   *320*
Consider Phlebas, who was once handsome and tall as you.

V. What the Thunder Said

After the torchlight red on sweaty faces
After the frosty silence in the gardens
After the agony in stony places

[300]**Margate Sands** an English seaside resort.   [307]**To Carthage then I came** Eliot's note: "V. St Augustine's *Confessions:* 'To Carthage then I came, where a cauldron of unholy loves sang all about mine ears.' "
[308]**Burning burning burning** Eliot's note to this line alludes to Buddha's Fire Sermon, without quoting any of it.   [309]**O Lord Thou pluckest me out** Eliot's note: "From St. Augustine's *Confessions* again. The collocation of these two representatives of eastern and western asceticism, as the culmination of this part of the poem, is not an accident."   **Death by Water** Eliot offered no notes for Part IV.   **What the Thunder Said** Eliot's note: "In the first part of V three themes are employed: the journey to Emmaus, the approach to the Chapel Perilous (see Miss Weston's book) and the present decay of Eastern Europe."   [322-327]**After the torchlight . . . distant mountains:** an allusion to Christ's agony in the garden of Gethsemane, his arrest, and his crucifixion.

The shouting and the crying   *325*
Prison and palace and reverberation
Of thunder of spring over distant mountains
He who was living is now dead
We who were living are now dying
With a little patience   *330*

Here is no water but only rock
Rock and no water and the sandy road
The road winding above among the mountains
Which are mountains of rock without water
If there were water we should stop and drink   *335*
Amongst the rock one cannot stop or think
Sweat is dry and feet are in the sand
If there were only water amongst the rock
Dead mountain mouth of carious teeth that cannot spit
Here one can neither stand nor lie nor sit   *340*
There is not even silence in the mountains
But dry sterile thunder without rain
There is not even solitude in the mountains
But red sullen faces sneer and snarl
From doors of mudcracked houses   *345*
                              If there were water
      And no rock
      If there were rock
      And also water
      And water   *350*
      A spring
      A pool among the rock
      If there were the sound of water only
      Not the cicada
      And dry grass singing   *355*
      But sound of water over a rock
      Where the hermit-thrush sings in the pine trees
      Drip drop drip drop drop drop drop
      But there is no water

Who is the third who walks always beside you?   *360*
When I count, there are only you and I together

---

³⁵⁷**hermit-thrush**   Eliot's note: "This is . . . the hermit-thrush which I have heard in Quebec Province. . . . Its water-dripping is justly celebrated."   ³⁶⁰**Who is the third . . . beside you?**   Eliot's note: "The following lines were stimulated by the account of one of the Antarctic expeditions (I forget which, but think one of Shackleton's): it was related that the party of explorers, at the extremity of their strength, had the constant delusion that there was *one more member* than could actually be counted." Also relevant is Luke 24:13–16, which describes Jesus on the way to Emmaus with two of his disciples who were unaware of who he was.

But when I look ahead up the white road
There is always another one walking beside you
Gliding wrapt in a brown mantle, hooded
I do not know whether a man or a woman   365
—But who is that on the other side of you?

What is that sound high in the air
Murmur of maternal lamentation
Who are those hooded hordes swarming
Over endless plains, stumbling in cracked earth   370
Ringed by the flat horizon only
What is the city over the mountains
Cracks and reforms and bursts in the violet air
Falling towers
Jerusalem Athens Alexandria   375
Vienna London
Unreal

A woman drew her long black hair out tight
And fiddled whisper music on those strings
And bats with baby faces in the violet light   380
Whistled, and beat their wings
And crawled head downward down a blackened wall
And upside down in air were towers
Tolling reminiscent bells, that kept the hours
And voices singing out of empty cisterns and exhausted wells.   385

In this decayed hole among the mountains
In the faint moonlight, the grass is singing
Over the tumbled graves, about the chapel
There is the empty chapel, only the wind's home.
It has no windows, and the door swings,   390
Dry bones can harm no one.
Only a cock stood on the rooftree
Co co rico co co rico
In a flash of lightning. Then a damp gust
Bringing rain   395

Ganga was sunken, and the limp leaves
Waited for rain, while the black clouds

367-370**What is that sound . . . Over endless plains**   Eliot's note quotes *A Glimpse of Chaos* by Hermann Hesse. In translation: "Already half of Europe, already at least half of Eastern Europe is on the way to Chaos, drives drunkenly in sacred madness along the edge of the abyss, and moreover, sings, sings drunken hymns as Dmitri Karamazov sang. The offended bourgeois laughs at these songs, the saint and seer hear them with tears."
396**Ganga**   the River Ganges, sacred in India.

Gathered far distant, over Himavant.
The jungle crouched, humped in silence.
Then spoke the thunder   *400*
DA
Datta: what have we given?
My friend, blood shaking my heart
The awful daring of a moment's surrender
Which an age of prudence can never retract   *405*
By this, and this only, we have existed
Which is not to be found in our obituaries
Or in memories draped by the beneficient spider
Or under seals broken by the lean solicitor
In our empty rooms   *410*
DA
Dayadhvam: I have heard the key
Turn in the door once and turn once only
We think of the key, each in his prison
Thinking of the key, each confirms a prison   *415*
Only at nightfall, aethereal rumours
Revive for a moment a broken Coriolanus
DA
Damyata: The boat responded
Gaily, to the hand expert with sail and oar   *420*
The sea was calm, your heart would have responded
Gaily, when invited, beating obedient
To controlling hands

                    I sat upon the shore
Fishing, with the arid plain behind me   *425*
Shall I at least set my lands in order?
London Bridge is falling down falling down falling down

---

[398]**Himavant**   a Himalayan mountain.   [402-419]**Datta . . . Dayadhvam . . . Damyata**   Eliot's note: "Datta, dayadhvam, damyata (Give, sympathize, control) The fable of the meaning of the thunder is found in Brihand-aranyaka, *Upanishad,* V, I. The fable describes how when the Creator speaks 'Da,' gods, men, and demons hear and respond to different commands."   [408]**Or in memories . . . beneficient spider**   Eliot's note: "Cf Webster, *The White Devil,* V, vi: 'they'll remarry / Ere the worm pierce your winding-sheet, ere the spider / Make a thin curtain for your epitaphs.' "   [412]**I have heard the key**   Eliot refers to Dante's *Inferno,* XXXIII, 46, which describes Ugolino and his children, who were locked in a tower to starve to death. Eliot quotes the Italian, which translates "And I heard below the door of the horrible tower being locked up." Eliot also quotes the philosopher F. H Bradley's *Appearance and Reality:* "My external sensations are no less private to myself than are my thoughts or my feelings. In either case my experience falls within my own circle, a circle closed on the outside, and, with all its elements alike, every sphere is opaque to the others which surround it. . . In brief, regarded as an existence which appears in a soul, the whole world for each is peculiar and private to that soul."   [417]**Coriolanus**   the tragic hero of Shakespeare's *Coriolanus,* a Roman general who, exiled from Rome, led the enemy against his former city.   [424-425]**sat upon the shore / Fishing**   Eliot's note: "V. Weston: *From Ritual to Romance,* chapter on The Fisher King."   [426]**Shall I at least set my lands in order?**   Cf. Isaiah: 38:1: "Thus saith the Lord. Set thine house in order for thou shalt die, and not live."

Poi s'ascose nel foco che gli affina
Quando fiam uti chelidon—O swallow swallow
Le Prince d'Aquitaine à la tour abolie   430
These fragments I have shored against my ruins
Why then Ile fit you. Hieronymo's mad againe.
Datta. Dayadhvam. Damyata.
            Shantih   shantih   shantih

                                                     [1922]

from *Four Quartets: Little Gidding*

I

Midwinter spring is its own season
Sempiternal though sodden towards sundown,
Suspended in time, between pole and tropic.
When the short day is brightest, with frost and fire,
The brief sun flames the ice, on pond and ditches,   5
In windless cold that is the heart's heat,
Reflecting in a watery mirror
A glare that is blindness in the early afternoon.
And glow more intense than blaze of branch, or brazier,
Stirs the dumb spirit: no wind, but pentecostal fire   10
In the dark time of the year. Between melting and freezing
The soul's sap quivers. There is no earth smell

THE WASTE LAND   **428Poi s'ascose . . . gli affina:** Eliot's note: "V. *Purgatorio* XXVI, 148." In the note, he quotes four lines that translate "Now I pray you by that virtue / that guides you to the top of the stair / be mindful in time of my suffering / Then he hid himself in the fire that refines them." In the poem, Eliot quotes only the last line of the four. The lines are spoken by the Provençal poet Arnaut Daniel, who was an important influence on Dante.   **429Quando fiam uti chelidon** Eliot's note: "V. *Pervigilium Veneris.* Cf. Philomela in Parts II and III." See note on lines 99–100. The line translates "She sings, when will my spring come?"   **430Le Prince d'Aquitaine à la tour abolie** Eliot's note: "V. Gerard de Nerval, sonnet *El Desdichado*" The title means "The Disinherited"; the line, "The Prince of Aquitaine at the ruined tower."   **432Hieronymo** Eliot's note: "V. Kyd's [1558–1594] *Spanish Tragedy* with the subtitle *Hieronymo's Mad Againe.*" In the play, Hieronymo avenges the murder of his son.   **434Shantih shantih shantih** Eliot's note: "Shantih. Repeated as here, a formal ending to an Upanishad. 'The Peace which passeth understanding' is our equivalent to this word."
LITTLE GIDDING   This is the last of Eliot's *Four Quartets.* Little Gidding was the name of an Anglican religious community founded in 1625 by Nicholas Ferrar. It lasted twenty-two years, until it was destroyed by the Puritans under Oliver Cromwell.   **10pentecostal fire** on the feast of Pentecost (the seventh Sunday after Easter) Christ's disciples were assembled when "suddenly there came a sound from heaven, as of a rushing mighty wind, and it filled all the house where they were sitting. And there appeared unto them cloven tongues, like as of fire. . . . And they were all filled with the Holy Ghost, and began to speak with other tongues, as the Spirit gave them utterance" (Acts 2:2–4).

Or smell of living thing. This is the spring time
But not in time's covenant. Now the hedgerow
Is blanched for an hour with transitory blossom   *15*
Of snow, a bloom more sudden
Than that of summer, neither budding nor fading,
Not in the scheme of generation.
Where is the summer, the unimaginable
Zero summer?   *20*

         If you came this way,
Taking the route you would be likely to take
From the place you would be likely to come from,
If you came this way in may time, you would find the hedges
White again, in May, with voluptuary sweetness.   *25*
It would be the same at the end of the journey,
If you came at night like a broken king,
If you came by day not knowing what you came for,
It would be the same, when you leave the rough road
And turn behind the pig-sty to the dull façade   *30*
And the tombstone. And what you thought you came for
Is only a shell, a husk of meaning
From which the purpose breaks only when it is fulfilled
If at all. Either you had no purpose
Or the purpose is beyond the end you figured   *35*
And is altered in fulfilment. There are other places
Which also are the world's end, some at the sea jaws,
Or over a dark lake, in a desert or a city—
But this is the nearest, in place and time,
Now and in England.   *40*

         If you came this way,
Taking any route, starting from anywhere,
At any time or at any season,
It would always be the same: you would have to put off
Sense and notion. You are not here to verify,   *45*
Instruct yourself, or inform curiosity
Or carry report. You are here to kneel
Where prayer has been valid. And prayer is more
Than an order of words, the conscious occupation
Of the praying mind, or the sound of the voice praying.   *50*
And what the dead had no speech for, when living,
They can tell you, being dead: the communication
Of the dead is tongued with fire beyond the language of the living.

---

[27]**a broken king**   King Charles I, who visited Little Gidding after a defeat in the English Civil War.

Here, the intersection of the timeless moment
Is England and nowhere. Never and always.   55

II

Ash on an old man's sleeve
Is all the ash the burnt roses leave.
Dust in the air suspended
Marks the place where a story ended.
Dust inbreathed was a house—   60
The wall, the wainscot and the mouse.
The death of hope and despair,
  This is the death of air.

There are flood and drouth
Over the eyes and in the mouth,   65
Dead water and dead sand
Contending for the upper hand.
The parched eviscerate soil
Gapes at the vanity of toil,
Laughs without mirth.   70
  This is the death of earth.

Water and fire succeed
The town, the pasture and the weed
Water and fire deride
The sacrifice that we denied.   75
Water and fire shall rot
The marred foundations we forgot,
Of sanctuary and choir.
  This is the death of water and fire.

In the uncertain hour before the morning   80
  Near the ending of interminable night
  At the recurrent end of the unending
After the dark dove with the flickering tongue
  Had passed below the horizon of his homing
  While the dead leaves still rattled on like tin   85
Over the asphalt where no other sound was
  Between three districts whence the smoke arose
  I met one walking, loitering and hurried
As if blown towards me like the metal leaves
  Before the urban dawn wind unresisting.   90
  And as I fixed upon the down-turned face

[80-151] Eliot imitates and varies Dante's *terza rima* in this section of the poem, which, he wrote, "cost me far more time and trouble and vexation than any passage of the same length I have ever written."

That pointed scrutiny with which we challenge
　　The first-met stranger in the waning dusk
　　I caught the sudden look of some dead master
Whom I had known, forgotten, half recalled　　　　　　　　95
　　Both one and many; in the brown baked features
　　The eyes of a familiar compound ghost
Both intimate and unidentifiable.
　　So I assumed a double part, and cried
　　And heard another's voice cry: "What! are *you* here?"　　　100
Although we were not. I was still the same,
　　Knowing myself yet being someone other—
　　And he a face still forming; yet the words sufficed
To compel the recognition they preceded.
　　And so, compliant to the common wind,　　　　　　　　105
　　Too strange to each other for misunderstanding,
In concord at this intersection time
　　Of meeting nowhere, no before and after,
　　We trod the pavement in a dead patrol.
I said: "The wonder that I feel is easy,　　　　　　　　110
　　Yet ease is cause of wonder. Therefore speak:
　　I may not comprehend, may not remember."
And he: "I am not eager to rehearse
　　My thoughts and theory which you have forgotten.
　　These things have served their purpose: let them be.　　115
So with your own, and pray they be forgiven
　　By others, as I pray you to forgive
　　Both bad and good. Last season's fruit is eaten
And the fullfed beast shall kick the empty pail.
　　For last year's words belong to last year's language　　　120
　　And next year's words await another voice.
But, as the passage now presents no hindrance
　　To the spirit unappeased and peregrine
　　Between two worlds become much like each other,
So I find words I never thought to speak　　　　　　　　125
　　In streets I never thought I should revisit
　　When I left my body on a distant shore.
Since our concern was speech, and speech impelled us
　　To purify the dialect of the tribe
　　And urge the mind to aftersight and foresight,　　　　130
Let me disclose the gifts reserved for age
　　To set a crown upon your lifetime's effort.
　　First, the cold friction of expiring sense

---

[129]**To purify the dialect of the tribe**　This line translates a line in Stéphane Mallarmé's "Le Tombeau d'Edgar Poe." See pp. 1074–1075.

Without enchantment, offering no promise
    But bitter tastelessness of shadow fruit   *135*
    As body and soul begin to fall asunder.
Second, the conscious impotence of rage
    At human folly, and the laceration
    Of laughter at what ceases to amuse.
And last, the rending pain of re-enactment   *140*
    Of all that you have done, and been; the shame
    Of motives late revealed, and the awareness
Of things ill done and done to others' harm
    Which once you took for exercise of virtue.
    Then fools' approval stings, and honor stains.   *145*
From wrong to wrong the exasperated spirit
    Proceeds, unless restored by that refining fire
    Where you must move in measure, like a dancer."
The day was breaking. In the disfigured street
    He left me, with a kind of valediction,   *150*
    And faded on the blowing of the horn.

III

There are three conditions which often look alike
Yet differ completely, flourish in the same hedgerow:
Attachment to self and to things and to persons, detachment
From self and from things and from persons; and, growing between them,
    indifference   *155*
Which resembles the others as death resembles life,
Being between two lives—unflowering, between
The live and the dead nettle. This is the use of memory:
For liberation—not less of love but expanding
Of love beyond desire, and so liberation   *160*
From the future as well as the past. Thus, love of a country
Begins as attachment to our own field of action
And comes to find that action of little importance
Though never indifferent. History may be servitude,
History may be freedom. See, now they vanish,   *165*
The faces and places, with the self which, as it could, loved them,
To become renewed, transfigured, in another pattern.

Sin is Behovely, but
All shall be well, and
All manner of thing shall be well.   *170*
    If I think, again, of this place,

[168–180]**Sin is Behovely . . . here and abroad**   Eliot took these lines from Dame Julian of Norwich, a fourteenth-century English mystic.

And of people, not wholly commendable,
Of no immediate kin or kindness,
But some of peculiar genius,
All touched by a common genius,   175
United in the strife which divided them;
If I think of a king at nightfall,
Of three men, and more, on the scaffold
And a few who died forgotten
In other places, here and abroad,   180
And of one who died blind and quiet,
Why should we celebrate
These dead men more than the dying?
It is not to ring the bell backward
Nor is it an incantation   185
To summon the specter of a Rose.
We cannot revive old factions
We cannot restore old policies
Or follow an antique drum.
These men, and those who opposed them   190
And those whom they opposed
Accept the constitution of silence
And are folded in a single party.
Whatever we inherit from the fortunate
We have taken from the defeated   195
What they had to leave us—a symbol:
A symbol perfected in death.
And all shall be well and
All manner of thing shall be well
By the purification of the motive   200
In the ground of our beseeching.

IV

The dove descending breaks the air
With flame of incandescent terror
Of which the tongues declare
The one discharge from sin and error.   205
The only hope, or else despair
   Lies in the choice of pyre or pyre—
   To be redeemed from fire by fire.

---

¹⁷⁷⁻¹⁷⁸**a king at nightfall . . . on the scaffold**   Charles I was beheaded, as were some of his followers.
¹⁸¹**one who died blind and quiet**   a reference to John Milton, a supporter of Cromwell.   ¹⁸⁶**specter of a Rose**   suggestive of both historical and symbolic considerations, the Tudor rose represented the English monarchy before the accession of the Stuart kings, of which Charles I was one.   ²⁰¹**In the ground of our beseeching**   Julian of Norwich held that "the ground of our beseeching is love."

Who then devised the torment? Love.
Love is the unfamiliar Name   210
Behind the hands that wove
The intolerable shirt of flame
Which human power cannot remove.
    We only live, only suspire
    Consumed by either fire or fire.   215

V

What we call the beginning is often the end
And to make an end is to make a beginning.
The end is where we start from. And every phrase
And sentence that is right (where every word is at home,
Taking its place to support the others,   220
The word neither diffident nor ostentatious,
An easy commerce of the old and the new,
The common word exact without vulgarity,
The formal word precise but not pedantic,
The complete consort dancing together)   225
Every phrase and every sentence is an end and a beginning,
Every poem an epitaph. And any action
Is a step to the block, to the fire, down the sea's throat
Or to an illegible stone: and that is where we start.
We die with the dying: 230
See, they depart, and we go with them.
We are born with the dead:
See, they return, and bring us with them.
The moment of the rose and the moment of the yew-tree
Are of equal duration. A people without history   235
Is not redeemed from time, for history is a pattern
Of timeless moments. So, while the light fails
On a winter's afternoon, in a secluded chapel
History is now and England.

With the drawing of this Love and the voice of this Calling   240

We shall not cease from exploration
And the end of all our exploring
Will be to arrive where we started
And know the place for the first time.

---

²¹²**The intolerable shirt of flame**   a reference to the shirt of Nessus, which Heracles's wife had him put on in the false hope she would win back her husband's love. The shirt burst into flames, adhered to his flesh, and caused agonizing pain as he was immolated.   ²⁴⁰**With the drawing . . . of this Calling**   from *The Cloud of Unknowing,* a fourteenth-century religious work.

Through the unknown, remembering gate   245
When the last of earth left to discover
Is that which was the beginning;
At the source of the longest river
The voice of the hidden waterfall
And the children in the apple-tree   250
Not known, because not looked for
But heard, half-heard, in the stillness
Between two waves of the sea.
Quick now, here, now, always—
A condition of complete simplicity   255
(Costing not less than everything)
And all shall be well and
All manner of thing shall be well
When the tongues of flame are in-folded
Into the crowned knot of fire   260
And the fire and the rose are one.

[1942]

JOHN CROWE RANSOM

[1888–1974]

Bells for John Whiteside's Daughter

There was such speed in her little body,
And such lightness in her footfall,
It is no wonder her brown study
Astonishes us all.

Her wars were bruited in our high window.   5
We looked among orchard trees and beyond
Where she took arms against her shadow,
Or harried unto the pond

The lazy geese, like a snow cloud
Dripping their snow on the green grass,   10
Tricking and stopping, sleepy and proud,
Who cried in goose, Alas,

LITTLE GIDDING   ²⁶¹**And the fire and the rose are one**   a reference to Dante's *Paradiso*, XXXIII, which, for Eliot, is "the highest point that poetry has ever reached or ever can reach."

For the tireless heart within the little
Lady with rod that made them rise
From their noon apple-dreams and scuttle   15
Goose-fashion under the skies!

But now go the bells, and we are ready,
In one house we are sternly stopped
To say we are vexed at her brown study,
Lying so primly propped.   20

[1924]

Piazza Piece

—I am a gentleman in a dust coat trying
To make you hear. Your ears are soft and small
And listen to an old man not at all,
They want the young men's whispering and sighing.
But see the roses on your trellis dying   5
And hear the spectral singing of the moon;
For I must have my lovely lady soon,
I am a gentleman in a dust coat trying.

—I am a lady young in beauty waiting
Until my truelove comes, and then we kiss.   10
But what gray man among the vines is this
Whose words are dry and faint as in a dream?
Back from my trellis, sir, before I scream!
I am a lady young in beauty waiting.

[1927]

CLAUDE McKAY

[1890–1948]

The Tropics in New York

Bananas ripe and green, and ginger-root,
    Cocoa in pods and alligator pears,
And tangerines and mangoes and grape fruit,
    Fit for the highest prize at parish fairs,

Set in the window, bringing memories   *5*
    Of fruit-trees laden by low-singing rills,
And dewy dawns, and mystical blue skies
    In benediction over nun-like hills.

My eyes grew dim, and I could no more gaze;
    A wave of longing through my body swept,   *10*
And hungry for the old familiar ways,
    I turned aside and bowed my head and wept.

                        [1922]

ARCHIBALD MacLEISH

[1892–1982]

Ars Poetica

A poem should be palpable and mute
As a globed fruit,

Dumb
As old medallions to the thumb,

Silent as the sleeve-worn stone   *5*
Of casement ledges where the moss has grown—

A poem should be wordless
As the flight of birds.

A poem should be motionless in time
As the moon climbs,   *10*

Leaving, as the moon releases
Twig by twig the night-entangled trees,

Leaving, as the moon behind the winter leaves,
Memory by memory the mind—

A poem should be motionless in time   *15*
As the moon climbs.

A poem should be equal to:
Not true.

For all the history of grief
An empty doorway and a maple leaf.   *20*

For love
The leaning grasses and two lights above the sea—

A poem should not mean
But be.

[1926]

EDNA ST. VINCENT MILLAY

[1892–1950]

Recuerdo

We were very tired, we were very merry—
We had gone back and forth all night on the ferry.
It was bare and bright, and smelled like a stable—
But we looked into a fire, we leaned across a table,
We lay on a hill-top underneath the moon;   *5*
And the whistles kept blowing, and the dawn came soon.

We were very tired, we were very merry—
We had gone back and forth all night on the ferry;
And you ate an apple, and I ate a pear,
From a dozen of each we had bought somewhere;   *10*
And the sky went wan, and the wind came cold,
And the sun rose dripping, a bucketful of gold.

We were very tired, we were very merry,
We had gone back and forth all night on the ferry.
We hailed, "Good morrow, mother!" to a shawl-covered head,   *15*
And bought a morning paper, which neither of us read;

And she wept, "God bless you!" for the apples and pears,
And we gave her all our money but our subway fares.

[1920]

WILFRED OWEN

[1893–1918]

Dulce et Decorum Est

Bent double, like old beggars under sacks,
Knock-kneed, coughing like hags, we cursed through sludge,
Till on the haunting flares we turned our backs
And towards our distant rest began to trudge.
Men marched asleep. Many had lost their boots   5
But limped on, blood-shod. All went lame; all blind;
Drunk with fatigue; deaf even to the hoots
Of tired, outstripped Five-Nines that dropped behind.

Gas! Gas! Quick, boys!—An ecstasy of fumbling,
Fitting the clumsy helmets just in time;   10
But someone still was yelling out and stumbling
And flound'ring like a man in fire or lime . . .
Dim, through the misty panes and thick green light,
As under a green sea, I saw him drowning.

In all my dreams, before my helpless sight,   15
He plunges at me, guttering, choking, drowning.

If in some smothering dreams you too could pace
Behind the wagon that we flung him in,
And watch the white eyes writhing in his face,
His hanging face, like a devil's sick of sin;   20
If you could hear, at every jolt, the blood
Come gargling from the froth-corrupted lungs,
Obscene as cancer, bitter as the cud
Of vile, incurable sores on innocent tongues,—
My friend, you would not tell with such high zest   25
To children ardent for some desperate glory,

DULCE ET DECORUM EST   "It is sweet and fitting to die for one's country." The title and last two lines
are from Horace, *Odes,* III, ii, 13.

The old Lie: *Dulce et decorum est*
Pro patria mori.

[1920]

E. E. CUMMINGS

[1894–1962]

Buffalo Bill's

Buffalo Bill's
defunct
          who used to
          ride a watersmooth-silver
                              stallion   5
and break onetwothreefourfive pigeons justlikethat
                              Jesus
he was a handsome man
                    and what i want to know is
how do you like your blueeyed boy   10
Mister Death

[1923]

may i feel said he

may i feel said he
(i'll squeal said she
just once said he)
it's fun said she

(may i touch said he   5
how much said she
a lot said he)
why not said she

(let's go said he
not too far said she   10
what's too far said he
where you are said she)

may i stay said he
(which way said she
like this said he   15
if you kiss said she

may i move said he
is it love said she)
if you're willing said he
(but you're killing said she   20

but it's life said he
but your wife said she
now said he)
ow said she

(tiptop said he   25
don't stop said she
oh no said he)
go slow said she

(cccome?said he
ummm said she)   30
you're divine!said he
(you are Mine said she)

[1935]

anyone lived in a pretty how town

anyone lived in a pretty how town
(with up so floating many bells down)
spring summer autumn winter
he sang his didn't he danced his did.

Women and men (both little and small)   5
cared for anyone not at all
they sowed their isn't they reaped their same
sun moon stars rain

children guessed (but only a few
and down they forgot as up they grew   10
autumn winter spring summer)
that noone loved him more by more

when by now and tree by leaf
she laughed his joy she cried his grief
bird by snow and stir by still   15
anyone's any was all to her

someones married their everyones
laughed their cryings and did their dance
(sleep wake hope and then) they
said their nevers they slept their dream   20

stars rain sun moon
(and only the snow can begin to explain
how children are apt to forget to remember
with up so floating many bells down)

one day anyone died i guess   25
(and noone stooped to kiss his face)
busy folk buried them side by side
little by little and was by was

all by all and deep by deep
and more by more they dream their sleep   30
noone and anyone earth by april
wish by spirit and if by yes.

Women and men (both dong and ding)
summer autumn winter spring
reaped their sowing and went their came   35
sun moon stars rain

[1940]

my father moved through dooms of love

my father moved through dooms of love
through sames of am through haves of give,
singing each morning out of each night
my father moved through depths of height

this motionless forgetful where   5
turned at his glance to shining here;

that if (so timid air is firm)
under his eyes would stir and squirm

newly as from unburied which
floats the first who,his april touch   *10*
drove sleeping selves to swarm their fates
woke dreamers to their ghostly roots

and should some why completely weep
my father's fingers brought her sleep:
vainly no smallest voice might cry   *15*
for he could feel the mountains grow.

Lifting the valleys of the sea
my father moved through griefs of joy;
praising a forehead called the moon
singing desire into begin   *20*

joy was his song and joy so pure
a heart of star by him could steer
and pure so now and now so yes
the wrists of twilight would rejoice

keen as midsummer's keen beyond   *25*
conceiving mind of sun will stand,
so strictly(over utmost him
so hugely)stood my father's dream

his flesh was flesh his blood was blood:
no hungry man but wished him food;   *30*
no cripple wouldn't creep one mile
uphill to only see him smile.

Scorning the pomp of must and shall
my father moved through dooms of feel;
his anger was as right as rain   *35*
his pity was as green as grain

septembering arms of year extend
less humbly wealth to foe and friend
than he to foolish and to wise
offered immeasurable is   *40*

proudly and (by octobering flame
beckoned) as earth will downward climb,
so naked for immortal work
his shoulders marched against the dark

his sorrow was as true as bread: 45
no liar looked him in the head;
if every friend became his foe
he'd laugh and build a world with snow.

My father moved through theys of we,
singing each new leaf out of each tree   50
(and every child was sure that spring
danced when she heard my father sing)

then let men kill which cannot share,
let blood and flesh be mud and mire,
scheming imagine,passion willed,   55
freedom a drug that's bought and sold

giving to steal and cruel kind,
a heart to fear,to doubt a mind,
to differ a disease of same,
conform the pinnacle of am   60

though dull were all we taste as bright,
bitter all utterly things sweet,
maggoty minus and dumb death
all we inherit,all bequeath

and nothing quite so least as truth   65
—i say though hate were why men breathe—
because my father lived his soul
love is the whole and more than all

                                                              [1940]

i thank You God for most this amazing

i thank You God for most this amazing
day:for the leaping greenly spirits of trees
and a blue true dream of sky;and for everything
which is natural which is infinite which is yes

(i who have died am alive again today,
and this is the sun's birthday;this is the birth
day of life and of love and wings:and of the gay
great happening illimitably earth)

how should tasting touching hearing seeing
breathing any—lifted from the no
of all nothing—human merely being
doubt unimaginable You?

(now the ears of my ears awake and
now the eyes of my eyes are opened)

[1950]

CHARLES REZNIKOFF

[b. 1894]

Kaddish

I

In her last sickness, my mother took my hand in hers
tightly: for the first time I knew
how calloused a hand it was, and how soft was mine.

II

Day after day you vomit the green sap of your life
and, wiping your lips with a paper napkin,
smile at me; and I smile back.
But, sometimes, as I talk calmly to others
I find that I have sighed—irrelevantly.

III

I pay my visit and, when the little we have to say is said,
go about my business and pleasures;

KADDISH   a portion of the ritual of the synagogue recited by mourners.

but you are lying these many weeks abed.
The sun comes out; the clouds are gone; the sky is blue;
the stars arise; the moon shines; and the sun shines anew
for me; but you are dying,
wiping the tears from your eyes—   15
secretly that I may go about my business and pleasures
while the sun shines and the stars rise.

IV

The wind that had been blowing yesterday has fallen;
now it is cold. The sun is shining behind the grove of trees
bare of every leaf (the trees no longer brown   20
as in autumn, but grayish—dead wood until the spring);
and in the withered grass the brown oak leaves are lying,
gray with frost.
"I was so sick but now—I think—am better."
Your voice, strangely deep, trembles;   25
your skin is ashen—
you seem a mother of us both, long dead.

V

The wind is crowding the waves down the river
to add their silver to the shimmering west.
The great work you did seems trifling now,   30
but you are tired. It is pleasant to close your eyes.
What is a street-light doing
so far from any street? That was the sun,
and now there is only darkness.

VI

Head sunken, eyes closed,   35
face pallid,
the bruised lips parted;
breathing heavily,
as if you had been climbing flights of stairs,
another flight of stairs—   40
and the heavy breathing
stopped.
The nurse came into the room silently
at the silence,
and felt your pulse,   45

and put your hand
beneath the covers,
and drew the covers to your chin,
and put a screen about your bed.
That was all: *50*
you were dead.

VII

Her heavy braids, the long hair of which she had been proud,
cut off, the undertaker's rouge
on her cheeks and lips,
and her cheerful greeting   *55*
silenced.

VIII

My mother leaned above me
as when I was a child.
What had she come to tell me
from the grave?   *60*

Helpless,
I looked at her anguish;
lifted my hand
to stroke her cheek,
touched it and woke.   *65*

IX
Stele

Not, as you were lying, a basin beside your head
into which you kept vomiting; nor, as that afternoon,
when you followed the doctor slowly with hardly the strength to stand,
small and shrunken in your black coat;
but, as you half turned to me, before you went through the swinging door,   *70*
and lifted your hand, your face solemn and calm.

X

We looked at the light burning slowly before your picture
and looked away;
we thought of you as we talked but could not bring ourselves to speak—

to strangers who do not care, yes,   *75*
but not among ourselves.

XI

I know you do not mind
(if you mind at all)
that I do not pray for you
or burn a light   *80*
on the day of your death:
we do not need these trifles
between us—
prayers and words and lights.

                                                  [1941]

JEAN TOOMER

[1894–1967]

Reapers

Black reapers with the sound of steel on stones
Are sharpening scythes. I see them place the hones
In their hip-pockets as a thing that's done,
And start their silent swinging, one by one.
Black horses drive a mower through the weeds,   *5*
And there, a field rat, startled, squealing bleeds,
His belly close to ground. I see the blade,
Blood-stained, continue cutting weeds and shade.

                                                  [1923]

ROBERT GRAVES

[1895–1985]

Down, wanton, down!

Down, wanton, down! Have you no shame
That at the whisper of Love's name,
Or Beauty's, presto! up you raise
Your angry head and stand at gaze?

Poor bombard-captain, sworn to reach   *5*
The ravelin and effect a breach—
Indifferent what you storm or why,
So that in the breach you die!

Love may be blind, but Love at least
Knows what is man and what mere beast;   *10*
Or Beauty wayward, but requires
More delicacy from her squires.

Tell me, my witless, whose one boast
Could be your staunchness at the post,
When were you made a man of parts   *15*
To think fine and profess the arts?

Will many-gifted Beauty come
Bowing to your bald rule of thumb,
Or Love swear loyalty to your crown?
Be gone, have done! Down, wanton, down!   *20*

[1933]

Symptoms of Love

Love is a universal migraine,
A bright stain on the vision
Blotting out reason.

Symptoms of true love
Are leanness, jealousy,   *5*
Laggard dawns;

Are omens and nightmares—
Listening for a knock,
Waiting for a sign:

For a touch of her fingers   10
In a darkened room,
For a searching look.

Take courage, lover!
Could you endure such pain
At any hand but hers?   15

[1938]

LOUISE BOGAN

[1897–1970]

Women

Women have no wilderness in them,
They are provident instead,
Content in the tight hot cell of their hearts
To eat dusty bread.

They do not see cattle cropping red winter grass,   5
They do not hear
Snow water going down under culverts
Shallow and clear.

They wait, when they should turn to journeys,
They stiffen, when they should bend.   10
They use against themselves that benevolence
To which no man is friend.

They cannot think of so many crops to a field
Or of clean wood cleft by an axe.
Their love is an eager meaninglessness   15
Too tense, or too lax.

They hear in every whisper that speaks to them
A shout and a cry.
As like as not, when they take life over their door-sills
They should let it go by.   20

[1923]

HART CRANE

[1899–1932]

from *The Bridge*

Proem: To Brooklyn Bridge

From going to and fro in the earth,
And from walking up and down in it.
—The Book of Job

How many dawns, chill from his rippling rest
The seagull's wings shall dip and pivot him,
Shedding white rings of tumult, building high
Over the chained bay waters Liberty—

Then, with inviolate curve, forsake our eyes   5
As apparitional as sails that cross
Some page of figures to be filed away;
—Till elevators drop us from our day . . .

I think of cinemas, panoramic sleights
With multitudes bent toward some flashing scene   10
Never disclosed, but hastened to again,
Foretold to other eyes on the same screen;

And Thee, across the harbor, silver-paced
As though the sun took step of thee, yet left
Some motion ever unspent in thy stride—   15
Implicitly thy freedom staying thee!

Out of some subway scuttle, cell or loft
A bedlamite° speeds to thy parapets,   madman
Tilting there momently, shrill shirt ballooning,
A jest falls from the speechless caravan.   20

Down Wall, from girder into street noon leaks,
A rip-tooth of the sky's acetylene,
All afternoon the cloud-flown derricks turn . . .
Thy cables breathe the North Atlantic still.

And obscure as that heaven of the Jews,   25
Thy guerdon . . . Accolade thou dost bestow

Of anonymity time cannot raise:
Vibrant reprieve and pardon thou dost show.

O harp and altar, of the fury fused,
(How could mere toil align thy choiring strings!)   30
Terrific threshold of the prophet's pledge,
Prayer of pariah, and the lover's cry—

Again the traffic lights that skim thy swift
Unfractioned idiom, immaculate sigh of stars,
Beading thy path—condense eternity: 35
And we have seen night lifted in thine arms.

Under thy shadow by the piers I waited;
Only in darkness is thy shadow clear.
The City's fiery parcels all undone,
Already snow submerges an iron year . . .   40

O Sleepless as the river under thee,
Vaulting the sea, the prairies' dreaming sod,
Unto us lowliest sometime sweep, descend
And of the curveship lend a myth to God.

[1930]

ROBERT FRANCIS

[1901–1987]

Cadence

Puckered like an old apple she lies abed,
Saying nothing and hearing nothing said,
Not seeing the birthday flowers by her head
To comfort her. She is not comforted.

The room is warm, too warm, but there is chill   5
Over her eyes and over her tired will.
Her hair is frost in the valley, snow on the hill.
Night is falling and the wind is still.

[1984]

LANGSTON HUGHES

[1902–1967]

"Poetry," Langston Hughes once remarked, "should be direct, comprehensible, and the epitome of simplicity." His poems illustrate these guidelines with remarkable consistency. Avoiding the obscure and the difficult, Hughes wrote poems that could be understood by readers and listeners who had little prior experience with poetry. He sought to write poems that were immediately understandable, poems that express concretely the concerns of daily black life.

Hughes's poetry offers a transcription of urban life through a portrayal of the speech, habits, attitudes, and feelings of an oppressed people. The poems do more, however, than reveal the pain of poverty. They also illustrate racial pride and dignity. Hughes's poems cling, moreover, to the spoken language. They derive from an oral tradition in which folk poetry is recited and performed, rather than published in written form. In the oral tradition poems are passed down from one generation to the next through performance and recitation. As a result Hughes's poems, more than most, need to be read aloud to be fully appreciated. Hughes himself became famous for his public readings, which were sometimes accompanied by a glee club or jazz combo.

Music, in fact, is a central feature of Hughes's poetry. And the kind of music most evident in his work is the blues, an important influence in the work of many modern black writers, especially those associated with the Harlem Renaissance, a flowering of artistic activity among black artists and writers of Harlem in the 1920s. Hughes once described the blues as "sad funny songs—too sad to be funny and too funny to be sad," songs that contain "laughter and pain, hunger and heartache." The bittersweet tone and view of life reflected in Hughes's perspective on the blues is consistently mirrored in his poems, which sometimes adapt the stanza form of the typical blues song. This stanza includes two nearly identical lines followed by a third that contrasts with the first two. "Same in Blues" (pp. 103–104) exhibits this characteristic with only slight modifications. In this and other poems, Hughes succeeds in grafting the inflections of the urban black dialect onto the rhythms of the blues.

But the blues is not the only musical influence on Hughes's poetry; his work also makes use of jazz as both subject and style, though Hughes's jazz poems are freer and looser in form than his blues poems. This difference reflects the improvisatory nature of jazz as well as its energy and vitality, which contrast with the more controlled idiom of the blues. The aggressive exuberance of jazz, its relaxed but vigorous informality is evident in poems like "Mulatto" and "Trumpet Player."

Hughes was a prolific writer whose published books span forty years (1926–1967). His output includes sixteen volumes of poems; two novels; three collections of short stories; four documentary works; three historical works; twenty dramatic pieces, including plays, musicals, and operettas; two volumes of autobiography; eight children's books; and twelve radio and television scripts. In addition, Hughes edited seven books—mostly collections of poems by black writers—and translated four others, including the poems of the renowned modern Spanish poet Federico García

Lorca (pp. 1093–1094). Such versatility established Hughes as an important man of letters, contributing to his stature as a leading figure in the arts, especially the theater, whose audience Hughes was instrumental in enlarging.

The writers who influenced Hughes included Paul Dunbar, whose poems re-created the black vernacular, and W. E. B. DuBois, whose collection of essays on Afro-American life, *The Souls of Black Folk,* exerted a lasting influence on many writers, including novelists Richard Wright and James Baldwin. Hughes was also strongly influenced by the democratic idealism of Walt Whitman and the populism of Carl Sandburg, whom Hughes designated his "guiding star." From Sandburg, Hughes learned to write free verse. From Dunbar, he learned a method of incorporating local dialect into poems. And from DuBois, he derived what later came to be called black pride. These influences were combined and amalgamated in myriad ways, resulting in poems that provided insight into urban life.

Hughes's life was as varied as his writing. Born in Joplin, Missouri, in 1902, Hughes lived in Kansas and Ohio before studying at Columbia University in New York and later and more fully at Lincoln University in Nebraska. He worked as a seaman and as a newspaper correspondent and columnist for the *Chicago Defender,* the *Baltimore Afro-American,* and the New York *Post.* He also worked briefly as a cook at a fashionable restaurant in France and as a busboy in a Washington, D.C., hotel. It was there that Hughes left three of his poems beside the plate of a hotel dinner guest, the poet Vachel Lindsay, who recognized their merit and helped Hughes to secure their publication.

Hughes also founded theaters on both coasts—the Harlem Suitcase Theatre (New York, 1938) and the New Negro Theatre (Los Angeles, 1939)—and, in the Midwest, the Skyloft Players (Chicago, 1941). He traveled extensively, visiting and at various times living in Africa and Europe, especially Italy and France, as well as in Cuba, Haiti, Russia, Korea, and Japan. His life and travels are richly and engagingly chronicled in his two volumes of autobiography, *The Big Sea* (1940) and *I Wonder As I Wander* (1956).

As a writer who believed it was his vocation to "explain and illuminate the Negro condition in America," Hughes captured the experience as "the hurt of their lives, the monotony of their jobs, and the veiled weariness of their songs." He accomplished this in poems remarkable not only for their directness and simplicity but for their economy, lucidity, and wit. Whether he was writing poems of racial protest like "Dream Deferred" and "Ballad of the Landlord" or poems of racial affirmation like "Mother to Son" (p. 15) and "The Negro Speaks of Rivers," Hughes was able to find language and forms to express not only the pain of urban life but also its splendid vitality.

The Negro Speaks of Rivers

I've known rivers:
I've known rivers ancient as the world and older than the flow of human blood in
   human veins.

My soul has grown deep like the rivers.

I bathed in the Euphrates when dawns were young.
I built my hut near the Congo and it lulled me to sleep.   5
I looked upon the Nile and raised the pyramids above it.
I heard the singing of the Mississippi when Abe Lincoln went down to New Orleans,
   and I've seen its muddy bosom turn all golden in the sunset

I've known rivers:
Ancient, dusky rivers.

My soul has grown deep like the rivers.   10

                                                [1926]

The Weary Blues

Droning a drowsy syncopated tune,
Rocking back and forth to a mellow croon,
      I heard a Negro play.
Down on Lenox Avenue the other night
By the pale dull pallor of an old gas light   5
      He did a lazy sway. . . .
      He did a lazy sway. . . .
To the tune o' those Weary Blues.
With his ebony hands on each ivory key
He made that poor piano moan with melody.   10
      O Blues!
Swaying to and fro on his rickety stool
He played that sad raggy tune like a musical fool.
      Sweet Blues!
Coming from a black man's soul.   15
      O Blues!
In a deep song voice with a melancholy tone
I heard that Negro sing, that old piano moan—
      "Ain't got nobody in all this world,
      Ain't got nobody but ma self.   20
      I's gwine to quit ma frownin'
      And put ma troubles on the shelf."
Thump, thump, thump, went his foot on the floor.
He played a few chords then he sang some more—
      "I got the Weary Blues   25
      And I can't be satisfied.

Got the Weary Blues
And can't be satisfied—
I ain't happy no mo'
And I wish that I had died."   30
And far into the night he crooned that tune.
The stars went out and so did the moon.
The singer stopped playing and went to bed
While the Weary Blues echoed through his head.
He slept like a rock or a man that's dead.   35

[1926]

Mulatto

I am your son, white man!

Georgia dusk
And the turpentine woods.
One of the pillars of the temple fell.

    You are my son!   5
    Like hell!

The moon over the turpentine woods.
The Southern night
Full of stars,
Great big yellow stars.   10
  What's a body but a toy?
    Juicy bodies
    Of nigger wenches
    Blue black
    Against black fences.   15
    O, you little bastard boy,
  What's a body but a toy?
The scent of pine wood stings the soft night air.
    What's the body of your mother?
Silver moonlight everywhere.   20

    What's the body of your mother?
Sharp pine scent in the evening air.
    A nigger night,
    A nigger joy,

A little yellow   25
Bastard boy.

Naw, you ain't my brother.
Niggers ain't my brother.

Not ever.
Niggers ain't my brother.   30

The Southern night is full of stars,
Great big yellow stars.
          O, sweet as earth,
          Dusk dark bodies
          Give sweet birth   35
To little yellow bastard boys.

          Git on back there in the night,
          You ain't white.

The bright stars scatter everywhere.
Pine wood scent in the evening air.   40
          A nigger night,
          A nigger joy.

     I am your son, white man!

          A little yellow
          Bastard boy.   45

                              [1926]

Trumpet Player

The Negro
With the trumpet at his lips
Has dark moons of weariness
Beneath his eyes
Where the smoldering memory   5
Of slave ships
Blazed to the crack of whips
About his thighs.

The Negro
With the trumpet at his lips   10
Has a head of vibrant hair
Tamed down,
Patent-leathered now
Until it gleams
Like jet—   15
Were jet a crown.

The music
From the trumpet at his lips
Is honey
Mixed with liquid fire.   20
The rhythm
From the trumpet at his lips
Is ecstasy
Distilled from old desire—

Desire   25
That is longing for the moon
Where the moonlight's but a spotlight
In his eyes,
Desire
That is longing for the sea   30
Where the sea's a bar-glass
Sucker size.

The Negro
With the trumpet at his lips
Whose jacket   35
Has a *fine* one-button roll,
Does not know
Upon what riff the music slips
Its hypodermic needle
To his soul—   40

But softly
As the tune comes from his throat
Trouble
Mellows to a golden note.

[1947]

Ballad of the Landlord

Landlord, landlord,
My roof has sprung a leak.
Don't you 'member I told you about it
Way last week?

Landlord, landlord,   5
These steps is broken down.
When you come up yourself
It's a wonder you don't fall down.

Ten Bucks you say I owe you?
Ten Bucks you say is due?   10
Well, that's Ten Bucks more'n I'll pay you
Till you fix this house up new.

What? You gonna get eviction orders?
You gonna cut off my heat?
You gonna take my furniture and   15
Throw it in the street?

Um-huh! You talking high and mighty.
Talk on—till you get through.
You ain't gonna be able to say a word
If I land my fist on you.   20

Police! Police!
Come and get this man!
He's trying to ruin the government
And overturn the land!

Copper's whistle!   25
Patrol bell!
Arrest.

Precinct Station.
Iron cell.
Headlines in press: 30

MAN THREATENS LANDLORD

TENANT HELD NO BAIL

JUDGE GIVES NEGRO 90 DAYS IN COUNTY JAIL

[1949]

Madam and the Rent Man

The rent man knocked.
He said, Howdy-do?
I said, What
Can I do for you?
He said, You know   5
Your rent is due.

I said, Listen,
Before I'd pay
I'd go to Hades
And rot away!   10

The sink is broke,
The water don't run,
And you ain't done a thing
You promised to've done.

Back window's cracked,   15
Kitchen floor squeaks,
There's rats in the cellar,
And the attic leaks.

He said, Madam,
It's not up to me.   20
I'm just the agent,
Don't you see?

I said, Naturally,
You pass the buck.
If it's money you want   25
You're out of luck.

He said, Madam,
I ain't pleased!
I said, Neither am I.

So we agrees!   30

[1949]

Dream Deferred

What happens to a dream
deferred:
Does it dry up
like a raisin in the sun?
Or fester like a sore—   5
And then run?
Does it stink like rotten meat?
Or crust and sugar over—
like a syrupy sweet?

Maybe it just sags   10
like a heavy load.

Or does it explode?

[1951]

Theme for English B

The instructor said,
  Go home and write
  a page tonight.
  And let that page come out of you—
  Then, it will be true.   5

I wonder if it's that simple?

I am twenty-two, colored, born in Winston-Salem.
I went to school there, then Durham, then here
to this college on the hill above Harlem.
I am the only colored student in my class.   10
The steps from the hill lead down into Harlem,
through a park, then I cross St. Nicholas,
Eighth Avenue, Seventh, and I come to the Y,
the Harlem Branch Y, where I take the elevator
up to my room, sit down, and write this page: 15

It's not easy to know what is true for you or me
at twenty-two, my age. But I guess I'm what

I feel and see and hear. Harlem, I hear you:
hear you, hear me—we two—you, me, talk on this page.
(I hear New York, too.) Me—who?   20

Well, I like to eat, sleep, drink, and be in love.
I like to work, read, learn, and understand life.
I like a pipe for a Christmas present,
or records—Bessie, bop, or Bach.
I guess being colored doesn't make me *not* like   25
the same things other folks like who are other races.

So will my page be colored that I write?
Being me, it will not be white.
But it will be
a part of you, instructor.   30
You are white—
yet a part of me, as I am a part of you.
That's American.
Sometimes perhaps you don't want to be a part of me.
Nor do I often want to be a part of you.   35
But we are, that's true!
As I learn from you,
I guess you learn from me—
although you're older—and white—
and somewhat more free.   40

This is my page for English B.

                                                              [1959]

STEVIE SMITH

[1902–1971]

Not Waving but Drowning

Nobody heard him, the dead man,
But still he lay moaning:
I was much further out than you thought
And not waving but drowning.

Poor chap, he always loved larking   5
And now he's dead

It must have been too cold for him his heart gave way,
They said.

Oh, no no no, it was too cold always
(Still the dead one lay moaning)   *10*
I was much too far out all my life
And not waving but drowning.

[1957]

COUNTEE CULLEN

[1903–1946]

Incident

Once riding in old Baltimore,
    Heart-filled, head-filled with glee,
I saw a Baltimorean
    Keep looking straight at me.

Now I was eight and very small,   *5*
    And he was no whit bigger,
And so I smiled, but he poked out
    His tongue and called me, "Nigger."

I saw the whole of Baltimore
    From May until December: *10*
Of all the things that happened there
    That's all that I remember.

[1925]

RICHARD EBERHART

[b. 1904]

The Groundhog

In June, amid the golden fields,
I saw a groundhog lying dead.
Dead lay he; my senses shook,
And mind outshot our naked frailty.

There slowly in the vigorous summer   *5*
His form began its senseless change,
And made my senses waver dim
Seeing nature ferocious in him.
Inspecting close his maggots' might
And seething cauldron of his being,   *10*
Half with loathing, half with a strange love,
I poked him with an angry stick.
The fever arose, became a flame
And Vigor circumscribed the skies,
Immense energy in the sun,   *15*
And through my frame a sunless trembling.
My stick had done nor good nor harm.
Then stood I silent in the day
Watching the object, as before;
And kept my reverence for knowledge   *20*
Trying for control, to be still,
To quell the passion of the blood;
Until I had bent down on my knees
Praying for joy in the sight of decay.
And so I left; and I returned   *25*
In Autumn strict of eye, to see
The sap gone out of the groundhog,
But the bony sodden hulk remained.
But the year had lost its meaning,
And in intellectual chains   *30*
I lost both love and loathing,
Mured up in the wall of wisdom.
Another summer took the fields again
Massive and burning, full of life,
But when I chanced upon the spot   *35*
There was only a little hair left,
And bones bleaching in the sunlight
Beautiful as architecture;
I watched them like a geometer,
And cut a walking stick from a birch.   *40*
It has been three years, now.
There is no sign of the groundhog.
I stood there in the whirling summer,
My hand capped a withered heart,
And thought of China and of Greece,   *45*
Of Alexander in his tent;
Of Montaigne in his tower,
Of Saint Theresa in her wild lament.

[1936]

KENNETH REXROTH

[1905–1982]

Floating

Our canoe idles in the idling current
Of the tree and vine and rush enclosed
Backwater of a torpid midwestern stream;
Revolves slowly, and lodges in the glutted
Waterlilies. We are tired of paddling.   5
All afternoon we have climbed the weak current,
Up dim meanders, through woods and pastures,
Past muddy fords where the strong smell of cattle
Lay thick across the water; singing the songs
Of perfect, habitual motion; ski songs,   10
Nightherding songs, songs of the capstan walk,
The levee, and the roll of the voyageurs.
Tired of motion, of the rhythms of motion,
Tired of the sweet play of our interwoven strength,
We lie in each other's arms and let the palps   15
Of waterlily leaf and petal hold back
All motion in the heat thickened, drowsing air.
Sing to me softly, Westron Wynde, Ah the Syghes,
Mon coeur se recommend à vous, Phoebi Claro;
Sing the wandering erotic melodies   20
Of men and women gone seven hundred years,
Softly, your mouth close to my cheek.
Let our thighs lie entangled on the cushions,
Let your breasts in their thin cover
Hang pendant against my naked arms and throat;   25
Let your odorous hair fall across our eyes;
Kiss me with those subtle, melodic lips.
As I undress you, your pupils are black, wet,
Immense, and your skin ivory and humid.
Move softly, move hardly at all, part your thighs,   30
Take me slowly while our gnawing lips
Fumble against the humming blood in our throats.
Move softly, do not move at all, but hold me,
Deep, still, deep within you, while time slides away,
As this river slides beyond this lily bed,   35
And the thieving moments fuse and disappear
In our mortal, timeless flesh.

[1944]

ROBERT PENN WARREN

[b. 1905]

Love and Knowledge

Their footless dance
Is of the beautiful liability of their nature.
Their eyes are round, boldly convex, bright as a jewel,
And merciless. They do not know
Compassion, and if they did,   5
We should not be worthy of it. They fly
In air that glitters like fluent crystal
And is hard as perfectly transparent iron, they cleave it
With no effort. They cry
In a tongue multitudinous, often like music.   10

He slew them, at surprising distances, with his gun.
Over a body held in his hand, his head was bowed low,
But not in grief.

He put them where they are, and there we see them:
In our imagination.   15

What is love?

One name for it is knowledge.

[1971]

W. H. AUDEN

[1907–1973]

The Unknown Citizen

(TO JS/07/M/378 THIS MARBLE MONUMENT IS ERECTED BY THE STATE)

He was found by the Bureau of Statistics to be
One against whom there was no official complaint,
And all the reports on his conduct agree

That, in the modern sense of an old-fashioned word, he was a saint,
For in everything he did he served the Greater Community.   5
Except for the War till the day he retired
He worked in a factory and never got fired
But satisfied his employers, Fudge Motors Inc.
Yet he wasn't a scab or odd in his views,
For his Union reports that he paid his dues,   10
(Our report on his Union shows it was sound)
And our Social Psychology workers found
That he was popular with his mates and liked a drink.
The Press are convinced that he bought a paper every day
And that his reactions to advertisements were normal in every way.   15
Policies taken out in his name prove that he was fully insured,
And his Health-card shows he was once in hospital but left it cured.
Both Producers Research and High-Grade Living declare
He was fully sensible to the advantages of the Installment Plan
And had everything necessary to the Modern Man,   20
A phonograph, a radio, a car and a frigidaire.
Our researchers into Public Opinion are content
That he held the proper opinions for the time of year;
When there was peace, he was for peace; when there was war, he went.
He was married and added five children to the population,   25
Which our Eugenist says was the right number for a parent of his generation.
And our teachers report that he never interfered with their education.

Was he free? Was he happy? The question is absurd:
Had anything been wrong, we should certainly have heard.

[1940]

In Memory of W. B. Yeats

[D. JANUARY 1939]

1

He disappeared in the dead of winter:
The brooks were frozen, the air-ports almost deserted,
And snow disfigured the public statues;
The mercury sank in the mouth of the dying day.
O all the instruments agree   5
The day of his death was a dark cold day.

Far from his illness
The wolves ran on through the evergreen forests,
The peasant river was untempted by the fashionable quays;
By mourning tongues   10
The death of the poet was kept from his poems.

But for him it was his last afternoon as himself,
An afternoon of nurses and rumours;
The provinces of his body revolted,
The squares of his mind were empty,   15
Silence invaded the suburbs,
The current of his feeling failed: he became his admirers.

Now he is scattered among a hundred cities
And wholly given over to unfamiliar affections;
To find his happiness in another kind of wood   20
And be punished under a foreign code of conscience.
The words of a dead man
Are modified in the guts of the living.

But in the importance and noise of to-morrow
When the brokers are roaring like beasts on the floor of the Bourse,   25
And the poor have the sufferings to which they are fairly accustomed,
And each in the cell of himself is almost convinced of his freedom;
A few thousand will think of this day
As one thinks of a day when one did something slightly unusual.
O all the instruments agree   30
The day of his death was a dark cold day.

2

You were silly like us: your gift survived it all;
The parish of rich women, physical decay,
Yourself; mad Ireland hurt you into poetry.
Now Ireland has her madness and her weather still,   35
For poetry makes nothing happen: it survives
In the valley of its saying where executives
Would never want to tamper; it flows south
From ranches of isolation and the busy griefs,
Raw towns that we believe and die in; it survives,   40
A way of happening, a mouth.

3

Earth, receive an honoured guest;
William Yeats is laid to rest:

Let the Irish vessel lie
Emptied of its poetry.   *45*

Time that is intolerant
Of the brave and innocent,
And indifferent in a week
To a beautiful physique,

Worships language and forgives   *50*
Everyone by whom it lives;
Pardons cowardice, conceit,
Lays its honours at their feet.

Time that with this strange excuse
Pardoned Kipling and his views,   *55*
And will pardon Paul Claudel,
Pardons him for writing well.

In the nightmare of the dark
All the dogs of Europe bark,
And the living nations wait,   *60*
Each sequestered in its hate;

Intellectual disgrace
Stares from every human face,
And the seas of pity lie
Locked and frozen in each eye.   *65*

Follow, poet, follow right
To the bottom of the night,
With your unconstraining Voice
Still persuade us to rejoice;

With the farming of a verse   *70*
Make a vineyard of the curse,
Sing of human unsuccess
In a rapture of distress;

In the deserts of the heart
Let the healing fountain start,   *75*

[55]**Kipling** Rudyard Kipling (1865–1936), British writer with imperialist views.   [56]**Paul Claudel** French
Catholic writer (1868–1955) who was extremely conservative politically.   [58-61]**In the nightmare . . . in its hate**
World War II broke out only a few months after Auden wrote this poem.

In the prison of his days
Teach the free man how to praise.

[1940]

The Shield of Achilles

She looked over his shoulder
    For vines and olive trees,
Marble well-governed cities
    And ships upon untamed seas,
But there on the shining metal   5
    His hands had put instead
An artificial wilderness
    And a sky like lead.

A plain without a feature, bare and brown,
    No blade of grass, no sign of neighborhood,   10
Nothing to eat and nowhere to sit down,
    Yet, congregated on its blankness, stood
    An unintelligible multitude,
A million eyes, a million boots in line,
Without expression, waiting for a sign.   15

Out of the air a voice without a face
    Proved by statistics that some cause was just
In tones as dry and level as the place:
    No one was cheered and nothing was discussed;
    Column by column in a cloud of dust   20
They marched away enduring a belief
Whose logic brought them, somewhere else, to grief.

She looked over his shoulder
    For ritual pieties,
White flower-garlanded heifers,   25
    Libation and sacrifice
But there on the shining metal
    Where the altar should have been,

THE SHIELD OF ACHILLES   In book 18 of *The Iliad,* Homer describes a shield made for Achilles by
Hephaestos at the request of Achilles' mother, Thetis. Much of what Thetis does not find on the shield described
in Auden's poem is present in Homer's description.

She saw by his flickering forge-light
   Quite another scene.   *30*

Barbed wire enclosed an arbitrary spot
   Where bored officials lounged (one cracked a joke)
And sentries sweated for the day was hot:
   A crowd of ordinary decent folk
   Watched from without and neither moved nor spoke   *35*
As three pale figures were led forth and bound
To three posts driven upright in the ground.

The mass and majesty of this world, all
   That carries weight and always weighs the same
Lay in the hands of others; they were small   *40*
   And could not hope for help and no help came:
   What their foes liked to do was done, their shame
Was all the worst could wish; they lost their pride
And died as men before their bodies died.

   She looked over his shoulder   *45*
     For athletes at their games,
   Men and women in a dance
     Moving their sweet limbs
     Quick, quick, to music,
     But there on the shining shield   *50*
   His hands had set no dancing-floor
     But a weed-choked field.

A ragged urchin, aimless and alone,
   Loitered about that vacancy; a bird
Flew up to safety from his well-aimed stone: *55*
   That girls are raped, that two boys knife a third,
   Were axioms to him, who'd never heard
Of any world where promises were kept,
Or one could weep because another wept.
     The thin-lipped armorer,   *60*
     Hephaestos, hobbled away,
   Thetis of the shining breasts
     Cried out in dismay
   At what the god had wrought
     To please her son, the strong   *65*
   Iron-hearted man-slaying Achilles
     Who would not live long.

                     [1955]

A. D. HOPE

[b. 1907]

Imperial Adam

Imperial Adam, naked in the dew,
Felt his brown flanks and found the rib was gone.
Puzzled he turned and saw where, two and two,
The mighty spoor of Jahweh marked the lawn.

Then he remembered through mysterious sleep   5
The surgeon fingers probing at the bone,
The voice so far away, so rich and deep:
"It is not good for him to live alone."

Turning once more he found Man's counterpart
In tender parody breathing at his side.   10
He knew her at first sight, he knew by heart
Her allegory of sense unsatisfied.

The pawpaw° drooped its golden breasts above   *a fruit tree*
Less generous than the honey of her flesh;
The innocent sunlight showed the place of love;   15
The dew on its dark hairs winked crisp and fresh.

This plump gourd severed from his virile root,
She promised on the turf of Paradise
Delicious pulp of the forbidden fruit;
Sly as the snake she loosed her sinuous thighs,   20

And waking, smiled up at him from the grass;
Her breasts rose softly and he heard her sigh—
From all the beasts whose pleasant task it was
In Eden to increase and multiply

Adam had learned the jolly deed of kind:°   *nature* 25
He took her in his arms and there and then,

IMPERIAL ADAM   8"It . . . alone"   "And the Lord said, It is not good that the man should be alone"
(Genesis 2:18).

Like the clean beasts, embracing from behind,
Began in joy to found the breed of men.

Then from the spurt of seed within her broke
Her terrible and triumphant female cry,   30
Split upward by the sexual lightning stroke.
It was the beasts now who stood watching by:

The gravid elephant, the calving hind,
The breeding bitch, the she-ape big with young
Were the first gentle midwives of mankind;   35
The teeming lioness rasped her with her tongue;

The proud vicuña nuzzled her as she slept
Lax on the grass; and Adam watching too
Saw how her dumb breasts at their ripening wept,
The great pod of her belly swelled and grew,   40

And saw its water break, and saw, in fear,
Its quaking muscles in the act of birth,
Between her legs a pigmy face appear,
And the first murderer lay upon the earth.

                                        [1955]

THEODORE ROETHKE

[1908–1963]

The Waking

I wake to sleep, and take my waking slow.
I feel my fate in what I cannot fear.
I learn by going where I have to go.

We think by feeling. What is there to know?
I hear my being dance from ear to ear.   5
I wake to sleep, and take my waking slow.

Of those so close beside me, which are you?
God bless the Ground! I shall walk softly there,
And learn by going where I have to go.

Light takes the Tree; but can who can tell us how?   *10*
The lowly worm climbs up a winding stair;
I wake to sleep, and take my waking slow.

Great Nature has another thing to do
To you and me; so take the lively air,
And, lovely, learn by going where to go.   *15*

This shaking keeps me steady. I should know.
What falls away is always. And is near.
I wake to sleep, and take my waking slow.
I learn by going where I have to go.

                                                  [1953]

Elegy for Jane

MY STUDENT, THROWN BY A HORSE

I remember the neckcurls, limp and damp as tendrils;
And her quick look, a sidelong pickerel smile;
And how, once startled into talk, the light syllables leaped for her,
And she balanced in the delight of her thought,
A wren, happy, tail into the wind,   *5*
Her song trembling the twigs and small branches.
The shade sang with her;
The leaves, their whispers turned to kissing;
And the mold sang in the bleached valleys under the rose.

Oh, when she was sad, she cast herself down into such a pure depth,   *10*
Even a father could not find her:
Scraping her cheek against straw;
Stirring the clearest water.

My sparrow, you are not here,
Waiting like a fern, making a spiny shadow.   *15*
The sides of wet stones cannot console me,
Nor the moss, wound with the last light.

If only I could nudge you from this sleep,
My maimed darling, my skittery pigeon.

Over this damp grave I speak the words of my love: 20
I, with no rights in this matter,
Neither father nor lover.

[1953]

CHARLES OLSON

[1910–1970]

Maximus, to Gloucester, Sunday, July 19

and they stopped before that bad sculpture of a fisherman

—"as if one were to talk to a man's house,
knowing not what gods or heroes are"—

not knowing what a fisherman is
instead of going straight to the Bridge 5
and doing no more than—saying no more than—
in the Charybdises of the
Cut waters the flowers tear off

the wreaths

the flowers 10
turn
the character of the sea The sea jumps
the fate of the flower The drowned men are undrowned
in the eddies
of the eyes 15
of the flowers
opening
the sea's eyes

The disaster
is undone 20

MAXIMUS: TO GLOUCESTER   Gloucester is a fishing town in Massachusetts, where Olson grew up. On July
19 the town holds a memorial service for fishermen lost at sea.   ⁷**Charybdis**   is a whirlpool that Odysseus, in
Homer's *Odyssey,* must sail around.

What was received as alien
—the flower
on the water, that a man drowns
that he dies in water as he dies on earth, the impossible
       that this gross fact can return to us   25
            in this upset
on a summer day
of a particular tide

that the sensation is true,
that the transformations of fire are, first of all, sea—   30
     "as gold for wares wares for gold"

     Let them be told who stopped first
     by a bronze idol

     A fisherman is not a successful man
     he is not a famous man he is not a man   35
     of power, these are the damned by God

II

whose surface bubbles
with these gimlets
which screw-in like

potholes, caustic   40
caked earth in painted
pools, Yellowstone

Park of holes
is death the diseased
presence on us, the spilling lesion   45

of the brilliance
it is to be alive: to walk onto it,
as Jim Bridger the first into it,

It is more true a scabious
field than it is a pretty   50
meadow

⁴⁸Jim Bridger   fur trader and Indian scout (1804–1881).

When a man's coffin is the sea
the whole of creation shall come to his funeral,

it turns out; the globe   55
is below, all lapis

and its blue surface golded
by what happened

this afternoon: there are eyes
in this water

the flowers   60
from the shore,

awakened
the sea

Men are so sure they know very many things,
they don't even know night and day are one   65

A fisherman works without reference to
that difference. It is possible he also

by lying there when he does lie, jowl
to the sea, has another advantage: it is said,

"You rectify what can be rectified," and when a man's heart   70
cannot see this, the door of his divine intelligence is shut

let you who paraded to the Cut today
to hold memorial services to all fishermen
who have been lost at sea in a year
when for the first time not one life was lost   75

radar sonar radio telephone good engines
bed-check seaplanes goodness over and
    under us

no difference
when men come back

                                                                                    [1953]

ELIZABETH BISHOP

[1911–1979]

Elizabeth Bishop's poems are rooted in precise observations. They are grounded in clarity and attentiveness. Bishop is noted for the purity and exactness of her language as well as for its range and unpredictability. Her poetry avoids the learned allusions to history and literature that characterize the poems of her contemporaries T. S. Eliot and Ezra Pound. Bishop also eschews the confessional, self-revelatory mode of Sylvia Plath. Her poems hold the private self in reserve. Their emotion is controlled and restrained.

Bishop's life was relatively quiet and undisturbed by the literary revolution that was occurring among her contemporaries. She was born in Massachusetts in 1911 and grew up in New England and Nova Scotia. Her father died before she reached her first birthday, and her mother was taken to a sanitarium when she was five. Bishop never saw her again. Educated at Vassar College, she later lived in Key West, Florida, and then for nearly seventeen years in Brazil. She served as poetry consultant to the Library of Congress, and she taught briefly at New York University, the University of Washington, the Massachusetts Institute of Technology, and at Harvard. She received numerous awards, including a Pulitzer Prize (1956) and a National Book Award (1970). In addition to her poetry, she wrote short fiction; she also translated Brazilian poetry.

Bishop's poetic subjects are conveniently indicated in the titles of her books, especially *North and South* (1946), *Questions of Travel* (1965), and *Geography III* (1976). Her poems, however, are not merely about the literal places that inspired them; they are more than pictures of those places. Characteristically speculative in tone, Bishop's poems raise questions about foreign landscapes and experiences, conveying a sense of their strangeness. In "Questions of Travel," for example, she asks whether it is right "to be watching strangers in a play / in this strangest of theatres?"—a foreign country. She also wonders whether it is a "lack of imagination that makes us come / to imagined places."

Bishop's poems exhibit a tendency to combine the factual with the fanciful, the imaginary with the real. Her poems are both realistic and surrealistic, a combination evident in the following lines from "The Monument":

> What is that?"
>   It is the monument.
> "It's piled-up boxes
> outlined with shoddy fret-work, half-fallen off,
> cracked and unpainted. It looks old."
> —The strong sunlight, the wind from the sea,
> all the conditions of its existence,
> may have flaked off the paint, if ever it was painted,
> and made it homelier than it was.

"Why did you bring me here to see it?
A temple of crates in cramped and crated scenery,
what can it prove?
I am tired of breathing this eroded air,
this dryness in which the monument is cracking."
It is an artifact
of wood. Wood holds together better
than sea or cloud or sand could by itself,
much better than real sea or sand or cloud.
It chose that way to grow and not to move.
The monument's an object, yet those decorations,
carelessly nailed, looking like nothing at all,
give it away as having life, and wishing;
wanting to be a monument, to cherish something.
The crudest scroll-work says "commemorate,"
while once each day the light goes around it
like a prowling animal,
or the rain falls on it, or the wind blows into it.
It may be solid, may be hollow.
The bones of the artist-prince may be inside
or far away on even drier soil.
But roughly but adequately it can shelter
what is within (which after all
cannot have been intended to be seen).
It is the beginning of a painting,
a piece of sculpture, or poem, or monument,
and all of wood. Watch it closely.

These lines invite the reader to watch closely—not just the monument but any object of perception—since the mind can transform reality, embroidering fact with fanciful imaginings. In the poem, Bishop's speaker demonstrates the process, commemorating both the unlikely monument itself and the act of imaginative perception whereby it is observed and transfigured. The acts of mind involved share something with the work of the naturalist observer who is part scientist and part visionary poet; for Bishop, Charles Darwin represents such a luminous conjunction of reality and imaginative vision. But Bishop's acts of seeing were more important than even this blending of reality and imagination would suggest. For Bishop, as Helen McNeil has pointed out, "to look was to act, an action that for her carried moral weight." The pleasures of perception thus extend beyond precision of seeing through dreamlike imagining and into moral imperative.

The qualities that distinguish Bishop's poetry include more, however, than her keen observations and imaginings. They extend, as Joseph Summers has noted, to an impeccable ear for language, a purity of diction, and a delicacy of tone that echo the work of the seventeenth-century metaphysical poet George Herbert. Like Herbert, (pp. 214–217) though not as extensively, Bishop wrote poems in a wide variety of forms—among them prose poems, blank verse, song, quatrain, sonnet, sestina, and villanelle. The following poem reveals both Bishop's attention to external detail and her precision of language. It also illustrates her striking ability to offer a fresh perspective—in this case, the point of view of a bird running along an ocean beach.

Sandpiper

The roaring alongside he takes for granted,
and that every so often the world is bound to shake.
He runs, he runs to the south, finical, awkward,
in a state of controlled panic, a student of Blake.

The beach hisses like fat. On his left, a sheet   5
of interrupting water comes and goes
and glazes over his dark and brittle feet.
He runs, he runs straight through it, watching his toes.

—Watching, rather, the spaces of sand between them,
where (no detail too small) the Atlantic drains   10
rapidly backwards and downwards. As he runs,
he stares at the dragging grains.

The world is a mist. And then the world is
minute and vast and clear. The tide
is higher or lower. He couldn't tell you which.   15
His beak is focussed; he is preoccupied,

looking for something, something, something.
Poor bird, he is obsessed!
The millions of grains are black, white, tan, and gray,
mixed with quartz grains, rose and amethyst.   20

[1965]

Bishop suggests the bird's acceptance of the way its "world is bound to shake" as the surf hits the beach. That the bird runs is not surprising and is easy enough to imagine. What is surprising is Bishop's description of that running as a "state of controlled panic" and as something "finical," an archaic word meaning finicky, or overdetailed. Equally original is the humorous allusion to William Blake, who wrote, in "Auguries of Innocence," that it is possible to see "a world in a grain of sand." Whereas for Blake such an act of imaginative perception was a sign of human wonder in the face of the splendor of nature, Bishop's ironic wit readapts Blake's perspective to illustrate the sandpiper's obsessive failure of imagination. The sandpiper is unable to see large things like the relative height of the tide because it is obsessed with minutiae like the grains of sand. Without Bishop's stating it directly, the poem describes the limitations of perception that result from a relentless preoccupation with detail, a focused narrowness that blocks the meditative imagination.

The details of stanza 2 are just as fresh: the beach hissing "like fat"; the "sheet" of sea water "interrupting" the sandpiper's watchful searching; the water glazing the bird's toes. Bishop's descriptive precision extends to the bird's direction: he runs south with the ocean on his left. And it accurately reflects the direction of the ocean's draining: "rapidly backwards and downwards"—from the bird's point of view. The linguistic precision includes the aptly chosen "dragging" to describe the grains of sand, and the repetition of "something, something, something" to mimic the sandpiper's obsessive looking. In noticing such attention to detail, we begin to appreciate Bishop's poetic accomplishment. Perhaps even more remarkable is the way Bishop surrenders herself to the object, an ability she shares with the great English Romantic poet John Keats, for whom this empathic capability was the essential poetic act. This imaginative empathy is among Bishop's most astonishing poetic qualities.

The Fish

I caught a tremendous fish
and held him beside the boat
half out of water, with my hook
fast in a corner of his mouth.
He didn't fight.   5
He hadn't fought at all.
He hung a grunting weight,
battered and venerable
and homely. Here and there
his brown skin hung in strips   10
like ancient wallpaper,
and its pattern of darker brown
was like wallpaper:
shapes like full-blown roses
stained and lost through age.   15
He was speckled with barnacles,
fine rosettes of lime,
and infested
with tiny white sea-lice,
and underneath two or three   20
rags of green weed hung down.
While his gills were breathing in
the terrible oxygen

—the frightening gills,
fresh and crisp with blood,   25
that can cut so badly—
I thought of the coarse white flesh
packed in like feathers,
the big bones and the little bones,
the dramatic reds and blacks   30
of his shiny entrails,
and the pink swim-bladder
like a big peony.
I looked into his eyes
which were far larger than mine   35
but shallower, and yellowed,
the irises backed and packed
with tarnished tinfoil
seen through the lenses
of old scratched isinglass.°   *mica* 40
They shifted a little, but not
to return my stare.
—It was more like the tipping
of an object toward the light.
I admired his sullen face,   45
the mechanism of his jaw,
and then I saw
that from his lower lip
—if you could call it a lip—
grim, wet, and weaponlike,   50
hung five old pieces of fish-line,
or four and a wire leader
with the swivel still attached,
with all their five big hooks
grown firmly in his mouth.   55
A green line, frayed at the end
where he broke it, two heavier lines,
and a fine black thread
still crimped from the strain and snap
when it broke and he got away.   60
Like medals with their ribbons
frayed and wavering,
a five-haired beard of wisdom
trailing from his aching jaw.
I stared and stared   65
and victory filled up
the little rented boat,
from the pool of bilge
where oil had spread a rainbow

around the rusted engine   70
to the bailer rusted orange,
the sun-cracked thwarts,
the oarlocks on their strings,
the gunnels—until everything
was rainbow, rainbow, rainbow!   75
And I let the fish go.

[1946]

The Monument

Now can you see the monument? It is of wood
built somewhat like a box. No. Built
like several boxes in descending sizes
one above the other.
Each is turned half-way round so that   5
its corners point toward the sides
of the one below and the angles alternate.
Then on the topmost cube is set
a sort of fleur-de-lys of weathered wood,
long petals of board, pierced with odd holes,   10
four-sided, stiff, ecclesiastical.
From it four thin, warped poles spring out,
(slanted like fishing-poles or flag-poles)
and from them jig-saw work hangs down,
four lines of vaguely whittled ornament   15
over the edges of the boxes
to the ground.
The monument is one-third set against
a sea; two-thirds against a sky.
The view is geared   20
(that is, the view's perspective)
so low there is no "far away,"
and we are far away within the view.
A sea of narrow, horizontal boards
lies out behind our lonely monument,   25
its long grains alternating right and left
like floor-boards—spotted, swarming-still,
and motionless. A sky runs parallel,
and it is palings, coarser than the sea's:

splintery sunlight and long-fibred clouds.   *30*
"Why does that strange sea make no sound?
Is it because we're far away?
Where are we? Are we in Asia Minor,
or in Mongolia?"
                    An ancient promontory,   *35*
an ancient principality whose artist-prince
might have wanted to build a monument
to mark a tomb or boundary, or make
a melancholy or romantic scene of it . . .
"But that queer sea looks made of wood,   *40*
half-shining, like a driftwood sea.
And the sky looks wooden, grained with cloud.
It's like a stage-set; it is all so flat!
Those clouds are full of glistening splinters!
What is that?"   *45*
                    It is the monument.
"It's piled-up boxes,
outlined with shoddy fret-work, half-fallen off,
cracked and unpainted. It looks old."
—The strong sunlight, the wind from the sea,   *50*
all the conditions of its existence,
may have flaked off the paint, if ever it was painted,
and made it homelier than it was.
"Why did you bring me here to see it?
A temple of crates in cramped and crated scenery,   *55*
what can it prove?
I am tired of breathing this eroded air,
this dryness in which the monument is cracking."

It is an artifact
of wood. Wood holds together better   *60*
than sea or cloud or sand could by itself,
much better than real sea or sand or cloud.
It chose that way to grow and not to move.
The monument's an object, yet those decorations,
carelessly nailed, looking like nothing at all,   *65*
give it away as having life, and wishing;
wanting to be a monument, to cherish something.
The crudest scroll-work says "commemorate,"
while once each day the light goes around it
like a prowling animal,   *70*
or the rain falls on it, or the wind blows into it.
It may be solid, may be hollow.
The bones of the artist-prince may be inside
or far away on even drier soil.

But roughly but adequately it can shelter   *75*
what is within (which after all
cannot have been intended to be seen).
It is the beginning of a painting,
a piece of sculpture, or poem, or monument,
and all of wood. Watch it closely.   *80*

[1946]

The Unbeliever

He sleeps on the top of a mast.
—Bunyan

He sleeps on the top of a mast
with his eyes fast closed.
The sails fall away below him
like the sheets of his bed,
leaving out in the air of the night the sleeper's head.   *5*

Asleep he was transported there,
asleep he curled
in a gilded ball on the mast's top,
or climbed inside
a gilded bird, or blindly seated himself astride.   *10*

"I am founded on marble pillars,"
said a cloud. "I never move.
See the pillars there in the sea?"
Secure in introspection
he peers at the watery pillars of his reflection.   *15*

A gull had wings under his
and remarked that the air
was "like marble." He said: "Up here
I tower through the sky
for the marble wings on my tower-top fly."   *20*

But he sleeps on the top of his mast
with his eyes closed tight.
The gull inquired into his dream,
which was, "I must not fall.   *25*
The spangled sea below wants me to fall.
It is hard as diamonds; it wants to destroy us all."

[1946]

Seascape

This celestial seascape, with white herons got up as angels,
flying as high as they want and as far as they want sidewise
in tiers and tiers of immaculate reflections;
the whole region, from the highest heron
down to the weightless mangrove island   5
with bright green leaves edged neatly with bird-droppings
like illumination in silver,
and down to the suggestively Gothic arches of the mangrove roots
and the beautiful pea-green back-pasture
where occasionally a fish jumps, like a wild-flower   10
in an ornamental spray of spray;
this cartoon by Raphael for a tapestry for a Pope:
it does look like heaven.
But a skeletal lighthouse standing there
in black and white clerical dress,   15
who lives on his nerves, thinks he knows better.
He thinks that hell rages below his iron feet,
and that is why the shallow water is so warm,
and he knows that heaven is not like this.
Heaven is not like flying or swimming,   20
but has something to do with blackness and a strong glare
and when it gets dark he will remember something
strongly worded to say on the subject.

                                                        [1946]

The Armadillo

FOR ROBERT LOWELL

This is the time of year
when almost every night
the frail, illegal fire balloons appear.
Climbing the mountain height,

rising toward a saint   5
still honored in these parts,
the paper chambers flush and fill with light
that comes and goes, like hearts.

Once up against the sky it's hard
to tell them from the stars—   *10*
planets, that is—the tinted ones:
Venus going down, or Mars,

or the pale green one. With a wind,
they flare and falter, wobble and toss;
but if it's still they steer between   *15*
the kite sticks of the Southern Cross,

receding, dwindling, solemnly
and steadily forsaking us,
or, in the downdraft from a peak,
suddenly turning dangerous.   *20*

Last night another big one fell.
It splattered like an egg of fire
against the cliff behind the house.
The flame ran down. We saw the pair

of owls who nest there flying up   *25*
and up, their whirling black-and-white
stained bright pink underneath, until
they shrieked up out of sight.

The ancient owls' nest must have burned.
Hastily, all alone,   *30*
a glistening armadillo left the scene,
rose-flecked, head down, tail down,

and then a baby rabbit jumped out,
short-eared, to our surprise.
So soft!—a handful of intangible ash   *35*
with fixed, ignited eyes.

Too pretty, dreamlike mimicry!
O falling fire and piercing cry
and panic, and a weak mailed fist
clenched ignorant against the sky!   *40*

[1965]

Questions of Travel

There are too many waterfalls here; the crowded streams
hurry too rapidly down to the sea,
and the pressure of so many clouds on the mountaintops
makes them spill over the sides in soft slow-motion,
turning to waterfalls under our very eyes.   5
—For if those streaks, those mile-long, shiny, tearstains,
aren't waterfalls yet,
in a quick age or so, as ages go here,
they probably will be.
But if the streams and clouds keep travelling, travelling,   10
the mountains look like the hulls of capsized ships,
slime-hung and barnacled.

Think of the long trip home.
Should we have stayed at home and thought of here?   15
Where should we be today?
Is it right to be watching strangers in a play
in this strangest of theatres?
What childishness is it that while there's a breath of life
in our bodies, we are determined to rush   20
to see the sun the other way around?
The tiniest green hummingbird in the world?
To stare at some inexplicable old stonework,
inexplicable and impenetrable,   25
at any view,
instantly seen and always, always delightful?
Oh, must we dream our dreams
and have them, too?
And have we room
for one more folded sunset, still quite warm?   30

But surely it would have been a pity
not to have seen the trees along this road,
really exaggerated in their beauty,
not to have seen them gesturing
like noble pantomimists, robed in pink.   35
—Not to have had to stop for gas and heard
the sad, two-noted, wooden tune
of disparate wooden clogs
carelessly clacking over
a grease-stained filling-station floor.   40
(In another country the clogs would all be tested.
Each pair there would have identical pitch.)

—A pity not to have heard
the other, less primitive music of the fat brown bird
who sings above the broken gasoline pump   *45*
in a bamboo church of Jesuit baroque:
three towers, five silver crosses.
—Yes, a pity not to have pondered,
blurr'dly and inconclusively,
on what connection can exist for centuries   *50*
between the crudest wooden footwear
and, careful and finicky,
the whittled fantasies of wooden cages.
—Never to have studied history in
the weak calligraphy of songbirds' cages.   *55*
—And never to have had to listen to rain
so much like politicians' speeches:
two hours of unrelenting oratory
and then a sudden golden silence
in which the traveller takes a notebook, writes: *60*

"Is it lack of imagination that makes us come
to imagined places, not just stay at home?
Or could Pascal have been not entirely right
about just sitting quietly in one's room?

Continent, city, country, society: *65*
the choice is never wide and never free.
And here, or there . . . No. Should we have stayed at home,
wherever that may be?"

[1965]

Sestina

September rain falls on the house.
In the failing light, the old grandmother
sits in the kitchen with the child
beside the Little Marvel Stove,
reading the jokes from the almanac,   *5*
laughing and talking to hide her tears.

She thinks that her equinoctial tears
and the rain that beats on the roof of the house
were both foretold by the almanac,
but only known to a grandmother.   *10*
The iron kettle sings on the stove.
She cuts some bread and says to the child,

It's time for tea now; but the child
is watching the teakettle's small hard tears
dance like mad on the hot black stove,   *15*
the way the rain must dance on the house.
Tidying up, the old grandmother
hangs up the clever almanac

on its string. Birdlike, the almanac
hovers half open above the child,   *20*
hovers above the old grandmother
and her teacup full of dark brown tears.
She shivers and says she thinks the house
feels chilly, and puts more wood in the stove.

It was to be, says the Marvel Stove.   *25*
I know what I know, says the almanac.
With crayons the child draws a rigid house
and a winding pathway. Then the child
puts in a man with buttons like tears
and shows it proudly to the grandmother.   *30*

But secretly, while the grandmother
busies herself about the stove,
the little moons fall down like tears
from between the pages of the almanac
into the flower bed the child   *35*
has carefully placed in the front of the house.

Time to plant tears, says the almanac.
The grandmother sings to the marvelous stove
and the child draws another inscrutable house.

                                         [1965]

In the Waiting Room

In Worcester, Massachusetts,
I went with Aunt Consuelo
to keep her dentist's appointment
and sat and waited for her
in the dentist's waiting room.   *5*

It was winter. It got dark
early. The waiting room
was full of grown-up people,
arctics and overcoats,
lamps and magazines.   *10*
My aunt was inside
what seemed like a long time

and while I waited I read
the *National Geographic*
(I could read) and carefully   15
studied the photographs:
the inside of a volcano,
black, and full of ashes;
then it was spilling over
in rivulets of fire.   20
Osa and Martin Johnson
dressed in riding breeches,
laced boots, and pith helmets.
A dead man slung on a pole
—"Long Pig," the caption said.   25
Babies with pointed heads
wound round and round with string;
black, naked women with necks
wound round and round with wire
like the necks of light bulbs.   30
Their breasts were horrifying.
I read it right straight through.
I was too shy to stop.
And then I looked at the cover:
the yellow margins, the date.   35

Suddenly, from inside,
came an *oh!* of pain
—Aunt Consuelo's voice—
not very loud or long.
I wasn't at all surprised;   40
even then I knew she was
a foolish, timid woman.
I might have been embarrassed,
but wasn't. What took me
completely by surprise   45
was that it was *me:*
my voice, in my mouth.
Without thinking at all
I was my foolish aunt,
I—we—were falling, falling,   50
our eyes glued to the cover
of the *National Geographic,*
February, 1918.

I said to myself: three days
and you'll be seven years old.   55
I was saying it to stop

the sensation of falling off
the round, turning world
into cold, blue-black space.
But I felt: you are an *I,*   60
you are an *Elizabeth,*
you are one of *them.*
Why should you be one, too?
I scarcely dared to look
to see what it was I was.   65
I gave a sidelong glance
—I couldn't look any higher—
at shadowy gray knees,
trousers and skirts and boots
and different pairs of hands   70
lying under the lamps.
I knew that nothing stranger
had ever happened, that nothing
stranger could ever happen.
Why should I be my aunt,   75
or me, or anyone?
What similarities—
boots, hands, the family voice
I felt in my throat, or even
the *National Geographic*   80
and those awful hanging breasts—
held us all together
or made us all just one?
How—I didn't know any
word for it—how "unlikely" . . .   85
How had I come to be here,
like them, and overhear
a cry of pain that could have
got loud and worse but hadn't?

The waiting room was bright   90
and too hot. It was sliding
beneath a big black wave,
another, and another.

Then I was back in it.
The War was on. Outside,   95
in Worcester, Massachusetts,
were night and slush and cold,
and it was still the fifth
of February, 1918.

                                              [1976]

ROBERT HAYDEN

[1913–1980]

Those Winter Sundays

Sundays too my father got up early
and put his clothes on in the blueblack cold,
then with cracked hands that ached
from labor in the weekday weather made
banked fires blaze. No one ever thanked him.   5

I'd wake and hear the cold splintering, breaking.
When the rooms were warm, he'd call,
and slowly I would rise and dress,
fearing the chronic angers of that house,

Speaking indifferently to him,   10
who had driven out the cold
and polished my good shoes as well.
What did I know, what did I know
of love's austere and lonely offices?

[1962]

MURIEL RUKEYSER

[1913–1980]

Myth

Long afterward, Oedipus, old and blinded, walked the
roads.   He smelled a familiar smell.   It was
the Sphinx.   Oedipus said, "I want to ask one question.
Why didn't I recognize my mother?"   "You gave the
wrong answer," said the Sphinx.   "But that was what   5
made everything possible," said Oedipus.   "No," she said.
"When I asked, What walks on four legs in the morning,
two at noon, and three in the evening, you answered,
Man.   You didn't say anything about woman."
"When you say Man," said Oedipus, "you include women   10
too. Everyone knows that."   She said, "That's what
you think."

[1973]

RANDALL JARRELL

[1914–1965]

The Death of the Ball Turret Gunner

From my mother's sleep I fell into the State,
And I hunched in its belly till my wet fur froze.
Six miles from earth, loosed from its dream of life,
I woke to black flak and the nightmare fighters.
When I died they washed me out of the turret with a hose.   5

[1945]

HENRY REED

[b. 1914]

Chard Whitlow

(Mr. Eliot's Sunday Evening Postscript)

As we get older we do not get any younger.
Seasons return, and today I am fifty-five,
And this time last year I was fifty-four,
And this time next year I shall be sixty-two.
And I cannot say I should care (to speak for myself)   *London subway*   5
Fidgeting uneasily under a drafty stair,
Or counting sleepless nights in the crowded Tube.°

There are certain precautions—though none of them very reliable—
Against the blast from bombs, or the flying splinter,
But not against the blast from Heaven, *vento dei venti*,   10
The wind within a wind, unable to speak for wind;

THE DEATH OF THE BALL TURRET GUNNER   Jarrell's note: "A ball turret was a plexiglass sphere set into the belly of a B-17 or B-24, and inhabited by two .50 caliber machine-guns and one man, a short small man. When this gunner tracked with his machine guns a fighter attacking his bomber from below, he revolved with the turret; hunched upside-down in his little sphere, he looked like the foetus in the womb. The fighters which attacked him were armed with cannon firing explosive shells The hose was a steam hose."
CHARD WHITLOW   **Mr. Eliot's . . . Postscript**   This combines two titles of poems by T. S. Eliot: "Mr. Eliot's Sunday Morning Service" and "The Boston Evening Transcript."   [10]**vento dei venti**   wind of winds.

And the frigid burnings of purgatory will not be touched
By any emollient.
              I think you will find this put,
Far better than I could ever hope to express it,   *15*
In the words of Kharma: "It is, we believe,
Idle to hope that the simple stirrup-pump
Can extinguish hell."
              Oh, listeners,
And you especially who have switched off the wireless,°   *radio*
And sit in Stoke or Basingstoke, listening appreciatively to the silence
(Which is also the silence of hell), pray not for yourselves but for your souls.   *20*

And pray for me also under the drafty stair.
As we get older we do not get any younger.

And pray for Kharma under the holy mountain.

                              [1946]

Naming of Parts

Today we have naming of parts. Yesterday,
We had daily cleaning. And tomorrow morning,
We shall have what to do after firing. But today,
Today we have naming of parts. Japonica
Glistens like coral in all of the neighboring gardens,   *5*
     And today we have naming of parts.

This is the lower sling swivel. And this
Is the upper sling swivel, whose use you will see,
When you are given your slings. And this is the piling swivel,
Which in your case you have not got. The branches   *10*
Hold in the gardens their silent, eloquent gestures,
     Which in our case we have not got.

This is the safety-catch, which is always released
With an easy flick of the thumb. And please do not let me
See anyone using his finger. You can do it quite easy   *15*
If you have any strength in your thumb. The blossoms
Are fragile and motionless, never letting anyone see
     Any of them using their finger.

And this you can see is the bolt. The purpose of this
Is to open the breech, as you see. We can slide it   *20*
Rapidly backwards and forwards: we call this
Easing the spring. And rapidly backwards and forwards
The early bees are assaulting and fumbling the flowers:
    They call it easing the Spring.

They call it easing the Spring: it is perfectly easy   *25*
If you have any strength in your thumb: like the bolt,
And the breech, and the cocking-piece, and the point of balance,
Which in our case we have not got; and the almond-blossom
Silent in all of the gardens and the bees going backwards and forwards,
    For today we have naming of parts.   *30*

           [1946]

WILLIAM STAFFORD

[b. 1914]

Traveling through the dark

Traveling through the dark I found a deer
dead on the edge of the Wilson River road.
It is usually best to roll them into the canyon:
that road is narrow; to swerve might make more dead.

By glow of the tail-light I stumbled back of the car   *5*
and stood by the heap, a doe, a recent killing;
she had stiffened already, almost cold.
I dragged her off; she was large in the belly.

My fingers touching her side brought me the reason—
her side was warm; her fawn lay there waiting,   *10*
alive, still, never to be born.
Beside that mountain road I hesitated.

The car aimed ahead its lowered parking lights;
under the hood purred the steady engine.
I stood in the glare of the warm exhaust turning red;   *15*
around our group I could hear the wilderness listen.

I thought hard for us all—my only swerving—,
then pushed her over the edge into the river.

           [1957]

DYLAN THOMAS

[1914–1953]

It is perhaps ironic that one of the leading twentieth-century heirs to Whitman's "barbaric yawp" was not from the New World but from the ancient country of Wales. Alive to the great oral tradition of bardic poetry, Dylan Thomas shaped a "tower of words" as intense, complex, and lyrical as the writings of the English devotional poets of the seventeenth century, as linguistically adventurous as the poetry of Gerard Manley Hopkins, and as modern as anything written by the French, Spanish, or Latin American Surrealists.

Often dismissed as an obscure poet, Dylan Thomas was nevertheless able to attract readers not normally interested in poetry. While it is true that some attended his very successful readings in America hoping to see the "bad boy" of modern verse reduced to alcoholism, a surprising number stayed to hear the poetry. Complimented both as a brilliant reader and also for having one of the best voices of his time, Thomas brought intense emotion to modern poetry, a poetry many had come to perceive as flat, cheerless, and overly intellectual.

Almost all of Thomas's poems celebrate the rightness of life. Even in the face of sorrow and death as in his "Do not go gentle into that good night," there is an echo of the "force that through the green fuse drives the flower." If a good many modern poets had come to agree with Freud that the most humanity could ever hope for was to transform its neurotic misery into everyday unhappiness, then Thomas, like Whitman, belonged to that handful of poets who counterbalanced Freud's grim prediction with the possibility of joy.

Much of the difficulty many readers experience with Thomas's poetry is lessened when we consider his beginnings as a poet. He writes, "I wanted to write poetry in the beginning because I had fallen in love with words." For Thomas, poetry begins not with the ideas a poem may convey, but with word-music. He goes on to state that as a child "words" themselves "were to me, as the notes of bells, the sounds of musical instruments, the noises of the wind, sea, and rain, the rattle of milkcarts, the clopping of hooves on cobbles, the fingering of branches on a window pane, might be to someone deaf from birth, who has miraculously found his hearing." Working in the oral tradition, Thomas often gave precedence to the sound of words over their meaning. Writing about words, he states, "The first thing was to feel and know their sound and substance; what I was going to make of them, what I was going to *say* through them, would come."

That Thomas intended his poems to have meaning is certain: "There must be a progressive line, or theme, of movement in every poem," he wrote. In fact, Thomas strongly suggested that he wanted his poems to be taken "literally." William York Tindall went so far as to assert that "close reading and comparison of texts proves Thomas as rational and orderly as any poet this side of Alexander Pope." For example, if we take a problematic image in Thomas and study it, we can as often as not make sense of it when we take Thomas's advice and read him literally. In "Fern

Hill," a carefully structured poem, Thomas writes of a "lilting house." Speech may have a lilt to it (as does Welsh) but houses, though they may tilt, never lilt. The lilt conveys a happy sound to the speaker, and this parallels the child's joy on the farm. The solution to the "lilting" house comes in the fourth stanza when Thomas writes of "the whinnying green stable." Thomas focuses the adult speaker's perceptions through the narcissistic distortions of early childhood. For the very young child, for whom the world is a lovely blur of images, no distinction is made between house and voice, between stable and its sounds. As a child, the speaker lived in a universe that didn't merely honor him but was, in fact, nothing more than a glorious reflection of his own sense of wonder. When he closes his eyes, the farm vanishes, but when he opens them he awakes to the farm "like a wanderer white / With the dew, come back, the cock on his shoulder. . . ."

This is not to suggest that all of Thomas's work will become instantly accessible if we look at it long enough; no poetry can be reduced to prose. But if we can imagine the poet as a "kind of poetic roving camera," as Stephen Spender once said, working in all five senses, bringing all the techniques of poetry into play, then Thomas becomes much less opaque. Every great poet demands a new way of reading, and Thomas is no exception.

Cultural considerations may also contribute to our difficulties in understanding Thomas. John Wain has suggested that what many hostile English critics objected to in Thomas is in fact his Welshness: "the open emotionalism, the large verbal gestures which seem to them mere rant, the rapt pleasure in elaborate craftsmanship, and above all the bardic tone." In the Celtic bardic tradition (pp. 947–966) the poet is not a man talking to other men as Wordsworth had suggested, but a man endowed with a special wisdom, a powerful imaginative strength and a mystical, religious vision. The bard reaches or quests after the unreachable. "My lines, *all* my lines," Thomas wrote, "are of the tenth intensity. They are not the words that express what I want to express. They are the only words I can find that come near to expressing a half." Furthermore, with Thomas the bardic scope is turned inward. As he states, his poems are "the record of my individual struggle from darkness towards some measure of light."

Born and reared in the port city of Swansea in southern Wales, a few miles east of his uncle's farm, Fern Hill, Dylan Marlais Thomas began writing poetry while still a child. He left school at age seventeen and shortly after began working as a reporter for the *South Wales Daily Post.* Many of the poems Thomas would finish later in life were begun during the years 1930 to 1934. In 1940 Thomas began writing scenarios for war documentaries which helped prepare him for his later involvement in film making. Though only one of Thomas's full-length features, *The Doctor and the Devils,* was ever produced, his *Under Milk Wood: A Play for Voices,* which starred fellow Welshman Richard Burton, is considered a minor masterpiece—as is his popular prose memoir *A Child's Christmas in Wales.*

Very few poets have been able to occasion the intensity and range of both popular and critical interest that Thomas has. Perhaps Edith Sitwell, who helped "discover" the young poet, best expressed Thomas's hold on his readers when she wrote after his death that "His voice resembles no other voice. . . . From the depths of Being, from the roots of the world, a voice speaks."

The force that through the green fuse drives the flower

The force that through the green fuse drives the flower
Drives my green age; that blasts the roots of trees
Is my destroyer.
And I am dumb to tell the crooked rose
My youth is bent by the same wintry fever. 5

The force that drives the water through the rocks
Drives my red blood; that dries the mouthing streams
Turns mine to wax.
And I am dumb to mouth unto my veins
How at the mountain spring the same mouth sucks. 10

The hand that whirls the water in the pool
Stirs the quicksand; that ropes the blowing wind
Hauls my shroud sail.
And I am dumb to tell the hanging man
How of my clay is made the hangman's lime. 15

The lips of time leech to the fountain head;
Love drips and gathers, but the fallen blood
Shall calm her sores.
And I am dumb to tell a weather's wind
How time has ticked a heaven round the stars. 20

And I am dumb to tell the lover's tomb
How at my sheet goes the same crooked worm.

[1933]

I see the boys of summer

I

I see the boys of summer in their ruin
Lay the gold tithings barren,
Setting no store by harvest, freeze the soils;
There in their heat the winter floods
Of frozen loves they fetch their girls, 5
And drown the cargoed apples in their tides.

These boys of light are curdlers in their folly,
Sour the boiling honey;

The jacks of frost they finger in the hives;
There in the sun the frigid threads   *10*
Of doubt and dark they feed their nerves;
The signal moon is zero in their voids.

I see the summer children in their mothers
Split up the brawned womb's weathers,
Divide the night and day with fairy thumbs;   *15*
There in the deep with quartered shades
Of sun and moon they paint their dams
As sunlight paints the shelling of their heads.

I see that from these boys shall men of nothing
Stature by seedy shifting,   *20*
Or lame the air with leaping from its heats;
There from their hearts the dogdayed pulse
Of love and light bursts in their throats.
O see the pulse of summer in the ice.

II

But seasons must be challenged or they totter   *25*
Into a chiming quarter
Where, punctual as death, we ring the stars;
There, in his night, the black-tongued bells
The sleepy man of winter pulls,
Nor blows back moon-and-midnight as she blows.   *30*

We are the dark deniers, let us summon
Death from a summer woman,
A muscling life from lovers in their cramp,
From the fair dead who flush the sea
The bright-eyed worm on Davy's lamp,   *35*
And from the planted womb the man of straw.

We summer boys in this four-winded spinning,
Green of the seaweeds' iron,
Hold up the noisy sea and drop her birds,
Pick the world's ball of wave and froth   *40*
To choke the deserts with her tides,
And comb the county gardens for a wreath.

In spring we cross our foreheads with the holly,
Heigh ho the blood and berry,
And nail the merry squires to the trees;   *45*
Here love's damp muscle dries and dies,

Here break a kiss in no love's quarry.
O see the poles of promise in the boys.

III

I see you boys of summer in your ruin.
Man in his maggot's barren.   *50*
And boys are full and foreign in the pouch.
I am the man your father was.
We are the sons of flint and pitch.
O see the poles are kissing as they cross.

[1934]

And death shall have no dominion

And death shall have no dominion.
Dead men naked they shall be one
With the man in the wind and the west moon;
When their bones are picked clean and the clean bones gone,
They shall have stars at elbow and foot;   *5*
Though they go mad they shall be sane,
Though they sink through the sea they shall rise again;
Though lovers be lost love shall not;
And death shall have no dominion.

And death shall have no dominion.   *10*
Under the windings of the sea
They lying long shall not die windily;
Twisting on racks when sinews give way,
Strapped to a wheel, yet they shall not break;
Faith in their hands shall snap in two,   *15*
And the unicorn evils run them through;
Split all ends up they shan't crack;
And death shall have no dominion.

And death shall have no dominion.
No more may gulls cry at their ears   *20*
Or waves break loud on the seashores;
Where blew a flower may a flower no more
Lift its head to the blows of the rain;
Though they be mad and dead as nails,
Heads of the characters hammer through daisies;   *25*

Break in the sun till the sun breaks down,
And death shall have no dominion.

[1936]

The hunchback in the park

The hunchback in the park
A solitary mister
Propped between trees and water
From the opening of the garden lock
That lets the trees and water enter   5
Until the Sunday sombre bell at dark

Eating bread from a newspaper
Drinking water from the chained cup
That the children filled with gravel
In the fountain basin where I sailed my ship   10
Slept at night in a dog kennel
But nobody chained him up.

Like the park birds he came early
Like the water he sat down
And Mister they called Hey mister   15
The truant boys from the town
Running when he had heard them clearly
On out of sound

Past lake and rockery
Laughing when he shook his paper   20
Hunchbacked in mockery
Through the loud zoo of the willow groves
Dodging the park keeper
With his stick that picked up leaves.

And the old dog sleeper   25
Alone between nurses and swans
While the boys among willows
Made the tigers jump out of their eyes
To roar on the rockery stones
And the groves were blue with sailors   30

Made all day until bell time
A woman figure without fault
Straight as a young elm

Straight and tall from his crooked bones
That she might stand in the night   35
After the locks and chains

All night in the unmade park
After the railings and shrubberies
The birds the grass the trees the lake
And the wild boys innocent as strawberries   40
Had followed the hunchback
To his kennel in the dark.

[1942]

A Refusal to Mourn the Death, by Fire, of a Child in London

Never until the mankind making
Bird beast and flower
Fathering and all humbling darkness
Tells with silence the last light breaking
And the still hour   5
Is come of the sea tumbling in harness

And I must enter again the round
Zion of the water bead
And the synagogue of the ear of corn
Shall I let pray the shadow of a sound   10
Or sow my salt seed
In the least valley of sackcloth to mourn

The majesty and burning of the child's death.
I shall not murder
The mankind of her going with a grave truth   15
Nor blaspheme down the stations of the breath
With any further
Elegy of innocence and youth.

Deep with the first dead lies London's daughter,
Robed in the long friends,   20
The grains beyond age, the dark veins of her mother,
Secret by the unmourning water
Of the riding Thames.
After the first death, there is no other.

[1946]

Poem in October

It was my thirtieth year to heaven
Woke to my hearing from harbour and neighbour wood
   And the mussel pooled and the heron
        Priested shore
      The morning beckon   *5*
With water praying and call of seagull and rook
And the knock of sailing boats on the net webbed wall
      Myself to set foot
        That second
In the still sleeping town and set forth.   *10*

    My birthday began with the water-
Birds and the birds of the winged trees flying my name
   Above the farms and the white horses
       And I rose
      In rainy autumn   *15*
And walked abroad in a shower of all my days.
High tide and the heron dived when I took the road
      Over the border
        And the gates
Of the town closed as the town awoke.   *20*

    A springful of larks in a rolling
Cloud and the roadside bushes brimming with whistling
   Blackbirds and the sun of October
        Summery
      On the hill's shoulder,   *25*
Here were fond climates and sweet singers suddenly
Come in the morning where I wandered and listened
      To the rain wringing
        Wind blow cold
In the wood faraway under me.   *30*

    Pale rain over the dwindling harbour
And over the sea wet church the size of a snail
   With its horns through mist and the castle
        Brown as owls
      But all the gardens   *35*
Of spring and summer were blooming in the tall tales
Beyond the border and under the lark full cloud.
      There could I marvel

My birthday
Away but the weather turned around.   *40*

It turned away from the blithe country
And down the other air and the blue altered sky
    Streamed again a wonder of summer
        With apples
      Pears and red currants   *45*
And I saw in the turning so clearly a child's
Forgotten mornings when he walked with his mother
      Through the parables
        Of sun light
    And the legends of the green chapels   *50*

    And the twice told fields of infancy
That his tears burned my cheeks and his heart moved in mine.
    These were the woods the river and sea
        Where a boy
      In the listening   *55*
Summertime of the dead whispered the truth of his joy
To the trees and the stones and the fish in the tide.
      And the mystery
        Sang alive
Still in the water and singingbirds.   *60*

    And there could I marvel my birthday
Away but the weather turned around. And the true
    Joy of the long dead child sang burning
        In the sun.
    It was my thirtieth   *65*
Year to heaven stood there then in the summer noon
Though the town below lay leaved with October blood.
      O may my heart's truth
        Still be sung
On this high hill in a year's turning.   *70*

[1946]

Fern Hill

Now as I was young and easy under the apple boughs
About the lilting house and happy as the grass was green,
    The night above the dingle starry,
      Time let me hail and climb

Golden in the heydays of his eyes,   *5*
And honored among wagons I was prince of the apple towns
And once below a time I lordly had the trees and leaves
        Trail with daisies and barley
     Down the rivers of the windfall light.

And as I was green and carefree, famous among the barns   *10*
About the happy yard and singing as the farm was home,
        In the sun that is young once only,
           Time let me play and be
        Golden in the mercy of his means,
And green and golden I was huntsman and herdsman, the calves   *15*
Sang to my horn, the foxes on the hills barked clear and cold,
          And the sabbath rang slowly
        In the pebbles of the holy streams.

All the sun long it was running, it was lovely, the hay
Fields high as the house, the tunes from the chimneys, it was air   *20*
        And playing, lovely and watery
          And fire green as grass.
        And nightly under the simple stars
As I rode to sleep the owls were bearing the farm away,
All the moon long I heard, blessed among stables, the night-jars   *25*
        Flying with the ricks, and the horses
          Flashing into the dark.

And then to awake, and the farm, like a wanderer white
With the dew, come back, the cock on his shoulder: it was all
        Shining, it was Adam and maiden,   *30*
          The sky gathered again
        And the sun grew round that very day.
So it must have been after the birth of the simple light
In the first, spinning place, the spellbound horses walking warm
        Out of the whinnying green stable   *35*
          On to the fields of praise.

And honored among foxes and pheasants by the gay house
Under the new made clouds and happy as the heart was long,
        In the sun born over and over,
          I ran my heedless ways,
          My wishes raced through the house high hay   *40*

And nothing I cared, at my sky blue trades, that time allows
In all his tuneful turning so few and such morning songs
    Before the children green and golden
        Follow him out of grace,   *45*

Nothing I cared, in the lamb white days, that time would take me
Up to the swallow thronged loft by the shadow of my hand,
    In the moon that is always rising,
        Nor that riding to sleep
    I should hear him fly with the high fields   *50*
And wake to the farm forever fled from the childless land.
Oh as I was young and easy in the mercy of his means,
        Time held me green and dying
    Though I sang in my chains like the sea.

                         [1946]

In my craft or sullen art

In my craft or sullen art
Exercised in the still night
When only the moon rages
And the lovers lie abed
With all their griefs in their arms,   *5*
I labour by singing light
Not for ambition or bread
Or the strut and trade of charms
On the ivory stages
But for the common wages   *10*
Of their most secret heart.

Not for the proud man apart
From the raging moon I write
On these spindrift pages
Nor for the towering dead   *15*
With their nightingales and psalms
But for the lovers, their arms
Round the griefs of the ages,
Who pay no praise or wages
Nor heed my craft or art.   *20*

                         [1946]

Do not go gentle into that good night

Do not go gentle into that good night,
Old age should burn and rave at close of day;
Rage, rage against the dying of the light.

Though wise men at their end know dark is right,
Because their words had forked no lightning they　　　5
Do not go gentle into that good night.

Good men, the last wave by, crying how bright
Their frail deeds might have danced in a green bay,
Rage, rage against the dying of the light.

Wild men who caught and sang the sun in flight,　　　10
And learn, too late, they grieved it on its way,
Do not go gentle into that good night.

Grave men, near death, who see with blinding sight
Blind eyes could blaze like meteors and be gay,
Rage, rage against the dying of the light.　　　15

And you, my father, there on the sad height,
Curse, bless, me now with your fierce tears, I pray.
Do not go gentle into that good night.
Rage, rage against the dying of the light.

[1952]

JUDITH WRIGHT

[b. 1915]

Eve to Her Daughters

It was not I who began it.
Turned out into draughty caves,
hungry so often, having to work for our bread,
hearing the children whining,
I was nevertheless not unhappy.　　　5
Where Adam went I was fairly contented to go.
I adapted myself to the punishment: it was my life.

But Adam, you know . . . !
He kept on brooding over the insult,
over the trick They had played on us, over the scolding.   *10*
He had discovered a flaw in himself
and he had to make up for it.

Outside Eden the earth was imperfect,
the seasons changed, the game was fleet-footed,
he had to work for our living, and he didn't like it.   *15*
He even complained of my cooking
(it was hard to compete with Heaven).

So he set to work.
The earth must be made a new Eden
with central heating, domesticated animals,   *20*
mechanical harvesters, combustion engines,
escalators, refrigerators,
and modern means of communication
and multiplied opportunities for safe investment
and higher education for Abel and Cain   *25*
and the rest of the family.
You can see how his pride had been hurt.

In the process he had to unravel everything,
because he believed that mechanism
was the whole secret—he was always mechanical-minded.   *30*
He got to the very inside of the whole machine
exclaiming as he went, So this is how it works!
And now that I know how it works, why, I must have invented it.
As for God and the Other, they cannot be demonstrated,
and what cannot be demonstrated   *35*
doesn't exist.
You see, he had always been jealous.

Yes, he got to the centre
where nothing at all can be demonstrated.
And clearly he doesn't exist; but he refuses   *40*
to accept the conclusion.
You see, he was always an egotist.

It was warmer than this in the cave;
there was none of this fall-out.
I would suggest, for the sake of the children,   *45*
that it's time you took over.
But you are my daughters, you inherit my own faults of character;

you are submissive, following Adam
even beyond existence.
Faults of character have their own logic   *50*
and it always works out.
I observed this with Abel and Cain.

Perhaps the whole elaborate fable
right from the beginning
is meant to demonstrate this; perhaps it's the whole secret.   *55*
Perhaps nothing exists but our faults?
At least they can be demonstrated.

But it's useless to make
such a suggestion to Adam.
He has turned himself into God,   *60*
who is faultless, and doesn't exist.

                                                              [1966]

ROBERT LOWELL

[1917–1977]

Skunk Hour

(FOR ELIZABETH BISHOP)

Nautilus Island's hermit
heiress still lives through winter in her Spartan cottage;
her sheep still graze above the sea.
Her son's a bishop. Her farmer
is first selectman in our village;   *5*
she's in her dotage.

Thirsting for
the hierarchic privacy
of Queen Victoria's century,
she buys up all   *10*
the eyesores facing her shore,
and lets them fall.

SKUNK HOUR   **⁵selectman**   senior town official.

The season's ill—
we've lost our summer millionaire,
who seemed to leap from an L. L. Bean   *15*
catalogue. His nine-knot yawl
was auctioned off to lobstermen.
A red fox stain covers Blue Hill.

And now our fairy
decorator brightens his shop for fall;   *20*
his fishnet's filled with orange cork,
orange, his cobbler's bench and awl;
there is no money in his work,
he'd rather marry.

One dark night,   *25*
my Tudor Ford climbed the hill's skull;
I watched for love-cars. Lights turned down,
they lay together, hull to hull,
where the graveyard shelves on the town. . . .
My mind's not right.   *30*

A car radio bleats,
"Love, O careless Love. . . ." I hear
my ill-spirit sob in each blood cell,
as if my hand were at its throat. . . .
I myself am hell;   *35*
nobody's here—

only skunks, that search
in the moonlight for a bite to eat.
They march on their soles up Main Street:
white stripes, moonstruck eyes' red fire   *40*
under the chalk-dry and spar spire
of the Trinitarian Church.

I stand on top
of our back steps and breathe the rich air—
a mother skunk with her column of kittens swills the garbage pail.   *45*
She jabs her wedge-head in a cup
of sour cream, drops her ostrich tail,
and will not scare.

[1957]

[15]**L. L. Bean** mail-order store in Maine specializing in camping and sports clothing and equipment. [18]**A . . . Hill** Lowell meant to suggest, he wrote, "the rusty, reddish color of autumn on Blue Hill, a Maine mountain." [35]**I . . . hell** cf. Milton, *Paradise Lost, IV, 75.*

For the Union Dead

"Relinquunt Omnia Servare Rem Publicam."

The old South Boston Aquarium stands
in a Sahara of snow now. Its broken windows are boarded.
The bronze weathervane cod has lost half its scales.
The airy tanks are dry.

Once my nose crawled like a snail on the glass;   5
my hand tingled
to burst the bubbles
drifting from the noses of the cowed, compliant fish.

My hand draws back. I often sigh still
for the dark downward and vegetating kingdom   10
of the fish and reptile. One morning last March,
I pressed against the new barbed and galvanized

fence on the Boston Common. Behind their cage,
yellow dinosaur steamshovels were grunting
as they cropped up tons of mush and grass   15
to gouge their underworld garage.

Parking spaces luxuriate like civic
sandpiles in the heart of Boston.
A girdle of orange, Puritan-pumpkin colored girders
braces the tingling Statehouse,   20

shaking over the excavations, as it faces Colonel Shaw
and his bell-cheeked Negro infantry
on St. Gaudens' shaking Civil War relief,
propped by a plank splint against the garage's earthquake.

Two months after marching through Boston,   25
half the regiment was dead;
at the dedication,
William James could almost hear the bronze Negroes breathe.

FOR THE UNION DEAD   This poem, which was originally entitled "Colonel Shaw and the Massachusetts 54," refers to a bronze relief by Augustus Saint-Gaudens (1848–1907), that depicts the commander of the first black regiment, Robert Gould Shaw (1837–1863), killed in a Civil War battle. The monument stands on Boston Common, opposite the Massachusetts State House. The epigraph is a Latin inscription on the monument, which translates "He leaves all behind to serve the Republic." [28]**William James** American philosopher and psychologist (1842–1910) who taught at Harvard

Their monument sticks like a fishbone
in the city's throat.   30
Its Colonel is as lean
as a compass-needle.

He has an angry wrenlike vigilance,
a greyhound's gentle tautness;
he seems to wince at pleasure,   35
and suffocate for privacy.

He is out of bounds now. He rejoices in man's lovely,
peculiar power to choose life and die—
when he leads his black soldiers to death,
he cannot bend his back.   40

On a thousand small town New England greens,
the old white churches hold their air
of sparse, sincere rebellion; frayed flags
quilt the graveyards of the Grand Army of the Republic.

The stone statues of the abstract Union Soldier   45
grow slimmer and younger each year—
wasp-waisted, they doze over muskets
and muse through their sideburns . . .

Shaw's father wanted no monument
except the ditch,   50
where his son's body was thrown
and lost with his "niggers."

The ditch is nearer.
There are no statues for the last war here;
on Boylston Street, a commercial photograph   55
shows Hiroshima boiling

over a Mosler Safe, the "Rock of Ages"
that survived the blast. Space is nearer.
When I crouch to my television set,
the drained faces of Negro school-children rise like balloons. 60

Colonel Shaw
is riding on his bubble,

⁵⁵**Boylston Street** a street in Boston

he waits
for the blessed break.

The Aquarium is gone. Everywhere,   65
giant finned cars nose forward like fish;
a savage servility
slides by on grease.

                                                                    [1964]

GWENDOLYN BROOKS

[b. 1917]

The Mother

Abortions will not let you forget.
You remember the children you got that you did not get,
The damp small pulps with a little or with no hair,
The singers and workers that never handled the air.
You will never neglect or beat   5
Them, or silence or buy with a sweet.
You will never wind up the sucking-thumb
Or scuttle off ghosts that come.
You will never leave them, controlling your luscious sigh,
Return for a snack of them, with gobbling mother-eye.   10

I have heard in the voices of the wind the voices of my dim killed children.
I have contracted. I have eased
My dim dears at the breasts they could never suck.
I have said, Sweets, if I sinned, if I seized
Your luck   15
And your lives from your unfinished reach,
If I stole your births and your names,
Your straight baby tears and your games,
Your stilted or lovely loves, your tumults, your marriages, aches, and your deaths,
If I poisoned the beginnings of your breaths,
Believe that even in my deliberateness I was not deliberate.   20
Though why should I whine,
Whine that the crime was other than mine?—
Since anyhow you are dead.
Or rather, or instead,
You were never made.   25

But that too, I am afraid,
Is faulty: oh, what shall I say, how is the truth to be said?
You were born, you had body, you died.
It is just that you never giggled or planned or cried.

Believe me, I loved you all.   *30*
Believe me, I knew you, though faintly, and I loved, I loved you
All.

[1945]

ROBERT DUNCAN

[1919–1988]

The Dance

from its dancers circulates among the other
                dancers. This
would-have-been feverish cool excess of
                movement makes
each man hit the pitch co-   *5*
                ordinate.

Lovely their feet pound the green solid meadow.
                The dancers
mimic flowers—root stem stamen and petal
                our words are,   *10*
our articulations,   our
                measures.

It is the joy that exceeds pleasure.

        You have passed the count, she said

or I understood from her eyes. Now   *15*
old Friedl has grown so lovely in my years,

        I remember only the truth.
        I swear by my yearning.

        You have conquerd the yearning, she said
        The numbers have enterd your feet   *20*

        turn   turn   turn

When you're real gone, boy, sweet boy . . .

Where have I gone, Beloved?

Into the Waltz, Dancer.

Lovely our circulations sweeten the meadow.   25
In Ruben's riotous scene the May dancers teach us our learning seeks abandon!
Maximus calld us to dance the Man.
We calld *him*   to call
        season   out of season-

d mind!   30
                    Lovely
join we to dance green to the meadow.

Whitman was right.   Our names are left
        like leaves of grass,
likeness and liking,   the human greenness   35

tough as grass that survives cruelest seasons.
            I see now a radiance.
            The dancers are gone.
            They lie in heaps, exhausted,
            dead tired we say.   40
            They'll sleep until noon.

            But I returned early
            for the silence,
            for the lovely pang that is
            a flower,   45
            returnd to the silent dance-ground.

(That was my job that summer. I'd dance until three, then up to get the hall swept before
nine—beer bottles, cigarette butts, paper mementos of the night before. Writing it down now,
it is the aftermath, the silence, I remember, part of the dance too, an articulation of the time
of dancing . . . like the almost dead sleeping is a step. I've got it in a poem, about Friedl,
moaning in the depths of. But that was another room that summer. Part of my description.
What I see is a meadow . . .

    I'll slip away before they're up . . .

        and see the dew shining.

                                                                        [1960]

LAWRENCE FERLINGHETTI

[b. 1919]

Constantly risking absurdity

Constantly risking absurdity
              and death
     whenever he performs
              above the heads
                    of his audience   5
the poet like an acrobat
           climbs on rime
              to a high wire of his own making
and balancing on eyebeams
           above a sea of faces   10
       paces his way
           to the other side of day
performing entrechats
         and slight-of-foot tricks
and other high theatrics   15
         and all without mistaking
     any thing
           for what it may not be
   For he's the super realist
           who must perforce perceive   20
     taut truth
       before the taking of each stance or step
in his supposed advance
        toward that still higher perch
where Beauty stands and waits   25
       with gravity
         to start her death-defying leap
     And he
   a little charleychaplin man
        who may or may not catch   30
   her fair eternal form
        spreadeagled in the empty air
   of existence

                           [1958]

MAY SWENSON

[b. 1919]

Women

Women   Or they
  should be   should be
  pedestals   little horses
  moving   those wooden
  pedestals   sweet   5
  moving   oldfashioned
  to the   painted
  motions   rocking
  of men   horses

        the gladdest things in the toyroom.   10

    the   feelingly
    pegs   and then
    of their   unfeelingly
    ears   To be
    so familiar   joyfully   15
    and dear   ridden
    to the trusting rockingly
  fists   ridden until
To be chafed   the restored

egos dismount and the legs stride away   20

Immobile   willing
  sweetlipped   to be set
  sturdy   into motion
  and smiling   Women
  women   should be   25
  should always   pedestals
  be waiting   to men

                                                    [1970]

The Centaur

The summer that I was ten—
Can it be there was only one
summer that I was ten? It must

have been a long one then—
each day I'd go out to choose   *5*
a fresh horse from my stable

which was a willow grove
down by the old canal.
I'd go on my two bare feet.

But when, with my brother's jack-knife,   *10*
I had cut me a long limber horse
with a good thick knob for a head,

and peeled him slick and clean
except a few leaves for the tail,
and cinched my brother's belt   *15*

around his head for a rein,
I'd straddle and canter him fast
up the grass bank to the path,

trot along in the lovely dust
that talcumed over his hoofs,   *20*
hiding my toes, and turning

his feet to swift half-moons.
The willow knob with the strap
jouncing between my thighs

was the pommel and yet the poll   *25*
of my nickering pony's head.
My head and my neck were mine,

yet they were shaped like a horse.
My hair flopped to the side
like the mane of a horse in the wind.   *30*

My forelock swung in my eyes,
my neck arched and I snorted.
I shied and skittered and reared,

stopped and raised my knees,
pawed at the ground and quivered.   *35*
My teeth bared as we wheeled

and swished through the dust again.
I was the horse and the rider,
and the leather I slapped to his rump

spanked my own behind.   40
Doubled, my two hoofs beat
a gallop along the bank,

the wind twanged in my mane,
my mouth squared to the bit.
And yet I sat on my steed   45

quiet, negligent riding,
my toes standing the stirrups,
my thighs hugging his ribs.

At a walk we drew up to the porch.
I tethered him to a paling.   50
Dismounting, I smoothed my skirt

and entered the dusky hall.
My feet on the clean linoleum
left ghostly toes in the hall.

Where have you been? said my mother.   55
Been riding. I said from the sink,
and filled me a glass of water.

What's that in your pocket? she said.
Just my knife. It weighted my pocket
and stretched my dress awry.   60

Go tie back your hair, said my mother,
and *Why is your mouth all green?*
*Rob Roy, he pulled some clover
as we crossed the field,* I told her.

[1970]

CHARLES BUKOWSKI

[b. 1920]

My Father

he carried a piece of
carbon, a blade and a whip
and at night he

feared his head
and covered it with blankets   5
until one morning in Los Angeles
it snowed
and I saw the snow
and I knew that my father
could control nothing,   10
and when
I got somewhat larger
and took my first boxcar
out, I sat there in
the lime   15
the burning lime
of having nothing
moving into the desert
for the first time
I sang.   20

[1963]

AMY CLAMPITT

[b. 1920]

Beach Glass

While you walk the water's edge,
turning over concepts
I can't envision, the honking buoy
serves notice that at any time
the wind may change,   5
the reef-bell clatters
its treble monotone, deaf as Cassandra
to any note but warning. The ocean,
cumbered by no business more urgent
than keeping open old accounts   10
that never balanced,
goes on shuffling its millenniums
of quartz, granite, and basalt.
                                        It behaves
toward the permutations of novelty—   15
driftwood and shipwreck, last night's
beer cans, spilt oil, the coughed-up
residue of plastic—with random

impartiality, playing catch or tag
or touch-last like a terrier,   20
turning the same thing over and over,
over and over. For the ocean, nothing
is beneath consideration.
　　　　　The houses
of so many mussels and periwinkles   25
have been abandoned here, it's hopeless
to know which to salvage. Instead
I keep a lookout for beach glass—
amber of Budweiser, chrysoprase
of Almadén and Gallo, lapis   30
by way of (no getting around it,
I'm afraid) Phillips'
Milk of Magnesia, with now and then a rare
translucent turquoise or blurred amethyst
of no known origin.   35
　　　　　The process
goes on forever: they came from sand,
they go back to gravel,
along with the treasuries
of Murano, the buttressed   40
astonishments of Chartres,
which even now are readying
for being turned over and over as gravely
and gradually as an intellect
engaged in the hazardous   45
redefinition of structures
no one has yet looked at.

[1991]

HOWARD NEMEROV

[1920–1991]

The War in the Air

For a saving grace, we didn't see our dead,
Who rarely bothered coming home to die
But simply stayed away out there
In the clean war, the war in the air.

BEACH GLASS   ²⁹⁻³⁰Budweiser . . . Almadén . . . Gallo   beer and wine bottles of colored glass.
³²⁻³³Phillips' Milk of Magnesia   a liquid laxative that was sold in a blue glass bottle.   ⁴⁰Murano   an island
off Venice famous for its glass products.   ⁴¹Chartres   cathedral famous for its stained glass windows.

Seldom the ghosts came back bearing their tales   5
Of hitting the earth, the incompressible sea,
But stayed up there in the relative wind,
Shades fading in the mind,

Who had no graves but only epitaphs
Where never so many spoke for never so few: 10
Per ardua, said the partisans of Mars,
Per aspera, to the stars.

That was the good war, the war we won
As if there were no death, for goodness' sake,
With the help of the losers we left out there   15
In the air, in the empty air.

[1977]

RICHARD WILBUR

[b. 1921]

Mind

Mind in its purest play is like some bat
That beats about in caverns all alone,
Contriving by a kind of senseless wit
Not to conclude against a wall of stone.

It has no need to falter or explore;   5
Darkly it knows what obstacles are there,
And so may weave and flitter, dip and soar
In perfect courses through the blackest air.

And has this simile a like perfection?
The mind is like a bat. Precisely. Save   10
That in the very happiest intellection
A graceful error may correct the cave.

[1956]

MARIE PONSOT
[b. 1922]

Summer Sestina

FOR ROSEMARY

Her daylilies are afloat on evening
As their petals, lemon- or melon-colored,
Dim and lift in the loosening grip of light
Until their leaves lie like their shadows, there
Where she had hid dry corms of them, in earth   5
She freed of stones, weeded, and has kept rich.

With dusk, the dense air rises unmixed, rich,
Around our bodies dim with evening;
Creek air pours up the cliff to her tilled earth
And we swim in cool, our thoughts so colored   10
They can haunt each other, speechless, there
Where bubbles of birdsong burst like mental light,

Among the isles of lilies soaked with light.
We wait for moonrise that may make us rich
With the outsight of insight, spilling there   15
On her meadow when the moon ends evening
And brings back known shapes, strangely uncolored,
To this earthly garden, this gardened earth.

Deep deep go these dug fertile beds of earth
Where mystery prepares the thrust for light.   20
Years of leaffall, raked wet and discolored
With winter kitchen scraps, make the mix rich;
The odds against such loam are evening,
Worked on by her intentions buried there.

Why she does it is neither here nor there—   25
Why would anyone choose to nurture earth,
Kneel to its dayneeds, dream it at evening,
Plan and plant according to soil and light,

Apple, basil, snowpea, each season rich—
What counts isn't that her world is colored   30

Or that by it our vision is colored,
But that the gardener who gardens there
Has been so gardened by her garden: grown rich,
Grown fruitful, grown to stand upon the earth
In answer to the ordering of light   35
She lends to us this August evening.

By her teaching there we are changed, colored,
Made ready for evening, reconciled to earth,
Gardened to richness by her spendthrift light.

[1981]

PHILIP LARKIN

[1922–1985]

Church Going

Once I am sure there's nothing going on
I step inside, letting the door thud shut.
Another church: matting, seats, and stone,
And little books; sprawlings of flowers, cut
For Sunday, brownish now; some brass and stuff   5
Up at the holy end; the small neat organ;
And a tense, musty, unignorable silence,
Brewed God knows how long. Hatless, I take off
My cycle-clips in awkward reverence,

Move forward, run my hand around the font.   10
From where I stand, the roof looks almost new—
Cleaned, or restored? Someone would know: I don't.
Mounting the lectern, I peruse a few
Hectoring large-scale verses, and pronounce
"Here endeth" much more loudly than I'd meant.   15
The echoes snigger briefly. Back at the door
I sign the book, donate an Irish sixpence.
Reflect the place was not worth stopping for.

Yet stop I did: in fact I often do,
And always end much at a loss like this,   *20*
Wondering what to look for; wondering, too,
When churches fall completely out of use
What we shall turn them into, if we shall keep
A few cathedrals chronically on show,
Their parchment, plate and pyx in locked cases,   *25*
And let the rest rent-free to rain and sheep.
Shall we avoid them as unlucky places?

Or, after dark, will dubious women come
To make their children touch a particular stone;
Pick simples° for a cancer; or on some   *medicinal herbs* *30*
Advised night see walking a dead one?
Power of some sort or other will go on
In games, in riddles, seemingly at random;
But superstition, like belief, must die,
And what remains when disbelief has gone?   *35*
Grass, weedy pavement, brambles, buttress, sky,

A shape less recognisable each week,
A purpose more obscure. I wonder who
Will be the last, the very last, to seek
This place for what it was, one of the crew   *40*
That tap and jot and know what rood-lofts were?
Some ruin-bibber, randy for antique,
Or Christmas-addict, counting on a whiff
Of gown-and-bands and organ-pipes and myrrh?
Or will he be my representative,   *45*

Bored, uninformed, knowing the ghostly silt
Dispersed, yet tending to this cross of ground
Through suburb scrub because it held unsplit
So long and equably what since is found
Only in separation—marriage, and birth,   *50*
And death, and thoughts of these—for whom was built
This special shell? For, though I've no idea
What this accoutred frowsty barn is worth,
It pleases me to stand in silence here;

A serious house on serious earth it is,   *55*
In whose blent air all our compulsions meet,
Are recognised, and robed as destinies.
And that much never can be obsolete,
Since someone will forever be surprising

A hunger in himself to be more serious,   *60*
And gravitating with it to this ground,
Which, he once heard, was proper to grow wise in,
If only that so many dead lie round.

                                                                    [1955]

A Study of Reading Habits

When getting my nose in a book
Cured most things short of school,
It was worth ruining my eyes
To know I could still keep cool,
And deal out the old right hook   *5*
To dirty dogs twice my size.

Later, with inch-thick specs,
Evil was just my lark:
Me and my cloak and fangs
Had ripping times in the dark.   *10*
The women I clubbed with sex!
I broke them up like meringues.

Don't read much now: the dude
Who lets the girl down before
The hero arrives, the chap   *15*
Who's yellow and keeps the store,
Seem far too familiar. Get stewed:
Books are a load of crap.

                                                                    [1964]

JAMES DICKEY

[b. 1923]

Buckdancer's Choice

So I would hear out those lungs,
The air split into nine levels,
Some gift of tongues of the whistler

BUCKDANCER'S CHOICE   A buckdancer is a traditional tap dancer.

In the invalid's bed: my mother,
Warbling all day to herself   5
The thousand variations of one song;

It is called Buckdancer's Choice.
For years, they have all been dying
Out, the classic buck-and-wing men

Of traveling minstrel shows;   10
With them also an old woman
Was dying of breathless angina,

Yet still found breath enough
To whistle up in my head
A sight like a one-man band,   15

Freed black, with cymbals at heel,
An ex-slave who thrivingly danced
To the ring of his own clashing light

Through the thousand variations of one song
All day to my mother's prone music,   20
The invalid's warbler's note,

While I crept close to the wall
Sock-footed, to hear the sounds alter,
Her tongue like a mockingbird's break

Through stratum after stratum of a tone   25
Proclaiming what choices there are
For the last dancers of their kind,

For ill women and for all slaves
Of death, and children enchanted at walls
With a brass-beating glow underfoot,   30

Not dancing but nearly risen
Through barnlike, theatrelike houses
On the wings of the buck and wing.

                                                      [1965]

The Heaven of Animals

Here they are. The soft eyes open.
If they have lived in a wood

It is a wood.
If they have lived on plains
It is grass rolling   5
Under their feet forever.

Having no souls, they have come,
Anyway, beyond their knowing.
Their instincts wholly bloom
And they rise.   10
The soft eyes open.

To match them, the landscape flowers,
Outdoing, desperately
Outdoing what is required:
The richest wood,   15
The deepest field.

For some of these,
It could not be the place
It is, without blood.
These hunt, as they have done,   20
But with claws and teeth grown perfect,

More deadly than they can believe.
They stalk more silently,
And crouch on the limbs of trees,
And their descent   25
Upon the bright backs of their prey

May take years
In a sovereign floating of joy.
And those that are hunted
Know this as their life,   30
Their reward: to walk

Under such trees in full knowledge
Of what is in glory above them,
And to feel no fear,
But acceptance, compliance.   35
Fulfilling themselves without pain

At the cycle's center,
They tremble, they walk

Under the tree,
They fall, they are torn,   *40*
They rise, they walk again.

[1967]

ALAN DUGAN

[b. 1923]

Love Song: I and Thou

Nothing is plumb, level or square:
    the studs are bowed, the joists
are shaky by nature, no piece fits
    any other piece without a gap
or pinch, and bent nails   *5*
    dance all over the surfacing
like maggots. By Christ
    I am no carpenter, I built
the roof for myself, the walls
    for myself, the floors   *10*
for myself, and got
    hung up in it myself. I
danced with a purple thumb
    at this house-warming, drunk
with my prime whiskey: rage.   *15*
    Oh I spat rage's nails
into the frame-up of my work:
    it held. It settled plumb,
level, solid, square and true
    for that great moment. Then   *20*
it screamed and went on through,
    skewing as wrong the other way.
God damned it. This is hell,
    but I planned it, I sawed it,
I nailed it, and I   *25*
    will live in it until it kills me.
I can nail my left palm
    to the left-hand cross-piece but

I can't do everything myself.
   I need a hand to nail the right,   *30*
a help, a love, a you, a wife.

                             [1961]

ANTHONY HECHT

[b. 1923]

The Dover Bitch: A Criticism of Life

FOR ANDREWS WANNING

So there stood Matthew Arnold and this girl
With the cliffs of England crumbling away behind them,
And he said to her, "Try to be true to me,
And I'll do the same for you, for things are bad
All over, etc., etc."   *5*
Well now, I knew this girl. It's true she had read
Sophocles in a fairly good translation
And caught that bitter allusion to the sea,
But all the time he was talking she had in mind
The notion of what his whiskers would feel like   *10*
On the back of her neck. She told me later on
That after a while she got to looking out
At the lights across the channel, and really felt sad,
Thinking of all the wine and enormous beds
And blandishments in French and the perfumes.   *15*
And then she got really angry. To have been brought
All the way down from London, and then be addressed
As a sort of mournful cosmic last resort
Is really tough on a girl, and she was pretty.
Anyway, she watched him pace the room   *20*
And finger his watch-chain and seem to sweat a bit,
And then she said one or two unprintable things.
But you mustn't judge her by that. What I mean to say is,
She's really all right. I still see her once in a while
And she always treats me right. We have a drink   *25*
And I give her a good time, and perhaps it's a year

THE DOVER BITCH   Cf. Matthew Arnold's "Dover Beach," pp. 458–459.

Before I see her again, but there she is,
Running to fat, but dependable as they come.
And sometimes I bring her a bottle of *Nuit d'Amour*.

[1967]

"More Light! More Light!"

FOR HEINRICH BLÜCHER AND HANNAH ARENDT

Composed in the Tower before his execution
These moving verses, and being brought at that time
Painfully to the stake, submitted, declaring thus:
"I implore my God to witness that I have made no crime."

Nor was he forsaken of courage, but the death was horrible,   5
The sack of gunpowder failing to ignite.
His legs were blistered sticks on which the black sap
Bubbled and burst as he howled for the Kindly Light.

And that was but one, and by no means one of the worst;
Permitted at least his pitiful dignity;   10
And such as were by made prayers in the name of Christ,
That shall judge all men, for his soul's tranquillity.

We move now to outside a German wood.
Three men are there commanded to dig a hole
In which the two Jews are ordered to lie down   15
And be buried alive by the third, who is a Pole.

Not light from the shrine at Weimar beyond the hill
Nor light from heaven appeared. But he did refuse.
A Lüger settled back deeply in its glove.
He was ordered to change places with the Jews.   20

Much casual death had drained away their souls.
The thick dirt mounted toward the quivering chin.

"MORE LIGHT! MORE LIGHT!"   reputed to have been the last words spoken by the German poet Goethe
as he lay dying.   **¹Tower**   the Tower of London, where political prisoners of importance were confined before
being executed.   **¹⁻⁸**Hecht has noted that the first two stanzas provide a conflation of stories of martyrdom.
¹³German wood   Buchenwald, where there was a German concentration camp.   **¹⁷Weimar**   German city,
home of Goethe.   **¹⁹Lüger**   a German automatic pistol.

When only the head was exposed the order came
To dig him out again and to get back in.

No light, no light in the blue Polish eye. *25*
When he finished a riding boot packed down the earth.
The Lüger hovered lightly in its glove.
He was shot in the belly and in three hours bled to death.

No prayers or incense rose up in those hours
Which grew to be years, and every day came mute *30*
Ghosts from the ovens, sifting through crisp air,
And settled upon his eyes in a black soot.

[1968]

DENISE LEVERTOV

[b. 1923]

O Taste and See

The world is
not with us enough.
O taste and see

the subway Bible poster said,
meaning *The Lord,* meaning *5*
if anything all that lives
to the imagination's tongue,

grief, mercy, language,
tangerine, weather, to
breathe them, bite, *10*
savor, chew, swallow, transform

into our flesh our
deaths, crossing the street, plum, quince,
living in the orchard and being

hungry, and plucking *15*
the fruit.

[1964]

LOUIS SIMPSON

[b. 1923]

American Poetry

Whatever it is, it must have
A stomach that can digest
Rubber, coal, uranium, moons, poems.

Like the shark, it contains a shoe.
It must swim for miles through the desert   5
Uttering cries that are almost human.

[1964]

My father in the night commanding No

My father in the night commanding No
Has work to do. Smoke issues from his lips;
    He reads in silence.
The frogs are croaking and the streetlamps glow.

And then my mother winds the gramophone;   5
The Bride of Lammermoor begins to shriek—
    Or reads a story
About a prince, a castle, and a dragon.

The moon is glittering above the hill.
I stand before the gateposts of the King—   10
    So runs the story—
Of Thule, at midnight when the mice are still.

And I have been in Thule! It has come true—
The journey and the danger of the world,
    All that there is   15
To bear and to enjoy, endure and do.

Landscapes, seascapes . . . where have I been led?
The names of cities—Paris, Venice, Rome—
    Held out their arms.
A feathered god, seductive, went ahead.   20

Here is my house. Under a red rose tree
A child is swinging; another gravely plays.
    They are not surprised
That I am here; they were expecting me.

And yet my father sits and reads in silence,   25
My mother sheds a tear, the moon is still,
    And the dark wind
Is murmuring that nothing ever happens.

Beyond his jurisdiction as I move
Do I not prove him wrong? And yet, it's true   30
    They will not change
There, on the stage of terror and of love.

The actors in that playhouse always sit
In fixed positions—father, mother, child
    With painted eyes.   35
How sad it is to be a little puppet!

Their heads are wooden. And you once pretended
To understand them! Shake them as you will,
    They cannot speak.
Do what you will, the comedy is ended.   40

Father, why did you work? Why did you weep,
Mother? Was the story so important?
    "Listen!" the wind
Said to the children, and they fell asleep.

        [1964]

DONALD JUSTICE

[b. 1925]

In Bertram's Garden

Jane looks down at her organdy skirt
As if *it* somehow were the thing disgraced,
For being there, on the floor, in the dirt,
And she catches it up about her waist,

Smooths it out along one hip,   5
And pulls it over the crumpled slip.

On the porch, green-shuttered, cool,
Asleep is Bertram, that bronze boy,
Who, having wound her around a spool,
Sends her spinning like a toy   10
Out to the garden, all alone,
To sit and weep on a bench of stone.

Soon the purple dark will bruise
Lily and bleeding-heart and rose,
And the little Cupid lose   15
Eyes and ears and chin and nose,
And Jane lie down with others soon
Naked to the naked moon.

                                        [1960]

Men at forty

Men at forty
Learn to close softly
The doors to rooms they will not be
Coming back to.

At rest on a stair landing,   5
They feel it
Moving beneath them now like the deck of a ship,
Though the swell is gentle.

And deep in mirrors
They rediscover   10
The face of the boy as he practices tying
His father's tie there in secret

And the face of that father,
Still warm with the mystery of lather.
They are more fathers than sons themselves now.   15
Something is filling them, something

That is like the twilight sound
Of the crickets, immense,

Filling the woods at the foot of the slope
Behind their mortgaged houses.   20

                                                                    [1967]

KENNETH KOCH

[b. 1925]

Variations on a Theme by William Carlos Williams

1

I chopped down the house that you had been saving to live in next summer.
I am sorry, but it was morning, and I had nothing to do
and its wooden beams were so inviting.

2

We laughed at the hollyhocks together
And then I sprayed them with lye.   5
Forgive me. I simply do not know what I am doing.

3

I gave away the money that you had been saving to live on for the next ten years.
The man who asked for it was shabby
and the firm March wind on the porch was so juicy and cold.

4

Last evening we went dancing and I broke your leg.   10
Forgive me. I was clumsy, and
I wanted you here in the wards, where I am the doctor!

                                                                    [1962]

You were wearing

You were wearing your Edgar Allan Poe printed cotton blouse.
In each divided up square of the blouse was a picture of Edgar Allan Poe.
Your hair was blonde and you were cute. You asked me, "Do most boys think that
    most girls are bad?"

VARIATIONS . . . WILLIAMS   Cf. W. C. Williams's "This is Just to Say" p. 586.

I smelled the mould of your seaside resort hotel bedroom on your hair held in place
   by a John Greenleaf Whittier clip.
"No," I said, "it's girls who think that boys are bad." Then we read *Snowbound*
   together   5
And ran around in an attic, so that a little of the blue enamel was scraped off my
   George Washington, Father of His Country, shoes.

Mother was walking in the living room, her Strauss Waltzes comb in her hair.
We waited for a time and then joined her, only to be served tea in cups painted
   with pictures of Herman Melville
As well as with illustrations from his book *Moby Dick* and from his novella, *Benito
   Cereno.*
Father came in wearing his Dick Tracy necktie: "How about a drink, everyone?"   10
I said, "Let's go outside a while." Then we went onto the porch and sat on the
   Abraham Lincoln swing.
You sat on the eyes, mouth, and beard part, and I sat on the knees.
In the yard across the street we saw a snowman holding a garbage can lid smashed
   into a likeness of the mad English king, George the Third.

                                                                                               [1962]

A . R . A M M O N S

[b. 1926]

Reflective

I found a
weed
that had a

mirror in it
and that   5
mirror

looked in at
a mirror
in

me that   10
had a
weed in it.

                                                                                               [1972]

Bonus

The hemlocks slumped
already as if bewailing
the branch-loading

shales of ice, the rain
changes and a snow   5
sifty as fog

begins to fall, brightening
the ice's bruise-glimmer
with white holdings:

the hemlocks, muffled,   10
deepen to the grim
taking of a further beauty on.

[1972]

ROBERT BLY

[b. 1926]

Driving to Town Late to Mail a Letter

It is a cold and snowy night. The main street is deserted.
The only things moving are swirls of snow.
As I lift the mailbox door, I feel its cold iron.
There is a privacy I love in this snowy night.
Driving around, I will waste more time.   5

[1984]

ROBERT CREELEY

[b. 1926]

After Lorca

FOR M. MARTI

The church is a business, and the rich
are the business men.
         When they pull on the bells, the

poor come piling in and when a poor man dies, he has a
    wooden   5
cross, and they rush through the ceremony.

But when a rich man dies, they
drag out the Sacrament
and a golden Cross, and go *doucement, doucement*
to the cemetery.   10

And the poor love it
and think it's crazy.

[1962]

I Know a Man

As I sd to my
friend, because I am
always talking,—John, I

sd, which was not his
name, the darkness sur-   5
rounds us, what

can we do against
it, or else, shall we &
why not, buy a goddamn big car,

drive, he sd, for   10
christ's sake, look
out where yr going.

[1962]

ALLEN GINSBERG

[b. 1926]

A Supermarket in California

What thoughts I have of you tonight, Walt Whitman, for I walked down the
sidestreets under the trees with a headache self-conscious looking at the full moon.

A SUPERMARKET IN CALIFORNIA   Cf. Whitman's "Crossing Brooklyn Ferry," pp. 442–446.

In my hungry fatigue, and shopping for images, I went into the neon fruit supermarket, dreaming of your enumerations!

What peaches and what penumbras! Whole families shopping at night! Aisles full of husbands! Wives in the avocados, babies in the tomatoes!—and you, Garcia Lorca, what were you doing down by the watermelons?

I saw you, Walt Whitman, childless, lonely old grubber, poking among the meats in the refrigerator and eyeing the grocery boys.

I heard you asking questions of each: Who killed the pork chops? What price bananas? Are you my Angel?   5

I wandered in and out of the brilliant stacks of cans following you, and followed in my imagination by the store detective.

We strode down the open corridors together in our solitary fancy tasting artichokes, possessing every frozen delicacy, and never passing the cashier.

Where are we going, Walt Whitman? The doors close in an hour. Which way does your beard point tonight?

(I touch your book and dream of our odyssey in the supermarket and feel absurd.)

Will we walk all night through solitary streets? The trees add shade to shade, lights out in the houses, we'll both be lonely.   10

Will we stroll dreaming of the lost America of love past blue automobiles in driveways, home to our silent cottage?

Ah, dear father, graybeard, lonely old courage-teacher, what America did you have when Charon quit poling his ferry and you got out on a smoking bank and stood watching the boat disappear on the black waters of Lethe?

                                                                                                              [1955]

JAMES MERRILL

[b. 1926]

The Pier: Under Pisces

The shallows, brighter,
Wetter than water,
Tepidly glitter with the fingerprint-
Obliterating feel of kerosene.

Each piling like a totem   5
Rises from rock bottom
Straight through the ceiling
Aswirl with suns, clear ones or pale bluegreen,

A SUPERMARKET IN CALIFORNIA   ¹²**Charon** mythological character who transported souls to the world of the dead.

And beyond! where bubbles burst,
Sphere of their worst dreams,   *10*
If dream is what they do,
These floozy fish—

Ceramic-lipped in filmy
Peekaboo blouses,
Fluorescent body   *15*
Stockings, hot stripes,

Swayed by the hypnotic ebb and flow
Of supermarket Muzak,
Bolero beat the undertow's
Pebble-filled gourds repeat;   *20*

Jailbait consumers of subliminal
Hints dropped from on high
In gobbets none
Eschews as minced kin;

Who, hooked themselves—bamboo diviner   *25*
Bent their way
Vigorously nodding
Encouragement—

Are one by one hauled kisswise, oh
Into some blinding hell   *30*
Policed by leathery ex-
Justices each

Minding his catch, if catch is what he can,
If mind is what one means—
the torn mouth   *35*
Stifled by newsprint, working still. If . . . if . . .

The little scales
Grow stiff. Dusk plugs her dryer in,
Buffs her nails, riffles through magazines,
While far and wide and deep   *40*

Rove the great sharkskin-suited criminals
And safe in this lit shrine
A boy sits. He'll be eight.
We've drunk our milk, we've eaten our stringbeans,

But left untasted on the plate   *45*
The fish. An eye, a broiled pearl, meeting mine,

I lift his fork . . .
The bite. The tug of fate.

[1985]

FRANK O'HARA

[1926–1966]

Autobiographia Literaria

When I was a child
I played by myself in a
corner of the schoolyard
all alone.

I hated dolls and I   5
hated games, animals were
not friendly and birds
flew away.

If anyone was looking
for me I hid behind a   10
tree and cried out "I am
an orphan."

And here I am, the
center of all beauty!
writing these poems!   15
Imagine!

[1967]

DAVID WAGONER

[b. 1926]

Walking in the Snow

". . . if the author had said, 'Let us put on appropriate galoshes,' there could, of course, have been no poem . . ."

—*An analysis of Elinor Wylie's "Velvet Shoes,"* College English, *March 1948, p. 319.*

Let us put on appropriate galoshes, letting them flap open,
And walk in the snow.

The eyes have fallen out of the nearest snowman;
It slumps in its shadow,
And the slush at the curb is gray as the breasts of gulls.   5
As we slog together
Past arbors and stiff trees, all knocked out cold
At the broken end of winter,
No matter what may be falling out of the sky
Or blowing sideways   10
Against our hearts, we'll make up our own weather.
Love, stamping our galoshes,
Let's say something inappropriate, something flat
As a scholar's ear
And, since this can't be a poem, something loud   15
And pointless, leading nowhere
Like our foot prints ducking and draking in the snow
One after the other.

                                                        [1976]

W . S . M E R W I N

[b. 1927]

Separation

Your absence has gone through me
Like thread through a needle.
Everything I do is stitched with its color.

                                                        [1963]

When you go away

When you go away the wind clicks around to the north
The painters work all day but at sundown the paint falls
Showing the black walls
The clock goes back to striking the same hour
That has no place in the years   5

And at night wrapped in the bed of ashes
In one breath I wake
It is the time when the beards of the dead get their growth
I remember that I am falling

That I am the reason 10
And that my words are the garment of what I shall never be
Like the tucked sleeve of a one-armed boy

[1967]

Elegy

Who would I show it to

[1970]

GALWAY KINNELL

[b. 1927]

Saint Francis and the Sow

The bud
stands for all things,
even for those things that don't flower,
for everything flowers, from within, of self-blessing;
though sometimes it is necessary 5
to reteach a thing its loveliness,
to put a hand on its brow
of the flower
and retell it in words and in touch
it is lovely 10
until it flowers again from within, of self-blessing;
as Saint Francis
put his hand on the creased forehead
of the sow, and told her in words and in touch
blessings of earth on the sow, and the sow 15
began remembering all down her thick length,
from the earthen snout all the way
through the fodder and slops to the spiritual curl of the tail,
from the hard spininess spiked out from the spine
down through the great broken heart 20
to the sheer blue milken dreaminess spurting and shuddering
from the fourteen teats into the fourteen mouths sucking and blowing beneath them:
the long, perfect loveliness of sow.

[1980]

SAINT FRANCIS AND THE SOW ¹²**Saint Francis** Saint Francis of Assisi (1182–1226) was famed for his
love of all creation, especially animals.

After Making Love We Hear Footsteps

For I can snore like a bullhorn
or play loud music
or sit up talking with any reasonably sober Irishman
and Fergus will only sink deeper
into his dreamless sleep, which goes by all in one flash,   5
but let there be that heavy breathing
or a stifled come-cry anywhere in the house
and he will wrench himself awake
and make for it on the run—as now, we lie together,
after making love, quiet, touching along the length of our bodies,   10
familiar touch of the long-married,
and he appears—in his baseball pajamas, it happens,
the neck opening so small
he has to screw them on, which one day may make him wonder
about the mental capacity of baseball players—   15
and flops down between us and hugs us and snuggles himself to sleep,
his face gleaming with satisfaction at being this very child.

In the half darkness we look at each other
and smile
and touch arms across his little, startlingly muscled body—   20
this one whom habit of memory propels to the ground of his making,
sleeper only the mortal sounds can sing awake,
this blessing love gives again into our arms.

                                                                      [1980]

RUTH F. EISENBERG

[b. 1927]

Jocasta

1

When she learned the king's power,
Jocasta lost delight in being queen.
Laius was a cold, dry man. Looking at him

JOCASTA   mother and wife of Oedipus. See Sophocles' play *Oedipus the King.*   ³**Laius**   father of Oedi-
pus.

brought the image of her baby, his feet
pierced and bound, her baby left to die   5
on the mountain slope. They would
have no other children.

     I remember Laius drunk that night, crying
     for Chrysippus, the source of his curse.
     Wanting his boy, he took me instead   10
     and threw me on my back to have his way.
     I am fifteen and afraid to resist
     and tell myself it is my husband's right;
     the gods decree a wife obey her spouse.

     Sober, Laius recalls Apollo's threat: 15
     our son will kill him, beget upon me.
     Nine months drag like oxen ploughing.
     With icy eyes Laius watches me swell.
     I fear the gods and beg Hera for a girl,
     but as foretold, I give birth to a son.   20
     Laius takes the child to bind its feet.
     The baby cries, and Laius turns away.
     He summons a servant and orders me to hand
     my baby over, threatening me when I cry.
     The king will keep his own hands clean.   25

  At the public altar, Laius
offered bulls and lambs in ritual
slaughter. The everburning fire raged
so the offerings charred, and Jocasta
trembled at the gods' displeasure.   30

     Upon the gates this dawn, a strange creature
     appeared and woke all Thebes. In raucous voice
     she cried, "A riddle. Who'll solve my riddle?"
     At first our people came to gawk, then marvel.
     Some trembled, children hid their heads and cried.   35
     I've heard old tales the minstrels sing of her,
     but never did expect to really see
     a Sphinx—part woman, bird, and lion too . . .
     And what she asks is strange as well: four legs,
     then two, then three. What can it be? No one   40
     knows the answer. No one.

---

[9]**Chrysippus** Laius's male lover.   [15]**Apollo** the sun god.   [19]**Hera** wife of Zeus, leader of the gods.

The Sphinx brought pestilence and
drought. Rivers and streams ran dry, vines
shriveled. But until her riddle was solved,
the creature would not leave. On the gates   *45*
she stayed, her destructive song echoing
from empty wells.

    My life is a toad. All day and all night
the Sphinx. We cannot escape her song.
Song! More like wail or whine or scream.   *50*
Laius is useless as always. Deceitful
man, I hate him, hate his touch.

    The land is parched; flocks die. Our people
haggard, starving, plead to ease their distress.
What can we do? Mortals cannot make the rain.   *55*
I suggest Laius seek Apollo's help.
To get away, he welcomes the idea to go
to Delphi and proclaims a pilgrimage.

On the sunswept road to Delphi,
Laius was killed. The servant reporting   *60*
the death begged Jocasta to let him tend
flocks in the hills. Sending him on his way,
she shut herself in the palace.

    The prophecy was false. How can that be
if gods control all things? For surely chance   *65*
does not . . . No, no. Yet Laius killed our son
and not the other way. That sin diseased
his soul. I bless the gods that I,
at last, am free.

    I dream of my baby night after night.   *70*
He is dancing for the gods with bound feet.
I do not understand how he can dance so.
When he jumps, he trips, falling in a heap.
The gods just laugh and turn away to drink.
I sit ravelling knots. The knots become rope.   *75*
I wake shaking and muffle my tears in the sheets.

2

    "Man" answered the young stranger
whose red hair caught the sun's rays,

and the riddle was solved. True to her
promise, the Sphinx dashed herself to   *80*
death. Thebes was free.

Hailing their hero, the people
elected Oedipus king. Gratefully,
he accepted the rule and with it the hand
of Thebes' queen, Jocasta.   *85*

I see young Oedipus in radiant
sunlight, Apollo blinding me to all
but young and vital strength. Deep in myself
I feel a pulsebeat, something asleep
begins to wake, as though a dormant seed   *90*
sends up a shoot, opens a leaf. That's how
Aphrodite touches me. I love this youth.
My sun, I rise to him and rise with him.

From a land of rock and misery, Thebes
became a bower. Brilliant poppies   *95*
dotted the land. The wells filled, crops
flourished, and the flocks grew fat again.

Before the people's eyes, Jocasta
became young. Her dark hair gleamed, her
eye was bright and her laughter cheered   *100*
the halls of the palace.

Oedipus has become my Apollo warming
my days and nights. I am eighteen again
with poppies in my hair. I am the poppies,
bright little blooms with milk in them.   *105*
Like them, I seem to spring from rocky ground.
Like their color and his hair, our love flames.

Sweet Aphrodite, you rush through me, a stream
until you burst like foam that crests the sea.
Your blessing washes what was once a barren   *110*
ground. I walk among the roses, feel
your blush upon my cheeks. Oh lovely goddess,
I send you swans and doves.

Thebes prospered these years:
the gnarled olive bent lower with fruit.   *115*
Lambs frisked in the fields and pipers'

songs rang through the hills. Jocasta had
four children. Psalms of joy were sung
and danced for the gods.

> With four children, the hours run away.   120
> Their hunger, games and tears take all my time.
> In bed, with Oedipus, I sleep in peace.
> He was at first my headstrong bull, but now
> he is what a man, a king, should be.
> I like to see him walking in the yard,   125
> his funny stiff gait, his hair burnished
> by Apollo's brilliant rays.

> Mine turns grey but he doesn't seem to mind.
> Our love has brought to me the joy I missed
> when I was young and thought I'd never know.   130
> At last, I lay to rest my little boy,
> his shadow vanished now from all my dreams.

3

Years of plenty at an end, Thebes
was inflicted with drought. The earth
burned as crops withered, cattle and   135
sheep sickened.

> While days were once too short, now each one drags
> a slow furrow, the earth heavy with heat,
> lament and prayer. When I go to the fields
> the women clutch my gown and plead my help.   140
> Too many children sicken. The healthy droop.
> At home, the girls sit listless, my sons tangle
> while Oedipus complains his ankles twinge.
> He limps and growls just like a wounded pup.

Jocasta, very grey now, walked   145
with a more measured step. More than
a loving wife, she was also counsellor
to Oedipus.

> Blaming himself because the land is parched,
> Oedipus frets alarmed he's failed the gods   150
> in some unknown way, searching within himself.
> In turn, I pray, lighting fire after fire,
> but none burn true. I call on Aphrodite

and offer her doves, but they flap their wings
and peck each others' eyes. When I ask Apollo   155
to dim his eye, his answer scalds.

    No relief at hand, Oedipus sought
aid from Delphi. The report came back
a confusing riddle about Laius' death.
Suspecting treason, Oedipus feared   160
conspiracy against his own throne.

        Oedipus needs someone to blame. He calls
Creon traitor, Tiresias false seer.
I take him in my arms and stroke his hair.
He tells me what Tiresias has foreseen.   165
I laugh and tell him I too once believed
that prophecy controlled our lives, that seers
had magic vision the rest of us did not.
I tell the story of Laius, how it
was foretold he would die at his son's hand   170
and how that baby died when one week old.

        As I speak I feel so strange, as though my tale
came from another life about someone else.

        My words do not comfort, they flame new fears.
He relates what drove him from home, tales that he   175
would kill his father and bring rank fruit
from his mother's womb. He fears he has
been cursed. Dear gods, how can I comfort him?

4

    From Corinth, a messenger
brought news of Polybus' death,   180
the king whom Oedipus called father.

        You say that Polybus is dead. Dare I
greet death with joy? Can that be blasphemy?
My heart flies into song: His father's dead—
my Oedipus lives safe. His prophecy   185
is false. Is false as Laius' was. Oh bless
your fate, dear love, you need no longer fear.

    Corinth wished Oedipus to return
and rule. Fearing he would sleep with

his mother, Oedipus refused. Nothing   190
to fear, the messenger assured. Merope
was a barren woman.

    Jocasta began to tremble. Her hands
rose to cover her mouth.

        What's this? What's this? What words do I hear?   195
        How can I shut his silly mouth, tell him
        Go. Leave. We will not heed your words.
        My tongue stops, rooted in my mouth.

        I look at Oedipus. He does not see
        me watching him. His face is strained, his eyes   200
        are glaring blue. I try to stop the questions.
        "Oedipus, I beg you, do not hear this out."

    When Oedipus insisted, the
messenger told the story of the king's
infancy,—how he, a shepherd then,   205
had helped to save the king's life
when a baby, a baby with bound feet.

        Oh God. Oh cold, gold God. Apollo,
        you chill me. My mind is ice, and I hear
        my mouth say freezing words to Oedipus.   210
        To my husband. My son. "God keep you from
        the knowledge of who you are. Unhappy,
        Oedipus, my poor, damned Oedipus,
        that is all I can call you, and the last thing
        I shall ever call you."   215

5

    Her face ashen, Jocasta rushed
into the palace, her hands showing her
the way to her own quarters. She
ordered the guards to let no one in.
Ignoring all offers of help, she commanded   220
her women to leave her alone.

        I can't believe. I can't believe. Oh God.
        He is my son. I've loved my son but not
        as mothers should, but in my bed, in me.
        All that I loved the most, his youth that made   225

our love the summer sun, wrong, all wrong.
Vile. He caressed me here and here. And I
returned his touch. Odious hands. My flesh
crawls with worms.

My God, we've had four children.   *230*

In her chamber, she looked at her
bed, sat on it, then jumped up as though
stung. Covering her eyes with her hands,
she shook her head back and forth, again
and again, her body rocking.   *235*

Oh, Oedipus, what good was our love if
it comes only to shame? To children whom
all Thebes can curse? Such children, even ours,
are rightly damned.

Although we could not know who we were   *240*
and loved in innocence, still we are monsters
in the eyes of god and man. Our names will mean
disgrace and guilt forever.

Walking to her dressing table,
she stood before it picking up small   *245*
objects: combs, a gold box, a pair of
brooches. Noticing a bracelet given her
by her father when she was a bride,
she let forth a dreadful groan.

Oh Laius, Laius, you brought this on me.   *250*
My fate was sealed my wedding day. Chrysippus
was innocent as I; for you this curse
was uttered, a curse that falls on me. Oh,
that I must bear the shame, that I must be
destroyed by your corruption. And our son,   *255*
because you sinned, is ruined, damned.

My marriage day . . . what choices did I have?
As many as the night you came to me.
The only choice a woman has is that she wed
accepting what the gods and men decree.   *260*
It is not just. It never can be right.

Moving decisively, she walked to the
doors and bolted them, straining against

their heavy weight. The women on the other
side called to her, but again she bade them   265
go away.

    Falling on her knees, she pummeled
her stomach as though to punish her
womb. As she did, she called her child-
ren's names, one name, Oedipus, again   270
and again.

        I thought him buried, forgotten. But no,
for countless days and nights these many years
he's thrust himself on me instead. My bed
once stained with birthing blood is now forever   275
stained; what once was love become a rank
corruption.

    Rising painfully, sore, she turned
to the small altar in her chamber.
Smashing a jar which held incense, she   280
began in a voice of char to call on
Apollo and Aphrodite.

    As she raised her eyes, she raised
her fist and shook it against
the silent air.   285

        Apollo, you blinded me to his scars,
his age, any resemblance to Laius.
And you, Aphrodite, cruel sister of the sun,
set my woman's body afire, matching my
ripe years and hungers with his youth and strength.   290
Paralyzing my mind, you inflamed my heart.

        The years I prayed to you and praised you
were all charade. You so enjoyed my dance.
We are your fools to trifle with, your joke.

        We tremble to question what the future holds.   295
As though it matters, we think asking will spoil
our luck, but your injustice mocks all hope.

        I hear a chant pounding inside my head.
Five babies. Five abominations.
As though a chorus raises call to prayer.   300
Five babies. Five abominations.

No call to prayer. It is a call to curse
the gods. No longer will I be their fool.

From her robe, she removed her
braided belt. As she looped its strands,   *305*
she heard, from the courtyard, a man's
voice scream in anguish. Undeflected, she
tied the necessary knots, slipping the loop
back and forth. Satisfied, she settled
the noose around her neck.   *310*

Five babies cursed by heavenly whim,
cursed in their lives without chance or hope.
Mothers ought not love their children so.

Gathering her skirts, she climbed
up on the stool.   *315*

And wives be more than merely bedside pawns.
Those who cannot shape their lives are better
dead.

She stepped onto the air.

[1986]

JOHN ASHBERY

[b. 1927]

The Painter

Sitting between the sea and the buildings
He enjoyed painting the sea's portrait.
But just as children imagine a prayer
Is merely silence, he expected his subject
To rush up the sand, and, seizing a brush,   *5*
Plaster its own portrait on the canvas.

So there was never any paint on his canvas
Until the people who lived in the buildings
Put him to work: "Try using the brush
As a means to an end. Select, for a portrait,   *10*
Something less angry and large, and more subject
To a painter's moods, or, perhaps, to a prayer."

How could he explain to them his prayer
That nature, not art, might usurp the canvas?
He chose his wife for a new subject,   *15*
Making her vast, like ruined buildings,
As if, forgetting itself, the portrait
Had expressed itself without a brush.

Slightly encouraged, he dipped his brush
In the sea, murmuring a heartfelt prayer: *20*
"My soul, when I paint this next portrait
Let it be you who wrecks the canvas."
The news spread like wildfire through the buildings:
He had gone back to the sea for his subject.

Imagine a painter crucified by his subject!   *25*
Too exhausted even to lift his brush,
He provoked some artists leaning from the buildings
To malicious mirth: "We haven't a prayer
Now, of putting ourselves on canvas,
Or getting the sea to sit for a portrait!"   *30*

Others declared it a self-portrait.
Finally all indications of a subject
Began to fade, leaving the canvas
Perfectly white. He put down the brush.
At once a howl, that was also a prayer,   *35*
Arose from the overcrowded buildings.

They tossed him, the portrait, from the tallest of the buildings;
And the sea devoured the canvas and the brush
As though his subject had decided to remain a prayer.

[1956]

JAMES WRIGHT

[1927–1980]

Lying in a Hammock at William Duffy's Farm in Pine Island, Minnesota

Over my head, I see the bronze butterfly,
Asleep on the black trunk,
Blowing like a leaf in green shadow.

Down the ravine behind the empty house,
The cowbells follow one another   5
Into the distances of the afternoon.
To my right,
In a field of sunlight between two pines,
The droppings of last year's horses
Blaze up into golden stones.   10
I lean back, as the evening darkens and comes on.
A chicken hawk floats over, looking for home.
I have wasted my life.

[1963]

A Blessing

Just off the highway to Rochester, Minnesota,
Twilight bounds softly forth on the grass.
And the eyes of those two Indian ponies
Darken with kindness.
They have come gladly out of the willows   5
To welcome my friend and me.
We step over the barbed wire into the pasture
Where they have been grazing all day, alone.
They ripple tensely, they can hardly contain their happiness
That we have come.   10
They bow shyly as wet swans. They love each other.
There is no loneliness like theirs.
At home once more,
They begin munching the young tufts of spring in the darkness.
I would like to hold the slenderer one in my arms,   15
For she has walked over to me
And nuzzled my left hand.
She is black and white,
Her mane falls wild on her forehead,
And the light breeze moves me to caress her long ear   20
That is delicate as the skin over a girl's wrist.
Suddenly I realize
That if I stepped out of my body I would break
Into blossom.

[1963]

DONALD HALL

[b. 1928]

My son, my executioner

My son, my executioner,
    I take you in my arms,
Quiet and small and just astir,
    And whom my body warms.

Sweet death, small son, our instrument   5
    Of immortality,
Your cries and hungers document
    Our bodily decay.

We twenty-five and twenty-two,
    Who seemed to live forever,   10
Observe enduring life in you
    And start to die together.

[1955]

PHILIP LEVINE

[b. 1928]

Starlight

My father stands in the warm evening
on the porch of my first house.
I am four years old and growing tired.
I see his head among the stars,
the glow of his cigarette, redder   5
than the summer moon riding
low over the old neighborhood. We
are alone, and he asks me if I am happy.
"Are you happy?" I cannot answer.
I do not really understand the word,   10

and the voice, my father's voice, is not
his voice, but somehow thick and choked,
a voice I have not heard before, but
heard often since. He bends and passes
a thumb beneath each of my eyes.   *15*
The cigarette is gone, but I can smell
the tiredness that hangs on his breath.
He has found nothing, and he smiles
and holds my head with both his hands.
Then he lifts me to his shoulder,   *20*
and now I too am there among the stars,
as tall as he. Are you happy? I say.
He nods in answer, Yes! oh yes! oh yes!
And in that new voice he says nothing,
holding my head tight against his head,   *25*
his eyes closed up against the starlight,
as though those tiny blinking eyes
of light might find a tall, gaunt child
holding his child against the promises
of autumn, until the boy slept   *30*
never to waken in that world again.

[1984]

ANNE SEXTON

[1928–1974]

Us

I was wrapped in black
fur and white fur and
you undid me and then
you placed me in gold light
and then you crowned me,   *5*
while snow fell outside
the door in diagonal darts.
While a ten-inch snow
came down like stars
in small calcium fragments,   *10*

we were in our own bodies
(that room that will bury us)
and you were in my body
(that room that will outlive us)
and at first I rubbed your   15
feet dry with a towel
because I was your slave
and then you called me princess.
Princess!

Oh then   20
I stood up in my gold skin
and I beat down the psalms
and I beat down the clothes
and you undid the bridle
and you undid the reins   25
and I undid the buttons,
the bones, the confusion,
the New England postcards,
the January ten o'clock night,
and we rose up like wheat,   30
acre after acre of gold,
and we harvested,
we harvested.

                                          [1969]

JOHN HOLLANDER

[b. 1929]

Adam's Task

"And Adam gave names to all cattle, and to the fowl of the air, and to every beast of the field . . ."
Gen. 2:20

Thou, paw-paw-paw; thou, glurd; thou, spotted
   Glurd; thou, whitesap, lurching through
The high-grown brush; thou, pliant-footed,
   Implex; thou, awagabu.

Every burrower, each flier   5
    Came for the name he had to give:
Gay, first work, ever to be prior,
    Not yet sunk to primitive.

Thou, verdle; thou, McFleery's pomma;
    Thou; thou; thou—three types of grawl;   10
Thou, flisket; thou, kabasch; thou, comma-
    Eared mashawk; thou, all; thou, all.

Were, in a fire of becoming,
    Laboring to be burned away,
Then work, half-measuring, half-humming,   15
    Would be as serious as play.

Thou, pambler; thou, rivarn; thou, greater
    Wherret, and thou, lesser one;
Thou, sproal; thou, zant; thou, lily-eater.
    Naming's over. Day is done.   20

[1971]

X . J . K E N N E D Y

[b. 1929]

First Confession

Blood thudded in my ears. I scuffed,
    Steps stubborn, to the telltale booth
Beyond whose curtained portal coughed
    The robed repositor of truth.

The slat shot back. The universe   5
    Bowed down his cratered dome to hear
Enumerated my each curse,
    The sip snitched from my old man's beer.

My sloth pride envy lechery,
    The dime held back from Peter's Pence   *10*
With which I'd bribed my girl to pee
    That I might spy her instruments.

Hovering scale-pans when I'd done
    Settled their balance slow as silt
While in the restless dark I burned   *15*
    Bright as a brimstone in my guilt

Until as one feeds birds he doled
    Seven Our Fathers and a Hail
Which I to double-scrub my soul
    Intoned twice at the altar rail   *20*

Where Sunday in seraphic light
    I knelt, as full of grace as most,
And stuck my tongue out at the priest:
    A fresh roost for the Holy Ghost.

                                         [1985]

In a prominent bar in Secaucus one day

TO THE TUNE OF "THE OLD ORANGE FLUTE" OR THE TUNE OF "SWEET BETSY FROM PIKE"

In a prominent bar in Secaucus one day
Rose a lady in skunk with a topheavy sway,
Raised a knobby red finger—all turned from their beer—
While with eyes bright as snowcrust she sang high and clear:

"Now who of you'd think from an eyeload of me   *5*
That I once was a lady as proud as could be?
Oh I'd never sit down by a tumbledown drunk
If it wasn't, my dears, for the high cost of junk.

"All the gents used to swear that the white of my calf
Beat the down of the swan by a length and a half.   *10*

In the kerchief of linen I caught to my nose
Ah, there never fell snot, but a little gold rose.

"I had seven gold teeth and a toothpick of gold,
My Virginia cheroot° was a leaf of it rolled   *cigar*
And I'd light it each time with a thousand in cash—   15
Why the bums used to fight if I flicked them an ash.

"Once the toast of the Biltmore, the belle of the Taft,
I would drink bottle beer at the Drake, never draft,
And dine at the Astor on Salisbury steak
With a clean tablecloth for each bite I did take.   20

"In a car like the Roxy I'd roll to the track,
A steel-guitar trio, a bar in the back,
And the wheels made no noise, they turned over so fast,
Still it took you ten minutes to see me go past.

"When the horses bowed down to me that I might choose,   25
I bet on them all, for I hated to lose.
Now I'm saddled each night for my butter and eggs
And the broken threads race down the backs of my legs.

"Let you hold in mind, girls, that your beauty must pass
Like a lovely white clover that rusts with its grass.   30
Keep your bottoms off barstools and marry you young
Or be left—an old barrel with many a bung.

"For when time takes you out for a spin in his car
You'll be hard-pressed to stop him from going too far
And be left by the roadside, for all your good deeds,   35
Two toadstools for tits and a face full of weeds."

All the house raised a cheer, but the man at the bar
Made a phonecall and up pulled a red patrol car
And she blew us a kiss as they copped her away
From that prominent bar in Secaucus, N.J.   40

[1985]

IN A PROMINENT BAR   [17-19]**Biltmore . . . Astor**   once-fine hotels in New York City.   [21]**Roxy**
a large, garish movie theater.

ADRIENNE RICH

[b. 1929]

For more than forty years now, Adrienne Rich's voice has been heard in poems, speeches, essays, reviews, and book-length studies of literary, social, and cultural ideas. Hers is a powerful voice, one that demands attention, an earnest, engaging voice passionately committed to the liberation of women and men from a prejudice that blinds perception and stunts the mind. Rich has become an important spokeswoman for feminist consciousness, especially for lesbianism, which according to her is considerably more than a matter of sexual preference. In seeing lesbianism as "a sense of desiring oneself, choosing oneself," Rich associates it with the formation of identity, with the power of the self to discover and define itself. But it is also, as she has remarked, "a primary intensity between women" that energizes them, propels them toward one another, both challenging and charging their imaginations.

And yet even though Rich has become associated with radical feminist ideology, she is not readily constrained by it. Her prose and poetry, while rooted in ideological concerns, nonetheless dramatize a self-discovering freedom in language and art. In her best writing, Rich is less a polemicist and publicist than an artist who challenges our preconceptions about women, especially their relationships with men and their responsibilities to one another. Her best work dramatically enacts the way she sees herself: as a writer who creates images that aid herself and others in understanding who they are. She describes this writerly instrumentality in a memorable image from one of her finest poems, "Planetarium":

> . . . I am an instrument in the shape
> of a woman trying to translate pulsations
> into images   for the relief of the body
> and the reconstruction of the mind.

One place to see Rich's own reconstruction of the mind is in her autobiographical writing. In "When We Dead Awaken: Writing as Re-Vision," Rich has charted the changing perception of herself as woman and poet. She describes how she needed to change the images that represented, for her, ideals of both woman and poet, since her images of both had been dominated by men. She explores the concept of "re-vision," which she considers "the act of looking back, of seeing with fresh eyes." It is an act essential for writers, both amateur and professional. It is also an essential act for readers if they want to avoid a paralyzed, ossified literary tradition. And as Rich insists, her version of re-vision is essential for women living in a male-dominated society. Re-vision is thus more than a mere chapter of cultural or literary history; rather, as Rich notes, "it is an act of survival." Rich uses her own experience as reader, poet, and woman to illustrate how such re-vision can and must occur.

Change became the lodestone of Rich's life and work. The title of her first book of poems, *A Change of World* (1951), ironically forecasts the driving impulse in Rich's life, an impulse manifested even more vigorously in the title of a later poetry collection, *The Will to Change* (1971), in which she celebrates power and self-determination as agents of that necessary change. Between these two volumes Rich revised both her life and her poetry. In 1953 she married Alfred Conrad, a Harvard economist, and bore three sons in four years. In her book *Of Woman Born: Motherhood as Experience and Institution* (1976) she described her seventeen years of marriage and motherhood as "a radicalizing experience." She writes: "I knew I had to remake my life; I did not then understand that we [middle-class women] were expected to fill both the part of the Victorian Lady of Leisure, the Angel in the House, and also of the Victorian cook, scullery maid, laundress, governess, and nurse." Rich initiated changes in both her life and her writing. In both her life and her art she moved out of the circle of the conventional and into new and unfamiliar territory.

Her poems vigorously reflect her new perspective on her identity and her poetic vocation. Rich's early poems were largely traditional in structure. "Aunt Jennifer's Tigers" (p. 11), one of her earliest, is cast in symmetrical four-line stanzas of rhyming iambic pentameter couplets. A slightly later poem, "The Knight," is also arranged in symmetrical stanzas. But with poems of the 60s and 70s such as "Snapshots of a Daughter-in-Law" (1963), "Planetarium" (1971), and "Diving into the Wreck" (1973), Rich broke through the poetic forms she associated with her male masters and precursors. In these poems rhyme has disappeared and along with it any semblance of stanzaic regularity. In their place we find abrupt shifts of tone and voice, extensive allusiveness and quotation, and a wider range and a greater intensity of imagery. The later poems seem more personal, more urgent and passionate, more immediately revelatory of the poet's thoughts and feelings.

Rich's critical writing reveals a similar transformation. In a seminal essay on Emily Dickinson, "Vesuvius at Home: The Power of Emily Dickinson," Rich performs a similar act of re-vision. Exploring Dickinson's poetry from a feminist perspective, Rich attends to Dickinson's compressed and varied language dense with implication, as well as to her eroticism and mysticism. She argues that Dickinson was the great female poet of "the intense inner event, the personal and psychological, *the* American poet whose work consisted in exploring states of psychic extremity." Her fresh, influential reading of Dickinson opened the way for subsequent feminist approaches to Dickinson's work. Rich's liberating critical essay is infused with cultural analysis and fueled by personal passion. Stressing the psychic energy of Dickinson's verse, Rich's analysis is a triumphant imaginative reconstruction of Dickinson's mind. It is also a revelation of her own.

In her prose pieces and in the many poems she has published, Rich writes out of an impassioned conviction that women's value lies not in their being mere appendages to men. Women's value resides in themselves as individuals who differ from men and from one another even while they share a sense of communal sisterhood. Her writing is urgent, forceful, occasionally angry in its denuncia-

tion of women's subjugation and humiliation. It is also assertive, even annuncia-
tory, in its insistence that conditions for living, working, and writing must be
improved. Through its anger and critical passion, however, sounds a note of
optimism, a belief that both men and women are listening and are ready for
change.

Storm Warnings

The glass has been falling all the afternoon,
And knowing better than the instrument
What winds are walking overhead, what zone
Of gray unrest is moving across the land,
I leave the book upon a pillowed chair   5
And walk from window to closed window, watching
Boughs strain against the sky

And think again, as often when the air
Moves inward toward a silent core of waiting,
How with a single purpose time has traveled   10
By secret currents of the undiscerned
Into this polar realm. Weather abroad
And weather in the heart alike come on
Regardless of prediction.

Between foreseeing and averting change   15
Lies all the mastery of elements
Which clocks and weatherglasses cannot alter.
Time in the hand is not control of time,
Nor shattered fragments of an instrument
A proof against the wind; the wind will rise   20
We can only close the shutters.

I draw the curtains as the sky goes black
And set a match to candles sheathed in glass
Against the keyhole draught, the insistent whine
Of weather through the unsealed aperture.   25
This is our sole defense against the season;
These are the things that we have learned to do
Who live in troubled regions.

[1951]

Snapshots of a Daughter-in-Law

1.

You, once a belle in Shreveport,
with henna-colored hair, skin like a peachbud,
still have your dresses copied from that time,
and play a Chopin prelude
called by Cortot: *"Delicious recollections*   5
float like perfume through the memory."

Your mind now, moldering like wedding-cake,
heavy with useless experience, rich
with suspicion, rumor, fantasy,
crumbling to pieces under the knife-edge   10
of mere fact. In the prime of your life.

Nervy, glowering, your daughter
wipes the teaspoons, grows another way.

2.

Banging the coffee-pot into the sink
she hears the angels chiding, and looks out   15
past the raked gardens to the sloppy sky.
Only a week since They said: *Have no patience.*

The next time it was: *Be insatiable.*
Then: *Save yourself; others you cannot save.*
Sometimes she's let the tapstream scald her arm,   20
a match burn to her thumbnail,

or held her hand above the kettle's snout
right in the woolly steam. They are probably angels,
since nothing hurts her anymore, except
each morning's grit blowing into her eyes.   25

3.

A thinking woman sleeps with monsters.
The beak that grips her, she becomes. And Nature,
that sprung-lidded, still commodious

SNAPSHOTS OF A DAUGHTER-IN-LAW   [4]**Chopin**   Frédéric François Chopin (1810–1849), Polish composer and pianist who settled in Paris in 1831.   [5]**Cortot**   Alfred Cortot (1877–1962), French pianist.
[5–6]**Delicious . . . memory**   Cortot's notation for Chopin's Prelude No. 7.

6.

When to her lute Corinna sings
neither words nor music are her own;   30
only the long hair dipping
over her cheek, only the song
of silk against her knees
and these
adjusted in reflections of an eye.   35

Poised, trembling and unsatisfied, before
an unlocked door, that cage of cages,
tell us, you bird, you tragical machine—
is this *fertilisante douleur?* Pinned down
by love, for you the only natural action,   40
are you edged more keen
to prise the secrets of the vault? has Nature shown
her household books to you, daughter-in-law,
that her sons never saw?

7.

"To have in this uncertain world some stay   45
which cannot be undermined, is
of the utmost consequence."
                                    Thus wrote
a woman, partly brave and partly good,
who fought with what she partly understood.
Few men about her would or could do more,   50
hence she was labeled harpy, shrew and whore.

8.

"You all die at fifteen," said Diderot,
and turn part legend, part convention.
Still, eyes inaccurately dream
behind closed windows blankening with steam.   55
Deliciously, all that we might have been,
all that we were—fire, tears,
wit, taste, martyred ambition—
stirs like the memory of refused adultery
the drained and flagging bosom of our middle years.   60

---

²⁹**When . . . sings** first line of a poem by Thomas Campion (1567–1620).   ³⁹**fertilisante douleur** French
for "fertilizing [or life-giving] sorrow."   ⁴⁵⁻⁴⁷**"To . . . consequence."**   Rich's note: "From Mary Wollstone-
craft, *Thoughts on the Education of Daughters*, London, 1787."   ⁵²**Diderot** Denis Diderot (1713–1784),
French philosopher, encyclopedist, playwright, and critic.

9.

Not that it is done well, but
that it is done at all? Yes, think
of the odds! or shrug them off forever.
This luxury of the precocious child,
Time's precious chronic invalid,—   65
would we, darlings, resign it if we could?
Our blight has been our sinecure:
mere talent was enough for us—
glitter in fragments and rough drafts.

Sigh no more, ladies.
                    Time is male   70
and in his cups drinks to the fair.
Bemused by gallantry, we hear
our mediocrities over-praised,
indolence read as abnegation,
slattern thought styled intuition,   75
every lapse forgiven, our crime
only to cast too bold a shadow
or smash the mold straight off.

For that, solitary confinement,
tear gas, attrition shelling.   80
Few applicants for that honor.

10.

                     Well,
she's long about her coming, who must be
more merciless to herself than history.
Her mind full to the wind, I see her plunge
breasted and glancing through the currents,   85
taking the light upon her
at least as beautiful as any boy
or helicopter,
                poised, still coming,
her fine blades making the air wince

[61-62]**Not . . . all?**   Samuel Johnson once remarked to James Boswell: "Sir, a woman's preaching is like a dog's walking on his hinder legs. It is not done well, but you are surprised to find it done at all." See *Boswell's Life of Johnson* for July 31, 1763.

but her cargo   *90*
no promise then:
delivered
palpable
ours.

[1963]

The Knight

A knight rides into the noon,
and his helmet points to the sun,
and a thousand splintered suns
are the gaiety of his mail.
The soles of his feet glitter   *5*
and his palms flash in reply,
and under his crackling banner
he rides like a ship in sail.

A knight rides into the noon,
and only his eye is living,   *10*
a lump of bitter jelly
set in a metal mask,
betraying rags and tatters
that cling to the flesh beneath
and wear his nerves to ribbons   *15*
under the radiant casque.

Who will unhorse this rider
and free him from between
the walls of iron, the emblems
crushing his chest with their weight?   *20*
Will they defeat him gently,
or leave him hurled on the green,
his rags and wounds still hidden
under the great breastplate?

[1963]

Orion

Far back when I went zig-zagging
through tamarack pastures

ORION   A constellation named for a mythical hunter. Stars in the constellation form his belt and sword

you were my genius, you
my cast-iron Viking, my helmed
lion-heart king in prison.   5
Years later now you're young

my fierce half-brother, staring
down from that simplified west
your breast open, your belt dragged down
by an oldfashioned thing, a sword   10
the last bravado you won't give over
though it weighs you down as you stride

and the stars in it are dim
and maybe have stopped burning.
But you burn, and I know it;   15
as I throw back my head to take you in
an old transfusion happens again:
divine astronomy is nothing to it.

Indoors I bruise and blunder,
break faith, leave ill enough   20
alone, a dead child born in the dark.
Night cracks up over the chimney,
pieces of time, frozen geodes
come showering down in the grate.

A man reaches behind my eyes   25
and finds them empty
a woman's head turns away
from my head in the mirror
children are dying my death
and eating crumbs of my life.   30

Pity is not your forte.
Calmly you ache up there
pinned aloft in your crow's nest,
my speechless pirate!
You take it all for granted   35
and when I look you back

it's with a starlike eye
shooting its cold and egotistical spear

---

⁵**lion-heart king**   Richard the Lion Hearted of England (1157–1199).

where it can do least damage.
Breathe deep! No hurt, no pardon   40
out here in the cold with you
you with your back to the wall

[1969]

Planetarium

THINKING OF CAROLINE HERSCHEL (1750–1848), ASTRONOMER,
SISTER OF WILLIAM; AND OTHERS.

A woman in the shape of a monster
a monster in the shape of a woman
the skies are full of them

a woman   "in the snow
among the Clocks and instruments   5
or measuring the ground with poles"
in her 98 years to discover
8 comets

she whom the moon ruled
like us   10
levitating into the night sky
riding the polished lenses

Galaxies of women, there
doing penance for impetuousness
ribs chilled   15
in those spaces   of the mind

An eye,

"virile, precise and absolutely certain"
from the mad webs of Uranusborg

encountering the NOVA

PLANETARIUM   Caroline . . . William   In helping her brother William (1738–1822), the discoverer of
Uranus, Caroline Herschel became a superb astronomer in her own right.   [18]"virile . . . certain"   language
used by the Danish astronomer Tycho Brahe (1546–1601) to describe his observations of the heavens.
[19]Uranusborg   Brahe's observatory was called Uranisborg, or "castle in the sky."

every impulse of light exploding   20
from the core
as life flies out of us

    Tycho whispering at last
    "Let me not seem to have lived in vain"

What we see, we see   25
and seeing is changing

the light that shrivels a mountain
and leaves a man alive

Heartbeat of the pulsar
heart sweating through my body   30

The radio impulse
pouring in from Taurus

    I am bombarded yet   I stand

I have been standing all my life in the
direct path of a battery of signals   35
the most accurately transmitted most
untranslatable language in the universe
I am a galactic cloud so deep so invo-
luted that a light wave could take 15
years to travel through me And has   40
taken I am an instrument in the shape
of a woman trying to translate pulsations
into images   for the relief of the body
and the reconstruction of the mind.

                                              [1971]

Trying to Talk with a Man

Out in this desert we are testing bombs,

that's why we came here.

Sometimes I feel an underground river
forcing its way between deformed cliffs

PLANETARIUM   ²⁴**Let . . . vain** Tycho Brahe's last words.   ³²**Taurus** The bull, a constellation in the
Northern Hemisphere, near Orion.

an acute angle of understanding   5
moving itself like a locus of the sun
into this condemned scenery.

What we've had to give up to get here—
whole LP collections, films we starred in
playing in the neighborhoods, bakery windows   10
full of dry, chocolate-filled Jewish cookies,
the language of love-letters, of suicide notes,
afternoons on the riverbank
pretending to be children

Coming out to this desert   15
we meant to change the face of
driving among dull green succulents
walking at noon in the ghost town
surrounded by a silence

that sounds like the silence of the place   20
except that it came with us
and is familiar
and everything we were saying until now
was an effort to blot it out—
coming out here we are up against it   25
Out here I feel more helpless
with you than without you
You mention the danger
and list the equipment
we talk of people caring for each other   30
in emergencies—laceration, thirst—
but you look at me like an emergency

Your dry heat feels like power
your eyes are stars of a different magnitude
they reflect lights that spell out: EXIT   35
when you get up and pace the floor

talking of the danger
as if it were not ourselves
as if we were testing anything else.

                                                    [1973]

Diving into the Wreck

First having read the book of myths,
and loaded the camera,
and checked the edge of the knife-blade,
I put on
the body-armor of black rubber   5
the absurd flippers
the grave and awkward mask.
I am having to do this
not like Cousteau with his
assiduous team   10
aboard the sun-flooded schooner
but here alone.

There is a ladder.
The ladder is always there
hanging innocently   15
close to the side of the schooner.
We know what it is for,
we who have used it.
Otherwise
it's a piece of maritime floss   20
some sundry equipment.

I go down.
Rung after rung and still
the oxygen immerses me
the blue light   25
the clear atoms
of our human air.

I go down.
My flippers cripple me,
I crawl like an insect down the ladder   30
and there is no one
to tell me when the ocean
will begin.

First the air is blue and then
it is bluer and then green and then   35
black I am blacking out and yet

my mask is powerful
it pumps my blood with power
the sea is another story
the sea is not a question of power   40
I have to learn alone
to turn my body without force
in the deep element.

And now: it is easy to forget
what I came for   45
among so many who have always
lived here
swaying their crenellated fans
between the reefs
and besides   50
you breathe differently down here.

I came to explore the wreck.
The words are purposes.
The words are maps.
I came to see the damage that was done   55
and the treasures that prevail.
I stroke the beam of my lamp
slowly along the flank
of something more permanent
than fish or weed   60

the thing I came for:
the wreck and not the story of the wreck
the thing itself and not the myth
the drowned face always staring
toward the sun   65
the evidence of damage
worn by salt and sway into this threadbare beauty
the ribs of the disaster
curving their assertion
among the tentative haunters.   70

This is the place.
And I am here, the mermaid whose dark hair
streams black, the merman in his armored body
We circle silently
about the wreck   75

we dive into the hold.
I am she: I am he

whose drowned face sleeps with open eyes
whose breasts still bear the stress
whose silver, copper, vermeil cargo lies   *80*
obscurely inside barrels
half-wedged and left to rot
we are the half-destroyed instruments
that once held to a course
the water-eaten log   *85*
the fouled compass

We are, I am, you are
by cowardice or courage
the one who find our way
back to this scene   *90*
carrying a knife, a camera
a book of myths
in which
our names do not appear.

[1973]

Rape

There is a cop who is both prowler and father:
he comes from your block, grew up with your brothers,
had certain ideals.
You hardly know him in his boots and silver badge,
on horseback, one hand touching his gun.   *5*

You hardly know him but you have to get to know him:
he has access to machinery that could kill you.
He and his stallion clop like warlords among the trash,
his ideals stand in the air, a frozen cloud
from between his unsmiling lips.   *10*

And so, when the time comes, you have to turn to him,
the maniac's sperm still greasing your thighs,
your mind whirling like crazy. You have to confess

to him, you are guilty of the crime
of having been forced.   15

And you see his blue eyes, the blue eyes of all the family
whom you used to know, grow narrow and glisten,
his hand types out the details
and he wants them all
but the hysteria in your voice pleases him best.   20

You hardly know him but now he thinks he knows you:
he has taken down your worst moment
on a machine and filed it in a file.
He knows, or thinks he knows, how much you imagined;
he knows, or thinks he knows, what you secretly wanted.   25

He has access to machinery that could get you put away;
and if, in the sickening light of the precinct,
and if, in the sickening light of the precinct,
your details sound like a portrait of your confessor,
will you swallow, will you deny them, will you lie your way home?   30

                                                       [1975]

For an Album

Our story isn't a file of photographs
faces laughing under green leaves
or snowlit doorways, on the verge of driving
away, our story is not about women
victoriously perched on the one   5
sunny day of the conference,
nor lovers displaying love:

Our story is of moments
when even slow motion moved too fast
for the shutter of the camera: 10
words that blew our lives apart, like so,
eyes that cut and caught each other,
mime of the operating room
where gas and knives quote each other
moments before the telephone   15

starts ringing: our story is
how still we stood,
how fast.

[1987]

from *An Atlas of the Difficult World*

II

Here is a map of our country:
here is the Sea of Indifference, glazed with salt
This is the haunted river flowing from brow to groin
we dare not taste its water
This is the desert where missiles are planted like corms   5
This is the breadbasket of foreclosed farms
This is the birthplace of the rockabilly boy
This is the cemetery of the poor
who died for democracy   This is a battlefield
from a nineteenth-century war   the shrine is famous   10
This is the sea-town of myth and story   when the fishing fleets
went bankrupt   here is where the jobs were   on the pier
processing frozen fishsticks   hourly wages and no shares
These are other battlefields   Centralia   Detroit
here are the forests primeval   the copper   the silver lodes   15
These are the suburbs of acquiescence   silence rising fumelike from the streets
This is the capital of money and dolor whose spires
flare up through air inversions whose bridges are crumbling
whose children are drifting blind alleys pent
between coiled rolls of razor wire   20
I promised to show you a map you say but this is a mural
then yes let it be   these are small distinctions
where do we see it from is the question

XIII (Dedications)

I know you are reading this poem
late, before leaving your office
of the one intense yellow lamp-spot and the darkening window
in the lassitude of a building faded to quiet
long after rush-hour.   I know you are reading this poem   5
standing up in a bookstore far from the ocean
on a grey day of early spring, faint flakes driven

across the plains' enormous spaces around you.
I know you are reading this poem
in a room where too much has happened for you to bear   10
where the bedclothes lie in stagnant coils on the bed
and the open valise speaks of flight
but you cannot leave yet.   I know you are reading this poem
as the underground train loses momentum and before running up the stairs
toward a new kind of love   15
your life has never allowed.
I know you are reading this poem by the light
of the television screen where soundless images jerk and slide
while you wait for the newscast from the *intifada*.
I know you are reading this poem in a waiting-room   20
of eyes met and unmeeting, of identity with strangers.
I know you are reading this poem by fluorescent light
in the boredom and fatigue of the young who are counted out,
count themselves out, at too early an age.   I know
you are reading this poem through your failing sight, the thick   25
lens enlarging these letters beyond all meaning yet you read on
because even the alphabet is precious.
I know you are reading this poem as you pace beside the stove
warming milk, a crying child on your shoulder, a book in your hand
because life is short and you too are thirsty.   30
I know you are reading this poem which is not in your language
guessing at some words while others keep you reading
and I want to know which words they are.
I know you are reading this poem listening for something, torn between bitterness
    and hope
turning back once again to the task you cannot refuse.   35
I know you are reading this poem because there is nothing else left to read
there where you have landed, stripped as you are.

[1991]

BRUCE DAWE

[b. 1930]

A Victorian Hangman Tells His Love

Dear one, forgive my appearing before you like this,
in a two-piece track-suit, welder's goggles
and a green cloth cap like some gross bee—this is the State's idea . . .

I would have come
arrayed like a bridegroom for these nuptials   5
knowing how often you have dreamed about this
moment of consummation in your cell.
If I must bind your arms now to your sides
with a leather strap and ask if you have anything to say
—these too are formalities I would dispense with: 10
I know your heart is too full at this moment
to say much and that the tranquilliser which I trust
you did not reject out of a stubborn pride
should by this have eased your ache for speech, breath
and the other incidentals which distract us from our end.   15
Let us now walk a step. This noose
with which we're wed is something of an heirloom, the last three
members of our holy family were wed with it, the softwood beam
it hangs from like a lovers' tree notched with their weight.
See now I slip it over your neck, the knot   20
under the left jaw, with a slip ring
to hold the knot in place . . . There. Perfect.
Allow me to adjust the canvas hood
which will enable you to anticipate the officially prescribed darkness
by some seconds.   25
The journalists are ready with the flash-bulbs of their eyes
raised to the simple altar, the doctor twitches like a stethoscope
—you have been given a clean bill of health, like any
modern bride.
        With this spring of mine   30
from the trap, hitting the door lever, you will go forth
into a new life which I, alas, am not yet fit to share.
Be assured, you will sink into the generous pool of public feeling
as gently as a leaf—accept your role, feel chosen.
You are this evening's headlines. Come, my love.   35

                          [1968]

DEREK WALCOTT

[b. 1930]

Codicil

Schizophrenic, wrenched by two styles,
one a hack's hired prose, I earn
my exile. I trudge this sickle, moonlit beach for miles,

tan, burn
to slough off   5
this love of ocean that's self-love.

To change your language you must change your life.

I cannot right old wrongs.
Waves tire of horizon and return.
Gulls screech with rusty tongues   10

Above the beached, rotting pirogues,
they were a venomous beaked cloud at Charlotteville.

Once I thought love of country was enough,
now, even I chose, there's no room at the trough.

I watch the best minds root like dogs   15
for scraps of favour.
I am nearing middle-

age, burnt skin
peels from my hand like paper, onion-thin,
like Peer Gynt's riddle.   20

At heart there's nothing, not the dread
of death. I know too many dead.
They're all familiar, all in character,

even how they died. On fire,
the flesh no longer fears that furnace mouth   25
of earth,

that kiln or ashpit of the sun,
nor this clouding, unclouding sickle moon
whitening this beach again like a blank page.

All its indifference is a different rage.   30

[1965]

CODICIL   ¹²**Charlotteville**   a town on the island of Tobago, in the West Indies.   ²⁰**Peer Gynt's riddle**
Peer Gynt, a character in a play by Henrik Ibsen, compares the layers he peels from an onion to aspects of his
character, only to discover that there is nothing at the center

TED HUGHES

[b. 1930]

Hawk Roosting

I sit in the top of the wood, my eyes closed.
Inaction, no falsifying dream
Between my hooked head and hooked feet:
Or in sleep rehearse perfect kills and eat.

The convenience of the high trees!   5
The air's buoyancy and the sun's ray
Are of advantage to me;
And the earth's face upward for my inspection.

My feet are locked upon the rough bark.
It took the whole of Creation   10
To produce my foot, my each feather:
Now I hold Creation in my foot

Or fly up, and revolve it all slowly—
I kill where I please because it is all mine.
There is no sophistry in my body: 15
My manners are tearing off heads—

The allotment of death.
For the one path of my flight is direct
Through the bones of the living.
No arguments assert my right: 20

The sun is behind me.
Nothing has changed since I began.
My eye has permitted no change.
I am going to keep things like this.

[1957]

GARY SNYDER

[b. 1930]

Prayer for the Great Family

AFTER A MOHAWK PRAYER

Gratitude to Mother Earth, sailing through night and day—
    and to her soil: rich, rare, and sweet
        in our minds so be it.

Gratitude to Plants, the sun-facing light-changing leaf
    and fine root-hairs; standing still through wind   5
    and rain; their dance is in the flowing spiral grain
        in our minds so be it.

Gratitude to Air, bearing the soaring Swift and the silent
    Owl at dawn. Breath of our song
    clear spirit breeze   10
        in our minds so be it.

Gratitude to Wild Beings, our brothers, teaching secrets,
    freedoms, and ways; who share with us their milk;
    self-complete, brave, and aware
        in our minds so be it.   15

Gratitude to Water: clouds, lakes, rivers, glaciers;
    holding or releasing; streaming through all
    our bodies salty seas
        in our minds so be it.

Gratitude to the Sun: blinding pulsing light through   20
    trunks of trees, through mists, warming caves where
    bears and snakes sleep—he who wakes us—
        in our minds so be it.

Gratitude to the Great Sky
    who holds billions of stars—and goes yet beyond that—   25
    beyond all powers, and thoughts
    and yet is within us—
    Grandfather Space.
    The Mind is his Wife.

        so be it.   30

[1974]

SYLVIA PLATH

[1932–1963]

Sylvia Plath emerges out of a tradition older than Euripides, one that includes Baudelaire, Poe, Dostoyevsky, and Kafka, among others. Exploring the innermost reaches of the mind, Sylvia Plath wrote a lyric poetry of the psyche's often painful journey toward self-actualization. Notable for its combination of powerful imagery and intense vision, her poetry is fueled by extravagance, irony, and wonder.

Plath's poems describe the truth of horror. The "boot in the face" we encounter in "Daddy" is reminiscent of Orwell's "boot stamping on a human face—forever" transposed from political to human relationships. Her speaker lives the "truth" of her terrifying struggle as an awakening self out of the psychological prison of her father's demands: "Daddy, I've had to kill you." Through Plath's poem, the reader can experience the powerful and sometimes terrible forces at play in the human mind.

But Plath did more than just paint the truth of horror; she also painted the horror of truth. For Plath, the truth sometimes meant a world in which people are pressed with humiliating questions about rubber breasts and crotches, as in "The Applicant," and where a suicidal patient glows "Bright as a Nazi lampshade" before the professional indifference of her doctors, as in "Lady Lazarus." It is a world in which we sometimes rage, delirious, as in "Fever 103°," a world that chokes "the aged and the meek."

And yet Plath was too honest and perceptive a poet to limit herself to a world of dread and aversion. Her poetry also acknowledges that "Miracles occur," as she stated in "Black Rook in Rainy Weather." And there are moments of wonder, as in "Crossing the Water" where "Stars open among the lilies" in the "silence of astounded souls."

For Sylvia Plath the truth and difficulty of self-realization also entailed the arduous and frustrating process of finding himself as woman. Helen McNeil suggests that we accept Plath's validity on the subject of women's struggle because of the intensity and honesty with which she depicted the plight of women caught remorselessly between the expectations associated with traditional roles of wife and mother and the driving force of her own poetic vocation. In this regard, Plath's commanding voice is assertive and authoritative. As the mother of two children and the wife of an accomplished poet, she expressed the irony, resentment, and anguish of women attempting to live their own lives while struggling with predetermined roles. Plath dealt with these competing roles, moreover, not only in her poetry but also in her novel, *The Bell Jar*. In that work, the protagonist, Esther Greenwood, a thinly disguised version of Plath herself, remembers once being told that when she had children she would no longer want to write poems.

Born in Boston in 1932, Sylvia Plath has been the subject of intensive biographical scholarship. What we have come to know of her background as a child offers only a few subtle clues to her tragic later life. Her father, Otto Plath, was of German descent and worked as a professor of biology and German at Boston University. He published a scholarly treatise on bees (a subject the poet went on to pursue later in life) and seems to have been a quiet, academically ambitious man. Colleagues remember how vehemently Professor Plath hated his Calvinistic schooling in the Midwest and how he detested the Nazis in Germany. Nevertheless, he was considered an "authoritarian head of the house." Plath went out of her way at an early age to earn his approval and became a "model child," and he is cited as the "panzer man" in her poem "Daddy." He died in November 1940, when his daughter was eight. Plath's mother, Aurelia Schober, who was of Austrian descent, met her husband while she was his student working on a master's degree in English and German. Upon their marriage, Aurelia Plath seemed content to play the role of academic wife and homemaker. She is remembered by her neighbors as an urbane, congenial, hardworking woman.

Sifting though these images of normalcy, many biographical and psychological critics have attempted to find associations between Plath's poems and her subsequent life. But surely biographical data only hint at future events. While still in high school, Plath wrote in a letter, "I have erected in my mind an image of myself—idealistic and beautiful. Is not that image, free from blemish, the true self—the true perfection? Am I wrong when this image insinuates itself between me and the merciless mirror?" Three years later she attempted suicide.

In 1955 Sylvia Plath graduated from Smith College, where she had written an honors thesis on Dostoyevsky, and then went to England as a Fulbright scholar. In June 1956 she married the English poet Ted Hughes, with whom she had two children. However, their marriage began to disintegrate, and in October 1962, Plath wrote home to her mother, "I am fighting now, against hard odds and alone." On the morning of February 11, 1963, Sylvia Plath attempted suicide again and this time succeeded.

Because we know a considerable amount about her troubled life, and because Plath, like so many other poets, drew from her own experiences, some critics treat her poetry, especially her later poems, as "confessional," emphasizing their biographical revelations rather than considering them as works of art. Such a restricted reading robs her poetry of its uniqueness. Her early poetry in *The Colossus* is complex, formal, and often brilliantly orchestrated. Her later poetry in *Ariel* is more direct and intense. Like the paintings of Hieronymus Bosch, her distortions and exaggerations seem much like the startling images of nightmares. We approach her poems with the expectation that we will find in them not the logical order of rational thought, but an urgently insistent retelling of the necessities of our often terrifying lives.

Black Rook in Rainy Weather

On the stiff twig up there
Hunches a wet black rook
Arranging and rearranging its feathers in the rain.

I do not expect miracle
Or an accident   5

To set the sight on fire
In my eye, nor seek
Any more in the desultory weather some design,
But let spotted leaves fall as they fall,
Without ceremony, or portent   10

Although, I admit, I desire,
Occasionally, some backtalk
From the mute sky, I can't honestly complain:
A certain minor light may still
Leap incandescent   15

Out of kitchen table or chair
As if a celestial burning took
Possession of the most obtuse objects now and then—
Thus hallowing an interval
Otherwise inconsequent   20

By bestowing largesse, honor,
One might say love. At any rate, I now walk
Wary (for it could happen
Even in this dull, ruinous landscape); skeptical,
Yet politic; ignorant.   25

Of whatever angel may choose to flare
Suddenly at my elbow. I only know that a rook
Ordering its black feathers can so shine
As to seize my senses, haul
My eyelids up, and grant   30

A brief respite from fear
Of total neutrality. With luck,
Trekking stubborn through this season
Of fatigue, I shall
Patch together a content   35

Of sorts. Miracles occur,
if you care to call those spasmodic

Tricks of radiance miracles. The wait's begun again,
The long wait for the angel,
For that rare, random descent.   *40*

[1956, 1971]

The Colossus

I shall never get you put together entirely,
Pieced, glued, and properly jointed.
Mule-bray, pig-grunt and bawdy cackles
Proceed from your great lips.
It's worse than a barnyard.   *5*

Perhaps you consider yourself an oracle,
Mouthpiece of the dead, or of some god or other.
Thirty years now I have labored
To dredge the silt from your throat.
I am none the wiser.   *10*

Scaling little ladders with gluepots and pails of Lysol
I crawl like an ant in mourning
Over the weedy acres of your brow
To mend the immense skull-plates and clear
The bald, white tumuli of your eyes.   *15*

A blue sky out of the Oresteia
Arches above us. O father, all by yourself
You are pithy and historical as the Roman Forum.
I open my lunch on a hill of black cypress.
Your fluted bones and acanthine hair are littered   *20*

In their old anarchy to the horizon-line.
It would take more than a lightning-stroke
To create such a ruin.
Nights, I squat in the cornucopia
Of your left ear, out of the wind,   *25*

Counting the red stars and those of plum-color.
The sun rises under the pillar of your tongue.
My hours are married to shadow.
No longer do I listen for the scrape of a keel
On the blank stones of the landing.   *30*

[1960]

Elm

FOR RUTH FAINLIGHT

I know the bottom, she says. I know it with my great tap root:
It is what you fear.
I do not fear it: I have been there.

Is it the sea you hear in me,
Its dissatisfactions?   5
Or the voice of nothing, that was your madness?

Love is a shadow.
How you lie and cry after it.
Listen: these are its hooves: it has gone off, like a horse.

All night I shall gallop thus, impetuously,   10
Till your head is a stone, your pillow a little turf,
Echoing, echoing.

Or shall I bring you the sound of poisons?
This is rain now, this big hush.
And this is the fruit of it: tin-white, like arsenic.   15

I have suffered the atrocity of sunsets.
Scorched to the root
My red filaments burn and stand, a hand of wires.

Now I break up in pieces that fly about like clubs.
A wind of such violence   20
Will tolerate no bystanding: I must shriek.

The moon, also, is merciless: she would drag me
Cruelly, being barren.
Her radiance scathes me. Or perhaps I have caught her.

I let her go. I let her go   25
Diminished and flat, as after radical surgery.
How your bad dreams possess and endow me.

I am inhabited by a cry.
Nightly it flaps out
Looking, with its hooks, for something to love.   30

I am terrified by this dark thing
That sleeps in me;
All day I feel its soft, feathery turnings, its malignity.

Clouds pass and disperse.
Are those the faces of love, those pale irretrievables?   35
Is it for such I agitate my heart?

I am incapable of more knowledge.
What is this, this face
So murderous in its strangle of branches?—

Its snaky acids kiss.   40
It petrifies the will. These are the isolate, slow faults
That kill, that kill, that kill.

                                                                    [1960]

Daddy

You do not do, you do not do
Any more, black shoe
In which I have lived like a foot
For thirty years, poor and white,
Barely daring to breathe or Achoo.   5

Daddy, I have had to kill you.
You died before I had time—
Marble-heavy, a bag full of God,
Ghastly statue with one grey toe
Big as a Frisco seal   10

And a head in the freakish Atlantic
Where it pours bean green over blue
In the waters off beautiful Nauset.
I used to pray to recover you.
Ach, du.   15

In the German tongue, in the Polish town
Scraped flat by the roller

DADDY   ¹³**Nauset** a beach north of Boston.   ¹⁵**Ach, du** German for "ah, you," a reference to Plath's
father.

Of wars, wars, wars.
But the name of the town is common.
My Polack friend   20

Says there are a dozen or two.
So I never could tell where you
Put your foot, your root,
I never could talk to you.
The tongue stuck in my jaw.   25

It stuck in a barb wire snare.
Ich, ich, ich, ich,
I could hardly speak.
I thought every German was you.
And the language obscene   30

An engine, an engine
Chuffing me off like a Jew.
A Jew to Dachau, Auschwitz, Belsen.
I began to talk like a Jew.
I think I may well be a Jew.   35

The snows of the Tyrol, the clear beer of Vienna
Are not very pure or true.
With my gypsy ancestress and my weird luck
And my Taroc pack and my Taroc pack
I may be a bit of a Jew.   40

I have always been scared of *you,*
With your Luftwaffe, your gobbledygoo.
And your neat moustache
And your Aryan eye, bright blue.
Panzer-man, panzer-man, O You—

Not God but a swastika
So black no sky could squeak through.
Every woman adores a Fascist,
The boot in the face, the brute
Brute heart of a brute like you.   50

---

[27]**Ich** German for "I."   [33]**Dachau, Auschwitz, Belsen** German concentration camps where millions of Jews were murdered during World War II.   [36]**Tyrol** in the Austrian Alps.   [39]**Taroc** tarot cards, used in fortunetelling.   [42]**Luftwaffe** German air force in World War II.   [45]**Panzer** German for "armor." "Panzer-man" is a reference to Hitler.

You stand at the blackboard, daddy,
In the picture I have of you,
A cleft in your chin instead of your foot
But no less a devil for that, no not
Any less the black man who   55

Bit my pretty red heart in two.
I was ten when they buried you.
At twenty I tried to die
And get back, back, back to you.
I thought even the bones would do.   60

But they pulled me out of the sack,
And they stuck me together with glue.
And then I knew what to do.
I made a model of you,
A man in black with a Meinkampf look   65

And a love of the rack and the screw.
And I said I do, I do.
So daddy, I'm finally through.
The black telephone's off at the root,
The voices just can't worm through.   70

If I've killed one man, I've killed two—
The vampire who said he was you
And drank my blood for a year,
Seven years, if you want to know.
Daddy, you can lie back now.   75

There's a stake in your fat black heart
And the villagers never liked you.
They are dancing and stamping on you.
They always *knew* it was you.
Daddy, daddy, you bastard, I'm through.   80

[1960]

Morning Song

Love set you going like a fat gold watch.
The midwife slapped your footsoles, and your bald cry
Took its place among the elements.

Our voices echo, magnifying your arrival. New statue.
In a drafty museum, your nakedness   5
Shadows our safety. We stand round blankly as walls.

I'm no more your mother
Than the cloud that distills a mirror to reflect its own slow
Effacement at the wind's hand.

All night your moth-breath   10
Flickers among the flat pink roses. I wake to listen:
A far sea moves in my ear.

One cry, and I stumble from bed, cow-heavy and floral
In my Victorian nightgown.
Your mouth opens clean as a cat's. The window square   15

Whitens and swallows its dull stars. And now you try
Your handful of notes;
The clear vowels rise like balloons.

                                                            [1961]

Edge

The woman is perfected.
Her dead

Body wears the smile of accomplishment,
The illusion of a Greek necessity

Flows in the scrolls of her toga,   5
Her bare

Feet seem to be saying:
We have come so far, it is over.

Each dead child coiled, a white serpent,
One at each little   10

Pitcher of milk, now empty.
She has folded

Them back into her body as petals
Of a rose close when the garden

Stiffens and odors bleed   15
From the sweet, deep throats of the night flower.

The moon has nothing to be sad about,
Staring from her hood of bone.

She is used to this sort of thing.
Her blacks crackle and drag.   20

[1965]

Words

Axes
After whose stroke the wood rings,
And the echoes!
Echoes travelling
Off from the center like horses.   5

The sap
Wells like tears, like the
Water striving
To re-establish its mirror
Over the rock   10

That drops and turns,
A white skull,
Eaten by weedy greens.
Years later I
Encounter them on the road—   15

Words dry and riderless,
The indefatigable hoof-taps.
While
From the bottom of the pool, fixed stars
Govern a life.   20

[1965]

The Applicant

First, are you our sort of a person?
Do you wear
A glass eye, false teeth or a crutch,
A brace or a hook,
Rubber breasts or a rubber crotch,   5

Stitches to show something's missing? No, no? Then
How can we give you a thing?
Stop crying.
Open your hand.
Empty? Empty. Here is a hand   10

To fill it and willing
To bring teacups and roll away headaches
And do whatever you tell it.
Will you marry it?
It is guaranteed   15

To thumb shut your eyes at the end
And dissolve of sorrow.
We make new stock from the salt.
I notice you are stark naked.
How about this suit—   20

Black and stiff, but not a bad fit.
Will you marry it?
It is waterproof, shatterproof, proof
Against fire and bombs through the roof.
Believe me, they'll bury you in it.   25

Now your head, excuse me, is empty.
I have the ticket for that.
Come here, sweetie, out of the closet.
Well, what do you think of *that*?
Naked as paper to start   30

But in twenty-five years she'll be silver,
In fifty, gold.
A living doll, everywhere you look.
It can sew, it can cook,
It can talk, talk, talk.   35

It works, there is nothing wrong with it.
You have a hole, it's a poultice.
You have an eye, it's an image.
My boy, it's your last resort.
Will you marry it, marry it, marry it.   *40*

                                                          [1966]

Lady Lazarus

I have done it again.
One year in every ten
I manage it—

A sort of walking miracle, my skin
Bright as a Nazi lampshade,   *5*
My right foot

A paperweight,
My face a featureless, fine
Jew linen.

Peel off the napkin   *10*
O my enemy.
Do I terrify?—

The nose, the eye pits, the full set of teeth?
The sour breath
Will vanish in a day.   *15*

Soon, soon the flesh
The grave cave ate will be
At home on me

And I a smiling woman.
I am only thirty.   *20*
And like the cat I have nine times to die.

This is Number Three.
What a trash
To annihilate each decade.

LADY LAZARUS   Lazarus was raised from the dead by Jesus (see John 11:1–45).   **⁵Nazi lampshade** the
skin of some Jewish victims of the Holocaust was made into lampshades.

What a million filaments.　　　　　　　　　　　　25
The peanut-crunching crowd
Shoves in to see

Them unwrap me hand and foot—
The big strip tease.
Gentlemen, ladies,　　　　　　　　　　　　　　30

These are my hands,
My knees.
I may be skin and bone,

Nevertheless, I am the same, identical woman.
The first time it happened I was ten.　　　　　　35
It was an accident.

The second time I meant
To last it out and not come back at all.
I rocked shut

As a seashell.　　　　　　　　　　　　　　　　40
They had to call and call
And pick the worms off me like sticky pearls.

Dying
Is an art, like everything else.
I do it exceptionally well.　　　　　　　　　　　45

I do it so it feels like hell.
I do it so it feels real.
I guess you could say I've a call.

It's easy enough to do it in a cell.
It's easy enough to do it and stay put.　　　　　50
It's the theatrical

Comeback in broad day
To the same place, the same face, the same brute
Amused shout:

"A miracle!"　　　　　　　　　　　　　　　　　55
That knocks me out.
There is a charge

For the eyeing of my scars, there is a charge
For the hearing of my heart—
It really goes.　　　　　　　　　　　　　　　　60

And there is a charge, a very large charge,
For a word or a touch
Or a bit of blood

Or a piece of my hair or my clothes.
So, so, Herr Doktor.   65
So, Herr Enemy.

I am your opus,
I am your valuable,
The pure gold baby

That melts to a shriek.   70
I turn and burn.
Do not think I underestimate your great concern.

Ash, ash—
You poke and stir.
Flesh, bone, there is nothing there—   75

A cake of soap,
A wedding ring,
A gold filling.

Herr God, Herr Lucifer,
Beware.   80
Beware.

Out of the ash
I rise with my red hair
And I eat men like air.

                                                                   [1966]

Fever 103°

Pure? What does it mean?
The tongues of hell
Are dull, dull as the triple

LADY LAZARUS   ⁶⁵Herr   German for "Mister."

Tongues of dull, fat Cerberus
Who wheezes at the gate. Incapable   5
Of licking clean

The aguey tendon, the sin, the sin.
The tinder cries.
The indelible smell

Of a snuffed candle!   10
Love, love, the low smokes roll
From me like Isadora's scarves, I'm in a fright

One scarf will catch and anchor in the wheel.
Such yellow sullen smokes
Make their own element. They will not rise,   15

But trundle round the globe
Choking the aged and the meek,
The weak

Hothouse baby in its crib,
The ghastly orchid   20
Hanging its hanging garden in the air,

Devilish leopard!
Radiation turned it white
And killed it in an hour.

Greasing the bodies of adulterers   25
Like Hiroshima ash and eating in.
The sin. The sin.

Darling, all night
I have been flickering, off, on, off, on.
The sheets grow heavy as a lecher's kiss.   30

Three days. Three nights.
Lemon water, chicken
Water, water make me retch.

FEVER 103°   **⁴Cerberus** in Greek mythology, the three-headed dog that guarded the gate to the Under-world. He also guards the gate of hell in Dante's *Inferno.*   ¹²⁻¹³**like Isadora's scarves . . . in the wheel** Isadora Duncan (1878–1927), dancer who was strangled when her long scarf caught in the wheel of her car.

I am too pure for you or anyone.
Your body   35
Hurts me as the world hurts God. I am a lantern—

My head a moon
Of Japanese paper, my gold beaten skin
Infinitely delicate and infinitely expensive.

Does not my heat astound you. And my light.   40
All by myself I am a huge camellia
Glowing and coming and going, flush on flush.

I think I am going up,
I think I may rise—
The beads of hot metal fly, and I, love, I   45

Am a pure acetylene
Virgin
Attended by roses,

By kisses, by cherubim,
By whatever these pink things mean.   50
Not you, nor him

Not him, nor him
(My selves dissolving, old whore petticoats)—
To Paradise.

                                                                    [1966]

Crossing the Water

Black lake, black boat, two black, tut-paper people.
Where do the black trees go that drink here?
Their shadows must cover Canada.

A little light is filtering from the water flowers.
Their leaves do not wish us to hurry: 5
They are round and flat and full of dark advice.

Cold worlds shake from the oar.
The spirit of blackness is in us, it is in the fishes.
A snag is lifting a valedictory, pale hand;

Stars open among the lilies.   *10*
Are you not blinded by such expressionless sirens?
This is the silence of astounded souls.

[1971]

PETER MEINKE

[b. 1932]

Advice to My Son

The trick is, to live your days
as if each one may be your last
(for they go fast, and young men lose their lives
in strange and unimaginable ways)
but at the same time, plan long range   *5*
(for they go slow: if you survive
the shattered windshield and the bursting shell
you will arrive
at our approximation here below
of heaven or hell).   *10*

To be specific, between the peony and the rose
plant squash and spinach, turnips and tomatoes;
beauty is nectar
and nectar, in a desert, saves—
but the stomach craves stronger sustenance   *15*
than the honied vine.

Therefore, marry a pretty girl
after seeing her mother;
show your soul to one man,
work with another;   *20*
and always serve bread with your wine.

But, son,
always serve wine.

[1981]

SANDRA SCHOR

[1932–1990]

At Point Hope on the Chukchi Sea

Senator Buckley admired the clear roles of men and women there. "Better than receiving welfare," he stated.

Eskimo girls
play hopscotch
on the ice,
the lines and squares
etched near   5
the edge of it
in sight of men
harpooning creatures
never hunted by
a woman.   10

Deep in the ice
the men lock the whale
hooked and butchered into
steaks, skin, blubber
enough to feed   15
a village for a year.
The women clean the blades
and far into the night,
over the fires they tend,
bend the iron rods.   20

Atop the ice
a sentry of birds in fur
takes the morning off
and happy men go down in sleds;
they trade oil and furs,   25
and toast a distant fair
in wirephotos.

But at the edge
the ice has voices.

The shoreline shifts   *30*
and campsites of women
keep on working,
for a footing if nothing else,
toes curled from infancies of hopscotch
against premonitions   *35*
of a slide.

[1993]

JOHN UPDIKE

[b. 1932]

The Mosquito

On the fine wire of her whine she walked,
Unseen in the ominous bedroom dark.
A traitor to her camouflage, she talked
A thirsty blue streak distinct as a spark.

I was to her a fragrant lake of blood   *5*
From which she had to sip a drop or die.
A reservoir, a lavish field of food,
I lay awake, unconscious of my size.

We seemed fair-matched opponents. Soft she dropped
Down like an anchor on her thread of song.   *10*
Her nose sank thankfully in; then I slapped
At the sting on my arm, cunning and strong.

A cunning, strong Gargantua, I struck
This lover pinned in the feast of my flesh,
Lulled by my blood, relaxed, half-sated, stuck   *15*
Engrossed in the gross rivers of myself.

Success! Without a cry the creature died,
Became a fleck of fluff upon the sheet.
The small welt of remorse subsides as side
By side we, murderer and murdered, sleep.   *20*

[1960]

ROBERT WALLACE

[b. 1932]

The Double-Play

In his sea lit
distance, the pitcher winding
like a clock about to chime comes down with

the ball, hit
sharply, under the artificial   5
banks of arc-lights, bounds like a vanishing string

over the green
to the shortstop magically
scoops to his right whirling above his invisible

shadows   10
in the dust redirects
its flight to the running poised second baseman

pirouettes
leaping, above the slide, to throw
from mid-air, across the colored tightened interval,   15

to the leaning-
out first baseman ends the dance
drawing it disappearing into his long brown glove

stretches. What
is too swift for deception   20
is final, lost, among the loosened figures

jogging off the field
(the pitcher walks), casual
in the space where the poem has happened.

[1965]

IMAMU AMIRI BARAKA

[b. 1934]

Preface to a Twenty Volume Suicide Note

FOR KELLIE JONES, BORN 16 MAY 1959

Lately, I've become accustomed to the way
The ground opens up and envelopes me
Each time I go out to walk the dog.
Or the broad edged silly music the wind
Makes when I run for a bus . . .   5

Things have come to that.

And now, each night I count the stars,
And each night I get the same number.
And when they will not come to be counted,
I count the holes they leave.   10

Nobody sings anymore.

And then last night I tiptoed up
To my daughter's room and heard her
Talking to someone, and when I opened
The door, there was no one there . . .   15
Only she on her knees, peeking into

Her own clasped hands.

[1961]

AUDRE LORDE

[b. 1934]

Now That I Am Forever with Child

How the days went
while you were blooming within me
I remember each upon each—

the swelling changed planes of my body
and how you first fluttered, then jumped   5
and I thought it was my heart.

How the days wound down
and the turning of winter
I recall, with you growing heavy
against the wind. I thought   10
now her hands
are formed, and her hair
has started to curl
now her teeth are done
now she sneezes.   15
Then the seed opened
I bore you one morning just before spring
My head rang like a fiery piston
my legs were towers between which
A new world was passing.   20

Since then
I can only distinguish
one thread within running hours
You, flowing through selves
toward You.   25

[1963]

MARY OLIVER

[b. 1934]

Poem for My Father's Ghost

Now is my father
A traveler, like all the bold men
He talked of, endlessly
And with boundless admiration,
Over the supper table,   5
Or gazing up from his white pillow—
Book on his lap always, until
Even that grew too heavy to hold.

Now is my father free of all binding fevers.
Now is my father   10
Traveling where there is no road.

Finally, he could not lift a hand
To cover his eyes.
Now he climbs to the eye of the river,
He strides through the Dakotas,   15
He disappears into the mountains. And though he looks
Cold and hungry as any man
At the end of a questing season,

He is one of *them* now:
He cannot be stopped.   20
Now is my father
Walking the wind,
Sniffing the deep Pacific
That begins at the end of the world.

Vanished from us utterly,   25
Now is my father circling the deepest forest—
Then turning in to the last red campfire burning
In the final hills,

Where chieftains, warriors and heroes
Rise and make him welcome,   30
Recognizing, under the shambles of his body,
A brother who has walked his thousand miles.

                                                                   [1976]

MARK STRAND

[b. 1934]

Eating Poetry

Ink runs from the corners of my mouth.
There is no happiness like mine.
I have been eating poetry.

The librarian does not believe what she sees.
Her eyes are sad   5
and she walks with her hands in her dress.

The poems are gone.
The light is dim.
The dogs are on the basement stairs and coming up.

Their eyeballs roll,   10
their blond legs burn like brush.
The poor librarian begins to stamp her feet and weep.

She does not understand.
When I get on my knees and lick her hand,
she screams.   15

I am a new man.
I snarl at her and bark.
I romp with joy in the bookish dark.

[1968]

Leopardi

The night is warm and clear and without wind.
The stone-white moon waits above the rooftops
and above the nearby river. Every street is still
and the corner lights shine down only upon the hunched shapes of cars.
You are asleep. And sleep gathers in your room   5
and nothing at this moment bothers you. Jules,
an old wound has opened and I feel the pain of it again.
While you sleep I have gone outside to pay my late respects
to the sky that seems so gentle
and to the world that is not and that says to me: 10
"I do not give you any hope. Not even hope."
Down the street there is the voice of a drunk
singing an unrecognizable song
and a car a few blocks off.
Things pass and leave no trace,   15
and tomorrow will come and the day after,
and whatever our ancestors knew time has taken away.

LEOPARDI   Giacomo Leopardi, Italian poet (1798–1837). See pp. 1057–1058.

They are gone and their children are gone
and the great nations are gone.
And the armies are gone that sent clouds of dust and smoke   *20*
rolling across Europe. The world is still and we do not hear them.
Once when I was a boy, and the birthday I had waited for
was over, I lay on my bed, awake and miserable, and very late
that night the sound of someone's voice singing down a side street,
dying little by little into the distance,   *25*
wounded me, as this does now.

[1980]

LUCILLE CLIFTON

[b. 1936]

Homage to My Hips

these hips are big hips.
they need space to
move around in.
they don't fit into little
pretty places. these hips   *5*
are free hips.
they don't like to be held back.
these hips have never been enslaved,
they go where they want to go
they do what they want to do.   *10*
these hips are mighty hips.
these hips are magic hips.
i have known them
to put a spell on a man and
spin him like a top!   *15*

[1972]

The Lost Baby Poem

the time i dropped your almost body down
down to meet the waters under the city
and run one with the sewage to the sea

what did i know about waters rushing back
what did i know about drowning   5
or being drowned

you would have been born into winter
in the year of the disconnected gas
and no car   we would have made the thin
walk over Genesee hill into the Canada wind   10
to watch you slip like ice into strangers' hands
you would have fallen naked as snow into winter
if you were here i could tell you these
and some other things

if i am ever less than a mountain   15
for your definite brothers and sisters
let the rivers pour over my head
let the sea take me for a spiller
of seas   let black men call me stranger
always   for your never named sake   20

[1972]

KATHLEEN FRASER

[b. 1937]

Poem in Which My Legs Are Accepted

Legs!
How we have suffered each other,
never meeting the standards of magazines
                        or official measurements.

I have hung you from trapezes,   5
        sat you on wooden rollers,
            pulled and pushed you
                            with the anxiety of taffy,
and still, you are yourselves!

Most obvious imperfection, blight on my fantasy life,   10
strong,
plump,

never to be skinny
or even hinting of the svelte beauties in history books
                                             or Sears catalogues.   *15*
Here you are—solid, fleshy and
white as when I first noticed you, sitting on the toilet,
                                             spread softly over the wooden seat,
having been with me only twelve years,
                                             yet   *20*
as obvious as the legs of my thirty-year-old gym teacher.

Legs!
O that was the year we did acrobatics in the annual gym show.
How you split for me!
                       One-handed cartwheels   *25*
                       from this end of the gymnasium to the other,
                       ending in double splits,
legs you flashed in blue rayon slacks my mother bought for the occasion
and tho you were confidently swinging along,
the rest of me blushed at the sound of clapping.   *30*

Legs!
How I have worried about you, not able to hide you,
embarrassed at beaches, in highschool
                       when the cheerleaders' slim brown legs
                                             spread all over   *35*
                                             the sand
                                             with the perfection
                                             of bamboo.

I hated you, and still you have never given out on me.

With you   *40*
I have risen to the top of blue waves,
with you
I have carried food home as a loving gift
                                             when my arms began
                                             unjelling like madrilene.   *45*
Legs, you are a pillow,
white and plentiful with feathers for his wild head.
You are the endless scenery
behind the tense sinewy elegance of his two dark legs.
You welcome him joyfully   *45*
and dance.

And you will be the locks in a new canal between continents.
                    The ship of life will push out of you
                and rejoice
                              in the whiteness,   *50*
                              in the first floating and rising of water.

                                                                  [1966]

D I A N E   W A K O S K I

[b. 1937]

Belly Dancer

Can these movements which move themselves
be the substance of my attraction?
Where does this thin green silk come from that covers my body?
Surely any woman wearing such fabrics
would move her body just to feel them touching every part of her.   *5*

Yet most of the women frown, or look away, or laugh stiffly.
They are afraid of these materials and these movements in some way.
The psychologists would say they are afraid of themselves, somehow.
Perhaps awakening too much desire—   *10*
that their men could never satisfy?

So they keep themselves laced and buttoned and made up
in hopes that the framework will keep them stiff enough not to feel
the whole register.
In hopes that they will not have to experience that unquenchable desire
for rhythm and contact.   *15*

If a snake glided across this floor
most of them would faint or shrink away.
Yet that movement could be their own.
That smooth movement frightens them—
awakening ancestors and relatives to the tips of the arms and toes.   *20*

So my bare feet
and my thin green silks
my bells and finger cymbals

offend them—frighten their old-young bodies.
While the men simper and leer—   25
glad for the vicarious experience and exercise.
They do not realize how I scorn them:
or how I dance for their frightened,
unawakened, sweet
women.   30

[1966]

MICHAEL S. HARPER

[b. 1938]

American History

FOR JOHN CALLAHAN

Those four black girls blown up
in that Alabama church
remind me of five hundred
middle passage blacks,
in a net, under water   5
in Charleston harbor
so *redcoats* wouldn't find them.
Can't find what you can't see
can you?

[1970]

CHARLES SIMIC

[b. 1938]

Stone

Go inside a stone
That would be my way.
Let somebody else become a dove

Or gnash with a tiger's tooth.
I am happy to be a stone.   5

From the outside the stone is a riddle:
No one knows how to answer it.
Yet within, it must be cool and quiet
Even though a cow steps on it full weight,
Even though a child throws it in a river;   10
The stone sinks, slow, unperturbed
To the river bottom
Where the fishes come to knock on it
And listen.

I have seen sparks fly out   15
When two stones are rubbed,
So perhaps it is not dark inside after all;
Perhaps there is a moon shining
From somewhere, as though behind a hill—
Just enough light to make out   20
The strange writings, the star-charts
On the inner walls.

[1971]

JAMES TYACK

[b. 1938]

For Neruda

I am entering this poem in a contest
& thought it should echo your voice,
reflect your tears like black grapes
catch light & hurl it back at the moon.
I want this poem to ring like   5
a grain of sun in the night,
have it hover & float as hazardous
as a moth beneath the beak of a bird,
but I know that's not possible.
Someone who knew you says you're not dead,

NERUDA   Pable Neruda (1904–1973) Chilean poet who won the Nobel prize for literature in 1971 See pp.
1095–1097.

but alive in Moscow inspiring ballerinas
with your tongue & I know this is true.
Whether I win this contest or not
I'll send woolen gloves to you there &
hope in the deepest of winter you are warm.   *15*

                                                              [1976]

MARGARET ATWOOD

[b. 1939]

Spelling

My daughter plays on the floor
with plastic letters,
red, blue & hard yellow,

learning how to spell,
spelling,   *5*
how to make spells.

                          •

I wonder how many women
denied themselves daughters,
closed themselves in rooms,
drew the curtains   *10*
so they could mainline words.

                          •

A child is not a poem,
a poem is not a child.
There is no either / or.
However.   *15*

                          •

I return to the story
of the woman caught in the war
& in labour, her thighs tied
together by the enemy
so she could not give birth.   *20*

Ancestress: the burning witch,
her mouth covered by leather
to strangle words.

A word after a word
after a word is power.   *25*

•

At the point where language falls away
from the hot bones, at the point
where the rock breaks open and darkness
flows out of it like blood, at
the melting point of granite   *30*
when the bones know
they are hollow & the word
splits & doubles & speaks
the truth & the body
itself becomes a mouth.   *35*

This is a metaphor.

•

How do you learn to spell?
Blood, sky & the sun,
your own name first,
your first naming, your first name,   *40*
your first word.

                                                             [1981]

RAYMOND CARVER

[1939–1988]

Late Fragment

And did you get what
you wanted from this life, even so?
I did.
And what did you want?
To call myself beloved, to feel myself   *5*
beloved on the earth.

                                                             [1988]

SEAMUS HEANEY

[b. 1939]

Like his great poetic predecessor William Butler Yeats, Seamus Heaney writes out of a rich Irish literary and folk tradition. It is a tradition that informs much of Heaney's work, and one to which he ascribes both his inspiration and his identity. Yet, though Irish history and legend, along with Ireland's land and people, animate Heaney's poetry, especially his early work, Heaney's devotion to his country's poetic tradition coexists with his participation in the tradition of English literature. Heaney himself has acknowledged his debt to both English and Irish literature. "I studied the Gaelic literature of Ireland," he has remarked, "as well as the literature of England, and since then I have maintained a notion of myself as Irish in a province that insists that it is British." And though this remark emphasizes Heaney's Irishness, Heaney voices his cultural identity by writing poems in English, poems that take their place as part of the tradition of English literature. Heaney, moreover, writes out of a literary tradition that links his poetry with that of William Wordsworth and John Keats in England and Robert Frost in America, as well as W. B. Yeats and Patrick Kavanaugh in his native Ireland.

Seamus Heaney was born in County Derry, Northern Ireland. He grew up there, attending Queens University in Belfast, from which he graduated with a B.A. He subsequently moved to the Dublin area, where he lives with his family. Since the early 1970s Heaney has been teaching in the United States part of the year. For the past dozen years he has been teaching during the spring term at Harvard University, where he is Boylston Professor of Rhetoric and Oratory. A celebrated member of the Irish Academy of Letters, in 1990 Heaney was appointed Professor of Poetry at Oxford University.

Including his first collection of poetry, *Death of a Naturalist* (1966), Heaney has published thirteen books—nine volumes of poems, two volumes of selected poems, and two collections of prose, *Preoccupations* (1978) and *The Government of the Tongue* (1987). Heaney's prose is instructive for what it reveals about his own poetry, not so much for his comments on particular poems but for his general approach to poetic art. Heaney's comments on Wordsworth and Hopkins, for example, illuminate his own poetic theory. So too do his more general remarks about writing poetry, such as his observation that poems are " 'made things,' self-delighting buds on the old bough of a tradition"; and his further observation that poems arise out of "impulses towards the satisfaction of aural and formal play." Comments like these suggest it is to Heaney's language and formal experimentation that we should look for an appreciation of his poetic accomplishment.

Heaney's earliest published poems are rooted in the life of rural Ireland. They spring from recollections of his boyhood on the family farm and are characterized by sharpness of detail and immediacy of image. The language of the early poems is alternately ornate and austere. In fact, Heaney's early poems lean in the direction of a lyrical intensity that he has consistently scaled back and chastened in his latest work.

The crisp, brisk diction of "Digging" is matched by the profuse copiousness of "Death of a Naturalist." These two impulses—toward luxuriousness and astringency—coexist harmoniously in Heaney's poetic oeuvre, lending it a variety amply revealed within his experimental linguistic versatility.

Heaney can write with the sensuous lushness of a Keats or the less adorned, more meditative reflectiveness of a Wordsworth. But whether he works in one mode or the other, Heaney's poetry consistently possesses an understated music that is a pleasure to hear. Even in the less ornate poems, which populate Heaney's work from 1975 on, we can hear a clear, lively music. Here, for example, is the opening of "Punishment," a poem inspired by the bog people, whose exhumed bodies Heaney saw in Denmark and read about in a book by the Danish archeologist P. V. Glob:

> I can feel the tug
> of the halter at the nape
> of her neck, the wind
> on her naked front.
>
> It blows her nipples
> to amber beads,
> it shakes the frail rigging
> of her ribs.
>
> I can see her drowned
> body in the bog,
> the weighing stone,
> the floating rods and boughs.

The short lines and the parallel grammatical structuring contribute to the sound effects of these lines. But their music is achieved more pronouncedly by echoes of assonance and alliteration. Moreover, these devices don't call as much attention to themselves as they do in a poem like "Death of a Naturalist," from Heaney's first book. In addition, Heaney varies his sound effects in virtuosic and risky ways by giving voice in the bog poems to the long-dead and -preserved figures themselves. In "Bog Queen," for example, the exhumed speaker tells her own story.

> I knew winter cold
> like the nuzzle of fjords
> at my thighs—
>
> the soaked fledge, the heavy
> swaddle of hides.
> My skull hibernated
> in the wet nest of my hair.

And in another bog poem, "The Grauballe Man," Heaney addresses his readers with questions while startling them with images.

Who will say "corpse"
to his vivid cast?
Who will say "body"
to his opaque repose?

And his rusted hair,
a mat unlikely
as a foetus's.
I first saw his twisted face

in a photograph,
a head and shoulder
out of the peat,
bruised like a forceps baby

The bog poems provide something of a way station, a balancing point in Heaney's poetic development. Before their publication in *North* (1975), Heaney's poetry had largely been located in the near past of his boyhood memories. The bog people took Heaney further back into the past and paradoxically much closer to the present as well. For Heaney used the images of the discovered dead to reflect on the contemporary Irish political situation, with bodies blown up for historical reasons of religious and ideological difference. (A poem like "Casualty," from Heaney's 1979 volume, *Field Work,* refers specifically to a contemporary political event—the murder of his cousin.) Moreover, the bog itself, as Robert F. Garratt has suggested, served Heaney as symbol of the rich loam of language, as an emblem of the unconscious, and as a hoard of history.

Throughout his poetic career, Heaney has continued to refashion himself, somewhat in the manner of Yeats (though Heaney has drawn literary inspiration less from Yeats, with his many masks and voices, than from the novelist James Joyce, who insisted on making a transcendent literature out of the local particulars of everyday Dublin life). Heaney has remarked that repeating himself for too long would be a poetic dead end, and he has suggested instead that "if you have managed to do one kind of poem in your own way, you should cast off that way and face into another area of your experience until you have learned a new voice." This Heaney has done with remarkable energy and virtuosity for a quarter century.

Two of his later volumes, *Station Island* (1984) and *Seeing Things* (1991), provide evidence that Heaney is continuing his versatile casting and gathering. *Seeing Things,* for example, includes poems that describe various marvels and apparitions. Our selection from this book reveals Heaney's ability to combine the legendary with the momentous, taking a simple story and, by inverting its terms, making it into something wondrous. Framing the marvels and apparitions that form the meat of the book are translations from Virgil and Dante, with Dante serving as Heaney's mentor, much as Dante made Virgil his own mentor in the *Commedia. Station Island* includes a long narrative poem in twelve assymetrical parts, four of them composed in variants of Dantean *terza rima.* This extended meditative monologue, moreover, reviews various stages of the poet–speaker's life by giving voice to a dozen ghosts

who inhabit the poem and who offer the speaker various admonitions. The most
striking of these is the ghost of James Joyce, who speaks these words in the poem's
final section:

"The main thing is to write
for the joy of it. Cultivate a work-lust
that imagines its haven like your hands at night

dreaming the sun in the sunspot of a breast.
You are fasted now, light-headed, dangerous.
Take off from here. And don't be so earnest,

so ready for the sackcloth and the ashes.
Let go, let fly, forget.
You've listened long enough. Now strike your note."

The advice of Joyce's ghost frees the poet–speaker of "Station Island" to find
what Heaney has called the "binding secret" of words that create, in Helen Ven-
dler's lovely formulation, "the intellectual and emotional consent between two
words . . . that rises from an arduous cooperation of mind and feeling and ear." This
blend of intellect and emotion, body and soul, voice and vision, makes Heaney's
poetry a rich harvest for contemporary readers.

Digging

Between my finger and my thumb
The squat pen rests; snug as a gun.

Under my window, a clean rasping sound
When the spade sinks into gravelly ground:
My father, digging. I look down   5

Till his straining rump among the flowerbeds
Bends low, comes up twenty years away
Stooping in rhythm through potato drills
Where he was digging.

The coarse boot nestled on the lug, the shaft   10
Against the inside knee was levered firmly.
He rooted out tall tops, buried the bright edge deep
To scatter new potatoes that we picked
Loving their cool hardness in our hands.

By God, the old man could handle a spade.   *15*
Just like his old man.

My grandfather cut more turf in a day
Than any other man on Toner's bog.
Once I carried him milk in a bottle
Corked sloppily with paper. He straightened up   *20*
To drink it, then fell to right away
Nicking and slicing neatly, heaving sods
Over his shoulder, going down and down
For the good turf. Digging.

The cold smell of potato mould, the squelch and slap   *25*
Of soggy peat, the curt cuts of an edge
Through living roots awaken in my head.
But I've no spade to follow men like them.

Between my finger and my thumb
The squat pen rests.   *30*
I'll dig with it.

[1966]

Mid-Term Break

I sat all morning in the college sick bay
Counting bells knelling classes to a close.
At two o'clock our neighbours drove me home.

In the porch I met my father crying—
He had always taken funerals in his stride—   *5*
And Big Jim Evans saying it was a hard blow.

The baby cooed and laughed and rocked the pram
When I came in, and I was embarrassed
By old men standing up to shake my hand

And tell me they were "sorry for my trouble."   *10*
Whispers informed strangers I was the eldest,
Away at school, as my mother held my hand

In hers and coughed out angry tearless sighs.
At ten o'clock the ambulance arrived
With the corpse, stanched and bandaged by the nurses.   *15*

Next morning I went up into the room. Snowdrops
And candles soothed the bedside; I saw him
For the first time in six weeks. Paler now,

Wearing a poppy bruise on his left temple,
He lay in the four-foot box as in his cot.
No gaudy scars, the bumper knocked him clear.

A four-foot box, a foot for every year.

[1966]

Death of a Naturalist

All year the flax-dam festered in the heart
Of the townland; green and heavy-headed
Flax had rotted there, weighted down by huge sods.
Daily it sweltered in the punishing sun.
Bubbles gargled delicately, bluebottles   *5*
Wove a strong gauze of sound around the smell.
There were dragonflies, spotted butterflies,
But best of all was the warm thick slobber
Of frogspawn that grew like clotted water
In the shade of the banks. Here, every spring   *10*
I would fill jampotfuls of the jellied
Specks to range on window-sills at home,
On shelves at school, and wait and watch until
The fattening dots burst into nimble-
Swimming tadpoles. Miss Walls would tell us how   *15*
The daddy frog was called a bullfrog
And how he croaked and how the mammy frog
Laid hundreds of little eggs and this was
Frogspawn. You could tell the weather by frogs too
For they were yellow in the sun and brown   *20*
In rain.

    Then one hot day when fields were rank
With cowdung in the grass the angry frogs

Invaded the flax-dam; I ducked through hedges
To a coarse croaking that I had not heard   25
Before. The air was thick with a bass chorus.
Right down the dam gross-bellied frogs were cocked
On sods; their loose necks pulsed like sails. Some hopped:
The slap and plop were obscene threats. Some sat
Poised like mud grenades, their blunt heads farting.   30
I sickened, turned, and ran. The great slime kings
Were gathered there for vengeance and I knew
That if I dipped my hand the spawn would clutch it.

[1966]

Bog Queen

I lay waiting
between turf-face and demesne wall,
between heathery levels
and glass-toothed stone.

My body was braille   5
for the creeping influences:
dawn suns groped over my head
and cooled at my feet,

through my fabrics and skins
the seeps of winter   10
digested me,
the illiterate roots

pondered and died
in the cavings
of stomach and socket.   15
I lay waiting

on the gravel bottom,
my brain darkening,
a jar of spawn
fermenting underground   20

dreams of Baltic amber.
Bruised berries under my nails,

the vital hoard reducing
in the crock of the pelvis.

My diadem grew carious,   *25*
gemstones dropped
in the peat floe
like the bearings of history.

My sash was a black glacier
wrinkling, dyed weaves   *30*
and Phoenician stitchwork
retted on my breasts'

soft moraines.
I knew winter cold
like the nuzzle of fjords   *35*
at my thighs—

the soaked fledge, the heavy
swaddle of hides.
My skull hibernated
in the wet nest of my hair.   *40*

Which they robbed.
I was barbered
and stripped
by a turfcutter's spade

who veiled me again   *45*
and packed coomb softly
between the stone jambs
at my head and my feet.

Till a peer's wife bribed him.
The plait of my hair,   *50*
a slimy birth-cord
of bog, had been cut

and I rose from the dark,
hacked bone, skull-ware,
frayed stitches, tufts,   *55*
small gleams on the bank.

                                                        [1975]

The Grauballe Man

As if he had been poured
in tar, he lies
on a pillow of turf
and seems to weep

the black river of himself.   *5*
The grain of his wrists
is like bog oak,
the ball of his heel

like a basalt egg.
His instep has shrunk   *10*
cold as a swan's foot
or a wet swamp root.

His hips are the ridge
and purse of a mussel,
his spine an eel arrested   *15*
under a glisten of mud.

The head lifts,
the chin is a visor
raised above the vent
of his slashed throat   *20*

that has tanned and toughened.
The cured wound
opens inwards to a dark
elderberry place.

Who will say "corpse"   *25*
to his vivid cast?
Who will say "body"
to his opaque repose?

And his rusted hair,
a mat unlikely   *30*
as a foetus's.
I first saw his twisted face

in a photograph,
a head and shoulder
out of the peat,   35
bruised like a forceps baby,

but now he lies
perfected in my memory,
down to the red horn
of his nails,   40

hung in the scales
with beauty and atrocity:
with the Dying Gaul
too strictly compassed

on his shield,   45
with the actual weight
of each hooded victim,
slashed and dumped.

                                        [1975]

Punishment

I can feel the tug
of the halter at the nape
of her neck, the wind
on her naked front.

It blows her nipples   5
to amber beads,
it shakes the frail rigging
of her ribs.

I can see her drowned
body in the bog,   10
the weighing stone,
the floating rods and boughs.

Under which at first
she was a barked sapling
that is dug up   15
oak-bone, brain-firkin:

her shaved head
like a stubble of black corn,
her blindfold a soiled bandage,
her noose a ring   *20*

to store
the memories of love.
Little adulteress,
before they punished you

you were flaxen-haired,   *25*
undernourished, and your
tar-black face was beautiful.
My poor scapegoat,

I almost love you
but would have cast, I know,   *30*
the stones of silence.
I am the artful voyeur

of your brain's exposed
and darkened combs,
your muscles' webbing   *35*
and all your numbered bones:

I who have stood dumb
when your betraying sisters,
cauled in tar,
wept by the railings,   *40*

who would connive
in civilized outrage
yet understand the exact
and tribal, intimate revenge.
                                                  [1975]

Casualty

I

He would drink by himself
And raise a weathered thumb
Towards the high shelf,

Calling another rum
And blackcurrant, without   5
Having to raise his voice,
Or order a quick stout
By a lifting of the eyes
And a discreet dumb-show
Of pulling off the top;   10
At closing time would go
In waders and peaked cap
Into the showery dark,
A dole-kept breadwinner
But a natural for work.   15
I loved his whole manner,
Sure-footed but too sly,
His deadpan sidling tact,
His fisherman's quick eye
And turned observant back.   20

Incomprehensible
To him, my other life.
Sometimes, on his high stool,
Too busy with his knife
At a tobacco plug   25
And not meeting my eye,
In the pause after a slug
He mentioned poetry.
We would be on our own
And, always politic   30
And shy of condescension,
I would manage by some trick
To switch the talk to eels
Or lore of the horse and cart
Or the Provisionals.   35

But my tentative art
His turned back watches too:
He was blown to bits
Out drinking in a curfew
Others obeyed, three nights   40
After they shot dead
The thirteen men in Derry.
PARAS THIRTEEN, the walls said,
BOGSIDE NIL. That Wednesday
Everybody held   45
His breath and trembled.

II

It was a day of cold
Raw silence, wind-blown
Surplice and soutane:
Rained-on, flower-laden   50
Coffin after coffin
Seemed to float from the door
Of the packed cathedral
Like blossoms on slow water.
The common funeral   55
Unrolled its swaddling band,
Lapping, tightening
Till we were braced and bound
Like brothers in a ring.

But he would not be held   60
At home by his own crowd
Whatever threats were phoned,
Whatever black flags waved.
I see him as he turned
In that bombed offending place,   65
Remorse fused with terror
In his still knowable face,
His cornered outfaced stare
Blinding in the flash.

He had gone miles away   70
For he drank like a fish
Nightly, naturally
Swimming towards the lure
Of warm lit-up places,
The blurred mesh and murmur   75
Drifting among glasses
In the gregarious smoke.
How culpable was he
That last night when he broke
Our tribe's complicity?   80
"Now, you're supposed to be
An educated man,"
I hear him say. "Puzzle me
The right answer to that one."

III

I missed his funeral,   85
Those quiet walkers

And sideways talkers
Shoaling out of his lane
To the respectable
Purring of the hearse . . .   90
They move in equal pace
With the habitual
Slow consolation
Of a dawdling engine,
The line lifted, hand   95
Over fist, cold sunshine
On the water, the land
Banked under fog: that morning
When he took me in his boat,
The screw purling, turning   100
Indolent fathoms white,
I tasted freedom with him.
To get out early, haul
Steadily off the bottom,
Dispraise the catch, and smile   105
As you find a rhythm
Working you, slow mile by mile,
Into your proper haunt
Somewhere, well out, beyond . . .

Dawn-sniffing revenant,   110
Plodder through midnight rain,
Question me again.

[1975]

The Skunk

Up, black, striped and damasked like the chasuble
At a funeral Mass, the skunk's tail
Paraded the skunk. Night after night
I expected her like a visitor.

The refrigerator whinnied into silence.   5
My desk light softened beyond the verandah.
Small oranges loomed in the orange tree.
I began to be tense as a voyeur.

After eleven years I was composing
Love-letters again, broaching the word "wife"   10

Like a stored cask, as if its slender vowel
Had mutated into the night earth and air

Of California. The beautiful, useless
Tang of eucalyptus spelt your absence.
The aftermath of a mouthful of wine   *15*
Was like inhaling you off a cold pillow.

And there she was, the intent and glamorous,
Ordinary, mysterious skunk,
Mythologized, demythologized,
Snuffing the boards five feet beyond me.   *20*

It all came back to me last night, stirred
By the sootfall of your things at bedtime,
Your head-down, tail-up hunt in a bottom drawer
For the black plunge-line nightdress.

[1979]

The Harvest Bow

As you plaited the harvest bow
You implicated the mellowed silence in you
In wheat that does not rust
But brightens as it tightens twist by twist
Into a knowable corona,   *5*
A throwaway love-knot of straw.

Hands that aged round ash plants and cane sticks
And lapped the spurs on a lifetime of gamecocks
Harked to their gift and worked with fine intent
Until your fingers moved somnambulant: *10*
I tell and finger it like braille,
Gleaning the unsaid off the palpable,

And if I spy into its golden loops
I see us walk between the railway slopes
Into an evening of long grass and midges,   *15*
Blue smoke straight up, old beds and ploughs in hedges,
An auction notice on an outhouse wall—
You with a harvest bow in your lapel,

Me with the fishing rod, already homesick
For the big lift of these evenings, as your stick   *20*

Whacking the tips off weeds and bushes
Beats out of time, and beats, but flushes
Nothing: that original townland
Still tongue-tied in the straw tied by your hand.

The end of art is peace   25
Could be the motto of this frail device
That I have pinned up on our deal dresser—
Like a drawn snare
Slipped lately by the spirit of the corn
Yet burnished by its passage, and still warm.   30

                                                         [1979]

from *Glanmore Sonnets*

X

I dreamt we slept in a moss in Donegal
On turf banks under blankets, with our faces
Exposed all night in a wetting drizzle,
Pallid as the dripping sapling birches.
Lorenzo and Jessica in a cold climate.   5
Diarmuid and Grainne waiting to be found.
Darkly asperged and censed, we were laid out
Like breathing effigies on a raised ground.
And in that dream I dreamt—how like you this?—
Our first night years ago in that hotel   10
When you came with your deliberate kiss
To raise us towards the lovely and painful
Covenants of flesh; our separateness;
The respite in our dewy dreaming faces.

                                                         [1979]

from *Station Island*

XII

Like a convalescent, I took the hand
stretched down from the jetty, sensed again
an alien comfort as I stepped on ground

to find the helping hand still gripping mine,
fish-cold and bony, but whether to guide   5
or to be guided I could not be certain

for the tall man in step at my side
seemed blind, though he walked straight as a rush
upon his ash plant, his eyes fixed straight ahead.

Then I knew him in the flesh   10
out there on the tarmac among the cars,
wintered hard and sharp as a blackthorn bush.

His voice eddying with the vowels of all rivers
came back to me, though he did not speak yet,
a voice like a prosecutor's or a singer's,   15

cunning, narcotic, mimic, definite
as a steel nib's downstroke, quick and clean,
and suddenly he hit a litter basket

with his stick, saying, "Your obligation
is not discharged by any common rite.   20
What you do you must do on your own.

The main thing is to write
for the joy of it. Cultivate a work-lust
that imagines its haven like your hands at night

dreaming the sun in the sunspot of a breast.   25
You are fasted now, light-headed, dangerous.
Take off from here. And don't be so earnest,

so ready for the sackcloth and the ashes.
Let go, let fly, forget.
You've listened long enough. Now strike your note."   30

It was as if I had stepped free into space
alone with nothing that I had not known
already. Raindrops blew in my face

as I came to and heard the harangue and jeers
going on and on: "The English language   35
belongs to us. You are raking at dead fires,

rehearsing the old whinges at your age.
That subject people stuff is a cod's game,
infantile, like this peasant pilgrimage.

You lose more of yourself than you redeem   *40*
doing the decent thing. Keep at a tangent.
When they make the circle wide, it's time to swim

cut on your own and fill the element
with signatures on your own frequency,
echo-soundings, searches, probes, allurements,   *45*

elver-gleams in the dark of the whole sea."
The shower broke in a cloudburst, the tarmac
fumed and sizzled. As he moved off quickly

the downpour loosed its screens round his straight walk.

[1984]

from *Lightenings*

VIII

The annals say: when the monks of Clonmacnoise
Were all at prayers inside the oratory
A ship appeared above them in the air.

The anchor dragged along behind so deep
It hooked itself into the altar rails   *5*
And then, as the big hull rocked to a standstill,

A crewman shinned and grappled down the rope
And struggled to release it. But in vain.
"This man can't bear our life here and will drown,"

The abbot said, "unless we help him." So   *10*
They did, the freed ship sailed, and the man climbed back
Out of the marvellous as he had known it.

[1991]

ROBERT PINSKY

[b. 1940]

Dying

Nothing to be said about it, and everything—
The change of changes, closer or further away:
The Golden Retriever next door, Gussie, is dead,

Like Sandy, the Cocker Spaniel from three doors down
Who died when I was small; and every day   *5*
Things that were in my memory fade and die.

Phrases die out: first, everyone forgets
What doornails are; then after certain decades
As a dead metaphor, *"dead as a doornail"* flickers

And fades away. But someone I know is dying—   *10*
And though one might say glibly, "everyone is,"
The different pace makes the difference absolute.

The tiny invisible spores in the air we breathe,
That settle harmlessly on our drinking water
And on our skin, happen to come together   *15*

With certain conditions on the forest floor,
Or even a shady corner of the lawn—
And overnight the fleshy, pale stalks gather,

The colorless growth without a leaf or flower;
And around the stalks, the summer grass keeps growing   *20*
With steady pressure, like the insistent whiskers

That grow between shaves on a face, the nails
Growing and dying from the toes and fingers
At their own humble pace, oblivious

As the nerveless moths, that live their night or two—   *25*
Though like a moth a bright soul keeps on beating,
Bored and impatient in the monster's mouth.

                                                            [1991]

ROBERT HASS

[b. 1941]

Meditation at Lagunitas

All the new thinking is about loss.
In this it resembles all the old thinking.
The idea, for example, that each particular erases
the luminous clarity of a general idea. That the clown-

faced woodpecker probing the dead sculpted trunk   *5*
of that black birch is, by his presence,
some tragic falling off from a first world
of undivided light. Or the other notion that,
because there is in this world no one thing
to which the bramble of *blackberry* corresponds,   *10*
a word is elegy to what it signifies.
We talked about it late last night and in the voice
of my friend, there was a thin wire of grief, a tone
almost querulous. After a while I understood that,
talking this way, everything dissolves: *justice,*   *15*
pine, hair, woman, you and *I.* There was a woman
I made love to and I remembered how, holding
her small shoulders in my hands sometimes,
I felt a violent wonder at her presence
like a thirst for salt, for my childhood river   *20*
with its island willows, silly music from the pleasure boat,
muddy places where we caught the little orange-silver fish
called *pumpkinseed.* It hardly had to do with her.
Longing, we say, because desire is full
of endless distances. I must have been the same to her.   *25*
But I remember so much, the way her hands dismantled bread,
the thing her father said that hurt her, what
she dreamed. There are moments when the body is as numinous
as words, days that are the good flesh continuing.
Such tenderness, those afternoons and evenings,   *30*
saying *blackberry, blackberry, blackberry.*

[1979]

WESLEY McNAIR

[b. 1941]

The Abandonment

Climbing on top of him and breathing
into his mouth this way she could be showing her
desire except that when she draws back
from him to make her little cries
she is turning to her young son just   *5*
coming into the room to find his father my brother
on the bed with his eyes closed and the slightest

smile on his lips as if when they
both beat on his chest as they do now
he will come back from the dream he is enjoying   *10*
so much he cannot hear her calling his name
louder and louder and the son saying get up
get up discovering both of them discovering
for the first time that all along
he has lived in this body this thing   *15*
with shut lids dangling its arms
that have nothing to do with him and everything
they can ever know the wife listening weeping
at his chest and the mute son who will never
forget how she takes the face into her hands now   *20*
as if there were nothing in the world
but the face and breathes oh
breathes into the mouth which does not breathe back.

            [1991]

MARILYN HACKER

[b. 1942]

Canzone

Consider the three functions of the tongue:
taste, speech, the telegraphy of pleasure,
are not confused in any human tongue:
yet, sinewy and singular, the tongue
accomplishes what, perhaps, no other organ   *5*
can. Were I to speak of giving tongue,
you'd think two things at least; and a cooked tongue,
sliced, on a plate, with caper sauce, which I give
my guest for lunch, is one more, to which she'd give
the careful concentration of her tongue   *10*
twice over, to appreciate the taste
and to express—it would be in good taste—

a gastronomic memory the taste
called to mind, and mind brought back to tongue.
There is a paucity of words for taste: *15*
sweet, sour, bitter, salty. Any taste,
however multiplicitous its pleasure,
complex its execution (I might taste

that sauce ten times in cooking, change its taste
with herbal subtleties, chromatic organ   20
tones of clove and basil, good with organ
meats) must be described with those few taste-
words, or with metaphors, to give
my version of sensations it would give

a neophyte, deciding whether to give   25
it a try. She might develop a taste.
(you try things once; I think you have to give
two chances, though, to know your mind, or give
up on novelties.) Your mother tongue
nurtures, has the subtleties which give   30
flavor to words, and words to flavor, give
the by no means subsidiary pleasure
of being able to describe a pleasure
and recreate it. Making words, we give
the private contemplations of each organ   35
to the others, and to others, organ-

ize sensations into thoughts. Sentient organ-
isms, we symbolize feeling, give
the spectrum (that's a symbol) each sense organ
perceives, by analogy, to others. Disorgan-   40
ization of the senses is an acquired taste
we all acquire; as speaking beasts, it's organ-
ic to our discourse. The first organ
of acknowledged communion is the tongue
(tripartite diplomat, which after tongu-   45
ing a less voluble expressive organ
to wordless efflorescences of pleasure
offers up words to reaffirm the pleasure).

That's a primary difficulty: pleasure
means something, and something different, for each organ;   50
each person, too. I may take exquisite pleasure
in boiled eel, or blancmange—or not. One pleasure
of language is making known what not to give.
And think of a bar of lavender soap, a pleasure
to see and, moistened, rub on your skin, a pleasure   55
especially to smell, but if you taste
it (though smell is most akin to taste)
what you experience will not be pleasure;
you almost retch, grimace, stick out your tongue,
slosh rinses of ice water over your tongue.   60

But I would rather think about your tongue
experiencing and transmitting pleasure
to one or another multi-sensual organ
—like memory. Whoever wants to give
only one meaning to that, has untutored taste.

[1980]

TESS GALLAGHER

[b. 1943]

Kidnaper

He motions me over with a question.
He is lost. I believe him. It seems
he calls my name. I move
closer. He says it again, the name
of someone he loves. I step back pretending   5

not to hear. I suspect
the street he wants
does not exist, but I am glad to point
away from myself. While he turns
I slip off my wristwatch, already laying a trail   10
for those who must find me
tumbled like an abandoned car
into the ravine. I lie

without breath for days among ferns.
Pine needles drift   15
onto my face and breasts
like the tiny hands
of watches. Cars pass.
I imagine it's him
coming back. My death   20
is not needed. The sun climbs again
for everyone. He lifts me
like a bride

and the leaves fall from my shoulders
in twenty-dollar bills.   25
"You must have been cold," he says
covering me with his handkerchief.
"You must have given me up."

[1976]

LOUISE GLÜCK

[b. 1943]

The Garden

1 The Fear of Birth

One sound. Then the hiss and whir
of houses gliding into their places.
And the wind
leafs through the bodies of animals—

But my body that could not content itself   5
with health—why should it be sprung back
into the chord of sunlight?

It will be the same again.
This fear, this inwardness,
until I am forced into a field   10
without immunity
even to the least shrub that walks
stiffly out of the dirt, trailing
the twisted signature of its root,
even to a tulip, a red claw.   15

And then the losses,
one after another,
all supportable.

2 The Garden

The garden admires you.
For your sake it smears itself with green pigment,   20
the ecstatic reds of the roses,
so that you will come to it with your lovers.

And the willows—
see how it has shaped these green
tents of silence. Yet   25
there is still something you need,
your body so soft, so alive, among the stone animals.

Admit that it is terrible to be like them,
beyond harm.

3 The Fear of Love

That body lying beside me like obedient stone—   *30*
once its eyes seemed to be opening,
we could have spoken.

At that time it was winter already.
By day the sun rose in its helmet of fire
and at night also, mirrored in the moon.   *35*
Its light passed over us freely,
as though we had lain down
in order to leave no shadows,
only these two shallow dents in the snow.
And the past, as always, stretched before us,
still, complex, impenetrable.   *40*

How long did we lie there
as, arm in arm in their cloaks of feathers,
the gods walked down
from the mountain we built for them?

4 Origins

As though a voice were saying   *45*
You should be asleep by now—
But there was no one. Nor
had the air darkened,
though the moon was there,
already filled in with marble.   *50*

As though, in a garden crowded with flowers,
a voice had said
How dull they are, these golds,
so sonorous, so repetitious
until you closed your eyes,   *55*
lying among them, all
stammering flame:

And yet you could not sleep,
poor body, the earth
still clinging to you—   *60*

5 The Fear of Burial

In the empty field, in the morning,
the body waits to be claimed.

The spirit sits beside it, on a small rock—
nothing comes to give it form again.

Think of the body's loneliness.   *70*
At night pacing the sheared field,
its shadow buckled tightly around.
Such a long journey.
And already the remote, trembling lights of the village
not pausing for it as they scan the rows.   *75*
How far away they seem,
the wooden doors, the bread and milk
laid like weights on the table.

[1980]

CRAIG RAINE

[b. 1944]

A Martian Sends a Postcard Home

Caxtons are mechanical birds with many wings
and some are treasured for their markings—

they cause the eyes to melt
or the body to shriek without pain.

I have never seen one fly, but   *5*
sometimes they perch on the hand.

Mist is when the sky is tired of flight
and rests its soft machine on ground:

then the world is dim and bookish
like engravings under tissue paper.   *10*

Rain is when the earth is television.
It has the property of making colours darker.

Model T is a room with the lock inside—
a key is turned to free the world

for movement, so quick there is a film   *15*
to watch for anything missed.

But time is tied to the wrist
or kept in a box, ticking with impatience.

In homes, a haunted apparatus sleeps,
that snores when you pick it up.   *20*

If the ghost cries, they carry it
to their lips and soothe it to sleep

with sounds. And yet, they wake it up
deliberately, by tickling with a finger.

Only the young are allowed to suffer   *25*
openly. Adults go to a punishment room

with water but nothing to eat.
They lock the door and suffer the noises

alone. No one is exempt
and everyone's pain has a different smell.   *30*

At night, when all the colours die,
they hide in pairs

and read about themselves—
in colour, with their eyelids shut.

[1979]

CATHY APPEL

[b. 1948]

Letters

Don't put your disembodied voice in an envelope—
send objects,
tangibles from Vermont, like the broken thread
from the last shirt button you've lost,
photographs of the house;   *5*

I should see you as you are.
What kind of soap is in your bathroom;
where do you keep your car keys? Send me
your favorite recipe, something from your pocket
like a ticket stub or tattered list.   *10*
I'll answer promptly
enclosing dust from my closet,
mud from the soles of my shoes.
Can you imagine me exhausted,
tissues tucked in a sleeve,   *15*
lying beside my husband, who, regardless,
caresses my hip? I could send you
a toenail clipping
or the umpteen odd barrettes, rubber bands,
unanswered letters scattered in my drawer.   *20*
Don't write in sentences.
No matter how we feel, send specifics—a branch
of your family's Christmas tree,
your daughter's loose tooth, crumbs
from the toast you ate this morning.   *25*
Send me what defies
language, something of which
there isn't any doubt.

                                                              [1993]

CAROLYN FORCHÉ

[b. 1950]

The Memory of Elena

We spend our morning
in the flower stalls counting
the dark tongues of bells
that hang from ropes waiting
for the silence of an hour.   *5*
We find a table, ask for *paella,*
cold soup and wine, where a calm
light trembles years behind us.

In Buenos Aires only three
years ago, it was the last time his hand   *10*

THE MEMORY OF ELENA   ⁶paella   Spanish dish of rice with meat, seafood, and vegetables.

slipped into her dress, with pearls
cooling her throat and bells like
these, chipping at the night—

As she talks, the hollow
clopping of a horse, the sound   *15*
of bones touched together.
The *paella* comes, a bed of rice
and *camarones*,° fingers and shells,   *shrimp*
the lips of those whose lips
have been removed, mussels   *20*
the soft blue of a leg socket.

This is not *paella,* this is what
has become of those who remained
in Buenos Aires. This is the ring
of a rifle report on the stones,   *25*
her hand over her mouth,
her husband falling against her.

These are the flowers we bought
this morning, the dahlias tossed
on his grave and bells   *30*
waiting with their tongues cut out
for this particular silence.

                                    [1981]

ROGER KAMENETZ

[b. 1950]

Christopher Magisto

I work in a theater
where the magic tricks
go too slowly for the audience
until they weep or cry out.
Always fooled   *5*
by their desire to know everything
they are as cruel as they are conscious.
When they ask for the trick
I empty my sleeves.

They close their eyes   *10*
and give me their dreams

which I turn into objects
that tumble down long shafts.
In the bright sunlight
they disappear.   *15*

The house lights come on
bringing deep clarity and regret.
The audience has aged.
Old women leave the places of young mothers.
Their children have become men.   *20*

They no longer care
how I do it.

                                                          [1985]

JORIE GRAHAM

[b. 1951]

Mind

The slow overture of rain,
each drop breaking
without breaking into
the next, describes
the unrelenting, syncopated   *5*
mind. Not unlike
the hummingbirds
imagining their wings
to be their heart, and swallows
believing the horizon   *10*
to be a line they lift
and drop. What is it
they cast for? The poplars,
advancing or retreating,
lose their stature   *15*
equally, and yet stand firm,
making arrangements
in order to become
imaginary. The city
draws the mind in streets,   *20*
and streets compel it
from their intersections
where a little

belongs to no one. It is
what is driven through   *25*
all stationary portions
of the world, gravity's
stake in things. the leaves,
pressed against the dank
window of November   *30*
soil, remain unwelcome
till transformed, parts
of a puzzle unsolvable
till the edges give a bit
and soften. See how   *35*
then the picture becomes clear,
the mind entering the ground
more easily in pieces,
and all the richer for it.

[1980]

JIMMY SANTIAGO BACA

[b. 1952]

from *Meditations on the South Valley*

XVII

I love the wind
when it blows through my barrio.
It hisses its snake love
down calles de polvo,
and cracks egg-shell skins   *5*
of abandoned homes.
Stray dogs find shelter
along the river,
where great cottonwoods rattle
like old covered wagons,   *10*
stuck in stagnant waterholes.
Days when the wind blows
full of sand and grit,
men and women make decisions
that change their whole lives.   *15*
Windy days in the barrio
give birth to divorce papers
and squalling separation. The wind tells us

what others refuse to tell us,
informing men and women of a secret,   *20*
that they move away to hide from.

                                                                [1979]

RITA DOVE

[b. 1952]

Canary

FOR MICHAEL S. HARPER

Billie Holiday's burned voice
had as many shadows as lights,
a mournful candelabra against a sleek piano,
the gardenia her signature under that ruined face.

(Now you're cooking, drummer to bass,   *5*
magic spoon, magic needle.
Take all day if you have to
with your mirror and your bracelet of song.)

Fact is, the invention of women under siege
has been to sharpen love in the service of myth.   *10*

If you can't be free, be a mystery.

                                                                [1989]

ALICE FULTON

[b. 1952]

Dance Script with Electric Ballerina

Here I am on this ledge again,
my body's five rays singing,
limbering up for another fling
with gravity. It's true,
I've dispensed with some conventions.   *5*
If you expected sleeping
beauty sprouting from a rococo

doughnut of tulle, a figurine
fit to top a music box, you might want
your money back. I'll take a getup   *10*
functional as light:
feet bright and precise as eggbeaters,
fingers quick as switch-
blades and a miner's lamp for my tiara.
You've seen kids on Independence Day, waving   *15*
sparklers to sketch their initials on the night?
Just so, I'd like to leave a residue
of slash and glide, a trace-
form on the riled air.
Like an action painter, tossing form on space   *20*
instead of oil on cloth,
I'm out to disprove the limited
orbit of fingers, swing some double-jointed
miracles, train myself to hover above ground
longer than the pinch of time allowed.   *25*
This stingy escarpment leaves so little
room to move!
But perhaps that's for the best. Despite brave talk
of brio and ballon, spectators prefer
gestures that don't endanger   *30*
body and soul. Equilibrium
is so soothing—while any strain is a reminder
of the pain that leads to grace:
muscles clenched like teeth to the shin, swollen
hubs of shoulder, ankle, wrist, and knee,   *35*
toes brown as figs from the clobbering
of poundage. In this game, lightness is all.
Here's another trick. When passing the critics
turn sideways to expose less
surface. Think like a knife   *40*
against the whetstone sneers: *unsympathetic*
in several minds   flat and hollow
at the core   shabby   too
flaccid   polishes off her pirouettes with
too assertive   *45*
a flick   ragged barbaric hysterical
needs to improve
her landings   technique   bullies
the audience into paying
attention   in short   *50*
does not really get around   lacking
assurance authority fluency restraint roundness
of gesture   something

of the air and manner of those who are ballerinas
by right rather than   55
assumption: one will say
I'm mildly impressed
by her good line and high extensions.
I can sense the movement
notators' strobe vision   60
picking the bones of flux into
positions. Can't they see the gulf
between gestures as a chance
to find clairvoyance—
a gift that thrives on fissures   65
between then and now and when?
If a complex network, a city, say
could be filmed for a millennium
and the footage shown
so in three hours it woke   70
from huts to wired shining,
its compressed assembling would be like this
dance: these air patterns
where I distill the scribbling moves
that start at birth   75
and dissolve in death.

Till then I'm signing space
in leaps angular and brief
as an electrocardiograph's beat.
Now as I settle on an ending   80
posture: my chest heaves,
joints shift, eyes dart—
and even at a stand-
still, I'm dancing.

                                                   [1983]

ALBERTO RIOS

[b. 1952]

A Dream of Husbands

Though we thought it, Doña Carolina did not die.
She was too old for that nonsense, and too set.
That morning she walked off just a little farther

into her favorite dream, favorite but not nice
so much, not nice and not bad, so it was not death.　　　　　　*5*
She dreamed the dream of husbands
and over there she found him after all the years.
Cabrón, she called him, *animal,* very loud
so we could hear it, for us it was a loud truck
passing, or thunder, or too many cats, very loud　　　　　　*10*
for having left her for so long and so far. Days now
her voice is the squeak of the rocking chair
as she complains, we hear it, it will not go
not with oils or sanding or shouts back at her.
But it becomes too the sound a spoon makes, her old　　　　*15*
very large wooden spoon as it stirs a pot of soup.
Dinnertimes, we think of her, the good parts, of her
cooking, we like her best then, even the smell of her.
But then, *cabrones* she calls us, *animales,* irritated,
from over there, from the dream, they come, her words　　*20*
they are the worst sounds of the street in the night
so that we will not get so comfortable about her,
so comfortable with her having left us
we thinking that her husband and her long dream
are so perfect, because no, they are not, not so much,　　　*25*
she is not so happy this way, not in this dream,
this is not heaven, don't think it. She tells us this,
sadness too is hers, a half measure, sadness at having
no time for the old things, for rice, for chairs.

　　　　　　　　　　　　　　　　　　　　　　　　[1985]

GERTRUDE SCHNACKENBERG

[b. 1952]

Signs

Threading the palm, a web of little lines
Spells out the lost money, the heart, the head,
The wagging tongues, the sudden deaths, in signs
We would smooth out, like imprints on a bed,

In signs that can't be helped, geese heading south,　　　*5*
In signs read anxiously, like breath that clouds

A mirror held to a barely open mouth,
Like telegrams, the gathering of crowds—

The plane's X in the sky, spelling disaster:
Before the whistle and hit, a tracer flare;   10
Before rubble, a hairline crack in plaster
And a housefly's panicked scribbling on the air.

                                                                              [1982]

ASKOLD MELNYCZUK

[b. 1954]

The Enamel Box

Given My Mother by a Visitor from Ukraine

It is a country and a house
I've never seen,
this trinket and odd record of humanity,
starfish, pewter, purple, green—
ancestral garden from a greener age—   5
and I turn outward to the oak which Spring
has, like a famished lover, licked
awake.

I imagine
somewhere beyond the tree   10
that house, the solitary, careful
child within,
and the dragonflies,
rising and falling like pistons
above a sputtering stream.   15

The mother bakes bread by an open
window, humming softly to a dying sun.
The father smokes a pipe,
instructs the child:
"Cultivate wheat and a conscience.   20
In a pinch, forfeit
the conscience,
but save that wheat."

It jars me, this lecture
I've imagined, because   25
there ought to be causes
worth dying for,
and my peasant says no.
Is it the mysteries of Eleusis
he's understood, while I,   30

battling each morning uncharitable
Aristotle,
worry the fine points,
obscure to the whole?
The old man says to the boy: 35
"Anyone tells you God cares
about anything except kindness
is a liar."

I imagine
a mother, a father, a child, a house: 40
eternal actors, paramours of joy and pain,
except the child, born all eyes,
who sits at the window
watching the dragonflies
and does not know   45
centuries are passing.

This is how they pass.

                                                                [1993]

CATHY SONG

[b. 1955]

Lost Sister

1

In China,
even the peasants
named their first daughters
Jade—
the stone that in the far fields   5
could moisten the dry season,

could make men move mountains
for the healing green of the inner hills
glistening like slices of winter melon.

And the daughters were grateful: 10
They never left home.
To move freely was a luxury
stolen from them at birth.
Instead, they gathered patience,
learning to walk in shoes   15
the size of teacups,
without breaking—
the arc of their movements
as dormant as the rooted willow,
as redundant as the farmyard hens.   20
But they traveled far
in surviving,
learning to stretch the family rice,
to quiet the demons,
the noisy stomachs.   25

2

There is a sister
across the ocean,
who relinquished her name,
diluting jade green
with the blue of the Pacific.   30
Rising with a tide of locusts,
she swarmed with others
to inundate another shore.
In America,
there are many roads   35
and women can stride along with men.

But in another wilderness,
the possibilities,
the loneliness,
can strangulate like jungle vines.   40
The meager provisions and sentiments
of once belonging—
fermented roots, Mah-Jong tiles and firecrackers—set but
a flimsy household
in a forest of nightless cities.   45
A giant snake rattles above,

spewing black clouds into your kitchen.
Dough-faced landlords
slip in and out of your keyholes,
making claims you don't understand,   *50*
tapping into your communication systems
of laundry lines and restaurant chains.

You find you need China:
your one fragile identification,
a jade link   *55*
handcuffed to your wrist.
You remember your mother
who walked for centuries,
footless—
and like her,   *60*
you have left no footprints,
but only because
there is an ocean in between,
the unremitting space of your rebellion.

[1983]

PART THREE

POEMS FROM
OTHER LANGUAGES

Hebrew Poetry

The Hebrew poetic tradition is an old one, going back more than three millennia. As with the poetry of other ancient civilizations such as that in mainland Greece, Hebrew poetry was closely affiliated with the religious, social, and military life of the culture it celebrated. War victories were enshrined in verse, as were various forms of achievement such as the freedom of the Hebrew slaves from their Egyptian masters. The oldest Hebrew poems, in fact, are celebrations of victorious accomplishments. The Bible's oldest recorded poem, "Song of Deborah" (Judges 5:1–31) describes how the Hebrew heroine Jael saves her people by killing the Canaanite military leader Sisera. Better known is the subject of the second oldest Hebrew verse performance, "Song of the Sea" (Exodus 15:1–18), which celebrates the destruction of the Egyptian pharaoh's army, especially its chariots and horsemen, in the Red Sea.

The most consistent and important aspects of ancient Hebrew poetry, however, were its religious and ethical impulses. These are splendidly and abundantly evident in the poetry of the Psalms, the prophecies of Isaiah, and the wisdom of Job. Complementing these ethically oriented and religiously grounded poetic works, other biblical poems display a more secular and less ostensibly religious cast (although these works, too, have been interpreted allegorically as being truly religious as well). The most beautiful and famous of these are "Song of Songs," also known as "Song of Solomon," and the Book of Ecclesiastes.

The Bible is thus the storehouse and source of much ancient Hebrew poetry. And since the Bible overall and biblical poetry in particular have had a tremendous influence on Western literature, we have included a range of examples. This range is also necessary because there is more than one genre, or type, of biblical poetry. And although we will describe characteristics of much biblical Hebrew poetry, it is important to note, for example, that the biblical poetic genres include love poetry, prophetic poetry, wisdom poetry, and psalms. Each of these genres can be further subdivided, as, for example, psalms into hymns, laments, thanksgivings, and others.

In addition to acknowledging the range and variety of ancient Hebrew poetry included in the Bible, we should also describe the characteristic features of ancient

Hebrew verse, especially since the stylistic features of ancient Hebrew poetry operate across the various types of poems included in the Bible.

The single most salient feature of biblical poetry is parallelism, or the repetition with variation of a linguistic pattern. This pattern of repetition with variation may occur in word, phrase, line, or sentence, as well as in larger poetic units. Literature generally relies heavily on parallelism in matters of structure as well as style, but biblical poetry thrives on it to such an extent that parallelism is a distinguishing feature. Parallelism in Hebrew poetry exists in two basic forms: synonymous and antithetical. In synonymous parallelism a unit, typically the idea of a poetic line (or a "stich," from the Greek *stichos,* for "line") is very nearly repeated, so as to create the effect of making the same point or expressing the same feeling or attitude in two similar ways. An example:

> The heavens are telling the glory of God,
> and the firmament proclaims his handiwork.
> (Psalm 19:1)

We should note, however, that this kind of synonymous parallelism is rare outside of the Psalms, and even there it is more characteristic of some psalms than others. What often passes for synonymity are lines that reveal not a mere repetition of idea from one line to another but usually an intensification, specification, or dramatization of one line by another. An example (one of many) from the Book of Job:

> Have you entered into the springs of the sea,
> or walked in the recesses of the deep?
> (Job 38:16)

Another form of parallelism, antithetical parallelism, establishes a contrast between the two lines:

> For the Lord knows the way of the righteous,
> but the way of the wicked will perish.
> (Psalm 1:6)

To acknowledge the importance of parallelism in ancient Hebrew poetry is not to suggest, however, that parallelism is its only poetic characteristic. Like poetry in most other languages, ancient Hebrew poetry organizes sound in distinctive rhythms, in patterns of repeating vowels and consonants, and in recurring variations of words with similar sounds but different meanings. Such patterns of sound and rhythm, of course, are not apparent in translation, and thus they are left for readers familiar with Hebrew to discern.

Of the biblical poetic texts we have selected, four are encased in works written partly in poetry and partly in prose. The Book of Exodus, for example, is a long narrative prose account of the emancipation of the Hebrews, or Israelites, from Egyptian bondage, their pilgrimage to and sojourn at Mt. Sinai, and the promulgation of a set of laws. "Song of the Sea" occupies a portion of a chapter about a third of the way into Exodus. The Book of Ecclesiastes is a much shorter book written hundreds of years later than Exodus (Exodus dates from c. 1000 B.C., Ecclesiastes from the third century B.C.). Though written largely in prose, portions of four chapters are in verse. The passage we have selected from Ecclesiastes is among the most famous in the book and among the best known of all passages from the Bible.

Like Ecclesiastes, the Book of Job is considered one of the wisdom books in the Hebrew Bible, the other being Proverbs. Unlike Ecclesiastes, however, Job is largely in verse, with the only prose passages being a framing narrative folktale that occupies the book's opening and closing chapters. A profound probing of faith and suffering, the Book of Job was written c. 900 B.C. Our selection comes from near the end of the book, when, after Job questions why God has made him suffer so extensively, God speaks out in response. We include two translations, the Revised Standard Version, produced by an ecumenical group of scholars, and a contemporary translation by Stephen Mitchell.

If Ecclesiastes and Job are part of the Bible's wisdom literature, Isaiah exemplifies one of its major prophetic voices, the other two major prophets being Ezekiel and Jeremiah. Isaiah is really three books in one, having been composed during three different periods by at least two and possibly three different writers. Our selection comes from the first Isaiah, who composed Chapters 1–39 around 700 B.C. A messianic passage that bears comparison with the "Fourth Eclogue" of Virgil (pp. 1013–1015), written hundreds of years later, Isaiah's poetic, prophetic utterance was especially valued by later biblical writers of the New Testament.

Perhaps the best-known poetry from the Bible occurs in the Psalms, which are used extensively in Hebrew and Christian liturgy. The Psalms were once thought to have been composed by King David (as Exodus was once attributed to Moses), but modern biblical scholars reject David's authorship of all but a few psalms. The other completely poetic book of the Bible is the "Song of Songs," once attributed to King Solomon. It is a collection of about twenty-five love lyrics, some of which are fragmentary. The book's imagery is erotic and a number of its allusions are pagan, referring to a god and goddess on whom the fertility of nature depends. Our selection from Chapter 7, consists of a dialogue between a female speaker (Verses 1–5 and 10–13) and a male speaker (6–9).

En route to a few Hebrew poems by twentieth-century poets, we have included a pair of poems by the medieval Hebrew poets Solomon ibn Gabirol and Judah Halevi. Solomon ibn Gabirol (c. 1022 – c. 1070) is famous for his secular poetry, especially poems about nature and love. He also composed highly liturgical poetry and a long philosophical poem, "The Kingly Crown," based on Neoplatonist, Midrashic, and Muslim astronomy. Judah Halevi (c. 1071 – c. 1141) grew up in Muslim Tudela on the borders of Christian Spain. He settled in Toledo, where he practiced medicine until he left for Córdoba due to attacks upon Jews by Christian mercenaries in Toledo. An ardent Hebrew nationalist, Halevi wrote passionately patriotic "Songs of Zion," which are among his most famous works, though he has also written highly regarded poems on both sacred and secular subjects.

Our modern poets include Rahel Bluwstein (1890–1931), who was born and raised in Russia. In 1909 she went to Palestine, where she became involved in agricultural work, later studying agronomy in France. Her contemporary David Vogel (1891–1944), also born in Russia, settled in Vienna in 1912. He suffered the ignominy of being imprisoned during World War I by the Austrians as a Russian national and during World War II by the French as an Austrian national. Arrested by the Nazis in 1944, he is believed to have perished in a concentration camp and left behind one slim volume of poems. Yocheved Bat-Miriam was born in Russia in 1901 and was educated in Russian and Hebrew. She settled in Palestine, where she was engaged in various literary pursuits. Leah Goldberg (1911–1970) grew up in Lithuania and emigrated to Palestine in 1935. Chair of the Department of Comparative Literature at Hebrew University, she made Hebrew translations of poems by the Italian poets Petrarch and Dante, the French poets Baudelaire and Verlaine, and the German poet Rilke, in addition to many poems from Russian and Lithuanian. Yehuda Amichai (b. 1924) went to Jerusalem from Würzburg in 1936. His understated, often ironic poems blend the vernacular with a more typically literary language. Dalia Ravikovitch (b. 1936), educated in Haifa and Jerusalem, has worked as a journalist and teacher. She published her first poems while serving in the Israeli army.

PSALM 23

The Lord is my shepherd

REVISED STANDARD VERSION

יהוה רֹעִי — לֹא אֶחְסָר:

[1]The Lord is my shepherd, I
    shall not want;

בִּנְאוֹת דֶּשֶׁא יַרְבִּיצֵנִי,

[2]he makes me lie down in green
    pastures.

עַל מֵי־מְנֻחוֹת יְנַהֲלֵנִי.

He leads me beside still waters;

נַפְשִׁי יְשׁוֹבֵב,

[3]he restores my soul.

יַנְחֵנִי בְמַעְגְּלֵי צֶדֶק

He leads me in paths of
    righteousness

לְמַעַן שְׁמוֹ.

    for his name's sake.

גַּם כִּי אֵלֵךְ

[4]Even though I walk through the
    valley of the shadow of death,

בְּגֵיא צַלְמָוֶת —

    I fear no evil;

לֹא אִירָא רָע,

for thou art with me;

כִּי אַתָּה עִמָּדִי.

    thy rod and thy staff,

שִׁבְטְךָ וּמִשְׁעַנְתֶּךָ
הֵמָּה יְנַחֲמֻנִי.

    they comfort me.

תַּעֲרֹךְ לְפָנַי שֻׁלְחָן   ⁵Thou preparest a table before me
נֶגֶד צֹרְרָי: in the presence of my enemies;
דִּשַּׁנְתָּ בַשֶּׁמֶן רֹאשִׁי,   thou anointest my head with oil,
כּוֹסִי רְוָיָה.   my cup overflows.
אַךְ טוֹב וָחֶסֶד יִרְדְּפוּנִי   ⁶Surely goodness and mercy shall
                 follow me
כָּל יְמֵי חַיָּי,   all the days of my life;
וְשַׁבְתִּי בְּבֵית יהוה   and I shall dwell in the house of the
                 Lord
לְאֹרֶךְ יָמִים.   for ever.

EXODUS 15:1–18

Song of the Sea

REVISED STANDARD VERSION

¹Then Moses and the people of Israel
   sang this song to the LORD, saying,
"I will sing to the Lord, for he has
   triumphed gloriously;
the horse and his rider he has
   thrown into the sea.
²The Lord is my strength and my song,
   and he has become my salvation;
this is my God, and I will praise him,
   my father's God, and I will exalt him.
³The Lord is a man of war;
   the Lord is his name.

⁴"Pharaoh's chariots and his host he
   cast into the sea;
and his picked officers are sunk in
   the Red Sea.
⁵The floods cover them;
   they went down into the depths like a stone.
⁶Thy right hand, O Lord, glorious
   in power,
   thy right hand, O Lord, shatters
   the enemy.

[7]In the greatness of thy majesty thou
overthrowest thy adversaries;
thou sendest forth thy fury, it
consumes them like stubble.
[8]At the blast of thy nostrils the
waters piled up,
the floods stood up in a heap;
the deeps congealed in the heart
of the sea.
[9]The enemy said, 'I will pursue, I
will overtake,
I will divide the spoil, my desire
shall have its fill of them.
I will draw my sword, my hand
shall destroy them.'
[10]Thou didst blow with thy wind,
the sea covered them;
they sank as lead in the mighty waters.

[11]"Who is like thee, O Lord, among
the gods?
Who is like thee, majestic in
holiness,
terrible in glorious deeds, doing
wonders?
[12]Thou didst stretch out thy right
hand,
the earth swallowed them.

[13]"Thou hast led in thy steadfast love
the people whom thou hast redeemed,
thou hast guided them by thy
strength to thy holy abode.
[14]The peoples have heard, they tremble;
pangs have seized on the
inhabitants of Philistia.
[15]Now are the chiefs of Edom dismayed;
the leaders of Moab, trembling
seizes them;
all the inhabitants of Canaan have
melted away.
[16]Terror and dread fall upon them;
because of the greatness of thy
arm, they are as still as a stone,
till thy people, O Lord, pass by,

till the people pass by whom thou
  hast purchased.
[17]Thou wilt bring them in, and plant
    them on thy own mountain,
  the place, O Lord, which thou
    hast made for thy abode,
  the sanctuary, O Lord, which thy
    hands have established.
[18]The Lord will reign for ever and ever."

ECCLESIASTES 1:2–11

Vanity of vanities

REVISED STANDARD VERSION

[2]Vanity of vanities, says the Preacher,
  vanity of vanities! All is vanity.
[3]What does man gain by all the toil
  at which he toils under the sun?
[4]A generation goes, and a generation comes,
  but the earth remains for ever.
[5]The sun rises and the sun goes down,
  and hastens to the place where it rises.
[6]The wind blows to the south,
  and goes round to the north;
 round and round goes the wind,
  and on its circuits the wind returns.
[7]All streams run to the sea,
  but the sea is not full;
 to the place where the streams flow,
  there they flow again.
[8]All things are full of weariness;
  a man cannot utter it;
 the eye is not satisfied with seeing,
  nor the ear filled with hearing.
[9]What has been is what will be,
  and what has been done is what
    will be done;
  and there is nothing new under the sun.
[10]Is there a thing of which it is said,
    "See, this is new"?

It has been already,
     in the ages before us.
[11]There is no remembrance of former things,
     nor will there be any remembrance
of later things yet to happen
     among those who come after.

ISAIAH 11:1–16

There shall come forth a shoot

REVISED STANDARD VERSION

[1]There shall come forth a shoot
     from the stump of Jesse,
     and a branch shall grow out of his
          roots.
[2]And the Spirit of the Lord shall
     rest upon him,
     the spirit of wisdom and
          understanding,
     the spirit of counsel and might,
     the spirit of knowledge and the
          fear of the Lord.
[3]And his delight shall be in the fear
     of the Lord.

He shall not judge by what his eyes see,
     or decide by what his ears hear;
[4]but with righteousness he shall
     judge the poor,
     and decide with equity for the
          meek of the earth;
and he shall smite the earth with the
     rod of his mouth,
     and with the breath of his lips he
          shall slay the wicked.
[5]Righteousness shall be the girdle of
     his waist,
     and faithfulness the girdle of his loins.

⁶The wolf shall dwell with the lamb,
   and the leopard shall lie down with the kid,
and the calf and the lion and the
      fatling together,
   and a little child shall lead them.
⁷The cow and the bear shall feed;
   their young shall lie down together;
   and the lion shall eat straw like the ox.
⁸The sucking child shall play over
      the hole of the asp,
   and the weaned child shall put his
      hand on the adder's den.
⁹They shall not hurt or destroy
   in all my holy mountain;
for the earth shall be full of the
      knowledge of the Lord
   as the waters cover the sea.
¹⁰In that day the root of Jesse shall stand as an
ensign to the peoples; him shall the nations
seek, and his dwellings shall be glorious.
¹¹In that day the Lord will extend his hand yet a
second time to recover the remnant which is
left of his people, from Assyria, from Egypt,
from Pathros, from Ethiopia, from Elam, from
Shinar, from Hamath, and from the coastlands
of the sea.
¹²He will raise an ensign for the
      nations,
   and will assemble the outcasts of
      Israel,
and gather the dispersed of Judah
   from the four corners of the earth.
¹³The jealousy of Ephraim shall depart,
   and those who harass Judah shall
      be cut off;
Ephraim shall not be jealous of Judah,
   and Judah shall not harass Ephraim.
¹⁴But they shall swoop down upon the
      shoulder of the Philistines in
      the west,
   and together they shall plunder
      the people of the east.
They shall put forth their hand
      against Edom and Moab,
   and the Ammonites shall obey them.

[15]And the Lord will utterly destroy
   the tongue of the sea of Egypt;
and will wave his hand over the River
   with his scorching wind,
and smite it into seven channels
   that men may cross dryshod.
[16]And there will be a highway from Assyria
   for the remnant which is left of
   his people,
as there was for Israel
   when they came up from the land
   of Egypt.

PSALM 13

How long, O Lord?

REVISED STANDARD VERSION

[1]How long, O Lord? Wilt thou
   forget me for ever?
  How long wilt thou hide thy
   face from me?
[2]How long must I bear pain in my soul,
   and have sorrow in my heart all
   the day?
  How long shall my enemy be exalted
   over me?

[3]Consider and answer me, O Lord
   my God;
  lighten my eyes, lest I sleep the
   sleep of death;
[4]lest my enemy say, "I have
   prevailed over him";
  lest my foes rejoice because I am
   shaken.

[5]But I have trusted in thy steadfast love;
   my heart shall rejoice in thy salvation.

⁶I will sing to the Lord,
    because he has dealt bountifully
      with me.

PSALM 137

By the waters of Babylon

REVISED STANDARD VERSION

¹By the waters of Babylon,
there we sat down and wept,
    when we remembered Zion.
²On the willows there
    we hung up our lyres.
³For there our captors
    required of us songs,
and our tormentors, mirth, saying,
    "Sing us one of the songs of
      Zion!"

⁴How shall we sing the Lord's song
    in a foreign land?
⁵If I forget you, O Jerusalem,
    let my right hand wither!
⁶Let my tongue cleave to the roof of
      my mouth,
    if I do not remember you,
if I do not set Jerusalem
    above my highest joy!

⁷Remember, O Lord, against the
      Edomites
    the day of Jerusalem,
how they said, "Rase it, rase it!
    Down to its foundations!"
⁸O daughter of Babylon, you devastator!
    Happy shall he be who requites you
    with what you have done to us!
⁹Happy shall he be who takes your
      little ones
    and dashes them against the rock!

SONG OF SONGS 7:1–13

How graceful are your feet in sandals

REVISED STANDARD VERSION

¹How graceful are your feet in
    sandals,
    O queenly maiden!
Your rounded thighs are like jewels,
    the work of a master hand.
²Your navel is a rounded bowl
    that never lacks mixed wine.
Your belly is a heap of wheat,
    encircled with lilies.
³Your two breasts are like two fawns,
    twins of a gazelle.
⁴Your neck is like an ivory tower.
Your eyes are pools in Heshbon,
    by the gate of Bath-rab'bim.
Your nose is like a tower of Lebanon,
    overlooking Damascus.
⁵Your head crowns you like Carmel,
    and your flowing locks are like purple;
    a king is held captive in the tresses.

⁶How fair and pleasant you are,
    O loved one, delectable maiden!
⁷You are stately as a palm tree,
    and your breasts are like its clusters.
⁸I say I will climb the palm tree
    and lay hold of its branches.
Oh, may your breasts be like
      clusters of the vine,
    and the scent of your breath like apples,
⁹and your kisses like the best wine
    that goes down smoothly,
    gliding over lips and teeth.

¹⁰I am my beloved's,
    and his desire is for me.
¹¹Come, my beloved,
    let us go forth into the fields,
    and lodge in the villages;

¹²let us go out early to the vineyards,
    and see whether the vines have budded,
whether the grape blossoms have opened
    and the pomegranates are in bloom.
There I will give you my love.
¹³The mandrakes give forth fragrance,
    and over our doors are all choice fruits,
new as well as old,
    which I have laid up for you, O
    my beloved.

J O B 38:1 – 40:5

Then the Lord answered Job out of the whirlwind

REVISED STANDARD VERSION

TRANSLATED BY STEPHEN MITCHELL

38¹Then the Lord answered Job
    out of the whirlwind:
²Who is this that darkens counsel
    by words without knowledge?
³Gird up your loins like a man,
    I will question you, and you shall declare to
    me.

⁴Where were you when I laid the foundation of
    the earth?
    Tell me, if you have understanding.
⁵Who determined its measurements—surely
    you know!
    Or who stretched the line upon it?
⁶On what were its bases sunk,
    or who laid its cornerstone,
⁷when the morning stars sang together,
    and all the sons of God shouted for joy?

⁸Or who shut in the sea with doors,
    when it burst forth from the womb;
⁹when I made clouds its garment,
    and thick darkness its swaddling band,
¹⁰and prescribed bounds for it,
    and set bars and doors,

Then the unnameable answered Job
    from within the whirlwind:
Who is this whose ignorant words
    smear my design with darkness?
Stand up now like a man;
    I will question you: please, instruct me.

Where were you when I planned the earth?
    Tell me, if you are so wise.
Do you know who took its dimensions,
    measuring its length with a cord?
What were its pillars built on?
    Who laid down its cornerstone,
while the morning stars burst out singing
    and the angels shouted for joy!

Were you there when I stopped the waters,
    as they issued gushing from the womb?
when I wrapped the ocean in clouds
    and swaddled the sea in shadows?
when I closed it in with barriers
    and set its boundaries, saying,

[11]and said, "Thus far shall you come, and no
    farther,
    and here shall your proud waves be stayed"?

"Here you may come, but no farther;
    here shall your proud waves break."

[12]Have you commanded the morning since
    your days began,
    and caused the dawn to know its place,
[13]that it might take hold of the skirts of the
    earth,
    and the wicked be shaken out of it?
[14]It is changed like clay under the sea and it is
    dyed like a garment.
[15]From the wicked their light is withheld,
    and their uplifted arm is broken.

Have you ever commanded morning
    or guided dawn to its place—
to hold the corners of the sky
    and shake off the last few stars?
All things are touched with color;
    the whole world is changed.

[16]Have you entered into the springs of the sea,
    or walked in the recesses of the deep?
[17]Have the gates of death been revealed to
    you,
    or have you seen the gates of deep darkness?
[18]Have you comprehended the expanse of the
    earth?
    Declare, if you know all this.

Have you walked through the depths of the ocean
    or dived to the floor of the sea?
Have you stood at the gates of doom
    or looked through the gates of death?
Have you seen to the edge of the universe?
    Speak up, if you have such knowledge.

[19]Where is the way to the dwelling of light,
    and where is the place of darkness,
[20]that you may take it to its territory
    and that you may discern the path to its
    home?
[21]You know, for you were born then,
    and the number of your days is great!

Where is the road to light?
    Where does darkness live?
(Perhaps you will guide them home
    or show them the way to their house.)
You know, since you have been there
    and are older than all creation.

[22]Have you entered the storehouses of the
    snow,
    or have you seen the storehouses of the hail,
[23]which I have reserved for the time of trouble,
    for the day of battle and war?
[24]What is the way to the place where the light
    is distributed,
    or where the east wind is scattered upon the
    earth?

Have you seen where the snow is stored
    or visited the storehouse of hail,
which I keep for the day of terror,
    the final hours of the world?
Where is the west wind released
    and the east wind sent down to earth?

[25]Who has cleft a channel for the torrents of
    rain,
    and a way for the thunderbolt,

Who cuts a path for the thunderstorm
    and carves a road for the rain—
to water the desolate wasteland,

²⁶to bring rain on a land where no man is,
on the desert in which there is no man;
²⁷to satisfy the waste and desolate land,
and to make the ground put forth grass?

²⁸Has the rain a father,
or who has begotten the drops of dew?
²⁹From whose womb did the ice come forth,
and who has given birth to the hoarfrost of
heaven?
³⁰The waters become hard like stone,
and the face of the deep is frozen.

³¹Can you bind the chains of the Pleiades,
or loose the cords of Orion?
³²Can you lead forth the Mazzaroth in their
season,
or can you guide the Bear with its children?
³³Do you know the ordinances of the heavens?
Can you establish their rule on the earth?

³⁴Can you lift up your voice to the clouds,
that a flood of waters may cover you?
³⁵Can you send forth lightnings, that they may
go
and say to you, "Here we are"?
³⁶Who has put wisdom in the clouds,
or given understanding to the mists?
³⁷Who can number the clouds by wisdom?
Or who can tilt the waterskins of the
heavens,
³⁸when the dust runs into a mass
and the clods cleave fast together?

³⁹Can you hunt the prey for the lion,
or satisfy the appetite of the young lions,
⁴⁰when they crouch in their dens,
or lie in wait in their covert?
⁴¹Who provides for the raven its prey,
when its young ones cry to God,
and wander about for lack of food?

39¹Do you know when the mountain goats
bring forth?
Do you observe the calving of the hinds?
²Can you number the months that they fulfil,
and do you know the time when they bring
forth,

the land where no man lives;
to make the wilderness blossom
and cover the desert with grass?

Does the rain have a father?
Who has begotten the dew?
Out of whose belly is the ice born?
Whose womb labors with the sleet?
(The water's surface stiffens;
the lake grows hard as rock.)

Can you tie the Twins together
or loosen the Hunter's cords?
Can you light the Evening Star
or lead out the Bear and her cubs?
Do you know all the patterns of heaven
and how they affect the earth?

If you shout commands to the thunderclouds,
will they rush off to do your bidding?
If you clap for the bolts of lightning,
will they come and say "Here we are"?
Who gathers up the stormclouds,
slits them and pours them out,
turning dust to mud
and soaking the cracked clay?

Do you hunt game for the lioness
and feed her ravenous cubs,
when they crouch in their den, impatient,
or lie in ambush in the thicket?
Who finds her prey at nightfall,
when her cubs are aching with hunger?

Do you tell the antelope to calve
or ease her when she is in labor?
Do you count the months of her fullness
and know when her time has come?
She kneels; she tightens her womb;
she pants, she presses, gives birth.

³when they crouch, bring forth their offspring,
    and are delivered of their young?
⁴Their young ones become strong,
      they grow up in the open;
    they go forth, and do not return to them.

Her little ones grow up;
    they leave and never return.

⁵Who has let the wild ass go free?
    Who has loosed the bonds of the swift ass,
⁶to whom I have given the steppe for his
      home,
    and the salt land for his dwelling place?
⁷He scorns the tumult of the city;
    he hears not the shouts of the driver.
⁸He ranges the mountains as his pasture,
    and he searches after every green thing.

Who unties the wild ass
    and lets him wander at will?
He ranges the open prairie
    and roams across the saltlands.
He is far from the tumult of cities;
    he laughs at the driver's whip.
He scours the hills for food,
    in search of anything green.

⁹Is the wild ox willing to serve you?
    Will he spend the night at your crib?
¹⁰Can you bind him in the furrow with ropes,
    or will he harrow the valleys after you?
¹¹Will you depend on him because his strength
      is great,
    and will you leave to him your labor?
¹²Do you have faith in him that he will return,
    and bring your grain to your threshing
      floor?

Is the wild ox willing to serve you?
    Will he spend the night in your stable?
Can you tie a rope to his neck?
    Will he harrow the fields behind you?
Will you trust him because he is powerful
    and leave him to do your work?
Will you wait for him to come back,
    bringing your grain to the barn?

¹³The wings of the ostrich wave proudly;
    but are they the pinions and plumage of
      love?
¹⁴For she leaves her eggs to the earth,
    and lets them be warmed on the ground,
¹⁵forgetting that a foot may crush them,
    and that the wild beast may trample them.
¹⁶She deals cruelly with her young, as if they
      were not hers;
    though her labor be in vain, yet she has no
      fear;
¹⁷because God has made her forget wisdom,
    and given her no share in understanding.
¹⁸When she rouses herself to flee,
    she laughs at the horse and his rider.

Do you deck the ostrich with wings,
    with elegant plumes and feathers?
She lays her eggs in the dirt
    and lets them hatch on the ground,
forgetting that a foot may crush them
    or sharp teeth crack them open.
She treats her children cruelly,
    as if they were not her own.
For God deprived her of wisdom
    and left her with little sense.
When she spreads her wings to run,
    she laughs at the horse and rider.

¹⁹Do you give the horse his might?
 Do you clothe his neck with strength?
²⁰Do you make him leap like the locust?
 His majestic snorting is terrible.
²¹He paws in the valley, and exults in his
  strength;
 he goes out to meet the weapons.
²²He laughs at fear, and is not dismayed;
 he does not turn back from the sword.
²³Upon him rattle the quiver,
 the flashing spear and the javelin.
²⁴With fierceness and rage he swallows the
  ground;
 he cannot stand still at the sound of the
  trumpet.
²⁵When the trumpet sounds, he says "Aha!"
 He smells the battle from afar,
 the thunder of the captains, and the
  shouting.

²⁶Is it by your wisdom that the hawk soars,
 and spreads his wings toward the south?
²⁷Is it at your command that the eagle mounts
  up
 and makes his nest on high?
²⁸On the rock he dwells and makes his home
 in the fastness of the rocky crag.
²⁹Thence he spies out the prey;
 his eyes behold it afar off.
³⁰His young ones suck up blood;
 and where the slain are, there is he.

40¹And the LORD said to Job:
²Shall a faultfinder contend with the Al-
  mighty?
He who argues with God, let him answer it.

³Then Job answered the LORD:
⁴Behold, I am of small account; what shall
  I answer thee?
 I lay my hand on my mouth.
⁵I have spoken once, and I will not answer;
 twice, but I will proceed no further.

Do you give the horse his strength?
 Do you clothe his neck with terror?
Do you make him leap like a locust,
 snort like a blast of thunder?
He paws and champs at the bit;
 he exults as he charges into battle.
He laughs at the sight of danger;
 he does not wince from the sword
or the arrows nipping at his ears
 or the flash of spear and javelin.
With his hooves he swallows the ground;
 he quivers at the sound of the trumpet.
When the trumpet calls, he says "Ah!"
 From far off he smells the battle,
 the thunder of the captains and the shouting.

Do you show the hawk how to fly,
 stretching his wings on the wind?
Do you teach the vulture to soar
 and build his nest in the clouds?
He makes his home on the mountaintop,
 on the unapproachable crag.
He sits and scans for prey;
 from far off his eyes can spot it;
his little ones drink its blood.
 Where the unburied are, he is.

Then the Unnameable Asked Job:
Has God's accuser resigned?
 Has my critic swallowed his tongue?

Job said to the Unnameable:
I am speechless: what can I answer?
 I put my hand on my mouth.
I have said too much already;
 now I will speak no more.

SOLOMON IBN GABIROL

[c. 1022 – c. 1070]

In Praise of God

TRANSLATED BY T. CARMI

Morning and evening I seek You,
spreading out my hands, lifting up my
face in prayer. I sigh for You with a
thirsting heart; I am like the pauper
begging at my doorstep. The heights of   5
heaven cannot contain Your presence,
yet You have a dwelling in my mind.
I try to conceal Your glorious name in
my heart, but my desire for You grows
till it bursts out of my mouth. There-   10
fore I shall praise the name of the Lord
as long as the breath of the living God
is in my nostrils.

JUDAH HALEVI

[c. 1071 – c. 1141]

The Pure Lover

TRANSLATED BY T. CARMI

Gently, my hard-hearted, soft-hipped
one, deal gently with me and let me
bow down before you. It is only my
eyes that were ravished by you; my
heart is pure, yes, but my eyes are not.   5
Oh, let my eyes pluck the roses and
lilies that were sown together in your
face! I rake the fire of your cheeks, to
put out fire with fire: and when I am
thirsty, it is there that I look for water.   10
Oh, I would suck your red lips that
flame like glowing coals, and my jaws
would be like tongs. My life hangs

upon the two scarlet threads [of your
lips], but my death lurks in the twilight   *15*
[of your hair]. Now the nights are
endless, though once no darkness came
between the days; Time was like clay
in my hands, and the zodiac turned
like a potter's wheel.   *20*

RAHEL BLUWSTEIN

[1890–1931]

Only of myself I knew how to tell

TRANSLATED BY RUTH FINER MINTZ

Only of myself I knew how to tell,
My world like the ant's compressed.
Also my burdens I carried like her.
Too many, too heavy for my thin shoulder.

Also my path—like hers to the treetop—   *5*
Was a path of pain, a path of toil.
A giant hand, sure and malicious,
A teasing hand lay over all.

All my ways trembled and wept
At this giant hand, in constant fright.   *10*
Why did you call me, shores of wonder?
Why disappoint me, distant lights?

DAVID VOGEL

[1891–1944]

[עָרֵי נְעוּרַי] *My childhood cities*

TRANSLATED BY T. CARMI

עָרֵי נְעוּרַי,
עַתָּה אֶת כֻּלָּן כְּבָר שָׁכַחְתִּי
וְאוֹתָךְ בְּאַחַת מֵהֶנָּה.

My childhood cities, by now I've
forgotten them all, and you in one of
them.

תּוֹךְ שְׁלוּלִית מֵי־גֶשֶׁם

You still dance on for me in a puddle

יָחֵפָה בִּשְׁבִילִי עוֹד תִּרְקְדִי —

of rainwater—but surely you're already

וְהִנֵּה וַדַּאי כְּבָר מַתּ.

dead.

מִתּוֹךְ יַלְדוּתִי הָרְחוֹקָה

How quickly I galloped out of my

לִדְהֹר אֵיךְ גֶחְפַּזְתִּי,

distant childhood, until I reached the

עַד בּוֹא אֶל הֵיכַל הַזִּקְנָה הַלָּבָן —

white palace of old age, and found it

וְהוּא רָחָב נֶרִיק.

wide and empty.

רֵאשִׁית דַּרְכִּי

I can no longer see my road's begin-

שׁוּב לֹא אֶרְאֶה,

ning; I cannot see you or the self that

וְאוֹתָךְ לֹא אֶרְאֶה,

I was.

וְלֹא אוֹתִי מֵאָז.

אֹרְחַת הַיָּמִים,

The caravan of days, from afar, will

מֵרָחוֹק,

move on its way, from nothingness to

לָנוּעַ תּוֹסִיף הָלְאָה,

nothingness, without me.

מֵאַיִן אֶל אָיִן,

בִּלְעָדִי.

YOCHEVED BAT-MIRIAM

[b. 1901]

Like this before you

TRANSLATED BY RUTH FINER MINTZ

Like this before you, just as I am:
Not charming, not painted with pink and blue
But wild and rebellious, very bad,
So do I wish to stand before you.

Thus and thus is the measure of my height,   5
And so my life upon earth must be.
A larger measure for my soul's ascent,
Wandering silent it escapes its captivity.

My words will not soar me up to the heights
My words melt, suddenly frightened away.   10

Is it so, is it so I will speak to you,
I who am dying from day to day?

From day to day, dry land and the sea
Arise and shine like visions in sleep:
Like white highways from nothing to nothing   15
They stretch through the blue of heights and deeps.

I shall not be, I am not already,
Across the boundary I flutter my course.
Here and beyond is the sin not atoned,
The punishment, vengeance, reward and remorse?   20

I stand before you, just as I am.
Wild and rebellious, I bitterly cry.
Harsh and barren the weeping enfolds me.
It is for my Self who shall not be I.

LEAH GOLDBERG

[1911–1970]

From My Mother's House

TRANSLATED BY T. CARMI

My mother's mother died in the spring
of her days. And her daughter did not
remember her face. Her image,
engraved upon my grandfather's heart,
was erased from the world of figures   5
after his death.

Only her mirror remained in the house,
grown deeper with age within its silver
frame. And I, her pale granddaughter,
who do not resemble her, look into it   10

today as if into a lake that hides its
treasures beneath the water.

Deep down, behind my face, I see a
young woman, pink-cheeked, smiling.
She is wearing a wig. Now she is   *15*
hanging a long earring from her ear
lobe, threading it through the tiny
opening in the dainty flesh of her ear.

Deep down, behind my face, glows the
clear golden speck of her eyes. And the   *20*
mirror carries on the family tradition:
that she was very beautiful.

YEHUDA AMICHAI

[b. 1924]

A Pity. We Were Such a Good Invention

TRANSLATED BY ASSIA GUTMANN

They amputated
your thighs off my hips.
As far as I'm concerned
they are all surgeons. All of them.

They dismantled us   *5*
each from the other.
As far as I'm concerned
they are all engineers. All of them.

A pity. We were such a good
and loving invention.   *10*
An airplane made from a man and wife.
Wings and everything.
We hovered a little above the earth.

We even flew a little.

DALIA RAVIKOVITCH

[b. 1936]

Mechanical Doll

TRANSLATED BY T. CARMI

On that night I was a mechanical doll
turning right and left, in all directions,
and I fell flat on my face and was
broken to bits, and they tried to put my
parts together with skilful hands.   5

And after that I again became a proper
doll, and my bearing, at all times, was
poised and submissive. But by then I
was already a different sort of doll, like
an injured twig, still held fast by a   10
tendril.

And afterwards I went to dance at a
ball, but they put me in the company
of cats and dogs, yet all my steps were
measured and fixed.   15

And I had golden hair and I had blue
eyes and I had a dress the color of
garden flowers and I had a straw hat
with an ornamental cherry.

Chinese Poetry

Few cultures have valued poetry as much as the Chinese. Prized from earliest times by field-workers and emperors alike, Chinese verse evolved from an oral poetry into an art form in which each word is written as a single, discrete calligraphic character that combines the beauty of painting with the functionality of language. As in the West, traditional Chinese poetry was often the result of a spontaneous overflow of powerful feelings or the reward of deliberate artifice. But unlike in the West, in China the writing of poetry was never considered the domain of a select, inspired few. Viewed simply as a daily part of living, poetry was even composed by civil servants, many of whom had to write poetry to pass an imperial exam for public office.

China's literary tradition is unusually humanistic in its choice of subjects and tone. It refuses to idealize such staples of Western poetry as war, heroic adventures, and even passionate love, choosing, instead, to focus on daily living. As such, traditional Chinese poetry is often startlingly modern. Even centuries-old works focus with a clear, intimate eye on the common occurrences of normal life: the meeting and parting of friends, aging, and the experiences of grief and loneliness. Readers who admire the poetry of William Carlos Williams (pp. 576–596), Charles Reznikoff (pp. 681–684), or Marianne Moore (pp. 627–638) will not only appreciate the subtle, discerning, and imagistic aesthetic of Chinese verse, but will also recognize it as a significant impulse in much modern American poetry.

Chinese poems are not limited to the strictly personal, however; many focus on public issues. According to Confucian philosophy, a ruler was to welcome moral and didactic poems that inventoried the griefs and complaints of his subjects. Though many Chinese officials who courageously upheld this Confucian ideal often found themselves sent into exile, the tradition of addressing public issues in poetry continues to the present day. The contemporary dissident poetry of Jiang He is a case in point. His "To the Execution Ground" eloquently captures the pressing political circumstances of today's China.

As Chinese poetry is often political or communal in spirit, scholars also suggest that the very nature of the Chinese written word furthers a sense of community. Because the forms of the calligraphic characters have changed over time, they constantly allude to China's collective cultural past. Conversely, these written or painted words also highlight each poet's individual artistry. For though an individual character keeps its shape regardless of its author, the quality of the brush strokes that make up a word will vary from one calligrapher to another. Most poets paint with a wolf-hair brush and pine-soot ink on absorbent mulberry-bark paper. The tensions between a calligraphic character's visual surface and its possible meanings become reflections of each artist's individual genius.

Customarily conservative in its use of metaphor, simile, personification, and other figures of speech associated with Western poetry, Chinese poetry creates much of its emotion through imagery, implying a great deal more than is stated. Nature imagery often functions on a symbolic level. For example, plum blossoms symbolize stamina and resolution; bamboo symbolizes principle and honesty. Similarly, a pine tree or a crane is a traditional emblem of a long life honorably lived.

The *Book of Odes* is considered China's first poetry anthology. It is believed to have been compiled by Confucius (551–479 B.C.) though many critics believe these poems were probably in existence several centuries before his birth. The 305-poem text is made up of folk songs such as "Near the East Gate" as well as of religious hymns and more stately odes celebrating the nobility. Another important anthology to emerge at the close of the Chou dynasty (1030–221 B.C.) is *The Elegies of Ch'u*, which is believed to have been composed or compiled by Ch'u Yüan (343–277 B.C.), a loyal minister who drowned himself after falling out of favor with the King of Ch'u.

The golden age of Chinese literature arrived during the T'ang dynasty (618–907), when Indian and Buddhist influences were strong. Nearly fifty thousand poems from this period have survived. Among the many gifted poets who wrote during the T'ang period, Li Po and Tu Fu were two of the greatest. Intolerant of restrictions, Li Po (701–762) approaches the Western idea of a romantic lyric poet. Leading a life that has inspired legends of wanderings and drinking bouts, Li Po wrote thousands of poems that were often playful and almost always eloquent. More concerned with intimate themes than with social and political ones, Li Po often drew on the traditional subjects of separation, commemoration, and celebrations for his inspiration, and is seen as a leading exponent of spiritual and imaginative freedom.

Li Po's younger friend, Tu Fu (712–770) may be viewed as Li Po's opposite. Whereas Li Po was celebrated in his lifetime, Tu Fu was neglected by his contemporaries. While Li Po led the kind of life that inspires legends, Tu Fu, disciplined and highly responsible, worked earnestly as a minor official personally committed to China's political struggles. Today, Tu Fu is remembered as the "poet sage" who brought a degree of candor, realism, verisimilitude, and humor to his meticulously crafted poems.

The decline of the T'ang dynasty witnessed the introduction of a poetry based on the meters of popular songs. One of China's greatest "tune" poets, Li Ching-chao (1081 – c. 1141), is one of China's most famous woman poets. A scholar as well as a poet, she employed "lyric" meters almost exclusively. Expanding on lyric meter, "aria poems," or "tone" poems, became the next major development in Chinese poetry. Arias were originally written for plays with alternating spoken and sung sections, but were soon composed independent of any plays. These poems, like the sung sections of the plays they emulated, were called "arias."

The subsequent Ming (1368–1644) and Ch'ing (1644–1911) periods saw no significant developments in China's poetic tradition. During the twentieth century the prevailing impact of the West on Chinese writers encouraged replacing the classical language with modern spoken Mandarin as the written medium. With the introduction of Western texts, influences on Chinese poets began to include such European schools of poetics as the Symbolists as well as more traditional sources. For example, consider "A Thought" by Li Chin-fa (1900?–) or "I think" by Tai Wang-shu (1905–1950). Both are evocative in the traditional manner, but the tone and imagery have expanded to include Western impressions. Other poets, such as Shen Yee-pin (1883–1968), continued to work in the tradition of Tu Fu and Li Ching-chao and focus with an unclouded, intimate eye on the familiar occurrences of ordinary life.

World War II and the succeeding civil war interrupted further literary exploration, but poets like Cheng Min (b. 1924) kept the tradition alive while still exploring new possibilities in her elegant and luminous poetry. Ironically, though Mao Tse-tung (1893–1976) was himself a poet who wrote in a highly orthodox manner, he sought to transform China's traditional culture into a revolutionary Communist society, suppressing any writing that emphasized China's links to the past. Recently, however, a new movement, "literature from the ruins," has emerged in the Confucian tradition of proclaiming injustice. "To the Execution Ground" by Jiang He (b. 1952) and "The Ruins of Gandan" by Yang Lain (b. 1955) fall into this category. There is little information on either poet except that Yang Lain's books have been banished since 1987. Bei Dao (b. 1949) is another revolutionary voice from contemporary China. Considered one of China's most gifted and controversial writers to emerge from the recent political upheavals, he has been both a Red Guard and political dissenter. His poetry simultaneously reflects and criticizes China's Cultural Revolution of the 60s and 70s.

ANONYMOUS (*CH'U TZ'U*)

[c. 300]

The Lord Among the Clouds

TRANSLATED BY BURTON WATSON

I bathe in orchid water,
    wash my hair with scents,
put on colored robes,
    flower-figured.
The spirit, twisting and turning,   5
    poised now above,

radiant and shining
  in endless glory,
comes to take his ease
  in the Temple of Long Life,   *10*
and with the sun and moon
  to pair his brilliance.
Riding his dragon chariot,
  drawn like a god,
he hovers and soars,   *15*
  roaming the vastness;
spirit majestic,
  but now descended,
swiftly rising
  far off to the clouds.   *20*
He looks down on Chi-chou,
  the regions beyond,
crosses to the four seas;
  what land does he not visit?
I think of you, Lord,   *25*
  sighing.
You afflict my heart
  sorely, sorely!

ANONYMOUS (SHIH CHING)

[c. 500]

Near the East Gate

TRANSLATED BY HENG KUAN

Near the East Gate
Young women go
Like so many clouds all day:
Like drifting clouds
A thought of them   *5*
Soon blows away.

    There. White robe
    and a blue scarf—
    she makes my day.

Near the Great Tower and Wall   10
Go slender girls
Like reeds by river's edge:
Like bending reeds
A thought of them
Soon passes by.   15

There. White robe
and a purple scarf—
she makes me rejoice.

LI PO

[701–762]

Autumn Cove

TRANSLATED BY BURTON WATSON

At Autumn Cove, so many white monkeys,
bounding, leaping up like snowflakes in flight!
They coax and pull their young ones down from the branches
to drink and frolic with the water-borne moon.

Poem No. 19 in the Old Manner

TRANSLATED BY BURTON WATSON

West ascending Lotus Flower Mountain,
far far away I saw the Bright Star maid;
with pale hands she plucked lotus blossoms,
with airy steps she walked the great clear void;
her rainbow skirts, their broad belt trailing,   5
dipped and fluttered as she strode up the sky.
She called me to climb with her to Cloud Terrace,
to lift hands in salutation to Wei Shu-ch'ing.
Dazed and enraptured, I went with her;
mounting a stork, we rode the purple gloom.   10

I looked down and saw the Lo-yang River,
barbarian troops marching in endless files;
streams of blood that stained the meadow grasses,
wildcats and wolves wearing the hats of men!

TU FU

[712–770]

Ballad of a Hundred Worries

TRANSLATED BY DAVID HINTON

Still a child's heart at fifteen. . . . I remember
running back and forth, sturdy as a brown calf.

And in September, courtyard dates and pears ripe,
I could scramble up a thousand trees in a day.

How suddenly it all passed. Already fifty, I rarely   5
walk, or even get up. If not asleep, I sit resting.

Today, forcing small talk and laughter for a host,
I grieve over the hundred worries crowding my life.

And when I return, the house bare as ever, my poor
wife mirrors the look she knows too well on my face.   10

Silly kids, still ignorant of courtesies due a father—
crying at the kitchen door, angry, they demand food.

Alone, Looking for Blossoms Along the River

TRANSLATED BY DAVID HINTON

1

The sorrow of riverside blossoms inexplicable,
And nowhere to complain—I've gone half crazy.

I look up our southern neighbor. But my friend in wine
Gone ten days drinking, I find only an empty bed.

2

A thick frenzy of blossoms shrouding the riverside,   5
I stroll, listing dangerously, in full fear of spring.

Poems, wine—even this profusely driven, I endure.
Arrangements for this old, white-haired man can wait.

3

A deep river, two or three houses in bamboo quiet,
And such goings-on: red blossoms glaring with white!   10

Among spring's vociferous glories, I too have my place:
With a lovely wine, bidding life's affairs *bon voyage*.

4

Looking east to Shao, its smoke filled with blossoms,
I admire that stately Po-hua wineshop even more.

To empty golden wine cups, calling such beautiful   15
Dancing girls to embroidered mats—who could bear it?

5

East of the river, before Abbot Huang's grave,
Spring is a frail splendor among gentle breezes.

In this crush of peach blossoms opening ownerless,
Shall I treasure light reds, or treasure them dark?   20

6

At Madame Huang's house, blossoms fill the paths:
Thousands, tens of thousands haul the branches down.

And butterflies linger playfully—an unbroken
Dance floating to songs orioles sing at their ease.

7

I don't so love blossoms I want to die. I'm afraid,   25
Once they are gone, of old age still more impetuous.

And they scatter gladly, by the branchful. Let's talk
Things over, little buds—open delicately, sparingly.

LI CHING-CHAO

[1081 – c. 1141]

From a flower-carrying pole

TO THE SHORT TUNE "THE MAGNOLIAS"

TRANSLATED BY KENNETH REXROTH AND LING CHUNG

From a flower-carrying pole
I bought a spray of Spring in bud,
All moist as if with tears,
Still holding the pink clouds of dawn
And traces of the morning dew.   5
Lest my lover should think
My face not as lovely as the flowers
I pin it slanting in my cloud like hair
And ask him to make a comparison.

Night comes

TO THE TUNE "TELLING OF INNERMOST FEELINGS"

TRANSLATED BY BURTON WATSON

Night comes and, drowsy with drink, I'm slow to shed my ornaments,
these plum petals stuck on a withered twig.
I wake from wine, its aroma scattering my spring sleep,
the dream grown distant—no returning there now.

No sound from anyone,   5
the moon still lingering,
kingfisher blinds lowered,
and once more I crush the withered stamens,
once more finger the fragrance left in them,
once more possess that time.   10

SHEN YEE-PING

[1883–1968]

Shutting the Door of a Tiny Study

SHUTTING THE DOOR OF A TINY STUDY, I ASK MY HUSBAND, WHO WORKS OUTSIDE IT, TO DO A PANEL IN GRASS WRITING. MAGIC ENTERS HIS WORD. IT IS WILD, CHANGED. I AM OVERJOYED.

TRANSLATED BY ROSABEL LU AND SANDRA SCHOR

As pirates from South River
overran the great Northeast
and as people flowed from the raging land,
precisely then I dared to name my house
"Contented Hut." And why must they despise   5
contentment snatched from the flames of war?
Oh, the heart's contentment
is never illicit. Both earth and sky
perceive no shame in contentment.
Must I walk in a mansion   10
down long corridors of rooms? My spare,
ordered house is snug as a simple boat.
In it, reading a small scroll
uplifts me. Nor do I read for reputation—
fame holds hands with slander. I overlook   15
fleet horses, tall silken carriages—
glory comes on foot. A spoon of rice,
something to drink: there's no shame
in frugality. Sometimes, as a poet
I become arrogant, bemoaning how bitterly   20
I work to make a poem
that will rival the great Tu Fu.
Frenzied, I extend a panel. I demand
you write upon it! Soon your brush begins—
a snake, a dragon. I am happy. Deep is my sigh   25
Yi yu shee! I attain unspeakable joy
as you throw your brush
and transform a single word
into a rainbow. One final sweep
and a living whale opens   30
the white sparkle of sea.

MAO TSE-TUNG

[1893–1976]

Sixteen-Syllable Stanza

TRANSLATED BY KAI-YU HSU

What hills!
I sped my steed over them without dismounting.
Looking back with a start
I saw them only three feet from the sky.

What hills!   5
Rising like angry waves in rivers and seas.
They rush by
As my horse immerses itself in the depth of battle.

LI CHIN-FA

[b. c. 1900]

A Thought

TRANSLATED BY KAI-YU HSU

Like fallen leaves
Splashing blood
On our feet,

SIXTEEN-SYLLABLE STANZA   **'I saw . . . the sky** Mao's note: A folk song says:
    The K'u-lou Mountain above
    The Pa-pao Mountain below,
    Only three feet from the sky.
    Man passing over them must duck his head,
    And the horse must shed its saddle.

Life is but
A smile on the lips   5
Of death.

Under a half-dead moon,
You drink and sing,
The sound splitting your throat
Disappears in the northern wind.   10
Ah!
Go and caress your beloved.
Open your doors and windows,
Make her timid, and
Let the dust of the road cover   15
Her lovely eyes.
Is this the timidity
And anger
Of life?
Like fallen leaves   20
Splashing blood
On our feet.

Life is but
A smile on the lips
Of death.   25

TAI WANG-SHU

[1905–1950]

I think

TRANSLATED BY KAI-YU HSU

I think, therefore I am a butterfly—

The little flowers' gentle call, after endless years,
Comes to vibrate my multicolored wings
Through the cloud of dreamless perpetual sleep.

CHENG MIN

[b. 1924]

A Glance

Rembrandt's "Young Girl at an Open Half Door"

TRANSLATED BY KAI-YU HSU

Exquisite are the shoulders receding into the shadow,
And the bosom, locked up, rich as a fruit-laden orchard.
The shining face, like the flush of dream,
Echoes the hands resting on the half door, so slender.

The river of time carries away another leaf from the tree of calendar,   5
Her half-closed eyes, like a riddle, speak of a blurred silence.
In the limited life the unchanging hurried pace is still too hurried,
She casts, in a casual evening, a lasting glance at the ever changing world.

BEI DAO

[b. 1949]

Declaration

FOR YU LUOKE

TRANSLATED BY BONNIE S. McDOUGALL

Perhaps the final hour is come
I have left no testament
Only a pen, for my mother
I am no hero
In an age without heroes   5
I just want to be a man

The still horizon
Divides the ranks of the living and the dead
I can only choose the sky
I will not kneel on the ground   10
Allowing the executioners to look tall
The better to obstruct the wind of freedom

From the star-like bullet holes shall flow
A blood-red dawn

JIANG HE

[b. 1952]

To the Execution Ground

TRANSLATED BY WIL-LIM YAP

Cheating winds muffle windows and eyes.
At this hour, killing is going on.
I cannot hide in the house.
My blood cannot let me remain this way.
Morning-like children cannot let me remain this way.   5
I am thrown into the prison.
Handcuffs and blood weave into a net upon my body.
My voice is cut off.
My heart is a ball of fire, burning silently upon my lips.
I am walking toward the execution ground, looking with scorn   10
Upon this historic night. In this corner of the world,
There is no other choice. I have chosen the sky
Because the sky will not rot.
Nothing but execution for me, otherwise darkness has nowhere to hide.
I was born in darkness, in order to create sun rays.   15
Nothing but execution for me, otherwise lies will be exposed.
I am all the people being milled by ancient rules and laws
Painfully watching
Myself being executed
Watching my blood flow, wave upon wave, till dried out.   20

YANG LAIN

[b. 1955]

The Ruins of Gandan

TRANSLATED BY GEREMIE BARMÉ AND J. MINFORD

For so it is: man is a sacrifice. He is the morning offering.
The Upanishads

Everywhere
        stone pillars
                erect wings spread to fly
Everywhere
        solitary crenellations   5
                unfathomable paths and voices of wind
A rough stillness has frozen the shapes of violence
This high peak, trapped by death,
        backdrop to a small stage

September,   10
        my autumn barren as this
Save for that azure blue
        which would recede at a touch
The sun unfolds, on an emptiness
        scrawled with the calligraphy of ruin   15
Breakers of rubble
        disintegrating hate and sorrow
Dusk, packs of dogs
        poke wet noses into history
Sniffing out the broken images beneath the earth   20

(Yesterday never passes, it is enfolded in today
The stars revolve, a single glance and primordial terror
Tumbles out of the darkness
All things complete at the same point of departure)

Japanese Poetry

The quest for agreement between life and art has lead over a million Japanese office workers, housewives, factory workers, students, policemen, and business executives to attend regularly scheduled group meetings where they may polish their haiku writing skills under the tutelage of an acknowledged master. Enthusiasm for poetry has even led newspapers and magazines to feature haiku columns and contests. In Japanese culture it is assumed that emperors as well as common soldiers will write love poems or poems about falling cherry blossoms.

The earliest surviving record of Japanese literature is *The Record of Ancient Matters* (712), followed by *The Collection of Ten Thousand Leaves* (760), a compendium of some 4,516 poems dating to the fourth century. Having absorbed much of Chinese civilization and Buddhism in the first five centuries A.D., the Japanese compiled these early works in the manner of Chinese models such as *The Book of Odes* and *The Elegies of Ch'u.*

One of the great poets included in *The Collection of Ten Thousand Leaves,* Kakinomoto no Hitomaro (c. 680 – c. 710), became known as the "saint of poetry." Combining lyricism, narrative forms, and complex parallelism, Hitomaro created a poetry of subtle ironies and luxuriant images still greatly admired today.

The next hundred years saw the emergence of classical Japanese literature in the Heian period (794–1192), also known as the Golden Age. This early classical period gave rise to several women poets considered the central figures of the Heian literary era. One such figure is the Lady Ōtomo no Sakanoe (c. 700–?) whose poetry was celebrated for its multiplicity of subjects, scholarly refinement, and verbal sheen. Another poet, the Lady Kasa (c. 700–?) wrote a series of poems to the poet Ōtomo no Yakamochi that made her one of the most famous of Japanese poets, though little else is known of her. Ono no Komachi (c. 834–?), served at the imperial court in what is now Kyoto, where she wrote her intricate, complex, and passionate poetry. Her devotion to technique and her philosophical depth helped direct Japanese poetry toward a more subjective and personal style. Her beauty and her forceful personality also made her the subject of a celebrated group of *Nō* plays. Another such poet, the Lady Izumi (c. 976–?) served as a lady-in-waiting. Committed to a life of both religious and erotic intensity, she gave voice to her life in a precise, lyrical, and highly intimate poetry recorded in her *Lady Izumi's Diary*.

The fourteenth century initiated the great dramatic works of *Nō* (or *Noh*) drama, a highly stylized dance drama with lyrical, poetic texts and masked actors that aroused significant interest in the modern West and influenced the dramatic lyrics of W. B. Yeats.

Another important development in Japanese poetry was "linked verse" or collaborative poetry that developed as a major medium for leading poets. In linked verse, classic poetry was divided into two "links," each written by a different poet. Two, three, or sometimes more poets worked together creating two to a hundred alternating five-seven-five and seven-seven syllable parts. The rules for "linked verse" poems are complex, but the underlying dictate is that any two consecutive parts must fashion a coherent whole. An early cultivator of this poetry was Monk Gusai (1282–1376) who set down many of the rudimentary rules of the form. His "Highly Renowned" (p. 938) was composed with the participation of ten other minor poets.

Haiku, a three-line poem consisting of seventeen syllables in a five-seven-five pattern, came into prominence through its mastery by Matsuo Bashō (1644–1694). Regarded by many as the finest haiku poet of all time, Bashō (the pseudonym of Matsuo Munefusa) served the local lord as a samurai. In 1667 he moved to Edo (now Tokyo), where he began to compose haiku that reflected the Zen Buddhist spirit of enlightenment. His attention to particulars and reverence for the natural world transformed haiku verse from an insignificant social pastime of the nobility into a major genre of Japanese poetry.

The essence of good haiku poetry is a momentary, implicitly spiritual insight presented imagistically and without moralizing. Haiku has a light touch, and when translating haiku, most poets admit that tone, texture, and feel are more important than any strict adherence to syllabic form. Bashō's most famous haiku (and perhaps the most famous of all haiku) focuses on a traditional Japanese subject: frog songs.

furuike ya	old pond . . .
kawazu tobikomu	a frog leaps in
mizu no oto	water's sound

In Japan, people study frog songs the way Westerners study bird calls. But Bashō's frog sings with his body as well as his voice. The poem records Bashō's spontaneous feeling as frog and water not only make one sound but literally become one. Expert at both lighthearted and more serious haiku, Bashō has been imitated the world over and has influenced such leading American poets as Ezra Pound, H.D., Wallace Stevens, and William Carlos Williams.

Tangiguchi Buson (1716–1783), later named Yosa Buson, another Japanese haiku poet and painter, is generally ranked second only to Matsuo Bashō. A gentleman scholar, Buson's technical skill as a painter in the southern Chinese style is also reflected in the sensual, objective quality of his poetry.

The third great haiku poet of the Tokugawa period, Kobayashi Issa (1763–1827), was the eldest son of a poor farmer. Suffering a cruel childhood, he went on to lead a life of poverty, studying the ways of small, seemingly inconsequential creatures. His poetry abounds with references to worms, flies, and grasshoppers. A rather unsophisticated figure compared to the rigorous, priestly Bashō and the cosmopolitan, scholarly Buson, Issa nevertheless ranks with them in greatness. His poetry is infused with humanity and compassion.

Modern Japanese poetry (1868 to the present) has absorbed the influence of Western European and American literature while still retaining a characteristically Japanese essence. Some Japanese poets, for example, have identified the French Surrealists, Ezra Pound, and T. S. Eliot as their "spiritual contemporaries." On the other hand, a poet like Miyazawa Kenji (1896–1933) remained closer to his Buddhist roots. Hardly acknowledged in his lifetime, his poetry is now prized for its acumen and freshness of imagery. Conversely, Kaneko Mitsuharu (1895–1975) wandered through Europe studying Whitman and Baudelaire. Relegated to obscurity during the 1930s for his critical attacks on Japanese militaristic policies, he emerged as a major postwar literary figure. Another important modern Japanese poet, Tomioka Taeko (b. 1935), brings a freshness of insight to psychological perspectives. She has also published novels, short stories, essays, and plays. The effect of her writings has often been compared to the biting ironies of the French film director René Clair.

KAKINOMOTO NO HITOMARO

[c. 680 – c. 710]

In Grief After His Wife's Death

TRANSLATED BY H. SATO AND B. WATSON

When she was alive, now a memory,
the two of us used to see, hand in hand,
the hundred-branch zelkova tree standing on the bank near us.
In as many ways as it sticks out its branches,
as luxuriantly as its leaves grow in spring,   5
I thought of my wife,
I depended upon her.
But because one cannot go against the way of the world,
in the wild field where heat haze flares
she hid herself with white-cloth scarves of heaven,   10
she rose and left with morning like a bird
and hid herself as the sun does, setting.
Each time the infant my lover left
as a keepsake for me cries, begging,
because I have nothing to give, nothing to leave with him,   15

though a man I lift him by his armpits.
In the bedroom with pillows
where my lover and I used to sleep,
I spend days, lonely, desolate till dark,
I spend nights, sighing till dawn.   20
I grieve but don't know what else to do,
I long for her but have no way of seeing her.
"Your wife you long for is seated
on Mount Wing of the great birds,"
someone says, so I come climbing over rocks   25
with difficulty. But there is nothing fortunate here,
with my wife who I thought was alive
lying in ashes.

A Strange Old Man

TRANSLATED BY KENNETH REXROTH

Masu kagami   A strange old man
Soko naru kage ni   Stops me,
Mukai ite miru   Looking out of my deep mirror.
Toki ni koso
Shiranu okina ni
Au kokochi sure

THE LADY ŌTOMO NO SAKANOE

[c. 700–?]

Love's Complaint

TRANSLATED BY H. SATO AND B. WATSON

Those sedges in light-flooded Naniwa—
you spoke as intimately as their clinging roots,
you said it would run deep into years, it would last long,
so I gave you my heart, as spotless
as a clear mirror.   5
          From that day,

unlike the seaweed that sways with the waves,
I did not have a heart that goes this way and that,
I trusted as one trusts a great ship.
But has a god, a rock-smasher, put us apart?   10
Or someone of this world interfered?
You used to come but you no longer do,
and no messenger bearing the catalpa branch appears.
Because of this there's nothing I can do.
All through the night black as leopard-flower seeds,   15
through the day till the red-rayed sun sets,
I grieve, but there's no sign,
I brood, but I don't know what to do.
They speak of "weak women"—I am just that,
weeping loudly like a child,   20
I go back and forth, waiting for your messenger—
will all this be in vain?

THE LADY KASA

[c. 700–?]

I dreamed I held

TRANSLATED BY KENNETH REXROTH

Tsurugi tachi	I dreamed I held
Mi ni tori sou to	A sword against my flesh.
Ime ni mitsu	What does it mean?
Nani no satoshi zomo	It means I shall see you soon.
Kimi ni awamu tame	

Like the crane whose cry

TRANSLATED BY H. SATO AND B. WATSON

Like the crane whose cry
I hear in the dark night,
I hear of you only
as someone far away—
we never so much as meet   5

ONO NO KOMACHI

[c. 834–?]

Submit to you

TRANSLATED BY H. SATO AND B. WATSON

Submit to you—
could that be what you're saying?
the way ripples on the water
submit to an idling wind?

They change

TRANSLATED BY H. SATO AND B. WATSON

They change,
though you can't see it
in the color of their faces—
these blossoms that are the hearts
of the people of this world   5

"Imagining her Death and Cremation"

TRANSLATED BY H. SATO AND B. WATSON

Sad—the end that waits me—
to think at last
I'll be a mere haze
pale green over the fields

THE LADY IZUMI

[c. 976–?]

Waiting for My Two Lovers Stationed in Distant Places

TRANSLATED BY H. SATO AND B. WATSON

Having waited for this one for this, that one for that, I can no longer tell which is who

To a Man Who Said, "You've Forgotten Me"

TRANSLATED BY H. SATO AND B. WATSON

Have I not forgotten you! If I hadn't, I certainly would, if I looked into your heart again!

Looking at My Grandchildren

TRANSLATED BY H. SATO AND B. WATSON

Having left us, which of us does she care for? I think more of my child, she, surely, of her children

MONK GUSAI

[1282–1376]

from *Highly Renowned*

(COMPOSED IN 1355 BY MONK GUSAI AND TEN OTHER POETS)

TRANSLATED BY H. SATO AND B. WATSON

Highly renowned, the cuckoo's voice cannot be topped   *Gusai*
lush trees—all of them are pines in a wind   *Yoshimoto*

by the mountain there's a cool water flow   *Eiun*

     the moon is best when at the ridge   *Shūa*

the autumn sun was just out of the clouds   *Soa*   5

     after a shower morning mists remain in the sky   *Gyōa*

the dew at evening does not settle on my sleeves   *Mokuchin*

     in any village there's that sound of beating cloth   *Shigekazu*

back from my travels—is her time of waiting long past?   *Gusai*

     from today on I won't count on any blossoms   *Yoshimoto*   10

though hazy, the winds still blow over the tree tops   *Chikanaga*

     the white snow remains in the shaded parts of the mountain   *Gyōa*

the moon upstream must freeze the water   *Gusai*

     as waves roll in, the cove grows cold   *Shūa*

the voices of plovers flying away are distant   *Ietada*   15

     friendless, yes, but evening still comes to a traveler   *Gusai*

though I've abandoned the world, let alone myself   *Yoshimoto*

     the melancholy of autumn lingers in this mountain village   *Eiun*

if you are dew, be mindful of my tearful sleeves   *Soa*

     wait, and the night you count on someone feels so long   *Gyōa*   20

though the wind stirring over rice stalks may reach the pines   *Gusai*

     the shore reeds by the waves have put out ears   *Soa*

MATSUO BASHŌ

[1644–1694]

The temple bell stops

TRANSLATED BY ROBERT BLY

The temple bell stops—
but the sound keeps coming
out of the flowers.

How rough a sea!

TRANSLATED BY HAROLD G. HENDERSON

How rough a sea!
and, stretching over Sado Isle,
the Galaxy . . .

Not even a hat

TRANSLATED BY HAROLD G. HENDERSON

Not even a hat—
and cold rain falling on me?
Tut-tut! think of that!

On a journey, ill

TRANSLATED BY HAROLD G. HENDERSON

On a journey, ill—
and my dreams, on withered fields
are wandering still.

TANGIGUCHI BUSON

[1716–1783]

The piercing chill I feel

TRANSLATED BY HAROLD G. HENDERSON

The piercing chill I feel:
my dead wife's comb, in our bedroom,
under my heel . . .

Blossoms on the pear

TRANSLATED BY HAROLD G. HENDERSON

Blossoms on the pear—
and a woman in the moonlight
reads a letter there.

KOBAYASHI ISSA

[1763–1827]

Awakened by a horse's fart

TRANSLATED BY H. SATO AND B. WATSON

> Awakened by a horse's fart,
> I see
> a firefly in the air

I look into a dragonfly's eye

TRANSLATED BY ROBERT BLY

> I look into a dragonfly's eye
> and see
> the mountains over my shoulder.

The old dog bends his head listening

TRANSLATED BY ROBERT BLY

> The old dog bends his head listening . . .
> I guess the singing
> of the earthworms gets *to* him.

The Pigeon Makes His Request

TRANSLATED BY ROBERT BLY

> Since it's spring and raining,
> could we have a little different expression,
> oh owl?

Falling leaves

TRANSLATED BY H. SATO AND B. WATSON

Falling leaves,
making no sound,
intensify the cold

KANEKO MITSUHARU

[1895–1975]

Mount Fuji

TRANSLATED BY E. D. SHIFFERT AND YUKI SAWA

The same as stacked lunchboxes
this Japan, narrow and confined.

From this corner to that corner, meanly and stingily
all of us are being counted up.
And, unlimited rudeness,   5
all of us are drafted—stupid idiots.

Birth certificates, they ought to be burned right away.
Nobody should remember my son.

My son,
be concealed away inside this hand.   10
Hide away for a while underneath a hat.

Both your father and mother in the house at the foot of the mountain
have talked about it all night long.

Soaking the withered forest at the foot of the mountain,
making sounds like twigs breaking, crackle, crackle,   15
the whole night rain was falling.

My son, you are soaked wet to the skin
carrying a heavy gun, gasping for breath,
walking along as if fallen into a trance. What place is it?

That place is not known. But for you   *20*
both your father and mother go outside to search aimlessly.

The night hateful with only such dreams,
the long anxious nighttime, at last ends.

The rain has let up.
In the sky vacant without my son,   *25*
well, how damnably disgusting,
like a shabby worn-out bathrobe,
Fuji!

MIYAZAWA KENJI

[1896–1933]

November 3rd

TRANSLATED BY H. SATO AND B. WATSON

neither yielding to rain
nor yielding to wind
yielding neither to
snow nor to summer heat
   with a stout body   *5*
        like that
without greed
never getting angry
always smiling quiet-
          ly   *10*
eating one and a half pints of brown rice
and bean paste and a bit of
            vegetables a day
in everything
not taking oneself   *15*
      into account
       looking listening understanding well
and not forgetting
living in the shadow of pine trees in a field
   in a small   *20*
     hut thatched with miscanthus

if in the east there's a
    sick child
going and nursing
        him   25
if in the west there's a tired mother
going and for her
    carrying
      bundles of rice
if in the south   30
  there's someone
          dying
going
  and saying
    you don't have to be   35
      afraid
if in the north
     there's a quarrel
        or a lawsuit
saying it's not worth it   40
      stop it
in a drought
  shedding tears
in a cold summer
  pacing back and forth   lost   45
called
  a good-for-nothing
     by everyone
neither praised
nor thought a pain   50
  someone
     like that
is what I want
    to be

TOMIOKA TAEKO

[b. 1935]

Just the Two of Us

TRANSLATED BY B. WATSON AND H. SATO

You'll make tea,
I'll make toast.

While we're doing that,
at times, early in the evening,
someone may notice the moonrise dyed scarlet   *5*
and at times visit us
but that'll be the last time the person comes here.
We'll shut the doors, lock them,
make tea, make toast,
talk as usual about how   *10*
sooner or later
there will be a time
you bury me,
and I bury you, in the garden,
and go out as usual to look for food.   *15*
There will be a time
either you or I
bury either me or you in the garden
and the one left, sipping tea,
then for the first time, will refuse fiction.   *20*
Even your freedom
was like a fool's story.

Between—

TRANSLATED BY H. SATO AND B. WATSON

There are two sorrows to be proud of

After slamming the door of the room behind me
After slamming the door
Of the entrance of the house behind me
And out on the street visibility zero because of the rain of the rainy season   *5*
When the day begins
What will I do
What am I going to do
To neither
Am I friend or enemy   *10*
Who can I ask
This concrete question
I hate war
And am no pacifist
The effort just to keep my eyes open   *15*
The sorrow that I can make only that effort

There are two sorrows to be proud of

I am with you
I don't understand you
Therefore I understand that you are
Therefore I understand that I am
The sorrow that I do not understand you
The sorrow that you are what you are

20

The Celtic Tradition

Our first knowledge of Celtic poetry comes from Latin writers such as Julius Caesar and Lucan. Caesar states that in the first century B.C. Celtic students were taught in an oral tradition in the druidic schools. Among the Celts, the druids were a class of priests and learned men who often rivaled kings and chiefs in prestige and status. Later, Lucan uses the term *bardi* as the recognized title of Celtic poets. Unfortunately, no examples of the poetry of this time survive. Most of the Celtic cultural and religious documents come to us much later, from Ireland, where they were written down under Christian auspices in the twelfth century A.D.

Though the word "bard" is often used today to designate any type of poet (especially a major poet), the term had (and still has) a very specific meaning in Ireland, Scotland, and Wales, where traditional Celtic bardic verse consisted mostly of eulogies, elegies, and satires recited in a highly poetic language defined by strict and intricate metrical patterns. Equally important, bardic verse was composed only by highly trained bards who were members of the bardic class, an entirely separate social stratum with the hereditary privilege to ensure the safe transmission of tribal literature. The bard was a historian, a teacher, and a celebrant, and according to "The Gododdin," *"Beirdd byd barnant wr o galon."* That is, a bard passed judgment on men of valor.

Though a bard's primary function was to celebrate the heroic chieftains and the warrior class, there were different categories to which a bard might belong. In Wales the categories for *bardd* included the *pencerdd,* or "chief of song," the *bardd teulu,* or "poet of the war-band," and the *cerddór,* or minstrel. In Ireland the bardic class included the *filí,* or seer, the *bárd,* the *brithen,* or judge, and the *senchaid,* or historian. Of these, the *filí* was considered to have magical powers, and his lampoon, or *áer,* might not only destroy a man's reputation but kill him as well. In the Highlands of Scotland, which had been settled by the Irish and where *Erse* or Irish was spoken until the end of the fifteenth century, the bardic hierarchy closely paralleled Ireland's.

Most bards were male, but there were women bards as well, the most note-worthy example of whom might be Ireland's Líadan of Corcaguiney (ninth century), a full member of the poet's guild. For a bard to have been a member of the guild meant that he or she had undergone as much as twelve years of training. Scholars are not certain exactly what such training encompassed, but according to Martin's *Description of the Western Islands of Scotland* (1703), training could be exceptional and even mysterious by today's standards.

> They shut their doors and windows for a day's time, and lie upon their backs with a stone upon their belly, and plaids about their heads, and their eyes being covered, they pump their brains for rhetorical encomium or panegyric; and indeed, they furnish such a style from this dark cell as is understood by very few.

Though the Celtic languages began to disappear from continental Europe in the late fifth century A.D., they nevertheless continued to survive in the British Isles. Insular Celtic, including Irish and Scottish Gaelic, is still spoken as a native language on the west and south coasts of Ireland. Scottish Gaelic has roughly 81,000 speakers living mainly in the Highlands and western islands of Scotland. British, which is spoken primarily in Wales, still has over half a million speakers. But the steady atrophy of Celtic culture brought on by political and social pressures helped induce the general collapse of the bardic orders. By the eighteenth century the bardic hierarchy had all but come to an end except in Wales, where the ancient *Eisteddfod*, an annual Welsh poetry contest and festival of the arts, was revived in 1822 and continues to the present. Today in Wales, the term "bard" means one who has participated in the *Eisteddfod*.

Through the years, as Celtic culture continued to give way to English influence, the Celtic tradition in poetry survived at the periphery of the English-dominated literary world. As such, most readers are more familiar with Anglo-Irish, Anglo-Scottish, and Anglo-Welsh writers than with poets who continued working in the Celtic language tradition.

For example, Irish literature encompasses poetry in two languages: Irish Gaelic and English. Most non-Irish readers, however, will be more familiar with such Anglo-Irish poets as Jonathan Swift and Oliver Goldsmith and less familiar with Irish poetry in the Celtic tradition. Irish Celtic poetry, however, begins with Amergin (sixth century ?), who is said to have been the *fili* of the Milesians and thus the first poet of Celtic Ireland. Irish Celtic poetry goes on to include such figures as the scholarly Sedulius Scottus (ninth century), one of the early "personal" or lyric poets. His poem "The Scholar and His Cat" has been described by Frank O'Connor as "the last word in humanist elegance and urbanity." "Líadan Laments Cuirithir," by Líadan of Corcaguiney, tells of her rejection of Cuirithir, another bard. Reminiscent of the Tristan and Iseult legend, the saga of Líadan and Cuirithir differs somewhat in that Líadan is wooed as an equal, and she finally declines Cuirithir's invitation to love because she chooses to pursue a life as a poet. Other important early figures in the Irish Celtic tradition include the courtly

Gerald Fitzgerald, Earl of Desmond (c. 1538–1583), and the very popular Thomas Moore (1780–1852), to name only two.

In the second half of the nineteenth century, however, as Ireland continued to press for independence, much of Irish literature began to take its inspiration from the Celtic tradition, culminating in an Irish literary renaissance. A champion of Celtic revivalism, William Butler Yeats asked, "Can we not build up a national literature which shall be none the less Irish in spirit from being English in language?" His answer was to write in English as it is spoken in Ireland, an "English which [had] an indefinable Irish quality of rhythm and style." Three other poets who worked with Yeats in shaping the Irish literary renaissance include the poet Æ, pseudonym of George William Russell (1867–1935), Padraic Colum (1881–1972), and Patrick Kavanagh (1904–1967). While Seamus Heaney is treated under his own expanded section, he as well as Paul Durcan (b. 1944) and Eavan Boland (b. 1945) epitomize many of the younger poets presently working within the Celtic tradition.

Scottish literature also includes a Gaelic heritage associated with the Scottish Highlands that is closely related to Celtic Irish poetry. Once again, however, most readers will be more familiar with the poetry of the Lowland Scots, a distinct, well-defined dialect of English made famous by the poetry of Robert Burns. Though the Celtic tradition never came to prominence in Scottish poetry as it did in Ireland, there are many who have written poetry in Gaelic, including George Campbell Hay (b. 1915) and Ian Crichton Smith (b. 1928) whose poetry suggests a strong affinity with oral as well as written Scottish Celtic literature. In addition to the above-mentioned poets, we have also included Hugh MacDiarmid, pseudonym of C. M. Grieve (1892–1978) in this selection from the Celtic. Though one might argue that MacDiarmid should technically be classified with the Lowland Scots poets, MacDiarmid's translations of Celtic poetry and his efforts to draw inspiration from all of Scottish culture certainly suggest a strong Celtic influence.

Turning to the Welsh Celtic tradition, we expect that many readers will be acquainted with the Welsh Celtic myth of King Arthur and the poet–wizard Merlin (Myrddin), first mentioned in the Welsh poem "The Gododdin." But this is misleading because Arthur was adopted early as an English folk hero despite his Celtic origins. These legends aside, many readers will once again find themselves more knowledgeable about such Anglo-Welsh poets as George Herbert, Henry Vaughan, and Wilfred Owen than with the bard Aneirin (sixth century), the influential Dafydd Ap Gwilym (1340–1370), or the modern poets Emyr Humphreys (b. 1919) and Bobi Jones (b. 1929). One notable exception to this tendency, of course, would have to be Dylan Thomas, who wrote in English rather than Welsh but whose poetry carries many bardic overtones.

It is far beyond the range of this introduction to attempt any characterization of any specific Celtic aesthetic or sensibility. The Irish, Scottish, and Welsh each have very distinct cultures, each of which must be explored individually. Scholarship does suggest, however, that Celtic culture reveres the poet as seer and enjoys a poetry that is often highly impressionistic while sensuously precise and full of sharp detail. Poems are often "stretched on a small canvas" and frequently use stylized and highly intricate metrical patterns, very often creating "a picture rounded off within a couplet or at least a quatrain," as Kurt Wittig suggests. Celtic poets tend to identify strongly with nature, and their range has expanded beyond the traditional categories of eulogies, elegies, and satires to include love poems, lyrics, clan poems, labor songs, political poetry, humorous poems, flyting (insult bouts in the form of dramatic verse dialogues), and even drinking songs. Despite suggestions that Celtic poetry is more often than not transcendental and even mystical, close readings suggest that it is often understated, ironic, and highly realistic.

IRISH POETRY

AMERGIN

[Sixth century ?]

The Muse of Amergin

TRANSLATED BY JOHN MONTAGUE

I speak for Erin,
Sailed and fertile sea,
Fertile fruitful mountains,
Fruitful moist woods,
Moist overflowing lochs,   5
Flowing hillside springs,
Springs of men assembling,
Assembling men at Tara,
Tara, hill of tribes,
Tribes of the sons of Mil,   10
Mil of boats and ships,
The high ship of Éire,
Eire of high recital,
Recital skilfully done,
The skill of the women   15
Of Breisi, of Buagnai;
That haughty lady, Éire,
By Eremon conquered,
Ir and Eber bespoken:
I speak for Erin.   20

SEDULIUS SCOTTUS

[Ninth century]

The Scholar and His Cat

TRANSLATED BY FRANK O'CONNOR

Meisse ocus Pangur Bán,
Cechtar nathar fria shaindán;
Bíth a menma-sam fri seilgg
Mo menma céin im shaincheird.

Each of us pursues his trade,
I and Pangur my comrade;
His whole fancy on the hunt,
And mine for learning ardent.

Caraim-se foss, ferr cach clú,   5
Oc mo lebrán léir ingnu;
Ní foirmtech frimm Pangur Bán,
Caraid cesin a maccdán.

More than fame I love to be
Among my books and study;
Pangur does not grudge me it,
Content with his own merit.

LÍADAN OF CORCAGUINEY

[Ninth century]

Líadan Laments Cuirithir

TRANSLATED BY JOHN MONTAGUE

Joyless
what I have done;
to torment my darling one.

But for fear
of the Lord of Heaven   5
he would lie with me here.

Not vain,
it seemed, our choice,
to seek Paradise through pain.

I am Líadan,   10
I loved Cuirithir
as truly as they say.

The short time
I passed with him
how sweet his company!   15

The forest trees
sighed music for us;
and the flaring blue of seas.

What folly
to turn him against me   20
whom I had treated most gently!

No whim
or scruple of mine
should have come between

Us, for above   25
all others, without shame
I declare him my heart's love.

A roaring flame
has consumed my heart:
I will not live without him.   30

GERALD FITZGERALD

[c. 1538–1583]

My love I gave for hate

TRANSLATED BY GEORGE CAMPBELL HAY

My love I gave for hate,
not long my days will be.
My curses lie on him
that loves her after me.

Calm eye and golden head,
speech sweet as cuckoo's stave;   5
to brows drawn fine as thread
my love for hate I gave.

White tongue and lips of red,
kind tongue and gentle gait,   10
'tis sad it should be said—
my love I gave for hate.

THOMAS MOORE

[1780–1852]

At the mid hour of night

At the mid hour of night, when stars are weeping,
   I fly to the lone vale we loved, when life shone warm in thine eye;
And I think oft, if spirits can steal from the regions of air,
To revisit past scenes of delight, thou wilt come to me there,
And tell me our love is remembered, even in the sky.

Then I sing the wild song 'twas once such pleasure to hear   5
When our voices commingling breathed, like one, on the ear;
And, as Echo far off through the vale my sad orison rolls,
I think, oh, my love! 'tis thy voice from the Kingdom of Souls,
Faintly answering still the notes that once were so dear.

Æ (GEORGE WILLIAM RUSSELL)

[1867–1935]

Exiles

The gods have taken alien shapes upon them
Wild peasants driving swine
In a strange country. Through the swarthy faces
The starry faces shine.

Under grey tattered skies they strain and reel there: *5*
Yet cannot all disguise
The majesty of fallen gods, the beauty,
The fire beneath their eyes.

They huddle at night within low clay-built cabins;
And, to themselves unknown,   *10*
They carry with them diadem and sceptre
And move from throne to throne.

PADRAIC COLUM

[1881–1972]

The Book of Kells

First, make a letter like a monument—
An upright like the fast-held hewn stone
Immovable, and half-rimming it
The strength of Behemoth his neck-bone,
And underneath that yoke, a staff, a rood   *5*
Of no less hardness than the cedar wood.

Then, on a page made golden as the crown
Of sainted man, a scripture you enscroll
Blackly, firmly, with the quickened skill
Lessoned by famous masters in our school,   *10*
And with an ink whose lustre will keep fresh
For fifty generations of our flesh.

And limn below it the Evangelist
In raddled coat, on bench abidingly,
Simple and bland: Matthew his name or Mark,   *15*
Or Luke or John; the book is by his knee,
And thereby its similitudes: Lion,
Or Calf, or Eagle, or Exalted Man.

The winds that blow around the world—the four
Winds in their colours on your pages join—   *20*

THE BOOK OF KELLS   an eighth-century illuminated copy of the Gospels in Latin; the book also contains
local records.

The Northern Wind—its blackness interpose;
The Southern Wind—its blueness gather in;
In redness and in greenness manifest
The splendours of the Winds of East and West.

And with these colours on a ground of gold   25
Compose a circuit will be seen by men
As endless patience, but is nether web
Of endless effort—a strict pattern:
Illumination lighting interlace
Of cirque and scroll, of panel and lattice.   30

A single line describes them and enfolds,
One line, one course where term there is none,
Which in its termlessness is envoying
The going forth and the return one.
With man and beast and beast and fish therein   35
Transformed to species that have never been.

With mouth a-gape or beak a-gape each stands
Initial to a verse of miracle,
Of mystery and of marvel (Depth of God!)
That Alpha or Omega may not spell,   40
Then finished with these wonders and these signs,
Turn to the figures of your first outlines.

Axal, our angel, has sustained you so
In hand, in brain; now to him seal that thing
With figures many as the days of man,   45
And colours, like the fire's enamelling—
That baulk, that letter you have greatly reared
To stay the violence of the entering Word!

PATRICK KAVANAGH

[1904–1967]

Tinker's Wife

I saw her amid the dunghill debris
Looking for things
Such as an old pair of shoes or gaiters.

She was a young woman,
A tinker's wife.   5
Her face had streaks of care
Like wires across it,
But she was supple

As a young goat
On a windy hill.   10

She searched on the dunghill debris,
Tripping gingerly
Over tin canisters
And sharp-broken
Dinner plates.   15

PAUL DURCAN

[b. 1944]

Tullamore Poetry Recital

It was a one-man show in Tullamore,
"The Sonnets of Shakespeare."
The newspaper advertisement bubbled:
"Bring Your Own Knitting."
The audience of twenty-five   5
Was devout, polite, attentive,
All with their knitting,
Men and women alike with their knitting.
I shut my eyes and glimpsed
Between the tidal breakers of iambic pentameter   10
The knitting needles flashing like the oars of Odysseus.

But as the evening wore on, and the centuries passed,
And the meditations, and the thanksgivings,
And darkness fell, and with it a fullish moon,
Not quite full but fullish,   15
Putting on weight by the teaspoonful,
One was aware of a reversal advancing,
Of incoming tides being dragged backwards.
The knitting needles were no longer oars
But fiddles in orchestras sawing to halts.   20

One became aware of one's own silence.
One was no longer where one thought one was.
One was alone in the pit of oneself, knitting needles.

E A V A N   B O L A N D

[b. 1945]

Anorexic

Flesh is heretic.
My body is a witch.
I am burning it.

Yes I am torching
her curves and paps and wiles.   5
They scorch in my self denials.

How she meshed my head
in the half-truths
of her fevers

till I renounced   10
milk and honey
and the taste of lunch.

I vomited
her hungers.
Now the bitch is burning.   15

I am starved and curveless.
I am skin and bone.
She has learned her lesson.

Thin as a rib
I turn in sleep.   20
My dreams probe

a claustrophobia
a sensuous enclosure.
How warm it was and wide

once by a warm drum,   25
once by the song of his breath
and in his sleeping side.

Only a little more,
only a few more days
sinless, foodless,   30

I will slip
back into him again
as if I had never been away.

Caged so
I will grow   35
angular and holy

past pain,
keeping his heart
such company

as will make me forget   40
in a small space
the fall

into forked dark,
into python needs
heaving to hips and breasts   45
and lips and heat
and sweat and fat and greed.

SCOTTISH POETRY

HUGH MacDIARMID (C. M. GRIEVE)

[1892–1978]

Hungry Waters

FOR A LITTLE BOY AT LINLITHGOW

The auld men o' the sea
Wi' their daberlack hair

HUNGRY WATERS   ²**daberlack**   seaweed.

Ha'e dackered the coasts
O' the country fell sair.

They gobble owre cas'les,   5
Chow mountains to san';
Or lang they'll eat up
The haill o' the lan'.

Lickin' their white lips
An' yowlin' for mair,   10
The auld men o' the sea
Wi' their daberlack hair.

GEORGE CAMPBELL HAY

[b. 1915]

The Two Neighbours

Two that through windy nights kept company,
two in the dark, two on the sea at the steering,
with aye one another's bow-wave and wake to see,
the neighbour's light away on the beam plunging and soaring.

Two on blind nights seeking counsel in turn—   5
"Where will we head now?"—sharing their care and labours,
spoke across plashing waters from stern to stern,
comrades in calm, fellows in storm, night-sea neighbours.

Dark and daybreak, heat and hail had tried
and schooled the two in the master glance for esteeming   10
the curve of the outgoing net, the set of the tide,
the drift of wind and sea, the airt where the prey was swimming.

Two on the sea. And the one fell sick at last,
"for he was weak, the soul, and old." And the other
watched long nights by his bed, as on nights that were past 15
he watched from the stern for his light, sea-neighbor, in ill a brother.

Watched by the peep of a lamp long nights by his side;
brightened his mood, talking their sea-nights over;
followed him to Cill Aindreis when he died,
and left him at peace in a lee that would feel no wind for ever. 20

HUNGRY WATERS   ³dackered   harried.   ⁴fell sair   very severely.   ¹⁰yowlin'   roaring.
THE TWO NEIGHBORS   ¹⁹Cill Aindreis   a graveyard.

IAN CRICHTON SMITH

[b. 1928]

Culloden and After

You understand it? How they returned from Culloden
over the soggy moors aslant, each cap
at the low ebb no new full tide could pardon:
how they stood silent at the end of the rope
unwound from battle: and to the envelope   5
of a bedded room came home, polite and sudden.

And how, much later, bards from Tiree and Mull
would write of exile in the hard town
where mills belched English, anger of new school:
how they remembered where the sad and brown   10
landscapes were dear and distant as the crown
that fuddled Charles might study in his ale.

There was a sleep. Long fences leaned across
the vacant croft. The silly cows were heard
mooing their sorrow and their Gaelic loss,   15
The pleasing thrush would branch upon a sword.
A mind withdrew against its dreamed hoard
as whelks withdraw or crabs their delicate claws.

And nothing to be heard but songs indeed
while wandering Charles would on his olives feed   20
and from his Minch of sherries mumble laws.

WELSH POETRY

ANEIRIN

[Sixth century]

from *The Gododdin*

TRANSLATED BY JOSEPH P. CLANCY

VIII

Men went to Catraeth, keen their war-band.
Pale mead their portion, it was poison.

Three hundred under orders to fight.
And after celebration, silence.
Though they went to churches for shriving,   5
True is the tale, death confronted them.

XI

Men went to Catraeth at dawn:
Their high spirits lessened their life-spans.
They drank mead, gold and sweet, ensnaring;
For a year the minstrels were merry.   10
Red their swords, let the blades remain
Uncleansed, white shields and four-sided spearheads,
Before Mynyddawg Mwynfawr's men.

XXI

Men went to Catraeth, they were renowned.
Wine and mead from gold cups was their drink,   15
A year in noble ceremonial,
Three hundred and sixty-three gold-torqued men.
Of all those who charged, after too much drink,
But three won free through courage in strife,
Aeron's two war-hounds and tough Cynon,   20
And myself, soaked in blood, for my song's sake.

DAFYOD AP GWILYM

[1340–1370]

The Girls of Llanbadarn

TRANSLATED BY ROLFE HUMPHRIES

I am one of passion's asses,
Plague on all these parish lasses!
Though I long for them like mad,
Not one female have I had,
Not a one in all my life,   5
Virgin, damsel, hag, or wife.
What maliciousness, what lack,
What does make them turn their back?
Would it be a shame to be
In a bower of leaves with me?   10
No one's ever been so bitched,
So bewildered, so bewitched

Saving Garwy's lunatics
By their foul fantastic tricks.

So I fall in love, I do,   15
Every day, with one or two,
Get no closer, any day,
Than an arrow's length away.
Every single Sunday, I,
Llanbadarn can testify,   20
Go to church and take my stand
With my plumed hat in my hand,
Make my reverence to the altar,
Find the right page in my psalter,
Turn my back on holy God,   25
Face the girls, and wink, and nod
For a long, long time, and look
Over feather, at the folk.
Suddenly, what do I hear?
A stage whisper, all too clear,   30
A girl's voice, and her companion
Isn't slow at catching on.

"See that simple fellow there,
Pale and with his sister's hair
Giving me those leering looks   35
Wickeder than any crook's?"

"Don't you think that he's sincere?"
Asks the other in her ear.
"All I'll give him is *Get out!*
Let the Devil take the lout!"   40

Pretty payment, in return
For the love with which I burn.
Burn for what? The bright girl's gift
Offers me the shortest shrift.
I must give them up, resign   45
These fear-troubled hopes of mine:
Better be a hermit, thief,
Anything, to bring relief.
Oh, strange lesson, that I must
Go companionless and lost,   50
Go because I looked too long,
I, who loved the power of song.

EMILY JANE PFEIFFER

[1827–1890]

A Song of Winter

Barb'd blossoms of the guarded gorse,
   I love thee where I see thee shine:
Thou sweetener of our common-ways,
And brightener of our wintry days.

Flower of the gorse, the rose is dead,   5
   Thou art undying, O be mine!
Be mine with all thy thorns, and prest
Close on a heart that asks not rest.

I pluck thee and thy stigma set
   Upon my breast and on my brow;   10
Blow, buds, and plenish so my wreath
That none may know the wounds beneath.

O crown of thorn that seem'st of gold,
   No festal coronal art thou;
Thy honey'd blossoms are but hives   15
That guard the growth of wingèd lives.

I saw thee in the time of flowers
   As sunshine spill'd upon the land,
Or burning bushes all ablaze
With sacred fire; but went my ways;   20

I went my ways, and as I went
   Pluck'd kindlier blooms on either hand;
Now of those blooms so passing sweet
None lives to stay my passing feet.

And still thy lamp upon the hill   25
   Feeds on the autumn's dying sigh,
And from thy midst comes murmuring
A music sweeter than in spring.

Barb'd blossoms of the guarded gorse,
   Be mine to wear until I die,   30
And mine the wounds of love which still
Bear witness to his human will.

EMYR HUMPHREYS

[b. 1919]

An Apple Tree and a Pig

Oian a parchellan, ni hawdd cysgaf
Rhag godwrdd y galar y sydd arnof.

1

All men wait for battle and when it comes
Pass along the sword's edge their resilient thumbs.

Men clasp in faithless arms their sobbing wives
Tasting even in the salt kiss the bliss pricking points of knives.

Men clip on armour and see in their children's eyes   5
Their swollen images, their godlike size.

Men assemble together, create a new sea
That floods into battle. Men become free

Of the dull bonds of life, become locked in a fight
In love in league with Death, lost in icy delight.   10

2

In such a frenzy I slaughtered my sister's son.
My sword cut open his face and I screamed as though I had won

Glory to nurse in the night, until I turned and saw
The flesh of Gwenddolau, the young king who loved me, raw

And Rhydderch's sword dull with Gwenddolau's blood   15
And his great mouth trumpeting joy. Ah then I understood

That rooted and nourished in my own affectionate heart
Was the spitting devil tearing our world apart.

3

When I fled to the wood, alone I lay under a tree
Still hearing the clash of our swords, still dumb in my agony.   20

AN APPLE TREE AND A PIG   **Oian . . . arnof.** Welsh for "Proclaiming his sorrow, the poet makes an
apostrophe to a pig."

So much despair had crowded into my heart
My tongue was cold, speech a forgotten art.

As I lay in the wood I suffered the germ of peace
To penetrate my veins like a lethal disease.

4

I have lost all desire to communicate with men.   25
My sighs do not disturb the building wren.

An apple tree and a pig: these are my friends
With whom I share my wisdom that no longer pretends

To be wise, since nothing my wisdom brings
Can restore the lost kingdom or challenge the armour of kings.   30

I have eaten the apple of knowledge and all I know
Is that love must fail and lust must overthrow

And in the nights of winter when the ice-winds howl
A pity and a terror fasten themselves on my soul

And I cry upon death to wrap his white redress   35
Without mercy about the stillness of the merciless
And remedy my madness with long silence.

BOBI JONES

[b. 1929]

Portrait of an Engine Driver

TRANSLATED BY JOSEPH P. CLANCY

Smoke contending with smoke which will be maddest;
Light chewing chunks in the cloud and then belching;
Blasphemous grunting in a garden of grease.
See the driver crouched singing in the steel ball
"And the lightning fading in the blood,"   5
Touching the plates and the gear, like a blackbird
Rubbing its herbal scent into every spot,
And his carnal filth on the wheels, his strength's stamp

With the furnace's mirth warm on the instruments.
Wil is the name,   10
Son of Ed Williams the Cwm and brother of Elen.
He orders the uproar's work in his own wilful way
And plants his green personality in the oil,
He who is utterly splendid to five children;
He plumbs his blood's clicking for the piston's vein   15
And tapeworms his terms through the metal.
Through the nights of their fellowship
And their diligent void
The machine has become a beautiful hill-breast home,
A sanctuary, since here he thought of God best,   20
God on the axle, and God in the crunching,
And gloried in them as his forebears did in a horse
Till he felt the newly-washed coal a petal in his nostrils,
And the iron cogs played at fondling his hard hands,
His happiness under his armpits.   25
(Yesterday my love came to buy a ready-made frock
And wore it and made it part of her own enchantment.)
Christmas today, the warmth of home on his cheek,
His children's sweat in place of the piston's laughter,
But at the same God's strong feet he cradles himself   30
Like a comely village in a mountain niche.

Scandinavian Poetry

In 1643, Brynjólfur Sveinsson, the Bishop of Skálholt, Iceland, discovered an ancient manuscript written in Old Norse during the Viking period by the Norwegian colonizers of Iceland. He named this collection of lays about the old Scandinavian gods and heroes the *Elder Edda*. The *Elder*, or poetic, *Edda* dates from roughly 1270 but focuses on pre-Christian Norwegian and Germanic myths. "Words of the High One," one of the two major subdivisions of the *Edda*, presents the chief god, Odin, initiating the Norse moral and social codes and is primarily didactic in tone. Another major section of the *Edda*, "Song of the Sibyl," tells of the origins of the world as well as of its end in "The Twilight of the Gods."

Some of the poets who composed sections of the *Elder Edda* were also court poets, or *skald*s. A more ornate and technically complicated poetry than that found in the *Edda*, skaldic literature was composed mainly in praise of the battle exploits of important chieftains. Fundamentally alliterative, most skaldic poetry demanded a combination of strict syllable count, alternating internal assonance and rhyme, and highly specific stanzaic patterns.

Unlike the Greek or Anglo-Saxon epics, the *Elder Edda* presents little epic narrative, though it often incorporates a considerable amount of dialogue. Two kinds of meter predominate in the *Edda*: epic meter and chant meter. Syntactically, an epic line normally contains four stresses that are evenly divided by a strongly marked caesura. The lines are mostly end-stopped and are grouped into stanzas of two to seven lines; the four-line stanza is most common. Chant meter, on the other hand is built from a standard epic line coupled (by alliteration) to a line of two or three stresses.

A Viking chieftain as well as an important skald, Egil Skallagrímsson (910–1004?) is thought to have been a major contributor to the *Elder Edda*, and he is also believed to be the first Norse poet to write end-rhymed verse. His poem "Head-Ransom" was supposedly composed in the course of one evening when Skallagríms-son attempted to ransom his own head by singing the praises of his enemy, King Eiríkur, the "Eric" referred to in the last line of the poem.

From the sixteenth through the eighteenth century, Norwegian literature was written in Danish, mainly by clerics and civil servants educated in Denmark. In response to Norway's independence from Denmark in 1814, Norwegian writers began to focus on the creation of a national literature. With the writings of the dramatist and poet Henrik Ibsen (1828–1906), Norway made an enduring contribution to world literature. Ibsen's reputation is usually attributed to his realistic plays. Nevertheless, many critics assert that Ibsen's two lyric dramas, *Brand* and *Peer Gynt*, would have been sufficient to establish Ibsen's renown as a major artist.

Another significant figure of Norwegian literature around the turn of the twentieth century was Knut Hamsun (1859–1952). World-renowned as a fiction writer who wrote prose that is almost pure poetry, Hamsun was also a highly influential lyric poet in his native Norway. His "Island off the Coast" explores the affinities between a mythic Norse past and modern realities. Known for his deep explorations of the "labyrinthine passages of the mind," Hamsun was awarded the Nobel Prize for literature in 1920. The Norwegian poet Rolf Jacobsen (b. 1907) often focuses on modern industrial life and brings his own close-up, photographic technique to a poetry rich in detail and unusual perspectives. He is considered Norway's first modern poet.

Swedish poetry is of relatively recent origin. Lars Wivallius (1605–1669) is considered Sweden's first lyric poet, but many scholars suggest that Georg Stiernhielm (1598–1672) was Sweden's first truly influential poet. He has been described as a poet "without finesse" and "without hesitation" who helped lead Swedish poetry away from Latin fixed measures by writing in natural stresses in his native Dalecarli dialect. "On Astrild, Honing His Arrows," for example, explores the psychology of erotic relationships through the metaphysical conceit of the grindstone. Though his elaborate metaphors suggest a Renaissance and even metaphysical influence, Stiernhielm's prosody is rooted in his native Swedish.

Another important figure of the century, August Strindberg (1849–1912), is often considered Sweden's greatest writer and the father of modern Swedish drama. Moving from naturalism to dreamlike symbolism, Strindberg foreshadowed modern Expressionism. "Street Scenes," for example, which is excerpted from his *Word Play and Minor Art,* appears to be a naturalistic description, but as the following passage to his wife indicates, Strindberg uses the realistic image as a way of approaching more expressionistic concerns.

> Might it be possible that my sufferings could be turned into joy for others? Well, let me suffer then! I think of that black electricity machine, placed down in the cellar on Gref Magnigatan, black and terrifying. It sits there, dark in the darkness, and grinds light for the whole block!

Strindberg's poem was published in 1902, eight years before Freud's announcement of the discovery of the unconscious. And yet, as Lars Gustafsson suggests, "Where could we find a better metaphor for Freud's subconscious than this generator, which like the libido, the elemental human drive, stands there black and terrible, humming in the darkness, yet still producing light for the entire area?" Strindberg's influence may still be seen in the work of such modern Swedish poets as Gunnar Ekelöf and Tomas Tranströmer.

Sometimes considered one of the more difficult of the prominent modern Swedish poets, Gunnar Ekelöf (1907–1968) was greatly influenced by Oriental and French poetry. His poem "Every human is a world" contains the mystical elements associated with Eastern thought as well as the surrealistic impulses of Arthur Rimbaud, whom he translated into Swedish.

Though relatively unknown outside her native Sweden, Elsa Grave (b. 1918) is sometimes compared to the American poet H.D. (pp. 625–626). Another celebrated Swedish poet, Tomas Tranströmer (b. 1931) often works in Sapphic stanzas, an unrhymed, fixed form associated with Sappho (p. 990) and Horace (p. 1022–1023). His poem "Storm" combines these elements with an apparent paradox: that which appears immobile (the constellations) is full of motion, while that which should be full of movement (the moose) is still. Influenced by Surrealism as well as Christianity, Tranströmer, a psychologist, also draws on the unconscious for the content of his poetry.

Although Danish poetry probably existed before the time of the Vikings, none of it was written down except for some versions rendered in Latin by Saxo Grammaticus during the twelfth century. Saxo's *Deeds of the Danes* records the early history of Denmark and includes the earliest version of the Hamlet story. Folk ballads, however, make up the greater part of medieval Danish poetry. Often introduced by a lyrical stanza suggesting character and mood, the ballads were epic in form and attempted to continue the Old Norse codes and legends. "The Death of Sir Stig," for example, is a stylized portrait of the ideal Danish knight. Modest, loyal, accepting death rather than surrender the flag, Sir Stig fights for Denmark, his king, and the glory of his betrothed.

The Danish poet Benny Andersen (b. 1929) earned his living from 1949 to 1962 by playing piano in nightclubs throughout Scandinavia, an unusual occupation for a poet and short story writer. His range as a poet is wide, encompassing the somber as well as the humorous. His metaphors often surprise and startle, and his poetry is often characterized by a rich tonal ambivalence, fusing emotions many people tend to segregate.

Our final poet, Gudrid Helmsdal-Nielsen (b. 1941) is a native of the Faeroe Islands, a group of islands in the north Atlantic Ocean located between Iceland and the Shetland Islands. Like Iceland, the Faeroe Islands were settled by Norwegian emigrants during the ninth century, though the islands eventually came under Danish rule. Despite these political affiliations, a native language developed and a native Faeroe literature began to flourish by the turn of the century. Helmsdal-Nielsen's "Thaw Night" touches on the complex relationship islanders have with water in its various manifestations of rain, ice, and ocean. The poem's eerie, mystical tone suggests that we may firmly place Helmsdal-Nielsen in the company of her fellow Scandinavian poets Rolf Jacobsen, Gunnar Ekelöf, and Tomas Tranströmer.

ICELANDIC POETRY

ANONYMOUS

from *Words of the High One*

TRANSLATED BY W. H. AUDEN AND PAUL B. TAYLOR

A snapping bow, a burning flame,
A grinning wolf, a grunting boar,
A raucous crow, a rootless tree,
A breaking wave, a boiling kettle,
A flying arrow, an ebbing tide,   5
A coiled adder, the ice of a night,
A bride's bed-talk, a broad sword,
A bear's play, a Prince's children,
A witch's welcome, the wit of a slave,
A sick calf, a corpse still fresh,   10
A brother's killer encountered upon
The highway, a house half-burned,
A racing stallion who has wrenched a leg,
Are never safe: let no man trust them.

ANONYMOUS

from *The Twilight of the Gods*

from Song of the Sibyl

TRANSLATED BY W. H. AUDEN AND PAUL B. TAYLOR

Now death is the portion of doomed men,
Red with blood the buildings of gods,
The sun turns black in the summer after,
Winds whine. *Well, would you know more?*

Earth sinks in the sea, the sun turns black,   5
Cast down from Heaven are the hot stars,
Fumes reek, into flames burst,
The sky itself is scorched with fire.

I see Earth rising a second time
Out of the foam, fair and green;   *10*
Down from the fells, fish to capture,
Wings the eagle; waters flow.

At Idavale the Aesir meet:
They remember the Worm of Middle Earth,
Ponder again the Great Twilight   *15*
And the ancient runes of the High God.

Boards shall be found of a beauty to wonder at,
Boards of gold in the grass long after,
The chess boards they owned in the olden days.

Unsown acres shall harvests bear,   *20*
Evil be abolished, Baldur return
And Hropt's Hall with Hödur rebuild,
Wise gods. *Well, would you know more?*

Haenir shall wield the wand of prophecy,
The sons of two brothers set up their dwelling   *25*
In wide Windhome. *Well, would you know more?*

Fairer than sunlight, I see a hall,
A hall thatched with gold in Gimlé:
Kind lords shall live there in delight for ever.

Now rides the Strong One to Rainbow Door,   *30*
Powerful from heaven, the All-Ruler:
From the depths below a drake comes flying,
The Dark Dragon from Darkfell,
Bears on his pinions the bodies of men,
Soars overhead. I sink now.   *35*

EGIL SKALLAGRÍMSSON

[910–1004?]

from *Head-Ransom*

TRANSLATED BY LEE M. HOLLANDER

I sailed to the West
and of Odin's breast

bear I the sea—
thus is't with me.
I put out to float,   5
at ice-break, my boat
freighted with load
of lofty ode.

At the king's behest
I came, as guest,   10
bearing Odin's lore
to England's shore.
A song in praise
of the prince I raise,
and him now pray   15
to hear my lay.

Give, thane, good heed
how that I read
of the sea-king's deed:
but I silence need.   20
Know folk, I ween,
how fought the keen;
but Fiolnir's seen
where fight has been.

Was lifted sword   25
'gainst linden-board
around the lord
as rushed he for'rd.
Was heard the roar
of raging war   30
as flowed wound-gore
on far-off shore.

Did the shower-of-darts
strike shield-ramparts
of the prince's array   35
as he plunged in the fray;
when on the sands
of surf-beaten strands,
brimming with blood,
the battle stood.   40

Did many a one sink
by the sea's low brink.
Great honor him gat
Eric by that.

NORWEGIAN POETRY

HENRIK IBSEN

[1828–1906]

Agnes

from Brand

TRANSLATED BY CHARLES WHARTON STORK

Agnes, my delicate butterfly,
Look out, for I mean to take you!
I'm weaving a net of the finest mesh,
Its threads are the songs I make you.

   "If I'm a butterfly, pretty and small,   5
   Then let me sip from the heather;
   Hunt if you will, you frolicsome boy,
   But do not catch me and tether!"

Agnes, my delicate butterfly,
Flitting will never save you;   10
Cunningly twined are the meshes now,
Soon in the net I'll have you.

   "If I'm a butterfly, see me soar,
   My gay fans merrily plying,
   And if you catch in the web of your net   15
   Mar not my wings for flying!"

No, I shall take you tenderly up
To lock in my heart, my fairest;
And there you shall play your whole life long
The gladdest of games and rarest.   20

KNUT HAMSUN

[1859–1952]

Island off the Coast

TRANSLATED BY MARTIN ALLWOOD

Now glides the boat to
the coastal island—
a blue sea island,
a verdant strand.

The flowers stand there   5
for no one's eyes,
they stand like strangers
and watch me land.

My heart becomes like
a magic garden,   10
with flowers just like
the island's now.

They speak together
and whisper strangely
like children meeting   15
who smile and bow.

Perhaps I was here
at the dawn of time,
a white Spiræa
that is no more.   20

I know the fragrance
from ancient times,
I tremble amid
these dreams of yore.

The night is thickening   25
over the island.
The sea is thundering
Nirvana thunder.

ROLF JACOBSEN

[b. 1907]

The Old Women

TRANSLATED BY ROBERT BLY

The girls whose feet moved so fast, where did they go?
Those with knees like small kisses and sleeping hair?

In the far reaches of time when they've become silent,
old women with narrow hands climb up stairs slowly

with huge keys in their bags and they look around   5
and chat with small children at cemetery gates.

In that big and bewildering country where winters are so long
and no one understands their expressions any more.

Bow clearly to them and greet them with respect
because they still carry everything with them, like a fragrance,   10

a secret bite-mark on the cheek, a nerve deep in
the palm of the hand somewhere betraying who they are.

SWEDISH POETRY

GEORG STIERNHIELM

[1598–1672]

Oppå Astrild, som står och slipar sine pilar	*On Astrild, Honing His Arrows*

TRANSLATED BY ROBERT T. ROVINSKY

Slipstenen intet skär; men skärper pilar och
   yxor:
samma natur min käresta bär; hon skärper
   och vässer
älskogen i mitt bröst; men själv är hon
   stumpar' än vätsten.

The grindstone can never cut; but it sharpens arrows
   and axes:
of similar nature is my beloved; she sharpens
   and hones
great love in my breast; herself she is duller than
   whetstone.

Mitt stolt' hjärta då gör hon vekt och sårar
  i älskog;
själver osargat och hel är hårdare flinto.   5
Själver är hon is och snö; men mig är
  hon hetar' än elden.
Kall är hon av sig själv; men mig hon bråder
  i älskog.
Allt vad hon yrker och gör, hon själv vart
  känner ell' av-vet:
mild är hon och spisar ut det hon själv vart
  äger ell' åtte.

My proud heart she then weakens and wounds in
  its love,
while hers, safe and sane, is harder than flintstone.
She herself is ice and snow; to me she is hotter
  than fire.
Frigid is she by nature; but me she does hurry to
  love her.
All she occasions and does, by her is unfelt or
  unknown:
mild is she and gives away what she neither owns
  nor ever was hers.

AUGUST STRINDBERG

[1849–1912]

Street Scenes III

from Word Play and Minor Art

TRANSLATED BY ROBERT T. ROVINSKY

Dark is the hill, dark the house—
but darkest is its cellar—
subterranean, windowless—
the staircase serves as door and window—
and down there deepest in the darkness   5
stands a humming dynamo,
sparks flying around its wheels:
black and horrifying, hidden,
it grinds light for the entire neighborhood.

GUNNAR EKELÖF

[1907–1968]

Every human is a world

TRANSLATED BY ROBERT T. ROVINSKY

Every human is a world, populated
by blind beings in dark revolt

against the ego, the king who rules over them.
In every soul a thousand souls are captive,
in every world a thousand worlds are hidden   5
and these blind, these lower worlds
are real and living, though premature,
as truly as I am real. And we kings
and princes of the thousand possible within us
are subjects ourselves, captive ourselves   10
in some greater being, whose ego and essence
we comprehend as little as our superior
his superior. From their death and love
our own feelings have received a coloring.

As when a great steamer passes by   15
far out, below the horizon, where it lies
so evening-smooth.—And we know nothing of it
until a swell reaches us here on the shore,
first one, then another, and many more
breaking and surging until everything is   20
as before.—Yet everything is different.

Thus we shadows are seized by a strange unrest
when something tells us that people have traveled on,
that some of the possible ones have gotten free.

ELSA GRAVE

[b. 1918]

Afterthought

TRANSLATED BY MARTIN ALLWOOD

And again they turn
their dark grey sails back
from air mass
after air mass
sailing counter-sunwise like silver vultures   5
spying over the icy wastes
and their hunger too
a slow swell

They have flown far
between winters and cardinal points   10
they have consumed streets
and solitude
and their cries of hunger
are long airy perspectives
behind the silence   15

TOMAS TRANSTRÖMER

[b. 1931]

Storm

TRANSLATED BY ROBERT T. ROVINSKY

Suddenly, here, the wanderer meets the ancient
giant oak tree, like a petrified moose with
mile-wide crown, before the September seascape's nightly green fortress

Northerly storm. It is the time when rowanberry
clusters ripen. Awake, one hears in the darkness   5
constellations stamping in their stables high over oak tree.

DANISH POETRY

ANONYMOUS

The Death of Sir Stig

TRANSLATED BY ALEXANDER GRAY

The *King* wad speak to *Sir Stig*. Quo' he:
"In the battle you'll carry my banner for me."
(It was mair than Stig cud manage.)

"I'm a sma' bit man, o' untried worth.
It's no for me to carry it furth." 5

"You may think you're a sma' and untried man;
But you'll carry my banner as weel as you can."

"Maun I bear the flag in the hot melee?
Then let a new banner be shapen for me.

Mak me a flag, blue, yellow and reid. 10
Thereunder there's mony will meet their deid!"

Furth they fared through a fremmyt land;
Ne'er did the banner quit *Stig*'s hand.

Thick, thick as hay the arrows flew,
And bluidily pierced *Stig's* airms richt through. 15

The arrows scorched like a burnin' brand,
And drave a wey through *Stig*'s white hand.

The *King* cried oot in the bluidy strife:
"Throw doon the banner, but save your life!"

"My love sanna hear the clash o' the toon, 20
That I feared for mysel', and cuist the flag doon.

My love sanna hear it clashed through the land,
That the *King*'s flag drapped frae my feckless hand."

In sair distress the *King* cried loud:
"*Sir Stig* lies deid, wi' his flag for his shroud!" 25

Victor was he in the bluidy strife;
But *Stig* the knicht maun tine his life.

The *King,* triumphant, raised his hand:
"The *Danes* hae conquessed a' this land!

Noo had I fared hame joyfully, 30
Had *Stig* but been o' my company."

---

[11]**deid** death (as well as dead). [12]**fremmyt** foreign. [20]**clash** gossip. [21]**cuist** cast. [27]**tine** lose.

As the *King* cam hame frae the wars again,
His sister gaed furth to meet him and his men.

"You're welcome, brither, and sae are you a'.
And hoo hae you fared, since you mairched awa'?"   *35*

"Weel hae I prospered. Oor men won the day,
But your true love fell deid in the thick o' the fray."

In dule she wrang her hands sae sair,
That her gowden rings loupt through the air.

"Be comforted, sweet sister dear!   *40*
The rich *Sir Karl* will be your fere."

Sabbin' the lassie spak. Quo' she:
"Ne'er will that man hae power ower me!

You ca' him 'the rich',—and you may be richt.
But he'll ne'er be the marrows o' *Stig,* the Knicht."   *45*
  (It was mair than Stig cud manage.)

BENNY ANDERSEN

[b. 1929]

High and Dry

TRANSLATED BY ALEXANDER TAYLOR

The spruce saws away at the horizon
while the dunes cautiously
peep out behind one another's shoulders.
Low tide. The scowling black stones
rise up and lick their lips   *5*
with tongues of seaweed.

Pale and bitter, the lighthouse stares
at the gloating jaws of the boats—

THE DEATH OF SIR STIG   **39loupt**   jumped, leaped.   **41fere**   companion.   **45marrows**   equal.

What distant shores have they tasted—
What place could be more beautiful than this? *10*

A dried up starfish
pointing in all directions.

FAEROESE POETRY

GUDRID HELMSDAL-NIELSEN

[b. 1941]

Thaw Night

TRANSLATED BY INGE KNUTSSON AND MARTIN ALLWOOD

And the rain came.
The drop that broke
the shell of ice.
The heavens breathed,
the heavens which had been held *5*
in the tight embrace of the cold.

Tonight winter lies
on its death-bed;
it draws its breath heavily,
sighing— *10*
like a huge animal
which has placed itself
round the world.

Greek Poetry

Greek poetry in written form begins with the two most famous epics in western literature, the *Iliad* and the *Odyssey,* which tradition credits to Homer, about whom we know nothing with certainty except his name—though early Greeks believed him to have been blind, and many scholars think that he lived in Ionia, in Asia Minor. Although both poems are considered to be based on a long oral tradition antedating their recorded written versions by hundreds of years, each of the Homeric epics is generally considered to bear the overall stylistic imprint and imaginative vision of a single resourceful poet, perhaps the same poet. As such the Homeric epics bring to a culmination the heroic oral tradition of epic verse.

Originally chanted or sung to a simple musical accompaniment at a rate of about five hundred lines an hour, the *Iliad* and *Odyssey* are most often thought to have been written down in the seventh century B.C., although some parts were probably added later. Containing many recurring lines and phrases suited to oral performance, both epics are written in dactylic hexameter, a six-foot line composed of dactyls (− ⌣ ⌣) varied with spondees (− −), though it is important to note that Greek poetic meter, unlike English meter, is based on the quantity or length of vowels rather than on stressed syllables. Both the *Iliad* and the *Odyssey* reflect their social context, a feudal, warring, aristocratic society in which honor, courage, heroism, and cunning are the most highly valued human virtues, though the gods and goddesses of the Greek pantheon also figure prominently in the Homeric epics. Each epic centers on a single heroic figure: the *Iliad* on the wrath of Achilles and its consequences for himself and his countrymen; the *Odyssey* on Odysseus, who after ten years of wandering and adventure returns from the Trojan War to reclaim his wife and home from an importunate group of Greek princes.

Homer's *Iliad* and *Odyssey* have been enormously influential in the history of Western poetry. Virgil's *Aeneid* aims to imitate Homer's epics, as does Milton's *Paradise Lost* in a different way, to cite only two famous examples. Yet, as influential as the epic tradition has been in Western literature, epic verse has now lain dormant for two centuries. Few epics were written after the eighteenth century. Other literary modes, especially lyric poetry, drama, and the novel, have been much more prevalent since then. The reasons for such changes in literary fashion are partly historical and partly sociological. With the advent of Romanticism, the nature lyric assumed prominence over most poetic genres, especially those involving long, complex poems. And with the emergence of the middle class and the increased size of the reading public, realistic drama and quasirealistic and sentimental fiction came to dominate the literary marketplace.

Other poetic genres also derive from ancient Greece. The earliest of these is lyric poetry, which arose as a written literary type not long after epic poetry, in the seventh century B.C. Like epic poetry, lyric poetry very likely antedated its original written formulations as oral folk verse. Unlike epic poetry, however, which was chanted, lyric poetry was originally sung, accompanied by a lyre, a stringed instrument from which the adjective "lyric" derives. And also unlike epic poetry, which flourished in Ionia, lyric poetry flourished on the island of Lesbos, the home of Sappho (c. 610 – c. 580 B.C.), whose expressive love lyrics brought her fame even during her own time. Sappho's poems consistently center on the power of Eros in all its tenderness, passion, and sublime exaltation. Unfortunately, only three of her poems survive in their entirety; the rest exist as fragments.

A third major type of Greek poetry is dramatic poetry, which became the dominant poetic form of Athens in the fifth century B.C. Greek tragic drama was written in verse and dealt with gods and heroes from the mythic or legendary past. Dialogue in Greek tragedy was usually written in a six-foot iambic line. Punctuating the dramatic dialogue was a series of choral lyrics, intricately wrought poetic performances, which in ancient times were sung as the chorus danced in a special area, called the *orchēstra,* or "dancing place." Choral lyrics employ an enormous variety of meters. The two tragic dramatic poets whose work we include here are Aeschylus (525–456 B.C.), generally considered the father of Greek tragedy, and Sophocles (c. 496–406 B.C.), whose plays remain well known today. Aeschylus is noted for the magnificence of his language and the richness and ingenuity of his metaphors. His great successor, Sophocles, of a generation later, became an even more popular and influential dramatist than Aeschylus. Sophocles' language is also widely appreciated, though his plays are celebrated even more for their emotional power and their portrayal of human nobility and grandeur in the face of suffering.

To conclude our selection of ancient Greek poetry, we have chosen examples of ode from Pindar (c. 522–438 B.C.) and epigram from Callimachus (c. 305 – c. 240 B.C.). Pindar is famed for the odes he wrote in honor of victorious athletes. His odes employ mythological allusion and an elaborate train of images. Their metrical structure is complex, like that of the tragic lyrics, and their language is stately and ceremonial. The epigrams of Callimachus belong to a quite different tradition of poetry, written in couplets, frequently elegiac. For the sake of consistency and unity we have chosen a series of Callimachus' epigrams on a single subject: death (though his poetic forms and subjects range considerably wider than our small selection of examples suggests). The language and tone of Callimachus' epigrams, however, illustrate still another dimension of the poetic achievement of the ancient Greeks: a directness, simplicity, and naturalness in the service of expressing emotion.

A scholar as well as a poet, Callimachus made an important contribution to the Hellenistic project of collecting and classifying valuable works of Greek cultural antiquity—a kind of "great works of ancient Greece." As a poet, Callimachus worked in forms of moderate length, often making use of his extensive knowledge of arcane myths. His influence extended to Latin poets such as Catullus and Propertius and well into Renaissance and neoclassical English poetry.

We have included these dozen examples of ancient Greek poetry largely because of their enormous influence. But we also think it important to indicate that Greek poetry continues to thrive in its modern forms. One major difference between ancient and modern Greek poetry derives from the nature of the Greek language, which exists in two forms: a classical and a demotic, or common, popular form. Modern poetry is typically written in demotic Greek, a language with a different vocabulary and grammatical structure than its classical predecessor.

We have included seven modern Greek poets. The earliest, C. P. Cavafy (Kónstantínos Kaváfis) (1863–1933), is recognized for his expression of the tragic sensuality of life. Born a generation later, George Seferis (Giorgios Seferiades) (1900–1971) is more a Symbolist poet of understatement and hesitation. Like his American counterpart T. S. Eliot, whose *The Waste Land* he has translated, Seferis' poems reflect the disintegration and disillusionment of modern life. Yannis Ritsos (1909–1940) is also a poet in the tradition of Cavafy. His poems often employ concrete images and a direct natural voice. Like the poems of both Seferis and Cavafy, those of Ritsos mask subtleties of feeling and nuances of thought, often tragically sad. Odysseus Elytis (b. 1912) is a more celebratory poet. In its free association of images, his verse, filled with the vitality and light of the Aegean Islands, occasionally borders on the surrealistic.

Our last three poets are less well known outside Greece than the Nobel Prize winners Seferis and Elytis or the internationally renowned Cavafy. Myrtiotissa, the pen name of Theoni Cracopolou, was born in Constantinople in 1882. An actress and professor of speech at the Conservatory of Athens, Myrtiotissa won a number of national poetry prizes. Eléni Vakaló, born in Athens in 1921, studied archaelogy at the University of Athens and art history in Paris. Author of eight volumes of poetry, Vakaló has taught art history and served as an art critic for Greek periodicals. Sophia Mavroidi Papadaky, born in Crete in 1905, studied at the Faculty of Letters in Athens and taught modern Greek literature. In addition to publishing poetry for more than half a century, Papadaky has written fiction and books for children and has also translated French and English fiction into Greek.

Like Greek architecture, philosophy, and mathematics, Greek poetry, especially in its ancient form, continues to be one of the glories of civilization.

HOMER

from *The Iliad*

from Book II, Hector and Andromache

TRANSLATED BY ROBERT FAGLES

Hector would always call the boy Scamandrius,
townsmen called him Astyanax, Lord of the City,
since Hector was the lone defense of Troy.

The great man of war breaking into a broad smile,
his gaze fixed on his son, in silence. Andromache,   5
pressing close beside him and weeping freely now,
clung to his hand, urged him, called him: "Reckless one,
my Hector—your own fiery courage will destroy you!
Have you no pity for him, our helpless son? Or me,
and the destiny that weighs me down, your widow,   10
now so soon. Yes, soon they will kill you off,
all the Achaean forces massed for assault, and then,
bereft of you, better for me to sink beneath the earth.
What other warmth, what comfort's left for me,
once you have met your doom? Nothing but torment!   15
I have lost my father. Mother's gone as well.
Father . . . the brilliant Achilles laid him low
when he stormed Cilicia's city filled with people,
Thebe with her towering gates. He killed Eetion,
not that he stripped his gear—he'd some respect at least—   20
for he burned his corpse in all his blazoned bronze,
then heaped a grave-mound high above the ashes
and nymphs of the mountain planted elms around it,
daughters of Zeus whose shield is storm and thunder.
And the seven brothers I had within our halls . . .   25
all in the same day went down to the House of Death,
the great godlike runner Achilles butchered them all,
tending their shambling oxen, shining flocks.
                                And mother,
who ruled under the timberline of woody Placos once—
he no sooner haled her here with his other plunder   30
than he took a priceless ransom, set her free
and home she went to her father's royal halls
where Artemis, showering arrows, shot her down.
You, Hector—you are my father now, my noble mother,
a brother too, and you are my husband, young and warm and strong!   35
Pity me, please! Take your stand on the rampart here,
before you orphan your son and make your wife a widow.
Draw your armies up where the wild fig tree stands,
there, where the city lies most open to assault,
the walls lower, easily overrun. Three times   40
they have tried that point, hoping to storm Troy,
their best fighters led by the Great and Little Ajax,
famous Idomeneus, Atreus' sons, valiant Diomedes.
Perhaps a skilled prophet revealed the spot—
or their own fury whips them on to attack."   45

   And tall Hector nodded, his helmet flashing:
"All this weighs on my mind too, dear woman.

But I would die of shame to face the men of Troy
and the Trojan women trailing their long robes
if I would shrink from battle now, a coward.   50
Nor does the spirit urge me on that way.
I've learned it all too well. To stand up bravely,
always to fight in the front ranks of Trojan soldiers,
winning my father great glory, glory for myself.
For in my heart and soul I also know this well: 55
the day will come when sacred Troy must die,
Priam must die and all his people with him,
Priam who hurls the strong ash spear . . .
                                        Even so,
it is less the pain of the Trojans still to come
that weighs me down, not even of Hecuba herself   60
or King Priam, or the thought that my own brothers
in all their numbers, all their gallant courage,
may tumble in the dust, crushed by enemies—
That is nothing, nothing beside your agony
when some brazen Argive hales you off in tears,   65
wrenching away your day of light and freedom!
Then far off in the land of Argos you must live,
laboring at a loom, at another woman's beck and call,
fetching water at some spring, Messeis or Hyperia,
resisting it all the way—   70
the rough yoke of necessity at your neck.
And a man may say, who sees you streaming tears,
'There is the wife of Hector, the bravest fighter
they could field, those stallion-breaking Trojans,
long ago when the men fought for Troy.' So he will say   75
and the fresh grief will swell your heart once more,
widowed, robbed of the one man strong enough
to fight off your day of slavery.
                        No, no,
let the earth come piling over my dead body
before I hear your cries, I hear you dragged away!"   80

    In the same breath, shining Hector reached down
for his son—but the boy recoiled,
cringing against his nurse's full breast,
screaming out at the sight of his own father,
terrified by the flashing bronze, the horsehair crest,   85
the great ridge of the helmet nodding, bristling terror—
so it struck his eyes. And his loving father laughed,
his mother laughed as well, and glorious Hector,
quickly lifting the helmet from his head,
set it down on the ground, fiery in the sunlight,   90

and raising his son he kissed him, tossed him in his arms,
lifting a prayer to Zeus and the other deathless gods:
"Zeus, all you immortals! Grant this boy, my son,
may be like me, first in glory among the Trojans,
strong and brave like me, and rule all Troy in power   95
and one day let them say, 'He is a better man than his father!'—
when he comes home from battle bearing the bloody gear
of the mortal enemy he has killed in war—
a joy to his mother's heart."
          So Hector prayed
and placed his son in the arms of his loving wife.   100
Andromache pressed the child to her scented breast,
smiling through her tears.

from *The Odyssey*

from Book XIII, The Cyclops

TRANSLATED BY ROBERT FITZGERALD

"Ὡς ἐφάμην, ὁ δὲ δέκτο καὶ ἔκπιεν· ἥσατο
   δ' αἰνῶς

ἡδὺ ποτὸν πίνων, καί μ' ἤτεε δεύτερον
   αὖτις·

⟨Δός μοι ἔτι πρόφρων, καί μοι τεὸν οὔνομα
   εἰπὲ

αὐτίκα νῦν, ἵνα τοι δῶ ξείνιον, ᾧ κε σὺ
   χαίρῃς.

καὶ γὰρ Κυκλώπεσσι φέρει ζείδωρος   5
   ἄρουρα

οἶνον ἐρισταφυλον, καί σφιν Διὸς ὄμβρος
   ἀέξει·

ἀλλὰ τόδ' ἀμβροσίης καὶ νέκταρός ἐστιν
   ἀπορρώξ.⟩

  "Ὡς ἔφατ'· αὐτάρ οἱ αὖτις πόρον αἴθοπα
   οἶνον·

τρὶς μὲν ἔδωκα φέρων, τρὶς δ' ἔκπιεν
   ἀφραδίῃσιν.

αὐτὰρ ἐπεὶ Κύκλωπα περὶ φρένας ἤλυθεν   10
   οἶνος,

καὶ τότε δή μιν ἔπεσσι προσηύδων
   μειλιχίοισι·

⟨Κύκλωψ, εἰρωτᾷς μ' ὄνομα κλυτόν; αὐτὰρ
   ἐγώ τοι

My moment was at hand, and I went forward

holding an ivy bowl of my dark drink,

looking up, saying: "Kyklops, try some wine.

Here's liquor to wash down your scraps of men.

Taste it, and see the kind of drink we carried

under our planks. I meant it for an offering

if you would help us home. But you are mad,

unbearable, a bloody monster! After this,

will any other traveler come to see you?"

He seized and drained the bowl, and it went
   down
so fiery and smooth he called for more:

"Give me another, thank you kindly. Tell me,

ἐξερέω· σὺ δέ μοι δὸς ξείνιον, ὥς περ
    ὑπέστης.
Οὖτις ἐμοί γ' ὄνομα· Οὖτιν δέ με
    κικλήσκουσι
μήτηρ ἠδὲ πατὴρ ἠδ' ἄλλοι πάντες   15
    ἑταῖροι.〉
  "Ὣς ἐφάμην, ὁ δέ μ' αὐτίκ' ἀμείβετο
    νηλέϊ θυμῷ·
〈Οὖτιν ἐγὼ πύματον ἔδομαι μετὰ οἷς
    ἑτάροισι,
τοὺς δ' ἄλλους πρόσθεν· τὸ δέ τοι ξεινήϊον
    ἔσται.
  Ἦ καὶ ἀνακλινθεὶς πέσεν ὕπτιος, αὐτὰρ
    ἔπειτα
κεῖτ' ἀποδοχμώσας παχὺν αὐχένα, κὰδ   20
    δέ μιν ὕπνος
ἥρει πανδαμάτωρ· φάρυγος δ' ἐξέσσυτο
    οἶνος
ψωμοί τ' ἀνδρόμεοι· ὁ δ' ἐρεύγετο
    οἰνοβαρείων.
καὶ τότ' ἐγὼ τὸν μοχλὸν ὑπὸ σποδοῦ
    ἤλασα πολλῆς,
ἧος θερμαίνοιτο· ἔπεσσί τε πάντας ἑταίρους
θάρσυνον, μή τίς μοι ὑποδείσας ἀναδύη.   25
ἀλλ' ὅτε δὴ τάχ' ὁ μοχλὸς ἐλάϊνος ἐν πυρὶ
    μέλλδν
ἅψεσθαι, χλωρός περ ἐών, διεφαίνετο δ'
    αἰνῶς,
καὶ τότ' ἐγὼν ἄσσον φέρον φέρον ἐκ
    πυρός, ἀμφὶ δ' ἑταῖροι
ἵσταντ'· αὐτὰρ θάρσος ἐνέπνευσεν μέγα
    δαίμων.
οἱ μὲν μοχλὸν ἑλόντες ἐλάϊνον, ὀξὺν ἐπ'   30
    ἄκρῳ,
ὀφθαλμῷ ἐνέρεισαν· ἐγὼ δ' ἐφύπερθεν
    ἐρεισθεὶς
δίνεον, ὡς ὅτε τις τρυπῶ δόρυ νήϊον ἀνὴρ
τρυπάνῳ, οἱ δέ τ' ἔνερθεν ὑποσσείουσιν
    ἱμάντι
ἁψάμενοι ἑκάτερθε, τὸ δὲ τρέχει ἐμμενὲς
    αἰεί·
ὡς τοῦ ἐν ὀφθαλμῷ πυριήκεα μοχλὸν   35
    ἑλόντες
δινέομεν, τὸν δ' αἷμα περίρρεε θερμὸν
    ἐόντα.

how are you called? I'll make a gift will please
    you.
Even Kyklopês know the wine-grapes grow

out of grassland and loam in heaven's rain,

but here's a bit of nectar and ambrosia!"

Three bowls I brought him, and he poured them
    down.
I saw the fuddle and flush come over him,

then I sang out in cordial tones: "Kyklops,

you ask my honorable name? Remember

the gift you promised me, and I shall tell you.

My name is Nohbdy: mother, father, and friends,

everyone calls me Nohbdy." And he said:

"Nohbdy's my meat, then, after I eat his friends.
Others come first. There's a noble gift, now."
Even as he spoke, he reeled and tumbled
    backward,
his great head lolling to one side: and sleep

took him like any creature. Drunk, hiccuping,

he dribbled streams of liquor and bits of men.

Now, by the gods, I drove my big hand spike

deep in the embers, charring it again,

and cheered my men along with battle talk
to keep their courage up: no quitting now.

The pike of olive, green though it had been,

reddened and glowed as if about to catch.

I drew it from the coals and my four fellows

πάντα σε οἱ βλέφαρ’ ἀμφὶ καὶ ὀφρύας εὖσεν
    ἀϋτμὴ

γλήνης καιομένης· σφαραγεῦντο δέ οἱ πυρὶ
    ῥίζαι.

ὡς δ’ ὅτ’ ἀνὴρ χαλκεὺς πέλεκυν μέγαν ἠὲ
    σκέπαρνον

εἰν ὕδατι ψυχρῷ βάπτῃ μεγάλα ἰάχοντα   40

φαρμάσσων· τὸ γὰρ αὖτε σιδήρου γε
    κράτος ἐστίν·

ὡς τοῦ σίζ’ ὀφθαλμὸς ἐλαϊνέῳ περὶ μοχλῷ.

σμερδαλέον δὲ μέγ’ ὤμωξεν, περὶ δ’ ἴαχε
    πέτρη,

ἡμεῖς δὲ δείσαντες ἀπεσσύμεθ’. αὐτὰρ ὁ
    μοχλὸν

ἐξέρυσ’ ὀφθαλμοῖο πεφυρμένον αἵματι   45
    πολλῷ.

τὸν μὲν ἔπειτ’ ἔρριψεν ἀπὸ ἕο χερσὶν
    ἀλύων,

αὐτὰρ ὁ Κύκλωπας μεγάλ’ ἤπυεν, οἵ ῥά μιν
    ἀμφὶς

οἴκεον ἐν σπήεσσι δι’ ἄκριας ἠνεμοέσσας.

οἱ δὲ βοῆς ἀΐοντες ἐφοίτων ἄλλοθεν ἄλλος,

ἱστάμενοι δ’ εἴροντο περὶ σπέος ὅττι ἑ   50
    κήδοι·

⟨τίπτε τόσον, Πολύφημ’, ἀρημένος ὧδ’
    ἐβόησας

νύκτα δι’ ἀμβροσίην, καὶ ἄϋπνους ἄμμε
    τίθησθα;

ἦ μή τίς σευ μῆλα βροτῶν ἀέκοντος
    ἐλαύνει;

ἦ μή τίς σ’ αὐτὸν κτείνει δόλῳ ἠὲ βίηφιν;⟩

    Τοὺς δ’ αὖτ’ ἐξ ἄντρου προσέφη   55
    κρατερὸς Πολύφημος·

    Οἱ δ’ ἀπαμειβόμενοι ἔπεα πτερόεντ’
    ἀγόρευον·

⟨εἰ μὲν δὴ μή τίς σε βιάζεται οἶον ἐόντα,

νοῦσόν γ’ οὔ πως ἔστι Διὸς μεγάλου
    ἀλέασθαι,

ἀλλὰ σὺ γ’ εὔχεο πατρὶ Ποσειδάωνι
    ἄνακτι.⟩

    “Ὣς ἄρ’ ἔφαν ἀπιόντες· ἐμὸν δ’   60
    ἐγέλασσε φίλον κῆρ,

ὡς ὄνομ’ ἐξαπάτησεν ἐμὸν καὶ μῆτις
    ἀμύμων.

---

gave me a hand, lugging it near the Kyklops

as more than natural force nerved them; straight

forward they sprinted, lifted it, and rammed it

deep in his crater eye, and I leaned on it
turning it as a shipwright turns a drill

in planking, having men below to swing
the two-handled strap that spins it in the groove.

So with our brand we bored that great eye socket

while blood ran out around the red hot bar.

Eyelid and lash were seared; the pierced ball

hissed broiling, and the roots popped. In a smithy

one sees a white-hot axehead or an adze
plunged and wrung in a cold tub, screeching
    steam—

the way they make soft iron hale and hard—:

just so that eyeball hissed around the spike.

The Kyklops bellowed and the rock roared round
    him,
and we fell back in fear. Clawing his face

he tugged the bloody spike out of his eye,
threw it away, and his wild hands went groping;

then he set up a howl for Kyklopês

who lived in caves on windy peaks nearby.
Some heard him; and they came by divers ways

to clump around outside and call: “What ails you,

Polyphêmos? Why do you cry so sore

in the starry night? You will not let us sleep.

Sure no man's driving off your flock? No man
has tricked you, ruined you?" Out of the cave
the mammoth Polyphêmos roared in answer:
65   "Nohbdy, Nohbdy's tricked me, Nohbdy's ruined
        me!"
To this rough shout they made a sage reply:
"Ah well, if nobody has played you foul
there in your lonely bed, we are no use in pain
given by great Zeus. Let it be your father,
70   Poseidon Lord, to whom you pray." So saying
they trailed away. And I was filled with laughter
to see how like a charm the name deceived them.

SAPPHO

[c. 610 – c. 580 B.C.]

Alone

TRANSLATED BY RICHMOND LATTIMORE

Δέδυκε μέν ἀ σέλαννα
χαὶ Πληίαδες, μέσαι δὲ
νύκτες, παρὰ δ᾽ ἔρχετ᾽ ὤρα,
ἔγω δὲ μόνα κατεύδω.

The moon and Pleiades
are set. Night is half
gone and time speeds by.
I lie in bed, alone.

Seizure

TRANSLATED BY RICHMOND LATTIMORE

Φαίνεταί μοι κῆνος᾽ἴσος δέοισιν
ἔμμεν ὤνηρ ὄττις ἐνάντιός τοι
ἰζάνει καὶ πλάσιον ἄδυ φωνεί-
σας ὐπακούει

To me that man equals a god
as he sits before you and listens
closely to your sweet voice

καὶ γελαίσας ἰμμέροεν, τό μ᾽ ἦ μὰν
κάρζαν ἐν στήδεσσιν ἐπεπτόασεν·   5
ὠς γὰρ ἔς τ᾽ ἴδω, βρόχε᾽, ὤς με φώνας
οὔδεν ἔτ᾽ ἴκει,

and lovely laughter—which troubles
the heart in my ribs. For now
as I look at you my voice fails,

ἀλλὰ κὰμ μὲν γλῶσσα Ζέαγε, λέπτον
δ᾽ αὔτικα χρῷ πῦρ ὐπαδεδρόμακεν,
ὀππάτσσι δ᾽ οὔδεν ὄρημ᾽, ἐπιρρόμ-
βεισι δ᾽ ἄκουαι,

my tongue is broken and thin fire
runs like a thief through my body.
My eyes are dead to light, my ears

ἀ δέ μ᾽ ἴδρως κακχέεται, τρόμος δὲ   *10*   pound, and sweat pours down over me.
παῖσαν ἄγρη, χλωροτέρα δὲ ποίας   I shudder, I am paler than grass,
ἔμμι, τεδνάκην δ᾽ ὀλίγω ᾽πιδεύϜην   and am intimate with dying—but
φαίνομαι—ἀλλὰ

πάντ [α νῦν τ] ολμάτε᾽, ἐπεὶ ᾽πένησα . . .   I must suffer everything, being poor.

AESCHYLUS

[525–456 B.C.]

from *Agamemnon*

TRANSLATED BY ROBERT FAGLES

Choral Ode: Fury

Who—what power named the name that drove your fate?—
what hidden brain could divine your future,
steer that word to the mark,
to the bride of spears,
   the whirlpool churning armies,   *5*
      Oh for all the world a Helen!
Hell at the prows, hell at the gates
hell on the men-of-war,
from her lair's sheer veils she drifted
   launched by the giant western wind,   *10*
    and the long tall waves of men in armor,
huntsmen trailing the oar-blades' dying spoor
slipped into her moorings,
   Simois' mouth that chokes with foliage,
      bayed for bloody strife,   *15*
for Troy's Blood Wedding Day—she drives her word,
her burning will to the birth, the Fury
late but true to the cause,
to the tables shamed
   and Zeus who guards the hearth—   *20*
    the Fury makes the Trojans pay!
Shouting their hymns, hymns for the bride
hymns for the kinsmen doomed
to the wedding march of Fate.
   Troy changed her tune in her late age,   *25*
    and I think I hear the dirges mourning

"Paris, born and groomed for the bed of Fate!"
They mourn with their life breath,
    they sing their last, the sons of Priam
        born for bloody slaughter.   *30*

    So a man once reared
a lion cub at hall, snatched
from the breast, still craving milk
    in the first flush of life.
A captivating pet for the young,   *35*
and the old men adored it, pampered it
    in their arms, day in, day out,
like an infant just born.
Its eyes on fire, little beggar,
fawning for its belly, slave to food.   *40*

    But it came of age
and the parent strain broke out
and it paid its breeders back.
    Grateful it was, it went
through the flock to prepare a feast,   *45*
an illicit orgy—the house swam with blood,
    none could resist that agony—
           massacre vast and raw!
From god there came a priest of ruin,
adopted by the house to lend it warmth.   *50*

And the first sensation Helen brought to Troy . . .
call it a spirit
    shimmer of winds dying
           glory light as gold
    shaft of the eyes dissolving, open bloom   *55*
    that wounds the heart with love.
But veering wild in mid-flight
she whirled her wedding on to a stabbing end,
slashed at the sons of Priam—hearthmate, friend to the death,
    sped by Zeus who speeds the guest,   *60*
a bride of tears, a Fury.

There's an ancient saying, old as man himself:
men's prosperity
    never will die childless,
           once full-grown it breeds.   *65*
    Sprung from the great good fortune in the race
    comes bloom on bloom of pain—
insatiable wealth! But not I,

I alone say this. Only the reckless act
can breed impiety, multiplying crime on crime, 70
   while the house kept straight and just
is blessed with radiant children.

      But ancient Violence longs to breed,
        new Violence comes
  when its fatal hour comes, the demon comes 75
  to take her toll—no war, no force, no prayer
   can hinder the midnight Fury stamped
  with parent Fury moving through the house.

     But Justice shines in sooty hovels,
       loves the decent life. 80
From proud halls crusted with gilt by filthy hands
  she turns her eyes to find the pure in spirit—
spurning the wealth stamped counterfeit with praise,
  she steers all things towards their destined end.

SOPHOCLES

[c. 496–406 B.C.]

Man

from Antigone

TRANSLATED BY DUDLEY FITTS AND ROBERT FITZGERALD

Numberless are the world's wonders, but none
More wonderful than man; the stormgrey sea
Yields to his prows, the huge crests bear him high;
Earth, holy and inexhaustible, is graven
With shining furrows where his plows have gone 5
Year after year, the timeless labor of stallions.

The lightboned birds and beasts that cling to cover,
The lithe fish lighting their reaches of dim water,
All are taken, tamed in the net of his mind;
The lion on the hill, the wild horse windy-maned, 10
Resign to him; and his blunt yoke has broken
The sultry shoulders of the mountain bull.

Words also, and thought as rapid as air,
He fashions to his good use; statecraft is his,

And his the skill that deflects the arrows of snow,   *15*
The spears of winter rain: from every wind
He has made himself secure—from all but one:
In the late wind of death he cannot stand.

O clear intelligence, force beyond all measure!
O fate of man, working both good and evil!   *20*
When the laws are kept, how proudly his city stands!
When the laws are broken, what of his city then?
Never may the anarchic man find rest at my hearth,
Never be it said that my thoughts are his thoughts.

PINDAR

[c. 522 – c. 438 B.C.]

Olympia XI

TRANSLATED BY RICHMOND LATTIMORE

There is a time when men need most favoring
gales; there is a time for water from the sky,
rain, child of cloud.
But if by endeavor a man win fairly, soft-spoken songs
are given, to be a beginning of men's   *5*
speech to come and a true seal on great achievements.

Abundant is such praise laid up for victories
Olympian. My lips have good will
to marshal these words; yet only
by God's grace does a man blossom in the wise turning of his thought. *10*
Son of Archestratos, know
that for the sake, Agesidamos, of your boxing

I shall enchant in strain of song a glory upon
your olive wreath of gold
and bespeak the race of the West Wind Lokrians.   *15*
There acclaim him; I warrant you,
Muses, you will visit no gathering cold to strangers
nor lost to lovely things
but deep to the heart in wisdom, and spearmen also. No thing, neither devious fox
nor loud lion, may change the nature born in his blood.   *20*

CALLIMACHUS

[c. 305 – c. 240 B.C.]

Epigrams

TRANSLATED BY STANLEY LOMBARDO AND DIANE RAYOR

1

News of your death.
    Tears, and the memory
of all the times we talked the sun down the sky.
    You, Herakleîtos of Halikarnássos,
once my friend, now vacant dust,   5
    whose poems are nightingales
beyond the clutch of the unseen god.

2

"Timónoë."
      Who are you, lady,
    besides a name on a tombstone   10
determined by other names:
                Timótheos,
your father, and Methýmna,
    your city, and your husband,
Euthýmenes,   15
      widowed and grieving.

3

The demon in the morning,
Unknown. Yesterday, Kharmis,
You were in our eyes. Today
We buried you. Yes, Kharmis,   20
You. Nothing
Your father has ever seen
Has caused him more pain.

4

He was twelve years old when his father laid him here,
    Philip's great hope, his son Nikóteles.   *25*

C. P. CAVAFY
(KONSTANTINOS KAVÁFIS)

[1863–1933]

πόλις   The City

TRANSLATED BY RAE DALVEN

Εἶπες᾿ ⟨θὰ πάγω σ᾿ ἄλλη γῆ, θὰ πάγω σ᾿
    ἄλλη θάλασσα.
Μιὰ πόλις ἄλλη θὰ βρεθῆ καλύτερη ἀπ᾿
    αὐτή.
Κάθε προσπάθειά μου μιὰ καταδίκη εἶναι
    γραφτή,
κι εἰν᾿ ἡ καρδιά μου, σὰν νεκρός, θαμμένη.
Ὁ νοῦς μου ὣς πότε μὲς στὸν μαρασμὸν
    αὐτὸν θὰ μένη;   5
Ὅπου τὸ μάτι μου γυρίσω, ὅπου κι ἄν σῶ,
ἐρείπια μαῦρα τῆς ζωῆς μου βλέπω ἐδῶ,
ποὺ τόσα χρόνια πέρασα καὶ
    ῥήμαξα καὶ χάλασα.⟩

Καινούριους τόπους δὲν θὰ βρῆς, δὲν θὰ
    βρῆς ἄλλες θάλασσες.
Ἡ πόλις θὰ σὲ ἀκολουθῆ. Στοὺς δρόμους θὰ
    γερνᾶς   10
τοὺς ἴδιους, καὶ στὲς γειτονιὲς τὲς ἴδιες θὰ
    γερνᾶς,
καὶ μὲς στὰ ἴδια σπίτια αὐτὰ θ᾿ ἀσπρίζης.
Πάντα στὴν πόλη αὐτὴ θα φτάνης. Γιὰ τὰ
    ἀλλοῦ—μὴ ἐλπίζης,—
δὲν ἔχει πλοῖο γιὰ σέ, δὲν ἔχει ὁδό.
Ἔτσι ποὺ τὴ ζωή σου ῥήμαξες εδῶ   15
στὴ κόχη τούτη τὴ μικρή, σ᾿ ὅλη τὴ γῆ
    χάλασες.

You said, "I will go to another land, I will go to another
    sea.
Another city will be found, a better one than this.

Every effort of mine is a condemnation of fate;

and my heart is—like a corpse—buried.
How long will my mind remain in this wasteland.

Wherever I turn my eyes, wherever I may look
I see black ruins of my life here,
where I spent so many years destroying and wasting."

You will find no new lands, you will find no other seas.

The city will follow you. You will roam the same

streets. And you will age in the same neighborhoods;

and you will grow gray in these same houses.
Always you will arrive in this city. Do not hope for any
    other—
There is no ship for you, there is no road.
As you have destroyed your life here
in this little corner, you have ruined it in the entire world.

MYRTIOTISSA (THEONI CRACOPOLOU)

[1882 – ?]

Women of Suli

TRANSLATED BY RAE DALVEN

(During the Greek War of Independence of 1821, all the women of Suli leaped to their death with their children in their arms from the cliffs of Zalongo in Epirus, rather than surrender to the Turks.)

Ah! You who wakened in my child's soul
the first quiver of phantasy and wonder,
who first opened the deeps of my heart
for the sublime breath of poetry to enter!

Ah! You who wakened in me a vast pride,   5
what if my life is a starless night,
what if a wasteland, bitter and black, surround me,
if only a drop of your blood beats in my heart!

As a child, I leaned on my grandmother's knee
to hear of princesses most fair and mighty kings,   10
but always at the end, I remembered to ask about you,
"Tell me your story, Grandma, the true story."

And as she began, I saw you passing before me,
one by one, like high-breasted, beautiful princesses,
and singing still, you plunged into the dragon's cave   15
imbedded at the base of the cliff.

Then terrified I closed my eyes and always
the moan of your wild song would reach my ears,
weaving a living circle in my mind,
yawning mouths of an unseen monster.   20

But though my early years were full of you, your meaning
escaped me, for it was greater than my mind could grasp,
I loved you with a seven year old heart
I thought of you with timid, quivering love.

As my emotion deepened and thought matured,   25
once as I stood beneath the spreading red-gold light

diffused over Zalongo before the sun went down,
I saw a miraculous vision of your tragic dance!

And I saw you like young does ascending
with your children, a sheer and rugged peak,   *30*
the sun crowning the serpents of your hair,
rags covering your bodies teeming with life.

And you tossed down your children, and ah me, the infants
seemed to be playing a happy mad game;
at the foot of the cliff were piled roses and lilies   *35*
that shone like an April garden, softly.

And then of a sudden you started a frenzied celebration,
One by one, dropping into space, you left the dance,
and you wheeled in ever narrowing circles
and the wind flailed many colored rags and hair!   *40*

Abruptly my heart shook, a worshipping bell,
for you were left the last, alone on the peak,
and I quaked like a terrified mother . . .
but you were rigid and still, last woman of Suli!

Ah! When your scream had trailed away, your feet were in space, *45*
when the tight-clenched fingers flew apart like birds,
and you saw about you only thorns and stones
in the frightful and infinite gloom enclosing you,

did horror not glide snake-like through your heart,
did doubt not face you for a moment   *50*
as you measured the yawning abyss before you,
did death not seem a foe worse than the Turk?

The others rested sweetly in the feathery arms of glory,
leaned down from the whirl of their sacred dance,
but you were awakened bitterly by silence   *55*
fixing its cold glance upon you.

Then, did your beloved country scenes not haunt you?
The rough path leading to the village?
Did you not feel your mother's trembling touch
under the pine shading your house, like a mighty guardian?   *60*

Did you not hear your dogs bay mournfully?
Did you not see the old folks left alone?

Did you not hear nature keening over you
through the crying of birds and the North Wind?

Your breasts that swelled with abundant milk, 65
your vigorous wholesome mountain body,
as you leaned far over the rocky hollow
did it not say *no* to you, did it not oppose you?

The sun set and with it the vision of you,
but I stood fixed as stone before the sacred mountain, 70
and for long I felt deeply throbbing within me
the warmth of your blood, the freshness of your hair,

Women of Suli! Where your bodies are one with the rocks,
the stony earth is adorned with wild flowers,
but on the peak there blooms a single lily to honor 75
the last Suli woman, foam of your fragrance.

GEORGE SEFERIS
(GIORGIOS SEFERIADES)

[1900–1971]

The Old Man

TRANSLATED BY EDMUND KEELEY AND PHILIP SHERRARD

So many flocks have passed so many poor
and rich riders, some
from distant villages had spent
the night in road-side ditches
lighting fires against the wolves: do you see 5
the ashes? Blackish circles cicatrized.
He's full of marks like the road.
In the dry well above they'd thrown the rabid
dogs. He's got no eyes, he's full
of marks, he's light; the wind blows; 10
he distinguishes nothing, knows everything,
empty sheath of a cicada on a hollow tree.
He's got no eyes, not even in his hands, he knows
dawn and dusk, knows the stars,

their blood doesn't nourish him, nor is   *15*
he dead, he has no race, he won't die,
they'll simply forget him, he has no ancestors.
His tired fingernails
inscribe crosses on decayed memories
while the wind blows darkly. It snows.   *20*

I saw the hoarfrost around the faces
I saw the lips wet, tears frozen
in the corner of the eye, I saw the line
of pain by the nostrils and the effort
at the roots of the hand, I saw the body come to an end.   *25*
He isn't alone, this shadow
bound to a dry inflexible stick
he doesn't bend to lie down, he can't:
sleep will have scattered his joints
as playthings into the hands of children.   *30*
He commands like dead branches
that break when night comes and the wind
wakes in the ravines
he commands the shades of men
not the man in the shadow   *35*
who hears nothing but the low voices
of earth and sea there where they mix
with the voice of destiny. He stands upright
on the bank, among piles of bones
among heaps of yellow leaves: *40*
empty cage that waits
for the hour of fire.

SOPHIA MAVROIDI PAPADAKY

[b. 1905]

Love Song

TRANSLATED BY RAE DALVEN

What is this thing that keeps me tirelessly waiting
        hours till you go by?
As if my heart were breaking, and I feel I turn pale
        when they mention your name?

Why should your shadow alone fill the world,   5
            you have but to appear
and I feel the wave of life seething
            ceaselessly within me!
Why should I lower my eyes beneath the glance
            I crave so much,   10
forget, when you spoke, the answer
            I had planned for days?
What is this thing assuming the guise of first love
            that comes at such a time?
A brilliant sun that, I know, always drags lightning behind,   15
            a downpour of rain?
If it is the last message of youth, I await it,
            I welcome it a thousand times
A triumphant twilight, sent by the light,
            before the night fades.   20

YANNIS RITSOS

[b. 1909]

The Meaning of Simplicity

TRANSLATED BY EDMUND KEELEY

I hide behind simple things so you'll find me;
if you don't find me, you'll find the things,
you'll touch what my hand has touched.
our hand-prints will merge.

The August moon glitters in the kitchen   5
like a tin-plated pot (it gets that way because of what I'm saying to you),
it lights up the empty house and the house's kneeling silence—
always the silence remains kneeling.

Every word is a doorway
to a meeting, one often cancelled,   10
and that's when a word is true: when it insists on the meeting.

ODYSSEUS ELYTIS

[b. 1912]

Drinking the Corinthian sun

TRANSLATED BY KIMON FRIAR

Drinking the Corinthian sun
Reading the marble ruins
Striding over vineyard seas
Aiming with my harpoon
At votive fish that elude me   5
I found those leaves that the psalm of the sun memorizes
The living land that desire rejoices
To open

I drink water, cut fruit
Plunge my hands through the wind's foliage   10
Lemon trees quicken the pollen of summer days
Green birds cut through my dreams
And I leave, my eyes filled
With a boundless gaze where the world becomes
Beautiful again from the beginning according to the heart's measure.

ELÉNI VAKALÓ

[b. 1921]

My Father's Eye

TRANSLATED BY KIMON FRIAR

My father had a glass eye.

On Sundays when he stayed at home he would take other eyes out of his pocket, polish them with the edge of his sleeve and then call my mother to make her choice. My mother would giggle.

In the mornings my father was well satisfied. He would toss the eye in his hand before he wore it and would say it was a good eye. But I did not want to believe him.

I would throw a dark shawl over my shoulders as though I were cold but this was that I might spy on him. At last one day I saw him weeping. There was no difference at all from a real eye.

> *This poem*
> *Is not to be read*
> *By those who do not love me*
> *Not even*
> *By those*
> *Who will not know me*
> *If they do not believe I existed*
> *Like themselves*

After this episode with my father
I became suspicious even of those who had real eyes.

Latin Poetry

Latin writers, like their counterparts in sculpture and architecture, owe an immense debt to their Greek predecessors. Like Roman artists, Latin writers imitated Greek models and emulated Greek standards of artistic achievement without either slavishly copying them or ever really equaling them, except perhaps in epic poetry. Latin poets almost always used Greek genres, except for satire, which they claim to have invented. They also sometimes adapted Greek plays, with varying degrees of ingenuity. In one early and important instance, a Latin poet, Lucretius (c. 99–c. 55 B.C.) wrote a long didactic poem, *De Rerum Natura* (On the Nature of Things), which is indebted to the Greek philosopher Empedocles and beyond him to Epicurus, whose philosophy of enjoying sensuous pleasures and avoiding unnecessary pain the poem espouses. Lucretius' ambitious unfinished poem attempts to clear the mind of superstition and ready it for reasoned explanation of the nature of things.

Latin poets, moreover, benefited from the tension their work displays toward celebrating their specifically Roman culture and emulating their Greek predecessors, who were foreign without being alien to their emerging, distinctively Roman literary tradition. The poet who best harmonized the two cultural and literary strains of the native Roman and the foreign Greek traditions was Virgil, whose *Aeneid* blends the strengths of both.

Publius Vergilius Maro (70–19 B.C.), known in English simply as Virgil, looms as Rome's greatest and most influential poet. His most important work is the *Aeneid,* an epic poem celebrating the founding of Rome and the development of a distinctive Roman culture. Although Virgil does indeed imitate Homer, making use of both the *Iliad* and the *Odyssey* in describing the fortunes of Aeneas, his epic hero, Virgil turns Homer's works to his own purposes while stamping the familiar heroic tales of the Greeks and Trojans with the distinctive imprint of his inimitable style. The famous opening line of his *Aeneid, arma virumque cano* ("arms and the man I sing"), echoes down through the centuries to be picked up nearly two thousand years later in the title of Bernard Shaw's play *Arms and the Man.*

The *Aeneid* describes the events that led to the founding of the city of Rome and the Roman empire, especially the suffering and loss involved in the accomplishment of heroic deeds. Like Homer's *Iliad,* Virgil's epic depicts both the horrors and the glories of war. Like the *Odyssey,* it describes its hero's adventures, both dangerous and amorous. Regardless of its debt to Greek epic, however, the *Aeneid* is a thoroughly Roman poem, one saturated in Roman traditions, marked at every turn by its respect for family and country, best characterized perhaps by the term *pietas,* or "piety." *Pietas* involves a devotion to duty, especially love and honor of one's family and country, all in the context of devotion to the gods.

Virgil's *Aeneid* exerted a powerful influence on European poetry—from the veneration of classical Roman writers to that of Dante in his *Commedia* through Milton in his epic *Paradise Lost,* and on into eighteenth- and nineteenth-century English poets, such as William Wordsworth and Alfred, Lord Tennyson, who were inspired perhaps even more by Virgil's pastoral *Eclogues* and didactic *Georgics* than they were by the *Aeneid.*

Besides the *Aeneid,* Virgil is also recognized as a pastoral poet of considerable distinction. We have selected one of his *Eclogues,* published in 37 B.C., to illustrate this dimension of his poetic achievement. The fourth eclogue has acquired considerable fame for its prophetic tone and temper. Some readers, moreover, have accentuated its celebration of the future achievements of a special male child to be born to the Roman rulers Octavia and Mark Antony. Known as the "Messianic" eclogue, it was interpreted by some Christian writers, notably Augustine, as prefiguring the birth of Christ. This Christian interpretation derives less from the poem's tone, however, than from its references to a virgin, a serpent, a primal crime of deceit, and similarities to biblical prophecies in the Book of Isaiah (p. 902). We might note, finally, that Virgil's eclogues also derive from Greek models, most importantly from the bucolic poetry of Theocritus, who flourished in the first half of the third century B.C. The pastoral idylls of Theocritus were widely imitated not only by Latin poets of Virgil's time, but by Renaissance English and Italian poets as well.

Another poetic genre important for Latin poetry was the ode, especially as practiced by Quintus Horatius Flaccus (65–8 B.C.), better known simply as Horace. Like Virgil, Horace was encouraged to write poetry by the Roman emperor Octavius. Of humble origins, Horace was nonetheless freed from economic worry when he was befriended by Virgil, who helped him secure the patronage of Maecenas, a wealthy patron of the arts. Horace's four books of odes, generally considered his best work, were written between 33 B.C. and 13 B.C. Though his poems lack the grandeur of Virgil's, they are celebrated for their precision of language and their perfection of form.

Horace's odes are also generally acknowledged as espousing a philosophy of moderation that derives from earlier Greek culture and which has been associated with the oracle of the god Apollo at Delphi. Horace's influence on English poetry was perhaps greatest during the sixteenth through eighteenth centuries, on poets such as Robert Herrick, Ben Jonson, John Dryden, and Alexander Pope. One of his most famous poems, entitled "Ars Poetica" (The Art of Poetry) was especially valued as a guide to poetic practice during the Renaissance and neoclassical periods.

But Latin poetry includes more than the eloquence of Virgil and the elegance of Horace. Although we can't sample the entire range of Latin poetry in the brief selection that follows, we can at least suggest something of its variety. One of the most consistently popular of Latin poets, Catullus (Gaius Valerius Catullus) was born about 84 B.C. Like the Greek poet Sappho before him, Catullus wrote passionate love poems, though his tone varies more widely than hers.

Although it is always dangerous to read a poet's biographical experience into his or her poems, we can be reasonably well assured that Catullus's poems about Lesbia (Clodia Pulchra) derive from his personal experience of pain and pleasure, delight and despair in their relationship. Yet on the other hand, we should be aware that Catullus, even at his most spontaneous and passionate, is a learned poet working within a well-established tradition of erotic lyric verse. Of course, Catullus himself influenced that tradition, with its high points of translation and imitation in the seventeenth century, when poets such as Robert Herrick and Ben Jonson both imitated and literally translated Catullus's witty, sparkling verse.

Two other poets who wrote about love deserve at least a brief note. The first, Sextus Propertius, was born about 50 B.C. Like Horace and Virgil, Propertius enjoyed the friendship of the wealthy patron Maecenas. Like Catullus, Propertius's intensely passionate erotic poems derive from his personal experience, though we do not have persuasive evidence concerning his poetic subjects. We have selected one of Propertius's elegies in a translation by the modern American poet Ezra Pound, who captures something of Propertius's vitality and spontaneity, though he takes a few liberties, including leaving out a few lines of the original poem.

If Catullus can be thought of as a passionate lyric poet of eroticism in the vein of Sappho, Ovid (Publius Ovidius Naso, 43 B.C.–17 A.D.) can be seen as a witty and ironic satirist of love. The very titles of some of Ovid's books reveal his persistent interest in the erotic—*Amores* (Loves) and *Ars Amatoria* (The Art of Love). His most famous and important work, *Metamorphoses,* is based on a series of stories about transformation, often with an erotic twist. Ovid's poetry combines skillful narrative with elegance and grace. He is generally recognized also as a keen analyst of love with a perceptive understanding of human experience. Though ironic, Ovid's poetry is not cruel or sarcastic; instead, Ovid seems almost compassionate towards his characters. Ovid's influence on English poetry has been extensive, with perhaps his greatest popularity extending from the Renaissance through the eighteenth century, though his appearance in the works of such twentieth-century masters as Yeats, Pound, and Eliot reveals a modern legacy. Our translation of the excerpt from his *Amores* is by the Renaissance poet Christopher Marlowe.

Finally, a word about one additional poet, neither an elegiac poet, an epic poet, nor a lyricist. Like his Greek predecessor Callimachus, Martial (Marcus Valerius Martialis, 38–104) is best known for his epigrams, brief pointed poems often of only two lines. Like Callimachus's epigrams, many of Martial's achieve the precision and economy of epitaphs, though the range of his epigrammatic subjects is wide.

Though Latin is no longer a living language since it is not actually spoken today, it is very much alive in these poems.

LUCRETIUS

[c. 99 – c. 55 B.C.]

from *On the Nature of Things*

TRANSLATED BY ROLFE HUMPHRIES

With loyal industry I shall begin
With a discussion of the scheme of things
As it regards the heaven and powers above,
Then I shall state the origin of things,
The seeds from which nature creates all things,   *5*
Bids them increase and multiply; in turn,
How she resolves them to their elements
After their course is run. These things we call
Matter, the life-motes, or the seeds of things,
(If we must find, in schools, a name for them),   *10*
Firstlings, we well might say, since every thing
Follows from these beginnings.

When human life, all too conspicuous,
Lay foully grovelling on earth, weighed down
By grim Religion looming from the skies,   *15*
Horribly threatening mortal men, a man,
A Greek, first raised his mortal eyes
Bravely against this menace. No report
Of gods, no lightning-flash, no thunder-peal
Made this man cower, but drove him all the more   *20*
With passionate manliness of mind and will
To be the first to spring the tight-barred gates
Of Nature's hold asunder. So his force,
His vital force of mind, a conqueror
Beyond the flaming ramparts of the world   *25*
Explored the vast immensities of space
With wit and wisdom, and came back to us
Triumphant, bringing news of what can be
And what cannot, limits and boundaries,
The borderline, the bench mark, set forever.   *30*
Religion, so, is trampled underfoot,
And by his victory we reach the stars.

I fear that, in these matters, you may think
You're entering upon a path of crime,

The ABC's of godlessness. Not so.   35
The opposite is true. Too many times
Religion mothers crime and wickedness.
Recall how once at Aulis, when the Greeks,
Those chosen peers, the very first of men,
Defiled, with a girl's blood, the altar-stone   40
Sacred to Artemis. The princess stood
Wearing the sacred fillets or a veil,
And sensed but could not see the king her father,
Agamemnon, standing sorrowful
Beside the altar, and the priests near-by   45
Hiding the knife-blade, and the folk in tears
At what they saw. She knelt, she spoke no word,
She was afraid, poor thing. Much good it did her
At such a time to have been the very first
To give the king that other title, *Father!*   50
Raised by men's hands and trembling she was led
Toward the altar, not to join in song
After the ritual of sacrifice
To the bright god of marriage. No; she fell
A victim by the sacrificing stroke   55
Her father gave, to shed her virgin blood—
Not the way virgins shed it—but in death,
To bring the fleet a happy exodus!
A mighty counselor, Religion stood
With all that power for wickedness.   60

                            You may,
Yourself, some time or other, feel like turning
Away from my instruction, terrified
By priestly rant. How many fantasies
They can invent to overturn your sense   65
Of logic, muddle your estates by fear!
And rightly so, for if we ever saw
A limit to our troubles, we'd be strong,
Resisters of religion, rant and cant,
But as things are, we have no chance at all   70
With all their everlasting punishments
Waiting us after death.

                            We do not know
The nature of the soul: is it something born
By, of, and for itself? Does it find its way   75
Into our selves when we are being born,
To die when we do? Or does it, after our death,
Tour Hell's tremendous emptiness and shadow?

Or does it, by divine commandment, find
Abode in lower beasts, as we are told   *80*
By Roman Ennius, the first of us
Chapleted with the green of Helicon,
Bright-shining through the realms of Italy?
But still, he also tells us, in his verse,
Immortal as it is, that Acheron   *85*
Has reaches where no souls or bodies dwell,
But only phantoms, pale in wondrous wise,
And that from there immortal Homer's image
(So Ennius says) transferred itself to him,
And wept, and talked about all kinds of things.   *90*
So, we had better have some principle
In our discussion of celestial ways,
Under what system both the sun and moon
Wheel in their courses, and what impulse moves
Events on earth; and, more than that, we must   *95*
See that our principle is shrewd and sound
When we consider what the spirit is,
Wherein the nature of the mind consists,
What fantasy it is that strikes our wits
With terror in our waking hours or sickness   *100*
Or in sleep's sepulcher, so that we see,
Or think we do, and hear, most audible,
Those whose dead bones earth holds in her enfolding.

I am well aware how very hard it is
To bring to light by means of Latin verse   *105*
The dark discoveries of the Greeks. I know
New terms must be invented, since our tongue
Is poor, and this material is new.
But I'm persuaded by your excellence
And by our friendship's dear expectancy
To suffer any toil, to keep my watch   *110*
Through the still nights, seeking the words, the song
Whereby to bring your mind that splendid light
By which you can see darkly hidden things.
Our terrors and our darknesses of mind
Must be dispelled, not by the sunshine's rays,   *115*
Not by those shining arrows of the light,
But by insight into nature, and a scheme
Of systematic contemplation. So
Our starting-point shall be this principle:
Nothing at all is ever born from nothing   *120*
By the gods' will. Ah, but men's minds are frightened
Because they see, on earth and in the heaven,

Many events whose causes are to them
Impossible to fix; so, they suppose,
The gods' will is the reason. As for us,   *125*
Once we have seen that *Nothing comes from nothing,*
We shall perceive with greater clarity
What we are looking for, whence each thing comes,
How things are caused, and no "gods' will" about it.

Now, if things come from nothing, all things could   *130*
Produce all kinds of things; nothing would need
Seed of its own. Men would burst out of the sea,
And fish and birds from earth, and, wild or tame,
All kinds of beasts, of dubious origin,
Inhabit deserts and the greener fields,   *135*
Nor would the same trees bear, in constancy,
The same fruit always, but, as like as not,
Oranges would appear on apple-boughs.
If things were not produced after their kind,
Each from its own determined particles,   *140*
How could we trace the substance to the source?
But now, since all created things have come
From their own definite kinds of seed, they move
From their beginnings toward the shores of light
Out of their primal motes. Impossible   *145*
That all things issue everywhence; each kind
Of substance has its own inherent power,
Its own capacity. Does not the rose
Blossom in spring, the wheat come ripe in summer,
The grape burst forth at autumn's urge? There must be   *150*
A proper meeting of their seeds in time
For us to see them at maturity
Grown by their season's favor, living earth
Bringing them safely to the shores of light.
But if they came from nothing, they might spring   *155*
To birth at any unpropitious time,—
Who could predict?—since there would be no seeds
Whose character rules out untimely union.
Thirdly, if things could come from nothing, time
Would not be of the essence, for their growth,   *160*
Their ripening to full maturity.
Babies would be young men, in the blink of an eye,
And full-grown forests come leaping out from the ground.
Ridiculous! We know that all things grow
Little by little, as indeed they must
From their essential nature.   *165*

CATULLUS

[c. 84 – c. 54 B.C.]

Vivamus, mea Lesbia, atque amemus

We should live, my Lesbia, and love

TRANSLATED BY GUY LEE

Vivamus, mea Lesbia, atque amemus	We should live, my Lesbia, and love
rumoresque senum seueriorum	And value all the talk of stricter
omnes unius aestimemus assis.	Old men at a single penny.
soles occidere et redire possunt;	Suns can set and rise again;
nobis, cum semel occidit brevis lux, 5	For us, once our brief light has set,
nox est perpetua una dormienda.	There's one unending night for sleeping.
da mi basia mille, deinde centum,	Give me a thousand kisses, then a hundred,
dein mille altera, dein secunda centum,	Then another thousand, then a second hundred,
deinde usque altera mille, deinde centum;	Then still another thousand, then a hundred;
dein cum milia multa fecerimus 10	Then, when we've made many thousands,
conturbabimus illa ne sciamus	We'll muddle them so as not to know
aut ne quis malus invidere possit	Or lest some villain overlook us
cum tantum sciat esse basiorum.	Knowing the total of our kisses.

Furius and Aurelius, companions of Catullus

TRANSLATED BY PETER GLASSGOLD

Furius and Aurelius, companions of Catullus
everywhere he goes: far to India's
shores, resounding wide with breakers
   battering eastward;
by chance to Hyrcania or lush Araby,   5
among nomad Sacae or bowmen of Parthia;
whether to the Nile, whose seven channels
   darken the flood plains,
or over the high Alps he marches,
taking in reminders of great Caesar,   10
the Gallic Rhine, even the Britons so
   distant and dreadful—
friends, ready to try all this together,

whatever the heavens' will, bring this
message to my girl, a few words   15
   and nothing witty.
Tell her live and good luck with her lovers,
all three hundred she holds in her arms now,
caring for none really but busting
   their balls forever;   20
and not be eager for my love as in past times
who by her own fault dropped it, like a flower
at meadow's edge that's been struck by
   a plough in passing.

Ille mi par esse *deo videtur*	*That man is seen by me* *as a God's equal*

TRANSLATED BY GUY LEE

Ille mi par esse deo uidetur,		That man is seen by me as a God's equal
ille, si fas est, superare diuos,		Or (if it may be said) the Gods' superior,
qui sedens aduersus identidem te		Who sitting opposite again and again
spectat et audit		Watches and hears *you*
dulce ridentem, misero quod omnis	5	Sweetly laughing—which dispossesses poor me
eripit sensus mihi: nam simul te,		Of all my senses, for no sooner, Lesbia,
Lesbia, aspexi, nihil est super mi		Do I look at you than there's no power left me
vocis in ore,		(Of speech in my mouth,)
lingua sed torpet, tenuis sub artus		But my tongue's paralysed, invisible flame
flamma demanat, sonitu suopte	10	Courses down through my limbs, with din
tintinant aures, gemina teguntur		of their own
lumina nocte.		My ears are ringing and twin darkness covers
		The light of my eyes.
otium, Catulle, tibi molestum est:		Leisure, Catullus, does not agree with you.
otio exsultas nimiumque gestis:		At leisure you're restless, too excitable.
otium et reges prius et beatas	15	Leisure in the past has ruined rulers and
perdidit urbes.		Prosperous cities.

THAT MAN IS SEEN BY ME   This poem, the first in the "Lesbia" sequence, records the poet's feelings at or near the beginning of his relationship with the woman usually identified as Clodia, a fashionable and emancipated beauty. The first three stanzas are a near-translation from a poem by Sappho—which survives only as a fragment ("He is more than a hero"). The Latin meter ("sapphics") is also derived from Sappho.

Odi et amo   I hate and love

TRANSLATED BY GUY LEE

Odi et amo. quare id faciam, fortasse requiris?   I hate and love. Perhaps you're asking why I do that?
nescio, sed fieri sentio et excrucior.   I don't know, but I feel it happening, and am
                                                             racked.

VIRGIL

The Fourth Eclogue

[70 – 19 B.C.]

TRANSLATED BY J. LAUGHLIN

Muses
Muses of Sicily
Now let us sing a serious song
There are taller trees than the apple and the crouching tamerisk
If we sing of the woods, let our forest be stately   5

Now the last age is coming
As it was written in the Sybil's book
The great circle of the centuries begins again
Justice, the Virgin, has returned to earth
With all of Saturn's court   10
A new line is sent down to us from the skies
And thou, Lucina, must smile
Smile for the birth of the boy, the blessed boy
For whom they will beat their swords into ploughshares
For whom the golden race will rise, the whole world new   15
Smile, pure Lucina, smile
Thine own Apollo will reign

And thou, Pollio
It is in thy term this glorious age begins

THE FOURTH ECLOGUE   [18]**Pollio** an important Roman politician of Virgil's time.

And the great months begin their march   *20*
When we shall lose all trace of the old guilt
And the world learn to forget fear
For the boy will become divine
He will see gods and heroes
And will himself be seen by them as god and hero   *25*
As he rules over a world of peace
A world made peaceful by his father's wisdom

For thee, little boy, will the earth pour forth gifts
All untilled, give thee gifts
First the wandering ivy and foxglove   *30*
Then colocasia and the laughing acanthus
Uncalled the goats will come home with their milk
No longer need the herds fear the lion
Thy cradle itself will bloom with sweet flowers
The serpent will die   *35*
The poison plant will wither
Assyrian herbs will spring up everywhere

And when thou art old enough to read of heroes
And of thy father's great deeds
Old enough to understand the meaning of courage   *40*
Then will the plain grow yellow with ripe grain
Grapes will grow on brambles
Hard old oaks drip honey

Yet still there must remain some traces of the old guilt
That lust that drives men to taunt the sea with ships   *45*
To circle cities with walls
And cut the earth with furrows
There must be another Tiphys
Another Argo carrying picked men
And there must be a war, one final war   *50*
With great Achilles storming a last Troy

But when thou hast grown strong and become a man
Then even the trader will leave the sea
His pine ship carry no more wares
And everywhere the land will yield all things that life requires   *55*
No longer need the ground endure the harrow
Nor the vine the pruning hook
The farmer can free his oxen from the yoke
Then colored cloths no longer will need lying dyes
For the ram in the field will change his own fleece   *60*

To soft purple or saffron yellow
Each grazing lamb will have a scarlet coat

"Onward, O glorious ages, onward"
Thus sang the fatal sisters to their spindles
Chanting together the unalterable Will 65

Go forward, little boy, to thy great honors
Soon comes thy time
Dear child of gods from whom a Jupiter will come
See how for thee the world nods its huge head
All lands and seas and endless depths of sky 70
See how the earth rejoices in the age that is to be

O may my life be long enough to let me sing of thee
With strength enough to tell thy deeds
With such a theme not even Thracian Orpheus could outsing me
Not Linus either, though Apollo prompted him 75
Help from Calliope herself could not make Orpheus' song the best
And even Pan, with Arcady as judge
Yes Pan, would fall before me when I sang of thee

Learn, little boy, to greet thy mother with a smile
For thee she has endured nine heavy months 80
Learn, little boy, to smile
For if thou didst not smile
And if thy parents did not smile on thee
No god could ask thee to his table
No goddess to her bed. 85

from *the Aeneid*

from Book I, Arms and the Man

TRANSLATED BY ROBERT FITZGERALD

Arma virumque cano, Trojae qui primus ab oris	I sing of warfare and a man at war.
Italiam fato profugus Lavinaque venit	From the sea-coast of Troy in early days
litora, multum ille et terris jactatus et alto	He came to Italy by destiny,
vi superum saevae memorem Junonis ob iram,	To our Lavinian western shore,
multa quoque et bello passus, dum couderet	A fugitive, this captain, buffeted
urbem 5	Cruelly on land as on the sea

inferretque deos Latio, genus unde Latinum
Albanique patres atque altae moenia Romae.
   Musa, mihi causas memora, quo numine
   laeso
quidve dolens regina deum tot volvere casus
insignem pietate virum, tot adire labores   *10*
impulerit. Tantaene animis caelestibus irae?
   Urbs antiqua fuit (Tyrii tenuere coloni),
Karthago, Italiam contra Tiberiaque longe
ostia, dives opum studiique asperrima belli,
quam Juno fertur terris magis omnibus unam   *15*
posthabita coluisse Samo; hic illius arma,
hic currus fuit; hoc regnum dea gentibus esse,
si qua fata sinant, jam tum tenditque fovetque.
Progeniem sed enim Trojano a sanguine duci
audierat, Tyrias olim quae verteret arces;   *20*
hinc populum late regem belloque superbum
venturum exscidio Libyae; sic volvere Parcas.
Id metuens veterisque memor Saturnia belli,
prima quod ad Trojam pro caris gesserat Argis
(necdum etiam causae irarum saevique dolores   *25*
exciderant animo; manet alta mente repostum
judicium Paridis sprētaeque injuria formae
et genus invisum et rapti Ganymedis
   honores)—
his accensa super, jactatos aequore toto
Troas, relliquias Danaum atque immitis
   Achilli,   *30*
arcebat longe Latio; multosque per annos
errabant acti fatis maria omnia circum.
Tantae molis erat Romaanam condere gentem.

By blows from powers of the air—behind them
Baleful Juno in her sleepless rage.
And cruel losses were his lot in war,
Till he could found a city and bring home,
His gods to Latium, land of the Latin race,
The Alban lords, and the high walls of Rome.
Tell me the causes now, O Muse, how galled
In her divine pride, and how sore at heart
From her old wound, the queen of gods compelled
   him—
A man apart, devoted to his mission—
To undergo so many perilous days
And enter on so many trials. Can anger
Black as this prey on the minds of heaven?
Tyrian settlers in that ancient time
Held Carthage, on the far shore of the sea,
Set against Italy and Tiber's mouth,
A rich new town, warlike and trained for war.
And Juno, we are told, cared more for Carthage
Than for any walled city of the earth,
More than for Samos, even. There her armor
And chariot were kept, and, fate permitting,
Carthage would be the ruler of the world.
So she intended, and so nursed that power.
But she had heard long since
That generations of Trojan blood
Would one day overthrow her Tyrian walls,
And from that blood a race would come in time
With ample kingdoms, arrogant in war,
For Libya's ruin: so the Parcae spun.
In fear of this, and holding in memory
The old war she had carried on at Troy
For Argos' sake (the origins of that anger,
That suffering, still rankled: deep within her,
Hidden away, the judgment Paris gave,
Snubbing her loveliness; the race she hated;
The honors given ravished Ganymede),
Saturnian Juno, burning for it all,
Buffeted on the waste of sea those Trojans
Left by the Greeks and pitiless Achilles,
Keeping them far from Latium. For years
They wandered as their destiny drove them on
From one sea to the next: so hard and huge
A task it was to found the Roman people.

from *The Aeneid*

from Book II, Dido and Aeneas

TRANSLATED BY ROBERT FITZGERALD

As to the cause
For a change of plan, they were to keep it secret,
Seeing the excellent Dido had no notion,
No warning that such love could be cut short;
He would himself look for the right occasion,   5
The easiest time to speak, the way to do it.
The Trojans to a man gladly obeyed.

The queen, for her part, felt some plot afoot
Quite soon—for who deceives a woman in love?
She caught wind of a change, being in fear   10
Of what had seemed her safety. Evil Rumor,
Shameless as before, brought word to her
In her distracted state of ships being rigged
In trim for sailing. Furious, at her wits' end,
She traversed the whole city, all aflame   15
With rage, like a Bacchantë driven wild
By emblems shaken, when the mountain revels
Of the odd year possess her, when the cry
Of Bacchus rises and Cithaeron calls
All through the shouting night. Thus it turned out   20
She was the first to speak and charge Aeneas:

"You even hoped to keep me in the dark
As to this outrage, did you, two-faced man,
And slip away in silence? Can our love
Not hold you, can the pledge we gave not hold you,   25
Can Dido not, now sure to die in pain?
Even in winter weather must you toil
With ships, and fret to launch against high winds
For the open sea? Oh, heartless!
                          Tell me now,   30
If you were not in search of alien lands
And new strange homes, if ancient Troy remained,
Would ships put out for Troy on these big seas?
Do you go to get away from me? I beg you,

By these tears, by your own right hand, since I   35
Have left my wretched self nothing but that—
Yes, by the marriage that we entered on,
If ever I did well and you were grateful
Or found some sweetness in a gift from me,
Have pity now on a declining house!   40
Put this plan by, I beg you, if a prayer
Is not yet out of place.
Because of you, Libyans and nomad kings
Detest me, my own Tyrians are hostile;
Because of you, I lost my integrity   45
And that admired name by which alone
I made my way once toward the stars.
                                                  To whom
Do you abandon me, a dying woman,
Guest that you are—the only name now left   50
From that of husband? Why do I live on?
Shall I, until my brother Pygmalion comes
To pull my walls down? Or the Gaetulan
Iarbas leads me captive? If at least
There were a child by you for me to care for,   55
A little one to play in my courtyard
And give me back Aeneas, in spite of all,
I should not feel so utterly defeated,
Utterly bereft."
                              She ended there.   60
The man by Jove's command held fast his eyes
And fought down the emotion in his heart.
At length he answered:
                              "As for myself, be sure
I never shall deny all you can say,   65
Your majesty, of what you meant to me.
Never will the memory of Elissa
Stale for me, while I can still remember
My own life, and the spirit rules my body.
As to the event, a few words. Do not think   70
I meant to be deceitful and slip away.
I never held the torches of a bridegroom,
Never entered upon the pact of marriage.
If Fate permitted me to spend my days
By my own lights, and make the best of things   75
According to my wishes, first of all
I should look after Troy and the loved relics
Left me of my people. Priam's great hall
Should stand again; I should have restored the tower

Of Pergamum for Trojans in defeat.   *80*
But now it is the rich Italian land
Apollo tells me I must make for: Italy,
Named by his oracles. There is my love;
There is my country. If, as a Phoenician,
You are so given to the charms of Carthage,   *85*
Libyan city that it is, then tell me,
Why begrudge the Teucrians new lands
For homesteads in Ausonia? Are we not
Entitled, too, to look for realms abroad?
Night never veils the earth in damp and darkness,   *90*
Fiery stars never ascend the east,
But in my dreams my father's troubled ghost
Admonishes and frightens me. Then, too,
Each night thoughts come of young Ascanius,
My dear boy wronged, defrauded of his kingdom,   *95*
Hesperian lands of destiny. And now
The gods' interpreter, sent by Jove himself—
I swear it by your head and mine—has brought
Commands down through the racing winds! I say
With my own eyes in full daylight I saw him   *100*
Entering the building! With my very ears
I drank his message in! So please, no more
Of these appeals that set us both afire.
I sail for Italy not of my own free will."

During all this she had been watching him   *105*
With face averted, looking him up and down
In silence, and she burst out raging now:

"No goddess was your mother. Dardanus
Was not the founder of your family.
Liar and cheat! Some rough Caucasian cliff   *110*
Begot you on flint. Hyrcanian tigresses
Tendered their teats to you. Why should I palter?
Why still hold back for more indignity?
Sigh, did he, while I wept? Or look at me?
Or yield a tear, or pity her who loved him?   *115*
What shall I say first, with so much to say?
The time is past when either supreme Juno
Or the Saturnian father viewed these things
With justice. Faith can never be secure.
I took the man in, thrown up on this coast   *120*
In dire need, and in my madness then
Contrived a place for him in my domain,

Rescued his lost fleet, saved his shipmates' lives.
Oh, I am swept away burning by furies!
Now the prophet Apollo, now his oracles,   125
Now the gods' interpreter, if you please,
Sent down by Jove himself, brings through the air
His formidable commands! What fit employment
For heaven's high powers! What anxieties
To plague serene immortals! I shall not   130
Detain you or dispute your story. Go,
Go after Italy on the sailing winds,
Look for your kingdom, cross the deepsea swell!
If divine justice counts for anything,
I hope and pray that on some grinding reef   135
Midway at sea you'll drink your punishment
And call and call on Dido's name!
From far away I shall come after you
With my black fires, and when cold death has parted
Body from soul I shall be everywhere   140
A shade to haunt you! You will pay for this,
Unconscionable! I shall hear! The news will reach me
Even among the lowest of the dead!'"

At this abruptly she broke off and ran
In sickness from his sight and the light of day,   145
Leaving him at a loss, alarmed, and mute
With all he meant to say. The maids in waiting
Caught her as she swooned and carried her
To bed in her marble chamber.
                              Duty-bound,   150
Aeneas, though he struggled with desire
To calm and comfort her in all her pain,
To speak to her and turn her mind from grief,
And though he sighed his heart out, shaken still
With love of her, yet took the course heaven gave him   155
And went back to the fleet. Then with a will
The Teucrians fell to work and launched the ships
Along the whole shore: slick with tar each hull
Took to the water. Eager to get away,
The sailors brought oar-boughs out of the woods   160
With leaves still on, and oaken logs unhewn.
Now you could see them issuing from the town
To the water's edge in streams, as when, aware
Of winter, ants will pillage a mound of spelt
To store it in their granary; over fields   165
The black battalion moves, and through the grass
On a narrow trail they carry off the spoil;

Some put their shoulders to the enormous weight
Of a trundled grain, while some pull stragglers in
And castigate delay; their to-and-fro   *170*
Of labor makes the whole track come alive.
At that sight, what were your emotions, Dido?
Sighing how deeply, looking out and down
From your high tower on the seething shore
Where all the harbor filled before your eyes   *175*
With bustle and shouts! Unconscionable Love,
To what extremes will you not drive our hearts!
She now felt driven to weep again, again
To move him, if she could, by supplication,
Humbling her pride before her love—to leave   *180*
Nothing untried, not to die needlessly.

"Anna, you see the arc of waterfront
All in commotion: they come crowding in
From everywhere. Spread canvas calls for wind,
The happy crews have garlanded the sterns.   *185*
If I could brace myself for this great sorrow,
Sister, I can endure it, too. One favor,
Even so, you may perform for me.
Since that deserter chose you for his friend
And trusted you, even with private thoughts,   *190*
Since you alone know when he may be reached,
Go, intercede with our proud enemy.
Remind him that I took no oath at Aulis
With Danaans to destroy the Trojan race;
I sent no ship to Pergamum. Never did I   *195*
Profane his father Anchisës' dust and shade.
Why will he not allow my prayers to fall
On his unpitying ears? Where is he racing?
Let him bestow one last gift on his mistress:
This, to await fair winds and easier flight.   *200*
Now I no longer plead the bond he broke
Of our old marriage, nor do I ask that he
Should live without his dear love, Latium,
Or yield his kingdom. Time is all I beg,
Mere time, a respite and a breathing space   *205*
For madness to subside in, while my fortune
Teaches me how to take defeat and grieve.
Pity your sister. This is the end, this favor—
To be repaid with interest when I die."

She pleaded in such terms, and such, in tears,   *210*
Her sorrowing sister brought him, time and again.

But no tears moved him, no one's voice would he
Attend to tractably. The fates opposed it;
God's will blocked the man's once kindly ears.
And just as when the north winds from the Alps   215
This way and that contend among themselves
To tear away an oaktree hale with age,
The wind and tree cry, and the buffeted trunk
Showers high foliage to earth, but holds
On bedrock, for the roots go down as far   220
Into the underworld as cresting boughs
Go up in heaven's air: just so this captain,
Buffeted by a gale of pleas
This way and that way, dinned all the day long,
Felt their moving power in his great heart,   225
And yet his will stood fast; tears fell in vain.

HORACE

[65 – 8 B.C.]

Eheu fugaces   Ah god how they race

TRANSLATED BY HELEN ROWE HENZE

Eheu fugaces, Postume, Postume,
labuntur anni nec pietas moram
    rugis et instanti senectae
        adferet indomitaeque morti;

non, si trecenis quotquot eunt dies,   5
amice, places inlacrimabilem
    Plutona tauris, qui ter amplum
        Geryonen Tityonque tristi

conpescit unda, scilicet omnibus
quicumque terrae munere uescimur   10
    enauiganda, siue reges
        siue inopes erimus coloni.

Ah god how they race, Postumus, Postumus,
how the years run out, and doing what is right
    will not delay wrinkles and age's
        onslaught and death who cannot be beaten;

no, dear friend, not even if every day
you tried with three hundred bulls to please Pluto,
    who has no tears, who holds in prison
        three-bodied Geryon and Tityos

by the sorrowful river whose crossing is
certain for those who live by the gifts of the earth,
    a must for all, the high and mighty
        and the poverty-stricken small farmers.

AH GOD HOW THEY RACE   ¹Postumus Unknown person; perhaps merely typical.   ⁸Geryon A giant with three bodies,
slain by Hercules.   Tityos Slain by Apollo and Diana; in the lower regions he covered nine acres of ground

frustra cruento marte carebimus	It will do no good to escape bloody Mars
fractisque rauci fluctibus Hadriae,	and breaking waves on the rough Adriatic,
frustra per autumnos nocentem 15	it will do no good to spend autumn
corporibus metuemus austrum:	in terror of sirocco and sickness:
uisendus ater flumine languido	we must see the dark waters of Cocytos
Cocytos errans et Danai genus	winding slowly, and the infamous daughters
infame damnatusque longi	of Danaus, and Sisyphus, son of
Sisyphus Aeolides laboris: 20	Aeolus, condemned to endless labor.
linquenda tellus et domus et placens	We must leave behind us earth and home and dear
uxor, neque harum quas colis arborum	wife, and of all the trees that you care for now,
te praeter inuisas cupressos	not one will follow you, so briefly
ulla breuem dominum sequetur.	its master, only the loathsome cypress.
absumet heres Caecuba dignior 25	An heir who deserves it will drink Caecuban
seruata centum clauibus et mero	you kept safe with a hundred keys, and he will
tinguet pauimentum superbus	soak the floor with magnificent wine,
pontificum potiore cenis.	finer than the priests drink at their festivals.

SEXTUS PROPERTIUS

[c. 50 – c. 15 B.C.]

Me happy, night, night full of brightness

TRANSLATED BY EZRA POUND

Me happy, night, night full of brightness;
Oh couch made happy by my long delectations;
How many words talked out with abundant candles;
Struggles when the lights were taken away;
Now with bared breasts she wrestled against me,   5
     Tunic spread in delay;

AH GOD HOW THEY RACE   [17]**Cocytos** A mythical river of the lower world.   [19]**Danaus** The Danaïdes, who killed their husbands on their wedding night.   **Sisyphus** The crafty king of Corinth, whose punishment in the underworld was to roll up a hill a huge stone which always slipped from his hands before he reached the top.   [25]**Caecuban** A very fine wine.

And she then opening my eyelids fallen in sleep,
Her lips upon them; and it was her mouth saying:
     Sluggard!

In how many varied embraces, our changing arms,   *10*
Her kisses, how many, lingering on my lips.
"Turn not Venus into a blinded motion,
    Eyes are the guides of love,
Paris took Helen naked coming from the bed of Menelaus,
Endymion's naked body, bright bait for Diana,"   *15*
     —such at least is the story.

While our fates twine together, sate we our eyes with love;
For long night comes upon you
         and a day when no day returns.
Let the gods lay chains upon us   *20*
     so that no day shall unbind them.

Fool who would set a term to love's madness,
For the sun shall drive with black horses,
       earth shall bring wheat from barley,
The flood shall move toward the fountain   *25*
     Ere love know moderations,
     The fish shall swim in dry streams.
No, now while it may be, let not the fruit of life cease.

Dry wreaths drop their petals,
      their stalks are woven in baskets,   *30*
To-day we take the great breath of lovers,
         to-morrow fate shuts us in.

Though you give all your kisses
         you give but few.

Nor can I shift my pains to other,   *35*
     Hers will I be dead,
If she confer such nights upon me,
       long is my life, long in years,
If she give me many,
       God am I for the time.   *40*

---

[14]**Paris took Helen . . . Menelaus** The abduction of Helen, wife of Menelaus, by Paris, a Trojan, sparked the hostilities that led to the Trojan War.

MARTIAL

[c. 38 – c. 104]

My friend, the things that do attain

TRANSLATED BY HENRY HOWARD, EARL OF SURREY

My friend, the things that do attain
The happy life be these, I find:
The riches left, not got with pain;
The fruitful ground; the quiet mind;

The equal friend; no grudge, no strife;   5
No charge of rule, nor governance;
Without disease, the healthy life;
The household of continuance;

The mean diet, no dainty fare;
Wisdom joined with simpleness;   10
The night dischargéd of all care,
Where wine the wit may not oppress;

The faithful wife, without debate;
Such sleeps as may beguile the night;
Content thyself with thine estate,   15
Neither wish death, nor fear his might.

You serve the best wine always, my dear sir

TRANSLATED BY J. V. CUNNINGHAM

You serve the best wine always, my dear sir,
And yet they say your wines are not so good.
They say you are four times a widower.
They say . . . A drink? I don't believe I would.

OVID

[43 B.C. – A.D. 17]

Siesta time in sultry summer

TRANSLATED BY GUY LEE

Siesta time in sultry summer.
I lay relaxed on the divan.

One shutter closed, the other ajar,
made sylvan semi-darkness,

a glimmering dusk, as after sunset,   5
or between night's end and day's beginning—

the half light shy girls need
to hide their hesitation.

At last—Corinna. On the loose in a short dress,
long hair parted and tumbling past the pale neck—   10

lovely as Lais of the many lovers,
Queen Semiramis gliding in.

I grabbed the dress; it didn't hide much,
but she fought to keep it,

only half-heartedly though.   15
Victory was easy, a self-betrayal.

There she stood, faultless beauty
in front of me, naked.

Shoulders and arms challenging eyes and fingers.
Nipples firmly demanding attention.   20

---

[12]**Semiramis**   Ninth-century Assyrian queen, famed for wisdom and beauty.

Breasts in high relief above the smooth belly.
Long and slender waist. Thighs of a girl.

Why list perfection?
I hugged her tight.

The rest can be imagined—we fell asleep.   *25*
Such afternoons are rare.

Russian Poetry

Although Russian folk poetry appears in the eleventh century in an oral tradition even before the development of an identifiable Russian literature, a written tradition of Russian poetry does not emerge until the seventeenth century. It was not until the eighteenth century, moreover, that numerous experiments in versification prepared for the richness and power of modern Russian poetry, which we sample here.

Our poets fall into two distinct groups. The first and older group consists of four poets, all born within a few years of one another: Anna Akhmatova (1889–1966), Boris Pasternak (1890–1960), Osip Mandelstam (1891–1938), and Marina Tsvetayeva (1892–1941). Akhmatova and Mandelstam considered themselves "Acmeists," in contradistinction to their precursors, the Symbolist poets. Acmeists like Akhmatova and Mandelstam sought to portray in their poems the very highest degree or essence of their subjects. They strove for precision of detail as contrasted with the more vaguely suggestive language of the Symbolists. The acmeists stressed craftsmanship in building poems that conveyed a precise expression of emotional experience. And finally, their poetry reflected a respect for the culture of the past, especially that of Europe.

Akhmatova and Mandelstam both suffered brutally under Stalinist repression during the 1930s. Akhmatova was prohibited from publishing her work for almost two decades. During the Stalinist purges both her husband and her son were arrested on political charges. This experience provided the stimulus for her powerful *Requiem,* which she composed from 1935 to 1940. This dirge to human suffering along with her late long work, *Poem Without a Hero,* and her lyrical love poems comprise the essence of her poetic legacy.

Like Akhmatova, Osip Mandelstam has been celebrated as one of the greatest of modern poets. Mandelstam was a literary theorist and prose writer as well as a poet. His essays "On the Nature of the Word" and "Conversation with Dante" explain his Acmeist principles. His poems on the great cathedrals of Notre Dame in Paris and Hagia Sophia in Istanbul, coupled with his celebrations of Dante, Homer, and François Villon, testify to his deep appreciation of classical and medieval culture.

Mandelstam was concerned with the present as well as the past. Although the bulk of his poetry is not avowedly and pointedly political, some of his poems reflect a decisive, unmitigatingly political point of view. Such is "The Stalin Epigram," which satirizes Stalin, a poem for which Mandelstam was arrested in 1934. After his release, Mandelstam lived in exile with his wife, Nadezhda. He continued to write poems, and though he couldn't publish them, Nadezhda committed them to memory. He was arrested a second time in 1938 and died in a prison camp later that year. The chronicle of Osip Mandelstam's last four years and the story of Nadezhda Mandelstam's ultimately successful attempt to rehabilitate her husband's reputation are movingly recounted in her extraordinary memoirs, *Hope Against Hope* and *Hope Abandoned*.

The other two important modern Russian poets included here, Boris Pasternak and Marina Tsvetayeva, shared some of the ignominy suffered by Mandelstam and Akhmatova. Like them, Pasternak suffered the indignity of being silenced. Although his poetry was not overtly critical of the political establishment, it was considered tainted by virtue of its lack of a positive, supportive political stance. Like Akhmatova and Mandelstam, Pasternak was compelled to earn his living by translating, since he could not support himself as a writer. One of the serendipitous benefits of this eventuality for the Russian people was a body of superb translations of German and English works, especially Romantic lyric poetry and the plays of Shakespeare, which remain the standard Russian editions to this day.

Like Akhmatova, Marina Tsvetayeva wrote prolifically, varying her style and experimenting with poetic language and form. Tsvetayeva and Pasternak admired each other's work and later became correspondents and then friends, though they were not as close as Akhmatova and Mandelstam, with whose widow Akhmatova was particularly friendly and with whom she lived for a number of years after Osip Mandelstam's death. Tsvetayeva is acknowledged as a remarkable poetic "ventriloquist." She has the ability to project a wide range of poetic voices. In "An Attempt at Jealousy" Tsvetayeva creates a bitterly taunting voice, one whose anger is fueled by vengefulness and scorn.

Boris Pasternak's poetry is of a different temperament. In "Winter Night" we glimpse a passion as intense as that expressed in Tsvetayeva's "Attempt at Jealousy," but the intensity is turned inward and finds expression in the image of an insistently burning candle rather than, as in "Attempt at Jealousy," in a scathing outburst into spoken discourse. Pasternak is recognized as an important figure in modern Russian literature as much for his controversial novel *Doctor Zhivago* as for his poetry. His poem "Hamlet" appears in an appended chapter of this novel.

Our second group of poets represents those born almost two generations after the earlier group. Each is considered a fresh, vigorous voice. Bella Akhmadulina (b. 1937), born and raised in Moscow, began publishing poetry at the age of eighteen. Her poems are notable for their wit, their humanity, and their concern with the act of poetic creation. Andrey Voznesensky (b. 1933), also born in Moscow, is more formally experimental than Akhmadulina, who tends to stay with traditional forms and meters. Voznesensky's poems can be shocking in their deliberately farfetched analogies and surprising in their juxtapositions of past and present. Yevgeny Yevtushenko (b. 1933) is one of Russia's most popular poets, performing his works in front of audiences in the thousands both at home and abroad. Like his contemporaries Voznesensky and Akhmadulina, Yevtushenko was raised in Moscow. Not as experimental as Voznesensky's in imagery and form, Yevtushenko's style is declamatory and oratorical, his typical poetic tone a mixture of combativeness and meditative reflection, as in his "Babii Yar," which is critical of Soviet anti-Semitism.

Whatever the direction Russian poetry may take in the politically open future, its past, from the Czarist-controlled Russia of Pushkin to the Communist-dominated world of Mandelstam, Akhmatova, Voznesensky, and Yevtushenko, suggests it will be illustrious, innovative, resilient, and enduring.

ANNA AKHMATOVA

[1889–1966]

Лотова жена

Lot's Wife

TRANSLATED BY STANLEY KUNITZ
AND MAX HAYWARD

И праведник шел за посланником Бога,	And the just man trailed God's shining agent,
Огромный и светлый, по черной горе.	over a black mountain, in his giant track,
Но громко жене говорила тревога:	while a restless voice kept harrying his woman:
Не поздно, ты можещь еще посмотреть	"It's not too late, you can still look back
На красные башни родного Содома,	at the red towers of your native Sodom,
На площадь, где пела, на двор где пряла,	the square where once you sang, the spinning-shed,
На окна пустые высокого дома,	at the empty windows set in the tall house
Где милому мужу детей родила.	where sons and daughters blessed your marriage-bed."
Взглянула,—и, скованы смертною болью,	A single glance: a sudden dart of pain
Глаза ее больше смотреть не могли;	stitching her eyes before she made a sound . . .
И сделалось тело прозрачною солью,	Her body flaked into transparent salt,
И быстрые ноги к земле приросли.	and her swift legs rooted to the ground.
Кто женщину эту оплакивать будет?	Who will grieve for this woman? Does she not seem
Не меньшей ли мнится она из утрат?	too insignificant for our concern?
Лишь сердце мое никогда не забудет	Yet in my heart I never will deny her,
Отдавшую жизнь за единственный взгляд.	who suffered death because she chose to turn.

Line numbers: 5, 10, 15

BORIS PASTERNAK

[1890–1960]

ЗИМНЯЯ НОЧЬ

Winter Night

TRANSLATED BY RICHARD MCKANE

Мело, мело по всей земле
во все прелелы.
Свеча горела на столе,
Свеча горела.

As in summer swarms   5
of midges fly to a flame,
snowflakes fluttered
around the windowframe.

Snow, snow over the whole land
across all boundaries.
The candle burned on the table,
the candle burned.

Как летом роем мошкара   5
Летит на пламя,
Слетались хлопья со двора
К оконной раме.

As in summer swarms
of midges fly to a flame,
snowflakes fluttered
around the windowframe.

Метель лепила на стекле
Кружки и стрелы.   10
Свеча горела на столе,
Свеча горела.

Blown snow stuck
rings and arrows on the glass.
The candle burned on the table,
the candle burned.

На озаренный потолок
Ложились тени,
Скрещенья рук, скрещенья ног,   15
Судьбы скрещенья.

Shadows were lying
on the lighted ceiling,
of crossed arms, crossed legs,
crossed destinies.

И падали два башмачка
Со стуком на пол.
И воск слезами с ночника
На платье капал.   20

Two shoes fell
noisily on the floor.
The night light wept
wax drops on a dress.

И все терялось в снежной мгле
Седой и белой.
Свеча горела на столе.
Свеча горела.

Everything was lost in the
greying white snow haze.
The candle burned on the table,
the candle burned.

На свечку дуло из угла,   25
И жар соблазна
вздымал, как ангел, два крыла
Крестообразно.

Draught at the candle from the corner,
the heat of temptation
angel-like raised two wings
in the form of a cross.

Мело весь месяц в феврале,
И то и дело   30
Свеча горела на столе,
Свеча горела.

Snow fell all February
and now and then
the candle burned on the table,
the candle burned.

OSIP MANDELSTAM

[1891–1938]

Ъессонница

Insomnia

TRANSLATED BY JOHN GLAD

Ъессонница. Гомер. Тугие паруса.	Insomnia. Homer. Taut sails.
Я список кораблей прочел до середины:	I have read the list of ships to the middle:
Сей длинный выводок, сей поезд журавлиный,	this migrant flight
Что над элладою когда-то поднялся.	that once winged over Hellas.
Как журавлиный клин в чужие рубежи— 5	What drives this wedge of cranes into alien borders?
на головах царей божественная пена—	What do you seek, Achean men?
Куда плывете вы? Когда бы не Елена,	Were it not for Helen,
Что Троя вам одна, ахейские мужи?	What need had you of Troy?
И море, и Гомер—все движется любовью.	Homer falls silent
Кого же слушать мне? И вот Гомер молчит, 10	And foam swirls from the heads of kings.
И море черное, витийствуя, шумит	Only the black sea rages
И с яжким грохотом подходит к изголовью.	And a heavy surf thunders against my pillow.

ANNA AKHMATOVA

Requiem
1935–1940

TRANSLATED BY STANLEY KUNITZ AND MAX HAYWARD

No foreign sky protected me,
no stranger's wing shielded my face.
I stand as witness to the common lot,
survivor of that time, that place.
—1961

Instead of a Preface

In the terrible years of the Yezhov terror I spent seventeen months waiting in line outside the prison in Leningrad. One day somebody in the crowd identified me. Standing behind me was a woman, with lips blue from the cold, who had, of course, never heard me called by name before. Now she started out of the torpor common to us all and asked me in a whisper (everyone whispered there): "Can you describe this?" And I said: "I can." Then something like a smile passed fleetingly over what had once been her face.

—Leningrad, 1 April 1957

Dedication

Such grief might make the mountains stoop,
reverse the waters where they flow,
but cannot burst these ponderous bolts
that block us from the prison cells
crowded with mortal woe. . . .   5
For some the wind can freshly blow,
for some the sunlight fade at ease,
but we, made partners in our dread,
hear but the grating of the keys,
and heavy-booted soldiers' tread.   10
As if for early mass, we rose
and each day walked the wilderness,
trudging through silent street and square,
to congregate, less live than dead.
The sun declined, the Neva blurred,   15
and hope sang always from afar.
Whose sentence is decreed? . . . That moan,
that sudden spurt of woman's tears,
shows one distinguished from the rest,
as if they'd knocked her to the ground   20
and wrenched the heart out of her breast,
then let her go, reeling, alone.
Where are they now, my nameless friends
from those two years I spent in hell?
What specters mock them now, amid   25
the fury of Siberian snows,
or in the blighted circle of the moon?
To them I cry, Hail and Farewell!

—March 1940

Prologue

That was a time when only the dead
could smile, delivered from their wars,   30

and the sign, the soul, of Leningrad
dangled outside its prison-house;
and the regiments of the condemned,
herded in the railroad-yards,
shrank from the engine's whistle-song   35
whose burden went, "Away, pariahs!"
The stars of death stood over us.
And Russia, guiltless, beloved, writhed
under the crunch of bloodstained boots,
under the wheels of Black Marias.   40

1

At dawn they came and took you away.
You were my dead: I walked behind.
In the dark room children cried,
the holy candle gasped for air.
Your lips were chill from the ikon's kiss,   45
sweat bloomed on your brow—those deathly flowers!
Like the wives of Peter's troopers in Red Square
I'll stand and howl under the Kremlin towers.

—1935

2

Quietly flows the quiet Don;
into my house slips the yellow moon.   50
It leaps the sill, with its cap askew,
and balks at a shadow, that yellow moon.

This woman is sick to her marrow-bone,
this woman is utterly alone,

with husband dead, with son away   55
in jail. Pray for me. Pray.

3

Not, not mine: it's somebody else's wound.
I could never have borne it. So take the thing
that happened, hide it, stick it in the ground.
Whisk the lamps away . . .   60
Night.

4

They should have shown you—mocker,
delight of your friends, hearts' thief,
naughtiest girl of Pushkin's town—
this picture of your fated years,   65
as under the glowering wall you stand,
shabby, three hundredth in the line,
clutching a parcel in your hand,
and the New Year's ice scorched by your tears.
See there the prison poplar bending!   70
No sound. No sound. Yet how many
innocent lives are ending. . . .

5

For seventeenth months I have cried aloud,
calling you back to your lair.
I hurled myself at the hangman's foot.   75
You are my son, changed into nightmare.
Confusion occupies the world,
and I am powerless to tell
somebody brute from something human,
or on what day the word spells, "Kill!"   80
Nothing is left but dusty flowers,
the tinkling thurible, and tracks
that lead to nowhere. Night of stone,
whose bright enormous star
stares me straight in the eyes,   85
promising death, ah soon!

6

The weeks fly out of mind,
I doubt that it occurred:
how into your prison, child,
the white nights, blazing, stared;   90
and still, as I draw breath,
they fix their buzzard eyes
on what the high cross shows,
this body of your death.

7

The Sentence

The word dropped like a stone   95
on my still living breast.

Confess: I was prepared,
am somehow ready for the test.

So much to do today:
kill memory, kill pain,   *100*
turn heart into a stone,
and yet prepare to live again.

Not quite. Hot summer's feast
brings rumors of carouse.
How long have I foreseen   *105*
this brilliant day, this empty house?
                            —Summer, 1939

                          8
                        To Death

You will come in any case—so why not now?
How long I wait and wait. The bad times fall.
I have put out the light and opened the door
for you, because you are simple and magical.   *110*
Assume, then, any form that suits your wish,
take aim, and blast at me with poisoned shot,
or strangle me like an efficient mugger,
or else infect me—typhus be my lot—
or spring out of the fairytale you wrote,   *115*
the one we're sick of hearing, day and night,
where the blue hatband marches up the stairs,
led by the janitor, pale with fright.
It's all the same to me. The Yenisei swirls,
the North Star shines, as it will shine forever;   *120*
and the blue luster of my loved one's eyes
is clouded over by the final horror.
                    —The House on the Fontanka,
                              19 August 1939

                          9

Already madness lifts its wing
to cover half my soul.
That taste of opiate wine!   *125*
Lure of the dark valley!

Now everything is clear.
I admit my defeat. The tongue

of my ravings in my ear
is the tongue of a stranger.   130

No use to fall down on my knees
and beg for mercy's sake.
Nothing I counted mine, out of my life,
is mine to take:

not my son's terrible eyes,   135
not the elaborate stone flower
of grief, not the day of the storm,
not the trial of the visiting hour,

not the dear coolness of his hands,
not the lime trees' agitated shade,   140
not the thin cricket-sound
of consolation's parting word.
                            —4 May 1940

10
Crucifixion

*"Do not weep for me, Mother,
when I am in my grave."*

I

A choir of angels glorified the hour,
the vault of heaven was dissolved in fire.
"Father, why hast Thou forsaken me?   145
Mother, I beg you, do not weep for me. . . ."

II

Mary Magdalene beat her breasts and sobbed,
His dear disciple, stone-faced, stared.
His mother stood apart. No other looked
into her secret eyes. Nobody dared.   150
                            —1940–1943

Epilogue
I

I have learned how faces fall to bone,
how under the eyelids terror lurks,
how suffering inscribes on cheeks

the hard lines of its cuneiform texts,
how glossy black or ash-fair locks   *155*
turn overnight to tarnished silver,
how smiles fade on submissive lips,
and fear quavers in a dry titter.
And I pray not for myself alone . . .
for all who stood outside the jail,   *160*
in bitter cold or summer's blaze,
with me under that blind red wall.

II

Remembrance hour returns with the turning year.
I see, I hear, I touch you drawing near:

the one we tried to help to the sentry's booth,   *165*
and who no longer walks this precious earth,

and that one who would toss her pretty mane
and say, "It's just like coming home again."

I want to name the names of all that host,
but they snatched up the list, and now it's lost.   *170*

I've woven them a garment that's prepared
out of poor words, those that I overheard,

and will hold fast to every word and glance
all of my days, even in new mischance,

and if a gag should blind my tortured mouth,   *175*
through which a hundred million people shout,

then let them pray for me, as I do pray
for them, this eve of my remembrance day.

And if my country ever should assent
to casting in my name a monument,   *180*

I should be proud to have my memory graced,
but only if the monument be placed

not near the sea on which my eyes first opened—
my last link with the sea has long been broken—

nor in the Tsar's garden near the sacred stump, *185*
where a grieved shadow hunts my body's warmth,

but here, where I endured three hundred hours
in line before the implacable iron bars.

Because even in blissful death I fear
to lose the clangor of the Black Marias, *190*

to lose the banging of that odious gate
and the old crone howling like a wounded beast.

And from my motionless bronze-lidded sockets
may the melting snow, like teardrops, slowly trickle,

and a prison dove coo somewhere, over and over, *195*
as the ships sail softly down the flowing Neva.
——March 1940

BORIS PASTERNAK

Hamlet

TRANSLATED BY JON STALLWORTHY AND PETER FRANCE

The buzz subsides. I have come on stage.
Leaning in an open door
I try to detect from the echo
What the future has in store.

A thousand opera-glasses level *5*
The dark, point-blank, at me.
Abba, Father, if it be possible
Let this cup pass from me.

I love your preordained design
And am ready to play this role. *10*
For this once let me go.

But the order of the acts is planned,
The end of the road already revealed.
Alone among the Pharisees I stand. *15*
Life is not a stroll across a field.

OSIP MANDELSTAM

The Stalin Epigram

TRANSLATED BY CLARENCE BROWN AND W. S. MERWIN

Our lives no longer feel ground under them.
At ten paces you can't hear our words.

But whenever there's a snatch of talk
it turns to the Kremlin mountaineer,

the ten thick worms his fingers,   5
his words like measures of weight,

the huge laughing cockroaches on his top lip,
the glitter of his boot-rims.

Ringed with a scum of chicken-necked bosses
he toys with the tributes of half-men.   10

One whistles, another meouws, a third snivels.
He pokes out his finger and he alone goes boom.

He forges decrees in a line like horseshoes,
One for the groin, one the forehead, temple, eye.

He rolls the executions on his tongue like berries.   15
He wishes he could hug them like big friends from home.

MARINA TSVETAYEVA

[1892 – 1941]

An Attempt at Jealousy

TRANSLATED BY BOB PERELMAN, SHIRLEY RIHNER, AND ALEXANDER PETROV

How is it with another woman?
Easier I bet.
One oar stroke! Did the memory
Of me (an island floating

In the sky not the sea) grow dim   5
Quickly like a coastline?
O souls, you will be sister and
Brother, not lovers!

How is it with a *normal* woman,
Rid of the divine?   10
Now that you've dethroned your queen
And given up your throne,

How is it? Do you keep busy?
Getting smaller? How
Do you get up? How are you able,   15
Poor man, to pay the cost

For her eternal boorishness?
"Enough of your hysterics,
I'm moving out!" How is it with
A woman who's just like   20

Any other, my chosen one?
Do you like her cooking?
When you're sick of it, don't whine!
How is it with a statue,

You who walked on Sinai?   25
How is it with a stranger,
A mortal? Tell me, do you love her?
Does shame, like Zeus's reins

Not lash your brow?
How is it? How's your health?   30
Still singing? Tell me, what do you do
About the wounds, poor fellow,

Of your stinking conscience? How is it
With a commodity?
Not easy, eh? Plaster of Paris   35
Isn't as good as marble

Of Carrara? (God was hewn
From it but he's smashed

To dust!) How is it with one
Of a hundred thousand,   40

You who have known Lilith? Are
You satisfied? Magicless?
How is it with a woman of earth,
Using five senses

Only? Well cross your heart, are you   45
Happy? No? In an endless pit
How is it, my love? Worse than for me
With another man?

ANDREY VOZNESENSKY

[b. 1933]

I am Goya

TRANSLATED BY STANLEY KUNITZ

I am Goya
of the bare field, by the enemy's beak gouged
till the craters of my eyes gape
I am grief

I am the tongue   5
of war, the embers of cities
on the snows of the year 1941
I am hunger

I am the gullet
of a woman hanged whose body like a bell   10
tolled over a blank square
I am Goya

O grapes of wrath!
I have hurled westward
                    the ashes of the uninvited guest!   15
and hammered stars into the unforgetting sky—like nails
I am Goya

YEVGENY YEVTUSHENKO

[b. 1933]

Babii Yar

TRANSLATED BY GEORGE REAVEY

No monument stands over Babii Yar.
A drop sheer as a crude gravestone.
I am afraid.
       Today I am as old in years
as all the Jewish people.   5
Now I seem to be
       a Jew.
Here I plod through ancient Egypt.
Here I perish crucified, on the cross,
and to this day I bear the scars of nails.   10
I seem to be
       Dreyfus.
The Philistine
       is both informer and judge.
I am behind bars.   15
Beset on every side.
Hounded,
       spat on,
          slandered.
Squealing, dainty ladies in flounced Brussels lace   20
stick their parasols into my face.
I seem to be then
       a young boy in Byelostok.
Blood runs, spilling over the floors.
The bar-room rabble-rousers   25
give off a stench of vodka and onion.
A boot kicks me aside, helpless.
In vain I plead with these pogrom bullies.

BABII YAR   **Babii**   Russian for "women's." **Yar**   Russian for "cliff" or "steep bank." Babii Yar is a place outside Kiev where thousands of Jews were slaughtered by the occupying Nazis. The poem first appeared in *Literaturnaya Gazeta*, September 19, 1961, and caused much controversy. It has been one of Yevtushenko's favorite reading pieces. Shostakovich used the poem in the opening movement of his *Thirteenth Symphony*. A monument, erected in 1991, now marks the place.   [12]**Dreyfus**   Alfred Dreyfus (1859–1935), a French artillery officer of Jewish descent who was sent to Devil's Island in 1894 for allegedly betraying military secrets. By 1914 he was finally cleared of the charges.   [23]**Byelostok**   a town, now in Soviet Byelorussia near the Polish frontier, which used to have a large Jewish population.

While they jeer and shout,
                    "Beat the Yids. Save Russia!"   30
some grain-marketeer beats up my mother.
O my Russian people!
                    I know
                    you
are international to the core.   35
But those with unclean hands
have often made a jingle of your purest name.
I know the goodness of my land.
How vile these antisemites—
                    without a qualm   40
they pompously called themselves
"The Union of the Russian People"!
I seem to be
          Anne Frank
transparent   45
          as a branch in April.
And I love.
          And have no need of phrases.
My need
          is that we gaze into each other.   50
How little we can see
                    or smell!
We are denied the leaves,
                    we are denied the sky.
Yet we can do so much—   55
                    tenderly
embrace each other in a dark room.
They're coming here?
                    Be not afraid. Those are the booming
sounds of spring: 60
                    spring is coming here.
Come then to me.
                    Quick, give me your lips.
Are they smashing down the door?
                    No, it's the ice breaking . . .   65
The wild grasses rustle over Babii Yar.
The trees look ominous,
                    like judges.
Here all things scream silently,
                    and, baring my head,   70

42"**The Union of the Russian People**" an ultranationalist organization under tsarism. It was responsible for the
"Black Hundreds"—gangs that carried out Jewish pogroms.

slowly I feel myself
                    turning gray.
And I myself
                    am one massive, soundless scream
above the thousand thousand buried here.   *75*
I am
        each old man
                        here shot dead.
I am
        every child   *80*
                    here shot dead.
Nothing in me
                    shall ever forget!
The "Internationale," let it
                            thunder   *85*
when the last antisemite on earth
is buried forever.
In my blood there is no Jewish blood.
In their callous rage, all antisemites
must hate me now as a Jew.   *90*
For that reason
                    I am a true Russian!

BELLA AKHMADULINA

[b. 1937]

The Bride

TRANSLATED BY STEPHAN STEPANCHEV

Oh to be a bride
Brilliant in my curls
Under the white canopy
Of a modest veil!

How my hands tremble,   *5*
Bound by my icy rings!
The glasses gather, brimming
With red compliments.

At last the world says yes;
It wishes me roses and sons.   10
My friends stand shyly at the door,
Carrying love gifts.

Chemises in cellophane,
Plates, flowers, lace . . .
They kiss my cheeks, they marvel   15
I'm to be a wife.

Soon my white gown
Is stained with wine like blood;
I feel both lucky and poor
As I sit, listening, at the table.   20

Terror and desire
Loom in the forward hours.
My mother, the darling, weeps—
Mama is like the weather.

. . . My rich, royal attire   25
I lay aside on the bed.
I find I am afraid
To look at you, to kiss you.

Loudly the chairs are set
Against the wall, eternity . . .   30
My love, what more can happen
To you and to me?

Italian Poetry

Italian poetry began as song, especially spiritual canticles or songs in praise of God. The earliest examples are the simple canticles of St. Francis of Assisi (1182–1226), though the more forceful poems of Jacopone da Todi (c. 1230–1306) were not far behind. The supreme Italian poet of the Middle Ages, however, was Dante Alighieri (1265–1321), whose *Divine Comedy* consummately reflects Medieval values. Coupled with Dante in importance is Francesco Petrarca, better known as Petrarch (c. 1304–1374). Petrarch did for Renaissance Italian poetry what Dante had done for Italian poetry of the Middle Ages.

Italian poetry had an enormous impact on the development of English poetry. Italian poets created *terza rima*, the octave, and the sonnet. The two greatest Italian poets, Dante and Petrarch, have been much admired and imitated by English and American poets. Percy Bysshe Shelley ("Ode to the West Wind") T. S. Eliot ("Little Gidding"), Robert Frost ("Acquainted with the Night"), and Seamus Heaney ("Station Island XII") to cite four examples, have imitated Dante's *terza rima*. Eliot, moreover, has celebrated Dante's use of language in a number of critical essays.

Petrarch has been imitated even more than Dante, for he was responsible for the introduction of the sonnet into English literature and must be credited with the eventual flowering of the sonnet during the Elizabethan age. Among those who translated and adapted Petrarch's sonnets were Sir Thomas Wyatt and Henry Howard, Earl of Surrey, whose renderings of Petrarch have become celebrated as English sonnets in their own right. And a generation later John Donne employed many Petrarchan lyric conventions in his witty and ingenious adaptations of the earlier Italian poet. The most famous English sonneteer, however, is William Shakespeare, who modified the Petrarchan sonnet form by increasing the number of rhymes and altering the sonnet's logical structure, while adhering to its length and meter.

As a medieval poet, Dante subscribed to a Catholic medieval theology, most fully documented in the *Summa Theologica* of the Dominican monk Thomas Aquinas (1225–1274). Petrarch, by contrast, a Renaissance poet, represented a set of changing attitudes toward, God, man, and the social world. Born in Florence in 1265, Dante Alighieri was involved in politics as well as literature. When a rival party seized power in 1302, Dante was exiled from his home city, never to return. His epic poem *The Divine Comedy* was completed in 1321, shortly before his death in Ravenna, where he was buried. The *Commedia* (the work's original Italian title) is divided into three parts: *Inferno* (Hell), *Purgatorio* (Purgatory), and *Paradiso* (Heaven). The entire poem contains one hundered cantos equally divided among the three sections, with the opening canto of the prologue prefacing the *Inferno*. Dante's elaborate attention to the poem's organization, especially its structural symmetry, is apparent in every aspect of the work, from the number of cantos (one hundred, or the square of ten) to the use of *terza rima,* a succession of three-line stanzas that rhyme *aba bcb cdc,* etc., where each stanza's unrhymed sound is picked up by the immediately succeeding stanza. Dante employs this harmonious pattern of interlocked rhyme for many thousands of lines through the entire length of the *Commedia.*

Dante's language ranges from the exalted to the disgusting, as his diction suits the various aspects of his subjects. In describing the carnal sinners in the third canto of the *Inferno,* for example, Dante employs coarse words and images appropriate for the punishment he creates for carnal sinners. Later, in the *Paradiso* (as well as in other cantos of the *Inferno*), Dante employs a more exalted diction, one better suited to his description of intellectual and spiritual matters. To suggest what Dante's language looks and sounds like, we provide one canto from the *Inferno* in Italian with a facing translation by John Ciardi into a modified English *terza rima.*

Although Petrarch was only forty years younger than Dante, he breathed the air of a time that had exhibited rapid and radical changes. Petrarch, in fact, can be considered the first Renaissance poet, one whose interests centered more on humanity than on God, and one whose poems owed more to the Greek and Latin past than to the theological and spiritual ideals of the Middle Ages. Unlike Dante, Petrarch was a humanist scholar, who devoted his life to rediscovering and rehabilitating great literary and philosophical works of Greco-Roman antiquity. It is Petrarch's poetry, however, rather than his scholarship that is important for the development of the English lyric tradition. For it was Petrarch who made himself and Laura, the woman he worshipped, the central dual subjects of his lyric poetry, especially his *Canzoniere.* Petrarch established the use of personal drama as a vital poetic element. He placed an increased emphasis on nature as the backdrop for his primary subject, love. And he emphasized the conflict between spiritual and temporal values, while stressing the need to find inner peace. The two sonnets included below can only suggest the impact Petrarch's work had on subsequent poetry in English, Italian, French, and Spanish, not only during the Renaissance but continuing into our own time as well.

We touch only lightly on the other Italian poets represented here. The first, after Petrarch, is Michelangelo Buonarotti (1475–1564), whose artistic genius found expression in literary form as well as in painting, sculpture, and architecture. The sonnet included here expresses Michelangelo's concept of inherent form, that is, his idea that sculpture releases the form of the object inherent in the marble that sculptors carve.

From the fifteenth century we jump to the early nineteenth to the poetry of Giacomo Leopardi (1798–1837), thus skipping over Ludovico Ariosto (1474–1533), famous for his lengthy narrative poem in *ottava rima, Orlando Furioso,* and Torquato Tasso (1544–1595), author of the epic *Gerusalemme Liberata.* Leopardi is considered one of the supreme lyric poets of Italy, on a level with Petrarch. Leopardi's poetry is meditative, reflective, and philosophical; it proffers a stoic disillusionment with life seeing its hopes and joys as temporal and illusory. The poems demonstrate a superb ear for sound and cadence. These qualities of temperament and style are especially evident in "Alla luna" (To the Moon) and "L'Infinito" (The Infinite), two of his most famous poems.

Our remaining poets are all twentieth-century figures: Gabriele D'Annunzio (1863–1938), Giuseppe Ungaretti (1888–1970), Eugenio Montale (1896–1981), Salvatore Quasimodo (1901–1968), and Amelia Rosselli (b. 1930). D'Annunzio's poems contain many that are sensual and effusive. We represent him, however, by a more emotionally reserved poem, though one of striking wit and imagination, "My Songs Are Children." Giuseppi Ungaretti, along with Eugenio Montale, began a literary movement known as "hermeticism," which represented a break with poems cast in traditional narrative or logical modes. Some of Ungaretti's early poems strip away so much of the older poetry's explanatory cast and its discursiveness that they resemble the minimalist imagist poems of Ezra Pound. One example is the following one-line poem entitled "Una Colomba" (A Dove):

D'altri diluvi una colomba ascolto.

I listen to a dove of other floods.

We have also included a longer and later poem, "You Shattered," which was inspired by the death of Ungaretti's son.

Ungaretti's contemporary Eugenio Montale was strongly influenced by T. S. Eliot, Ezra Pound's friend and contemporary. Montale's poems are characterized by a reliance on stark images, especially images of aridity, suggested in the title of an early collection, *Ossi di Seppia* (Sepia Bones). We include his playful and hopeful "L'Anguilla" (The Eel).

Of our final poets, Salvatore Quasimodo won the Nobel Prize in 1959. He is represented by "Letter to My Mother." Amelia Rosselli, born in Paris in 1930, has studied music throughout Europe and has written music for theater and film. She is represented by "Snow."

ST. FRANCIS OF ASSISI

[1182–1226]

Il cantico delle Creature

The Canticle of the Creatures

TRANSLATED BY ELEANOR L. TURNBULL

Altissimu, onnipotente, bon Signore,
    tue son le laude, la gloria e l'onore et onne
    benedictione.
    Ad te solo Altissimo, se konfano
    et nullu omu ene dignu Te mentovare.
Laudato si, mi Signore, cum tucte le tue
    creature,
    spetialmente messor lo frate sole,
    lo quale jorna, et illumini per lui;
    et ellu è bellu e radiante cum grande
    splendore;
    de Te, Altissimo, porta significatione.
Laudato si, mi Signore, per sora luna e le stelle;
    in celu l'ài formate clarite et pretiose et
    belle.
Laudato si, mi Signore, per frate vento
    et per aere et nubilo et sereno et onne
    tempo,
    per le quale a le tue creature dai susten-
    tamento.
Laudato si, mi Signore, per sor' acqua,
    la quale è multo utile, et humele, et pretiosa
    et casta.
Laudato si, mi Signore, per frate focu,
    per lo quale ennallumini la nocte,
    et ello è bellu, et jucundo, et robustoso et
    forte.
Laudato si, mi Signore, per sora nostra matre
    terra,
    la quale ne sustenta e governa,
    e produce diversi fructi, con coloriti fiori et
    herba.
Laudato si, mi Signore, per quilli, che per-
    donano per lo tuo amore
    e sostengo infirmitate et tribulatione.
    Beati quilli, che sosterrano in pace,
    ka de Te, Altissimo, sirano incoronati.

O Most High, Omnipotent, Good Lord; Thine be
the praise, the glory and the honor; to Thee be
every blessing. To Thee alone, Most Highest, are
they due, and there is no man worthy to speak
of Thee.

Be praised, O Lord, with all Thy creatures, especially
my lord Brother Sun, who gives the day, and by
whom Thou showest light. He is beautiful and
shining with great splendor; of Thee, Most
Highest, he is the symbol.

Be praised, O Lord, for Sister Moon and the stars;
Thou hast formed them in the heavens, clear,
precious and beautiful.

Be praised, O Lord, for Brother Wind and for air and
cloud, for fair and for all weather by which Thou
givest Thy creatures sustenance.

Be praised, O Lord, for Sister Water, the which is so
useful, humble, precious and chaste.

Be praised, O Lord, for Brother Fire, by which Thou
lightest up the night. He is beautiful and gay,
vigorous and strong.

Be praised, O Lord, for our Sister Mother Earth, the
which supports and nourishes us and produces
diverse fruits, with brilliant flowers and grass.

Be praised, O Lord, for those, who for love of Thee
forgive, who bear sickness and tribulation; blessèd
those who in peace shall endure, for by Thee,
Most High, they shall be crowned.

Laudato si, mi Signore, per sora nostra morte
  corporale,
  da la quale nullu homo vivente po skappare.
  Guai a quilli, ke morrano ne le peccata
  mortali.
  Beati quilli, che se trovarà ne le tue sanctis-
  sime voluntati;
  ka la morte secunda nol farrà male.
Laudate et benedicete mi Signore,
  e rengratiate,
  e serviteli cum grande humilitate.

Be praised, O Lord, for our Sister Death of the
Body, from the which no man living may escape;
woe to them who shall die in mortal sin and
blessèd those who shall be found in Thy most holy
will, for the second death shall work them no
harm.

Give praises and blessings and render thanks to my
Lord, and serve Him with great humility.

DANTE ALIGHIERI

[1265–1321]

The Inferno

TRANSLATED BY JOHN CIARDI

CANTO III

PER ME SI VA NE LA CITTÀ DOLENTE,
PER ME SI VA NE L'ETTERNO DOLORE,
PER ME SI VA TRA LA PERDUTA GENTE.
  GIUSTIZIA MOSSE IL MIO ALTO FATTORE;
FECEMI LA DIVINA PODESTATE,   5
LA SOMMA SAPIENZA E 'L PRIMO AMORE.
  DINANZI A ME NON FUOR COSE CREATE
SE NON ETTERNE, E IO ETTERNO DURO.
LASCIATE OGNE SPERANZA, VOI CH'INTRATE.
  Queste parole di colore oscuro   10
vid' ïo scritte al sommo d'una porta;
per ch'io: "Maestro, il senso lor m'è duro."
  Ed elli a me, come persona accorta:
"Qui si convien lasciare ogne sospetto;
ogne viltà convien che qui sia morta.   15
  Noi siam venuti al loco ov' i' t'ho detto
che tu vedrai le genti dolorose
c'hanno perduto il ben de l'intelletto."

I AM THE WAY INTO THE CITY OF WOE.
  I AM THE WAY TO A FORSAKEN PEOPLE.
  I AM THE WAY INTO ETERNAL SORROW.
SACRED JUSTICE MOVED MY ARCHITECT.
  I WAS RAISED HERE BY DIVINE OMNIPOTENCE,   5
  PRIMORDAL LOVE AND ULTIMATE INTELLECT.
ONLY THOSE ELEMENTS TIME CANNOT WEAR
  WERE MADE BEFORE ME, AND BEYOND TIME I STAND.
  ABANDON ALL HOPE YE WHO ENTER HERE.
These mysteries I read cut into stone   10
  above a gate. And turning I said: "Master,
  what is the meaning of this harsh inscription?"
And he then as initiate to novice:
  "Here must you put by all division of spirit
  and gather your soul against all cowardice.   15
This is the place I told you to expect.
  Here you shall pass among the fallen people,
  souls who have lost the good of intellect."

THE INFERNO   [7] **THOSE ELEMENTS TIME CANNOT WEAR**   The Angels, the Empyrean, and the First Matter are the elements time cannot wear, for they will last to all time. Man, however, in his mortal state, is not eternal The Gate of Hell, therefore, was created before man.   [8]**BEYOND TIME I STAND**   So odious is sin to God that there can be no end to its just punishment.   [9]**ABANDON . . . HERE** The admonition, of course, is to the damned and not to those who come on Heaven-sent errands Translator's notes.

E poi che la sua mano a la mia puose
con lieto volto, ond' io mi confortai,   20
mi mise dentro a le segrete cose.

   Quivi sospiri, pianti e alti guai
risonavan per l'aere sanza stelle,
per ch'io al cominciar ne lagrimai.

   Diverse lingue, orribili favelle,   25
parole di dolore, accenti d'ira,
voci alte e fioche, e suon di man con elle

   facevano un tumulto, il qual s'aggira
sempre in quell' aura sanza tempo tinta,
come la rena quando turbo spira.   30

   E io ch'avea d'orror la testa cinta,
dissi: "Maestro, che è quel ch'i' odo?
e che gent' è che par nel duol sì vinta?"

   Ed elli a me: "Questo misero modo
tegnon l'anime triste di coloro   35
che visser sanza 'nfamia e sanza lodo.

   Mischiate sono a quel cattivo coro
de li angeli che non furon ribelli
né fur fedeli a Dio, ma per sé fuoro.

   Caccianli i ciel per non esser men belli,   40
né lo profondo inferno li riceve,
ch'alcuna gloria i rei avrebber d'elli."

   E io: "Maestro, che è tanto greve
a lor che lamentar li fa sì forte?"
Rispuose: "Dicerolti molto breve.   45

   Questi non hanno speranza di morte,
e la lor cieca vita è tanto bassa,
che 'nvidiosi son d'ogne altra sorte.

   Fama di loro il mondo esser non lassa;
misericordia e giustizia li sdegna: 50
non ragioniam di lor, ma guarda e passa."

   E io, che riguardai, vidi una 'nsegna
che girando correva tanto ratta,
che d'ogne posa mi parea indegna;

   e dietro le venìa sì lunga tratta   55
di gente, ch'i' non averei creduto
che morte tanta n'avesse disfatta.

   Poscia ch'io v'ebbi alcun riconosciuto,
vidi e conobbi l'ombra di colui
che fece per viltade il gran rifiuto.   60

So saying, he put forth his hand to me,
   and with a gentle and encouraging smile   20
   he led me through the gate of mystery.
Here sighs and cries and wails coiled and recoiled
   on the starless air, spilling my soul to tears.

   A confusion of tongues and monstrous accents toiled
in pain and anger. Voices hoarse and shrill   25
   and sounds of blows, all intermingled, raised
   tumult and pandemonium that still
whirls on the air forever dirty with it
   as if a whirlwind sucked at sand. And I,
   holding my head in horror, cried: "Sweet Spirit,   30
what souls are these who run through this
   black haze?"
   And he to me: "These are the nearly soulless
   whose lives concluded neither blame nor praise.
They are mixed here with that despicable corps
   of angels who were neither for God nor Satan,   35
   but only for themselves. The High Creator
scourged them from Heaven for its perfect beauty,
   and Hell will not receive them since the wicked
   might feel some glory over them." And I:

"Master, what gnaws at them so hideously   40
   their lamentation stuns the very air?"
   "They have no hope of death," he answered me,
"and in their blind and unattaining state
   their miserable lives have sunk so low
   that they must envy every other fate.   45
No word of them survives their living season.
   Mercy and Justice deny them even a name.
   Let us not speak of them: look, and pass on."
I saw a banner there upon the mist.
   Circling and circling, it seemed to scorn all pause.   50
   So it ran on, and still behind it pressed
a never-ending route of souls in pain.
   I had not thought death had undone so many
   as passed before me in that mournful train.
And some I knew among them; last of all   55
   I recognized the shadow of that soul
   who, in his cowardice, made the Great Denial.

[56-57]**that soul . . . the Great Denial**   This is almost certainly intended to be Celestine V, who became Pope in 1294. He was a man of saintly life, but allowed himself to be convinced by a priest named Benedetto that his soul was in danger since no man could live in the world without being damned. In fear for his soul he withdrew from all worldly affairs and renounced the papacy. Benedetto promptly assumed the mantle himself and became Boniface VIII, a Pope who became for Dante a symbol of all the worst corruptions of the church. Dante also blamed Boniface and his intrigues for many of the evils that befell Florence. We learn in Canto XIX that the fires of Hell are waiting for Boniface in the pit of the Simoniacs, and we are given further evidence of his corruption in Canto XXVII. Celestine's great guilt is that his cowardice (in selfish terror for his own welfare) served as the door through which so much evil entered the church.

Incontanente intesi e certo fui
che questa era la setta d'i cattivi,
a Dio spiacenti e a' nemici sui.

   Questi sciaurati, che mai non fur vivi,
erano ignudi e stimolati molto   65
da mosconi e da vespe ch'eran ivi.

   Elle rigavan lor di sangue il volto,
che, mischiato di lagrime, a' lor piedi
da fastidiosi vermi era ricolto.

   E poi ch'a riguardar oltre mi diedi,   70
vidi genti a la riva d'un gran fiume;
per ch'io dissi: "Maestro, or mi concedi
   ch'i' sappia quali sono, e qual costume
le fa di trapassar parer sì pronte,
com' i' discerno per lo fioco lume."   75

   Ed elli a me: "Le cose ti fier conte
quando noi fermerem li nostri passi
su la trista riviera d'Acheronte."

   Allor con li occhi vergognosi e bassi,
temendo no 'l mio dir li fosse grave,   80
infino al fiume del parlar mi trassi.

   Ed ecco verso noi venir per nave
un vecchio, bianco per antico pelo,
gridando: "Guai a voi, anime prave!

   Non isperate mai veder lo cielo: 85
i' vegno per menarvi a l'altra riva
ne le tenebre etterne, in caldo e 'n gelo.

   E tu che se' costì, anima viva,
pàrtiti da cotesti che son morti."
Ma poi che vide ch'io non mi partiva,   90

   disse: "Per altra via, per altri porti
verrai a piaggia, non qui, per passare:
più lieve legno convien che ti porti."

   E 'l duca lui: "Caron, non ti crucciare:
vuolsi così colà dove si puote   95
ciò che si vuole, e più non dimandare."

   Quinci fuor quete le lanose gote
al nocchier de la livida palude,
che 'ntorno a li occhi avea di fiamme rote.

   Ma quell' anime, ch'eran lasse e nude,   100
cangiar colore e dibattero i denti,

At once I understood for certain: these
   were of that retrograde and faithless crew
   hateful to God and to His enemies.   60
These wretches never born and never dead
   ran naked in a swarm of wasps and hornets
   that goaded them the more they fled,
and made their faces stream with bloody gouts
   of pus and tears that dribbled to their feet   65
   to be swallowed there by loathsome worms and
     maggots.
Then looking onward I made out a throng
   assembled on the beach of a wide river,
   whereupon I turned to him: "Master, I long
to know what souls these are, and what strange usage
   makes them as eager to cross as they seem to be
   in this infected light." At which the Sage:
"All this shall be made known to you when we stand
   on the joyless beach of Acheron." And I
   cast down my eyes, sensing a reprimand   75
in what he said, and so walked at his side
   in silence and ashamed until we came
   through the dead cavern to that sunless tide.
There, steering toward us in an ancient ferry
   came an old man with a white bush of hair,   80
   bellowing: "Woe to you depraved souls! Bury
here and forever all hope of Paradise:
   I come to lead you to the other shore,
   into eternal dark, into fire and ice.
And you who are living yet, I say begone   85
   from these who are dead." But when he saw me stand
   against his violence he began again:
"By other windings and by other steerage
   shall you cross to that other shore. Not here! Not here!
   A lighter craft than mine must give you passage."
And my Guide to him: "Charon, bite back your spleen:
   this has been willed where what is willed must be,
   and is not yours to ask what it may mean."
The steersman of that marsh of ruined souls,
   who wore a wheel of flame around each eye,   95
   stifled the rage that shook his woolly jowls.
But those unmanned and naked spirits there
   turned pale with fear and their teeth began to chatter

---

[80] **an old man**   Charon. He is the ferryman of dead souls across the river Acheron.

[88-90] **"By other . . . you passage."**   Charon recognizes Dante not only as a living man but as a soul in grace, and knows, therefore, that the Infernal Ferry was not intended for him. He is probably referring to the fact that souls destined for Purgatory and Heaven assemble not at his ferry point, but on the banks of the Tiber, from which they are transported by an Angel.

ratto che 'nteser le parole crude.

Bestemmiavano Dio e lor parenti,
l'umana spezie e 'l loco e 'l tempo e 'l seme
di lor semenza e di lor nascimenti.   *105*

Poi si ritrasser tutte quante insieme,
forte piangendo, a la riva malvagia
ch'attende ciascun uom che Dio non teme.

Caron dimonio, con occhi di bragia
loro accennando, tutte le raccoglie;   *110*
batte col remo qualunque s'adagia.

Come d'autunno si levan le foglie
l'una appresso de l'altra, fin che 'l ramo
vede a la terra tutte le sue spoglie,

similemente il mal seme d'Adamo   *115*
gittansi di quel lito ad una ad una,
per cenni come augel per suo richiamo.

Così sen vanno su per l'onda bruna,
e avanti che sien di là discese,
anche di qua nuova schiera s'auna.   *120*

"Figliuol mio," disse 'l maestro cortese,
"quelli che muoion ne l'ira di Dio
tutti convegnon qui d'ogne paese;

e pronti sono a trapassar lo rio,
ché la divina giustizia li sprona,   *125*
sì che la tema si volve in disio.

Quinci non passa mai anima buona;
e però, se Caron di te si lagna,
ben puoi sapere omai che 'l suo dir suona."

Finito questo, la buia campagna   *130*
tremò sì forte, che de lo spavento
la mente di sudore ancor mi bagna.

La terra lagrimosa diede vento,
che balenò una luce vermiglia
la qual mi vinse ciascun sentimento;   *135*

e caddi come l'uom cui sonno piglia.

---

at sound of his crude bellow. In despair
they blasphemed God, their parents, their time on earth,
the race of Adam, and the day and the hour

and the place and the seed and the womb that gave
them birth.
But all together they drew to that grim shore
where all must come who lose the fear of God.

Weeping and cursing they come for evermore,   *105*
and demon Charon with eyes like burning coals
herds them in, and with a whistling oar
flails on the stragglers to his wake of souls.

As leaves in autumn loosen and stream down
until the branch stands bare above its tatters   *110*
spread on the rustling ground, so one by one
the evil seed of Adam in its Fall

cast themselves, at his signal, from the shore
and streamed away like birds who hear their call.
So they are gone over that shadowy water,   *115*
and always before they reach the other shore
a new noise stirs on this, and new throngs gather.

"My son," the courteous Master said to me,
"all who die in the shadow of God's wrath
converge to this from every clime and country.   *120*
And all pass over eagerly, for here

Divine Justice transforms and spurs them so
their dread turns wish: they yearn for what they fear.
No soul in Grace comes ever to this crossing;
therefore if Charon rages at your presence   *125*
you will understand the reason for his cursing."

When he had spoken, all the twilight country
shook so violently, the terror of it
bathes me with sweat even in memory:
the tear-soaked ground gave out a sigh of wind   *130*
that spewed itself in flame on a red sky,

and all my shuttered senses left me. Blind,
like one whom sleep comes over in a swoon,
I stumbled into darkness and went down.

[99-100]**In despair/they blasphemed God** 7. The souls of the damned are not permitted to repent, for repentance is a divine grace.
[123]**they yearn for what they fear** Hell (allegorically Sin) is what the souls of the damned really wish for. Hell is their actual and deliberate choice, for divine grace is denied to none who wish for it in their hearts. The damned must, in fact, deliberately harden their hearts to God in order to become damned. Christ's grace is sufficient to save all who wish for it. [132-4]**Blind . . . went down** This device (repeated at the end of Canto V) serves a double purpose. The first is technical: Dante uses it to cover a transition. We are never told how he crossed Acheron, for that would involve certain narrative matters he can better deal with when he crosses Styx in Canto VII. The second is to provide a point of departure for a theme that is carried through the entire descent: the theme of Dante's emotional reaction to Hell. These two swoons early in the descent show him most susceptible to the grief about him. As he descends, pity leaves him, and he even goes so far as to add to the torments of one sinner. The allegory is clear: we must harden ourselves against every sympathy for sin.

FRANCESCO PETRARCH

[c. 1304–1374]

Amor, che nel penser mio vive e regna

Amor, che nel penser mio vive e regna
E 'l suo seggio maggior nel mio cor tène,
Talor armato ne la fronte vène,
Ivi si loca, et ivi pon sua insegna.

Quella ch'amare e sofferir ne 'nsegna   5
E vòl che 'l gran desio, l'accesa spene,
Ragion, vergogna e reverenza affrene,   *shamefaced*
Di nostro ardir fra se stessa si sdegna.

Onde Amor paventoso fugge al core,
Lasciando ogni sua impresa, e piange,   *10*
  e trema;   *complain*
Ivi s'asconde, e non appar piú fòre.

Che poss'io far, temendo il mio signore,
Se non star seco in fin a l'ora estrema?
Ché bel fin fa chi ben amando more.

HENRY HOWARD, EARL OF SURREY *

[1517–1547]

Love, that doth reign and live within my thought

Love, that doth reign and live within my thought,
And built his seat within my captive breast,
Clad in the arms wherein with me he fought,
Oft in my face he doth his banner rest.

But she that taught me love and suffer pain,
My doubtful hope and eke my hot desire
With shamefast° look to shadow and refrain,
Her smiling grace converteth straight to ire.

And coward Love, then, to the heart apace
Taketh his flight, where he doth lurk
  and plain,°
His purpose lost, and dare not show his face.

For my lord's guilt thus faultless bide I pain,
Yet from my lord shall not my foot remove:
Sweet is the death that taketh end by love.

THOMAS WYATT *

[1503–1542]

The long love that in my thought doth harbor

The long love that in my thought doth harbor,
And in my heart doth keep his residence,
Into my face presseth with bold pretense
And there encampeth, spreading his banner.
She that me learns° to love and suffer   *teaches* 5
And wills that my trust and lust's negligence
Be reined by reason, shame, and reverence
With his hardiness takes displeasure.
Wherewithal unto the heart's forest he fleeth,
Leaving his enterprise with pain and cry,   *10*

*Surrey's and Wyatt's sonnets are adaptations, or loose translations, of Petrarch's sonnet.

And there him hideth, and not appeareth.
What may I do, when my master feareth,
But in the field with him to live and die?
For good is the life ending faithfully.

FRANCESCO PETRARCH

<table>
<tr><td>

Passa la nave mia colma d'oblio

</td><td>

My ship is sailing, full of mindless woe

</td></tr>
</table>

TRANSLATED BY ANNA MARIA ARMI

<table>
<tr><td>

Passa la nave mia colma d'oblio
Per aspro mare, a mezza notte il verno,
Enfra Scilla e Caribdi; et al governo
Siede 'l signore, anzi 'l nimico mio;

A ciascun remo un penser pronto e rio   5
Che la tempesta e 'l fin par ch'abbi a scherno;
La vela rompe un vento umido, eterno,
Di sospir, di speranze, e di desio;

Pioggia di lagrimar, nebbia di sdegni
Bagna e rallenta le giá stanche sarte,   10
Che son d'error con ignoranzia attorto.

Celansi i duo mei dolci usati segni;
Morta fra l'onde è la ragion e l'arte,
Tal ch'i' 'ncomincio a desperar del porto.

</td><td>

My ship is sailing, full of mindless woe,
Through the rough sea, in winter-midnight drear,
Between Scylla and Charybdis; there to steer
Stands my master, or rather stands my foe.

At each oar sits a rapid wicked thought
Which seems to scoff at storms and at their end;
The sail, by wet eternal winds distraught,
With hopes, desires and sighs is made to rend.

A rain of tears, a fog of scornful lines,
Washes and tugs at the too sluggish cords
Which by error with ignorance are wound.

Vanished are my two old beloved signs,
Dead in the waves are all reason and words,
And I despair ever to reach the ground.

</td></tr>
</table>

THOMAS WYATT*

[1503–1542]

My galley charged with forgetfulness

My galley charged with forgetfulness
Thorough sharp seas in winter nights doth pass
'Tween rock and rock; and eke mine enemy, alas,
That is my lord, steereth with cruelness;
And every oar a thought in readiness,   5
As though that death were light in such a case.

*Wyatt's sonnet adapts and translates Petrarch's.

And endless wind doth tear the sail apace
Of forced sighs, and trusty fearfulness.
A rain of tears, a cloud of dark disdain,
Hath done the wearied cords great hinderance;   *10*
Wreathed with error and eke with ignorance,
The stars be hid that led me to this pain;
Drowned is reason that should me consort,
And I remain despairing of the port.

MICHELANGELO BUONAROTTI

[1475–1564]

The best of artists never has a concept

TRANSLATED BY MICHAEL CREIGHTON

The best of artists never has a concept
A single marble block does not contain,
Inside its husk, but to it may attain
Only if hand follows the intellect.
The good I pledge myself, bad I reject.   *5*
Hide, O my Lady, beautiful, proud, divine,
Just thus in you, but now my life must end,
Since my skill works against the wished effect.
It is not love then, fortune or your beauty,
Or your hardness and scorn, in all my ill   *10*
That are to blame, neither my luck nor fate,
If at the same time both death and pity
Are present in your heart, and my low skill,
Burning, can grasp nothing but death from it.

GIACOMO LEOPARDI

[1798–1837]

L'Infinito

The Infinite

TRANSLATED BY
JOHN HEATH-STUBBS

Sempre caro mi fu quest'ermo colle,
E questa siepe, che da tanta parte
Dell'ultimo orizzonte il guardo esclude.
Ma sedendo e mirando, interminati

This lonely hill was always dear to me,
And this hedgerow, that hides so large a part
Of the far sky-line from my view. Sitting and gazing,
I fashion in my mind what lies beyond—

Spazi di là da quella, e sovrumani   5
Silenzi, e profondissima quiete
Io nel pensier mi fingo; ove per poco
Il cor non si spaura. E come il vento
Odo stormir tra queste piante, io quello
Infinito silenzio a questa voce   10
Vo comparando: e mi sovvien l'eterno,
E le morte stagioni, e la presente
E viva, e il suon di lei. Così tra questa
Immensità s'annega il pensier mio:
E il naufragar m'è dolce in questo mare.

Unearthly silences, and endless space,
And very deepest quiet; then for a while
The heart is not afraid. And when I hear
The wind come blustering among the trees
I set that voice against this infinite silence:
And then I call to mind Eternity,
The ages that are dead, and the living present
And all the noise of it. And thus it is
In that immensity my thought is drowned:
And sweet to me the foundering in that sea.

Alla luna

O graziosa luna, io mi rammento
Che, or volge l'anno, sovra questo colle
Io venia pien d'angoscia a rimirarti:
E tu pendevi allor su quella selva
Siccome or fai, che tutta la rischiari.   5
Ma nebuloso e tremulo dal pianto
Che mi sorgea sul ciglio, alle mie luci
Il tuo volto apparia, che travagliosa
Era mia vita: ed è, né cangia stile,
O mia diletta luna. E pur mi giova   10
La ricordanza, e il noverar l'etate
Del mio dolore. Oh come grato occorre
Nel tempo giovanil, quando ancor lungo
La speme e breve ha la memoria il corso,
Il rimembrar delle passate cose,
Ancor che triste, e che l'affanno duri!

To the Moon

O gracious Moon, I call to mind again
It was a year ago I climbed this hill
To gaze upon you in my agony;
And you were hanging then above that wood,
Filling it all with light, as you do now.
But dim and tremulous your face appeared,
Seen through the tears that rose beneath my eyelids,
My life being full of travail; as it is still—
It does not change, O my sweet Moon. And yet
Remembrance helps, and reckoning up
The cycles of my sorrow. How sweet the thought
That brings to mind things past, when we are
          young—
When long's the road for hope, for memory brief—
Though they were sad, and though our pain
          endures.

GABRIELE D'ANNUNZIO

[1863–1938]

My songs are children

TRANSLATED BY OLGA RAGUSA

My songs are children
of the forest,
others of the waves,
others of the sands,

others of the sun,   *5*
others of the wind Argestes.
My words
are deep
like earthen
roots,   *10*
others serene
like firmaments,
ardent like the veins
of adolescents,
rough like the brier,   *15*
confused like jumbled
smoke,
clear as the crystals
of the mountain,
tremulous as the fronds   *20*
of the poplar,
turgid as the nostrils
of horses
on the gallop,
fleeting as perfumes   *25*
diffused,
virgin as calices
barely opened,
nocturnal as the dews
of the skies,   *30*
mournful as the asphodels
of Hades,
flexible as the willows
of the pond,
tenuous like the web   *35*
the spider weaves
between two reeds.

GIUSEPPE UNGARETTI

[1888–1970]

You Shattered

TRANSLATED BY ALLEN MANDELBAUM

1

That swarm of scattered, huge, gray stones
Still quivering in secret slings

Of stifled flames of origin
Or in the terrors of virgin torrents
Plunging in implacable caresses—   5
Rigid on the sands that dazzled
In a dull horizon, don't you remember?

And where it opened toward the only
Gathering of shadows in the valley,
The leaning araucaria, huge with longing,   10
Its lonely fibers thrust into hard flint,
More stubborn than the other damned,
Its mouth cool with butterflies and grass
Where it parted from its roots—
Don't you remember it, frenzied, silent,   15
Above three spans of a rounded rock
In perfect balance
Magically present?

From branch to branch, light gold-crest wren,
Your eager eyes drunk with amazement,   20
You won its speckled summit,
Rash and musical child,
Simply to see again—along the gleaming bed
Of a deep and tranquil gulf—
Fabulous tortoises   25
Reawakening among the seaweed.

Nature's final tension
And the undersea processions,
Fatal admonitions.

2

You raised your arms like wings   30
And you gave birth back to the wind
Running in the weight of the motionless air.

Your foot—so light in dance that no one
Ever saw it touch the ground.

3

Happy grace,   35
How could you not have shattered
In a blindness so inflexible,
You, simple breath and crystal,

Too-human dazzling for the ruthless,
Savage, droning, tenacious   *40*
Roar of a naked sun.

EUGENIO MONTALE

[1896–1981]

The Eel

TRANSLATED BY JOHN FREDERICK NIMS

The eel, the
siren of sleety seas, abandoning
the Baltic for our waters,
our estuaries, our
freshets, to lash upcurrent under the brunt   *5*
of the flood, sunk deep, from brook to brook and then
trickle to trickle dwindling,
more inner always, always more in the heart
of the rock, thrusting
through ruts of the mud, until, one day,   *10*
explosion of splendor from the chestnut groves
kindles a flicker in deadwater sumps,
in ditches pitched
from ramparts of the Apennine to Romagna;
eel: torch and whip,   *15*
arrow of love on earth,
which nothing but our gorges or bone-dry
gutters of the Pyrenees usher back
to edens of fertility;
green soul that probes   *20*
for life where only
fevering heat or devastation preys,
spark that says
the whole commences when the whole would seem
charred black, an old stick buried;   *25*
brief rainbow, twin
to that within your lashes' dazzle, to that
you keep alive, inviolate, among

the sons of men, steeped in your mire—in this
not recognize a sister?   30

SALVATORE QUASIMODO

[1901–1968]

Letter to My Mother

TRANSLATED BY ALLEN MANDELBAUM

"*Mater dulcissima,* now the mists descend,
the Naviglio dashes against its dikes,
the trees swell with water, burn with snow;
I am not sad in the North: I am not
at peace with myself, but I expect   5
pardon from no one, many owe me tears,
as man to man. I know you are not well, that you live
like all the mothers of poets, poor
and just in the measure of their love
for distant sons. Today it is I   10
who write to you."—At last, you will say, two words
from that boy who fled by night in a short coat,
a few lines in his pocket. Poor, so quick of heart,
one day they'll kill him somewhere.
"Surely, I remember, I left from that gray station   15
of slow trains that carried almonds and oranges,
at the mouth of the Imera, river full of magpies,
salt, of eucalyptus. But now I thank you—
this I would—for the irony you laid upon
my lips, mild as your own.   20
That smile has saved me from laments and griefs.
And it matters not if now I've some tears for you,
for all who wait—like you—
and know not what they wait. Ah, gentle death,
don't touch the clock in the kitchen that ticks on the wall;   25
all my childhood has passed on the enamel
of its face, upon those painted flowers:
don't touch the hands, the heart of the dead.
Perhaps someone will answer? O death of mercy,
death of modesty. Farewell, dear one, farewell, my *dulcissima mater.*"   30

AMELIA ROSSELLI

[b. 1930]

Neve

Snow

TRANSLATED BY LAWRENCE R. SMITH

Sembrano minuscoli insetti festeggianti	They seem to be tiny insects celebrating
uno sciame di motori squillanti, una	a swarm of shrill motors, a
pena discissa in faticose attenzioni	pain split into difficult attentions
e una radunata di bravate.	and a gathering of daring actions.
Nevica fuori; e tutto questo rassomiglia	Snow outside; and all this resembles
ad una crisi giovanile di pianto se	a youthful crisis of tears if
non fosse che ora le lacrime sono asciutte	it weren't for the fact that now the tears are dry
come la neve.	as the snow.
Un esperto di questioni meteorologiche	An expert on meteorological questions
direbbe che si tratta di un innamoramento	would say that this had to do with an infatuation
ma io che sono un esperto in queste	but I who am expert in these
cose direi forse che si tratta di una	things would say that it has to do with an
imboscata!	ambush!

(line numbers in margin: 5, 10)

French Language Poetry

The first major Anglo-Norman poet is France's first woman poet, Marie de France (1140–1200) who lived and wrote at the court of Henry II of England. Her *lais,* dedicated to the king, defined the genre of the *lai* as a highly personal romantic narrative in verse, of alterable length, and in the tradition of the Roman poet Ovid (p. 1026), or as some sources suggest, inspired by the ancient lays of Breton harpists.

One of the most colorful poets ever, François de Montcorbier (1431–1463?), was born into a poor family and adopted the name of his patron, Guillaume de Villon, as a young man. An intense poet, he wrote from his experiences as a student at the Sorbonne as well as from his fellowship with the nobility, prostitutes, and thieves of Paris. Although he left only a slim body of verse, Villon records his wit and grief with humor and great lyrical intensity. Reflecting the Christian mysteries and metaphysics of the times, Villon's poetry also focuses on its vanities, wars, and famines. Convicted of murdering a priest in a street brawl in 1455, Villon was nevertheless granted a royal pardon. It is worth noting that Villon was three times under the sentence of death, and his poem "I am Francis," written in Paris in 1462 while he was awaiting execution, is literally an example of gallows humor.

Another early poet who was influenced by Marie de France as well as by Villon, Jean de La Fontaine (1621–1695) made the fable an important poetic genre. Combining naiveté with a cultured, sophisticated taste, he brought a musical intensity to traditional folk themes and animal tales to create incomparable, deceptively simple poetic masterpieces of humor and incisive psychological observation. He is considered the world's consummate fabulist and has been brilliantly translated by such poets as Marianne Moore.

More modern poets of particular interest to readers of English poetry would include the French Symbolists. We have come to understand the Symbolists mostly in terms of their theories on the nature of poetry. Influenced by the German composer Richard Wagner, who stated that the best poetry would be a "perfect music," the Symbolists were equally influenced by Edgar Allan Poe, who insisted that poems must be "written solely for the poem's sake." Rejecting pedantry, eloquence, political affiliation, melodramatic emotion, and objective description, the Symbolists chose to create poetic impressions through suggestion and a subtle, sensuous revery of images. Working toward a musical "fluidity," the Symbolists chose to evoke rather than crystallize, to suggest rather than describe. As Stéphane Mallarmé, one of the leaders of the French Symbolists, wrote, "To name an object is to do away with three-quarters of the enjoyment of the poem, which is derived from the satisfaction of guessing little by little; to suggest it, to evoke it; this is what charms the imagination." For the Symbolists, reality was to be conveyed by intuition, impression, and sensation because reality was highly personal. A poet's images were inspired symbols of the soul rather than representational creations.

Charles Baudelaire (1821–1867) is considered the first great Symbolist and the greatest French poet of the second half of the nineteenth century. As such, he is also regarded as a central figure at the inception of modern poetry. He invented the term "modernism" and declared the modern poet to be an exile who should attempt to reconcile the human spirit through art. This highly influential theme of artistic exile is echoed in his well-known poem "The Albatross" (p. 1067), in which the poet is seen as disabled and ridiculed on earth though majestic in flight. Ironically, this theme was also literally dramatized for Baudelaire in 1857 when he was charged with obscenity upon the publication of his now famous *Flowers of Evil*. A profound psychologist, aesthetician, and poet of lyric melancholy and subtle rhythms, Baudelaire greatly influenced such major modern poets as William Butler Yeats, Ezra Pound, T. S. Eliot, and Wallace Stevens.

Stéphane Mallarmé (1842–1898), another important Symbolist, pursued the ideal of a pure poetry in which metaphor was free of logic and obvious explanations. This demanding goal limited Mallarmé's published output to a little over a thousand lines. Lyrical, evocative, and highly condensed, Mallarmé's poetry often casts the poet as a magician in search of his own innermost being, unwilling to compromise with reality. Aware of the dangers inherent in this kind of poetry, Mallarmé nevertheless chose to "purify the language of the tribe," which is, as he states in "The Tomb of Edgar Poe," the poet's ultimate function.

Paul Verlaine (1844–1896) remains a unique, somewhat autonomous figure among French poets. Arguably the most popular of the Symbolists within his lifetime, he remains a tragic and mysterious figure as well as a poet of the first order. Highly impressionable, he was able, as Keats prompted, "to let the mind be a thoroughfare for all thoughts." Many readers associate Verlaine with Arthur Rimbaud (1854–1891), another Symbolist poet of great originality. One of the most dramatic figures in French poetry, Rimbaud abandoned poetry by age nineteen for the life of a gunrunner and explorer in Africa. Often identified as one of the originators of free verse because of his rhythmic experiments in *Illuminations,* Rimbaud is also seen as a precursor of Surrealism. His "The Drunken Boat" is perhaps the most famous French poem ever written. Invoking seemingly random imagery, the seventeen-year-old poet fashions, in marvelous rhetoric, a stream of furious, exotic, and scattered images all reflecting the central symbol, the drunken boat, drifting free of moorings and anchors, rushing toward the undiscovered truth of itself. For Rimbaud poetry did not "teach and delight" but served as a preface to change; he wanted to create a poetry of revolt that transcended the senses, translating the absolutely human into a language of illumination.

One of the last of the great French Symbolist poets, Paul Valéry (1871–1945), placed more emphasis on technique than on inspiration. He wrote poetry that drew on classical prosody as well as on the unconscious. He saw symbols as establishing a link between the reader and the universe, and as such, his is a poetry of meditation. Although he admired Poe, especially Poe's theories on poetry, we can see his approach to the poem as more meditative than celebratory when we compare his "Hélène" (p. 1079) with Poe's "To Helen" (p. 380). Like Mallarmé, his mentor, Valéry perfected a small body of poems and remained indifferent to his poetry reading public.

A less academic figure than Valéry and a leader of the French avant-garde of the early twentieth century, Guillaume Apollinaire (1880–1918) is frequently linked with such diverse movements as Cubism and Futurism. Born Wilhelm Apollinaris de Kostrowitzki, Apollinaire was a self-conscious and highly inventive modernist who rebelled against the artifice of the Symbolist poets, insisting on more worldly sources for his lyrics. An immediate forerunner of the antirationalist line, Apollinaire nevertheless continued to see poetry as a means of knowing the self and the world in the midst of change. As eager to see automobiles and airplanes in poetry as he was eager to see them in the streets and skies, Apollinaire preferred democracy to any elitist "tradition." His diction is rich in idioms, and his imagery and his experiments in form and punctuation all combined to fulfill his motto "I astonish." His insistence on the modern also led him to promote such painters as Pablo Picasso and Georges Braque.

Coining the term "Surrealist," Apollinaire also helped usher in the influential movement in art and literature that evolved in the mid-1920s from Freud's theories of the unconscious as much as from Symbolist poetry. Surrealists sought to give expression to the "real functioning of thought" through dreams, hallucinations, and automatic writing, anything that liberated the mind from conscious thought and rational control.

As modern French poetry continued to develop ideas introduced by the Symbolists and Surrealists, politics also came to play a more important role in its formation. After confronting the tragic realities of war, Paul Éluard (1895–1952) turned to Surrealism as a sanctuary from the inanities and cruelties of the times, but then broke with Surrealism in 1938 to become politically and humanistically assertive. Embracing the essential rightness of life, Éluard felt that love should once again become a fundamental theme of poetry. He wrote, "The time has come when all poets have the right and the duty to proclaim that they are deeply committed to the lives of other men, to life in common."

A poet who bridges the gap between classical French Surrealism and contemporary poetry, Blaise Cendrars (1887–1961) explores American as well as African culture in his spirited writing. Born Frédéric Sauser in Switzerland, in 1912 he moved to Paris, where he associated with Apollinaire, Chagall, and other surrealists. Innovative, experimental, and urbane, as his poem "Me Too Boogie" (its original title) suggests, Cendrars helped further the idea of a multicultural poetry.

Often using Surrealist techniques to express political insights, French-language Négritude poets sought to restore cultural individuality to survivors of the great African diaspora. The movement was launched by Aimé Césaire (b. 1913), one of the most important poets from the French-speaking West Indies, along with Léopold Sédar Senghor (b. 1906), and Léon Damas (1912–1978). Césaire originally used the term "Négritude" in his *Return to My Native Land* and defined it as "the simple recognition of the fact of being a Negro and the acceptance of this fact and of its cultural and historical consequences." Central to Césaire's technique is his steadfast adaptation of surrealism to black "history, traditions, and languages, to the culture which truly expresses [the African] soul."

Another important Négritude poet, Léon Gontran Damas (1912–1978), was born in French Guiana but studied in Paris. His outrage at the treatment of blacks in a white culture inspired the social and racial protest that is a central theme in his poetry. One of Damas's most notable works is *Pigments,* a collection of poems composed in jazz rhythms that comments bitterly on racial injustice.

Finally, Yves Bonnefoy (b. 1923) is an important modern French poet whose work is often compared to that of Paul Valéry. Frequently concerned with themes of death and transformation, he has also published essays on poetry and art, including studies of Arthur Rimbaud. He has taught at several universities in the United States and has translated works by Shakespeare, Seferis, and Yeats.

CHARLES BAUDELAIRE

[1821–1867]

L'Albatros

The Albatross

TRANSLATED BY RICHARD WILBUR

Souvent, pour s'amuser, les hommes d'équipage
Prennent des albatros, vastes oiseaux des mers,
Qui suivent, indolents compagnons de voyage,
Le navire glissant sur les gouffres amers.

Often, for pastime, mariners will ensnare
The albatross, that vast sea-bird who sweeps
On high companionable pinion where
Their vessel glides upon the bitter deeps.

A peine les ont-ils déposés sur les planches,   5
Que ces rois de l'azur, maladroits et honteux,
Laissent piteusement leurs grandes ailes blanches
Comme des avirons traîner à côté d'eux.

Torn from his native space, this captive king
Flounders upon the deck in stricken pride,
And pitiably lets his great white wing
Drag like a heavy paddle at his side.

Ce voyageur ailé, comme il est gauche et veule!
Lui, naguère si beau, qu'il est comique et laid!   10

This rider of winds, how awkward he is, and weak!
How droll he seems, who lately was all grace!

L'un agace son bec avec un brûle-gueule,	A sailor pokes a pipestem into his beak;
L'autre mime, en boitant, l'infirme qui volait!	Another, hobbling, mocks his trammeled pace.
Le Poëte est semblable au prince des nuées	The Poet is like this monarch of the clouds,
Qui hante la tempête et se rit de l'archer;	Familiar of storms, of stars, and of all high things;
Exilé sur le sol au milieu des huées, 15	Exiled on earth amidst its hooting crowds,
Ses ailes de géant l'empêchent de marcher.	He cannot walk, borne down by his giant wings.

MARIE DE FRANCE

[c. 1140 – c. 1200]

The Nightingale

TRANSLATED BY PATRICIA TERRY

The story I shall tell today
Was taken from a Breton lay
Called Laustic in Brittany,
Which, in proper French would be
Rossignol. They'd call the tale   5
In English lands *The Nightingale*.

There was, near Saint Malo, a town
Of some importance and renown.
Two barons who could well afford
Houses suited to a lord   10
Gave the city its good name
By their benevolence and fame.
Only one of them had married.
His wife was beautiful indeed
And courteous as she was fair,   15
A lady who was well aware
Of all that custom and rank required.
The younger baron was much admired,
Being, among his peers, foremost
In valor, and a gracious host.   20
He never refused a tournament,
And what he owned he gladly spent.
He loved his neighbor's wife. She knew

That all she heard of him was true,
And so she was inclined to be   25
Persuaded when she heard his plea.
Soon she had yielded all her heart
To his real merit and, in part,
Because he lived not far away.
Fearful that they might betray   30
The love that they had come to share,
They always took the greatest care
Not to let anyone detect
Anything that might be suspect.
And it was easy enough to hide;   35
Their houses were almost side by side
With nothing between the two at all
Except a single high stone wall.
The baron's wife need only go
And stand beside her bedroom window   40
Whenever she wished to see her friend.
They would talk for hours on end
Across the wall, and often threw
Presents through the window too.
They were much happier than before,   45
And would have asked for nothing more;
But lovers can't be satisfied
When love's true pleasure is denied.
The lady was watched too carefully
As soon as her friend was known to be   50
At home. But still they had the delight
Of seeing each other day or night
And talking to their heart's content.
The strictest guard could not prevent
The lady from looking out her window;   55
What she saw there no one could know.
Nothing came to interfere
With their true love until one year
In the season when the summer grows
Green in all the woods and meadows,   60
When birds to show their pleasure cling
To flower tops and sweetly sing.
Then those who were in love before
Do, in love's service, even more.
The baron, in truth, was all intent   65
On love; the messages he sent
Across the wall had such replies
From his lady's lips and from her eyes,
He knew that she felt just the same.

Now she very often came   70
To her window lighted by the moon,
Leaving her husband's side as soon
As she knew that he was fast asleep.
Wrapped in a cloak, she went to keep
Watch with her lover, sure that he   75
Would be waiting for her faithfully.
To see each other was, despite
Their endless longing, great delight.
She went so often and remained
So long, her husband soon complained,   80
Insisting that she must reply
To where she went at night and why.
"I'll tell you, my lord," the lady answered;
"Anyone who has ever heard
The nightingale singing will admit   85
No joy on earth compares with it.
That music just outside my window
Gives me such pleasure that I know
I cannot go to sleep until
The sweet voice in the night is still."   90

The baron only answered her
With a malicious raging laughter.
He wrought a plan that could not fail
To overcome the nightingale.
The household servants all were set   95
To making traps of cord or net;
Then, throughout the orchard, these
Were fixed to hazel and chestnut trees,
And all the branches rimmed with glue
So that the bird could not slip through.   100
It was not long before they brought
The nightingale who had been caught
Alive. The baron, well content,
Took the bird to his wife's apartment.
"Where are you, lady? Come talk to me!"   105
He cried, "I've something for you to see!
Look! Here is the bird whose song
Has kept you from your sleep so long.
Your nights will be more peaceful when
He can't awaken you again!"   110

She heard with sorrow and with dread
Everything her husband said,
Then asked him for the bird, and he

Killed it out of cruelty;
Vile, with his two hands he wrung   *115*
Its neck, and when he finished, flung
The body at his wife. The red
drops of blood ran down and spread
Over the bodice of her dress.
He left her alone with her distress.   *120*
Weeping, she held the bird and thought
With bitter rage of those who brought
The nightingale to death, betrayed
By all the hidden traps they laid.
"Alas!" she cried. "They had destroyed   *125*
The one great pleasure I enjoyed.
Now I can no longer go
And see my love outside my window
At night the way I used to do!
One thing certainly is true: *130*
He'll think that I no longer care.
Somehow he must be made aware
Of what has happened. It will be clear
Then why I cannot appear."

And so she began at once to write   *135*
On a piece of gold-embroidered samite.
When it couldn't hold another word
She wrapped it around the little bird.
Then she called someone in her service
Whom she could entrust with this,   *140*
Bidding him take without delay
Her message to her chevalier.
Thus he came to understand
Everything, just as she planned.
The servant brought the little bird;   *145*
And when the chevalier had heard
All that he so grieved to know,
His courteous answer was not slow.
He ordered made a little case,
Not of iron or any base   *150*
Metal, but fine gold embossed
With jewels—he did not count the cost.
The cover was not too long or wide.
He placed the nightingale inside
And had the casket sealed with care!   *155*
He carried it with him everywhere.
Stories like this can't be controlled,
And it was very promptly told.

Breton poets rhymed the tale,
Calling it *The Nightingale*.   160

FRANÇOIS VILLON

[1431–1463?]

Ballade

Ballade of the Ladies of Bygone Time

TRANSLATED BY NORMAN CAMERON

Tell me but where, beneath what skies
Is lovely Roman Flora ta'en?
Tell me where Archipiada lies,
Or Thais (they were kin, these twain);
Or Echo, answering again   5
Across the river and the mere,
Beauty of more than human strain?
Where are the snows of yesteryear?

Where is the learned Eloise,
For whom Pierre Abelard, her swain,   10
Became a monk at Saint Denis,
And had for her his manhood slain?
Where is the queen who did ordain
That Buridan, her sometime dear,
Should perish coldly in the Seine?   15
Where are the snows of yesteryear?

Queen Blanche, white as a fleur-de-lys,
Who sang like sirens o'er the main?
Bertha the Broadfoot, Beatrice,
Or Erembourg who held the Maine;   20
Or Joan, sweet lady of Lorraine,
For whom the English drop no tear:
Where are they, Virgin sovereign?
Where are the snows of yesteryear?

Prince, do not ask where they are lain,   25
Ask not the week, ask not the year,
Lest you remember this refrain:
Where are the snows of yesteryear?

I Am Francis

TRANSLATED BY NORMAN CAMERON

Francis by name, France's by birth
(I've never had much luck on earth),
At Paris first I op'd my eyes
(It is a hamlet near Pontoise);
And soon my neck, to end the farce,   5
Must learn how heavy is my arse.

JEAN DE LA FONTAINE

[1621–1695]

The Grasshopper and the Ant

TRANSLATED BY MARIANNE MOORE

Until fall, a grasshopper
Chose to chirr;
With starvation as foe
When northeasters would blow,
And not even a gnat's residue   5
Or caterpillar's to chew,
She chirred a recurrent chant
Of want beside an ant,
Begging it to rescue her
With some seeds it could spare   10
Till the following year's fell.
"By August you shall have them all,
Interest and principal."
Share one's seeds? Now what is worse
For any ant to do?   15
Ours asked, "When fair, what brought you through?"
—"I sang for those who might pass by chance—
Night and day. Please do not be repelled."
—"Sang? A delight when someone has excelled.
A singer! Excellent. Now dance."   20

CHARLES BAUDELAIRE

[1821–1867]

Correspondences

TRANSLATED BY RICHARD WILBUR

Nature is a temple whose living colonnades
Breathe forth a mystic speech in fitful sighs;
Man wanders among symbols in those glades
Where all things watch him with familiar eyes.

Like dwindling echoes gathered far away   5
Into a deep and thronging unison
Huge as the night or as the light of day,
All scents and sounds and colors meet as one.

Perfumes there are as sweet as the oboe's sound,
Green as the prairies, fresh as a child's caress,   10
—And there are others, rich, corrupt, profound

And of an infinite pervasiveness,
Like myrrh, or musk, or amber, that excite
The ecstasies of sense, the soul's delight.

STÉPHANE MALLARMÉ

[1842–1898]

The Tomb of Edgar Poe

TRANSLATED BY DAISY ALDAN

TRANSLATED BY STÉPHANE MALLARMÉ;
THE FOOTNOTES ARE HIS OWN

Even as Eternity brings him at last to Himself,
The Poet revives with a naked sword his age
Aghast at having failed to be aware
Of a triumph over death in that strange voice!

Such as into himself at last Eternity changes him,
The Poet arouses with a naked hymn
His century overawed not to have known
That death extolled itself in this strange voice:

THE TOMB OF EDGAR POE   [2]**naked hymn**   meant when
the words take in death their absolute value   [4]**this**   means his
own.

They, like a hydra's vile start once having heard   5
The angel give a purer meaning to the words
  of the tribe
Loudly proclaimed that witchery imbibed
In the dishonored flow of some foul brew.

From hostile soil and cloud, O grief!
If our idea cannot carve out a bas-relief   10
To adorn the dazzling monument of Poe,

Silent stone fallen here below from some dim
  disaster,
May at least this granite forever be a bourne
To the black flights that Blasphemy may
  spread hereafter.

But, in a vile writhing of an hydra, (they) once
  hearing the Angel
To give too pure a meaning to the words of the tribe,
They (between themselves) thought (by him) the
  spell drunk
In the honorless flood of some dark mixture

Of the soil and the ether (which are) enemies, o
  struggle!
If with it my idea does not carve a bas-relief
Of which Poe's dazzling tomb be adorned,

(A) Stern block here fallen from a mysterious
  disaster,
Let this granite at least show forever their bound
To the old flights of Blasphemy (still) spread in the
  future

[5] **the Angel** means the above said Poet.   [6] **to give** means giving.   [7] in plain prose: charged him with always being drunk.   [11] **dazzling** means with the idea of such a bas-relief.   [14] **Blasphemy** means against Poets, such as the charge of Poe being drunk.

PAUL VERLAINE

[1844–1896]

Sentimental Dialogue

TRANSLATED BY MURIEL KITTEL

In the old park, frozen and deserted,
Two shapes have just slipped by.

Their eyes are dead and their lips are limp,
And their words can scarcely be heard.

In the old park, frozen and deserted,   5
Two wraiths have recalled the past.

"Do you remember our old delight?"
"Whyever should I remember it?"

"Does your heart still throb at my very name?
Do you still see my soul in your dreams?" "No."   10

"Ah, the fine days of unspeakable joy
When our lips met!" "Perhaps."

"How beautiful the sky was, how great our hope!"
"Hope has fled, defeated, to the dark sky."

They wandered on through the wild oats   15
And only the night listened to their words.

ARTHUR RIMBAUD

[1854–1891]

The Drunken Boat

TRANSLATED BY STEPHEN STEPANCHEV

As I descended black, impassive Rivers,
I sensed that haulers were no longer guiding me:
Screaming Redskins took them for their targets,
Nailed nude to colored stakes: barbaric trees.

I was indifferent to all my crews;   5
I carried English cottons, Flemish wheat.
When the disturbing din of haulers ceased,
The Rivers let me ramble where I willed.

Through the furious ripping of the sea's mad tides,
Last winter, deafer than an infant's mind,   10
I ran! And drifting, green Peninsulas
Did not know roar more gleefully unkind.

A tempest blessed my vigils on the sea.
Lighter than a cork I danced on the waves,
Those endless rollers, as they say, of graves: 15
Ten nights beyond a lantern's silly eye!

Sweeter than sourest apple-flesh to children,
Green water seeped into my pine-wood hull
And washed away blue wine stains, vomitings,
Scattering rudder, anchor, man's lost rule.   *20*

And then I, trembling, plunged into the Poem
Of the Sea, infused with stars, milk-white,
Devouring azure greens; where remnants, pale
And gnawed, of pensive corpses fell from light;

Where, staining suddenly the blueness, delirium,   *25*
The slow rhythms of the pulsing glow of day,
Stronger than alcohol and vaster than our lyres,
The bitter reds of love ferment the way!

I know skies splitting into light, whirled spouts
Of water, surfs, and currents: I know the night,   *30*
The dawn exalted like a flock of doves, pure wing,
And I have seen what men imagine they have seen.

I saw the low sun stained with mystic horrors,
Lighting long, curdled clouds of violet,
Like actors in a very ancient play,   *35*
Waves rolling distant thrills like lattice light!

I dreamed of green night, stirred by dazzling snows,
Of kisses rising to the sea's eyes, slowly,
The sap-like coursing of surprising currents,
And singing phosphors, flaring blue and gold!   *40*

I followed, for whole months, a surge like herds
Of insane cattle in assault on the reefs,
Unhopeful that three Marys, come on luminous feet,
Could force a muzzle on the panting seas!

Yes, I struck incredible Floridas   *45*
That mingled flowers and the eyes of panthers
In skins of men! And rainbows bridled green
Herds beneath the horizon of the seas.

I saw the ferment of enormous marshes, weirs
Where a whole Leviathan lies rotting in the weeds!   *50*
Collapse of waters within calms at sea,
And distances in cataract toward chasms!

Glaciers, silver suns, pearl waves, and skies like coals,
Hideous wrecks at the bottom of brown gulfs
Where giant serpents eaten by red bugs   55
Drop from twisted trees and shed a black perfume!

I should have liked to show the young those dolphins
In blue waves, those golden fish, those fish that sing.
—Foam like flowers rocked my sleepy drifting,
And, now and then, fine winds supplied me wings.   60

When, feeling like a martyr, I tired of poles and zones,
The sea, whose sobbing made my tossing sweet,
Raised me its dark flowers, deep and yellow whirled,
And, like a woman, I fell on my knees . . .

Peninsula, I tossed upon my shores   65
The quarrels and droppings of clamorous, blond-eyed birds.
I sailed until, across my rotting cords,
Drowned men, spinning backwards, fell asleep! . . .

Now I, a lost boat in the hair of coves,
Hurled by tempest into a birdless air,   70
I, whose drunken carcass neither Monitors
Nor Hansa ships would fish back for men's care;

Free, smoking, rigged with violet fogs,
I, who pierced the red sky like a wall
That carries exquisite mixtures for good poets,   75
Lichens of sun and azure mucus veils;

Who, spotted with electric crescents, ran
Like a mad plank, escorted by seahorses,
When cudgel blows of hot Julys struck down
The sea-blue skies upon wild water spouts;   80

I, who trembled, feeling the moan at fifty leagues
Of rutting Behemoths and thick Maelstroms, I,
Eternal weaver of blue immobilities,
I long for Europe with its ancient quays!

I saw sidereal archipelagoes! and isles   85
Whose delirious skies are open to the voyager:
—Is it in depthless nights you sleep your exile,
A million golden birds, O future Vigor?—

But, truly, I have wept too much! The dawns disturb.
All moons are painful, and all suns break bitterly:　　　　90
Love has swollen me with drunken torpors.
Oh, that my keel might break and spend me in the sea!

Of European waters I desire
Only the black, cold puddle in a scented twilight
Where a child of sorrows squats and sets the sails　　　　95
Of a boat as frail as a butterfly in May.

I can no longer, bathed in languors, O waves,
Cross the wake of cotton-bearers on long trips,
Nor ramble in a pride of flags and flares,
Nor swim beneath the horrible eyes of prison ships.　　　　100

PAUL VALÉRY

[1871–1945]

Hélèn

TRANSLATED BY ANDREW CHIAPPE

Azure! behold me . . . I come from the caverns of death
To hear once more the measured sounding of waves,
And once more I see long galleys in the dawn
Revive from darkness in a file of golden oars.

My solitary hands call forth those monarchs　　　　5
Whose beards of salt entwined my simple fingers.
I wept. They sang of their obscure triumphs
And of buried seas in the wake of their barques.

I hear deep hollow shells and the compelling
Clarions of war, pacing the flight of the oars—　　　　10
The clear song of the oarsmen chains this tumult.

And gods raised high on the Heroic prow,
Their ancient smile insulted by the spray,
Hold forth toward me forgiving sculptured arms.

GUILLAUME APOLLINAIRE

[1880–1918]

The Mirabeau Bridge

TRANSLATED BY W. S. MERWIN

Under the Mirabeau Bridge the Seine
Flows and our love
Must I be reminded again
How joy came always after pain

Night comes the hour is rung   5
The days go I remain

Hands within hands we stand face to face
While underneath
The bridge of our arms passes
The loose wave of our gazing which is endless   10

Night comes the hour is rung
The days go I remain

Love slips away like this water flowing
Love slips away
How slow life is in its going   15
And hope is so violent a thing

Night comes the hour is rung
The days go I remain

The days pass the weeks pass and are gone
Neither time that is gone   20
Nor love ever returns again
Under the Mirabeau Bridge flows the Seine

Night comes the hour is rung
The days go I remain

BLAISE CENDRARS

[1887–1961]

Mee Too Boogie

TRANSLATED BY RON PADGETT

As among the Greeks it is believed that every well-bred man ought to
    know how to pluck the lyre
Give me that fango-fango
So I can press it to my nose
A sound soft and resonant
From the right nostril   5
There are descriptions of landscapes
The story of past events
A telling of distant lands
Bolotoo
Papalangi   10
The poet describes among other things the animals
The houses are turned over by enormous birds
The women have on too many clothes
Rhymes or measures lacking
If you don't count a little exaggeration   15
The man who cut off his own leg succeeded in a light and simple genre
Mee low folla
Mareewagee beats the drum at the entrance to his house

PAUL ÉLUARD

[1895–1952]

Lady Love

TRANSLATED BY SAMUEL BECKETT

She is standing on my lids
And her hair is in my hair
She has the colour of my eye
She has the body of my hand

In my shade she is engulfed   *5*
As a stone against the sky

She will never close her eyes
And she does not let me sleep
And her dreams in the bright day
Make the suns evaporate   *10*
And me laugh cry and laugh
Speak when I have nothing to say

LÉON GONTRAN DAMAS

[1912–1978]

There Are Nights

FOR ALEJO CARPENTIER

TRANSLATED BY E. C. KENNEDY

There are nights with no name
There are nights with no moon
when a clammy
suffocation
nearly overwhelms me   *5*
the acrid smell of blood
spewing
from every muted trumpet

On those nights with no name
on those nights with no moon   *10*
the pain that inhabits me
presses
the pain that inhabits me
chokes

Nights with no name   *15*
nights with no moon
when I would have preferred
to be able no longer to doubt
the nausea obsesses me so
a need to escape   *20*
with no name

with no moon
with no moon
with no name
on nights with no moon   25
on nameless nameless nights
when the sickness sticks within me
like an Oriental dagger.

AIMÉ CÉSAIRE

[b. 1913]

First Problem

TRANSLATED BY CLAYTON ESHLEMAN AND DENIS KELLY

When they grab my leg
I hurl back a jungle of lianas
Let them lynch me
I vanish into a row of figs

The weakness of most men   5
they don't know how to become a stone or tree

Sometimes I stick tinder between my fingers
for the sole pleasure of breaking out
fresh poinsettia all night long
reds, greens flaming in the wind   10
like our dawn in my throat.

YVES BONNEFOY

[b. 1923]

True Name

TRANSLATED BY GALWAY KINNELL

I will name wilderness the castle which you were,
Night your voice, absence your face,
And when you fall back into sterile earth
I will name nothingness the lightning which bore you.

Dying is a country which you loved. I approach   5
Along your dark ways, but eternally.
I destroy your desire, your form, your trace in me,
I am your enemy who shows no mercy.

I will name you war and I will take
With you the liberties of war, and I will have   10
In my hands your dark-crossed face,
In my heart this land which the storm lights.

Spanish Language Poetry

The recently rediscovered Spanish language poet of the seventeenth century, Sor Juana Inés de la Cruz (1648–1695) was born not on the Iberian peninsula but in New Spain, southeast of Mexico City. Hailed as the "Phoenix of Mexico, America's Tenth Muse" during her lifetime, she was shortly thereafter forgotten. Nevertheless, she is now considered one of the finest Hispanic poets of her time. Speaking to our present interest in the self-realization of women, her poetry is considered spirited and complex in its use of images and subtle rhythms, often drawing on African as well as Nahuatl sources.

Modern Iberian Spanish poetry begins with Antonio Machado (1875–1939), the first great Spanish poet to emerge after the Spanish-American War. Born in Seville, he evokes the parched landscape of Castile, his setting for a poetry that often describes a people's isolated and difficult life. Machado states in his prologue to *Solitudes* that he considered the essence of poetry "the deep palpitation of the spirit." Combining the meters of popular Spanish literature and traditional forms with intensely human themes, Machado's poetry marks the beginnings of a "dialogue of a man with his time." The Spanish prize him as a poet of wit, gravity, and the dream.

More drawn to the ideal than to themes of human struggle, Juan Ramón Jiménez (1881–1958) was greatly influenced by the French Symbolists. He is considered a pure lyric poet and often compared to W. B. Yeats (pp. 501–524) and Rainer Maria Rilke (pp. 1109–1111). Jiménez stated that he lived in "spiritual asceticism;" nevertheless, he produced over forty volumes of poetry during his fifty years as a writer. A Platonist who believed that "Ideas" of Beauty, Love, and God literally exist, Jiménez wrote within traditional as well as modern forms. He was awarded the Nobel Prize for Literature in 1956.

The first Spanish American writer to be awarded the Nobel Prize for Literature took the pen name of Gabriela Mistral. Born Lucila Godoy Alcayaga (1889–1957) in an impoverished part of Chile, Mistral began teaching in rural schools at age fifteen, working for the social and psychological liberation of Spanish American women. By 1922 she was already the most widely read Spanish American poet. As an artist, Mistral's poems focus on nature, biblical motifs, platonic love, mother-child relationships, and especially on her love of children and the disinherited. Truly a populist poet, Mistral also worked as an international educator and with Madame Curie and Henri Bergson, in the League of Nations. A collection of her poetry was translated into English in 1957 by Langston Hughes (pp. 689–698).

Unlike Mistral, Jorge Luis Borges (1889–1986) often used complex enigmas to dramatize what he considered our near inability to achieve awareness. His lyric poetry shows a strong metaphysical pre-disposition, and its tone is often elegiac. The epitome of the artist–intellectual, Borges was born in Buenos Aires, Argentina, and is also considered a foremost Spanish American writer of essays and short stories. Despite Borges's deeply rooted skepticism, his poetry is often witty and humorous, and his translucent, labyrinthine and verbal structures often achieve an unusual level of intimacy.

Counterbalancing Borges's intellectual achievements, the driving passion of César Vallejo (1892–1938), another Spanish American poet, records an equally arresting vision of modern experience. The youngest of eleven children, Vallejo was born in dire poverty into a family of Inca and Spanish descent in Northern Peru. The theme of human suffering underlies his first book, *The Black Riders*, published when he was twenty-six. Influenced by Walt Whitman (pp. 424–458) and Charles Baudelaire (p. 1074), Vallejo rebelled against convention, often working with the interior monologue, often disregarding grammar, syntax, and logic. Much of the passion and strong political undercurrents associated with modern Spanish American Surrealism can trace their roots to Vallejo's intense, powerful voice and vision.

Federico García Lorca (1898–1936) is perhaps the best known of the modern Spanish Iberian poets and dramatists. An intuitive genius, Lorca often combined Surrealist techniques with folk structures to create a sweeping, impassioned lyric poetry more emotionally coherent than much of the French Surrealist poetry of his time. With Lorca, as with Vallejo, Surrealism became a way of understanding experience and emotion as well as a way of understanding the mind. Fascinated by human vitality, Lorca is the poet of passion and blood, of the human animal oblivious of social constraint. His "Somnambule Ballad," for example, uses the rhythms of the traditional Spanish ballad form while exploring the secretive, peripheral society of Andalusian gypsies. A supporter of Walt Whitman, Lorca insisted on the total personal liberty of the individual. He was assassinated at age thirty-eight during the Spanish Civil war.

Spanish American poetry glories in the joyful, dramatic lyrics of Pablo Neruda (1904–1973), the pen name of Ricardo Eliezer Neftali Reyes y Basoalto. Born in Chile and greatly influenced by Walt Whitman and the French and Spanish Surrealists, Neruda detailed the social and psychological dramas confronting modern humanity in general and Spanish America in particular in a poetry as rich in humor as it is in tragedy and pathos. More than a poet of solitude, Neruda was also considered a political activist and diplomat, who used the apparent irrationality of Surrealism to great advantage in his attacks on social injustice. Translated into most modern languages, his poetry is often considered the best Surrealist work written in any Western language. He was awarded the Nobel Prize for Literature in 1971.

Surrealism and native Mexican mythology combine with Oriental philosophies in the poetry of Octavio Paz (b. 1914). Considered one of the strongest voices in Spanish American poetry today, Paz often fuses Aztec myths of fate and the soul with a surrealist and mystical aesthetic. "When I am writing a poem," he states, "it is to make something, an object or organism that will be whole and living, something that will have a life independent of me." Serious and often tragic in tone, his poetry reflects and redefines the changing Latin American culture as well as his own artistic intentions. Paz writes, "I am the shadow my words cast." A close friend of Elizabeth Bishop (pp. 714–728), who translated his poetry into English, Paz was born in Mexico City and has also worked as a diplomat, serving as Mexico's ambassador to India. He was awarded the Nobel Prize for Literature in 1990.

SOR JUANA INÉS DE LA CRUZ

[1648–1695]

| *Encarece de Animosidad la Elección de Estado Durable Hasta la Muerte* | *She Ponders the Choice of a Way of Life Binding Until Death* |

TRANSLATED BY ALAN S. TRUEBLOOD

Si los riesgos del mar considerara,
ninguno se embarcara; si antes viera
bien su peligro, nadie se atreviera
ni al bravo toro osado provocara.

Si del fogoso bruto ponderara   5
la furia desbocada en la carrera
el jinete prudente, nunca hubiera
quien con discreta mano lo enfrenara.

Pero si hubiera alguno tan osado
que, no obstante el peligro, al mismo Apolo   10
quisiese gobernar con atrevida

mano el rápido carro en luz bañado,
todo lo hiciera, y no tomara sólo
estado que ha de ser toda la vida.

If men weighed the hazards of the sea,
none would embark. If they foresaw
the dangers of the ring, rather than taunt
the savage bull, they'd cautiously withdraw.

If the horseman should prudently reflect
on the headlong fury of the steed's wild dash,
he'd never undertake to rein him in
adroitly, or to wield the cracking lash.

But were there one of such temerity
that, facing undoubted peril, he still planned
to drive the fiery chariot and subdue

the steeds of Apollo himself with daring hand,
he'd stop at nothing, would not meekly choose
a way of life binding a whole life through.

She Demonstrates the Inconsistency of Men's Wishes in Blaming Women for What They Themselves Have Caused

TRANSLATED BY ALAN S. TRUEBLOOD

Silly, you men—so very adept
at wrongly faulting womankind,
not seeing you're alone to blame
for faults you plant in woman's mind.

After you've won by urgent plea   5
the right to tarnish her good name,
you still expect her to behave—
you, that coaxed her into shame.

You batter her resistance down
and then, all righteousness, proclaim   10
that feminine frivolity,
not your persistence, is to blame.

When it comes to bravely posturing,
your witlessness must take the prize:
you're the child that makes a bogeyman,   15
and then recoils in fear and cries.

Presumptuous beyond belief,
you'd have the woman you pursue
be Thais when you're courting her,
Lucretia once she falls to you.   20

For plain default of common sense,
could any action be so queer
as oneself to cloud the mirror,
then complain that it's not clear?

Whether you're favored or disdained,   25
nothing can leave you satisfied.
You whimper if you're turned away,
you sneer if you've been gratified.

With you, no woman can hope to score;
whichever way, she's bound to lose;   30
spurning you, she's ungrateful;
succumbing, you call her lewd.

Your folly is always the same:
you apply a single rule
to the one you accuse of looseness   35
and the one you brand as cruel.

SHE DEMONSTRATES THE INCONSISTENCY   [19]Thais   Athenian courtesan who accompanied Alexander the Great on his Asiatic conquests.

What happy mean could there be
for the woman who catches your eye,
if, unresponsive, she offends,
yet whose complaisance you decry?   40

    Still, whether it's torment or anger—
and both ways you've yourselves to blame—
God bless the woman who won't have you,
no matter how loud you complain.

    It's your persistent entreaties   45
that change her from timid to bold.
Having made her thereby naughty,
you would have her good as gold.

    So where does the greater guilt lie
for a passion that should not be: 50
with the man who pleads out of baseness
or the woman debased by his plea?

    Or which is more to be blamed—
though both will have cause for chagrin:
the woman who sins for money   55
or the man who pays money to sin?

    So why are you men all so stunned
at the thought you're all guilty alike?
Either like them for what you've made them
or make of them what you can like.   60

    If you'd give up pursuing them,
you'd discover, without a doubt,
you've a stronger case to make
against those who seek you out.

    I well know what powerful arms   65
you wield in pressing for evil:
your arrogance is allied
with the world, the flesh, and the devil!

ANTONIO MACHADO

[1875–1939]

Daydreams have endlessly turning

TRANSLATED BY ROBERT BLY

Daydreams have endlessly turning
paths going over the bitter
earth, winding roads,
parks flowering, in darkness and in silence;

deep vaults, ladders against the stars;   5
scenes of hopes and memories.
Tiny figures that walk past and smile
—sad playthings for an old man—,

friends we think we see
at the flowery turn in the road,   10
and imaginary creatures
that show us roads . . . far off . . .

JUAN RAMÓN JIMÉNEZ

[1881–1958]

I shall run through the shadow

TRANSLATED BY W. S. MERWIN

I shall run through the shadow,
sleeping, sleeping, to see
if I can come where you are
who died, and I did not know.

Wait, wait; do not run;   5
wait for me in the dead water
by the lily that the moon
makes out of light; with the water
that flows from the infinite
into your white hand!   10
         Wait;
I have one foot already through the black
mouth of the first nothing,
of the resplendent and blessed dream,
the bud of death flowering!   15

GABRIELA MISTRAL

[1889–1957]

Absence

TRANSLATED BY KATE FLORES

My body leaves you drop by drop.
My face leaves in a deaf anointment;

My hands are leaving in loosed mercury;
My feet leave in two tides of dust.

Everything leaves you, everything leaves us!   5

My voice is leaving, that made you a bell
Closed to all except ourselves.
My gestures leave, that before your eyes
Round on spindles wound themselves,
And the gaze is leaving that fixed on you   10
Gave forth juniper and elm.

With your very breathing I am leaving you:
I am exuded like your body's mist.
Asleep and waking I am leaving you,
And in your most faithful recollection I am already blurred,   15
And in your memory faded with those
Born in neither field nor wood.

Would I were blood, and leaving in the palms
Of your labor, and in your mouth of attar of grape.
In your sinews I should leave, and be burned   20
In your motions I could never hear again,
And in your passion pounding in the night
Like the dementia of lonely seas!

Everything leaves us, everything leaves us!

JORGE LUIS BORGES

[1889–1986]

Amorous Anticipation

TRANSLATED BY PERRY HIGMAN

Not the intimacy of your forehead clear as a celebration
nor the prize of your body, still mysterious and tacit and childlike
nor the sequence of your life showing itself in words or silence
will be so mysterious a favor
as to watch your dream implied   5
in the vigil of my arms.

Miraculously virgin again through the absolving virtue of sleep,
quiet and resplendent like a lucky choice of memories,
you will give me those far reaches of your life that you yourself do not have.

Cast into stillness,   *10*
I will perceive that ultimate strand of your being
and will see you for the first time, perhaps
as God must see you,
the fiction of Time destroyed,
without love, without me.   *15*

CÉSAR VALLEJO

[1892–1938]

The Black Riders

TRANSLATED BY ROBERT BLY

There are blows in life so violent—I can't answer!
Blows as if from the hatred of God; as if before them,
the deep waters of everything lived through
were backed up in the soul . . . I can't answer!

Not many; but they exist . . . They open dark ravines   *5*
in the most ferocious face and in the most bull-like back.
Perhaps they are the horses of that heathen Attila,
or the black riders sent to us by Death.

They are the slips backward made by the Christs of the soul,
away from some holy faith that is sneered at by Events.   *10*
These blows that are bloody are the crackling sounds
from some bread that burns at the oven door.

And man . . . poor man! . . . poor man! He swings his eyes, as
when a man behind us calls us by clapping his hands;
swings his crazy eyes, and everything alive   *15*
is backed up, like a pool of guilt, in that glance.

There are blows in life so violent . . . I can't answer!

FEDERICO GARCÍA LORCA

[1898–1936]

Somnambule Ballad

TRANSLATED BY STEPHEN SPENDER AND J. L. GILI

Green, how much I want you green.
Green wind. Green branches.
The ship upon the sea
and the horse in the mountain.
With the shadow on her waist   5
she dreams on her balcony,
green flesh, hair of green,
and eyes of cold silver.
Green, how much I want you green.
Beneath the gypsy moon,   10
all things look at her
but she cannot see them.

Green, how much I want you green.
Great stars of white frost
come with the fish of darkness   15
that opens the road of dawn.
The fig tree rubs the wind
with the sandpaper of its branches,
and the mountain, a filching cat,
bristles its bitter aloes.   20
But who will come? And from where?
She lingers on her balcony,
green flesh, hair of green,
dreaming of the bitter sea.

—Friend, I want to change   25
my horse for your house,
my saddle for your mirror,
my knife for your blanket.

Friend, I come bleeding,
from the passes of Cabra.   30
—If I could, young man,
this pact would be sealed.

But I am no more I,
nor is my house now my house.
—Friend, I want to die   35
decently in my bed.
Of iron, if it be possible,
with sheets of fine holland.
Do you not see the wound I have
from my breast to my throat?   40
—Your white shirt bears
three hundred dark roses.
Your pungent blood oozes
around your sash.
But I am no more I,   45
nor is my house now my house.
—Let me climb at least
up to the high balustrades:
let me come! Let me come!
up to the green balustrades.   50
Balustrades of the moon
where the water resounds.

Now the two friends go up
towards the high balustrades.
Leaving a trail of blood,   55
leaving a trail of tears.
Small lanterns of tin
were trembling on the roofs.
A thousand crystal tambourines
were piercing the dawn.   60

Green, how much I want you green,
green wind, green branches.
The two friends went up.
The long wind was leaving
in the mouth a strange taste   65
of gall, mint and sweet-basil.
Friend! Where is she, tell me,
where is your bitter girl?
How often she waited for you!
How often did she wait for you,   70
cool face, black hair,
on this green balcony!

Over the face of the cistern
the gypsy girl swayed.

Green flesh, hair of green,   75
with eyes of cold silver.
An icicle of the moon
suspends her above the water.
The night became as intimate
as a little square.   80
Drunken civil guards
were knocking at the door.
Green, how much I want you green.
Green wind. Green branches.
The ship upon the sea.   85
And the horse on the mountain.

PABLO NERUDA

[1904–1973]

Ode to My Socks

TRANSLATED BY ROBERT BLY

Maru Mori brought me
a pair
of socks
which she knitted herself
with her sheepherder's hands,   5
two socks as soft
as rabbits.
I slipped my feet
into them
as though into   10
two
cases
knitted
with threads of
twilight   15
and goatskin.
Violent socks,
my feet were
two fish made
of wool,   20

two long sharks
sea-blue, shot
through
by one golden thread,
two immense blackbirds,   25
two cannons:
my feet
were honored
in this way
by   30
these
heavenly
socks.
They were
so handsome   35
for the first time
my feet seemed to me
unacceptable
like two decrepit
firemen, firemen   40
unworthy
of that woven
fire,
of those glowing
socks.   45
Nevertheless
I resisted
the sharp temptation
to save them somewhere
as schoolboys   50
keep
fireflies,
as learned men
collect
sacred texts,   55
I resisted
the mad impulse
to put them
into a golden
cage   60
and each day give them
birdseed
and pieces of pink melon.
Like explorers
in the jungle who hand   65

over the very rare
green deer
to the spit
and eat it
with remorse,   70
I stretched out
my feet
and pulled on
the magnificent
socks   75
and then my shoes.

The moral
of my ode is this:
beauty is twice
beauty   80
and what is good is doubly
good
when it is a matter of two socks
made of wool
in winter.   85

OCTAVIO PAZ

[b. 1914]

The Key of Water

TRANSLATED BY ELIZABETH BISHOP

After Rishikesh
The Ganges is still green.
The glass horizon
Breaks among the peaks.
We walk upon crystals.   5
Above and below
Great gulfs of calm.
In the blue spaces
White rocks, black clouds.
You said: 10
    Le pays est plein de sources.
That night I dipped my hands in your breasts.

THE KEY OF WATER   [11]**Le pays . . . sources** French for "the country is full of resources."

The Street

TRANSLATED BY MURIEL RUKEYSER

Here is a long and silent street.
I walk in blackness and I stumble and fall
and rise, and I walk blind, my feet
trampling the silent stones and the dry leaves.
Someone behind me also tramples, stones, leaves: 5
if I slow down, he slows;
if I run, he runs. I turn: nobody.
Everything dark and doorless,
only my steps aware of me,
I turning and turning among these corners   10
which lead forever to the street
where nobody waits for, nobody follows me,
where I pursue a man who stumbles
and rises and says when he sees me: nobody.

The Day in Udaipur

TRANSLATED BY ELIOT WEINBERGER

White palace,
white on the black lake.
Lingam and yoni.

                    As the goddess to the god,
                    you surround me, night.   5

Cool terrace.
You are immense, immense—
made to measure.

                    Inhuman stars.
                    But this hour is ours.   10

THE DAY IN UDAIPUR   ³**Lingam and yoni**   Sanskrit words for phallus and vulva.

I fall and rise,
I burn, drenched.
Are you only one body?

        Birds on the water,
        dawn on eyelids.   15

Self-absorbed,
high as death,
the marble bursts.

        Hushed palaces,
        whiteness adrift.   20

Women and children
on the roads:
scattered fruit.

        Rags or rays of lightning?
        A procession on the plain.   25

Silver running cool
and clanking:
ankle and wrist.

        In a rented costume
        the boy goes to his wedding.   30

Clean clothes
spread out on the rocks
Look at them and say nothing.

        On the little island
        monkeys with red asses screech.   35

Hanging from the wall,
a dark and angry sun:
wasps' nest.

        And my head is another sun,
        full of black thoughts.   40

Flies and blood.
A small goat skips
in Kali's court.

Gods, men and beasts
eat from the same plate.   *45*

Over the pale god
the black goddess dances,
decapitated.

Heat, the hour split open,
and those mangoes, rotten . . .   *50*

Your face, the lake:
smooth, without thoughts.
A trout leaps.

Lights on the water:
souls sailing.   *55*

Ripples:
the golden plain—and the crack . . .
Your clothes nearby.

I, like a lamp
on your shadow body.   *60*

A living scales:
bodies entwined
over the void.

The sky crushes us,
the water sustains us.   *65*

I open my eyes:
so many trees
were born tonight.

What I've seen here, what I say,
the white sun erases.   *70*

German Language Poetry

Modern German language poetry finds its earliest voice in the poetry of Johann Wolfgang von Goethe (1749–1832). Viewing all his writings as "part of a great confession," Goethe began his career as a fiery, impatient youth who nevertheless combined passion with discipline. In time, however, his writings grew more formal as he matured into a shrewd, classically stylized man of letters who stressed the importance of technique, as shown in his "Nature and Art." Recognized as one of the most versatile European writers and thinkers, he is credited with setting the tone for entire literary movements, including German Romanticism.

Friedrich Johann Christoph von Schiller (1759–1805) also survives as one of Germany's leading *Dichter,* or important figure of letters. A major dramatic author, poet, philosopher, and historian, Schiller stressed liberty and dignity as the entitlement of all humanity, and his tragedies mark the zenith of the eighteenth-century German classic tradition. Among his best-known works are *William Tell,* a drama that serves as a paradigm for the struggle of the oppressed, and his passionate and forceful "Ode to Joy," set to music by Beethoven in his monumental Ninth Symphony.

A poet who admired both Schiller and Goethe but whom Goethe failed to recognize, Friedrich Hölderlin (1770–1843) was marked by an individualism that made him an isolated figure in the history of German literature. With the striking exception of Friedrich Nietzsche, who greatly admired him, Hölderlin was "discovered" in the twentieth century. Unlike much of the German poetry of his age, Hölderlin's open-form verse stressed cadence and imagery and sprang from his intense love of ancient Greek poetry. Seeing Greek culture as an outburst of primordial forces dominated by Dionysus, he viewed Hellenism as the very incarnation of all beauty and harmony. A friend of the German philosopher Hegel, Hölderlin remains a poet of intellectual passion and humanitarian ideals.

Counterbalancing Hölderlin's idealism, Annette von Droste–Hülshoff (1797–1848) brought a legacy of spirituality to her observations of nature. Fusing realism with a romantic temperament, her poetry often explores the seemingly insignificant lives of such creatures as insects, toads, and mice. Her poetry, however, is marked by lyrical strength, metrical freedom, realism, bold imagery, and a symbolism that anticipates later trends in German poetry. As well as an important novelist, she is considered Germany's greatest woman poet.

A contemporary of Annette von Droste–Hülshoff, Heinrich Heine (1797–1856) is deemed by many critics to be the last poet of the German Romantic Age and one of the greatest and most controversial German writers of the nineteenth century. Early in life, Heine mastered a bittersweet poetry rich in irony and sorrow, the best-known example of which is "The Lorelei." Composers including Schubert, Schumann, Mendelssohn, Liszt, Brahms, and Wagner set many of these early lyrics to music. Later in life, as a member of the factional *Jung Deutschland* group, Heine developed into a highly committed, radical political thinker, counting Karl Marx (who knew many of Heine's poems by heart) among his friends. Scholars even suggest that Karl Marx was quoting (actually, slightly misquoting) Heine when he claimed "Religion is the opiate of the people." Also considered one of Germany's wittiest satirists, Heine was included in Metternich's 1835 ban on the "Young German" writers.

More concerned with the inner life than with politics, the greatest German language poet of modern times was born in Prague, Czechoslovakia. Formulating a poetry of flawless alliterations, assonance, rhyme, and rhythm, Rainer Maria Rilke (1875–1926) has long been a poet of international stature. No other modern German language poet is as well known to the English reading public. As a poet, Rilke chose to transform private suffering into public language, into what he termed "hard words as the stone-mason of a cathedral obstinately translates himself into the equanimity of the stone." The longing for transcendence and transformation is also a theme of Rilke's "Archaic Torso of Apollo," (p. 86) which Rilke composed after studying the fragmentary sculpture at the Louvre. Contemplating the object, Rilke senses the spirit of its ancient maker and draws forth the torso's essential directive: "You must change your life." Associated with the French Symbolists and with German Impressionism, a literary movement that set out to describe complex subjective emotional states by employing symbolic imagery, Rilke possessed a vision that recognized the centrality of the unconscious.

Often compared to Rilke and Hölderlin, Georg Trakl (1887–1914) foreshadows expressionistic concerns by focusing on death, decay, and the despondency of civilization. His poetry is greatly influenced by that of Baudelaire (p. 1074) and Rimbaud (pp. 1076–1079) and often centers on disintegrating worlds. Moving beyond Expressionism, the painter, graphic artist, sculptor, and highly experimental poet Hans (Jean) Arp (1887–1966) became a leading figure in the early twentieth-century European avant-garde. Disgusted with war and bored with the dominant literary fashions, Arp advocated an artistic nihilism that emphasized the illogical, the absurd, and the importance of chance in artistic creation. His poetry often took liberties with conventional syntax and with grammatical connections and was often "transcribed directly, unreflected, and uncorrected" to the page.

Another important figure in the German avant-garde, Bertolt Brecht (1898–1956) is most widely known as a playwright and as the author of *The Threepenny*

Opera (with score by Kurt Weill). Much of Brecht's poetic vitality springs from deeply felt social concerns. Like Heine, Brecht underscored his cynicism, irony, and despair with an earthy humanism, writing a poetry that he hoped would show that social change was both necessary and possible. In language that is often harsh and always direct, Brecht rebelled against what he considered to be the esoteric aesthetics of the Symbolist poets and the insistent subjective experiences that culminated in Surrealism.

The post–World War II poet Leonie Nelly Sachs (1891–1970) is one of the most prominent German poets of the mid–twentieth century. Persecuted by the Nazis as a Jew, she fled to Sweden, where her memories of the Holocaust forced her to find a means of expression that would "make the unspeakable bearable." An intensely spiritual awareness and a sense of grieving pervades her unrhymed poetry. Her often-quoted poem, "O the chimneys," in which the smoke from the chimneys of Nazi extermination camps symbolizes Israel's body, provided the title for the first selection of her poems in English (1967). She shared the Nobel Prize for literature in 1966 with Shmuel Yosef Agnon, a writer of fiction.

Similarly, Paul Celan (1920–1970) also endured great tragedy at the hands of the Nazis. Born Paul Antschel in Romania of Jewish parents, Celan went on to lose both his parents in a concentration camp. Profoundly moved by the horrors forced on Jews, Celan wrote his intense and compelling "Fugue of Death" as an evocation of Auschwitz, reaching the zenith of German poetic Surrealism in this visionary poem.

JOHANN WOLFGANG VON GOETHE

[1749–1832]

Nature and Art

TRANSLATED BY JOHN FREDERICK NIMS

Genius, technique—you'd swear the pair unsuited,
Yet here they stand together, hand in hand.
Nature's in love with art. Their widely bruited
Hassle's a lie, I've come to understand.

Poet, there's one thing only works: to work.   5
Hours of the sweaty effort day and night
Trying it this way, that way—going berserk.
Then you can be spontaneous. You've the right.

Habits of mind we earn. To earn's laborious.
Small chance they'll make it to a difficult goal,   10
Those do-as-you-like "free spirits," la-dee-dee!

Nose to the grindstone first, if aims are glorious.
Mastery's much in little, tight control.
Rules! They're a springboard only, and we're *free!*

FRIEDRICH VON SCHILLER

[1759–1805]

Ode to Joy

TRANSLATED BY NORMAN MACLEOD AND ALEXANDER GODE–VON AESCH

Joy, of flame celestial fashioned,
    Daughter of Elysium,
By that holy fire impassioned
    To thy sanctuary we come.
Thine the spells that reunited   5
    Those estranged by Custom dread,
Every man a brother plighted
    Where thy gentle wings are spread.
        Millions in our arms we gather,
            To the world our kiss be sent!   10
            Past the starry firmament,
        Brothers, dwells a loving Father.

Who that height of bliss has provèd
    Once a friend of friends to be,
Who has won a maid belovèd   15
    Join us in our jubilee.
Whoso holds a heart in keeping,
    One—in all the world—his own—
Who has failed, let him with weeping
    From our fellowship begone!   20
        All the mighty globe containeth
            Homage to Compassion pay!
            To the stars she leads the way
        Where, unknown, the Godhead reigneth.

All drink joy from Mother Nature,   25
    All she suckled at her breast,
Good or evil, every creature,
    Follows where her foot has pressed.
Love she gave us, passing measure,
    One Who true in death abode,   30
E'en the worm was granted pleasure,
    Angels see the face of God.
        Fall ye millions, fall before Him,
           Is thy Maker, World, unknown?
           Far above the stars His throne   35
        Yonder seek Him and adore Him.

Joy, the spring of all contriving,
    In eternal Nature's plan,
Joy set wheels on wheels a-driving
    Since earth's horologe began;   40
From the bud the blossom winning
    Suns from out the sky she drew
Spheres through boundless ether spinning
    Worlds no gazer's science knew.
        Gladsome as her suns and glorious   45
           Through the spacious heavens career,
           Brothers, so your courses steer
        Heroes joyful and victorious.

She from Truth's own mirror shining
    Casts on sages glances gay,   50
Guides the sufferer unrepining
    Far up Virtue's steepest way;
On the hills of Faith all-glorious
    Mark her sunlit banners fly,
She, in death's despite, victorious,   55
    Stands with angels in the sky.
        Millions, bravely sorrows bearing,
           Suffer for a better time!
           See, above the starry clime
        God a great reward preparing.   60

Men may never match Immortals;
    Fair it is like Gods to be
Welcome to our joyous portals
    Sons of Want and Poverty.
Rancor and resentment leaving,   65
    Be our mortal foe forgiven,

Not a sorrow for his grieving,
  Not a tear to mar his heaven!
    Pardon every debt ungrudging,
      Let all nations be atoned!   70
      God above the stars enthroned
  Judges us, as we are judging.

Savages drink gentler notions
  While the meek learn to be bold
Through the joy of sparkling potions   75
  In the goblet's liquid gold.
Brothers, rise! In kindred feeling
  Let the goblet make the rounds.
While the foam spurts to the ceiling,
  Drink to Him whose love abounds.   80
    Him whose praise through stellar spaces
      Like a seraphs' chorus sounds,
      Drink to Him whose love abounds,
    Praise Him by your joyous faces.

Hearts in direst need unquailing,   85
  Aid to Innocence in woe,
Troth eternally unfailing,
  Loyalty to friend and foe!
Fronting kings, a manly spirit,
  Though it cost our wealth and blood!   90
Crowns to nought save noblest merit,
  Death to all the Liars' brood!
    Close the holy circle. Ever
      Swear it by the wine of gold,
      Swear these sacred vows to hold,   95
    Swear it by the stars' Lawgiver.

FRIEDRICH HÖLDERLIN

[1770–1843]

Fall

TRANSLATED BY HEDWIG HELLMANN

This is the Fall, which yet will break your heart!
Fly away, fly away!—
The sun creeps to the hills

And climbs and climbs
And rests with every step. 5

How wilted grew the world!
On wearily strung threads the wind
Intunes its song.
Hope has fled,
Wind mourns for her. 10

This is the Fall, which yet will break your heart!
Fly away, fly away!—
Fruit of the tree,
You tremble, fall?
What secret must have taught to you the night 15
That icy shudders cover
Your cheek, the purple cheek?

You stay mute, you answer not?
Who is it speaks?
This is the Fall, which yet will break your heart! 20
Fly away, fly away!—
"I am not handsome,"
The aster tells me,
"Yet I love mankind
And comfort mankind, 25
They shall see flowers still now
And bend down for me
Alas! and pick me—
Then from their eyes remembrance
Glitters forth, 30
Remembrance of more handsome things than I:—
I see it, see it, and thus I die."

This is the Fall, which yet will break your heart!
Fly away, fly away!

ANNETTE VON DROSTE-HÜLSHOFF

[1797–1848]

On the Tower

TRANSLATED BY JAMES EDWARD TOBIN

I stand high in the belfry tower,
Where starlings scream and swirl in air;

As though I were a maenad, Storm,
You run your fingers through my hair.
O spirit free, entrancing youth,   5
Here at the very railing, I
Would wrestle, hip to hip, against
Your hold; become alive—or die.

Below, along the sandy beach,
I see the whitecaps leap in play   10
Like frisky hounds tumbling the surf,
Darting in hissing, sparkling spray.
Oh, I would join them in their game,
Pursuing walrus, sportive prey,
Leading the romping pack through glades   15
Of coral, hunting dolphins gay.

Far off I see a pennant stream,
Bold as an admiral's banner;
I watch the masts bob in the sea,
From safe in my high-towered manor.   20
Oh, I would rule that tossing ship
And hold helm firm and guide her true,
Skim lightly over foaming reefs
As brushing wings of seagulls do.

If I could hunt the open fields,   25
Or march to war, a soldier tall,
If heaven listened to my plea,
Made me a man, even though small!
Instead, I sit here—delicate,
Polite, precise, well-mannered child.   30
Dreams shake my loosened hair—the wind
Lone listener to my spirit wild.

HEINRICH HEINE

[1797–1856]

Die Lore-Ley	*The Lorelei*

TRANSLATED BY EDWIN MORGAN

Ich weiß nicht, was soll es bedeuten,	Whit wey° is my hert sae eerie?	*why, how*
Daß ich so traurig bin;	I speir,° but I speir in vain.	*ask*
Ein Märchen aus alten Zeiten,	An auld auld tale has seized me	
Das kommt mir nicht aus dem Sinn.	And it winna° leave my brain.	*will not*

Die Luft ist kühl und es dunkelt,	In the caller° air o the gloamin	cool, fresh 5
Und ruhig flieβ der Rhein;	The Rhine slides lown° and quaet;°	calm/quiet
Der Gipfel des Berges funkelt	Westlins° the sun gangs rovan	westward
Im Abendsonnenschein.	And the hill-taps glint wi't.	
Die schönste Jungfrau sitzet	There's a ferlie° up yonder, a lassie	marvelous thing
Dort oben wunderbar,	As fair as the day sits there;	10
Ihr goldnes Geschmeide blitzet,	Her gowdie-gauds° skimmer°	golden jewelry/sparkle
	and dazzle	
Sie kämmt ihr goldenes Haar.	As she kaims her gowden hair.	
Sie kämmt es mit goldenem Kamme,	She kaims wi a gowden kaimie,°	comb
Und singt ein Lied dabei;	And whiles she sings a sang;	
Das hat eine wundersame,	Its ringan melodie dazes	15
Gewaltige Melodei.	As it echoes lang and lang.	
Den Schiffer im kleinen Schiffe	The boatman's taen by her music,	
Ergreift es mit wildem Weh;	He stoonds° to the wild wild notes,	thrills, throbs
Er schaut nicht die Felsenriffe,	His een are abune in his furie,	
Er schaut nur hinauf in die Höh.	He seesna the scaurs° whaur he floats.	rocks 20
Ich glaube, die Wellen verschlingen	But I see the chiel at his driftin,	
Am Ende Schiffer und Kahn;	And his boat, baith droont in the swaw.°	wave
Und das hat mit ihrem Singen	And this was the end o her liltin,	
Die Lore-Ley getan.	The Lorelei wan° them awa.	won

RAINER MARIA RILKE

[1875–1926]

## Der Panther	## The Panther
IM JARDIN DES PLANTES, PARIS	IN THE JARDIN DES PLANTES, PARIS
	TRANSLATED BY STEPHEN MITCHELL

Sein Blick ist vom Vorübergehn der Stäbe		His vision, from the constantly passing bars,
so müd geworden, daβ er nichts mehr hält.		has grown so weary that it cannot hold
Ihm ist, als ob es tausend Stäbe gäbe		anything else. It seems to him there are
und hinter tausend Stäben keine Welt.		a thousand bars; and behind the bars, no world.
Der weiche Gang geschmeidig starker	5	As he paces in cramped circles, over and over,
Schritte,		
der sich im allerkleinsten Kreise dreht,		the movement of his powerful soft strides

ist wie ein Tanz von Kraft um eine Mitte,
in der betäubt ein großer Wille steht.

Nur manchmal schiebt der Vorhang der
    Pupille
sich lautlos auf—. Dann geht ein Bild hinein,   10
geht durch der Glieder angespannte Stille—
und hört im Herzen auf zu sein.

is like a ritual dance around a center
in which a mighty will stands paralyzed.

Only at times, the curtain of the pupils

lifts, quietly—. An image enters in,
rushes down through the tensed, arrested muscles,
plunges into the heart and is gone.

The Cadet Picture of My Father

ADAPTED BY ROBERT LOWELL

There's absence in the eyes. The brow's in touch
with something far. Now distant boyishness
and seduction shadow his enormous lips,
the slender aristocratic uniform
with its Franz Josef braid; both the hands bulge   5
like gloves upon the saber's basket hilt.
The hands are quiet, they reach out toward nothing—

I hardly see them now, as if they were
the first to grasp distance and disappear,
and all the rest lies curtained in itself,   10
and so withdrawn, I cannot understand
my father as he bleaches on this page—

Oh quickly disappearing photograph
in my more slowly disappearing hand!

Buddha in Glory

TRANSLATED BY STEPHEN MITCHELL

Center of all centers, core of cores,
almond self-enclosed and growing sweet—
all this universe, to the furthest stars
and beyond them, is your flesh, your fruit.

Now you feel how nothing clings to you;   5
your vast shell reaches into endless space,
and there the rich, thick fluids rise and flow.
Illuminated in your infinite peace,

a billion stars go spinning through the night,
blazing high above your head.   10
But *in* you is the presence that
will be, when all the stars are dead.

GEORG TRAKL

[1887–1914]

Decline

TO KARL BORROMÄUS HEINRICH

TRANSLATED BY MICHAEL HAMBURGER

Over the white pond
The wild birds have traveled on.
In the evening an icy wind blows from our stars.

Over our graves
The broken brow of the night inclines.   5
Under oak trees we sway in a silver boat.

Always the town's white walls resound.
Under arches of thorns,
O my brother, blind minute-hands,
We climb towards midnight.   10

HANS (JEAN) ARP

[1887–1966]

Kaspar Is Dead

TRANSLATED BY JOACHIM NEVGROSCHELL

alas our good kaspar is dead.
who will conceal the burning banner in the cloud's pigtail now and blackly thumb
   his daily nose.

who will run the coffee grinder in the primeval cask now.
who will entice the idyllic deer out of the petrified bag.
who will blow the noses of ships umbrellas beekeepers ozone-spindles and bone the
    pyramids.   5
alas alas alas our good kaspar is dead. goodness gracious me kaspar is dead.
the hay-fish in the bell-barns chatter heartbreakingly whenever his first name is uttered.
    that's why i keep on sighing his surname kaspar kaspar kaspar.
why hast thou forsaken us. into what shape has your great wonderful soul migrated.
    are you a star now or a chain of water on a hot cyclone or an udder of
    black light or a transparent brick on the moaning drum of craggy existence.
now our crowns and our soles are drying up and the fairies are lying half-charred
    at the stake.
now the black bowling alley is booming behind the sun and no one is winding the
    compasses or the handbarrow wheels any more.   10
who will eat with the phosphorescent rat at the lonesome barefoot table.
who will drive out the siroccoco-devil when he tries to lure the horses away.
who will interpret the monograms in the stars for us.
his bust will grace the mantels of all truly noble men but that's no solace or snuff
    for a death's-head.

LEONIE NELLY SACHS

[1891–1970]

O the chimneys

TRANSLATED BY MICHAEL ROLOFF

And though after my skin worms destroy this
body, yet in my flesh shall I see God.
          —JOB 19:26

O the chimneys
On the ingeniously devised habitations of death
When Israel's body drifted as smoke
Through the air—
Was welcomed by a star, a chimney sweep,   5
A star that turned black
Or was it a ray of sun?

O the chimneys!
Freedomway for Jeremiah and Job's dust—
Who devised you and laid stone upon stone   10
The road for refugees of smoke?

O the habitations of death,
Invitingly appointed
For the host who used to be a guest—
O you fingers   15
Laying the threshold
Like a knife between life and death—

O you chimneys,
O you fingers
And Israel's body as smoke through the air!   20

BERTOLT BRECHT

[1898–1956]

Song on Black Saturday at the Eleventh Hour of the Night Before Easter

TRANSLATED BY LESLEY LENDRUM

1

In spring between green skies and wild
Enamoured winds part animal already
I went down into the black cities
Papered inside with chilly words to say.

2

I filled myself with animals of asphalt
I filled myself with screaming and with water
But, my dear fellow, all that left me cold
I stayed as light and empty as before.

3

They came and battered holes right through my walls
And crawled with curses out of me again:

Nothing inside but masses of space and silence
They cursed and screamed: I must be a paper man.

4

Grinning I rolled downwards between houses
Out into the open. The grave soft wind
Now ran more swiftly through my walls
It was still snowing. Into me it rained.

5

The wretched snouts of cynical fellows have
Discovered how empty I must be.
Wild pigs have coupled in me. Ravens
Of the milky sky pissed often into me.

6

Weaker than clouds are! Lighter than the winds!
Invisible! Solemn, brutish, light
Like one of my own poems I flew through the sky
Along with a stork of somewhat faster flight!

PAUL CELAN

[1920–1970]

Fugue of Death

TRANSLATED BY DONALD WHITE

Coal-black milk of morning we drink it at sundown
we drink it at noon and at dawning we drink it at night
we drink it and drink it
we'll shovel a grave in the heavens there's no crowding there
A man's in the house he plays with his serpents he writes   5
he writes back home when the dark comes your golden hair Margareta
he writes it and then leaves the house and the stars are atwinkle he whistles
   his dogs to come near
he whistles his Jews to come here and shovel a grave in the earth
he commands us play sweet now for dancing

Coal-black milk of morning we drink thee at night   10
we drink thee at dawning at noontime we drink thee at sundown

we drink thee and drink thee
A man's in the house he plays with his serpents he writes
he writes back home when the dark comes your golden hair Margareta
your ashen hair Shulamite we'll shovel a grave in the heavens there's
   no crowding there   15

He shouts you there get the earth open deeper you here sing and play for the dance
he grabs at the gun in his belt he lifts it his eyes are bright blue
you there get the earth open faster you others play on now for dancing

Coal-black milk of morning we drink thee at night
we drink thee at noon and at dawning we drink thee at sundown   20
we drink thee and drink thee
a man's in the house your golden hair Margareta
your ashen hair Shulamite he plays with his serpents

He shouts play death very sweet now Death is a proud German master
he shouts make the fiddles sing darker you'll rise as grey smoke in the air   25
your grave will be high in the clouds there's no crowding there

Coal-black milk of morning we drink thee at night
we drink thee at noontime and Death is a proud German master
we drink thee at dawning and sundown we drink thee and drink thee
and Death is a proud German master his eyes are bright blue   30
he'll get you with missile of lead he will pierce you right through
a man's in the house your golden hair Margareta
he'll sic his big dogs on us all he'll give us a grave in the sky
he plays with his snakes he dreams nightly and Death is a proud German master

your golden hair Margareta   35
your ashen hair Shulamite

Todesfuge

Schwarze Milch der Frühe wir trinken sie abends
wir trinken sie mittags und morgens wir trinken sie nachts
wir trinken und trinken
wir schaufeln ein Grab in den Lüften da liegt man nicht eng
Ein Mann wohnt im Haus der spielt mit den Schlangen der schreibt
der schreibt wenn es dunkelt nach Deutschland dein goldenes Haar Margarete
er schreibt es und tritt vor das Haus und es blitzen die Sterne er pfeift seine Rüden
   herbei

er pfeift seine Juden hervor läßt schaufeln ein Grab in der Erde
er befiehlt uns spielt auf nun zum Tanz

Schwarze Milch der Frühe wir trinken dich nachts
wir trinken dich morgens und mittags wir trinken dich abends
wir trinken und trinken
Ein Mann wohnt im Haus der spielt mit den Schlangen der schreibt
der schreibt wenn es dunkelt nach Deutschland dein goldenes Haar Margarete
Dein aschenes Haar Sulamith wir schaufeln ein Grab in den Lüften da liegt man nicht
    eng

Er ruft stecht tiefer ins Erdreich ihr einen ihr andern singet und spielt
er greift nach dem Eisen im Gurt er schwingts seine Augen sind blau
stecht tiefer die Spaten ihr einen ihr andern spielt weiter zum Tanz auf

Schwarze Milch der Frühe wir trinken dich nachts
wir trinken dich mittags und morgens wir trinken dich abends
wir trinken und trinken
ein Mann wohnt im Haus dein goldenes Haar Margarete
dein aschenes Haar Sulamith er spielt mit den Schlangen

Er ruft spielt süßer den Tod der Tod ist ein Meister aus Deutschland
er ruft streicht dunkler die Geigen dann steigt ihr als Rauch in die Luft
dann habt ihr ein Grab in den Wolken da liegt man nicht eng

Schwarze Milch der Frühre wir trinken dich nachts
wir trinken dich mittags der Tod ist ein Meister aus Deutschland
wir trinken dich abends und morgens wir trinken und trinken
der Tod ist ein Meister aus Deutschland sein Auge ist blau
er trifft dich mit bleierner Kugel er trifft dich genau
ein Mann wohnt im Haus dein goldenes Haar Margarete
er hetzt seine Rüden auf uns er schenkt uns ein Grab in der Luft
er spielt mit den Schlangen und träumet der Tod ist ein Meister aus Deutschland

dein goldenes Haar Margarete
dein aschenes Haar Sulamith

Native American Poetry

Native American poetry begins as incantation, chant, and song often associated with the dance, where the dancer's motion emphasizes his or her oneness with the earth. The poem–dance, moreover, also kinetically expresses the Native American's bond with life beyond the senses. Varying in length from a few words to ceremonial productions that might run for days, Native American poems were presumed to have been inspired by the gods, and correspondingly were often used to evoke a god's help. As one Native American has commented, "If a man is to do something more than human, he must have more than human power."

Since Native American poetry was a component of daily tribal life, everyone was considered a poet. Songs and poems, however, were rarely used for entertainment. Instead, they were associated with important aspects of daily life. There were sacred songs to greet the sun, to ease labor, to guide the medicine man's healing ritual, to plant seeds, to raise the spirits of warriors before battle, and to curse an enemy or charm a lover. Poetry marked the marriage of husband and wife and ushered in the birth of a child. Mothers crooned to their babies, and every man acknowledged death, even his own, with a poem.

Native American poetry is a poetry of many different languages and of many different peoples. It is estimated that over two thousand separate languages were spoken by Native American peoples at the time of European contact; many of these languages show as great a difference between them as do French and German. Today five hundred or so of America's native languages are still spoken.

Considering the diversity of Native American cultures and languages, it is no wonder that the themes and content of tribal poetry vary as much as they do. For example, poetry from Southwestern peoples often emphasizes ritual and group solidarity, as befits a farming community. Plains, plateau, and prairie Native Americans, who were hunters, have left a body of literature that is often more personal and individualistic. Poetry from Northwestern peoples, in turn, stresses trade and town life. Still, the differences among the cultures do not outweigh their great similarities.

Recent study focuses on these similarities by stressing certain recurring aspects of Native American poetry. For example, a strong faith in the power of words to affect the cosmos surfaces in such repeated expressions as "Drink my blood!" and "my god descended." Here language is not a preface to action; it *is* action. To speak the words is to achieve the magic. Similarly, much Native American poetry also underscores the spirit life of objects, animals, and nature as exemplified in the phrase "Now the wind begins singing." Though this may at first glance appear to be mere personification, it would be more accurate to read such a line as the person literally listening to the song of a god. Along the same lines, spirits might inspire a person through dreams or visions. Once the dream is spoken, its power is made operative. Finally, another common theme in Native American poetry is the un-self-conscious life of personal anonymity in which the human voice is experienced as an extension of tribal culture. As such, individual authorship is impossible, and all poetry is communal property.

Because most Native American poetry was in the oral tradition, few ancestral songs of the many languages spoken survive. The Aztecs, however, not only recorded their poetry but conducted schools for poets known as "houses of song." These academies trained poets and sponsored poetry contests. Cherokee formulas, Iroquois mnemonic beads, Mayan stone glyphs, and Mextec codices (bark-paper books painted with glyphs) also recorded poetry and were translated or transposed into Spanish and English by Native Americans who had learned the Latin alphabet. Much of Native American poetry, however, has come to us through translations by ethnologists like Henry Rowe Schoolcraft, whose study of Native American poetry in 1851 included this Chippewa text with an accompanying literal translation.

Chant to the Fire-fly

> *Wau tay see!*
> *Wau tay see!*
> *E mow e shin*
> *Tahe bwau ne baun-e wee!*
> *Be eghaun-be eghaun-ewee!*
> *Wau tay see!*
> *Wau tay see!*
> *Was sa koon ain je gun.*
> *Was sa koon ain je gun.*

Flitting-white-fire-insect! waving-white-fire-bug! give me light before I go to bed! give me light before I go to sleep. Come, little dancing white-fire-bug! Come, little flitting white-fire-beast! Light me with your bright white-flame-instrument your little candle.

Of the poetry that does survive, we can see that its stylistic techniques include rhythm (often associated with elaborate drum beats), motif, imagery, contrast, repetition, variation, personification, euphony, onomatopoeia, and various melodic schemes. Structure in a poem often takes the pattern of paired words or "rhyming thoughts" such as light and dark, sun and rain, Father Sky and Mother Earth. However, the range and structures of tribal poetry cannot be fully understood in terms of the closed definitions of European-rooted formal poetry. Tribal poetry often employed mixed media, and as such might better be approached in the spirit of modern open-form poetry and experimental intermedia poetry.

Presently, Native American life and poetry are in a state of transition. Native American Indian poets now write in the same styles as other modern American poets. Though their subject matter may be Native American, they may draw as much on imagism, symbolism, surrealism, and modernist theory as on techniques associated with tribal composition.

Among the Native American poets writing today, N. Scott Momaday (b. 1934) won a Pulitzer Prize in 1969 for his novel *House Made of Dawn*. Combining myth and history in another book, *The Way to Rainy Mountain*, Momaday tells the story of his tribe, the Kiowas. In his poem "Angle of Geese," Momaday focuses on the inadequacy of language to contend with dying. Often writing in the tradition of the Symbolists, Momaday has published several books of poetry, including *The Angle of Geese and Other Poems*, *The Gourd Dancer*, and *The Names*.

Duane Niatum (b. 1938), a graduate of the Johns Hopkins Writing Seminars, is a member of the Klallam tribe, whose ancestral lands are on the Washington Coast along the Strait of Juan de Fuca. Seeing his Native American ancestry as central to his poetry, he writes, "My roots are in the earth and sky philosophies and arts of my ancestors." Intensely lyrical and often bordering on mysticism, Niatum quotes Andrew Joe of the Skagit Tribe to sum up the Native American sensibility: "When we can understand animals, we will know the change is halfway. When we can talk to the forest, we will know that change has come." Duane Niatum's books include *After the Death of an Elder Klallam*, *Ascending Red Cedar Moon*, *Digging Out the Roots*, and *Songs for the Harvester of Dreams*.

Influenced by the poetry of César Vallejo (who was half Native American), James Welch (b. 1940) often fuses the traditional Native American practice of dream writing with modern surrealism, as in his "Magic Fox." A Blackfoot on his father's side and a Gros Ventre on his mother's, James Welch's books include a volume of poetry, *Riding the Earthboy 40*, and two novels, *Winter in the Blood* and *The Death of Jim Lonely*.

A contemporary Native American poet known primarily as a fiction writer, Leslie Marmon Silko (b. 1948) often conveys the continuity of life beyond the individual in her writings. Focusing on themes of transformation, her poetry is both narrative and lyrical, direct and imagistic. Her books include *Laguna Woman*, the novel *Ceremony*, and the collection of stories *Storyteller*.

A fiction writer as well as a poet, Louise Erdrich (b. 1954) grew up in North Dakota near the Turtle Mountain Reservation. Drawing on her Chippewa background, she often combines Native American mythology with contemporary narrative technique, allowing her characters to unfold as complex psychological entities. She is the author of a collection of poetry, *Jacklight*, and two novels, *Love Medicine*, winner of the National Book Critics' Circle Award and the American Academy of Arts and Letters prize, and *The Beet Queen*. A graduate of the Johns Hopkins Writing Seminars, she presently lives in Cornish, New Hampshire.

MAYAN

The moon and the year

TRANSLATED FROM THE SPANISH BY JOHN BIERHORST

The moon and the year
travel and pass away:
also the day, also the wind.
Also the flesh passes away
to the place of its quietness.   5

AZTEC

A Woman's Complaint

TRANSLATED BY MIGUEL LÉON-PORTILLA

What shall I do? My man compares me
to a wild red flower.
When I have withered in his hands,
he will leave me.

The artist

TRANSLATED BY DENISE LEVERTOV

The artist: disciple, abundant, multiple, restless.
The true artist: capable, practicing, skillful;
maintains dialogue with his heart, meets things with his mind.
The true artist: draws out all from his heart,

works with delight, makes things with calm, with sagacity,   5
works like a true Toltec, composes his objects, works dexterously, invents;
arranges materials, adorns them, makes them adjust.

The carrion artist: works at random, sneers at the people,
makes things opaque, brushes across the surface of the face of things,
works without care, defrauds people, is a thief.   10

CHIPPEWA

Dream Song

TRANSLATED BY FRANCES DENSMORE

Sometimes
I go about pitying myself
While I am carried by the wind
Across the sky

WHITE MOUNTAIN APACHE

What Happened to a Young Man in a Place Where He Turned to Water

TRANSLATED BY ANSELM HOLLO, AFTER PLINY EARLE GODDARD

1

no sleep for twelve days
then found himself in a circle of water girls
"come dance with us"
water people
they say   5
were dancing with him

ahead of the water they came
they were water
the water's soft feathers were theirs

closer they came
and to the very end of the water   10
closer and closer
their hands were electric

fog people
danced with him they say   15
where the fog was a wall
they came
they were fog
the fog's soft feathers
were theirs   20

closer they came
to the very end of the fog
closer and closer
their hands were electric

the moon before him they say   25
high as a woman's head
or no higher

the sun before him they say
no higher than a man's head
or as high   30

"come dance with us"

again no sleep for twelve days

2

he woke up and saw
only one had stayed
(remembered stumbling   35
over her foot in the dance)

they say those two
went away
to where the country is great with maize
there they sat down   40

they went
where the country grows beautiful pumpkins
there they lay down

great maize
            strong roots   45
                  big stalks

big pumpkin
            long tendrils
                  wide leaves
where the sun rises   50
as soon as it sets

yellow-top pumpkin
            big-bellied
strong maize
            with a bushy tassel   55

pollen
    and
        dew

3

he came back here
where people were living   60
his mother was angry but she forgave him
he went and hunted the deer with his brother

PIMA

Song of the Fallen Deer

TRANSLATED BY FRANK RUSSELL

At the time of the White Dawn;
    At the time of the White Dawn,
I arose and went away.
    At Blue Nightfall I went away.

I ate the thornapple leaves   5
    And the leaves made me dizzy.
I drank the thornapple flowers
    And the drink made me stagger.

The hunter, Bow-Remaining,
    He overtook and killed me,   10

Cut and threw my horns away.
   The hunter, Reed-Remaining,
He overtook and killed me,
   Cut and threw my feet away.

Now the flies become crazy   *15*
   And they drop with flapping wings.
The drunken butterflies sit
   With opening and shutting wings.

ARAPAHO

I Gave Them Fruits

TRANSLATED BY JAMES MOONEY

1

My children, when at first I liked the whites,
My children, when at first I liked the whites,
I gave them fruits,
I gave them fruits.

2

Father, have pity on me,   *5*
Father, have pity on me;
I am crying for thirst,
I am crying for thirst;
All is gone—I have nothing to eat,
All is gone—I have nothing to eat.   *10*

N. SCOTT MOMADAY

[b. 1934]

Angle of Geese

   How shall we adorn
   Recognition with our speech?—
   Now the dead firstborn
   Will lag in the wake of words.

Custom intervenes;   *5*
We are civil, something more:
   More than language means,
The mute presence mulls and marks.

Almost of a mind,
We take measure of the loss;   *10*
   I am slow to find
The mere margin of repose.

And one November
It was longer in the watch,
   As if forever,   *15*
Of the huge ancestral goose.

So much symmetry!
Like the pale angle of time
   And eternity.
The great shape labored and fell.   *20*

Quit of hope and hurt,
It held a motionless gaze,
   Wide of time, alert,
On the dark distant flurry.

DUANE NIATUM

[b. 1938]

Chief Leschi of the Nisqually

He awoke this morning uneasily from a dream;
Thunderbird had crashed through
the jail wall like a club.
And from its circle, Nisqually women

led him back to their river, the dance of its song.   *5*
For a few changes in the wind
he burned in the forest like a red cedar,

his branches fanning blue flames
toward the white men taking the camas valley
for their pigs and cows.   10
Musing over wolf tracks, the offspring of snow,
the memory of his wives and children
keeps him mute. Flickering in the dawn embers,
his faith grows grizzly, tricks the soldiers
like a fawn, sleeping as the brush.   15
The soldiers make jokes about his fate,
frozen as a bat against their throat.
Still, death will take him

only to his father's burial mound,
past the rope's sinewy snap.   20
The bars lock in but his tired body; he will
eat little and speak less before he hangs.

JAMES WELCH

[b. 1940]

Magic Fox

They shook the green leaves down,
those men that rattled
in their sleep. Truth became
a nightmare to their fox.
He turned their horses into fish,   5
or was it horses strung
like fish, or fish like fish
hung naked in the wind?

Stars fell upon their catch.
A girl, not yet twenty-four   10
but blonde as morning birds, began
a dance that drew the men in
green around her skirts.
In dust her magic jangled memories
of dawn, till fox and grief   15
turned nightmare in their sleep.

And this: fish not fish but stars
that fell into their dreams.

LESLIE MARMON SILKO

[b. 1948]

Slim Man Canyon

FOR JOHN, MAY 1972

700 years ago
        people were living here
        water was running gently
        and the sun was warm on pumpkin flowers.
It was 700 years ago   5
        I remember
they were here
        deep in this canyon
        with sandstone walls rising high above them.
The rock, the silence, tall sky and flowing water   10
        sunshine through cottonwood leaves
        the willow smell in the wind
                    700 years ago.

The rhythm,
        the horses' feet, moving strong through   15
            white deep sand.
Where I come from is like this
        the warmth, the fragrance, the silence.
Blue sky and rainclouds in the distance
        we ride together   20
past the cliffs with the stories
        the songs painted on rocks. . . .
        There was a man who loved a woman
        seven hundred years ago.

LOUISE ERDRICH

[b. 1954]

Indian Boarding School: The Runaways

Home's the place we head for in our sleep.
Boxcars stumbling north in dreams
don't wait for us. We catch them on the run.
The rails, old lacerations that we love,

shoot parallel across the face and break   *5*
just under Turtle Mountains. Riding scars
you can't get lost. Home is the place they cross.

The lame guard strikes a match and makes the dark
less tolerant. We watch through cracks in boards
as the land starts rolling, rolling till it hurts   *10*
to be here, cold in regulation clothes.
We know the sheriff's waiting at midrun
to take us back. His car is dumb and warm.
The highway doesn't rock, it only hums
like a wing of long insults. The worn-down welts   *15*
of ancient punishments lead back and forth.

All runaways wear dresses, long green ones,
the color you would think shame was. We scrub
the sidewalks down because it's shameful work.
Our brushes cut the stone in watered arcs   *20*
and in the soak frail outlines shiver clear
a moment, things us kids pressed on the dark
face before it hardened, place, remembering
delicate old injuries, the spines of names and leaves.

African Poetry

An old Peulh proverb, from Africa, defines poetry as "words pleasing to the heart and ear." Although some African poetry was written down more than a thousand years ago, until recently, the majority of African poetry was part of the oral tradition. As such, poetry played an important role in daily tribal life, often taking the form of proverb and song. Poems recorded tribal history and philosophy, celebrated warriors, satirized enemies, honored leaders, and revered the gods. Work songs strengthened farmers as they planted seeds or tapped palm trees for wine, and songs heartened canoe paddlers on their journeys across lakes and down rivers. Women chanted poems while weaving, and they sang to their children at play. Poems would register a person's birth and rites of passage to adulthood, marriage, and eventual death. Consider, for example, the following traditional Ewe mourning poem, or lament, which is part of a burial ceremony:

Na ye e e!   *Mother dear!*

TRANSLATED BY GEORMBECYI ADALI—MORTTY

Na ye e e!   Mother dear!
  Na mumũa na 'mela   Mother, who freely gives of what she has:
  Ɖaɖa na 'mela   fresh food and cooked meals alike.
Na mlenuɖee   Mother, who never deserts the hearth,
Na yɔ mele!   5   Mother, hearken to me!
  Azi favi megbea na yɔɔ o.   The crying child will call after its mother.
  Mele na yɔɔ metoa nam o.   How is it that mother does not answer me when I call?

  Dzre wɔɔ míle dzã?   Are we quarrelling?

The poem's ideas are arranged in pairs, not unlike the "rhyming thoughts" in traditional Native American poetry. The poem also uses assonance to stress the mourner's cry. Addressing the corpse, the speaker forcefully understates the grief and confusion associated with the death of the mother, asking "Are we quarrelling?"

Techniques associated with traditional African oral poetry incorporate most of those identified with traditional European and American poetry, including the regular as well as irregular line, imagery, metaphor, allegory, and motif. Sound devices include rhythm, rhyme, meter, assonance, alliteration, and onomatopoeia. Traditional African poetry, however, often stresses improvisation, and a person's ability to compose poetry during communal functions has long been greatly valued. Still, many poems were memorized and handed down from one *griot*, or virtuoso poet, to another.

Recent scholarship suggests that there are literally hundreds of languages spoken in Africa today—including Sesotho, Xhosa, Zulu, Nyanja, Bemba, Shona, Swahili, Luganda, Yoruba, Asante-Twi, and Ewe, to mention a few. Thus we need to remember that the term "African poetry" refers to the poetry of many diverse cultures. This diversity of indigenous languages and cultures is further complicated by the European cultures that set out to colonize the African continent. When we turn to modern African poetry, therefore, we find that much of it is written in two European languages—notably French (called Francophone) and English (called Anglophone). (Poetry is also being written in Portuguese—called Lusophone—but it is not as well known outside Africa.) Each of these cultures, in turn, has added its own sense of what a poem might be to any existing indigenous understanding of poetry. This great diversity and transplantation of cultures forces modern readers to reconsider exactly who an African poet might be. Aimé Césaire (p. 1083), for example, is one of the founders of Négritude and is considered both a French poet living in Paris and an African poet, though he was born in Martinique in the French Caribbean. (See the introduction to "French Language Poetry," (pp. 1064–1067) we have selected only those poets born in Africa for this section of the book.)

Enriched by many languages and diverse societies, modern African poetry has gained international recognition within the last sixty years by producing poets of the highest caliber. Jean-Joseph Rabéarivelo (1901–1937), for example, was the first modern African poet to publish in French. Born in Madagascar, he published his first book, *The Cup of Ashes*, at age twenty-four. A great admirer of the French poet Charles Baudelaire (p. 1074) and influenced by Walt Whitman (pp. 424–428), Rabéarivelo went on to master open-form poems of unique and compelling power. His highly evocative poetry is not concerned with social or political themes but explores the boundaries between objective and subjective realities that, as he writes, "rustle with what is unreal / unreal from being too real / like dreams." A life of isolation eventually overwhelmed Rabéarivelo with despair, and he committed suicide in 1937, when French authorities refused to let him travel to France. His books include *Little Poems* and *Scrolls*.

Francophone poetry as a literary movement, however, did not attract international attention until African and Caribbean students in Paris launched a literary and philosophical movement known as Négritude. This highly compelling movement sought to restore the cultural individuality and dignity of black Africans of the great diaspora. Influenced by Surrealism as well as by Langston Hughes (pp. 689–698) and the Harlem Renaissance, Négritude poets emphasized African humanity and individuality. One of Négritude's founders, Léopold Sédar Senghor (b. 1906), described the African's predicament under European colonial rule when he wrote that, according to Europeans, "We had neither carved, painted nor sung." A Senegalese poet and diplomat, by the end of World War II Senghor had already published his first volumes of verse, edited an influential anthology of Négritude poetry, and helped establish *Présence Africaine* as one of the most important literary journals in the black world. After the war he went on to lead the Senegalese struggle for independence and became president of Senegal from 1960 to 1980. A scholar and philosopher as well as a poet, he was elected to the French Academy of Moral and Political Sciences and, in 1984, became the first black member of the French Academy. Primarily a lyric poet, his books include *Songs of the Shade, Éthiopiques,* and *On African Socialism.*

Another Senegalese poet, Birago Diop (b. 1906), grew up on the northwest coast of Senegal. Writing in French, Diop nevertheless drew heavily on indigenous Senegalese sources, including traditional oral forms, rhythms, narratives, and themes. His poem "Diptych" is considered a haunting summoning of ancient African religious beliefs, drawing on African reverence for the dead and the belief in their power to influence the living. His books include *Gleams and Glimmers* and a collection of fables and legends, *Tales of Amadou Koumba.*

Another African poet of international stature, Tchicaya U Tam'si (b. 1929) was born in the Congo Republic and is considered the major Francophone poet now writing. A novelist, playwright, and short story writer as well as a poet, U Tam'si is an international figure and world traveler who describes himself as a cultural "pillager." He writes, "Europe went to the four corners for what it needed . . . I would like to bring the Rhine to the Congo, the Louvre to the Congo. I would like us to be rich with everything mankind has ever produced." Seeing Arthur Rimbaud (p. 1076) as the "essential poet," U Tam'si made his first book of poetry, *Bad Blood,* a response to Rimbaud's *A Season in Hell.* Senghor has stated that U Tam'si's poetry has "the most authentic qualities of African poetry . . . For the image is the only thread that leads from one heart to another, the only flame that consumes and consummates the soul." U Tam'si's books of poetry include *Brush Fire* and *Bow Harp.*

Shifting now to African poetry written in English, we can state that the Anglophone literary movement emerged later than the French, with the first major works appearing in the 1950s. Primarily interested in reexamining African history from an indigenous point of view rather than filtering it through a Eurocentric aesthetic, these poets concentrated on the dignity of the African past without idealizing it. Today the literary accent in West Africa focuses on the present.

Wole Soyinka (b. 1934), a Nigerian poet, novelist, and playwright, often focuses on the contradictory forces that shape human life. Drawing on African and European influences, Soyinka melds Western poetic and dramatic techniques with African philosophies. His pantheon includes Shakespeare as well as traditional

Yoruba gods. As such, the imagistic qualities of his native speech combine with traditional Yoruba insights to produce a highly original poetry that speaks as eloquently to the world as it does to modern Africa. His books of poetry include *Poems from Prison* (1969) and *A Shuttle in the Crypt* (1972). He was awarded the 1986 Nobel Prize for Literature.

Another English language poet writing in Africa today, Kofi Awoonor (b. 1935), is also a novelist, playwright, and scholar. Often drawing on imagery from oral vernacular poetry, Awoonor urges a return to the culture of his forefathers. His poetry blends a sense of traditional oral culture and language with a powerful and uniquely flowing voice. He has taught at several American universities and at Ghana's University of Cape Coast and has edited the literary journal *Okyeame*. His books include *Rediscovery and Other Poems, Night of My Blood, Ride Me, Memory, The House by the Sea, This Earth, My Brother,* and *Fire in the Valley*. In 1983 he became Ghana's ambassador to Brazil.

Another African poet who wrote in English, Arthur K. Nortje (1942–1970) was born in Cape Province, South Africa, and attended the Government High School for Coloureds. In 1965 he attended Jesus College, Oxford, to study English literature. His poetry first appeared in *Black Orpheus* in 1961. After teaching in Canada, Nortje returned to England to continue his studies but committed suicide in 1970. *Dead Roots,* his only collection of poetry, was published posthumously in 1973.

JEAN-JOSEPH RABÉARIVELO

[1901–1937]

She

TRANSLATED BY GERALD MOORE AND ULLI BEIER

She
whose eyes are prisms of sleep
and whose lids are heavy with dreams,
she whose feet are planted in the sea
and whose shiny hands appear   5
full of corals and blocks of shining salt.

She will put them in little heaps beside a misty gulf
and sell them to naked sailors
whose tongues have been cut out,
until the rain begins to fall.   10

Then she will disappear
and we shall only see

her hair spread by the wind
like a bunch of seaweed unravelling,
and perhaps some tasteless grains of salt.   *15*

The black glassmaker

TRANSLATED BY GERALD MOORE AND ULLI BEIER

The black glassmaker
whose countless eyeballs none has ever seen,
whose shoulders none has overlooked,
that slave all clothed in pearls of glass,
who is strong as Atlas   *5*
and who carries the seven skies on his head,
one would think that the vast river of clouds might carry him away,
the river in which his loincloth is already wet.

A thousand particles of glass
fall from his hands   *10*
but rebound towards his brow
shattered by the mountains
where the winds are born.

And you are witness of his daily suffering
and of his endless task;   *15*
you watch his thunder-riddled agony
until the battlements of the East re-echo
the conches of the sea—
but you pity him no more
and do not even remember that his sufferings begin again   *20*
each time the sun capsizes.

LÉOPOLD SÉDAR SENGHOR

[b. 1906]

Night of Sine

TRANSLATED BY GERALD MOORE AND ULLI BEIER

Woman, rest on my brow your balsam hands, your hands gentler than fur.
The tall palmtrees swinging in the nightwind
Hardly rustle. Not even cradlesongs,
The rhythmic silence rocks us.

Listen to its song, listen to the beating of our dark blood, listen   5
To the beating of the dark pulse of Africa in the mist of lost villages.
Now the tired moon sinks towards its bed of slack water,
Now the peals of laughter even fall asleep, and the bards themselves
Dandle their heads like children on the backs of their mothers.
Now the feet of the dancers grow heavy and heavy grows the tongue of the singers.   10
This is the hour of the stars and of the night that dreams
And reclines on this hill of clouds, draped in her long gown of milk.
The roofs of the houses gleam gently. What are they telling so confidently to the stars?
Inside the hearth is extinguished in the intimacy of bitter and sweet scents.
Woman, light the lamp of clear oil, and let the children in bed talk about
     their ancestors, like their parents.   15
Listen to the voice of the ancients of Elissa. Like we, exiled,
They did not want to die, lest their seminal flood be lost in the sand.
Let me listen in the smoky hut for the shadowy visit of propitious souls,
My head on your breast glowing, like a kuskus ball smoking out of the fire,
Let me breathe the smell of our dead, let me contemplate and repeat their
     living voice, let me learn   20
To live before I sink, deeper than the diver, into the lofty depth of sleep.

Paris in the Snow

TRANSLATED BY GERALD MOORE AND ULLI BEIER

Lord, you visited Paris on the day of your birth
Because it had become paltry and bad.
You purified it with incorruptible cold,
The white death.
This morning even the factory funnels hoisted in harmony   5
The white flags.
"Peace to all men of good will."
Lord, you have offered the divided world, divided Europe,
The snow of peace.
And the rebels fired their fourteen hundred cannons   10
Against the mountains of your peace.
Lord, I have accepted your white cold that burns worse than salt.
And now my heat melts like snow in the sun.
And I forget
The white hands that loaded the guns that destroyed the kingdoms,   15
The hands that whipped the slaves and that whipped you
The dusty hands that slapped you, the white powdered hands that slapped me

The sure hands that pushed me into solitude and hatred
The white hands that felled the high forest that dominated Africa,
That felled the Sara, erect and firm in the heart of Africa, beautiful like the first men
    that were created by your brown hands. 20
They felled the virgin forest to turn into railway sleepers.
They felled Africa's forest in order to save civilization that was lacking in men.
Lord, I can still not abandon this last hate, I know it, the hatred of diplomats
    who show their long teeth
And who will barter with black flesh tomorrow.
My heart, oh lord, has melted like the snow on the roofs of Paris 25
In the sun of your Goodness,
It is kind to my enemies, my brothers with the snowless white hands,
Also because of the hands of dew that lie on my burning cheeks at night.

BIRAGO DIOP

[b. 1906]

Diptych

TRANSLATED BY ELLEN CONROY KENNEDY

The Sun, hung by a string
deep in the indigo calabash,
boils up the kettleful of day.
The Darkness, frightened at the coming
of the Daughters-of-Fire, burrows 5
at the foot of fenceposts.
The savanna is bright and crisp,
shapes and colors, sharp.
But in distressing silences filled with hummings
and noises neither muffled nor shrill 10
a heavy mystery hovers,
a secret, shapeless mystery
frightens and surrounds us.

Nailed on with fiery nails, the dark cloth
spread above the earth covers up the bed of night. 15
Frightened at the coming of the Daughters-of-Darkness,
dogs bark, horses whinny,
man burrows deep within his hut.

The savanna is dark
shapes and colors, all are black.   20
But in distressing silences filled with hummings
pathways thick with mystery
slowly become visible
to those who have departed
and to those who will return.   25

TCHICAYA U TAM'SI

[b. 1929]

Brush Fire

TRANSLATED BY SANGODARE AKANJI

the fire the river that is to say
the sea to drink following the sand
the feet the hands
within the heart to love
this river that lives in me repeoples me   5
only to you I said around the fire
my race
it flows here and there a river
the flames are the looks
of those who brood upon it   10
I said to you
my race
remembers
the taste of bronze drunk hot.

WOLE SOYINKA

[b. 1934]

Hamlet

He stilled his doubts, they rose to halt and lame
A resolution on the rack. Passion's flame
Was doused in fear of error, his mind's unease
Bred indulgence to the state's disease

Ghosts embowelled his earth; he clung to rails   5
In a gallery of abstractions, dissecting tales
As "told by an idiot." Passionless he set a stage
Of passion for the guilt he would engage.

Justice despaired. The turn and turn abouts
Of reason danced default to duty's counterpoint   10
Till treachery scratched the slate of primal clay
Then Metaphysics waived a thought's delay—
It took the salt in the wound, the "point
Envenom'd too" to steel the prince of doubts.

KOFI AWOONOR

[b. 1935]

Song of War

I shall sleep in white calico;
War has come upon the sons of men
And I shall sleep in calico;
Let the boys go forward,
Kpli and his people should go forward;   5
Let the white man's guns boom,
We are marching forward;
We all shall sleep in calico.

When we start, the ground shall shake;
The war is within our very huts;   10
Cowards should fall back
And live at home with the women;
They who go near our wives
While we are away in battle
Shall lose their calabashes when we come.   15

Where has it been heard before
That a snake has bitten a child
In front of its own mother;
The war is upon us
It is within our very huts   20

And the sons of men shall fight it
Let the white man's guns boom
And its smoke cover us
We are fighting them to die.

We shall die on the battlefield   25
We shall like death at no other place,
Our guns shall die with us
And our sharp knives shall perish with us
We shall die on the battlefield.

The Sea Eats the Land at Home

At home the sea is in the town,
Running in and out of the cooking places,
Collecting the firewood from the hearths
And sending it back at night;
The sea eats the land at home.   5
It came one day at the dead of night,
Destroying the cement walls,
And carried away the fowls,
The cooking-pots and the ladles,
The sea eats the land at home;   10
It is a sad thing to hear the wails,
And the mourning shouts of the women,
Calling on all the gods they worship,
To protect them from the angry sea.
Aku stood outside where her cooking-pot stood,   15
With her two children shivering from the cold,
Her hands on her breast,
Weeping mournfully.
Her ancestors have neglected her,
Her gods have deserted her,   20
It was a cold Sunday morning,
The storm was raging,
Goats and fowls were struggling in the water,
The angry water of the cruel sea;
The lap-lapping of the bark water at the shore,   25
And above the sobs and the deep and low moans,
Was the eternal hum of the living sea.
It has taken away their belongings
Adena has lost the trinkets which

Were her dowry and her joy,   *30*
In the sea that eats the land at home,
Eats the whole land at home.

ARTHUR K. NORTJE

[1942–1970]

Up Late

Night here, the owners asleep upstairs:
the room's eyes shut, its voices dead,
though I admire it when its mirrors
oblige me with my presence. Looking ahead
needs glancing back to what I once   *5*
was, the time that mischance
borrowed my body to break it by terror.

Now the cameras rest in their elegant
leather coffins, having caught
the whirl of streets before the wheels go silent.   *10*
Rain trickles as the red biro writes my heart:
time demands no attention of the will,
the clock is yellow with black numerals.
The icebox resumes its purring descant.

This picture opens on the past. I rise   *15*
to study a calendar scene from what was home:
an old white mill, sentimental, South African Airways
(the blue lithe buck), peaceful, implausible. Some
fugitive sense holds back the bruising wave:
that gift to spend, my song where I arrive,   *20*
didn't I take it from the first dispiriting wilderness?

My mind burned and I shackled it
with squalid love, the violence of the flesh.
The quiet scars over my veins bit
less deep now than the knife or lash   *25*
could feel content about:
no longer need I shout
freedom in the house. I sit in light

here, the refugee's privilege. Nor do I want
fruit in a bowl, banana pleasure, the skin   *30*
that slides from my fingers, spent
because the soft heart only must be eaten.
Give me the whole experience to savour
who have known waste and also favor:
time to come may find me eloquent   *35*

in other rooms, that reminisce
of this one so composed in silence. Love,
the necessary pain, has spurred a search.
Moving from place to place I always have
come some way closer to knowing   *40*
the final sequence of song that's going
to master the solitudes night can teach.

CRITICAL
COMMENTS
ON POETRY

PLATO

[428–348 B.C.]

Poetry and Inspiration

from The Dialogues of Plato

For all good poets, epic as well as lyric, compose their beautiful poems not by art, but because they are inspired and possessed. And as the Corybantian revelers when they dance are not in their right mind, so the lyric poets are not in their right mind when they are composing their beautiful strains: but when falling under the power of music and meter they are inspired and possessed; like Bacchic maidens who draw milk and honey from the rivers when they are under the influence of Dionysus but not when they are in their right mind. And the soul of the lyric poet does the same, as they themselves say; for they tell us that they bring songs from honeyed fountains, culling them out of the gardens and dells of the Muses; they, like the bees, winging their way from flower to flower. And this is true. For the poet is a light and winged and holy thing, and there is no invention in him until he has been inspired and is out of his senses, and reason is no longer in him: no man, while he retains that faculty, has the oracular gift of poetry.

Many are the noble words in which poets speak concerning the actions of men; but like yourself when speaking about Homer, they do not speak of them by any rules of art: they are simply inspired to utter that to which the Muse impels them, and that only; and when inspired, one of them will make dithyrambs, another hymns of praise, another choral strains, another epic or iambic verses, but not one of them is of any account in the other kinds. For not by art does the poet sing, but by power divine; had he learned by rules of art, he would have known how to speak not of one theme only, but of all; and therefore God takes away reason from poets, and uses them as his ministers, as he also uses the pronouncers of oracles and holy prophets, in order that we who hear them may know them to be speaking not of themselves, who utter these priceless words while bereft of reason, but that God himself is the speaker, and that through them he is addressing us. And Tynnichus the Chalcidian affords a striking instance of what I am saying: he wrote no poem that anyone would care to remember but the famous paean which is in everyone's mouth, one of the finest lyric poems ever written, simply an invention of the Muses, as he himself says. For in this way God would seem to demonstrate to us and not to allow us to doubt that these beautiful poems are not human, nor the work of man, but divine and the work of God; and that the poets are only the interpreters of the gods by whom they are severally possessed.

ARISTOTLE

[384–322 B.C.]

The Causes of Poetry

from The Poetics

Poetry in general seems to have sprung from two causes, each of them lying deep in our nature. First, the instinct of imitation is implanted in man from childhood, one difference between him and other animals being that he is the most imitative of living creatures, and through imitation learns his earliest lessons; and no less universal is the pleasure felt in things imitated. We have evidence of this in the facts of experience. Objects which in themselves we view with pain, we delight to contemplate when reproduced with minute fidelity: such as the forms of the most ignoble animals and of dead bodies. The cause of this again is, that to learn gives the liveliest pleasure, not only to philosophers but to men in general; whose capacity, however, of learning is more limited. Thus the reason why men enjoy seeing a likeness is, that in contemplating it they find themselves learning or inferring, and saying perhaps, "Ah, that is he." For if you happen not to have seen the original, the pleasure will be due not to the imitation as such, but to the execution, the coloring, or some such other cause.

Imitation, then, is one instinct of our nature. Next, there is the instinct for "harmony" and rhythm, metres being manifestly sections of rhythm. Persons, therefore, starting with this natural gift developed by degrees their special aptitudes, till their rude improvisations gave birth to Poetry.

Poetry now diverged in two directions, according to the individual character of the writers. The graver spirits imitated noble actions, and the actions of good men. The more trivial sort imitated the actions of meaner persons, at first composing satires, as the former did hymns to the gods and the praises of famous men. A poem of the satirical kind cannot indeed be put down to any author earlier than Homer; though many such writers probably there were. But from Homer onward, instances can be cited,—his own Margites, for example, and other similar compositions. The appropriate metre was also here introduced; hence the measure is still called the iambic or lampooning measure, being that in which people lampooned one another. Thus the older poets were distinguished as writers of heroic or of lampooning verse.

SIR PHILIP SIDNEY

[1554–1586]

from *An Apology for Poetry*

But now, let us see how the Greeks named it, and how they deemed of it. The Greeks called him "a poet," which name hath, as the most excellent, gone through other languages. It cometh of this word *Poiein,* which is "to make": wherein, I know not whether by luck or wisdom, we Englishmen have met with the Greeks in calling him "a maker": which name, how high and incomparable a title it is, I had rather were known by marking the scope of other sciences than by my partial allegation.

There is no art delivered to mankind that hath not the works of Nature for his principal object, without which they could not consist, and on which they so depend, as they become actors and players, as it were, of what Nature will have set forth. So doth the astronomer look upon the stars, and, by that he seeth, setteth down what order Nature hath taken therein. So do the geometrician and arithmetician in their diverse sorts of quantities. So doth the musician in times tell you which by nature agree, which not. The natural philosopher thereon hath his name, and the moral philosopher standeth upon the natural virtues, vices, and passions of man; and "follow Nature" (saith he) "therein, and thou shalt not err." The lawyer saith what men have determined; the historian what men have done. The grammarian speaketh only of the rules of speech; and the rhetorician and logician, considering what in Nature will soonest prove and persuade, thereon give artificial rules, which still are compassed within the circle of a question according to the proposed matter. The physician weigheth the nature of a man's body, and the nature of things helpful or hurtful unto it. And the metaphysic, though it be in the second and abstract notions, and therefore be counted supernatural, yet doth he indeed build upon the depth of Nature. Only the poet, disdaining to be tied to any such subjection, lifted up with the vigor of his own invention, doth grow in effect another nature, in making things either better than Nature bringeth forth, or, quite anew, forms such as never were in Nature, as the Heroes, Demigods, Cyclopes, Chimeras, Furies, and such like: so as he goeth hand in hand with Nature, not enclosed within the narrow warrant of her gifts, but freely ranging only within the zodiac of his own wit.

SAMUEL JOHNSON

[1709–1784]

from *The Metaphysical Poets*

Wit, like all other things subject by their nature to the choice of man, has its changes and fashions, and at different times takes different forms. About the beginning of the seventeenth century appeared a race of writers that may be termed the *metaphysical poets,* of whom, in a criticism on the works of Cowley, it is not improper to give some account.

The metaphysical poets were men of learning, and to show their learning was their whole endeavor; but, unluckily resolving to show it in rhyme, instead of writing poetry they only wrote verses, and very often such verses as stood the trial of the finger better than of the ear; for the modulation was so imperfect, that they were only found to be verses by counting the syllables.

If the father of criticism[1] has rightly denominated poetry τέχνη μιμητικὴ, an imitative art, these writers will, without great wrong, lose their right to the name of poets, for they cannot be said to have imitated anything; they neither copied nature for life, neither painted the forms of matter, nor represented the operations of intellect.

Those, however, who deny them to be poets, allow them to be wits. Dryden confesses of himself and his contemporaries, that they fall below Donne in wit, but maintains that they surpass him in poetry.

If wit be well described by Pope, as being "that which has been often thought, but was never before so well expressed,"* they certainly never attained, nor ever sought it; for they endeavored to be singular in their thoughts, and were careless of their diction. But Pope's account of wit is undoubtedly erroneous: he depresses it below its natural dignity, and reduces it from strength of thought to happiness of language.

If by a more noble and more adequate conception that be considered as wit which is at once natural and new, that which, though not obvious, is, upon its first production, acknowledged to be just; if it be that which he that never found it wonders how he missed, to wit of this kind the metaphysical poets have seldom risen. Their thoughts are often new, but seldom natural; they are not obvious, but neither are they just; and the reader, far from wondering that he missed them, wonders more frequently by what perverseness of industry they were ever found.

But wit, abstracted from its effects upon the hearer, may be more rigorously and philosophically considered as a kind of *discordia concors;* a combination of dissimilar images, or discovery of occult resemblances in things apparently unlike. Of wit, thus defined, they have more than enough. The most heterogeneous ideas are yoked by violence together; nature and art are ransacked for illustrations, comparisons, and allusions; their learning instructs, and their subtlety surprises; but the reader commonly thinks his improvement dearly bought, and, though he sometimes admires, is seldom pleased.

WILLIAM BLAKE

[1757–1827]

Art and Imagination

I feel very sorry that your Ideas & Mine on Moral Painting differ so much as to have made you angry with my method of Study. If I am wrong, I am wrong in good company. I had hoped your plan comprehended All Species of this Art, &

THE METAPHYSICAL POETS   [1]Aristotle   *Johnson approximates but misquotes Popes lines: "What oft was thought but ne'er so well expressed." See Popes "Essay on Criticism," pp. 272–280.

Expecially that you would not regret that Species which gives Existence to Every other, namely, Visions of Eternity. You say that I want somebody to Elucidate my Ideas. But you ought to know that What is Grand is necessarily obscure to Weak men. That which can be made Explicit to the Idiot is not worth my care. The wisest of the Ancients consider'd what is not too Explicit as the fittest for Instruction, because it rouzes the faculties to act. I name Moses, Solomon, Esop, Homer, Plato. I know that This World Is a World of imagination & Vision. I see Every thing I paint In This World, but Every body does not see alike. To the Eyes of a Miser a Guinea is more beautiful than the Sun, & a bag worn with the use of Money has more beautiful proportions than a Vine filled with Grapes. The tree which moves some to tears of joy is in the Eyes of others only a Green thing that stands in the way. Some See Nature all Ridicule & Deformity, & by these I shall not regulate my proportions; & Some Scarce see Nature at all. But to the Eyes of the Man of Imagination, Nature is Imagination itself. As a man is, So he Sees. As the Eye is formed, such are its Powers. You certainly Mistake, when you say that the Visions of Fancy are not to be found in This World. To Me This World is all One continued Vision of Fancy or Imagination, & I feel Flatter'd when I am told so. What is it sets Homer, Virgil & Milton in so high a rank of Art? Why is the Bible more Entertaining & Instructive than any other book? Is it not because they are addressed to the Imagination, which is Spiritual Sensation, & but mediately to the Understanding or Reason? Such is True Painting, and such was alone valued by the Greeks & the best modern Artists. Consider what Lord Bacon says: "Sense sends over to Imagination before Reason have judged, & Reason sends over to Imagination before the Decree can be acted."

WILLIAM WORDSWORTH

[1770–1850]

Poetry and Feeling

from Preface to the Lyrical Ballads

I have said that poetry is the spontaneous overflow of powerful feelings: it takes its origin from emotion recollected in tranquillity: the emotion is contemplated till, by a species of reaction, the tranquillity gradually disappears, and an emotion, kindred to that which was before the subject of contemplation, is gradually produced, and does itself actually exist in the mind. In this mood successful composition generally begins, and in a mood similar to this it is carried on; but the emotion, of whatever kind, and in whatever degree, from various causes, is qualified by various pleasures, so that in describing any passions whatsoever, which are voluntarily described, the mind will, upon the whole, be in a state of enjoyment. If Nature be thus cautious to preserve in a state of enjoyment a being so employed, the Poet ought to profit by the lesson held forth to him, and ought especially to take care, that, whatever passions he communicates to his Reader, those passions, if his Reader's mind be sound and vigorous, should always be accompanied with an overbalance of pleasure. Now the music of harmonious metrical language, the sense of difficulty overcome, and the blind association of pleasure which has been previously received from works of rhyme or metre of the same or similar construction, an indistinct perception perpetually renewed of language closely resembling that of real life, and yet, in the circumstance of meter, differing from it so widely—all these imperceptibly make up a complex feeling of delight, which is of the most important use in tempering the painful feeling always found intermingled with powerful descriptions of the deeper passions. This effect is always produced in pathetic and impassioned poetry; while, in lighter compositions, the ease and gracefulness with which the Poet manages his numbers are themselves confessedly a principal source of the gratification of the Reader. All that it is *necessary* to say, however, upon this subject, may be effected by affirming, what few persons will deny, that, of two descriptions, either of passions, manners, or characters, each of them equally well executed, the one in prose and the other in verse, the verse will be read a hundred times where the prose is read once.

SAMUEL TAYLOR COLERIDGE

[1772–1834]

The Poet, the Imagination

from Biographia Literaria

The poet, described in *ideal* perfection, brings the whole soul of man into activity, with the subordination of its faculties to each other, according to their relative worth and dignity. He diffuses a tone and spirit of unity, that blends, and (as it were) *fuses,* each into each, by that synthetic and magical power, to which we have exclusively appropriated the name of imagination. This power, first put in action by the will and understanding, and retained under their irremissive, though gentle and unnoticed, control *(laxis effertur habenis)* reveals itself in the balance or reconciliation of opposite or discordant qualities: of sameness, with difference; of the general, with the concrete; the idea, with the image; the individual, with the representative; the sense of novelty and freshness, with old and familiar objects; a more than usual state of emotion, with more than usual order; judgement ever awake and steady self-possession, with enthusiasm and feeling profound or vehement; and while it blends and harmonizes the natural and the artificial, still subordinates art to nature; the manner to the matter; and our admiration of the poet to our sympathy with the poetry. . . .

The IMAGINATION then, I consider either as primary, or secondary. The primary IMAGINATION I hold to be the living Power and prime Agent of all human Perception, and as a repetition in the finite mind of the eternal act of creation in the infinite I AM. The secondary Imagination I consider as an echo of the former, coexisting with the conscious will, yet still as identical with the primary in the *kind* of its agency, and differing only in *degree,* and in the *mode* of its operation. It dissolves, diffuses, dissipates, in order to recreate; or where this process is rendered impossible, yet still at all events it struggles to idealize and to unify. It is essentially *vital,* even as all objects (*as* objects) are essentially fixed and dead.

PERCY BYSSHE SHELLEY

[1792–1822]

Poets and Language

from A Defence of Poetry

Poets, according to the circumstances of the age and nation in which they appeared, were called, in the earlier epochs of the world, legislators, or prophets: a poet essentially comprises and unites both these characters. For he not only beholds intensely the present as it is, and discovers those laws according to which present things ought to be ordered, but he beholds the future in the present, and his thoughts are the germs of the flower and the fruit of latest time. Not that I assert poets to be prophets in the gross sense of the word, or that they can foretell the form as surely as they foreknow the spirit of events: such is the pretence of superstition, which would make poetry an attribute of prophecy, rather than prophecy an attribute of poetry. A poet participates in the eternal, the infinite, and the one; as far as relates to his conceptions, time and place and number are not. The grammatical forms which express the moods of time, and the difference of persons, and the distinction of place, are convertible with respect to the highest poetry without injuring it as poetry; and the choruses of Aeschylus, and the book of *Job,* and Dante's *Paradise,* would afford, more than any other writings, examples of this fact, if the limits of this essay did not forbid citation. The creations of sculpture, painting, and music, are illustrations still more decisive.

Language, colour, form, and religious and civil habits of action, are all the instruments and materials of poetry; they may be called poetry by that figure of speech which considers the effect as a synonym of the cause. But poetry in a more restricted sense expresses those arrangements of language, and especially metrical language, which are created by that imperial faculty, whose throne is curtained within the invisible nature of man. And this springs from the nature itself of language, which is a more direct representation of the actions and passions of our internal being, and is susceptible of more various and delicate combinations, than colour, form, or motion, and is more plastic and obedient to the control of that faculty of which it is the creation. For language is arbitrarily produced by the imagination, and has relation to thoughts alone; but all other materials, instruments, and conditions of art, have relations among each other, which limit and interpose between conception and expression. The former is as a mirror which reflects, the latter as a cloud which enfeebles, the light of which both are mediums of communication. . . .

Poets are the hierophants of an unapprehended inspiration; the mirrors of the gigantic shadows which futurity casts upon the present; the words which express what they understand not; the trumpets which sing to battle, and feel not what they inspire; the influence which is moved not, but moves. Poets are the unacknowledged legislators of the world.

JOHN KEATS

[1795–1821]

The Authenticity of the Imagination

[NOVEMBER 22, 1817]

My dear Bailey,
. . . O I wish I was as certain of the end of all your troubles as that of your momentary start about the authenticity of the Imagination. I am certain of nothing but of the holiness of the Heart's affections and the truth of Imagination—What the imagination seizes as Beauty must be truth—whether it existed before or not—for I have the same Idea of all our Passions as of Love they are all in their sublime, creative of essential Beauty—In a Word, you may know my favorite Speculation by my first Book and the little song I sent in my last—which is a representation from the fancy of the probable mode of operating in these Matters—The Imagination may be compared to Adam's dream—he awoke and found it truth. I am the more zealous in this affair, because I have never yet been able to perceive how any thing can be known for truth by consequitive reasoning—and yet it must be—Can it be that even the greatest Philosopher ever arrived at his goal without putting aside numerous

objections—However it may be, O for a Life of Sensations rather than of Thoughts! It is "a Vision in the form of Youth" a Shadow of reality to come—and this consideration has further convinced me for it has come as auxiliary to another favorite Speculation of mine, that we shall enjoy ourselves here after by having what we called happiness on Earth repeated in a finer tone and so repeated—And yet such a fate can only befall those who delight in sensation rather than hunger as you do after Truth—Adam's dream will do here and seems to be a conviction that Imagination and its empyreal reflection is the same as human Life and its spiritual repetition. But as I was saying—the simple imaginative Mind may have its rewards in the repetition of its own silent Working coming continually on the spirit with a fine suddenness—to compare great things with small—have you never by being surprised with an old Melody—in a delicious place—by a delicious voice, felt over again your very speculations and surmises at the time it first operated on your soul—do you not remember forming to yourself the singer's face more beautiful than it was possible and yet with the elevation of the Moment you did not think so—even then you were mounted on the Wings of Imagination so high—that the Prototype must be here after—that delicious face you will see—What a time! I am continually running away from the subject—sure this cannot be exactly the case with a complex Mind—one that is imaginative and at the same time careful of its fruits—who would exist partly on sensation partly on thought—to whom it is necessary that years should bring the philosophic Mind—such an one I consider yours and therefore it is necessary to your eternal Happiness that you not only drink this old Wine of Heaven which I shall call the redigestion of our most ethereal Musings on Earth; but also increase in knowledge and know all things. I am glad to hear you are in a fair Way for Easter—you will soon get through your unpleasant reading and then!—but the world is full of troubles and I have not much reason to think myself pesterd with many—I think Jane or Marianne has a better opinion of me than I deserve—for really and truly I do not think my Brother's illness connected with mine—you know more of the real Cause than they do—nor have I any chance of being rack'd as you have been—you perhaps at one time thought there was such a thing as Worldly Happiness to be arrived at, at certain periods of time marked out—you have of necessity from your disposition been thus led away—I scarcely remember counting upon any Happiness—I look not for it if it be not in the present hour—nothing startles me beyond the Moment. The setting sun will always set me to rights—or if a Sparrow come before my Window I take part in its existince and pick about the Gravel. The first thing that strikes me on hearing a Misfortune having befalled another is this. "Well it cannot be helped.—he will have the pleasure of trying the resourses of his spirit, and I beg now my dear Bailey that hereafter should you observe any thing cold in me not to but it to the account of heartlessness but abstraction—for I assure you I sometimes feel not the influence of a Passion or Affection during a whole week—and so long this sometimes continues I begin to suspect myself and the genuiness of my feelings at other times—thinking them a few barren Tragedy-tears.

Your affectionate friend . . .

John Keats

EDGAR ALLAN POE
[1809–1849]

True Poetry
from The Poetic Principle

I hold that a long poem does not exist. I maintain that the phrase, "a long poem," is simply a flat contradiction in terms.

I need scarcely observe that a poem deserves its title only inasmuch as it excites, by elevating the soul. The value of the poem is in the ratio of this elevating excitement. But all excitements are, through a psychal necessity, transient. That degree of excitement which would entitle a poem to be so called at all, cannot be sustained throughout a composition of any great length. After the lapse of half an hour, at the very utmost, it flags—fails—a revulsion ensues—and then the poem is, in effect, and in fact, no longer such.

There are, no doubt, many who have found difficulty in reconciling the critical dictum that the "Paradise Lost" is to be devoutly admired throughout, with the absolute impossibility of maintaining for it, during perusal, the amount of enthusiasm which that critical dictum would demand. This great work, in fact, is to be regarded as poetical, only when, losing sight of that vital requisite in all works of Art, Unity, we view it merely as a series of minor poems. If, to preserve its Unity—its totality of effect or impression—we read it (as would be necessary) at a single sitting, the result is but a constant alternation of excitement and depression. After a passage of what we feel to be true poetry, there follows, inevitably, a passage of platitude which no critical pre-judgment can force us to admire; but if, upon completing the work, we read it again; omitting the first book—that is to say, commencing with the second—we shall be surprised at now finding that admirable which we before condemned—that damnable which we had previously so much admired. It follows from all this that the ultimate, aggregate, or absolute effect of even the best epic under the sun, is a nullity:—and this is precisely the fact. . . .

On the other hand, it is clear that a poem may be improperly brief. Undue brevity degenerates into mere epigrammatism. A *very* short poem, while now and then producing a brilliant or vivid, never produces a profound or enduring effect. There must be the steady pressing down of the stamp upon the wax.

WALT WHITMAN
[1819–1892]

The Poem of America
from Preface to the 1855 Edition of Leaves of Grass

The Americans of all nations at any time upon the earth have probably the fullest poetical nature. The United States themselves are essentially the greatest poem. In the history of the earth hitherto the largest and most stirring appear tame and orderly to their ampler largeness and stir. Here at last is something in the doings of man that corresponds with the broadcast doings of the day and night. Here is not merely a nation but a teeming nation of nations. Here is action untied from strings necessarily blind to particulars and details magnificently moving in vast masses. Here is the hospitality which forever indicates heroes. . . . Here are the roughs and beards and space and ruggedness and nonchalance that the soul loves. Here the performance disdaining the trivial unapproached in the tremendous audacity of its crowds and groupings and the push of its perspective spreads with crampless and flowing breadth and showers its prolific and splendid extravagance. One sees it must indeed own the riches of the summer and winter, and need never be bankrupt while corn grows from the ground or the orchards drop apples or the bays contain fish or men beget children upon women.

Other states indicate themselves in their deputies . . . but the genius of the United States is not best or most in its executives or legislatures, nor in its ambassadors or authors or colleges or churches or parlors, nor even in its newspapers or inventors . . . but always most in the common people. Their manners speech dress friendships—the freshness and candor of their physiognomy—the picturesque looseness of their carriage . . . their deathless attachment to freedom—their aversion to anything indecorous or soft or mean—the practical acknowledgment of the citizens of one state by the citizens of all other states—the fierceness of their roused resentment—their curiosity and welcome of novelty—their self-esteem and wonderful sympathy—their susceptibility to a slight—the air they have of persons who never knew how it felt to stand in the presence of superiors—the fluency of their speech—their delight in music, the sure symptom of manly tenderness and native elegance of soul . . . their good temper and openhandedness—the terrible significance of their elections—the President's taking off his hat to them not they to him—these too are unrhymed poetry. It awaits the gigantic and generous treatment worthy of it.

EMILY DICKINSON

[1830–1886]

On Her Poems

TO T. W. HIGGINSON

15 April 1862

Mr Higginson,

Are you too deeply occupied to say if my Verse is alive?

The Mind is so near itself—it cannot see, distinctly—and I have none to ask—

Should you think it breathed—and had you the leisure to tell me, I should feel quick gratitude—

If I make the mistake—that you dared to tell me—would give me sincerer honor—toward you—

I enclose my name—asking you, if you please—Sir—to tell me what is true?

That you will not betray me—it is needless to ask—since Honor is it's own pawn—

TO T. W. HIGGINSON

25 April 1862

Mr Higginson,

Your kindness claimed earlier gratitude—but I was ill—and write today, from my pillow.

Thank you for the surgery—it was not so painful as I supposed. I bring you others—as you ask—though they might not differ—

While my thought is undressed—I can make the distinction, but when I put them in the Gown—they look alike, and numb.

You asked how old I was? I made no verse—but one or two—until this winter—Sir—

I had a terror—since September—I could tell to none—and so I sing, as the Boy does by the Burying Ground—because I am afraid—You inquire my Books—For Poets—I have Keats—and Mr and Mrs Browning. For Prose—Mr Ruskin—Sir Thomas Browne—and the Revelations. I went to school—but in your manner of the phrase—had no education. When a little Girl, I had a friend, who taught me Immortality—but venturing too near, himself—he never returned—Soon after, my Tutor, died—and for several years, my Lexicon—was my only companion—Then I found one more—but he was not contented I be his scholar—so he left the Land.

You ask of my Companions Hills—Sir—and the Sundown—and a Dog—large as myself, that my Father bought me—They are better than Beings—because they know—but do not tell—and the noise in the Pool, at Noon—excels my Piano. I have a Brother and Sister—My Mother does not care for thought—and Father, too busy with his Briefs—to notice what we do—He buys me many Books—but begs me not to read them—because he fears they joggle the Mind. They are religious—except me—and address an Eclipse, every morning—whom they call their "Father." But I fear my story fatigues you—I would like to learn—Could you tell me how to grow—or is it unconveyed—like Melody—or Witchcraft?

You speak of Mr Whitman—I never read his Book—but was told that he was disgraceful—

GERARD MANLEY HOPKINS

[1844–1889]

Sprung Rhythm

I had long had haunting my ear the echo of a new rhythm which now I realised on paper. To speak shortly, it consists in scanning by accents or stresses alone, without any account of the number of syllables, so that a foot may be one strong syllable or it may be many light and one strong. I do not say the idea is altogether new; there are hints of it in music, in nursery rhymes and popular jingles, in the poets themselves, and, since then, I have seen it talked about as a thing possible in critics. Here are instances— *"Díng, dóng, béll; Pússy's ín the wéll; Whó pút her ín? Little Jóhnny Thín. Whó púlled her óut? Little Jóhnny Stóut."* For if each line has three stresses or three feet it follows that some of the feet are of one syllable only. So too *"Óne, twó, Búckle my shóe"* *passim.* In Campbell you have "And their fléet alóng the *déep próudly* shóne"—"Ít was tén of Ápril *mórn bý* the chíme" etc; in Shakspere "Whý shd. *this* désert bé?" corrected wrongly by the editors; in Moore a little melody I cannot quote; etc. But no one has professedly used it and made it the principle throughout, that I know of. Nevertheless to me it appears, I own, to be a better and more natural principle than the ordinary system, much more flexible, and capable of much greater effects. However I had to mark the stresses in blue chalk, and this and my rhymes carried on from one line into another and certain chimes suggested by the Welsh poetry I had been reading (what they call *cynghanedd*) and a great many more oddnesses could not but dismay an editor's eye, so that when I offered it to our magazine the *Month,* though at first they accepted it, after a time they withdrew and dared not print it. After writing this I held myself free to compose, but cannot find it in my conscience to spend time upon it; so I have done little and shall do less. But I wrote a shorter piece on the Eurydice, also in "sprung rhythm," as I call it, but simpler, shorter, and without marks, and offered the *Month* that too, but they did not like it either. Also I have written some sonnets and a few other little things; some in sprung rhythm, with various other experiments—as "outriding feet," that is parts of which do not count in the scanning (such as you find in Shakspere's later plays, but as a licence, whereas mine are rather calculated effects); others in the ordinary scanning *counterpointed* (this is counterpoint: *"Hóme to* his móther's hóuse *private* retúrned" and *"Bút to vánquish* by wísdom héllish wíles" etc); others, one or two, in common uncounterpointed rhythm.

WILLIAM BUTLER YEATS

[1865–1939]

The First Principle

from Essays and Introductions

A poet writes always of his personal life, in his finest work out of its tragedy, whatever it be, remorse, lost love, or mere loneliness; he never speaks directly as to someone at the breakfast table, there is always a phantasmagoria. Dante and Milton had mythologies, Shakespeare the characters of English history or of traditional romance; even when the poet seems most himself, when he is Raleigh and gives potentates the lie, or Shelley "a nerve o'er which do creep the else unfelt oppressions of this earth," or Byron when "the soul wears out the breast" as "the sword outwears its sheath," he is never the bundle of accident and incoherence that sits down to breakfast; he has been reborn as an idea, something intended, complete. A novelist might describe his accidence, his incoherence, he must not; he is more type than man, more passion than type. He is Lear, Romeo, Oedipus, Tiresias; he has stepped out of a play, and even the woman he loves is Rosalind, Cleopatra, never The Dark Lady. He is part of his own phantasmagoria and we adore him because nature has grown intelligible, and by so doing a part of our creative power. "When mind is lost in the light of the Self," says the Prashna Upanishad, "it dreams no more; still in the body it is lost in happiness." "A wise man seeks in Self," says the Chandogya Upanishad, "those that are alive and those that are dead and gets what the world cannot give." The world knows nothing because it has made nothing, we know everything because we have made everything.

PAUL VALÉRY

[1871–1945]

Poetry, Prose, Song

TRANSLATED BY DENISE FOLLIOT

The passage from prose to verse, from speech to song, from walking to dancing—a moment that is at once action and dream.

The aim of the dance is not to transport me from one point to another; nor of pure verse, nor of song.

But they exist to make me more present to myself, more entirely given up to myself, expending my energy to no useful end, replacing myself—and all things and sensations have no other value. A particular movement sets them free; and infinitely mobile, infinitely present, they hasten to serve as fuel to a fire. Hence metaphors, those stationary movements!

Song is more real than level speech, for the latter is of value only by a substitution and a deciphering operation, whereas the former stirs and provokes imitation, arouses desire, causes a vibration as though its variation and substance were the law and matter of my being. It stands in my stead; but level speech is on the surface, it sets out external things, divides and labels them.

One can get a wonderful conception of this difference by observing the efforts and inventions of those who have tried to make music speak and language sing or dance.

*

Poetry. Those ideas which cannot be put into prose are put into verse. If one finds them in prose, they demand verse and have the air of verse that has not yet been able to take shape. What ideas are these?

They are ideas that are possible only in very lively, rhythmic, or spontaneous movements of thought.

Metaphor, for example, marks in its naïve principle a *groping,* a hesitation between several different expressions of one thought, an explosive incapacity that surpasses the *necessary* and *sufficient* capacity. Once one has gone over and made the thought rigorously precise, restricted it to a single object, then the metaphor will be effaced, and prose will reappear.

These procedures, observed and cultivated for their own sake, have become the object of a study and an employment: poetry. The result of this analysis is that poetry's special aim and own true sphere is the expression of what cannot be expressed in the finite functions of words. The proper object of poetry is what has no single name, what in itself provokes and demands more than one expression. That which, for the expression of its unity, arouses a plurality of expressions.

R O B E R T   F R O S T

[1874–1963]

from *The Figure a Poem Makes*

It should be of the pleasure of a poem itself to tell how it can. The figure a poem makes. It begins in delight and ends in wisdom. The figure is the same as for love. No one can really hold that the ecstasy should be static and stand still in one place. It begins in delight, it inclines to the impulse, it assumes direction with the first line laid down, it runs a course of lucky events, and ends in a clarification of life—not necessarily a great clarification, such as sects and cults are founded on, but in a momentary stay against confusion. It has denouement. It has an outcome that though unforeseen was predestined from the first image of the original mood—and indeed from the very mood. It is but a trick poem and no poem at all if the best of it was thought of first and saved for the last. It finds its own name as it goes and discovers the best waiting for it in some final phrase at once wise and sad—the happy-sad blend of the drinking song.

No tears in the writer, no tears in the reader. No surprise for the writer, no surprise for the reader. For me the initial delight is in the surprise of remembering something I didn't know I knew. I am in a place, in a situation, as if I had materialized from cloud or risen out of the ground. There is a glad recognition of the long lost and the rest follows. Step by step the wonder of unexpected supply keeps growing. The impressions most useful to my purpose seem always those I was unaware of and so made no note of at the time when taken, and the conclusion is come to that like giants we are always hurling experience ahead of us to pave the future with against the day when we may want to strike a line of purpose across it for somewhere. The line will have the more charm for not being mechanically straight. We enjoy the straight crookedness of a good walking stick. Modern instruments of precision are being used to make things crooked as if by eye and hand in the old days. . . .

More than once I should have lost my soul to radicalism if it had been the originality it was mistaken for by its young converts. Originality and initiative are what I ask for my country. For myself the originality need be no more than the freshness of a poem run in the way I have described: from delight to wisdom. The figure is the same as for love. Like a piece of ice on a hot stove the poem must ride on its own melting. A poem may be worked over once it is in being, but may not be worried into being. Its most previous quality will remain its having run itself and carried away the poet with it. Read it a hundred times: it will forever keep its freshness as a metal keeps its fragrance. It can never lose its sense of a meaning that once unfolded by surprise as it went.

RAINER MARIA RILKE

[1875–1926]

from *Letters to a Young Poet*

TRANSLATED BY M.D. HERTER NORTON

Viareggio, near Pisa (Italy),
April 5th, 1903

Irony: Do not let yourself be governed by it, especially not in uncreative moments. In creative moments try to make use of it as one more means of grasping life. Cleanly used, it too is clean, and one need not be ashamed of it; and if you feel you are getting too familiar with it, if you fear this growing intimacy with it, then turn to great and serious objects, before which it becomes small and helpless. Seek the depth of things: thither irony never descends—and when you come thus close to the edge of greatness, test out at the same time whether this ironic attitude springs from a necessity of your nature. For under the influence of serious things either it will fall from you (if it is something fortuitous), or else it will (if it really innately belongs to you) strengthen into a stern instrument and take its place in the series of tools with which you will have to shape your art.

ANTONIO MACHADO

[1875–1939]

Problems of the Lyric

TRANSLATED BY REGINALD GIBBONS

We do not say much, nor do we say nearly enough, when we hold that it is sufficient for the poet to feel strongly and deeply, and to express his feeling clearly. In affirming this we are assuming, without even having mentioned them, that a great many problems are already resolved.

Feelings are not the creation of the individual subject, a sincere [*cordial*] elaboration of the "I" out of materials from the exterior world. They always contain a collaboration with a "You"—that is, with other subjects. One cannot arrive at this simple formula: my heart, confronting a landscape, produces a feeling; and once it is produced, I communicate it to my neighbor by means of language. My heart, confronting a landscape, would barely be able to feel cosmic terror, because even this elemental feeling requires the anguish of other hearts caught in the middle of a natural world not fully understood. My feeling in the face of the exterior world, which I am here calling a landscape, does not arise without an invigorating atmosphere. My feeling, in sum, is not exclusively mine, but rather *ours*. Without going out of myself, I note that in my feeling other feelings are vibrating as well, and that my heart is always singing in a chorus, although its own voice may be, for me, the best. That it also be the best for others—*that* is the problem of lyrical expression.

A second problem: in order to express my feelings I have language. But language is already much *less mine* than are my feelings. For after all I have had to acquire it, learn it from others. Before being *ours*—because it will never be *mine* alone—it was theirs; it belonged to that world which is neither subjective nor objective, to that third world to which psychology has not yet paid sufficient attention, the world of *other I's*.

WALLACE STEVENS

[1879–1955]

Reflections on Poetry

from Adagia

Literature is the better part of life. To this it seems inevitably necessary to add, provided life is the better part of literature.

*

After one has abandoned a belief in God, poetry is that essence which takes its place as life's redemption.

*

Accuracy of observation is the equivalent of accuracy of thinking.

*

The relation of art to life is of the first importance especially in a skeptical age since, in the absence of a belief in God, the mind turns to its own creations and examines them, not alone from the aesthetic point of view, but for what they reveal, for what they validate and invalidate, for the support that they give.

What we see in the mind is as real to us as what we see by the eye.

One reads poetry with one's nerves.

Every poem is a poem within a poem: the poem of the idea within the poem of the words.

*

Poetry is the gaiety (joy) of language.

*

To be at the end of fact is not to be at the beginning of imagination but it is to be at the end of both.

*

There is a nature that absorbs the mixedness of metaphors.

*

Imagination applied to the whole world is vapid in comparison to imagination applied to a detail.

*

Poetry is a response to the daily necessity of getting the world right.

EZRA POUND

[1885–1972]

Kinds of Poetry

The mastery of any art is the work of a lifetime. I should not discriminate between the "amateur" and the "professional." Or rather I should discriminate quite often in favor of the amateur, but I should discriminate between the amateur and the expert. It is certain that the present chaos will endure until the Art of poetry has been preached down the amateur gullet, until there is such a general understanding of the fact that poetry is an art and not a pastime; such a knowledge of technique; of technique of surface and technique of content, that the amateurs will cease to try to drown out the masters.

If a certain thing was said once for all in Atlantis or Arcadia, in 450 Before Christ or in 1290 after, it is not for us moderns to go saying it over, or to go obscuring the memory of the dead by saying the same thing with less skill and less conviction.

My pawing over the ancients and semi-ancients has been one struggle to find out what has been done, once for all, better than it can ever be done again, and to find out what remains for us to do, and plenty does remain, for if we still feel the same emotions as those which launched the thousand ships, it is quite certain that we come on these feelings differently, through different nuances, by different intellectual gradations. Each age has its own abounding gifts yet only some ages transmute them into matter of duration. No good poetry is ever written in a manner twenty years old, for to write in such a manner shows conclusively that the writer thinks from books, convention and *cliché,* and not from life, yet a man feeling the divorce of life and his art may naturally try to resurrect a forgotten mode if he finds in that mode some leaven, or if he think he sees in it some element lacking in contemporary art which might unite that art again to its sustenance, life. . . .

That is to say, there are three "kinds of poetry":

MELOPŒIA, wherein the words are charged, over and above their plain meaning, with some musical property, which directs the bearing or trend of that meaning.

PHANOPŒIA, which is a casting of images upon the visual imagination.

LOGOPŒIA, "the dance of the intellect among words," that is to say, it employs words not only for their direct meaning, but it takes count in a special way of habits of usage, of the context we *expect* to find with the word, its usual concomitants, of its known acceptances, and of ironical play. It holds the aesthetic content which is peculiarly the domain of verbal manifestation, and cannot possibly be contained in plastic or in music. It is the latest come, and perhaps most tricky and undependable mode.

The *melopœia* can be appreciated by a foreigner with a sensitive ear, even though he be ignorant of the language in which the poem is written. It is practically impossible to transfer or translate it from one language to another, save perhaps by divine accident, and for half a line at a time.

Phanopœia can, on the other hand, be translated almost, or wholly, intact. When it is good enough, it is practically impossible for the translator to destroy it save by very crass bungling, and the neglect of perfectly well-known and formulative rules.

Logopœia does not translate; though the attitude of mind it expresses may pass through a paraphrase. Or one might say, you can *not* translate it "locally," but having determined the original author's state of mind, you may or may not be able to find a derivative or an equivalent.

T. S. ELIOT

[1888–1965]

The Poet and the Tradition

from Tradition and The Individual Talent

Tradition is a matter of much wider significance. It cannot be inherited, and if you want it you must obtain it by great labor. It involves, in the first place, the historical sense, which we may call nearly indispensable to anyone who would continue to be a poet beyond his twenty-fifth year; and the historical sense involves a perception, not only of the pastness of the past, but of its presence; the historical sense compels a man to write not merely with his own generation in his bones, but with a feeling that the whole of the literature of Europe from Homer and within it the whole of the literature of his own country has a simultaneous existence and composes a simultaneous order. This historical sense, which is a sense of the timeless as well as of the temporal and of the timeless and of the temporal together, is what makes a writer traditional. And it is at the same time what makes a writer most acutely conscious of his place in time, of his contemporaneity.

No poet, no artist of any art, has his complete meaning alone. His significance, his appreciation is the appreciation of his relation to the dead poets and artists. You cannot value him alone; you must set him, for contrast and comparison, among the dead. I mean this as a principle of aesthetic, not merely historical, criticism. The necessity that he shall conform, that he shall cohere, is not one-sided; what happens when a new work of art is created is something that happens simultaneously to all the works of art which preceded it. The existing monuments form an ideal order among themselves, which is modified by the introduction of the new (the really new) work of art among them. The existing order is complete before the new work arrives; for order to persist after the supervention of novelty, the *whole* existing order must be, if ever so slightly, altered; and so the relations, proportions, values of each work of art toward the whole are readjusted; and this is conformity between the old and the new. Whoever has approved this idea of order, of the form of European, of English literature, will not find it preposterous that the past should be altered by the present as much as the present is directed by the past. And the poet who is aware of this will be aware of great difficulties and responsibilities.

In a peculiar sense he will be aware also that he must inevitably be judged by the standards of the past. I say judged, not amputated, by them; not judged to be as good as, or worse or better than, the dead; and certainly not judged by the canons of dead critics. It is a judgment, a comparison, in which two things are measured by each other. To conform merely would be for the new work not really to conform at all; it would not be new, and would therefore not be a work of art.

FEDERICO GARCÍA LORCA

[1898–1936]

Play and Theory of the Duende

TRANSLATED BY CHRISTOPHER MAURER

Whoever finds himself on the bull's hide stretched between the Júcar, Guadalfeo, Sil, and Pisuerga rivers—not to mention the great streams that meet the tawny waves churned by the Plata—often hears people say, "This has much duende." Manuel Torre, great artist of the Andalusian people, once told a singer, "You have a voice, you know the styles, but you will never truimph, because you have no duende."

All over Andalusia, from the rock of Jaén to the whorled shell of Cádiz, the people speak constantly of the "duende," and identify it accurately and instinctively whenever it appears. The marvelous singer El Lebrijano, creator of the debla, used to say, "On days when I sing with duende, no one can touch me." The old Gypsy dancer La Malena once heard Brailowsky play a fragment of Bach and exclaimed, "Olé! That has duende!" but was bored by Gluck, Brahms, and Darius Milbaud. Manuel Torre, who had more culture in the blood than any man I have ever known, prononuced this splendid sentence on hearing Falla play his own *Nocturno del Generalife:* "All that has black sounds has duende." And there is no greater truth.

These black sounds are the mystery, the tools fastened in the mire that we all know and all ignore, the mire that gives us the very substance of art. "Black sounds," said that man of the Spanish people, concurring with Goethe, who defined the duende while speaking of Paganini: "A mysterious power which everyone senses and no philosopher explains."

The duende, then, is a power, not a work; it is a struggle, not a thought. I have heard an old maestro of the guitar say, "The duende is not in the throat; the duende climbs up inside you, from the soles of the feet." Meaning this: it is not a question of ability, but of true, living style, of blood, of the most ancient culture, of spontaneous creation.

This "mysterious power which everyone senses and no philosopher explains" is, in sum, the spirit of the earth, the same duende that scorched the heart of Nietzsche, who looked for its external forms on the Rialto Bridge and in the music of Bizet, without ever finding it and without knowing that the duende he was pursuing had leaped straight from the Greek mysteries to the dancers of Cádiz or the beheaded, Dionysian scream of Silverlo's siguiriya.

GEORGE SEFERIS

[1900–1971]

Poetry and Human Living

from A Poet's Journal

TRANSLATED BY ATHAN ANAGNOSTOPOULOS

Among the many ways that there are to study poets, the simplest, it seems to me, is the best: to look at what their works show us. And it is not improbable that they show things which we were looking for; "which we would not have sought if we had not found them already," as someone else says; or, to remember the ancient sage, "knowledge is memory." Thus, poets complement us and we complement them. I do not intend to advise arbitrariness when we read poems. A poem is not reason enough for us to unleash our imagination in reckless wanderings. Rather, what I want to say is this: that poets, if their poetry is good, draw on a deep-rooted experience of life, which all of us, young and old, have within ourselves; how much we feel this, I don't know. These are the roots through which they communicate with us. What forms, what vestments this common experience, this common feeling of life, will take in a historical moment no one can tell. It depends, I think, not only upon the idiosyncrasy of the individual who expresses himself but also upon many intellectual, social, and political mores of the time. A poem written from a purely erotic impulse may become in another era the expression of the feeling of human humiliation, of deceit, of degradation, because the era in some way has brought such sentiments to the surface; it has made them, let's say, public. And the praise of a rose or a ray of sunlight may convey the impression of human grandeur at moments when human grandeur flashes like lightning, as Solomos would say. These variations, as time passes, indicate that poems are alive and are nourished; they have the power to complement us and they ask us to complement them. If poetry were not sustained by this kind of human solidarity, in this human community, it wouldn't have lived very long. Poetry does not express truths in the scientific meaning of the word, nor does it discover philosophies and life theories. It uses science *and* the philosophy of others, if it needs them. Poetry is not for personal confessions; if it makes them, it is not they that save it. It does not try to express the personality of the poets, but, as Eliot has written, tries rather to abolish it. But in doing this, it expresses another personality that belongs to everyone; whosoever loses his life will find it, the Gospel says. Thus, let us not ask from the poet, in order to understand him, the petty, everyday details of his life which we think he is expressing. These petty events, if they have become poetry, are events belonging to you and me, and to those who have gone before, and to those who will come after us. If it were not so, poetry would not exist. You can make the experiment yourselves. Read a rhapsody of Homer and see if whether, at the parts that move you, what you feel is merely an archaeological reference alone, or if perhaps it is a sentiment nurtured by all the human experience that has occurred from that ancient era down to your present moment.

OSIP MANDELSTAM

[1891–1938]

On Classical Poetry

TRANSLATED BY SIDNEY MONAS

Poetry is the plow that turns up time so that the deep layers of time, the black soil, appear on top. There are epochs, however, when mankind, not content with the present, longing for time's deeper layers, like the plowman, thirsts for the virgin soil of time. Revolution in art inevitably tends to Classicism. Not because David reaped Robespierre's harvest, but because that is how the earth would have it.

One often hears: that might be good, but it belongs to yesterday. But I say: yesterday hasn't been born yet. It has not yet really come to pass. I want Ovid, Pushkin, Catullus afresh, and I will not be satisfied with the historical Ovid, Pushkin, Catullus.

In fact, it's amazing how everybody keeps fussing over the poets and can't seem to have done with them. You might think, once they'd been read, that was that. Superseded, as they say now. Nothing of the sort. The silver horn of Catullus—*"Ad claras Asiae volemus urbes"*—frets and excites more powerfully than any futuristic mystification. It doesn't exist in Russian, and yet it must. I picked a Latin line so that the Russian reader would see that it obviously belongs to the category of Duty; the imperative rings more resonantly in it. Yet this is characteristic of any poetry that is Classical. Classical poetry is perceived as that which must be, not as that which has already been.

Not a single poet has yet appeared. We are free of the weight of memories. For all that, how many rare presentiments: Pushkin, Ovid, Homer. When in the silence a lover gets tangled up in tender names and suddenly remembers that all this has happened before, the words and the hair, and the rooster that crowed outside the window had been crowing in Ovid's *Tristia,* a deep joy of repetition seizes him, a head-spinning joy—

Like dark water I drink the dimmed air,
Time upturned by the plow; that rose was once the earth.

So that poet, too, has no fear of repetition and gets easily drunk on Classical wine.

E. E. CUMMINGS

[1894–1962]

Mostpeople and Ourselves

from Poems 1923–1954

The poems to come are for you and for me and are not for mostpeople
　—it's no use trying to pretend that mostpeople and ourselves are alike. Mostpeople have less in common with ourselves than the squarerootofminusone. You and I are human beings;mostpeople are snobs.
　Take the matter of being born. What does being born mean to mostpeople? Catastrophe unmitigated. Socialrevolution. The cultured aristocrat yanked out of his hyperexclusively ultravoluptuous superpalazzo,and dumped into an incredibly vulgar detentioncamp swarming with every conceivable species of undesirable organism. Mostpeople fancy a guaranteed birthproof safetysuit of nondestructible selflessness. If mostpeople were to be born twice they'd improbably call it dying—
　you and I are not snobs. We can never be born enough. We are human beings;for whom birth is a supremely welcome mystery,the mystery of growing: the mystery which happens only and whenever we are faithful to ourselves. You and I wear the dangerous looseness of doom and find it becoming. Life, for eternal us, is now; and now is much too busy being a little more than everything to seem anything, catastrophic included.
　Life,for mostpeople,simply isn't. Take the socalled standardofliving. What do mostpeople mean by "living"? They don't mean living. They mean the latest and closest plural approximation to singular prenatal passivity which science,in its finite but unbounded wisdom,has succeeded in selling their wives. If science could fail,a mountain's a mammal. Mostpeople's wives can spot a genuine delusion of embryonic omnipotence immediately and will accept no substitutes.
　—luckily for us,a mountain is a mammal. The plusorminus movie to end moving,the strictly scientific parlourgame of real unreality,the tyranny conceived in misconception and dedicated to the proposition that every man is a woman and any woman a king,hasn't a wheel to stand on. What their most synthetic not to mention transparent majesty,mrsandmr collective foetus,would improbably call a ghost is walking. He isn't an undream of anaesthetized impersons,or a cosmic comfortstation,or a transcendentally sterilized lookiesoundiefeelietastiesmellie. He is a healthily complex,a naturally homogeneous,citizen of immortality. The now of his each pitying free imperfect gesture,his any birth or breathing,insults perfected inframor-

tally millenniums of slavishness. He is a little more than everything, he is democracy; he is alive: he is ourselves.

PABLO NERUDA

[1904–1973]

The Word

TRANSLATED BY HARDI ST. MARTIN

. . . You can say anything you want, yessir, but it's the words that sing, they soar and descend . . . I bow to them . . . I love them, I cling to them, I run them down, I bite into them, I melt them down . . . I love words so much . . . The unexpected ones . . . The ones I wait for greedily or stalk until, suddenly, they drop . . . Vowels I love . . . They glitter like colored stones, they leap like silver fish, they are foam, thread, metal, dew . . . I run after certain words . . . They are so beautiful that I want to fit them all into my poem . . . I catch them in mid-flight, as they buzz past, I trap them, clean them, peel them, I set myself in front of the dish, they have a crystalline texture to me, vibrant, ivory, vegetable, oily, like fruit, like algae, like agates, like olives . . . And then I stir them, I shake them, I drink them, I gulp them down, I mash them, I garnish them, I let them go . . . I leave them in my poem like stalactites, like slivers of polished wood, like coals, pickings from a shipwreck, gifts from the waves . . . Everything exists in the word . . . An idea goes through a complete change because one word shifted its place, or because another settled down like a spoiled little thing inside a phrase that was not expecting her but obeys her . . . They have shadow, transparence, weight, feathers, hair, and everything they gathered from so much rolling down the river, from so much wandering from country to country, from being roots so long . . . They are very ancient and very new . . . They live in the bier, hidden away, and in the budding flower . . . What a great language I have, it's a fine language we inherited from the fierce conquistadors . . . They strode over the giant cordilleras, over the rugged Americas, hunting for potatoes, sausages, beans, black tobacco, gold, corn, fried eggs, with a voracious appetite not found in the world since then . . . They swallowed up everything, religions, pyramids, tribes, idolatries just like the ones they brought along in their huge sacks . . . Wherever they went, they razed the land . . . But words fell like pebbles out of the boots of the barbarians, out of their beards, their helmets, their horseshoes, luminous words that were left glittering here . . . our language. We came up losers . . . We came up winners . . . They carried off the gold and left us the gold . . . They carried everything off and left us everything . . . They left us the words.

OCTAVIO PAZ

[b. 1914]

from *The Other Voice*

TRANSLATED BY HELEN LANE

Between revolution and religion, poetry is the *other* voice. Its voice is *other,* because it is the voice of the passions and of visions. It is otherworldly and thisworldly, of days long gone and of this very day, an antiquity without dates. Heretical and devout, innocent and perverted, limpid and murky, aerial and subterranean, of the hermitage and of the corner bar, within hand's reach and always beyond. . . .

The operative mode of poetic thought is imagining, and imagination consists, essentially, of the ability to place contrary or divergent realities in relationship. All poetic forms and all linguistic figures have one thing in common: They seek, and often find, hidden resemblances. In the most extreme cases, they unite opposites. Comparisons, analogies, metaphors, metonymies and the other devices of poetry— all tend to produce images in which this and that, the one and the other, the one and the many are joined. The poetic process conceives of language as an animated universe traversed by a dual current of attraction and repulsion. In language, the unions and the divisions, the love affairs and the separations of stars, cells, atoms and men are reproduced. Each poem, whatever its subject and form and the ideas that shape it, is first and foremost a miniature animated cosmos. The poem unites the "ten thousand things that make up the universe," as the ancient Chinese put it.

The relationship between man and poetry is as old as our history: it began when human beings began to be human. The first hunters and gatherers looked at themselves in astonishment one day, for an interminable instant, in the still waters of a poem. Since that moment, people have not stopped looking at themselves in this mirror. And they have seen themselves, at one and the same time, as creators of images and as images of their creations. For that reason I can say, with a modicum of certainty, that as long as there are people there will be poetry. The relationship, however, may be broken. Born of the human imagination, it may die if imagination dies or is corrupted. If human beings forget poetry, they will forget themselves. And return to original chaos.

DYLAN THOMAS

[1914–1953]

from *Notes on the Art of Poetry*

You want to know why and how I just began to write poetry, and which poets or kinds of poetry I was first moved and influenced by.

To answer the first part of this question, I should say I wanted to write poetry in the beginning because I had fallen in love with words. The first poems I knew were nursery rhymes, and before I could read them for myself I had come to love just the words of them, the words alone. What the words stood for, symbolised, or meant, was of very secondary importance. What mattered was the *sound* of them as I heard them for the first time on the lips of the remote and incomprehensible grown-ups who seemed, for some reason, to be living in my world. And these words were, to me, as the notes of bells, the sounds of musical instruments, the noises of wind, sea, and rain, the rattle of milkcarts, the clopping of hooves on cobbles, the fingering of branches on a window pane, might be to someone, deaf from birth, who has miraculously found his hearing. I did not care what the words said, overmuch, nor what happened to Jack and Jill and the Mother Goose rest of them; I cared for the shapes of sound that their names, and the words describing their actions, made in my ears; I cared for the colours the words cast on my eyes. I realise that I may be, as I think back all that way, romanticising my reactions to the simple and beautiful words of those pure poems; but that is all I can honestly remember, however much time might have falsified my memory. I fell in love—that is the only expression I can think of—at once, and am still at the mercy of words, though sometimes now, knowing a little of their behaviour very well, I think I can influence them slightly and have even learned to beat them now and then, which they appear to enjoy. . . .

To your third question—Do I deliberately utilise devices of rhyme, rhythm, and word-formation in my writing—I must, of course, answer with an immediate, Yes. I am a painstaking, conscientious, involved and devious craftsman in words, however unsuccessful the result so often appears, and to whatever wrong uses I may apply my technical paraphernalia. I use everything and anything to make my poems work and move in the direction I want them to: old tricks, new tricks, puns, portmanteau-words, paradox, allusion, paronomasia, paragram, catachresis, slang, assonantal rhymes, vowel rhymes, sprung rhythm. Every device there is in language is there to be used if you will. Poets have got to enjoy themselves sometimes, and the twisting and convolutions of words, the inventions and contrivances, are all part of the joy that is part of the painful, voluntary work.

DENISE LEVERTOV

[b. 1923]

Some Notes on Organic Form

So—as the poet stands open-mouthed in the temple of life, contemplating his experience, there come to him the first words of the poem: the words which are to be his *way in* to the poem, if there is to be a poem. The pressure of demand and the meditation on its elements culminate in a moment of vision, of crystallization, in which some inkling of the correspondence between those elements occurs; *and it occurs as words.* If he forces a beginning before this point, it won't work. These words sometimes remain the first, sometimes in the completed poem their eventual place may be elsewhere, or they may turn out to have been only forerunners, which fulfilled their function in bringing him to the words which are the actual beginning of the poem. It is faithful attention to the experience from the first moment of crystallization that allows those first or those forerunning words to rise to the surface: and with that same fidelity of attention the poet, from that moment of being *let in* to the possibility of the poem, must *follow through,* letting the experience lead him through the world of the poem, its unique inscape revealing itself as he goes.

During the writing of a poem the various elements of the poet's being are in communion with each other, and heightened. Ear and eye, intellect and passion, interrelate more subtly than at other times; and the "checking for accuracy," for precision of language, that must take place throughout the writing is not a matter of one element supervising the others but of intuitive interaction between all the elements involved.

In the same way, content and form are in a state of dynamic interaction; the understanding of whether an experience is a linear sequence or a constellation raying out from and in to a central focus or axis, for instance, is discoverable only *in the work,* not before it.

Rhyme, chime, echo, repetition: they not only serve to knit the elements of an experience but often are the very means, the sole means, by which the density of texture and the returning or circling of perception can be transmuted into language, apperceived. *A* may lead to *E* directly through *B, C,* and *D:* but if then there is the sharp remembrance or revisioning of *A,* this return must find its metric counterpart. It could do so by actual repetition of the words that spoke of *A* the first time (and if this return occurs more than once, one finds oneself with a refrain—not put there because one decided to write something with a refrain at the end of each stanza but directly because of the demand of the content). Or it may be that since the return to *A* is now conditioned by the journey through *B, C,* and *D,* its words will not be a simple repetition but a variation. . . . Again, if *B* and *D* are of a complementary nature, then their thought- or feeling-rhyme may find its corresponding word-rhyme. Corresponding images are a kind of non-aural rhyme. It usually happens that within the whole, that is between the point of crystallization that marks the beginning or onset of a poem and the point at which the intensity of contemplation has ceased, there are distinct units of awareness; and it is—for me anyway—these that indicate the duration of stanzas. Sometimes these units are of such equal duration that one gets a whole poem of, say, three-line stanzas, a regularity of pattern that looks like, but is not, predetermined.

WENDELL BERRY

[b. 1934]

Poetry and Song

Song is natural; we have it in common with animals. It is also traditional; it has to be sung *to* someone, who will have to recognize it as a song. Rhythm is fundamental to it, and is its profoundest *reference*. The rhythm of a song or a poem rises, no doubt, in reference to the pulse and breath of the poet, as is often said, but that is still too specialized an accounting; it rises also in reference to daily and seasonal—and surely even longer—rhythms in the life of the poet and in the life that surrounds him. The rhythm of a poem resonates with these larger rhythms that surround it; it fills its environment with sympathetic vibrations. Rhyme, which is a function of rhythm, may suggest this sort of resonance; it marks the coincidences of the rhythm of the structure with the rhythm of the lines, or the coincidences of smaller structures with larger ones, as when the day, the month, and the year all end at the same moment. Song, then, is a force opposed to specialty and to isolation. It is the testimony of the singer's inescapable relation to the world, to the human community, and also, I think, to tradition.

MARK STRAND

[b. 1934]

Poetry, Language, and Meaning

What is known in a poem is its language, that is, the words it uses. Yet those words seem different in a poem. Even the most familiar will seem strange. In a poem, each word, being equally important, exists in absolute focus, having a weight it rarely achieves in fiction. (Some notable exceptions can be found in the works of Joyce, Beckett, and Virginia Woolf.) Words in a novel are subordinate to broad slices of action or characterization that push the plot forward. In a poem, they *are* the action. That is why poems establish themselves right away—in a line or two—and why experienced readers of poetry can tell immediately if the poem they are reading possesses any authority. On the other hand, it would be hard to know much about a novel on the basis of its first sentence. We usually give it a dozen or so pages to earn its right to our attention. And, paradoxically, it has our attention when its language has all but disappeared into the events it generated. We are much more comfortable reading a novel when we don't feel distracted by its language. What we want while reading a novel is to get on with it. A poem works the opposite way. It encourages slowness, urges us to savor each word. It is in poetry that the power of language is most palpably felt. . . .

Poetry is language performing at its most beguiling and seductive while being, at the same time, elusive, even seeming to mock one's desire for reduction, for plain and available order. It is not just that various meanings are preferable to a single dominant meaning; it may be that something beyond "meaning" is being communicated, something that originated not with the poet but in the first dim light of language, in some period of "beforeness." It may be, therefore, that reading poetry is often a search for the unknown, something that lies at the heart of experience but cannot be pointed out or described without being altered or diminished—something that nevertheless can be contained so that is it not so terrifying. It is not knowledge, at least not as I conceive knowledge, but rather some occasion for belief, some reason for assent, some avowal of being. It is not knowledge because it is never revealed. It is mysterious or opaque, and even as it invites the reader, it wards him off. This unknown can make him uncomfortable, force him to do things that would make it seem less strange; and this usually means inventing a context in which to set it, something that counteracts the disembodiedness of the poem. As I have suggested, it may have to do with the origin of the poem—out of what dark habitation it emerged. The contexts we construct in our own defense may shed some light, may even explain parts or features of the poem, but they will never replace it in the wholeness of its utterance. Despite its power to enchant, the poem will always resist all but partial meanings.

A U D R E   L O R D E

[b. 1934]

from *Poems Are Not Luxuries*

For women, then, poetry is not a luxury. It is a vital necessity of our existence. It forms the quality of the light within which we predicate our hopes and dreams toward survival and change, first made into language, then into idea, then into more tangible action. Poetry is the way we help give name to the nameless so it can be thought. The farthest external horizons of our hopes and fears are cobbled by our poems, carved from the rock experiences of our daily lives.

As they become known and accepted to ourselves, our feelings, and the honest exploration of them, become sanctuaries and fortresses and spawning grounds for the most radical and daring of ideas, the house of difference so necessary to change and the conceptualization of any meaningful action. Right now, I could name at least ten ideas I would once have found intolerable or incomprehensible and frightening, except as they came after dreams and poems. This is not idle fantasy, but the true meaning of "It feels right to me." We can train ourselves to respect our feelings and to discipline (transpose) them into a language that catches those feelings so they can be shared. And where that language does not yet exist, it is our poetry which helps to fashion it. Poetry is not only dream or vision, it is the skeleton architecture of our lives.

S E A M U S   H E A N E Y

[b. 1939]

from *Feelings into Words*

"Digging," in fact, was the name of the first poem I wrote where I thought my feelings got into words, or, to put it more accurately, where I thought my *feel* had got into words. Its rhythms and noises still please me, although there are a couple of lines in it that have the theatricality of the gunslinger rather than the self-absorption of the digger. I wrote it in the summer of 1964, almost two years after I had begun to dabble in verses, and as Patrick Kavanagh said, a man dabbles in verses and finds they are his life. This was the first place where I felt I had done more than make an arrangement of words: I felt that I had let down a shaft into real life. The facts and surfaces of the thing were true, but more important, the excitement that came from naming them gave me a kind of insouciance and a kind of confidence. I didn't care who thought what about it: somehow, it had surprised me by coming out with a stance and an idea that I would stand over:

> The cold smell of potato mold, the squelch and slap
> Of soggy peat, the curt cuts of an edge
> Through living roots awaken in my head.
> But I've no spade to follow men like them.
>
> Between my finger and my thumb
> The squat pen rests.
> I'll dig with it.

As I say, I wrote it down ten years ago; yet perhaps I should say that I dug it up, because I have come to realize that it was laid down in me years before that even. The pen/spade analogy was the simple heart of the matter, and *that* was simply a matter of almost proverbial common sense. People used to ask a child on the road to and from school what class you were in and how many slaps you'd got that day, and invariably they ended up with an exhortation to keep studying because "learning's easy carried" and "the pen's lighter than the spade." And the poem does no more than allow that bud of wisdom to exfoliate, although the significant point in this context is that at the time of writing I was not aware of the proverbial structure at the back of my mind. Nor was I aware that the poem was an enactment of yet another digging metaphor that came back to me years later. This was a rhyme that also had a currency on the road to school, though again we were not fully aware of what we were dealing with:

> "Are your praties dry
> And are they fit for digging?"

"Put in your spade and try,"
Says Dirty-Face McGuigan.

Well, digging there becomes a sexual metaphor, an emblem of initiation, like putting your hand into the bush or robbing the nest, one of the various natural analogies for uncovering and touching the hidden thing. I now believe that the "Digging" poem had for me the force of an initiation: the confidence I mentioned arose from a sense that perhaps I could work this poetry thing, too, and having experienced the excitement and release of it once, I was doomed to look for it again and again.

ROBERT HASS

[b. 1941]

Images

Images haunt. There is a whole mythology built on this fact: Cézanne painting till his eyes bled, Wordsworth wandering the Lake Country hills in an impassioned daze. Blake describes it very well, and so did the colleague of Tu Fu who said to him, "It is like being alive twice." Images are not quite ideas, they are stiller than that, with less implication outside themselves. And they are not myth, they do not have that explanatory power; they are nearer to pure story. Nor are they always metaphors; they do not say this is that, they say this is. In the nineteenth century one would have said that what compelled us about them was a sense of the eternal. And it is something like that, some feeling in the arrest of the image that what perishes and what lasts forever have been brought into conjunction, and accompanying that sensation is a feeling of release from the self. Antonio Machado wrote, *"Hoy es siempre todavía."* Yet today is always. And Czesław Miłosz, *"Tylko trwa wieczna chwila."* Only the moment is eternal.

DIANE ACKERMAN

[b. 1943]

What a Poem Knows

A poem tells us about the subtleties of mood for which we have no labels. The voluptuousness of waiting, for instance: how one's whole body can rock from the heavy pounding of the heart. It knows extremes of consciousness, knows what the landscape of imagination looks like when the mind is at full-throttle, or beclouded, or cyclone-torn. Especially it tells us about our human need to make treaties. Often a poem is where an emotional or metaphysical truce takes place. Time slow-gaits enough in the hewing of the poem to make a treaty that will endure, in print, until the poet disowns it, perhaps in a second treaty called a "palinode." A poem knows about illusion and magic, how to glorify what is not glorious, how to bankrupt what is. It displays, in its alchemy of mind, the transmuting of the commonplace into golden saliences. It takes two pedestrian items, claps them together, and comes out with something finer than either one, makes them unite in a metaphor's common cause. . . . It *accretes* life, which is why different people can read different things in the same poem. It freezes life, too, yanks a bit out of life's turbulent stream, and holds it up squirming for view, framed by the white margins of the page. Poetry is an act of distillation. It takes contingency samples, is selective. It telescopes time. It focuses what most often floods past us in a polite blur.

Glossary

Allegory A symbolic narrative in which the surface details imply a secondary meaning, often both generalized and moral.

Alliteration The repetition of consonant sounds, especially at the beginning of words.

Allusion A reference to a person, event, or literary work outside the poem.

Anapest Two unaccented syllables followed by an accented one, as in cŏmprĕhénd or ĭntĕrvéne.

Archetype An image, character, or event recurring in literature and suggestive of mythological patterns of experience.

Assonance The repetition of similar vowel sounds in a sentence or a line of poetry, as in "I rose and told of him of my woe."

Aubade A love lyric in which the speaker complains about the arrival of the dawn, when he must part from his lover.

Ballad A narrative poem written in four-line stanzas, characterized by swift action and narrated in a direct style.

Blank verse A line of poetry or prose in unrhymed iambic pentameter.

Caesura A strong pause within a line of verse.

Closed form A type of form or structure in poetry characterized by regularity and consistency in such elements as rhyme, line length, and metrical pattern.

Connotation The personal and emotional associations called up by a word.

Convention A customary feature of a literary work, such as the use of iambic pentameter in a sonnet.

Couplet A pair of rhymed lines that may or may not constitute a separate stanza in a poem.

Dactyl A stressed syllable followed by two unstressed ones, as in flúttĕrĭng or blúebĕrrў.

Denotation The dictionary meaning of a word.

Diction The selection of words in a literary work.

Dramatic monologue A type of poem in which a speaker addresses a silent listener.

Elegy A lyric poem that laments or memorializes the dead.

Elision The omission of an unstressed vowel or syllable to preserve the meter of a line of poetry.

Enjambment A run-on line of poetry in which logical and grammatical sense carries over from one line into the next. An enjambed line differs from an end-stopped line, in which the grammatical and logical sense is completed within the line.

Epic A long narrative poem that records the adventures of a hero. Epics typically chronicle the origins of a civilization and embody its central values.

Epigram A brief, witty poem, often satirical.

Falling meter Poetic meters such as trochaic and dactylic that move, or fall, from a stressed to an unstressed syllable.

Figurative language A form of language use in which writers and speakers intend something other than the literal meaning of their words. See *hyperbole, metaphor, metonymy, simile, synecdoche,* and *understatement.*

Foot A metrical unit composed of stressed and unstressed syllables. For example, an *iamb,* or *imabic foot,* is represented by ⌣ ′, that is, by an unaccented syllable followed by an accented one. See the chart on p. 55.

Free verse Poetry without a regular pattern of meter or rhyme.

Hyperbole A figure of speech involving exaggeration.

Iamb An unstressed syllable followed by a stressed one, as in tŏdáy.

Image A concrete representation of a sense impression, a feeling, or an idea. Imagery refers to the pattern of related details in a work.

Irony A contrast or discrepancy between what is said and what is meant or between what happens and what is expected to happen. In verbal irony, characters say the opposite of what they mean. In irony of circumstance or situation, the opposite of what is expected happens. In dramatic irony, a character speaks in ignorance of a situation or event known to the audience or to other characters.

Literal language A form of language in which writers and speakers mean exactly what their words denote.

Lyric poem A type of poem characterized by brevity, compression, and the expression of feeling.

Metaphor A comparison between essentially unlike things without a word such as *like* or *as* to designate the comparison. An example: "My love is a red, red rose."

Meter The measured pattern of rhythmic accents in poems.

Metonymy A figure of speech in which a closely related term is substituted for an object or idea. An example: "We have always remained loyal to the crown."

Narrative poem A poem that tells a story.

Narrator The voice and implied speaker (often called a *speaker*) of a literary work, to be distinguished from the actual living author.

Octave An eight-line unit, which may constitute a stanza or a section of a poem, as in the octave of a sonnet.

Ode A long, stately poem in stanzas of varied length, meter, and form. Usually a serious poem on an exalted subject.

Onomatopoeia The use of words to imitate the sounds they describe. *Buzz* and *crack* are onomatopoeic.

Open form A type of literary structure or form in poetry characterized by freedom from regularity and consistency in such elements as rhyme, line length, and metrical pattern.

Parody A humorous, mocking imitation of a literary work.

Personification The endowment of inanimate objects or abstract concepts with animate or living qualities. An example: "The yellow leaves flaunted their color gaily in the wind."

Quatrain A four-line stanza in a poem.

Rhyme The matching of final vowel or consonant sounds in two or more words. Masculine rhymes end with a stressed syllable, feminine rhymes with an unstressed one. Approximate or imperfect rhymes are called "slant" or "near" rhymes.

Rhythm The recurrence of accent or stress in lines of verse.

Rising meter Poetic meters such as iambic and anapestic that move, or ascend, from an unstressed to a stressed syllable.

Satire A literary work that criticizes human misconduct and ridicules vice, stupidity, and folly.

Sestet A six-line unit of verse constituting a stanza or section of a poem; the last six lines of an Italian sonnet.

Sestina A poem of thirty-nine lines written in iambic pentameter. Its six-line stanzas repeat in an intricate and prescribed order the last six words of each line in the opening stanza. After the sixth stanza there is a three-line *envoi* (or envoy) which uses the six repeating words, two to a line.

Simile A figure of speech involving a comparison between unlike things using *like, as,* or *as though.* An example: "My love is like a red, red rose."

Sonnet A fourteen-line poem in iambic pentameter. The *Shakespearean,* or *English, sonnet* is arranged as three quatrains and a couplet, rhyming *abab cdcd efef gg.* The *Petrarchan,* or *Italian, sonnet* divides into two parts: an eight-line octave and a six-line sestet, rhyming *abbaabba cde cde* or *cd cd cd.*

Spondee A metrical foot represented by two stressed syllables, such as kníck-knáck.

Stanza A division or unit of a poem that is repeated in the same form, with similar or identical patterns of rhyme and meter.

Structure The design of form of a literary work.

Style The way an author chooses words, arranges them in sentences or lines, and develops actions, ideas, and forms.

Symbol An object or action in a literary work that means more than itself, that stands for something beyond itself.

Synecdoche A figure of speech in which a part is substituted for the whole. An example: "Lend me a hand."

Synesthesia An attempt to fuse different senses by describing one in terms of another.

Syntax The grammatical order of words in a sentence or line of verse or dialogue.

Tercet A three-line stanza.

Terza rima Interlocking tercets rhyming *aba bcb cdc.* . . .

Theme The idea of a literary work abstracted from its details of language, character, and action, and cast in the form of a generalization.

Tone The implied attitude of a poet toward the subject and materials of a poem.

Understatement A figure of speech in which a writer or speaker says less than what he or she means; the converse of exaggeration, or *hyperbole.*

Villanelle A nineteen-line lyric poem that relies heavily on repetition. The first and third lines alternate throughout the poem, which is structured in six stanzas—five tercets and a final quatrain.

ACKNOWLEDGMENTS

McGraw-Hill, Inc., wishes to thank the copyright owners who have granted permission for use of the following copyrighted poetry and prose:

Diane Ackerman, "What a Poem Knows" from *The Writer on Her Work.* Diane Ackerman is the author of 10 books of poetry and prose, including *A Natural History of the Senses, Jaguar of Sweet Laughter: New and Selected Poems,* and *The Moon by Whale Light.*

Aeschylus, *Agamemnon:* Choral Ode, "Fury" from *The Oresteia.* Translated by Robert Fagles. Translation copyright © 1966, 1967, 1975 by Robert Fagles. Used by permission of Viking Penguin, a division of Penguin Books, Inc., and George Borchardt, Inc.

Bella Akhmadulina, "The Bride" from *Harpers Magazine.* Translated by Stephen Stepanchev. Translation reprinted by permission of Stephen Stepanchev.

Anna Akhmatova, "Lot's Wife" (original and translation) and "Requiem" from *Poems of Akhmatova.* Selected, translated, and introduced by Stanley Kunitz and Max Hayward. Copyright © 1973 by Stanley Kunitz and Max Hayward. Originally published in the *Atlantic.* By permission of Little, Brown and Company.

Dante Alighieri, "Inferno: Canto III" from the John Ciardi translation of *The Divine Comedy.* Copyright © 1954, 1957, 1959, 1960, 1961, 1965, 1967, 1970 by John Ciardi. Reprinted by permission of W. W. Norton & Company, Inc.

Amergin, "The Muse of Amergin" from *The Book of Irish Verse: An Anthology of Irish Poetry from the Sixth Century to the Present.* Translated by John Montague. Copyright © 1974 by John Montague. Reprinted by permission of Harold Matson Company, Inc.

Yehudai Amichai, "A Pity. We Were Such a Good Invention" from *Love Poems: A Bilingual Edition.* English language translation copyright © 1968 by Assia Gutmann. Copyright © 1981 by Yehudai Amichai. Reprinted by permission of HarperCollins Publishers, Inc., and by Olwyn Hugues, London.

A. R. Ammons, "Reflective" and "Bonus" from *The Selected Poems 1951–1977.* Copyright © 1977, 1975, 1974, 1972, 1971, 1970, 1966, 1965, 1964, 1955, by A. R. Ammons. Reprinted by permission of W. W. Norton & Co., Inc.

Benny Anderson, "High and Dry" from *Benny Anderson: Selected Poems.* Translated by Alexander Taylor. Copyright © 1975 by Princeton University Press. Reprinted by permission of Princeton University Press.

Aneirin, "The Gododdin" from *The Earliest Welsh Poetry* (St. Martin's Press, 1970). Translated by Joseph P. Clancy. Copyright © by Joseph Clancy. Reprinted by permission.

Anonymous (Shih Ching), "Near the East Gate" from *Sunflower Splendor: Three Thousand Years of Chinese Poetry.* Translated by Heng Kuan. Copyright © 1975 by Wu-chi Liu and Irving Lo. All rights reserved.

Anonymous (Ch'u Tz'u), "The Lord among the Clouds" from *The Columbia Book of Chinese Poetry: From Early Times to the Thirteenth Century.* Translated by Burton Watson. Copyright © Columbia University Press, New York. Used with permission of the publisher.

Anonymous, "The Words of the High One" and "Twilight of the Gods" from "Song of the Sybil" from *The Elder Edda.* Translated by W. H. Auden and Paul B. Taylor. Copyright © 1967, 1968, 1969 by Paul B. Taylor and W. H. Auden. Reprinted by permission of the publisher, Faber & Faber Ltd., and Curtis Brown, Ltd.

Anonymous, "The Death of Sir Stig" from *Historical Ballads of Denmark.* Translated by Alexander Gray. Reprinted by permission of Alexander Gray and Edinburgh University Press, 22 George Square, Edinburgh EH8 9LF, Scotland.

Anonymous, "Ewe Mourning Poem" from *Introduction to African Literature.* Translated by Geormbeeyi Adali-Mortty.

Apache, "What Happened to a Young man in a Place Where He Turned to Water" from *Shaking the Pumpkin: Traditional Poetry of the Indian North Americas.* Translated by Anselm Hollo; based on Pliny Goddard; edited by Jerome Rothenberg. Reprinted by permission of Sterling Lord Literistic, Inc. Copyright © by Jerome Rothenberg.

Guillaume Apollinaire, "The Mirabeau Bridge," "Miroir," "La Tour Eifell" from *Selected Translations, 1948–1968.* Translated by W. S. Merwin. Copyright © 1968 by W. S. Merwin. Reprinted by permission of George Borchardt, Inc., and David Higham Associates, Ltd.

Cathy Appel, "Letters" from *Raccoon* (poetry journal, issue 20, 1986). "Letters" was first published in *Raccoon 20.* Reprinted by permission of Raccoon Books, Inc.

Aristotle, "The Causes of Poetry" from *Aristotle's Theory of Poetry and Fine Art.* Edited by S. H. Butler. Reprinted by permission of Dover Publications, Inc.

Hans (Jean) Arp, "Kaspar is Dead" from *Arp on Arp: Poems, Essays, Memories* and from *Collected French Writings of Jean (Hans) Arp* (published in England by Calder & Boyous, Ltd., London) by Marcel Jean (editor). Translated by Joachim Neugroschell. Translation copyright © 1969, 1972 by the Viking Press, Inc. Used by permision of Viking Penguin, a division of Penguin Books USA, Inc., and Calder Educational trust, London.

John Ashbery, "The Painter" from *Some Trees.* (New York: The Ecco Press, 1977). Copyright © 1956 by John Asbery. Reprinted by permission of George Borchardt, Inc., for the author and by Carcanet Press.

Margaret Atwood, "Spelling" from *True Stories.* Reprinted by permission of Margaret Atwood; copyright © 1966, 1981.

W. H. Auden, "Musée des Beaux Arts," "The Shield of Achilles," "The Unknown City," "In Memory of W. B. Yeats," from *W. H. Auden: Collected Poems.* Copyright © 1940, 1952, and renewed 1968 by W. H. Auden. Reprinted by permission of Random House, Inc., and Faber & Faber, Ltd.

W. H. Auden, excerpt from "New Year Letter" from" *W. H. Auden: Collected Poems,* edited by Edward Mendelson. Copyright © 1941 and renewed 1969 by permission of Random House, Inc., and Faber & Faber, Ltd.

Kofi Awoonor, "The Sea Eats the Land at Home" and "Song of War" from *The Penguin Book of Modern African Poetry. Okyeame I* (Accra, 1961).

Aztec, "A Woman's Complaint" from *Pre-Columbian Literature of Mexico.* Translated by Miguel Léon Portilla. Copyright 1969 by the University of Oklahoma Press. Reprinted by permission of Oklahoma Press.

Aztec, "The Artist" from *Shaking the Pumpkin: Traditional Poetry of the Indian North Americas.* Edited by Jerome Rothenberg. Translated by Denise Levertov. Copyright © by Jerome Rothenberg. Reprinted by permission of Sterling Lord Literistic, Inc.

Jimmy Santiago Baca, "Meditations on the South Valley XVII" from *Martin and Meditations on the South Valley.* Copyright © 1986, 1987 by Jimmy Santiago Baca. Reprinted by permission of New Directions Publishing Corporation.

Imamu Amiri Baraka, "Preface to a Twenty Volume Suicide Note" from *Preface to a Twenty Volume Suicide Note.* Copyright © 1967 by Amiri Baraka. Reprinted by permission of Sterling Lord Literistic, Inc.

Matsuo Bashō, "Old Pond" from *The Haiku Handbook: How to Write, Share, and Teach Haiku* by William J. Higginson with Penny Harter, published in 1985 by McGraw-Hill, New York, and in 1989 by Kodansha International, Tokyo. Translated by William J. Higginson. Copyright © 1985 by William J. Higginson. Reprinted by permission of the translator.

Matsuo Bashō, "The Temple Bell Stops" from *The Sea and the Honeycomb,* Beacon Press, Boston, 1971. Translated by Robert Bly. Copyright © 1966 by Robert Bly. Reprinted by his permission.

Matsuo Bashō, "Not Even a Hat" from *An Introduction to Haiku* by Harold G. Henderson. Translated by Harold Henderson. Copyright © 1958 by Harold G. Henderson. Reprinted by permission of Doubleday, a division of Bantam Doubleday Dell Publishing Group, Inc.

Matsuo Bashō, "On a Journey, Ill" and "How Rough a Sea!" from *Anthology of Japanese Literature from the Earliest Ear to the Mid-Nineteenth Century,* edited by Donald Keene. Translated by Harold G. Henderson. Copyright © 1955 by Grove Press, Inc. Used by permission of Grove Press, Inc.

Yocheved Bat-Miriam, "Like this before you" from *Modern Hebrew Poetry: A Bilingual Anthology.* Translated by Ruth Finer Mintz. Copyright © 1966 The Regents of the University of California. Reprinted by permission of the University of California Press.

Charles Baudelaire, "The Albatross" and "Correspondences" from *Flowers of Evil.* Translated by Richard Wilbur. Copyright © 1955, 1962 by New Directions Publishing Co. Reprinted by permission of New Directions Publishing Corporation.

Benson, Larry D. (Editor), *The Riverside Chaucer,* Third Edition. Copyright © 1987 by Houghton Mifflin Company. Used with permission.

Wendell Berry, "Poetry and Song" from *The Specialization of Poetry* in *The Hudson Review.* Reprinted by permission from *Hudson Review,* vol. XXVIII, no. 1 (Spring 1975). Copyright © by The Hudson Review, Inc.

Holy Bible, Song of Songs 7: 1–13: "How graceful are your feet in sandals," Psalm 23: "The lord is my shepherd," Job 38: 1–40: 5, "The Lord answered Job out of the whirlwind," Psalm 137: "By the waters of Babylon," Psalm 13: "How long, O Lord wilt thou forget me?" Isaiah 11: 1–6, "There shall come forth a shoot," Ecclesiastes 1: 2–11: "Vanity of vanities," Ecclesiastes 3: 1–8, Psalm 9: 1, excerpts from Psalm 19:1, Job 38:16, Psalm 1:6 from *The Holy Bible–Revised Standard Version.* Copyright © 1946, 1952, 1971 by The Division of Christian Education of The National Council of The Churches of Christ in the USA, and used by permission.

Holy Bible, "Exodus 15: 1–18, Moses' Victory Song" from *The Oxford Annotated Bible.* Permission by the National Council of Churches.

Holy Bible, "Song of Songs 7: 1–13, How graceful are your feet in sandals" from *Bible/The Penguin Book of Hebrew Verse.* Translated by T. Carmi. Copyright © 1981 by T. Carmi. First published by the Viking Press in 1981. Reprinted by permission of Penguin Books, Ltd.

Holy Bible, "Job 38: 1–40: 5, The Lord answered Job out of the whirlwind" from *The Book of Job.* Translated by Stephen Mitchell. Copyright © 1979 by Stephen Mitchell. Revised edition and introduction copyright © 1987 by Stephen Mitchell. Reprinted by permission of HarperCollins Publishers and Michael Katz.

Elizabeth Bishop, "First Death in Nova Scotia," "The Armadillo," "The Fish," "In the Waiting Room," "The Monument," "One Art," "Sandpiper," "Questions of Travel," "Seascape," "Sestina," "The Unbeliever" from *The Complete Poems: 1927–1979.* Copyright © 1979, 1983 by Alice Helen Methfessel. Reprinted by permission of Farrar, Straus & Giroux, Inc.

William Blake, "Art and Imagination" from "A Letter to Dr. Trusler on August 23, 1979," in *The Letters of William Blake.* Edited by Geoffrey Keynes. Reprinted by permission of Oxford University Press.

Rahel Bluwstein, "Only of myself I knew how to tell" from *Modern Hebrew Poetry: A Bilingual Anthology.* Translated by Ruth Finer Mintz. Copyright © 1966 The Regents of The University of California. Reprinted by permission of the University of California Press.

Robert Bly, "Driving to Town to Mail a Letter" from *Silence in the Snowy Fields* (Wesleyan University Press, Middleton, CT). Copyright 1962 by Robert Bly. Reprinted by permission of Robert Bly.

Louise Bogan, "Woman" from *The Blue Estuaries.* Copyright © 1957, 1958, 1962, 1963, 1964, 1965, 1966, 1967, 1968 by Louise Bogan. Reprinted by permission of Farrar, Straus & Giroux, Inc.

Eavan Boland, "Anorexic" from *In Her Own Image.* Copyright © 1989 Eavan Boland. Reprinted by permission of Carcaret Press, Ltd.

Yves Bonnefoy, "True Name" from *On the Motion and Immobility of Douve.* Translated by Galway Kinnell. Original copyright © 1953 by Mercure de France: translation copyright © 1991 by Galway Kinnell. Reprinted with permission of the Ohio University Press, Athens.

Jorge Luis Borges, "Amorous Anticipation" from *Love Poems from Spain and Spanish America.* Translated by Perry Higman. Copyright © 1986 by Perry Higman. Reprinted by permission of City Light Books.

Bertold Brecht, "Song on Black Saturday at Eleventh Hour of the Night Before Easter" from *Bertold Brecht, Poems 1913–1956.* Translated by Lesley Lendrum. Copyright © 1976 by Eyre Methuen, Ltd. Reprinted by permission of Methuen London and Routledge, Chapman & Hall.

Gwendolyn Brooks, "The mother" from *Blacks.* Copyright © 1991 by Gwendolyn Brooks. Formerly (1987) published by The David Company (Chicago) reissued by Third World Press, 7524 S. Cottage Grove, Chicago, IL 60619. Reprinted by permission.

Gwendolyn Brooks, "We Real Cool the Pool Players. Seven at the Golden Shovel" from *Blacks.* Copyright © 1991 by Gwendolyn Brooks; reissued by Third World Press, Chicago. Reprinted by permission.

Charles Bukowski, "My father" from *Burning in Water, Drowning in Flame.* Copyright © 1974 by Charles Bukowski. Reprinted with the permission of Black Sparrow Press.

Michelangelo Buonarotti, "Sonnet CXLIX" ["The Best of Artists . . ."] from *Complete and Selected Letters of Michelangelo,* (Princeton University Press). Translated by Greighton Gilbert. Reprinted by permission.

Tangiguchi Buson, "The piercing chill I feel" and "Blossoms on the pear" from *An Introduction to Haiku,* by Harold G. Henderson. Translated by Harold G. Henderson. Copyright © 1958 by Harold G. Henderson. Reprinted by permission of Doubleday, a division of Bantam Doubleday Dell Publishing, Inc.

Callimachus, "Epigrams" from *Callimachus: Epigrams.* Stanley Lombardo and Diane Rayor, editors and translators. Callimachus: Hymns, Epigrams, Select Fragments. The John Hopkins University Press, Baltimore/London, 1988, pp. 43–61. Reprinted by permission.

Raymond Carver, "Photograph of My Father in His Twenty-second Year" from *Fires.* Copyright © 1983 by Raymond Carver Estate. Reprinted by permission of Capra Press, Santa Barbara.

Raymond Carver, "Late fragment" from *A New Path to the Waterfall.* Copyright © 1989 by the Estate of Raymond Carver. Used by permission of Atlantic Monthy Press.

Catullus, "We should live, my Lesbia, and love" from *The Poems of Catullus.* Translated by Guy Lee. Reprinted by permission of Oxford University Press.

Catullus, "(11), Furius and Aurelius, companions of Catullus." Translated by Peter Glassgold. Copyright © 1988 by Peter Glassgold. Reprinted by permission.

Catullus, "(85), I Hate and I Love." Translated by Guy Lee. Reprinted by permission of Oxford University Press.

C. P. Cavafy, excerpt from "As Much as You Can" from *The Complete Poems of Cavafy.* Translated from the Greek. Copyright © 1961 and renewed 1989 by Rae Dalven. Reprinted by permission of Harcourt, Brace, Jovanovich, Inc. and Rogers, Coleridge & White, Ltd.

C. P. Cavafy, (original and translation) "The City" from *The Complete Poems of Cavafy.* Translated by Rae Dalven. Copyright © 1976 by Rae Dalven. Reprinted by permission of Harcourt, Brace, Jovanovich, Inc.

Paul Celan, "Todesfuge" from *Mohn und Gedachtnis.* Copyright © 1952 by Deutsche Verlags–Anstalt Gmbh, Stuttgart. Reprinted by permission.

Paul Celan, "Fugue of Death" from *Modern European Poetry.* (Bantam Books) Translated by Donald White.

Blaise Cendrars, "Mee Too Boogie" from *Complete Poems.* Translated by Ron Padgett. Copyright © 1922 Ron Padgett, © 1947 Editions Denoel. Reprinted by permission of the University of California Press.

Aimé Césaire, "First Problem" from *The Negritude Poets,* edited by Ellen Conroy Kennedy. Translated by Clayton Eshleman and Dennis Kelly. Copyright © 1975 by Ellen Conroy Kennedy. Used by permission of the publisher, Thunder's Mouth Press.

Helen Chasin, "The Word *Plum"* from *Coming Close and Other Poems.* Published by Yale University Press and reprinted by permission.

Geoffrey Chaucer, "Prologue to the Canterbury Tales" and "The Pardoner's Tale" from *The Canterbury Tales.* Translated by Nevill Coghill (Penguin Classics, 1951, 1958, 1960), copyright © Nevill Coghill, 1951, 1958, 1960. Reprinted by permission of Penguin Books, Ltd.

Li Chin-fa. "A Thought" from *The Chinese Twentieth Century Poetry.* Translated by Kai Yu Hsu.

Li Ch'ing-chao, Tune: "Telling of Innermost Feelings" from *The Columbia Book of Chinese Poetry: From Early Times to the Thirteenth Century.* Translated by Burton Watson. Reprinted by permission of The Columbia University Press.

Li Ch'ing-chao, "To the Short Tune 'The Magnolias' " from *The Orchid Boat: Women Poets of China.* Translated by K. Rexroth and Ling Chung. Copyright © 1972 by Kenneth Rexroth and Ling Chung. Reprinted by permission of New Directions Publishing Corporation.

Amy Clampitt, "Beach Glass" from *The Kingfisher.* Copyright © 1983 by Amy Clampitt. Reprinted by permission of Alfred A. Knopf and Faber & Faber, Ltd.

Lucille Clifton, "The Lost Baby Poem" and "Homage to My Hips" from *Good Woman: Poems and a Memoir, 1969–1980.* Copyright © 1987 by Lucille Clifton. Reprinted with the permission of BOA Editions, Ltd., 92 Park Avenue, Brockport, NY 14420.

Padraic Colum, "The Book of Kells" from *The Book of Irish Verse: An Anthology of Irish Poetry from the Sixth Century to the Present.* Copyright © The Estate of Padraic Colum "Glandor," Stradbrook Rd., Blackrock Co., Dublin, IRELAND. Reprinted by permission.

Hart Crane, "To Brooklyn Bridge" from *The Complete Poems and Selected Letters and Prose of Hart Crane.* Copyright © 1933, 1958, 1966 by Liveright Publishing Co. Reprinted by permission of Liveright Publishing Corporation.

Robert Creeley, "I Know a Man" and "After Lorca" from *Collected Poems: 1945–1975.* Copyright © 1983 The Regents of The University of California. Reprinted by permission of University of California Press.

Countee Cullen, "Incident" from *Color.* Copyright © 1925 by Harper & Brothers; copyright © 1953 by Ida M. Cullen. Reprinted by permission of GRM Associates, Inc., Agents for the Estate of Ida M. Cullen.

e. e. cummings, "Me up at Does," "1(a)," "may i feel said he," "anyone lived in a pretty how town," "my father moved toward dooms of love," "i thank You God for most this amazing," "Buffalo Bill's," and introduction to *New Poems* from *Complete Poems, 1913–1962.* Copyright © 1923, 1925, 1931, 1935, 1938, 1939, 1940, 1944, 1945, 1946, 1947, 1948, 1949, 1950, 1951, 1952, 1953, 1954, 1955, 1956, 1957, 1958, 1960, 1961, 1962 by e. e. cummings. Copyright © 1961, 1963, 1968 by Marion Morehouse Cummings. Reprinted by permission of Liveright Publishing Corporation and MacGibbon & Kee, an imprint of HarperCollins Publishers, Ltd.

Vinnie-Marie D'Ambrosio, "The Painter Yearning for Her Lake (to Suzanne Gilliard)." Reprinted by permission of the author.

Gabriele D'Annunzio, "My songs are children" from *Twentieth-Century Italian Poetry.* Translated by Olga Ragusa. Copyright © Gabriele D'Annunzio. Reprinted by permission of Olga Ragusa.

Léon Gontran Damas, "There Are Nights" from *The Negritude Poets*. Translated by E. C. Kennedy. Edited by Ellen Conroy Kennedy. Copyright © 1975 by Ellen Conroy Kennedy. Used by permission of the Publisher, Thunder's Mouth Press.

Bei Dao, "Declaration" from *The August Sleepwalker*. Translated by Bonnie S. McDougall. Copyright © 1988 by Bei Dao. Reprinted by permission of New Directions Publishing Corporation.

Bruce Dawe, "A Victorian Hangman Tells His Love" from *Condolences of the Season*. Reprinted by permission of Longman Cheshire Pty. Limited.

James Dickey, "The Heaven of Animals" from *Poems: 1957–1967*. Copyright © 1961 by James Dickey; first appeared in the New Yorker. Reprinted by permission of the University Press of New England.

James Dickey, "Buckdancer's Choice" from *Buckdancer's Choice*. Copyright © 1965 by James Dickey; first appeared in *The New Yorker*. Reprinted by permission of the University Press of New England.

Emily Dickinson, "I cannot dance upon my Toes," "There is a pain—so utter," "My Life has stood—A Loaded Gun," "After great pain, a formal feeling comes" from *The Complete Poems of Emily Dickinson*. Edited by Thomas H. Johnson. Copyright © 1929 by Martha Dickinson Bianche. Copyright renewed © 1957 by Mary L. Hampson. Reprinted by permission of Little, Brown and Company.

Emily Dickinson, "Letter to T. W. Higginson 15 April 1862," "Letter to T. W. Higginson 25 April 1862" from *The Letters of Emily Dickinson,* Thomas E. Johnson, ed., Cambridge, Mass.: The Belknap Press of Harvard University Press. Copyright © 1958, 1986 by the President and Fellows of Harvard College. Reprinted by permission of the publishers.

Emily Dickinson, "The Soul selects her own Society," "Wild Nights—Wild Nights!" "I like a look of Agony," "I'm 'Wife'— I've finished that," "There's a certain Slant of light," "I felt a Funeral, in my Brain," "I died for Beauty—but was scarce," "I heard a Fly buzz—when I died," "The Heart asks Pleasure—first," "Pain—has an element of Blank," "Because I could not stop for Death," "Remorse—is Memory—awake," "A narrow Fellow in the Grass," "The Bustle in a House," "The last Night that She lived," "Apparently with no surprise," "My life closed twice before its close," "Tell all the Truth but tell it slant" from *The Poems of Emily Dickinson,* Thomas H. Johnson, ed., Cambridge, Mass.: The Belknap Press of Harvard University Press. Copyright © 1951, 1955, 1979, 1983 by the President and Fellows of Harvard College. Reprinted by permission of the publishers and the Trustees of Amherst College.

Birago Diop, "Diptych" from *The Negritude Poets,* edited by Ellen Conroy Kennedy and translated by Ellen Conroy Kennedy. Copyright © 1975 by Ellen Conroy Kennedy. Used by permission of the publisher, Thunder's Mouth Press.

Reinhard Döhl, "Pattern Poem with Elusive Intruder." Reprinted by permission of the author.

H. D. (Hilda Doolittle), "Helen" and "Heat" from *Selected Poems*. Copyright © 1982 by the Estate of Hilda Doolittle. Reprinted by permission of New Directions Publishing Corporation and Carcanet Press, Ltd.

Rita Dove, "Canary" from *Grace Notes*. Copyright © 1989 by Rita Dove. Reprinted by permission of W. W. Norton & Company.

Alan Dugan, "Love Songs: I and Thou" from *New and Collected Poems, 1961–1983,* first published by Ecco Press in 1983. Copyright © 1961, 1962, 1968, 1972, 1973, 1974, 1983 by Alan Dugan. Reprinted by permission.

Robert Duncan, "The Dance" from *The Opening of the Field*. Copyright © 1960 by Robert Duncan. Reprinted by permission of New Directions Publishing Corporation.

Paul Durcan, "Tullamore Poetry Recital" from *Daddy, Daddy*. Reprinted by permission of The Black Staff Press, Ltd.

Richard Eberhart, "The Groundhog" from *The Collected Poems, 1930–1976.* Copyright © 1976 by Richard Eberhart. Reprinted by permission of Oxford University Press, Inc.

Ruth F. Eisenberg, "Coventry Cathedral" first publication and "Jocasta." Reprinted by permission of the author.

Gunnar Ekelof, "Every Human Is a World" from *Forays into Swedish Poetry* by Lars Gustavsson. Translated by Robert T. Rovinsky. Copyright © 1977 by permission of the University of Texas Press.

T. S. Eliot, "The Love Song of J. Alfred Prufrock," "Preludes," "The Wasteland," "Gerontion" from *Collected Poems: 1909–1962.* Copyright © 1936 by Harcourt Brace Jovanovich, Inc., copyright © 1963, 1964, by T. S. Eliot. Reprinted by permission of Harcourt Brace Jovanovich, Inc., and Faber & Faber, Ltd.

T. S. Eliot, "Little Gidding" from *Four Quartets* and *Collected Poems, 1909–1962.* Copyright © 1943 by T. S. Eliot and renewed 1971 by Esme Valerie Eliot. Reprinted by permission of Harcourt Brace Jovanovich, Inc., and Faber & Faber, Ltd.

T. S. Eliot, "Tradition and the Individual Talent" from *Selected Essays.* Copyright © 1950 by Harcourt Brace Jovanovich, Inc., and renewed 1978 by Esme Valerie Eliot. Reprinted by permission of Harcourt Brace Jovanovich, Inc., and Faber & Faber, Ltd.

Paul Eluard, "Lady Love" from *Collected Poems in English and French.* Translated by Samuel Beckett. Copyright © 1977 by Samuel Beckett. Used by permission of Grove Press, Inc.

Odysseus Elytis, "Drinking the Corinthian sun" from *Modern European Poetry.* (Bantam Books) Translated by Kinmon Friar.

Louise Erdrich, "Indian Boarding School: The Runaways" from *Jacklight.* Translated by Louise Erdrich. Copyright © 1984 by Louise Erdrich. Reprinted by permission of Henry Holt and Company, Inc.

Robert Fagles, "The Starry Night" from *I Vincent: Poems from the Pictures of Van Gogh.* Copyright © by Princeton University Press. Reprinted by permission of Princeton University Press.

Lawrence Ferlinghetti, "Constantly risking absurdity" from *A Coney Island of the Mind.* Copyright © 1958 by Lawrence Ferlinghetti. Reprinted by permission of New Directions Publishing Corporation.

Gerald Fitzgerald, "My love I gave for hate" from *The Book of Irish Verse: An Anthology of Irish Poetry from the Sixth Century to the Present.* Translated by George Campbell Hay.

Robert Fitzgerald, "Cobb Would Have Caught It" from *In the Rose of Time.* Copyright 1943 by Robert Fitzgerald. Reprinted by permission of New Directions Publishing Corp.

Jean de la Fontaine, "The Grasshopper and the Ant" from *The Fables of la Fontaine* by Marianne Moore, translator, translated by Marianne Moore. Translation copyright © 1952, 1953, 1954; © 1964 by Marianne Moore; renewed © 1980, 1981, 1982 by Lawrence E. Brinn and Louise Crane, executors of the Estate. Used by permission of Viking Penguin, a division of Penguin Books USA, Inc.

Carolyn Forché, "The Memory of Elena" from *The Country Between Us.* Copyright © 1982 by Carolyn Forché. Reprinted by permission of HarperCollins Publishers, Inc. Copyright © 1981 by Carolyn Forché. Reprinted by arrangement with Virginia Barber Literary Agency, Inc. All rights reserved.

Marie de France, "The Nightingale" from *Lays of Courtly Love.* Translated by Patricia Terry.

Robert Francis, "Pitcher" from *The Orb Weaver.* Copyright © 1960 by Robert Francis. Reprinted by permission of The University Press of New England.

Kathleen Fraser, "Poem in Which My Legs Are Accepted" from *What I Want.* Copyright © 1974 by Kathleen Fraser.

Robert Frost, "The Need of Being Versed in Country Things," "Once by the Pacific," "Departmental," "On Looking up by Chance at the Constellations," "Nothing Gold Can Stay," "Tree at my window," "Desert Places," "Acquainted with the night," "Dust of Snow," "To Earthward," "Provide, Provide," "The Silken Tent," "The Most of It," "For Once, then, Something," "Neither

Out Far Nor in Deep," "The Span of Life" from *The Poetry of Robert Frost*, edited by Connery Lathem. Copyright 1923 © 1969 by Holt Rinehart and Winston. Copyright 1936, 1951 by Robert Frost. Copyright © 1964, 1970 by Lesley Frost Ballantine. Reprinted by permission of Henry Holt and Company, Inc., and by permission of Jonathan Cape.

Robert Frost, "To Earthward," "The Most of It," "The Need of Being Versed in Country Things," "The Silken Tent" from *The Poetry of Robert Frost*, edited by Edward Connery Lathem. Copyright 1936, 1942, 1956 by Robert Frost. Copyright 1923, 1928, © 1969 by Holt Rinehart and Winston. Copyright © 1964, 1970 by Lesley Frost Ballantine. Reprinted by permission of Henry Holt and Company, Inc.

Robert Frost, "Design," "Fire and Ice," "Stopping by Woods on a Snowy Evening" from *The Poetry of Robert Frost*, edited by Edward Connery Lathem. Copyright 1923 © 1969 by Holt Rinehart and Winston. Copyright © 1964 by Lesley Frost Ballantine. Reprinted by permission of Henry Holt and Company, Inc., and Jonathan Cape.

Robert Frost, "The Figure a Poem Makes" from *Selected Prose of Robert Frost*, edited by Hyde Cox and Edward Connery Lathem. Copyright © 1967 by Holt, Rinehart and Winston. Reprinted by permission.

Robert Frost, "Two Look at Two" from *Complete Poems of Robert Frost.* Copyright 1916, 1921, 1923, 1928, 1930, 1934, 1939, 1943, 1945, 1947, 1949 © 1967 by Holt Rinehart and Winston. Copyright 1936, 1942, 1945, 1947, 1948 by Robert Frost. Copyright renewed 1944, 1951 © 1956, 1958, 1962 by Robert Frost. Copyright renewed © 1964 by Weiley Frost Ballantine. Reprinted by permission of Henry Holt and Company, Inc.

Alice Fulton, "Dance Script with Electric Ballerina" from *Dance Script with Electric Ballerina* (University of Pennsylvania Press). Copyright © 1983 by Alice Fulton. Reprinted by permission of the author.

Solomon Ibn Gabirol, "In Praise of God" from *The Penguin Book of Hebrew Verse.* Translated by T. Carmi.

Tess Gallagher, "Kidnapper" from *Amplitude.* Copyright © 1987 by Tess Gallagher. Reprinted from *Amplitude* with the permission of Graywolf Press, Saint Paul, Minnesota.

Allen Ginsberg, "A Supermarket in California" from *Collected Poems of Allen Ginsberg: 1947–1980.* Copyright © 1955, 1980 by Allen Ginsberg. Reprinted by permission of HarperCollins Publishers, Inc., and of Penguin Books, Ltd.

Louise Glück, "The Garden" from *Descending Figure,* first published by Ecco Press in 1980. Copyright © 1976, 1977, 1978, 1979, 1980 by Louise Gluck. Reprinted by permission.

Lea Goldberg, "From My Grandmother's House" from *The Penguin Book of Hebrew Verse.* Translated by T. Carmi. Reprinted by permission of Acum Books, Ltd.

Jane Graham, "Mind" from *Hybrids from Plants and Ghosts.* Reprinted by permission of Princeton University Press, 1980.

Robert Graves, "Down, Wanton, Down!," and "Symptoms of Love" from *Collected Poems 1975.* Copyright © 1975 by Robert Graves. Reprinted by permission of Oxford University Press, Inc., and by permission of A. P. Watt, Ltd., on behalf of The Trustees of the Robert Graves Copyright Trust.

Elsa Grave, "Afterthought" from *Modern Scandinavian Poetry.* Translated by Martin Allwood. Reprinted by permission of Martin Allwood.

Monk Gusai, excerpt from "Highly Renowned" from *From The Country of Eight Islands: An Anthology of Japanese Poetry* by Hiroaki Sato and Burton Watson. Translated by H. Sato and B. Watson. Copyright © 1981 by Hiroaki Sato and Burton Watson. Used by permission of Doubleday, a division of Bantam Doubleday Dell Publishing Group, Inc.

Woody Guthrie, "This Land Is Your Land." Copyright © 1956 (renewed), 1958 (renewed), and 1990, Ludlow Music, Inc., New York, NY. Used by permission.

Dafydd ap Gwilym, "The Girls of Llandbadarn" from *Nine Thorny Thickets: Selected Poems of Dafydd ap Gwilym,* 1970. Translated by Rolfe Humphries. Reprinted by permission of the Kent State University Press.

Marilyn Hacker, "Canzone" from *Taking Notice.* Reprinted by permission of Frances Collin, literary agent.

Judah Halevi, "The Pure Lover" from *The Penguin Book of Hebrew Verse.* Translated by T. Carmi. Reprinted by permission of Penguin Books, Ltd.

Donald Hall, "My Son, My Executioner" from *Old and New Poems.* Copyright © 1990 by Donald Hall. Reprinted by permission of Ticknor and Fields, a Houghton Mifflin Company imprint. All rights reserved.

Knut Hamsun, "Island Off the Coast" from *Modern Scandinavian Poetry.* Translated by Martin Allwood. Reprinted by permission of Martin Allwood.

Thomas Hardy, "Channel Firing," "During Wind and Rain," "Neutral Tones," "The Man He Killed," "The Oxen," "The Ruined Maid" from *The Complete Poems of Thomas Hardy,* edited by James Gibson (New York: Macmillan, 1978). Reprinted by permission of Macmillan Publishing Company.

Michael S. Harper, "American History" from *Images of Kin.* Reprinted by permission of the University of Illinois.

Robert Hass, "Meditation at Lagunitas" from *Praise,* published by Ecco Press. Copyright © 1974, 1975, 1976, 1977, 1978 by Robert Hass. Reprinted by permission.

Robert Hass, "Images" from *Twentieth Century Pleasures,* first published by the Ecco Press in 1984. Copyright © 1984 by Robert Hass. Reprinted by permission.

George Campbell Hay, "The Two Neighbours" from *Oxford Book of Scottish Verse.*

Robert Hayden, "Those Winter Sundays" from *Angle of Ascent, New and Selected Poems.* Copyright © 1975, 1972, 1970, 1966 by Robert Hayden. Reprinted by permission of Liveright Publishing Corporation.

Jiang He, "To the Execution Ground" from *Seeds of Fire: Chinese Voices of Conscience,* edited by Geremie Barme and John Minford. Translated by Wai-lim Yap. Copyright © 1988 by Geremie Barme and John Minford. Reprinted by permission of Hill and Wang, a division of Farrar, Straus & Giroux, Inc., and by permission of Bloodaxe Books, Ltd. (Bloodaxe Books, 1989).

Seamus Heaney, "Digging," "Mid-Term Break" from *Poems, 1965–1975* and *Death of a Naturalist.* Copyright © 1966, 1969, 1972, 1975, 1980 by Seamus Heaney. Reprinted by permission of Farrar, Straus & Giroux, and Faber & Faber, Ltd.

Seamus Heaney, from "Feelings into Words" from *The Poet's Work* and *Preoccupations.* Copyright © 1980 by Seamus Heaney. Reprinted by permision of Farrar, Straus & Giroux, and Faber & Faber, Ltd.

Seamus Heaney, "Seeing Things" from *Seeing Things.* Copyright © 1991 by Seamus Heaney. Reprinted by permission of Farrar, Straus & Giroux, and Faber & Faber, Ltd.

Seamus Heaney, "Bog Queen," "Casualty," "Untitled Sonnet," "Death of a Naturalist," "Glanmore Sonnets III," "The Grauballe Man," "The Harvest Bow," "Punishment," "The Skunk," "Station Island" from *Selected Poems: 1966–1987.* Copyright © 1990 by Seamus Heaney. Reprinted by permission of Farrar, Straus & Giroux, and Faber & Faber, Ltd.

Anthony Hecht, "More Light! More Light!" and "The Dover Bitch: A Criticism of Life" from *Collected Earlier Poems.* Copyright © 1990 by Anthony E. Hecht. Reprinted by permission of Alfred A. Knopf, Inc.

Heinrich Heine, "The Lorelei" from *An Anthology of German Poetry from Holderlin to Rilke* (Anchor Books). Translated by Edwin Morgan. Reprinted by permission of the Estate of Angel Flores.

Gudrid Helmsdal-Nielsen, "Thaw Night" from *Modern Scandinavian Poetry.* Translated by Inge Knutsson and Martin Allwood. Reprinted by permission of Martin Allwood.

Kakinomoto no Hitomaro, "In Grief after His Wife's Death" from *From the Country of Eight Islands: An Anthology of Japanese Poetry.* Translated by Hiroaki Sato and Burton Watson. Copyright © 1981 by Hiroaki Sato and Burton Watson. Used by permission of Doubleday, a division of Bantam Doubleday Dell Publishing Group, Inc.

Kakinomoto no Hitomaro, "A Strange Old Man" from *One Hundred Poems from the Japanese.* Translated by Kenneth Rexroth. Reprinted by permission of New Directions Publishing Corporation. All rights reserved.

Friedrich Holderlin, "Fall" from *Anthology of German Poetry Through the Nineteenth Century* by Gode. Translated by Hedwig Hellmann. Copyright © 1964 by Gode. Reprinted by permission of The Continuum Publishing Company.

Billie Holiday and Arthur Herzog, Jr., "God Bless the Child." Copyright © 1941—Edward B. Marks Music Company, copyright renewed. Used by permission. All rights reserved.

John Hollander, "Rhyme's Reason" from *Rhyme's Reason.* Copyright © 1981, 1989 by John Hollander. Reprinted by permission of Yale University Press.

John Hollander, "Adam's Task" from *The Night Mirror.* Copyright © 1971 by John Hollander. Used by permission.

John Hollander, "Swan and Shadow" from *Types of Shape.* Reprinted by permission of Yale University Press.

Homer, excerpt from "Hector and Andromache" from *Iliad: Book II,* (Greek original) from *The Penguin Book of Greek Poetry.* Edited by Constantine A. Trypanis. Copyright © Constantine A. Trypanis, 1971. Reprinted by permission of Penguin Books, Ltd.

Homer, excerpt from "Hector and Andromache" from *The Iliad.* Robert Fagles (translator). Translated by Robert Fagles. Translation copyright © 1990 by Robert Fagles. Introduction and Notes, Copyright © 1990 by Bernard Knox. Used by permission of Viking Penguin, a division of Penguin Books USA, Inc.

Homer, excerpt from "The Cyclops" from *Odyssey: Book XIII* from *The Penguin Book of Greek Poetry.* (Greek original) Edited by Constantine A. Trypanis. Copyright © Constantine A. Trypanis, 1971. Reprinted by permission of Penguin Books, Ltd.

Homer, "Cyklops" from *Odyssey: Book XIII.* Translated by Robert Fitzgerald. Copyright © 1961, 1963 by Robert Fitzgerald. Copyright renewed © 1989 by Benedict R. C. Fitzgerald Children. Reprinted by permission of Alfred A. Knopf, Inc.

A. D. Hope, "Imperial Adam" from *Collected Poems, 1930–1965.* Reprinted by permission of Collins/Angus and Robertson Publishers.

Horace, "Odes II, 14" from *The Odes of Horace* by Helen Rowe Henze. Translated by Helen Rowe Henze. Copyright © 1961 by the University of Oklahoma Press.

A. E. Housman, "Is My Team Ploughing?" "To an Athlete Dying Young," "With rue my heart is laden" from *Collected Poems of A. E. Housman.* Copyright 1939, 1940, © 1965 by Holt Rinehart and Winston. Copyright © 1967, 1968 by Robert E. Symons. Reprinted by permission of Henry Holt and Company.

Langston Hughes, "Ballad of the Landlord," "Same in Blues," "Theme for English B" from *Montage of a Dream Deferred.* Copyright 1951 by Langston Hughes, renewed 1979 by George Houston Bass. Reprinted by permission of Harold Ober Associates, Inc.

Langston Hughes, "I, Too," "Mother to Son," "My People," "The Weary Blues" from *Selected Poems.* Copyright 1926 by Alfred A. Knopf, Inc., and renewed 1954 by Langston Hughes. Reprinted by permission of the publisher.

Langston Hughes, "Mulatto" from *Selected Poems.* Copyright 1927 by Alfred A. Knopf, Inc., and renewed 1955 by Langston Hughes. Reprinted by permission of Alfred A. Knopf, Inc.

Langston Hughes, "Madame and the Rent Man" and "Trumpet Player" from *Selected Poems.* Copyright 1947 by Langston Hughes. Reprinted by permission of Alfred A. Knopf, Inc.

Langston Hughes, "The Negro Speaks of Rivers" from *Selected Poems.* Copyright © 1959 by Langston Hughes. Reprinted by permission of Alfred A. Knopf.

Langston Hughes, "Dream Deferred" from *The Panther and the Lash.* Copyright 1951 by Langston Hughes. Reprinted by permission of Alfred A. Knopf, Inc., and Harold Ober Associates, Inc.

Ted Hughes, "Hawk Roosting" from *New Selected Poems* and *Lupercal.* Copyright © 1982 by Ted Hughes. Reprinted by permission of HarperCollins Publishers, Inc., and Faber & Faber, Ltd.

Emyr Humphreys, "An Apple Tree and a Pig" from *Ancestor Worship* (Gee and Son, 1970), also found in *The Oxford Book of Welsh Verse in English,* edited by Gwyn Jones. Reprinted by permission.

Henrik Ibsen, "Agnes" from *Anthology of Norwegian Lyrics.* Translated by Charles Wharton Stork. Reprinted by courtesy of the American Scandinnavian Foundation.

Kobayashi Issa, "I look into a dragonfly's eye," "The old dog bends his Head listening," "The Pigeon Makes His Request" from *The Sea and the Honeycomb.* Translated by Robert Bly. Copyright © 1966 by Robert Bly. Reprinted by permission.

Kobayashi Issa, "Awakened by a horse's fart" and "Falling leaves" from *The Country of Eight Islands: An Anthology of Japanese Poetry.* Translated by Hiroaki Sato and Burton Watson. Copyright © 1981 by Hiroaki Sato and Burton Watson. Used by permission of Doubleday, a division of Bantam Doubleday Dell Publishing Group, Inc.

Lady Izumi, "Looking at my grandchildren," "To a man who said, 'You've forgotten me,' " "Waiting for my two lovers stationed at distant places" from *From the Country of Eight Islands: An Anthology of Japanese Poetry.* Translated by Hiroaki Sato and Burton Watson. Copyright © 1981 by Hiroaki Sato and Burton Watson. Used by permission of Doubleday, a division of Bantam Doubleday Dell Publishing Group, Inc.

Rolf Jacobsen, "The Old Women" from *Twenty Poems of Rolf Jacobsen,* Seventies Press, Moose Lake, MN, 1977. Translated by Robert Bly. Copyright © 1977 by Robert Bly. Reprinted with permission.

Randall Jarrell, "The Death of the Ball Turret Gunner" from *The Complete Poems.* Copyright © 1945, renewal copyright © 1972 by Mrs. Randall Jarrell. Reprinted by permission of Farrar, Straus & Giroux, Inc., and Faber & Faber, Ltd.

Juan Ramón Jimenez, "I shall run through the shadow" from *Roots and Wings: Poetry from Spain, 1900–1975,* edited by Hardie St. Martin. Translated by W. S. Merwin. Copyright © 1976 by Hardie St. Martin. Reprinted by permission of HarperCollins Publishers.

Bobi Jones, "Portrait of an Engine Driver" from *Y Gan Gyntaf* (1957). Translated by Joseph P. Clancy. Reprinted in *Twentieth Century Welsh Poems* (Gomer Press) and *Bobi Jones: Selected Poems* (Christopher Davies, Ltd., 1987). Copyright © Joseph P. Clancy. Reprinted by permission.

Sor Juana Inés de la Cruz, "She Ponders the Choice of a Way of Life Binding until Death," "In a Lighter Vein" from *A Sor Juana Anthology.* Translated by Alan S. Trueblood. Cambridge, Mass: Harvard University Press. Copyright © by the President and Fellows of Harvard College. Reprinted by permission of the publishers.

Donald Justice, "Men at Forty" from *Night Life.* Copyright © 1981 revised edition by Donald Justice. Reprinted by permission of the University Press of New England.

Donald Justice, "In Bertram's Garden" from *The Summer Anniversaries.* Copyright © 1981 by Donald Justice. Reprinted by permission of the University Press of New England.

Rodger Kamenetz, "Christopher Magisto" from *Nympholepsy (Dryad Press).* "Christopher Magisto" appeared previously in *The Ardis Anthology of New American Poetry.* Copyright © 1985 Rodger Kamenetz. Reprinted by permission.

The Lady Kasa, "I dreamed I held" from *One Hundred Poems from the Japanese* by Kenneth Rexroth. Translated by Kenneth Rexroth. Reprinted by permission of New Directions Publishing Corporation. All rights reserved.

The Lady Kasa, "Like the crane whose cry" from *From the Country of Eight Islands: An Anthology of Japanese Poetry.* Translated by Hiroaki Sato and Burton Watson. Copyright © 1981 by Hiroaki

Sato and Burton Watson. Used by permision of Doubleday, a division of Bantam Doubleday Dell Publishing Group, Inc.

Patrick Kavanagh, "Tinker's Wife" from *Collected Poems.* Copyright by the Devin-Adair Publishers. Reprinted by permission.

Miyazawa Kenji, "November 3rd" from *From the Country of Eight Islands: An Anthology of Japanese Poetry.* Translated by Hiroaki Sato and Burton Watson. Copyright © 1981 by Hiroaki Sato and Burton Watson. Used by permission of Doubleday, a division of Bantam Doubleday Dell Publishing Group, Inc.

X. J. Kennedy, "First Confession," "In a prominent bar in Secaucus one day" from *Cross Ties.* Reprinted by permission of the University of Georgia Press.

X. J. Kennedy, "Nude Descending a Staircase" from *Nude Descending a Staircase.* Copyright © 1956 by X. J. Kennedy. Reprinted by permission of Curtis Brown, Ltd.

Galway Kinnell, "Saint Francis and the Sow" and "After Making Love We Hear Footsteps" from *Mortal Acts, Mortal Wounds.* Copyright © 1980 by Galway Kinnell. Reprinted by permission of Houghton Mifflin Co. All rights reserved.

Kenneth Koch, "Variations on a Theme by Williams Carlos Williams," "You were wearing" from *Thank You and Other Poems.* Copyright © 1962, 1985 by Kenneth Koch. Reprinted by permission of the author.

Ono no Komachi, "Imagining her death and cremation," "Submit to you," "They Change" from *From the Country of Eight Islands: An Anthology of Japanese Poetry.* Translated by Hiroaki Sato and Burton Watson. Copyright © 1981 by Hiroaki Sato and Burton Watson. Used by permission of Doubleday, a division of Bantam Doubleday Dell Publishing Group, Inc.

Yang Lain, "The Ruins of Gandan" from *Seeds of Fire: Chinese Voices of Conscience,* edited by Gérémie Barmé and John Minford. Translated by Gérémie Barmé and John Minford. Copyright © 1988 by Gérémie Barmé and John Minford. Reprinted by permission of Hill and Wang, a division of Farrar, Straus & Giroux, Inc., and Bloodaxe Books, Ltd. (Bloodaxe Books, 1989).

Philip Larkin, "A Study of Reading Habits" from *Collected Poems* Copyright © 1988, 1989 by the Estate of Philip Larkin. Reprinted by permission of Farrar, Straus & Giroux, Inc.

Philip Larkin, "Church Going" from *The Less Deceived.* Reprinted by permission of the Marvell Press, England.

D. H. Lawrence, "Humming-bird," "Love on the Farm," "Piano," "Snake," "The Elephant Is Slow to Mate," "When I read Shakespeare" from *The Complete Poems of D. H. Lawrence.* Copyright © 1964, 1971 by Angelo Ravagli and C. M. Weekley, Executors of the Estate of Frieda Lawrence Ravagli. Used by permission of Viking Penguin, a division of Penguin Books USA, Inc., Laurence Pollinger, Ltd., and the Estate of Frieda Lawrence Ravagli.

Giacomo Leopardi, "The Infinite" and "To the Moon" from *Selected Prose and Poetry.* Translated by Iris Origo and John Heath-Stubbs. Translation copyright © 1966 by Oxford University Press. Used by permission of New American Library, a division of Penguin USA, Inc. and David Higham Associates, Ltd.

Denise Levertov, "O Taste and See" from *O Taste and See.* Copyright © 1964 by Denise Levertov. Reprinted by permission of New Directions Publishing Corporation.

Denise Levertov, "Some Notes on Organic Form" from *The Poet in the World.* Copyright © 1965 by Denise Levertov Goodman. First printed in *Poetry.* Reprinted by permission of New Directions Publishing Corporation.

Philip Levine, "Starlight" from *Ashes.* Atheneum Publishers, 1979. Copyright © Philip Levine. Reprinted by permission.

Li Po, "Autumn Cove," "Poem No. 19 in the Old Manner" from *The Columbia Book of Chinese Poetry: From Early Times to the Thirteenth Century.* Translated by Burton Watson. Columbia University Press, New York. Used by permission of the publisher.

Líadan of Corcaguiney, "Líadan Laments Cuithirir" from *The Book of Irish Verse: An Anthology of Irish Poetry from the Sixth Century to the Present.* Translated by John Montague. Copyright © 1974 by John Montague. Reprinted by permission of Harold Matson Company, Inc.

Federico Garcia Lorca, "Play and Theory of the Duende" from *Deep Prose and Other Prose.* (New Directions) Translated by Christopher Maurer. Copyright © 1975 by the Estate of Federico Garcia Lorca. Copyright © 1975, 1976, 1980 by Christopher Maurer. Reprinted by permission of Kosmas and Miller, London.

Federico Garcia Lorca, "Somnambule Ballad" from *Selected Poems.* Translated by Stephen Spender and J. L. Gili. Copyright © 1955 by New Directions Publishing Corporation. Reprinted by permission of New Directions Publishing Corporation.

Audre Lorde, "Now That I Am Forever with Child" from *Chosen Poems, Old and New.* Copyright © 1982, 1976, 1974, 1973, 1970, 1968 by Audre Lorde. Reprinted by permission of W. W. Norton & Company, Inc., and by permission of Audre Lorde.

Audre Lorde, "Poems Are Not Luxuries" from *Claims for Poetry,* edited by Donald Hall. Copyright © 1978 by Audre Lorde. Reprinted by permission of Charlotte Sheedy Literary Agency, Inc.

Amy Lowell, "Patterns" from *The Complete Poetical Works of Amy Lowell.* Copyright © renewed 1983 by Houghton Mifflin Co., Brinton P. Roberts, and G. D'Anedlot Belin, Esquire. Reprinted by permission of Houghton Mifflin Co. All rights reserved.

Robert Lowell, "For the Union Dead," "Skunk Hour" from *Selected Poems.* Copyright © 1976 by Robert Lowell. Reprinted by permission of Farrar, Straus & Giroux, Inc., and Faber & Faber, Ltd.

Lucretius, excerpt from "On the Nature of Things" from *The Way Things Are.* Translated by Rolfe Humphries. Reprinted by permission of Indiana University Press.

Claude McKay, "The Tropics in New York" from *Selected Poems of Claude McKay.* Reprinted by permission of the Estate of Claude McKay.

Wesley McNair, "The Abandonment" from *The Best of American Poetry.* Reprinted by permission of David R. Godine, Publisher, Inc.

Hugh MacDiarmid, "Hungry Waters" from *Hugh MacDiarmid: Selected Poems.* Edited by Michel Grieves and W. R. Aitken, 1978. First published by Martin Brian and O'Keeffe, Ltd. Copyright © 1978. Christopher Murray Grieves.

Don MacLean, "Vincent." Words and music by Don McLean © 1971, 1972 by Music Corporation of America and Benny Bird Music. All rights administered by MCA Music Publishing, a division of MCA, Inc. New York, NY 10019. Reprinted by permission of Music Corporation of America.

Archibald MacLeish, "Ars Poetica" from *Collected Poems.* Copyright © 1985 by the Estate of Archibald MacLeish. Reprinted by permission of Houghton Mifflin Co. All rights reserved.

Antonio Machado, "Problems of the Lyric" from *Obras Completas of Antonio Machado.* Translated by Reginald Gibbons. Copyright © 1979 Reginald Gibbons. Reprinted by permission of Reginald Gibbons.

Antonio Machado, "Daydreams have endlessly turning paths" from *Roots and Wings: Poetry from Spain, 1900–1975,* edited by Hardie St. Martin. Translated by Robert Bly. Copyright © 1976 by Hardie St. Martin. Reprinted by permission of HarperCollins Publishers, Inc.

Stephane Mallarmé, "The Tomb of Edgar Poe" from *An Anthology of French Poetry from Nerval to Valery in English Translation with French Originals* (Anchor Books). Translated by Daisy Aldan. Reprinted by permission of the estate of Angel Flores.

Osip Mandelstam, "Insomnia" (Russian original) from *Russian Poetry: The Modern Period.* Reprinted by permission of Princeton University Press.

Osip Mandelstam, "Insomnia" from *Russian Poetry: The Modern Period,* edited by John Glad and Daniel Weissbert. Translated by John Glad. Copyright © 1978 by the University of Iowa Press. Reprinted by permission of the University of Iowa Press.

Osip Mandelstam, "On Classical Poetry" from *Selected Essays of Osip Mandelstam,* University of Texas

Press, publisher. Translated by Sidney Monas. Copyright © 1977 by the University of Texas Press. Reprinted by permission of the publisher.

Osip Mandelstam, "The Stalin Epigram" from *Selected Poems.* Translated by Clarence Brown and W. S. Merwin. English translation copyright © 1973 by Clarence Brown and W. S. Merwin. Reprinted by permission of Atheneum Publishers, an imprint of Macmillan Publishing Company and Oxford University Press.

Walter de la Mare, "The Listeners" from *Collected Poems, 1942.* The Literary Trustess of Walter de la Mare and the Society of Authors as their representative. Reprinted by permission.

Martial, "Epigrams IV, 69: You Serve the Best Wine Always . . ." from *Latin Poetry in Verse Translation,* edited by J. R. Lind, Riverside edition. Translated by J. V. Cunningham. Copyright © 1957 by Houghton Mifflin Company. Used with permission.

John Masefield, "Cargoes" from *Poems.* The Society of Authors as the literary representative of the Estate of John Masefield. Reprinted by permission.

Maya, "The moon and the year" from *In the Trail of the Wind: American Indian Poems and Ritual Orations,* edited by John Bierhorst. Translated by John Bierhorst. Copyright © 1971 by John Bierhorst. Reprinted by permission of Farrar, Straus & Giroux, Inc.

Peter Meinke, "Advice to My Son" from *Trying to Surprise God.* Copyright © 1965 by the Antioch Review, Inc. First appeared in the *Antioch Review,* Vol. 25, no. 3 (Fall, 1965). Reprinted by permission of the editors.

Askold Melnyczuk, "The Enamel Box." First appeared in *MSS,* 1982. Reprinted by permission of Agni.

James Merrill, "The Pier: Under Pisces" from *Selected Poems: 1946–1985.* Copyright © 1992 by James Merrill. Reprinted by permission of Alfred A. Knopf.

W. S. Merwin, "When You Go Away" from *The Lie.* Copyright © 1963, 1964, 1965, 1966, 1967 by W. S. Merwin. Reprinted by permission of George Borchardt, Inc.

W. S. Merwin, "Separation" from *The Moving Target.* Copyright © 1960, 1961, 1962, 1963 by W. S. Merwin. Reprinted by permission of George Borchardt, Inc.

W. S. Merwin, "Elegy" from The *Carrier of Ladders.* Copyright © 1967, 1968, 1969, 1970 by W. S. Merwin. Reprinted by permission of George Borchardt, Inc.

Edna St. Vincent Millay, Sonnet XXX of *Fatal Interview,* "What Lips My Lips Have Kissed," "Recuerdo" from *Collected Poems,* HarperCollins. Copyright © 1922, 1923, 1931, 1950, 1951, 1958 by Edna St. Vincent Millay and Norma Millay Ellis. Reprinted by permission of Elizabeth Barnett, literary executor.

Cheng Min, "A Glance" from *Twentieth Century Chinese Poetry: An Anthology.* Translated by Kai-yu Hsu. Copyright © 1963 by Kai-yu Hsu. Used by permission of Doubleday, a division of Bantam Doubleday Dell Publishing Group, Inc.

Gabriela Mistral, "Absence" from *An Anthology of Spanish Poetry from Garciloso to Garcia Lorca* (Anchor Books). Translated by Kate Flores. Reprinted by permission of the Estate of Angel Flores.

Stephen Mitchell, "Vermeer" from *Parables and Portraits.* Copyright © 1990 by Stephen Mitchell. Reprinted by permission of HarperCollins Publishers, Inc.

Kaneko Mitsuharu, "Mount Fuji" from *Anthology of Modern Japanese Poetry.* Translated by E. D. Shiffert and Yuki Sawa. Reprinted by permission of Charles E. Tuttle Co., Inc., of Tokyo, Japan.

Scott Momaday, "A Simile," "Angle of Geese" from *American Indian Literature: An Anthology.* Reprinted by permission of Scott Momaday.

Eugenio Montale, "The Eel" from *Sappho to Valery.* Translated by John Frederick Nims. Copyright © 1990. Reprinted by permission of the University of Arkansas Press.

Marianne Moore, "Critics and Connoisseurs," "Poetry," "The Fish," "The Monkeys," "The Past

Is the Present," "To a Snail," from *Collected Poems of Marianne Moore.* Copyright 1935 by Marianne Moore. Reprinted by permission of Macmillan Publishing Company and Faber & Faber, Ltd.

Marianne Moore, "Nevertheless," "The Mind Is an Enchanting Thing" from *Collected Poems of Marianne Moore.* Copyright 1944, and renewed 1972 by Marianne Moore. Reprinted by permission of Macmillan Publishing Company and Faber & Faber, Ltd.

Marianne Moore, "Propriety" from *Collected Poems of Marianne Moore.* Copyright 1951 by Marianne Moore, renewed 1979 by Lawrence E. Brinn and Louise Crane. Reprinted by permission of Macmillan Publishing Company and Faber & Faber, Ltd.

Marianne Moore, "The Steeple-jack" from *The Complete Poems of Marianne Moore.* Copyright 1951 © 1970 by Marianne Moore, © renewed 1979 by Lawrence Brinn and Louise Crane, Executors of the Estate of Marianne Moore. Used by permission of Viking Penguin, a division of Penguin Books USA, Inc. and Faber & Faber Ltd.

Myrtiotissa, "Women of Suli" from *Modern Greek Poetry.* Translated by Rae Dalven. Reprinted by permission of the Estate of Rae Dalven.

Howard Nemerov, "The War in the Air" from *The Collected Poems of Howard Nemerov.* Reprinted by permission.

Pablo Neruda, "The Word" from *Memoirs.* Translated by Hardie St. Martin. Copyright © 1976 by Farrar, Straus & Giroux, Inc. Reprinted by permission of Farrar, Straus & Giroux and Souvenir Press, Ltd.

Pablo Neruda, "Ode to My Socks," "Walking Around" from *Neruda and Vallejo: Selected Poems.* Translated by Robert Bly. Copyright © 1971 by Robert Bly. Reprinted by his permission.

Duane Niatum, "Chief Leschi of the Nisqually" from *Drawing of the Song Animals: New and Selected Poems.* Copyright © by the author. Reprinted by permission of the author.

K. A. Nortje, "Up Late" from *Modern Poetry from Africa.* Reprinted by permission of Penguin Books, Ltd.

Frank O'Hara, "Autobiographica Literaria" from *The Collected Poems.* Copyright © 1967 by Maureen Granville-Smith, Administratrix of the Estate of Frank O'Hara. Reprinted by permission of Alfred A. Knopf, Inc.

Mary Oliver, "Poem for My Father's Ghost" from *Twelve Moons.* Copyright © 1976 by Mary Oliver. First appeared in *Prairee.* Reprinted by permission of Little, Brown, and Company.

Charles Olson, "Maximus, to Gloucester, Sunday, July 19" from *Selected Writings.* Copyright © 1951, 1966 by Charles Olson. Reprinted by permission of New Directions Publishing Corporation.

Ovid, excerpt from "The Story of Daedalus and Icarus" from *Metamorphoses.* Translated by Rolfe Humphries, reprinted by permission of Indiana University Press.

Ovid, excerpts from "Amores I,5" from *Ovid's Amores.* Translated by Guy Lee. Reprinted by permission of John Murray Publishers, Ltd.

Wilfred Owen, "Dulce et Decorum Est" from *Collected Poems of Wilfred Owen,* edited by C. Day Lewis. Copyright © 1963 by Chatto and Windus, Ltd. Reprinted by permission of the Estate of the author, New Directions Publishing Corporation, and Hogarth Press, Ltd.

Sophia Mavroidi Papadaky, "Love Song" from *Modern Greek Poetry.* Translated by Rae Dalven. Reprinted by permission of the Estate of Rae Dalven.

Boris Pasternak, "Winter Night"(original) from *Modern Russian Poetry.* Reprinted by permission of Feltrivelli Editor. Edited by David Weissbort.

Boris Pasternak, "Winter Night" from *Postwar Russian Poets.* Copyright © 1974 Daniel Weissbort. Translated by Richard McKane.

Boris Pasternak, "Hamlet" from *Selected Poems.* Translated by John Stallworthy and Peter France. Copyright © 1982 Jon Stallworthy and Peter Fraure. Reprinted by permission of Penguin Books, Ltd.

Octavio Paz, "The Key of Water" from *The Complete Poems: 1927–1979.* Translated by Elizabeth Bishop. Copyright © 1979, 1983 by Alice Helen Methfessel. Reprinted by permission of Farrar, Straus & Giroux, Inc., and Carcanet Press, Ltd.

Octavio Paz, "The Day in Udaipur" from *The Collected Poems: 1957–1987.* Translated by Eliot Weinberger. Copyright © 1972, 1986 by Octavio Paz and Eliot Weinberger. Reprinted by permission of New Directions Publishing Corporation.

Octavio Paz, "The Street" from *Selected Poems of Octavio Paz,* Indiana University Press, Bloomington, 1963. Translated by Muriel Rukeyser. Copyright © 1963, 1973 Octavio Paz and Muriel Rukeyser. Reprinted by permission of William L. Rukeyser and New Directions Publishing Corporation and Carcanet Press, Ltd.

Octavio Paz, "The Other Voice" from *The Other Voice,* 1991. Copyright © 1990 Octavio Paz. Translation copyright © 1991 by Harcourt Brace Jovanovich, Inc.

Pindar, "Olympia XI" from *The Odes of Pindar.* Translated by Richmond Lattimore. Reprinted by permission of the University of Chicago Press.

Robert Pinsky, "Dying" from *The History of My Heart,* published by the Ecco Press. Copyright © 1984 by Robert Pinsky. Reprinted by permission.

Sylvia Plath, "Black Rook in Rainy Weather," "Daddy," "Edge," "Elm," "Fever 103°," "Lady Lazarus," "Metaphors," "Morning Song," "The Applicant," "Words," "Crossing the Water" from *The Collected Poems of Sylvia Plath,* edited by Ted Hughes. Copyright © 1960, 1961, 1962, 1963, 1981 by the Estate of Sylvia Plath and Ted Hughes. Reprinted by permission of HarperCollins Publishers, Inc., and Faber & Faber, Ltd.

Sylvia Plath, "The Colossus" from *The Colossus and Other Poems.* Copyright © 1961 by Sylvia Plath. Reprinted by permission of Alfred A. Knopf, Inc., and Faber & Faber, Ltd.

Plato, "The Ion" from *The Dialogues of Plato,* (The Clarendon Press, 4th edition, 1953). Translated by Benjamin Jowett. Reprinted by permission of Oxford University Press.

Marie Ponsot, "Summer Sestina" from *Admit Impediment.* Copyright © 1977 by Marie Ponsot. Reprinted by permission of Alfred A. Knopf, Inc.

Ezra Pound, "Canto I," "Canto XII: Kung Walked," "Canto XLV," "Canto LXXXI" from *The Cantos of Ezra Pound.* Copyright © 1934, 1937, 1948, 1962, 1971 by Ezra Pound. Reprinted by permission of New Directions Publishing Corporation and Faber & Faber, Ltd.

Ezra Pound, "A Pact," "Epitaphs," "Hugh Selwyn Mauberley (Life and Contacts)," "In a Station of the Metro," "Portrait D'une Femme," "Sestina: Altaforte," "The Garden," "The Return," The River-Merchant's Wife: A Letter," "The Seafarer," "The White Stag" from *Personae* and *Collected Shorter Poems.* Copyright 1926 by Ezra Pound. Reprinted by permission of New Directions Publishing Company Corporation and Faber & Faber, Ltd.

Ezra Pound, "A Retrospect" from *Literary Essays of Ezra Pound.* Copyright 1935 by Ezra Pound. Reprinted by permission of New Directions Publishing Corporation and Faber & Faber, Ltd.

Sextus Propertius, "Section VII of Homage to Sextus Propertius" from *Personae* and *Collected Shorter Poem* by Ezra Pound. Translated by Ezra Pound. Copyright 1926 by Ezra Pound. Reprinted by permission of New Directions Publishing Corporation and Faber & Faber, Ltd.

Alexander Pushkin, "Old Man" from *The Poems, Prose and Plays of Alexander Pushkin.* Translated by Babette Deutsch. Copyright © 1936 and renewed 1964 by Random House, Inc. Reprinted by permission of Random House, Inc.

Salvatore Quasimodo, "Letter to My Mother" from *Selected Writings of Salvadore Quasimodo.* Translated by Allen Mandelbaum. Copyright © 1971 by Arnoldo Mondadori Editore Spa, Milano. Reprinted by permission.

Jean-Joseph Rabéarivelo, "The Black Glassmaker" from *Modern Poetry of Africa.* Translated by Gerald Moore and Ulli Beier.

Jean-Joseph Rabéarivelo, "She" from *Modern Poetry from Africa.* Translated by Gerald Moore and Ulli Beier. Reprinted by permission of the Presse Universitaires de France.

Craig Raine, "A Martian Sends a Postcard Home" from *A Martian Sends a Postcard Home.* Copyright © 1979 by Craig Raine. Reprinted by permission of Oxford University Press.

John Crowe Ransom, "Bells for John Whiteside's Daughter," "Piazza Piece" from *Selected Poems.* Copyright 1924 by Alfred A. Knopf, Inc., and renewed 1955 by John Crowe Ransom. Reprinted by permission of Alfred A. Knopf, Random House, Inc., and Carcanet Press, Ltd.

Lutz Rathenow, "For Uwe Gressman" from *Contacts/Kontakt: Poems and Writings by Lutz Rathenow.* Copyright © Boria Sax. Reprinted by permission of Boria Sax. Translated by Boria Sax.

Dalia Ravikovitch, "Mechnical Doll" from *The Penguin Book of Hebrew Verse.* Translated by T. Carmi. Reprinted by permission of Acam Ltd.

Henry Reed, "Chard Whitlow" and "Naming of Parts" from *Collected Poems,* edited by Jon Stallworthy (1991). Copyright © the Executor of Henry Reed's Estate. Reprinted by permission of Oxford University Press.

Kenneth Rexroth, "Floating" from *Collected Shorter Poems of Kenneth Rexroth.* Copyright 1944 by New Directions Publishing Corporation. Reprinted by permission of New Directions Publishing Corporation.

Charles Reznikoff, "Kaddish" from *By the Waters of Manhattan.* Copyright © 1959 by Charles Reznikoff. Reprinted by permission of New Directions Publishing Corporation.

Adrienne Rich, "Aunt Jennifer's Tigers," "Diving into the Wreck," "Orion," "Planetarium," "Rape," "Snapshots of a Daughter-in-Law," "Storm Warnings," "Trying to Talk with a Man," The Knight" from *The Fact of the Doorframe, Poems Selected and New: 1950–1984.* Copyright © 1984 by Adrienne Rich. Copyright © 1975, 1978 by W. W. Norton & Company, Inc. Copyright © 1981 by Adrienne Rich. Reprinted by permission of W. W. Norton & Company, Inc.

Adrienne Rich, "For an Album" from *Time's Power Poems, 1985–1988.* Copyright © 1989 by Adrienne Rich. Reprinted by permission of W. W. Norton & Company, Inc.

Adrienne Rich, "Here is a Map of Our Country" and "(Dedications) I Know You Are Reading This Poem" from *An Atlas of The Difficult World.* Copyright © 1991 by Adrienne Rich. Reprinted by permission of W. W. Norton and Co., Inc.

Rainer Maria Rilke, "Der Panther" (German original) from *Rainer Maria Rilke: Samtliche Werke.* Reprinted by permission of Insel Verlag.

Rainer Maria Rilke, "The Cadet Picture of My Father" from *Imitations.* Translated by Robert Lowell. Copyright © 1958, 1959, 1960, 1961 by Robert Lowell. Renewal copyright © 1986, 1987, 1989 by Caroline Lowell, Harriet Lowell, and Sheridan Lowell. Reprinted by permission of Farrar, Straus & Giroux, Inc., and Faber & Faber, Ltd.

Rainer Maria Rilke, "Letter, April 5th, 1903" from *Letters to a Young Poet.* Translated by M. D. Herter Norton. Copyright 1934 by W. W. Norton & Company, Inc. Copyright renewed 1962 by M. D. Herter Norton. Revised edition copyright 1954 by W. W. Norton & Company, Inc. Copyright renewed 1982 by M. D. Herter Norton. Reprinted by permission of W. W. Norton & Company, Inc.

Rainer Maria Rilke, "Archaic Torso of Apollo," "Buddha in Glory," "Self Portrait," "The Panther" from *The Selected Poetry of Rainer Maria Rilke.* Translated by Stephen Mitchell. Copyright © 1982 by Stephen Mitchell. Reprinted by permission of Random House, Inc.

Arthur Rimbaud, "The Drunken Boat" from *An Anthology of French Poetry from Nerval to Valery in English Translation with French Originals.* Translated by Stephen Stepanchev. Translation copyright © 1958 by Stephen Stepanchev. Reprinted by permission of Stephen Stepanchev.

Alberto Rios, "A Dream of Husbands" from *Whispering to Fool the Wind,* published by Sheepmeadow Press. Copyright © 1985 by Alberto Rios. Reprinted by permission.

Yannis Ritsos, "The Meaning of Simplicity" from *Yannis Ritsos: Selected Poems.* Translated by Kimon Friar and Kostas Myrsiades. Copyright © 1989 by Kimon Friar. Reprinted with the permission of Boa Editions, Ltd., 92 Park Avenue, Brockport, NY 14420.

Edwin Arlington Robinson, "Richard Cory" from *The Children of the Night* (New York: Charles Scribner's Sons, 1897). Reprinted by permission.

Edwin Arlington Robinson, "Miniver Cheevy" from *The Town Down the River* (New York: Charles Scribner's Sons, 1910). Reprinted by permission.

Theodore Roethke, "Elegy for Jane" from *The Collected Poems of Theodore of Theodore Roethke.* Copyright 1950 by Theodore Roethke. Used by permission of Doubleday, a division of Bantam Doubleday Dell Publishing Group, Inc., and Faber & Faber, Ltd.

Theodore Roethke, "My Papa's Waltz" from *The Collected Poems of Theodore Roethke.* Copyright 1942 by Hearst Magazines, Inc. Used by permission of Doubleday, a division of Bantam Doubleday Dell Publishing Group, Inc., and Faber & Faber, Ltd.

Theodore Roethke, "The Waking" from *The Collected Poems of Theodore Roethke.* Copyright 1953 by Theodore Roethke. Used by permission of Doubleday, a division of Bantam Doubleday Dell Publishing Group, Inc., and Faber & Faber, Ltd.

Amelia Rosselli, "Neve" (Italian original) from *Documento 1966–1973.* Reprinted by permission of Garzanti Editore.

Amelia Rosseli, "Snow" from *New Italian Poetry, 1945 to the Present: A Bilingual Anthology.* Edited and translated by Lawrence R. Smith. Copyright © 1981 by the Regents of the University of California.

Muriel Rukeyser, "Myth" from *Out of Silence.* Copyright © 1992 Muriel Rukeyser. Tri-Quarterly Books, Evanston, IL, 1992. Reprinted by permission of William L. Rukeyser.

George William Russell, (Æ), "Exiles" from *The Book of Irish Verse: An Anthology of Irish Poetry from the Sixth Century to the Present.* Copyright George William Russell, A. M. Heath & Co., Ltd. Reprinted by permission of Diarmuid Russell and A. M. Heath.

Nelly Sachs, "O the chimneys" from *O the Chimneys.* Translated by Michael Roloff. Copyright © 1967 by Farrar, Straus & Giroux, Inc. Reprinted by permission and Joan Daves Agency.

Natalie Safir, "Matisse's Dance." Copyright © Natalie Safir. Reprinted by permission of the author.

St. Francis of Assisi, "Canticle of the Creatures" from *Lyric Poetry of Italian Renaissance* (Yale University Press). Translated by Eleanor L. Turnbull. Copyright 1954 by L. R. Lind. Reprinted by permission.

The Lady Ōtomo no Sakanoe, "Love's Complaint" from *From the Country of Eight Islands: An Anthology of Japanese Poetry.* Translated by Hiroaki Sato and Burton Watson. Copyright © 1981 by Hiroaki Sato and Burton Watson. Used by permission of Doubleday, a division of Bantam Doubleday Dell Publishing Group, Inc.

Carl Sandburg, "Chicago" from *Chicago Poems.* Copyright 1916 by Holt, Rinehart and Winston, Inc., and renewed 1944 by Carl Sandburg. Reprinted by permission of Harcourt Brace Jovanovich, Inc.

Sappho, "Alone" and Seizure" (Greek original) from *Greek Lyrics.* Translated by R. Lattimore.

Sappho, "Alone" and "Seizure" from *Greek Lyric Poetry.* Translated by Willis Barstone.

Friedrich Schiller, "Ode to Joy" from *Friedrich Schiller: An Anthology of Our Time with Account of His Life and Work,* by Frederick Ungar. Translated by Norman MacLeod and Alexander Gode–van Aesch. Copyright © by Frederick Ungar Publishing Company. Reprinted by permission of the Continuum Publishing Company.

Gertrude Schnackenberg, "Signs" from *The Lamplit Answer.* Copyright © 1982, 1985 by Gertrude Schnackenberg. Reprinted by permission of Farrar, Straus & Giroux, Inc.

Sandra Schor, "At Point Hope on the Chukchi Sea." Copyright © 1975 by Sandra M. Schor. Reprinted by permission of Joseph M. Schor.

Sedulius Scottus, "The Scholar and His Cat" from *A Short History of Irish Literature: A Backward Look by Frank O'Connor.* Translated by Frank O'Connor. Reprinted by permission of Joan Daves, Inc.

Pete Seeger, "Turn! Turn! Turn!" (To everything there is a reason), words from the book of Ecclesiastes. Adaptation and music by Pete Seeger. Copyright © 1962 (renewed) Melody Trails, Inc., New York, NY. Used by permission.

George Seferis, "Poetry and Human Living" from *A Poet's Journal: Days of 1945–1951*. Translated by Athan Anagnostopoulos. Cambridge, Mass. The Belknap Press of Harvard University Press. Copyright © 1974 by the President and Fellows of Harvard College. Reprinted by permission.

George Seferis, "The Old Man" from *Six Poets of Modern Greece*. Translated by Edmond Keeley and Philip Sherrard. Reprinted by permission of Thames & Hudson, London.

Léopold Sédar Senghor, "Night of Sine" and "Paris in the Snow" from *Modern Poetry from Africa*. Translated by Gerald Moore and Ulli Beier. Reprinted by permission of Oxford University Press.

Anne Sexton, "The Starry Night" and "To a Friend Whose Work Has Come to Triumph" from *All My Pretty Ones*. Copyright © 1962 by Anne Sexton. Reprinted by permission of Houghton Mifflin Co. and Sterling Lord Literistic, Inc. All rights reserved.

Anne Sexton, "Us" from *Love Poems*. Copyright © 1967, 1968, 1969 by Anne Sexton. Reprinted by Houghton Mifflin Co. and Sterling Lord Literistic, Inc. All rights reserved.

Shen Yee-Ping, "Shutting the door of a tiny study." Translated by Rosabel Lu and Sandra Schor. Copyright © 1975 by Sandra Schor. Reprinted by permission of Joseph M. Schor.

Leslie Marmon Silko, "Slim Man Canyon" from *Come to Power: Eleven Contempory American Indian Poets*, edited by Dick Lourie. Translated by Leslie Silko. Copyright © 1974 by the Crossing Press. Reprinted by permission of Wylie, Aitken & Stone, Inc.

Charles Simic, "Stone" from *Dismantling the Silence*. Copyright © 1971 by Charles Simic. Reprinted by permission of George Braziller, Inc.

Paul Simon, "Richard Cory." Reprinted by permission of Paul Simon Music. Copyright © 1966 by Paul Simon. Used by permission of the Publisher.

Louis Simpson, "American Poetry" and "My Father in the Night Commanding No" from *At the End of the Open Road*. Copyright © 1963 by Louis Simpson. Reprinted by permission of the University Press of New England.

Louis Simpson, "The Heroes" from *People Live Here: Selected Poems, 1949–1953*. Reprinted by permission of Louis Simpson.

Egil Skallagrimsson, "Head-Ransom" from *The Skalds*. Translated by Lee M. Hollander. Reprinted by permission of the American Scandinavian Foundation.

Ian Crichton Smith, "Culloden and After" from *Collected Poems* (Eyre & Spottiswoode, Ltd., 1961). Reprinted by permission of Carcanet Press, Ltd.

Bessie Smith, "Lost Your Head Blues." © 1925 Frank Music Corp, © renewed 1953 Frank Music Corp. International Copyright secured. All rights reserved. Used by permission.

Stevie Smith, "Not Waving but Drowning" from *Collected Poems of Stevie Smith*. Copyright © 1972 by Stevie Smith. Reprinted by permission of New Directions Publishing Corporation.

Gary Snyder, "Prayer for the Great Family" from *Turtle Island*. Copyright © 1974 by Gary Snyder. Reprinted by permission of New Directions Publishing Corporation.

Cathy Song, "Lost Sister" and "Girl Powdering her Neck" from *Picture Bride*. Reprinted by permission of Yale University Press.

Sophocles, "Ode I" from *The Antigone of Sophocles*. Translated by Dudley Fitts and Robert Fitzgerald. Copyright 1939 by Harcourt, Brace Jovanovich, Inc., and renewed 1967 by Dudley Fitts and Robert Fitzgerald. Reprinted by permission of Harcourt Brace Jovanovich, Inc.

Wole Soyinka, "Hamlet" from *A Shuttle in the Crypt*. Copyright © 1972 by Wole Soyinka. Reprinted by permission of Hill and Wang, a division of Farrar, Straus & Giroux, Inc., and Rex Collings, Ltd.

William Stafford, "Traveling through the dark" from *Stories that Could Be True*, Harper and Row, 1977. Copyright by William Stafford. Reprinted by permission of William Stafford.

Gertrude Stein, "A Petticoat" from *Selected Writings of Gertrude Stein*, edited by Carl Van Vechten.

Copyright 1946 by Random House, Inc. Reprinted by permission of Random House, Inc., and the Estate of Gertrude Stein.

Wallace Stevens, "Anecdote of the Jar," "Bantams in Pine-Woods," "Peter Quince at the Clavier," "Sunday Morning," "The Snow Man," "Thirteen Ways of Looking a Black Bird" from *Collected Poems*. Copyright 1923 and renewed 1951 by Wallace Stevens. Reprinted by permission of Alfred A. Knopf, Inc., and Faber & Faber, Ltd.

Wallace Stevens, "The Idea of Order at Key West," "The Man with the Blue Guitar" from *Collected Poems*. Copyright 1936 by Wallace Stevens and renewed 1964 by Holly Stevens. Reprinted by permission of Alfred A. Knopf, Inc., and Faber & Faber, Ltd.

Wallace Stevens, "Of Modern Poetry" and "The Poems of Our Climate" from *Collected Poems*. Copyright 1942 by Wallace Stevens and renewed 1970 by Holly Stevens. Reprinted by permission of Alfred A. Knopf, Inc., and Faber & Faber, Ltd.

Wallace Stevens, "The house was quiet and the world was calm" from *Collected Poems*. Copyright 1947 by Wallace Stevens. Reprinted by permission of Alfred A. Knopf, Inc. and Faber & Faber, Ltd.

Wallace Stevens, untitled poem from *Collected Poems*. Copyright 1954 by Wallace Stevens. Reprinted by permission of Alfred A. Knopf, Inc., and Faber & Faber, Ltd.

Wallace Stevens, "Adagia" from *The Necessary Angel*. Copyright 1951 by Wallace Stevens. Reprinted by permission of Alfred A. Knopf, Inc., and Faber & Faber, Ltd.

Georg Stiernhielm, "On Astrild, Honing His Arrows" (Swedish original and translation) from *Forays into Swedish Poetry* by Lars Gustafsson. Translated by Robert T. Rovinsky. Copyright © 1977. Reprinted by permission of the University of Texas Press.

Mark Strand, "Eating Poetry," "Leopardi," from *Selected Poems*. Copyright © 1979, 1980 by Mark Strand. Reprinted by permission of Alfred A. Knopf, Inc.

Mark Strand, "Poetry, Language, and Meaning" from *The Best American Poetry 1991, Introduction*. Copyright 1991 Mark Strand. Reprinted by permission of Mark Strand.

August Strindberg, "Street Scenes III" from *Forays into Swedish Poetry,* by Lars Gustafsson. Translated by Robert T. Rovinsky. Copyright © 1977. Reprinted by permission of the University of Texas Press.

May Swenson, "How Everything Happens" from *New and Selected Things Taking Place*. Copyright © 1969. Used with the permission of the Literary Estate of May Swenson.

May Swenson, "The Centaur" from *New and Selected Things Taking Place*. Copyright © 1956 and renewed 1984. Used with permission of the Literary Estate of May Swenson.

May Swenson, "Women" from *New and Selected Things Taking Place*. Copyright © 1968. Used with the permission of the Literary Estate of May Swenson.

Tomioka Taeko, "Between" from *From the Country of Eight Islands: An Anthology of Japanese Poetry*. Translated by Hiroaki Sato and Burton Watson. Copyright © 1981 by Hiroaki Sato and Burton Watson. Used by permission of Doubleday, a division of Bantam Doubleday Dell Publishing Group, Inc.

Tomioka Taeko, "Just the Two of Us" from *From the Country of Eight Islands: An Anthology of Japanese Poetry*. Translated by Hiroaki Sato and Burton Watson. Reprinted by permission of Hiroaki Sato.

Tchicaya U Tam'si, "Brush Fire" from *The Negritude Poets,* edited by Ellen Conroy Kennedy. Translated by Sangodare Akanji. Copyright © 1975 by Ellen Conroy Kennedy. Used by permission of the publisher, Thunder's Mouth Press.

Dylan Thomas, "And death shall have no dominion," "A Refusal to Mourn the Death by Fire, of a Child in London," "Do not go gentle into that good night," "Fern Hill," "In my craft or sullen art," "I see the boys of summer," "Poem in October," "The force that through the green fuse drives the flower," "The hunchback in the park" from *Poems of Dylan Thomas*. Copyright 1939, 1943, 1946 by New Directions, 1945 by the Trustees for the Copyrights of Dylan Thomas, 1952 by Dylan Thomas. "Poem in October" was first published in *Poetry*. Reprinted by permission of New Directions Publishing Corporation and David Higham Associates, Ltd.

Dylan Thomas, "Notes on the Art of Poetry" from *Poems of Dylan Thomas.* Copyright © 1964 by New Directions Publishing Corporation. Reprinted by permission of New Directions Publishing Corporation and David Higham Associates, Ltd.

Jean Toomer, "Reapers" from *Cane.* Reprinted by permission of Liveright Publishing Co.

Georg Trakl, "Decline" from *German Poetry: 1910–1975.* Translated by Michael Hamburger. Reprinted by permission of Michael Hamburger.

Tomas Tranströmer, "Storm" from *Forays into Swedish Poetry,* by Lars Gustafsson. Translated by Robert T. Rovinsky. Copyright © 1977. Reprinted by permission of the University of Texas Press.

Mao Tse-tung, "Sixteen-Syllable Stanza" from *Twentieth Century Chinese Poetry: An Anthology.* Translated by Kai-yu Hsu. Copyright © 1963 by Kai-yu Hsu. Used by permission of Doubleday, a division of Bantam Doubleday Dell Publishing Group, Inc.

Marina Tsvetayeva, "An Attempt at Jealousy" from *Russian Poetry: The Modern Period,* John Glad and Daniel Weissbort (editors). Translated by Bob Perlman, Shirley Rihner, Alexander Petrov. Copyright 1978 by the University of Iowa Press. Reprinted by permission of the University of Iowa Press.

Tu Fu, "Alone Looking for Blossoms along the River" and "Ballad of a Hundred Worries" from *Selected Poems of Tu Fu.* Translated by Daniel Hinton. Copyright © 1988, 1989 by Daniel Hinton. Reprinted by permission of New Directions Publishing Corporation.

Jim Tyack, "For Neruda" from *The Rented Tuxedo* (Street Press). Copyright © 1976 by Jim Tyack. Reprinted by permission of the author.

Giuseppe Ungaretti, "You Shattered" from *Selected Poems of Giuseppe Ungaretti.* Translated and edited by Allen Mandrelbaum. Copyright © 1975 by Cornell University. Used by permission of the publisher, Cornell University Press.

John Updike, "The Mosquito" from *Telephone Poles and Other Poems.* Originally appeared in *The New Yorker.* Copyright © 1960 by John Updike. Reprinted by permisison of Alfred A. Knopf, Inc., and Penguin Books, Ltd.

Éleni Vakaló, "My Father's Eye" from *Modern European Poetry.* (Bantam Doubleday Dell Publishing Group). Translated by Kimon Friar.

Paul Valéry, "Hélèn" from *An Anthology of French Poetry from Nerval to Valery in English Translation with French Originals,* (Anchor Books). Translated by Andrew Chiappe. Reprinted by permission of the Estate of Angel Flores.

Paul Valéry, "Poetry, Prose, Song" from *The Art of Poetry,* volume 1. Translated by Denise Folliot. Copyright © 1958 by Princeton University Press, renewed 1986. Reprinted by permission of Princeton University Press.

César Vallejo, "The Black Riders" from *Neruda and Vallejo: Selected Poems,* Beacon Press, 1976. Translated by Robert Bly. Reprinted by permission of Robert Bly.

Paul Verlaine, "Sentimental Dialogue" from *An Anthology of French Poetry from Nerval to Valery in English Translation with French Originals* (Anchor Books). Translated by Muriel Kittel. Reprinted by permission of the Estate of Angel Flores.

François Villon, "Ballade of the Ladies of Bygone Time" and "I Am Francis" from *Poems of François Villon.* Translated by Norman Cameron. Reprinted by permission of Jonathan Cape, Ltd.

Virgil, "Arms and the Man" from *The Aeneid: Book I,* and "Dido and Aeneas" from *The Aeneid: Book IV.* Translated by Robert Fitzgerald. Translation copyright © 1980, 1982, 1983 by Robert Fitzgerald. Reprinted by permission of Random House, Inc.

Virgil, "The Fourth Eclogue" from *Virgil: The Eclogues.* Translated by Guy Lee. Reprinted by permission of Penguin Books, Ltd.

David Vogel, "My Childhood Cities" from *The Penguin Book of Hebrew Verse.* Translated by T. Carmi. Reprinted by permission of Acum Books, Ltd.

Annette von Droste–Hülshoff, "On the Tower" from *An Anthology of German Poetry From Hölderlin to Rilke* (Anchor Books). Translated by James Edward Tobin. Reprinted by permission of the Estate of Angel Flores.

Johann Wolfgang von Goethe, "Nature and Art" from *Sappho to Valery.* Originally appeared in *College English.* Translated by John Frederick Nims. Copyright 1990 by Frederick Nims. Reprinted by permission of the University of Arkansas Press.

Andrey Voznesensky, "I Am Goya" (Russian original and translation) from *Antiworlds and the Fifth Ace.* Edited by W. H. Auden. Translated by Stanley Kunitz. Copyright © 1966 by Basic Books, Inc. Reprinted by permission of Basic Books, a division of HarperCollins Publishers.

David Wagoner, "Walking in the Snow" from *Staying Alive.* Published by Poetry Northwest, 1965. Copyright David Wagoner. Reprinted by permission of David Wagoner.

Diane Wakoski, "Belly Dancer" from *Emerald Ice: Selected Poems, 1962–1987.* Copyright © 1966 by Diane Wakoski. Reprinted by permission of Black Sparrow Press.

Derek Walcott, "Codicil" from *Collected Poems.* Copyright © 1982, 1983, 1984 by Derek Walcott. Reprinted by permission of Farrar, Straus & Giroux, Inc., and Faber & Faber, Ltd.

Robert Wallace, "The Double-Play" from *Views of a Ferris Wheel.* Copyright © 1961 by Robert Wallace. Reprinted by permission of the author.

Tai Wang-shu, "I Think" from *Twentieth Century Chinese Poetry: An Anthology,* by Kai-yu Hsu. Translated by Kai-yu Hsu. Copyright© 1963 by Kai-yu Hsu. Used by permission of Doubleday, a division of Bantam Doubleday Dell Publishing Group, Inc.

Robert Penn Warren, "Love and Knowledge" from *New and Selected Poems, 1923–1985.* First appeared in *The New Yorker.* Copyright © 1969 by Robert Penn Warren. Reprinted by permission of Random House, Inc., and William Morris agency, New York.

James Welch, "Magic Fox" from *American Indian Literature: An Anthology,* edited by Alan R. Velie. Translated by James Welch. Reprinted by permission of James Welch.

Richard Wilbur, "Mind" from *Things of the World.* Copyright © 1956 and renewed 1984 by Richard Wilbur. Reprinted by permission of Harcourt Brace Jovanovich, Inc.

William Carlos Williams, "Book II: Sunday in the Park" from *Paterson.* Copyright 1948 by William Carlos Williams. Reprinted by permission of New Directions Publishing Corporation and Carcanet Press, Ltd.

William Carlos Williams, "At the Ball Game," "Danse Russe," "January Morning," "Nantucket," "Queen Anne's Lace," "Spring and All," "The Last Words of My English Grandmother," "The Red Wheelbarrow," "The Young Housewife," "This Is Just to Say," "To a Poor Old Woman," "To Elsie," "Winter Trees" from *The Collected Poems of William Carlos Williams: 1909–1939,* volume II. Copyright 1938 by New Directions Publishing Corporation. Reprinted by permission of New Directions Publishing Corporation and Carcanet Press, Ltd.

William Carlos Williams, "A Sort of a Song," "Landscape with the Fall of Icarus," "The Dance," "The Sparrow" from *The Collected Poems of William Carlos Williams: 1939–1962,* volume II. Copyright © 1944, 1948, 1962 by William Carlos Williams. Reprinted by permission of New Directions Publishing Corporation and Carcanet Press, Ltd.

James Wright, "Blessing" and "Lying in a Hammock at William Duffy's Farm in Pine Island, Minnesota" from *Collected Poems.* Copyright 1971 by James Wright. Reprinted by permission of University Press of New England.

Judith Wright, "Eve to Her Daughters" from *Collected Poems, 1942–1970.* Copyright © 1971. Reprinted by permission of Collins/Angus & Robertson Publishers.

William Butler Yeats, "Essays and Introduction" from *Essays and Introductions.* Copyright © 1961 by W. B. Yeats. Reprinted by permission of Macmillan Publishing Company.

William Butler Yeats, "An Irish Airman Forsees His Death," "The Scholars," "The Wild Swans at Coole" from *The Poems of W. B. Yeats: A New Edition,* edited by Richard J. Finneran. Copyright 1919 by Macmillan Publishing Company, renewed 1947 by Bertha Georgie Yeats. Reprinted by permission of Macmillan Publishing Company.

William Butler Yeats, "A Prayer for My Daughter," "Easter 1916," "The Second Coming" from *The Poems of W. B. Yeats: A New Edition,* edited by Richard J. Finneran. Copyright 1924 by Macmillan Publishing Company, renewed 1952 by Bertha Georgie Yeats. Reprinted by permission of Macmillan Publishing Company.

William Butler Yeats, "Among School Children," "Leda and the Swan," "Sailing to Byzantium" from *The Poems of W. B. Yeats: A New Edition,* edited by Richard J. Finneran. Copyright 1928 by Macmillan Publishing Company, renewed 1956 by Bertha Georgie Yeats. Reprinted by permission of Macmillan Publishing Company.

William Butler Yeats, "Byzantium," "Crazy Jane Talks with the Bishop" from *The Poems of W. B. Yeats: A New Edition,* edited by Richard J. Finneran. Copyright 1933 by Macmillan Publishing Company, renewed 1961 by Bertha Georgie Yeats. Reprinted by permission of Macmillan Publishing Company.

William Butler Yeats, "Lapis Lazuli," "Long-Legged Fly," "Politics," "The Circus Animals' Desertion" "Under Ben Bulben" from *The Poems of W. B Yeats,* edited by Richard J. Finneran. Copyright 1940 by Bertha Georgie Yeats, renewed 1968 by Bertha Georgie Yeats, Michael Butler Yeats, and Anne Yeats. Reprinted by permission of Macmillan Publishing Company.

William Butler Yeats, "A Coat," "Adam's Curse," "No Second Troy," "The Lake Isle of Innisfree," "The Song of Wandering Aengus," "When You Are Old" from *The Poems of W. B. Yeats: A New Edition,* edited by Richard J. Finneran (New York: Macmillan, 1983). Reprinted by permission of Macmillan Publishing Company.

Yevgeny Yevtushenko, "Babii Yar" from *Yevtushenko's Reader,* translated by various translators. Translation copyright © 1962, 1963, 1965, 1967, 1972 by E. P. Dutton. English translation, copyright © 1967 by George Reavey. Used by permission of the publisher, Dutton, an imprint of New American Library, a division of Penguin Books USA, Inc.

INDEX

Italics are used for titles of poems and songs. Quotation marks are used for titles of essays. Pages in italics refer to discussion of poem; an *n.* after a page number refers to a note.